CW01084652

1,000,000 Books

are available to read at

www.ForgottenBooks.com

Read online
Download PDF
Purchase in print

ISBN 978-1-5278-0094-6
PIBN 10901746

This book is a reproduction of an important historical work. Forgotten Books uses
state-of-the-art technology to digitally reconstruct the work, preserving the original format
whilst repairing imperfections present in the aged copy. In rare cases, an imperfection in
the original, such as a blemish or missing page, may be replicated in our edition. We do,
however, repair the vast majority of imperfections successfully; any imperfections that
remain are intentionally left to preserve the state of such historical works.

Forgotten Books is a registered trademark of FB &c Ltd.
Copyright © 2018 FB &c Ltd.
FB &c Ltd, Dalton House, 60 Windsor Avenue, London, SW19 2RR.
Company number 08720141. Registered in England and Wales.

For support please visit www.forgottenbooks.com

1 MONTH OF
FREE
READING

at

www.ForgottenBooks.com

By purchasing this book you are eligible for one month membership to ForgottenBooks.com, giving you unlimited access to our entire collection of over 1,000,000 titles via our web site and mobile apps.

To claim your free month visit:
www.forgottenbooks.com/free901746

* Offer is valid for 45 days from date of purchase. Terms and conditions apply.

English
Français
Deutsche
Italiano
Español
Português

www.forgottenbooks.com

Mythology Photography **Fiction**
Fishing Christianity **Art** Cooking
Essays Buddhism Freemasonry
Medicine **Biology** Music **Ancient**
Egypt Evolution Carpentry Physics
Dance Geology **Mathematics** Fitness
Shakespeare **Folklore** Yoga Marketing
Confidence Immortality Biographies
Poetry **Psychology** Witchcraft
Electronics Chemistry History **Law**
Accounting **Philosophy** Anthropology
Alchemy Drama Quantum Mechanics
Atheism Sexual Health **Ancient History**
Entrepreneurship Languages Sport
Paleontology Needlework Islam
Metaphysics Investment Archaeology
Parenting Statistics Criminology
Motivational

CATALOGUE

OF

SEALS

IN THE

DEPARTMENT OF MANUSCRIPTS

IN THE

BRITISH MUSEUM

BY

W. DE G. BIRCH,

ASSISTANT IN THE DEPT. OF MSS.

VOLUME II.

PRINTED BY ORDER OF THE TRUSTEES.

SOLD AT THE BRITISH MUSEUM;

AND BY

LONGMANS AND CO., 39 PATERNOSTER ROW; B. QUARITCH, 15 PICCADILLY;
ASHER AND CO., 13 BEDFORD STREET, COVENT GARDEN; AND
KEGAN PAUL, TRENCH, TRÜBNER AND CO., PATERNOSTER HOUSE,
CHARING CROSS ROAD.

1892.

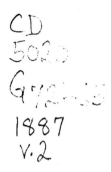
CD
50..
G7...
1887
V.2

LONDON:
PRINTED BY WILLIAM CLOWES AND SONS, Limited,
STAMFORD STREET AND CHARING CROSS.

NOTICE.

THE present volume continues the series of English and Welsh seals. The descriptions are arranged under the headings—Local, Princes of Wales, Equestrian, Noble and other Ladies, and Heraldic—the last class being carried only to the end of letter **F.**

The Catalogue is the work of Mr. Walter de Gray Birch, 1st Class Assistant in the Department.

EDWARD SCOTT.

DEPT. OF MSS.,
20th August, 1892.

TABLE OF CONTENTS.

———◆◇◆———

SEALS OF ENGLAND AND WALES—*(continued).*

———

LIST OF PLATES.

CATALOGUE OF SEALS.

ENGLAND.

LOCAL SEALS.

ABINGDON, *co. Berks.*

4579. [A.D. 1605.] Recent impression in red sealing-wax from the silver matrix. 1¾ in. [xxxvii. 53.]

A shield of arms: a cross patonce betw. four crosses pattées, BOROUGH OF ABINGDON.

S ✸ MAIORIS ✸ BALLIVORV̄ ✸ ET ✸
BVRGENS ✸ ABENDONIE ⋈ ✸ ⋈ ✸

At the end of the legend a butterfly.

Cf. S. Lewis, *Topogr. Dict.*, vol. i., p. 3, for a different seal with same arms.

ALBEMARLE. (*Lands of the Earldom in Yorkshire and Lincolnshire.*)

Bailiff of the Honour.

4580. [A.D. 1412.] Red: fine. 1⅜ in. [Slo. ch. xxxiii. 58.]

The Bailiff of the Honour, standing turned to the l. ; in the r. h. by a strap, a shield of arms : a fess betw. two chevrons ; in the l. h. a staff. Field diapered lozengy.

✠ S' BALL' HONORIS ALBIMARLE.

The letters OR in *honoris,* and AR in *Albimarle* are conjoined.

ALDBOROUGH, or ALDEBURGH, *co. Suffolk.*

4581. [A.D. 1708.] Red: *en placard.* ⅞ × ¾ in. [Add. ch. 13,640.]

Oval: a three-masted ship of war, with mainsail set, sailing on the sea to the l.

✠ . ALDBURGHE . ∼ . IN . ∼ . SVFF.

Cf. S. Lewis, *Topogr. Dict.*, vol. i., p. 16, for a different seal with similar design and variant legend.

ALNWICK, *co. Northumberland.*

4582. [14th cent.]   Sulph. cast from the matrix.   2⅛ in.
[lxx. 1.]

Michael the Archangel, with expanded wings, in the l. h.
a shield of arms charged with an ornamental cross, in the r. h.
a long cross, held obliquely, with which he is piercing the
head of a Dragon under his feet.   The Dragon is set on a
carved mount or corbel.

✠ S' COMVNE BURGI · DE ALNEWIKE ♠

The letters UR of *Burgi* are conjoined.
Beaded borders.

ALVERSTOKE LIBERTY, *ço. Southampton.*

4583. [13th cent.]   Sulph. cast from the matrix.   2⁷⁄₁₆ in.
[xxxvi. 185.]

St. Swithun, Bishop of Winchester, seated on a carved
throne, slightly turned to the r., with mitre, in the r. h. a
pastoral staff curved outwards, in the l. h. a book.   Feet on a
projecting foot-board.   Field replenished with pierced roses
and cinquefoils.

✠ SIGILL' · COMVNE : HOMINVM · PRIORIS :
SCI SWITHVNI DE ALWARESTOKE.

The letters N are reversed: the letters PR and OR in
prioris, TH and UN in *Swithuni*, DE in *de*, and AL and OK
in *Alwarestoke*, are respectively conjoined.
Beaded borders.
The living of this parish is a rectory in the peculiar jurisdiction of the Bishop of Winchester.   *See* LYDD.

Journ. Brit. Arch. Assoc., vol. xlii., 1886, p. 130 ; *Arch. Journ.*
vol. *Winchester*, 1846, p. 111.

ANDOVER, *co. Southampton.*

4584. [16th cent.]   Sulph. cast from the matrix.   1⁵⁄₁₆ ×
1⅛ in. [lxiii. 78.]

Oval : on a mount a lion of ENGLAND statant guardant
beneath a tree.

✠ SIGILL'. COMMVNE · VILLE · DE · ANDEVER.

Beaded borders.

S. Lewis, *Topogr. Dict.*, vol. i., p. 34.

Mayor, Aldermen and Councillors.

4585. [18th cent.] Sulph. cast from the matrix. 1⅝ ×
1¾ in. [lxiii. 79.]
- Rectangular with rounded corners : on a mount a lion
statant guardant with tail extended, beneath a tree.

MAYOR ALDERMEN & COUNCILLORS OF THE BOROUGH
OF ANDOVER.

Uncertain Seal.

4586. [16th cent.] Sulph. cast from fine impression.
1¼ in. [lxiii. 80.]
A shield of arms : three fusils in fess. Crest on a helmet
and mantling, on a wreath two maces in saltire.
Carved border.

APPLEBY, *co. Westmorland.*

Corporation.

4587. [13th cent.] Sulph. casts from the matrix. 2½ in.
[D. C., F. 631, 632.]
Ø. On an elaborately carved symmetrical apple-tree of
seven branches laden with fruit, a shield of Royal Arms of
ENGLAND for Henry III., who established here a Court of
Exchequer.

❀ SIGILLVM : COMMVNITATIS : BVRGII : DE : APPILBI.

℞. The Martyrdom of St. Lawrence, on a gridiron over
burning coals, betw. two executioners, at the head and feet.
Overhead a banner-flag, charged with the Royal Arms of
ENGLAND, and a demi-angel, issuing from clouds on the r.,
with expanded wings, carrying up the soul of the Saint in a
cloth. In the field under the banner-flag three estoiles, and
over the head of the executioner on the l. an apple, slipped.

❀ HIC · IACET :· LAVRENCIVS · IN · CRATICVLA : POSITVS ᴀ
Beaded borders.

S. Lewis, *Topogr. Dict.*, vol. i., p. 37.

Grammar School, A.D. 1574.

4588. Sulph. cast from the matrix, tinted red. 2 in.
[xxxv. 120.]

A stag tripping or at speed, on a plinth bearing the names of the principal benefactors :—LANGTON · SPENSER · for Robert Langton, and Dr. Miles Spencer. The field replenished with elegant and conventional foliage and flowers.

✠ SIGILLVM ✱ APPELBIANÆ ✱ SCHOLÆ ✱ HARTLEY.

The name *Hartley* is in reference to Rainold Hartley, benefactor, A.D. 1589.

4589. Another. [xlvii. 739.]

N. Carlisle, *Endowed Grammar Schools*, vol. ii., p. 694 ; Laing's *MS. Catal.*, No. 299.

ARUNDEL, *co. Sussex.*

Burgesses.

4590. [17th cent.] Sulph. cast from the matrix. 2 in. [lxxii. 73.]

On a fleur-de-lis, slipped on a spiral stem issuing from the base, a swallow, or *hirondelle*, (by way of *rebus* on the name of the town,) rising, contourné, with wings expanded, arms of ARUNDEL. Across the face of the seal, which appears to have been cracked, the date "8th September 1835," in a running hand.

✫ ✛ ✠ SIGILLVM ✫ BVRGENSIVM ✫ BVRGI ✫ DE ✫ ARVNDEL.

Beaded borders.

Dallaway, *History of Western Sussex*, vol. ii., p. 1 ; and *New Add.*, p. 207.

ASHBORNE, *co. Derby.*

Grammar School, A.D. 1585.

4591. Sulph. cast from the matrix ; tinted red. $3\frac{3}{8} \times 2\frac{3}{4}$ in. [xxxv. 121.]

Pointed oval : in the upper part, on an embroidered dais, Qu. Elizabeth, enthroned, with crown, sceptre and orb, overhead a curtained baldachin. At her side a deputation of the founders kneeling. In base, a view of the interior of the school, with a body of teachers and scholars.

SIGILLV · LIBERAE · SCHOLAE · GRAMATICALIS · ELIZABETHÁE · REGINAE · ANGLIAE · IN · VILLA · DE · ASHBVRNE · IN · COMITATV · DERBIAE.

N. Carlisle, *Endowed Grammar Schools*, vol. i., p. 206.

4592. Another. [xlvii. 741.]

Laing's *MS. Catal.*, No. 274.

ASHBURTON, *co. Devon.*

Provost or Portreeve and Corporation.

4593. [14th cent.] Sulph. cast from fine but imperfect impression. 1⅜ in. [lxi. 50.]

A church-like edifice, with central spire. In the field, on the r. h. a saltire cross of St. Andrew, patron saint of the parish church ; on the l. a tree of three branches. In the field over the church, on the l. an estoile of six points wavy, on the r. a crescent.

.... [P]REPOSITI ET COMM .   AYSHB'T . . . .

Cf. S. Lewis, *Topogr. Dict.*, vol. i., p. 46, for a seal of different type.

Borough.

4594. [17th cent.] Sulph. cast from the matrix. 1⅜ in. [lxi. 51.]

An imitation of the older seal, No. 4593. The tree on the l. resembles a corn-plant with three wheat ears.

SIGILLVM ✿ BVRGI ✿ DE ✿ AYSHEBERTON ✿

Inner border beaded, outer border carved with the egg and tongue pattern.

S. Lewis, *Topogr. Dict.*, vol. i., p. 46.

ASKRIGG, *co. York.*

4595. [17th cent.] Sulph. cast from the matrix. 2 in. [lxxiv. 12.]

A cross of Calvary on three steps ; betw. two floral scrolls. Legend in two concentric rings :

(1.) · SIGILLVM COMMUNE INHABITANTIUM

(2.)   VILLÆ DE ASKRIGG ·.·

ATHERSTONE, *co. Warwick.*

Free Grammar School, A.D. 1608.

4596. Sulph. cast from the matrix, tinted red. 1 in. [xxxv. 122.]

A rectangular *stone* slab, about it seven *adders*, forming a *rebus* on the name of the town. In the field above, the date 1608.

· OIC · SIGIL' SCHOLÆ · ADDERSTONIEN ·

N. Carlisle, *Endowed Grammar Schools*, vol. ii., p. 615.

4597. Another. [xlvii. 742.]

Laing's *MS. Catal.*, No. 294.

AXBRIDGE, *co. Somerset.*

First Corporation Seal.

4598. [13th cent.] Sulph. cast from fine impression, chipped. 1¾ in. [lxxi. 47.]

An Agnus Dei, contourné, reguardant.

S' COMMVNITATIS BVRGI DE AXEBRVGE.

Modern Seal.

4599. Sulph. cast from the matrix. 1⅜ in. [lxxi. 48.]

An Agnus Dei, on a mount, with nimbus.

S · ✸ COMMVNITATIS BURGI DE AXBRIDGE.

S. Lewis, *Topogr. Dict.*, vol. i., p. 67.

BANBURY, *co. Oxon.*

Corporation.

4600. [16th cent.] Sulph. cast from the matrix. 1¼ in. [lxx. 64.]

A carved ornamental shield of arms : a sun in radiance, on a field *or*, TOWN OF BANBURY.

Legend on a riband :—

SIGILLVM · BVRGI · DE · BANBVRI · DOMINVS · NOBIS · SOL · & · SCVTVM.

S. Lewis, *Topogr. Dict.*, vol. i., p. 78.

Another Seal.

4601. [16th cent.] Faded red : injured by pressure. 1⅛ in. [xxxvi. 45.]

A rose-tree with three branches, with flowers on a stand. In base the letters S.A.

✸ THYS · YS · THE · SEALE · OF · THE · TOWNE · OF · BANBVREY.

Mayor.

4602. [16th cent.] Sulph. cast from the matrix. ⅞ in. [lxx. 65.]

A carved ornamental shield of arms : as before, No. 4600.

✷ SIGILLVM · MAIORIS · DE · BANBVRY.

BARNARD-CASTLE, *co. Durham.*

4603. [16th cent.] Sulph. cast. 2¼ in. [lxii. 83.]

A cross pattée, betw. a crescent on the l. and an estoile of seven points wavy on the r.

♠ SIGILL · COMMVNE · BVRGENSIVM · DE · CASTRO · BARNARD.

The letters MM in *commune* are conjoined.

BARNSTAPLE, *or* BARUM, *co. Devon.*

Corporation.

4604. [13th cent.] Sulph. cast from the matrix. 2 in. [lxi. 52.]

An eagle, rising with expanded wings, contourné.

✠ SIGILLVM : COMMVNE : BVRGI : BARNASTAPOLIE.

Mayor.

4605. [A.D. 1571.] Red: indistinct. $\frac{7}{8}$ in. [Add. ch. 13,087.]

A triple-towered embattled castle, with round-headed doorway, Town of Barnstaple.

✠ S' MAIORIS BARNESTAPVLIE.

4606. [17th cent.] Sulph. cast from the matrix. $1\frac{5}{8}$ in. [lxi. 54.]

On a mount a triple-towered embattled castle, with round-headed doorway and quatrefoiled windows, Town of Barnstaple. Within a beaded and engrailed border.

❀ SIGILLVM · AD · ARMA · PRO · MAIORE · ET · CORPORACIONE · VILLE · BARVM.

The letters MA in *arma* and *Maiore*, and NE in *corporacione*, are conjoined.

Cf. S. Lewis, *Topogr. Dict.*, vol. i., p. 88, for variant seal of arms.

Bridge Seal.

4607. [15th cent.] Sulph. cast from the matrix. $2\frac{3}{4}$ in. [lxi. 53.]

A bridge of six arches, over waves, for the river Taw. Above the bridge an eagle displayed, betw. a chapel or church with spire topped with a cross on the l., and a cross of Calvary on four steps on the r., from which a long pennon, charged with a cross, floats over the field.

❀ SIGILLUM : LONGI : PONTIS : UILLE : BARNESTAPOLIE : IN COMIT' DEUONIE.

Cabled borders.

Royal Court of Sessions.

4608. [17th cent.] Sulph. cast from the matrix. $1\frac{3}{8} \times \frac{7}{16}$ in. [lxi. 55.]

Oval: a shield of the Royal Arms of Great Britain as borne by K. James I., ensigned with a royal crown.

Legend on a scroll :—

SIGIL' + REGAL + CVR + BARVM.

Court of the Recorder.

4609. [18th cent.] Sulph. cast from the matrix. 1¼ × 1 in. [lxi. 56.]

Oval: a shield of the ROYAL ARMS OF GREAT BRITAIN as borne by QU. ANNE before the Union in A.D. 1707, ensigned with a royal crown.

SIGIL : CVR : RECORDᴏʀ · CORP · BARVᴍ.

BASINGSTOKE, *co. Southampton.*

4610. [15th cent.] Sulph. cast. from the matrix. 1⅜ in. [xxxvii. 14.]

The Combat of St. Michael the Archangel with the Dragon.

SIGILLVM ✿ CŌE ✿ VILLE ✿ DE ✿ BASINGSTOKE ✿ ⁊ +.

Cf. engraving of a later seal in S. Lewis, *Topogr. Dict.*, vol. i., p. 95.

BATH, *co. Somerset.*

Corporation.

4611. [13th cent.] Red: imperfect. 2³⁄₁₆ in. Enclosed in a tin box. [xlviii. 20.]

An embattled precinct or enclosure, straight in front, circular in the rear, with masoned walls, enclosing a small building, perhaps intended for the building on the site of the bath.

+ SIGILLVM : CIVIVM : VRBIS : BATHONIE :

4612. Sulph. cast from the matrix. [lxxi. 52.]

S. Lewis, *Topogr. Dict.*, vol. i., p. 100 ; *Journ. Brit. Arch. Assoc.*, vol. xxxi., p. 317.

Mayor.

4613. [A.D. 1363.] Dark-green: a fragment. About 1¼ in. when perfect. [Eg. ch. 336.]

Portion of an embattled castle or doorway.

. . . . SIGILL' M . . . .

Journ. Brit. Arch. Assoc., vol. xxxi., p. 317, *pl. fig.* I.

Later Seal.

4614. [17th cent.] Sulph. cast from the matrix. 1⅛ in. [lxxi. 53.]

A castle gateway, with portcullis, side-towers, and embattled walls. Above, in the field the letter ♭'.

🞲 SIGILLVM ✿ MAIORIS ✿ DE ✿ BAṬOMA (*sic*).

Cf. *Journ. Brit. Arch. Assoc.*, *l.c., fig.* 2.

BECCLES, *co. Suffolk.*

The new Incorporation for the Fen, A.D. 1584.

4615. Sulph. cast from the matrix. 1¾ in. [lxxii. 22.]

An octagonal enclosure of hurdles, within it a horse, an ass, and an ox, standing on fen-ground. In the background a house. In the field the date 15–84.

Legend on a riband :—

SIGILLŪ + COĒ + NOVE + INCORPORACŌIS + Ɛ̃ · BECCLES · FFĒNE.

S. Lewis, *Topogr. Dict.*, vol. i., p. 116. Qu. Elizabeth's Charter to the Corporation of Beccles was issued in A.D. 1584.

BEDFORD, *co. Bedford.*

Corporation.

4616. [15th cent.] Sulph. cast from the brass matrix. 2⅛ in. [lviii. 26.]

A towered castle of three storeys, masoned and embattled, with portcullis in round-headed portal. All upon an eagle displayed, head to the l., crowned.

ⱥ SIGILLŪ ⱥ COMUNTATIS (*sic*) ⱥ VILLE ⱥ BEDEFOR ⱥ DIE ⱥ

Cabled border.

S. Lewis, *Topogr. Dict.*, vol. i., p. 113.

Mayor's First Seal.

4617. [13th cent.] Sulph. cast from an impression, indistinct and injured in places. 1⅝ in. [lviii. 27.]

An embattled castle, with tall centre tower, and a smaller turret at each side. In the field on each side a wyvern, holding a sprig of foliage in the jaws, tail nowed.

✿ S' MAYORITATIS · VILLE · BEDEFORDIE.

Later Seal.

4618. Sulph. cast from the brass matrix. 1½ in. [lviii. 28.]

This is a badly designed and blundered copy of No. 4617.

✿ S' IMAVOMTIITT · VILLEB · IIIFOIRT · ⱥ ✿

BEDWYN, GREAT, *co. Wilts.*

Corporation.

4619. [17th cent.] Sulph. cast from the matrix. 1⁹⁄₁₆ in. [lxxiii. 69.]

An ornamental shield of arms : a tower, domed, masoned

and embattled, TOWN OF GREAT BEDWYN. Crest on a helmet, mantling, and wreath, a griffin.

: ✿ : THE · COMMON · SEALE · OF · THE · CORPORATION · OF · GREAT · BEDWIN.

S. Lewis, *Topogr. Dict.*, vol. i., p. 118.

BENYNGTON,* *co. Surrey.*

Seal of the Parish " ad Causas."

4620. [A.D. 1372.] Green : chipped. About ¾ in. when perfect. [Add. ch. 23,136.]

Across the field in two lines the final word of the legend :

+ S[IG]ILLVM AD CAV-SAS.

BERKSHIRE,

ANTHONY BRIDGES, *Sheriff.*

4621. [A.D. 1575.] Dark-green : much injured by compression. About 1⅛ in. when perfect. [Add. ch. 13,653.]

A triple-towered castle, the central tower domed, the side towers pinnacled ; betw. the initials of the name of the sheriff, A. B.

BERWICK-UPON-TWEED, *co. Berwick.*

Mayoralty, with counterseal of GEORGE MORTON, *Mayor.*

4622. [A.D. 1569.] Dark-green : fine. 1¾ in. [Add. ch. 19,882.]

Ø. In a carved gothic panel, on a mount, a *bear* passant, beneath a tree of three branches, betw. two shields of arms : quarterly, 1, 4, FRANCE (MODERN), 2, 3, ENGLAND. Above, in a small carved niche with ogee-arched canopy, betw. two carved circular openings, our Lord, seated, lifting up the r. h. in benediction, in the l. h. an orb with long cross.

Fourteenth century style of work.

SIGILLŪ : MAIORATUS : VILLA : BERWICI : SUPER ꞉ TWEDAM ꞉· ⚘

℞. A smaller counterseal. ¾ in. A monogram or merchant's mark ; incorporating the initial letter G. Within a cusped or denticulated bordure.

4623. Sulph. cast from an impression injured in places. [lxx. 4.]

Cf. S. Lewis, *Topogr. Dict.*, vol. i., p. 133, for drawing of the arms, which resembles the design of this seal.

---

* Perhaps Beddington, in the hundred of Wallington, with which this seal may be connected. For other seals of hundreds, etc., with legends across the field, see Bindon, Flaxwell, South Erpingham, Staplehou, and Wangford. Cf. *Arch. Journ.* x. 12 ; xi. 31.

Royal Seal for the Chamberlain within the Town.

4624. [A.D. 1565.] Uncoloured : very indistinct. 3¼ in. [Add. ch. 983.]

Ø. Within a cusped gothic six-foil, carved and trefoiled, a shield of the ROYAL ARMS used from HENRY V. down to QU. ELIZABETH ; above it a royal crown.

+ HENRICUS : DEI : GRACIA : REX : ANGLIE : ET : FRANCIE : ET : DOMINUS : HIBERNIE :

℞. Resembles the *rev.* of No. 753. The legend probably adapted, but too indistinct to be read.

For other seals of this class, see Nos. 750–754.

BEVERLEY, *co. York.*

Corporation.

4625. [A.D. 1425.] Red : fine, edge chipped. 2⁷⁄₁₆ in. [Add. ch. 15,888.]

St. John of Beverley, Archbishop of York, seated on a carved throne, somewhat resembling that on the great seal of K. Edward I. (*see* No. 132), with mitre and pall, lifting up the r. h. in benediction, in the l. h. a crozier, his feet on a projecting footboard, and under his feet a fox. In the field, on each side a tree, and overhead on the l. a crescent, on the r. an estoile. Thirteenth century style of work.

+ SIGILLVM : COMMVNITATIS : BVRG[ENCIV]M : BEVERLACI ⋈

4625*. Sulph. cast from fine but chipped impression. [lxxiv. 13.]

.. + ... GILL .... ATI ..... VRGENCIUM : BE ... R · ACI.

G. Poulson, *Beverlac*, London, 4to., 1829, pl., p. 771.

Another state of the Seal, A.D. 1501–1507.

4626. Sulph. cast from indistinct impression. ₁2⁷⁄₁₆ in. [D.C., E. 32.]

Generally resembles the preceding seal, with addition of a shield of arms in the field on each side ; l. an eagle displayed ; r., per pale, *dex.*, SEE OF YORK, *sin.*, a pale lozengy, for THOMAS SAVAGE, Archbishop of York, A.D. 1501–1507.

✠ SIGILLVM : COMMVNITATIS : BVRGENCIUM : BEUERLACI ⋈ ,

Drake, *Eboracum*, pl. ci., appendix, fig. xxv.

Mayor's First Seal.

4627. [A.D. 1648.] Red, covered with paper before impression. 2¼ in. [Add. ch. 5820.]

A carved shield of arms: three bars wavy, on a chief a *beaver*, for TOWN OF BEVERLEY. Background of foliage.

✠ SIGIL' · MAIOR' · GVBERNAT' · ET · BVRGENS' · VILLÆ · ÐE ·
          .... ERLA.

4628. [A.D. 1656–7.] Red: fine, but fragmentary. [Add. ch. 5823.]

. . . . L' MAIOR' · GVBERNAT . . . . EN . . . VILLÆ · DE . . . . . .

Second Seal.

4629. [late 17th cent.] Sulph. cast from the matrix. 2¼ in. [lxxiv. 16.]
A copy of the preceding seal, No. 4627.

✠ SIGIL' · MAIOR GVBERNAT · ET · BVRGENS · VILLÆ · DE ·
          BEVERLA'.

Inner border beaded, outer border carved.

Town Seal.

4630. [18th cent.] Sulph. cast from the matrix. 1¼ in. [lxxiv. 17.]
A shield of arms of the TOWN OF BEVERLEY as in No. 4627.

THE SEALE OF THE TOWN OF BEVERLEY.

Signet.

4631. [15th cent.] Sulph. cast from the matrix. 1 in. [lxxiv. 14.]
A shield of arms : three bars wavy, on a chief a peacock in his pride, betw. on the *dex.* a fleur-de-lis, on the *sin.* a lion passant, a variant form of the arms of.the TOWN OF BEVERLEY.

Another Signet.

4632. [17th cent.] Sulph. cast from the matrix. ¾ in. [lxxiv. 15.]
A shield of arms of the TOWN OF BEVERLEY, as in No. 4627.

✠ BEVERLEY.

Official of the Provost Court.

4633. [14th cent.] Sulph. cast from fine impression. 1⅝ × 1 in. [lxxiv. 18.]
Pointed oval: St. John of Beverley, Archbishop of York, seated in a carved and canopied niche, with mitre, lifting up the r. h. in benediction, in the l. h. a crozier. In base under an arch, an official kneeling in prayer to the r.

S' · OFFICIALITAT' · ꝐPOSITVRE · BEVERLACI ·

Seal of uncertain use.

4634. [17th cent.] Sulph. cast from the matrix. · 1⅛ × 1 in. [lxxiv. 19.]

Oval: the front of a castle, with two round-towers, each domed and bearing a flag, round-headed doorway with portcullis down, curtain-wall masoned and embattled, and having two quatrefoiled windows. Over the battlements, on a wreath a dexter hand couped at the wrist, grasping an olive branch. This type resembles the seals used by sheriffs.

BEWDLEY, *co. Worcester.*

Corporation.

4635. [17th cent.] Sulph. cast from the matrix. 1⅜ in. [lxxiii. 89.]

An anchor, ringed, over all a fetterlock containing on the *dex.* a sword erect, on the *sin.* a rose, TOWN OF BEWDLEY.

❀ SIGILLVM ✩ LIBERTATIS ✩ BVRGI DE ✩ BEWDLEY.

Inner border cabled, outer border carved.

S. Lewis, *Topogr. Dict.*, vol. i., p. 139.

Official Seal.

4636. [17th cent.] Sulph. cast from the matrix. ¾ in. [lxxiii. 90.]

Device of the armorial charges of the TOWN OF BEWDLEY, as in No. 4635.

✵ SIGILLVM · OFFICIALE · DE · BEWDLEY.

BIDEFORD, *co. Devon.*

Corporation.

4637. [15th cent.] Sulph. east. 2¼ in. [D.C., G. 271.]

On a bridge of four round-headed arches, with a river (the Torridge) flowing in base ; on the l. a chapel with bell-cote and bell ; on the r. a chapel with tall spire ; in the centre, on a cross pattée standing on a tall stem, the Virgin and Child, the Virgin being Patron Saint of the parish. Field diapered with foliage and flowers.

SIGILLUM ⚮ VILLA ⚮ DE ⚮ BYDEFORD ⚮ IN ⚮ COM ⚮ DEVON ⚮

Inner border cabled.

Common Seal, A.D. 1577.

4638. Sulph. cast from the matrix.   1-³⁄₁₀ in.   [lxi. 63.]
A bridge of one whole and two demi-arches, masoned and with parapet, over the river Torridge, with a ship of one mast passing under the central arch.

+ SIGILLVM · COMVNE · DE · BEDIIFORDE. 1577.

S. Lewis, *Topogr. Dict.,* vol. i., p. 143.

Bridge Estate.

4639. [17th cent.] Sulph. cast.   ⅞ in.   [lxi. 64.]
A reduced design derived from that described in No. 4637.

BRIDGE TRUST · BIDEFORD.

BINDON LIBERTY, *co. Dorset.*

Seal for Labourers' Passes.

4640. [15th cent.] Recent impression in red sealing-wax, from the matrix.   1 in.
The inscription BYNEDON, across the field, betw. two parallel lines, with a fascicle of sprigs above, and another below.

✿ COMITATUS ⚜ ⚜ DORS' ⚜

Beaded border.

BIRMINGHAM, *co. Warwick,* A.D. 1838.

4641. [19th cent.] Sulph. cast from the matrix.   2¼ in. [lxxiii. 2.]
An ornamental shield of arms: quarterly, 1, 4, az. five lozenges in bend sinister, or, BURMICHAME ; 2, 3, per pale indented, arg. and sa., BERMINGHAM. Motto on a scroll below :—FORWARD. All encircled with a branch of myrtle or laurel on the l., and a branch of oak on the r. fructed ; interlaced with a ribbon inscribed :—INCORPORATED BY ROYAL CHARTER, 1838.
Legend on a buckled strap :

COMMON SEAL OF THE MAYOR ALDERMEN & BURGESSES OF THE BOROUGH OF BIRMINGHAM.

For a variant form of the arms, cf. S. Lewis, *Topogr. Dict.,* vol. i., p. 154.

Free Grammar School.

First Seal, A.D. 1552.

4642. Sulph. cast from the matrix, tinted red. 1¼ in. [xxxv. 123.]

Five persons seated at a rectangular board or table; the three who are in the front have the arms based and extended to the table.

··S : COMVNE : LIBERE : SCOLE : EDWARDI : VI : IИ : BIRMIИGHM.

Beaded borders.

N. Carlisle, *Endowed Grammar Schools*, vol. ii., p. 620.

4643. Another. [xlvii. 748.]

Laing's *MS. Catal.*, No. 295.

Second Seal, A.D. 1685.

4644. Sulph. cast from the matrix, tinted red. 2¼ in. [xxxv. 124.]

K. Edward VI., Royal Founder, seated in majesty on a canopied throne; on each side two persons kneeling, the two nearest to the king holding books. In the field two royal badges, l. a fleur-de-lis; r. a rose *en soleil.*

✠ SIGILLVM ✤ ♣ ✤ CŌE ✤ ♣ ✤ G ♣ P ♣ LIBERE ♣ SCOLE ♣ EDWARDI ♣ VI ♣ IN ✤ ♣ ✤ BRIMICHAM.

G. P. appears to stand for *Gubernatorum possessionum.*

N. Carlisle, *Endowed Grammar Schools*, vol. ii., p. 628.

4645. Another. [xlvii. 746.]

˙ Laing's *MS. Catal*, No. 296. ·

BISHOP'S CASTLE, *co. Salop*, A.D. 1609.

4646. Sulph. cast from the matrix. 1⅛ × 1 in. [lxxi. 12.]

Oval: the front of a castle, with two round towers, each domed and bearing a flag, round-headed doorway with portcullis half-down; curtain-wall masoned and embattled, and having a dome of four segments, topped with a flag on a staff, between the initial letters I. R. for *Jacobus Rex.* In base the date of the confirmation by K. James I. of the ·Royal Charter granted to the inhabitants by Qu. Elizabeth, .A.D. 1609.·

Cabled border.

S. Lewis, *Topogr. Dict.*, vol. i., p. 159. ·

BLANDFORD-FORUM, *co. Dorset.*

Corporation.

4647. [17th cent.] Sulph. cast from the matrix.. 1¾ in. [lxxii. 25.]

A carved shield of arms : ENGLAND with a label of three points, for the DUCHY OF LANCASTER. The carved work of the shield at each side includes, by way of supporter, an ostrich feather of the DUCHY. In the field at the sides the initial letters D. L. (*Ducatus Lancastriæ.*)

☻ SIGILLVM ☆ BVRGENTIVM ☆ VILLAE ☆ DE ☆ BLANFORD ☆ F.ORVM.

S. Lewis, *Topogr. Dict.*, vol. i., p. 169.

Mayor.

4648. [18th cent.] Sulph. cast from the matrix. 1 × ⅞ in. [lxii. 26.]

Oval : a shield of arms : DUCHY OF LANCASTER, as in No. 4647, hanging from a riband tied in a double bow-knot.

BLYTHING HUNDRED, *co. Suffolk.*

Bailiff.

4649. [17th cent.] Sulph. cast, tinted brownish-red, from an impression belonging to the Earl of Leicester. +⅛ in. [lxxvi. 35.]

A castle, with round-headed doorway, portcullis half-down, and two round side-towers, with domes and flags. In base the inscription :

BLITH.

The letters TH are conjoined.

BODMIN, *co. Cornwall.*

First Common Seal.

4650. [14th cent.] Sulph. cast from fine impression. 1⅞ × 1¼ in. [D.C., G. 56.] .

Pointed oval : a king, perhaps Ethelred, or Edward the Elder, seated on a throne under a canopy, resembling a triple-towered castle, supported on slender columns, in the r. h. a sceptre fleury. Field hatched or diapered lozengy.

S' COMVNE : BVRGENCIVM : BODMINIE.

Second Seal.

4651. [17th cent.] Sulph. cast from the matrix. $1\frac{7}{8} \times 1\frac{3}{8}$ in. [lxi. 4.]

Pointed oval : a king, seated on a throne under a canopy, resembling a triple-towered castle, with crown, in the r. h. a sceptre fleury.

SIGILL. COMVNE BVRGENSIVM BODMINIE.

- Cabled borders.

S. Lewis, *Topogr. Dict.*, vol. i., p. 178.

BOLTON, *co. Lancaster.*

Corporation.

4652. [19th cent.] Sulph. cast from the matrix $2\frac{1}{4}$ in. [lxvi. 23.]

A carved shield of arms : on a mount an elephant with an embattled tower on its back, TOWN OF BOLTON. Encircled with a branch of oak on the l., and a branch of myrtle or laurel on the r., fructed, tied with a riband.

Legend on a buckled strap :—

SEAL OF THE MUNICIPAL CORPORATION OF THE
BOROUGH OF BOLTON.

For the arms, cf. S. Lewis, *Topogr. Dict.*, vol. i., p. 183.

Mayor.

4653. [19th cent.] Sulph. cast from the matrix. $1\frac{5}{8} \times 1\frac{1}{4}$ in. [lxvi. 24.]

A shield of arms of the TOWN OF BOLTON, as in No. 4652 ; encircled with the branches as before.

BOROUGH OF BOLTON.
MAYOR'S SEAL.

BOSSINEY *with* TREVENA, *in the Parish of* TINTAGEL, *co. Cornwall.*

4654. [16th cent.] Sulph. cast from the matrix. $1\frac{5}{8}$ in. [lxi. 6.]

K. Arthur's castle, with three towers, the principal one domed, and embattled walls, set upon the sea, with a flight of four steps leading down from the central doorway into the water.

✠ SIGILLVM · MAIORIS · ET · BVRGIENSIV' · BVRGI ·
DE · TINTAIOEL ·

Cabled borders.

S. Lewis, *Topogr. Dict.*, vol. i., p. 190.

BOSTON, *co. Lincoln.*

Mayor and Burgesses.

4655. [17th cent.] Sulph. cast from the matrix.   1¾ in.
[lxvi. 83.]

A shield of arms : three crowns in pale, TOWN OF BOSTON.
Betw. three ornamental branches of foliage.   In the field on
the l. the letter B, on the r. a *tun*, by way of *rebus.*

☆ SIGIL̅ · C̅O̅E · MAIOR̅ · ET · BVRGEN · BVRGI · DE ·
BOSTON · IN · COM · LINCOLN.

S. Lewis, *Topogr. Dict.,* vol. i., p. 192.

Mayor of the New Borough.

4656. [16th cent.] Sulph. cast from the matrix.   1 in.
[lxvi. 84.]

An ornamental shield of arms : TOWN OF BOSTON, as in
No. 4655.

♠ SIGILLV̅ ♠ MAIORS ☆ NOVI ♠ BVRGI ☆ DE ☆ BOSTON.
Inner border beaded.

Admiralty Court, A.D. 1573.

4657. Sulph. cast from impression, chipped.   1¾ in.
[D.C., H. 176.]

A three-masted ship on the sea ; the mainsail set and
charged with a shield of arms of the TOWN OF BOSTON.

SIGILLV̂ · CONCERN' · CAVSAS · MARINAS . MAIORATVS ·
BVRGI · DE · BOSTON · 1573.

S. Lewis, *Topogr. Dict.,* vol. i., p. 191.

Wool Staple.

4658. [14th cent.]   Sulph. cast from fine impression.
1¼ in.   [lxvi. 85.]

In a carved gothic panel, St. Botulph, standing, in the r. h.
a pastoral staff, in the l. h. a book.   Before him a wool-pack.

SIGIL' ☆ STAPULE ☆ DE ☆ SANCTO ☆ BOTULFO.

4659. Another.   [D.C., F. 45.]

BOXFORD. *co. Suffolk.*

Queen Elizabeth's Free Grammar School.

4660. Sulph. cast.   1¼ in. [lxxii. 19.]

A shield of arms : three ˏdexter hands, issuing from clouds at the dexter, sinister and base, grasping a closed book.

✠ SIG : LIBERE : SCH : GRAM : REGI : ELIZ : IN : BOXFORD :
IN · COM · SVFF.

Cabled borders.

BRACKLEY, *co. Northampton.*

4661. [16th cent.] Sulph. cast from the matrix. 1⅜ in. [lxx. 44.]

A shield of arms : quarterly, 1, 4, a lion rampant between three pheons, EGERTON, EARL OF BRIDGWATER, for TOWN OF BRACKLEY ; 2, 3, on a bend, three buck's heads cabossed, bend-wise, STANLEY. Crests, (1.) on a wreath a lion rampant holding an arrow ; (2.) on a chapeau turned up erm. an eagle preying on an infant swaddled, STANLEY.

Legend on a riband :—

SIGILLVM · BVRGI · DE · BRACKLEY.

S. Lewis, *Topogr. Dict.*, vol. i., p. 202.

BRENTWOOD, *co. Essex.*

Free Grammar School, A.D. 1557.

4662. Sulph. casts from the silver matrix. 1½ in. [xxxv. 125. A, B.]

Ø. An ornamental shield of arms : the Trinity. Background replenished with elegant arabesque design of foliage.

℞. An ornamental shield of arms, shaped as in the *obv.*; per pale, *dex.*, a chevron betw. three lions' gambs erect and erased within a bordure, on a chief an eagle displayed, armed and crowned, a fleur-de-lis for difference, SIR ANTHONY BROWNE, knt., founder ; *sin.*, quarterly, 1. 4, [on] a chevron betw. three leopards' faces [as many bombs, fired], FARRINGTON ; 2, three cinquefoils, two and one, FARRINGTON ; 4. a cross engrailed between four roundles, CLAYTON. Background as in *obv.*

N. Carlisle, *Endowed Grammar Schools*, vol. i., p. 408.

4663. Another. [xlvii. 753, 754.]

Laing's *MS. Catal.*, No. 279.

C 2

BRIDGNORTH, *co. Salop.*

4664. [12th cent.] Sulph. cast from fine impression. 2¼ in. [lxxi. 13.]

A triple-towered castle, embattled wall and turrets, round-headed doorway, three flat-headed and two circular windows.

    ✱ SIGILLVM COMVNE VILLÆ DE BRIDGNORTH.

Cabled borders.

S. Lewis, *Topogr. Dict.*, vol. i., p. 227 ; cf. a variant seal, somewhat resembling the above, in *Archæologia*, vol. xv., p. 380.

4665. [A.D. 1724.] Red wax, covered with paper before impression. [Add. ch. 19,411.]

In the body of this document the seal is called that of the Bailiffs' office, cf. No. 4666.

Bailiffs of the Liberty.

4666. [15th cent.] Sulph. cast from fine impression. 2 in. [D.C., G. 275.]

On a rocky mount replenished with flowers, an embattled castle, with central turret and two round towers, and round-headed doorway, with portcullis half-down. In the field two shields of arms: l. a cross of St. George ; r., quarterly, 1, 4 FRANCE (MODERN), 2, 3, ENGLAND. Inner edge of the field engrailed.

    ✠ SIGILLUM : OFFICIJ : BALLIUOR : LIBERTATIS : VILLE :
                DE : BRUGES.

Cabled borders.

Archæologia, vol. xv., pp. 380, 400, 401.

4667. Another. [xlvii. 755.]

Laing's *MS. Catal.*, No. 378.

Municipal Council of the Borough.

4668. Red sealing-wax from the matrix. 2 in. [xliv. 227.]

Modern copy of preceding seal of the Bailiffs' office with legend substituted.

    ✠ SEAL : OF : THE : MUNICIPAL : COVNCIL : OF : THE :
                BOROVGH : OF : BRIDGNORTH.

Cabled borders.

BRIDGWATER, *co. Somerset.*

4669. [A.D. 1398.] Red : fine ; very imperfect. About
2 in. when perfect. [Cott. ch. xv. 17.]
On a bridge of four round-headed arches, over the river
Parret, a castle, with three tiers or storeys of walling, masoned
and embattled, and with round-headed doorway. Twelfth
century style of work.

✠ SIGILL : COM . . . . GE · WA . . . .

4670. Sulph. cast of No. 4669, before it had been so much
injured. [D.C., F. 634.]
4671. Another. [lxxi. 54.]

Mayor, Bailiffs, and Burgesses.

4672. [15th cent.] Sulph. cast from the matrix. 2¼ in.
[lxxi. 55.]
On a bridge of five pointed arches over the river, a castle
with three tiers or storeys of walling, masoned and embattled,
and at each side a round tower or turret, with round-headed
doorway, portcullis half-down, below it a head. In the field
above on the l. an estoile, on the r. a fleur-de-lis. This
design forms the charges on the shield of arms of the TOWN
OF BRIDGWATER.

❀ SIGILLUM ❀ MAIORIS ❀ BALLIUOR ❀ ET BVRGENC' ❀
WILLE ❀ DE BRIGEWATER ❀

Cabled borders.

S. Lewis, *Topogr. Dict.*, vol. i., p. 230.

BRIDPORT, *co. Dorset.*

First Common Seal.

4673. [17th cent.] Sulph. cast from the matrix. 1¾ in.
[D.C., H. 186.]
A castle, standing on water (the River Bride), masoned
and embattled, with a round tower at each side, over each a
fleur-de-lis of FRANCE. In the field betw. the towers a lion
passant guardant of ENGLAND, crowned. In the round-
headed doorway three stanchions. This design forms the
charges on the shield of arms of the TOWN OF BRIDPORT.

✠ SIGILLVM ❀ COMVNE ❀ VILLÆ ❀ DE ❀ BRYDEPORTE.

Inner border cabled.

S. Lewis, *Topogr. Dict.*, vol. i., p. 232.

Later Common Seal, A.D. 1836.

4674. Red sealing-wax, recent impression from the matrix. 2 in. [xxxvi. 196.]

An ornamental carved shield of arms with the heraldic colours indicated : gu., a castle with two side towers, arg., over each a fleur-de-lis, or, in chief a lion passant guardant, crowned of the last, the base barry wavy of eight, arg. and az., TOWN OF BRIDPORT.

SIGILLVM COMVNE VILLÆ DE BRYDEPORTE
+ 1836 +

Mayor, A.D. 1836.

4675. Recent impression in red sealing-wax from the matrix. 1¼ in. [xxxvi. 197.]

A shield of arms of the TOWN OF BRIDPORT, as in No. 4674.

SEAL OF THE MAYOR OF BRIDPORT
· 1836 ·

Mayor's Signet.

4676. [17th cent.] Sulph. cast from matrix. ⅞ in. [lxii. 27.]

On a wreath a castle, embattled and masoned, with two round side-towers, domed ; betw. them a lion passant.

Beaded border.

Bailiff's Signet.

4677. [17th-18th cent.] Sulph. cast from matrix. ⅞ in. [lxii. 29.]

A castle, embattled and masoned, with two round side-towers, domed ; betw. them, on a wreath, a hand and arm in armour grasping a sword in bend.

BRIGHTFORD HUNDRED, *co. Sussex, in the Rape of Bramber.*

4678. [16th cent.] Sulph. cast from fine impression. 2 × 1¾ in. [lxxii. 80.]

Shield-shaped : a shield of arms : a fess betw. a lion rampant in chief, and in base a griffin's head erased.

+ SVSSEX · R · BRAMBOR + HVИDRED DE· + BYRTFORD'.

BRISTOL, *cos. Gloucester and Somerset.*

First Common Seal.

4679. [14th cent.] Recent impressions in red sealing-wax from the matrix. 2⅞ in., shewing marks of the pins employed in the matrix to steady it. [xlv. 18, 19.]

∅. View of Bristol Castle, an elaborately designed edifice on waves, with outer bailey and walls embattled and masoned, round-headed windows and doorway, lofty tower on the r., somewhat lower tower on the l., with a watchman on it, half-length, to the r., blowing a long trumpet; at each side a smaller tower.

+ SIGILLVM : COMMVNE : BVRGENSIVM : BRISTOLLIE :

℞. On the r. a one-masted ship, with mainsail set, steered over the waves by a mariner holding a rudder or sweep over the side, towards a round-headed archway at the corner of a building on the l. ; on the embattled summit of the building the head and r. h. of a watchman who is pointing out the way to the steersman. In the foreground on the beach a large conger-eel to the l.

Legend in two rhyming hexameters :—

+ SECRETI CLAVIS SV̄ PORT⁹ NAVITA NAVIS
PORTĀ CVSTODIT PORT⁹ VIGIL INDICE ⊕DIT.

The letters OR in *portam* are conjoined.

Beaded borders.

Journ. Brit. Arch. Assoc., vol. xxxi., pp. 180-183; cf. Ducange, *Glossarium*, s.v. " Clavis," a place closed by a key, hence a "key" or "quay," in which signification the word is probably here employed.

4680. Plaster cast, tinted red, of the rev. only. [xlv. 20.]
4681. [A.D. 1496.] Bronze-green: fine, chipped at the edges. [Add. ch. 26,476.]
4682. [A.D. 1553.] Red: fine, imperfect. [Add. ch. 26,500.]

Second Common Seal, A.D. 1569.

4683. Sulph. cast from the matrix in possession of the Corporation. 3¼ in. [lxiii. 42, 43.]

∅. On a mount replenished with tufts of herbage a shield of arms: on the *sin.*, on a mount, a castle, with two towers, domed, on each a pennon : the *dex.* base barry wavy, thereon a three-masted ship sailing from behind the castle, the fore and main masts in sight, on the first a sail, CITY OF BRISTOL. Crest upon a helmet mantling and wreath, two arms embowed, and interlaced in saltire, issuing from clouds, in the *dex.* a snake, in the *sin.* a balance. Supporters, two unicorns sejant.

❀ : SIGILLVM : ❀ : COMMVNE · ❀ · MAIORIS : ❀ · ET + ❀ +
COMMVNITATIS + ❀ + CIVITATIS + ❀ + BRISTOLLIAE ✖
A.o + DOMINI · 1569.

℞. A copy of the *rev.* of the first seal, No. 4679.

❀ : NISI ✖ ❀ ✪ DOMINVS ·: ❀ ·:· CVSTODIERIT ❀ CIVITATEM ✖
❀ ✖ FRVSTRA ✖ ❀ ✖ VIGILAT ·: ❀ ·:· QVI ✪ ✪ ✪ CVSTODIT :
✖ : EAM ✖ 1569 :   Psalm cxxvi. 1.)

S. Lewis, *Topogr. Dict.*, vol. i., p. 240.

4684. [A.D. 1616.]   Bronze-green : indistinct and injured
by pressure.   About 3¼ in.   [Harl. ch. 58 E. 15.]

4685. [A.D. 1620.]   Bronze-green : very imperfect and indistinct.   [Harl. ch. 58 E. 21.]

Seal of Arms.

4686. [17th cent.]   Recent impression in red sealing-wax,
from matrix.   1¾ × 1⁷⁄₁₆ in.   [xlv. 23.]

Oval : a shield of arms of the CITY OF BRISTOL, crest, and
supporters, as described in No. 4683.

Cabled border.

Mayoralty.

First Seal.

4687. [14th cent.]   Sulph. cast from fine impression.
1⅛ inch.   [lxiii. 49.]

On the l. a view of Bristol castle, with four embattled
towers.   The secret quay, see No. 4679, is open, and a ship is
sailing out, bearing a flag of the ROYAL ARMS, ENGLAND
only.   Betw. the flag and the ship, in the field the letter B.

✪ SIGILLVM · MAIORITATIS · VILLE · BRISTOLLIE.

Second Seal.

4688. [14th cent.]   Recent impression in red sealing-wax,
from matrix.   1¾ in.   [xlv. 21.]

On the l. a view of Bristol castle, with three storeys of
embattled masonry, on one of the corner towers a watchman,
half-length to the l., blowing a horn, on the battlements a
flag charged with a cross, on another turret another watchman blowing a horn.   The secret quay, see No. 4679, is open,
and a ship is sailing out from behind the castle, with high
forecastle and flag of the ROYAL ARMS OF ENGLAND, as
used by EDWARD III., viz., quarterly, 1, 4, five fleurs-de-lis,
for FRANCE, 2, 3, ENGLAND.   In the field over the forecastle
the initial letter B.

✪ SIGILL' · MAIORITATIS · VILLE · BRISTOLLIE ·:·

Iourn. Brit. Arch. Assoc., vol. xxxi., p. 180.

4689. Red : fine, cut from a charter dated A.D. 1340. [xxxvi. 43.]

4690. Red : fine, cut from a charter. [xxxvi. 222.]

4691. [A.D. 1414.] Red : fine. [Add. ch. 26,469.]

4692. Sulph. cast from fine impression of *obv.* only. [D.C., G. 270.]

With counterseal of JOHN STANLEY, *Mayor.*

4693. [A.D. 1444.] Red : fine. [Add. ch. 26,471.]

Ø. As before, No. 4688.

℞. A small oval signet, $\frac{1}{2} \times \frac{3}{8}$ in., from a ring. On a shield a merchant's mark, betw. the initial letters, I. S.

Cabled border.

4694. [A.D. 1444.] Red : fine, with the counterseal as above. [Add. ch. 26,472.]

With counterseal of WILLIAM CANYNGES, *Mayor.*

4695. [A.D. 1449.] Red : the edge injured. [Harl. ch. 112 D. 40.]

Ø. As before, No. 4688.

℞. A small round signet, $\frac{1}{4}$ in., from a chased ring. A wing ? In the field an indistinct word .. NYN .. Perhaps the·name of the mayor.

Cabled border.

With counterseal of PHILIP MEEDE, *Mayor.*

4696. [A.D. 1459.] Red. [Add. ch. 26,474.]

Ø. As before, No. 4688.

℞. A small round signet, $\frac{3}{8}$ in., from a chased ring. An eagle rising with expanded wings, cf. crest of MEADE, an eagle displayed with two heads. Betw. two indistinct initial letters in black letter.

The Jurats.

4697. [A.D. 1536.] Red : fine, injured. $\frac{3}{4}$ in. [Harl. ch. 76 H. 24.]

A lion passant guardant of· ENGLAND, in the fore paw a sword erect. In the field a crown of three points. Fourteenth century style of work.

✠ S' IVRAT . . . . ISTOLLE.

Admiralty and Maritime Affairs.

4698. [16th cent. ?] Recent impression in red sealing-wax, from a worn leaden matrix ?   2 in.   [xlv. 22.]

A one-masted ship on waves; with mainmast, shrouds, · mainsail set and charged with foliage and devices 'now obliterated, crenellated poop, and prow, on the one a flag charged with a cross, on the other a flag of the ROYAL ARMS OF ENGLAND, coarsely and erroneously engraved.   Field replenished with sprigs of foliage.

4699. Sulph. cast.   [lxiii. 44.]

Mayor of the Staple.

4700. [14th cent.] Sulph. cast from fine impression.   [D.C., E. 713.]

A lion's face, enraged, within a cordon of eight fleurs-de-lis.

✚ · S' · MAIOR : STAPVLE : B'RSTOLL'.

Beaded borders.

Seal "*pro recognitione debitorum,*" see Nos. 1066–1068.

BRUTON, *or* **BREWTON,** *co. Somerset.*

Free Grammar School, A.D. 1520.

4701. Sulph. cast from the matrix, tinted red.   1¼ in. [xxxv. 126.]

A *tun*, with branches of vine and grapes springing therefrom ; forming a *rebus* on the name of the town in conjunction with the legend.

✩ THE ✩ SEALLE ✩ OF ✩ THE ✩ SKOLLE ✩ OF ✩ BREW

Outer border carved.

N. Carlisle, *Endowed Grammar Schools,* vol. ii., p. 412.

4702. Another. [xlvii. 756.]

Laing's *MS. Catal.,* No. 289.

BUCKINGHAM, *co. Buckingham.*

4703. [17th cent.] Sulph. cast from the matrix.   1¾ in. [lix. 78.]

A carved shield of arms : per pale, a swan with wings expanded, ducally gorged and chained, TOWN OF BUCKINGHAM.

☓ SIGIL' : COMVN : BALLI : ET : BVRGENS : DE : BVCK.

Carved border.

S. Lewis, *Topogr. Dict.,* vol. i., p. 265.

BUCKINGHAMSHIRE.

PETER DE SALFORD, *Sheriff.*

4704. [A.D. 1365.] Brown: injured by pressure. ⅜ in.
[Harl. ch. 86 D. 44.]
A stag's head cabossed, with the initial letter B betw.
the attires.

S' VIC' B' ЄT B'.

(*Sigillum Vicecomitis Bedfordie et Buckinghamie.*)

BURFORD, *co. Oxon.*

4705. [13th cent.] Sulph. cast from the matrix. 2 × 1¼ in.
[lxxi. 6.]
Pointed oval : a lion rampant guardant contourné.

+ SIGILL' COMMVNE · BVRGENSIVM · DE · BVREFORD.
Beaded border.

S. Lewis, *Topogr. Dict.*, vol. i., p. 275.

A Counterseal.

4706. Sulph. cast from matrix. ¾ in. [lxxi. 7.]
A lion rampant.

BURY ST. EDMUND'S, *co. Suffolk.*

Free Grammar School.

4707. [16th cent.] Sulph. cast from the matrix. 2⅛ in.
[lxxi. 98.]
Our Lord, three-quarters length, with nimbus of radiant
lines, before a group of the disciples, blessing a child, whose
head only is shown. In base, an ornamentally carved
entablature inscribed :—

· + SINITE + · · · PARVVLOS · · ✿ VENIRE ✿ · AD · · ME · .
—Marc. x. 14.

· SIGIL · CŌE · GVBER · LIBERE · SCHOLÆ · GRAM · REGIS ·
EDWARDI · VI · BVRIÆ.

CASTRUM LEONIS (CAERLEON, CASTELL-LLEON, *or* HOLT), *co. Denbigh.*

Exchequer.

(*Duke of Norfolk, Edward Neville, Edmund Lentall.*)

4708. [A.D. 1450.] Red : fine, but imperfect. About 1¼ in.
when perfect. [Add. ch. 8640.]
Within a finely carved gothic trefoil or trilobe of tracery, a
shield of arms : chequy, WARREN, borne by the HOWARDS,
DUKES OF NORFOLK.

✠ SIGILLU DUC' NORFF EDWARDI NEVYLL' EDMUNDI
LENTALL'.

Carved border.

4709. [A.D. 1450.] Red: fine, chipped and injured. [Add. ch. 8639.]

✠ SIGILLU : . . . . EVYLL' EDMVNDI LENTALL'.

4710. [A.D. 1451.] Red: fine, but fragmentary. [Harl. ch. 58 F. 36.]

. . . . I NEVY . . . .

4711. [A.D. 1456.] Red: injured by pressure. [Add. ch. 8641.]

✪ SIGILLU · D . . . . . . WARDI NEVYLL' EDMUNDI LENTALL'.

4712. [A.D. 1470.] Red: fine, but very imperfect. [Add. ch. 8636.]

. . . . . . ILLU DU . . . . EDMUNDI LENT . . . .

First Seal of Henry VIII.

4713. [A.D. 1520.] Red: fine.   1⅜ in.   [Add. ch. 8647.]

A lion passant, over it an open crown of three fleurs-de-lis. Inner border partly engrailed.   Poor style of art.

+ SIGILLŪ DŇI REGIS S̄C̄II CASTRILEONŪ.

4714. [A.D. 1530.] Red: fine, chipped.   [Add. ch. 8648.]

Second Seal.

4715. [A.D. 1546.] Red: fine, the sides broken off.   2⅜ in. [Add. ch. 8649.]

On a mount, a lion passant.   Over it a jewelled coronet of three crosses pattées, and two fleurs-de-lis.   Inner border partly engrailed.

S' HENR̄ · R · . . . . DŇI · HIB̄ · ET · CASTELL
. . . . V FIL · TAL.

The letters HE in *Henr* are conjoined.

CAERLEON, *co. Monmouth.*

Mayoralty.

4716. [14th–15th cent.] Sulph. cast from imperfect impression.   1¼ in.   [lxvii. 51.]

A triple-towered castle, masoned and embattled, round-headed doorway.   On a field or, background semé-de-lis.

. . . . . . : MAIORITA . . . . E : KAIRLION ✸

Inner border beaded.

CAMBRIDGE, *co. Cambridge.*

First Corporation Seal.

4717. [14th cent.] Sulph. cast from indistinct impression. 1⅝ in. [lx. 5.]

On a bridge of four complete and two incomplete arches, embattled, with the R. Cam flowing in base, a shield of arms : quarterly, 1, 4, FRANCE (MODERN), 2, 3, ENGLAND, supported by two kneeling angels.

Legend on a riband :—

       S' : COMMUNITATIS : VILLE : CANTEBRIGE ⱥ

Second Seal.

4718. [17th cent.] Sulph. cast from the matrix. 2⅛ in. [lx. 6.]

An ornamental shield of arms : on a fess three towers arched, masoned and embattled, in chief a fleur-de-lis betw. two roses, in base a river, thereon three ships, each with one mast and yard, TOWN OF CAMBRIDGE. Crest on a helmet, mantling, and narrow wreath, on a mount a quadrangular castle, with five (for four) domed towers, in front two portals. Supporters two seahorses. In base a riband not inscribed.

   ✠ SIGILLVM · COMMVNITATIS · VILLÆ · CANTABRIGIÆ.

S. Lewis, *Topogr. Dict.*, vol. i., p. 308.

Mayoralty.

4719. [17th cent.] Sulph. cast from the matrix. 1⅝ × 1⅝ in. [lx. 9.]

Oval : a shield of arms : TOWN OF CAMBRIDGE, as before, differently treated.

Legend on a band :—

   ❋ SEAL OF THE MAYORALTY OF THE BOROUGH OF CAMBRIDGE.

Carved border.

Mayor.

4720. [17th cent.] Sulph. cast. 1¼ × 1⅛ in. [lx. 7.]

Oval : a shield of arms, TOWN OF CAMBRIDGE.

Another Seal.

4721. [17th cent.] Sulph. cast. 1¼ × 1 1/16 in. [lx. 8.]

Oval : a shield of arms, TOWN OF CAMBRIDGE, a variant.

CAMBRIDGE UNIVERSITY.

First Seal.

4722. [*c.* A.D. 1261.] Sulph. cast from fine impression, chipped at the edge. 2⅜ × 1↓↓ in. [lx. 10.]

Pointed oval: the Chancellor, seated on a throne or chair, with flat cap and academical gown, holding a book, betw. two scholars, standing, in disputation. All in a niche, with carved church-like canopy above it, on the l. an estoile of six points, on the r. a crescent. In base, over the R. Cam, a bridge with sloping sides, on four carved pointed arches; in the water three fish naiant, two and one.

SIGILLVM [: VNI]VERSITATIS : CANTEBRIGIE .

Proc. Soc. Antiq., 2nd series, vol. x., 1885, pt. III., pp. 226, 229.

Second Seal.

4723. [*c.* A.D. 1410.] Sulph. cast from fine impression. 2¼ × 1⅜ in. [lx. 15.]

Pointed oval: in three carved niches, with canopies pinnacled and crocketed, the Chancellor, seated, with fur-tippet, hood and cap, holding in the l. h. a book, betw. two scholars, standing, in disputation, each with gown and hood. The background of the niches, and field outside, diapered with wavy sprigs of foliage. In base, over the R. Cam, a border of three pointed arches, with masoned walls at the sides, and crenellated parapet; in the water two fish naiant in fess.

SIGILLUM ❃ VNIUERSITATIS ❃ CANTEBRIGGIE .

Proc. Soc. Antiq., 2nd series, vol. x., 1885, pt. III., pp. 227, 229.

Third Seal, A.D. 1580.

4724. Sulph. cast from the silver matrix. 3¾ × 2¼ in. [lx. 13.]

Pointed oval: the Chancellor, seated on a canopied chair, with shell-shaped back and fluted pilasters of the style of the Renaissance, wearing gown, fur-tippet, and hood, betw. two masters-of-arts, wearing gown and hood, the one on the l. carrying a chained book of the Statutes of the University, the other an open book. These are probably the proctors. Over the chair the trilingual name of the Almighty :—יְהֹוָה ΘΕΟΣ · DEVS, in three lines, surrounded by a radiant glory. At each side of this, a shield of the ROYAL ARMS OF ENGLAND as used by QU. *ELIZABETH.* In base, a shield of arms: on a cross ermine, cantoned with four lions of

*E*NGLAND, a book clasped and garnished, UNIVERSITY OF CAMBRIDGE. The shield is placed betw. branches of flowers and foliage, and the date 15–80. Over the shield on a riband, the inscription :—

☆ MARS ☆ MVSAS ☆

☀ SIGILLVM ☀ CŌE ☀ CANCELLARII ☀ M͠RŌR̃ ☀ ET ☀ SCHOLARIV̄ ☀ VNIVERSITAT̄ ☀ CANTEBRIGIE.

Proc. Soc Antiq., 2nd series, vol. x., 1885 ; pt. III., p. 227. Where the back of the matrix is said to bear the following inscription :

GVLIELMVS ☆ FARRAND ☆ PROCVRATOR ☆ DEDIT ☆ MATERIAM .
MATTHÆVS ☆ STOKIS ⚹ BEDELLVS ☆ DEDIT ☆ FORMAM ☆ 1580 ☆

4725. [A.D. 1630.] Light brown : fine fragments. [Add. ch. 5523.]

. . . . VERSITAT ☆ CANTEB . . . .

4726. [A.D. 1661.] Red : fine fragments. [Add. ch. 6035.]

. . . . VNIVERSITAT ☆ CANTEBR . . . .

4727. [A.D. 1670.] Red : injured by pressure ; app. by pink and green silk ribands. [Add. MS. 8129 B.]

Chancellor.

4728. [13th cent.] Sulph. cast from fine impression, the edge chipped. 2 × 1¼ in. [lx. 12.]
Pointed oval': bust of the Chancellor, to the r., wearing a flat cap, betw. two flowering branches, on a masoned bridge of four carved pointed arches, over the R. Cam. In the water two fishes embowed and addorsed. All within an elegantly carved and pointed double quatrefoil.

☆ S' CANCELLARII VNIVERSITATIS CANTEBRIGIE

Proc. Soc. Antiq., 2nd series, vol. x., pt. III., p. 228.

4729. [A.D. 1316.] Dark-green : originally fine, now fragmentary. [Harl. ch. 111 C. 25.]

. . . . VNIVERSIT . . . .

Official Seal of the Chancellor, A.D. 1580.

4730. Sulph. cast from fine impression, chipped at the edge. 2¾ × 1⅞ in. [lx. 14.]
Pointed oval : the Chancellor, with gown, fur-tippet with hanging tails, and flat square cap, holding a book ; in a carved pulpit on a reeded corbel, betw. two branches of laurel. From his mouth a label issues, inscribed :— ☆ ☆ DOMINVS ☆ PROPE . EST ☆ ☆ —*Philipp*. iv. 5. Over head a crowned shield

of the ROYAL ARMS OF ENGLAND as used by QU.
ELIZABETH. In base, a carved shield of arms: UNIVERSITY
OF CAMBRIDGE, betw. the date 15–80.

✠ SIGILLVM ✿ OFFICII ✿ CANCELLARII ✿ ALMÆ ✿
VNIVERSITATIS ✿ CANTEBRIGIE ✿

Proc. Soc. Antiq., 2nd series, vol. x., pt. III., p. 228, where the back
of the matrix is said to bear the following inscription

: EX : DONO ⁖ D : EDW : LEEDYS : IVRIS ⁖ CIVILIS :
DOCTORIS :

and in the centre, M. S. for Matthew Stokis, Bedell, see No. 4724.

Official Seal of the Vice-Chancellor, A.D. 1580.

4731. Sulph. cast from the gold signet ring. 1 × ¾ in.
[lix. 11.]
Oval: a carved shield of arms: UNIVERSITY OF CAM-
BRIDGE, see No. 4724.

Proc. Soc. Antiq., 2nd series, vol. x., pt. III., p. 229, where the ring is
said to bear inside the initials of Matthew Stokis, Bedell, see No.
4724.

Michael-House,
or House of the Scholars of St. Michael, A.D. 1324;
afterwards incorporated into Trinity College, A.D. 1546.

4732. Sulph. cast from fine impression, edge chipped.
1⅜ in. [lx. 51.]
St. Michael the Archangel, with expanded wings, in the
l. h. a shield of early form charged with a cross, trampling
on the dragon, and piercing his head with a long cross held
in the r. h.

✿ S' : MAG̅RI ET : SCOLARIV̅ · DOM' : SC̅I : MICH'IS : CANTEBR'.

Proc. Soc. Antiq., 2nd series, vol. x., pt. III., p. 232.

King's Hall, A.D. 1337;
afterwards incorporated into Trinity College, A.D. 1546.

4733. Sulph. cast from fine impression, chipped at the
edge. 2¼ in. [lx. 32.]
On a low carved pedestal in a carved and canopied gothic
niche with open sides, K. Edward III., founder, seated with
crown, holding in the l. h. a model of a church, with the r. h.
presenting foundation-charter to the Master, kneeling on
the l., outside the pale of the niche. In base, under five

carved arches of a pent-house, three three-quarter-length, and two half-length suppliants with upraised hands. On each side, on a mount, an oak-tree, on which is suspended a shield of arms : l., ENGLAND ; r., quarterly 1, 4, FRANCE (ANCIENT), 2, 3, ENGLAND, for Edward III.

: SIGILLŪ : COMUNE : CUSTODIS ET SCOLA[RI]UM AULE :
REGIS : CANTEBRIGGIE ⚜ ⚜ ⚜

Proc. Soc. Antiq., 2nd series, vol. x., pt. III., p. 232.

Clare Hall,
now Clare College, A.D. 1326.*
First Seal.

4734. Sulph. cast from the silver matrix. 2½ × 1⅜ in. [lx. 18.]
Pointed oval : in a carved gothic niche, with triple canopy, the Lady Elizabeth [de Burgh], sister and co-heir of Gilbert, Earl of Clare, foundress, standing, turned to the l., a book of Statutes in the l. h., and with the r. h. presenting the charter of foundation to a body of nine kneeling representatives of the foundation and scholars. Background of the niche replenished with large roses. Overhead, in three small canopied niches, three-quarter-length effigies of the Virgin and Child betw. St. John Baptist with the Agnus Dei on the l., and St. John the Evangelist ? with an eagle and a palm branch on the r. On the tabernacle work at each side of the principal niche a shield of arms : l., ENGLAND ; r., quarterly, CASTILE and LEON, for K. EDWARD I., and QU. ELEANOR of CASTILE, maternal grandparents of the foundress. In base, betw. two slipped flowers a shield of arms : per pale, *dex.*, three chevrons, CLARE, *sin.*, a cross, BURGH, within a bordure [guttée ?], CLARE COLLEGE. For remarks on this bordure, which has been conjectured to be guttée, but is very indistinct, and at one part seems to bear a castle, rather than a goutte, see *Proc. Soc. Antiq. l. c.*, p. 233.

· · AULA · CLARE · PIA · REGE · SEMPER · VIRGO · MARIA.

Proc. Soc. Antiq., 2nd series, vol. x., pt. III., p. 233.

Second Seal.

4735. [18th cent.] Sulph. cast from the silver matrix. 2¹³⁄₁₆ × 2⅛ in. [lx. 19.]
· Oval : a copy, badly proportioned, of the preceding seal, No. 4734.
Beaded border.

Proc. Soc. Antiq., 2nd series, vol. x., pt. III., p. 234.

* Or A.D. 1333–9, *Proc. Soc. Antiq. l. c.*

Master, A.D. 1742.

4736. Sulph. cast from the matrix. $1\frac{9}{16} \times 1$ in. [lx. 20.]
Oval: an elegantly carved shield of arms, CLARE COLLEGE,
see No. 4734.

Pembroke, or Valence-Mary Hall,
now College, A.D. 1347.
First Seal.

4737. Sulph. cast from the matrix. $2\frac{1}{4} \times 1\frac{1}{2}$ in. [lx.
35.]
Pointed oval: on a mount replenished with flowers, Aymer
de Valence, Earl of Pembroke, on the l., and Mary de St. Paul,
his Countess, on the r., standing side by side, each one holding
up the interior hand to a church or college-building overhead,
on the roof of which is a seated figure of Our Lord with
cruciform nimbus lifting up the hands in benediction betw.
two cinquefoils in the field. On each side of the mount a
forked tree, on which is slung by the strap a shield of arms:
l., eight barrulets (for barry of ten), an orle of nine martlets,
VALENCE ; r., per pale, *dex.*, VALENCE (as in the other shield),
sin., three pales vair, on a chief a label of three points, each
dimidiated, ST. PAUL, PEMBROKE COLLEGE. Background
faintly hatched.

    ❖ S'. CVSTODIS : ET : SCOLARIV̄ : DOMVS : DE : VALENCE :
        MARIE : IN : CANTEBRIG'.

Proc. Soc. Antiq., 2nd series, vol. x., pt. III., p. 234.

Secretum or Privy Seal, A.D. 1347.

4738. Sulph. cast from fine impression, edge chipped.
1 in. [lx. 38.]
The Trinity, in a finely traced gothic panel.

    SECRETV̄ · AVLE · VALENCE · MARIE · CANTABRIḠ.

Proc. Soc. Antiq., 2nd series, vol. x., pt. III., p. 235.

Seal of Arms, A.D. 1649.

4739. Sulph. cast from the silver matrix. $1\frac{7}{8} \times 1$ in. [lx.
37.]
Oval: a shield of arms, PEMBROKE COLLEGE, see No. 4737.

    SIGILL : AVLÆ PEMBROCHIÆ CANTABRIGIÆ.

Inner border beaded, outer border carved.

Proc. Soc. Antiq., 2nd series, vol. x., pt. III., p. 235.

Later Seal of Arms, A.D. 1844.

4740. Sulph. cast from the steel matrix. $1\frac{1}{8} \times \frac{7}{8}$. [lx. 36.]

Oval : a shield of arms, PEMBROKE COLLEGE, see No. 4737, suspended by a strap from a tree.

Proc. Soc. Antiq., 2nd series, vol. x., pt. III., p. 235.

Gonville Hall,
or Hall of the Annunciation of the Virgin Mary,
A.D. 1348 ; afterwards refounded as Gonville and
Caius College, A.D. 1558.

4741. Sulph. cast from fine impression, chipped at the edges. $2\frac{1}{3} \times 1\frac{3}{8}$ in. [lx. 52.]

Pointed oval : the Annunciation of the Virgin in a carved niche, with elegantly carved triple arched canopy pinnacled and crocketed. In base, a bishop, (for William Bateman, Bishop of Norwich, A.D. 1344–1354, who established the College for the founder, Edmund de Gonville, rector of Terrington and Rushworth) with mitre and pastoral staff, kneeling in adoration to the r., betw. six other kneeling personages.

S' C̄OE . AVLE . ĀN̄VCIACŌIS : B̄Ē : MARIE . CANTEBRI . . .

Proc. Soc. Antiq., 2nd series, vol. x., pt. III., p. 237.

Gonville and Caius College, A.D. 1558.

4742. Sulph. cast from the silver matrix. $2\frac{7}{8} \times 1\frac{1}{4}$ in. [lx. 16.]

Pointed oval : the Annunciation of the Virgin, under an elegantly carved arch of the Italian style, supported on slender shafts. In base an oval shield with carved work, and having indistinct charges ; between the letter B on the l. and a mitre on the r., for William Bateman, Bishop of Norwich, A.D. 1344–1354. See No. 4741.

SIGILL' COLLEG . DE . GONEVIL ET CAIVS . FVND . T̂ . HO .

AN . B . MA . VIR . T̂ . VN̄ITE C̄ATA [B.]

Proc. Soc. Antiq., 2nd series, vol. x., pt. III., p. 250.

Trinity Hall,
or Hall of the Holy Trinity of Norwich, A.D. 1350.
First Seal.

4743. Sulph. cast from the silver matrix. $2\frac{1}{4}$ in. [lx. 43.]

The Trinity in a heavily canopied niche. At each side a

D 2

wavy branch or sprig enclosing ten small heads, full-face, to represent the host of heaven. In base, a small shield of arms : a crescent ermine within a bordure engrailed, WILLIAM BATEMAN, Bishop of Norwich, A.D. 1344–1354, founder ; the arms are borne by TRINITY HALL.

> ✠ S' COLLEGII : SCOLARIŪ : AULE : SCĒ : TRINITATIS : DE : NORWICO : IN : VNIUERSITATE . CANTEBR :

Proc. Soc. Antiq., 2nd series, vol. x., pt. III., p. 237.

4744. [18th cent.] Sulph. cast from a matrix. $\frac{9}{16}$ in. [lx. 46.]
A shield of arms, TRINITY HALL, (*Sa.* field).

> TRIN : AVL : CANT ;

Master, A.D. 1350.

4745. Sulph. cast from the silver matrix. $1\frac{3}{4} \times \frac{7}{8}$ in. [lx. 44.]
Pointed oval : the Trinity in a canopied niche with tabernacle work at the sides. In base a shield of arms, TRINITY HALL, see No. 4743.

> SIGILLŪ CUSTODIS COLLEGII SCĒ TRINITAT' CANTEBRIG'.

Cabled borders.

Proc. Soc. Antiq., 2nd series, vol. x., pt. III., p. 238.

STEPHEN GARDINER, *Master.*   A.D. 1525–1549, 1553–1555.
(Bishop of Winchester, A.D. 1531–1550, 1553–1555.)

4746. Sulph. cast from the brass matrix. $\frac{7}{8}$ in. [lx. 45.]
A shield of arms : TRINITY HALL, see No. 4743.

> SIGILLUM ⚜ STEPHANI ⚜ MAKSAY ⚜

Proc. Soc. Antiq., 2nd series, vol. x., pt. III., p. 238, where the name at the end of the legend is read, M.A.TR.CAN. (*i.e.*, Magister Aulæ Trinitatis Cantebrigie).

HENRY HERVYE, *or* HARVEY, *LL.D., Master.*

4747. [A.D. 1580.] Light-brown : fine. $\frac{11}{16}$ in. [Add. ch. 15,009.]
The monogram Hҍ, for H. H., initials of the master. In the field the motto :—☆ OS · MENS · MANVS.
Beaded border.

Corpus Christi College, A.D. 1352.

4748. [Late 14th cent.] Sulph. cast from the matrix. $2\frac{3}{4} \times 1\frac{1}{4}$ in. [D.C., F. 62.]

· Pointed oval : in a carved niche, with canopy pinnacled and crocketed, the Coronation of the Virgin. Below this the shields of arms : l., the ARMS OF THE TRINITY ; r., the symbols of the Passion, for JESUS CHRIST. In base, two figures representing the two gilds which founded the College, holding up a model church, betw. three half-length worshippers.

S' · CŌE · DOMUS · CORPORIS · XPI · ᴢ · BĒ · MARIE · CANTEBRIGGIE.

4749. Another. [lx. 21.]

4750. Recent impression in red sealing-wax from the matrix. [xxxv. 62.]

4751. [A.D. 1567.] Red : app. by a plaited cord, green and white, and enclosed in a tin-box. [Add. ch. 26,723.]

4752. Light-brown : fine, but imperfect at the edge. [xl. 9.]

∅. As before, No. 4748.

℞. A small round counterseal, from a signet-ring. ⅝ in. A shield of arms : quarterly, 1, 4, a pelican in her piety, 2, 3, three lilies, slipped, two and one, CORPUS CHRISTI COLLEGE.

Proc. Soc. Antiq., 2nd series, vol. x., pt. III., p. 239.

God's House, A.D. 1442.

4753. Sulph. cast from imperfect impression. 1¾ in. [lx. 47.]

The field divided by a horizontal line ; in the upper part the Ascension of our Lord, in the lower part the Nativity.

SIGILLUM ⚜ [COMMUNE ⚜ COLLEGII ⚜ DE ⚜] GODES · HOUS ⚜ [CANTEBRIGI]E ⚜

Proc. Soc. Antiq., 2nd series, vol. x., pt. III., p. 239.

Seal ad Causas.

See Monastic Seals, No. 2826.

King's College, A.D. 1441.

Second state [A.D. 1449] *of the seal of the Refoundation,* A.D. 1443.

4754. [15th cent.] Sulph. cast from the silver matrix. 2⅞ in. [D.C., G. 31.]

The Assumption of the Virgin, in a vesica of clouds, upheld by the Almighty and four angels at the top, and two angels below ; in a heavily canopied niche. On each side, in a smaller niche similarly canopied, on the l., on a pedestal, a bishop, St. Nicholas, full-length with mitre, lifting up the r. h. in benediction, in the l. h. a pastoral staff curved outwards : on the r., on a pedestal, Henry VI. with crown, hands elevated in prayer.   Outside these, on each side a small pent-house, in which is an angel or shield-bearer, holding in front a shield of arms : l., FRANCE (MODERN), for Henry VI. as King de'facto, r., quarterly, 1, 4, FRANCE (MODERN), 2, 3, ENGLAND, for Henry VI.   In base, under a depressed arch, with carved and arcaded corbel table behind and at the sides, a shield of arms : three roses, two and one, on a chief per pale a fleur-de-lis on the dex., and a lion passant guardant on the sin., KING'S COLLEGE.

SIGILLŪ : CŌE PREPOSITI · ᷦ · SCOLARIUM : COLLEGII : REGALIS ḆE MARIE ᷦ SC̄I NICHOLAI DE CANTEBR̄

4755. Another. [lx. 31.]

4756. Yellow or uncoloured : fine but imperfect. [xxxv. 25.]

. . . . . RIUM : CO . . . . LIS ḆE MARIE ᷦ SC̄I NICHO . . . . . .

Proc. Soc. Antiq., 2nd series, vol. x., pt. III., pp. 240, 241 ; where a notice is given of the shield of arms found in the first state of this seal.

JAMES FLETEWOOD, S.T.P., Provost.

4757. [A.D. 1664.]   Red : injured by pressure. $\frac{7}{8}$ in. [Harl. ch. 111 G. 16.]

A shield of arms, KING'S COLLEGE, as in No. 4754. Above it the date 1588.

Cabled border. _____

Queens' College,
of SS. Margaret and Bernard, A.D. 1448.

4758. Sulph. cast from fine, but chipped impression. $2\frac{3}{8}$ in. [lx. 39.]

In two canopied niches, full-length figures of St. Margaret holding a book and trampling on a Dragon, whose head she is piercing with a long cross, on the l. ; and St. Bernard with pastoral staff and book on the r.   At each side a small open pent-house, on a bracket, containing a kneeling angel.   In base, betw. the President, kneeling in adoration on the r. and four kneeling fellows of the College on the l., a shield of arms of six quarterings : 1, Barry of eight (for six), HUNGARY ; 2, semé-de-lis, a label of three points, NAPLES ; 3, a cross potent betw. four crosses crosslet or potent, JERUSALEM ; 4, semé-de-lis, within a bordure, ANJOU ; 5, Crusily fitchy, two barrs or barbel fishes addorsed, BAR ; 6, on a bend three eaglets, LORRAINE.   MARGARET OF ANJOU, (for QUEENS' COLLEGE.)

SIGILLŪ CŌE P̄SIDENT' ꝛ SOCIOꝜ : COLLEGII REGINALIS SC̄E MARGARETE ꝛ SC̄I BERNAR[DI DE CANTEBRIG'.]

Proc. Soc. Antiq., 2nd series, vol. x., pt. III., p. 242.

Later Seal, A.D. 1675.

4759. Sulph. cast. $2\frac{3}{4} \times 2$ in. [D.C., H. 59.]

Pointed oval: Qu. Margaret, wife of K. Henry VI., first foundress, or Qu. Elizabeth, wife of K. Edward IV., second foundress, standing on a bracket, with crown, turned to the l., in her r. h. a sceptre, in the l. h. an orb.

✿ SIGILLVM · ⁝ · COLLEGII · ⁝ · REGINALIS · ⁝ · CANTABRIG · ⁝ · 1675.

Carved border.

4760. Another. [lx. 41.]

4761. Cast in lead. [Slo. xxxiv. 70.]

Proc. Soc. Antiq., 2nd series, vol. x., pt. III., p. 244.

Seal of Arms, A.D. 1575.

4762. Sulph. cast from the matrix. $1 \times \frac{7}{8}$ in. [lx. 40.]

Oval: a shield of arms, MARGARET OF ANJOU, see No. 4758, within a bordure, QUEENS' COLLEGE, granted by Rob. Cooke, A.D. 1575. Above the shield the initial letters, Q. C.

Beaded border.

Proc. Soc. Antiq., 2nd series, vol. x., pt. III., p. 244.

St. Catharine's Hall or College, A.D. 1473.

4763. Sulph. cast from the silver matrix. $2\frac{1}{10} \times 1\frac{1}{4}$ in. [lx. 29.]

Pointed oval: St. Catharine standing in a canopied niche, with tabernacle work at the sides, and carved bracket in base, with crown, in the r. h. a sword, in the l. h. a Catharine wheel.

SIGILL' CŌIE ✥ COLLEGIJ SIUE AULE SC̄E KATERINE VIRḠIS ✥ DE CĀTEBREGIA.

Cabled borders.

Proc. Soc. Antiq., 2nd series, vol. x., pt. III., p. 244.

Master's Seal.

4764. Sulph. cast from the silver matrix. $1 \times \frac{7}{8}$ in. [lx. 30.]

Oval: a shield of arms: gu. a Catharine wheel, ST. CATHA-
RINE'S COLLEGE OR HALL.

Cabled border.

Proc. Soc. Antiq., 2nd series, vol. x., pt. III., p. 244.

Jesus College, A.D. 1496.
From the Benedictine Priory of St. Radegund.
Priory Seal.

4765. [12th cent.] Sulph. cast from a fine impression.
$2\frac{3}{8} \times 1\frac{3}{4}$ in. [lx. 48.]

Pointed oval: St. Radegund, standing, head turned to the
r., with staff, wallet and book. Archaic style.

⚜ SIGILLVM SAИCTE RADEGVNDIS.

Another.

4766. Sulph. cast from fine impression. $2\frac{3}{8} \times 1\frac{3}{4}$ in.
[lx. 49.]

This very closely resembles the previous seal, No. 4765, but
is not from the same matrix.

Common Seal, A.D. 1496.

4767. Sulph. cast from the silver matrix. $2\frac{3}{8} \times 1\frac{3}{4}$ in.
[lx. 23.]

Pointed oval: in three heavily canopied niches, Our Lord,
standing on a pedestal, with cruciform nimbus, lifting up the
r. h. in benediction, in the l. h. an orb topped with a long
cross, betw. the Virgin, with crown and nimbus, hands in
prayer, on the l.; and St. John the Evangelist, with nimbus,
in the r. h. a chalice, in the l. h. a palm-branch, on the r. In
base, under an arch with sides of masonry, an angel supporting in front a shield of arms: the five wounds of Our Lord,
viz., a human heart betw. two hands and two feet in saltire,
gouttée de sang, for JESUS CHRIST.

· SIGILLUM : COLLEGIJ : IH̅U : MARIE : ET : JOH̅IS : EV̅A̅G' :
CANTEBR'.

Proc. Soc. Antiq., 2nd series, vol. x., pt. III., p. 245.

Seal ad Causas, A.D. 1586.

4768. Sulph. cast from the silver matrix. $2\frac{1}{4} \times 1\frac{3}{4}$ in.
[lx. 24.]

Oval: a shield of arms: a fess betw. three cock's heads
erased, all within a bordure charged with ten crowns, for John

ALCOCK,.Bishop of Ely, and JESUS COLLEGE. Above in radiant clouds the Hebrew inscription יְגֻן‬ probably intended for יְהֹוָה‬ In base, on a carved ante-fixal ornament or tablet, the date 1586.

✠ SIGILLVM · COLLEGII ✸ IHESV · CANTABRIG ✸ QVO ✸ AD ✸ CAVSAS ᴀ

Proc. Soc. Antiq., 2nd series, vol. x., pt. III., p. 245.

Master.

4769. [17th cent.] Sulph. cast from the silver matrix. 1 × ⅞ in. [lx. 25.]

Oval : a carved shield of arms, JESUS COLLEGE, see No. 4768. (Eight crowns only.)

Christ's College, A.D. 1505.
Master.

4770. Sulph. cast from the silver matrix. 1⅜ in. [lx. 17.]

An heraldic antelope lodged, on a mount. The field replenished with the royal badges, the rose and portcullis, for MARGARET BEAUFORT, Countess of Richmond and Derby, mother of K. Henry VII., and foundress.

+ SIGILLŪ + CUSTODIS + COLLEGIJ + CRISTI + CANTIBRIGIE

Proc. Soc. Antiq., 2nd series, vol. x., pt. III., p. 246. Cf. the seal of Countess Margaret in Sandford, *Geneal. Hist.*, p. 246.

St. John's College, A.D. 1511.

4771. Sulph. cast from fine but imperfect impression. 2¼ in. [lx. 26.]

St. John the Evangelist, seated to the l., in a canopied chair writing his gospel on a desk, over which hangs a roll. In the field, on the l. an eagle with nimbus, rising with expanded wings, and a quatrefoil flower, slipped and leaved ; on the r. a portcullis, ringed and chained, an heraldic antelope, (see No. 4773), and a marguerite-flower.

✸ ✸ : COLLEGY · ✸ A · IOHAN[I]⅗ EV]ANGELI⅗TE [· z · MA]RGARETAM · [RICH]EMOT ⅗

Proc. Soc. Antiq., 2nd series, vol. x. pt. III., pp. 246, 247.

4772. [A.D. 1568.] Light-brown or uncoloured : very imperfect and indistinct. [Harl. ch. 79 A. 33.]

. . . . . . z . MAR . . . .

4773. [A.D. 1649.]   Light brownish-red : fine, very imper-. fect and indistinct.   [Add. ch. 15,685.]

This impression shews the portcullis and antelope, wanting in the previous seal, No. 4772.

     . . . . HANIS · EV[ANG]ELISTE · ᙆ · MA . . ,

Another Seal ?

4774. Sulph. cast from imperfect impression.   About $2\frac{1}{2}$ × $1\frac{1}{4}$ in. when perfect.   [lx. 27.]

Pointed oval : an eagle of St. John the Evangelist, rising reguardant with expanded wings, in a carved border or frame.

ᙏ IN : ᙏ PRINCIPIO : ᙏ ERAT : ᙏ [VERB]UM : ᙏ —Joh. i. 1.

Signet, or Master's Seal.

4775. [16th cent.] Sulph. cast from the silver matrix. $\frac{13}{16}$ × $\frac{13}{16}$ in.   [lx. 28.]

Oval : a portcullis, ringed and chained, surmounted by a crown.

Proc. Soc. Antiq., 2nd series, vol. x., pt. III., p. 247.

Magdalene College, A.D. 1519.

4776. [17th cent.] Sulph. cast from the silver matrix. $1\frac{1}{4}$ × $1\frac{1}{4}$ in.   [lx. 33.]

Oval : a carved shield of arms : quarterly per pale indented, on a bend betw. two eagles displayed a fret betw. two martlets, for THOMAS AUDLEY, (afterwards 1st Baron Audley), founder, and MAGDALENE COLLEGE.   On a label above the shield the motto :—GARDE · TA · FOY.

Proc. Soc. Antiq., 2nd series, vol. x., part III., p. 248.

Another.

4777. [18th cent.] Sulph. cast from the silver matrix. $1\frac{1}{8}$ in.   [lx. 34.]

A carved shield of arms, as in No. 4776, wreathed and garlanded.   In the carving over the shield a cherub's head. In the field above, the motto as in No. 4776.

Proc. Soc. Antiq., 2nd series, vol. x., pt. III., p. 248.

Trinity College, A.D. 1546.

4778. Light-brown, uncoloured : fine, but imperfect. $3\frac{3}{16}$ in. when perfect.   [xl. 11.]   . . . . .   .

∅. The Baptism of Our Lord ; a dove with nimbus and expanded wings descending from rays of light in the upper part. Over the dove, on a scroll, the inscription :—

[HIC EST FILIVS] MEVS DELECT' [I IPSVM AVDITE.]

✠ SIIGILLVM : COLLEGII : TRINITATIS : CANTABRIGIAE : FVNDATORE : HENRICO : OCTAVO.]

℞. K. Henry VIII., seated, with royal robes, sceptre, orb, and crown ; in a niche of debased style, with round-headed canopy and carved scroll-work at the sides. [Field diapered with a rose in each space, in two of which, one on each side of the king, the initial letters R. H. are substituted for the roses.]

: SE[RVIRE : ✶ : DEO : ✶ : REGNARE : ✶ : EST : ✶ : FAC]TVM : ✶ : [ANNO : ✶ : GRACIE : ✶ : 1546 : HENRICI : 8 : 3]8.

This *rev.* and legend has much in common with *rev.* of the seal of Christ Church, Oxford, made in the same year. See No. 2139.

Proc. Soc. Antiq., 2nd series, vol. x., pt. III., p. 249, where the copper-gilt matrix is described. The engraver has erroneously substituted the words "ipsum audite," from the passage relating to the Transfiguration, for the words "quo mihi complacui," of the Baptism.

Emmanuel College, A.D. 1584.

Master.

4779. Sulph. cast from the silver matrix. 1 × ⅞ in. [lx. 22.]

Oval : on a wreath, a lion rampant, (crest of SIR WALTER MILDMAY, Kt., founder,) holding a chaplet, out of the mouth a scroll inscribed :—EMMANOYHΛ. This is the bearing of the shield of arms of EMMANUEL COLLEGE.

Proc. Soc. Antiq., 2nd series., vol. x., pt. III., p. 250.

Sidney Sussex College, A.D. 1598.

Master.

4780. Sulph. cast from the silver matrix. 1 in. [lx. 42.]

A lozenge-shaped shield of arms : quarterly of eight pieces, for LADY FRANCES SYDNEY, widow of Thomas Ratcliffe, 3rd Earl of Sussex, *ob.* A.D. 1569. Ensigned with a coronet of five pearls. In the field around, the motto :—

DE · CALVMNIEZ · DIEV · ME · GARDE.

Proc. Soc. Antiq., 2nd series, vol. x., pt. III., p. 251.

CAMELFORD, *co. Cornwall.*

4781. [17th cent.]   Sulph. cast from the matrix.   1¼ in. [lxi. 7.]

A *camel* passing a *ford*, to the l., forming a *rebus* on the name of the town.

⚹ SIGILLVM ⚹ VILL : DE ⚹ CAMILLFORD.

S. Lewis, *Topogr. Dict.*, vol. i., p. 333.

CANTERBURY, *co. Kent.*
First Corporation Seal, A.D. 1318.

4782. [A.D. 1357.]   Red: fine.   3¼ in.   [Cott. ch. xxi. 10.]

Ø. An elaborately designed castle, with three embattled towers, each of two stories, with windows, masoned walls, and inclined causeway. In base, a shield of arms of ENGLAND ; within a finely carved and cusped gothic rosette of eight points, with a lion of ENGLAND in each spandril. Field diapered lozengy, with a small quatrefoil in each space, and with five cinquefoils, one in each of the five uppermost cusps.

⁑ ⁑ ⁑ ISTVD ⁑ EST ⁑ SIGILLVM ⁑ COMMVNE ⁑ CIVIVM ⁑ CIVITATIS ⁑ CANTVARIE.

℞. A section of the Cathedral, elegantly carved, showing in a large central niche, with ogee-arch, Becket's martyrdom. In a smaller niche on each side, a king, with crown and sceptre. In base, under a carved gothic arcade, the middle arch of ogee shape, Our Lord, half-length, lifting up the r. h. in benediction, in the l. h. an orb. Field hatched ; over the roof, on the l. a crescent, on the r. a cinquefoil.

Legend in two rhyming hexameter verses :—

ICTIBVS : INMEИS : THOMAS : QVI : CORRVIT : EИS : TVTOR : AB : OFFENS : VRBIS : SIT : CANTVRIENS.

Beaded border.

Legend on the rim of the seal, in two rhyming hexameter verses :—

⁕ ANNO : MILLENO : XP̄I : DECAS : OCTO : TRICENO : REGIS : Ƶ · VNDENO : FIT · HOC · EDWARDI · S . . MEN[O]

S. Lewis, *Topogr. Dict.*, vol. i., p. 340, engraves the *obv.*, and the new *rev.* adapted from the above *rev.* by substituting a shield of arms of the City in the place of the Martyrdom, and removing the legend, which is replaced by a coarsely carved border. ·   .

Seal of arms.

4783. [15th cent.] Sulph. cast from the ivory matrix. 1⅜ in. [lxv. 8.]

. A shield of arms : three Cornish choughs, on a chief a lion passant guardant, CITY OF CANTERBURY. Foliage above, and at the sides of the shield.

✠ CIVITAS CANTVAR.

Inner border cabled.

Mayor.

4784. [14th cent.] Sulph. cast from the silver matrix. 1 11/16 in. [D.C., F. 627.]

A triple-towered castle, masoned and embattled, at each side a small tower. Within a trefoil, with a lion of ENGLAND in each spandril.

✠ SIGILLVM : MAIORIS : CIVITATIS : CANTVARIE.

The word *Maioris* has been engraved in the matrix over the word *Ballivorum*, erased.

Signet.

4785. [17th-18th cent.] Sulph. cast from the matrix. 1 3/16 in. [lxv. 9.]

A shield of arms, CITY OF CANTERBURY, see No. 4783.

SIGILL' · MAIOR · CIVIT · CANT'

The new silver matrix, made in 1832, superseded this signet, which it closely resembles.

Chamberlain.

4786. [17th-18th cent.] Sulph. cast from the silver matrix. 1 3/8 in. [lxv. 10.]

A shield of arms, CITY OF CANTERBURY, see No. 4783.

SIGILL' · CAMBR' · CIVIT · CANT.

St. Augustine's Lathe and the Eastern Division.

4787. [18th-19th cent.] Sulph. cast from the matrix. ⅞ × ¾ in. [lxv. 11.]

·Oval : on an estrade, St. Augustine standing, with mitre and cloak, to the l., lifting up the r. h. in benediction, in the l. h. a pastoral staff.

ST AVSTINS LTH & EASTRN DIVISN.

Seal "pro recognitione debitorum," see No. 1069.

CARDIFF, *co. Glamorgan.*

Chancery.

(*Seal of* HENRY VII. *as Lord of Glamorgan and Morgan.*)

4788. [A.D. 1503.] Light-brown: fine, but imperfect. About 3¼ in. when perfect. [Harl. ch. 75 E. 19.]

Ø. On a rocky mount replenished with herbage, the King, armed *cap-à-pie*, with a shield of arms slung over the r. shoulder, riding to the r. on a caparisoned horse with a plume of three ostrich feathers on its head. The armorial bearings of the shield and caparisons are: quarterly, 1, 4, FRANCE (MODERN), 2, 3, *E*NGLAND. Background replenished with sprigs of foliage and flowers. Compare *rev.* of the great seals of Edward IV., Edward V., Richard III., and Henry VII., Nos. 300–324.

SIGI . . . . [RE]GIS : HENRICI . . . . . . [HIB]ERNIE [D]OMIN[I] DE] GLAMOR[GAN] . . . [M]ORGA[N] . . . .

R. A shield of the ROYAL ARMS OF *E*NGLAND, as in the *obv.*, betw. three sprigs of foliage, encircled with a garter inscribed with the motto of the order. Crest, on a helmet and ornamental mantling of foliage, on a chapeau a lion statant guardant, *E*NGLAND.

SIG[ILL' C]ANCELLARI . . . .
. . . . NOK.

4789. Creamy-white: cracked and imperfect. [xxxvi. 8.]

4790. Sulph. cast of the *rev.* only of the preceding seal, No. 4788. [D.C., A. 111*.]

Corporation.

4791. [14th cent.] Red: 1¼ in. [xxxvi. 44.]

On a pyramidal mount, or cairn of stones, two lions rampant combatant, supporting aloft a shield of arms: three chevrons, TOWN OF CARDIFF.

Legend in ornamental letters :—

S' COMVNE DE KERDIF.
Beaded borders.

Cf. Add. MS. 6,331, f. 15.

CARLISLE, *co. Cumberland.*

4792. [13th cent.] Sulph. cast from the matrix. 3 in. [lxi. 31, 32.]

Ø. The Virgin, with nimbus and crown, seated on a throne, in the r. h. an ornamental fleur-de-lis, and supporting with the l. h. on her knee the Child, with cruciform nimbus, lifting up the r. h. in benediction, in the l. h. a book.

Legend in two concentric circles within beaded annuli.

Inner circle :—AVE MARIA : GRACIA PLENA.

Outer circle :—✠ S' · COMMVNIS : CIVIVM : KARLIOLENSIS·

℞. A cross, slightly pattée, charged with a six-foil rose at the crossing of the arms, and cantoned with four similar roses.

✠ S' COMMVNIS : CIVIVM : KARLIOLENSIS ♣

- Beaded borders.

4793. [A.D. 1415.] White : fine, very imperfect ; r. h. side wanting. [Harl. ch. 83 D. 20.]

Ø.   . AVE MARIA : GR . . . . , ...

         ✠ . . . . . V . . . KARLIOLENSIS . .

℞.   ✠ S' COMMVNIS : CIVIVM . . . . . .

4794. Sulph. cast of the *obv.* only of No. 4793. [D.C., G. 14.]

CARMARTHEN, *co. Carmarthen.*

4795. [16th cent.] Sulph. cast from fine impression or the matrix. 2¼ in. [D.C., G. 272.]

A triple-towered castle, masoned and embattled, with ornamental carving, tall narrow windows, round-headed doorway with a flight of steps and portcullis. On each of the side towers an eagle. In the field, on each side an ostrich feather, labelled. In base, a lion passant reguardant contourné.

✠ : SIGILLVM : COMMVNITATIS : VILLE : DE : KERMERDYNN : Inner border beaded.

CASTLE-RISING, *co. Norfolk.*

4796. [17th cent.] Sulph. cast from the matrix. 1⅜ in. [lxix. 13.]

A castle, with three domed towers, each topped with a flag ; round-headed doorway with portcullis down.

✿ THE ✿ BOROVGH OF · CASTLE · RYDING ✦

S. Lewis, *Topogr. Dict.,* vol. i., p. 358.

CHARD, or CHERDE, *co. Somerset.*

4797. [A.D. 1400.] Green : fine, but imperfect. About 2¼ × 1½ in. when perfect. [Harl. ch. 49 A. 18.]

Pointed oval : an ornamental flowering tree, on it two eagles.

✿ S' CO . . . . RGI DE SERDA ✦

Beaded borders.

CHESTER, *County.*
RICHARD, *Prince of Wales, Duke of Cornwall, and Earl of Chester, afterwards Richard II.*
(*Seal of his Chester Exchequer.*)

4798. [A.D. 1377.] Uncoloured, opaque: fine, the edge chipped. 1⅝ in. [Add. ch. 6103.]

Within an elaborately carved gothic trefoiled panel, a shield of arms: quarterly, 1, 4, FRANCE (ANCIENT), 2, 3, *E*NGLAND, over all a label of three points, RICHARD, PRINCE OF WALES.

✠ ⚘ : SIGILLUM : RICARDI : ⚘ COMITIS : ⚘ CESTRIE : ⚘

COUNTY PALATINE OF CHESTER.
EDWARD IV., A.D. 1461–1483.

4799. Sulph. cast, tinted greenish-brown, from fine but imperfect impression. 3¼ in. [lxvi, 92, 93.]

∅. The king, armed *cap-à-pie*, with plate armour, helmet closed, chapeau and crest, a lion statant guardant crowned, the tail extended; sword held aloft in the r. h., in the l. h. a shield of arms slung with a strap over the r. shoulder; riding to the r. on a caparisoned horse, galloping on a mount replenished with herbage and flowers. The armorial bearings of the shield and caparisons are the ROYAL ARMS OF ENGLAND as borne by EDWARD IV. The background is replenished with wavy branches of foliage.

SIGILLVM : EDWARDI : DEI : GRA . . . . . . NGLIE ᵶ FRANCIE :
DN̄I : HIBERNIE ᵶ COMITIS : CESTRIE.

Beaded border.

℞. A shield of arms: per pale, *dex.*, ROYAL ARMS as in the *obv.;* *sin.*, three garbs, two and one, CHESTER. Ensigned with an open jewelled coronet of five fleurs-de-lis and four trefoil leaves disposed alternately. Supporters: *dex.*, a lion; *sin.*, a bull. The background is replenished with wavy branches of foliage.

SIGILLVM ⦂ EDWARDI ⦂ DEI ⦂ GRACIA ⦂ REGIS ⦂ ANGLIE . . . . .
. . . OMINI ⦂ HIBERNIE ⦂ ET ⦂ COMITIS ⦂ CESTRIE ⦂

Inner border carved and ornamented with quatrefoils or ball-flowers.

HENRY VII., A.D. 1485–1509.

4800. Sulph. casts, tinted dark-green, from fine but cracked impression, with the edge chipped. 3¼ in. [lxxvi. 94, 95.]

∅. The king, armed *cap-à-pie*, with plate armour, helmet closed, chapeau and crest, a lion statant guardant crowned, the tail extended ; sword held aloft in the r. h., in the l. h. a shield of arms slung with a strap over the r. shoulder ; riding to the r. on a caparisoned horse, galloping on a mount replenished with herbage and flowers, resembling that used on the *rev.* of the Great Seal of the king, see No. 324. The armorial bearings of the shield and caparisons are : per pale, *dex.*, the ROYAL ARMS OF ENGLAND, as borne by HENRY VII. ; *sin.*, three garbs, two and one, CHESTER. The background is replenished with branches of foliage elegantly designed.

SIGILLŪ : HENRICI : DEI : GRACIA : REGIS : ANG . . . . ɀ : FRANCIE : DNI : HIBERNIE : ɀ COMITIS : CESTRIE.

℞. A shield of arms, as in the preceding seal of Edward IV., ensigned as before, and placed betw. two ostrich feathers, with the quill stuck through a label.

♠ SIGILLŪ : HENRICI : DEI : GRACIA : REGIS : ANGLIE ɀ FRANCIE : DÑI : HIBERNIE ɀ COMITIS : CESTRIE : м

Inner border carved and ornamented with quatrefoils or ball-flowers, and having a cusp of tracery on each side of the base of the shield below the feather.

4801. Sulph. casts from chipped impression, somewhat indistinct in places. [lxxvi. 96, 97.]

HENRY VIII., A.D. 1509–1547.

4802. Sulph. casts, tinted red, from fine impression, indistinct in places. 3¾ in. [lxxvi. 98, 99.]

∅. The king, armed *cap-à-pie*, as in the preceding seal of Henry VII., riding to the r. on a caparisoned horse, with plume of three feathers on the head, galloping to the r. The armorial bearings of the shield and caparisons are the ROYAL ARMS OF ENGLAND as borne by HENRY VIII., with a label of three points. The background of the seal is composed of a very elegant diaper lozengy, the knot or intersection in each case being covered with a fleur-de-lis of France ; in each space an ostrich feather.

SIḠ : HENR̄ : DEI : GRA : REGIS : ANGL : ET : FRANC : ɀ : DÑI : HIBN̄ : COMITATVS : PALATINI : SVI : CESTRIE.

℞. A shield of arms : per pale, *dex.*, as in the *obv. ; sin.*, three garbs, two and one, CHESTER. Ensigned with a covered crown of five roses and four fleurs-de-lis alternately disposed. Supporters, two dragons or wyverns sejant addorsed, each supporting an ostrich feather with label inscribed:—ICH DIEN.

SIGILL : HENRICI : DEI : GRA : REGIS : ANGL : Z : FRANC : ɀ : DÑI : HIB'NIE : COMITATVS : PALAT' : SVI : CESTRIE.

Inner border carved and ornamented with quatrefoils or ball-flowers.

4803. Sulph. casts, tinted green from very fine impression, with the edge chipped off. [lxxvi. 100, 101.]

EDWARD VI., A.D. 1547–1553.

4804. Yellow: fine, imperfect at the bottom. $3\frac{5}{16}$ in. [xxxvi. 33.]

Ø. The king, armed *cap-à-pie*, with plate armour, helmet closed, chapeau, and crest, a lion statant guardant crowned, the tail extended; sword held aloft in the r. h., in the l. h. a shield of arms slung with a strap over the r. shoulder; riding to the r. on a caparisoned and armoured horse, with a plume of three ostrich feathers on the head. The armorial bearings of the shield and caparisons are: ROYAL ARMS OF ENGLAND, as borne by EDWARD VI., with a label of three points for PRINCE OF WALES. The background of the seal is composed of a very elegant diaper lozengy, the knot or intersection in each case being covered with a fleur-de-lis of FRANCE; in each space an ostrich feather, either straight or curling to the *dex.* or *sin.*, WALES.

SIGILLV : EDOARDI : DEI : GRA : AGL' : FRA : ℨ : H . . . .
S . . : ET : IN : TERRIS : ❀ : ❀ :

R. A shield of arms: per pale, *dex.*, quarterly, 1, 4, FRANCE (MODERN), 2, 3, ENGLAND; *sin.*, three garbs, two and one, CHESTER. Ensigned with a crown of five roses and four fleurs-de-lis, alternately disposed. Supporters, two dragons or wyverns sejant addorsed, each supporting an ostrich feather, with label inscribed :—ICH · DIEN.

Legend following from *obv.* :—

ECCLESIE : ❀ : ANGLICANE : ❀ : ET : ❀ H . . . CE : ❀ :
SVPREMI : ❀ : CAPIT' : ❀ : P : ❀ : COM : ❀ :
PALATINI ❀ SVI ❀ CESTRE .

Carved borders.

COUNTY PALATINE OF CHESTER AND COUNTY OF FLINT.

ELIZABETH, A.D. 1558–1603.

4805. Light-brown opaque, uncoloured: fine, showing marks of the studs or pins used to steady the matrix. $3\frac{1}{4}$ in. [xxvii. 68.]

Ø. On a mount replenished with herbage and flowers, the Queen, in embroidered attire, with crown and sceptre, riding to the l., on a pacing horse with embroidered reins, breast-band and saddle-cloth. The saddle-cloth is diapered lozengy, with a fleur-de-lis or a rose in alternate spaces. Back-ground enriched with a diaper lozengy, with a fleur-de-lis on each knot of the reticulation and a labelled ostrich feather in each space.

♠ SIGILLUM : ❋ : ELIZABETHE : ❋ : DEI : ❋ : G̅RA : ❋ :
ANGLIE : ❋ : FRANCIE : ❋ : ET : ❋ : HIBERNIE : ❋
FIDEI : ❋ : DEFENSOR .

℞. A shield of arms: per pale, *dex.*, quarterly, 1, 4, FRANCE (MODERN), 2, 3, ENGLAND, with a label of three points for PRINCE OF WALES ; *sin.*, three garbs, two and one, CHESTER, ensigned with a royal crown. Supporters, two dragons sejant addorsed, each holding up an ostrich feather with a label inscribed :— ICH · DIEN. In the field above, the initial letters E. R.

♠ · COMITATVS : ❋ PALANTINI : ❋ SVI : ❋ : CESTRIE : ❋ :
·· ET : ❋ COMITATVS : ❋ : SVI : ❋ FLINT .

4806. Light-brown, opaque, uncoloured : fine, showing marks of the studs or pins used to steady the matrix ; originally applied to a charter by black and white silk ribbons plaited together. [xxxvii. 69.]

4807. Casts in sulph., tinted green. [lxxvi. 57, 58.]

JAMES I., A.D. 1603.

4808. Light yellowish-brown, opaque, uncoloured : fine, showing marks of the studs or pins used to steady the matrix. 3¾ in. [xxxvii. 61.]

∅. On a mount replenished with herbage and flowers, the king, armed *cap-à-pie* in plate armour, with cuirass, helmet, crown, plume of five ostrich feathers, and sword ; riding to the l. on a caparisoned and armoured horse, with ostrich plume and aigrette. The caparisons are diapered lozengy, with an ostrich feather in each space, and border of various badges.

♠ SIGILLVM ❋ IACOBI ❋ DEI ❋ GRACIA ❋ ANGLIÆ ❋
SCOTIÆ ❋ FRANCIÆ ❋ ET ❋ HIBERNIÆ
❋ REGIS ❋ FIDEI ❋ DEF :

℞. A shield of arms : per pale, *dex.*, ROYAL ARMS OF K. JAMES I., see No. 522, with label of three points for PRINCE OF WALES ; *sin.*, three garbs, two and one, CHESTER. En-signed with a royal crown, jewelled, with three crosses pattées and two fleurs-de-lis. Supporters, two dragons sejant addorsed, each holding an ostrich feather.

COMITATVS ❋ PALATINI ❋ SVI ❋ CESTRIÆ ❋ ET ❋ COMITATVS ❋
SVI ❋ FLINT ❋ Aᵒ ❋ DNI ❋ 1603.

Carved borders.

E 2

CHARLES, *Prince of Wales, Duke of Cornwall and York, Earl of Chester, etc.*, A.D. 1616, *afterwards Charles I.*

4809. Light yellowish-brown, opaque, uncoloured : fine, showing marks of the studs or pins used to steady the matrix. 3¾ in. [xxxvii. 62.]

∅. A copy, with variant details, of the *obv.* of the preceding seal of James I., No. 4808. On the helmet an open coronet, in the l. h. a shield of arms : three garbs, two and one, CHESTER. The devices in the diaper-work are garbs, ostrich feathers and fleurs-de-lis.

♠ SIGILLVM ✿ CAROLI ✿ PRINCIPIS ✿ WALLIÆ ✿ DVCIS ✿ CORNVBIÆ ✿ ET ✿ EBORVM ✿ ET ✿ COMITIS ✿ CESTRIÆ.

R. A shield of arms, CHESTER, see *obv.* Ensigned with a jewelled coronet of four fleurs-de-lis, and five pearls on rays. Supporters as in the preceding seal, No. 4808.

♠ · COMITATVS ✿ PALATINI ✿ SVI ✿ CESTRIÆ ✿ ET ✿ FLINT ✿ ANNO 1616.
Carved borders.

COMMONWEALTH, A.D. 1648.

4810. Sulph. casts from the *obv.* and *rev.* of a fine impression. 3¾ in. [lx. 67, 68.]

∅. An elaborately detailed representation of Chester Castle, with an ornamental shield of arms on each of the side round-towers, *dex.*, ENGLAND (COMMONWEALTH), *sin.*, IRELAND. Overhead, clouds ; in base, water.

THE ✿ ORIGINALL ✿ SEALE ✿ FOR ✿ THE ✿ COVNTY ✿ PALATINE ✿ OF ✿ CHESTER ✿ AND ✿ FLINT ✿ 1648.

R. A representation of the interior of the House of Commons during session. In base, an ornamentally carved shield of arms, couché, ENGLAND (COMMONWEALTH) ; cf. No. 598.

✿ IN ✿ THE ✿ FIRST ✿ YEARE ✿ O[F ✿ F]REEDOME ✿ BY ✿ GODS ✿ BLESSING ✿ RESTORED ✿ 1648.

CHESTER, *co. Chester.*

4811. [17th cent.] Sulph. cast from the silver matrix. 2⅞ in. [lx. 70.]

An elaborate representation of a castle, walls masoned and embattled, six towers, portal with folding doors closed and portcullis half-down. In the field over it, a lion of ENGLAND betw. two garbs of CHESTER.

✿ SIGILLVM COMVNE MAIORIS ET CIVIVM CIVITATIS CESTRIE.

Inner border beaded, outer border carved.

S. Lewis, *Topogr. Dict.*, vol. i., p. 399.

Privy Seal of the Mayor.

4812. [13th cent.] Sulph. cast from the matrix, or from fine impression. 1⅞ in. [lx. 71.]

A shield of arms, *E*NGLAND, with a label of five points. Suspended by a strap from a loop ; with a garb of CHESTER on each side.

🕀 SIGILLVM : SECRETI : MAIORIS : CESTRIE.

Beaded borders.

Chamberlain or Sheriff.

4813. [A.D. 1280.] Light-green or uncoloured: the edge chipped. 1½ in. [Add. ch. 20,484.]

A shield of arms, *E*NGLAND, within a finely carved gothic rosette of eight points, with a countersunk trefoil in each cusp.

. . . . . ANGL' . . . . CESTR.

(? *Sigillum Regis Angliæ* . . . . .)

Seal " pro recognitione debitorum," see No. 1070.

CHESTERFIELD, *co. Derby.*

4814. [17th cent.] Sulph. cast from the matrix. 1¼ in. [D.C., H. 152.]

An ornamental shield of arms : on a fess a lozenge.

· ✵ · BVRG DE CHESTERFIELD.

Carved borders.

S. Lewis, *Topogr. Dict.*, vol. i., p. 403.

Smaller Seal.

4815. [17th cent.] Sulph. cast from the matrix. ¾ in. [lxi. 38.]

Shield of arms, and legend as before, No. 4814.

CHEVELEY, *co. Cambridge.*
Free Grammar School.

4816. [16th cent.] Sulph. cast. 1¾ × 1⅝ in. [lx. 54.]

Oval : a book, with ornamental cover and clasps. Field replenished with sprigs of wavy foliage.

🕀 SIGILLVM · COMVNE · PRO · SCHOLA · IOH̄IS · RAY · IN CHEVELEY ✻

CHICHESTER, *co. Sussex.*
First Corporation Seal.

4817. [13th cent.] Recent impression in red sealing-wax, from the matrix. 2½ × 1½ in. [xxxvi. 191.]

Pointed oval : an eagle, rising reguardant contourné, holding in the beak a fleur-de-lis. In the field, an estoile of eight points wavy.

⚜ SIGILLVM · CIVIVM · CICESTRIE.

Beaded borders.

Later Corporation Seal.

4818. [17th cent.] Recent impression in red wax, from the matrix. 3¼ in. [xxxvi. 192.]

A triple-towered castle, embattled and masoned, the crenellations of the wall charged alternately with a cross, rose, fleur-de-lis, and lion's face, and similar devices are placed on the face of the wall, and crenellations of the towers. Portal with embattled wall, and portcullis down, surmounted with a large shield of arms : guttée de poix, on a chief a lion of England, CITY OF CHICHESTER.

✱ ❧ SIGILLVM ❧ ✱ ❧ COMMVNE ❧ ✱ ❧ CIVITATIS ❧ ✱ ❧
CICESTRIÆ.

Carved border.

S. Lewis, *Topogr. Dict.*, vol. i., p. 408.

Seal of Arms.

4819. [17th cent.] Recent impression in red sealing-wax, from the matrix. 1¾ × 1¼ in. [xxxvi. 193.]

Oval ; a shield of arms, CITY OF CHICHESTER, see No. 4818.

: ✿ : SIGILLVM ✿ CIVITATIS ✿ CICESTRIÆ.

Carved border.

CHIPPENHAM, *co. Wilts.*

4820. Sulph. cast from the matrix. 1½ in. [lxxiii. 47.]

A tree of three branches, eradicated, betw. two suspended shields of arms : l. ten billets in pile, four, three, two, and one, in chief a label of five points ; r. three human legs couped at the thigh in bend, two and one.

+ BVRGI + DE + CHIPPENHAM.

S. Lewis, *Topogr. Dict.*, vol. i., p. 416.

CHIRBURY CASTLE, *co. Salop.*

4821. Sulph. cast from fine impression on the matrix. $2\frac{1}{8}$ in. [D.C., A. 107*.]

A portcullis, the royal badge of HENRY VIII., barbed, studded, chained and ringed. Ensigned with a royal crown, jewelled, of three crosses pattées and two fleurs-de-lis.

✿ S · HENR · VIII · DEI · GRA · REG · ANGL · FRA · Ƶ · DÑI · HIBE · P · CASTELL' · DOMI · SVE · CHIR.

CLITHEROE, *co. Lancaster.*

4822. [17th cent.] Sulph. cast from the matrix. $1\frac{5}{16}$ in. [lxvi. 29.]

A triple-towered castle, embattled and masoned. The towers are circular, domed, each topped with a flag. Round-headed portal, with portcullis half-down.

SIGILLVM · BVRGI · DE · CLIDEROWE IN COM : LANC.
Beaded borders.

S. Lewis, *Topogr. Dict.*, vol. i., p. 446.

Signet.

4823. [17th cent.] Sulph. cast, from the matrix. $1\frac{3}{4}$ in. [lxvi. 30.]

A double cinquefoiled rose, *en soleil*, barbed and seeded.

✠ SIGИVM · DE · CLITHEROW · IИ · LAИCAS.

COCKERMOUTH, *co. Cumberland.*

4824. [18th cent.] Sulph. cast from the matrix. $1\frac{1}{16}$ × $\frac{7}{8}$ in. [lxi. 33.]

Oval: on an oval shield enriched with carved scrolls and festoons, the cypher C. L. C., repeated in reverse. Over the shield a basket of flowers.

COLCHESTER, *co. Essex.*
First Corporation Seal.

4825. [13th cent.] Casts in red composition from fine but imperfect impression. About $3\frac{3}{4}$ in. when perfect. From a deed dated A.D. 1379. [lxxv. 95, 96.]

Ø. A triple-towered castle, masoned and embattled. The round-headed doorway with valve-doors, with ornamental hinges, being opened by the porter. In base, a bridge of three arches over a stream, with a fish naiant under each arch. Background coarsely diapered lozengy, with a leaf or pellet in each space. Peculiar and coarse style of work.

. OLCESTRENSIS : S . . . : BV . . GI : C . . . . .

℞. St. Helena the Empress, a native of this town, with crown, seated on a carved throne, under a canopy supported on architectural buttresses, in the r. h. a long cross, her emblem, in the l. h. some indistinct emblems. Background diapered as in the *obv.*

✠ : QVAM : CRVX : INSIGNIT : HELENAM : COLECESTRIA GIIGNIT .

Proc. Soc. Antiq., 1885, vol. x., pp. 344, 345.

4826. Casts in red composition, of a suggested restoration of the seal. [lxxv. 95*, 96*.]

   Ø. ✠ : COLCESTRENSIS : SVM : BVRGI : COMMVNE :
            SIGILLVM :
  ℞. ✠ : QVAM : CRVX : INSIGNIT : HELENAM : COLCESTRIA :
            GIGNIT.

Second Seal.

4827. [15th cent.] Sulph. cast, tinted grey, from fine impression. 3¼ in. [xlvii. 758, 759.]

Ø. St. Helena, with crown, holding the cross, seated on a throne, in a heavily canopied niche, with Our Lord, half-length in a small niche overhead. On each side, a similar niche, smaller, with canopy and turret of two storeys; in each niche, on a balcony, an angel with expanded wings holding a shield of arms: l. a cross; r. quarterly, 1, 4, FRANCE (MODERN), 2, 3, ENGLAND; outside these, on each side, a penthouse. In base, under a flat arch, a shield of arms: a cross raguly betw. three crowns, the one in base enfiling the cross, TOWN OF COLCHESTER. Supported by two lions.

✯ ⦂ SIGILLŪ ⦂ COMMUNE ⦂ BALLIUORŪ ⦂ ᴢ ⦂ COMMUNITATIS ⦂
    VILLE ⦂ DOMINI ⦂ REGIS ⦂ COLCESTRIE +

℞. An elaborately detailed representation of a castle, or castellated town, with a flight of steps leading from the round-headed doorway over water in base. On each side, a lion statant, and in the field a wavy branch of flowers and foliage.

⦂ INTRAUIT ⦂ IH̄C ⦂ INI⦂ QUODDAM ⦂ CASTELLUM ⦂ ET ⦂
   MULIER ⦂ QUEDAM ⦂ EXCEPIT ⦂ ILLUM ⋈

                     —Luc. x. 38.

Carved borders.

S. Lewis, *Topogr. Dict.*, vol. i., p. 458 ; Laing's *MS. Catal.*, Nos. 379, 380.

4828. Sulph. casts. [D.C., G. 8, 9.]

4829. Red : very fine, but imperfect, cracked, and chipped. [xxxvii. 83.]

Bailiffs' Office.

4830. [15th cent.] Sulph. cast from the matrix. 2¼ in. [lxiii. 6.]

A castle, masoned and embattled, the central tower hexagonal, the side towers circular and topped with flags. In the central tower in a carved round-headed niche, St. Helena the Empress, standing, with crown, in the r. h. a book, in the l. h. a long cross. The round-headed portal has the portcullis half down, and is flanked with two small circular towers, on each a head.

⚜ SIGILLVM : OFFICII : BALLIUORUM : VILLE : COLCESTRIE : ⚜

Outside the legend a broad border of fourteen cinquefoil roses alternately disposed with vesical frames, foliated, each enclosing a fleur-de-lis.

Warden of the Gate.

4831. [A.D. 1348.] Red : fine, edge chipped. 2 in. [L.F.C., xxiii. 14.]

An eagle of St. John the Evangelist, to the r.

[✠S]IGILL' · CVSTOÐ · PORT̄ · CO[L]ECEST . : . . . .

4832. Sulph. cast from No. 4831. [lxiii. 15.]

Castle.

4833. [A.D. 1441.] Red : injured by pressure. ⅞ in. [Add. ch. 24,671.]

A triple towered castle, with round-headed doorway. Early 14th cent. style of work.

✠ CASTRVM · COLECESTR'.

Another Seal.

4834. [14th cent.] Sulph. cast from fine impression. ⅞ in. [lxiii. 7.]

A shield of arms : a chevron gules betw. three billets. Over the shield a triple-towered castle, masoned, with round-headed doorway.

S' · CASTRI · COLECESTR'.

CONGLETON, *co. Chester.*

4835. [15th cent.] Sulph. cast from the matrix. $1\frac{7}{8}$ in. [lx. 88.]

On waves a *tun* or barrel betw. two *conger* eels erect, forming a *rebus* on the name of the town.   Above the tun a lion of *E*NGLAND.

✠ : SIGILLVM ✠ COMUNE ✠ VILLE : ✠ : DE : ✠ CONGULTON ✠ :

Beaded borders, the inner one also partly engrailed.

S. Lewis, *Topogr. Dict.*, vol. i., p. 473.

CORBRIDGE or CORFBRIDGE, *co. Northumberland.*

4836. [12th cent.] Sulph. cast from imperfect and injured impression. $1\frac{7}{8}$ in.   [lxx. 10.]

A cross of ornamental design, cantoned with four human heads erased.

    + SIGILL' COMMVNE CORFBRIGIE.

CORFE-CASTLE, *co. Dorset.*

4837. [15th cent.]   Sulph. cast from fine but chipped impression. $2\frac{1}{8}$ in.   [lxii. 32.]

On a mount a triple towered castle, embattled and masoned, in each round tower a square window of four lights ; round-headed doorway with portcullis half down, below it a *corve* or *corbeau,* by way of *rebus* on the name of the town. On each of the towers an ostrich feather.   The field diapered lozengy, with each space charged with a fleur-de-lis and martlet or corbeau, alternately.

✠ SIGILL' ✠ MAIORIS : ET : BARONŪ ✠ VILLE ✠ DE ✠ CORFF ✠
          CASTELL'. ✠ :

S. Lewis, *Topogr. Dict.*, vol. i., p. 478 (very incorrect).

CONWAY, *co. Carnarvon.*
Provostship.

4838. [14th cent.] Red : fine. $1\frac{3}{4}$ in.   [xxxvii. 76.]

On waves, a triple-towered castle, masoned and embattled, pointed doorway.

    + S' : PROVESTRIE : DE : CONEWEY.

CORNWALL.

Subsidy of Cornwall and Plymouth, co. Devon.

4839. [15th cent.] Sulph. cast from fine impression. 1¾ in. [lxi. 100.]

A shield of arms : ENGLAND. Inner border engrailed, with a pellet in each cusp.

: SIGILLUM ⚜ SUB̄S ⚜ CORNUBY ⚜ ET ⚜ PLYMOUTH' ⚜

Corporation of "Stannators" of the Stannaries.

4840. [13th cent.] Sulph. cast from fine impression, edge chipped. 2 in. [lxi. 1.]

On a platform two miners, to the l., working ; the one on the r. has a spade with triangular blade and single shoulder, the other on the l. a mattock. In the centre a lion's face, the tongue protruded. Background diapered lozengy, with a rose in each space.

⚜ S' COMVNITATIS · STANGNATORVM . CORNVBIE.

SIR WALTER RALEGH, KNT.

Warden of the Stannaries of Cornwall and Devon, Captain of the Royal Guard, and Governor of the Island of Jersey.

c. A.D. 1600.

4841. Sulph. cast. 1⅖ in. [D.C., H. 82.]

The Warden, in plate armour, with plumed helmet, sword, and shield of arms, riding to the l. on a galloping horse, caparisoned and plumed. The armorial bearings of the shield and caparisons are : five lozenges in bend, RALEGH. Border of two concentric circles beaded.

Legend in two concentric circles :—

(1.) ⚜ SIGILL · DÑI · WALTERI : RALEGH : MILITIS : GARDIAN : STANNAR : CORNVB : ET : DEVON :

(2.) ⚜ CAPITAN : GARD : REG : ET : GVBERNATOR : INSVLÆ : DE : IERSEY : ⚜

Outer border beaded.

Gent. Mag., vol. lvii., p. 459.

DUCHY OF CORNWALL.

Cokett Seal.

4842. [14th cent.] Sulph. cast from the matrix. 1⅛ in. [lxi. 3.]

Bust of a king, with crown of three points fleury, drapery fastened on the breast with a fibula betw. two sprigs of foliage.

✠ SIGILLŪ · DE · COKETT' · DUCAT' · CORNUB'.

Cabled borders.

Office of the Cokett.

Seal of HENRY, PRINCE OF WALES, *Duke of Cornwall, and Earl of Chester, afterwards Henry V.*

4843. [*c.* A.D. 1399–1413.] Sulph. cast from the matrix. 2⅛ in. [lxi. 2.]

In a quadrilobe, a shield of arms: quarterly, 1, 4, FRANCE (MODERN), 2, 3, ENGLAND, over all a label of three points, each indistinctly charged, HENRY PRINCE OF WALES. Betw. two ostrich feathers labelled ; over the shield a swan rising.

♠ S' HENRIC' PRINCIPIS WALL' DUC' CORNUB' ꝫ COMIT' CESTR' DE OFFICIO COKETTI DUCATUS CORNUBIE ꞥ

Cabled borders.

4844. Another. [D.C., G. 137.]

Letter Seal of ALBERT EDWARD, PRINCE OF WALES, K.G.

4845. [A.D. 1842.] Red sealing-wax, impression from a letter. 1 × ⁹⁄₁₀ in. [xlix. 41.]

Rectangular with rounded corners : an oval shield of the ROYAL ARMS OF GREAT BRITAIN, with an escutcheon of SAXONY and label of three points for difference, PRINCE OF WALES. The shield is encircled with a Garter, inscribed with the motto of the Order, and ensigned with a prince's crown and plume of three ostrich feathers. Supporters of GREAT BRITAIN, each with a label as above, and placed on carved scrolls. In base a riband bearing the motto :—ICH DIEN. The whole within a bordure bezantée, for CORNWALL, inscribed in base :—

DUCHY OF CO[RNWALL].

Secretary's Letter Seal.

4846. [A.D. 1842.] Red sealing-wax, impression from a letter. 1 × ⅞ in. [xlix. 42.]

Oval : an oval shield of the arms described in No. 4845, encircled with a Garter inscribed with the motto of the Order, and ensigned with a crown as before. Supporters of GREAT BRITAIN, each with a label, and placed on a riband bearing the motto :—ICH DIEN. entwined with the rose, thistle and shamrock.

Inscription in the field above :—

DUCHY OF CORNWALL.

Below, on a plinth,

SECRETARY.

COVENTRY, *co. Warwick.*
Mayoralty.

4847. [From a charter dated A.D. 1618.] Light brown : injured by pressure and slipped when being made. About 2 in. [xxxvi. 46.]

On a mount replenished with foliage, and betw. two trees, an elephant, bearing on his back a triple-towered castle, topped with a flag [bearing three scimitars in fess, handles downward.]

⚜ SIGI[LLUM · MAIO]RATUS · CIUITATIS · COUENTRIE.

S. Lewis, *Topogr. Dict.*, vol. i., p. 497.

Seal " pro recognitione debitorum," see No. 1071.

CREDITON, *co. Devon.*
Free Grammar School, A.D. 1674.

4848. Sulph. cast, tinted red. 1⅝ in. [xxxv. 127.]

The Almighty, standing, slightly turned to the l., with radiant nimbus, lifting up the r. h. in benediction, in the l. h. an orb topped with a cross.

⚓ SIG · XII · GVBER : BONOR · ECLE · S · CRVCIS DE · CREDITON : 1674.

Inner border beaded, outer border carved.

N. Carlisle, *Endowed Grammar Schools*, vol. i., p. 254.

4849. Another. [xlvii. 761.]

Laing's *MS. Catal.*, No. 275.

CUMBERLAND.
A Sheriff's Seal ?

4850. [A.D. 1668.] Red : imperfect, *en placard.* About ¾ in. when perfect. [Add. ch. 17,178.]

A portcullis, ringed and chained. In the field below, the inscription :—

CVMBR . . . . . .

4851. [A.D. 1668.] Another. [Add. ch. 17,181.]
Legend wanting.

DARTMOUTH, or CLIFTON-DARTMOUTH,
co. Devon.

4852. [Late 13th cent.] Sulph. cast from the matrix. 2⅛ in. [lxi. 67.]

A ship on waves, containing the full-face bust of a king, crowned, betw. two lions passant guardant of *E*NGLAND.

In the field overhead, on the l. a crescent, on the r. an estoile of six points.

✠ SIGILLVM : COMMVNE : DE CLIFTONE : DERTEMVTHE.

Cf. S. Lewis, *Topogr. Dict.*, vol. ii., p. 9.

Later Seal, A.D. 1836.

4853. Sulph. cast from the matrix. 2¼ in. [lxii. 20.]

Resembles the preceding seal in design, but very inferior in execution. The king has a fur-tippet and collar.

Legend in two concentric circles :—
Outer circle.—✯ THE · COMMON · SEAL · OF · THE · MAYOR · ALDERMEN · AND · BURGESSES.

Inner circle.—OF · THE · BOROUGH · OF · CLIFTON · DARTMOUTH · HARDNESS.
✠ 1836 ✠ .
Cabled borders.

Signet.

4854. Sulph. cast from the matrix. ⅞ in. [lxii. 21.]

In a warship without masts, on waves, the king, half-length, with crown and fur-tippet, in the r. h. a sceptre fleury.
Beaded border.

Mayor.

4855. [14th cent.] Sulph. cast. 1¾ in. [lxi. 68.]

A ship with embattled castles, but without masts, on waves, therein a king, full-face, half-length, with crown, in the l. h. a sceptre fleury. In the field on the l., a crescent.

✯ S' + MAIORIS + DE + CLIFTONE + DERTEMVTHE + H'.

The letter H, at the end of the legend, probably stands for Hardness, the third town included in the corporation. See No. 4853.

Steward.

4856. [15th cent.]   Sulph. cast.   1⅝ in.   [lxi. 69.]

Three piles, meeting in base, enfiled with a horn garnished. This device is probably in allusion to the arms of BRYAN, three piles, and to the crest of the same, on a chapeau or bugle-horn sans strings.

⚜ PRO · OFFICIO · SENESCALLI · DE · DERTEMUTH'
CLIFT' · H.

Port.

4857. [17th cent.]   Sulph. cast from the matrix.   1⅜ in. [lxi. 70.]

An oval shield of the ROYAL ARMS OF GREAT BRITAIN, as used by JAMES I.

⚜ SIGILLVM : OFFICI : PORTVS ⁝ DARTMOVTH :
Carved border.

DAVENTRY, *co. Northampton.*

4858· Sulph. cast from the matrix.   1⅝ in.   [lxix. 70.]

A *Dane* or woodman, standing, holding an axe, on the l., a *tree* on the r., by way of *rebus* on the name of the town. Across the field the date 15–95.

⚜ SIGILLVM · COMVNE · BVRGI · DE · DANETRE · N · S.

S. Lewis, *Topogr. Dict.*, vol. ii., p. 11.

Smaller Seal.

4859. Sulph. cast from the matrix.   1 1/16 in.   [lxix. 71.]
Same design and legend as in No. 4858.
Cabled borders.

DEAL, *co. Kent.*
Corporation, A.D. 1699.

4860. Sulph. cast from the matrix.   2¼ in.   [lxv. 38.]
The field contains the charges of the shield of arms of the CINQUEPORTS; per pale, three demi-lions passant guardant, each united to a demi-hulk, in pale.

⚜ SIGILL : MAIOR : IVRAT : ET : COIAT : VILL : ET · BVRG :
DE · DEAL · IN · COM : KANC :

Inner border beaded, outer border carved with a chain pattern.

Mayor, A.D. 1699.

4861. Sulph. cast from the matrix.   1¼ in.   [lxv. 39.]

A three-masted ship of war, with flags at stem and stern, sailing on waves to the l.   In base on a mount, two castles or round towers embattled.

Legend commences with an escallop :—

: SIGILL : MAIORIS : DE · DEAL : 1699 :

Inner border beaded, outer border carved.

DEPTFORD-STROND, *co. Kent.*

Corporation of the Master, Wardens and Assistants of the Trinity House, A.D. 1513.

4862. [A.D. 1727.] Paper impression : very indistinct. 2½ in. [Add. ch. 26,398.]

A shield of arms : a cross betw. four ships of three masts [each under full sail].   Crest, on a helmet, mantling, and wreath, a demi-lion rampant guardant regally crowned, holding in the dexter paw a sword erect.

Legend indistinct.

DERBY, *co. Derby.*

4863. Sulph. cast from the matrix.   1⅜ in.   [lxi. 40.]

A *deer*, lodged, in a park or *by*, enclosed in a double cordon of foliage and berries.

⚜ SIGILLUM ⚜ ❀ COM̄UNE ⚜ ❀ WILLE ⚜ ❀ DE ⚜ ❀
DERBI ⚜ ❀.

Beaded borders.

S. Lewis, *Topogr. Dict.*, vol. ii., p. 24.

4864. Sulph. cast from impression injured in parts by pressure.   [D.C., G. 277.]

DEVIZES, *co. Wilts.*

4865. Sulph. cast from the matrix.   2½ in.   [lxxiii. 49.]

A castle, with embattled and masoned walls, two round-towers, each domed and topped with a flag, at the corners, central tower or keep, and round-headed doorway.   On the interior side of the wall, at the sides of the central tower, two estoiles of six points wavy. In base the date 1608.

✠ SIG' · COMVNE · MAIORIS · ET . BURGENSI̅ · BVRGI · DN̄I' · REGIS · DE · DEVIZES · IN · CŌM' WILT.

Inner border beaded, outer border carved.

S. Lewis, *Topogr. Dict.*, vol. ii., p. 35.

Another Seal.

4866. Sulph. cast from cracked impression. $2\frac{3}{8}$ in. [lxxiii. 51.]

A castle, resembling in general design that described in No. 4865; the round towers are finished with a knob instead of a flag, portcullis in doorway half-down, and a ladder or grating across.

✠ SIGILLUM COMMUNE BURGEINSIUM DN̄I REGIS DIUISAR

Beaded borders.

Mayor.

4867. [16th cent.] Sulph. cast from the matrix. $1\frac{5}{8}$ in. [lxxiii. 50.]

A castle, resembling in general design that described in No. 4865; the round towers are finished with a knob instead of a flag, and the estoiles are not wavy; no windows; portcullis in doorway.

✠ SIGILL ✡ OFFICII ✡ MAIOR ✡ BVRGI ✠ DN̄E ✡ REGI DIVISAR.

DEVONSHIRE.

Seal for the Stannaries.

4868. [16th cent.] Sulph. cast. $1\frac{3}{4}$ in. [lxi. 71.]

A shield of arms with a carved scroll at each side: fifteen bezants in pile, five, four, three, two, and one, COUNTY OF CORNWALL. Above the shield a duke's coronet of five strawberry leaves.

· PRO · STANNARIIS · IN · COMITAT · DEVŌ.

Beaded border.

DODFORD MANOR, *co. Northampton.*

HENRY BENSON, Lord of the Manor, ob. A.D. 1725.

4869. Sulph. cast. $1\frac{1}{4}$ in. [lxix. 72.]

A shield of· arms : on a chevron, betw. three goats' heads, erased, as many escallops, BENSON.

In base the legend :—

DODFORD.

Baker, *Hist. of Northamptonshire*, vol. i., p. 361.

DORCHESTER, *co. Dorset.*

First Corporation Seal.

4870. [14th cent.] Sulph. casts from the matrix. 1¼ in. [lxii. 33, 34.]

∅. A shield of the ROYAL ARMS OF ENGLAND for EDWARD II., betw. three wavy sprigs of berries.

✠ S' COMMVNITATIS BVRGI DORCESTRIE.

℞. Bust of EDWARD II., full-face, couped at the neck, crowned ; in a quatrefoil with a small trefoiled sprig in each spandril.

✠ CAPVT DOMINI EDWARDI REGIS ANGLIE.

Beaded borders.

4871. Recent impression in red sealing-wax, of the *obv.* of No. 4870. [xlix. 46.]

4872. Recent impression in red sealing-wax, of the *rev.* of No. 4870. [lxxvi. 36.]

Second Corporation Seal.

4873. [17th cent.] Sulph. cast from impression with edge chipped. 1¾ in. [lxii. 36.]

On a mount a triple-towered castle of two storeys, masoned and embattled, on the curtain wall a shield of the ROYAL ARMS OF GREAT BRITAIN as used by JAMES I. This design forms the bearings of the shield of arms of the town.

✰ SIG : MAIOR · BAL : ALD : ET· BVRGI : DE ·
DORCHESTER · C' · DORSET.

Carved borders.

S. Lewis, *Topogr. Dict.*, vol. ii., p. 56.

Third Corporation Seal, A.D. 1836.

4874. Sulph. cast from the matrix, 1¾ in. [lxii. 40.]

A copy of the preceding seal, No. 4873.

THE MAYOR ALDERMEN & BURGESSES OF DORCHESTER
DORSET · 1836.

Carved borders.

Mayor.

4875. Sulph. cast from the matrix. 1 in. [lxii. 37.]

A shield of arms, TOWN OF DORCHESTER, see No. 4873. The edge of the shield hidden in places by the inner annulus of the legend.

❖ SIG . MAIORIS · DE · DORCHESTER.

Beaded borders.

Bailiffs.

4876. [A.D. 1368.] Green : edge indistinct. ⅞ in. [Harl. ch. 85 D. 28.]

A shield of arms : a lion passant guardant crowned. Within a carved and pointed gothic quatrefoil of tracery.

♢ S'. BALLIWORVM · DORCESTR'.

4877. Sulph. cast of No. 4876. [D.C., F. 461.]

Second Seal.

4878. [Late 14th or early 15th cent.] Sulph. cast from the matrix. 1¼ in. [lxii. 35.]

A triple-towered castle, masoned and embattled, no windows ; on the curtain-wall, a shield of the ROYAL ARMS OF ENGLAND as borne by K. EDWARD III., viz., quarterly 1, 4, FRANCE (ANCIENT), 2, 3, ENGLAND.

SIGILLVM : BALLIVORVM : DORCESTRE.

Beaded borders.

Another Seal or Signet.

4879. [17th cent.] Sulph. cast. ⅜ in. [lxii. 38.]

A cinquefoil rose, *en soleil*, barbed and seeded.

♢ BALL · DE · DORCHESTER.

Beaded border.

Bailiffs and Burgesses.

4880. [17th cent.] Sulph. cast from the matrix. 2¼ × 2⅛ in. [lxii. 39.]

Oval : on a rocky mount a triple-towered castle, masoned and embattled. The towers domed, and each having a flag charged with a cross ; round-headed and embattled portal with portcullis half-down ; round windows with gratings in the wall, quatrefoil opening in the two side round towers ; in the upper tower a round-headed door or window with portcullis half-down.

❊ SIGILLVM · BALLIORVM · ET · BVRGENSIVM · BVRGI · DE · DORCHESTER · IN · COMITATV · DORSET.

The letters TE in *Dorchester* are conjoined.

Carved borders.

F 2

DORSETSHIRE.
JOHN DE LA HALE, *late Sheriff.*

4881. [A.D. 1365.] Red : small fragment, about ⅞ in. when perfect. [Harl. ch. 51 B. 36.]

An embattled tower or castle. Beneath it an eagle displayed ; and in base, the initial letter I.

Legend destroyed.

DOUGLAS, *Isle of Man.*
High Bailiff, A.D. 1777.

4882. Recent impression in red sealing-wax from the matrix. 1¼ in. [xxxvi. 178.]

A cusped shield of arms of nine points, or (for gules) three legs conjoined in the fess point, in armour, garnished and spurred, ISLE OF MAN.

✠ HIGH · BAILIFF · DOUGLAS · 1777

DOVER, *co. Kent.*
Corporation Seal, A.D. 1305.

4883. Sulph. casts, chipped, from the brass matrix. 3 in. [D.C., F. 628, 629.]

∅. A one-masted ship on the waves ; mainsail furled, embattled crow's nest, flag and triple pendant ; on the embattled and arcaded forecastle, a banner flag of ENGLAND ; on a similar castle at the stern, two mariners standing, each blowing a long trumpet ; in the ship on the left two mariners, one hauling in the bowsprit, the other coiling a rope ; on the r. two other mariners, one climbing the rigging, the other managing a sweep or side rudder.

SIGILLVM ⦂ COMMVNE ⦂ BARONVM ·⦂· DE · DOVORIA.

℞. St. Martin, with nimbus, seated on a horse walking to the l., and dividing by his sword his cloak with a beggar standing under the doorway of a triple-towered castle, embattled and with pointed windows, embattled walls, and portcullis half-door in the gate. The inner edge of the field on the l. h. side is elegantly cusped or engrailed. Below the horse a platform or plinth ornamented with three quatrefoiled openings, and resting on an arcade.

In place of legend the annulus bears a cordon of twelve lions passant guardant of ENGLAND, arranged in six pairs counter-passant.

W. Boys, *History of Sandwich*, vol. ii., p. 797, fig. 1 ; S. Lewis, *Topogr. Dict.*, vol. ii., p. 67.

4884. Sulph. casts. [lxv. 42, 43.]

Mayoralty of the Port.

4885. Sulph. cast from the matrix. 1⅜ in. [lxv. 44.]

St. Martin, with nimbus, seated on a horse walking to the l., and dividing by the sword his cloak with a beggar half-length on the r. On the l., in the field a man's head. In a carved and trefoiled gothic quatrefoil of tracery, with a demi-lion passant guardant conjoined to a demi-hulk—(the charge in the shield of arms of the CINQUE-PORTS)—in each spandril.

✠ SIGILLVM · MAIORATVS · PORTVS · DOVORIE ·

• W. Boys, *History of Sandwich*, vol. ii., p. 797 ; fig. 4.

Second Seal, A.D. 1572.

4886. Sulph. cast from the matrix. [D.C., H. 46.]

St. Martin, with nimbus, seated on a horse walking to the l. on an ornamented geometrical pavement ; and dividing his cloak with a wooden-legged beggar on the r. Field replenished with a cinquefoil, slipped trefoils, and small flowers.

SIGILLVM · MAIORATVS · PORTVS · DOVORIÆ 1572 :

With a man's face after the first, and a lion's face after the second and third words.

Beaded borders.

Third Seal, A.D. 1748.

4887. Sulph. cast from the steel matrix. 1¼ × 1 in. [D.C., H. 61.]

Oval : on a mount, St. Martin with plumed helmet, seated on a horse, to the l., dividing his cloak with a beggar.

✠ SIGILLUM MAIORATUS PORTUS DOVORIÆ.

Boys, *History of Sandwich*, vol. ii., p. 797, ng. 2.

Signet, A.D. 1749.

4888. Sulph. cast from matrix. 1³⁄₁₆ × 1 in. [D.C., H. 62.]

Oval : on a mount, St. Martin with plumed helmet, seated on a horse springing to the r. On the r. a beggar, standing, holding out the r. h., in the l. h. a crutch.

In the field overhead : ST. MARTIN. In base: 1749.

Harbour Seal, A.D. 1646.

4889. Sulph. cast, chipped, from the matrix. $2\frac{11}{16} \times 2\frac{5}{16}$ in. [D.C., H. 149.]

Oval : a shield of arms : CINQUE-PORTS, see No. 4885.

❋ DOVOR ❋ HARBOVR ❋ ANO ❋ DOM ❋ 1646.

Inner border beaded, outer border carved.

4890. Sulph. cast. [lxv. 45.]

Boys, *History of Sandwich*, vol. ii., p. 797, fig. 8 ; S. Lewis, *Topogr. Dict.*, vol. ii., p. 64.

Great Seal of the Castle and Courts of the Cinque-Ports.

4891. [18th cent.] Sulph. cast from the matrix. $2\frac{1}{8}$ in. [lxv. 46.]

On the l. Dover castle on a rock, with a flag charged with a cross and saltire united ; in the foreground the town ; on the r. a three-masted ship of war under sail to the r., flags charged with a cross.

Legend on a riband with wavy ends :—

MAG · SIGILL · CASTR · DOVER · ET · CVRIARVM · CANCELL · ET · ADMIR · QVINQ · PORT.

Carved border.

W. Boys, *History of Sandwich*, vol. ii., p. 797, fig. 6.

A seal or badge.

4892. Sulph. cast from the matrix or a die. $2\frac{3}{4}$ in. [lxvi. 21.]

St. Martin, on a horse walking to the l. on a mount replenished with foliage. On the r. a beggar with wooden leg, and behind him the church of St. Mary and two trees. In the field overhead a riband inscribed : DOVOR.

In place of the legend a carved border.

DROITWICH, *co. Worcester.*

4893. [15th cent.] Sulph. cast. $2\frac{1}{8}$ in. [lxxiii. 95.]

A shield of arms : per pale, *dex.,* a sword of state palewise, handle in chief, surmounted of two lions passant in pale, *sin.*

quarterly, 1, 4, chequy, 2, 3, two barrows palewise in fess, TOWN OF DROITWICH. Inner edge of the field engrailed.

+ SIGILLUM ⚭ COMMUNE ⚭ VILLE ⚭ WYCHIE ⚭
Beaded borders.

Later Seal.

4894. Sulph. cast from the matrix. 2 in. [lxxiii. 96.]
A shield of arms : TOWN OF DROITWICH, see No. 4893.

~ + ~ SIGILLVM ⌒ + ~ COMMVNE ⌒ + ~ VILLE ⌒ + ~ WYTCHIE.

The letters IE, of *Wytchie*, appear to have been filled up in the matrix.

S. Lewis, *Topogr. Dict.*, vol. ii., p. 75.

Small Seal.

4895. Sulph. cast from the matrix. 1¾ in. [lxxiii. 97.]
A shield of arms : TOWN OF DROITWICH, as in No. 4894.

⌒ + ~ SIGILLVM ⌒ + ~ COMMVNE ⌒ + ~ VILLE ⌒ + ~ WYTCH.

DUNWICH, *co. Suffolk.*
Corporation Seal.

4896. [12th–13th cent.] Sulph. cast from the matrix. 3 × 2¼ in. [lxxi. 107.]
Lozenge-shaped : a one-masted ship on the sea, in which are five fishes ; mainsail furled by a mariner on board ; embattled crow's nest, topped with a lance-flag, charged with three demi-lions (?) ; at each end an embattled castle, ornamented with a fret-work and topped with a lance-flag, that on the l. charged with two chevrons, that on the r. indistinct ; in each castle a mariner ; at the side four port-holes, closed, and on the l. a side-rudder. In the field above, on the l., a crescent, on the r. a radiant sun or roundle with eight rays.

SIGILL' : BVRGI : DE : DONEWIZ.

Bailiffs.

4897. [A.D. 1688.] Red : covered with paper before impression ; very indistinct. 2 in. [Add. ch. 10,445.]
Lozenge-shaped : bust of a king, full-face, with crown, in a boat on the waves. In the field on each side an estoile. 14th cent. style of work.

✠ SIGILLUM ⚭ BALLIUORUM ⚭ DE ⚭ DONEWICU ⚭

Another Seal.

4898. Sulph. cast from fine impression. [lxxi. 108.]

Lozenge-shaped: resembles the preceding seal, No. 4897, but is not from the same matrix.

⊕ SIGILLUM ⋈ BALLIUORUM ⋈ ⋈ DE ⋈ DONEWICO.

S. Lewis, *Topogr. Dict.*, vol. ii., p. 87 ; *Add. MS.* 5,524, ff. 76 *b*, 121.

DURHAM, *co. Durham.*

4899. [16th cent.] Sulph. cast from the matrix. 2¼ in. [D.C., H. 54.]

A bishop with mitre, standing in a niche with trefoiled arch supported on slender shafts ; the canopy resembles a church with tall spire. Lifting up the r. h. in benediction, in the l. h. a pastoral staff held obliquely. In the field, over the canopy on the l. an estoile of six points, on the r. a crescent. At each side in the field a shield of arms : ENGLAND, surmounted by a mitre. In base a shield of arms : a cross fimbriated, perhaps for Bishop SKIRLAW. See No. 2469.

⊕ : S' : COMVNE ·:· CIVITAT̄ ·:· DVNELMIE ·:· ⋈

S. Lewis, *Topogr. Dict.*, vol. ii., p. 90.

ELY, *co. Cambridge.*
Governors for the Townland.

4900. [18th cent.] Sulph. cast from the matrix. 1½ in. [lx. 57.]

A shield of arms : a chevron betw. three crowns, CITY OF ELY, derived from the arms of THE SEE, viz. three crowns.

THE SEAL OF THE GOVERNORS FOR THE TOWNLAND OF ELY.

The word *the*, which occurs three times, is a monogram.

S. Lewis, *Topogr. Dict.*, vol. ii., p. 131.

Clerk of the Crown and Assizes within the Isle of Ely.

4901. [Late 16th cent.] Red : recent impression. 2⅛ in. [xxxv. 359.]

A shield of arms : SEE OF ELY, betw. the initial letters I. G. and three ornamental sprigs of foliage.

· S' OFFICI ⁞ CLERICI ⁞ CORONÆ ⁞ ET ⁞ ASSISAR ⁞ ETO ⁞ INFRA ⁞ INSVLAM ⁞ ELIEN ⁞ IN ⁞ COM ⁞ CANTEBRIGIÆ.

Official Seal of the Liberty.

4902. [16th cent.] Red sealing-wax, from the matrix. 1¼ in. [xxxv. 63.]

The Trinity, represented with three faces, one full, two in profile, with radiant nimbus and mound, and wearing a pall, lifting up the r. h. in benediction. In the field, two wings erect.

+ SIGIL . . . . ICII · LIBERTAT · ELIENS.

Beaded borders.

ERPINGHAM, SOUTH, HUNDRED, *co. Norfolk.*

4903. [15th cent.] Recent impression in red sealing-wax, from the matrix. $1\frac{1}{8}$ in. [xxxv. 361.]

Across the field the inscription in three lines :—

HUNDR̄ · DE — SOUTHERPYN — GHAM.

Ensigned with an open crown of three points, fleury. Within a border of three slightly raised cusped points.

S : REGIS : IN : COMIT : NORFF ·

The letters DE in *de*, and HE in *Southerpyngham*, are conjoined.

ESSEX.

SIR MAURICE BRUYÑ, *Sheriff.*

4904. [A.D. 1436.] Green : fine, but imperfect. 1 in. [Harl. ch. 55 E. 7.]

A tower or castle masoned, with round-headed doorway and portcullis. In the field over the central tower the initial letter M, and on each side a wing erect.

4905. Sulph. cast from No. 4904. [D.C., G. 283.]

ETON, *co. Buckingham.*

Royal College of St. Mary, A.D. 1440.

First Seal.

4906. [A.D. 1446.] Red : impression blurred in many places by the matrix shifting during use. $2\frac{1}{4}$ in. [Add. ch. 7210.]

The Coronation of the Virgin, who is standing supported by three angels, with expanded wings, on each side. Overhead the Almighty, with nimbus, placing a crown on the Virgin's head with the l. h., the r. h. lifted up in benediction, the crown supported by two angels. On each side an angel standing with expanded wings, holding a shield of arms : l. FRANCE (MODERN) ; r., quarterly, 1, 4, FRANCE (MODERN)

2, 3, ENGLAND, for HENRY VI., Founder.   Below the Virgin's
feet, a shield of arms : three lilies slipped and leaved, two and
one, a chief per pale, on the *dex.* side a fleur-de-lis, on the *sin.*
a lion passant guardant, ETON COLLEGE.   On the l. a queen,
on the r. an altar.

Legend on a scroll :—

SIGILLŪ · COMMUNE · PREPOSITI · COLLEGII · REGALIS ·
BEATE · MARIE · DE · ETOÑ.

Carved borders.

4907. Sulph. cast from No. 4906.   [lix. 54.]

Second Seal.

4908. [16th cent.]   Red: fine, edge chipped, and the l.
side imperfect.   2¼ in.   [Add. ch. 15,571.]

The Assumption of the Virgin Mary, standing crowned,
with hands in prayer, surrounded by a band of angels in
radiance within a bordure or cordon of clouds.   At her feet a
shield of the ROYAL ARMS, as described in No. 4906,
supported by two lions sejant guardant.

[SIGILLŪ : COMMVNE] PREPOSITI ET COLLEGII : REGALIS
BEATE MARIE DE ETOÑ.

Beaded borders.

N. Carlisle, *Endowed Grammar Schools*, vol. i., p. 48.

4909. Sulph. cast, tinted red, from fine impression.   [xxxv.
128.]

4910. Another.   [xlvii. 792.]

Laing's *MS. Catal.*, No. 271.

4911. Sulph. cast from fine impression.   [lix. 83.]

4912. [A.D. 1716.]   Red: covered with paper before impression.   [Add. ch. 15,572.]

4913. [A.D. 1740.]   Red: *en placard*, covered with paper
before impression.   [Add. ch. 15,573.]

Provost.

4914. [16th cent.]   Sulph. cast, tinted red, from cracked
impression.   2⅛ × 1¾ in.   [xxxv. 129.]

Oval : an ornamental shield of arms : ETON COLLEGE, see
No. 4906, betw. the initial letters E. C.

♠ SIGILLVM · PRAEPOSITI · COLLEGII · REGALIS · ETONIENSIS.

Cf. Carlisle, *Endowed Grammar Schools*, vol. i., p. 90.

4915. Another.   [xlvii. 794.]

Laing's *MS. Catal.*, No. 272.

ETON, *or* NUN-EATON, *co. Warwick.*
Free Grammar School, A.D. 1553.

4916. Sulph. cast from the matrix. 2⅛ × 1¼ in. [xlvii. 793.]

Pointed oval: a cross springing from a leafy ornament. Above, the date 1553. Below, a skull.

✠ SEGILLVM · SCOLA · DE · ETOИE.

Cabled borders.

Laing's *MS. Catal.,* No. 297 ; N. Carlisle, *Endowed Grammar Schools,* vol. ii., p. 655.

4917. Another. [xxxv. 145.]

EVESHAM, *co. Worcester.*

4918. [A.D. 1604.] Sulph. cast from the matrix. 2¼ in. [lxxiii. 98, 99.]

∅. A shield of arms: a prince's coronet betw. in chief two ostrich feathers jewelled, and in base a garb, within a bordure bezantée, BOROUGH OF *E*VESHAM.

✾ SIGILLVM · ✾ · BVRGI · ✾ · EVESHAMIENSIS ⁑ + ℳ

℞. A town, with round domed tower in the centre, two embattled towers with tall spires, houses, embattled doorway, and round domed towers at the sides. In base, on a label with scroll-ends, the inscription EVESHAM, with a palm-branch on the r. and a laurel branch on the l. In the field above a radiant sun ; in base a rose, slipped and leaved.

LIBER ·✰· AB ·✰· HENRICO ·✰· FACTVS ·✰· SVM ·✰· PRINCIPE ·✰· BVRGVS ✰ 1604. ℳ ✾

Inner border beaded, outer border carved.

S. Lewis, *Topogr. Dict.,* vol. ii., p. 148.

EXETER, *co. Devon.*

4919. [13th cent.] Sulph. cast from the matrix. 2¼ in. [lxi. 74.]

An elaborate building of two storeys with pent roof and two flags, placed betw. two circular embattled towers enriched with numerous string-courses and two arcades of round-headed arches. The towers are united at the base with an embattlement, and outside the towers two small arcades or double doorways, with flory ironwork hinges, also embattled. In the field, over the building, a sun, betw. an estoile of ten points on the l. and a crescent on the r.; at the sides two keys, handles downwards; in base a fleur-de-lis, betw. two wyverns with their tails flory.

Legend in ornamental letters :—

✠ SIGILLVM : CIVITATIS : EXONIE ⱥ .

S. Lewis, *Topogr. Dict.*, vol. ii., p. 154.

Mayoralty.

4920. [13th cent.] Sulph. cast from the matrix. 1¼ × 1⅛ in. [D.C., E. 48.]

Pointed oval : an archbishop or bishop? with crown and mitre, half-length, in a canopied niche of elegant design, with trefoiled arch, crocketed, and tabernacle work at the sides ; in the r. h. a model of a church, in the l. h. a crozier. Below him a wall with round-headed doorway, doors opened. In base, under an arch, a lion's face, crowned. In the field out- side the niche, on the r. the keys of St. Peter, on the l. the sword of St. Paul, patron saints of the city.

✿ S' MAIORATVS : CIVITATIS : EXONIE ✿ .

4921. Another. [lxi. 75.]

Mayor of the Staple.

4922. [14th cent.] Sulph. cast. 1⅛ in. [lxi. 77.]

A triple-towered and embattled castle ; in the doorway, under a portcullis, a lion sejant guardant, the r. paw raised, collared and lined ; in base a small fleur-de-lis. Background hatched or reticulated.

✿ S' MAIORIS STAPVLE CIVITATIS EXON'.

Provosts.

4923. [13th cent.] Sulph. cast from fine impression. 1½ in. [lxi. 75.]

Octagonal : an embattled tower of two storeys, with round- headed doorway and trefoiled opening betw. the round-headed windows of the upper storey. On the battlements a lion passant contourné betw. two flags. On each side a wall, masoned and embattled, and above it an estoile wavy of eight points. In base two lions passant addorsed.

✠ S' PREPOSITORVM · CIVITATIS · DE · EXONIA.

Seal " pro recognitione debitorum," see No. 1072.

Seal of the Free Grammar School. See Hospital of St. John the Baptist, Exeter, Nos. 3129–3136.

EYE, *co. Suffolk.*

4924. [15th cent.] Sulph. cast from the matrix. 1⅛ in. [lxxi. 110.]

The name EYE in black letter, ensigned with a crown, within a cordon of pellets.

❀ SIGILLVM ✩ COMVNE ✩ BVRGI ✪ DE · EYE.

Cabled borders.

S. Lewis, *Topogr. Dict.,* vol. ii., p. 160.

Smaller Seal.

4925. Sulph. cast from the matrix. 1 in. [lxxi. 111.]

Similar in design to, but smaller than, the previous seal, No. 4924.

Burgesses.

4926. [15th cent.] Sulph. cast from the matrix. 1 in. [lxxiii. 37.]

The name EYE with the initial E, of larger dimensions than the rest of the lettering, ensigned with a crown of three points fleury. This is to be read as the last word of the legend

❀ SIGILLŪ + COM̄E ⚜ BURGENCIAR · DE .

FAVERSHAM, or FEVERSHAM, *co. Kent.*

4927. [12th cent.] Sulph. cast from fine, but imperfect, impression. 2¾ in. [lxv. 55.]

A one-masted ship on the sea, with sails furled, stern and forecastle embattled.

+ SI . . . . SHAM.

Cf. *Add. MS.* 6,331, f. 127.

Later Seal.

4928. [13th cent.] Sulph. casts from the matrix. 2¼ in. [lxv. 56, 57.]

Ø. A ship of war, with one mast, on the sea ; two sailors sitting on the yard furling the mainsail, a mariner in the embattled crow's nest, five soldiers, with weapons, and a captain in the body of the vessel, two trumpeters in the embattled stern-castle, with a flag charged with three chevronels. In the embattled forecastle a flag with a cross of St. George. In the upper part of the field a large rose *en soleil.*

❀ SIGILLVM BARONVM ·:· DE ·:· FAVERSHAM.

R. A large shield of arms of ENGLAND, betw. three wyverns, tails fleury.

✠ REGIS : VT : ARMA : REGO : LIBERA : PORTVS : EGO.

Beaded borders.

Jacob, *History of Faversham*, p. 17, pl. iii. ; *Add. MS.* 6,331, f. 128 ; S. Lewis, *Topogr. Dict.*, vol. ii., p. 175.

4929. Sulph. cast of the *rev.* only. [D.C., E. 340.]

Mayoralty.

First Seal.

4930. [14th cent.] Sulph. cast from the matrix. 1½ in. [xlvii. 796.]

The Virgin, with crown, seated on a carved throne, in a niche with trefoiled canopy and tabernacle work at the sides, on her l. knee the Child, in her r. h. a fleur-de-lis. In base, a shield of arms, CINQUE-PORTS, see No. 4885. Background diapered lozengy.

✠ SIGILLVM · MAIORATVS · VILLE · DE · FAVERSHAM.

Jacob, *History of Faversham*, p. 17, pl. iii. ; *Add. MS.*, 6,331, f. 128 ; Laing, *MS. Catal.*, No. 381.

4931. Another. [lxv. 58.]

Second Seal.

4932. [A.D. 1573.] Red : injured by pressure. 1⅛ in. [Harl. ch. 85 D. 39.]

A copy of the previous seal, with details differently treated.

SIGILLU MAIORATVS · VILLE · DE · FEUERSHAM.

4933. Sulph. cast of No. 4932. [D.C., H. 47.]

Court of the Portmote.

4934. [16th cent.] Sulph. cast. 1¼ in. [xlvii. 797.]

A demi-lion passant guardant conjoined to the hulk of a ship, one of the charges in the shield of arms of the CINQUE-PORTS.

SIGILLVM : CVR PORTMOT' DE FFEVERSHAM.

Jacob, *History of Faversham*, p. 17, pl. iii., f. 3 ; Laing, *MS. Catal.*, No. 382.

FLAXWELL, *co. Lincoln.*

Seal of the Wapentake for Passes, or "Pro Servis."

4935. [15th cent.] Recent impression in black wax, from the matrix. 1¼ in. [lxxvi. 31.]

Across the field, in two lines, the word:— FLAX-WELL, with a sprig of foliage above, and another below.

✠ SIGILL' · COM̄ · LINCOL'N · ꝑ · S'VIS.

4936. Impression in green wax, from a block. [lxxvi. 32.]

Thompson, *History of Boston*, fol. ed., p. 302; *Journ. Brit. Arch. Assoc.*, vol. xxxii., p. 120.

FOLKESTONE, *co. Kent.*

4937. [13th cent.] Sulph. cast from the matrix. 1$\frac{1}{16}$ in. [xlvii. 799.]

A one-masted ship of war, on the waves, mainsail furled, embattled crow's nest, and fore- and stern-castles, with a mariner's head in each castle. In the body of the vessel a mariner's head and hand; in the stern another mariner steering.

SIGILL' BARONVM FOLKESTANIE.

W. Boys, *History of Sandwich*, p. 811; S. Lewis, *Topogr. Dict.*, vol. ii., p. 190; Laing, *MS. Catal.*, No. 621.

4938. Another. [lxv. 63.]

Mayoralty.

4939. [15th cent.] Sulph. cast. 1⅜ in. [xlvii. 800.]

The Abbess and Patron Saint Eanswitha, standing crowned, in the r. h. a book, in the l. h. a pastoral staff richly ornamented, and curved outwards, betw. two fishes hauriant embowed. Field replenished with small cinquefoils.

✠ SIGILLŪ ✠ OFFICIJ ✠ MAIORATUS ✠ FOLKESTANIE.

Inner border cabled.

W. Boys, *History of Sandwich*, p. 811; Laing, *MS. Catal.*, No. 622.

4940. Another. [lxv. 64.]

FOLSTON or FOLKESTONE HUNDRED, *co. Kent.*

4941. [A.D. 1540.]   Red. $\frac{4}{8}$ in.   [Harl. ch. 78 G. 29.]
The initial letters I. B., perhaps of John Boys, one of the parties in the charter.

HUNDERD OF FOLSTŌ.

The letters DE of *Hunderd* are conjoined.

FORDWICH, *co. Kent.*

4942. [12th cent.]   Sulph. cast from the matrix. $2\frac{1}{8}$ in. [lxv. 66.]
A one-masted ship, with mainsail furled, on waves.

+ SIGILLVM BARONVM DE FORWIZ.

W. Boys, *History of Sandwich*, pp. 806, 816.

Another Seal.

4943. [12th cent.]   Sulph. cast from imperfect impression. $2\frac{1}{8}$ in.   [lxv. 67.]
Same design as the preceding seal, No. 4942, but with details differently proportioned.

... ILLVM : BARON ..... DE .... WIZ.

Mayor.

4944. [13th cent.]   Sulph. cast from the matrix. $1\frac{1}{8}$ in. [xlvii. 801.]
A lion passant guardant of ENGLAND, on an oval enclosure set with an antique oval intaglio gem, bearing a fish naiant on a wave.

✠ S' MAIORIS : DE : FORDWICO.

Laing's *MS. Catal.*, No. 623.

FRAMLINGHAM CASTLE, *co. Suffolk.*

4945. [15th cent.]   Sulph. cast.   1 in.   [lxxi. 113.]
A triple-towered castle, masoned and embattled, with square-headed doorways, betw. the initial letters W. B.

FRANCHEWILLE, or NEWTOWN, *Isle of Wight,*
co. Southampton.

4946. [13th cent.]   Recent impression in red sealing-wax from the matrix. $1\frac{7}{8}$ in.   [xxxvii. 77.]

A one-masted ship on the waves, mainsail furled, embattled stern- and fore-castles. Behind the mast in the field a lion passant guardant of ENGLAND. On the r. a shield of arms : a cross. Overhead, on the l. an estoilé of six points, on the r. a crescent.

✠ S' COĪTATIS . DE : FRANCHEWILLE : DE : LILE : DE : WYHT ✠

S. Lewis, *Topogr. Dict.*, vol. iii., p. 375.

⁻ **4947.** Sulph. cast. [lxiii. 95.]

GATESHEAD, *co. Durham*.

4948. [16th cent.] Sulph. cast. 1¼ in. [lxii. 86.]
An embattled gateway or tower with three doors, that in the centre round-headed.

SIGILLVM BVRGI DE GATESHEAD.

S. Lewis, *Topogr. Dict.*, vol. ii., p. 216.

GLOUCESTER, *co. Gloucester*.
Mayoralty.

4949. [A.D. 1492.] Red : fine, but fragmentary. About 1⅛ in. when perfect. [Add. ch. 23,845.]
A shield of arms : a sword in bend, hilt downwards, betw. six horseshoes and ten horse-nails.

Legend broken away.

Cf. Burke, *General Armory, s. v.;* Fosbrooke, *History of Gloucester*, p. 203 ; cf. also Add. ch. 19,564.

Bailiffs.

4950. [13th cent.] Sulph. cast from a matrix. 1¾ in. [D.C., G. 276.]
A triple-towered castle, masoned, with round-headed doorway, side towers embattled, central tower with pent-roof, flying buttresses, and quatrefoiled window. In base wavy lines representing the River Severn. In the field above the towers, two estoiles of six points.

✠ SIGILL' : BALLIVOR' : GLOVCESTRIE.

Beaded borders.

S. Lewis, *Topogr. Dict.*, vol. ii, p. 230.

Seals, "pro recognitione debitorum," see Nos. 1073, 1074.

GODMANCHESTER, *co. Huntingdon.*
Free Grammar School, A.D. 1580.

4951. Sulph. cast, tinted red. 1⅜ in. [xxxv. 131.]
An ornamental fleur-de-lis, seeded.

⫶ COMMVNE SIGILLVM GVMECESTRE.

Beaded borders.

N. Carlisle, *Endowed Grammar Schools,* vol. i., p. 555 ; *Gent. Mag.,* vol. lxviii., p. 293 ; S. Lewis, *Topogr. Dict.,* vol. ii., p. 241.

4952. Another. [xlvii. 808.]

Laing's *MS. Catal.,* No. 281.

GRAMPOUND, *co. Cornwall.*

4953. Sulph. cast from the matrix. 1⅞ in. [lxi. 10.]
A bridge, masoned, of two arches, over a torrent. On the r. a tree. On the wall a shield of arms : a lion rampant within a bordure charged with eleven roundles, JOHN PLANTAGENET of Eltham, Earl of Cornwall.

✿ SIGILLVM : MAIORIS · & · BVRGENSIVM : BVRGE · DE · GRANDPONT · ALS : PONSMVR.

S. Lewis, *Topogr. Dict.,* vol. ii., p. 249.

GRANTHAM, *co. Lincoln.*

4954. Sulph. cast from the matrix. 2⅜ in. [lxvi. 98.]
A shield of arms : chequy, on a bordure eleven trefoils slipped, TOWN OF GRANTHAM.

✿ SIGILLVM ✖ BVRGENCIVM ✖ ET ✖ COMMVNITATIS ✖ VILLE ✖ DE ✖ GRANTHAM.

Carved borders.

Cf. S. Lewis, *Topogr. Dict.,* vol. ii., p. 250.

Another Seal.

4955. Sulph. cast from the matrix. 2⅜ in. [lxvi. 99.]
An ornamental estoile or rosette of six leaves enclosed in a cusped sixfoil panel, with fleury points. The spandrils carved with foliage.

✿ SIGILL' ✖ BVRGENSIVMIERR (*sic*) ✖ CAMERARI ✖ DE GRAHAM.

Carved borders.

*Seal of the Office of the Soke, used by the Free
.Grammar School*, A.D. 1528.

4956. .Sulph. cast, tinted red. .1 in.. [xxxv. 132.] ꞏ.

A shield of arms: chequy, a bordure charged with eight
.trefoils slipped, TOWN OF GRANTHAM.

.✠ SIGILLVM · OFFICII · GRANTHAMIE · CVM · SOCA.

'N. Carlisle, *Endowed Grammar Schools*, vol. i., p. 804 ; S. Lewis,
Topogr. Dict., vol. ii., p. 250.

4957. Another. [xlvii. 809.]

Laing's *MS. Catal.*, No. 284.

GRIMSBY, *co. Lincoln.*

4958. [13th cent.] Recent impression in red sealing-wax
from the matrix. 2 in. [xxxv. 79.]

The merchant Gryem, with sword and shield, to the r.,
with a hand of blessing over his head, betw. Habloc holding
an axe on the l. and Goldesburch on the r. crowned, holding
a sceptre fleury. Below, the hat of Gryem. In the field the
names ✠ GRYEM—HABLOC—GOLDESBVRCH.

✠ SIGILLVM : COMMVNITATIS : GRIMEBYE.

Beaded borders.

Oliver, *History of Great Grimsby ; British Topographer ;* S. Lewis,
Topogr. Dict., vol. ii., p. 264 ; Sir Frederic Madden, *Introduction to
Legend of Havelock* (Roxburgh Club).

4959. Sulph. cast from matrix. [xlvii. 810.]

Laing's *MS. Catal.*, No. 479.

4960. Another. [D.C., E. 294.]

Mayoralty.

4961. [14th cent.] Recent impression in red sealing-wax
from the matrix. 1½ in. [xxxv. 80.]

A boar-hunt, the boar running to the r. pursued by a
huntsman blowing a horn, and dog ; in background a forked
tree with an eagle on the foliage.

✠ SIGILLVM : MAIORITATIS : DE : GRIMESBY.

Oliver, *History of Great Grimsby*, p. 13, pl. II., fig. 2 ; *Gent. Mag.*,
1828, p. 401.

GUERNSEY, *Island of.*

Royal Seal for the Bailiwick.

Seal used by HENRY SPIGOURNEL, *Justice in Eyre.*

4962. [A.D. 1323.] Dark-green : fine, the edge chipped. 1¾ in. [Add. ch. 19,809.]

A shield of arms : *E*NGLAND. Upon a branch of foliage.

〔✠ S' · B〕ALL〔IVI〕E · I〔NSVL〕E · DE · GERNESEYE.

Beaded borders.

S. Lewis, *Topogr. Dict.*, vol. ii., p. 268.

EDWARD III.

Seal used by PIERREZ de BEAUÑ, *Bailiff.*

4963. [A.D. 1347.] Dark-green : fine, the edge chipped. 1¾ in. [Add. ch. 19,811.]

A shield of arms : *E*NGLAND. Upon a branch of foliage.

〔✠〕 S' BALLIVIE · INSVLE · DE · GE〔R〕NESEYE.

Perhaps from the same matrix as No. 4962, the preceding seal, but the beaded borders and other details are worn out in the matrix from which this impression was derived.

HENRY VIII.

Seal used by JOHAN HARYVEL ? *Bailiff.*

4964. [A.D. 1548.] Dark-green : imperfect at the upper part. [Add. ch. 19,812.]

Same as No. 4963, the preceding seal.

. . . . . . IE INSVLE DE GERNES . . . . . .

JAMES I.

Seal used by AMICE DE CARTERET, *Esquire, Bailiff.*

4965. [A.D. 1612.] Dark-green : only fragment of the centre. [Add. ch. 19,814.]

The shield of arms only. Legend wanting, Apparently from the same matrix as the preceding seal, No. 4964.

Official Seal of DENIS LE MARCHANT, *Seneschal of the Court of the "Priourtey" of St. Michael du Valle.*

4966. [A.D. 1439.] Green : indistinct. 1⅛ in. [Add. ch. 19,810.]

- Michael the Archangel, in combat with a horned devil, and piercing him with a long cross.

.... ⚜ SCEAU ⚜ DU ⚜ UILLE ⚜ ....

HALIFAX, *co. York.*

4967. [A.D. 1662.] Recent impression in red sealing-wax from the matrix. 1⅜ in. [xlix. 136.]

· On a mount a tree of three branches ; on the **r.** a man standing, with flat hat, holding a fruit in the r. h. ; on the l. a woman hanging by the neck from a branch. This is probably designed to represent the "Gibbet Law" of the Forest of Hardwick, a district co-extensive with the Parish of Halifax.

⚜ SIGILL' · CORP · APVD · HALLIF · 1662.

Outer border carved.

Cf. Lewis, *Topogr. Dict.*, vol. ii., p. 295.

Later Seal.

4968. [19th cent.] Recent impression in gutta percha, tinted red, from the matrix. 2¾ in. [xxxvi. 223.]

The Head of St. John Baptist with three gouttes dropping from the neck, and encircled with an ornamental nimbus with five cusps, betw. the words HALIG–FAX. Background diapered lozengy with a reticulated pattern. All within an elegantly carved gothic panel of tracery, enriched with quatrefoils, over which, on each side, a label inscribed, l. :— WARREN, r. :—LEWYS.

The legend commences with a lamb sejant for initial stop :—

SIGILLUM · COMMUNITATIS · BURGENSIUM · DE · HALIFAX.

Free Grammar School, A.D. 1585.

4969. Sulph. cast, tinted red. 2 × 1¾ in. [xxxv. 133.]

Pointed oval: an open book inscribed :—QUI MIHI DISCIPULUS' PUER ES SAPIS ATQ3. Above, a cinquefoiled rose, *en soleil*, betw. the date 15–97 ; in base a portcullis.

· SIGIL · LIBE · GRAM : SCHOL · R · ELIZ · VICARIAT · HALIFAX.

N. Carlisle, *Endowed Grammar Schools*, vol. ii., p. 808.

4970. Another. [xlvii. 815.]

Laing's *MS. Catal.*, No. 303.

HARLECH, *co. Merioneth.*

Corporation, A.D. 1286.

4973. [A.D. 1529.] Bronze-green : fine, but imperfect. 1½ in. [Add. ch. 8486.]

A triple-towered castle, masoned and embattled, round-headed doorway. Field at the sides, diapered lozengy.

[✠ SI]GILLV : COMMVNE : DE : HAR . . . .

HARROW-ON-THE-HILL, *co. Middlesex.*

Free Grammar School.

4971. [*c.* A.D. 1590.] Sulph. cast, tinted red. 1⅜ × 1¼ in. [xxxv. 134.]

Oval: a lion rampant, being a *rebus* on the name of the founder, John Lyon.

·:· DONORVM DEI DISPENSATIO FIDELIS.

Carved border.

N. Carlisle, *Endowed Grammar Schools*, vol. ii., p. 125.

4972. Another. [xlvii. 816.]

Laing's *MS. Catal.*, No. 287.

HARTLEBURY, *co. Worcester.*

Free Grammar School, A.D. 1558.

4974. Sulph. cast, tinted red. 2¼ × 1⅞ in. [xxxv. 135.]

Pointed oval : the Virgin and Child, under a dome-shaped canopy with curtains, of the style of the Renaissance, on carved pillars.

In base a flowering branch.

SIGILLV̄ : GVBERNATORV̄ · LIBERE : SCOLE : IN :
HARTILBVRY · Aᴼ. 1558.

Inner border beaded.

N. Carlisle, *Endowed Grammar Schools*, vol. ii., p. 757.

4975. Another. [xlvii. 817.]

Laing's *MS. Catal.*, No. 301.

HARTLEPOOL, *co. Durham.*

4976. [13th cent.] Sulph. cast from the matrix. 2 in.
[lxii. 87.]

In a *pool*, a *hart* at gaze to the r., on its haunches a deer-
hound. In the field on the r. a wavy sprig of foliage.

✠ S' COMMVNITATIS : DE : HERTERPOL. ✠

Beaded borders.

S. Lewis, *Topogr. Dict.*, vol. ii., p. 327.

Counterseal.

4977. [13th cent.] Sulph. cast from the matrix. 2 in.
[lxii. 88.]

For description of this seal, see vol. i., p. 806, No. 4328,
where another example is attributed, erroneously, to the
Benedictine abbey of SS. Peter and Hilda of Whitby, co.
York.

SVBVENIAT FAMVL' NOBIL' : HILDA SVIS.

Beaded borders.

4977*b*. Sulph. cast from a fine impression, or the matrix,
see No. 4977. [D.C., E. 39.]

Mayor.

4978. [13th cent.] Sulph. cast from the matrix. 1⅜ in.
[lxii. 89.]

On a stag lodged, and beneath three canopies supported on
slender shafts, St. Hilda, standing with a book in the r. h.
and a pastoral staff curved outwards in the l. h., betw. two
bishops, each lifting up the r. h. in benediction, a pastoral staff
in the l. h. Tabernacle-work at the sides.

S' OFFICII · MAIORIS · ✸ ✠ ✸ DE · HERTILPOL.

HASTINGS, *co. Sussex.*

4979. [13th cent.]   Sulph. casts from the matrix. $3\frac{1}{8}$ in.
[lxxii. 84, 85.]

Ø.   A one-masted ship of war, sailing on the waves, main-sail set by a mariner with coif of mail.   In the stern, under an arch with crenellated ridge, a mariner with similar coif, steering the rudder ; over the ridge a banner flag charged with the arms of ENGLAND.   On the prow a banner flag charged with the arms of the CINQUE-PORTS, see No. 4885. This vessel is ramming another of similar shape without banner flags, which is cut down to the edge of the water. In the waves in base, the head of a man with similar coif overboard.

SIGILLVM : COMMVNE BARONVM : DE HASTINGGIS.

The legend ends with a bird holding a wavy branch in its beak.

℞. Michael the Archangel, with nimbus and round shield charged with a cross betw. twelve pellets, three in each canton, turned slightly to the l., trampling on a Dragon and piercing his head with a long cross held in the r. h.

✠ : DRACO : CRVDELIS : TE VINCET : VIS : MICAELIS.

The legend ends with a bird and branch as in the *obv.*
Beaded borders.

S. Lewis, *Topogr. Dict.*, vol. ii., p. 336.

4980. [A.D. 1361.]   Green : fine, but imperfect.   [Add. ch. 15,872.]

Ø.   . . . . NVM : DE HASTINGGI . .

℞.   . . . . O : CRVDELI . . . . VINCE . . . .

Mayor.

4981. [17th cent.]   Sulph. cast. from the matrix. $1\frac{1}{2}$ in. [lxxii. 86.]

A shield of arms with carved scrolls of foliage at top and sides : CINQUE-PORTS ; with the variation that the lion in the centre is not dimidiated with a hulk but entire.

✠ SIGILLVM · OFFICII · MAIORIS · DE · HASTING.

Inner border beaded.

HAVERING-ATTE-BOWER MANOR, *co. Essex.*

4982. [14th cent.]   Sulph. cast from indistinct impression. $1\frac{1}{2}$ and $1\frac{1}{8}$ in.   [D.C., H. 163.]

Pointed oval : a triple-towered castle, centre tower domed, embattled, and topped with a cross ; side towers pinnacled, portcullis in the round-headed doorway. In base a *ring*, or annulet.

⚘ SIGILLVM · MANERII · DE · HAVERING · ATTE · BOWRE.

The letters TT in *atte* are conjoined.

Ogbourne, *History of Essex*, p. 186.

Another Seal.

4983. Sulph. cast from indistinct impression. 1½ × 1¼ in. [D.C., H. 164.]

Copy of the preceding seal, No. 4982, but the details slightly larger in some parts.

HEDON, *co. York.*

4984. [A.D. 1598.] Sulph. cast. 1 in. [lxxiv. 54.]

A one-masted ship, with mainsail and maintopsail set, sailing to the r., on the poop a mariner standing turned to the l.

H · CAMERA ·:· REGISS : 1598.

Beaded border.

S. Lewis, *Topogr. Dict.*, vol. ii., p. 352.

Later Seal.

4985. [17th cent.] Sulph. cast from the matrix. 1¾ in. [lxxiv. 55.]

A decked-boat with one mast and two sails set, on board two mariners, at the stern a flag charged with a cross.

⚘ SIG : VIL : DE : HEDON : CAMERA : REGIS ❋

HELSTON or HELLESTON, *co. Cornwall.*

4986. [15th cent.] Sulph. cast from the matrix. 2 in. [lxi. 8.]

On an embattled arcade, betw. two embattled octagon towers, with domed roofs, Michael the Archangel, with expanded wings and nimbus, in the l. h. a shield of arms of ENGLAND ; trampling on a dragon and piercing his head with a long spear. In the field on each side, a cinquefoil.

⚘ SIGILLUM : COMUNITATIS : UILLE : DE : HELLESTONE : BURGTH.

Beaded border.

S. Lewis, *Topogr. Dict.*, vol. ii., p. 356.

: *Later Seal.*

4987. [17th cent.] Sulph. cast from the matrix.
A late copy of the preceding seal, No. 4986, poorly designed.

THE SEAL OF THE BOROUGH OF HELLESTON.

HEMEL-HEMPSTEAD, *co. Hertford.*

4988. [16th cent.] Sulph. cast from the matrix. 1¼ ×
1⅛ in. [lxiv. 63.]

Oval : bust of Henry VIII., in whose reign the town was
incorporated, in flat cap and ermine tippet, with gold collar
and breast ; the face turned slightly to the r.

SIGIL · CORP · HEMEL · HEMPSTEAD.

S. Lewis, *Topogr. Dict.*, vol. ii., p. 358.

HEMSWORTH, *co. York.*
Hospital or Free Grammar School, 1637.

4989. Sulph. cast, tinted red, from the silver matrix. 3⅛ ×
2⅛ in. [xxxv. 136.]

Pointed oval : two keys with ornamental wards and handles
in saltire, handles downwards, betw. two crosses crosslets
fitchées in allusion to the arms of the SEE OF YORK, the school
having been founded by Archbishop Holgate, A.D. 1545–1554,
and the date 16–37. In chief, rays of light descending from
clouds ; in base, a mount replenished with flowers.

✠ SI · COME · HOSTLIS · ROBTI · HOLGATE · QvOD · ARCHI ·
EBOR · IN · HIMSWORTH ·
C · EB·

*(Sigillum Commune Hospitalis Roberti Holgate quondam
Archiepiscopi Eboracensis in Himsworth, co. Ebor.)*

Inner border beaded, outer border carved.

N. Carlisle, *Endowed Grammar Schools*, vol. ii., p. 821.

4990. Another. [xlvii. 818.]

Laing, *MS. Catal.*, No. 304,

HENLEY-IN-ARDEN, *co. Warwick.*

4991. [15th cent.] Sulph. cast from impression chipped
at the edge. 1¾ in. [lxxiii. 13.]

The Trinity in a niche with trefoiled canopy, pinnacled and crocketed : on each side in a smaller niche a saint ; l. St. John Baptist with **A**gnus Dei ; r. St. John the Evangelist with book and eagle on the r. h., and in the l. h. a palmbranch. In the field on each side, a branch of foliage.

✠ : SIGILLUM ✠ : ✠ BURGEN . . . . . . US : ✠ DE ✠ HENLEYE : ✠

HENLEY-UPON-THAMES, *co. Oxon.*

4992. [17th cent.] Sulph. cast from the matrix. $1\frac{3}{16}$ in. [lxxi. 8.]

A lion rampant.

✠ SIGILLVM : COMVNE : VILLÆ : DE : HENLEE.

Beaded borders.

S. Lewis, *Topogr. Dict.*, vol. ii , p. 361.

HEREFORD, *co. Hereford.*

4993. [12th cent.]. Sulph. cast from fine, but chipped, impression. $2\frac{1}{4}$ in. [lxiv. 42.]

A shield of arms of early form : three lions passant guardant in pale, enfiling a banner-flag.

✠ SIGILL' COMVNE : CIVIVM : HEREFORD.

Beaded borders.

Later Seal.

4994. [18th cent.] Sulph. cast from the matrix. $2\frac{3}{4}$ in. [lxiv. 43.]

A shield of arms : three lions passant guardant in pale within a bordure charged with ten saltires, CITY OF HEREFORD. Crest, on a helmet, mantling, and wreath, a lion statant guardant, in the dexter paw a sword erect. Supporters two lions rampant guardant, each gorged with a collar charged with three buckles. In base, on a riband the inscription :—INVICTÆ FIDELITATIS PRŒMIVM.

Beaded and carved borders.

S. Lewis, *Topogr. Dict.*, vol. ii., p. 365.

4995. Recent impression in red sealing-wax. [xxxiv. 63.]

Bailiffs.

4996. [14th cent.] Sulph. cast from the matrix. $1\frac{7}{8}$ in. [D.C., F. 338.]

A shield of arms: three lions passant guardant in pale, ENGLAND, or perhaps CITY OF HEREFORD, cf. No. 4994, betw. three pierced cinquefoils. Within a finely carved and traced gothic sexfoil.

✠ S' BALLIUORVM : CIUITATIS : HEREFORDIE :

Staple.

4997. [18th cent.] Sulph. cast from cracked impression. 1 in. [lxiv. 44.]

A shield of arms as in the preceding seal, No. 4996.

SIGILL' ·:· CIVIT ·:· HEREF' ·:·

Seal "pro recognitione debitorum," see No. 1075.

HERTFORD, *co. Hertford.*

4998. Sulph. cast from the matrix. $1\frac{1}{4}$ in. [lxiv. 64.]

A rose *en soleil*, or rosette of five double leaves, barbed and seeded, within a loosely cabled bordure.

✠ BVRGVS ✠ DE HERTFORD 1608.

The letters TF in *Hertford* are conjoined.

Later Seal.

4999. [16th cent.] Sulph. cast from the matrix. $2\frac{3}{8}$ in. [lxiv. 65.]

A *hart* standing in a *ford*, forming a *rebus* on the name of the town, betw. its antlers a long cross pattée fitchée. On the further bank, on the r. h. a triple-towered castle, each tower domed, embattled and topped by a cross, portcullis half-down in the round-headed doorway ; on the l. a tree.

✠ R · D · G · THE · SEALE · OF · THE BOROVGHE · TOWNE · OF · HARTFORDE ✠✿

S. Lewis, *Topogr. Dict.*, vol. ii., p. 375.

Small Seal.

5000. Sulph. cast from the matrix. $\frac{7}{8}$ in. [lxiv. 66.]

A copy of the preceding seal, No. 4999, with details differently proportioned.

BOROUGH OF HERTFORD.

HIGHGATE, *co. Middlesex.*
Free Grammar School, A.D. 1600.

5001. Recent impression in red sealing-wax from the matrix. 2⅛ in. [xxxvi. 181.]

A shield of arms : a sword in fess betw. in chief a helmet in base a griffin's head erased, HIGHGATE SCHOOL. In allusion to the arms of SIR ROGER CHOLMELEY, *Knt.* founder, whose shield bears two garbs in place of the griffin's head. Over the shield the date 1600.

✠ SIGILL' : LIɃE : SCOLÆ : GRAM' : ROGER : CHOLMLEY : MIL' : IN · HIGAT · IN : COM⁹ : MID.

HOLDERNESS WAPENTAKE, *co. York.*

5002. [16th cent.] Sulph. cast from the matrix. ⅞ in. [lxxiv. 58.]

A shield of arms : barry of six ensigned with an open coronet (a viscount's) of seven pearls, and betw. the initials R D with a small crosslet above and a cinquefoil below each letter.

✩ WAPENTAG · DE · HOLDERNES.

HOLT, *co. Denbigh.* (See CASTRUM LEONIS, *Caerleon.*)

HONITON, *co. Devon.*

5003. [17th cent.] Sulph. cast from the matrix. 1⅝ × 1¼ in. [lxi. 91.]

Oval : on the l. h. side the upper part of a human body, the trunk erased, over it a hand of blessing ; below it a flowering branch, on the r. h. side a man draped in profile to the l. praying.

✠ SIGILLVM : COMMVNE : DE : BVRGO : DE : HONITON : CÕ : DEVOI.

Inner border beaded, outer border carved.

S. Lewis, *Topogr. Dict.,* vol. ii., p. 409.

HUNTINGDON, *co. Huntingdon.*

5004. [A.D. 1628.] Sulph. cast from chipped impression. 2½ in. [lxiv. 81.]

On a rocky mount, with a large branching tree in the foreground, and with a bird on a low branch, a bowman blowing a horn, cheering on two dogs at a stag at speed to the l.

✠ SIGILLVM · COMMVNITATIS · DE · HVNTIRISOVNE (*sic*) . 16

Cabled borders.

S. Lewis, *Topogr. Dict.*, vol. ii., p. 436.

Small Seal, A.D. 1634.

5005. Sulph. cast from indistinct impression.   1 $\frac{3}{16}$ in. [lxiv. 82.]

Same design as the previous seal, No. 5004.

Legend indistinct, but apparently same as in No. 5004, with date altered to 1634.

HYTHE, *co. Kent.*

5006. [12th–13th cent.]   Sulph. cast from the matrix.   3 $\frac{1}{8}$ in. [lxv. 69.]

A one-masted ship on waves in which are seven fishes. Two mariners on the yard furling up the mainsail. Embattled castles at each end. On board, a trumpeter on the l., and a steersman on the r. In the field four small quatrefoils, two at each end of the ship.

☩ SIGILLVM |�| COMMVNE |�| BARONVM. |�| DE HETHE |�|

Beaded borders.

W. Boys, *History of Sandwich*, p. 811 ; S. Lewis, *Topogr. Dict.*, vol. ii., p. 446.

Jurats.

5007. [15th cent.] Sulph. cast from the matrix.   1 $\frac{1}{8}$ in. [lxv. 70.]

An eagle rising with expanded wings, contourné, in the beak a long riband inscribed :— ᛗ Є ᛗ ᛘ C ᛗ ᛘ C ᛗ ᛘ Є ᛗ ᛘ

S⋯IURATORŪ VILLE HEDE.

Customs.

5008. [Late 14th, or 15th cent.]   Recent impression in red sealing-wax from the matrix, found at Goudhurst, Kent, in 1868.   1 $\frac{1}{8}$ in. [xliii. 31.]

On waves in base, a demi-lion passant guardant conjoined to a hulk, from the arms of the CINQUE-PORTS ; ensigned with a crown fleury of three points. All within a cordon of fleurs-de-lis.

✠ ❚ SIGILLŪ ❚ CUSTUM' ❚ DE ❚ HETH ᛘ

Archæologia Cantiana, vol. vii., p. 342, (1868).

ILCHESTER, or IVELCHESTER, *co. Somerset.*

5009. [13th cent.] Sulph. cast from chipped and imperfect impression. 1¾ in. [lxxi. 64.]

A crescent enclosing an estoile of eight points wavy.

· ✠ S' BVRGEN . . . . GI . IVELCESTRIE.

Cf. S. Lewis, *Topogr. Dict.*, vol. ii. p. 450.

Later Seal.

5010. [17th cent.] Sulph. cast from the matrix. 1¾ in [lxxi. 65.]

A crescent enclosing an estoile of sixteen points alternately wavy and plain.

: · : SIGILLUM : BURGI : DE : IVELCHESTER.

Beaded borders.

S. Lewis, *Topogr. Dict.*, vol. ii., p. 450.

ILMINSTER, *co. Somerset.*

Free Grammar School, A.D. 1550.

5011. Sulph. cast from the matrix. 2⅛ in. [xxxv. 137.]

An open book encircled with a radiant aureole, and inscribed :—LEAR-NINGE—GAY-NETH—HO-NOR.

✠ · SIGILLVM + SCHOLE + ILMINSTERII +

N. Carlisle, *Endowed Grammar Schools*, vol. ii., p. 427.

5012. Another. [xlvii. 819.]

Laing, *MS. Catal.*, No. 305.

IPSWICH, *co. Suffolk.*

5013. [13th cent.] Sulph. cast from the matrix. 2⅝ in. [lxxi. 118, 119.]

Ø. A one-masted ship on the waves, mainsail furled, flag charged with a cross, and having a pennon of three streamers, embattled stern, and rudder of large dimensions on the l., octagon castle on the r., two mariners on board hauling at ropes.

Legend commences with an estoile wavy of eight points.

S' COMVNITATIS · VILLE : GYPEWICI :

℞. A church, with central spire topped with a cross, round-headed doorway in the middle, two smaller doorways with folding doors at the sides. In the pediments over the doors a trefoiled opening in the middle, at each side a quatrefoil. In the clerestory three windows each with three lights, and with a trefoiled opening in the pediment over each window. On the l. h. wall a wavy estoile of eight points; on the r. a quatrefoil opening. Background and base replenished with foliage in an elegant arabesque pattern.

The space for legend is also replenished with a similar pattern of foliage.

Beaded borders.

S. Lewis, *Topogr. Dict.*, vol. ii., p. 459.

5014. [A.D. 1349.] Dark-green: fine, but very imperfect, only central part remaining. [Add. ch. 10,130.]

5015. [A.D. 1599.] Red : much injured by pressure. [Add. ch. 10,241.]

ELIAS, son of TURSTIN of IPSWICH.
Called a Seal of the Town.

5016. [12th cent.] Sulph. cast from indistinct impression. 1⅝ in. [lxxi. 116.]

A one-masted ship with mainsail furled, mainmast topped with a cross. In the ship a mariner on each side.

✠ SIGILL' ELIE FIL' TVRSTINI DE GIPEWICH'.

Another Seal.

5017. [A.D. 1332.] Bronze-green: fine, but imperfect. About 1¾ × 1¼ in. when perfect. [Add. ch. 9952.]

Pointed oval : a one-masted ship on waves, mainsail furled, flag and streamers. In the field on the l. two keys, on the r. a key and sword ; emblems of SS. Peter and Paul, Patrons of the town.

. . . . GILLVM · BAL . . . . GIPE . . . .

Bailiffs.

5018. [14th–15th cent.] Sulph. cast from fine impression. 1¾ in. [lxxi. 117.]

A one-masted ship on the waves, mainsail furled, crow's nest, and at the top of the mast a cross and pennon with three streamers. In the field on each side a mullet, and below it a key for St. Peter ; on the r. side also a sword for St. Paul.

SIGIⲄLUM ⚜ OFFICII ⚜ BALLIUOR ⚜ UILLE ⚜ GIPPOICII. (sic)

Another Seal.

5019. [A.D. 1432.] Red: fine, but imperfect. [Add. ch. 10,143.]

Resembles the preceding seal, No. 5018, but is from a different matrix.

... GILLUM ⚜ OFFICII ⚜ BALLI ......

Cabled borders.

Mayor of the Staple.

5020. [14th cent.] Sulph. cast from the matrix. 1⅜ in. [lxxi. 20.]

A lion sejant guardant crowned, pierced through the neck with an arrow fess-wise. Within a carved gothic panel of three round cusps and one ogee cusp at the top, ornamented with tracery in the spandrils, and ball-flowers.

⚜ : SIGILLUM : MAIORATUS : STAPULE : GIPPEWICI : ⚜

5021. Recent impression in red sealing-wax, much injured by the melting of the wax. [xxxv. 65.]

Seal of Arms, A.D. 1561.

5022. [17th cent.] Sulph. cast from the matrix. 1⅛ × ⅞ in. [lxxii. 1.]

Oval: a shield of arms: per pale, *dex.*, a lion rampant guardant; *sin.*, three demi-hulks of ships in pale, joined to the impaled line, TOWN OF IPSWICH. Crest, on a helmet, mantling, and wreath a demi-lion rampant, in his gamb a ship of three masts, sails furled, [round the top of the third, on the maintopmast head, a pennon.]

Port of Ipswich.

5023. [17th cent.] Sulph. cast from cracked impression. 1⅜ in. [lxxii. 2.]

Three lions rampant, two and one.

❀ SIGIL ✪ OFFICII ✪ PORTVS ✪ IPSWICH :

Inner border beaded, outer border cabled.

JERSEY, *Island of.*
Royal Seal for the Bailiwick.
EDWARD I., A.D. 1279.

5024. Recent impression in red sealing-wax from the matrix. 1⅜ in. [xxxix. 51.]

A shield of arms, *E*NGLAND.

✪ S' BALLIVIE : INSVLE : DE : IERSEYE.

H

With a transcript of the Grant of this seal by K. Edward I.
A.D. 1279, the date of this matrix, and of that described in
No. 4962, for Guernsey.

S. Lewis, *Topogr. Dict.*, vol. ii., p. 472.

ELIZABETH.

Seal used by GEORGE POULET, *Bailly.*

5025. [A.D. 1601.]   Green : imperfect.   [Add. ch. 11,203.]
Ø. A shield of arms, ENGLAND, as before, No. 5024.

.... BAL .... EY ..

R. A small oval counterseal.   ⅞ × ¾ in.   An ornamentally
carved shield of arms : three swords in pile, points meeting in
base, in chief two mullets, POULET.   Betw. the initial letters
G. P.

CHARLES II.

Seal used by EDWARD CARTERET, *Bailly.*

5026. [A.D. 1670.]   Green : indistinct. [Add. ch. 18,101.]
Ø. A shield of arms, ENGLAND, as before, No. 5024.

S'BALLIVIE .... IER ......

R. A small oval counterseal.   ⅞ × ¾ in.   An oval shield of
arms : four fusils in fess, CARTERET.   Crest on a helmet,
wreath and mantling, a squirrel.   Supporters, two stags.   In
base, an indistinct motto.

KENDAL, *co. Westmorland.*

5027. [A.D. 1576.]   Sulph. cast from the matrix.   1⅜ in.
[lxxiii. 41.]
A view of the town, churches and houses having flags and
crosses.   In the background a triple-towered castle in a moat.
In the field five birds.   In base the initial letters, K. K., for
KIRKBY KENDAL, betw. the date 15–74.

S. Lewis, *Topogr. Dict.*, vol. ii., p. 478.

Later Seal.

5028. Sulph. cast from the matrix.   1¼ in.   [lxxiii. 42.]
A half-length figure of K. Charles I., with crown, and royal

vestments, turned slightly to the l. In the r. h. a drawn sword, in the l. h. an orb or mound.

· THE · SEALE · OF · THE · TOWNE · OF · KIRKBY · KENDALL.

Carved border.

KIDDERMINSTER, *co. Worcester.*
Free Grammar School, A.D. 1619.

5029. Sulph. cast, tinted red, from fine impression or the matrix. $1\frac{7}{16}$ in. [xxxv. 138.]

A symmetrical mark or monogram ⊞, betw. in chief the date 1619, at each side a sword, point downwards, in base a *kid* couchant, by way of *rebus* on the name of the town.

SIGLVM · FRATERNITATIS · FIDEI : COMIS · ʿEIE · LVDI · LIBERI · DE · KIDDERMINSTER.

The letters TE, in *Fraternitatis*, and *Kidderminster*; ID in *fidei*, and IN in *Kidderminster*, are conjoined; COMIS · ʿEIE is probably a blunder for COMISARIE.

Carved border.

5030. Another. [xlvii. 831.]

Laing's *MS. Catal.*, No. 302.

KINGSTON-UPON-HULL, *co. York.*

5031. [Temp. Edw. I.] Sulph. cast from the matrix. $2\frac{5}{16}$ in. [lxxiv. 60.]

K. Edward I. standing with crown and long mantle, in the hands a sceptre fleury, topped by a dove. Under his feet a lion couchant guardant. In the field on each side a lion passant guardant of *E*NGLAND.

SIGILLVM : COMVNE : DE ⚔ KYNGISTON̄ · SVPER HVLL'.

The letters ER of *super* are conjoined.

Beaded borders.

S. Lewis, *Topogr. Dict.*, vol. ii., p. 516.

Mayoralty.

5032. [Late 14th, or 15th cent.] Sulph. cast from fine, but chipped, impression. $1\frac{1}{16}$ in. [lxxiv. 61.]

A shield of arms: three crowns or coronets in pale, TOWN OF KINGSTON-UPON-HULL. Within a cusped and pointed

H 2

quatrefoil enriched with carved ball-flower ornamentation. Field replenished with sprigs of foliage.

S' OFFICII **❉** MAIORATUS **❉** VILLE **❉** D[E **❉**] . . . . GSTON **❉** SUPER HULL **✠**

Cf. S. Lewis, *Topogr. Dict.*, vol. ii., p. 512.

Mayor or Bailiffs, A.D. 1685–1688.

5033. [17th cent.] Sulph. cast from the matrix. $1\frac{1}{8}$ × 1 in. [lxxiv. 62.]

An oval carved shield of arms, TOWN OF KINGSTON-UPON-HULL, as in No. 5032.

❀ SIG VILLÆ KINGSTON SVPER HULL.

Another Seal or Signet.

5034. Sulph. cast from the matrix. $\frac{7}{8}$ × $\frac{5}{8}$ in. [lxxiv. 64.]

Oval : a shield of arms, TOWN OF KINGSTON-UPON-HULL, as in No. 5032. Betw. a palm-branch on the l., and a laurel branch on the r. tied in base.

Another Seal.

5035. [17th cent.] Sulph. cast from the matrix. $1\frac{5}{16}$ × $1\frac{1}{16}$ in. [lxxiv. 63.]

A castle with embattled wall and side-towers : round-headed doorway closed. Above in the field, the three crowns, in pale, of the arms of the Town, see No. 5032.

❀ ✠ KINGSTON ✫ SVP ✫ HVLL **✠ ❀**

Admiralty.

5036. [15th cent.] Sulph. cast from fine impression or the matrix. $1\frac{11}{16}$ in. [lxxiv. 65.]

A one-masted ship on waves, mainsail charged with a shield of arms, TOWN OF KINGSTON-UPON-HULL, as in No. 5032. Crow's nest, pennon at the mast-head, high poop and prow.

S' OFFICIJ **✠** ADMIRALLITATIS **✠** UILLE **✠** . . . . H . . LL'

Cabled borders.

KINGSTON-UPON-THAMES, *co. Surrey.*

5037. Sulph. cast from the matrix. 2 in. [D.C., F. 337.]

A shield of arms : three salmons naiant in pale, in base

the initial letter K, Town' of Kingston-upon-Thames. (Burke, *General Armory*, and Papworth, *Ordinary of British Armorials*, state that the salmons are *hauriant*, in error.) Betw. three lions rampant guardant of England, within a cusped and pointed gothic quatrefoil with carved spandrils.

�֍ S' COMVNITATIS VILLE DE KYNGGESTONE : SVPER : TAMICIAM �֍

S. Lewis, *Topogr. Dict.*, vol. ii., p. 518.

5038. [A.D. 1549.] Red : imperfect and indistinct. [Add. ch. 5628.]

S' . . . . TONE . . . . .TAMICIAM

5039. [A.D. 1613.] Red : chipped and indistinct in parts. [Add. ch. 5636.]

�֍ S' COMVNITATIS VILLE DE . . . . .ESTONE : SVPER : TAM . . . . . .

KIRKBY-IN-LONSDALE, *co. Westmorland.*
Free Grammar School, A.D. 1591.

5040. Sulph. cast from the matrix, tinted red. $1\frac{9}{16}$ in. [xxxv. 139.]

A schoolmaster, seated on a chair, turned to the r., with cap and robes, instructing two pupils from an open book.

Legend, an elegiac distich, in two concentric annuli :—

(I.) �֍ STET ✭ SCHOLA ✭ DE ✭ KIRKBY ✭ IN ✭ LONSDAL ✭ DEVS ✭ ET ✭ PIA ✭ PRINCEPS : ✭ :

(2.) DY ✭ FAVEANT ✭ PVERIS ✭ ELISABETA ✭ SCOLIS : ✭ :

5041. Another. [xlvii. 837.]

Laing, *MS. Catal.*, No. 300.

KIRKBY KENDAL, *co. Westmorland*, see KENDAL.

KIRKBY-RAVENSWORTH, *co. York.*
Almshouse of St. John Baptist and Free Grammar
School, A.D. 1555.

5042. Sulph. cast from the matrix, tinted red. $2\frac{3}{16}$ × $1\frac{3}{4}$ in. [xxxv. 140.]

Oval : St. John Baptist in the wilderness, standing with

nimbus and cloak, in the r. h., holding the Agnus Dei on a plaque, and pointing to it with the l. h. In base the date 1555.

✠ + S + ELEMOSINARIE + S + IOHANNIS · BABTISTE · DE · KIRKBI RAVESWATH.

5043. Another. [xlvii. 838.]

Laing, *MS. Catal.*, No. 307.

LANCASTER, *County of.*
NICHOLAS TOWNLEY, *Sheriff*, A.D. 1632.

5044. Sulph. cast from the matrix. 1¼ in. [lxvi. 39.]

A castle gateway, with two domed towers, on each a flag, round-headed portal with portcullis ; over the doorway an estoile of eight points ; over the battlements, on a helmet and wreath a hawk, in allusion to the crest of TOWNLEY, viz., on a perch a hawk belled, round the perch a riband. At the sides the initial letters ʍ. T. Below each, a circular mark in matrix. In base the word LAʍC.

Carved border.

Cf. *Add. MS.* 26,741, f. 521.

LANCASTER, *co. Lancaster.*

5045. [15th cent.] Recent impression in red sealing-wax from the matrix. 1¾ in. [xlviii. 10.]

A triple-towered castle of coarse design, with two storeys, embattled and masoned. In base, on the l. a lion passant guardant (with tail extended and fourchée) of ENGLAND, on the r. a fleur-de-lis of FRANCE, (see next seal, No. 5047). Rude workmanship. The King mentioned in the legend is probably Henry IV.

✠ S' HENR : DE G ʍ RE ʍ ANGLE : ⚥ : FRANCE ʍ DNS : HIBE.

S. Lewis, *Topogr. Dict.*, vol. iii., p. 21.

5046. Sulph. cast. [lxvi. 36.]

Burgesses, or Borough.

5047. [16th cent.] Sulph. cast from the matrix. 1$\frac{5}{16}$ in. [lxvi. 37.]

A shield of arms : in chief a fleur-de-lis of FRANCE ; in base a lion rampant guardant of ENGLAND, TOWN OF LANCASTER.

⁎ SIGILLVM COMVNE BVRG' SIVE VILL LANCASTRIE.

LANGPORT-EAST-OVER, *co. Somerset.*

5048. [A.D. 1617.] Sulph. cast from the matrix. $1\frac{11}{16}$ × $1\frac{1}{4}$ in. [D.C., H. 181.]

Oval : a blackamoor's head to the left, filleted, the bust draped with a laced collar.

SIG' : PREPOS · ET : COMVNI : BVRGI : DE · LANG' · ESTO ·

Carved border.

S. Lewis, *Topogr. Dict.*, vol. iii., p. 28.

5049. Another. [lxi. 12.]

LEACH, NORTH, *co. Gloucester.*
Free Grammar School, A.D. 1559.

5050. Sulph. cast from the matrix, tinted red. $1\frac{1}{8}$ in. [xlvii. 847.]

A shield of arms ornamentally carved with flowers and fruits : three estoiles or mullets of six points, a canton ermine, WESTWOOD, founder.

SIGILLVM · HVGO · WESTWOOD · IN · COM · GLOC.

Beaded borders.

N. Carlisle, *Endowed Grammar Schools,* vol. i., p. 454 ; Laing's *MS. Catal.*, No. 280.

LEEDS, *co. York.*
First Corporation Seal, A.D. 1626.

5051. Sulph. cast from the matrix. $1\frac{1}{4}$ in. [lxxiv. 75.]

On a mount a shield of arms : a fleece, suspended by strap and chain. Crest a chaplet. Supporters two owls crowned,. TOWN OF LEEDS.

⚘ SIGILLVM · · BVRGI : DE · · LEEDES. 1626.

Inner border cabled, outer border carved.

Second Corporation Seal, A.D. 1662.

5052. Sulph. cast from the matrix. $1\frac{9}{10}$ in. [lxxiv. 76.].

An ornamental shield of arms : a fleece (see No. 5051) in·a chief three mullets, TOWN OF LEEDS.

�֎ SIGILLVM . BVRGI . DE . LEEDES · 1662.

Carved border.

Another, A.D. 1662.

5053. Sulph. cast from the matrix. 1½ in. [lxxiv. 77.]

An oval shield of arms, ornamentally carved, TOWN OF LEEDS, as in the preceding seal No. 5052.

☆ SIGILLVM ☆ BVRGI ☆ DE ☆ LEEDS ☆ 1662.

S. Lewis, *Topogr. Dict.,* vol. iii., p. 46.

Third Corporation Seal, A.D. 1836.

5054. Sulph. cast from the matrix. 1 9/16 in. [lxxiv. 78.]

An ornamental shield of arms, TOWN OF LEEDS, as in No. 5052. Crest, on a wreath, an owl. Supporters, two owls, crowned, standing on carved scrolls with a leopard's head in base.

SIGILLVM BVRGI DE LEEDS · 1836 ·

LEWES, *co. Sussex.*

5055. [15th cent.] Sulph. cast from the matrix. 1¾ in. [lxxii. 92.]

A shield of arms : chequy in the sinister chief on a canton a lion rampant betw. eight crosses crosslets, TOWN OF LEWES. Betw. three palm branches.

☆ ⚜ SIGILLUM : ⚜ : COMVNE · ⚜ : BURGI : ⚜ : DE · ⚜ : LEWYS · ⚜ :

Inner border carved and enriched with ball-flowers, outer border beaded.

Another

5056. [15th cent.] Sulph. cast from the matrix. 1 1/16 in. × 1 in. [lxxii. 93.]

A copy, but smaller, of the design of the preceding seal, No. 5055.

❀ ⚜ SIGILLVM ❀ ❖ BVRGI ❀ DE ❀ LEWYS ❖ + ❀

S. Lewis, *Topogr. Dict.,* vol. iii., p. 67.

LEICESTER, *co. Leicester.*

Mayor.

5057. [17th cent.] Sulph. cast from the matrix. 1¼ in. [lxvi. 59.]

The Virgin, crowned, seated in a canopied niche with tabernacle-work at the sides, the Child on the l. arm, in the

r. h. a sceptre. In base, under an imperfect arch with masonry at the sides, a shield of arms: a cinquefoil, TOWN OF LEICESTER.

SIGILL STAT MAIO BVRGI LEICESTRI.

LEOMINSTER, *co. Hereford.*

5058. [13th cent.] Sulph. cast from the matrix. 1⅞ × 1 in. [lxiv. 54.]

Pointed oval: St. Peter, one of the Patron Saints of the parish, standing, in the r. h. two keys, in the l. h. a book. The figure perhaps has been copied from an earlier seal.

✠ SIGILLVM : COMMVNE : LEOMINSTRIE.

S. Lewis, *Topogr. Dict.*, vol. iii., p. 63.

LICHFIELD, *co. Stafford.*

5059. [A.D. 1688.] Sulph. cast from the matrix. 2⅜ in. [lxxii. 50.]

A battle-field strewn with three dead bodies and weapons, a flag, and a crown, in allusion to the name of the town *Lich-* (*i.e.* lic, *Anglo-Sax.*, a corpse)-*field.*

✿ SIGILLVM COMMVNE CIVITATIS DE LICHFEILD + + AN : D' : 1688.

S. Lewis, *Topogr. Dict.*, vol. iii., p. 72.

LINCOLNSHIRE.

G—— W——, *Sheriff.*

5060. Sulph. cast from the matrix. 1¼ in. [lxvii. 13.]

A castle with two side towers, domed and topped by a flag; round-headed portal with portcullis down. Betw. the tower, over the battlements, on a wreath a demi-eagle. In the field the initials Ġ. W. In base the word :—LINC'·

Carved border.

P—— G——, *Sheriff.*

5061. Sulph. cast. 1⅛ × 1 in. [lxvii. 14.]

Oval: a castle with two side towers domed, and topped by a flag, roundheaded portal. Betw. the towers, over the battlements, on a wreath a lion's head erased. In the field the initials P. G. In base the word :—LINC.

LINCOLN, *co. Lincoln.*

First Corporation Seal.

5062. [A.D. 1511.] Red: fine, chipped and imperfect on the r. side.   About 3¼ in. when perfect.   (Stowe Collection: Burton charters.)

A castle of elaborate design in three storeys, curtain wall diapered lozengy, five towers, with short spires topped with weather vanes, and quatrefoiled openings; round-headed portal closed, portcullis one-third down.   On the curtain-wall a shield of arms: on a cross a fleur-de-lis, CITY OF LINCOLN. At each side a wall, shown obliquely, with crenellated ridge, over it on the l., a fleur-de-lis; the corresponding device on the r. is wanting.

SIG. . . . . . . UNE ⚜ CIVITATIS ⚜ LINÇOLNIE ⚜

Second Corporation Seal, c. A.D. 1628.

5063. Recent impression in red sealing-wax from the matrix.   2⅝ in.   [l. 23.]

A copy of the design of the preceding seal with details differently treated.   On each side of the portal a circular opening; over the portal a shield of arms, CITY OF LINCOLN, see No. 5061.   In the field over the towers four fleurs-de-lis; on each side another.

THE · COMMON · SEALE · OF · THE · CIT̄ : LIN̊COLN̊ᴇ.

Carved borders.

S. Lewis, *Topogr. Dict.*, vol. iii., p. 80.

Mayoralty.

5064. [13th cent.] Sulph. cast from the matrix.   1⅜ in. [lxvii. 11.]

The Virgin, standing on a carved corbel under a trefoiled arch crocketed and supported on architectural piers; with crown, the Child with nimbus on the l. arm, in the r. h. a ball. In the field on each side a lion passant guardant of ENGLAND.

SIGILL' MAIORITATIS LINCOLNIE.

Beaded borders.

Wool Staple.

5065. [14th cent.] Sulph. cast from the matrix.   1 9⁄16 in. [lxvii. 12.]

The Virgin, with crown, standing on a wool-sack, in a canopied niche with tabernacle work at the sides; the Child on the r. arm.

S' ⚌ OFFICII ⚌ STAPVLE ⚌ CIVITAT' + LINCOLN' ·
Beaded borders.

Seal for delivery of Wool and Hides, see No. 1159.

Seals "pro recognitione debitorum," see Nos. 1076–1079.

LISKEARD, *co. Cornwall.*

5066. [17th cent.] Sulph. cast from the matrix. 2 ×
1⅜ in. [lxi. 15.]

Pointed oval: a fleur-de-lis of elegant design (by way of
rebus); thereon two birds. In the field on each side an
annulet and an ostrich feather; probably in reference to
RICHARD PLANTAGENET, Earl of Cornwall, who enfranchised
the Borough in A.D. 1240, and to Q. Elizabeth.

❋ SIGILLVM · COMMVNE · BVRGI · DE · LISKEARD.

Carved border.

S. Lewis, *Topogr. Dict.,* vol. iii., p. 94.

LIVERPOOL, *co. Lancaster.*

5067. [14th cent.] Sulph. cast from the matrix. 2⅛ ×
1¼ in. [lxvi. 35.]

Pointed oval: an eagle, rising contourné with expanded
wings, holding in its beak a trefoiled sprig. On the foot a
scroll inscribed :— IOH'IS. In the field a crescent enclosing
an estoile of six points.

✿ SIGILL' COMMVNE ✿ BORGESIV̄ D̄ LEVE ꓭ.

Beaded borders.

S. Lewis, *Topogr. Dict.,* vol. iii., p. 105 ; Picton, *Memorials of Liverpool,*
vol. i., pp. 17, 18.

LONDON, *co. Middlesex.*

5068. [13th cent.] Sulph. casts from fine, but chipped,
impression. 2⅝ in. [lxviii. 18, 19.]

∅. St. Paul, Patron Saint of the City, with nimbus, in the
r. h. a drawn sword erect, in the l. h. a banner-flag, charged with
the arms of ENGLAND (reversed); standing on the tower of
St. Paul's Cathedral, over a gateway in the embattled wall of
the city. Within the *enceinte* of the wall is a view of the city
with several tall spires of churches, and at each side two

square-towered churches.   In front of the wall, the R. Thames.
The round-headed doorway is filled up with the heraldic
device of, quarterly, in the fess point a pierced mullet.

· SIGILLVM : BARONVM : LONDONIARVM.

℞. St. Thomas, Archbishop of Canterbury, with mitre and
pall, lifting up the r. h. in benediction, in the l. h. a long crozier
held obliquely, seated on a carved throne, betw. two groups of
worshippers, those on the r. h. side, with hoods, are probably
monks or clergy, those on the l. h. side, laymen.   Across the
field the inscription :—sĉs · THOM̂ · AR.   In base, under a
semicircular arch of large span, a representation of the City of
London with St. Paul's Cathedral in the middle, tall pointed
spires on each side and at the end, on each side a church
with square embattled tower, all enclosed within an embattled
wall with gateway and towers.

Legend, a rhyming verse :—

ME · QV . . . . . .˙. . . . MA : TV . . . . .

Later Seal.

5069. [A.D. 1670.] Red : covered with paper before impression.   2¹¹⁄₁₆ in. [Add. ch. 1683.]

∅. A copy of the *obv.* of the preceding seal, No. 5068.   The
armorial charges in the doorway are here replaced by the
line or rabbet of the folding doors with a rose, boss, or knocker
in the centre.

SIGILLVM : BARONVM : LONDONIARVM.

℞. A shield of arms, *couché* : a cross quarterly, in the dexter
chief a sword hilt downwards, CITY OF LONDON.   Crest, on a
helmet, tasselled mantling, and wreath, a cross betw. two
dragons' wings.

✣ LONDINI ✣ DEFENDE ✣ TVOS ✣ DEVS ✣ OPTIME ✣ GIVES ✣

S. Lewis, *Topogr. Dict.*, vol. iii., p. 136.

5070. [A.D. 1791.] Another. [xliii. 177.]

5071. *Rev.* only, on a wafer covered with paper before impression *en placard*. Cut from a parchment deed. [xliii. 158.]

5072. Another *rev.* similar to the preceding. [xliii. 159.]

Corporation for the Poor of the City.

5073. [A.D. 1699.] Red : fine, imperfect in places. Covered
with paper before impression, *en placard*, on a label.   2¼ in.
[Add. ch. 19,740.]

Ø. A shield of arms : a cross, in the dexter chief a sword, hilt downward, CITY OF LONDON. The shield richly carved with scroll-work, foliage and flowers.

[THE · SEAL · OF ·] THE · CORPORATION · FOR · THE · POOR · OF · [THE · CITY · OF · LONDON.]

℞. An emblematical shield of arms : a field of ripe corn, on a chief semé of bees a beehive. Crest on a helmet, mantling of foliage, and wreath, a lamb sejant or couchant. Supporters, *dex.*, a boy ; *sin.*, a girl, each on a mount.

✸ GOD ✸ GIVES ✸ PEACE . . . .˙. . Y (*? and plenty*) ✸ TO ✸ INDUSTRY.

Carved borders.

Mayoralty.

First Seal.

5074. [14th cent.] Red : fine. Cut from a charter bearing date A.D. 1544. 2¼ in. [xxxvi. 41.]

This design appears to have been the work of the goldsmith who executed some of the great seals of Edward III. and Richard II. See Nos. 231, etc. Stow, *Survey of London* (Candlewick Ward), p. 237, ed. 1933, states that this seal was made in A.D. 1380.

In a central niche of three bays (the two side bays richly canopied, the middle bay groined and supporting a smaller niche in the upper part), on the l. St. Thomas, Archbishop of Canterbury, with mitre and pall, seated on a bench, lifting up the r. h. in benediction, in the l. h. a long crozier ; on the r. St. Paul, holding in the r. h. a drawn sword, in the l. h. a book, similarly seated on a bench, beneath his feet a prostrate figure of Elymas the sorcerer. In the smaller niche overhead, the Virgin, crowned, seated, holding the Child standing on her l. knee, in her r. h. a book. On each side of this central niche a canopied niche, containing in a balcony a half-length man-at-arms with low cap, holding a mace or club. Above, on each side on a pedestal or bracket, an angel kneeling, with wings expanded, hands in prayer. In base, in a compartment with flat head, a shield of arms : CITY OF LONDON, as in No. 5073, supported by two demi-lions, rampant guardant, each under a round-headed arch. At the sides outside all, tabernacle work.

SIGILL' . MAIORATUS : CIUITATIS : LONDON :

Arch. Journ., vol. iii., p. 74, fig. 2.

5075. Sulph. cast from imperfect and indistinct impression. [D.C., F. 56.]

. . . . ITATIS : LONDON :

5076. [A.D. 1389.] Red : very fine, very imperfect. [Add. ch. 6046.]

. . . . CIUITATIS : LONDON :

5077. [A.D. 1449.] Red: fine, very imperfect, only central part remaining. [Add. ch. 22,642.]

5078. [A.D. 1452.] Red: good, but imperfect, the edge very much injured. [Stowe Collection : Burton Charters.]

Second state of the First Seal.

5079. Sulph. cast from the matrix. [lxvii. 20.]

This is from the same matrix as the preceding seal, No. 5074, but shows the greatly worn condition of the matrix, which appears in some places to have been retouched by the goldsmith.

Later Seal, or
Design for a new Seal.

5080. [17th cent.] Sulph. cast from the matrix. $2\frac{1}{4}$ in. [lxviii. 21.]

This is a design which owes its origin to the previous seal, No. 5075, but has been executed with a view to supersede the Gothic architecture by substituting the Italian style. In the centre in a niche with three round-headed arches, on the l. St. Thomas the Archbishop seated with mitre and long cross or crozier, on the r. a king seated, crowned, with drawn sword in the r. h., and orb and cross in the l. h., betw. the two figures a vase. Above, in smaller niche, with double arch, the Virgin and Child ; smaller niche on each side, and an angel on each side outside the niches. At each side of the central niche, a niche with round-headed arch containing a man-at-arms, half-length. In base, a shield of arms as before, supported by two sea-lions, crowned, each in a niche with round-headed arch. Under the men-at-arms on each side a shield of arms : l., two lions passant guardant in pale, perhaps for one of the Mayors, or for NORMANDY ; r., ENGLAND.

⚜ SIGILL' MAIORATUS CIVITATIS LONDON.

Archæol. Journ. vol. iii., p. 74.

ELIAS, *Town Clerk.*

5081. [12th cent.] Sulph. cast from fine impression. $1\frac{1}{4} \times \frac{3}{4}$ in. [lvii. 6.]

Pointed oval : the clerk, seated on a carved chair with scroll-shaped back, to the r., reading a book on a lectern.

✠ S' ELIE LONDONIARV'. CL'ICI.·

Beaded border.

5082. Another. [D.C., E 303.]

Chamberlain, A.D. 1589.

5083. Red: fine. $1\frac{1}{4} \times \frac{7}{8}$ in. [Harl. ch. 56 E. 20.]

Oval: on the l. a sword of St. Paul, handle downward, on the r. two keys interlinked at the handles, of St. Peter. Across the field the date :—1-5-8-9. Above, an open jewelled crown of three points fleury and two pearls ; below, a lion passant guardant of ENGLAND.

S' CAMERE LONDONIAR'.

5083*. Sulph. cast of No. 5083. [D.C., H. 180.]

5084. Red: a fragment, detached from its charter. [Box with Harl. ch. 47 D. 50.]

Another Seal, A.D. 1589.

5085. Sulph. cast from the matrix or fine impression. $\frac{7}{8} \times \frac{3}{4}$ in. [lxviii. 96.]

Oval: same design as the previous seal, No. 5083, but smaller.

S · CAMERÆ · LONDINI.

Later Seal, A.D. 1720.

5086. Sulph. cast from the matrix. $1\frac{1}{8}$ in. [lxviii. 62.]

Same design as the previous seal, No. 5083, but larger. Across the field the date :—1-7-2-0.

SIG · CAMERÆ · LONDINI.

Seal "pro recognitione debitorum," see No. 1080.

Seal of the Port of London, see No. 1157.

Seal of the Collectors of the subsidy for rebuilding London Bridge, see No. 1167.

Heralds' College or College of Arms.

5087. [16th cent.] Sulph. cast from the matrix. $2\frac{5}{16}$ in. [lxviii. 66.]

On a mount with herbage, a shield of arms : a cross betw. four doves, the wings expanded and inverted, HERALDS' COLLEGE. Crest, on a helmet and mantling, in a ducal coronet a dove rising. Supporters, two lions rampant guardant ducally gorged.

✠ SIGILLVM · COMVNE · CORPORACIONIS · OFFICII · ARMORVM ·

Kings of Arms.

SIR EDWARD WALKER, *Garter.*

5088. [A.D. 1660.]   Red: fine, app. by plaited strands of blue and yellow silk, and enclosed in a tinned iron box of contemporary make.   2⅛ in.   [Wol. ch. iv. 67.]

A shield of arms, of ornamental design, with carved scrolls and festoons of flowers and fruit: per pale, *dex.* St. George's Cross, on a chief a coronet or open crown within the Garter of the order, betw. a lion of ENGLAND and a fleur-de-lis of FRANCE, OFFICE OF GARTER KING OF ARMS; *sin.,* on a chevron ringed at the point, betw. three crescents, a crescent for difference, WALKER.

ᴕ SIG · DÑI · EDI · WALKER · EQVITIS · AV · GARTERII · PRINCIPALIS · REGIS · ARMOR · ANGLI.

Carved borders.

M. Noble, *History of the College of Arms,* p. 278.

SIR HENRY ST. GEORGE, *Garter.*

5089. [A.D. 1711.]   Red: fine, app. by ribands of blue and white silk, and enclosed in a tinned iron box of contemporary make.   2⅛ in.   [Add. ch. 16,284.]

A shield of arms of ornamental design, as in No. 5088, with a lion's face over it.   The armorial bearings are: per pale, *dex.,* OFFICE OF GARTER KING OF ARMS, see No. 5088; *sin.,* a chief, over all a lion rampant, on an escutcheon three ducal coronets, two and one, ST. GEORGE.

+ SIG · DÑI · HEN · SAINT · GEORGE · MIL · GARTER · PRINC · REGIS · ARMORVM · ANGL.

Carved borders.

Official Seal used by
JOHN ANSTIS, *Garter.*

5090. [A.D. 1741.]   Red: fine, app. by ribands of green and yellow silk, and enclosed in a tinned iron box of contemporary make.   2¼ in.   [Add. ch. 27,004.]

A shield of arms of ornamental design, as in No. 5088, OFFICE OF GARTER KING OF ARMS.

+ SIGILL · OFFICII · GARTERII · PRINCIPALIS · REGIS · ARMORVM · ANGLICORVM.

Carved borders.

ROBERT COOKE, *Clarenceux.*

5091. [A.D. 1563.] Red: cracked, enclosed in a turned wooden box. 1¾ in. [Add. ch. 15,557.]

A shield of arms : arg. St. George's cross. In the dexter chief a fleur-de-lis of FRANCE, on a chief gu. a lion of ENGLAND, crowned with an open crown, OFFICE OF CLARENCEUX KING OF ARMS. Betw. two crosses crosslet fitchées, and over it a lion rampant.

    ✠ S' : OFFICII : CLARENCIEVLX : REGIS : ARMORVM : ETᶜ :
           AVSTRAL' :

5092. [A.D. 1577.] Red : fine, injured in places ; enclosed in a turned wooden box. [Add. ch. 13,612.]

5093. [A.D. 1577.] Red : fine, enclosed in a turned wooden box. [Wol. ch. xi. 88.]

5094. [A.D. 1592.] Red : fine, enclosed in a turned wooden box. [Harl. ch. 111 C. 9.]

5095. Sulph. cast from an indistinct impression. [D.C., H. 128.]

SIR JOHN VANBRUGH, *Clarenceux.*

5096. [A.D. 1711.] Red : fine ; app. by ribands of blue and white silk, and enclosed in a tinned iron box of contemporary make. 2 in. [Add. ch. 16,284.]

An ornamental shield of arms : per pale, *dex.*, OFFICE OF CLARENCEUX KING OF ARMS, as in No. 5092, *sin.*, quarterly, 1, 4, on a fess three barrulets, in chief a demi-lion rampant issuing, VANBRUGH ; 2, 3, on a bend three mascles, CARLETON.

    👑 SIGILL' : IOHAN : VANBRUGH : ARM : CLARENCEUX : REGIS :
           ARMORUM.
Carved border.

M. Noble, *History of the College of Arms*, p. 355 ; the official arms ; described on p. 62, do not agree altogether with those on this seal.

KNOX WARD, *Clarenceux.*

5097. [A.D. 1741.] Red : fine ; app. by ribands of green and yellow silk, and enclosed in a tinned iron box of contemporary make. 2¼ in. [Add. ch. 27,004.]

A shield of arms of ornamental design : with carved scrolls and festoons of flowers and fruit : *dex.*, OFFICE OF CLARENCEUX KING OF ARMS, as in No. 5091, but without the fleur-de-lis in the dexter chief ; *sin.*, erm. a cross flory cantoned with four annulets, WARD. Over the shield an open crown of five leaves.

: SIGILL : KNOX WARD ARM : CLARENCEUX REGIS ARMORUM.

Carved border.

PETER, "*Rex Hyraudorum citra aquam de Trente ex parte boriali*," *Norroy*.

5098. [A.D. 1276.] Green : only a fine fragment. About 1 in. when perfect. [Harl. ch. 54 G. 44.]

A shield of arms : three crowns, two and one.

. . . . VRV . . . . . .

SIR JOHN BOROUGH, *Norroy*.

5099. [A.D. 1625.] Red : cracked ; app. by ribands of faded red silk, and enclosed in an ornamented tinned iron box of contemporary make. 1⅞ in. [Harl. ch. 111 C. 10.]

A shield of arms : St. George's cross, on a chief, per pale, a lion passant guardant of ENGLAND, betw. a fleur-de-lis of FRANCE, and a key, OFFICE OF NORROY KING OF ARMS.

S · S · OFFICII · NORROY · REGIS · ARMORVM · BOREALIS.

The letters LIS of *Borealis* are in the field over the shield.

M. Noble, *History of the College of Arms*, p. 62.

5100. Sulph. cast from No. 5099. [D.C., H. 139.]

PETER LE NEVE, *Norroy*.

5101. [A.D. 1711.] Red : fine ; app. by ribands of blue and white silk, and enclosed in a tinned iron box of contemporary make. 2 in. [Add. ch. 16,284.]

An ornamental shield of arms : per pale, *dex.*, OFFICE OF NORROY KING OF ARMS, as in No. 5099 ; *sin.*, on a cross five fleurs-de-lis, LE NEVE, in dexter chief a crescent for difference.

SIGILL · PETRI · LE NEVE · ARMIG · NORROY · REGIS · ARMORUM.

Carved borders.

Royal Mint.

Warden and Workmen.

5102. [18th cent.] Recent impression in red sealing-wax from the matrix. $2\frac{3}{8}$ in. [xxxv. 349.]

On a mount an embattled fortress of elaborate design, with central tower having dome and side turrets, betw. two shields of arms: l., ENGLAND ; r., quarterly 1, 4, quarterly i., iv., ENGLAND, ii., iii., SCOTLAND, 2, FRANCE (MODERN), 3, IRELAND. Below the shields the Royal initials G. R.

> ❀ SIGIL : COR : CVSTODIS : CAMB : OPERAT : ET : ALIORVM : MINIST.

Carved border.

Ruding, *Annals of the English Coinage*, vols. i., p. 40 *n.* ; vi., map.

The Royal Society, A.D. 1663.

5103. Leaden impression, very much oxidised. [Slo. xxxiv. 40.]

Too much defaced to be described.

Engr. in Vertue, *Simons' Works*, pl. xxxi.

The Royal College of Physicians of London, A.D. 1523.

5104. [18th cent.] Proof impression in red sealing-wax from the matrix : enclosed in a box. $2\frac{1}{4}$ in. [Slo. xxxiv. 39.]

St. Luke, with nimbus, seated in a chair to the l., at a round table, writing in a book. In a hall, paved, panelled, and ornamented with festoons of flowers. At the r. h. side a curtain looped up. Above, an ornamentally carved shield of arms with an escallop at the top and a lion's face at the bottom, and a palm branch on each side. The armorial bearings are : a dexter hand issuing out of clouds in chief rayonnés, feeling the pulse of a dexter hand and arm in fess issuing from the *sin.* side of the shield, vested : in base a pomegranate slashed and seeded, slipped and leaved ; all within five demi-fleurs-de-lis bordering the edge of the shield, (field hatched with crossing lines for sable), ROYAL COLLEGE OF PHYSICIANS OF LONDON.

Legend on a scroll :—

SIGILLUM · COMMUNE · COL . REG . MEDICORUM LONDIN.

Carved border.

Small Seal.

5105. [18th cent.] Sulph. cast from the matrix. $\frac{7}{8} \times \frac{3}{4}$ in. [lxviii. 94.]

Oval: an ornamental shield of arms as in No. 5104, with a bordure, ROYAL COLLEGE OF PHYSICIANS OF LONDON.

Legend on a scroll :—

O · BIOC · BPAXYC · H · ΔE · TEXNH · MAKPH.

British Museum, A.D. 1753.

5106. Recent proof impression in red sealing-wax from the matrix. 3¼ in. [xxxv. 57.]

An Ionic edifice or temple, tetrastyle, approached by a flight of three steps, and having a triangular pediment, in which is a radiant head, and a doorway with panelled folding-doors and pediment above them. Over the doorway a plain blank oval, with festoons over it. Betw. the two l. h. pillars, RHEA or CYBELE, standing with mural or crenellated crown, a pine cone slipped, in the r. h., a sickle in the l. h., at her feet two lions crouching. On the l., in a corresponding position, MINERVA, helmeted, in the r. h. a scroll, in the l. h. a long spear ; at her feet, on the l. an owl, on the r. an oval shield charged with Medusa's head and snakes. In the exergue the motto :—

BONARVM · ARTIVM
CVLTORIBVS.

✳ SIGILLVM · CVRATORVM · MVSEI · BRITANNICI · EX · SENATVS
CONSVLTO · CONDITI · A · D · MDCCLIII.

Carved border.

Museum Minervæ.

A Literary Institution founded by Sir Francis Kynaston, Knt., Esquire of the Body to Charles I., in Covent Garden, London.

5107. [A.D. 1632–1642.] Recent impression in red sealing-wax. 1½ × 1⅛ in. [xlix. 47.]

Oval: Sir Francis Kynaston, knt., founder, half-length, to the l., with an armoured cuirass of damascened work, and collar. On his l. arm a shield of arms, ENGLAND, ensigned with a royal crown. In the exergue the letters T. R:, for Thomas Rawlins, Engraver to the Mint in 1643, see Grueber, *Medallic Illustrations*, vol. ii., p. 736.

FRA · KINASTON · EQV · AVRAT · REGII · CORP · ARG.

Chalmers, *Biogr. Dict.*, vol. xix., p. 435.

Christ's Hospital, A.D. 1553.

5108. Sulph. cast, tinted red, from the matrix. $\frac{7}{8} \times \frac{3}{4}$ in. [xxxv. 141.]

Oval: an ornamental shield of arms with carved scrolls and flowers; a cross quarterly, in the dexter chief a sword erect, on a chief a rose of five leaves, barbed and seeded betw. two fleurs-de-lis, CHRIST'S HOSPITAL.

5109. Another. [xlvii. 851.]

Laing's *MS. Catal.*, No. 286.

The Foundling Hospital.

5110. Sulph. cast from the matrix. $2\frac{1}{4}$ in. [lxviii. 95.]

An ornamental shield of arms : [per fess] in chief a crescent betw. two estoiles or mullets of six points, in base an infant exposed, recumbent, stretching upwards the r. h., FOUNDLING HOSPITAL. Crest, on a wreath, a lamb statant [holding in the mouth a sprig of laurel]. Supporters, two emblematical figures, *dex.*, NATURE, *sin.*, WISDOM according to Burke, *Gen. Armory*, s.v., but somewhat doubtful, if rightly depicted in this seal. Motto on a carved scroll in base :—HELP.

Carved border.

Brewers' Company.

5111. [15th cent.] Sulph. cast. $2\frac{1}{4}$ in. [D.C., G. 51.]

The Assumption of the Virgin, standing, crowned, hands in prayer, surrounded by radiance, upheld by three demi-angels with expanded wings on each side, and one, with arms extended, in base. Overhead in clouds the head of the Almighty. All within a carved panel of circular form with cusped lobe at the top.

SIGILLUM : COMMUNITATIS : MISTERII : BRACIATORUM :
LONDINI. *m*

At the end of the legend a long sprig with four ears of barley.

Drapers' Company, A.D. 1439.

5112. [15th cent.] Sulph. cast from fine impression. $3\frac{5}{8}$ in. [lxviii. 61.]

The Virgin, with triple crown or tiara, three-quarters-length, in the r. h. a sceptre, in the l. h. a palm-branch, on each side a group of persons sheltered under her cloak, surrounded by

radiance and supported by four angels with expanded wings.
Over her head the Almighty, half-length, lifting up the r. h.
in benediction, with the l. h. placing the crown on the Virgin's
head; above him the Dove of the Spirit. In base, a shield
of arms : three clouds, radiated in base, each surmounted with
a triple crown, DRAPERS' COMPANY OF LONDON.

SIGILLŪ ⚜ CŌMUNE ⚜ FRATERNITAT' ⚜ BE ⚜ MARIE ⚜
MISTERE ⚜ PANNARIOᴿ ⚜ LONDON'.

Carved borders.

Noorthouck, *History of London*, pl. I., p. 888.

Girdlers' Company, A.D. 1449.

5113. [A.D. 1509.] Red : fine, imperfect on the lower part
of the l. h. side. 1⅛ in. [Harl. ch. 45 C. 23.]

A shield of arms, couché : per fess, a pale counterchanged,
three gridirons, GIRDLERS' COMPANY OF LONDON. Crest,
on a helmet, and ornamental mantling, a demi-man, representing St. Lawrence, with nimbus, issuing out of clouds, girt
round the body with a girdle, holding in the r. h. a gridiron
and in the l. h. a book.

Legend on a riband :—

S' COĪE · ARTIS · ZONARIOᴿ . . . . ATIS · LONDON ·

For arms see Noorthouck, *Hist. of London*, pl. II.

5114. Sulph. cast from No. 5113. [D.C., H. 86.]

Glovers' Company, A.D. 1638.

5115. Sulph. cast from the matrix. 1¹³⁄₁₆ × 1½ in. [lxviii.
64.]

Oval : a shield of arms : per fess, a pale counterchanged,
three rams salient, two and one, GLOVERS' COMPANY OF
LONDON. Crest on a helmet, ornamental mantling and wreath,
a ram's head issuing from a basket, betw. a pair of wings.

◆ SIGILLVM ✰ CHIROTHECAREORVM ✰ LONDON ✰

Beaded border.

Noorthouck, *History of London*, pl. I., p. 888.

Leathersellers' Company, A.D. 1442.

5116. Sulph. cast from imperfect and indistinct impression.
2⅛ in. [D.C., G. 50.]

The Assumption of the Virgin, with crown, hands in prayer, surrounded by radiance, upheld by two demi-angels, with expanded wings, issuing from clouds, on each side. Above, two half-length figures of the Father and the Son, crowned, in clouds, placing the crown on the Virgin's head ; over her head the Dove of the Spirit. In base, a shield of arms : three stags, tripping, reguardant, LEATHERSELLERS' COMPANY OF LONDON. Supporters, two angels, kneeling, very indistinct.

SIGILLUM : COE : ART' : SIUE : MISTERIJ : DE : LETHER-
SELLARS · LONDON.

Noorthouck, *History of London*, pl. II.

Mercers' Company, A.D. 1393.

5117. Sulph. cast from fine impression, injured in places. $1\frac{1}{16}$ in. [lxviii. 63.]

Bust of the Virgin, full-face, with a crown of five points fleury, the charge in the shield of arms of the MERCERS' COMPANY OF LONDON.

Legend on a riband or scroll, with curled ends :

SIGILLUM : COMMUNITATIS : MYSTERE : MERCERIE : LONDON' (?)

Cf. the arms in Noorthouck, *History of London*, pl. I., p. 888.

Merchant-Taylors' Company, A.D. 1466.

5118. Pale-red : fine. $2\frac{1}{8}$ in. [xxxv. 258.]

St. John Baptist, with nimbus, holding the Agnus Dei in the l. h. and pointing with the r. h. to it ; standing on a mount in a wilderness, with two trees on each side, a lion on the r. and an unicorn on the l. In base a shield of arms : per chief, (or a chief, over all) a royal tent betw. two parliament robes, in chief an Agnus Dei in a glory, ancient arms of the MERCHANT TAYLORS' COMPANY OF LONDON. Background diapered lozengy with a fleur-de-lis or rose in each space.

S' COE ⚬ MCATOR ⚬ SCISSOR ⚬ FRATNITAT' ⚬ SCI ⚬ IOHIS ⚬
BAPTE ⚬ LODON.

Cf. the modern arms in Noorthouck, *History of London*, pl. I.

5119. Sulph. cast. [lxviii. 65.]

Skinners' Company, A.D. 1327.

5120. [A.D. 1327.] Light-brown : cut from a deed. $1\frac{13}{16}$ in. [xxxvi. 47.]

An ornamental shield of arms: ermine, on a chief three princes' crowns, of crosses pattées and fleurs-de-lis, with tasselled caps, SKINNERS' COMPANY OF LONDON. Crest, on a helmet, ornamental mantling and wreath, an heraldic lizard wreathed round the neck with laurel leaves purfled. Supporters, *dex.*, a lizard of Norway, rampant guardant, *sin.*, a martin, each gorged with a laurel wreath, purfled.

On a scroll in base the inscription :—ÆR' · I · III · R.—(? Anno regni I Edw. III. Regis.)

Noorthouck, *History of London*, pl. I.

Staple Merchants.

5121. [14th cent.] Red: fine, much injured. About 1 in. when perfect. [xl. 21.]

A shield of arms: barry nebulée of four or six (?) on a chief a lion passant guardant, STAPLE MERCHANTS OF LONDON.

SIGILL . . . . TA . . . .

Tallow-Chandlers' Company, A.D. 1463.

5122. Sulph. cast from the matrix. 1¼ in. [D.C., G. 252.]

A shield of arms, couché: per fess, a pale counterchanged, three doves, in the beak of each an olive branch, TALLOW CHANDLERS' COMPANY OF LONDON. Crest, on a helmet, ornamental mantling and wreath, a demi-angel issuing from clouds, vested, wings expanded, and crined, on his head a cap surmounted by a cross pattée, holding a circular dish containing the head of St. John Baptist.

Legend on a scroll or riband curled and waved :—

SIGILLŪ + CŌE + CŌITATIS + MISTERE + TALOUGH + CHANDLERS + CŪTAT⁹ + LONDONIARUM.

Cf. Noorthouck, *History of London*, pl. III., p. 888.

Wax-Chandlers' Company, A.D. 1483 (?)

5123. Sulph. cast from imperfect and indistinct impression. 1¼ in. [lxviii. 30.]

Our Lord, full-length, with nimbus, lifting up the r. h. in benediction, in the l. h. an orb topped with a long cross; surrounded with radiance. Overhead, the Almighty Father, half-length, with nimbus, hands uplifted in benediction. At the sides two angels ? half-length, issuing from clouds. Below these, three saints, each with nimbus.

Legend on a scroll :—

SIGILLUM : COMUNE : MISTERII .... NDELERS : CIUITAT' : LONDŌ.

Society of Mineral and Battery Works, A.D. 1568.

5124. Cast in red earth or composition : chipped.   1½ in. [xxxv. 54.]

A shield of arms : on a mount a brazen pillar supported on the *dex.* side by a lion rampant reguardant, on the *sin.* side by a griffin or dragon segreant, on the pillar a coil of wire tied betw. a bezant and a plate in chief, THE SOCIETY. Crest on a helmet, wreath, and ornamental mantling of foliage, two arms embowed, vested at the shoulder, the hands holding up a calamine stone.   Supporters, *dex.*, SCIENCE as a female figure vested, in her r. h. a pair of compasses, on her head a crescent ; *sin.*, LABOUR, as an old man, vested, in his l. h. a hammer, on his head a crescent.

SIGIL · MINERARIOR · ET · METALL · CVSOR · IN · ANGLIA · DO · TER⁻ · HIBERNIAQ · ANO .... NA.

Cf. the arms in Noorthouck's *History of London*, pl. III.

New-River Company, A.D. 1612.

5125. [A.D. 1678.] Red : each side covered with paper before impression.   2⅙ in.   [Harl. ch. 77 D. 28.]

Ø. View of the city of London, with St. Paul's Cathedral and other churches ; in the foreground an embattled tower and wall.   Above it a dexter hand issuing from the clouds, and scattering rain on the city.

ET PLVI SVPER VNAM CIVITATEM ⚹ .
—Amos iv. 7.

Inner border beaded, outer border carved.

℞. A fleur-de-lis surrounded by the legend given below, in three concentric circles.

Outer circle.   ♠ THE SEALE OF THE COMPANIE OF THE NEW RIVER.

Second circle.   ♠ BROVGHT FROM CHADWEL AND AM·

Inner circle.   ♠ VVELL TO LONDON.

Beaded border.

5126. [A.D. 1697.] Another.   [Lansd. ch. 662.]

Company for Making Hollow Sword-Blades in England.

5127. [A.D. 1704.] Wafer: covered with paper before impression. 1⅞ in. [Add. ch. 24,474.]

A carved shield of arms ornamented with scrolls and festoons of flowers and fruit : BRITANNIA seated before an altar on which are two "hollow sword-blades" in saltire, and holding over them with the r. h. a royal crown.

THE · SEALE · OF · THE · GOVERNER · & COMPANY · FOR · MAKING · HOLLOW · SWORD · BLADES · IN · ENGLAND.

Carved border.

LOOE, EAST, *co. Cornwall.*

5128. [13th cent.] Sulph. cast from the matrix. 1 in. [lxi. 16.]

A one-masted ship, with embattled castles at stern and prow, two mariners on board. Over the side three similar shields of arms : three bends.

✠ S' COMMVNETATIS : DE : LOO.

¡ S. Lewis, *Topogr. Dict.*, vol. iii., p. 165.

LOOE, WEST, PORT PIGHAM, *or* PORT VICHAN, *co. Cornwall.*

5129. [16th cent.] Sulph. cast from the matrix. 1¾ × 1¼ in. [lvi. 17.]

Oval : an archer, standing, full-face, in the r. h. a bow, in the l. h. an arrow ; in his belt a sword.

✠ POR ✸ TV ✸ AM ✸ OTHER ✸ WYS ✸ CALLED ✸ WESTLO.

The letters HE in *other* conjoined.

S. Lewis, *Topogr. Dict.*, vol. iii., p. 166.

LOSTWITHIEL, *and* PENKNETH *or* PENKNIGHT, *co. Cornwall.*

5130. [A.D. 1732.] Sulph. cast from the matrix. 2⅜ in. [lxi. 18.]

A shield of arms : on the sea, in which are two fishes naiant in fess, a castle of three round towers, each masoned and having three tall turrets, betw. two thistle trees, slipped and leaved, LOSTWITHIEL BOROUGH. Over the shield the date 1732,-

SIGILLVM BVRGI DE LOSTWITHYEL ET PENKNIGHT IN
CORNVBIA.

Cabled borders.

S. Lewis, *Topogr. Dict.*, vol. iii., p. 167.

Small Seal of Arms.

5131. Sulph. cast from the matrix. $\frac{7}{8}$ in. [lxi. 19.]

A shield of arms of the BOROUGH OF LOSTWITHIEL, etc., as in No. 5130. The fishes are naiant contournés in fess.

SIG' BVRGI DE LOSTWITHYELL.

Beaded border.

Mayoralty.

5132. [A.D. 1427.] Red : fine, injured by pressure at the sides. $1\frac{1}{4}$ in. [Add. ch. 13,046.]

On the sea, in which is a large fish naiant contourné, a triple-towered castle, betw. two trees. This design was afterwards adopted as the charge on the shield of arms of the Borough, see Nos. 5130, 5131.

. . . . . M · DE MA . . . . LOS . . TEEL.

5133. [A.D. 1441.] Red : chipped and the edge injured. [Add. ch. 19,512.]

SIGL'M · DE . . . . . . LOS . . TEEL.

LOUTH PARK, *or* DE PARCO LUDE, *co. Lincoln.*

Common Seal of the Abbat and Convent used by the Grammar School.

5134. [14th cent.] Sulph. cast from imperfect impression. $1\frac{5}{8}$ in. [lxvii. 20.]

The Virgin, standing, with crown, in a carved niche with trefoiled canopy, crocketed, the Child on the l. arm. Background hatched, and replenished with sprigs of foliage. On each side a tree, representing the *park.*

S' COMMVNE · ABĒIS · ET CONVE . . . . DE · PARCO ·
LVDE.

N. Carlisle, *Endowed Grammar Schools*, vol. i., p. 835.

LOWESTOFT, *co. Suffolk.*

5135. [17th cent.]   Sulph. cast from fine impression.
1¾ in. [lxxii. 7.]

A saint, half-length, with nimbus and cloak, holding in
front an ornamental shield of arms : a rose, *en soleil*, ensigned
with a crown.

☆ VILLA ☆ LOWISTOFT ☆ SOFFOCHE ☆ ☆ ☆.

Beaded border.

LUDLOW, *co. Salop.*

5136. [15th cent.] Sulph. cast from fine impression.   2 in.
[lxxi. 20.]

A shield of arms : a lion couchant guardant betw. three
double heraldic roses, TOWN OF LUDLOW.   Inner border
of the field indented.

Legend on a scroll :—

⚔ SIGILLUM ⚔ BURGENTIUM ⚔ VILLÆ ⚔ DE ⚔ LUDLOW ⚔.

Another Seal.

5137. [15th cent.] Sulph. cast from fine impression.   1⅞ in.
[lxxi. 21.]

Same design as the preceding seal, No. 5136, but from a
different matrix.   The field of the shield powdered for *or.*

Legend on a scroll :—

⚔ SIGILLUM ⚔ BURGENSIBUS ⚔ VILLE ⚔ DE ⚔ LUDELOW ⚔

Small Seal.

5138. [16th cent.]   Sulph. cast from fine impression.
1¼ in. [lxxi. 23.]

A double heraldic cinquefoiled rose *en soleil*, barbed and
seeded.

SIGILLVM : BVRGENS : VILLÆ : DE : LVDLOW.

Beaded borders.

Bailiffs, Burgesses, and Commonalty.

5139. [Late 17th cent.] Sulph. cast from the matrix.
1⅞ in. [lxxi. 22.]

An ornamental shield of arms of the TOWN OF LUDLOW,
as in No. 5136, carved with scrolls and festoons of flowers and

fruit. The field of the shield lined horizontally for *az.*, which is the right tincture for the arms.

> THE · SEAL · OF · THE · BAYLIFFS · BURGESSES · & · COMONALTY · OF · LUDLOW.

Bailiffs and Burgesses.

5140. [17th cent.] Sulph. cast from the matrix. 1¼ in. [lxxi. 24.]

An ornamental shield of arms of the TOWN OF LUDLOW, as in the preceding seal, No. 5139, carved with scrolls. In base the word :— LUDLOW.

> ❀ SIGL' · BALLIVORUM · ET · BURGENSIUM.

S. Lewis, *Topogr. Dict.*, vol. iii., p. 176.

Mayor, Aldermen, and Burgesses, A.D. 1836.

5141. Sulph. cast from the matrix. 1⁵⁄₁₆ in. [lxxi. 26.]

An ornamental shield of arms of the TOWN OF LUDLOW, carved with scrolls. In base the word :—LUDLOW.

> MAYOR ALDERMEN AND BURGESSES · 1836 ·

Court of Record.

5142. [16th cent.] Sulph. cast from the matrix. 2¼ in. [lxxi. 25.]

A shield of arms of the TOWN OF LUDLOW, field powdered. The shield surrounded with carved scrolls and foliage.

> SIGILL' : EXEMPLIFIC' · CVΓIE : DE·: REϹϹOΓD ! VILLE : DE ·: LVDLOW :· ᴀᴋ

Beaded border.

LYDD, *co. Kent.*

5143. [13th cent.] Sulph. cast from the matrix. 2⅞ in. [lxv. 80.]

On the sea in base, on the l. a church with tall spire topped with a cross and flag, on the r. a one-masted ship of war, issuing from behind the church, mainsail furled, crow's nest and flag on the mast-head, trumpeter standing on the embattled forecastle ; in the field over the church, and suspended by the strap from a hook, a shield of arms : quarterly, four lions rampant.

> S' : COMVNɆ : BARONṼ : DOMINI : REGIS : ANGLIɆ DɆ : LYDE ᴀᴋ ᴀᴋ

S. Lewis, *Topogr. Dict.*, vol. iii., p. 185 ; W. Boys, *History of Sandwich*, pl. p. 806, and p. 821.

Bailiffs.

5144. [15th cent.] Sulph. cast from the matrix.   1⅜ in.
[lxv. 81.]

A shield of arms reversed: CINQUE-PORTS, see No. 4885;
ensigned with a crown.   Supporters, *dex.*, a lion, *sin.*, a fox,
their tails looped together in base.

     ✠ SIGILLŪ · OFFICIJ ⚜ · BALIVI · DE ⚜ LED'.

W. Boys, *History of Sandwich*, pp. 806 and 821.

Free Tenants of the Archbishop of Canterbury.

5145. [15th cent.] Sulph. cast from the matrix.   1¼ in.
[lxv. 82.]

In a rudely carved bilobe, a mitre labelled.

    ✠ S' FRAUNCETENENTIB⁹ : VILLE : DE : LYDE : IN
      ARC · HE · PISCOPATV · CANTUARE.

The living of this Parish is a Vicarage in the Peculiar
Jurisdiction and Patronage of the Archbishop of Canterbury.
See ALVERSTOKE, No. 4583.

W. Boys, *History of Sandwich*, p. 806.

LYME-REGIS, *co. Dorset.*

5146. [13th cent.] Sulph. cast from the matrix.   2 in.
[D.C., F. 641.]

On the sea, a one-masted ship, mainyard lowered and
mainsail furled.   On the r. a banner flag charged with the
armorial bearings of ENGLAND, on the l. a similar banner,
charged with the armorial bearings of CASTILE and LEON,
quarterly; for EDWARD I. and his Queen, ELEANOR OF
CASTILE, by whom the incorporation was granted.   The
flag at the masthead is charged with a cross, and has three
streamers.   The ship has a figure-head of a dragon's head, at
each end.   In the field over the ship; on the r. Our Lord on
the cross, betw. St. John the Evangelist on the r., and the
Virgin Mary on the l.; on the r. Michael the Archangel the
Patron Saint of the town and parish, with expanded wings,
in the l. h. a shield charged with a cross, in the r. h. a long
cross held obliquely with which he is piercing the head of a
Dragon under his feet.   Overhead on the l. an estoile or sun
of six points wavy, on the r. a crescent enclosing an estoile.

    ✠ SIGILLVM : COMVNE : DE LIM ✠

Beaded borders.

S. Lewis, *Topogr. Dict.*, vol. iii., p. 188.

5147. [A.D. 1398.] Red : fine, very fragmentary. [Harl. ch. 47 D. 5.]

LYMINGTON, *co. Southampton.*

5148. [Late 15th cent.] Sulph. cast from fine impression, chipped and cracked. 1¾ in. [xxxvii. 13.]

On the sea, a one-masted ship, mainsail furled ; from the mast a shield of arms slung from a rope : three torteaux, in chief a label of as many points, COURTENAY, perhaps for PETER COURTENAY, Bishop of Winchester, A.D. 1487–1492.

SIGILLVM : BVRGI : DE : LYMINGTON : · :

S. Lewis, *Topogr. Dict.*, vol. iii., p. 189.

LYNN REGIS, *or* KING'S LYNN, *co. Norfolk.*

5149. [13th cent.] Dark-bronze green : fine, chipped and rubbed in places ; cut from a charter. 2⅞ in. [xxxv. 254.]

Ø. The Eagle of St. John the Evangelist, rising reguardant contourné, with beaded nimbus, and grasping in its talons a scroll inscribed with the commencing words of the Gospel of St. John :—IN PRINCIPIO ERAT. Within a cusped panel or compartment of eight points, with a countersunk trefoil in each spandril.

✠ : SIGILLUM : COMMVNITATIS : LENNIE :

℞. St. Margaret, the Patron Saint of the town and parish, standing, in the l. h. a book, in the r. h. a long cross, with which she is piercing the head of a Dragon under her feet, its tail also bearing a head. Under an elaborately carved trefoiled arch, crocketed, supported on two richly carved towers, with three storeys of windows, pinnacled and crocketed.

SUB · MARGARETA : TERITUR : DRACO : STAT :
CRVCE : LETA.

Beaded borders.

Blomefield, *History of Norfolk*, vol. viii., p. 476.

5150. Sulph. casts of the *obv.* and *rev.* from the matrix. [lxix. 52, 53.]

5151. Red, covered with paper before impression : very imperfect. [xliii. 146.]

Privy Seal of the Mayoralty.

5152. [Early 15th cent.] Red: fine, chipped and rubbed in places. 2 in. [xxxv. 255.]

St. Margaret, with crown and nimbus, standing, in the l. h. a book, in the r. h. a long cross, with which she is piercing the head of a Dragon under her feet. Under an elaborately carved canopy, supported on two richly carved side towers of tabernacle work. The base is semi-octagonal, and on the masonry is a shield of arms: three conger eels' heads erased and erect, in the mouth of each a cross crosslet fitchée, TOWN OF LYNN REGÎS. Inside edge of field engrailed.

☙ SIGILLUM . . . . M ⚶ ⚶ MAIORATUS ⚶ LENNIE ⚶

Cabled border.

Second state of the Seal.

5153. Sulph. cast from chipped impression. 2 in. [D.C., G. 44.]

This appears to be an impression from the same matrix as the preceding seal, No. 5152, after having been worn down very considerably by use, and retouched and some lines deeply cut by an engraver.

☙ SIGILLUM ⚶ SECRETUM ⚶ ⚶ MAIORATUS ⚶ LENNIE ⚶

5154. Another. [lxix. 36.]

Seal for the delivery of wool and hides, see No. 1160.

Guardians of the Poor.

5155. Sulph. cast from chipped impression. 1¾ × 1⅓ in. [lxix. 33.]

Oval: a man, bearded, three-quarters-length, in the r. h. a long staff, in the l. h. a shield of arms, TOWN OF LYNN REGIS, as in No. 5152.

GARDIAN · PAVP ⚶ ⚶ ⚶ ⚶ LENNÆ · REGIS.

Beaded border.

MACCLESFIELD, *co. Chester.*

5156. [17th cent.] Sulph. cast from the matrix. 1¾ in. [lx. 89.]

A lion rampant, in its forepaws a garb of CHESTER.

SIGILLUM BVRGI DE MACCLESFIELD.

Beaded borders.

S. Lewis, *Topogr. Dict.*, vol. iii., p. 196.

Smaller Seal.

5157. [17th cent.] Sulph. cast from the matrix. ¾ in. [lx. 90.]

Design similar to that of the preceding seal, No. 5156.

No legend.

Free Grammar School, A.D. 1552.

5158. Sulph. cast from the matrix, tinted red. About 1½ × ¾ in. [xxxv. 142.]

Pointed oval: a pedagogue, with birch-rod held aloft in the r. h., an open book in the l. h., seated on a bench. In the field overhead the letters E. R. (*Edwardus Rex*), and in base the royal badge, a rose of five leaves *en soleil.*

✲ SIGILLUM ✲ LIBERE ✲ SCOLE ✲ DE ✲ MACCLEFFELD.

N. Carlisle, *Endowed Grammar Schools*, vol. i., p. 117.

5159. Another. [xlvii. 852.]

Laing's *MS. Catal.*, No. 273.

MAIDENHEAD, *co. Berks.*

5160. Sulph. cast from the brass matrix. 1½ × 1 in. [lix. 68.]

Pointed oval: a *maiden's head,* in allusion, by way of *rebus,* to the name of the borough, full-face, couped at the neck, long hair, nimbus; overhead a small estoile of six points.

+ S' IOH'IS · GODAYHCARTHIERR. ?

S. Lewis, *Topogr. Dict.*, vol. iii., p. 200.

MAIDSTONE, *co. Kent.*

5161. [16th cent.] Sulph. casts of *obv.* and *rev.* from chipped impression. 2⅝ in. [lxv. 83, 84.]

Ø. A view of the town, with churches and houses, on a river, with a bridge of two round-headed arches.

✠ : SIGILL' . COM . . . . . . REGIS : DE : MAYDSTON :

℞. A shield of arms: a fess wavy, betw. three roundles; on a chief a lion passant guardant of *E*NGLAND, TOWN OF MAIDSTONE.

✠ : SIGILL' : COM : VILLE : REGIS : DE : MAYDSTON.

Rev. only engraved in S. Lewis, *Topogr. Dict.*, vol. iii., p. 202.

Seal of Arms.

5162. [16th cent.] Sulph. cast. $2\frac{5}{16} \times 1\frac{3}{4}$ in.   [lxv. 85.]

Shield-shaped : a shield of arms ; as in the previous seal No. 5161.

No legend.

Mayoralty, A.D. 1567 [8].

5163. Sulph. cast from the matrix. $1\frac{7}{8}$ in.   [lxv. 86.]

A *maid* undraped, standing on an orb or *stone*, in allusion, by way of *rebus*, to the name of the Town ; in the r. h. an orb or stone, in the l. h. a branch of foliage.

✠ SIGILLVM · MAIORAT · VILLE · DE · MAYDSTONE · MVTATVM ⚭

and across the field in two horizontal lines the continuation of the legend :—

20 · DIE · FEBR · ANO · 1567.

MALDON, *co. Essex.*

5164. [A.D. 1562.]   Red : fine fragment of the *obv.* and *rev.* [Harl. ch. 58 F. 3.]

∅. On the waves a one-masted ship, mainsail furled, with embattled castle at poop and at prow.

Legend wanting.

℞. A shield of arms : three lions passant guardant in pale, ENGLAND, and TOWN OF MALDON.

Legend wanting.

5165. Sulph. cast of the *obv.* only of the preceding seal, No. 5164.   [D.C., H. 174.]

Second Seal.

5166. [17th cent.]   Sulph. casts of the *obv.* and *rev.* from the matrix. $2\frac{7}{8}$ in.   [lxiii. 22, 23.]

∅. On the sea, a one-masted ship, mainsail furled, embattled castle on the r. with a banner-flag charged with the arms of ENGLAND, or MALDON.

♠ · SIGILLVM ·⋮· COMMVNE ·⋮· CORP ·⋮· VILLÆ ·⋮·DE ·⋮· MALDON ··

℞. A shield of arms : three lions passant reguardant in pale.

✿ · SIGILLVM ·⋮· COMMVNE ·⋮· CORP ·⋮· VILLÆ ·⋮· DE ·⋮· MALDON ·⋮·

Carved borders.

S. Lewis, *Topogr. Dict.*, vol. iii., p. 206.

MALMESBURY, *co. Wilts.*.

5167. [Late 17th cent.] Sulph. cast from the matrix.
1¾ in. [lxxiii. 65.]

On a mount a triple-towered castle, masoned and embattled, with central tower domed and topped with a flag,
round-headed doorway with portcullis half-down. On each
side a corn plant with three ears of corn. In base the sea,
indicated by a heraldic representation of barry wavy of six.
In the field on the l. an estoile of six points, on the r. an increscent. There are also three pellets placed irregularly in
the field.

    � SIGIL · COM · ALDRI · ET · BVRGEN · BVRGI · DE ·
    MALMESBVRY · IN · COM · WILTS.

Beaded border.

S. Lewis, *Topogr. Dict.*, vol. iv., p. 208, engraves a seal, of similar
design but different legend, bearing date A.D. 1615.

Smaller Seal.

5168. Sulph. cast from the matrix. 1⁵⁄₁₆ in. [lxxiii. 66.]

This is similar in design to the preceding seal, No. 5167, but
smaller. The position of the pellets is reversed.

    · SIGIL · COM · ALDRI ET CAPITAL BVRGEN BVRGI DE
    MALMESBVRY.

Inner border cabled, outer border beaded.

MAN, ISLE OF.

5169. [18th cent.] Recent impression in red sealing-wax,
from the matrix. 1³⁄₈ × 1³⁄₁₀ in. [xxxvi. 177.]

Oval: an ornamental shield of arms: three legs conjoined
in the fess point in armour, garnished and spurred, ISLE OF
MAN.

    ✿ QUOCUNQUE IECERIS STABIT.

Carved borders.

S. Lewis, *Topogr. Dict.*, vol. iii., p. 213.

MANSFIELD, *co. Nottingham.*

Free Grammar School, A.D. 1561 ; *and Corporation,*

A.D. 1556.

5170. Sulph. cast, tinted red, from the matrix. 1¼ in.
[xxxv. 143.]

K 2

St. Peter, with nimbus, holding a book and key, seated on
the l., and St. Paul, with nimbus, holding a sword and book,
seated on the r.

⽊ SIGILL' ♠ COMME ♠ DE ♠ MANNYSFEL.

N. Carlisle, *Endowed Grammar Schools*, vol. ii., p. 261.

5171. Another.   [xlvii. 854.]

Laing's *MS. Catal.*, No 288.

5172. [A.D. 1785.]   Red : *en placard*, edge imperfect.
[Add. ch. 13,940.]

MARAZION, *co. Cornwall.*
Mayor.

5173. [? 12th cent.] Sulph. cast from the matrix.   1¼ in.
[lxi. 20.]

A triple-towered castle, domed, the side towers topped
with a flag.   Coarse work.

⽊ SIGILL' · MAIORIS · VILLE · ET · BOROV · DE · MARGHASION.

S. Lewis, *Topogr. Dict.*, vol. iii., p. 250.

MARKET-BOSWORTH, *co. Leicester.*
Free Grammar School, A.D. 1593.

5174. Sulph. cast, tinted red, from the matrix.   1¼ in.
[xxxv. 144.]

On a wreath a leopard sejant, ducally gorged.   Crest of Sir
WOLSTAN DIXIE, Knt., founder.

⽊ SIG' · SCHOLÆ · GRAM : WOLSTANI · DIXIE · MIL' ·
DE · MARKET · BOSWORTH.
Carved borders.

N. Carlisle, *Endowed Grammar Schools*, vol. i., p. 753.

5175. Another.   [xlvii. 750.]

Laing's *MS. Catal.*, No. 283.

5176. Sulph. cast.   [lxvi. 45.]

MARLBOROUGH, *co. Wilts.*

5177. [13th cent.] Sulph. cast from fine, but very imperfect, impression.   1⅞ in. [lxiii. 41.]

A triple-towered castle, embattled and masoned, long round-headed windows, round-headed doorway with hinged door closed.

... IG ... L' .... ARLEBERG ....

5178. Another. [D.C., F. 633.]

5179. [A.D. 1532.] Red: very imperfect and injured by pressure. [Add. ch. 5695.]

✠ S .... MVN ... E : MARLEBERGE :

5180. [A.D. 1532.] Red: cracked and injured by pressure. [Add. ch. 5696.]

✠ SIGILL' · COMMVNE : DE : MARLEBERGE :

Later Seal, A.D. 1714.

5181. Sulph. cast from the matrix. $1\frac{7}{8}$ in. [lxxiii. 67.]

A shield of arms: per saltire, *gu.* and *az.*, in chief a bull passant, in fess two cocks or capons, in base three grey-hounds courant in pale, on a chief *or*, a tower betw. two roses of five leaves barbed and seeded, TOWN OF MARLBOROUGH. According to Burke, *Gen. Armory*, the tower is on a pale. Crest, on a helmet and ornamental mantling, a tower.

SIGILLVM MAIORIS & BURGENS · BURGI & VILLÆ DE MARLEBERG · 1714.

Carved border.

S. Lewis, *Topogr. Dict.,* vol. iii., p. 257.

Mayor.

5182. Sulph. cast from the matrix. $1\frac{1}{4}$ in. [lxxiii. 68.]

A shield of arms as in the preceding seal, No. 5181.

❀ SIGILLVM MAIORIS BURGI DE MARLEBERG.

MELCOMBE-REGIS, *see* **WEYMOUTH,** *co. Dorset.*

MIDDLETON, *co. Lancaster.*

Free Grammar School, A.D. 1572.

5183. Sulph. cast from the matrix. 3 × 2 in. [D.C., H. 68.]

Pointed oval: Qu. Elizabeth, in royal robes, with crown, sceptre fleur-de-lizé and orb, seated under a rectangular tester canopy with embroidered back, on a pavement ornamented with geometrical diaper, each space enclosing alternately a small cinquefoil or pellet.   Over the canopy a carved entablature, hanging from a ring, and bearing the inscription :—

· REG · ELIZABETH ·

At each side an elegantly designed scroll of foliage. In base, on an arcade of round-headed arches, and betw. two trefoils, a shield of arms: a brazen-nose, in allusion to BRASENOSE COLLEGE, Oxford.

✠ SIGILL ✩ COLL ✩ REG ✩ DE ✩ BRASEN ✩ NOSE ✩ IN ✩ OXON ✩ GVBERNATOR ✩ LIBERÆ ✩ SCHOLÆ ✩ IN MIDLETON.

SOUTH MOLTON LIBERTY, *co. Devon.*

5184. [17th century.]   Sulph. cast from the matrix.   1¾ in. [lxi. 93.]

A fleece, betw. a royal crown, (for Charles II.), in chief, and a stringed and jewelled mitre (for the Bishop of Exeter) in base.   Below the mitre, a label inscribed :—FIAT IVSTITIA.

LIBERTAS ✩ DE ✩ SOVTH MOLTON.

Inner border beaded, outer border carved.

S Lewis, *Topogr. Dict.,* vol. iii., p. 314.

Another Seal.

5185. [17th cent.]   Sulph. cast from the matrix.   1⅜ in. [lxi. 94.]

A royal crown.

LIBERTY OF SOUTH MOLTON.

Inner border beaded, outer border carved.

MONMOUTH, *co. Monmouth.*

5186. [13th . cent.]   Sulph. cast from a fine impression, chipped and indistinct in places.   1⅜ in.   [D.C., E. 628.]

An ancient ship, with one mast, flag and streamers, each end of the ship having the figure head of an animal.

✠ CONMVNE SIGILL' MONEMVTE.

Cf. S. Lewis, *Topogr. Dict.,* vol. iii., p. 317, for a later seal.

NEWARK-UPON-TRENT, *co. Nottingham.*

5187. [A.D. 1723.]   Sulph. cast from the matrix.   2¾ in. [lxx. 63.]

An ornamentally carved shield of arms : barry wavy of six, on a chief wavy a peacock in his pride betw. a fleur-de-lis and a lion passant guardant, TOWN OF NEWARK-UPON-TRENT. Crest on a helmet, mantling, and wreath, a martlet holding a snake in its beak. Supporters, two bears.

· ♠ · SIGILLUM ✿ COMMUNE ✿ BURGI ✿ DE ✿ NEWARKE ✿ SUPER ✿ TRENT ✿ 1723.

S. Lewis, *Topogr. Dict.*, vol. iii., p. 346.

NEWBOROUGH, *co. Anglesey.*

5188. [A.D. 1426.] Red : injured by pressure, and the edge imperfect. 1¼ in. [Add. ch. 8642.]

On the sea a ship with one mast, mainsail set, high at each end, castles, crow's nest, and split flag at the masthead.

SIGILLU : COMUNITATIS : DE : NEUBURGH :

Beaded borders.

NEWBURY, *co. Berks.*

5189. [17th cent.] Sulph. cast from the matrix. ⅞ × ¾ in. [lix. 69.]

Oval : a castle, masoned and embattled, central tower domed.

BURROUGH OF NEWBURY.

Carved border.

Cf. S. Lewis, *Topogr. Dict.*, vol. iii., p. 351.

NEWCASTLE-UNDER-LYME, *co. Stafford.*

5190. [13th cent.] Sulph. cast from the matrix. 1¾ in. [lxxii. 51.]

On waves, a low embattled wall, enclosing an edifice with two gable-ends at each side, on the central embattled tower a banner flag betw. a man-at-arms holding a battleaxe on the l., and a man-at-arms blowing a horn on the r. On the frieze below the battlements three shields of arms : 1. a lion rampant contourné within a bordure charged with roundles, probably for EDMUND, EARL of CORNWALL ; 2. ENGLAND ? 3. CHESTER ?

SIGILL'. : COMVNE : BVRGENSIVM : NOVI : CASTELLI.

Beaded borders.

S. Lewis, *Topogr. Dict*, vol. iii., p. 353

Small Seal.

5191. [Modern.] Sulph. cast from the matrix. $\frac{7}{8}$ in.
[lxxii. 52.]

Design copied from that on the preceding seal, No. 5190.
Legend in black letter capitals :—

✿ NEWCASTLE UNDER LYME.

Another Seal.

5192. [17th cent.] Sulph. cast from a fine impression.
1¼ in. [lxxii. 53.]

An embattled castle.

✿ · NEWCASTLE · ✿ · VNDER · ✿ · LYNE ·

Carved borders.

NEWCASTLE-UPON-TYNE, *co. Northumberland.*

5193. [13th cent.] Sulph. cast from fine impression.   2 in.
[lxx. 20.]

An embattled castle, the wall ornamented with a lozengy
pattern, central doorway round-headed, with closed doors ;
on the tower two shields of early form.

✿ COMMVNE : SIGILL' : ИOVI : CASTRI SVP TIИAM.

Brand, *History of Newcastle,* vol. ii., pl. 1, f. 13.

With Counterseal of NICHOLAS LESCOT, *Mayor.*

5194. [A.D. 1321.] Dark green : fine, but very imperfect.
[Add. ch. 20,535.]

∅. As before, No. 5193.

.... VI CAST ......

R. A small round counterseal of the Mayor. About $\frac{7}{8}$ in.
when perfect. A shield of arms : a chevron (fretty ?) betw.
three escallops.

✿ SIGILL'V NICHO . . . . T.

Later Seal.

5195. [18th cent.] Sulph. cast from the matrix.   2¾ in.
[lxx. 21.]

A shield of arms of ornamental shape : three castles or
towers, two and one, TOWN OF NEWCASTLE-UPON-TYNE.
Crest, on a helmet, ornamental mantling, and wreath, a
tower, thereon a demi-lion issuing rampant reguardant, holding

a split banner ensigned with the arms of· St. George. Supporters, two sea-horses. In base, on a riband, the motto :—
FORTITER · DEFENDIT · TRIUMP:HANS.

    ✠ COMMUNE · SIGILLUM · VILLE · NOVICASTRI · SUPER ·
                TINAM.

Brand, *History of Newcastle*, vol. ii., pl. I, f. 8 ; S. Lewis, *Topogr. Dict.*, vol. iii., p. 354.

Privy Seal.

5196· [14th cent.] Sulph. cast from fine, but chipped, impression. $1\frac{5}{8}$ in. [lxx. 22.]

On waves, a triple-towered castle, masoned and embattled. In the doorway, the portcullis partly down, on the threshold a lion passant guardant of ENGLAND. In the field on each side a fleur-de-lis of FRANCE. Inner border of the field enriched with small quatrefoils or ball-flowers.

    ✠ SIGILL͞V · SE . . . . VILLE . . OVI : CASTRI · SV̶P · TYN͞A.

Mayoralty.
First Seal, or Seal ad Causas.

5197. [13th cent.] Sulph. cast from fine impression. $1\frac{5}{8}$ in. [lxx. 23.]

On an embattled bridge with two ogee arches over a river, a triple-towered castle, with embattled parapets, quatrefoil windows, and closed doorway, betw. two supporting lions, that on the l. passant guardant, that on the r. passant. Background faintly hatched.

    ✠ S' : MAIORAT' : VILLE : NOVI : CAST' : SV̶P : TINAM : AD :
                CAVSAS.

Brand, *History of Newcastle*, vol. ii., pl. II., f. 2.

Second Seal.

5198. [17th cent.] Sulph. cast from fine impression. $1\frac{4}{8}$ in. [D.C., H. 153.]

A shield of arms, TOWN OF NEWCASTLE-UPON-TYNE. Over the shield two carved scrolls of conventional foliage. Supporters, two lions rampant guardant. In base a riband, not inscribed.

    SIGIL : MAIORALITAT : VILLÆ : NOVICASTR' · SVP · TINA.

Another Seal.

 5199. [18th cent.] Sulph. cast, chipped, from the matrix. 2 in. [D.C., H. 162.]

A shield of arms : *gu.* three castles or towers triple-towered, two and one, TOWN OF NEWCASTLE-UPON-TYNE. Crest on a helmet, ornamental mantling, and wreath, a tower as in the shield, thereon a demi-lion issuant rampant guardant holding a split banner ensigned with arms of St. George. Supporters, two sea-horses, crined and finned.   In base a riband, not inscribed.

✠ [SIGI]LLUM · MAIORALITATIS · VILLE · NOVICASTRI · SUPER · TINAM.

Cf. S. Lewis, *Topogr. Dict.*, vol. iii., p. 354, where a seal resembling this, but with variant legend, is engraved.

5200. Another, in better preservation.   [lxx. 24.]

Another Seal.

5201. [18th cent.]   Sulph. cast from the matrix.   **2** in. [lxx. 25.]

Resembles the preceding seal, No. 5199, but is cut in lower relief.

Fraternity of the Ostmen.

5202. [18th cent.]   Sulph. cast from the matrix.   **2** in. [lxx. 26.]

On a geometrical pavement, the Master of the Ostmen with long furred coat, on the l., receiving an "oste" on the r., with their r. hands clasped : each holds a low crowned hat.   On a scroll proceeding from the mouth of the Master the inscription :— WELCOME · MY · OSTE.   The letters ME in *welcome* are conjoined.

⚮ THE · SEALE · OF · THE · FRETERNITY · OF · THE · OSTMEN · OF · THE · TOWNE · OF · NEWCASTLE · VPON · TINE.

Several pairs of letters are conjoined.

Inner border cabled, outer border carved.

See Brand, *History of Newcastle*, vol. ii., p. 269.

5203. Another.   [D.C., H. 73.]

Statute-Merchant.

5204. [A.D. 1650.]   Red : imperfect and indistinct.   1⅜ in. [Eg. ch. 307.]

A shield of arms, TOWN OF NEWCASTLE-UPON-TYNE. Above it, a royal crown betw. the initials E–R, each crowned. On the l. the royal badge a rose, crowned ; on the r. a portcullis, crowned.   Sixteenth century work.

✠ SIGILL . . . . . MERCAT . . . . NOV . . CASTR : SVP · TINAM.

Trinity House, A.D. 1584.

5205. Sulph. cast from the matrix.   2¼ × 1¾ in.   [D.C., H. 154.]

Oval : a shield of arms : on the sea a three-masted ship of war, sailing under full sail to the l., the flag at each mast-head charged with a cross. Crest on a helmet, ornamental mantling and wreath, an eagle displayed.

❋ · THIS · IS · THE · SEALE · OF · THE · TRINITIE · HOVSE · IN · NEWCASTLE · VPON · TINE.

The letters N E in *Tine* are conjoined.
Inner border beaded, outer border carved.

Antiquarian Society, A.D. 1813.

5206. Red : fine, cracked, enclosed in a turned wooden box. 2 in. [Add. ch. 7085.]

On an estrade, a figure of MINERVA or ANTIQUITY (?), to the r., seated on the capital of an Ionic column, and draped in classical style, writing on an opened scroll. Before her a wine jar, and an altar with a lamp on it and inscribed in incised characters :—LAMIIS TRIBVS. In the exergue the motto :—SCRIPTA MANENT. The base of the altar bears the engraver's name :—T. WYON.

SIGILLVM SOCIETATIS ANTIQVARIORVM PONTIS ÆLII MDCCCXIII.

NEWPORT, *Isle of Wight, co. Southampton.*

5207. [15th cent.] Sulph. cast from fine impression. 1⅞ in. [xxxvii. 15.]

On the sea, a one-masted ship with mainsail set, flag with cross of St. George and streamers, embattled forecastle, small flag and cross at the stern.

SIGILLUM : COMUNE : UILLE : DE : NEUPORT : IN : INSULA : DE : WIGHT.

S. Lewis, *Topogr. Dict.,* vol. iii., p. 371.

Later Seal.

5208. [18th cent.] Sulph. cast from the matrix. 1⅛ in. [lxiii. 94.]

A three-masted ship of war, sails set, embattled round-tops, high deck at poop and prow ; on the mainsail a lion passant guardant of *E*NGLAND.

SIGILLVM COMVNE VILLÆ DE NEWPORT IN INSVLA VECTIS.

The letters IN in *insula* are conjoined.
Beaded border.

Small Seal.

5209. [18th cent.]   Sulph. cast.   1 in.   [xxxvii. 22.]
Somewhat resembles the previous seal, No. 5208, but with different details.

SIGILLVM COMVNE VILLE DE NEVPORT IN INSVLA VECTIS·

The letters NE in *commune* are conjoined.
Beaded border.

Seal of the Statute Merchant, see No. 1093.

NEWPORT, *co. Monmouth.*

5210. [18th cent.]   Sulph. cast from the matrix.   1⅛ in.
[lxxi. 27.]
Three fishes naiant in pale, *or*, not on a shield.   Background wavy.

✛ . ❖ . NOVA . ⋮ ❖ . BVRGA . . ❖ .

Inner border beaded, outer border carved.
An uncertain seal.

NEWTOWN, *Isle of Wight, co. Southampton, see* FRANCHEWILLE.

NORFOLK.

THOMAS DE MORIEUX, *or* MORVEUX, *Sheriff.*

5211. [A.D. 1355.]   Brown.   ⅞ in.   [Cotton ch. xxvii. 152.]
A triple-towered castle, betw. the initial letters T. M., and four small quatrefoils.
In place of a legend a wavy scroll of foliage.

GUYDO DE SEYNTCLER, *Sheriff.*

5212. [A.D. 1357.]   Brown.   ⅞ in. [Add. ch. 14,972.]
Oval: a shield of arms: a lion rampant, tail nowed and fourchée, ST. CLERE.   Ensigned with the barbican of a castle, and between two crosses pattée.   Background diapered.

NORTHAMPTONSHIRE.

JOHN CARNELL, *Late Sheriff.*

5213. [A.D. 1378.]   Green: very imperfect.   ⅞ in.   [Add. ch. 21,791.]

A triple-towered castle.

Legend destroyed.

JOHN MALORRE, *Sheriff.*

5214. [A.D. 1393.] Red. $\frac{4}{8}$ in. [Add. ch. 6047.]

Octagonal : a triple-towered castle, in the doorway an ermine spot.

Beaded border.

5215. Sulph. cast from No. 5205. [lxix. 81.]

SIR WILLIAM PARR, *Sheriff.*

5216. [A.D. 1522.] Green. $\frac{4}{8}$ in. [Add. ch. 22,416.]

An embattled castle of two storeys.

NORTHAMPTON, *co. Northampton.*

5217. [13th cent.] Sulph. cast from fine impression. $1\frac{4}{8}$ in. [lxix. 78.]

An embattled tower with closed portal, the walls and battlements charged with fourteen quatrefoils. Over the battlements the head of a knight, to the l., who is holding a cross-bow and a banner-flag. In the field a sprig and leaves of foliage.

SIGILLVM : COMMVNE : NORHAMPTONE :

Beaded borders.

5218. [A.D. 1683.] Red : *en plaque*, on a label. [Add. ch. 6132.]

Mayoralty.

5219. [14th cent.] Sulph. cast from the matrix. $1\frac{4}{8}$ in. [lxix. 79.]

A triple-towered castle, walls masoned and embattled : doors open. Supported by two lions passant guardant of ENGLAND. In the field above, a reticulated pattern.

✠ S' MAIORITATIS VILLE NORHAMTONIE.

Beaded borders.

5220. [A.D. 1337.] Dark-green : fine, but very imperfect. [Add. ch. 729.]

. . . . LL . . . . . . AMTO . .

5221. [A.D. 1390.] Dark-green : fine, but imperfect. [Add. ch. 22,368.]

. . . . . MAIORITATIS VILLE N . . . .

5222. [A.D. 1402.] Dark-green : fine, but very imperfect. [Add. ch. 22,371.]

. . . . MAIORITATIS VIL . . . .

5223. [A.D. 1406.] Brown: cracked and chipped. [Add. ch. 730.]

✠ S' MAIORITATIS VILLE NORHAMTONIE.

5224. [A.D. 1406.] Green: fine, chipped and imperfect. [Add. ch. 731.]

. . . ITATIS . . . . NOR . A . . .

5225. [A.D. 1410.] Red: fine fragment. [Add. ch. 21,816.]

. . . AIORITATIS . . .

5226. [A.D. 1440.] Red: fine, injured by pressure in places. [Add. ch. 732.]

✠ S' MAIORITATIS VILLE NORHAMTONIE.

5227. [A.D. 1444.] Red: cracked and injured. [Add. ch. 735.]

. . . . RITATIS VI . . . . HAM . .

Seal "pro recognitione debitorum," see Nos. 1081, 1082.

NORTHUMBERLAND.

JOHN DE COUPLAND, *Escheator.*

5228. [A.D. 1355.] Dark-brown: much injured. [Harl. ch. 48 I. 20.]

Oval: a triple-towered castle, embattled.

NORWICH, *co. Norfolk.*

5229. [A.D. 1559.] Red: very fragmentary. [Add. ch. 14,230.]

For description see following seal, No. 5230, which represents the second or altered state of the matrix, which had originally on the *rev.* (here only indicated by portions of drapery) a representation of the Trinity, removed in A.D. 1573, and the inscribed entablature engraved instead over it.

Blomefield, *Hist. of Norfolk*, vol. iv., plan at end, Nos. 174, 175; see also p. 574.

Second State of the Seal, A.D. 1753.

5230. Sulph. cast of the *obv.* and *rev.*, from fine, but chipped, impression. 2¼ in. [lxix. 38.]

Ø. A castle, with outer walls and keep embattled and masoned, round-headed portal and portcullis half-down. Below it a lion passant guardant of ENGLAND. In base a cinquefoiled flower, slipped and leaved, on each side a branch of flowers and foliage. The castle and lion are now the armorial charges of the shield of arms of the CITY OF NORWICH.

SIGILLUM ✠ [C]OMUNE ✠ CIUITATIS ✠ NORWICI ✠.

℞. A niche with elaborate canopy of two stages or tiers, pinnacled and crocketed, containing an ornamentally carved entablature, inscribed in four lines: IM-MA-NV-EL On a semi-hexagonal plinth in base the date 1573.* On each side, in a pent-house, on a corbel of masonry, a demi-angel with wings expanded, leaning forward to the central subject, (see previous seal, No. 5229), and holding in front a shield of arms : l., ROYAL ARMS of K. HENRY IV., who extended the constitution of the city in A.D. 1403 : r., diapré, a cross.

Legend as in *obv.*

S. Lewis, *Topogr. Dict.*, vol. iii., p. 423 ; Blomefield, *History of Norfolk*, vol. iv., p. 574.

5231. Red : fair, chipped and indistinct in places. [xxxv. 244.]

Φ and ℞. SIGILLUM ✠ COMUNE ✠ CIVITATIS ✠ NORWICI ✠

5232. Red : fine, chipped and injured in places by pressure. [xxxv. 245.]

Castle.

5233. [A.D. 1356.] Dark-green :. fine, cracked and imperfect. 1⅛ in. [Add. ch. 27,370.]

A triple-towered castle, masoned and embattled ; round-headed doorway. In the field, on each side a wavy sprig of flowers.

✠ SI]GILLVM · CASTRI · NORWYCI.

Bailiffs, A.D. 1223–1403.

5234. [A.D. 1226.] ·Dark mottled-green : fine, chipped at the edge. Cut from a dated charter. 2⅛ in. [xxxv. 241.]

A representation of Norwich Castle, showing the large keep, with two tiers of windows, battlements, side towers, and embattled outer wall with round-headed doorway. In the doorway a man half-length to the l. In base, a river.

✠ SIGILLVM : BALLIVORVM : [NORWIC]I ⁑

Beaded borders.

Blomefield, *History of Norfolk*, vol. iv., plan at end, No. 171 ; see also p. 574.

---

* Blomefield, *Hist. of Norf.* iv. 574, states that the alteration was effected in A.D. 1686.

Second State of the Seal.

5235. [14th cent.] . Red: fine, chipped and imperfect. [xxxv. 242.]

Ø. As before, No. 5234, but appears to have been retouched in some of the lines of the masonry, and the mullions of the lower arcaded window of keep.

✠ S . . . . . LLVM : BALLIVORVM : NORWICI ⚜

R. On a mount, a lion passant guardant of ENGLAND, designed in a bold and spirited manner. The lion was granted, as an addition to the city arms, by Edward III.

✠ CVM SC . . NO NO[V]UM TIBI SUM NORWYCE (?) SIGILLUM.

The M of *cum* has a bar through its second upright stroke. The legend is deciphered by Blomefield, vol. iv., p. 574, to read: " Cum isto signo novum tibi sum Norwyce sigillum."

Blomefield, *History of Norfolk*, vol. iv., plan at end, Nos. 171, 172.

Mayoralty, A.D. 1403.

5236. Red: fine, edge much chipped. 2 in. [xxxv. 245.]

The Trinity, on a semi-hexagonal masoned plinth, in a carved niche with elegant canopy, on which is a shield of the ROYAL ARMS of K. Henry IV. At each side on tabernacle-work a shield of arms: l. CITY OF NORWICH, see No. 5230; r. a cross.

✠ SIGILLUM ⚜ OFFICII ⚜ [MAIORATU]S ⚜ [CI]VITAT[IS ⚜ N]ORWICI ⚜

This seal was altered at the Reformation by substituting a representation of the Resurrection of Our Lord in the place of the Trinity. See Blomefield, *History of Norfolk*, vol. iv., p. 574 ; plan at end, No. 176.

Sheriffs, A.D. 1403.

5237. Sulph. cast from chipped impression. 1 in. [lxix. 39.]

On a castle with walls masoned and embattled, round-headed doorway, with portcullis and a fleur-de-lis of FRANCE, a lion passant guardant of ENGLAND.

✠ SIGILL' · OFFICII · VICECOMIT' · CIVITATIS · N[ORWICI].

Blomefield, *History of Norfolk*, vol. iv., plan at end, No. 178, and see p. 575.

Chamberlain, A.D. 1448.

5238. Red : fine. 1¼ × 1 in. [xxxv. 247.]

Oval : a triple-towered castle, in base a lion passant guardant of ENGLAND. The armorial bearings of the CITY OF NORWICH. On the side towers the initials **. t. t̃ .** (?)

✠ S' : ᴏꜰꜰ'ᴄɪɪ : CAMERAR̃ · CIVITATIS · NORWICI. Cabled borders.

Blomefield, *History of Norfolk*, vol. iv., plan at end, No. 179 ; p. 595.

Second State.

5239. Sulph. cast from fine impression. [lxix. 40.]

Similar to the preceding No. 5238, with addition of a small fleur-de-lis under the portcullis of the castle.

Seal "pro recognitione debitorum," see Nos. 1083, 1084.

Seal for delivery of wool and hides, see Nos. 1161, 1162.

NOTTINGHAMSHIRE.

SIR JOHN PORTER, *Sheriff,* A.D. 1554.

5240. Sulph. cast from fine impression. 1⅜ in. [lxx. 49.]

A shield of arms : three bells, and a canton erm., PORTER. Crest on a helmet and ornamental mantling, a portcullis chained.

. . VIC . . NOTT . .

Cf. Harl. *MS.* 259, f. 57.

NOTTINGHAM, *co. Nottingham.*

5241. [15th cent.] Recent impression in red sealing-wax, from the matrix. 2⅝ in. [xl. 24.]

A castle, of four round towers embattled, domed, and topped with a knob. Ogee arched doorway, with portcullis half down. In the field above, on the l. a crescent, on the r. an estoile of seven points wavy. Background diapered with foliage.

✠ SIGILLN ⚜ CVMMVNE ⚜ WILLE ⚜ NOTINGHAMIE. ⚜

Thoroton, *History of Nottinghamshire,* vol. ii., p. 148 ; S. Lewis, *Topogr. Dict.,* vol. iii., p. 430.

5242. Sulph. cast from the matrix. [lxx. 48.]

Seal "pro recognitione debitorum," see No. 1085.

NUNEATON, *see* ETON.

OAKHAMPTON, *co. Devon.*

5243. [18th cent.] Sulph. cast from the matrix. 1⅛ in. [lxi. 95.]

An oval shield of arms, enriched with carved scrolls and branches of flowers and foliage : chequy *or* and *az.*, two bars, TOWN OF OAKHAMPTON. Crest, on a wreath an embattled tower.

S. Lewis, *Topogr. Dict.*, vol. iii., p. 442.

ORFORD, *co. Suffolk.*
Mayor, A.D. 1579.

5244. Sulph. cast from the matrix. 1⅜ in. [lxxii. 11.]

On a mount an embattled tower, masoned, round-headed doorway, portcullis half down. In base on the mount, the date 1579.

✠ SIGILLVM OFFICII MAIORIS BVRGI OREFORD.

ORLINGBURY, *or* ORLIBERE HUNDRED,
co. Northampton.

5245. [16th cent.] Sulph. cast from cracked impression. 1½ in. [lxix. 93.]

✠ HVNDREDE OF ORLIBERE ·
NORTH-AMTVN'

The letter R, with open top, resembles K. The last word in two lines across the field.

Cf. seal of the Wapentake of Flaxwell, No. 4935.

OSWESTRY, *co. Salop.*

5246. [13th cent.] Sulph. cast from fine impression. 2 in. [lxxi. 28.]

St. *Oswald,* King and Martyr, Patron Saint of the town, with crown, seated on a carved throne, in the r. h. a drawn sword erect ; in the l. h. he grasps a *tree*, on the r. The whole forms a *rebus* on the name of the town. Background on the l. h. side diapered lozengy with a leaf or small device in each space.

✶ SIGILLVM · COMMVNE · DE · OSWALDESTRE ✶

Beaded border.

S. Lewis, *Topogr. Dict.*, vol. iii., p. 458.

OUNDLE, *co. Northampton.*
Hospital for Poor Widows.

5247. [A.D. 1601.] Sulph. cast from the matrix. $1\frac{1}{4} \times 1\frac{1}{16}$ in. [lxix. 86.]

Oval: an eagle preying on a child wrapped in swaddling-clothes. Crest of Rev. NICHOLAS LATHAM, founder. In the field above, the date :—1601 ; in base the initial letters of the founder's name :—N. L.

✠ THE · WIDOWES · MITE.

Second Seal.

5248. [A.D. 1611.] Sulph. cast from the matrix. $1\frac{1}{4} \times 1\frac{1}{16}$ in. [lxix. 87.]

Oval: design similar to that of the preceding seal, No. 5247 ; from a different matrix. In the field above, the date 1611 ; in base the initial letters of the founder's name as before :—N. L.

✠ QVOD ✿ DEDI ✿ ACCEPI.

—1 Chron. xxix. 14.

OXFORD, *co. Oxon.*

5249. [A.D. 1812.] Wafer, covered with paper before impression. About $2\frac{1}{8}$ in. [Add. ch. 6313.]

∅. A shield of arms: an *ox*, passing a *ford* of water in base, CITY OF OXFORD. Crest, a helmet, mantling and wreath, a demi-lion rampant guardant, holding betw. his paws a rose charged with another. Supporters, *dex.*, an elephant, collared and lined, *sin.*, a beaver, ducally collared and lined. In base on a scroll the motto :—FORTIS EST VERITAS.

℞. A smaller round counterseal. $1\frac{3}{16}$ in. The armorial bearings of the shield as in the *obv.* In the field above, an uncertain inscription.

S. Lewis, *Topogr. Dict.*, vol. iii., p. 469 (*obv.* only).

5250. [14th cent.] Sulph. cast from fine impression. $1\frac{3}{8}$ in. [lxx. 85.]

An *ox* passing a *ford* of water, the armorial bearings of the CITY OF OXFORD, by way of *rebus* on the name of the city. In the background an oak-tree. On the r., in the field, a shield of arms: a cross. Background replenished with sprigs of foliage.

+ SIGILLUM ⚬ MAIORIS ⚬ OXONIE ⚬

Cabled borders.

L 2

5251. Sulph. cast from chipped and imperfect impression. [D.C., F. 677.]

　　　+ SIGILLUM ⋈ + MAIOR . . . . . XONIE ⋈

5252. Another. [lxx. 86.]

———

Seal "pro recognitione debitorum," *see* Nos. 1086, 1091, 1092.

———

OXFORD UNIVERSITY.
Chancellor.

5253. [13th cent.] Sulph. cast from matrix or fine impression. $3\frac{1}{16} \times 1\frac{3}{4}$ in. [D.C., E. 47.]

Pointed oval: the Chancellor, in academical dress, seated on a bench, with his feet on a platform, under a trefoiled arch, with church-like canopy of pinnacled turrets, and holding a book: on each side, three scholars in academical dress, seated on a chair-like bench, under a pointed arch, with pinnacled canopy. In base, six other scholars seated on similar benches, in two tiers, the two scholars on the lower tier hold an open book betw. them. Background partially hatched.

　　SIGILL' · CANCELLARII : ET : UNIUERSITATIS :
　　　　　　　　OXONIENS ⋈

Beaded borders.

Vetusta Monumenta, vol. i., pl. 62.

Official or Smaller Seal.

5254. [13th cent.] Sulph. cast from fine, but chipped, impression. $2\frac{1}{8} \times 1\frac{1}{4}$ in. [lxx. 84.]

Pointed oval: the Chancellor, seated on a bench under a carved cinquefoiled arch, betw. two scholars, each holding a book, facing to centre. In base under the platform an *ox* passing a *ford*, the armorial bearings of the shield of arms of the CITY OF OXFORD.

　　SIGILLVM : OFFICII : CANCELLARII : VNIVERSITATIS :
　　　　　　OXONIE ◡.

Later Seal.

5255. [15th cent.] Sulph. cast from fine, but very imperfect, impression. About $3\frac{1}{4} \times 2$ in. when perfect. [D.C., F. 59.]

Pointed oval: the Chancellor in academical dress, seated in a canopied niche, holding a book. In a smaller canopied niche overhead a shield of arms: an open book, betw. three crowns, UNIVERSITY OF OXFORD. On each side in similar, but smaller niches, two scholars seated, in academical dress, the one on the l. with an open book on his knees ; overhead, on each side, in a similar, but smaller niche, a proctor or bedell, three-quarters length, holding a wand or staff of office. In base, under a carved round-headed arch, with a wall of masonry and arcaded screenwork on each side, a shield of arms, CITY OF OXFORD, see No. 5249.

- Legend wanting, except the imperfect word :—

. . . . UNIUERS . . . . . .

Another Seal.

5256. [15th cent.] Sulph. cast from fine impression. 3¼ × 2¼ in. [lxx. 91.]

A close copy of the preceding seal, No. 5255.

: SIGILLUM : OFFICII : CANCELLARIATUS ꝳ : STUDIJ [?] : UNIUERSITATIS ✠ OXONIE : ꝛ

Signet.

5257. [17th cent.] Red: *en placard*, covered with paper before impression. 1 in. [Cott. ch. iv. 49.]

A shield of arms, UNIVERSITY OF OXFORD, *see* No. 5255.

VERITAS · REGNABIT · VERITAS · LIBERABIT (?)

Seal of the Proctors.

5258. [18th cent.] Sulph. cast from the matrix. 1⅜ in. [lxx. 87.]

K. Alfred, founder, with crown and sceptre, seated in a canopied niche. On each side in a smaller niche a scholar, three-quarters length. Below, under a round-headed arch, a female, half-length, with three children ; on each side, under smaller arches, a scholar as before. Outside, tabernacle-work.

· SIG · PROC · COLL · MAG · AUL · UNIV · OXON.

University College, A.D. 1249.

Durham Hall, afterwards University College.

5259. [13th cent.] Sulph. cast from fine impression. 2¼ × 1½ in. [lxx. 94.]

Pointed oval : St. Cuthbert the Bishop, seated on a throne consisting of two lions statant guardant, with mitre, lifting up the r. h. in benediction, in the l. h. the crowned head of St. Oswald, king and martyr, and a pastoral staff held obliquely. In the lower part, under two round-headed cinquefoiled arches, with three countersunk trefoils in the spandrils, the founder, William, Archdeacon of Durham, turned to the r., three-quarters length, a book in the r. h., the l. h. raised, in converse with a group of four scholars on the r.

> ✠ S' COMMVNE · SCOLARIVM ATRI
> WILL'I DE DVNELMIA STVDENCIV OXON.

The N's are reversed.

St. Edmund, or Canterbury Hal, t. Hen. III.

5260. [14th cent.] Sulph. cast from fine, but very imperfect, impression. About 2 in. when perfect. [xlvii. 862.]

Becket's Martyrdom, within a border enriched with roses; in allusion to St. Edmund Rich, Archbishop of Canterbury, A.D. 1234, founder.

> . . . . LE ⚜ CANTUARI . . . .

Laing's *MS. Catal.*, No. 374.

Balliol College, A.D. 1260.

5261. Sulph. cast from the matrix. $2\frac{7}{8} \times 1\frac{13}{16}$ in. [xlvii. 860.]

Pointed oval: the Virgin, crowned, seated on a throne under a trefoiled arch, with church-like canopy elaborately detailed; holding on her l. knee the Child, with nimbus, in her r. h. a ball or orb. On each side, on the shaft which supports the trefoiled arch, a shield of arms; l. three garbs, r. two piles meeting towards the base. Below, two kneeling figures, that on the r. John Balliol, of Barnard Castle, founder, in armour, with a shield of arms: an orb, BALLIOL; that on the l. his wife, the lady Devorguilla, holding by the l. h. a shield of arms: a lion rampant, GALLOWAY. Each of these figures is holding up the hand, supporting a model of the Collegiate buildings (thereby indicated to be dedicated to the Virgin), which has a bold trefoiled arch for its base, two tiers of upright beams or timber work, and over the roof, along the ridge, a frieze or entablature inscribed :—

> DOM'S SCOLARIV D' BALL'O.

The letters AR in *Scolarium* and AL in *Ball'o* are respectively conjoined. Background behind the figure of the

Virgin, hatched lozengy. In the lower half of the seal, and over the canopy, the background is replenished with sprigs of foliage.

S' · 9̄ē ⠶ D' ⠶ BALL' : SCVTA : NOTĀT : ᴀᴧ ST̄
PIA : VGO : DOMV̄ · T · D̄ATES ·

i.e.; Sigillum Commune de Balliolo.

Scuta notant stantes, pia Virgo, domum tibi dantes.

⁻ The letters AL in *Ball'* are conjoined.

Laing's *MS. Catal.*, No. 468.

Seal ad Causas.

5262. [15th cent.] Recent impression in red sealing-wax from the matrix. $1\frac{7}{8} \times 1\frac{1}{8}$ in. [xlvii. 861.]

Pointed oval: St. Katharine, with crown, standing in a niche, with carved canopy, pinnacled and crocketed, in her r. h. a Katharine wheel, in the l. h. a palm branch. Tabernacle-work at sides ; carved corbel. Background replenished with sprigs of foliage.

✠ SIGILLUM ᴀᴧ ❀ AD ᴀᴧ ❀ CAUSAS ❀ ᴀᴧ ❀ AULE ❀ ᴀᴧ ❀
BALIOLI ❀ ᴀᴧ ❀ OXON ❀ ᴀᴧ ❀

Laing's *MS. Catal.*, No. 469.

Merton College, A.D. 1264.
Seal of the Scholars ad Causas.

5263. Sulph. cast from the matrix. $2 \times \frac{1}{4}$ in. [lxx. 95.]

Pointed oval : the Virgin seated on an elegantly ornamented throne, the Child, with nimbus, on the l. knee. Overhead a trefoiled roof or canopy. At the l. corner of the throne a wavy branch of foliage, perhaps a vine ; on the r. a fleur-de-lis on a short stem. In base, under a round-headed arch with arcade work at the sides, a man kneeling in prayer to the l.

S' SCOLARIVM D' MERTONA · AD CÃS.

Beaded borders.

5264. Another. [D.C., E. 143.]

Later Seal.

5265. [17th cent.] Sulph. cast from the matrix. $1\frac{3}{16}$ in. [lxx. 96.]

Our Lord, seated, with nimbus, his feet on a platform or footboard, holding up a cloth containing five half-length figures, representative of the Resurrection; the cloth or napkin is inscribed with an indistinct legend :—

DÑI EST ASSVMTIO NRA.
—Psal. lxxxviii. 19.
SIGILLVM SCHOLARIVM DE MERTON.

Beaded border.

5266. Another. [D.C., G. 38.]

Stapledon Hall (afterwards removed to Exeter College), A.D. 1314.

5267. [18th cent.] Sulph. cast, tinted red. 2¾ × 1¼ in. xlvii. 863.]

Pointed oval : in the upper part, the Virgin with crown and nimbus of rays, seated in a canopied niche, the Child on the l. knee. Below, a bishop, for Walter Stapleton, or Stapledon, Bishop of Exeter, A.D. 1308–1326, founder, with mitre and pastoral staff, kneeling to the r. in adoration ; betw. the two keys of St. Peter on the l., and the sword of St. Paul on the r., cf. No. 1554 (rev.). These emblems are in allusion to the shield of arms of the See of Exeter, viz., a sword in pale, point towards the chief, surmounted of two keys in saltire. In base, a shield of arms : two bands wavy or nebuly, STAPLE-TON, and EXETER COLLEGE.

Bedford (*Blazon of Episcopacy*, p. 44), refers to two variant coats of arms attributed to Bishop Stapledon.

S · RECTORIS · ET · SCOLARIUM · DE · STAPELDON · HAL · OXON.

Inner border beaded, outer border carved.

Laing's *MS. Catal.*, No. 373.

Oriel College, A.D. 1326.

5268. Sulph. cast, from fine impression, chipped at the edge. 2⅛ × 1¼ in. [lxx. 97.]

Pointed oval: the Annunciation of the Virgin ; in the centre a large jar with one handle, out of which springs a fleur-de-lis, slipped on a long stem and leaved ; on the r. the Virgin lifting up the r. h., in her l. h. a book ; on the l. the Archangel Gabriel with expanded wings, holding a scroll inscribed (in reverse order of lettering) :—AVE M'. Within a niche, with a canopy of two trefoiled arches, pinnacled and crocketed. Over the canopy on each side, a small bird ; on the

l. an'estoile of six points, on the r. a crescent. In base, under a round-headed cinquefoiled arch, with a demi-arch on each side, and countersunk trefoil in each spandril, the founder and first Provost, Adam de Brome, Almoner of K. Edward II., in gown and hood, kneeling in prayer to the l. The frieze over his head is inscribed :—ADAM DE BROM.

     ✠ + S' COMMVNE · DOMVS · SCOLARIVM · BEATE ·
         MARIE · OXONI . . . ⋈

5269. Another. [D.C., F. 14.]

Later Seal of arms.

5270. [15th. cent.] Sulph. cast from the matrix. 1 in. [lxx. 98.]

A shield of arms, ENGLAND, for EDWARD III., benefactor, within a bordure invecked, ORIEL COLLEGE. Betw. three small trefoils, slipped from the inner edge of the field.

Beaded border.

Queen's College, A.D. 1340.

5271. Recent impression in red sealing-wax from the matrix. 1½ in. [xxxv. 164.]

Qu. Philippa of Hainault, wife of K. Edward III., Patroness, standing, with crown and sceptre fleur-de-lizé, in a carved niche with ogee-arched canopy, pinnacled and crocketed, the inner border enriched with ball-flower ornamentation, and the field replenished with roses. On elegant tabernacle-work of similar character, on each side, a shield of arms ; r., quarterly, 1, 4, FRANCE (ANCIENT), 2, 3, ENGLAND, for EDWARD III. ; l., quarterly, 1, 4, ENGLAND, 2, 3, four lions rampant, HAINAULT, see No. 801. In base a shield of arms : three eagles displayed, two and one, ROBERT DE EGLESFIELD or EGGLESFIELD (rector of Brough, co. Westmorland, and confessor to Qu. Philippa), and QUEEN'S COLLEGE.

     S' COMVNE · PREPOSITI · ET · SCOLARIV̄ · AVLE ·
         REGINE ⋮ DE · OXONIA.

Beaded borders.

5272. Sulph. cast. [D.C., F. 47.]

Second Seal,

after the establishment by Qu. Elizabeth.

5273. Sulph. cast, from fine impression, chipped and bent. 1⅞ in. [lxxi. 5.]

Qu. Elizabeth, standing, turned to the l., in embroidered dress, with crown and ruff, in the r. h. a sceptre fleur-de-lizé, in the l. h. an orb.   In the field on each side an eagle displayed, and over it the royal Tudor badge—a rose.   In base an ornamental shield of arms, EGLESFIELD, as in No. 5271.

S' · PREP' · ET · SCHOL' · COL' · REGINAL' · DE : OXON' · STABILIT' · PER · REGIN' · ELIZAB'.

Carved border.

New College, A.D. 1386.

5274. [Before A.D. 1542.] Bright red : fine, injured by pressure, and bent at the top.   2½ in. [xxxvi. 48.]

∅. For description see next seal, No. 5275.

℞. A small round counterseal, about ⅞ in. when perfect. A shield of arms, NEW COLLEGE, see No. 5275. Above the shield a sprig of foliage ; at the sides the initials I. L. for JOHN LONDON, J. C. D., Canon of Windsor, York, and Lincoln, Warden of the college, A.D. 1526–1542.

✠ + MANNER + MAKYTH + MAN +

5275. Sulph. cast of the *obv.*, from the matrix. [lxx. 99.]

In two niches with canopies, on the r. a bishop with mitre and pastoral staff, lifting up the r. h. in benediction, for St. Swithun ; on the l. a bishop with mitre and pastoral staff, kneeling in adoration, for William of Wykeham, Bishop of Winchester, A.D. 1367, founder. Over these, in a niche with ogee-arched and arcaded canopy, the Annunciation of the Virgin, with a lily flower growing in a pot betw. the Virgin on the r., and the Archangel Gabriel on the l., holding a scroll inscribed :—AUE MARIA. On each side, in a canopied niche, with tabernacle-work outside, a saint standing ; l. St. Peter with a key, r. St. Paul with a sword. The plinth or string-course below these niches is inscribed :—WYKHAM : EPS FŪDATOR. In base, betw. two small roses, a shield of arms : two chevronels betw. three roses, Bishop WILLIAM OF WYKEHAM, and NEW COLLEGE. Supporters, two lions sejant guardant.

SIGILLUM : COMUNE : COLLEGII : SCE : MARE : OF : WYNCHESTRE : IN : OXONIA.

Beaded borders.

5276. Sulph. cast, from an impression injured in places. [D.C., F. 76.]

Journ. Brit. Archæol. Assoc., vol. xii., p. 18.   Cf. the seal of Winchester College of St. Mary, co. Southampton. [D.C., F. 77.]

Lincoln College, A.D. 1427.

Seal ad Causas.

5277. Sulph. cast from the matrix. 1¾ × 1 in. [D.C., G. 28.]

Pointed oval : St. Hugh, Bishop of Lincoln, standing in a canopied niche, with mitre and pastoral staff held obliquely, lifting up the r. h. in benediction. On the corbel the inscription :—S · HUGO.

SIGILLŪ COLLEGIJ LYNCOLNIE IN OXONIA AD CAUSAS.

Inner border beaded and engrailed, outer border beaded.

All Souls' College, A.D. 1437.

5278. Sulph. cast, from fine impression, injured by pressure in places. 2¼ in. [lxx. 92.]

Our Lord, seated in a carved niche with trefoiled arch and heavy canopy, with cruciform nimbus, lifting up the hands to enter into Judgment. On each side, in a canopied niche a number of personages, including a king crowned, kneeling, a pope with tiara and patriarchal cross, an archbishop with mitre and crozier, on the l. ; a cardinal and bishops on the r. Outside these, tabernacle-work. In base, a number of souls rising from their graves at the Day of Judgment, betw. two shields of arms: l., quarterly, 1, 4, FRANCE (MODERN), 2, 3, ENGLAND, for K. HENRY VI., co-founder ; r., per pale, *dex.*, SEE OF CANTERBURY, *sin.*, a chevron betw. three cinquefoils, Archbishop HENRY CHICHELEY, A.D. 1414–1443, founder, see No. 1241, *et seq.*

✠ SIGILLŪ : COMUNE COLLEGII ANIMAR ŌIM FIDELIUM DEFUNCTORUM DE OXONIA.

Brasenose College, A.D. 1509.

5279. Sulph. cast from the matrix. 2⅞ × 1¾ in. [D.C., H. 6.]

Pointed oval : in three canopied niches of late gothic style, supported on four twisted columns, the Trinity, betw. a sainted bishop with mitre, pall, pastoral staff, and book on the l., and another ; with mitre, pall, and pastoral staff, feeding a swan, on the r., probably for St. Chad of Lichfield, and St. Hugh of Lincoln. In base, betw. two carved scrolls of foliage, a shield

of arms : a chevron betw. three roses, for WILLIAM SMITH
(Bishop of Lichfield and Coventry A.D. 1491, and of Lincoln
A.D. 1496–1514) and BRASENOSE COLLEGE.

SIGILLŪ · COIE · COLEGII · REGALIS ⚊ DE · BRASIN ·
NOSE · IN · OXONIA ·

Christ Church, A.D. 1547.

5280. Sulph. cast, from fine, but chipped, impression. 4 in.
[lxx. 93.]

The Trinity in a round-headed niche of the style of the
Renaissance. The figure of the Almighty is enveloped in a
large cloak, within the folds of which are three personages on
each side, among them a king, an archbishop, and a cardinal.
Cf. No. 5278.

On each side a smaller niche, containing on the l. the
Virgin, standing, with crown and nimbus, the Child with
nimbus on the l. arm ; on the r. a saint with crown and
nimbus, in the r. h. a pastoral staff, in the l. h. a book, at the
feet an ox couchant. The columns are enriched with capitals
of carved foliage ; over the small niche on each side a
dolphin. In base, under the platform, which is supported by
four carved corbels, an ornamental shield of arms : THOMAS
WOLSEY, Cardinal Archbishop of York, as in No. 2338. Supporters two griffins, each holding a baton.

SIGILLV̂ · COÊ · COLLEGII · THOME · WVLCY · CARDINAL ·

EBOR · T̂ · ÂGLIA · A · LATERE · LEGATI.

Vetusta Monumenta, vol. i., pl. LIX., f. 1.

Deans and Canons.

5281. Sulph. cast, from chipped and indistinct impression.
2⅞ in. [lxx. 90.]

The Trinity in a round-headed niche of the style of the
Renaissance. On each side a lamp or torch, on a stand. In
base, a shield of ROYAL ARMS of HENRY VIII., crowned.
Supporters, *dex.*, a griffin, *sin.*, a greyhound collared and
lined.

S' COMMVNE · DECANI · ET · CANONICORVM · COLLEGII ·
R[EGIS HENR]ICI · OCTAVI · IN · OXONIA.

For common seal of the DEAN AND CHAPTER see. Ecclesi-
astical Seals, Nos. 2138, 2139.

PEMBROKESHIRE.

Chancery.

WILLIAM DE BEAUCHAMP, *Knt., Custos of the County of Pembroke.*

5282. [A.D. 1387.] Creamy-white : fine, but very imperfect, only the centre part remaining. About 2½ in. when perfect. [Slo. ch. xxxi. 19.]

Ø. The Custos of the County, in armour, with hauberk, surcoat, broad sword in r. h. chained to wrist, shield of arms slung over the r. shoulder and held in l. h., riding to the r. on a caparisoned horse. The armorial bearings of the shield and caparisons are : on a fess betw. three crosses crosslets, a crescent for difference, BEAUCHAMP.

Legend wanting.

℞. Within a finely carved and traced gothic trefoil, a shield of arms as in *obv.* Background replenished with sprigs of foliage.

Legend wanting.

HUMPHREY PLANTAGENET, *youngest son of K. Henry IV., Duke of Gloucester, Earl of Pembroke, Chamberlain of England.*

5283. [A.D. 1424.] Light brown, opaque : fine, but imperfect, wanting in several places. About 3¾ in. when perfect. [Slo. ch. xxxi. 9.]

Ø. On a mount, replenished with herbage and flowers, the Earl, armed *cap-à-pie*, with hauberk, helmet with chapeau and crest, a lion of ENGLAND, broad-sword in the r. h., shield of arms slung over the r. shoulder by a strap and held in the l. h., riding to the r. on a caparisoned and armoured horse with panache plume. The armorial bearings of the shield and caparisons are as described below for the *rev.* Background replenished with sprigs of the broom-plant for PLANTAGENET.

S' H[ŪFRIDI : D]E : LĀCASTRI : FILII : ⁊ : FR[AT]RIS : REG[Ū : A]NGL : ⁊ : FRAÑE : CAM'AR᷉ : ANG᷉ : ⁊ : DÑI : PEÑ.

℞. A demi-angel issuing from clouds, and with expanded wings, the hands in prayer, round the neck a beaded strap supporting a large shield of arms which occupies the centre of the seal : quarterly, 1, 4, FRANCE (MODERN), 2, 3, ENGLAND, within a bordure, HUMPHREY, DUKE OF GLOUCESTER. On each side (that on the left wanting), a curved ostrich feather, the shaft labelled, and charged along the quill with twenty-one fleurs-de-lis. Background replenished as on the *obv.*

[S'] HŪFRIDI : DE : LĀCASTRI : FILII : ᴣ : FRATRIS : [RE]GŪ : AN . . . : ᴣ : FRAÑE CAM . . . . .

Carved borders.

5284. [A.D. 1426.] Light-brown, opaque: fine originally, edge now very imperfect. [Add. ch. 6,000.]

Ø. This side shows more distinctly than the former seal, No. 5283 the details of the flowers, the armorials, and the peculiar form of the horse's plume and head-gear.

. . . . REGŪ : ANGL' : ᴣ : FRAÑE : CAM'AR̄ : ANGL . . . .

℟. This shows the l. h. ostrich feather which is wanting in the former seal.

. . . . LAC̄ASTRI : FILII : ᴣ : FRATRIS : REGŪ : ANGL̄ . . . .

WILLIAM DE LA POLE, 1*st Marquess and* 4*th Earl of Suffolk, Earl of Pembroke, and Great Chamberlain of England.*

5285. [A.D. 1448.] Creamy-white: fine, very imperfect, only the centre part remaining. About 3¼ in. when perfect. [Slo. ch. xxxii. 5.]

Ø. The Earl, armed *cap-à-pie*, with hauberk, surcoat with open sleeves, helmet, [sword,] and shield of arms slung over the r. shoulder, riding to the r. on a caparisoned horse with plume on head. The armorial bearings of the shield and caparisons are as described below for the *rev.* Background replenished with sprigs of foliage and flowers.

Legend wanting.

℟. On an ornamental tree of conventional foliage, and with a central flower, a shield of arms: quarterly, 1, 4, a fess betw. three leopards' heads, DE LA POLE, 2, 3, a chief, and over all a lion rampant queue fourchée, CHAUCER. Supporters, two wild boars collared.

Legend wanting.

PENRITH, *co. Cumberland.*

5286. [13th cent.] Sulph. cast from imperfect and injured impression. 2¼ in. [D.C., D. 297.]

A saltire cross of St. Andrew, Patron Saint of the parish and town, betw. a carved trefoil in chief and base, and an ornamental double quatrefoil at each side.

SIGILLVM : COMMVNE : VILLE : DE : PENRETH.

Cabled borders.

PENRYN, *co. Cornwall.*

5287. [16th cent.] Sulph. cast from the matrix. $1\frac{3}{8}$ in. [lxi. 21.]

A shield of arms: a laureated bust in profile to the l., draped and filleted.

✠ PENRYN BVRGVS.

S. Lewis, *Topogr. Dict.*, vol. iii., p. 520.

PENZANCE, *co. Cornwall.*

5288. [A.D. 1614.] Sulph. cast from the matrix. $1\frac{1}{8}$ in. [lxi. 22.]

In an oval dish of vesical form, the head of St. John Baptist, in allusion to the annual and customary Midsummer-eve ceremonies and Midsummer-day fair carried on in the town.

Legend on a riband :—

❀ ✠ ❀ PENSANS ANNO DOMINI 16-14.

The date is placed across the field.

S. Lewis, *Topogr. Dict.*, vol. iii., p. 522.

PETERSFIELD, *co. Southampton.*

5289. [16th cent.] Sulph. cast. $1\frac{1}{2}$ in. [xxxvii. 18.]

Within a rudely invecked border, a pointed quatrefoil or quadrilobe containing a shield of arms: an annulet betw. three pellets, TOWN OF PETERSFIELD. The correct arms are : on a rose of six leaves, barbed, an escutcheon charged with an annulet betw. four pellets in saltire.

PETERSFELD.

Betw. the letters are devices of annulets, pellets, trefoils, etc.

Cf. S. Lewis, *Topogr. Dict.*, vol. iii., p. 527.

PEVENSEY, *co. Sussex.*

5290. [13th cent.] Sulph. casts from the matrix. 2¼ in. [lxxii. 94, 95.]

Ø. On the sea, a one-masted ship, with flag and streamers at the main-top, main-sail furled, a mariner clinging to the ropes, four mariners on deck, two and two, hauling ropes, on embattled castle at the stern two trumpeters, and below, under an arch, a half-length knight; embattled forecastle with fleur-de-lis and banner flag, side rudder or sweep. In the field overhead: on the l. a crescent, on the r. an estoile of six points; and below the mainsail a shield of arms, ENGLAND.

SIGLL'V : BARONVM · DOMINI · REGIS · ANGLIE DE PEVENES'

Cabled borders.

R. On the waves, two ships of one-mast each, with sails furled and the clew-lines hanging down loosely, the mainmast topped with flag, streamers and cross. In the ship on the l., which appears to be in collision with the other, St. Nicholas, patron saint of the town and parish, with mitre and pastoral staff, lifting up the r. h. in benediction. In the field overhead, on the l. a crescent.

SCE · NICOLAE · DVC · NOS · SPONTE · TRAHE : PEV'.

The N's reversed in the two legends.

Beaded borders; outside, a wavy scroll of foliage.

Obv. only, in W. Boys, *History of Sandwich*, p. 811; cf. *Sussex Archæol. Collections*, vol. i., p. 21.

Customs Seal of the Port.

5291. [Late 14th cent.] Sulph. cast. 1½ in. [lxxii. 96.]

Two ostrich feathers in fess, ensigned with an open crown of three fleurs-de-lis. Background faintly diapered with sprigs of foliage.

S' ᴀ THE · CUSTUM : SELLE · OF · THE · PORTE · OF · PEMSE.

Sussex Archæol. Collections, vol. i., p. 21; *Archæologia Cantiana*, vol. vii., 342.

PLYMOUTH, *co. Devon.*

5292. [16th cent.] Sulph. cast from the matrix. 2⅝ in. [lxi. 101.]

St. Andrew the Apostle, Patron Saint of the town and parish, seated in a heavily-canopied niche, with nimbus, in the r. h. a saltire cross, in the l. h. a book and orb. On each side, in a smaller but similar niche, with tabernacle-work outside, an angel, with expanded wings, a diadem of pearls, and a large cloak, holding in front a shield of arms : l., the UNION CROSS as on the ROYAL FLAG ; r. quarterly, 1, 4, FRANCE (MODERN), 2, 3, ENGLAND. In base, on a mount, a shield of arms : a St. Andrew's cross betw. four castles, TOWN OF PLYMOUTH. Supporters, two lions passant guardant.

THE : COMEN : SELLE : OF : THE : BOROVGH : ʒ :
COMENALTE : OF : Yᴱ KYNGS : TOWNE : OF : PLYMOTHE.

Beaded borders.

S. Lewis, *Topogr. Dict.*, vol. iii., p. 544.

Mayoralty.

5293. [16th cent.] Sulph. cast from the matrix. 1¾ in. [lxi. 102.]

Within a carved trefoil, a shield of arms : TOWN OF PLYMOUTH, as in No. 5292 ensigned with an open crown of five large, and four small fleurs-de-lis.

S' OFFICIJ · MAIORATUS · BURGI · UILLE* . . . . DE .
PLYMOUTH.

Carved border.

Privy Seal of the Mayor, A.D. 1595.

5294. Sulph. cast from the matrix. 1⅛ × 1₇⁄₁₆ in. [lxi. 103.]

Slightly oval, a shield of arms, TOWN OF PLYMOUTH, as in No. 5292. Over the shield the date 1595.

Beaded border.

New Seal of the Mayor, Aldermen, and Burgesses, A.D. 1835.

5295. Sulph. cast from the matrix. · 2⅛ in. [lxi. 104.]

This is a device combining the ancient and modern arms of the TOWN OF PLYMOUTH, viz., on the sea, a ship with embattled gunwale, flag with cross of St. George at the prow, three masts each with a round-top, the centre one having also a fire-beacon. This portion of the device is in reference to the ANCIENT ARMS, viz., a ship with three masts without sails and yard-arms, on the round-top a fire-beacon, the base of the shield barry wavy of six. In the centre of the field on a carved scroll or bracket, a shield of arms, MODERN PLYMOUTH, as in No. 5292 ensigned with a coronet from which

* An erased word here. D . . . G . .

springs a sheaf of flags, three on each side, each charged with the modern arms.

Legend in two concentric circles :—

Inner circle:—   ᴧ ❋ TURRIS ❋ FORTISSIMA ❋ EST ❋ NOMEN ❋ JEHOVA ❋

Cf. Prov. xviii. 10.

Outer circle:—COMMON SEAL OF THE MAYOR ALDERMEN & BURGESSES OF THE BOROUGH OF PLYMOUTH ❋ 1835 ❋

PLYMPTON, EARL'S, *co. Devon.*

5296. Sulph. cast from the matrix. 1 × ⅞ in. [lxii. 1.] Oval : an eagle rising.

❋ SIGILL' : BVRG : DE : PLYMPT : COMIT.

S. Lewis, *Topogr. Dict.*, vol. iii., p. 545.

POCKLINGTON, *co. York.*
Free Grammar School, bef. A.D. 1526.

5297. Sulph. cast, tinted red, from the matrix. 2¼ in. [xxxv. 146.]

On a geometrical pavement, a scene or *tableau*, representing John Doweman, Archdeacon of Suffolk, founder of the school, kneeling in prayer at a desk, before which, on a lozenge, is a shield charged with a monogram composed of the initials of his name :—I. D. Before him are three carved brackets or corbels, each containing a standing figure on it. In the centre, Our Lord, as a child with cruciform nimbus, and naked, lifting up the hands in benediction ; on the l., the Virgin crowned, the Child on the r. arm ; on the r., St. Nicholas, Bishop of Myra, with mitre, in the r. h. a pastoral staff, the l. h. lifted up in benediction, at his l. side three youths in a tub, one of the emblems of the saint. In the field, which is replenished with triform tongues of fire, the holy name ſ ɥ ʊ repeated five times.

❋ SIGILLŪ ⦂ COīE + FRATēē + NōīS + IĦʊ + BīE + MARIE + SōI + NICHI + DE POKLINGTON.

Several pairs of letters are conjoined.

N. Carlisle, *Endowed Grammar Schools*, vol. ii., p. 863.

5298. Another. [xlvii. 869.]

Laing's *MS. Catal.*, No. 305.

PONTEFRACT, *co. York.*

5299. [14th cent.] Sulph. cast from the matrix. 2⅛ in. [D.C., F. 626.]

On a mount a triple-towered castle, embattled, masonry of an ornamental character with wide joints and an annulet in each square block, tall round-headed windows, pointed doorway with portcullis half down. At side a small wing or gable. In the field over the side towers the initial letters P.-P. Background partly hatched.

⚜ SIGILLVM : COMMVNE : BVRGENCIVM : PONTISFRACTI.

Beaded borders.

S. Lewis, *Topogr. Dict.,* vol. iii., p. 549.

5300. Another. [lxxiv. 93.]

Mayoralty.

5301. [17th cent.] Sulph. cast from the matrix. 1¼ in. [D.C., H. 188.]

The field divided by a cross quarterly : 1, in the first quarter a triple-towered castle, of the corporation seal, No. 5299, 2, a bridge of three piers in allusion to the name of the town, or perhaps an heraldic label of three points, in allusion to [St.] Thomas, the canonised Earl of Lancaster, lord of the castle,
border of these two quarters enriched with foliage.

⚜ SIGILL : OFFIC' : MAIORAL : VILL · PONT :

5302. Another. [lxxiv. 94.]

Smaller Seal of the Mayoralty.

5303. Sulph. cast from the matrix. 1⅛ in. [lxxiv. 95.]

A copy of the preceding seal, No. 5301 in a carved circular panel.

SIGILL'. OFFIC. MAIORAL. VILL. PONT.

POOLE, *co. Dorset.*
Common seal ; used for the Admiralty Court.

5304. [13th cent.] Sulph. cast from fine impression or the matrix. 2¼ in. [D.C., F. 640.]

In a quatrefoil or quadrilobe, with carved trefoils in the spandrils, on the sea, a one-masted ship, mainsail furled, anchor and bowsprit on the r., an arcaded and embattled

M 2

castle at each end, with a course of roses or quatrefoils in panels below the battlements. On the mast a flag or embattled crow's nest. In the field betw. the mast and the stern a shield of arms : a sword in pale, hilt downward, for WILLIAM LONGESPEE, lord of the Manor of Canford, of which Poole formed part, *temp.* Ric. I.

❉ SIGILLVM ✿ COMMVNE · DE : LAPOLE 🞄

Beaded borders.

S. Lewis, *Topogr. Dict.*, vol. iii., p. 553.

Mayoralty.

5305. [14th–15th cent.] Sulph. cast from fine impression. 1¼ in. [D.C., H. 110.]

Within an engrailed border, a shield of arms : barry wavy a dolphin embowed naiant, on a chief wavy in chief three escallops, TOWN OF POOLE.

🞄 : SIGILLŪ ·:· MAIORITATIS ·:· WILLE ·:· DE ·:· POLE.

Staple.

5306. [14th cent.] Sulph. cast from fine, but chipped, impression. ⅞ in. [lxii. 44.]

A lion's face, enraged, betw. three fleurs-de-lis ; within a quadrilobe.

🞄 SIGILL' STAPULE IN PORTU DE POLE.

The letters DE of *de* are conjoined.

Comptroller.

5307. [14th–15th cent.] Sulph. cast from fine impression. 1¹³⁄₁₆ in. [lxii. 43.]

A lion statant guardant enraged, the tail reflexed betw. the hind legs.

Legend on a riband.

S' : CONTRAR 🞄 DE 🞄 POOL 🞄

Beaded border.

Corporation Seal of Arms.

5308. [16th cent.] Sulph. cast from fine impression, chipped. 1¼ in. [D.C., H. 120.]

A shield of arms, TOWN OF POOLE, see No. 5305. Over the shield a wavy line.

AD · MOREM VILLÆ DE POOLE.

Later Seal of Arms.

5309. [17th cent.] Sulph. cast from the matrix. $1\frac{3}{16}$ in. [lxii. 45.]

An ornamental shield of- arms, TOWN OF POOLE, see No. 5305. The *barry* wavy here becomes three *bars* wavy. Crest, on a helmet and ornamental mantling, a mermaid holding in the r. h. an anchor in pale, cabled, without a beam, the l. h. extended holding a ball.

In base the legend :—

AD MOREM VILLÆ DE POOLE.

Mayor.

5310. [18th–19th cent.] Sulph. cast from the matrix. $1\frac{1}{4}$ in. [lxii. 46.]

An ornamental shield of arms of TOWN OF POOLE as in the preceding seal No. 5309. Crest on a helmet and ornamental mantling as before.

BOROUGH OF POOLE . MAYOR.

Beaded border.

Sheriff.

5311. [18th–19th cent.] Sulph. cast from the matrix. $1 \times \frac{7}{8}$ in. [lxii. 47.]

Oval : an ornamental shield of arms, helmet, mantling and crest, as before.

SHERIFF OF POOLE.

Beaded border.

Town Clerk's office.

5312. [18th–19th cent.] Sulph. cast from· the matrix. $\frac{7}{8}$ in. [lxii. 48.]

An ornamental shield of arms, helmet, mantling and crest as before.

Legend on a riband, above :—TOWN CLERKS OFFICE.

Below, in field :—POOLE.—·

PORTSMOUTH, *co. Southampton.*

5313. [13th cent.] Sulph. cast from the matrix. 3 in. [lxiii. 96, 97.]

Ø. On the sea, a one-masted ship, two mariners on the yard furling the mainsail, in the· embattled forecastle two trumpeters, an embattled castle at the stern, in the hold two mariners hauling up the anchor. .

SIGILLVM ⚹ COMMVNE ⚹ DE ⚹ PORTEMVTHA.

. ℞. In a church-like building of elegant architectural details, with pointed arches, pinnacled and crocketed, the Virgin, standing, crowned, the Child on the l. arm; under similar but smaller arches in perspective at the sides, on the l. St. Thomas, Archbishop of Canterbury, with mitre, lifting up the r. h. in benediction, on the r. St. Nicholas, with mitre and pastoral staff, lifting up the r. h. in benediction.

PORTVM : VIRGO : IVVA · NICHOLAE : FOVE : ROGE *(sic)* [*i.e.* Rege] : THOMA.

The letters OR of *Portum* are conjoined:

S. Lewis, *Topogr. Dict.*, vol. iii., p. 561.

Provost.

5314. Sulph. cast from ·chipped impression. $1\frac{1}{8}$ in. [xxxvii. 19.]

A crescent enclosing an estoile of seven points wavy, the armorial bearings of the TOWN OF PORTSMOUTH.

S' PREPOSITI DE PORTESMVE.

Beaded border.

Cf. S. Lewis, *Topogr. Dict.*, vol. iii., p. 559.

PRESTON, *co. Lancaster.*

5315. [A.D. 1376.] Bronze-green: fine, the edge chipped, $2\frac{1}{4}$ in. [Add. ch. 20,519.]

An Agnus Dei, statant reguardant, with banner-flag; on its shoulder a shield of arms couché: ENGLAND, with a label of three points for DUCHY OF LANCASTER.

Legend on a raised rim, carved on the inside edge with small quatrefoils or ball-flowers :—

🌼 SIGILL' COMVNE BVRGENCIVM DE PRESTON.

Later Seal.

5316. [17th cent.] Sulph. cast from the matrix. $1\frac{9}{16}$ in. [xlvii. 871.]

A shield of arms : an Agnus Dei, with nimbus, statant reguardant, with banner-flag of shield shape, TOWN OF

PRESTON. The shield betw. two tied branches of laurel, leaved and fructed.

No legend.

Laing's *MS. Catal.*, No. 484.

5317. Another. [lxvi. 40.]

Another Seal.

5318. [17th–18th cent.] Sulph. cast from the matrix. $1\frac{9}{16}$ in. [xlvii. 870.]

A shield of arms : an Agnus Dei, with nimbus, couchant, and with banner-flag, a variant form of the arms of the TOWN OF PRESTON.

✿ SIGILLVM · COMVNE · VILLÆ · DE · PRESTON.

Laing's *MS. Catal.*, No. 483 ; S. Lewis, *Topogr. Dict.*, vol. iii., p. 567.

READING, *co. Berks.*

5319. [13th cent.] Sulph. cast from the matrix. $1\frac{3}{4} \times 1\frac{3}{8}$ in. [lix. 70.]

Pointed oval : a crowned head with long hair, couped at the neck, betw. four heads with long hair, couped at the neck, turned three-quarters to the centre. The shield of arms granted in 1566 to the town is derived from the device on this seal, and bears also the letters R. E., for Rex Edwardus, at the sides of the crowned head. See S. Lewis, *Topogr. Dict.*, vol. iii., p. 590, Burke, *Gen. Arm., s. v.*

+ ·S· : COMMVNITATIS : RADINGIE.

S. Lewis, *Topogr. Dict.*, vol. iii., p. 592.

RETFORD, EAST, *co. Nottingham.*

5320. [13th–14th cent.] Sulph. cast from fine impression or the matrix. $1\frac{7}{8}$ in. [lxx. 61.]

Two eagles with expanded wings, combatant.

✿ ISTVT : SIGILLV ꞉ ESTE ꞉ RETTFVRTHE.

S. Lewis, *Topogr. Dict.*, vol. iii., p. 600.

Signet.

5321. [Modern.] Sulph. cast from the matrix. $\frac{3}{4} \times \frac{3}{8}$ in. [lxx. 62.]

Oblate octagonal: an ornamental shield of arms: two eagles with expanded wings, combatant, TOWN OF EAST RETFORD.

Legend on a garter :—

EAST RETFORD.

RICHMOND HONOUR, *co. York.*
WILLIAM DE LA POLE, *4th Earl of Suffolk,*
Lord of the Honour.
[A.D. 1415-1444.]

5322. Sulph. cast from the matrix.   1⅝ in.   [D.C., G. 210.]

A shield of arms: chequy, a canton erm., and bordure charged with lions? or other indistinct devices, RICHMOND. The shield placed upon a pedestal or dwarfed column, and supported by the royal supporters, *dex.*, an antelope, *sin.*, a lion. Background faintly diapered lozengy. All within a border ornamented with carved quatrefoils or ball-flowers, and engrailed at the upper part, over the shield of arms.

   ⚙ SIGILL' · WILL'MI · COMITIS : SUFFOLCHIE:
      z · DⁿS (*sic for* DⁿI) · HONORIS · RICHMŌD.

Carved border.

Cf. Clarkson, *History of Richmond*, p. 21.

SIR THOMAS STANLEY, *Second Lord Stanley,*
(*First Earl of Derby in* A.D. 1485), *ob.* A.D. 1504, *and*
Lady MARGARET, *his wife, daughter of John*
Beaufort, Duke of Somerset.
Lord and Lady of the Liberty of the Honour.

5323. Sulph. cast from the matrix.   1¾ in.   [xlvii. 1801.]

A shield of arms, couché: per pale, *dex.*, per fess, in chief, MAN, see No. 4882; in base quarterly, 1, 4, on a bend three stags' heads cabossed, STANLEY of Stanley; 2, 3, on a chief indented three annulets, (for roundles) LATHOM of Lathom: *sin.*, quarterly, 1, 4, FRANCE (MODERN) 2, 3, ENGLAND, within a bordure compony, BEAUFORT. Crest, on a helmet, mantling, and wreath, an eagle in its nest, preying on an infant in swaddling clothes, STANLEY. Field replenished with branches of cinquefoil roses, slipped and leaved.

Legend on scroll :—

   SIGILLŪ : DⁿI : z : DⁿE : LIB'TAT' · HONORIS ·
        RICHMOUNDI.

Laing's *MS. Catal.*, No. 318.

RICHMOND, *co. York.*

5324. [A.D. 1531.] Red: very imperfect and indistinct.
[Eg. ch. 279.]

For description see next seal, No. 5325.

5325. Sulph. cast from fine impression or the matrix.
1¼ in. [lxxiv. 98.]

The Trinity, on a carved corbel in a canopied niche; at
each side, under a similar but smaller canopy, a shield of
arms: l., quarterly 1, 4, FRANCE (MODERN), 2, 3, ENGLAND;
r., chequy, a canton erm., RICHMOND. Below each shield a
sprig of foliage.

✤ SIGILLVM ✤ CŌE ✤ BVRGENSIṼ ✤
VILLE ✤ RICHEMOND'.

Beaded border.

S. Lewis, *Topogr. Dict.*, vol. iii., p. 605 ; Clarkson, *History of Richmond*,
p. 110 ; *Add. MS.* 28,017, f. 115.

Signet, or Minor Seal, A.D. 1603.

5326. [16th cent.] Sulph. cast from the matrix. 1 in.
[lxxxiv. 99.]

A double cinquefoil rose, barbed and seeded, for union of
the white and red roses of York and Lancaster by Henry VII.
as explained by the elegiac distich :—

" Nostra nec albescit rubicunda, nec alba rubescit,
Facta sed ex gemino nostra colore rosa est."

+ SIGILLVM · BVRGI · RICHMONDII.

Beaded border.

Clarkson, *History of Richmond*, pp. 110, 111 ; *Add. MS.* 28,017, f. 115.

Royal Seal for Recognisances within the Borough, temp.
WILLIAM WETWANG, *1st Mayor,* A.D. 1668.

5327. Sulph. cast from the matrix. 2⅞ × 2⅛ in. [lxxv.
60.]

Pointed oval: an ornamentally carved shield of arms: an
orle, over all on a bend, five ermine spots bendwise, TOWN
OF RICHMOND. Over the shield, impressed by a small
matrix, introduced into the face of the other, and of the shape
of an inverted shield, by way of a crest, a double cinquefoil

rose *en soleil*, ensigned with a royal crown. This movable portion could be used separately by the Town Clerk.

　　　❹ S' DN̄I · R · AD · CAP · RECO : INFRA · BVRG :
　　　RICHM' · CONCS : TEMP : WIL' : WETWANG · PRI :
　　　　　　　　MAIR · I̠BM.

.　Inner border beaded, outer border carved.

Clarkson, *History of Richmond*, p. 110, cf. p. 84; *Add. MS.* 28,017, f. 115.

Free Grammar School, A.D. 1567.

　5328. [16th cent.] Sulph. cast, from cracked impression. 2¼ × 1¼ in. [lxxiv. 100.]

Pointed oval: St. James the Greater, the apostle, in pilgrim's habit, barefoot, to the r., with round hat (on which is an escallop), cloak, wallet, and staff, holding in the l. h. a small water barrel (?) and a rosary. In the field on each side, an ornamental shield of arms : quarterly, 1, 4, FRANCE, (MODERN), 2, 3, ENGLAND. In the field also are three small fleurs-de-lis of FRANCE and two lions passant guardant of ENGLAND.

　　🏵 S|GILLVM · COMVNE · LIBERE · SCOLE · BVRGENSIVM ·
　　　　　　　　DE · RICHMOND.

The letters NE in *comune*, and HM and ND of *Richmond*, are conjoined.

N. Carlisle, *Endowed Grammar Schools*, vol. ii., p. 875 ; Clarkson, *History of Richmond*, pp. 110, 193 ; *Add. MS.* 28,017, f. 115.

RIVINGTON, *co. Lancaster.*
Free Grammar School, A.D. 1566, 1586.

　5329. Sulph. cast, tinted red, from the matrix. 3 × 2¼ in. [xxxv. 147.]

Oval : a rudely carved shield of arms : per pale, *dex.* SEE OF DURHAM, see No. 2475, *sin.*, a cross patonce voided, on a chief three suns in fesse radiated, JAMES PILKINGTON, Bishop of Durham, founder. Over the shield a scroll or riband inscribed :—S . . . . TVI RO . . . . . EI . T . Above this, a pedagogue, or perhaps the founder, half-length, with cap and gown, in the r. h. a birch-rod, in the l. h. an open book inscribed with an indistinct legend, and near it the date 1566. In the field overhead the date 1586, and at the sides the initial letters I. D. for JACOBUS DUNELMENSIS. There is also an imperfect cordon of pellets round the field.

Legend engraved in reverse :—

∴ SIGILLVM ✠ SCHOLARCHARVM ∴ DE ∴ RIVIGTON.

Inner border beaded. ·

N. Carlisle, *Endowed Grammar Schools*, vol. i., p. 714.

5330. Another. [xlvii. 877.]

Laing's *MS. Catal.*, No. 282.

ROCHESTER, *co. Kent.*

5331. [13th cent.] Sulph. casts of the *obv.* and *rev.* from the matrix. 3 in. [lxv. 92, 93.]

Ø. On waves, for the R. Medway, Rochester castle, with a banner-flag of ENGLAND over the entrance to the keep, on the r. a gateway with two round towers embattled, on the l. h. side tower a trumpeter.

✠ SIGILLVM ⚭ CIVIVM ⚭ ROFENSIS.

Ŗ. The crucifixion of St. Andrew, treated in an artistic manner.

✠ SIGILLVM COMMVNE : CIVITATIS ROFENSIS.

Beaded borders ; the annulus of the legend replenished with groups of small pellets disposed irregularly.

S. Lewis, *Topogr. Dict.*, vol. iii., p. 620 ; *Archæologia*, vol. xlix., pt. I., (appendix).

5332. Plaster casts of the *obv.* and *rev.*, tinted red. [lxxii. 23, 24.]

Mayoralty.

5333. [16th cent.] Sulph. cast from the matrix. $1\frac{7}{8}$ in. [lxv. 94.]

An ornamentally carved shield of arms : on a cross, the text letter ℭ; on a chief a lion passant guardant of ENGLAND, CITY OF ROCHESTER.

·×· SIGILL · OFF · × ⁚ MAIORATVS⁚ CIVITAT : × : ROFFEN.

Inner border beaded, outer border carved.

Castle.

5334. [15th cent.] Sulph. cast from the matrix. $1\frac{1}{8}$ in. [xlvii. 878.]

On a mount, an embattled castle of two storeys, with four turrets on the lower wall, round-headed portal with portcullis half-down.

SIG : CASTRI . ROFFENSIS.

Beaded borders.

Laing's *MS. Catal.*, No. 384 ; *Gent. Mag.*, 1772.

5335. Another.   [D.C., G. 284.]

Bridge Wardens.

5336. [15th cent.] Sulph. cast from fine, chipped, impression. $1\frac{3}{8}$ in.   [lxv. 98.]

On a bridge of seven pointed arches, through which flows the R. Medway, a carved and canopied niche with ogee arch, crocketed, containing the Trinity ; tabernacle-work at the sides.

SIGILLŪ : GARDIANORŪ : COMUNITATIS : PONTIS : ROFFENSIS.

Later Seal, A.D. 1576.

5337. Sulph. cast from the matrix.   2 in.   [lxv. 97.]

On an embattled bridge of six round-headed arches, with draw-bridge in the middle, a view of the cathedral tower, and other details of the City of Rochester.   In base the river.   In the field above, the date 1576.

·: ✠ :· SIGILVM ✿ COMVNE ✿ PONTIS ✿ ROFFENSIS.

The N's in *comune* and *Roffensis* are reversed.

Beaded border.

Admiralty, A.D. 1606.

5338. Sulph. cast from fine, but cracked, impression. $1\frac{1}{4}$ in. [lxv. 95.]

On the waves, a three-masted ship of war, sailing to the r., flag at mizen-top charged with the cross of St. George, guns run out from the portholes.

SIGILL · ADMIRAL · CIVITAT · ROFFEN · 1606.

S. Lewis, *Topogr. Dict.*, vol. iii., p. 620.

Fishery, A.D. 1606.

5339. Sulph. cast from the matrix. $\frac{15}{16}$ in.   [lxv. 96.]

A pike-fish, embowed.   In the field below, the inscription :—

S · C
ROFFEN
1606.

· ROMNEY, *co. Kent*, A.D. 1558.

5340. Sulph. cast from the matrix.   2¼ in.   [xlvii. 879.]

On the sea, a one-masted ship, with mainsail furled on the yard, which is furnished with a large ring where it meets the mast.   The centre of the seal has a slight circular depression, about ½ in. wide.   In the field the date A⁰ 15–58, in reference to the year 1558, when a new charter was granted by Q. Elizabeth.   The figure 5 is in both cases badly cut.

☆ ƧIGILLVM · BARONVM DE RONEMEY ⸿

Beaded borders.

Laing's *MS. Catal.*, No. 620 ; S. Lewis, *Topogr. Dict.*, vol. iii., p. 627.

Another Seal.

5341. Sulph. cast from the matrix.   2⅜ in.   [lxv. 99.]

This is a coarsely executed copy of the preceding seal, No. 5340, with legend wrongly copied.

🏵 ƧIGILLVM · BARONVM DE RONEMEV ⸿

Cabled borders.

W. Boys, *History of Sandwich*, p. 806, for suggested date of A.D. 1358 ; and pl. fig. 2.

Another Seal.

5342. Proof impression on red paper.   2⅜ in.   [xliv. 221.]

A copy of the first seal, the main-sail furled, but without the ring on the yard.   There are nine oar-holes in the side of the ship.

🏵 ～ SIGILLVM BARONVM DE ROИEMEY ～

· Inner border beaded, outer border cabled.

Mayoralty.

5343. [17th cent.]   Sulph. cast from the matrix.   1⅝ in. [lxvi. 1.]

Three lions passant guardant in pale, not on a shield.   The armorial bearings of the TOWN OF NEW ROMNEY.

🏵 SIGILLVM · OF : MAIORATVS : PORTVS · DE · ROMENE .

Beaded borders.

W. Boys, *History of Sandwich*, pl. p. 808.

Another Seal.

5344. [17th cent.]   Sulph. cast from the matrix.   1¼ in. [lxvi. 2.]

Same design as the preceding seal, No. 5343, but different matrix.

✠ SIGILLVM · OF : MAIORATVS · PORTVS · DE · ROMENᵛE.

Inner border beaded.

Signet ?

5345. [17th cent.] Sulph. cast from the matrix.   1¹⁄₁₆ in.
[lxv. 100.]

A double cinquefoil rose *en soleil*, barbed and seeded.

✰ VILLA ✰ DE ✰ NOVA ✰ ROMÑEY.

Beaded border.

ROMNEY-MARSH, *co. Kent.*

Bailiff, Jurats, and Commonalty of the Liberty, A.D. 1560.

5346. [A.D. 1622.]   Red: very indistinct and imperfect.
About 1¾ in. when perfect.   [Harl. ch. 75 D. 50.]

A church, with tall spire, crosses at the gable-ends, and round-headed doorway.   Over it the date 15–60.   In base a shield of the ROYAL ARMS of QU. *ELIZABETH.*   Supporters, two angels, each with a nimbus.

✠ SIGILLVM CO........ DE RVMNE .

Small Seal.

5347. [16th cent.]   Sulph. cast from the matrix.   1⅛ in.
[lxvi. 3.]

A church-like building, as in No. 5346.   In base a small plain shield.

ROMNEY MARSH.

W. Boys, *History of Sandwich,* p. 806.

Common Seal, A.D. 1665.

5348.   Recent impression in red sealing-wax, from the matrix.   2¼ in.   [xliv. 1.]

A view of the "Marsh," with a church having embattled tower, spire surmounted by a cross, and a cross at the gable end of the nave.   In the background the sea, with a three-masted ship of war, with high quarter-deck, sails furled, flags at each masthead and at the bow, charged with a cross of St. George.

✠ SIGILLVM COMMVNE DE RVMNEY MARSHE : AN : 1665.ᵛ]

The letters . NE' in *commune* and in *Rumney,* and HE in *marshe*, are conjoined.

W. Boys, *History of Sandwich*, p. 806, pl. fig. 1.

ROMSEY INFRA, *co. Southampton.* [A.D. 1578.]

5349. Sulph. cast from the matrix. 1⅛ in. [xxxvii. 21.]
A portcullis, chained and ringed, over it the date, 1578.

    ⊕ SIGILLVM · DE · ROMSEY · INFRA.

S. Lewis, *Topogr. Dict.*, vol. iii., p. 628·

RUGBY, *co. Warwick.*
Free Grammar School, A.D. 1567.

5350. [18th cent.] Sulph. cast, tinted red, from the matrix. 1⅛ in. [xxxv. 148.]

An ornamental shield of arms, with sprigs and festoons of flowers and foliage at the sides : on a fess betw. three griffins' heads erased, a fleur-de-lis betw. two cinquefoils, LAWRENCE SHERIFF, founder. Crest on a wreath, a lion's gamb erect and erased, holding a date branch.

Legend in two concentric circles :—

Outer circle :— ❀ THE · TRUSTEES · OF · THE · RUGBY · CHARITY.

Inner circle :— FOUNDED · BY · LAWRENCE · SHERIFF.

N. Carlisle, *Endowed Grammar Schools*, vol. iii., p. 662.

5351. Another. [xlvii. 844.]

Laing's *MS. Catal.*, No. 298.

RYE, *co. Sussex.*

5352. [15th cent.] Sulph. casts from the *obv.* and *rev.* of the matrix. 2⅞ in. [lxxii. 101, 102.]

∅. On the waves, a one-masted ship, square mainsail set, sailing to l., with three rows of reef-points, embattled crow's-nest and flag with a cross of St. George and streamers on the mast, embattled forecastle, with banner flag of St. George, and larger embattled poop or stern-castle, with a standard-bearer wearing a cuirass or jupon, camail, and bascinet, and holding a similar banner flag. In the hold a mariner half-length.

SIGILLUM : ⚥ ⚥ : BARONUM : ⚥ ⚥ : DE : ⚥ ⚥ : RYA : ⚥

℞. An elevation of a church, probably St. Mary's, Rye, with embattled and masoned wall, spire topped with a cross, two side pinnacles crocketed, arcaded clerestory, six-pointed windows, each gable topped with a cross. In the centre on a carved corbel a canopied niche with the sides ornamented with ball-flowers, the Virgin, standing, the Child on the l. arm, in the r. h. a flowering branch. In the field overhead, on the l. a radiant sun or estoile of twelve points, on the r. a crescent, each accompanied by seven stars.

: AVE : MARIA : GRACIA : PLENA : DN̄S : TECUM : BENEDICTA :
TU : IN : MULIERIBVS : ⚥

Cabled borders.

S. Lewis, *Topogr. Dict.*, vol. iii., p. 650 ; *Sussex Archæol. Collections*, vol. i., p. 16 (with date, *temp.* Henry V., suggested.)

5353. Sulph. cast of the *rev.* only, indistinct. [xlvii. 729.]

Laing's *MS. Catal.*, No. 655.

Mayor.

First Seal, now used by Deputy Mayor.

5354. [15th cent.] Sulph. cast from the matrix. 1⅛ in. [lxxii. 103.]

A shield of arms, CINQUE-PORTS, see No. 4885, betw. three wyverns.

⚹ : SIGILLUM : OFFICII : MAIORIS : VILLE : DE : RYA :

W. Boys, *History of Sandwich*, p. 782, pl. fig. 4 ; and p. 814.

5355. [A.D. 1450.] Red : fine, but very imperfect. [Add. ch. 973.]

⚹ : SI . . . . CII : MA . . . . . . ILLE : DE : RYA :

Later Seal, A.D. 1574.

5356. Sulph. cast from the matrix. 1⅛ in. [lxxii. 104.]

A copy of the preceding seal, No. 5354. The wyverns obscurely designed.

ϑ SIGILLVM ϑ OFFICII ϑ MAIORIS ϑ VILLE ϑ DE ϑ RYA ϑ ⚥

Sussex Archæol. Collections, vol. i., p. 19, and pl. f. 7 ; W. Boys, *History of Sandwich*, p. 782, pl. fig. 1, and p. 814.

SAFFRON-WALDEN, *co. Essex.*
Mayor and Aldermen.

5357. [17th cent.] Sulph. cast from the matrix. 1¾ in. [lxiii. 34].

A castle-frontage, with two round side-towers, masoned and embattled, and embattled *enceinte*, or surrounding wall, with two similar round towers. In the enclosed area, three *saffron* plants in flower, *walled in :* by way of a *rebus* on the name of the town.

    ✠ COMM͂IE : SIGILL : MAIORIS · ET · ALDERMAND · VILLE · DE · SAFFRON · WALDEN · IN · COND : ESSEX.

Carved border.

S. Lewis, *Topogr. Dict.*, vol. iv., p. 364.

ST. ALBANS, *co. Hertford.*

5358. [17th cent.] Sulph. cast from the matrix. 1₁₆/₃ in. [lxiv. 57.]

An ornamental shield of arms : a saltire, TOWN OF ST. ALBANS.

    ✠ S · CŌMVNE · VILLE · SANCTI · ALBANI · :

S. Lewis, *Topogr. Dict.*, vol. i., p. 12.

ST. IVES, *co. Cornwall.*

5359. [A.D. 1690.] Sulph. cast from the matrix. 1¾ in. [lxi. 25.]

An ornamentally carved shield of arms : an *ivy* branch overspreading the whole field, TOWN OF ST. IVES.

    ✠ SIGILLVM · BVRGI · ST · IVES · IN · COM · CORNVB : 1690.

S. Lewis, *Topogr. Dict.*, vol. ii., p. 469.

5360. Another. [D.C., H. 194.]

SALISBURY, *co. Wilts.*

5361. [13th cent.] Sulph. cast from a fine, but chipped, impression. 2⅛ in. [lxxiii. 71.]

The Virgin, with crown, in the r. h. a sceptre fleur-de-lizé, on the l. arm the Child, with nimbus ; seated on a castle with two embattled side-towers, on each a bird, two round turrets with pointed roofs behind, each topped with cross and knop. In the field above, a crescent on each side, and an estoile also on the r. In base, under a trefoiled arch, a bishop, half-length, with mitre, and pastoral staff held obliquely, lifting up the r. h. in benediction.

✠ SIGILL' NOVE : CIVITATIS : SARESBVRIE :

5362. Sulph. cast from imperfect impression. [D.C., E. 51.]

✠ SIGILL' N . . . . . CIVITATIS : SARESBVRIE :

5363. [A.D. 1397.] Red : fine, but very imperfect. [Add. ch. 17,424.]

. . . . ATIS : SARESBVR . . .

Mayor.

5364. [13th cent.] Sulph. cast from fine, but chipped, impression. 1¾ × 1⅛ in. [lxxiii. 72.]

Pointed oval : the Annunciation of the Virgin, under a trefoiled arch with church-like canopy. In base, under a round-headed arch, the mayor, kneeling in prayer to the r.

· ✠ · S' · MAIORIS · SARRVM ᴹ

Second Seal.

5365. [14th cent.] Sulph. cast from fine, but chipped, impression. 1³⁄₁₆ in. [lxxiii. 73.]

The Annunciation of the Virgin, in a niche with two pointed arches, pinnacled and crocketed. In base, under a carved round-headed arch, the mayor, half-length, in prayer to the r.

SIGILLŪ MAIORIS ✶ SARRVM · ✶ ·

Third Seal.

5366. [A.D. 1416.] Red : fine, chipped on the l. h. side. 1¾ in. [L.F.C., viii. 8.]

The Annunciation of the Virgin : with a lily flower of three sprays growing out of a pot, betw. the Virgin with nimbus, holding up the hands on the r., and the Archangel Gabriel holding a scroll inscribed :-AVE MAR', on the l., in a niche with two carved canopies, having a crocketed finial betw. them, and tabernacle-work at the sides. In base, under a round-headed arch, betw. two half arches, the mayor, half-length, in prayer.

SIGILLUM ; MAIORIS : NOVE : SA . . . . .   .I Ɛ

5367. [A.D. 1421.] Red : fine, injured by a plaited rush having been pressed over it when newly made. [L.F.C., viii. 9.]

Legend indistinct.

With Counterseal of JOHN HALLE, *Mayor.*

⸗ **5368.** [A.D. 1465.] Red: fine, slightly chipped. [Harl. ch. 78 I. 55.]

Ø, ⸱ SIGILLUM ː MAJORIS : NOVE ː SARUM : ʍ ·

⸲ R. A small oval counterseal, or signet, from a ring. About ¾ × ⅜ in. Impression of an antique oval intaglio gem of the Gnostic period. St. John Baptist, with camel's hair coat, and nimbus, holding in the r. h. towards his breast the Agnus Dei, and lifting up the l. h. in benediction ; under his feet, an indistinct object—perhaps an asp.

✠ SIGILLUM ☆ IOHANYS ☆ HALLA.

5369. Sulph. cast of the third seal as in No. 5366. [D.C., G. 70.]

Seal "pro recognitione debitorum," see No. 1087.

New Corporation of the City of New Sarum,
A.D. 1658.

⸲ **5370.** Sulph. cast from the matrix. 1⅞ in. [D.C., H. 158.]

An ornamentally carved shield of arms : four bars, CITY OF NEW SARUM. (*Visitation,* 1565.)

✿ THE : CITIE : OF : NEW : SARVM : 1·6·5·8 : ʍ ✿.

Carved borders.

S. Lewis, *Topogr. Dict.,* vol. iv., p. 74.

Smaller Seal of Arms.

5371. [17th cent.] Sulph. cast from the matrix. 1 in. [lxxxiii. 74.]

An ornamentally carved shield of arms : barry of six, er-roneously for four bars, CITY OF NEW SARUM.

· ✤ · CIVITAS : NOVE : SARVM.

Another Seal.

5372. [17th cent.] Sulph. cast from the matrix. 1 in. [lxxiii. 75.]

A shield of arms : barry of eight, erroneously for four bars, CITY OF NEW SARUM ; suspended by a riband from a festoon of flowers and foliage. Supporters, on brackets, two double-headed eagles displayed, gorged with coronets. In base, two palm-branches, tied.

+ CIVITAS NOVÆ SARUM.

N 2

Weavers' Company.

5373. [17th cent.] Sulph. cast from cracked impression. 2 in. [D.C., H. 165.]

A lion's head, affrontée, crowned with the coronet of seven points, with six pearls alternately disposed, in the mouth a shuttle (?).

✠ SIGILLVM ◇ TEXTORVM ◇ CIVITATIS ◇ NOVE ◇ SARVM.

The letters TE in *textorum*, and VE in *nove* are conjoined. Beaded borders.

SALTASH, *co. Cornwall.*

5374. [14th cent.] Sulph. cast from the matrix. $1\frac{9}{16}$ in. [lxi. 23.]

Within a cusped border of six points, a shield of arms: a lion rampant, within a bordure charged with thirteen roundles, for the EARLS OF CORNWALL, and TOWN OF SALTASH. Over the shield an open crown of three points; at each side an ostrich feather labelled, and a sprig of foliage; in base, wavy lines representing the sea.

✠ SIGILLVM : SALTASCHE : IN : CORNWAILE.

S. Lewis, *Topogr. Dict.*, vol. iv., p. 7.

SANDWICH, *co. Kent.*

5375. [13th cent.] Sulph. casts of the *obv.* and *rev.*, from the matrix. $2\frac{9}{16}$ in. [D.C., E. 626, 627.]

∅. On the sea, in which are several fishes, a one-masted ship with three guns in the hull, mainsail being furled by two mariners sitting on the yard, embattled crow's nest, forecastle and stern-castle, streamer at the masthead, flag at the forecastle, and two flags at the stern; in the hold two half-length mariners, one holding an axe, the other a flag charged with two estoiles of six points. There is also a small boat on board at the foot of the mast. In the stern the head of the steersman is seen, and near him a boat-hook, erect.

SIGILL' ✠ CONSILII ✠ BARONVM ✠ DE ✠ SANDWICO ✠

R. A lion passant guardant crowned. The field filled with two trees of elegant design, with trefoiled leaves and of conventional character.

✠ QVI ✠ SERVARE ✠ GREGEM ✠ CELI ✠ SOLET ✠ INDICO ✠ REGEM' ✠

Beaded borders.

W. Boys, *History of Sandwich*, pp. 769, 789 ; S. Lewis, *Topogr. Dict.*, vol. iv., p. 14.

Mayoralty.

5376. [15th cent.] Sulph. cast from the matrix. 1⅛ in. [lxvi. 5.]

Within an engrailed border, the three demi-lions passant guardant conjoined to as many hulks, in pale, which form the armorial bearings on the shield of arms of the CINQUE-PORTS.

✠ SIGILLU ⚹ COMMŪE ⚹ MAIORAT' ⚹ UILLE ⚹ SANDUICH ⚹

Another Seal.

5377. [15th cent.] Sulph. cast from the matrix. 1⅛ in. [lxvi. 6.]

Within a cusped or engrailed border a similar design to that of the preceding seal, No. 5376.

❀ SIGILLUM ❀ OFFICII ❀ MAIORATUS ❀ ⚹ ⚹ ⚹ VILLE ❀
SANDEWICI ❀ ⚹ ❀ ⚹

The space betw. the third and fourth words appears to have contained a word now erased in the matrix.

W. Boys, *Hist. of Sandwich*, p. 844.

Comptroller of the Port.

5378. [*temp.* Car. I.] Sulph. cast from the matrix. 1 9/16 in. [lxvi. 7.]

The Royal Badge of a double cinquefoiled rose, barbed and seeded. Above it a royal crown. In the field the initial letters C. R. and six fleurs-de-lis.

❀ S' · OFF : CONTRAROT : PORTVS · SANDWICH ·

Inner border beaded, outer border carved.

Free Grammar School, A.D. 1563.

5379. Sulph. cast from the matrix. 2¾ in. [lxvi. 11.]

Our Lord, with a nimbus or corona of rays, seated under a round-headed arch of masonry, with book on his lap and l. h. extended, teaching. On the l. a group of five disciples ; at his feet an infant ; on the r. a pedagogue, under a smaller arch, and five children, two of them carrying books under the arm. In base, under the plinth or platform a shield of arms :

two pales engrailed, on a chief a demi-lion rampant issuing, a crescent for difference, ROGER MANWOOD, founder. On a looped riband at each side of the shield the inscription :—

     ✿ ʍ AD ME VENIRE SINITE PARVVLOS ʍ ✿

                  —Marc. x. 14.

✠ SIGILLVM ✿ CÕE ✿ GVB̃NAT ✿ LIB̃E ✿ SCOLE ✿ GRAMATICE ✿ ROGERI ✿ MANVVOOD ✿ IN ✿ SANDWICO.

The letters ND in *Sandwico* are conjoined.

N. Carlisle, *Endowed Grammar Schools*, vol. i., p. 594 ; W. Boys, *History of Sandwich*, pp. 244, 790.

SCARBOROUGH, *co. York.*

5380. [13th cent.] Sulph. cast from the matrix. 2¼ in. [lxxv. 61.]

An embattled castle of two storeys, with masoned walls, round-headed portal, the doors closed, two narrow round-headed windows and two circular windows in the lower storey, two quatrefoiled windows in the upper storey, over the battlements the helmeted head of a castellan. At the back and l. h. side of the castle the sea. On the l. a one-masted ship with embattled crow's nest, and the heads of two mariners on board. In the field overhead an estoile of eight points wavy.

    ✠ SIGILLVM : CÕMVNE : BVRGENSIV̄ : DE : SCARDEBVRG.

The letters AR of *Scardeburg* are conjoined.

Beaded borders.

S. Lewis, *Topogr. Dict.*, vol. iv., p. 21.

Later Seal.

5381. [18th cent.] Sulph. cast from the matrix. 1¼ in. [lxxv. 7.]

On the sea, a ship of war, with a beacon of three points on the mast, betw. two embattled round-towers, each bearing a flag charged with the cross of St. George, the hull containing two rows of circular port-holes.

    ✿ ✤ SIGILLVM ✤ VILLE ✤ DE ✤ SCARDEBROVGH ✤

Beaded border.

SEAFORD, *co. Sussex.*

5382. [16th cent.] Sulph. casts from the *obv.* and *rev.* of the matrix. 1¼ in. [lxxii. 106, 107.]

Ø. An eagle, rising reguardant with expanded wings.

✠ SIGILLVM BVRGENSIVM : DE SAFFORDIA.

The S's reversed.

℞. On the sea, a three-masted ship of war of antique shape, with mainsail set, fore and mizen sails furled, a circular crow's nest and flag on each mast.

WITH SVTONII ✫ ✫ ET ✫ CHVNGTON.

W. Boys, *History of Sandwich*, p. 814 ; S. Lewis, *Topogr. Dict.*, vol. iv., p. 29.

Bailiff.

5383. [15th cent.] Sulph. cast from the matrix. 1 in. [lxxii. 105.]

An eagle displayed.

✿ SIGILLVM ✿ BALLIVI ✿ DE ✿ SEFORDE.

Cabled borders.

SEVENOAKS, *co. Kent.*
Free Grammar School, A.D. 1560.

5384. Sulph. cast from the matrix. 3⅜ × 3 in. [lxvi. 12.]

Pointed oval : beneath a reeded baldachin, topped with a cross, and supported by two turned columns each topped with a similar cross, the pedagogue, with academical cap and gown, seated in a carved chair with two similar columns at the sides, in the r. h. a birch-rod, in the l. h. an open book. At each side a scholar, the one on the left holding a book. In the field the letters R. B. for Sir Ralph Bosville, knt., benefactor. On the flagged pavement in the foreground six scholars, four with books. In base, in three lines, the inscription :—

✫ SERVIRE ✫ DEO — REGNARI ✫ — ✫ EST.

For this motto, cf. No. 2139.

✠ · SIGILLVM ✫ COMMVNE ✫ SCOLE · GRAMATICALIS ✫.
DE ✫ SEVENOK ✫ IN ✫ COM ✫ KANCE.

The N's reversed.

SHAFTESBURY, *co. Dorset.*
Mayoralty.

5385. [A.D. 1434.] Red : fine but very fragmentary. About 1⅜ in. when perfect. [Harl. ch. 80 D. 51.]

A shield of arms : a cross betw. in the 1st and 4th quarters a fleur-de-lis, in the 2nd and 3rd, a lion's face, TOWN OF SHAFTESBURY. ' Inner border carved and enriched with ball-flowers.

SIG . . . .

Second Seal, A.D. 1570.

5386. [17th cent.] Sulph. cast from the matrix. 1⅜ in. [lxii. 51.]

A carved shield of arms : a cross quarterly, betw. in the 1st and 4th quarters a fleur-de-lis, in the 2nd and 3rd quarters a lion's face, TOWN OF SHAFTESBURY. Over the shield the date 1570 .·.

❈ SIGILLVM + OFFICII + MAIORATVS + BVRGI + SHASTON.

Cabled borders.

Court of Record, A.D. 1570.

5387. Sulph. cast from the matrix. ⅞ in. [lxii. 52.]

A shield of arms : a tree eradicated, the lower branches pruned and sprouting afresh, in the branches a bird, on the *dex.* a lion leaping up towards the bird. Betw. the initial letters B. S. Over the shield the date, 1570.

SHEFFIELD, *co. York.*

5388. [A.D. 1554.] Sulph. cast from the matrix. 2 in. [D.C., H. 172.]

A *sheaf* of fifteen arrows arranged saltire-wise, tied with a tasselled cord, betw. two pheons.

❈ : SIGILLVM : · : VILLA : · : DE : · : SHEFFELDE : · :
ANNO : · : 1554 :

S. Lewis, *Topogr. Dict.*, vol. iv., p. 48.

Free Grammar School, A.D. 1603 or 1604.

5389. Sulph. cast from the matrix, varnished. 2¼ × 1⅞ in. [D.C., H. 70.]

Pointed oval : on a mount a scholar standing, an open book in the r. h. The background or *field* replenished with a *sheaf* of twelve arrows radiating from the centre, points in base.

❈ LVCERNA PE ✹ DIBVS MEIS ✹ VERBVM TVVM.

—Psalm cxviii. 105.

5390. Sulph. cast, tinted red. [xxxv. 149.]
5391. Sulph. cast, tinted red. [xlvii. 905.]

Laing's *MS. Catal.*, No. 306 ; N. Carlisle, *Endowed Grammar Schools*, vol. ii., p. 896.

SHOREHAM, co. Sussex.

Seal for delivery of Wool and Hides, see No. 1163.

SHREWSBURY, co. Salop.
Bailiffs.

5392. [13th cent.] Sulph. cast from fine impression. $1\frac{5}{8}$ in. [lxxi. 32.]

A shield of arms : ENGLAND. Betw. three oak-trees.

        ☩ SIGILLVM : BALLIVORV̄ : SALOPIE.

Beaded borders.

Corporation, A.D. 1425.

5393. Sulph. cast from the matrix. 3 in. [D.C., G. 264.]

A view of the town, with houses, churches, and a large church of cruciform plan with tall spire topped with a cross in the middle, within an embattled wall with four round towers embattled, and a central round-headed doorway and two similar side doorways leading to bridges over the R. Severn. Over the central doorway a shield of arms : ENGLAND ; on the walls on each side a shield of arms : l. diapré, a cross of St. George ; r. three leopards' heads, two and one, TOWN OF SHREWSBURY.

SIGILLŪ + COMUNE + LIBERTATIS + VILLE + SALOPESBURIE + FAOTŪ + AÑO + GR̄E + M + CCCC + XXV.

Beaded border.

  S. Lewis, *Topogr. Dict.*, vol. iv., p. 72 ; [Hugh Owen], *Some Account of . . . Shrewsbury*, 1808, *frontispiece.*

5394. Another, fine. [lxxi. 30.]

Seal of Arms.

5395. [17th cent.] Sulph. cast from the matrix. $1\frac{1}{4}$ in. [lxxi. 33.]

An ornamental shield of arms : TOWN OF SHREWSBURY, as in No. 5393. In base, on a scroll the legend :—

        VILLA SALOPIÆ.

S. Lewis, *Topogr. Dict.*, vol. iv., p. 69.

Manor of Foregate Monachorum belonging to Shrewsbury Abbey.

5396. [13th cent.] Sulph. cast from the matrix or a fine impression. 2¼ × 1⁵⁄₁₆ in. [D.C., E. 690.]

Pointed oval : a. baton, with the ends and centre beaded and ringed, betw. on the l. a dexter hand and vested arm, holding a jewelled pastoral staff in pale, on the r. a dexter hand and arm vested with a hauberk-sleeve of ring-mail, holding a drawn broad-sword in pale. In the field two six-foils, a smaller one, and a quatrefoil.

    ✠ S' COMMVNE · DE · FFORYATE MONACHORYM.

Beaded borders.

[Hugh Owen], *Some Account of . . . Shrewsbury*, 1808; p. 135 ; Dugdale, *Mon. Angl.*, vol. iii., p. 516.

Drapers' Company.

5397. [15th cent.] Sulph. cast from the matrix. 1⅞ in. [lxxi. 36.]

The Almighty Father, with nimbus and radiant lines round the head, seated, lifting up the hands in benediction ; on the lap a staff set obliquely ; across the breast, the word DEUS. Behind, the field replenished with tongues of fire or rays, set horizontally. The legend following is connected by a line at the end with the mouth of the Father.

    ✠ PATER : DE CELIS : FILI : REDEMPTOR : MVDI : SPIRITUS : SCI (*sic*) : SCA : T'NITAS : VN'.

Cabled borders.

Smaller Seal or Counterseal.

5398. Sulph. cast from the matrix. 1¼ in. [lxxi. 37.]

The Almighty as in the preceding seal, No. 5397, without the staff and the name on the breast.

    S' FRAT'NITATIS PANNARIOR DE SENOPIA :

The letters OR in *pannariorum*, and DE in *de* are conjoined.

Free Grammar School, A.D. 1798.

5399. Sulph. cast from the matrix. 2⅞ in. [xxxv. 150.]

In a hall, with geometrical pavement, two low pointed arches on clustered shafts, and an ogee-arched window of five lights, on the l., K. EDWARD VI. presenting the foundation chaŕter of A.D.. 1552' to the promoters, Hugh'.Edwards and Richard Whitacre. · ·

In base, the inscription in three lines:— FUNDAT · 1552.— AUCT ·.AB ELIZABETH · 1571.—REPARAT · 1798 .

In the exergue, on the r., W. BOWLEY · F ·

SIGILL · GVBERNATORVM ET. FIDE COMM · LIBERAE SCHOLAE · GRAMM · R · EDWARDI · VI · SALOP.

At the commencement of the legend a shield of arms : three leopards' heads, TOWN OF SHREWSBURY, see No. 5393.

5400. Another. - [xlvii. 906.]

Laing's *MS. Catal.*, No. 290 ; N. Carlisle, *Endowed Grammar Schools*, vol. ii., p. 377.

SOUTHAMPTON, *County of.* ·

JOHN UVEDALE, *Sheriff*, A.D. 1387–1388.

5401. Red ' sealing-wax, from fine impression. ¾ in. [xliii. 5.]

A shield of arms : a cross moline, UVEDALE, ensigned with a castle as used in sheriffs' seals. In the field on the r., in base the initial letter R. All within a finely carved and traced gothic panel.

JOHN GIFFORD, *Sheriff*, A.D. 1494–5.

5402. Sulph. cast from fine impression. 1 in. [lxiv. 11.]

A triple-towered castle, embattled walls masoned, on the portal a shield of arms, couché : ten torteaux, four, three, two, and one, in pile, GIFFORD. Betw. the initial letters I. G. Cabled border.

SIR JOHN BRUYN or BRUNE, *Sheriff*, A.D. 1554–5.

5403. Sulph. cast from imperfect impression. 1 in. [lxiv. 9.]

A triple-towered castle, embattled, narrow round-headed windows, round-headed portal with portcullis half-down. On the portal a shield of arms, couché : quarterly, 1, 4, a cross moline, (cf. No. 5401), 2, 3, lozengy, BRUNE. At the sides two branches of foliage ; above, two cusps and two leaves slipped.

Another Seal, or a Counterseal.

5404. Sulph. cast. ⅞ × ¾ in. [lxiv. 10.]

Oval : upon a triple-towered castle, embattled and with walls masoned, a shield of arms, couché, lozengy, BRUNE.

Royal Seal of Henry V. (?) for the Subsidy on Cloth in
co. Southampton.

5405. Sulph. cast.   1¼ in.   [lxiv. 12.]

The king's head, full face, crowned, and collared, betw. two ostrich feathers labelled.

S : SVBSIDIVM : PANNORVM : SVTH'T.

Coarse style.   For other seals of this class, see Nos. 1060-1063.

SOUTHAMPTON, *co. Southampton.*

5406. [13th cent.]   Sulph. cast from fine impression.   2½ in.   [lxiv. 4.]

On the sea, a one-masted ship, triangular sail set and charged with two crosses pattées, embattled stern-castle, side sweep or rudder, flag and streamers at the mast-head.

SIGILLVM · VILLE · SVTHAMTONIE.

Second Seal.

5407. [13th cent.]   Sulph. cast of the *obv.* only.   3⅛ in. [D.C., F. 639.]

On the sea a one-masted ship, mainsail furled, embattled crow's nest, and castles, in the hold a mariner holding a spar and lifting up the r. h., in the castle at the stern two trumpeters, flag at the mast-head.   In the field a crescent and two estoiles.

SIGILLVM ✸ COMVNITATIS ✸ SVTHAMTONE : ℭ ✠ .

Cf. S. Lewis, *Topogr. Dict.*, vol. ii., p. 119, for a seal very similar, but with variant details and legend.

5408. Sulph. cast of the *rev.* only.   3⅛ in.   [lxiv. 3.]

Three carved gothic niches, with ogee arched canopies, pinnacled and crocketed, containing the Virgin, crowned, the Child on the l. arm, betw. two angels turned towards her, with expanded wings, swinging censers, tabernacle-work at the sides.   Background coarsely hatched with diagonal lines. In base, under a string-course ornamented with ball-flowers, an arcade of eight round-headed arches containing two lions' faces, as many fleurs-de-lis, and as many roundles or roses.

☋ MATER ✸ VIRGO ✸ DEI ✸ TV ✸ MISERERE ✸ NOBIS ✠

S. Lewis, *Topogr. Dict.*, vol. ii., p. 119.

Later Seal.

5409. [17th cent.]   Sulph. cast from the matrix.   3⅛ in. [lxiv. 6.]

On the sea, a three-masted ship of war, two decks of guns, fully rigged, sailing to the l., on the mainsail an ornamental shield of arms: per fess, three cinquefoil roses, barbed and seeded, TOWN OF SOUTHAMPTON. Foremast and mainmast heads carry on the flag the cross of St. George.

    ::; ♠ ::: SIGILLVM : COMMVNE : VILLÆ : SOVTHAMTONIÆ .

Seal of Arms.

5410. [17th cent.] Sulph. cast from the matrix. ⅞ in. [lxiv. 5.]

An ornamental shield of arms: a fess or barrulet betw. three cinquefoil roses barbed and seeded, for per fess three roses, TOWN OF SOUTHAMPTON.

    ⌘ VILLA ⚕ SVTHAMPTON.

Beaded border.

Official Seal.

5411. [16th cent.] Sulph. cast from chipped impression. 1⅛ in. [lxiv. 8.]

A castle gateway, with two round towers, masoned and embattled,. round-headed portal with portcullis half-down. In the field above, a rose of five points, from the arms of the TOWN OF SOUTHAMPTON. In base the legend :—SOVTHTON·

Beaded border.

Mayoralty.

5412. [15th cent.] Sulph. cast from fine, but slightly chipped, impression. 1¼ in. [lxiv. 7.]

On the sea, a one-masted ship, with mainsail furled, embattled castles at each end. In the field on the r. an estoile of six points.

    : ⚕ SIG' : MAIORITATIS : VILLE : DE : SUTHAMPTON . ⚕ :

Another Seal.

5413. [15th cent.] Sulph. cast from fine impression, chipped. 2 in. [D.C., G. 263.]

On the sea, a one-masted ship of peculiar style, mainsail furled, embattled castles at each end; flag at the bowsprit, charged with the cross of St. George and with streamers. In the field over the deck a cinquefoil rose, barbed and seeded, as in the arms of the TOWN OF SOUTHAMPTON; on the r. a crescent; on the l. an estoile of six points.

    : ⚕ SIGILLVM : MAIORATUS : VILLE : SUTHAMPTONE BENES (?)

5414. [A.D. 1545.]   Red : fine fragments.   [Add. ch. 7219.]
Legend wanting. ..

Bailiffs.

5415. [13th cent.]   Sulph. cast from fine impression.
$1\frac{1}{2}$ × 1 in.   [lxiv. 13.]

Pointed oval : on the sea a one-masted ship with mainsail
furled, rudder at the starboard side.

S' BALLIVOR SVTAMTOÑIE: :

Another Seal.

5416. [13th cent.]   Sulph. cast from fine impression.
$1\frac{1}{2}$ × 1 in.   [lxiv. 14.]

Pointed oval : apparently a copy of the preceding seal,
No. 5415.   In the field on the l. an estoile of six points.

S' BALLIVORVM SVTHAMTONIE.

The letters AM in *Suthamtonie* are conjoined.

Provostry.

5417. [13th cent.]   Sulph. cast from fine impression,
chipped at the edge. $1\frac{7}{8}$ × $1\frac{1}{4}$ in.   [lxiv. 15.]

Pointed oval : on the sea a one-masted ship, with mainsail
furled, a cross at the mast-head, rudder at the starboard side.
This appears to be a similar design to that on the seal of the
Bailiffs, No. 5415.

☒ S' PREPO[SI]TVRE : SVTHAMTON'.

Another Seal.

5418. [13th cent.]   Sulph. cast from fine impression,
slightly chipped. $1\frac{7}{8}$ × $1\frac{1}{4}$ in.   [lxiv. 16.]

Pointed oval : this is a copy of the preceding seal, No. 5417,
with the additions in the field of an estoile of six points wavy
on the l., and a crescent on the r. over the deck.

✠ S' . PREPOSITVRE : SYTHAMTONE.

Another Seal.

5419. [13th cent.]   Sulph. cast from fine impression,
slightly chipped. $1\frac{7}{8}$ × $1\frac{1}{4}$ in.   [lxiv. 17.]

Pointed oval : a copy of the designs of the two previous seals,
Nos. 5417, 5418, with larger castles at stern and stem.   The
position of the estoile and crescent in the field is transposed.

✠ S' : PREPOSITVRE : SVTHAMTONE :

Staple.

5420. [13th–14th cent.] Sulph. cast from fine impression. 1¼ in. [D.C., F. 688.]

Within a finely traced and carved gothic rosette of four pointed and two semicircular lobes, a leopard's face, enraged, between two fleurs-de-lis at the sides, and four small roses.

☆ SIGILLUM ፧ OFFICIJ ፧ STAPULLE (*sic*) ፧ UILLE ፧ ᶜ SUTHAMPTONIJ ፧

Seal "pro recognitione debitorum," see No. 1088.

Free Grammar School, A.D. 1584?

5421. Red: fine originally, now chipped and injured. 1¾ in. [xxxv. 260.]

Qu. Elizabeth, standing, in royal robes, slightly turned to the l., in the r. h. an orb, in the l. h. a sceptre. In the field on each side, a shield of the ROYAL ARMS of the Queen, couché, suspended by a looped riband. In base an ornamental shield of arms: three eagles displayed, two and one.

Legend on a scroll:—

S . . . . IN VILLA SOVTH' . . . . [STA]BILIT' · PER · ELIZAB' · REGIN'. 1584 (?)

5422. Sulph. cast. [lviii. 25.]

5423. Another. [lxiv. 23.]

SOUTHWARK, *co. Surrey.*

St. Olave's Free Grammar School, A.D. 1570.

5424. Sulph. cast from the matrix. 1¾ in. [D.C., H. 177.]

A view of the interior of the school, with master seated on a chair before a table on which is a birch-rod and open book, before him five scholars. The pavement is flagged with lozenge-shaped slabs; the window is of five lights, below it on a string-course the date : ✿ : 1576 : .

✠ THE SEALE OF Yᴱ FREE SCHOOLE OF Yᴱ · PARISHONERS OF Sᵀ OLAVES SOVTHᵂ FOVNDED BY Q. ELZ.

Carved borders.

St. Mary Overey's or St. Saviour's Free Grammar School, A.D. 1573.

5425. Sulph. cast from the matrix, tinted red. 1⅞ in. [xxxv. 151.]

In a niche of the style of the Renaissance, with carved plinth, columns with spiral fluting, and triangular pediment or canopy with ornamental back, the master, seated on a chair, to the r., instructing a class of scholars on the r. Background partly diapered lozengy. At the sides the initials T. C., for Thomas Cure, one of the co-founders. In base, a birch-rod.

✠ SIGILLVM ✠ SCOLLAE ✠ SANTÆ (*sic*) ✠ SALVATORIS · 1573 ʍ

The letters TÆ in *santæ* are conjoined.
Beaded borders.

N. Carlisle, *Endowed Grammar Schools*, vol. ii., p. 582.

5426. Sulph. cast. [xlvii. 903.]

Laing's *MS. Catal.*, No. 293.

5427. Another. [lxxii. 69.]

SPALDING, *co. Lincoln.*
Portreeve.

5428. [17th cent.] Sulph. cast from the matrix. $1\frac{5}{16}$ in. [D.C., H. 187.]

A portcullis, chained and ringed; over it the initial letters C. R. [Carolus Rex.]

   ✝ SIGIL : OFFICII : PORT : SPALDEN.

Cabled borders.

Free Grammar School, A.D. 1668.

5429. Sulph. cast from the matrix, tinted red. $1\frac{1}{4}$ in. [xxxv. 152.]

A shield of arms: on a chief three mallets, a coat founded on that of three mallets, JOHN GAMLYN or GAMBLYN, one of the co-founders.

  ※ SIG · LIB · SOHO · GRA · IN : SPALDING · IN · COM · LINC.

Beaded borders.

N. Carlisle, *Endowed Grammar Schools*, vol. i., p. 843.

5430. Another. [xlvii. 907.]

Laing's *MS. Catal.*, No. 285.

5431. Sulph. cast. [lxvii. 31.]

STAFFORD, *co. Stafford.*

First Corporation Seal, also used by the Free Grammar School.

5432. [13th cent.] Sulph. cast, cracked, from fine impression ; tinted red. 2 in. [xxxv. 153]

A triple-towered castle, masoned and embattled, quatrefoiled windows, doors thrown back, in the portal a portcullis half-down. In the field on each side, two lions passant guardant of ENGLAND in pale ; in base, in water a fish naiant contourné. All within a carved sixfoil, with trefoiled tracery in the spandrils, and a trefoil slipped and leaved, attached to the cusp betw. the lions on each side ; the inner edge ornamented with ball-flowers.

✿ SIGILLVM ✿ COMUNITATIS ✿ VILLE ✿ STAFFORDIE.

Beaded border.

S. Lewis, *Topogr. Dict.*, vol. iv., p. 144 ; *Journ. Brit. Arch. Assoc.,* vol. xii., pl. 32, fig. 4 ; N. Carlisle, *Endowed Grammar Schools*, vol. ii., p. 491.

5433. Sulph. cast, tinted red, from fine impression. [xlvii. 908.]

Laing's *MS. Catal.*, No. 292.

5434. Sulph. cast from cracked impression. [lxxii. 39.]
5435. Another. [D.C., F. 630.]

Later Seal, A.D. 1826.

5436. Sulph. cast from the matrix. 2 in. [lxxii. 40.]
A modern copy of the preceding seal.

✿ SIGILLVM COMMUNITATIS VILLÆ STAFFORDIÆ ✿ 1826.

5437. Another. [D.C., H. 197.]

STAMFORD, *co. Lincoln.*

5438. [14th cent.] Red sealing-wax, from the matrix. 2¾ in. [xliii. 137.]
The Virgin, with crown, seated in a finely carved niche with ogee-arched canopy, pinnacled and crocketed, supported on two side-towers of tabernacle-work enriched with cinquefoil roses, the Child on the l. arm. Background at sides diapered lozengy, with a small cinquefoil in each space. In base, under a carved ogee-arch with a trefoiled opening in each spandril, an ecclesiastic kneeling in prayer to the l.

STAVNFORD ✿ BVRGENSES ✿ VIRGO ✿ FVNDVNT ✿ TIBI · PRECES.

The N's reversed.

Beaded borders.

Cf. Peck, *History of Stamford*, vol. iii., p. 33.

5439. Sulph. cast. [xlvii. 909.]

Laing's *MS. Catal.*, No. 385.

5440. Another. [D.C., F. 34.]

Later Seal.

5441. [17th cent.] Sulph. cast from the matrix.   2 in. [lxvii. 36.]

A shield of arms : per pale, *dex.*, ENGLAND, *sin.*, chequy, WARREN. Over the shield two oak-leaves, at each side a wyvern with a peacock's tail.

SIGILLUM COMMUNE BURGI STAMFORDIÆ.

Cf. S. Lewis, *Topogr. Dict.*, vol. iv., p. 157.

STAPELHOU HUNDRED, *co. Cambridge.*

5442. [14th cent.] Sulph. cast. 1⅛ in. [lx. 59.]

Across the field in two lines, the inscription :—STAP–YLHO with a sprig of foliage above, and another below it.

S̄ : COM̄ : CANTEBRYGG :

STOCKPORT, *co. Chester.*

5443. [19th cent.] Sulph. cast from the matrix.   2¼ in. [lx. 93.]

On a mount replenished with foliage and flowers an orna- mental shield of arms : three lozenges betw. nine crosses crosslet, TOWN OF STOCKPORT. Lewis describes the crosslets as fitchées. Over the shield a riband ensigned with a mural crown, and inscribed— · · · · CORPORATE · · · POR · · 185 · · ·

THE COMMON SEAL OF THE BOROUGH OF STOCKPORT ❀

S. Lewis, *Topogr. Dict.*, vol. iv., p. 182.

STOCKTON-ON-TEES, *co. Durham.*

Corporation.

5444. [18th cent.] Sulph. cast from the matrix. 1¼ in. [lxii. 93.]

f An anchor, lined, surmounted by a castle, embattled and masoned.

✿ SIG' : CORP : DE · STOCKTON · IN · COM : PAL : DUNELM.

S. Lewis, *Topogr. Dict.*, vol. iv., p. 185.

STOKE-COURCY, *co. Somerset.*

5445. [12th–13th cent.] Sulph. cast from fine impression. 2 in. [lxxi. 71.]

An embattled tower of four diminishing storeys, walls masoned, a round tower at each angle, portal with valve doors closed.

✿ SIGILL' COMMVNE : BVRGENSIVM ·:· DE : STOKES · CVRCI ·:·

SUFFOLK, *County of.*
SIR SYMONDS D'EWES, *Bart., Sheriff*, A.D. 1640.

5446. Red : fragmentary. [Harl. ch. 49 F. 1.]

Oval : a triple-towered castle, masoned and embattled. In the field above, portion of the base of a shield of arms : three quatrefoils, two and one, D'*E*WES.

EDMUND TYRELL, *Sheriff*, A.D. 1774.

5447. Red : very indistinct ; *en placard* on a broad riband of yellow silk. ¾ in. [Add. ch. 10,518.]

Oval : a triple-towered castle, masoned and embattled, on each side-tower a dome topped with a flag. At the sides the initial letters :— E. T. In base the legend :—SUFF.

JOHN WENYEVE, *Sheriff*, A.D. 1784.

5448. Red : fine impression, edge imperfect ; *en placard* on a tape. 1¾ in. [Add. ch. 10,519.]

Oval : a triple-towered castle, masoned and embattled, on each side-tower a dome topped with a flag. Above, on a wreath, on a mount a bird rising, with a sprig of foliage in its beak, Crest of WENYEVE ? At the sides the initial letters :— I. W. In base the legend :—SUFF.

SURREY, *County of.*
Coroner.

5449. [Modern.] Sulph. cast from the matrix. 1 × ⅞ in. [lxxii. 71.]

O 2

Oval: a rose, slipped and leaved, ensigned with a royal crown.

> SIGILLVM · CORONATOR · COM · SVRRY.

SUTTON-COLDFIELD, *co. Warwick.*

Seal of the separate jurisdiction.

5450. [16th cent.] Sulph. cast from the matrix. 2¼ in. [lxxiii. 36.]

A double cinquefoiled rose, *en soleil*, barbed and seeded: one of the royal badges of K. Henry VIII.

> ⁑ ✿ ⁑ SIGILLV ✿ GARDIANI ⁑ C ⁑ SOCIETAT' ⁑ DE ⁑
>   SVTTON ⁑ ✿ COLFYLD.

Cabled border.

S. Lewis, *Topogr. Dict.*, vol. iv., p. 250.

TAMWORTH, *cos. Warwick and Stafford.*

5451. [17th cent.] Sulph. cast from the matrix. 2¼ in. [lxxii. 54.]

A fleur-de-lis, diapered.

Legend on a riband with wavy ends :—

> SIG · BVRGI · DE · TAMWORTH · IN · COMITAT · WARWIC ·
>   ET · STAF.

Carved border.

S. Lewis, *Topogr. Dict.*, vol. iv., p. 264.

TAUNTON, *co. Somerset.*

5452. [13th cent.] Sulph. cast from fine impression. 2¼ in. [lxxi. 72.]

A castle of peculiar and elaborate style, having a house of two storeys, in the middle two flags on the roof, two round side-towers, each topped with a fleur-de-lis ; outside these, on an embattled wall, with round-headed arches, on each side a pastoral staff. In base, a fleur-de-lis betw. two birds. The field contains several groups of pellets arranged three by three in clusters.

> ✿ : SIGILLVM : COMMVNE ·∴· BVRGI : TANTONIE.

Beaded borders.

Cf. the seal of Exeter, No. 4919.

TAVISTOCK LIBERTY, *co. Devon.*

5453. Sulph. cast from the matrix. $1\frac{1}{8} \times \frac{7}{8}$ in. [lxii. 5.]
Oval: a shield of arms: a lion rampant, on a chief three escallops, RUSSELL, Duke of Bedford. Ensigned with an earl's coronet of five pearls.

✠ ARMA · DNI : LIBERT' · DE · TAVISTOCKE.
Carved border.

S. Lewis, *Topogr. Dict.*, vol. iv., p. 273.

TENTERDEN TOWN AND HUNDRED, *co. Kent.*

5454. [15th cent.] Sulph. casts of the *obv.* and *rev.* from the matrix. $2\frac{3}{8}$ in. [lxvi. 15, 16.]

∅. On the waves, a one-masted ship of war, mainsail charged with the armorial bearings of the shield of arms of the CINQUE-PORTS, flag of St. George on the castle at the stern, round crow's nest. In the field on the l. a crescent, on the r. an estoile of eight points. Inner border of the field partially engrailed.

⋈ SIGILLUM ⋈ COMUNE ⋈ VILLE ⋈ ET ⋈ HUNDREDE ⋈
DE ⋈ TENTERDEN : ⋈

℞. St. Mildred, Patroness of the Church and Town, crowned, in the r. h. a book, in the l. h. a pastoral staff, standing in a carved niche with octagon plan, and with heavy canopy, and tabernacle-work at the sides; background diapered with vertical stripes enclosing rows of quatrefoils; on the plinth, or string-course below, the inscription **l : SC̄A : t̄ : MILDREDA : l ⋈.** In base, under a depressed arch, carved, with masonry at the sides, a shield of arms: on a bend betw. four lions' heads erased, enraged, three estoiles, PILLESDEN ?·

✠ ORA : PRO NOBIS : B̄A MILDREDA ⋈ · VT · DIGNI ·
EFFIGIA̅ · ⸬PMISCŌIB3 : XPI :

W. Boys, *History of Sandwich*, p. 814; S. Lewis, *Topogr. Dict.*, vol. ii., p. 278.

5455. [A.D. 1479.] Red: a fragment. [Add. ch. 16,328.]

Mayor.

5456. [17th cent.] Sulph. cast from the matrix. $1\frac{1}{4}$ in. [lxvi. 17.]

On the sea, a one-masted ship of war, the mainsail charged with the armorial bearings described on the shield in the previous seal, No. 5454.

SIGILV̄ · OFFICII · MAIOR · VILLE · HVNDREDE · DE
TENTERDEN.

Later Seal of the Mayoralty.

5457. [17th cent.] Sulph. cast from the matrix. 2 in. [lxvi. 18.]

On the sea, a three-masted ship of war in full sail to the l.

☆ : S' · OFFICII MAIORATVS VIL : ET HVND : DE
TENTERDEN :

Carved border.

THETFORD, *co. Norfolk.*

5458. [A.D. 1313.] Mottled-green : originally fine, edge chipped away. About 2⅜ in. when perfect. [Add. ch. 17,207.]

An embattled castle of elaborate design, the walls diapered, lozengy in a rough manner, keep triple-towered [with a flag; on the topmost tower], on a small side tower on the l. a knight with shield of arms and sword, on a similar tower on the r. [a trumpeter].   Thirteenth century style of work.

Legend wanting.

Cf. Blomefield, *History of Norfolk*, vol. ii., p. 134 ; Add. MS. 23,014, f. 70 *b.*

Second state.

5459. Sulph. cast from the matrix, which has been re-touched with deep outlines. 2⅜ in. [lxix. 46.]

This shows many details of the architecture wanting in the previous seal.   The shield of the knight is ornamented with a fretty device.

SIGILLVM · COMMVNE · BVRGENCIVM · DE · THEFORD · ☾ .

Beaded borders.

Cf. S. Lewis, *Topogr. Dict.*, vol. iv., p. 287.

Second Seal.

5460. [A.D. 1661.] Red : cracked and imperfect. ⅞ in. [Add. ch. 24,245.]

A triple-towered castle, charged with a shield of arms ; per pale, *dex.*, three lions passant guardant in pale, in chief a label of three points, THETFORD OF BATISHALL, *sin.*, chequy, THETFORD CANONS.

SIGILLVM · B   THETFORD.

TONBRIDGE, co. *Kent.*

A Doubtful Seal or Counterseal.

5461. Sulph. cast. ¼ in. [lxii. 94.]

A *rebus*, consisting of a *tun* surmounted by the letter T, and below it the word BRVGE. In the field, a sprig and two slipped leaves.

Free Grammar School, A.D. 1552.

5462. Sulph. cast from bent impression. 1⅜ in. [lxvi. 19.]

A shield of arms : a fess raguly betw. three boars' heads couped, SIR ANDREW JUDDE, knt., founder.

SIGILLVM · GVBER · LIBERÆ · SCOLÆ · ANDREÆ · JVDDE · MIL'.

Carved border.

TORRINGTON, *or* CHIPPING TORRINGTON,
co. *Devon.*

5463. [Early 15th cent.] Sulph. cast from the matrix. 1⁷⁄₁₆ in. [lxii. 11.]

On waves, a fleur-de-lis of elegant proportions, betw. two small text letters F, and two very small crosslets. The upper part of the border of the field is cusped or engrailed with ten points, eight of which are enriched with clusters of three pellets each.

: SIGILLŪ : CŌE · DE · CHIPYNGTORITON : COM̄ : DEVON.

The legend is preceded by a leopard's face, enraged. The letters DE, in *de* and *Devon*, are conjoined

Cabled borders.

S. Lewis, *Topogr. Dict.*, vol. iv., p. 324.

Borough.

5464. Sulph. cast from the matrix. ⅝ in. [lxii. 12.]

Design similar to that of the preceding seal. Two large and two small crosslets in the field.

❀ BOROUGH ❀ OF GREAT TORRINGTON.

TOTNES, co. *Devon.*

5465. Sulph. cast from fine, but cracked, impression. 2⅛ in. [lxii. 18.]

A triple-towered castle, masoned and domed, the side-towers topped with a knob, portcullis half-down. In the field on each side, a key. Background diapered with foliage.

    ❀ SIGILLUM ❀ COMUNITAT' ❀ MAGNE ❀ TOTTONIE ᴀᴋ

S. Lewis, *Topogr. Dict.*, vol. iv., p. 326.

Mayor.

5466. [15th cent.] Sulph. cast from chipped and indistinct impression. 1¼ in. [lxii. 17.]

On a mount, a castle, with embattled tower and walls, round-headed doorway with portcullis up, side towers spired ; in the field on each side, a beacon.

    SIGILLUM : OFFICIJ : MAIORATUS . TOTTONIE.

TRELLECK, *co. Monmouth.*

5467. [13th cent.] Sulph. cast from fine impression.   1⅛ in. [lxii. 19.]

A shield of arms : three chevrons, CLARE. Above the shield a trefoiled sprig, on the l. a crescent, on the r. a mullet with wavy points.

    ❀ S' : COMMVNITATIS : BVRGI · DE TRILL'.

Inner border beaded.

5468. Another. [D.C., F. 340.]

TRURO, *co. Cornwall.*

5469. [18th cent.] Sulph. cast from the matrix. 1 in. [lxi. 26.]

An ornamentally carved shield of arms : the base wavy, thereon a ship of three masts under sail, on each top-mast a banner of St. George, on the waves in base two fishes naiant in pale, TOWN OF TRURO.

S. Lewis, *Topogr. Dict.*, vol. iv., p. 336.

TUTBURY HONOUR, *cos. Stafford, Derby, etc.*

5470. [A.D. 173–] Red : *en placard* on a label. 1⅛ × 1 in. [Wol. ch. xi. 60.]

Oval : on a torse or wreath a hunting-horn of the Honour stringed and garnished, Crest of AGARD ; surmounted by a shield of arms : per pale, *dex.*, 1, 4. FRANCE (MODERN), 2, 3, ENGLAND, for HENRY IV. ; *sin.*, vair or vairé, FERRARS.

Motto in the field above :—EFFIGIS CORNV.

For a description of the horn and shield of arms, see Shaw, *History of Staffordshire,* vol. i., p. 44.

TWYNHAM, *co. Southampton.*

5471. [Late 13th cent.] Sulph. cast from the matrix. 2 in. [lxiv. 30.]

Our Lord, with cruciform nimbus, seated on a throne in a carved niche, with cinquefoiled arch crocketed and tabernacle-work of two orders at the sides ; lifting up the r. h. in benediction, in the l. h. a book. The base masoned ; field at the sides diapered lozengy.

S' : COMVNE : VILLE : XPI : ECCL'IE : DE : TWYNHAM.

Beaded borders.

S. Lewis, *Topogr. Dict.,* vol. i., p. 421.

Another Seal.

5472. Sulph. cast from a matrix. [lxiv. 31.]

This appears to be an unfinished copy of the previous seal, No. 5471, with slight variations.

No legend.

WALLINGFORD, *co. Berks.*

5473. [15th cent.] Sulph. cast from the matrix in possession of the corporation. 2⅜ in. [lviii. 55.]

A king, (perhaps intended to represent Edward the Confessor, in whose reign Wallingford became a royal prescriptive borough,) in plate armour with helmet, chapeau ; crest a lion of ENGLAND statant guardant crowned, the tail extended ; sword chained to neck, shield of arms : quarterly 1, 4, FRANCE (MODERN), 2, 3, ENGLAND ; riding a caparisoned horse at full speed to the r. over a *ford*, in allusion to the name of the town. In the field, over the horse's neck, the letter *t*, under the neck, the letter *h*.

SIGILLUM ✿ ⚜ ⚜ ✿ ⚜ ✿ ⚜ ✿ ⚜ ✿ COMUNE ⚜ ✿ DE ⚜ ✿ ⚜ ✿ ✿ ⚜ ⚜ ✿ WALLINGFORD ✿ ⚜ ⚜ ✿

Cabled borders.

S. Lewis, *Topogr. Dict.,* vol. iv., p. 368.

Later Seal.

5474. [18th cent.] Sulph. cast from the matrix. $1\frac{3}{8} \times 1\frac{1}{4}$ in. [lix. 71.]

Oval : an oval shield of arms elegantly carved : a portcullis, chained and ringed.

❀ THE · SEAL · OF · THE · BOROUGH · OF · WALLINGFORD.

WALSALL, *co. Stafford.*

5475. [Late 15th cent.] Sulph. cast from a fine impression, or the matrix. $1\frac{1}{8}$ in. [lxxii. 55.]

A shield of arms : quarterly, 1, 4, FRANCE (MODERN), 2, 3, *E*NGLAND, for Henry V. or VI. ? ensigned with an open coronet of five fleurs-de-lis. Supporters, two lions sejant guardant tails flory interlinked in base.

S' CŌE MAIORIS ᶎ COMUNITATIS VILLE DÑI REG' DE WALSAL.

Carved border.

S. Lewis, *Topogr. Dict.*, vol. iv., p. 372.

WANGFORD, *or* WAYNFORD HUNDRED, *co. Suffolk.*

5476. [15th cent.] Sulph. cast. 1 in. [lxxii. 21.]

Across the field in two lines the legend HUNDR——DE WAYNFORD. Over the legend a crown fleury of three points with a cusp in the field on each side. Below the legend a third cusp from which spring two slipped trefoils.

· S : REGIS : IN.: COMIT' . SUFF .

Archæol. Journ., vol. xi., 31.

WANTAGE, *or* WANTING, *co. Berks.*
Seal of the Town Lands for the Free Grammar School, A.D. 1598.

5477. Sulph. cast, tinted red, from the matrix. $1\frac{3}{8}$ in. [xxxv. 154.]

On the r. a man, standing turned to the l., with hat and tunic, giving a coin to a beggar, kneeling, and holding out his hat to receive it ; on a mount replenished with herbage and flowers.

Legend in two concentric circles :—

Outer circle :—⚜ THE + SEALE + OF + THE + TOWNE + LANDES + OF + WANTING.

Inner circle :—B A R K S. ˙ The letters .alternating with a Bourchier knot,.above and below, and 'a water-bouget on each side.

N. Carlisle, *Endowed Grammar Schools,* vol. i., p. 43 ; W. N. Clarke, *Paroch. Topogr. of the Hund. of Wanting,* 1824, p. 184.

5478. Another. [xlvii. 915.]

Laing's *MS. Catal.,* No. 270. ˙

. · · · . **WAREHAM.** *co. Dorset.*

5479. [18th cent.] Sulph. cast from the matrix. ˙1⅛ in. [lxii. 58.]

An .ornamental shield of arms : a crescent. enclosing an estoile of six points betw. three fleurs-de-lis: reversed, TOWN OF WAREHAM.. · · · .

· ⚜ SIGILLVM : VILLÆ : & : BVRGI : DE WAREHAM. ˙

Carved border. ·

S. Lewis, *Topogr. Dict.,* vol. iv., p. 386.

WARWICK, *co. Warwick.*

˙**5480.** [13th cent.]˙ Sulph. cast from fine impression, or the matrix. 2½ in. [lxxiii. 35.]

A castle, with masoned and embattled wall, round side-towers with tall round-headed windows and battlements, and circular wall masoned and embattled in base. The central tower or keep is of peculiar form, and is charged with a shield of arms : a bar, betw. in chief three crosslets, in base chequy a chevron. This is a compound coat, the chief referring to BEAUCHAMP, and the base to GUY, EARL OF WARWICK. On each side of the central tower a spire topped with a cross. On each of the side-towers a watchman, half-length, blowing a horn ; that on the l. has the appearance of being double. The doorway has a pointed arch. In the field on the l. an estoile of six points, on the r. a crescent, each betw. two small :pierced sixfoils in pale.

⚜ SIGILLVM COMMVNITATIS · WARWYCHIE ⚜

At the end of the legend, on the sprig a small bird. ˙ ˙

Carved borders.

S. Lewis, *Topogr. Dict.,* vol. iv., p. 396.- ——--

WELLS, *co. Somerset.*

5481. [13th cent.] Recent impressions in red sealing-wax from the matrix. 2¼ in. With marks of the studs used for steadying the two sides. [xxxv. 364 A. B.]

∅. The city of Wells represented by a bridge of three round-headed arches and with houses upon it; behind are five niches with round-headed arches, the two outside niches containing doors, the central one, a man standing; over them four towers. Over these Our Lord, half-length, with cruciform nimbus, issuing from clouds, betw. the sun as a human head, full-face, surrounded by an invecked nimbus, on the l., and the crescent moon, as a head in profile, on the r.

SIGILLUM : COMMVNE : BVRGI : WELLIE : ⚓

℞. In base, a *well* or fountain with water issuing thereout, in which is a pike or lucy naiant to the r. and a crane pecking it on the r. Over the well, on a mount a tree of elaborate design with twisted branches and large trefoiled leaves. On the foliage and in the field are eight birds of varying sizes.

✠ ANDREA : FAMVLOS : MORE : TVERE : TVOS ⚓

Beaded borders.

Small Seal.

5482. [18th cent.] Sulph. cast from the matrix. 1³⁄₁₆ × 1 in. [lxxi. 75.]

Oval: an ornamentally carved shield of arms : per fess in base three *wells* two and one, masoned, in chief a tree issuant from the fess line, CITY OF WELLS.

HOC FONTE DERIVATA COPIA IN PATRIAM POPULUMQUE RUIT.

Cf. Horat. *Carm.* iii., 6, 19.

S. Lewis, *Topogr. Dict.*, vol. iv., p. 418.

Steward's Office.

5483. [14th cent.] Sulph. cast from the matrix. 1½ in. [lxxi. 74.]

A tree with five small birds on the branches. In base, a *well* with a pike naiant, and two birds pecking at it.

✠ S' OFFICII SENESCALLI COMVNITATIS BVRGI WELLIE.

Inner border carved.

WENLOCK, *co. Salop.*

5484. [15th cent.] Sulph. cast from the matrix. 1¾ in. [lxxi. 38.]

In three niches with carved canopies, the Trinity, betw. on the l., St. Milburga, Patroness of the town and abbey, standing crowned, in the r. h. a book, in the l. an ornamental pastoral staff, at her feet a lion or other animal sejant; on the r., St. Michael the Archangel, with expanded wings, shield charged with a cross, and sword, in combat with the Dragon. In base, on herbage under three round-headed arches, as many shields of arms: centre, a lion rampant, ROGER DE MONTGOMERY, benefactor; l., a stag tripping; r., a chevron betw. three blackamoors' heads, WENLOCK. In the field outside the niches, on the l., a stag's head erased and the legend ROG', on the r., a crutch or bracket and the legend HOLA.

✠ SIGILLUM : CŌMUNE : BURGI : DE ⁚ WENLOK :

Cabled borders.

S. Lewis, *Topogr. Dict.*, vol. iv., p. 425.

WESTBURY, *co. Wilts.*

5485. [16th cent.] Sulph. cast from the matrix. 1¾ × 1⅝ in. [lxxiii. 87.]

Oval: a shield of arms: quarterly, a cross, alternately fleury and patonce, within a bordure charged with twenty lioncels rampant, all counterchanged, TOWN OF WESTBURY. Background coarsely hatched.

✠ SIGILLVM ✲ MAIORIS ✲ ET ✲ BVRGEN ✲ DE ✲ WESTBVRIE.

Carved border, with four flowers in cross.

S. Lewis, *Topogr. Dict.*, vol. iv., p. 428.

WESTMINSTER, *co. Middlesex.*

Seals of the Statute Staple, see Nos. 1095–1106.

WEYMOUTH, *including* MELCOMBE-REGIS, *co. Dorset.*

Common Seal of Melcombe Regis.

5486. [Early 14th cent.] Sulph. cast from fine impression, or the matrix. 1⅞ in. [lxii. 59.]

An ancient ship, with starboard rudder on the r., single mast with embattled crow's nest and two castles, at each end a fir-tree or sprig. In the field on each side of the mast a shield of arms : quarterly, 1, 4, a lion rampant, LEON, 2, 3, a triple-towered castle, CASTILE, in reference to King Edward II., in whose time the town attained importance.

✚ SIGILLVM : COMVNIE : DE MELCOMA :

Mayoralty of Melcombe-Regis.

5487. [13th cent.] Sulph. cast from the matrix. 1½ in. [lxii. 60.]

A shield of arms of ENGLAND, suspended by a hanked strap betw. two floral devices.

⚲ SIGILL: · MAIORATVS · VILL' · D: MELCOVB REG'.

Town of Weymouth and Melcombe-Regis.

5488. [17th cent.] Sulph. cast from the matrix. 2¼ in. [lxii. 61.]

A shield of arms : on the waves of the sea in base, a ship of three masts tackled and rigged, on the fore and mizen masts two square banners, on the first three lions passant guardant, in pale, ENGLAND ; on the second, quarterly, 1, (4), a lion rampant, 2, (3), a castle, (the 3rd and 4th left blank), for Edward II., see the preceding seal, No. 5486. On the hull of the vessel an escutcheon, per fess, in chief three chevrons, in base as many lions passant guardant in pale, UNITED TOWNS OF WEYMOUTH AND MELCOMBE-REGIS.

✚ SIGILLVM ☆ WILLE ☆ DE ☆ WAYMOTH ☆ ET ☆ MELCOMBE ⚲ REGIS.

Beaded borders.

Mayor of Weymouth and Melcombe-Regis.

5489. [17th cent.] Sulph. cast from the matrix. 2¼ in. [lxii. 64.]

An ornamental shield of arms : a bridge of three arches, masoned and double embattled, standing in the sea, in chief an escutcheon bearing in chief three chevronels, in base as many lions passant guardant in pale, cf. No. 5488.

✚ SIGILLVM ⚲ MAYIOR (*sic*) ⚲ DE ⚲ WAYMOTH ⚲ ET. ⚲ MELCOMBE ⚲ REGIS.

Beaded borders.

Another Seal.

5490. [17th cent.] Sulph. cast from fine impression. 1¾ in. [lxii. 62.]

An ornamental shield of arms: a bridge of three arches, faintly masoned and double embattled, standing in the sea, in chief an escutcheon bearing three lions passant guardant in pale.

✠ WAYMOVTH ❀ AND ❀ MELCOMBE ❀ REGIS ❀

Carved borders.

Cf. S. Lewis, *Topogr. Dict.*, vol. iv., p. 444.

Another Seal.

5491. [17th cent.] Sulph. cast from the matrix. 1¼ in. [lxii. 63.]

A shield of arms as in the preceding seal, No. 5490. Betw. three cherubim.

❀ WAYMOVTH AND MELCOMB REGIS.

Carved border.

S. Lewis, *Topogr. Dict.*, vol. iv., p. 444.

Admiralty of Melcombe-Regis.
First Seal.

5492. [16th cent.] Sulph. cast from fine impression. 1⅚ in. [D.C., H. 175.]

A three-masted rigged ship of war on the sea, yards set obliquely, sails furled, beacon or crow's nest on the maintop, on the foremast a flag charged with the cross of St. George, the other masts bear each a plain flag. On the mainmast a shield of arms, as described in No. 5488.

No legend.

Carved border.

S. Lewis, *Topogr. Dict.*, vol. iv., p. 442.

Later Seal for Weymouth and Melcombe-Regis.

5493. [17th cent.] Sulph. cast from the matrix. 2¼ in. [lxii. 65.]

A three-masted rigged ship of war on the sea, fore and mizen yards set obliquely and sails furled, main-sail set, charged with the armorial bearings described in the previous seal, No. 5489. Each mast topped with a cross and flag, and having a round-top garnished with handspikes. The anchor is hanging over the bows. Figure-head, a dragon's head.

SIGILLVM ♣ ADMIRALIS ♣ DE ♣ WAYMOUTH ✰ ET ✰ MELCOMBE ✰ REGIS.

Inner border cabled, outer border beaded.

WIGAN, *co. Lancaster.*

5494. [13th cent.]   Sulph. cast from the matrix.   I⅛ in.
[lxvi. 43.]

A church-like building, perhaps a town hall, with central
spire topped with a cross, betw. two trees.

✠ SIGILLUM : DE : WYGAN.

Cf. S. Lewis, *Topogr. Dict.*, vol. iv., p. 468.

Later Seal.

5495. [17th cent.]   Sulph. cast from cracked impression.
2 × I½ in.   [lxvi. 44.]

Oval: a church-like building, with square windows, bell-
tower in centre, and at the gables, on the l. a knob, on the r.
a flag; set on an arcade of three round-headed arches, with
a half-arch on each side.   In foreground a cross on four
steps.

: ✿ : SIGILLVM . COMVNE VILLÆ ET BVRGI DE WIGAN.

Cabled borders.

S. Lewis, *Topogr. Dict.*, vol. iv., p. 468.

WILTON, *co. Wilts.*

5496. [Late 14th cent.]   Recent impression in red sealing-
wax, from the matrix.   I½ × I¹¹⁄₁₆ in.   [xxxix. 52.]

Pointed oval: a shrine, elegantly ornamented, in a canopied
shrine.   Above it an angel, swinging a censer, and a shield of
arms of ENGLAND.   Background replenished with sprigs of
foliage and flowers.   In base, under a round-headed arch
with masonry at the side, a female figure, half-length, with
cap and mantle, praying.   Inner border of the field engrailed.

✠ SIGILLŪ ✠ COMUNE ✠ BURGENS' ✠ DE ✠ WILTON ✠.

Cabled borders.

S. Lewis, *Topogr. Dict.*, vol. iv., p. 479.

5497. Sulph. cast from injured impression.   [xlvii. 919.]

Laing's *MS. Catal.*, No. 387.

Mayoralty.

5498. [Late 14th cent.]   Recent impression in red wax,
from the matrix.   I¾ in.   [xxxiv. 53.]

The coronation of the Virgin, in a carved niche with triple canopy and tabernacle-work at the side. Over the canopy a shield of arms : *E*NGLAND.

S : MAⁱORITATIS : BURG DE WILTON.

The letters DE, of *de*, are conjoined.

5500. Sulph. cast from fine impression. [lxxiii. 88.]

WILTSHIRE.

ROBERT DYNLEY, *Sheriff*, A.D. 1392.

5501. Brown : very imperfect, and injured by pressure. ¾ in. [Harl. ch. 49 G. 13.]

A shield of arms, couché to the left : a fess (or two bars), in chief two mullets, DYNELEY, surmounted by a triple-towered castle, betw. the initial letters : R. D. On each side of the shield a small sprig of foliage.

Seal for the subsidy on cloth, see No. 1062.

WINCHELSEA, *co. Sussex*.

5502. [Late 13th cent.] Pale-brown wax, varnished a dark-brown colour : chipped. 3½ in. [Egert. ch. 396.]

∅. On waves, a one-masted ship, with mainsail furled on the yard, a mariner climbing up the rigging, castle at the fore and stern embattled ; in the forecastle, which is on the r., a flag, on the castle at the stern two trumpeters, and below them, under a pointed arch, the steersman directing the side rudder, three mariners on board hauling ropes. In the field a shield of arms : ENGLAND ; above the yard on the l. a crescent, on the r. an estoile.

SIGILLVM : BARONVM : DOMINI : REGIS :
ANGLIE : DE : WINCHELLESE :

℞. An elaborate design representing on waves in base a tower of two storeys. In the lower storey, the pointed arched doorway is open and contains an ecclesiastic, seated, to the r. and a suppliant, with hands uplifted in prayer before him, on the r. This subject appears to have been impressed deeply by a moveable and separate part of the matrix. Above, in the second storey, a narrow rectangular window, also apparently impressed by a moveable matrix, a saint standing full-length, holding a palm-branch. Over this, an angular embattled tower, on which is a banner-flag charged with three chevrons, and also a watchman, half-length to the l., holding a lantern.

Before him, on the l. in the field a shield of arms of ENGLAND. On each side of this tower, in base, are houses representing the town of Winchelsea. On the l. h. side of the tower two gothic niches with pointed arches, canopies pinnacled and crocketed, on that on the l. a bird, behind the other a tall spire, pinnacled and crocketed, and topped with a cross. The two niches contain on the r. St. GILES, seated to the l., with a fawn leaping up to him, and a tree, on the l. a huntsman with a bow in the l. and a horn in the r. h., and a tree, from moveable matrices. On the r. h. side of the tower three gothic niches with pointed arches, canopies pinnacled and crocketed, and behind the middle niche a tall spire. These three niches contain a representation of THOMAS BECKET'S martyrdom. This also appears to be from a moveable matrix. Cf. Nos. 1373, 1374 and 1377 in Vol. I., Plate ix.; 2688, 2799, and 4061.

Legend on a bevelled edge indistinct in places, but, when perfect, it reads in two rhyming hexameter verses :—

⁜ EGIDIO : THOME : LAVDVM : PLEBS : CANTICA : PME : NE : SIT : IN : ANGARIA : GREX : SVVS : AMNE : VIA.

Beaded borders.

W. Boys, *History of Sandwich*, pp. 814, 815.

5503. [A.D. 1329.] Green: fine fragments. [Add. ch. 20,166.]

5504. [A.D. 1342.] Green: fine fragment. [Add. ch. 20,174.]

Second Seal.

5505. [14th cent.] Green: fine originally, now cracked and chipped, and drilled with a large hole at the top for suspension. [L. ii.]

Ø. As before.

R. A close copy of the *rev.* of the preceding seal with some slight differences of measurement. The figures in the moveable parts of the central tower are differently designed, and on the l., in the place of the huntsman, the figures of St. Giles and the fawn have been repeated. The depths of the parts which are from moveable matrices in the first seal, here are much less, and the designs are probably not separable.

W. Boys, *History of Sandwich*, pl. p. 782, p. 815; Add. MS. 6331, f. 142, fig. 6; S. Lewis, *Topogr. Dict.*, vol. iv., p. 493.

5506. Recent impression in red sealing-wax from the " brass matrix in possession of Mr. Dean, 1 Upper Wimpole Street, 11th April, 1832." [xxxv. 92.]

5507. Sulph. cast. [lxxii. 112.]

Mayoralty.

5508. [15th cent.] Sulph. cast from the matrix. 1⅛ in. [lxxii. 100.]

A shield of arms: CINQUE PORTS, see No. 4885. Betw. three wyverns.

✠ : SIGILLVM : *æ* : MAIORATVS : *æ* : VILLE :·*æ* : DE : *æ* : WYNCHELSE :

W. Boys, *History of Sandwich*, pl. p. 772, fig. 7.

Seal of the Ports of Winchelsea, Rye, and ————.

5509. [A.D. 1366.] Green: fine, but very imperfect. About 1 in. when perfect. [Add. ch. 20,189.]

A shield of arms: field diapered lozengy, a fleur-de-lis. Betw. three sprigs of foliage.

. . . . . [P]ORTVB$ · DE · WYNCHILSE · RY . . . .

WINCHESTER, *co. Southampton.*

Mayoralty.

5510. [17th cent.] Sulph. cast from chipped impression. 1 in. [xxxvii. 20.]

A triple-towered castle, masoned and embattled, round-headed doorway, out of each side tower a demi-lion rampant, with the paw placed on a central pinnacle topped with a cross.

SIGILLVM · MAIORATVS · WINTONIE.

Seal " pro recognitione debitorum," see No. 1089.

Seal for delivery of wool and hides, see No. 1164.

Winchester College of St. Mary, A.D. 1387.

5511. Sulph. cast from the matrix. 3 in. [D.C., F. 77.]

Pointed oval: in two niches with canopies, on the r. St. Paul, seated with sword and book, on the l. St. Peter with key and book. Over these, in a niche with pinnacled and crocketed canopy betw. two carved and lower canopies, the Annunciation of the Virgin, with a lily-flower growing in a pot betw. the Virgin on the r., standing, and the archangel Gabriel, with wings expanded, kneeling, on the l., holding a scroll inscribed :—AUE MARIA. On the tabernacle-work at the sides, two shields of arms : two chevronels betw. three roses, Bishop WILLIAM OF WYKEHAM. The plinth or string-course, below the niche, is inscribed :—WIKEH'M · EPS ·. FVDATOR. In base

P 2

under a carved round-headed arch, the bishop-founder, half-length, with mitre and pastoral staff, in prayer. On each side, in a round-headed window, a half-length figure in prayer, with nimbus. Outside, on each side a slipped rose.

SIG' : CŌE : COLLEGII : VOCATI : SCE : MARIE : COLLEGIE : OF . WYNCHESTRE : PPE : WYNTON.

Cf. the seal of New College, Oxford, No. 5275.

WINDSOR, *co. Berks.*

5512. [Late 13th cent.]   Sulph. cast from the matrix. 2¼ in.   [lviii. 57.]

A triple-towered castle, masoned and embattled. In the field on each side a shield of arms : l., ENGLAND for EDWARD I. ; r. per pale, *dex.*, ENGLAND dimidiated, *sin.*, per fess, in chief LEON, in base CASTILE, for Qu. ELEANOR OF CASTILE, being a dimidiation of her whole shield of quarterly LEON and CASTILE.

S' ꙮ COMMVNE ꙮ BVRGENSIVM ꙮ WYND'LSORIE.

Beaded borders.

S. Lewis, *Topogr. Dict.*, vol. iv., p. 513.

Mayor of the Borough of New Windsor.

5513. [15th cent.]   Sulph. cast from the matrix.   1¾ in. [lviii. 58.]

A castle in base, embattled and surmounted by three towers, the middle tower or keep of two storeys. In the centre over the castle a stag's head cabossed, and having betw. the antlers a shield of arms : quarterly, 1, 4, FRANCE, (MODERN), 2, 3, ENGLAND ; on the l. in the field, the letter W, on the r., B.   Background replenished with sprigs of foliage.

SIGILLŪ MAIORIS BURGI DE NOVA WYNDESORE.

Beaded borders.

S. Lewis, *Topogr. Dict.*, vol. iv., p. 507.

Windsor Castle.

5514. [15th cent.]   Plaster cast from mould.   1¼ in. [xxxvi. 175.]

A stag's head cabossed, having betw. the antlers a triple-towered castle, masoned and embattled, with round-headed portal.   Inner edge cusped.

• SIGILLVM : CASTRI : DE : WYNDESORE.

College Seal, ad causas.

5515. [15th cent.] Sulph. cast from somewhat indistinct impression. 2⅛ × 1¼ in. [lix. 73.]

Pointed oval : within a cusped border a shield of arms : a cross of St. George. Encircled by a garter inscribed with the motto of the Order.

HONY · SOIT · QE · MAL · I · PENSE.

The whole upheld by an angel descending from clouds, with expanded wings. Above the angel an uncertain design, perhaps an Agnus Dei.

    SIGILLVM : COLLEGII : DE : WYNDESORES : AD : CAUSAS.

WIRKSWORTH, *co. Derby.*

Free Grammar School, c. A.D. 1565.

5516. Sulph. cast tinted red, from a cracked mould made from the matrix. 2⅜ × 1¾ in. [xxxv. 155.]

Oval : the founder, Anthony Gell of Hopton, Esq., standing with the r. h. raised, in the l. h. a glove, and wearing flat cap, academical gown, and ruff collar. In base, a carved shield of arms : three mullets in bend, (pierced and counterchanged), GELL. Crest, on a wreath a greyhound statant.

Legend on a raised band :—

✸ : IMAGO : ANTHONII : GELL : ✿ ✿ : DE : HOPTON : ARMIGERI.

N. Carlisle, *Endowed Grammar Schools*, vol. i., p. 239.

5517. Another. [xlvii. 916.]

Laing's *MS. Catal.*, No. 276.

5518. Sulph. cast. [D.C., H. 74.]

WISBECH, *co. Cambridge.*

5519. [16th cent.] Sulph. cast from the matrix. 1¾ in. [xlvii. 920.]

In a double niche of late style, with triangular pediments and turned columns, full-length figures of St. Peter with nimbus, book, and key on the l., and St. Paul with nimbus, sword, and book on the. r. The background of the seal replenished with wavy sprigs of foliage.

9 SIGILLVM 9 COMMVNE 9 9 INHABITANCIVM 9 VILLE 9
DE 9 WISBECHE.

Laing's *MS. Catal.*, No. 386 ; S. Lewis, *Topogr. Dict.*, vol. iv., p. 523.

5520. Another, fine. [lx. 61.]

.**5521.** Another, from an impression injured in parts by pressure. [D.C., H. 48.]

Mayor, A.D. 1740.

5522. Sulph. cast from the matrix. $1\frac{1}{8}$ in.   [lx, 62.]

Two keys with ornamental handles, in saltire, wards in chief ; betw. the figures of the date 174, in chief, o in base. Beaded border.

Privy Seal of the Mayor.

5523. Sulph. cast from the matrix. $\frac{7}{8}$ in. [lx. 63.]

Two keys in saltire, as in the preceding seal.

Town Clerk.

5524. Sulph. cast from the matrix. · $\frac{7}{8} \times \frac{4}{5}$ in.   [lx. 64.]

Oval : on a carved shield, two keys in saltire, as before. Legend on a buckled strap :—

BOROUGH OF WISBECH.

Castle.

Used by Sir John Colvile, Governor, A.D. 1409.

5525. Recent impression in red sealing-wax, (from the matrix belonging to C. R. Colvile, Esq., 1860.) 1 in. [xxxix. 58.]

A castle with two side towers and a keep of three towers, masoned and embattled, the windows of a peculiar quatrefoiled shape.

ᴋ SIGILLVM ᴋ ᴋ CASTRI ᴋ DE ᴋ WISEBECH ᴋ

Beaded borders.

WOKINGHAM, co. Berks.

5526. [17th cent.]   Sulph. cast. $\frac{7}{8}$ in.   [lix. 74.]

An acorn, slipped and leaved.

WOKINGHAM.

Carved border.

S. Lewis, *Topogr. Dict.*, vol. iv., p. 535.

WOLVERHAMPTON, co. Stafford.

5527. [Modern.]   Recent proof impression in red sealing-wax from the matrix. $2\frac{1}{4}$ in. [xliv. 155.]

Within a carved quatrefoil, and on a back-ground replenished with sprigs of trefoiled foliage, an allegorical shield of arms : on a chevron, betw. two cressets in chief and the "Wolverhampton cross" in base, an escutcheon charged with a saltire, on a canton a cross charged with a key. Behind the shield a mace and sword in saltire surmounted with a mural crown, and over them a Stafford knot. In base, two keys of St. Peter, patron saint of the town, with handles interlinked, upright in fess, on a scroll inscribed :—E TENEBRIS ORITUR LUX. On each side a shield of arms : l., EDWARD THE CONFESSOR, ensigned with an antique crown of five points ; r. quarterly 1, 4, barry of eight, a cross flory, GOWER, 2, 3, three leaves, LEVESON, ensigned with a coronet of five leaves. The heraldic colours on the three shields are indicated in the usual manner.

✤ THE : SEAL : OF : THE : MAYOR : ALDERMEN : AND : BURGESSES : OF : THE : BOROUGH : OF : WOLVERHAMPTON.

WORCESTER, *co. Worcester.*

5528. [13th cent.] Sulph. cast from the matrix ; chipped. 2$\frac{7}{16}$ in. [D.C., F. 635.]

A peculiar and irregular view of the cathedral, with central spire topped with an orb and cross, round-headed doorway with hinged folding doors closed, two spires with large crosses, two with small crosses and three storeys of arcaded work. In base a round wall, embattled and masoned.

SIGILLVM : COMMVNE : CIVIVM : WIGORNIE · ᴙ

Beaded borders.

Valentine Green, *History of Worcester*, vol. ii., p. 113 ; S. Lewis, *Topogr. Dict.*, vol. iv., p. 563.

5529. Another, fine. [lxxiv. 4.]

Seal of the Statute Merchant, see No. 1094.

WYCOMBE, HIGH-WYCOMBE, *or* CHIPPING-WYCOMBE, *co. Buckingham.*

5530. [16th cent.] Sulph. cast from the matrix. 1$\frac{3}{8}$ in. [lix. 85.]

A swan rising, with expanded wings, ducally gorged, chained and ringed, BUCKINGHAM.

BVRGVS · DE · CHEPINGE · WICOMBE · IN · COM · BVCK ✿ · . · ✿ · . · ✿

Carved borders.

Another Seal.

5531. Sulph. cast from the matrix.　1⅜ × 1¼ in.
Oval : a swan, as before.

✠ BVRGVS DE CHEPPING WYCOMBE IN COM BVCK.

S. Lewis, *Topogr. Dict.*, vol. iv., p. 584.

YARMOUTH, *I. of Wight, co. Southampton.*

5532. [18th cent.]　Sulph. cast from the matrix.　1⁷⁄₁₆ in.
[lxiv. 35.]

On the sea, a three-masted ship of war, sails furled.

✠ S . COMMV ·:· HG ·:· DE ·:· ERE : MVE ᴍ ᴍ
Beaded border. ·

S. Lewis, *Topogr. Dict.*, vol. iv., p. 591.

YARMOUTH, *co. Norfolk.*

5533. [13th cent.]　Sulph. cast from the *obv.* only of the
matrix, which appears to be very much worn.　2⅜ in.　[lxix.
61.]

∅. On the waves, with three fishes (herrings ?) naiant, two
and one, a ship of one mast, with embattled crow's-nest, and
castle, two sailors on the yard, furling the main-sail, trumpeter
in the castle on the r., and below him the steersman governing
the rudder, one mariner on board hauling a rope.

SIGILLVM : COMVNITATIS : DE : GERNEMVTHA :

5534. Sulph. cast of the *rev.* only.　[D.C., E. 50.]

℞. St. Nicholas, the Archbishop, patron saint of the town
and parish, seated on a carved bench, with mitre, lifting up
the r. h. in benediction, in the l. h. a pastoral staff.　Feet on
a projecting foot-board.　On each side a flying angel, with
flowing drapery and expanded wings, swinging a censer.

✠ O : PASTOR : VERE : TIBI : SVBIECTIS : MISERERE ᴍ ᴍ

W. Boys, *History of Sandwich*, vol. ii., p. 774, fig. 1; S. Lewis, *Topogr.
Dict.*, vol. iv., p. 593.

Bailiffs.

5535. [15th cent.]　Sulph. cast from the matrix.　2¹⁄₁₆ in.
[lxix. 62.]

On the sea, a one-masted ship of war, round-top and
pennon, flag at the peak, charged with a cross of ST.

GEORGE, flag at stern with arms of the CINQUEPORTS, mainsail set, charged with the ROYAL ARMS OF ENGLAND used in the fifteenth century, viz., quarterly, 1, 4, FRANCE (MODERN), 2, 3, ENGLAND. Anchor hanging over the side. The field replenished with flowers and foliage, wheatears, etc.

IHC ⚹ ✿ SIGILLUM ⚹ ✿ OFFICIJ ⚹ ✿ BALLIUOR ⚹ ✿
VILLE ⚹ ✿ MAGNE ⚹ ✿ JERNEMUTH ⚹ ✿

- Coloured drawing in Add. MS. 23,023, f. 159 *b* (Blomefield's *Norfolk*).

5536. [A.D. 1522.] Red: only a fragment of the central part. [Add. ch. 14,967.]

. . . . . . VILL . . . .

Comptroller, or the Herring Chamber.

5537. [15th cent.] Recent impression in red sealing-wax from the matrix. 1 in. [xxxv. 177.]

A shield of arms: a herring hauriant in pale, contourné. Within a pointed trefoil.

S' · OFIC : CŌT' ROTULAT Ī : NAUE : ZERNMUTH.

Cabled borders.

Coloured drawing in Add. MS. 23,023, f. 131 (Blomefield's *Norfolk*).

YEOVIL, *co. Somerset.*

5538. [15th cent.] Sulph. cast from the matrix. $2\frac{5}{16}$ in. [D.C., G. 43.]

In a carved niche, of late style, with trefoiled canopy pinnacled and crocketed, St. John Baptist, patron saint of the church and town, standing on a corbel, the Agnus Dei on a plaque in the l. h., and pointing to it with the r. h. In the field on each side, a conventional tree.

✠ SIGILLUM : COMUNITATIS + UILLE + DE + YEUELE +
FACTUM + IN + HONORE + SC̄I + IOH̄IS.

Beaded borders.

S. Lewis, *Topogr. Dict.*, vol. iv., p. 597.

5539. Another. [lxxi. 79.]

YORK, *County of.*
RICHARD HASTYNGES, *Sheriff,* A.D. 1426.

5540. Dark-green: imperfect and indistinct. About $\frac{3}{4}$ in. when perfect. [Add. ch. 16,911.]

A shield of arms, *couché*: a maunch, HASTINGS. Over the shield, a castle or gateway betw. two side towers. In the field on each side, a sprig.

Cabled border.

ROBERT CONSTABLE, *Sheriff*, A.D. 1461.

5541. Dark-green : a fragment. About ¾ in. when perfect. [Add. ch. 16,952.]

A triple-towered castle, embattled, round-headed portal, portcullis half-down. In the field on each side an initial, that on the r. wanting, on the l. b.

YORK, *co. York.*

5542. [A.D. 1100–1108.] Dark-green : fine, cracked and imperfect at the edges. 2¼ in. App. by closely woven bobbin, faded colours. [Add. ch. 10,636.]

Ø. A triple-towered castle of peculiar and archaic design, the wall diapered lozengy with embattled parapet, the towers embattled, each of the two at the sides having an arcade and gallery under the parapet, and being attached to the central tower by a flying buttress also embattled ; the central tower is enriched with lattice work or carved work in small squares betw. the battlements and the arcade, and below its arcade down to the base.

    ✠ [SI]GILLVM : EOL'E : SAN[CTI] : PET]RI : CAT . . . .
              EBORAC . . . .

R. St. Peter, patron of the cathedral and city, standing with nimbus, in the r. h. two keys over the shoulder, in the l. h. a long cross and banner flag.

    ✠ SIGILLVM · CIVIVM · EBORACI · FIDELES · R[EG]IS.

Figured from this impression, when not so imperfect as it now is, in Drake, *Eboracum*, appendix, pl. p. ci., fig. xxiii. ; cf. also *ib.*, p. 313, and pl. p. 381, fig. 1.

Second Seal.

5543. [13th cent.] Sulph. cast of the *obv.* and *rev.* from fine impression. 2⅜ in. [lxxv. 22, 23.]

Ø. A triple-towered castle of elaborate design, with embattled keep masoned and embattled ; the towers with pointed roofs, ornamental tiles or shingles, and each side tower topped with a flag split into three streamers, round-headed doorway in each tower, at each side a projecting stage, or bracket, also embattled.

    ✠ : SIGILLVM : CIVIVM : EBORACI

℞. St. Peter, standing on a carved bracket, in the r. h. two long keys with interlinked handles, over the shoulder, in the l. h. a banner flag, with three streamers, topped with a cross. On each side, on a bracket, an angel standing with expanded wings, and nimbus, holding a tall candle in a candlestick. Each of the brackets is united to the central one by a round-headed arch on which is a double fleur-de-lis.

✠ . : S' · B̄ . I ⦂ PETRI ⦂ PRINCIPIS · ⦂ · APOSTOLOR'.

Beaded borders.

Drake, *Eboracum*, pl., p. 381, fig. 1.

Privy Seal of the City.

5544. [15th cent.] Sulph. cast from imperfect impression. 1⅛ in. [lxxv. 26.]

A triple-towered castle, masoned and embattled, round-headed doorway with a key of St. Peter in it. Background diapered lozengy with a reticulated pattern. On each side a lion's face.

✿ S . . . . Є CIVITATIS ЄBO[R]ACI.

Beaded border.

Privy Seal of the Mayoralty.

5545. [15th cent.] Sulph. cast from fine impression or the matrix. 2 in. [D.C., G. 231.]

A shield of arms : diapré, on a cross five lioncels passant guardant, CITY OF YORK. Ensigned with an open coronet of three fleurs-de-lis and two triplets of pearls. Supporters, two ostrich feathers labelled.

SIGIL ✿ LUM ⦂ SECRETUM : OFFICI : MAIORATUS : CIUITAT⁹ : EBORACI.

Cabled borders.

Drake, *Eboracum*, pl., p. 381, fig. 3.

Seal of the Sessions.

5546. [17th cent.] Sulph. cast from the matrix. 1⅛ × 1 in. [lxxv. 27.]

Oval : a carved shield of arms : CITY OF YORK. As in No. 5545, but field plain.

✿ SIGNACVLVM ✿ EBORACENSIVM.

Cabled border.

Drake, *Eboracum*, pl., p. 381, fig. 4.

Seal "pro recognitione debitorum," see No. 1090.

Seal for customs, see No. 1166.

WALES.

PRINCES.

(including Princes and Principality of North Wales.)

LLEWELLYN, *Prince of North Wales.*

5547. [*circ.* A.D. 1222.] Creamy-white : fine, but very imperfect. About 3¼ in. when perfect. [Cott. ch. xxiv. 17.]

Ø. To the r. In armour : hauberk, surcoat, round helmet, broad sword in r. h., and scabbard at the waist, shield slung by a strap over the r. shoulder. Horse galloping with saddle, breast-band, and reins.

⊞ SIG . . . . LIE.

℞. A small oval counterseal. With mark of the handle. 1¼ × 1 in. Impression of an antique oval intaglio gem. A boar passant to the r. under a tree.

⊞ SIGILLUM SECRETVM LEWLINI.

5548. Sulph. casts of *obv.* and *rev.* of the preceding No. 5547. [D.C., D. 119, 120.]

EDWARD, *Prince of Wales, Earl of Chester, Count of Ponthieu and Montreuil, eldest son of King Edward I.; afterwards King of England.*

5549. Plaster casts, from fine, but chipped, impression. 3⅜ in. [lxxx. 48, 49.]

Ø. To the r. In armour : hauberk of mail, flowing surcoat, helmet with vizor closed, fan plume, sword, shield of arms slung by a strap over the r. shoulder. Horse galloping, caparisoned and plumed. Arms : ENGLAND, with a label of three points for difference.

EDWARDVS ILLVSTRIS REGIS ANGLIE FILIVS.

℞. Within a carvèd rosette 'of eight semicircular cusps, with a sunken trefoil in each spandril, and suspended by the strap or *guige* from an oak-tree between two slipped branches of the same, a shield of arms : ENGLAND, with a label of five points.

[ED]WARDVS PRINCEPS + WALLIE COMES CESTRIE ET
PONT . . IVI . .

Sandford, *Geneal. Hist.*, p. 122.

5550. [A.D. 1305.] Light-brown : fine, very imperfect. About 3¼ in. when perfect. [Harl. ch. 43 D. 12.]

Ø. . . . . LIE . . . .·. VS.

℞. . . . . EDW . . . . . . PRI . . . .

EDWARD, *Prince of Aquitaine and Wales, Duke of Cornwall, and Earl of Chester : " The Black Prince,"*
A.D. 1343–1376.

Great Seal.

5551. Plaster casts from fine impression. 3¼ in. [lxxx. 52, 53.]

Ø. The Prince, seated, with bordered robe, mantle, and sceptre, under an elaborately carved canopy with tabernacle work at the sides, enriched with pinnacles and crocketings. In the field on each side an ostrich feather labelled, over them the initial letters E. P.

S' . EDVARDI : PRIMOGENITI : REGIS : ANGL' : P'NCIPIS :
AQVITANNIE : ET : WALLIE : DVCIS : CORNVBIE : ET : COMITIS :
CESTRIE.

℞. To the l. In armour : coat of arms, helmet with chapeau and crest of England (the tail of the lion extended), sword, shield of arms. Horse, armorially caparisoned, galloping over broken ground. Arms : quarterly, FRANCE (ANCIENT), and ENGLAND, [a label of three points].

S'. EDVARDI : PRIMOGENITI : REGIS : ANGL' : P'NCIPIS :
AQVITANNIEꞮ: ET : WALLIE : DVCIS : CORNVBIE : ET : COMITIS :
CESTRIE ·

Sandford, *Geneal. Hist.*, p. 125, figs. 1, 2.

Another Seal.

5552. [A.D. 1360.] Sulph. cast, from fine impression. 2 in. [xlvii. 50.]

A shield of arms, as before, *couché;* crest on a helmet, and chapeau turned up ermine, a lion of ENGLAND as before ;

betw. two tall ostrich feathers, their tips bent outwards. All within a very elaborately carved gothic panel enriched with cusped tracery, and with ball-flowers along the edge.

: S : Edwardi Pmogeniti Regis Angl' Pncipis Wallie Duc' Cornub' : z Coil . Cestr'.

5553. Plaster cast, from chipped impression. [lxxx. 51.]

Seal of Arms.

5554. [A.D. 1350.] Plaster cast, from fine impression. 2 in. [lxxx. 71.]

A shield of arms *couché;* quarterly, FRANCE (ANCIENT), and ENGLAND, with a label of three points, for PRINCE EDWARD, crest on a helmet, damascened, and chapeau, turned-up ermine, a lion of ENGLAND, statant guardant crowned, the tail extended ; supported by two ostrich feathers labelled, their tips bent slightly outwards. All within a very elaborately carved gothic panel enriched with cusped tracery, and with ball-flowers along the edge.

[S'] . edwardi : primogeniti : regis : angl' : z : franc' : principis : wall' : ducis : cornub': z : comit' : cestr'.

Beaded borders.

Sandford, *Geneal. Hist.*, p. 125, fig. 3.

Another Seal.

5555. [A.D. 1360.] Red : very fine, edge chipped and imperfect. 1⅜ in. [Add. ch. 11,308.]

Within an elaborately carved gothic quatrefoiled panel, with tracery in the spandrils, and ball-flower ornamentation on the edge, a shield of arms: quarterly, 1, 4, FRANCE (ANCIENT), 2, 3, ENGLAND, over all a label of three points, EDWARD, PRINCE OF WALES. The shield upheld by a demi-angel, draped, and with expanded wings, under a carved canopy of three arches, pinnacled and crocketed. In the field on each side of the shield an ostrich feather.

✱Sigillu[m]✲✱Edward[i✲✱P]rincipis✲✱Wa . . . .

5556. Plaster cast, from fine impression, chipped at edge. [lxxx. 73.]

Another Seal.

5557. [A.D. 1361.]   Plaster cast, from fine impression.
1⅞ in.   [lxxx. 72.]

A shield of arms, as before, *couché;* helmet, chapeau, and crest as before, within a very finely carved gothic panel, with flowers and foliage branching out into the field.

-**S' Edwardi Pmogēiti regis Angl' z Frā Pncipis Wall' Ducis Cornub' z Coīt' Ceſt'.**

Another Seal.

5558. Plaster cast, from fine impression.   1½ in. [lxxx. 74.]

A shield of arms as before; above it a small lion rampant; at the sides two oak branches.   All within a finely carved gothic panel of eight cusps, traced, and enriched with ball-flower ornaments.

S' Edwardi P'mogēiti Regis Angl' z Franc' P'ncipis Wall' Ducis Cornub' z Comit' Ceſtr'.

HENRY IV—VII.

Seal for the Principality of North Wales.

5559. Uncoloured, opaque, somewhat darkened: fine, the lower part chipped.   With marks of the four pins used to steady the matrices during the making of the impression. 3¼ in. [xxxvii. 66.]

∅. To the r. on a field diapered lozengy with a reticulated pattern, enriched with a fleur-de-lis at each point of intersection, and with an ostrich feather labelled in each space (some of those at the sides truncated).   The Prince, in armour *cap-à-pie,* hauberk, cuirass, elbow and knee-plates; helmet closed, with the Crest of England, a lion statant guardant, crowned, tail extended; spurs, broad-sword brandished aloft in r. h., shield of arms slung by a strap over r. shoulder. Horse caparisoned with plate armour on neck and face, plume of three ostrich feathers on head, and ornamental breast-band and reins.   Arms: three lions passant reguardant in pale, tails placed betw. the hind legs and then up over the back, NORTH WALES.

z **Sig : henrici : Dei : grā : regis : angl' : z : franc' : z : Dñi : hibn]ie : principalitat' : sui : northwallie.**

℞. A shield of arms, as described in *obv.*, ensigned with cap-shaped coronet of five cinque-foiled roses, alternated, disposed with four fleurs-de-lis on nine engrailings or cusps. Supporters : in the field, on each side of the shield, a dragon, sejant addorsed, tail nowy, holding up an ostrich feather, labelled.

𝕾𝖎𝖌 : 𝖍𝖊𝖓𝖗𝖎𝖈': 𝖉𝖊𝖎 : 𝖌𝖗̄𝖆 : 𝖗𝖊𝖌𝖎𝖘 : 𝖆𝖓𝖌𝖑' . . . . 𝖘 :
𝖆 : 𝖉𝖓̄𝖎 : 𝖍𝖎𝖇𝖓𝖎𝖊 : 𝖕𝖗𝖎𝖓𝖈𝖎𝖕𝖆𝖑𝖎𝖙𝖆𝖙' : 𝖘𝖚𝖎 : 𝖓𝖔𝖗𝖙𝖍𝖜𝖆𝖑𝖑𝖎𝖊.

Inner borders carved and enriched with ball-flower ornamentation, with an inner beaded ring.

5560. Creamy-white : fine, but imperfect, the l. h. side wanting. [xlviii. 148.]
Legend indistinct in places.

5561. Creamy-white : fine, but imperfect, the lower part wanting. [xliii. 149.]

5562. Uncoloured, opaque : very imperfect, the lower part wanting. [Detached in box, Add. ch. 22,617—22,670.]

EDWARD, *Prince of Wales, Duke of Cornwall, and Earl of Chester, eldest son of King Edward IV. ; afterwards King Edward V.*
Seal for the Principality of North Wales.

5563. [A.D. 1476.] Light-brown : fine, much injured and very imperfect, edge and legend flaked away. About 3¼ in. when perfect. [Add. ch. 8526.]

∅. A copy of the *obv.* of preceding seal, with variations of detail, *viz.* roses in place of fleurs-de-lis on the diaper work, and one feather instead of three on the horse's head.

. . . . . 𝖜𝖆𝖗𝖉𝖎 : 𝖕𝖗𝖎 . . . .

℞. A copy of *rev.* of preceding seal, with lions guardant with tail between the hind legs, in place of dragons, supporting the shield.

Legend wanting.

JAMES I., *King of England.*
Seal for Wales. A.D. 1603–1610.

5564. Reddish-brown : fine, the *rev.* only. About 3 in. when perfect. [xlviii. 155.]

A shield of the ROYAL ARMS of ENGLAND as used by James I.; see No. 522, ensigned with a jewelled crown with coronet of three crosses pattées and two fleurs-de-lis, betw.

the initial letters, I. R.   In base on a mount replenished with herbage, the supporters, two lions sejant guardant, tail between the legs as in No. 5559, holding up an ostrich feather.   The sinister supporter wanting.

IA . . . . G ✰ FRA . . . . FIDEI ✰ DE[FENSOR✰].

Carved borders.

CHARLES, *Prince of Wales*,
Duke of York, Duke of Cornwall, Earl of Chester, &c.,
afterwards Charles I.

Great Seal.

5565. [A.D. ·1616–1625.]   Bronze-green : fine, injured in places, lower part of edge chipped.   4⅜ in.   [xlv. 15.]

Ø. To the r. on a mount replenished with herbage and flowering plants.   In plate armour *cap-à-pie* with cuirass, elbow and knee plates, glove, helmet open, coronet of five crosses pattées, (or perhaps three crosses and two fleurs-de-lis as below), broadsword brandished aloft in the r. h., shield of arms held in front over breast.   Horse caparisoned with plate armour on neck and face, plume of three ostrich feathers on head, sharp-pointed spur-like projections on forehead and back, and ornamental breast-band and reins.   Arms: quarterly, four lions passant guardant, counterchanged, LLEWELLYN AP GRIFFITH, last PRINCE OF NORTH-WALES.   The caparisons and harness, embroidered with a bordering of roses, bear, on the flank, a shield of arms: three garbs, CHESTER, over it a cordelière knot.   On the withers a shield of arms: fifteen bezants, five, four, three, two, and one in pile, CORNWALL.   In the field on the l., over the horse, a shield of the ROYAL ARMS OF ENGLAND, as borne by K. JAMES I., with a label of three points, PRINCE CHARLES, ensigned with a jewelled coronet of three crosses pattées and two fleurs-de-lis.

No legend, but a thick carved border.

℞. On a mount replenished with herbage and flowering plants, a shield of arms, as described in the *obv.* for PRINCE CHARLES, ensigned as before.   Royal supporters : *dex.*, a lion rampant guardant crowned, *sin.*, a wyvern or dragon, tail nowy, each with a label of three points for difference.   In base, on the mount, a plume of three ostrich feathers, within a coronet as above, and tied below with a scroll or label charged with an indistinct motto.

✿ MAGNVM · SIGILLVM · CAROLI · PRINCIPIS · WALLI . . .
· . . . . EBORVM · ET COMITIS
CESTRIÆ · ET C'.

Carved borders.

CHARLES II.
Seal for the Council of the Marches.

5566. [A.D. 1660–1685.]   Sulph. cast from fine impression. 1¾ in.   [D.C., A. 144.]

An oval shield of the ROYAL ARMS OF GREAT BRITAIN as used by Charles II., encircled with a Garter inscribed with the motto of the Order, over it a royal crown and the three ostrich feathers of the PRINCE OF WALES, between the initials C.R.   In base, on a scroll or label the inscription :—CON· CILIVM · MARCHIAR :

CAROLVS · II · D · G · MAG · BRIT · FRA · ET · HIB · REX · F · D ·

Carved border.

FREDERIC LOUIS *of Brunswick-Lunenburgh, Duke of Gloucester, Edinburgh, etc., Prince of Wales and Earl of Chester, Duke of Cornwall and Rothsay, K.G., son of K. George II.*

Seal for the Council.

5567. [A.D. 1729–1751.]   Recent impression in red sealing-wax from the matrix.   1¼ in.   [xxxvii. 35.]

The three ostrich-feathers of the PRINCE OF WALES, within an open jewelled coronet of three crosses pattées and two fleurs-de-lis, and a scroll or label inscribed with the motto :— ICH · DIEN.   All within a border of thirty-two rays alternately wavy and plain.

✠ PRO · CONSILIO · FREDERICI · PRINCIPIS · WALLIÆ · ET°.

GEORGE AUGUSTUS FREDERIC, *Prince of Wales and Earl of Chester,* A.D. 1762, *Duke of Cornwall and Rothsay, K.G., afterwards George IV.*

5568. [A.D. 1790.]   Red : imperfect and injured by pressure, *en placard* on a red silk riband.   1 × ¾ in.   [Egert. ch. 337.]

Oval: an oval shield of the ROYAL ARMS OF GREAT BRITAIN used by K. GEORGE III. before the Union, with a label of three points, for PRINCE GEORGE ; encircled with a Garter inscribed with the motto of the order, and ensigned with a cap-shaped coronet of three crosses pattées and two fleurs-de-lis.   Royal supporters : *dex.*, a lion rampant guardant crowned, *sin.*, an unicorn, gorged with a coronet, each differenced with a label of three points. In base, a scroll or label inscribed with the motto :—ICH DIEN.

Another Seal.

5569. [A.D. 1801–1820.] 1 × ⅞ in. [xliv. 23.]

Oval : an oval shield of the ROYAL ARMS OF GREAT BRITAIN, used by K. GEORGE III. after the Union with Ireland and discarding the arms of France in the second quarter, with a label of three points for PRINCE GEORGE, encircled with a Garter inscribed with the motto of the Order, and ensigned with a cap-shaped coronet as before. Royal supporters as in No. 5568, each differenced as above. In base a scroll or label inscribed with the usual motto.

ROYAL JUDICIAL SEAL FOR THE COUNTIES OF BRECKNOCK, RADNOR, AND GLAMORGAN.
JAMES I., A.D. 1603–1625.

5570. [A.D. 1606.] Bronze-green : imperfect and indistinct. [Add. ch. 26,508.]

For description see next seal, No. 5571.

5571. Bronze-green : fine, edge injured in places by pressure. About 3¾ in. when perfect. [xliii. 10.]

∅. To the l., on a mount replenished with herbage and flowers. In plate armour *cap-à-pie* with crown, holding aloft a sword in the r. h. Horse with plume of three ostrich feathers on the head, embroidered caparisons, and armourplates on head and neck, the tail bound with two tassels. In the field on the r., over the tail of the horse, the royal badge, a portcullis, chained and ringed, and ensigned with the crown

♣ IACOBVS ✿ DEI ✿ GRATIA ✿ ANGLIÆ ✿ SCOTIÆ ✿ FRANCIÆ ✿ ET ✿ HIBERNIÆ ✿ REX ✿ FIDEI ✿ DEFENSOR ✿

℞. A shield of the ROYAL ARMS OF ENGLAND as borne by K. JAMES I., see No. 522, ensigned with a royal crown. Supporters : *dex.*, a greyhound collared and ringed, *sin.*, an antelope, collared and chained. In base the PRINCE OF WALES' plume and crest of three ostrich feathers, labelled, the label inscribed, ICH · DIEN.

✿ SIGILLVM ✿ IVDICIALE ✿ PRO ✿ COMITATIBVS ✿ BREKNOK ✿ RADNOR ✿ ET ✿ GLAMORGAN. ✿

Carved borders.

ROYAL JUDICIAL SEAL, ETC., FOR THE COUNTIES OF CARMARTHEN, CARDIGAN, AND PEMBROKE.

EDWARD II.

Seal for livery of wool and hides at Carmarthen.

5572. Red sealing-wax impressions from the matrix in Dept. of British and Mediæval Antiquities.   1⅛ in.   [lxii. 79, 80.]

Ø. A shield of arms: ENGLAND, suspended by a strap from a hook, and betw. two wavy rose-branches.

✠ SIGILL' ✸ EDWARDI ✸ REGIS ✸ ANGL' ✸ APVD ✸ KERMERDYN ✸

R. Three lions passant guardant in pale, the charges in the armorial bearings of ENGLAND, not on a shield.

✠ PRO ✸ LANIS ✸ ET ✸ COREIS ✸ LIBERANDIS.

Beaded borders.

For other seals of this class, see Nos. 1159, *et seq.*

HENRY, *Prince of Wales, Duke of Aquitaine, Lancaster, and Cornwall, Earl of Chester, and Lord of Carmarthen, afterwards K. Henry V.*

5573. Sulph. cast of *obv.* only, from a fine impression or the matrix.   2⅝ in.   [D.C., 3 G. 82.]

To the r., on a hummocky or rocky mount. In armour, *cap-à-pie*, hauberk, helmet, with chapeau, and crest a lion of England, crowned, sword in the r. h., shield of arms, slung over the r. shoulder by a strap, and held in the l. h.   Horse caparisoned and armoured, with fan plume, and ridge down the nose of peculiar shape.   Arms: the later ROYAL ARMS OF ENGLAND, as borne by HENRY IV. with the fleurs-de-lis of FRANCE in the second and third quarters reduced to three, a change which took place between A.D. 1406 and 1409, with a label of three points for PRINCE HENRY.   Background replenished with sprigs of the broom-plant of PLANTAGENET.

s' . henr' . principis . wall' . duc' . acquit' . lancastr' . ⁊ . cornub' . comes . cestr . de : dñio . de . kermerdyne .

Carved borders.

5574. Plaster cast. ˙ [lxxx. 50.]

ELIZABETH.

5575. Sulph. casts, tinted green, from a cracked impression.   2¾ in.   [lxxvi. 90, 91.]

Ø. Queen, with sceptre, on a horse pacing to the l., on a mount with herbage. In the field on the r. the royal badge, a portcullis, ensigned with a royal crown, chained and ringed.

⚛ ♦ ELIZABETH.· DEI · GRACIA · ANGLIE · FRANCIE · ET · HIBERNIE · REGINA · FIDEI · DEFENSOR ♦

℞. A shield of the ROYAL ARMS OF ENGLAND as used by the Queen, see No. 442, ensigned with a jewelled crown. Supporters: *dex.*, a dragon, tail recurved betw. the hind legs, *sin.*, an heraldic antelope. (?) In base, under the shield the plumè of three ostrich feathers within a scroll or label, with split ends, inscribed:—ICH DIEN, for the PRINCE OF WALES.

S · IVDICIALE : DOMINE : REGINE : PRO : COMITATIBVS : CARMERDEN : CARDIGAN : ꝣ : PEMBROK'.

JAMES I.

5576. [A.D. 1613.] Bronze-green : fine, cracked, portions of the edge wanting. 3¾ in. [Add. ch. 979.]

Ø. To the l., on a mount replenished with herbage and flowers. Armed *cap-à-pie*, in plate armour: helmet with crest of England, and ostrich feathers of the Prince of Wales, scabbard at side. Horse caparisoned and partly armoured, with plume of four ostrich feathers and aigrette, the caparisons diapered lozengy, and enriched with crosslets at the knots, and little bells in the spaces of the reticulation, the border being ornamented with the fleur-de-lis, portcullis in a quatrefoil, etc. ; embroidered reins.

♦ IACOBVS ❇ DEI ❇ GRACIA ❇ ANGLIÆ ❇ SCOTIÆ ❇ FRANCIÆ ❇ ET ❇ HIBERNIÆ ❇ REX ❇ FIDEI ❇ D[EFENS]OR.

℞. A shield of the ROYAL ARMS OF ENGLAND, as used by· JAMES I., see No. 522, ensigned with a royal jewelled crown. Supporters : *dex.*, a dragon, tail nowy, *sin.*, a goat. In base, under the shield the plume of three ostrich feathers, within a scroll or label inscribed :—ICH DIEN, for the PRINCE OF WALES..

SIGI[LLVM] ❇ IVDICIALE ❇ PRO ❇ COMITATIBVS ❇ CARMERTHEN ❇ CARDIGAN ❇ ET ❇ PEMBROOK ❇

Carved border.

CHARLES II.
Chancery Seal.

5577. Recent impressions in red sealing-wax from *obv.* and *rev.* of matrix. 4 in. [xxxvi. 183, 184.]

Ø. To the l., on a mount replenished with herbage and flowers, with a dwarfed oak-tree in the background. Armed *cap-à-pie*, round cap-shaped helmet, with peak and ostrich plume, long fringed sash, streaming out to the l., sword in r. h. held over the head, carved oval shield of the ROYAL ARMS OF ENGLAND, see No. 522, in l. h.   Horse prancing, without caparisons.

✠ CAROLVS · II · DEI · GRACIA · MAG : BRITTANIÆ · FRANCIÆ · ET · HIBERNIÆ · REX · FIDEI · DEFENSOR · ⁞ · : ♦ ⁞ ♦ ⁞ ♦ :

℞. A poorly executed copy of *rev.* of Judicial Seal of ·James I. for these counties ; see preceding seal, No. 5576.

· ❀ · SIG ♦ PRO ♦ CANCELLARIA ♦ PRO ♦ COMITATIBVS ♦
CARMERTHEN ♦ CARDIGAN ♦ ET ♦ PEMBROOK .

Carved borders.

ROYAL JUDICIAL SEAL FOR THE COUNTIES OF CARNARVON, MERIONETH AND ANGLESEA.

EDWARD VI.

5578. Dark bronze-green : indistinct in several places. 2¾ in. [xxxvii. 60.]

∅. To the r., on a mount replenished with herbage and flowers.   Armed *cap-à-pie*, helmet, crown, crest of ENGLAND, sword, shield of the ROYAL ARMS OF ENGLAND, as in No. 407.   Horse prancing, caparisoned and armoured, with ostrich plume and frontal spike, ornamental reins, and a knob on the back.   Arms on the caparisons as above, reversed.

❀ EDWARD⁹ · VI⁹ · DEI · GR̄A · ANGL' · FRANC' · ET · HIB'NIE ·
REX · FIDEI · DEFENSOR · ET · IN · T'RA · ÆCCL'IÆ ·
ANGL' . . . . NC . . . .SVP̄M · CAPVT.

℞. A shield of the ROYAL ARMS OF ENGLAND as above, ensigned with a royal crown.   Supporters : *dex.*, a greyhound, *sin.*, a stag.   In base, the plume of three ostrich feathers, within a scroll or label inscribed :—ICH DIEN, for the PRINCE OF WALES.

SIGILLVM · IVDICIALE · DOMINI · REGIS · PRO · COMITATIBVS ·
C'NARV̄N · MERION̄ · ET · ANGLESER ♣

CHARLES I.

5579. Bronze-green : fine, showing the marks made by the studs or pins used to steady the matrix. 3¾ in. [xxxvii. 73.]

∅. To the l., on a mount replenished with herbage and flowers, with a greyhound coursing a hare in the foreground.

Armed *cap-à-pie*, helmet, crown, plume of five ostrich feathers, with aigrette, sword. Horse prancing, plumed, caparisoned and armoured ; the ornamentation of the caparisons includes fleurs-de-lis, roses, cushions, and pairs of annulets.

    🔥 CAROLVS ✿ DEI ✿ GRACIA ✿ MAGNIÆ (*sic*) ✿ BRITANIÆ ✿
       FRANCIÆ ✿ ET ✿ HIBERNIÆ ✿ REX ✿ FIDEI ✿
               DEFENSOR ✿ &ᶜ.

℞. A shield of the ROYAL ARMS OF GREAT BRITAIN, as first used by JAMES I.—see No. 522. Ensigned with a royal crown. Supporters : *dex.*, a greyhound, *sin.*, a stag. In base, the plume of three ostrich feathers, within a scroll or label inscribed :—ICH DIEN, for the PRINCE OF WALES.

    ✿ 🔥 ✿ SIGILL ✿ IVDICIALE ✿ PRO ✿ COMITATIBVS ✿
       CARNARVAN ✿ MERIONETH ✿ ET ✿ ANGLESEA.

Carved borders.

COMMONWEALTH. A.D. 1648.

5580. Bronze-green : fine, showing the marks made by the studs or pins used to steady the matrix. 3⅞ in. [xxxvii. 75.]

∅. Map of British Isles ; in the seas several ships. At the top a carved shield of arms : cross of St. George, for ENGLAND. In base a similar shield of arms of IRELAND.

    SIGILLVM ✿ IVDICIALE ✿ PRO ✿ COMITATIBVS ✿
       CARNARVAN ✿ MERIONETH ✿ ET ✿
          ANGLESEA ✿ 1648.

℞. Representation of interior of House of Commons during Session.

    IN ✿ THE ✿ FIRST ✿ YEARE ✿ OF ✿ FREEDOME ✿ BY ✿
       GODS ✿ BLESSING ✿ RESTORED ✿ 1648.

Carved borders.

For Royal Seals for the County Palatine of Chester and County of Flint, see CHESTER, Nos. 4805–4810.

ROYAL JUDICIAL SEAL FOR THE COUNTIES OF DENBIGH, MONTGOMERY, AND FLINT.

HENRY VIII.

5581. [A.D. 1545.] Bronze-green : fine, showing marks of the studs or pins used to steady the matrix. 2¾ in. [Add. ch. 8650.]

Ø. To the r., on a mount replenished with herbage and flowers. Armed *cap-à-pie*, in plate armour, helmet, coronet, crest of England, a lion statant guardant crowned, the tail extended ; in the r. h. a long sword, in the l. h. a shield of arms. Horse caparisoned and armoured, with plume of three ostrich feathers, frontal spike, and knob on back. Arms : quarterly FRANCE (MODERN) and ENGLAND, those on the caparisons being reversed.

     ♠ HENRIO͞! · VIII · DEI · GR̂A · ANGLIE · FRÂC · ꝝ ·
        HIB̂NE · REX · FIDEI · DEFÊS' · ET · IN ·
     T'RA ECCL · ĀGL · (?) ꝝ HIB̂NICE · SVPREM̄ · CAPVT.

Some words in legend indistinct and uncertain. Some pairs of letters conjoined.

℞. A shield of the ROYAL ARMS, as above, ensigned with a royal crown, of three crosses pattées and two fleurs-de-lis alternately disposed, with points of three pearls each betw. each. Supporters : *dex.*, a lion rampant guardant crowned, *sin.*, a stag gorged with a coronet and chained, the tails flory and between the legs. In base, the plume of three ostrich feathers with label inscribed :—ICH DIEN.

     ⛪ S + IVDICIALE + DÑI + REGIS + PRO COMITATI[BVS +
     DEN]BIGHE + MONTGOMERI + ET + FLINT.

EDWARD VI.

5582. [A.D. 1551.] Bronze-green : fine and sharp, showing marks of the studs or pins used to steady the matrix. 2¾ in. [Add. ch. 8528.]

Ø. Resembles *obv.* of preceding seal of Henry VIII., No. 5581.

     ✿ EDWARD' · VI · D̄I · GR̄A, etc., as in No. 5581.

℞. As in No. 5581.

5583. Casts in dark-green wax from No. 5582. [lxxvi. 55, 56.]

ELIZABETH.

5584. Bronze-green : fine, indistinct in places, with marks of the studs or pins used to steady the matrix. 2¾ in. [xxxvii. 70.]

Ø. To the r., on a mount replenished with herbage and flowers. In plate armour, helmet, crown, crest of England, sword, shield. Horse caparisoned and armoured, plume of ostrich feathers on head. Arms : quarterly, 1, 4, FRANCE (MODERN), 2, 3, ENGLAND, those on the caparisons being reversed.

     ✿ ELIZABETH ✿ DEI ✿ GRA ✿ ANGLIE ✿ FRANCIE ✿ ET ✿
     HIBERNIE ✿ REGINA ✿ FIDEI ✿ DEFENS̄.

℞. A shield of arms, crown, supporters, and plume, as in the seal of Henry VIII., No. 5581, but not from the same matrix.

♠ S ❀ IVDICIALE ❀ DNE ❀ REGINE ❀ PRO ❀ COMTIBᴣ ❀
DENBIGHE ❀ MOVNGOM'I ❀ ᴣ ❀ FLĪT.

5585. [A.D. 1597.] Bronze-green: indistinct in places, with marks of the studs as before. [Add. ch. 8534.]

- **5586.** [A.D. 1600.] Bronze-green: indistinct in places, marks of the studs as before. [Add. ch. 8656.]

5587. Bronze-green: fine, edge injured by pressure in places. [xxxvii. 59.]

JAMES I. A.D. 1603.

5588. [A.D. 1619.] Bronze-green: fine, edge slightly imperfect. 3¼ in. [Add. ch. 8657.]

∅. Resembles the *obv.* of James I.'s seal for the County Palatine of Chester and County of Flint, No. 4808, but with variation of small details in foliage, diaper and other parts.

❀ IACOBVS ❀ DEI ❀ GRACIA ❀ ANGLIÆ ❀ SCOTIÆ ❀ FRANCIÆ ❀
ET ❀ HIBERNIÆ ❀ REX ❀ FIDEI ❀ DEFENSOR ❀

℞. A shield of the ROYAL ARMS OF ENGLAND as used by James I. Ensigned with a royal crown; supporters, *dex.*, a lion rampant guardant crowned, *sin.*, an heraldic antelope, gorged with a coronet, chained and ringed. In base, the plume of three ostrich feathers within a scroll or label inscribed :— ICH DIEN.

SIGILLVM ❀ IVDICIALE ❀ PRO ❀ COMITATIBVS ❀ DENBIGH ❀
MONTGOMERI ❀ ET ❀ FLINT ❀ 1603 ❀

Carved borders.

5589. [A.D. 1619.] Bronze-green: fine, edge imperfect in places, showing marks of the studs or pins used to steady the matrix. [Add. ch. 8658.]

5590. Bronze-green, speckled: fine, cracked, and imperfect in places. [xxxvii. 71.]

5591. Bronze-green: imperfect on the r. h. side, and injured in parts. [xxxvii. 72.]

CHARLES I. A.D. 1626.

5592. Bronze-green: injured in parts by pressure. 3¾ in. [xxxvii. 74.]

Ø. To the l., on a mount replenished with herbage and flowers. In plate armour, helmet, crown, plume of five ostrich feathers, sword, scabbard, etc. Horse caparisoned and armoured, with plume of ostrich feathers and aigrette. The caparisons diapered with arabesques and bordered.

⚜ CAROLVS ❀ DEI ❀ GRACIA ❀ MAGNÆ ❀ BRITANNIÆ ❀ FRANCIÆ ❀ ET HIBERNIÆ ❀ REX ❀ FIDEI ❀ DEFENSOR.

℞. A shield of the ROYAL ARMS OF GREAT BRITAIN, as used by CHARLES I., ensigned with a royal crown betw. the initial letters C. R. Supporters and plume in base, as in the preceding seal of James I., No. 5588.

SIGILLVM ❀ ❀ IVDICIALE ❀ PRO COMITATIBVS ❀ DENBIGH ❀ MONTGOMERI ❀ ET ❀ FLINT ❀ 1626 ❀

5592*. Casts in green composition, of the *obv.* and *rev.* of No. 5592. [lxxvi. 59, 60.]

CHARLES II. A.D. 1661.

5593. Sulph. cast, tinted green, from fine impression. 3⅜ in. [lxxvi. 39, 40.]

Ø. To the l., in plate armour, plume of ostrich feathers, sash, long scabbard, in the r. h. a drawn sword erect. Horse prancing. In the background an indistinct landscape. In the field on the r. a coroneted plume of three ostrich feathers for the PRINCE OF WALES; below it a riband inscribed with the usual motto.

· CAROLVS · II · DEI · GRATIA · MAGNÆ · BRITANNIÆ · FRANCIÆ · ET · HIBERNIÆ · REX · FIDEI · DEFENS ·

℞. A carved shield of the ROYAL ARMS OF GREAT BRITAIN, as used by K. Charles II., see No. 614, ensigned with a royal crown. Supporters: *dex.*, a lion rampant guardant crowned, *sin.*, an antelope, gorged with a coronet. In base, the coronet, plume and inscribed riband as in the *obv.*

SIGILLVM · IVDICIALE · PRO · COMITATIBVS · DENBIGH · MONTGOMERI · ET · FLINT · 1661.

EQUESTRIAN SEALS.

Rogō de Abbernon, [*of Ockshot, co. Surr.*]
5594. [Late 12th cent.]   Dark-green: very fine, shewing mark of the handle of the matrix.   1¾ in.   [Add. ch. 5529.]

To the r.   In armour: hauberk of mail, surcoat, flat helmet, sword, convex shield of arms slung with strap over the r. shoulder.   Arms: a lion rampant.   *See At tur Collections Online seal cast LDSAL2020.F7.5*

✠ SIGILL' ⦂ ROGŌ ⦂ DE ⦂ ABB̄ NŌ.

Surrey Archæol. Collections, vol. v., p. 56.   *drawing   and see conventional seal below*
Cf. Add. ch. 5528, *temp.* Joh.

Walterus de Ab(b)ernun, [*of Leicroht, co. Devon ?*]
5595. [Late 12th cent.]   Greenish-brown: very imperfect. About 1¾ in. when perfect.   [Add. ch. 27,527.]

To the r.   In armour: coat of mail diapered lozengy, sword, long convex shield with central boss.

. . . . Ε AB . . ERИV . . .

Surrey Archæol. Collections, vol. v., p. 57.
Cf. Add. ch. 5531; 5532, 5537, 5540, 5541, 5542, 5562, *temp.* Hen. III.

Ingerramus de Abernun, [*son of Walter de Abernun, of Stoke d'Abernon, co. Surr.*]
5596. [Early Hen. III., before A.D. 1235.]   Green: fine, the edge chipped.   1¼ in.   [Add. ch. 5540.]

Ø. To the r.   In armour: hauberk of mail, surcoat, flat helmet, sword, and shield of arms slung with strap over r. shoulder; horse galloping.   Arms: a chevron.

S[I]GILL[V]M ⦂ IN[GE]RRAMI ⦂ DE ⦂ ABERN . . . . .

℞. Smaller counterseal.   1 in.   A shield of arms, as in the *obv.*

✠ SIGILLVM ⦂ INGERRAMI ⦂ DE ⦂ ABERNVN.

Beaded borders.

Cf. Add. ch. 5531, 5532, 5541, 5549.
Surrey Archæol. Collections, vol. v., p. 59.

Reginaldus de Acleya, [*of Rockingham, co. Northt.*]
5597. [Late 12th cent.]   Mottled green: the upper part and l. side wanting.   1⅞ in.   [Harl. ch. 45 B. 9.]

To the r.   In armour: hauberk, surcoat, sword, shield bearing a form of escarbuncle with central boss.

. . . GILL' REGINALDI ⦂ DE . . . .

5598. Sulph. cast. [D.C., D. 192.]
Cf. Reginald de Acle, witness in Add. ch. 19,909, before A.D. 1184.

Willelmus de Adelvaldeleie, [*son of* AISOLLE DE
ADWALDLAYA, *or Adwaldley, co. York.*]
5599. [Early 13th cent.]   Brownish-green : a thick mass,
well preserved. 2 in. [Add. ch. 7451.]
To the l. In armour : hauberk, surcoat, cap-like helmet,
long convex shield with central spike ; hawk held by the
jesses on the l. h. Horse with ornamental breast-band.
✠ SIGILL' · WILLI · DE · ADELV · ALDE · LEIE.

Walterus de Aincurt, [*of Holmesfield, co. Derby.*]
5600. [*circ.* A.D. 1156–1165.] ' Light-brown, covered with
a reddish-brown varnish, which has peeled away in places.
About 2¾ × 2 in. when perfect.   App. by a woven bobbin of
faded colours. [Wolley ch. x. 1.]
Pointed oval. To the r. In armour : hauberk of mail,
conical helmet, sword, long narrow convex shield.
. . . . . . LVM . . . .
Cf. *Liber Niger Scaccarii,* ed. Hearne, 1774, vol. i., p. 268. For an
earlier Walter de Aincurte, A.D. 1087, 1088, cf. Cotton ch. xvi. 32.

Reginaldus de Albemare.
5601. [12th cent.]   Plaster cast, from chipped impression.
1⅞ in. [lxxviii. 10.]
To the r. In armour : hauberk, surcoat, sword, conical
helmet, convex shield with central spike. Horse galloping.
✠ SIGILLVM REGINALDI DE ALB . . MARE.

Helias de Albeni, [*or* ALBENIACO, *of Scampton, co. Linc.*]
5602. [*circ.* A.D. 1175.]   Dark mottled green : fine, the
edge imperfect. 2⅓ × 1¾ in. [Harl. ch. 45 B. 28.]
Pointed oval. To the l. In long surcoat ; a hawk on the
l. fist. Horse springing. In the foreground two hounds.
✠ SIGILLVM · HELIE · DE · ALBENI :
5602*. Sulph. cast. [D.C., D. 118.]
5603. [A.D. 1163–1182.]   Creamy-white : the edge imperfect. App. by a plaited hempen cord. [Harl. ch. 45
B. 27.]
✠ SIGILLVM . . . . . I . . .

Willelmus de Albeni, [*Earl of Sussex, and Earl of Arundel,*
A.D. 1176–1222.]
5604. [*circ.* A.D. 1180.]   Creamy-white : fine, very im-'
perfect. About 3 in. when perfect. [Add. ch. 19,603]
∅. To the r. In armour : hauberk of mail, surcoat with

long pleated skirt and large maunch, sword, long convex shield
of arms: a lion rampant. The curved toe of the r. foot is
placed in a square stirrup of peculiar form. In the field on
the r., in front of the horse, a wyvern with tail nowy.

.. IGILLVM . . . .

℞. A small round counterseal. 1 in. A lion passant
reguardant.

[✠ SIGI]LLVM · SECRETI.

Nigellus de Albinneio.

5605. [*temp.* Steph.] Plaster cast from fine impression
chipped at the edge. 2⅜ in. [lxxviii. 11.]
To the r. In armour: hauberk of mail, sword, kite-shaped
shield showing interior side held by a short strap.

✠ SIGILLVꟿ NIGELLI DE ALBINNEIO.

See Dugdale, *Baronage*, vol. i., p. 121.

Radulfus de Alchtunia, [*or* HALTON *of Halton, co. Linc.*]

5606. [*circ.* A.D. 1150.] Dark-green, a thick mass: fine,
with mark of handle of matrix. 2¼ in. [Harl. ch. 51 B. 50.]
To the l. In armour: surcoat, a hawk on the l. hand.
Horse springing, with ornamental breast-band.

SIGILLVM · RADVLFI · ALCHTVꟼIA.

5607. Sulph. cast. [D.C., D. 67.]

Willelmus de Aldri, [*of Drayton, co. Northt. ?*]

5608. [*circ.* A.D. 1184–1219.] Dark-green: very imperfect.
About 2 in. when perfect. App. by a hempen string
[Harl. ch. 45 B. 37.]
To the r. In armour : hauberk, sword, long narrow shield.

... IGILLVM WILLEL . . . . DR . . . .

5609. Sulph. cast. [D.C., D. 161.]

Petrus de Altaripa, [*of co. York ?*]

5610. [Late 12th cent.] Plaster cast from chipped impression. 1¾ in. [lxxviii. 13.]
To the r. In armour: hauberk of mail, coif, sword, long
convex shield with central boss or spike. Horse galloping.

✠ SI . . . . . ꟿ : PETRI : DE : A . . . . . . IPA.

Cf. *Rotuli de Oblatis temp. Joh.*, ed. T. D. Hardy, p. 152 ; A.D. 1201.

Amundevilla (Rob. de). *v.* Mundevile (Rob. de).

Hada Amomavila, [*son of* (ROBERT ? and) BEATRIX DE AMUNDEVILLA, *of co. Linc.*]

5611. [Early 13th cent.] Light-brown: fine, varnished.
2¼ in. [Harl. ch. 45 C. 32.]

To the r. In armour: hauberk, surcoat, conical helmet with nasal, sword, long convex shield ornamented with rays and central boss. Horse prancing, with caparisons ornamented with a kind of vair or papillonné work.

⊕ SIGILLVM HADE AMOMAVILA.

Cf. *Rotuli de Oblatis temp. Joh.*, ed. T. D. Hardy, p. 580; A.D. 1216.

5612. Sulph. cast. [D.C., D. 129.]

Hubertus de Anesti, [*or* ANESTIA, *son of* RICHARD DE ANESTIA, *of Nutfield, co. Surrey.*]

5613. [*circ.* A.D. 1190.] Light mottled green: fine, but very imperfect. About 2 in. when perfect. [Add. ch. 24,607.]

Ø. To the r. In armour: hauberk, surcoat, helmet, sword, convex shield of arms. Horse galloping. Arms: a fess.

Legend wanting.

℞. A smaller round counterseal. 1¾ in. With mark of the handle of the matrix. An early-shaped shield of arms: a fess, charged with some indistinct bearings.

⊕ SECRETVM · HVBERTI · DE ANESTI.

Manning and Bray, *History of Surrey*, vol. ii., p. 267.

5614. Another, light mottled green: very imperfect. [Add. ch. 24,606.]

Ø. SIG . . . .

℞. ⊕ SECRET . . . . ANESTI.

Ricardus de Anestia, [*of Nutfield, co. Surrey.*]

5615. [Late 12th cent.] Mottled green: very imperfect and indistinct. About 1⅜ in. when perfect. [Add. ch. 24,607.]

To the r. In armour: hauberk, surcoat, conical helmet, sword, convex shield.

⊕ SIGILLVM . . . . · H . . . .

Manning and Bray, *History of Surrey*, vol. ii., p. 267.

Ansketillus, [*of Newbold-Verdon, co. Leicester.*]

5616. [12th cent.] Light-brown, covered with a dark varnish: very imperfect. About 2¼ in. when perfect. [Harl. ch. 45 C. 40.]

To the r. In armour: hauberk of mail, surcoat, helmet, [sword,] large pointed convex shield with central spike. Horse prancing.

Legend wanting.

Madoc ap Griffin, [*of Stratamarcella, co. Montgom.*]

5617. [? Late 12th cent.] Plaster cast from imperfect impression. About 2⅜ in. when perfect. [lxxix. 30.]

To the r. In armour: hauberk of mail, coif, flat-topped helmet, sword, scabbard, shield slung by a strap round the neck. Horse galloping.

Legend wanting.

Hugo de Ardena, [*of Rothley, co. Leic.*]

5618. [*Temp.* Hen. II.] Light orange-coloured: fine, the edge injured. About 2¼ in. when perfect. [Harl. ch. 45 C. 47.]

To the r. In armour: hauberk of mail, surcoat, helmet with a crescent-shaped plume, sword, long convex shield strengthened with rays and having a central spike. Horse with an ornamental breast-band of pendent balls.

SIGILLVM H[VGO]NIS DE AR . . . .

5619. Sulph. cast. [D.C., D. 95.]

Osbertus de Ardene, [*of co. Warw.*]

5620. [*Temp..* Hen. I.] Dark-green: very imperfect, injured by fire; app. by a parchment label and also by a plaited cord. About 2¼ in. when perfect. [Cott. ch. xxii. 2.]

To the r. In armour: hauberk, surcoat, [sword,] long convex shield strengthened with a star-shaped ornament.

Legend wanting.

Willelmus de Ardena, [*of Hampton, co. Warw.*]

5621. [A.D. 1198–1216.] Creamy-white: injured and indistinct. About 1¾ in. [Cott. ch. xxii. 4.]

To the r. In armour: sword, long convex shield strengthened with a star-like ornament.

. . . IGILL' · W . . . .

Philip de Areci, *or* **Arecy,** [*of Killingholm, co. Linc.*]

5622. [13th cent.] Dark bronze-green: fine, but imperfect. 1 in. [Harl. ch. 49 C. 37.]

To the r. In armour: hauberk, surcoat, flat-topped helmet, sword, shield of arms. Horse caparisoned. Arms: three cinquefoils (?).

✠ SIGILL' PHILIP . . . .

5623. Brown: a fragment. [Harl. ch. 49 C. 38.]

Reginaldus Arsie, [*of Selverleia, co. Cambr. ?*]

5624. [Early 13th cent.] Pale greenish-white: fine, very imperfect. About 3 in. when perfect. [Add. ch. 28,340.]

To the r. In armour: hauberk, surcoat with flowing skirts, [sword], long convex shield. Horse with ornamental breast-band. Armorial bearings very indistinct, apparently a dragon or wyvern segreant with wings expanded.

Legend wanting.
Cf. Cott. ch. xxii. 7.

Reginaldus de Ashburnham.

5625. [12th cent.] Plaster cast from indistinct impression. 2¼ in. A doubtful seal. [lxxviii. 15.]

To the r. In armour: hauberk, surcoat, conical helmet, sword, convex shield with central spike.

· ... REGINALDVS .. STRI ...

Engraved from a clearer impression in Drummond, *History of Noble Families,* "Ashburnham," p. 1.

Aswelle (Joh. de). *v.* Filius Lambardi (Ivo.)

Eustacius [*fil.* EUSTACII] **de Athde** [*i.e. Wathford, of Wathford, co. Northt.*]

5626. [13th cent.] Faded green: with imperfect raised rim. 1½ in. [Add. ch. 22,510.]

To the r. In armour: hauberk, surcoat, flat helmet, sword, shield. Horse galloping.

✠ SIGILL' EVSTACII DE ATH DE.

The letters TH conjoined.

Nicholaus de Audeleye [*8th Baron Audley, of Heleigh, co. Staff.*]

5627. [A.D. 1314.] Red: very fine. 1 in. [Add. ch. 20,558.]

To the r. In armour: hauberk of mail, surcoat, sword, shield of arms, plumed helmet. Horse galloping, caparisoned and plumed. Armorial bearings of hauberk, shield, and caparisons: fretty, AUDLEY.

S' NICHOLAI · DE · AVDELEYE.

Beaded borders.

Ydo de Aufort [*EUDO, son of* HENRY DE BROCLOSBI, *or* AUFORT, *of co. Lincoln.*]

5628. [A.D. 1186–1200.] Dark-green: indistinct. 1½ in. With mark of the handle of the matrix. [Harl. ch. 47 C. 22.]

. To the r. In armour: hauberk, surcoat, sword, long convex shield with central spike, circular helmet with nasal.

✠ SIGILLVM · YDONIS · DE · AVFORT.

5629. Sulph cast. [D.C., D. 160.]

5630. [Late 12th cent.] Light-brown, varnished: imperfeet and indistinct. [Harl. ch. 47 C. 23.]

5631. Sulph. cast. [D.C., D. 159.]

5632. Mottled green: fair, with mark of the handle. [Harl. ch. 45 E. 42.]

5633. Sulph. cast. [D.C., D. 158.]

Another Seal.

5634. [Late 12th or early 13th cent.] Light-brown, varnished: fine. 1¾ in. [Harl. ch. 45 E. 41.]

To the r. In armour: hauberk, surcoat, sword, shield of

convex lozenge-form strengthened with a star-like or radiated ornament, and round cap or helmet with long ties behind. Horse galloping.

☩ SIGILLVM IDONIS DE AVFORT.

5635. Sulph. cast. [D.C., D. 157.]

5636. [Late 12th or early 13th cent.] Dark-green: very fine, well preserved, with mark of handle. [Harl. ch. 45 E. 43.]

5637. [Late 12th or early 13th cent.] Opaque brown: fine, but imperfect; l. side wanting. [Harl. ch. 45 E. 45.]

Willelmus Ambesas, [*or* Aumbesas, *of Carshalton, co. Surr.*]

5638. [A.D. 1307.] Dark-green: fine, but very imperfect, l. side and lower parts wanting. 1¼ in. when perfect. [Add. ch. 23,355.]

To the r. In armour: [hauberk,] surcoat, conical helmet with the vizor down, [sword,] shield of arms. Horse caparisoned. Armorial bearings of shield and caparisons: a lion rampant within a bordure engrailed?

S' WIL . . . .

5639. [A.D. 1319.] Dark-green: fine, chipped and injured in places. [Add. ch. 23,365.]

S' WILLELMI AMBESAS. ⋈

Cf. Manning and Bray, *History of Surrey*, vol. ii., p. 508.

R[obertus ?] Avenelle, [*of Thorncombe, co. Dev.*]

5640. [12th cent.] Discoloured white: very imperfect and indistinct. About 1¾ in. when perfect. [L.F.C., viii. 11.]

To the r. In armour: sword, shield showing only the interior surface.

Legend wanting.

Cf. Robert Auenell, A.D. 1129-1135, Harl. ch. 58 H. 37 ; and Robert Avenel, A.D. 1166-1170, Cott. ch. xviii. 13, 14.

Johannes fil. Galfridi de Badele, [*of Great Waldingfield, co. Suff.*]

5641. [*Temp.* Hen. III.] Mottled green: very fine, the edge chipped. 1⅛ in. [Harl. ch. 45 F. 9.]

To the l. In armour: hauberk, surcoat, plumed helmet with vizor down, sword, shield of which only the interior side is shown, with a strap over the l. shoulder.

☩ S' IOH'IS · FIL' · GALFRIDI · DE · . . . . LE.

5642. Sulph. cast. [D.C., E. 232.]

Bernardus de Baillol, [*of Gainford, co. Durh.*]

5643. [A.D. 1186-1188.] Light-brown, varnished: very imperfect. About 2½ in. when perfect. [Cott. ch. v. 75.]

To the r. In armour : hauberk of mail, surcoat, [sword, helmet,] long convex shield with central spike. Horse galloping.

　　　　　　⳨ S . . . .

Hugo de Baiocis, [*of Sempringham, co. Linc.*]

5644. [*Temp.* Hen. II.] Light reddish-brown : fine, edge chipped. About 2¼ in. when perfect. [Harl. ch. 45 F. 20.]

To the r. In armour : hauberk of mail, surcoat, conical helmet with nasal, sword, long convex shield with central spike. Horse galloping.

　　　　　⳨ SIG . . . VM HVGO : DE : . . . . . . OCIS.

The C is square.

5645. Sulph. cast. [D.C., D. 146.]

Johannes de Balun, [*of Merkeley, co. Heref.*]

5646. [A.D. 1210–1245.] Dark-green : injured and chipped ; app. by a plaited cord of variegated silks. 2 in. [Harl. ch. 111 D. 18.]

To the r. In armour : hauberk, surcoat, conical helmet with nasal, sword, shield. Horse galloping. Arms indistinct, perhaps ermine, a bend.

　　　　　⳨ SIGILLVM · IOHANNIS . . . . VN.

5647. Sulph. cast. [D.C., E. 218.]

Barbeaverill (Willelmus), *v.* No. 5813.

Willelmus fil. Roberti de Barcheword, [*of Barkwith, co. Linc.*]

5648. [*Temp.* Hen. II.] Red : fine, now fragmentary. About 2⅜ in. when perfect. [Add. ch. 20,682.]

To the r. In armour : hauberk of mail represented by a lozengy diaper.

　　　. . . . . . · W . . . . ILII · ROBER . . . .

Cf. Harl. ch. 52 G. 24.

Barri (Radulfus), *v.* Stantune (Radulfus de).

Radulfus de Baskervilla, *or* Baschavilla, [*of Bredwardine, co. Heref.*]

5649. [Late Hen. II.] Creamy-white : very imperfect and indistinct. About 2 in. when perfect. [Add. ch. 20,408.]

To the r. In armour : hauberk, surcoat. Other details wanting.

Legend wanting.

5650. [Late 12th cent.] . Creamy-white : fine, imperfect. [Add. ch. 20,410.]

In this impression the sword, helmet and convex shield with metal rim and central spike remain.

☫ SI . . . .

Gilebert Baset, [*of cos. Midd. and Oxon.*]

5651. [A.D. 1182.] Dark-green : fine. 2¼ in. [Add. ch. 10,595.]

To the r. In armour : hauberk, conical helmet with back-sweep and nasal, large sword, convex shield ornamented with a kind of orle or bordure ; horse springing, with loose frontlet on the forehead.

☫ SIGILLVM · GILEBERT · BASET.

5652. [A.D. 1182.] Dark-green: very imperfect and in-distinct. [Add. ch. 10,593.]

5653. [*Temp*. Hen. II.] Pale mottled green : fine, edge chipped in places. [Add. ch. 10,597.]

☫ SIGI . . . . ERT . . . ASET.

5654. [*Temp*. Hen. II.] Dark-green : only fragment of the centre ; app. by a closely woven bobbin of various colours. [Add. ch. 9211.]

Amauri Bataile, [**Almaric Bellum,** *of Bradwell-juxta-mare, co. Ess.*]

5655. [*Temp*. Hen. III.] Dark-green: chipped. 1½ in. [Harl. ch. 45 I. 44.]

To the r. In armour : hauberk, surcoat, conical helmet with nasal, sword, convex shield, with central spike. Horse galloping.

☫ SIGILL' AMAVRI BATAILE.

5656. Sulph. cast. [D.C., D. 167.]

——— o **Campo.**

5657. [12th cent.] Light-brown varnished : very im-perfect and indistinct. About 2¼ in. when perfect. [xxxix. 61.]

To the r. In armour : hauberk, surcoat, helmet, large sword, convex shield, ornamented with an escarbuncle and central boss. Horse springing.

☫ SIG . . . ⋮ . . . M · DN . . . . O CAMPO.

BEAUCHAMP.

Guido de Bello campo, [*9th Earl of Warwick,* A.D. 1298–1315.]

5658. [A.D. 1301.] Plaster cast from fine, but imperfect, impression. 2¼ in. [lxxviii. 22, 23.]

Ø. To the l. In armour : hauberk of mail, surcoat, helmet plumed and with lambrequin, sword, shield of arms. Horse

R 2

caparisoned. Arms: a fess between six crosses crosslet, BEAUCHAMP.

... GW .. DON' · DE · BELLOCAM ....

Beaded borders.

R. A shield of arms : chequy, a chevron ermine, WARWICK. Suspended by a loop from a hook, and betw. two lions passant guardant.

.... AMPO COM' · WARREWYK' ..

Hugo de Bellocampo, [*of Melbourne, co. Derb.*]

5659. [*Temp.* Hen. II.] Mottled brown, opaque : fine. 2¾ in. [Add. ch. 7081.] *temp Hen. II (?)   Hugo II c1180 - 1217*

To the r. In armour : hauberk, conical helmet, broad sword, shield of arms ; fretty. Horse galloping.   *AES pDIh*

SIGILLVM · HVGONIS · DE . BELLOCAMPO.

Cf. *Rotuli de Oblatis temp. Joh.*, ed. T. D. Hardy, p. 310, A.D. 1205.

Philippus de Bellocampo, [*of Stebbing, co. Ess.*]

5660. [12th–13th cent.] Creamy-white : very imperfect and indistinct. 1¾ in. [Add. ch. 28,365.]

To the r. In armour : sword, large convex shield over the back, showing the interior side. Horse galloping.

Legend obliterated.

[✠ SIG]ILL' PHIL ....

5661. Another. [Add. ch. 28,366.] .

✠ SIGILL' PHILIPPI DE ....

Thomas [de Bellocampo, 12*th*] *Earl of Warwick.*

5662. [A.D. 1343–4.] Recent impressions in red sealing-wax, from the matrix. 3¼ in. [xliii. 18, 19.]

∅. To the r. On a rugged mount, in armour : hauberk of mail, surcoat of arms, sword chained to the shoulder, shield, helmet ; coronet of three leaves, out of which rises the crest, a swan's neck. Horse caparisoned. Arms : a fess between six crosses crosslet, BEAUCHAMP.

S' : THŌE : COMITIS : WARRWYCHIE : AИИO : REGNI : REGIS : E : T'CII.

R. Within an elaborately carved gothic rosace of twenty-four cusps,—the points trefoiled, in each of the twelve spandrils a rose of six points, in the twelve heads of the tracery as many quatrefoils, the borders enriched with ball flowers, a shield of arms : chequy on a chevron five ermine spots, GUY OF WARWICK.

Legend continued from the *obv.* :—

✠ POST : CŌQVESTV . AИGLIE : SEPTĪO : DECĬO : ET : REGИI : SVI : FRAИCIE : QVARTO :

Carved borders.

5663. Sulph. cast of the *rev.* only. [D.C., F. 169.]

Willelmus de Bellocampo, [*of Gislingham, co. Suff.*]

5664. [Early 13th cent.] Creamy-white: very imperfect and indistinct. About 2 in. when perfect. [Harl. ch. 45 I. 14.]

To the r. In armour: a shirt of mail, sword, kite-shaped shield showing interior side.

Legend indistinct.

Johannes de Belloforti,
[*Beaufort, Duke and Earl of Somerset,
Earl of Kendal, Lord of Corfe.*]

5665. [A.D. 1443.] Red: fragment of fine large seal. About 3 in. when perfect. [Add. ch. 12,212.]

To the r. In armour.

. . . . . EL . . . .

BEAUMONT.

Gualerannus, *Count of Mellent* [*in Normandy*],
Earl of Worcester, [*son and heir of Robert* DE BELLOMONTE,
Earl of Leicester, etc.]

5666. [*circ.* A.D. 1144–1166.] Red: fine, chipped at the edges. 3¾ in. [Harl. ch. 45 I. 30.]

Ø. To the r. In armour: hauberk, coif, surcoat with long skirt, bag-shaped maunch on the r. wrist, conical helmet with nasal, long lance-flag with chequy device and three wavy streamers, convex shield with central spike. Horse with ornamental saddle and breast-band.

⊕ SIGILLVM · G[VA]LERANNI · COMITIS · WIGORNIE ·

R. To the r. In armour: hauberk, coif, surcoat, conical helmet with nasal and back-ties, sword, convex shield with central spike. Horse springing, with ornamental saddle of chequy design, fringed.

⊕ SIGILLVM · GVALERANNI · CO . . . IS . MELLENTI.

Beaded borders.

5667. Sulph. casts. [D.C., D. 70, 71.]

5668. [A.D. 1138?] Red: imperfect; app. by a folded bobbin of faded red stuff. [Add. ch. 20,419.]

Robertus [de Bossu, 2nd] Earl of Leicester,
[*son of* ROBERT DE BELLOMONTE, 1*st Earl.*]

5669. [*circ.* A.D. 1147.] Light-brown, varnished: fine, edge imperfect. About 3 in. when perfect. [Harl. ch. 84 H. 19.]

Ø. To the l. In armour: hauberk of mail, long kite-shaped shield.

. . . . . . M · RO . . . . COMITIS LEGRECESTR . . .

Beaded borders.

R. Small oval counterseal. 1⅛ × 1 in. Victory, holding a

rudder to the l.   From an antique oval intaglio gem, set in a
metal rim bearing the legend :—
     ✠ SECRETVM ROBERTI COITIS LEIRCESTRIE.
The letters TR in *Leircestrie* conjoined.

5670. Sulph. casts of the *obv.* and *rev.* of No. 5669. [D.C.,
D. 59, 60.]

5671. [*circ.* A.D. 1147.]   Another, very fragmentary, in an
old stuff bag. [Harl. ch. 84 H. 18.]

Robertus de Bellomonte, *Count of Mellent,*
[*afterw. Earl of Leicester.*]

5672. [A.D. 1170–1178.]   Dark-red : fine, speckled, and edge
chipped.   App. by strands of red silk, with marks of the nicks
in the matrices for steadying them.   3¼ in. [L. F. C., xxii. 1.]

  Ø. To the r.   In armour : hauberk, long surcoat, conical
helmet with nasal and long lambrequins, lance flag with ornamental device and streamers ; convex shield with central
spike and ornamental star or escarbuncle.
     [✠ SI]GILLVM : ROBERTI · DOMINI · BELLOMONTIS.

  R. In armour, as in the *obv.*, with sword in place of the
lance-flag.
       SIGILLVM · ROBERTI · COMITIS · MELL[EN].

5673. Plaster casts from the above impression, before it
was chipped. [lxxx. 5, 6.]

Robertus [Fitz-Parnell de Bellomonte,
4*th*] *Earl of Leicester* [A.D. 1190–1204],
with counterseal of ROBERT DE BRETUEL. *or* BRETBY.

5674. [A.D. 1195.]   Plaster cast of fine impression.   2¾ in.
[lxxviii. 25, 26.]

  Ø. To the r.   In armour : hauberk of mail, long surcoat,
coif, cap-shaped helmet, sword, convex shield.   Horse springing.   In the field on each side a fleur-de-lis.
     ✠ SIGILLVM ROBERTI COMITIS LEICESTRIE.

  R. A smaller round counterseal.   1⅛ in. diam.   A shield of
arms : chequy.
       ✠ SECRETVM : ROBERTI DE : BRETVEL. (?)

  Cf. the arms of BRETBY, or BRETTY, which are chequy
argent and azure.

Henri de Beaumont, *Constable of England.*

5675. [A.D. 1322.]   Red : fine, the edge chipped.   About
1¼ in. when perfect. [Add. ch. 21,506.]

  Within an engrailed bordure, on a field replenished with
wavy sprigs of foliage, to the r.   In armour : hauberk of
mail, surcoat, helmet with vizor down, and plumed, short
broad sword, shield, square shoulder-pieces.   Horse capa-

risoned and at full speed. Arms : semé-de-lis, a lion rampant, over all a bend, BEAUMONT.

. . . . . . I : DE : . . . .

Willelmus de Beaumunt, [*or* de Bellomonte, *of Battisford, co. Suff.*]

5676. [*Temp.* Hen. III.] Mottled green : fine, injured in places. 1⅜ in. [Add. ch. 9826.]

To the r. In armour : hauberk, surcoat, sword, shield, flat helmet. Horse galloping.

✠ SIGILL WILL' DE BEAVMVNT.

Robertus de Becchering, [*of Waddingworth, co. Linc.*]

5677. [Late 12th cent.] Creamy-white : fine, but very imperfect. About 1⅞ in. when perfect. [Harl. ch. 44 A. 21.]

To the r. In armour : hauberk, surcoat (helmet broken away), sword, long convex shield with central spike. Horse galloping.

. . . . . LLV . . ROBE . . . .

Petrus de Bekerighe, [*or* de Bekeringe, *of Faldingworth, co. Linc.*]

5678. [Early 13th cent.] Light yellowish-brown, mottled : fine, edge imperfect. About 1⅞ in. when perfect. [Harl. ch. 45 H. 28.]

To the r. In armour : hauberk, surcoat, round-topped helmet with nasal, sword, long convex shield with central spike. Horse springing.

✠ SIGILLVM PETRI DE BEKERIGHE.

Cf *Rotuli de Oblatis temp. Joh.*, ed. T. D. Hardy, p. 588, A.D. 1216.

5679. Sulph. cast. [D.C., D. 206.]

Goyfredus de Becco, [*of Hatton, co. Derb.*]

5680. [*Temp.* Hen. II.] Pale reddish-white : fine, but very imperfect and cracked. 2¼ in. [Harl. ch. 45 H. 5.]

To the r. In armour : hauberk, surcoat, conical helmet with nasal, sword, long convex shield.

. . . . DVS · DE . . . .

5681. Sulph. cast. [D.C., D. 88.]

Walterus Bech, [*of Kirkstead, co. Linc.*]

5682. [Late 12th cent.] Light reddish-brown : fine, varnished. 2¼ in. [Harl. ch. 45 H. 6.]

To the r. In armour : hauberk of mail, conical helmet with nasal, sword, shield with central spike. Horse springing. The saddle cloth fringed with five tassels.

✠ SIGILLVM WALTERI BECH.

5683. Sulph. cast. [D.C., D. 89.]

Cf. *Rotuli de Oblatis temp. Joh.*, ed. T. D. Hardy, p. 370, A.D. 1206.

Warnerius de Begalaia, [of Beely, co. Derb.]

5684. [Early 13th cent.] Dark mottled green: fine, much injured. About $1\frac{7}{8}$ in. when perfect. [Woll. ch. i. 13.]

To the r. In armour: hauberk, conical helmet with nasal, sword, shield with central spike. Horse galloping.

✠ SIGIL . . . .

Gilbertus de Benigwore, Benigwrd or Benigwurthe, [of Alton, etc., co. Linc.]

5685. [Late 12th and early 13th centt.] Brown, opaque: fine, edge slightly chipped. About $2\frac{1}{8}$ in. [Harl. ch. 45 I. 53.]

To the r. In armour: hauberk, surcoat, round-topped helmet with back-ties and nasal, sword, long convex shield.

✠ SIGILLVM GILBERTI DE BENINGWORE.

5686. Light-brown: fine, but imperfect, r. side wanting. [Harl. ch. 45 I. 52.]

5687. Dark-green: fine, showing mark of handle. [Harl. ch. 45 I. 54.]

5688. Dark-green: fine, slightly chipped. [Harl. ch. 45 I. 56.]

5689. Dark-green: very fine, showing the composition of the leathern surcoat with quilted work (cf. J. Hewitt, *Ancient Armour in Europe*, vol. i., p. 126). [Harl. ch. 46 A. 1.]

5690. Sulph. cast from No. 5689. [D.C., E. 201.]

5691. Plaster cast from fine example, chipped. [lxxviii. 29.]

5692. Pale greenish-white, varnished: very imperfect, lower part wanting. [Harl. ch. 46 A. 2.]

5693. Dark-green: fine, slightly chipped. [Harl. ch. 46 A. 5.]

5694. Dark-brown, opaque: imperfect and edge chipped. [Harl. ch. 46 A. 7.]

Cf. *Rotuli de Oblatis temp. Joh.*, ed. T. D. Hardy, p. 369, A.D. 1206 ; p. 459, A.D. 1207 ; p. 589, A.D. 1216.

Matheus de Beningworth.

5695. [12th cent.] Plaster cast from chipped and indistinct impression. $1\frac{7}{8}$ in. [lxxviii. 28.]

To the r. In armour: hauberk of mail, conical helmet, sword, convex shield.

✠ SIGILLVM MATHEV DE . . . .

Robertus de Berevilla, [of Scopwick, co. Linc.]

5696. [Early Hen. II.] Greenish-brown: fine. 2 in. [Add. ch. 20,863.]

To the r. In armour: hauberk and coif of mail, surcoat, conical helmet with nasal, sword, long convex shield with star-like ornament.

✠ SIGILLVM ROBERTI DE BEREVILLA.

Robertus de Berchelaya *or* Berkelai, [*ob.* $\overset{Suce\ 1190}{\text{A.D.}}$ 1219.]
5697. [Late 12th cent.] Plaster cast from chipped impression. 2⅜ in. [lxxix. 60.]
∅. To the r. In armour: hauberk of mail, cap-like helmet with nasal, sword, scabbard, shield of arms: a chevron. Horse galloping.

     ✠ SIGILLV .... OBERTI · DE · BERCHELAYA.

R. A smaller oval counterseal. 1½ × 1⅜ in. A warrior, riding to the l. on a galloping horse. From a fine antique oval intaglio gem, set in a metal rim bearing the legend:—

     ✠ SIGILLVM : ROBERTI : DE : BERKELAI.

Radulfus de Berneres II., [*of Great Waldingfield, co. Suff.*]
5698. [*Temp.* Hen. III.] Creamy-white: indistinct; app. by a plaited cord of variously coloured silk strands. 1⅝ in. [Harl. ch. 46 D. 2.]
To the r. In armour: hauberk, surcoat, flat-topped helmet, sword, shield. Horse galloping.

     ✠ SIGILL' · RADVLFI · DE B .. E .... SECVNDI.

Willelmus Berner, [*son of* HUGH BERNER,
of Haburc or Habrough, co. Lincoln.]
5699. [A.D. 1147–1168.] Light-red, mottled: fine, with mark of handle of matrix. 2 in. [Harl. ch. 46 B. 2.]
To the r. In armour: hauberk of mail, conical helmet with nasal, sword, long convex shield with central spike.

     ✠ SIGILLVM WILLELMI BERИER.

5700. Sulph. cast. [D.C., D. 99.]
5701. [A.D. 1147–1168.] Green, discoloured: the edge chipped. [Harl. ch. 46 B. 3.]

James [**Bertie,** 1*st*] *Earl of Abingdon,*
Baron Norreys of Rycott. [A.D. 1682–1699.]
5702. Proof impression in reddish-brown wax from matrix. 2¼ in. [xxxix. 40.]
To the l. On a mount, replenished with foliage. In plate armour: plumed helmet, sash, sword. Horse springing.

✿ SIGILLVM · PRÆNOBILIS · IACOBI · COMITIS · DE · ABINGDON ·
     ET · BARONIS · NORREYS · DE · RYCOTT.

Carved borders.

Montague [**Bertie-Venables,** 2*nd*] *Earl of Abingdon,*
Baron Norreys of Rycott. [A.D. 1699–1743.]
Constable of the Tower, Lord Lieut. of the Tower Hamlets.
5703. [A.D. 1702.] Red, covered with paper, before impression: indistinct. 2¼ in. [Add. ch. 13,630.]

∅. Apparently same as *obv.* of preceding seal, No. 5702, with legend altered.

    ✿ SIGILLVM · PRÆNOBILIS · MONTAG · COMITIS · DE · ABINGDON · ET · BARONIS · NORREYS · DE · RYCOTT.

℞. A shield of arms of six quarterings : 1. quarterly, i., iv., two bars, VENABLES ; ii., iii., three battering-rams barwise in pale, headed and garnished, BERTIE ; 2. quarterly, in the second and third quarters a fret, over all a fess, NORREYS ; 3. Semé of fleurs-de-lis a lion rampant ; 4. quarterly, in the first quarter a pierced mullet ; 5. a fess betw. three crescents, LEE ; 6. a chevron betw. three mullets, DANVERS. Ensigned with an earl's coronet. Supporters, *dex.* a friar with crutch and rosary, *sin.* a savage wreathed about the temples and middle.

On a scroll in base, the motto : VIRTVS · ARIETE · FORTIOR. Carved border.

5704. [A.D. 1702.] Another. [Add. ch. 13,631.]

5705. [A.D. 1712.] Another, pressed. [Add. ch. 13,642.]

Cf. Add. ch. 13,644 ; where the *rev.* is used separately as a shield of arms.

Rogerus Bertram, *Lord of Mitford,* [*co. Northumb.*]

5706. [A.D. 1267–1269.] Dark-green : fine. App. by a closely woven cord of variegated silk. 1⅞ in. [Harl. ch. 46 D. 15.]

∅. To the r. In armour : hauberk of mail, surcoat, flat-topped helmet with vizor closed, sword, shield of arms. Horse caparisoned. Arms : an orle betw. eleven crosses crosslet, BERTRAM.

    ✠ S' ROGERI · B'TRAM · DÑI · D' · MIDFORD.

℞. Small counterseal. 1 in. A shield of arms, as in *obv.*

    ✠ SIGILLVM : SECRETI : ᴍ

5707. Sulph. casts of the *obv.* and *rev.* [D.C., E. 262, 263.]

Rogerus Bigod, [*4th*] *Earl of Norfolk.* [A.D. 1225–1270.]

5708. [A.D. 1232–1234.] Creamy-white : fine, cracked and imperfect. About 2¾ in. when perfect. [Add. ch. 17,735.]

∅. To the r. In armour : hauberk of mail, surcoat, flat-topped helmet with vizor down, sword, shield of arms : a cross, in base, a lion passant.

    ✠ SIGI .... CO .... HIE.

℞. A smaller counterseal. 1⅞ in. A shield of arms : a cross, BIGOD.

    ✠ SECRETVM · ROGERI · COMITIS · NORFOLCHIE.

Privy Seal, as Marshal of England.

5709. [A.D. 1255.] Dark-green : fine, edge chipped. 1 in. [Add. ch. 7207.]

To the r. In armour : hauberk of mail, surcoat, flat-topped

helmet with vizor down, sword, shield of arms. Horse caparisoned. Arms : a cross, BIGOD.

✠ SECR · R · COMITIS · INORIF' · MAR' · ANGLIE .

Beaded borders.

Cf. *Vetusta Monumenta*, vol. i., p. 29. Notes to Upton, *De Studio militari*, p. 40.

Another Seal ?

5710. [A.D. 1259.] Plaster cast from indistinct impression. 1 in. [lxxix. 62.]

To the r. In armour : hauberk, flat-helmet, sword, shield of arms. Horse caparisoned. Very similar to the preceding.

.. SEOR' R' COMITIS NORF' MAR' ANG' ...

Radulfus fil. Idonis de Bilesbi, [*of Huttoft, co. Linc.*]

5711. [Early Hen. III.] Dark-green : indistinct, edge very imperfect. About 2¼ in. when perfect. [Harl. ch. 47 F. 22.]

To the r. In armour : hauberk or shirt of mail, conical helmet with nasal, sword, long convex shield with central spike. Horse galloping.

SIGIL..... V .. I FILII IDONIS DE BIL ....

5712. Sulph. cast. [D.C., D. 180.]

Henricus Biset, [*of Fordingbridge, co. Hants.*]

5713. [Early 13th cent.] Brown : only a fragment of the centre. About 1¾ in. when perfect. [Harl. ch. 46 E. 5.]

To the r. In armour.

Legend wanting.

Cf. *Rotuli de Oblatis temp. Joh.*, ed. T. D. Hardy, pp. 4, 44, 399, 458.

Ricardus de Blevile, [*of Blofield ?, co. Norf*]

5714. [Early 13th cent.] Brownish-white, or discoloured : indistinct and edge imperfect. 2¼ in. [Harl. ch. 46 E. 23.]

To the r. In armour : hauberk, surcoat, helmet, broadsword, shield. Horse springing.

.... IGILL ....

Cf. *Rotuli de Oblatis temp. Joh.*, ed. T. D. Hardy, pp. 327, 537.

5715. Sulph. cast. [D.C., D. 201.]

Alanus de Blez.

5716. [Late 12th cent.] Plaster cast from indistinct impression. 1¼ in. [lxxviii. 31.]

To the r. In armour: hauberk of mail, cap-like helmet, sword, shield.

✠ SIGILLVM ALANI DE BLEZ.

Ricardus de Blukeville, [*son of* ROGER DE BLUKEVILLE, *of Winwick, co. Northants.*]

"*New Seal.*"

5717. [*circ.* A.D. 1225.] Dark-green : fine, edge chipped. 1½ in. [Add. ch. 22,544.]

To * the r. In armour : hauberk, surcoat, cap-shaped helmet, sword, shield. Horse springing.
❈ SIGILLVM RICADI (*sic*) DE BLVKEVILL'.

Willelmus Blunde, [*of Ixworth, co. Suff.*]

5718. [Early 13th cent.] Discoloured green : very imperfect and indistinct. About 1¾ in. when perfect. [Harl. ch. 46 E. 31.]
To the r. In armour.
Legend wanting.

Ricardus de Blunvi.

5719. [Late 12th cent.] Plaster cast from fine impression. 1⅝ in. [lxxviii. 32.]
To the r. In armour : hauberk of mail, surcoat, conical helmet, sword, kite-shaped shield with central spike. Horse galloping.
❈ SIGILL' RICARDI DE BLVNVI.

Humfridus de Bohun, *or* Boun, [2*nd*] *Earl of Hereford,*
[A.D. 1220–1275,] and [1*st*] *Earl of Essex.*

5720. [A.D. 1259.] Plaster casts from chipped and some-what indistinct impression. 2⅓ in. [lxxviii. 36, 37.]
Ø. To the r. In armour : hauberk of mail, surcoat, flat helmet, sword, shield of arms (see *rev.*). Horse galloping. In base, a bifurcated tree. Fine style of workmanship.
❈ SIGILLV · HVMFRIDI · DE · BOVN · COMITIS · HERFOR
. . . . . ESSESIE.
R. A shield of arms : a bend cotised betw. six lioncels, BOHUN. Above the shield an estoile of eight points, on each side a small shield of arms : quarterly, FITZ-PIERS, Earl of Essex, his maternal arms.
❈ SIGILL . . . . E · BOV . . OMITIS · HERFORDIE ET
ESS . . . IE.

Smaller Equestrian Seal.

5721. [A.D. 1274.] Plaster cast from fine impression, chipped at the lower l. h. side. 1⅛ in. [lxxviii. 38.]
To the l. In a fur mantle, with conical cap, on l. wrist a hawk.
S'. H̄ : DE : BOHVN : COMITIS : HERF . . . . [E]T : ESSEXIE.
Beaded borders.

Humfridus de Bohun, [4*th*] *Earl of Hereford, Earl of Essex,*
and *Lord High Constable.* [A.D. 1297–1301.]

5722. [A.D. 1301.] Plaster cast from fine impression, chipped at the bottom. 2¾ in. [lxxviii. 39, 40.]

---

* The following paragraph, towards the end of the charter, bears on the history of the seal :—" Set quia per consilium mutavi sigillum meum quod prius fuit : *Secretum Ricardi de Blukeville*, feci eciam omnes cartas suas, quas eis feci, in presentem cartam redigere, et eam *sigillo* meo *novo* signavi."

Ø. To the r. In armour: hauberk of mail, surcoat, helmet with vizor down and fan plume, sword, shield of arms. Horse galloping, caparisoned and plumed. Arms: BOHUN, see No. 5720.

S' H' DE BOHVN : COMITIS . . . . ET : ⁹STABVLAR' · ANGL'.

The letters AB and AR, in *Constabular*', conjoined.

Ŗ. A shield of arms: BOHUN, sustained by a loop over a swan. On each side a shield of arms: FITZ-PIERS, surmounted by a slipped trefoil.

✠ : S' : HVMFRIDI : DE : BOHV . . . . [C]OMITIS : HEREFORDIE : ET : ESSEXIE :

Herebertus de Bolebec, [*of Hampden, co. Buck.*]

5723. [Early 13th cent.] Creamy-white: imperfect and indistinct. About 1¾ in. when perfect. [Slo. ch. xxxii. 58.]

To the r. In armour: sword, shield. Horse galloping.

SIGILL . . . . DE BOLEB . . . . .

Cf. *Rotuli de Oblatis temp. Joh.*, ed. T. D. Hardy, p. 68, A.D. 1200.

Johanes de Bolebi, [*of Bulby, co. Linc.*]

5724. [A.D. 1170–1190.] Greenish-brown: fine, well preserved. 2¼ in. [Add. ch. 20,622.]

To the r. In armour: hauberk of mail, surcoat, conical helmet with nasal, sword, long convex shield.

SIGILLVM IOHAИIS DE BOLEBI.

5725. Another. [Add. ch. 20,623.]

5726. Another. Dark greenish-brown: fine. [Add. ch. 20,701.]

5727. [A.D. 1167–1174.] Another. Green. [Add. ch. 20,624.]

Gillebertus de Bulonia, *or* Bolonia, [*of co. Linc.*]

5728. [13th cent.] Cast in red composition from original seal bel. to Hon. E. Stanhope (No. 3). [lii. 2.]

To the r. In armour: hauberk, surcoat, round-topped helmet, sword, long convex shield with central spike. Horse galloping.

✠ SIGILLVM GILLEBERTI DE BVLONIA.

Willelmus de Bolonia, [*of Alfladwick, co. Hert.*]

5729. [Late 12th cent.] Creamy-white: indistinct, and imperfect. 1¼ in. [Add. ch. 28,346.]

To the r. looking back. In long surcoat, with hawk on l. fist.

. . . . LL'MI D . . . .

Ranulfus de Bonekil.

5730. [Late 12th cent.] Plaster cast from fine impression. 1¾ in. [lxxviii. 43.]

·To the r. In armour: hauberk of mail, surcoat, flat cap-like helmet with nasal, sword, kite-shaped shield without spike.

      ✠ SIGILL' RANVLFI DE BONEKIL :

Ernaldus de Bosco, *or* **de Nemore,** [*of Syresham,*
co. Northt., &c.]

5731. [*circ.* A.D. 1147.]   Greenish-brown : fine, chipped ; app. by a green silk cord.   2⅛ in. [Harl. ch. 84 H. 46.]
To the r. In armour: hauberk, conical helmet with nasal, sword, kite-shaped shield showing only the interior side. Horse springing.

     ✠ SIGILLVM ERN . . . .

5732. Sulph. cast.   [D.C., D. 63.]
5733. [A.D. 1147.]   Discoloured, varnished brown : imperfect and indistinct.   [Harl. ch. 84 H. 45.]

        . . . . I DE . . . .

5734. Sulph. cast.   [D.C., D. 62.]

Another Seal.

5735. [*Temp.* Hen. II.]   Reddish-yellow : fine, cracked and imperfect.   About 3 in. when perfect.   [Harl. ch. 84 H. 47.]
To the l. In armour: hauberk of mail, conical helmet, long lance and flag, sword in belt, long kite-shaped shield. Horse galloping, with saddle and breastband.

      . . . ILL . . . . . DE NEMORE.

5736. Sulph. cast.   [D.C., D. 64.]
5737. [*Temp.* Hen. II.] Dark red, varnished: very imperfect. [Harl. ch. 84 H. 48.]

       . . . . E.

5738. Pale yellow : fine, but edge entirely destroyed.

       . . . . ORE.

5739. Sulph. cast.   [D.C., D. 65.]

Ernaldus de Bosco, *or* **de Nemore,** (*a later*) [*of Houghton,*
co. Northt.]

5740. [End of 12th cent.]   Green, mottled : fine, edge imperfect, with mark of the handle.   About 2 in. when perfect. [Harl. ch. 84 H. 52.]
Ø. To the r. In armour: hauberk and coat of mail, nasal, sword, long kite-shaped shield strengthened with an ornament like an escarbuncle.   Horse springing.

     ✠ SIGILLVM ERNALDI DE NEMORE.

R. Small oval counterseal.   1¾ × 1⅛ in. Impression of an antique oval intaglio gem, set in a metal rim. A classical subject of three figures, one with helmet and shield, on an estrade.

     ✠ SECRETVM · HERNALDI · DE · BOSCO.

Beaded border.

5741. Sulph. cast of the *rev.* only. [D.C., D. 66.]

5742. [Late 12th cent.] Dark-green, mottled: originally fine, very imperfect. App. by faded purple silk strands. [Harl. ch. 84 H. 51.]

✠ SIGILL . . . . RE.

No counterseal.

5743. [Beg. 13th cent.] Opaque yellow uncoloured: fine. Mark of handle. [Harl. ch. 84 H. 53.]

✠ SIGILLVM ERNALDI DE NEMORE.

No counterseal.

Henricus fil. Rogeri de Bosco, [*of Flixton, co. Suff.*]

5744. [*Temp.* Hen. III.] Dark reddish-brown: fine, chipped at the edge. 1⅞ in. [L.F.C., i. 21.]

To the r. In armour: surcoat of mail, here indicated in a curious manner by a chequy or hatched pattern, square-topped helmet; reaching out the r. hand. In the field on the l. a spear, obliquely set, and over it a shield of arms: an escutcheon and chief.

✠ SIGILLVM . . . NRICI FIL' RO . . ER' DE B'SCO.

5745. White: very imperfect and indistinct. [Stowe Collection: Flixton Charters, 14.]

. . . LLVM . . . . . NRI . . . . DE B'SCO.

Willelmus de Bosco Roardi (?).

5746. [Late 12th cent.] Plaster cast from good but chipped impression. 1¼ in. [lxxviii. 44.]

To the r. In armour: hauberk, round flat cap, sword, kite-shaped shield. Horse galloping.

✠ SIGILL' WILLELMI DE BOSCO ROARDI (?)

Rogerus de Brai, [*of Dunton, co. Bedford.*]

5747. [*Temp.* Rich. I.] Brownish-red: fine. 2⅛ in. [Harl. ch. 83 A. 47.]

To the r. In armour: hauberk of mail, conical helmet with nasal, sword, shield with ornamental bands for support.

✠ SIGILLVM ROGERI DE BRAI.

5748. Sulph. cast. [D.C., D. 121.]

Another Seal.

5749. [Early 13th cent.] Uncoloured, varnished: edge chipped. 2 in. [Harl. ch. 84 I. 20.]

To the r. In armour: hauberk, round-topped helmet, sword, convex shield strengthened with a cross or escarbuncle, and central spike.

✠ SIGILLVM ROGERI DE BRAI

5750. Sulph. cast. [D.C., D. 122.]

Braibroc (Robertus de). *v.* Filius Ingebaldi (Robertus).

Wilem fil. Bernardi de Breclosbi, [*of Brocklesby, co. Linc.*]
5751. [A.D. 1153–1168.] Reddish-brown : fine, cracked, with mark of the handle. 2 in. [Harl. ch. 47 C. 20.]
To the r. In armour : hauberk, conical helmet with nasal, sword, convex shield with central spike. Horse prancing.
✠ SIGILLVM : WILEM · FILIV : BERNARDI : DE BRECLOSBI.
5752. Sulph. cast. [D.C., D. 83.]

Willelmus de Breosa, *juvenis.*
5753. [Early 13th cent.] Plaster cast from fine impression, chipped on the r. h. side. 2¾ in. [lxxviii. 51.]
To the r. In armour : hauberk of mail, conical helmet and nasal, sword, convex shield with central boss and radiating lines in form of an estoile of eight points. Horse galloping.
SIG . . . . . . LELMI DE BREOSA IVVENIS.
Cf. *Rotuli de Oblatis temp. Joh.*, ed. T. D. Hardy, p. 460, A.D. 1208.

Simon le Breth, *or* Brito, [*of co. Som. ?*]
5754. [*Temp.* John.] Plaster cast from fine but imperfect impression. 2¼ in. [lxxviii. 45.]
To the r. In armour : hauberk of mail, surcoat, sword, convex shield with spike. Horse galloping.
. . . GILLV . . SIMONIS · LE · BR . . . . .
5755. Another, from chipped impression. [lxxviii. 47.]
This shows the head with conical helmet.
✠ SIGILLVM SIMONIS . . . . BRI . . .

Bretby *or* Bretuel (Robert de).
v. Bellomonte (Robertus Fitz-Parnell de).

Willelmus Brito, [*or* Le Bretun *of Tecken', Teton, co. Northt.*]
5756. [13th cent.] Red : fine but imperfect, with mark of the handle. About 2⅛ in. when perfect. [Add. ch. 22,479.]
·To the r. In armour : hauberk, surcoat, helmet, sword, shield with central spike. Horse galloping.
✠ . . . . I BRIT[ON]IS.

Conanus [Le Petit,] *Duke of Brittany and* [*5th*] *Earl of Richmond.* [A.D. 1165–1171.]
5757. Dark-red : a small fragment. [Harl. ch. 48 G. 43.]
∅. To the r. In hauberk of mail. Horse with ornamental saddle.
. . . . [COMIT]IS RIC[HEMVNDIE].
℞. Similar to the *obv.*
. . . . . [CON]ANI . . . .

5758. Creamy-white: fine, but very imperfect. About 3¾ in. when perfect. [Add. ch. 28,335.]

5759. Uncoloured, creamy-white: fine, the lower r. h. side broken off. App. by a skein of faded silks. [Harl. ch. 48 G. 40.]

Ø. To the r. In armour: hauberk of mail, continuous coif, surcoat, conical helmet and nasal, long convex shield with broad bordure and ornamental bands; in the r. h. a long lance with flag and streamers overhead. Horse galloping.

✠ SIGILLVM CONANI DVCIS BRITAJNNIE.

R. To the r. In armour: hauberk of mail, and continuous coif, conical helmet, kite-shaped shield, showing interior side, ornamented with diaper work and a broad bordure, sword, sash or baldric. Horse with ornamental saddle.

✠ SIGILLVM [CONANI COMITIJS RICHEMVNDIE.

The letter S in *Sigillum* and *Ducis*, reversed.

5760. Sulph. casts of the *obv.* and *rev.* [D.C., D. 109, 110.]

Engr. apparently from this example, when it was perfect, in the *Registrum Honoris de Richmond*, London, 1722, folio, pl. fig. iii. See also Add. MS. 6728, f. 15; and Douët D'Arcq, *Collection de Sceaux*, No. 531.

Ra[nnulph] del Broc, [" *Hostiarius*" and] *Marshal of King* [*Henry II.*]

5761. [12th cent.] Sulph. cast from imperfect impression. About 2 in. when perfect. [D.C., D. 162.]

To the r. In armour: hauberk, surcoat, conical helmet with nasal, sword, long convex shield. Horse galloping.

✠ SIGILLV RA . . . . . . DEL BROC MARESCALLI REGI.

The S in *Sigillu* is reversed.

5762. Plaster cast. [lxxix. 66.]

R. de Broc, Hostiarius, etc., occurs in the *Rotuli de Oblatis temp. Joh.*, ed. T. D. Hardy, p. 339, A.D. 1206.

Broclosbi (Eudo, *son of* HENRY DE). *v.* Aufort (Ido de).

Henricus Clericus [fil. Nigelli] de Brocelausbi, [*of Brocklesby, co. Linc.*]

5763. [A.D. 1153–1168.] Light reddish-brown: fine, with mark of the handle, edge chipped. 2 in. [Harl. ch. 47 C. 21.]

To the r. In armour: hauberk, surcoat with long maunch on the r. wrist, conical helmet with nasal, long convex shield with central spike, lance with flag and split streamers (the flag bears a saltire).

✠ SIGILLVM HENRICI CLERICI DE BROCELAVSBI

5764. Sulph. cast. [D.C., D. 82.]

VOL. II.

Radulffus de Buctun, [or BUCHETUN, *of Ancaster, co. Linc.*]

5765. [13th cent.] Dark-green: fine, with mark of the handle. 1⅞ in. [Eg. ch. 509.]

To the r. In armour: hauberk of mail, conical helmet with nasal, sword, long convex shield. Horse springing.

✠ SIGILLVM RADVLFFI · DE · BVCTVN.

Johannes Bucuinte, [*son of* GEOFFREY BUCOINTE, *of London.*]

5766. [Late 12th cent.] Dark-green, mottled: fine, but imperfect; app. by a finely woven hollow bobbin of green taffeta. 2 in. [Add. ch. 1046.]

To the r. In armour: hauberk, surcoat, helmet with nasal, sword, shield with bordure. Horse galloping. In base a wyvern, tail flory and nowed, wings expanded.

.... ILL' · IOHANNIS F .... BVCVINTE—

The letters NN in *Johannis*, and TE in *Bucuinte*, respectively conjoined.

Geof. Bokointe occurs *temp. Joh.*

Johannes Bucuinte.

5767. [Late 12th cent.] Plaster cast from fine impression. 2⅛ in. [lxxviii. 53.]

To the r. In armour: hauberk of mail, surcoat, conical helmet, sword, convex shield with central spike.

✠ SIGILLVM IOHANNIS BVCVINTE.

Godardus de Buiun ...

5768. [Late 12th cent.] Plaster cast from a chipped impression. 1⅝ in. [lxxviii. 42.]

To the r. In armour: hauberk of mail, surcoat, conical helmet, sword, convex shield. Horse galloping.

SIGILLVM · GODARDI · DE · BVIVN ...

Hubertus de Burgo, [*Earl of Kent, Justice of England.*]

5769. [A.D. 1227–1233.] Pale-green: fine, very imperfect; app. by a finely woven hollow bobbin of green taffeta. About 2¼ in. when perfect. [Add. ch. 20,407.]

∅. To the r. In armour: hauberk of mail, surcoat, sword, shield of arms. Horse caparisoned. Arms: seven lozenges, three, three, and one vairé (or lozengy of fifteen pieces), BURGH.

Legend destroyed.

℞. A shield of arms as described in the *obv.*

Legend destroyed.

5770. [A.D. 1227–1229.] Dark-green: fine, very imper-

fect; app. by a finely woven cord of faded purple taffeta.
[L. F. C., ii. 12.]

Legend destroyed.

Cf. *Journ. Brit. Arch. Assoc.*, vols. ix., p. 371, xiv. pl. xvi.

Another Seal.

5771. Plaster casts from fine but imperfect impression, the
edge entirely gone. [lxxviii. 55.]

Ø. To the r. In armour: hauberk of mail, surcoat of arms:
round cap, sword, shield of arms. Horse caparisoned. Arms
as in the *rev.*

Legend wanting.

R. A kite-shaped shield of arms: masculy or lozengy of
nineteen pieces, five, three, and one, vairé, BURGH. This is
a variant of the arms on the preceding *rev.*, where the mascles
or lozenges are only three in number in the row in chief.

Legend wanting.

Johannes de Burgo, [*son and heir of* HUBERT DE
BURGO, *of Banstead, co. Surr.*]

5772. [A.D. 1269.] Bronze-green: fine, but imperfect.
2½ in. [Harl. ch. 47 E. 35.]

Ø. To the r. In armour: hauberk of mail, surcoat, flat-
topped helmet, sword, shield of arms slung by a band over
the r. shoulder. Horse caparisoned. Arms: lozengy, [gu.]
and vairé, BURGH.

[·❁· SIG]I[LL]VM [❁ I]IOHANNIS ·❁· DE ·❁· BVRGO ❁

R. Small round counterseal. 1 1/16 in. A shield of arms, as
described in the *obv.*

+ SIGILLVM SECRETI.

Carved borders.

5773. Sulph. cast of the *obv.* only. [D.C., E. 264.]

5774. Sulph. cast of the *rev.* only. [D.C., E. 387.]

5775. [Late Hen. III.] Mottled green: fine, edge injured;
app. by a woven bobbin of green stuff. [Harl. ch. 47 E. 36.]

Ø. This shows a plume of flowers on the helmet, and some
parts of the legend wanting in the previous seal, No. 5772.

·❁· SIGILLVM ❁ IOHANNIS ·❁· DE ·❁· BVRGO ❁

R. As before.

Robertus de Burun, [*of Ossington, co. Nott.*]

5776. [*Temp.* Hen. III.] Pale-yellow, uncoloured, opaque:
fine, imperfect on the l. h. side. 1⅞ in. [Toph. ch. 14.]

·To the r. In armour: hauberk of mail, surcoat, [sword],
shield. Horse galloping. In base a wyvern, to the l., with
expanded wings.

❁ SIGILLVM · ROBERTI · DE . . . .

5777. Sulph. cast. [D.C., E. 233.]

Rogerus de Buterleye, [*fil.* STEPHANI DE BUTERLEYE, *Mil.*]
5778. [13th cent.]   Dark-green : imperfect and indistinct.
1¼ in. [Add. ch. 27,186.]
Ø. To the l.   In armour : surcoat, sword, shield of arms.
Horse caparisoned.   Arms : a fesse between three roses.
. . . . SIЄ S . . . .
R. Small round counterseal, of which nothing remains but
the legend :—
. . . . [S]ЄCRET . . . .

Butiler (William le). *v.* (Pincerna) Willelmus.

Ricardus fil. Johannis de Birun, *Mil.* [*Lord of Cadney,*
                                co. Linc.]
5779. [A.D. 1342.]. . Cast in pale red composition.   1 in.
[lxxviii. 7.]
To the r.   In armour : hauberk, surcoat, crested helmet,
sword, shield of arms.   Horse crested and caparisoned, galloping.   Arms : three bendlets, BYRON.   Crest, a mermaid
with comb and mirror, BYRON.
                S' RICARDI · · DE · BIRVN ·
5780. [A.D. 1340.]   Red : fine, but very fragmentary.
About 1 in.   [Add. ch. 21,449.] ·
. . . . . RDI · DE · BIRVN.

Doubtful, perhaps one of the **Byr**on *Family.*
5781. [Late 13th cent.]   Sulph. cast from fine impression.
1 in. [D.C., F. 154.]
To the l.   In armour : hauberk of mail, flat-topped helmet,
sword, shield of arms.   Horse caparisoned.   Arms : bendy
of six, BYRON ?
The legend consists of a cross, the letter P reversed, fol-
lowed by seven roses of fine points pierced, and as many
fleurs-de-lis, arranged alternately.

Walterus de Cadomo, *or* **Caen.**
5782. [Late 12th or 13th cent.]   Plaster cast from fine
impression.   1⅝ in.   [lxxvii. 58.]
To the r.   In armour : hauberk, surcoat, cap-shaped helmet,
sword, convex shield.   Horse galloping.
        ✠ SIGILLV WALTERI DE CADOMO.
Walter de Cadomo occurs under Yorkshire, in the *Rotuli de Oblatis,*
temp. Joh., ed. T. D. Hardy, p. 52, A.D. 1200.

Morganus Cam, [*of co. Glamorgan.*]
5783. [A.D. 1234.]   Dark-green : fragmentary.   About
1¼ × 1 in. when perfect.   [Harl. ch. 75 A. 25.] .

Pointed oval. To the l. In armour : tunic, helmet, sword.
. . . . ANI · C . . . . . .
5784. [A.D. 1234.] Dark-green : very imperfect· [Harl.
ch. 75 B. 40.]
. . SIGILLV . . . . GANI CA . . .
5785. Sulph. cast. [D.C., E. 214.]

Cam (Morganus.) *v.* Gam (Morganus).

Thomas, [*fil.* **Hamonis] de Camera, [** *of Gt. Totham, co. Ess.*]
5786. [Early 13th cent.] Pale-red :. fine, but imperfect.
2⅛ in. [Harl. ch. 83 E. 1.]
To the r. In armour : hauberk of mail, surcoat, round-
topped helmet with nasal, sword, long convex shield. Horse
springing.
✠ SIG . . . . . . TH . . . . . M.
5787. Sulph. cast. [D.C., D. 174.]

Stephanus Camerarius, [*of Wikingesbi, Wickenby, co. Linc.*]
5788. [A.D. 1187.] Dark-green : imperfect and indistinct.
About 2 in. when perfect. [Harl. ch. 47 I. 9.]
To the r. In armour : surcoat. Horse galloping.
. . . . . ANI CA . . . .

Henricus Camberli . . . ., [*or* **Camerarius,** *of*
Wykingby, Wickenby. co. Linc.]
5789. [*Temp.* Hen. III.] Dark-green : fine edge chipped.
1¾ in. [Harl. ch. 47 I. 21.]
∅ To the r. In armour : hauberk of mail, surcoat, flat-
topped helmet, sword, shield of arms. Horse caparisoned.
Arms : a roundle (?).
S' HERICI CAMBERLI . . . .
R. Small oval counterseal, from a ring, with mark of the
handle. ⅝ × ¼ in. Impression of an antique oval intaglio
gem. VICTORY to the l., with trophies, sacrificing (?)
SIGILLVM SECRETI.
5790. Sulph. cast of *obv.* only. [D.C., E. 228.]

Warnerius de la Campani[a, *of Barrow, co. Linc.*]
5791. [A.D. 1152–1175.] Greenish-brown : fine, with mark
of the handle. 1⅞ in. [Harl. ch. 47 I. 33.]
To the r. In armour : hauberk, conical helmet with nasal,
sword, long convex shield with central spike. Horse
galloping. ✠ SIGILLVM WARNERII DE LA CAMPANI.
5792. Sulph. cast. [D.C., D. 125.]

Petrus de Campania, [*son of* PETER DE CAMPANIA, *of Killingholm, co. Linc.*]

5793. [Early 14th cent.] Light-brown : fine, with marks of the setting as a ring. $\frac{5}{16}$ in. [Harl. ch. 47 I. 37.]

To the r. In armour : hauberk of mail, surcoat, helmet, sword, shield. Horse caparisoned. The seal is remarkable for the smallness of its size in comparison with other seals of this class.

The legend is complete, but very small and faintly impressed.

      ❀ S' BON . . . . SLI . . . . . .

Gerardus de Campo (?).

5794. [13th cent.] Sulph. cast from imperfect impression. About $2\frac{1}{4}$ in. when perfect. [D.C., D. 179.]

To the r. In armour : hauberk, conical helmet and nasal, sword, long convex shield. Legend wanting.

(Attributed by Doubleday to Gerard, son of Wlric de Campo, whose seal, an ornamental design, is attached to Harl. ch. 47 G. 10.)

Martinus de la Chapele, [*or* **de Capella,** *of Denham, co. Buck.*]

5795. [*circ.* A.D. 1176–1191.] Light-brown : fine, edge chipped. $1\frac{3}{4}$ in. [Harl. ch. 111 C. 38.]

To the r. In armour : hauberk of mail, furnished with a long loose tail or flap, conical helmet, with nasal, sword, convex shield with strengthening bands and central spike. Horse springing, elegantly designed, somewhat resembling the Greek style.

      ❀ SIGILLV . . . . . TINI : DE : LA : CHAPELE.

5796. Sulph. cast. [D.C., D. 151.]

Ernolphus de Certrifelt (? Cestrefelde.)
(A doubtful seal.)

5797. [A.D. 1143.] Plaster cast from fine impression, the edge chipped. 2 in. [lxxviii. 77.]

To the r. In armour : hauberk, continuous coif, conical helmet, sword, kite-shaped shield showing interior side bordered, and held by a short strap.

      ❀ SIGILLVM ERNOLPHI · DE · CERTRIFELT.

Robertus Chambort, *or* **Chambord** [*of Cowton, cc. York.*]

5798. [Early Hen. II.] Red : with mark of the handle. $1\frac{3}{4}$ in. [Add. ch. 20,564.]

To the r. In armour : hauberk of mail, surcoat, conical helmet and nasal, sword, long convex shield.

      ❀ SIGILLVM ROBE . . . . CHA . . . ORT.

Walterus de Chanci, [*of Skirpenbeck, co. York.*]

5799. [A.D. 1207.] Green: large and thick mass, as is usually found with the charters of Byland Abbey, of which this is one. 1¾ in. [Add. ch. 20,589.]

To the r. In armour: hauberk of mail, conical helmet with nasal, sword, shield with bordure, central spike, and ornamental bands of strengthening. Horse galloping.

✠ SIGILL' WALTERI DE CHANCI.

The letter N is reversed.

Ricardus de Chandos, [*of Wilmarston, co. Heref.*]

5800. [Early 13th cent.] Pale-green: originally fine, now very imperfect on the l. h. side. About 1⅞ in. [Add. ch. 20,416.].

To the r. In armour: hauberk of mail, surcoat, helmet with nasal, sword, shield with ornamental strengthening like a star or escarbuncle. Horse galloping.

✠ SIGILL' : RICARDI : DE . . . . . . A·

Robertus de Chaucumba.

5801. [Late 12th cent.] Plaster cast from fine but chipped impression. 1¾ in. [lxxviii. 62.]

To the r. In flowing surcoat, and with round cap, a falcon by the jesses on the r. wrist.

✠ SIGILL' ROBERTI DE CHAVCVMBA.

Paganus de Chaorciis, [*or* Chaurciis, *of Kempsford, co. Glouc.*]

5802. [Early 13th cent.] Dark mottled green: fine, the edge chipped. 2¾ in. [L. F. C., vii. 2.]

∅. To the r. In armour: hauberk of mail, surcoat, flat helmet, sword, shield of arms. Arms appear to be: barry of eight. The arms of CHAWORTH are: barry an orle of martlets.

✠ SIGILL' PA[G]A[N]I DE CHAORCIIS.

The letter N is reversed.

℞. A smaller counterseal. 1⅜ in. A shield of arms much defaced, but apparently: barry unnumbered.

✠ SECRETVM PAGANI· DE CHAORCIIS.

Paganus de Chaurciis [*or* Paen de Chaworth, *Chev.*].

5803. [A.D. 1270.] Green: fine, very imperfect. About 1¼ in. when perfect. [Add. ch. 19,829.]

To the r. In armour: hauberk of mail, surcoat, sword, [shield of arms]. Horse caparisoned. Arms: barry, an orle of martlets, CHAWORTH.

. . . . [CH]AVRC[IIS]·

CHESTER.
Rannulphus [de Meschines, 3rd] Earl of Chester.
[A.D. 1119–1128.]

5804. Plaster cast from imperfect impression. 3 in. [lxxx. 7.]

To the r. With sword.

...... VM RANNVL .... RE ....

Journ. Brit. Arch. Assoc., vol. v., p. 241, *obv.* only. The seal is here wrongly attributed to Ranulf II., or de Gernons.

Ranulfus, [or Randle de Gernons, 4th] Earl of Chester.
[A.D. 1128–1153.]

5805. Sulph. cast from fine impression. 3 in. [D.C., D. 73.]

To the r. full-face. In a surcoat, with sword. Horse with plain saddle and breast-band.

✠ SIGILLVM RANVLFI COMITIS CESTRIENSIS.

5806. Cast in white plaster. [xxxiv. 29.]

Archæolog., vol. iv., p. 120 ; *Journ. Brit. Arch. Assoc.*, vol. v., p. 241.

Hugo [Cyvelioc, 5th] Earl of Chester. [A.D. 1153–1180.]
FIRST SEAL.

5807. [A.D. 1155–1168.] Light-brown, with dark-brown varnish : fine, very imperfect, only centre remaining. [Harl. ch. 52 A. 13.]

∅. For description see No. 5809.

℞. Two impressions of an oval counterseal, very imperfect. About 1½ × 1⅛ in. when perfect. Impression of an antique oval intaglio gem : two nude athletes in combat, one kneeling on the other, who is falling backward.

[✠] CONTRA SI[GILLVM DO]MINI CESTRIE.

Beaded borders.

The gem in this counterseal was used (according to Randle Holme) by Ranulph or Randle II., de Gernons, 4th Earl of Chester, father of this Hugh, see woodcuts of his seal and counterseal in *Journ. Brit. Arch. Assoc.*, vol. v., p. 241 (J. R. Planché, *On the seals of the Earls of Chester*), but with a different legend. Holme, however, is mistaken in attributing the seal to R. de Gernons.

5808. [A.D. 1163–1185.] Light-brown, with a dark-brown varnish : fine, very fragmentary, only centre remaining. [Stowe Collection, Repyngdon charters, No. 3.]

∅. For description see next seal.

℞. A small oval counterseal. About 1¼ × 1 in. Impression of an antique oval intaglio gem : uncertain subject, perhaps a gnostic gryllus or nondescript emblematical figure.

..... S . E .... TVE .....

5809. Light-brown, with a dark-brown varnish : imperfect. 3¼ in. [Stowe Collection, Burton Charters, No. 3.]

Ø. To the r. In armour: hauberk and coif of mail, embroidered surcoat with long skirt, and full maunch on r. wrist, conical helmet with nasal, in the r. h. a lance with square flag and long streamers: the flag chequy of nine pieces with a roundle in each square, in the l. h. a long convex shield strengthened with an ornamental escarbuncle, and slung round the neck. Horse with ornamental saddle.

[✠ SIG]IL[LV]M · H[VG]ONI2 COMITI2 .CE2TRIE.

The letter S reversed.

℞. Two impressions of a small oval counterseal as described in the next or second seal.

SECOND SEAL.
With counterseal of **Willielmus Barbeaverill.***

5810. [A.D. 1153–1181.] Bright-red: fine, only the centre remaining. About 3 in. when perfect. App. by a diapered bobbin of finely woven threads. [Harl. ch. 83 F. 32.]

Ø. To the r. In armour: hauberk of mail, long pleated surcoat, [helmet, sword,] shield ornamented with a bordure, ornamental strengthenings of a star-like or escarbuncle form. Horse galloping, with saddle, saddle-cloth diapered lozengy with a small cross in each space, and fringed, and ornamental breast-band with pendent pellets.

Legend wanting.

℞. Small oval counterseal. $1\frac{1}{10} \times \frac{7}{10}$ in., with marks of a curiously carved handle. Impression of an antique oval intaglio gem: a gryllus of two human faces conjoined, on the l. Silenus, on the r. Mercury?

✠ SIGILLVM WILELMI BARBEAṼILL.

5811. Sulph. casts of the *obv.* and *rev.* [D.C., D. 114, 115.] *Obv.* in *Journ. Brit. Arch. Assoc.*, vol. v., p. 243.

5812. [A.D. 1175–1180.] Dark-green: very imperfect. [The *obv.* formerly detached and numbered xxxv. 19 (o), but now rejoined to the Cotton ch. x. 7, to which it belongs.]

Ø. As before, the long sword, and some other parts wanting in the preceding seal are shown in this example.

. . . . CO[MITIS] . . . .

℞. Two smaller counterseals:

(1) Heart-shaped: about $1 \times \frac{3}{4}$ in. Impression of an antique oval intaglio gem: a human face. Legend indistinct.

(2.) Oval: slightly larger, the impression of another antique oval intaglio gem. The subject defaced. Legend indistinct. Beaded border.

---

* Cf. Radulphus Barba ap'l', among the witnesses to Stowe ch. Repyngdon, No. 3.

Ranulfus [Blundeville, *6th*] *Earl of Chester,* [*and 4th*]
         Earl of Lincoln. [A.D. 1180–1232.]

5813. [A.D. 1216–1232.]   Creamy-white : fine, imperfect at
the lower part.   3¼ in. when perfect.   [Harl. ch. 52 A. 16.]

Ø. To the r. In armour : hauberk of mail, surcoat, flat-
topped helmet with vizor closed, sword, shield of arms. Horse
caparisoned, galloping.   Arms : three garbs, two and one,
CHESTER.

⊕ SIGI . . . . COM´. . . . . NIE.

℞. Small round counterseal.   1¼ in. A shield of arms as
in the *obv.*

⊕ SECRETVM : RANVLFI : COMITIS : CESTRIE : ET : LINCOLNIE.

Madox, *Formulare Anglicanum; Journ. Brit. Arch. Assoc.,* vol. v.,
p. 246.

5814. Sulph. casts of *obv.* and *rev.*   [D.C., E. 212, 213.]

5815. [A.D. 1231.]   Bronze-green : fine originally, now
injured ; app. by a plaited cord of faded silk. [Cott. ch.
xxiv. 16.]

Journ. Brit. Arch. Assoc., vol. v., p. 246.

Willelmus de Cheurevile, [*or* de **Caravilla,** *of Raydon,*
            co. Suff.]

5816. [A.D. 1281.]   Creamy-white : now indistinct and imperfect.   1¾ in. [Harl. ch. 48 B. 1.]

To the r. In armour : hauberk, surcoat, helmet, sword,
shield.   Horse springing.

. . . . HEVREVILE.

5817. Sulph. cast.   [D.C., E. 272.]

5818. [A.D. 1286.]   Creamy-white : indistinct. [Harl. ch.
47 G. 43.]

. . . . . ELMI : DE : CHE . . . .

Robertus de Chetwode, [*of Horton, co. Northt.*]

5819. [Early 13th cent.]   Dark-green : fine.   1⅛ in. [Harl.
ch. 85 A. 59.]

To the r. In armour : hauberk of mail, surcoat, round-
topped helmet with nasal, sword, long convex shield.   Horse
galloping, with ornamental breast-band.

⊕ SIGILLVM · ROBERTI · DE · CHETWODE.

5820. Sulph. cast.   [D.C., D. 195.]

Philippus de Chime, [*or* **Kyma,** *of co. Linc.*]

5821. [*circ.* A.D. 1172.]   Light-brown, varnished : originally good, now the edge chipped.   About 2¼ in. when perfect.
[Harl. ch. 52 G. 36.]

To the r. In armour: hauberk and coif of mail, surcoat, conical helmet and nasal, long convex shield with ornamental bordure and central boss.

✠ SIGILLV . . . . LIPI DE CHIME.

5822. Sulph. cast. [D.C., D. 105.]

5823. Bright-red, mottled: fine, edge chipped. [Harl. ch. 52 G. 31.]

✠ SIGIL . V . . . . . HI . . . . . DE CHIME.

5824. Dark-red: only a fragment containing the l. h. side. [Harl. ch. 52 G. 32.]

. . . . HIL . . DE CHIME.

5825. Creamy-yellow: very imperfect, edge wanting. [Harl. ch. 52 G. 33.]

Legend wanting.

5826. Light-brown: very imperfect. [Harl. ch. 52 G. 34.]

✠ SIGI . . . . ME.

5827. [*circ.* A.D. 1172.] Light-brown, varnished of a dark colour: only centre part remaining. [Harl. ch. 52 G. 35.]

Legend wanting.

5828. [*circ.* A.D. 1172.] Brown: originally good, now very imperfect, r. h. side and bottom part wanting. [Harl. ch. 52 G. 37.]

. . . . CHIME.

v. Kima (Philippus de).

Willelmus fil. Alani de Claxebi, [*co. Linc.*]

5829. [Early 13th cent.] Brown, mottled, semi-opaque: fine, with mark of handle. 1¾ in. [Harl. ch. 48 B. 39.]

To the r. In armour: hauberk, helmet, sword, long convex shield with central spike, star-like ornament, and bordure.

✠ SIGILL' WILLELMI FILLII ALANI Đ CLAXEBI.

5830. Sulph. cast. [D.C., D. 134.]

5831. [Early 13th cent.] Dark-green: indistinct in places. [Harl. ch. 48 B. 40.]

5832. [Early 13th cent.] Dark-green, mottled: fine. [Harl. ch. 48 B. 41.]

Gilbertus de Clare II. (?), [*called " Strongbow," Earl of Pembroke and Striguil, i.e. Chepstow*], *etc.* [*ob.* A.D. 1148], *or*
Gilbertus de Clare, [*3rd Earl of Clare,* A.D. 1152.]

5833. [*Temp.* Steph.] Plaster cast from fine impression, chipped round the edge. About 3 in. when perfect. [lxxviii. 63.]

To the r. In armour: hauberk of mail and continuous coif, conical helmet and nasal, sword, long convex kite-shaped shield on which are faint traces of the armorial bearings of chevronelly, for CLARE.

[SIGILLV] M · GV . . . . . . LE . . . . . (?)

Gilebertus de Clara, [5*th Earl of Hertford and Gloucester,*
A.D. 1218–1229.]

5834. [A.D. 1218.] Light-brown : fine, now very imperfect,
only centre remaining ; app. by a plaited cord of variegated
threads. About 3 in. when perfect. [Harl. ch. 75 B. 37.]

∅. To the r. In armour : hauberk of mail, surcoat, shield
of arms. Horse caparisoned. Arms : three chevrons, CLARE.
Legend wanting.

R. A smaller counterseal. 1 in. A shield of arms as above.
　　　⚜ SIGILL' GILEBERTI DE CLARA.

5835. [A.D. 1218–1230.] Dark-green : fine, but fragmentary. [Harl. ch. 75 B. 38.]

∅. . . SIGILL' G . . . .

R. As before. _____

Gilebertus de Clare, [7*th*] *Earl of Hertford and Gloucester,*
[A.D. 1261–1295.]

5836. [A.D. 1262–1295.] Dark-green : fine, chipped. 3 in.
[L.F.C., xii. 5.]

∅. To the l. In armour : hauberk of mail, surcoat, flat
helmet with vizor down, sword, shield of arms. Horse
galloping. Arms : three chevrons, CLARE.
　　SIGILL' GILEBERTI · DE · CLARE : COMITIS : . . . . VERNIE.

R. To the r. In armour : hauberk of mail, surcoat, flat
helmet with vizor down, sword, shield of arms. Horse
caparisoned, galloping. Arms : CLARE.
　　SIGILL' : GIL . . . RTI : DE : CLARE : COMITIS : HERTFORDIE.
Beaded borders.
Sandford, *General Hist.,* p. 139 ; Spelman, *Aspilogia, Notæ in Upton,*
p. 68.

5837. [Early Edw. I.] Green : fine, but very fragmentary ;
app. by a closely plaited cord of various colours. [Add.
ch. 20,398.]

5838. [A.D. 1292.] Dark-green : fine, but very fragmentary.
[Cott. ch. xviii. 48.]　　　　　　　　　　　　　　·

_____

Ricardus de Clare, [*of Saltrey, co. Hunt., and*
·　　*Buckenham Parva, co. Norf*]

5839. [*Temp.* Joh.] Green, mottled : indistinct in places.
1⅜ in. [Harl. ch. 83 A. 54.]

To the r. In armour : hauberk, surcoat, sword, shield.
Horse galloping.
　　. . . . ILLVM RICARDI · DE CLARE.

5840. Sulph. cast. [D.C., D. 145.] _____

Ricardus de Clare, [4*th Earl of Hertford,* A.D. 1172–1218.]

5841. Dark-green, mottled : only a fragment of the upper
part. About 2 in. when perfect. [Harl. ch. 111 E. 45.]

To the r. In hauberk, surcoat, conical helmet, sword, kite-shaped shield.

Legend wanting.

Ricardus de Clare, [6th] *Earl of Hertford* [and 6th] *Earl of Gloucester.* [A.D. 1230–1262.]

5842. [*circ.* A.D. 1250.]˙ Creamy-white : fine originally, now very imperfect, only centre remaining. About 2¾ in. when perfect. [Add. ch. 16,531.]

Ø. To the r. In armour : hauberk of mail, surcoat, [flat helmet], sword, shield of arms. Horse caparisoned. Arms : three chevrons, CLARE.

Legend wanting.

℞. A shield of arms of CLARE, as in *obv.*, suspended by a strap, and supported by two lions rampant addorsed.

Legend wanting.

5843. [*circ.* A.D. 1250–1260.] Creamy-white : fine, very imperfect. [Add. ch. 20,039.]

Ø. This shows the helmet and other details wanting in the previous seal.

✠ SIG . . . . IE.

℞ This shows the ornamental foliage at the top of the shield and the strap.

✠ SIG . . . . CAR . . . . E.

Beaded borders.

5844. Plaster casts from fine impression, very much chipped at the edges. [lxxviii. 64, 65.]

Ø. ✠ SIG . . . . CLARE : C[O]MITIS : HERTFORDIE.

℞. ✠ SIGILLVM : RICARDI : DE : CLA . . . . IS : GLO . . . . . . E.

A member of the CLARE *Family.**

5845. Plaster casts from fine impression, edge entirely wanting. About 3¼ in. when perfect. [lxxviii. 66, 67.]

Ø. To the r. In armour : hauberk of mail, surcoat, sword, shield of arms. Horse caparisoned. Arms : three chevrons, CLARE.

Legend wanting.

℞. A shield of arms, CLARE : the chevrons diapré, with wavy scrolls of foliage. Background hatched. Within a broad circle of elegantly designed wavy scrolls of foliage.

Legend wanting.

Clericus de Brocelausbi (Henricus). *v.* Brocelausbi (Henricus Clericus de).

---

* Called by Doubleday, Gilbert de Clare, E. of Gloucester and Hertford.

Ricardus Clericus, [of Branteston, co. Norf, son of BALDEWINE CLERICUS, of the same.]

5846. [13th cent.] Pale-green, discoloured : very imperfect. About 1¾ in. when perfect. [Harl. ch. 48 C. 6.]

To the l. In armour.

Legend wanting.

Radulfus de Climtun.

5847. [Late 12th cent.] Plaster cast from chipped impression. 1¼ in. [lxxviii. 69.]

To the r. In armour : hauberk, surcoat, conical helmet and nasal, sword, shield. Horse galloping.

⊕ SIGILL' RADVLFI [D]E CLIMTVИ.

Radulfus de Clintunia P.

5848. [Late 12th cent.] Plaster cast from indistinct impression. 1¼ in. [lxxviii. 68.]

To the r. In armour : conical helmet, sword, shield. Horse galloping.

⊕ SIGILL' RADVLFI DE CL .... VNIA (?).

Petrus de Codingtun.

5849. [12th cent.] Plaster cast from imperfect impression. 2¼ in. [lxxviii. 70.]

To the l. In armour : hauberk of mail, surcoat, long spear held horizontally, long convex triangular shield.

SIGILLVM PETRI DE CODIИ . . . . .

Roaldus, [son of ALAN, Constabularius] Richemundie, co. York.

5850. [Early 13th cent.] Recent cast in green composition, from original seal bel. to Hon. E. Stanhope ; very imperfect, l. h. side wanting. About 1¼ in. when perfect. [lii. 22, 23.]

Ø. To the r. In armour : kite-shaped shield.

SIGILL' ROALD . . . .

℞. A smaller counterseal. 1 in. A shield of arms of an early character : two bars and a chief.

⊕ S' RO . . . . RICHEMVИDIE.

Also called Reulend, or Ruold fil. Alani, Constabularius Richemund', in *Rotuli de Oblatis, temp. Joh.*, pp. 569, 603.

Radulfus de C[ornhill P].

5851. [Early 13th cent.] Plaster cast from imperfect impression. 2¼ in. [lxxix. 94.]

To the r. In armour : convex shield slung by a strap round the shoulders. Horse galloping. In the field, below the horse, an elegantly designed flower.

⊕ SIGILLVM RADVLFI DE C . . . .

Robertus de Curtenai, [COURTENAY, *of co. Cumb.?*].
5852. [Early 13th cent.] Plaster cast from fine but
chipped impression. 2 in. [lxxviii. 76.]
To the r. In armour: hauberk, surcoat, flat helmet, sword,
shield. Horse galloping.

⁜ SIGILLVM .. BER ... Є CVRTЄNAI.

- **Rogerus de Creft,** [*or* CREFTH, *of Helmedon, co. Northt.*]
5853. [*circ.* A.D. 1225.] Dark-green : fine, with mark of
the handle. 2¼ in. [Harl. ch. 85 B. 51.]
To the l. In armour: hauberk, surcoat, conical helmet
with nasal, long lance or spear in the r. h., long kite-shaped
shield in the l. h.

⁜ SIGILLVM ROGERI DE CREFT.

5854. [*circ.* A.D. 1225–1230.] Dark-green : fine, with mark
of the handle. [Harl. ch. 85 B. 52.]
5855. [*circ.* A.D. 1225–1230.] Dark-green : very fine and
sharp. [Harl. ch. 85 B. 53.]
5856. Sulph. cast of the previous seal, No. 5855. [D.C.,
D. 164.]

Hamo, [*fil.* ECARDI] **de Crevequer,** [*of Blean, co. Kent.*]
5857. [Early Hen. III.] Green, mottled: fine, edge
chipped. 1¾ in. [Add. ch. 919.]
To the right. In armour: hauberk, surcoat, round-topped
helmet, sword, convex shield. Horse galloping.

⁜ SIGILL' HAMONIS DE CREVEPVER :

5858. Plaster cast from very fine impression, which appears
to be from a very close copy of the seal, rather than from the
same matrix. [lxxviii. 81.]

Mauricius de Creun, [*of Butterwick, co. Lincoln.*]
5859. [A.D. 1158.] Red: fine, edge chipped ; app. by
cords of closely plaited or woven threads. 2¼ × 1¾ in. [Harl.
ch. 49 A. 1.]
Pointed oval. To the r. In armour: hauberk and continuous coif of mail, conical helmet with nasal, sword, kite-
shaped shield very indistinctly cut. Horse galloping, with
ornamental breast-band.

. . . IGILL' . . . . . . MAVRICI DE . . . . REV . . . . .
For another pointed oval seal of this class, cf. Harl. ch. 45 B. 27.
5860. Sulph. cast. [D.C., D. 78.]

Another Seal.

5861. [Early Hen. II.] Creamy-white, varnished brown.
1¾ in. [Add. ch. 20,591.]

To the r. In armour : hauberk, conical helmet and nasal, sword, long convex shield with central spike. Horse galloping.

.... MA ..... Є ....

Johannes de Criail.

5862. [Late 12th cent.] Plaster cast from fine impression. 1¾ in. [lxxviii. 79.]

To the r. In armour : hauberk of mail, cap-like helmet, sword, convex kite-shaped shield. Horse galloping.

✠ SIGILL' · IOH'IS · D' CRIAIL.

Johannes de Criol.

5863. [12th cent.] Plaster cast from indistinct impression. 2⅛ in. [lxxviii. 78.]

To the r. In armour : hauberk of mail, coif, cap-shaped helmet with nasal, sword, convex shield with central spike and rays.

✠ SIGILLVM · IOHANNIS · DE ORIOL.

Walterus Croc.

5864. [Early 13th cent.] Plaster cast from good impression. 1¾ in. [lxxviii. 80.]

To the r. In armour : hauberk of mail, surcoat, round cap-like helmet, sword, shield. Horse galloping.

✠ SIGILLVM : WALTERI : CROC :

Walterus Croc, [*son of* WALTER CROC, *of Wadwick, co. Wilts.*]

5865. [Late 12th cent.] Pale greenish-brown : fine, lower part chipped. 2¼ in. [L.F.C., xiii. 11.]

To the r. In armour : hauberk of mail, surcoat, round cap-like helmet, sword, shield with central spike. Horse galloping.

✠ SIGILLV .... I · CROC.

Robertus fil. Ricardi de Crocstun, [*of Habrough, co. Linc.*]

5866. [12th–13th cent.] Creamy-white, discoloured : fine, edge chipped. Marks of the handle. 2 in. [Add. ch. 20,741.]

To the r. In armour : hauberk of mail, conical helmet and nasal, sword, long convex shield with central spike. Horse galloping.

✠ SIGILL' ROBERTI FILII RICARDI DE CROCSTVN.

The letters TUN, of *Crocstun*, placed in the field.

Willelmus fil. Walteri de Cukeleya, [*of Cookley, co. Suff.*]

5867. [Early 13th cent.] White, discoloured and varnished : indistinct and imperfect. 1¼ in. [Harl. ch. 83 E. 28.]

To the r. In armour: round-topped helmet, sword, convex shield. Horse galloping.

✠ SIGILL . . . . I · FIL . . . .

5868. Sulph. cast. [D.C., D. 193.]

Robertus de Curli.

5869. [12th cent.] Plaster cast from chipped impression. 2¼ in. [lxxviii. 82.]

˙ To the r. In armour: surcoat, conical helmet, sword, kite-shaped shield.

SIGILLVM . . . OBERTI . . . CVRLI.

Willelmus de Curchi, [*of Spaxton, co. Som.*]

5870. [*circ.* A.D. 1136–1165.] Red, discoloured: originally fine, imperfect. [Harl. ch. 49 B. 23.]

To the r. In armour: hauberk diapered, conical helmet, sword.

✠ . . . G . . . . CI · DA . . . .

Stephanus de Curzun, [*of Diseworth, co. Leic.*]

5871. [*circ.* A.D. 1180.] Red: fine, but imperfect. 2 in. [Cott. ch. v. 49.]

To .the r. In armour: hauberk of mail, conical helmet with nasal, sword, kite-shaped shield, with star-like ornamentation and central spike. Horse galloping.

SIGILLVM STE . . . . VRƷVN.

5872. Sulph. cast. [D.C., D. 182.]

Johannes Danecurt, [*or* DE DAIENCURT, *of Granby, co. Nott.*]

5873. [A.D. 1170–1184.] Dark reddish-brown: fine, indistinct in parts. 2⅜ in. [Add. ch. 20,738.]

To the r. In armour: hauberk, surcoat, conical helmet, nasal, sword, long convex shield.

✠ SIGILLVM · IOHANNES DANECVRT.

The C is square.

Maneserus de Danmartin, [*of Mendlesham, co. Suff.*]

5874. [A.D. 1171–1172.] Red: originally fine, chipped at the edge. 2⅜ in. [Harl. ch. 49 C. 1.]

To the r. In armour: hauberk, surcoat, conical helmet and nasal, sword, shield.

SIGIL . . . . ANESER' : D . . . . MARTIИ.

Normannus de Darci, [*son of* PHILIP DE ARCY, *knt.,* *of Stallingborough, co. Linc.*]

5875. [*Temp.* Edw. I.] Dark-green: fine. 1 in. [Harl. ch. 49 C. 46.]

· To the r., In armour: surcoat, helmet with vizor down, shield of arms, sword. Horse caparisoned. Arms: three roses of six leaves, DARCY.

S' NORMANNI · DE DARCI.

5876. Sulph. cast. [D.C., E. 276.]

Philippus de Davintria, [*of Thurnby, co. Northt.*]

5877. [A.D. 1194?]. Red: fine fragment. About 2¼ in. when perfect. [Add. ch. 22,474.]

To the r. In armour: surcoat, sword.

Legend wanting.

Mateus de Da[u]ntn.

5878. [Late 12th cent.] Plaster cast from chipped impression. 2¼ in. [lxxviii. 83.]

To the l. In armour: hauberk of mail, flowing coat, helmet, sword, kite-shaped shield with projecting spike.

Legend reversed:—

✠ SIGILLVM · MATEVS · DE · DA[V]NTN.

Galfridus de Dearleeia.

5879. [12th cent.] Plaster cast from chipped impression. 2¼ in. [lxxviii. 85.]

To the r. In armour:. hauberk of mail, cap-like helmet with nasal, short sword; no shield.

✠ SIGILLVM GALFRIDI DE DEARLEEIA.

The letters AR of *Dearleeia* conjoined.

Willelmus [*fil.* JOHANNIS] **de Dinigtuna,** [*Clerk, of Dinnington, W. R., co. York,*]

5880. [Late 13th cent.] Dark-green: good. ⅟₁₆ in. [Add. ch. 21,575.]

To the l. With a hawk, held by the jesses, in the l. hand.

S' · WILLELMI · DE · DINIGTVNA.

Beaded borders.

Gregorius de Diva, [*of Ashby Ledgers, co. Northt.*]

5881. [Late Hen. II.] Creamy-white: fine, but indistinct, edge chipped; app. by a woven riband of green thread. 2 in. [Add. ch. 21,516.]

To the r. In armour: hauberk, surcoat, conical helmet and nasal, sword, convex shield with central spike. Horse galloping. In front of the rider an uncertain object.

. . . . DI . . . . .

Hugo de Dive, [*fil.* WILL. DE DIVE, *of cos. Northt. and Sussex*].

5882. [A.D. 1200–1210.] Pale-red: originally fine, now fragmentary. About 2 in. when perfect. [Add. ch. 21,879.]

To the r. In armour : with surcoat.

.... HVGONIS ....

Willelmus de Dive, [*fil.* HUGONIS DE DIVE, *of Nortoft, co. Northt.*]

5883. [Late 12th cent.] Uncoloured : imperfect and indistinct. 2½ in. [Harl. ch. 49 F. 12.]

To the r. In armour : hauberk, conical helmet and nasal, sword, shield.

........,........VA.

John de Dreux, [*Duke of Brittany, 6th (7th) Earl of Richmond.*]

5884. [A.D. 1279.] White : only fragment of the central part. [Add. ch. 7756.]

Ø. To the r. In armour. Horse caparisoned. Arms as on *rev.*

Legend wanting.

℞. A smaller counterseal. 1¼ in. diam. A shield of arms : chequy, a canton, BRITTANY.

Legend wanting.

Trésor de Numismatique, Sc. des Rois, pp. 19, 20.

John de Dreux, [*Duke of Brittany, 8th (9th) Earl of Richmond, and Lord of the Rape of Hastings, co. Sussex,* A.D. 1306–1334.]

5885. [A.D. 1315.] Red : very fine, edge chipped; enclosed in a case of red leather lined with diapered stuff, and edged with variegated silk stitches. About $2\frac{7}{10}$ in. when perfect. [Egert. ch. 399.]

Ø. To the r. In armour : hauberk, surcoat, helmet with vizor down, shield of arms. Horse caparisoned, with fan plume. Arms : chequy, *or* and *az.* a bordure *gu.*, charged with lions of ENGLAND, over all a canton, *erm.*, BRITTANY. Background diapered lozengy, with a small pierced cinque-foil in each space.

.... NDIE.

℞. Small round counterseal. ⅞ in. Within a pointed gothic quatrefoil, with sunk trefoil openings in the spandrils, a shield of the arms as described on the *obv.*, suspended by the guige or strap from a trifurcated tree.

Registrum Honoris de Richemond, pl. ad init.

T 2

· **Robertus Dudley, K.G.,** *Earl of Leicester, etc.*

5886. [A.D. 1577.]　Red: fine.　3 in.　[Add. ch. 8487.]
Ø. To the l. on a mount.　In plate armour: plumed helmet, and sword.　Horse caparisoned.　On the trappings a bear statant, surrounded by a Garter, and a lion passant within a collar of the Order of ST. MICHAEL.

In place of a legend a collar of the above Order of St. Michael.　Outside this an ornamental border of pearls in small oval links.

· R. Within a Garter, bearing the motto of the Order, and surmounted by an earl's coronet, on a carved escutcheon a shield of arms: quarterly of eight pieces, 1. a lion rampant queue fourchée, SUTTON ; 2. two lions passant, DUDLEY ; 3. a cinquefoil, erm., PAGANELL ; 4. Barry of six in chief three roundles, a label of as many points, GREY ; 5. ? Barry of ten an orle of martlets, VALENCE ; 6. a lion rampant within a bordure engrailed, TALBOT : 7. a fess between six crosses crosslet, BEAUCHAMP ; 8. chequy a chevron, WARWICK.　In the nombril point a crescent for difference.　Supporters, *dex.*, a bear erect on its hind legs, collared and chained, and charged with the above difference ; *sin.*, a lion rampant crowned.

　　✠ ROBERTVS · COMES · LEYCESTRI[E · BAR]O · DE ·
　　DENBIGHE · VTRIVSQVE · ORDINIS · GARTERII ·
　　　　ET · SANCTI · MICH · MILES. ⚜ ⚜ ⚜ ⚜
The letters HE in *Denbighe* are conjoined.

5887. Red : fine, cut from a charter and pierced for suspension.　[xxxv. 345.]

5888. Sulph. casts of *obv.* and *rev.* from good impression.
[D.C., H. 79, 80.]

Aggelram de Dumart, *or* **Ingelram de Dumard,**
　　　　[of Faxton, etc., co. Northt.]
5889. [12th–13th cent.]　Green, varnished : very indistinct, edge chipped.　2 in.　[Harl. ch. 49 F. 53.]
To the r.　In armour : hauberk, surcoat, conical helmet and nasal, sword, long convex shield with central spike.　Horse galloping.
　　　　✠ S . . . . GERAM . . . . RT.
5890. Plaster cast from chipped impression.　2 in.
[lxxviii. 88.]
　　　　✠ SIGILLVM : AGGELRAM . . . .

Ralph de [D]unstanscot (?)
5891. [12th cent.]　Plaster cast from chipped impression.
1⅞ in.　[lxxix. 45.]
To the l.　In armour : hauberk of mail, coif, surcoat, helmet, sword, long shield.　Horse galloping.
　　　　✠ SIGILL' RADVL . . . VИSTAИSCOT.

Willelmus de Echingeham, [*Miles, of Etchingham, co. Suss.*]

5892. [*circ.* A.D. 1307–8.] Bronze-green : fine, but chipped.
1¾ in. [Egert. ch. 398.]

∅. To the r. In armour : hauberk, surcoat, conical helmet
with fan plume, sword, shield. Horse galloping, caparisoned and plumed. Arms : a fret, or fretty, ECHINGHAM.
In the field four shields of arms, two above, two below
-the horse : 1. as No. 4 in the *rev.;* 2. as No. 2 in the *rev.;*
3. three bars, over all a bend ; 4. as No. 4 in the *rev.*

    S' DOMINI ✽ WILLELMI ✽ DE ✽ ECHINGEHAM.

℞. Four shields of arms in cross, the points meeting at the
centre. 1. fretty, ECHINGHAM ; 2. three crescents, over all a
canton ; 3. lozengy ; 4. on a chief two pierced mullets.

    ⚥ : S' WILL'I : DE : ECHINGHAM.

5893. [A.D. 1319.] Bronze-green : fine, chipped at the
edge. [Egert. ch. 400.]

Petrus de Eclisfeld.

5894. [A.D. 1185–1201]. Discoloured : a fragment. About
2 in. when perfect. [Harl. ch. 43 A. 54.]

To the r. In armour : conical helmet and nasal.

    ✠ SIGIL . . . .

Fulcherus, Dominus de Ednesouria, [*or* EDENSOR, *co. Derby.*]

5895. [Late 12th cent.] Light-brown, thickly varnished :
imperfect ; app. by a diapered ribbon of plaited threads.
2½ in. [Harl. ch. 111 F. 59.]

To the r. In armour : hauberk, surcoat, conical helmet
with nasal, sword, long convex shield.

    . . . . IGI . . . . . . L . . . . . . ⚥

5896. Sulph. cast. [D.C., D. 92.]

Henricus [*fil.* VITALIS] Engainne, [*or* ENGAYNE, *of Laxton, co. Northt.*]

5897. [A.D. 1248–1261.] Green : fine, but chipped ; app.
by green silk cords. 1¾ in. [Add. ch. 22,080.]

To the l. In armour : hauberk, surcoat, flat-topped helmet,
spear, shield of arms. Horse galloping, with ornamental
breast band. Arms : a fess dancettée betw. six crosses
crosslet, ENGAINE.

    S' HE[N]RICI : EN ⚥ GAINNE :

Beaded borders.

5898. Another, on a label, sewn to the cords of the above
impression. [Add. ch. 22,080.]

    S' HEN . . . . . I : EN ⚥ GAINNE :

Willelmus, [*Count of Boulogne and Warrenne, youngest son of King Stephen.*]

5899. [A.D. 1146–1159.] Green, with a brown varnish: fine but imperfect. About 2½ in. when perfect. [Harl. ch. 83 A. 25.]

Ø. To the r. three-quarters. In armour: hauberk, conical helmet, lance and flag in the r. h., and kite-shaped shield, showing interior side on the l. h.

⚹ S . . . .

R. Small oval counterseal. ⅜ × ½ in. Impression of an antique oval intaglio gem: an indistinct warrior, with a shield and lance, set in a metal rim, with indistinct legend.

5900. Sulph. cast of the *obv.* only. [D.C., D. 80.]

Johannes de Estoutevilla, [*Miles, of Eckington, co. Derby.*]

5901. [A.D. 1255.] Creamy-white: fine, imperfect. About 2¼ in. when perfect. [Add. ch. 20,486.]

Ø. To the l. In armour: hauberk, flat-topped helmet, sword, shield of arms. Horse caparisoned. Arms: barry of twelve, over all a lion rampant, ESTOUTEVILLE. (Cf. Add. MS. 17,732.)

SIGILLVM · IOH[A]NNIS · DE ES[TOV]TEVIL . . .

R. A smaller counterseal. 1¼ in. A shield of arms, as in the *obv.*, suspended by a loop, and betw. three round buckles.

Willelmus de Estuteville, [*of Upsall, etc., co. York.*]

5902. [Late 12th cent.] Dark-green, varnished brown: very imperfect. About 2⅛ in. when perfect. [Add. ch. 19,922.]

To the r. In armour: hauberk, surcoat, flat helmet, sword, convex shield with central spike.

. . . . IGILL . . . .

Almaricus [**D'Evereux,** *4th Earl of Gloucester, Count-Earl of Evreux.* A.D. 1192–1216.]

5903. Plaster cast from fine impression. 2¼ in. [lxxviii. 93.]

To the r. In armour: hauberk of mail, caplike helmet, with nasal and pendants, shield with central boss. Horse with ornamental saddle. Beneath the horse a fleur-de-lis.

⚹ SIGILLVM · AMARICI : COMITIS : EBROICENSIS.

Cf. Douët d'Arcq, *Collection de Sceaux*, No. 10,139.

Petrus de Falkenberge, [*of Mablethorpe, co. Linc.*]

5904. [Early 13th cent.] Light-green: very imperfect, and the face peeled off in places. About 2¼ in. when perfect. [Harl. ch. 49 I. 16.]

To the r. In armour: hauberk, flat-topped helmet, long convex shield.

✠ SI .... PE .... E.

Walterus de Enle, *or* Fenle, (Faucumberge),
[*of Mablethorpe. co. Linc.*]

5905. [Early 13th cent.] Light-brown: fine, but imper-feet. About 2⅜ in. when perfect. [Harl. ch. 49 I. 17.]

∅. To the r. In armour: hauberk, sword, shield. Horse galloping. Arms appear to be: a fess, and label of three points.

... GIL .... ERI DE ENLE, *or* D'FENLE.

℞. Small pointed oval counterseal, with mark of the handle. 1¼ × ¾ in. An eagle displayed, head turned to the r.

✠ SIGILLVM SECRETI.

Cf. *Rotuli de Oblatis, temp. Joh.*, ed. T. D. Hardy, p. 253, A.D. 1205.

Basil [FEILDING, 2*nd*] *Earl of Denbigh.* [A.D. 1643–1675?]

5906. Cast in lead from fine impression. 2⅛ in. [Slo. xxxiv. 31.]

To the l., on a mount. In plate armour: with an ostrich plume. Horse caparisoned. Arms: on a fess three lozenges, FEILDING. In the background, on the r., a palm-tree. In the foreground, an eagle rising reguardant, in allusion to the arms.

✠ SIGILLVM ⁙ BASILII ⁙ COMITIS ⁙ DENBIGH.

Outer border carved.

5907. Sulph. cast. [D.C., H. 83.]

Robertus fil. D. Will. de Ferrariis, [ROBERT DE FERRERS,
8*th Earl of Derby.* A.D. 1254–1278.]

5908. [*circ.* A.D. 1265.] Green: very fine, chipped, with marks of the four studs used to steady the matrix. 2⅜ in. [Add. ch. 20,459.]

∅. To the r. In armour: hauberk, surcoat, flat-topped helmet with vizor down, sword, shield slung by a strap over the shoulder. Horse galloping, caparisoned. Arms: vairé, FERRERS.

✠ ROBS · FIL' · ET · HERES · DÑI : WILL'I : DE · FERRAR' · QŌDA' · COMITIS · DERBEYE.

The letters ER in *heres* and *Derbeye*, conjoined.

℞. A large shield of arms: vairé (in fourteen rows), for FERRERS, suspended by a strap from an elegantly designed conventional tree, and betw. two finely drawn wavy branches of foliage and flowers.

✠ SIGILLVM · ROBERTI · DE [FERRAR]IIS · COMITIS : DERBEYE.

Beaded borders.

5909. [A.D. 1262.]   Mottled-green : fine, but imperfect ;
. app. by cords of plaited thread.   [Wol. ch. 6. 48.]

Ø. . . . . . . I : WILL'I . . . . S · DERB . . . .

R. . . . IGILLV . . . . ERRARIIS · COM . . . .

5910. Mottled-green : fine, but very imperfect, only centre
remaining.   [Wol. ch. 9. 67.]

5911. [A.D. 1262.]   Mottled-green : fine, but very imperfect.
[*Egert.* ch. 443.]

Legend wanting.

5912. Sulph. casts of *obv.* and *rev.* from fine and perfect
impression.   [D.C., E. 256, 257.]

5913. Sulph. cast of *obv.* only from fine impression.   [xlvii.
1065.]

5914. Plaster casts from fine impressions.   [lxxviii. 99,
100.]

Willelmus de Ferariis, [*Miles, Lord of Groby or Grooby, co. Leic.*]

5915. [Early 13th cent.]   Light-brown, varnished : fine,
but imperfect, only centre remaining.   About $2\frac{1}{4}$ in. when
perfect.   [Harl. ch. 111 G. 4.]

To the r.   In armour : hauberk and surcoat.   Horse caparisoned.   Arms : mascles (number uncertain), for FERRERS.

Legend wanting.

Willelmus, Comes de Ferrariis, [*Earl of Ferrers and 6thEarl of Derby, son of William de Ferrers, 5th Earl of Derby.* A.D. 1191–1246.]

5916. [A.D. 1191–1199.]   Red : fine and very heavy, chipped.   About $2\frac{1}{8}$ in. when perfect.   [Egert. ch. 437.]

To the r.   In armour : hauberk, surcoat, sword, long convex
shield.   Horse galloping.

. . . . . . WILL . . . . . CO . . . . ERR[A]RIIS.

Another seal.

5917. Dark mottled-green : fine, but imperfect.   About
$2\frac{1}{8}$ in. when perfect.   [Wol. ch. 2. 1.]

Ø. To the r.   In armour : hauberk, surcoat, flat-topped
helmet, sword, shield of arms : vairé, FERRERS.

. . . . IS . . . .

R. Small oval counterseal. $1\frac{1}{4} \times 1$ in.   With mark of
the handle.   Impression of an antique oval intaglio gem.   A
lion devouring a stag.

✠ S' WILLELMI COMITIS DERBEIE.

5918. Sulph. casts of *obv.* and *rev.*   [D.C., E. 241, 242.]

5919. [A.D. 1200–1225.]   Green, fragmentary.   [Add. ch.
24,201.]

5919.* Plaster cast of *obv.* only, from chipped impression. [lxxviii. 95.]

⛨ . . . . FERR . . . .

Willelmus [de Ferrariis, *7th*] *Earl of Derby.*
[A.D. 1246–1254.]

5920. [A.D. 1254.] Light-green : fine, upper part chipped. About 1⅛ in. [*Egert.* ch. 442.]

∅. To the r. In armour : hauberk, surcoat, shield, sword. Horse galloping. Fine style of workmanship.

. . . . WI . . . . . . T' · DE · F . . . . . .

℞. Small round counterseal. ¾ in. A shield of arms : vairé, on a bordure eight horse-shoes.

⛨ S WILL'I ⦂ COMITIS ⦂ DERB'.

Second Counterseal.

5921. Plaster cast from fine, but chipped, impression, showing parts wanting in the previous seal. [lxxviii. 97, 98.]

∅. As before.

⛨ SIGILLVM WILLEL[M] · · · · · · Є · FERRARIIS.

℞. Small round counterseal. 1⅛ in. A shield of arms as before, but from different and larger matrix.

⛨ FRANGE LEGE TEGE.

(Here begins the series of Seals arranged under FILIUS.*)*

Herbertus *filius* ADALARDI, *of co. Linc.*

5922. [Late 12th cent.] Light-brown : indistinct in places, and imperfect. About 2¼ in. when perfect. [*Harl.* ch. 54 E. 5.]

To the r. In armour : hauberk, surcoat, round-topped helmet, sword, kite-shaped convex shield with radiating ornament and central spike. Horse galloping with ornamental breast-band.

⛨ SI . . . . VM · H . . . . LII . . . . . RDI.

5923. Sulph. cast. [D.C., D. 202.]

Patricius *filius* ADÆ.

5924. [Early 13th cent.] Plaster cast from fine impression, chipped and rubbed. 2 in. [lxxix. 1.]

To the r. In armour : hauberk of mail, cap-like helmet with ties behind, sword, convex shield. Horse with fringed saddle-cloth.

⛨ SIGILL' · PATRICII · FILII · ADE.

Johannes *filius* ALANI [DE WLURINGTON, (*Wolwardington, Walrington,* or *Wolverton,*) co. *Warw.*]

5925. [13th cent.] Dark-green : fine and perfect. 1½ in. [*Harl.* ch. 86 F. 61.]

To the r. In armour : hauberk, surcoat, flat-topped helmet, sword, shield of arms.   Horse galloping.   Arms : bendy, uncertain in number ; probably bendy of six or of ten, for WOLWARDINGTON or WALRINGTON, of co. Warwick.

✠ SIGILL' · IOHANNIS : FILI · ALANI ⋈

5926. Sulph. cast. [D.C., E. 265.]

5927. Mottled-green : fine, slightly chipped. [Harl. ch. 86 F. 62.]

5928. [A.D. 1272.] Dark-green, slightly mottled with red grains : very fine and perfect. [Harl. ch. 86 G. 1.]

5929. Sulph. cast. [D.C., E. 266.]

5930. Dark-green, slightly mottled : lower part chipped. [Harl. ch. 86 G. 2.]

Ricardus [FITZ-ALAN, *7th*] *Earl of Arundel.* [A.D. 1267–1301.]

5931. [A.D. 1301.] Plaster cast from fine, but chipped, impression. 2 in. [lxxix. 2.]

To the r. In armour : hauberk of mail, surcoat, helmet with fan plume, sword, shield of arms.   Horse galloping, caparisoned and plumed. Arms : a lion rampant.

SIGILLVM : RICARDI : COMITIS : DE : ARONDEL.

Willelmus *filius* ALANI [*of Woodbridge, co. Suff.*]

5932. [Early 13th cent.] Light-green : indistinct and imperfect. About 1¾ in. when perfect. [Harl. ch. 50 A. 1.]

To the r. In armour : hauberk and shield.

. . . GILLV . . . . M . . . .

5933. Sulph. cast. [D.C., D. 142.]

Willelmus *filius* WILLELMI *filii* ALANI [*of Brockton, co. Salop.*]

5934. [Early 13th cent. ?] Light-brown : fine, but imperfect. About 2¾ in. when perfect. [Harl. ch. 50 A. 2.]

To the r. In armour : hauberk, surcoat, conical helmet and nasal, sword, long convex shield with central spike. Archaic design.

✠ SIGILL . . . . ALAɅI ✠

The N in *Alani* reversed.

5935. Sulph. cast. [D.C., E. 206.]

Galfridus *filius* ALBRI[CI *of Marton, co. Linc.*]

5936. [13th cent.] Dark-green, discoloured at the bottom : fine, with mark of the handle. 1¾ in. [Cott. ch. xxvii. 62.]

To the r. In armour : hauberk, helmet and nasal, sword, shield.· Horse galloping.

✠ SIGILLVM GALFRIDIDI (*sic*) FILII ALBRI.

5937. Sulph. cast. [D.C., D. 191.]

Robertus *filius* WALTERI, *filii* ALUEREDI [*of co. Linc.*]

5938. [A.D. 1147–1160.]   Light-brown, mottled : edge imperfect.   2 in.   [Harl. ch. 50 A. 6.]

To the r.   In armour: conical helmet, sword, long convex shield with central spike.

.. SIG[ILLVM] ROBERT' · FI[L]II WALTERI.

5939. Sulph. cast.   [D.C., D. 81.]

.. SIG .. LVM · ROBERT' · FI[L]II WALTERI.

Rogerus *filius* ALUREDI [*of co. York.*]

5940. [Late 12th cent.]   Greenish-white: very indistinct. About 1¾ in. when perfect.   [Add. ch. 8117.]

To the r.   In armour : hauberk, surcoat, sword, shield. Legend defaced.

W · · · · · : *filius* BALDEWINI, [*of co. Nott. ?*]

5941. [Early 13th cent.]   Sulph. cast.   1⅞ in.   [D.C., D. 166.]

To the r.   In armour : hauberk, surcoat, conical helmet and nasal, sword, long convex shield with central spike.

✠ SIGILL' W . . . . . . II BALDEWI.

Cf. *Rotuli de Oblatis, temp. Joh.*, ed. T. D. Hardy, p. 51, A.D. 1200 ; p. 446, A.D. 1207.

Alanus *filius* BRIANI, [*Lord of Bedale,*
of North Cowton, co. York.]

5942. [*circ.* A.D. 1250.]   Dark-green : fine.   1¼ in.   [Cott. ch. ix. 9.]

To the r.   In armour : hauberk, surcoat, flat helmet plumed, sword, shield of arms.   Horse caparisoned.   Arms : barry.

✠ SIGILL' · ALANI · FILII · BRIANI.

5943. Sulph. cast.   [D.C., E. 227.]

Cadwalan *filius* CARATOCI, *of S. Wales.*

5944. [*circ.* A.D. 1200.]   Bright reddish-yellow: fine, imperfect at the lower part.   2¼ in.   [Harl. ch. 75 B. 29.]

To the r.   In armour : hauberk and coif of mail, surcoat, conical helmet and nasal, sword, long convex shield with ornamental border and central spike.   Horse galloping.

✠ SIGILL' CADW .: .. NI FI . . . . RATOCI.

5945. Sulph. cast.   [D.C., D. 85.]

Marganus *filius* CARADOCI, [*of Aberafon, co. Glamorg.*]

5946. [12th or 13th cent.]   Bright reddish-yellow : imperfect on the r. h. side.   2 in.   [Harl. ch. 75 B. 29.]

To the r.   In armour : hauberk of mail, surcoat, round-topped helmet and nasal, sword, shield of large dimensions, convex, round-topped, ornamented with star and central spike. Horse galloping.

⊕ S . . . . . AⱲI · FILII . . . . . . CI.

The letter N reversed.

5947. Sulph. cast. [D.C., D. 86.]

Marganus *filius* CARADOCI, [*of Aberafon, co. Glamorg.*]
(*Perhaps same person as the last.*)

5948. [A.D. 1205.] Bright-red: indistinct and chipped, with mark of the handle. 2⅛ × 2 in. [Harl. ch. 75 B. 30.]

Oval to the r. In armour: hauberk, round-topped helmet, sword, shield.

⊕ ƧIGILLVM MARGANI FILII CA . . . . CI.

The letter S reversed.

5949. Sulph. cast. [D.C., E. 197.]

5950. [A.D. 1205.] Bright-red: indistinct and imperfect. [Harl. ch. 75 B. 31.]

⊕ ƧIGILLVM MARG . . . .

Robertus *filius* HUGONIS [*filii* EUDONIS, *of Tattershall, co. Linc.*]

5951. [12th cent.] Light-red: fine, but imperfect. About 2¾ in. when perfect. [Harl. ch. 56 H. 10.]

To the r. In armour: hauberk of mail and continuous coif, tall round-topped helmet, sword, shield of arms. Horse with ornamental breast-band. Arms: chequy, a chief indistinctly charged. The stirrup of peculiar form.

⊕ SI[GILLVM] . . . . S.

5952. Sulph. cast from another imperfect impression. [D.C., D. 149.]

⊕ SIGIL' . . . . ERT . . . . ·. . . S.

Hugo *filius* EUDONIS [*of Tattershall, co. Linc.*]

5953. [12th cent.] Dark-red, varnished: fine, but imperfect. About 2¼ in. when perfect. [Harl. ch. 56 H. 9.]

To the r. In armour: hauberk, surcoat, conical helmet, sword, shield.

⊕ SIGILLVM . . . .

5954. Sulph. cast. [D.C., D. 132.]

Willelmus *filius* GREGORII, [*of Finmere, co. Oxon.*]

5955. [*circ.* A.D. 1189.] Light-brown: indistinct and imperfect. About 1¾ in. when perfect. [Harl. ch. 84 D. 15.]

To the r. In armour: hauberk, surcoat, sword, shield. Horse galloping.

Legend wanting.

See *Pipe Roll*, co. Wilts., 1 Ric. I.

Petrus *filius* GRENTE, [*of Carlton, co. York.*]
5956. [A.D. 1183–1184.] Self-coloured, varnished : fine, but imperfect. With mark of handle. 1¾ in. [Add. ch. 20,562.]
To the r. In armour : hauberk and continuous coif with ties, surcoat, conical helmet with nasal, sword, convex shield with central spike. Horse with ornamental breast-band.
⠂ ⁚ SIGIL[LVM] PETRI FILII G[R]EИTE.
The N reversed.

Madoc *filius* GRIFUD, [*of Ekal, co. Montgom. ?*]
5957. [A.D. 1228.] Light-yellow : fine originally, now very imperfect. About 2½ in. when perfect. [Add. ch. 10,637.]
Ø. To the r. In armour : hauberk of mail, surcoat, flat-helmet, sword, shield. Horse galloping.
Legend wanting.
R. Small oval counterseal, with mark of the handle. 1⅛ × 1 in. Impression of an antique oval intaglio gem : a bust in profile to the r.
. . . . . ADOCI FILII GRIF . . . .

Thomas *filius* WILLELMI *fil.* HACONIS [*of Grimsby, co. Linc.*]
5958. [Early 13th cent.] Brown : fine, with mark of handle. 1¾ in. [Harl. ch. 50 C. 23.]
To the r. In armour : hauberk, helmet with nasal, sword, shield. Horse galloping.
SIGILVM · THOME · FILII · WILL'I · FILII · HACONIS.
5959. Sulph. cast. [D.C., D. 175.]
5960. Light brown, varnished : only a fragment of the lower part. [Harl. ch. 50 C. 24.]

Osmund *filius* HAMONIS.
5961. [13th cent.] Plaster cast from fine impression. 2¾ in. [lxxix. 5.]
To the r. In armour : hauberk of mail, surcoat, conical helmet with ties behind, sword, shield of arms. Horse galloping, with fringed breast-band and saddle-cloth.
✠ SIGILL' OSMVNDI FILII HAMOИIS.

Philippus *filius* HAMONIS.
5962. [12th century.] Plaster cast from fine, but chipped, impression. 2⅛ in. [lxxix. 6.]
To the r. In armour : hauberk, surcoat, cap-like helmet with ties behind, sword, kite-shaped convex shield, bordered.
SIGILLVM ⁚ . . . . . . PI ⁚ FILII ⁚ HAMONIS.

Willermus *filius* HAMUN, [*of Wolverton, co. Buck.*]

5963. [13th · cent.]   Mottled-green : fine, well-preserved. 1¾ in. [Harl. ch. 85 D. 43.]

To the r.   In armour : hauberk, surcoat, round-topped helmet and nasal, sword, shield.   Horse galloping.

SIGILLVM WILLERMI FILII HAMVN.

5964. Sulph. cast.   [D.C., E. 223.]

5965. Mottled-green : fine, chipped.   [Harl. ch. 85 D. 42.]

5966. Mottled-green : fine, chipped ; app. by a woven tape of damask thread.   [Harl. ch. 85 D. 44.]

5967. Pale yellowish - brown : imperfect at the base. [Harl. ch. 85 D. 46.]

5968. Dark-green : indistinct.   [Harl. ch. 86 F. 60.]

5969. Sulph. cast.   [D.C., E. 224.]

Ricardus *filius* HARDINGI, *or* RICHARD DE M - - - - -.

5970. [*Early* 13th cent.]   Plaster cast from chipped impression.   1¾ in.   [lxxix. 7.]

To the l.   In armour : long coat ornamented with stripes, embroidered cap, a falcon on the l. wrist.

SIGILLVM : RICARDI : DE : M . . . . I.

Conanus *filius* HELIÆ.

5971. [Late 12th cent.]   Plaster cast from imperfect and indistinct impression.   2 in.   [lxxix. 8.]

To the r.   In armour : hauberk, coif, surcoat, cap-like helmet with nasal, sword, kite-shaped shield.   Horse galloping.

✠ SIGIL . . M : CONANI FILII HELIE.

Osbertus *filius* HUGONIS.

5972. [Late 12th cent.]   Cast in plaster, tinted light yellowish-brown, from fine, but imperfect, impression.   About ·2¼ in. when perfect.   With mark of handle.   [xliii. 51.]

.To the r.   In armour : hauberk, surcoat, conical helmet and nasal, sword, long convex shield with central spike. Horse galloping.

✠ SIGILL . . . . . BERTI . . . . . ONIS.

5973. Pale greenish-brown : fine, but fragmentary.   [Harl. ch. 50 A. 45.]

. . . . . ILLV . . . . TI . . . .

Adam *filius* ILBERTI.

5974. [12th cent.]   Plaster cast from fine, but chipped, impression.   2¼ in.   [lxxix. 4.]

To the r. In armour: hauberk of mail, conical cap, sword, kite-shaped convex shield with central spike.

      ✠ SIGILLVᴍ : ADE : FILII : ILBERTI.

5975. Another. From a fine impression. [lxxix. 9.]

Robertus *filius* INGEBALDI, [*of Braybrook, co. Northt.*]

5976. [A.D. 1183–1184.] Dark-yellow: fine, somewhat injured. 2¼ in. [Harl. ch. 47 B. 3.]

- To the r. In armour: hauberk, surcoat, round-topped helmet, sword, long convex shield. Horse galloping, with· an ornamental breast-band.

      ✠ SIGILLVM : ROBERTI FILII INGEBALDI.

  Cf. *Rotuli de Oblatis, temp. Joh.*, ed. T. D. Hardy, p. 289, A.D. 1205.

Howel *filius* KATWALLAUN, [*of Dolgeneru, co. Radn.*]

5977. [Late 12th cent.] Light-brown: very imperfect and indistinct. About 2 in. when perfect. [Add. ch. 26,727.]

  To the r. In armour. Horse galloping.

      . . SIGILLVM . . . .

Cunei *filius* JOHANNIS, *filii* MEGHI, [*of Westfield, co. Norf.*]

5978. [*Temp.* Hen. I.–Steph.] Light-brown, semi-opaque: a fragment. About 2¼ in. when perfect. [Add. ch. 26,726.]

  To the r. In armour: hauberk of mail, coif, helmet and nasal, sword, shield.

      SI . . . . Mɛ . . . .

Ivo *filius* LA[M]BARDI, [*seal used by* JOHN DE ASWELLE.]

5979. [13th cent.] Brown: indistinct, edge much injured. 1¾ in. [Harl. ch. 45 E. 29.]

  To the r. In armour: hauberk, surcoat, sword, convex shield, with uncertain charges somewhat resembling two bars. Horse galloping.

      SIGILLV IVO . . . . FIL' LABARD . . .

Leisan *filius* MORGANI, [*of Pultimore, co. Glam.*]

5980. [A.D. 1215–1221.] Dark-green: fine, well preserved, with mark of the handle. 2 in. [Harl. ch. 75 C. 35.]

  To the r. In armour :· hauberk of mail, continuous coif, round-topped helmet with nasal, sword, long convex shield with central spike. Horse galloping.

      SIGILLWM : LɛISAVN : FILII : MORGAN.

5981. Sulph. cast. [D.C., E. 225.]

Another Seal.

5982. [Early. 13th cent.] Light-brown, uncoloured: edge imperfect. 2 in. [Harl. ch. 75 C. 34.]

An abbess or religious woman, wearing a tall head-dress and wimple, seated on a cushioned throne with carved panels and footboard, holding up the r. h. in benediction ; in the l. h. a book bound in an ornamental cover. On the l. h. side before her, the owner of the seal kneeling in supplication.

..GILLVM LEISAN : FI...........

Rogerus *filius* NICHOLAI, [*of Everton, co. Hunt.*]

5983. [Early 13th cent.]   Light-brown, varnished: fine, chipped at edges.   1⅞ in. [Harl. ch. 83 B. 13.]

To the r.   In armour : hauberk and continuous coif, surcoat, round-topped helmet and nasal, sword, triangular convex shield with borders and central spike or boss.   Horse galloping, with ornamental breast-band.

SIGILLVM . RO ...... FILII : NICNOLAI. (*sic*)

5984. Sulph. cast.   [D.C., D. 176.]

Willelmus *filius* OTUERI, [*of co. Lincoln.*]

5985. [Late 12th cent.]   Light-brown, varnished : very indistinct.   1⅞ in. [Harl. ch. 50 B. 15.]

To the r.   In armour : hauberk, conical helmet, kite-shaped shield.   Horse with ornamental breast-band.

✠ SIGILLVM WILL ... FILII OTVERI. (?)

5986. Sulph. cast.   [D.C., D. 124.]

Radulfus *filius* PETRI DE SAIDENE?

5987. [Late 12th cent.]   Plaster cast from fine impression. 1⅛ in. [lxxix. 10.]

To the r.   In armour : hauberk, conical helmet, sword, kite-shaped shield.

✠ SIGILL' . RADVLFI . FILII . PETRI ..

Simon *filius* PETRI, [*of Preston, co. Northt.*]

5988. [Late 12th or early 13th cent.]   Red : chipped, edges imperfect.   2¾ in. [Harl. ch. 85 D. 49.]

To the r.   In armour : hauberk, surcoat, conical helmet, sword, shield.   Horse galloping, with ornamental breast-band.

✠ SIGILL[V]M : SIMONIS : FILII : PETRI.

5989. Sulph. cast.   [D.C., D. 131.]

Hugo *filius* PINCEONIS, *Lord of Eresby,* [*co. Linc.*]

5990. [*Temp.* Steph. or Hen. II.]   Light-brown, varnished : cracked and very imperfect.   About 2¼ in. when perfect. [Harl. ch. 50 B. 18.]

To the r.   In armour : hauberk, surcoat, sword, shield. Horse galloping.

Legend wanting.

Osbern *filius* PONTII, [*of Longney, co. Glouc.*]

5991. [*circ.* A.D. 1100.] Light-red : edge chipped. 2 in. [Harl. ch. 50 B. 22.]

To the l. In armour : cap-like helmet, a hawk with ex-panded wings on the l. hand. In the field on the l. a bird flying.

✠ SIGILLVM OSBERNI . . .NZ(?)I.

-**5992·** Sulph. cast. [D.C., D. 90.]

Brianus *or* **Brientius** *filius* RADULFI, [*of Steeple, co. Ess.*]

5993. [*Early* 13th cent.] Dark-green : fine, edge chipped. 2 in. [Harl. ch. 83 E. 39.]

To the r. In armour : hauberk, surcoat, round-topped helmet and nasal, sword, shield with ornamental border and central spike. Horse galloping, with bordered breast-band.

✠ SIGILL' · BRIANI · FILII · RADVLF[I].

5994. Sulph. cast. [D.C., D. 205.]

Geroldus *filius* RADULFI, [*of Dowgate, London.*]

5995. [12th cent.] Green, mottled : fine, edge slightly chipped. 2¾ in. [Harl. ch. 50 B. 24.]

To the r. In armour : hauberk, surcoat, conical helmet and nasal, sword, long convex shield with central spike. Horse galloping.

✠ SIGILL' · GEROLDI · FILII · RADVLFI.

5996. Sulph. cast. [D.C., D. 141.]

Hugo *filius* RADULFI, *brother of* WILLIAM DE MUNGAY, [*of Yeldersley, co. Derby.*]

5997. [*Early* 13th cent.] Creamy-white : imperfect and indistinct. About 1⅞ in. when perfect. [Wol. ch. 9. 7.]

To the l. In surcoat, with hawk on the l. hand.

✠ SIGILL . . . . NIS DE . . . . . .

- - - - - - - *filius* RADULFI.

5998. [Late 12th or early 13th cent.] Red : fine, but im-perfect. About 2¼ in. when perfect. [xxxv. 17 B.]

To the r. In armour : hauberk, surcoat, helmet, sword, long kite-shaped shield with vertical bar ornament.

S . . . . I . . . RADVLFI.

Johannes *filius* REGINALDI, [*Lord of Blakeney, co. Norf.*]

5999. [A.D. 1301.] Plaster cast from fine impression. 1¼ in. [lxxix. 11.]

To the r. In armour : hauberk, surcoat, helmet with

VOL. II.   U

grating, sword, shield of arms.   Horse caparisoned.   Arms :
three lions rampant, FITZ-RAYNALD.

✠ S' IOH'IS FIL'I REGINALDI.

Beaded borders.

Galfridus <i>filius</i> RICARDI.

6000. [12th cent.]   Plaster cast from fine, but chipped,
impression.   [lxxix. 12.]

To the r.   In armour : hauberk of mail, helmet, sword,
shield with central spike.   Horse galloping.

✠ SIGILLVM · GALFRIDI · FILII · RICARDI.

Maurice <i>filius</i> ROBERTI [DE TOTHAM, <i>co. Essex.</i>]

6001. [<i>circ.</i> A.D. 1150–1175.]   Light-brown, varnished :
fine originally, now indistinct in places, and chipped at edge.
2⅜ in. [Harl. ch. 84 A. 58.]

To the r.   In armour : hauberk, surcoat, conical helmet and
nasal, sword, long convex shield with radiating ornament and
central spike.   Horse galloping, covered with a large housing,
except the nose and feet.

✠ SIGILLVM · MAVRICII FI[L]II ROB]ERTI.

6002. Sulph. cast.   [D.C., E. 268.]

6003. Creamy-white : imperfect   at   the   lower   part   and
edge chipped.   [Harl. ch. 84 A. 59.]

Walterus <i>filius</i> ROBERTI, [<i>of co. Ess.</i>]

6004. [A.D. 1250?]   Light yellowish - brown, varnished :
fine, edge chipped away.   Nearly 3 in. when perfect.   [Add.
ch. 918.]

To the r.   In armour : hauberk of mail, sword, shield.
Horse caparisoned ; the caparisons are charged with chevrons,
or chevronelly, in allusion to the arms of FITZ-ROBERT, two
chevrons.

Legend wanting.

Robertus <i>filius</i> ROGERI.

6005. [12th cent.]   Plaster cast from fine, but chipped,
impression.   2⅞ in.   [lxxix. 14.]

To the r.   In armour : hauberk of mail, coif, surcoat, cap-
like helmet, sword, shield of arms.   Horse galloping, with
fringed breast-band.   Arms : quarterly, a bend, FITZ-ROGER.
Fine style of workmanship.

✠ SIGILLVM ROBERTI FIL[II] ROGERI ✸

Robertus <i>filius</i> ROGERI.

6006. [Late 13th cent.] . Plaster cast from fine impression.
2 in.   [lxxix. 13.]

To the r. In armour: hauberk of mail, surcoat, plumed helmet, sword, shield of arms. Horse galloping, caparisoned and plumed. Arms: quarterly, a bend, FITZ-ROGER. Fine style of workmanship.

: SIGILLVM : ROBERTI : FILII : ROGERI.

Robertus *filius* ROGERI, *or* WILLELMUS *filius* PETRI DE EDISFELD.

6007. [*Early* 13th cent.] Discoloured white: a fragment. About 2¼ in. when perfect. [Harl. ch. 50 B. 32.]

To the r. In armour: with sword.

Legend wanting.

Filippus *filius* SIMONIS.

6008. [Late 12th cent.] Plaster cast from chipped and partly indistinct impression. 2 in. [lxxix. 16.]

To the r. In armour: hauberk of mail, coif with ties behind, conical helmet, sword, bordered kite-shaped shield. Horse with ornamental breast-band and saddle.

SIGILLVM : FILIPPI : FILII : SIMONIS.

Galfridus *filius* [T]ERICI *et Ceciliæ filiæ Sabeline,* ·[? *of Southwark, co. Surr.*]

6009. [Late 12th cent.] Greenish-brown: fine, very imperfect ; app. by closely-woven brown taffeta cord. About 2½ in. when perfect. [Harl. ch. 50 B. 33.]

To the r. In armour: hauberk, surcoat, flat-topped helmet, sword, convex shield with ornamental rib. Horse springing.

..... LLV .... LFR ...... FIL' .... ERICI.

6010. Sulph. cast. [D.C., D. 147.]

Robertus *filius* THOLI, [*of co. Derb.*]

6011. [Late 12th cent.] White: imperfect. About 2 in. when perfect. [Wol. ch. 9. 2.]

To the l. With a hawk on the l. hand.

Legend wanting.

Robertus *filius* TOMÆ.

6012. [12th cent.] Plaster cast from fine impression. 1¾ in. [lxxix. 17.]

· To the r. In armour: hauberk of mail, surcoat, cap-like helmet, sword, convex shield. Horse galloping.

✠ SIGILLVM ROBERTI FILII TOME.

The letters ME in *Tome* conjoined.

Robertus *filius* TURHETINI, *al.* TURKETINI, [*of co. Linc.*]

6013. [*circ.* A.D. 1155–1168.] Bright - red : fine, edge

chipped ; app. by a diapered bobbin of variegated colours.
2 in. [Harl. ch. 50 B. 44.]

To the r. In armour : hauberk of mail, conical helmet and
nasal, lance, kite-shaped shield.

⊕ SIGILLVM ROBERTI : FILII TVRHETINI.

Osbertus *filius* WALCHERI, [*of Soham, co. Suff.*]

6014. [Mid. 12th cent.] Light-brown, varnished : fine, but
very imperfect. About 2 in. when perfect. [Harl. ch. 83 E. 41.]

To the r. In armour, hauberk, conical helmet.

Legend wanting.

Robertus *filius* WALTERI, [*3rd Baron Fitz-Walter.*
A.D. 1198–1234.]

6015. [12th cent.] Discoloured green : very indistinct.
About 1¾ in. when perfect. [Harl. ch. 50 C. 2.]

To the r. In armour : hauberk of mail, sword, kite-shaped
shield showing strap on the inside.

Legend wanting.

Second Seal of the same ?

6016. Recent cast in bronzed gutta-percha, from the matrix
in the Dept. of Antiquities. 2¾ in. [xxxvii. 1.]

To the r. In armour : hauberk and chaussées of mail, with
continuous coif, surcoat, flat-topped helmet with vizor closed,
sword, shield of arms. Horse caparisoned, with diapered
head-cloth. Arms : a fess betw. two chevrons, FITZ-
WALTER. In the field, in front of the horse, a shield of
arms : seven mascles, three, three, and one, DE QUINCY.
Below the horse, in the foreground, a wyvern reguardant, tail
flory. Fine workmanship.

⊕ SIGILLVM : ROBERTI : FILII : WALTERI :

Beaded borders.

6017. Recent impression in red sealing-wax from the
matrix. [xliv. 226.]

Simon *filius* WALTERI, [*of Redbourne, co. Linc.*]

6018. [*circ.* A.D. 1156.] Light-brown : imperfect.. About
2¼ in. when perfect. [Harl. ch. 50 C. 1.]

To the r. In armour : hauberk of mail, continuous coif,
conical helmet, sword, long convex shield with central spike.
Horse galloping.

. . . . IS · FILII · W . . . . . .

6019. Sulph. cast. [D.C., D. 77.]

Walterus *filius* WALTERI [DE TATERSALE, *co. Linc.*]

6020. [Late 12th cent.] Dark-green : fine, with mark of
handle. 1½ in. [Harl. ch. 56 H. 12.]

To the r. In armour: hauberk, surcoat, cap-like helmet, sword, convex shield. Horse galloping.

✠ SIGILL' WALTERI FIL' WALTERI.

The letters TE in *Walteri* in both cases conjoined.

6021. Sulph. cast. [D.C., E. 230.]

Fulco *filius* WARINI, [*of Alveston, co. Glouc.*]

6022. [*Temp.* Henry III.] Creamy-white, discoloured and varnished: very imperfect. About 2 in. when perfect. [Harl. ch. 50 C. 15.]

∅. To the r. In armour: hauberk, surcoat, flat-topped helmet with vizor down, sword, shield of arms. Horse galloping, with ornamental breast-band. Fine workmanship.

SIGI . . . . ONIS . . . .

℞. Within a pointed and carved quatrefoil, and on an elegantly designed tree, a shield of arms: quarterly, per fess indented, FITZ-WARIN, or FITZ-WARREN, betw. two wavy branches of foliage.

✠ SIG . . . . CO . . . . NI.

Beaded borders.

6023. Sulph. casts of the *obv.* and *rev.* [D.C., F. 155, 156.]

Alan *filius* WILL. *fil.* WARINI, *Miles*, [*of Wileby, co. Northt.*]

6024. [A.D. 1312.] Dark-green: fine, slightly chipped. 1 in. [Add. ch. 22,535.]

To the r. In armour: hauberk of mail, surcoat, helmet and plume, sword, shield of arms. Horse galloping, caparisoned and plumed. Arms: quarterly, per fess indented, FITZ-WARIN.

S' ALANI FILII WARINI.

Beaded borders.

6025. Plaster cast. [lxxxi. 22.]

Willelmus *filius* WILL. *fil.* WARINI, [*of Pershore, co. Worc.*]

6026. [A.D. 1175–1198.] Green: fine, left side chipped. With mark of handle. 2¾ in. [Add. ch. 20,425.]

To the r. In armour: hauberk of mail, surcoat, round-topped helmet, sword, shield with radiating ornament, border, and central knob. Horse galloping.

✠ SIGILLVM · W · FILII · [W ·] FILII [WAR]INI.

Willelmus *filius* WIBERTI, [*of Westfield, co. Suss.*]

6027. [*circ.* A.D. 1107–1124.] Pale-green, varnished: much rubbed and injured. About 1¼ in. when perfect. [Add. ch. 20,161.]

To the r. In armour: hauberk of mail.

Legend wanting.

Herveus *filius* WILLELMI, [*of Welleford, co. Northt.*]
6028. [Late 12th cent.] Red: only a fragment of the
r. h. side.   About 1¾ in. when perfect.   [Add. ch. 22,514.]
    To the l. In cap, and shield (?), a hawk on the l. hand.
          ✠ SIGILLVM : H . . . . MI. .
The borders are composed of annulets.

Hugo *filius* WILLELMI, [*of Hatton, co. Warw.*]
6029. [*Temp.* Joh.]   Creamy-white: fine, but chipped.
1⅛ in.   [Cott. ch. xxv. 26.]
    To the r. In armour: hauberk, surcoat, round-topped
helmet, sword, shield with chevronelly ornament, border and
central spike.   Horse galloping.
          ✠ SIGILL' [H]VGONIS . FILII ·' WILLELMI.
Beaded border.
6030. Creamy-white: indistinct.   [Cott. ch. xxiv. 20.]
∅. As before.
          ✠ SIGIL . . . . . . GON . . . . LMI.
R. Small oval counterseal.   With mark of handle.   1 × ⅞ in.
Impression of an antique oval intaglio gem : a lion passant.
          ✠ S' HVGONIS · FIL' WILL'I. ·

Ranulfus *filius* WILLELMI.
6031. [Late 12th cent.] Plaster cast from fine impression.
2 in.   [lxxix. 65.]
    To the r. In armour: hauberk, coif, surcoat, conical helmet
with ties behind, sword, long convex shield with central spike.
Horse galloping.
          ✠ SIGILLVM : RANVLFI : FILII : WILLELMI.

Ricardus *filius* WILLELMI, [*of Sulby, co. Northt.*]
6032. [Early 13th cent.]   Dark-green: fine, edge chipped.
2⅛ in.   [Add. ch. 22,421.]
    To the r. In armour: hauberk of mail, continuous coif,
surcoat, conical helmet and nasal, sword, long convex shield
with radiating ornament and central spike.   Horse with
large caparison covering all except the nose, the lower edge
invecked.
          ✠ SIGILLVM RICA[RD]I FILII WILLELMI :

Robertus *filius* WILLELMI ; *al.* ROBERTUS MEPERSALTUS,
          [*Lord of Bitlesden, co. Buck.*]
6033. [*circ.* A.D. 1147.]   Light - brown, varnished : fine,
chipped at the top.   2¼ in.   [Harl. ch. 85 G. 48.]
    To the r. In armour: hauberk of mail, continuous coif,
round-topped helmet, sword, long kite-shaped shield with

vertical rib. Horse springing, with ornamental breast-band.

Legend on raised rim.

✠ SIGILLVM ROBERTI FI .... WILELMI.

6034. Sulph. cast. [D.C., D. 68.]

Willelmus *filius* WILLELMI, [*Lord of Emley, co. York.*]

6035. [13th cent.] Dark-green, mottled : app. to a charter *circ.* A.D. 1385. [Add. ch. 7478.]

To the r. In armour : hauberk, surcoat, round-topped helmet, sword, long convex shield. Horse galloping.

✠ SIGILL' WIL.............

Peter de Flota (?).

6036. [13th cent.] Plaster cast from fine, but very imperfect, impression. About 2⅛ in. when perfect. [lxxix. 19.]

To the r. In armour : hauberk of mail, surcoat, plumed helmet with vizor down, sword, shield of arms. Horse galloping, caparisoned and plumed. Arms : six combs or floats, two and two in pale, on a chief a demi-lion rampant issuing.

.... II.

Willelmus Folet, [*of Longdon, co. Worc.*]

6037. [*Temp.* Hen. II.] Dark-green, mottled : fine, with mark of handle, chipped at the edge. 2¼ in. [Harl. ch. 83 B. 16.]

To the r. In armour : hauberk of mail, continuous coif, surcoat, conical helmet and nasal, sword, long convex shield with ornament of rays, border, and central spike. Horse with ornamental breast-band.

✠ SIGILLVM WILELMI FOLET.

Another Seal.

6038. [Late 12th cent.] Bright-red : fine, with mark of handle. 2¼ in. [Harl. ch. 83 B. 17.]

To the r. In armour : hauberk of mail and continuous coif, conical helmet, sword, long convex shield with ornaments and central spike. Horse galloping.

✠ SIGILLVM WILLELMI FOLE[T.]

6039. Sulph. cast. [D.C., D. 130.]

6040. Creamy-white : fine, edge chipped ; app. by a woven bobbin diapered with three colours. [Harl. ch. 83 B. 15.]

William Foliot, [*of Malvern, co. Worc.*]

6041. [Early 13th cent.] Creamy-white : fine, very imperfect. About 2¼ in. when perfect. [Harl. ch. 83 B. 14.]

To the r. In armour: hauberk, surcoat, conical helmet, sword, long convex shield. Horse galloping.

✠ SIGILL ...... ILL .... IOT.

6042. Sulph. cast. [D.C., D. 113.]

Willelmus Foliot.

6043. [Late 12th cent.] Plaster cast from chipped impression. About 2 in. [lxxix. 20.]

To the r. In armour: hauberk, surcoat, conical helmet, sword, convex shield. Horse galloping.

✠ SIGILL' WILLELMI FOLIOT.

Willelmus de Fortibus, [3rd] Earl of Albemarle.
[A.D. 1241–1259.]

6044. [A.D. 1251.] Dark-green: fine, very imperfect, speckled. About 3⅛ in. when perfect. [Harl. ch. 50 D. 38.]

∅. To the r. In armour: hauberk and coif of mail, flat-topped helmet with vizor closed, [sword], shield of arms suspended by an embroidered strap round his neck. Horse galloping with ornamental breast-band. Arms as in *rev.*

.. SIG ....

℞. A shield of arms: a cross formée vairée, DE FORTIBUS; suspended by the strap on an ornamental tree of conventional and elegant design, betw. two wavy branches of foliage.

Legend wanting.

Beaded borders.

6045. Sulph. casts of *obv.* and *rev.* [D.C., E. 251, 252.]

6046. Plaster casts from very fine impression, slightly chipped at edge. [lxxix. 21, 22.]

∅. ⟳ SIGILLVM WILLELMI DE FORTIBVS CO[MI]TIS ALBEMARLIE.

The letters AL in *Albemarlie* conjoined.

℞. ⟳ SIGILLVM WILLELMI DE FORTIBVS COMITIS ALBEMARLIE.

Rogo *or* [Rorgo] de Freuvilla, [*of Filsham, co. Suss.*]

6047. [Early 13th cent.] Dark-green: fine, with mark of handle. 1⅞ in. [L. F. C., xxv. 6.]

To the r. In armour: surcoat, conical helmet, lance, kite-shaped shield. Horse galloping.

✠ SIGILLVM ROGONIS DE .... VILLA (?).

Gerardus *fil.* Gerardi [DE FURNIVALLE, *of Caldecote Manor, co. Herts.*]

6048. [*Temp.* Edw. I.] Green: very fine, the l. h. side wanting. 1¾ in. [Add. ch. 19,958.]

Ø. To the r. In armour: hauberk of mail, flat - topped helmet with vizor down, sword, shield of arms. Horse caparisoned. Arms: a bend betw. six martlets, FURNIVAL.

✠ S' GERARDI : FILII : GERA . . . .

Beaded borders.

R. Small oval counterseal. $\frac{7}{8} \times \frac{3}{4}$ in. Impression of an antique oval intaglio gem. A female bust in profile to the r., the hair tied in a knot behind.

✠ SECRETVM : GERARDI.

6049. Bronze-green : fine, very imperfect, edge chipped away. [Harl. ch. 50 E. 55.]

Ø. As before.

. . . . DI . . . .

R. As before, cracked.

✠ SECRETVM : GERARDI.

Beaded border.

6050. Sulph. cast of *obv.* only. [D.C., E. 240.]

Reginaldus Furo.

6051. [12th cent.] Plaster cast from indistinct and chipped impression. $1\frac{3}{4}$ in. [lxxix. 23.]

To the r. In armour: hauberk, surcoat, conical helmet, sword. Horse galloping.

✠ SIGILL' REGINALDI FVRO (?).

Morganus Gam, [or Kam, of Aberafon, co. Glam.]
(? Same as Morgan Cam. See No. 5783.)

6052. [Early Hen. III.] Dark-green : fine, edge slightly chipped. $1\frac{1}{2}$ in. [Harl. ch. 75 C. 21.]

To the r. In armour: hauberk, surcoat, flat-topped helmet, sword, shield with star-like ornament and central spike. Horse galloping.

✠ SIGILLVM : MORGANI : GAM ✳

6053. Sulph. cast. [D.C., E. 215.]

Gilebertus de Gant.

6054. [A.D. 1146–1154.] Light - brown : fine, very imperfect. About $2\frac{3}{4}$ in. when perfect. [Harl. ch. 83 E. 54.]

To the r. In armour: hauberk, sword, shield. Horse galloping.

. . . . . GILEBERTI DE GA . . . .

6055. [A.D. 1146–1156.] Another: fragmentary. [Harl. ch. 83 E. 52.]

Gillebertus de Gant, Earl of Lincoln.

6056. [A.D. 1142–1156.] Pale creamy-white : originally fine, now soft and the surface flaked away. [Harl. ch. 50 F. 31.]

To the r. In armour : hauberk, long surcoat and maunches (see the seal of Hugh Cyvelioc, Earl of Chester, No. 5812), helmet and nasal, sword, long convex shield with central spike.

Legend wanting.

J. G. Nichols, *Topographer*, vol. i., p. 317.

6057. Sulph. cast. [D.C., D. 76.]

Willelmus de Gedding, [*of Polstead, co. Suffolk.*]

6058. [*Temp.* Hen. III.] Pale-green : very imperfect and indistinct. About 2⅛ in. when perfect. [Harl. ch. 50 G. 4.]

To the r. In armour: hauberk, helmet, sword, shield.

. . . . W . . . . DE · G :: DD . . . . . Є . . .

Galfridus de Geinvile [*or* GEYNVILLE], *Lord of "Wallis-Colorum," [of co. Meath.]*

6059. [A.D. 1259.] Dark bronze-green : fine. 1⅞ in. [Harl. ch. 50 G. 38.]

Ø. To the r. In armour : hauberk of mail, surcoat. flat helmet and vizor down, sword, shield of arms. Horse caparisoned, galloping at full speed. For arms, see the description of *rev.*

✠ S' . GALFRIDI : DE : GEINVILE : DN̄I : DE : WALLE : COLOR'.

R. 1¼ in. Within a pointed gothic quatrefoil, and suspended by the loop from a hook betw. two sprigs of foliage, a shield of arms : three horses' bits, on a chief a demi lion issuant, GENEVILL.

✠ SIGILLVM : SECRETI : MEI :

6060. Sulph. cast of *obv.* only. [D.C., E. 253.]

6061. Sulph. cast of *rev.* only. [D.C., E. 382.]

Robertus de Ghines, [*Miles, of Tolleshunt, co. Ess.*]

6062. [*circ.* A.D. 1245–1250.] Greenish-white : originally fine, now cracked and edge injured ; app. by a plaited cord of red silk. 1⅞ in. [Harl. ch. 50 G. 39.]

Ø. To the r. In armour: hauberk of mail, short surcoat, flat helmet with vizor closed, sword, shield of arms. Horse galloping with ornamental breast-band. For arms, see description of *rev.*

✠ S' DOMINI · ROBERTI · DE · GHINES.

R. A smaller counterseal. 1⅛ in. A shield of arms : a chief vairé, GHINES.

✠ S' ROBERTI : ✱ : DE : GHINES :

Beaded borders.

6063. Sulph. casts of *obv.* and *rev.* [D.C., E. 245, 246.]

Milo de Gloecestria, [*afterwards Earl of Hereford.*
A.D. 1140–1143.]

6064. Recent impression, in red sealing-wax, from silver matrix. 2½ in. With mark of handle. [xxxv. 56.]

To the r. In armour: hauberk and coif of mail, conical helmet and nasal, banner flag and other streamers, kite-shaped shield showing the inside strap. Horse with ornamental breast-band.

⊕ SIGILLVM MILONIS DE GLOECESTRIA.

Gent. Mag., vol. lxv., p. 737 ; *Archæologia*, vol. xv., p. 276.

6065. Sulph. cast. [xlvii. 923.]

Laing's *MS. Catal.*, No. 313.

Peres de Goldintune, *or* Petrus de Goldintona,
[of Coton-under-Guilsborough, co. Northt.]

6066. [Late 12th cent.] - Light-brown, varnished red : indistinct in parts. 2¼ in. [Add. ch. 20,451.]

To the r. In armour: hauberk and coif of mail, surcoat, conical helmet and nasal, sword, long convex shield with ornamental border. Horse springing.

⊕ SIGILLVM · PERES . . . . . DINTVNE.

Another Seal.

6067. [Late 12th cent.] Pale greenish-brown : very imperfect ; app. by a woven bobbin of purple and yellow threads. About 2⅜ in. when perfect. [Add. ch. 22,343.]

To the r. In armour: hauberk of mail, spear or lance, long convex shield. Horse galloping.

. . . . PETRI DE GO . . . . . . INTON . . .

The letter N reversed.

Gwilliam de Goram.

6068. [*circ.* A.D. 1190.] Sulph. cast from fine impression. With mark of handle. 1¾ in. [xxxvi. 199.]

To the r. In armour: hauberk of mail, surcoat, helmet, sword, shield ornamented with a cross-like ornament. Horse galloping, with ornamental breast-band.

⊕ SIGILLVM : GWILL'I DE GORAM.

6069. Plaster cast. [lxxix. 68.]

Radulfus de Goran.

6070. [*circ.* A.D. 1210.] Sulph. cast from fine, but very imperfect, impression. About 2¼ in. when perfect. [xxxvi. 200.]

To the r. In armour: round-topped helmet, sword, shield with ornaments. Horse galloping.

⊕ S' : RADVLFI DE GORAИ.

The letter N reversed.

6071. Plaster cast. [lxxix. 67.]

Petrus de Gousla, [GOLSA, GOSLA, *or* GAUSLA,
of Newsham, etc., co. Lincoln.]

6072. [*circ.* A.D. 1150.] Dark-green : indistinct in parts. 2¼ in. [Harl. ch. 50 H. 58.]

To the r. In armour : a lance and flag, kite-shaped shield showing the inside.

✠ SIGILLVM PETRI DE GOVSLA.

6073. Sulph. cast. [D.C., D. 58.]

Albertus Grelle.

6074. [Late 12th cent.] Plaster cast from indistinct impression chipped at edges. 2⅙ in. [lxxix. 26.]

To the r. In armour : hauberk of mail, coif, conical helmet, sword, convex kite shield.

✠ SIGILLVM ALBERTI GRELLE.

Robertus Grellei.

6075. [12th cent.] Plaster cast from fine, but chipped, impression. 2¼ in. [lxxix. 27.]

To the r. In armour: hauberk of mail, conical helmet and nasal, sword, shield bearing central spike and a fretty device.

✠ SIGILLVM ROBERTI GRELLEI.

Willelmus de Gresleia, [of Wetley, co. Staff.]

6076. [Early 13th cent.] Dark-green : fine, with mark of handle. 1⅞ in. [Woll. ch. v. 33.]

To the r. In armour: hauberk, surcoat, round-topped helmet, sword, long convex shield. Horse galloping.

✠ SIGILL' WILLELMI DE GRESLEIA.

6077. Sulph. cast. [D.C., D. 197.]

Ricardus de Greai, [or GREY, "Consiliarius Regis Angliæ," English Plenipotentiary at Paris.]

6078. [A.D. 1255.] Bronze-green : fine, well preserved, chipped at top. 2 in. [Add. ch. 11,295.]

To the r. In armour: hauberk of mail, flat cap-like helmet with vizor down, sword, shield of arms. Horse galloping. Arms : barry of six, GRAY or GREY. Fine work.

SIGILLVM : RICARDI : DE : GREAI.

Beaded borders.

6079. Plaster cast from fine, but chipped, impression. [lxxix. 28.]

Robertus Grimbaut, [or GRIMBAUD, Lord of Houghton, co. Northt.]

6080. [A.D. 1260.] Dark-green : fine, slightly chipped. 1⅛ in. [Harl. ch. 86 C. 43.]

To the r. In armour: hauberk of mail, flat cap-like helmet

with vizor down, sword, shield of arms. Horse caparisoned galloping. Arms: two bars, within a bordure, GRIMBAUD.

✠ S' ROBERTI · GRIMBAVT.

Beaded borders.

6081. Sulph. cast. [D.C., E. 254.]

Willelmus Grymbaud, [*Miles, son of Robert Grymbaud, of co. Northt.*]

6082. [A.D. 1288.] Dark-green: fine fragment. About 1¾ in. when perfect. [Harl. ch. 50 I. 53.]

To the r. In armour: hauberk of mail, surcoat, shield of arms. Horse caparisoned. Arms: barry, within a bordure, for GRIMBAUD.

Legend wanting.

Eudo de Grenesbi, [*founder of Greenfield Abbey, co. Linc.*]

6083. [*circ.* A.D. 1150.] Brown, varnished: very imperfect. About 2⅜ in. when perfect. [Harl. ch. 50 I. 30.]

To the r. In armour: hauberk and continuous coif of mail, conical helmet with ties and nasal, sword, shield.

. . . . DE : GRENESBI.

Willelmus Gubaltus, [*or* GUBALD, *of Rippingale, co. Linc.*]

6084. [Late 12th cent.] Brown, semi-opaque: good, with mark of handle. 2 in. [Add. ch. 21,096.]

To the r. In armour: hauberk of mail, round-topped helmet and nasal, sword, shield of convex form with ornamental bands. Horse galloping.

✠ SIGILLVM · WILLELMI : GVBALTI.

Rogerus *filius* - - - - - **de Guige',** [*or* GUIGES, *of London.*]

6085. [A.D. 1201.] Brownish-green: edge chipped, indistinct in parts. 1⅞ in. [*Egert.* ch. 510.]

To the r. In armour: hauberk, conical helmet and nasal, sword, long convex shield with central spike. Horse galloping.

✠ SIG' ROGERI FILII · IV . . . DOMÏI DE G . ، GE'.

Robert Hagat, [*or* HACET, *of Feltwell, co. Norf*]

6086. [A.D. 1170.] Light-brown: fine, the l. h. side wanting. 1⅞ in. [Harl. ch. 112 D. 58.]

To the r. In armour: hauberk, surcoat, conical helmet and nasal, sword, convex shield with engrailed bordure of ornamentation and central spike. Horse galloping.

✠ SIGILLVM ROBERT . . . . Ṫ.

Another Seal.

6087. [A.D. 1179.]   Creamy-white : fine, indistinct in parts. [Harl. ch. 111 G. 50.]

Similar in appearance to preceding seal.

⊕ SIGILLVM ROBBERTI · HAGAT.

6088. Sulph. cast.   [D.C., D. 156.]

Rollandus Haget, [*of Brightwell, co. Berk.*]

6089. [Late 12th cent.]   Creamy-white : very fragmentary. About 1¼ in. when perfect.   [Harl. ch. 83 F. 10.]

To the r.   In armour : hauberk, long shield.   Horse galloping.

Legend wanting.

R——— de Haia, [*of Authorpe, co. Linc.*]

6090. [Late 12th cent.]   Pale creamy-white, varnished : the face peeled off in parts, very imperfect.   About 2¼ in. when perfect.   [Harl. ch. 51 D. 22.]

To the r.   In armour : hauberk, surcoat, conical helmet and nasal, sword, long shield.   Horse galloping, with long caparisons invecked at the bottom, covering the whole of the body.   See Nos. 6001, 6032, etc.

Legend wanting.

Haltun (Radulfus de).   *v.* Alchtunia (Radulfus de).

Jehan de Hardredishill, [*or* HARDESHULLE, *Chev.,*
of Great Paxton, co. Hunt.]

6091. [A.D. 1360.]   Red : fine, edge imperfect on the r. h. side.   1⅛ in.   [Add. ch. 22,611.]

To the r.   In armour : hauberk of mail, surcoat, conical helmet with fan plume, and vizor down, sword, shield of arms.   Horse galloping, caparisoned and plumed.   Arms : a chevron betw. five martlets in chief and three in base. HARDESHULL.   Background diapered.

S' .... Є HARDREDISHILL.

6092. [A.D. 1367.]   White : fine fragment.   About 1¼ in. when perfect.   [Harl. ch. 76 E. 26.]

To the r.   In armour : shield of arms.   Horse caparisoned. Arms : a chevron betw. eight martlets, five in chief, three in base, HARDESHULL.   Perhaps same as last.

Legend wanting.

———trop Hasd———.
(*A doubtful seal.*)

6093. [Late 12th cent.]   Light red : fine, imperfect.   About 2⅛ in. when perfect.   [xxxvi. 54.]

To the r. In armour: hauberk, surcoat, round-topped helmet with nasal, sword, shield with ornamental border and central spike. Horse galloping, with ornamental breast-band.

✠ SI . . . . . M . . . . . TROP : HASD . . . .

6094. Plaster cast. [lxxix. 35.]

Henricus de Hastings.

˙**0095˙** [12th cent] Plaster cast from chipped impression. 1¾ in. [lxxix. 36.]

To the r. In armour: hauberk, surcoat, helmet, sword, convex shield with central spike. Horse .

✠ SIGIL . . . . ENRICI DE . . . . ǥalloping

Henricus de Hastings, [*son of* WILLIAM DE HASTINGS, *of Odstone, co. Leic.*]

6096. [Late 12th cent.] Greenish-white, varnished: very imperfect, edge chipped away; app. by a woven cord or bobbin of diapered pattern. About 2 in. when perfect. [Add. ch. 21,390.]

To the r. In armour: hauberk, surcoat, cap-shaped helmet and nasal, sword, long convex shield. Horse galloping.

✠ . . . . . . RICI D . . . .

Henry Hastings, 5*th Earl of Huntingdon; Baron Hastings, Hungerford, Botreaux, Moleyns, and Moels.*

6097. [A.D. 1631.] Cast in red composition from fine impression, the sides broken away. 2½ in. [lxxv. 68, 69.]

∅. A shield of arms of twelve quarterings:—1. HASTINGS; 2. HEYTESBURY; 3. BOTREAUX; 4. MOLEYNS; 5. MOELS or HUNGERFORD; 6. POLE; 7. GEORGE DUKE of CLARENCE; 8. NEVILLE of *Warwick;* 9. MONTAGU; 10. BEAUCHAMP; 11. DESPENSER; 12. CLARE. (Cf. Doyle, *Official Baronage,* vol. ii. p. 239.) Crest, out of a coronet of five pearls and four strawberry leaves, on a helmet, mantling, and wreath, a bull's head, erased, gorged with a coronet. Supporters broken off. Motto in base on a ribbon.

[HONORAN]TES · ME · HONORA[BO.]

Cf. 1 Sam. ii. 30.

. . . . I ✠ CO . . . . ✠

Inner border beaded, outer border carved.

℞. To the l. On a mount with flowering plants, armed *cap-à-pie,* with plate armour, helmet ornamented with ostrich plumes, in the r. h. a sword held overhead. Horse caparisoned. On the flank the maunch of HASTINGS, on the fore quarter the crest as in the *obv.*

✠ BAR[O] . . . .

Laurentius de Hastyngs, *Earl of Pembroke, Lord of Weysford and of Bergavenny.*

6098. [A.D. 1340.]   Creamy-white : fine originally, now very imperfect on the l. h. side, and the face flaked away. About 2¾ in. when perfect. [Add. ch. 6027.]

Ø. To the r.   In armour : hauberk, surcoat, sword, shield of arms (see *rev.*).   Horse caparisoned.

. . . . . . ES . . . . . .

R. An eagle displayed, charged on the breast with a large shield of arms : quarterly 1, 4. a maunch, HASTINGS ; 2, 3. Barry of uncertain number, an orle of martlets, for PEMBROKE.

. . . . . . REN . . . . . DE · HAS . . . . . .

Willelmus Le Hauburge, [*of Kelmarsh, co. Northt.*]

6099. [Early 13th cent.]   Yellowish-red : chipped on the l. h. side.   1¾ in. [Add. ch. 20,524.]

To the r.   In armour : hauberk, surcoat, flat or crown-shaped helmet, sword, shield with ornamental border and central spike.   Horse galloping.   In base, below the horse, an ornamental fleur-de-lis.

SIGILL' WILL'I LE HAVB . . . . . .

Willelmus *filius* Radulfi de Hauville, [*of Takeley, co. Oxon.*]

6100. [Late 12th cent.]   Discoloured white : very imperfeet and indistinct.   About 2 in. when perfect. [Harl. ch. 51 D. 10.]

To the l.   A hawk on the l. hand.

Legend wanting.

Henricus, Comes Northumberlandiæ, *filius* DAVID [I.,] *Regis Scotiæ.*   [A.D. 1140–1152.]

6101. Sulph. cast tinted red, from fine impression, chipped at the lower part, cracked.   2⅞ in. [xlvii. 9.]

To the r.   In armour : hauberk and coif of mail, with ties, surcoat, conical helmet, sword, long kite-shaped shield with vertical ridge.   Horse with fringed saddle cloth and ornamental breast-band.

✠ SIGILLVM HENRICI COMITIS NORI . . . . ANDIE
FILII REGIS SCOCIE.

Laing's *Suppl. Catal. of Scottish Seals*, No. 2.

Willelmus [de Westbi] *filius* Rodberti de Herrierbi, [*of co. Linc.*]

6102. [*circ.* A.D. 1172.]   Dark-green, speckled : fine, with raised edge, chipped, and mark of handle.   2¼ in. [Egert. ch. 434.]

To the r. In armour: hauberk, conical helmet and nasal, sword, shield with central boss.

✠ SIGILLVM · WIL . . . . . . I · FILII · RODB'TI DE HERRIERBI.

Another Seal.

6103. [*circ.* A.D. 1172.] Green: fine, edge chipped. 2¼ in. [Egert. ch. 433.]

To the r. In armour: hauberk of mail, conical helmet and nasal, sword, long convex shield with central spike. Horse with ornamental breast-band.

✠ SIGILL͞V · WIL . . . . ILII ROBE . . . . DE HERIERBI.

Tomas, *fil.* Roberti de Heri[n]gtu[n].

6104. [Early 13th cent.] Plaster cast from fine impression, face corroded. 1⅜ in. [lxxix. 39.]

To the r. In armour: hauberk, surcoat, flat helmet, sword, shield.

✠ SIGILL' TOME FILII · ROBERTI D' HERIGTV'.

Rikardus de Hintona, [*of Charwelton, co. Northt.*]

6105. [Early 13th cent.] Brown, mottled: good, lower part imperfect. 1¾ in. [Harl. ch. 84 D. 22.]

To the r. In armour: hauberk of mail, surcoat, cap-shaped helmet, sword, shield with ornamental bordure and central spike. Horse galloping.

SIGILL' RIKARD . . . . TONA.

6106. Sulph. cast. [D.C., E. 229.]

Robertus de Hintuna.

6107. [13th cent.] Light yellowish-brown: rubbed and injured. 1⅞ in. [xxxvi. 52.]

To the r. In armour: conical helmet with long ties, sword, long convex shield with star-like ornament. Horse galloping.

✠ SIGILLVM ROBERTI DE HINTVNA.

Willelmus de Yspania, [Hispania ?] [*of Willingale-Spain, co. Essex.*]

6108. [Early 12th cent.] Creamy-white: originally fine, edge imperfect. About 2½ × 1¾ in. when perfect. [Add. ch. 28,347.]

Pointed oval. To the l. In armour: conical helmet, kite-shaped shield, spear?

✠ SIG . . . . PANIA.

Willelmus de Hocretona, [*of Hockerton, co. Northt.*]

6109. [Late 12th or early 13th cent.] Brownish-red: indistinct, chipped. 1⅜ in. [Harl. ch. 83 F. 23.]

To the r. In armour: hauberk, surcoat, helmet, sword, shield. Horse galloping.
Legend

          . . . . W . . . . . .

6110. Sulph. cast. [D.C., D. 188.]

Henricus de Hoctun.

6111. [13th cent.] Plaster cast from fine impression. $\frac{7}{8}$ in. [lxxix. 40.]
To the r. In armour: hauberk of mail, surcoat, flat helmet, sword, shield. Horse galloping.

    ✠ SIGILLVM : HENRICI : DE : HOCTVN.
Beaded border.

Radulfus, [*fil.* RADULFI] de Holandia, [*of Wyberton, co. Linc.*]

6112. [Late 12th or early 13th cent.] Green, mottled: fine originally, now imperfect on r. h. side. $2\frac{1}{8}$ in. [Harl. ch. 58 A. 24.]
To the r. In armour: hauberk and coif of mail, cap-like helmet and nasal, in the l. h. a lance with banner flag, charged with an uncertain pattern or chequy device. In the field on the l., over the horse, a rosette or flower of eight leaves.

    SIGILL . . . . DE HOLANDIA.

6113. Sulph. cast. [D.C., D. 94.]

Radulfus, [*fil.* STEPHANI] de Hoilandia, [*or* OILANDIA, *of Snelland, co. Linc.*]

6114. [12th cent.] Brown: fine, well preserved. $2\frac{1}{4}$ in. [Harl. ch. 54 D. 31.]
To the r. In armour: hauberk and coif, conical helmet and nasal, sword, long kite-shaped shield with ornamental border, vertical rib and central spike.

    SIGILL' · RADVLFI · DE . HOILANDIA.

6115. Sulph. cast. [D.C., D. 93.]

Willelmus de Holt. (P)

6116. [Late 12th cent.] Sulph. cast from chipped and indistinct impression. $1\frac{3}{4}$ in. [D.C., D. 186.]
To the r. In armour: hauberk, surcoat, helmet, sword, long shield. Horse galloping.

    ✠ SIGI . . . . LLI DE HOLT (?)

Rogerus de Hoo, [*Miles, of Shelfhanger, co. Norf.*]

6117. [Early Hen. III.] Light brown, varnished red: originally fine, now only lower half remaining. About 2 in. when perfect. [Harl. ch. 83 F. 36.]
To the r. In armour: hauberk. Horse galloping.

    . . . . M ROGERI . . . .

Simun de Hórbelig, [*or* **Horbeling,** *of Reasby, co. Linc.*]
6118. [Late 12th cent.] Brown, mottled and varnished. 1⅝ in. [Harl. ch. 51 G. 16.]
To the r. In armour: hauberk, surcoat, cap-like helmet, sword, shield. Horse galloping.

※ SIGILLVM · SIMVN DE HORBELIG.

The N in *Simun* and D in *de*, reversed.
- **6119.** Sulph. cast. [D.C., D. 185.]

Ricardus de Hotun, [*or* HUTUN], *fil.* **Pigoti.**
[*of Newton, co. Linc.*]
6120. [13th cent.] Light brown: edge chipped and indistinct in places. 2 in. [Harl. ch. 52 A. 45.]
To the r. In armour: surcoat, conical helmet, shield with central spike, hawk on r. hand.

※ SIGILLVM RICARDI DE HOT . . . . FILI PIGOTI.

6121. Sulph. cast. [D.C., D. 181.]

Asctin de Huc, *or* **Haschetillus de Huch,** [*of Swinfleet, co. York.*]
6122. [End of the 12th cent.] Brown, semi-opaque: with mark of the handle. 1⅜ in. [Harl. ch. 52 A. 10.]
To the r. In armour: hauberk of mail, cap-like helmet, sword, shield. Horse galloping.

※ SIGILLVM · ASCTIN DE HVC.

The C's are square.
6123. Sulph. cast. [D.C., D. 79.]

Ricardus de Humetis, [*or* **Richard de Humez,** *Constable of the king,* i.e. *Constable of Normandy.*]
6124. [A.D. 1154–1180.] Green: originally fine, edge broken away in places. About 2¾ in. [Harl. ch. 83 A. 6.]
To the r. In armour: hauberk and continuous coif of mail, conical helmet, nasal, long sword, kite-shaped shield showing the interior strap by which it is held. Horse galloping with ornamental breast-band and fringed saddle cloth. In the field are several stars, and below the r. elbow of the rider a small cross or star.

※ SIGILLVM RICJARDII DE HVJMETIS.

6125. Sulph. cast. [D.C., D. 108.]
6126. White: very imperfect at lower part, originally fine. [Harl. ch. 83 B. 35.]

※ SIGILLV . . . . ETIS.

6127. Green: originally fine, chipped and repaired. [Harl. ch. 83 B. 36.]

. . . . . . LVM RICARDI DE HV . : . . . . .

6128. Sulph. cast before the cracked pieces were lost. [D.C., D. 107.]

⊕ SIGILLVM RICARDI DE HVMETIS.

Willelmus de Hummetis [*or* Humez], *Constable [of Normandy.]*

6129. [A.D. 1180–1189.]   Green: fine, very imperfect, chipped at the edge: originally app. by a diapered riband. 2¼ in. [xxxix. 64,]

Ø. To the r.   In armour: hauberk of mail, surcoat, cap-like helmet, sword, shield of arms.   Horse galloping.   Arms appear to be: bezanty a bordure, for *argent* a bordure *gu.* bezanty, HUMEZ.

. . . . DE · HVM . . . . CONES . . ABVL . . .

R. Small oval counterseal.   1⅛ × 1¾ in.   Impression of an antique oval intaglio gem: a horseman riding to the l.

. . . . VMET . . . .

Another Seal.

6130. Plaster cast from fine impression.   2¾ in.   [lxxix. 44.]

To the r.   In armour: hauberk of mail, coif, conical helmet, sword, kite-shaped shield, seen from the inner side, with border, and held by a short strap or *enarme*.   Horse galloping with fringed saddle cloth.   In the field at the side of the rider's head an estoile, and below the horse two others.

⊕ SIGILLVM WILLELMI DE HVMMETIS.

Rogerus de Huntingfeld, [*of cos. Linc. and Suff.*]

6131. [Late 13th cent.]   Plaster cast from fine impression. 1⅞ in.   [lxxix. 46.]

To the r.   In armour: hauberk of mail, surcoat, plumed helmet affronté with vizor closed, sword, shield of arms, shoulder-pieces with arms thereon.   Horse galloping, capari-soned and plumed.   In the field over the neck of the horse a maunch.   Arms: on a fess three roundles.

SIGILL' ⊕ ROGERI ⊕ DN̄I ⊕ DE ⊕ HVNTINGFELD'.
Cf. *Inq. p. mort.*, 41 Hen. III.

Nigellus, *fil.* Alexandri de Ingoldesbi, [*of Ingoldsby, co. Linc.*]

6132. [Early 13th cent.]   Red: originally fine, chipped in places.   2¾ in.   [Add. ch. 20,580.]

To the r.   In armour: hauberk, cap-like helmet and nasal, sword, long convex shield with central spike.   In the field on the r., two estoiles of six points.

⊕ SIGILL' NIGELLI FILL'I ALEXANDRI DE ING . . . . ı.
The N's reversed.

O[s]bertus, *fil.* **Ne** [- - - - -] **de Ingoudeby**, [*co. Linc.*]
6133. [Early 13th cent.] Creamy-white : edge chipped.
1⅜ in. [Add. ch. 20,538.]

To the r. In armour : hauberk, surcoat, conical helmet and nasal, sword, shield charged with an ornament resembling a cross moline. Horse galloping.

✠ SIGILLVM : OBERTI FILII NE . . ϵ . .

The N reversed.

Willelmus de Insford.

6134. [12th cent.] Plaster cast from indistinct impression.
1¾ in. [lxxix. 69.]

To the r. In armour : hauberk, conical helmet with nasal, lance-flag with four streamers, convex shield with central spike. Horse galloping.

✠ SIGILL' WILLELMI DE INSFOR . . LETIR (?)

Walterus de Insula.

6135. [Late 12th cent.] Plaster cast of indistinct and imperfect impression. About 1½ in. when perfect. [lxxix. 72.]

To the l. A hawk on his l. h. Horse springing.

✠ SIGILL . . . . LA.

Ranulfus, (de Isert P)

6136. [Late 12th cent.] Plaster cast from indistinct impression. 1⅝ in. [lxxix. 70.]

To the r. In armour : hauberk, surcoat, round cap-like helmet, sword, shield.

✠ SIGILLVM RANVLFI . . . IS . . B' (?)

Kalverleia (Rogerus de) *v.* Scot (Rogerus).

Walterus de Kamville, [*of Crick, co. Northt. ?*]

6137. [Late 12th cent.] Brown : imperfect and indistinct.
About 2⅛ in. when perfect. [Harl. ch. 47 G. 16.]

To the r. In armour : hauberk, surcoat, conical helmet and nasal, sword, shield.

. . . . ALT . . . .

Willelmus de Kel', [*of Coningsby, co. Linc.*]

6138. [Late 12th or early 13th cent.] Brown, varnished : only a fragment of r. h. side. About 2 in. when perfect. [Harl. ch. 52 D. 21.]

To the r. with shield.

. . . IGILLV . . . .

Ridellus de Kesibi, [*fil.* THOMÆ COLUMBEIN, *et nepos Ridel Papallun de Kisebi, of Keisby, co. Linc.*]

6139. [Late Hen. II.] Brown : fine, with mark of handle

and raised rim, edge chipped on the r. h. side. $1\frac{7}{8}$ in. [Add. ch. 20,907.]

To the r. In armour : hauberk, surcoat, cap-like helmet, sword, long convex shield with central spike. Horse galloping.

SIGILLVM RIDEL DE KESIBI.

6140. Brown : fine, but chipped and injured. [Add. ch. 20,908.]

---

v. Papallun (Ridelus) de Cesebi.

Adam de Killingworth, *Miles.*

6141. [14th cent.] Sulph. cast from a chipped impression. About 1 in. when perfect. [D.C., F. 162.]

To the r. In armour : surcoat, flat-topped helmet, standing before a lady full-length, who is presenting to him a lance-flag and shield of arms. Horse caparisoned. Arms : three cinquefoils pierced, KILLINGWORTH?

✠ S' ADE KIL . . . . ITIS.

Rogerus de Kivelīwort', [*fil.* ROGERI DE KYVILLINGWRTH, *Kilworth, co. Leic.*]

6142. [A.D. 1229.] Light red : chipped. $1\frac{3}{4}$ in. [Add. ch. 21,273.]

To the r. In armour : hauberk, surcoat, round-topped helmet, sword, convex shield. Horse galloping.

✠ SIGILL' ROGERI DE KIVE . . . . T.

6143. Creamy - white : imperfect and indistinct. [Add. ch. 21,271.]

. . . . LIWORT'.

6144. Creamy-white : edge chipped and indistinct. [Add. ch. 21,299.]

✠ SIGILL' ROGERI DE KIVELĪWORT'.

6145. Light red : good originally, edge chipped. [Add. ch. 21,301.]

✠ SIGILL' ROGERI DE KIVELĪWORT'.

Kima, (Philippus de) *v.* Chime (Philippus de).

Philippus de Kima, [*or* **Kyma.**]

6146. [*circ.* A.D. 1191.] Brown : fine, edge imperfect. $2\frac{1}{4}$ in. [Harl. ch. 52 G. 39.]

To the r. In armour : hauberk and coif, surcoat, cap-shaped helmet and nasal, sword, long convex shield with central spike. Horse galloping.

✠ SIGILLVM . . HILIPPI DE KIMA.

6147. Discoloured : fine, edge chipped. [Harl. ch. 52 G. 38.]

✠ SIGILLVM. PH .... PI DE KIMA.

6148. [*circ.* A.D. 1172–1200.] Discoloured-white : imperfect and indistinct. [Harl. ch. 52 G. 40.]

✠ SIGILLVM PHILIP ....

: 6149. Light brownish - white : indistinct, edge chipped. [Harl. ch. 52 G. 41.]

.. SIGILLVM PH .... PI .. E KIMA.

v. Chime (Philippus de).

Philippus de Kyme, [*son of* D. WILLIAM DE KYMA, *of co.·Linc.*]

6150. [End of the 13th cent.] Dark brown : fine, chipped at top, injured by casting. 1⅛ in. [Harl. ch. 52 H. 6.]

To the r. In armour : hauberk. of mail, plumed helmet, sword,. shield. .of arms. Horse galloping. caparisoned and plumed. Arms : a chevron betw. ten crosses crosslet, KYME.

S′ PHILIPPI DE KYME :

6151. Sulph. cast. [D.C., D. 170.]

6152. Dark green : somewhat indistinct in places. [Harl. ch. 52 H. 4.]

6153. Dark green : fine, cracked and injured. [Harl. ch. 52 H. 6.]

Simon de Kyma, [*of Elkington, etc., co. Linc.*]

6154. [*circ.* A.D. 1200.][1] Yellowish-brown, varnished with a dark glaze : fine, but very imperfect ; app. by a closely woven cord of twilled threads striped with various colours. About 2⅜ in. when perfect. [Add. ch. 20,605.]

Ø. To the r. In armour : hauberk, surcoat, cap-shaped helmet, sword, shield of arms. Horse galloping with ornamental breast-band. Arms : a chevron, for KYME.

✠..I .... IS · DE ......

℞. Small oval counterseal. ⅝ × ¾ in. Impression of an antique oval intaglio gem. Bust of PALLAS ATHENE, helmeted, to the r.

✠ SE′VO SECRETA DM MEI.

6155. Discoloured, varnished : very imperfect. [Harl. ch. 52 G. 43.]

Ø. .... NIS ......

No counterseal.

Henricus de Laci, [*3rd*] *Earl of Lincoln, Constable of Chester.*

6156. [A.D. 1290.] Reddish-brown, grained : fine, chipped in places at the bottom. 2⅝ in. [Add. ch. 15,310.].

Ø. To the r. In armour : hauberk of mail, surcoat, plumed

helmet with vizor closed, sword, shield of arms. Horse galloping, caparisoned and plumed. Arms : a lion rampant, LACY.

S' HENRICI · DE · LACI · COM . . . . E[T]

CONSTABVLAR' CESTR'.

The letters NR in *Henrici*, and AB and AR in *constabular'*, conjoined.

Beaded borders.

℞. Small round counterseal. 1⅛ in. A shield of arms as in *obv.*, suspended by the strap from a tree of three branches, and supported by two lions rampant guardant addorsed.

SIGILLVM · SECRETI.

The letters LL of *sigillum* conjoined.

6157. [A.D. 1303.] Bronze green : very fine, much injured, edge nearly all destroyed. [Add. ch. 11,304.]

∅. . . . . TIS LINCOL . . . .

. . . . STR'.

℞. A variant counterseal. 1⅛ in. A shield of arms, LACY, as before, see No. 6156, suspended by the strap from a tree of three branches, and supported by two wyverns *sans* wings.

SIGILLVM SECRETI.

Beaded borders. . . .

6158. Plaster cast from fine impression. 2⅝ in. [lxxix. 81, 82.]

∅. To the r. In armour : hauberk of mail, surcoat, helmet with vizor down, fan plume, sword chained to shoulder, shield of arms. Horse galloping, caparisoned and plumed. Arms : a lion rampant.

S' HENRICI · DE · LACI · COMITIS : LINCOLNIE · ET

CONSTABVLAR' OESTR'.

℞. Counterseal, as in No. 6157.

Another Seal.

6159. [*circ.* A.D. 1300.] Dark green, a large mass : fine, well preserved. 2⅜ in. [Add. ch. 7438.]

∅. To the r. In armour : hauberk of mail, surcoat, plumed helmet, sword, and shield of arms. Horse galloping, caparisoned. Arms : quarterly, a bend, over all in chief a label of three points.

S' HENRICI DE LACI COMIT' LINCOLINE ET

CONSTABVLAR' CESTR'.

The letters AB and AR in *Constabular'* conjoined.

℞. Small counterseal. ¾ in. A shield of arms, as in *obv.* betw. two garbs for CHESTER.

Legend indistinct, but appears to read :—

SECRETVM · HENRICI : DE : LACI. (?)

Beaded borders.

. **Johannes de Lascy,** [1*st*] *Earl of Lincoln, and Constable of Chester.* [A.D. 1232–1240.]

6160. Plaster cast from fine impression. 2¾ in. [lxxix. 77, 78.]

∅. To the r. In armour: hauberk of mail, surcoat, flat-topped helmet, sword, kite-shaped shield of arms: as in the *rev.* Horse galloping. In the field, below the horse, a cinquefoil.

✠ S' : IOH'IS : DE : LASCY : COMITIS : LINCOLN' : ET : CO[NSTA]BVL' : CESTRIE.·

℞. A smaller round counterseal. 1½ in. A shield of arms: quarterly, over all a bend, in chief a label of four points.

✠ SECRETV̄ : IOH'IS : DE : LASCI : COM̄ : LINC̄ : ET ΘSTAB' CESTE.

Beaded borders.

Johannes de Lacy, *Constable of Chester ?* [1*st Earl of Lincoln,* A.D. 1232–1240.]

6161. Plaster cast from fine but indistinct impression, chipped at the edges. 2½ in. [lxxix. 76.]

To the r. In armour: hauberk, surcoat, flat-topped helmet, sword, shield of arms (indistinct charges). Horse galloping. In the field, below the horse, a large cinquefoil.

✠ SIGILLVM IOH . . . .

Walterus de Lacy, [*ob.* A.D. 1241.]

6162. [13th cent.] Plaster cast from fine impression. 2¼ in. [lxxix. 75.]

To the r. In armour: hauberk, surcoat, cap-like helmet, sword, shield of arms slung over the shoulder by a strap. Horse galloping with broad breast-band. Arms: a fess.

✠ SIGILLVM VVALTERI DE LACI.

Johannes de La Hay, *Miles,* [*Lord of Burwell, co. Linc.*]

6163. [A.D. 1281.] Greenish-brown: fine, slightly chipped at the top. 1⅛ in. [Harl. ch. 51 D. 32.]

To the r. In armour: hauberk of mail, surcoat, plumed helmet with vizor down, sword, shield of arms. Horse galloping, caparisoned. Arms: an estoile of twelve points, DE LA HAY.

S' · IOHANNIS · DE · LA HAYΘ · MILITIS.

6164. Sulph. cast. [D.C., E. 273.]

6165. Yellowish-brown: good, chipped at the top. [Harl. ch. 51 D. 30.]

6166. [A.D. 1283–1311.] Green: fine, but very imperfect. [Harl. ch. 51 D. 31.]

·Galfridus de La Mare, *Miles,* [*son and heir of .*
PETER DE LA MARE, *Miles, of Sawbridgeworth, co. Hertf.*]
   6167. [A.D. 1302.]   Green: fine, well preserved. 1 in.
[Cott. ch. xxvii. 33.]
   To the r. In armour: hauberk of mail, surcoat, plumed
helmet with the vizor down, sword, shield of arms. Horse
galloping, caparisoned. Arms: a fesse double cotised, DE
LA MARE.
                  : S' GALFRIDI : DE : LAMARE :
   Beaded borders.
   6168. Sulph. cast.   [D.C., F. 147.]

Willelmus de La Mara,
[*son of* ALAN *and* BEATRIX DE LA MARE, *of co. Lincoln ?*]
   6169. [*circ.* A.D. 1147–1166.]   Discoloured, varnished: indistinct. 1¾ in. [Cott. ch. xxvii. 34.]
   To the r. In armour: hauberk, conical helmet of peculiar
shape with nasal, lance-flag, shield.
         ⊕ SIGILLVM : WIL . . LMI DE LA MARA.
   6170. Sulph. cast.   [D.C., D. 100.]

Willelmus de Lancastre.
   6171. [13th cent.]   Plaster cast from chipped impression.
2 in. [lxxix. 84.]
   To the r. In armour: hauberk of mail, surcoat, helmet
with vizor down, sword, shield of arms. Horse galloping.
Arms: two bars, on a canton a crescent or some other uncertain charge, LANCASTER.
         SIGL . . . . E LANCASTRE.
   Cf. *Rot. de Oblatis,* p. 570, A.D. 1216 ; and *Inq. p. mort.,* 31 Hen. III.

Radulfus de Landa, [*of Langdon, co. Warw.*]
   6172. [*Temp.* Joh.]   Creamy-white: imperfect and indistinct. 1¾ in. [Cott. ch. xxvi. 37.]
   To the r. In armour: hauberk, surcoat, helmet, sword,
shield. Horse galloping.
   Legend wanting.
   Cf. *Rot. de Oblatis,* p. 540, A.D. 1214.

Nigellus de Langeford, [*of Langford, co. Derby.*]
   6173. [A.D. 1269.]   Green, mottled: originally fine, chipped,
1 in. [Wol. ch. ix. 59.]
   To the r. In armour: hauberk, surcoat, flat-topped helmet
with an ornament resembling three annulets rising out of it,
sword, shield of arms. Horse caparisoned. Caparisons apparently charged with paly of six.
            S' · NIGELLI.: DE : LA . . . . . : ORD :
   The letters O R conjoined.

Robertus, *fil.* **Roberti de Langtuna,** [*of Bulby, co. Linc.*]

6174. [Late' 12th cent.] Red: fine, edge slightly chipped.
1⅞ in. [Add. ch. 20,630.]

To the l. In long surcoat, a hawk on the l. h.

✠ SIGILLVM · ROBERTI · FIL'I · ROBERTI · DE · LANGTVNA.

The letters N reversed.

6175. Green, mottled: with marks of handle, the raised
edge and part of the legend broken away. [Add. ch. 20,629.]

✠ SIGILLVM · ROBERTI · FIL'I . . . . DE · LANGTVNA.

Thomas Le Latimer, [*of Ilketshall, co. Suff.*]

6176. [*Temp.* Hen. III.] Dark green: imperfect and indistinct. 1½ in. [Harl. ch. 83 G. 13.]

To the r. In armour: hauberk, surcoat, cap-like helmet
with nasal, sword, long convex shield with ornaments. Horse
galloping.

✠ SIGIL . . . . ME LE LATIMER.

6177. Sulph. cast. [D.C., E. 222.]

Cf. *Rotuli de Oblatis temp. Joh.*, ed. Hardy, p. 462, A.D. 1208.

Gido de Laval, *Junior* [*of Naseby, co. Northt.*]

6178. [A.D. 1200.] Dark. greenish-brown: good, edge
chipped, and imperfect on the r. h. side; app. by a woven
cord of various colours. 2½ in. [Harl. ch. 52 A. 15.]

Ø. To the r. In armour: hauberk of mail, coif, surcoat,
cap-like helmet, sword, long convex shield with star-like
ornament and central spike. Horse galloping.

✠ SIGIL . . . : GIDONIS : IVNI . . . . . . L.

℞. Small counterseal. 1 in. A wolf? passant, contourné.

ANTE SIGILL GI.

6179. Sulph. cast of *obv.* only. [D.C., D. 196.]

6180. Bright red: fine, edge chipped on r. h. side. [Add.
ch. 22,323.]

Ø. ✠ SIGILLVM : GIDONIS : IVNIORIS : DE LAVAL.

℞. As before.

6181. Creamy-white: fine, but edge chipped. [xxxvi. 55.]

Ø. ✠ SIGILL[VM] : GIDONIS : IVNIORIS : DE LAVAL.

℞. As before.

6182. Plaster cast of *obv.* only, from fine but chipped impression. [lxxviii. 84.]

✠ SIGILLVM : GIDONIS : IVNIORIS : DE LAVAL.

Henricus, *fil.* **Li - - - de La Wik.**

6183. [12th cent.] Plaster cast from chipped impression.
1¾ in. [lxxix. 38.]

To the r. In armour: hauberk of mail, coif, conical helmet, sword, long convex shield with star-like pattern. Horse galloping.

✠ SIGILLVM HEИRICI FILL' LI .... DE LA WIK.

Matheus de Leiham, [*of Boxford, co. Suff.*]
6184. [13th cent.] Discoloured white: good. 1⅞ in. [Harl. ch. 53 A. 25.]
To the r. In armour: hauberk, surcoat, cap-like helmet, sword, shield with fretty ornament. Horse galloping.

✠ SIGILLVM ⦂ MATHEI ⦂ DE ⦂ LEIHAM.

The letters DE in *de* conjoined.
6185. Sulph. cast. [D.C., E. 231.]

Hugo de Lile, *or* **Hugo de Insula,** [*of Barby, co. Northt.*]
6186. [Early 13th cent.] Light brown: edge chipped. 1⅝ in. [Add. ch. 21,531.]
To the r. In armour: hauberk, surcoat, conical helmet and nasal, sword, shield charged with an ornament resembling an escarbuncle. Horse galloping.

✠ SIGILL' HVGONIS DE LILE.

The DE of *de* conjoined.
6187. Plaster cast. [lxxix. 93.]

Hugo de Linco - - - -
6188. [Late 13th cent.] Plaster cast from chipped impression. 1⅝ in. [lxxix. 92.]
To the r. In armour: sword, long convex shield. Horse springing.

.... L · HVGONIS DE LINCO ....

Robertus de Lindholt, [*of Boxford, co. Suff.*]
6189. [*Temp.* Hen. III.] Green, mottled: edge imperfect. About 2 in. when perfect. [Harl. ch. 53 A. 31.]
To the r. In armour: hauberk, surcoat, cap-like helmet, sword, convex shield with central spike. Horse galloping.

✠ SIG ...... BERTI DE LINDHOLT.

6190. White wax: indistinct, the face flaked in places. [Harl. ch. 53 A. 32.]

✠ SIG .... RT ...... NDHO ....

Willelmus de Longespeie, [*Earl of Salisbury.*
Ob. A.D. 1226.]
6191. [A.D. 1219.] Plaster casts from very imperfect impression. About 3 in. when perfect. [lxxix. 95, 96.]
Ø. To the l. In armour: hauberk of mail, flat helmet with

vizor closed, sword, scabbard, shield of arms. Horse caparisoned. Arms: six lioncels rampant, three, two, and one, LONGESPEE ; on the caparisons, a lion rampant.

SIGILL' WLL' .... BERI.

℞. Small round counterseal. 1¼ in. A sword erect, hilt upwards, garnished with a belt.

SI .... LI LONGESPEIE.

Bowles, *Annals of Lacock Abbey*, p. 147.

Matheus de Lumlehe.

6192. [13th cent.] Plaster cast from fine impression. 1⅝ in. [lxxx. 1.]

To the l. with head turned to the r. In loosely-fitting surcoat, on his l. h. a falcon.

✠ SIGILL' MATHEI DE LVMLEHE.

Robertus Luvel, [*son of* ADAM LUVEL.]

6193. [Early 13th cent.] Cast in brownish-red composition. 1¾ in. [xlix. 13.]

To the r. In armour: hauberk of mail, cap-like helmet, sword, shield with ornamental border and central spike. Horse galloping.

✠ SIGILL' ... OBERTI · LWEL.

Cf. *Rot. de Oblatis*, p. 462, A.D. 1208.

Ricardus Malebise, [*of co. York.*]

6194. [Early 13th cent.] Plaster cast from fine impression. 2⅜ in. [lxxx. 2.]

To the r. In armour: hauberk of mail, surcoat, coif, cap-like helmet with ties behind and nasal, sword, triangular shield with radiating lines. Horse with a breast-band ornamented with pendants. In the field, below the horse, an increscent.

✠ SIGILL' RICARDI MALEBISE.

Cf. *Rot. de Oblatis*, pp. 41, 55, etc., A.D. 1199–1208.

Johannes Maleð, [*of co. Northt.?*]

6195. [12th or early 13th cent.] Green, mottled : a fragment. [Add. ch. 22,012.]

To the r.

Legend wanting.

Robertus Malet, [*of Walpole, co. Suff.*]

6196. [13th cent.] Greenish-white, varnished yellow: chipped. 2 in. [Harl. ch. 83 G. 33.]

To the r. In armour: hauberk, helmet, sword, convex shield. Horse galloping.

✠ SIGILLVM ROB .... LET.

6197. Sulph. cast. [D.C., D. 194.]

Petrus de Malo Lacu, *Tercius.*

6198. [Late 13th and early 14th cent.]   Plaster casts from
fine impressions.   2⅜ in.   [lxxx. 3, 4.]

Ø. To the r.   In armour : hauberk of mail, surcoat, helmet
with vizor closed and fan plume, shield of arms, sword.
Horse caparisoned.   Arms : diapré, a bend, MAULEY.

S' PETRI : DE MALO : LACV . TERCII.

R. A shield of arms as in *obv.*, betw. three lions rampant
guardant.

✠ SEEL PRIVE : SVY : APELE.

Beaded borders.

Gaufridus de Mandeville, [2*nd*] *Earl of Essex,*
[*ob.* A.D. 1167.]

6199. [*circ.* A.D. 1156–1163.] Light red : originally fine,
now chipped at edges and lower part imperfect.   About
3⅛ in. when perfect.   [Slo. ch. xxxii. 64.]

To the r.   In armour : hauberk and continuous coif of
mail, surcoat, conical helmet and nasal, sword, long convex
shield with star-like ornament in a bordure.   In base, below
the horse, an animal of uncertain form, perhaps a lion.

. . IGIL . . GAVFRIDI . . . . IT . . . . .

Willelmus de Mandeville, [3*rd*] *Earl of Essex.*

6200. [A.D. 1167–1190.] Pale yellow : fine, very imperfect.
About 3 in. when perfect.   [Cott. ch. x. 1.]

To the r.   In armour : hauberk, surcoat with long folds,
conical helmet and nasal, sword, long convex shield with
central spike.   Horse galloping with ornamental breast-band.

✠ SIG . . . VM . . . . . . LMI COM . . . . . DE ESSEX.

6201. [A.D. 1167–1190.] Pale creamy-yellow : fine originally, the lower part now wanting.   [Harl. ch. 53 C. 50.]

✠ SIGILLVM · W . . . . TIS : DE ESSEX . .

6202. Sulph. cast.   [D.C., D. 150.]

Rogerus, *fil.* Lett. [DE MARA.]

6203. [Late 12th or early 13th cent.]   Plaster cast from
imperfect impression.   1½ in.   [lxxx. 12.]

To the r.   In armour : hauberk, sword, convex shield with
central spike.   Horse galloping.

✠ SIGILL' ROGERI . . . . I.

Perhaps identical with Roger de Mara, of co. Salop, in *Rotuli de
Oblatis temp. Joh.,* ed. Hardy, p. 544, A.D. 1214.   Doubleday attributes
this seal to *circ.* A.D. 1221–1228.

Walterus Marescallus, [7*th*] *Earl of Pembroke.*

6204. [A.D. 1241–1245.] Green : fine, but imperfect ; app.
by cords of thread, red and yellow, closely woven.   The
upper part wanting.   1 in.   [Harl. ch. 83 B. 38.]

To the r. In armour : hauberk, surcoat, flat-topped helmet with vizor down, sword, shield with indistinct device or ornament, slung round the neck by a strap.

.... LTERI MARESCALLI COM·······

6205. Sulph. cast. [D.C., D. 57.]

Robertus Marmium, [*Lord of Tamworth.*]

6206. [Before A.D. 1217.] Sulph. cast in tinted pale green, from original impression, imperfect at sides and indistinct. 3 in. [lii. 35.]

To the r. In armour : hauberk, long surcoat, helmet, sword, shield. Horse galloping.

...... OBERTI MARMIVM.

Robertus Marmium.

6207. [A.D. 1226.] Green : fine, very imperfect, the r. h. side wanting. About $1\frac{7}{8}$ in. when perfect. [xxxix. 68.]

∅. To the r. In armour : hauberk, flat-topped helmet, sword, shield. Horse galloping.

※ .... I MARMIVM.

℞. An oval counterseal. About $1\frac{3}{8} \times 1\frac{1}{8}$ in. Impression of an antique oval intaglio gem. FORTUNE, seated, holding a helmeted NIKE, at her feet a shield. The gem appears to have been cracked across.

※ S' ROBERTI .. MAR .... M.

Willelmus Maskerel, [*of Brook, Isle of Wight.*]

6208. [12th–13th cent.] · Light reddish-yellow : fine, but very imperfect ; app. by two closely-woven bobbins of diapered stuff. About 2 in. when perfect. [Add. ch. 15,686.]

To the l. In a tunic fastened over the l. shoulder, a hawk on the l. hand. Horse galloping.

Legend wanting.

Thomas de Mendham, [*of Livermere, co. Suff.*]

6209. [Late 12th or early 13th cent.] Dark green : originally fine, now very imperfect. About 2 in. when perfect. [Add. ch. 7209.]

To the r. In armour : hauberk of mail, sword, convex shield with central spike. Horse galloping.

Legend wanting.

Henricus de Mere, [*of Raydon, co. Suff.*]

6210. [*Temp.* Joh.] Green, mottled : fine. $1\frac{7}{8}$ in. [Cott. ch. xii. 14.]

To the r. In armour: hauberk of mail, surcoat, cap-like
helmet, sword, shield. Horse galloping.

    ✠ SIGILL' HENRICI DE MERC :·

6211. Sulph. cast. [D.C., D. 135.]

Engellramus de Mercellis, [*of Killingholme, co. Linc.*]

6212. [Late 12th or early 13th cent.] Creamy-white: fine
fragment. About 2¼ in. when perfect. [Cott. ch. xxvii. 99.]

To the r. In armour: hauberk, surcoat, sword, [shield?]
Legend wanting.

Symon, *fil.* Henrici de Messingham,
[*of Scotter, co. Linc.*]

6213. [Early Hen. III.] Light brown, semi-opaque: imperfect on r. h. side. About 2 in. when perfect. [Add. ch.
19,820.]

To the r. In armour: hauberk, cap-like helmet and nasal,
sword, shield.

    . . SI . . . . M[G]HAM.

Henricus Miles, *Dominus de Rokeby,* [co. York.]

6214. [Late 13th cent.] Creamy-white: imperfect and indistinct. About 1¾ in. when perfect. [Add. ch. 20,584.]

To the r. In armour: hauberk, flat-capped helmet, sword,
shield of arms. Horse galloping. Arms too indistinct to
be read.

    SIG . . . . . CI DE . . . . .

Nigellus de Molbrai, [*or* **Mubrai,** *3rd Baron Mowbray.*]

6215. [Late 12th cent.] Sulph. cast, tinted pale green,
from fine impression, chipped at edge. About 2¾ in.
[xlix. 12.]

To the r. In armour: hauberk of mail, surcoat, cap-like
helmet with nasal, sword, shield ornamented with bordure and
escarbuncle with central spike. Horse with ornamental breast-
band and diapered saddle.

    ✠ SIGILLVM NIGELLI : DE MOLBRAI.

6216. White: imperfect; app. by a cord bobbin. [Add.
ch. 20,607.]

Legend wanting.

Nigellus de Molbrai, [*or* **Nigel.** *fil.* WILL. DE MUBRAI,
Lord of Axholme, co. Linc.]
(*? 5th Baron.*)

6217. [*circ.* A.D. 1222–1228.] Creamy-white: originally
fine, now imperfect at lower part. [Add. ch. 21,088.]

To the r. In armour: hauberk, helmet, sword, shield with central spike. Horse galloping. Very similar in design to the previous seal, but the proportions vary.

IGI . . . . OLBR . . . . . .

6218. [A.D. 1145.] Plaster east from chipped impression, showing several details in fine preservation. [lxxx. 25.]

SIGILLVM . . . . MOLB . . . . .

Rogerus de Molbrai, [2nd Baron Mowbray, of cos. York and Linc.]

6219. [12th cent.] Bright red: fine, slightly chipped at edges. 3¼ in. [Harl. ch. 83 C. 38.]

To the r. In armour: hauberk of mail, surcoat with ornamentation of a fleury, vairy, or cruzily pattern intended for leather work, cap-like helmet with nasal, plain goad spur, scabbard, sword, long maunch on the r. wrist, shield of convex form with large central boss, ornamented like the surcoat. Horse galloping with ornamental breast-band. The shield and helmet charged, as the surcoat.

✠ SIGILLVM ROGERI DE MOLBRAI.

6220. Sulph. east. [D.C., D. 91.]

6221. Sulph. cast, tinted red from very fine impression, showing the peculiar ornamentation of the helmet, shield, and surcoat, the r. h. side wanting. [xlix. 11.]

. . . . MOLBRAI.

6222. Creamy-white: very imperfect. [Add. ch. 20,847.] Legend wanting.

6223. [12th cent.] Brown, varnished: indistinct and edge chipped away. [Egert. ch. 585.]

6224. [A.D. 1145.] Plaster cast from fine but imperfect impression. [lxxx. 23.]

SIGILLV . . . . ERI DE MOLBRAI.

Robert Monahus, al. MONACHUS, of Kisebi [Keisby, co. Linc.]

6225. [circ. A.D. 1170.] Light brown, semi-opaque: fine. 2 in. [Add. 20,901.]

To the r. In armour: hauberk of mail, coif, conical helmet and nasal, sword, shield with central spike.

✠ SIGILLVM ROBERTI MONAHI DE KISEBI.

6226. Light brown: imperfect at top, and edge injured. [Add. ch. 20,903.]

6227. Pale yellowish-brown, semi-opaque: fine. [Add. ch. 20,905.]

Baderon de Monemuda, [3rd Baron Monmouth.]

6228. [Temp. Hen. II.] Plaster east from indistinct and imperfect impression. 2 in. [lxxx. 11.]

To the r. In armour: hauberk, sword, kite-shaped shield showing the interior side.

.. SIG ... BADERONIS DE MONEMVD ....

Gilbertus de Monemue, [4*th Baron Monmouth.*]
6229. [Late 12th cent.] Creamy-yellow: very indistinct. About 2¼ in. when perfect. [Cott. ch. xxvii. 124.]
To the r. In armour: hauberk, surcoat, flat-capped helmet, sword, long convex shield with central spike. Horse galloping.

SIGILLVM ... ILB ...... MVE.

Gillebertus [*fil.* BADERONIS] **de Monemuta,** [*of Hadnock, co. Glouc.*]
(*Another seal of the same person as above.*)
6230. [Late Hen. II.] Greenish-white: a fragment of the central part. About 2 in. when perfect. [Add. ch. 7012.]
To the r. In armour: hauberk, shield with bordure and star-like ornament.
Legend wanting.

Willelmus de Monteacuto, [4*th*] *Earl of Sarum, Lord of Denbigh and the Isle of Man.* [A.D. 1337-1344.]
6231. [A.D. 1338.] Plaster cast from very fine impression. 2¾ in. [lxxx. 13.]
To the r. In armour: hauberk of mail, surcoat, helmet crested: out of a coronet, a griffin's head betw. two wings, sword chained to the shoulder, scabbard in belt, shield of arms. Horse galloping, caparisoned and plumed. Arms: three fusils or lozenges conjoined in fess, MONTACUTE. The background, diapered with carved quatrefoils, has a cinquefoil rose in each interstitial space.

SIGILLŪ : WILLELMI · DE : MŌTEACUTO : CŌITIS : SARŪ : DŃI : DE · DȲBI : Z : MĀNIE.

Rogerus de Munbegums, *or* **Montebegonis,** [*of co. Northt.*]
6232. [*Temp.* Joh.] Creamy-yellow: fine originally, now imperfect. About 2½ in. when perfect. [Harl. ch. 53 E. 14.]
To the r. In armour: hauberk, surcoat, cap-like helmet, sword, shield of arms. Horse galloping. Arms: apparently, bendy sinister of six, an orle of roundles.

✠ SIGILLVM ..... OGE ...... GVMS.

6233. Sulph. cast. [D.C., D. 140.]

Simon de Monteforti, [*Lord of Montfort in France ?*]
6234. [Late 12th cent.] Plaster cast. 2¼ in. [lxxx. 15.]
To the r. In armour: flat cap, in the r. h. a kite-shaped

shield of arms, a lion rampant, and with the left holding a
hunting horn to his mouth. Horse galloping. In base, two
greyhounds at speed. In the background, at the sides, three
trees.

✠ SIGILLVM : SIMONIƧ · DE · MONTE · FORTI.

The first and third s in the legend reversed.

Symon de Monteforti, [*afterwards* 1*st Earl of Leicester.*]
6235. [Early 13th cent.]· Plaster casts from fine but
chipped impression. 2¾ in. [lxxx. 17, 18.]

Ø. To the l. full face. In a dress girded at the waist,
blowing a horn held to the mouth by the r. hand. Horse
galloping, with diapered saddle and high crupper. Below,
in the foreground, a hound standing with head bent to the
ground. On the r. h. side an ornamental and conventional
tree.

✠ SIGILL' · SIMONIS · DE · MONTE FORTI ✹

Beaded borders.

℞. A smaller round counterseal. 1¼ in. An early shaped
shield of arms : a lion rampant contourné, queue fourchée,
MONTFORT.

Symon de Monteforti, [2*nd Earl of Leicester.*]
6236. [A.D. 1258.] Bronze-green : very fine, the edge
chipped. 2⅞ in. [Add. ch. 11,296.]

Ø To the l. In a dress girded at the waist, blowing a horn
held to the mouth by the r. hand. Horse galloping on a hilly
mount replenished with flowers and herbage. Below, in the
foreground, a hound at speed : on the right a tree of two
branches in the background.

✠ SIGILLVM ✹ SYMONIS ✹ DE ✹ MONTE ✹ FORTI.

℞. A small counterseal. 1¼ in. A shield of arms : a lion
rampant, queue fourchée, MONTFORT.

✠ S' SYMONIS : DE : MONTE : FORTI :

Beaded borders.

6237. [A.D. 1255.] Light-brown, semi-opaque : fine, but
very imperfect. [Add. ch. 11,294.]

Ø. Legend wanting.

℞. As in No. 6236.

6238. [A.D. 1236–1264.] Light brownish-yellow, mottled :
very imperfect. [Harl. ch. 83 G. 45.]

Ø. ✠ S . . . .

℞. Cracked and indistinct, as in No. 6236.

6239. Sulph. casts of *obv.* and *rev.* [D.C., E. 260, 261.]

Counterseal only.

6240. [A.D. 1258.] Bronze-green : fine, edge chipped.
[Add. ch. 11,297.]

Y 2

Radulfus de Monthermer, *Earl of Gloucester and Hertford,*
[A.D. 1297–1307 ; *Earl of Athol ;*
Baron de Monthermer, etc., A.D. .1309–1323.]

6241. [A.D. 1301.] Plaster casts from fine but very imperfect impression. 3 in. [lxxx. 19, 20.]

∅. A shield of arms, as in *rev.,* suspended by a loop from a forked tree, and betw. two wyverns with tails floriated.

　　　　[. . . . CO]M' : G[L]OV'NIE : HERTF[OR]D' . . . .

℞. To the l. In armour : hauberk of mail, surcoat, helmet with vizor down and furnished with a lambrequin (the crest, an eagle displayed, see Doyle, *Off. Baron.,* ii. 16, is wanting), sword, shield of arms. Horse galloping, caparisoned and plumed, with the crest of an eagle displayed. Arms : an eagle displayed, MONTHERMER.

　　　　. . . . . RTFORD : KILKENI 𝔷 D̄N̄I GLA . . . .
Beaded borders.

Rogerus de Mortuo Mari, [*of Bisley, co. Glouc.*]

6242. [*circ.* A.D. 1180.] Bright red : chipped at bottom and edge imperfect. 2¾ in. [Sloane ch. xxxiii. 4.]

To the r. In armour : hauberk, surcoat, cap-like helmet and nasal, sword, shield. Horse galloping, with ornamental breast-band and stirrup of peculiar form.

　　　　✠ SIGILLV . . . . ORTVOMARI.

6243. Sulph. cast. [D.C., D. 138.]

Johannes de Moubray, *or* **Moumbray,** [*Lord of the Isle of Haxiholme, co. Linc., and of the Honours of Brembre and Gouher.*]

6244. [A.D. 1334.] Dark-green : fine, imperfect ; app. by closely plaited cords of green stuff. About 4 in. when perfect. [Add. ch. 1252.]

∅. To the r. In armour : hauberk of mail, surcoat, coneal helmet with vizor closed, sword chained to the arm, shield of arms. Horse galloping, caparisoned. Arms : a lion rampant, MOUBRAY. Background faintly hatched.

Legend on a band or bordure, in form of a quatrefoil, with carved cusps.

　　　　[✠ S]IGILLVM [IOH]ANNI[S DE M]OV[BR]AY. ✱

℞. A shield of arms as in *obv.* Above the shield a feathered serpent or cockatrice volant, wings extended ; below it a wyvern reguardant, tail nowy ; on the *dexter* the head and arms of a man-at-arms holding a lance-flag charged with three chevronels, for CLARE ; on the *sin.* another, similar, with semé of crosses crosslet a lion rampant, BRAOSE.

Background diapered lozengy, with a small flower in each space. Legend as in *obv.*

... LV ... OHANN .... ✻ MOVBRA ...

Collectanea Topographica, vol. iv., p. 32. ·

Thomas de Moulton.

6245. [Late 13th cent.] Plaster cast from fine impression. 1¼ in. [lxxx. 10.]

To the r. In armour: hauberk of mail, surcoat, helmet with vizor down and fan plume, sword, shield of arms. Horse galloping, caparisoned and plumed. Arms: three bars, MOULTON.

SIGILLVM THOME ✩ DE ✩ MOVLTOŇ.

Beaded borders.

Thos. de Molton of Gillesland, co. Cumberl., *ob.* 21 Edw. I. See *Inquis. p. mort.*, vol. i., p. 114, col. 1.

Willelmus de Mubrai, [*of Thirsk, co. York.*]

6246. [*Temp.* Joh.] Pale greenish-white: imperfect and indistinct. 2⅜ in. [Harl. ch. 83 G. 53.]

To the r. In armour: hauberk, surcoat, flat-cap or helmet, sword, shield. Horse galloping.

.... MI DE M ... R . I.

6247. Sulph. cast. [D.C., E. 209.]

Radulfus de Mumpinsun.

6248. [Early 13th cent.] Plaster cast from fine but chipped impression. 2 in. [lxxx. 24.]

To the r. In armour: hauberk of mail, surcoat, cap-shaped helmet, sword, convex shield with central boss and radiating lines. Horse galloping.

⊞ SIGILL' RADVLFI DE MVMPINSVN.

Walerannus de Munceaus, [*or* Waleran, *fil.* IDONEÆ DE HERSTE, *of Broomhill, co. Kent.*]

6249. [Early Hen. III.] Light-brown, mottled: good. 1¾ in. [L. F. C., xxv. 10.]

To the r. In armour: hauberk of mail, conical helmet and nasal, sword, shield with ornamental bordure and central spike. Horse galloping.

⊞ SIGILL' · WALERANNI DE MVNCEAVS.

For Waleran de Munceaus, of co. Southampton, see *Rotuli de Oblatis temp. Joh.*, ed. Hardy, pp. 310, 448, A.D. 1205, 1207.

Ingelram de Munceus, [*of Cuxwold, co. Linc.*]

6250. [Late 12th cent.] Pale greenish-white: very imperfect. About 1¾ in. when perfect. [Add. ch. 20,503.]

To the r. In armour: helmet, shield. Horse galloping.

SIGILL' ING ....

Robertus de Mundevile, *or* **Amundevilla,** [*of co. Lincoln.*]
   6251. [*Temp.* Joh. or Hen. III.]   Dark-green : fine, well
preserved. . 1¾ in. [Harl. ch. .45 C. 31.]. .
   To the r.   In armour : hauberk, surcoat. .conical helmet
with nasal, sword, long narrow convex shield with central
boss.   Horse prancing.
         ✠ SIGIGILL' (*sic*) ROBERTI .DE MVИDEVILE.
   6252. Sulph. cast.   [D.C., D. 133.]
   Cf. *Rotuli de Oblatis temp. Joh.*, ed. T. D. Hardy, p. 580, A.D. 1216.

   Radulfus Murdac, [*of Black-Bourton, co. Oxon.*]
   6253. [Late 12th cent.]   Light-brown, varnished : chipped
at edge.   2 in.   [Add. ch. 20,292.]
   To the r.   In armour? : long surcoat, a hawk on the r. hand.
         ✠ SIGILLVM : RADVL . . . . . . DAC.
   6254. Plaster east.   [lxxx. 26.]
   Occurs in A.D. 1200, see *Rotuli de Oblatis temp. Joh.*, ed. Hardy,
p. 48.

   Hugo de Muscam, [*of Muskham, co. Notts.*]
   6255. [A.D. 1147–1153.]   Reddish-brown : fine ; app. by
cords of closely woven red and ẏellow threads.   1¾ in. [Harl.
ch. 83 G. 55.]
   To the r.   In armour : hauberk of mail, conical helmet with
nasal, sword, long convex shield with central spike.   Horse
galloping.
         ✠ SIGILLVM HVGONIS DE MVSCAM.
   6256. Sulph. cast.   [D.C., D. 74.]

   Lisiardus de Musters, [*of cos. Nottingham and York.*]
   6257. [*circ.* A.D. 1200–1207.]   Plaster cast from good impression with chipped edge.   2⅛ in.   [lxxx. 30.]
   To the r.   In armour : hauberk, surcoat, conical helmet,
sword, convex shield with border and central spike.   Horse
galloping.
         ✠ SIGILLVM LISIARDI DE MVSTERS.

   Nemore, (**Ernaldus de**) *v.* Bosco (Ernaldus de).

   Ricardus Nevil, *Earl of Warwick.*   [A.D. 1449–1471.]
   6258. Recent impression in gilded gutta percha, from
matrix in Dept. of Antiquities.   3¼ in.   [xxxiv. 33.]
   To the r.   In plate armour : breastplate, helmet with vizor
down, crest out of a ducal coronet a swan's neck, sword, shield
of arms : a saltire and label of the three points compony,
NEVILLE. ' Horse galloping, armoured and caparisoned, on a
mount of herbage and flowers.   Caparisons charged with the

armorials: on the neck, quarterly, 1, 4, an eagle displayed, MONTHERMER, 2, 3, three fusils in fess, a label of as many points, MONTACUTE. On the flanks: quarterly, 1, 4 quarterly, i. iv. BEAUCHAMP, ii. iii. GUY OF WARWICK; 2, 3, quarterly, i. iv. CLARE, ii. iii. quarterly in the 2nd and 3rd quarters a fret, over all a bend, DESPENCER. Background replenished with wavy branches of foliage and flowers.

: SIGILLVM : RICARDI : NEVIL : : COMITIS : WARWICI :
DNI : GLAMORGANCIE ET MORGANCIE.

Beaded borders.

Drummond, *Hist. of Noble Families*, p. 10 ; Rowlands, *Hist. Acc. of the Nevilles*, No. 5.

6259. Sulph. cast. [xlvii. 1680.]

Laing's *MS. Catal.*, No. 324.

6260. Sulph. cast. [D.C., G. 85.]

Walterus de Nevilla, [*or* **Nefwilla,** *of Redburn, co. Linc.*]

6261. [Late 12th cent.] Light-brown, mottled: good. 2 in. [Harl. ch. 54 B. 29.]

To the r. In armour: hauberk, cap-like helmet, sword, long convex shield.

⊕ SIGILLVM WALTERI DE NEVILLA.

The letter N reversed.

Rogerus de Novoburgo, [*2nd Earl of Warwick.* A.D. 1123–1153.]

6262. Light uncoloured, semi-opaque: a fragment. About 2¼ in. when perfect. [Add. ch. 21,493.]

To the l. In armour: hauberk of mail, conical helmet, long kite-shaped shield with a kind of lozengy or fretty orna-mentation. Horse with ornamental breast-band.

. . . . WA . . . .

Walerannus de Novoburgo, [*Earl of Warwick.* A.D. 1184–1205.]

6263. [*Temp.* Rich. I.] Green, mottled: very fine, chipped all round and cracked. About 3 in. when perfect. [Cott. ch. xi. 16.]

To the r. In armour: hauberk of mail, surcoat, damasked sword, plain shield of convex form, slung from a strap round the neck. Horse, with ornamental breast-band, and diapered saddle with bordure and fringe.

SIG . . . . WALERANNI · COM . . IS . . . . .

The letters NN conjoined.

6264. Sulph. cast. [D.C., E. 205.]

6265. Pale-green: fine fragment of upper part. [Cott. ch. xi. 39.]

SIGILL . . . .

Thomas [de Newburgh, 6*th*] *Earl of Warwick.*
[A.D. 1229–1242.]

6266. Bright-red: fine originally, sides chipped. 2¼ in. [Add. ch. 20,452.]

To the r. In armour: hauberk of mail, surcoat, flat-topped helmet, sword, shield with strengthening rib. Horse galloping.

☩ SI . . . . OME GOMIT . . . . . WARWIC.

6267. Sulph. cast. [D.C., F. 168.]

6268. Dark-green, speckled: edge very imperfect; app. by plaited cords of green and purple silk. [Harl. ch. 45 I. 31.]

☩ SIGIL . . . . Є COMI . . . . RWIC.

Willelmus, *fil.* Rogeri de Nordintu[n].

6269. [Early 13th cent.] Plaster cast from fine but chipped impression. 2 in. [lxxx. 34.]

To the r. In armour: hauberk, surcoat, conical helmet, sword, convex shield.

☩ S[IGI]LL' WILLEMI FI . . . . GERI DE NORDINTV.

Gaufridus de Novilla, [*of co. Linc.*]

6270. [A.D. 1148–1166.] Creamy-white in a thick brown mass: indistinct. With mark of the handle. 1⅜ in. [Harl. ch. 54 B. 7.]

To the r. In armour: hauberk, conical helmet, sword, shield.

☩ SIGILLVM GAVFRIDI DE NOVILLA.

6271. Sulph. cast. [D.C., D. 101.]

Oilandia (Radulfus, *fil.* Steph. de) *v.* Hoilandia (Radulfus, *fil.* Steph. de).

Henricus [*fil.* ROBERTI] de Oilli, *Constable of King Henry II.*

6272. [*circ.* A.D. 1155–1157.] Creamy-white: originally good, now indistinct and chipped. 2¾ × 2¼ in. [Add. ch. 20,462.]

Oval. To the r. In armour: hauberk and coif of mail, conical helmet with nasal, sword, long convex shield with star-like ornament. Horse galloping, with ornamental breast-band.

SI . . . . O . . . CONSTAB . . . . REGIS · H'.

Willelmus de Orkesdena, [*of co. Surr.*]

6273. [*Temp.* Hen. III.] Brownish-white: indistinct fragment. About 2 in. when perfect. [Harl. ch. 54 D. 40.]

To the r. In armour: shield. Horse galloping.

Legend wanting.

Johannes de Orrebi, [*of Blackwell, co. Derb.*]

6274. [Early 13th cent.] Creamy-white: fine fragment. About 2¼ in. when perfect. [Harl. ch. 54 E. 12.]

To the r. In armour: hauberk and coif of mail, sword, shield of arms. Horse galloping, with ornamental breast-band and saddle. Arms: a fleur-de-lis betw. two chevrons, which have some affinity to the shield borne by the ORBY families.

. . . . ESV . . . .

Willelmus Painel, [*of co. Linc.*]

6275. [*Temp.* Hen. III.] White, varnished: imperfect and indistinct. About 2 in. when perfect. [Harl. ch. 54 E. 54.]

To the r. In armour: hauberk, surcoat, helmet, sword, long convex shield with ornamental bordure and central boss. Horse galloping.

. . . . LI . . . .

Willelmus Pantul, [*of Somerby, etc., co. Leic.*]

6276. [12th cent.] Thick greenish-brown: app. by closely woven cord of greenish threads. 2⅛ in. [Cott. ch. v. 62.]

To the r. In armour: hauberk, surcoat, cap-like helmet, sword, long convex shield.

Legend very indistinct.

. . . . VL . . . . . AN . . . .

6277. Sulph. cast. [D.C., D. 55.]

Ridelus Papallun de Cesebi, [*Keisby, co. Linc.*]

6278. [Late 12th cent.] Brown: originally good, now injured and indistinct in parts. 2 in. [Add. ch. 20,906.]

To the r. In armour: hauberk and coif of mail, conical helmet and nasal, sword, long convex shield with central spike. Horse galloping, with ornamental breast-band.

✠ SIGILLVM : RIDELVS : PAPALLVN DE CESEBI.

v. Kesibi (Ridellus de).

Halennot Papilun, [*or* Halenald Papilio, *of Great Addington, co. Northt.*]

6279. [Early Hen. II.] Greenish-white, varnished: edge chipped. 2 in. [Add. ch. 21,512.]

To the r. In armour: hauberk and coif of mail, cap-like helmet and nasal, sword, long convex shield with ornament of rays and central spike. Horse with ornamental breast-band and fringed saddle.

SIGILLVM HALENⲘOT PAPILVN.

The second L is enclosed in the first.

Paganus de Parles (P).

6280. [Early 13th cent.] Plaster east from an indistinct impression. $1\frac{7}{8}$ in. [lxxx. 35.]

To the r. In armour: hauberk of mail, surcoat, conical helmet and nasal, sword, convex shield with central boss. Horse galloping, with breast-band ornamented with pendants.

✠ SIGILLV PAGANI DE PARLES (?)

Radulfus de Parnelia, [*of co. Linc.*]

6281. [*circ.* A.D. 1200.] Green: edge chipped. About $2\frac{1}{4}$ in. when perfect. [Egert. ch. 507.]

To the r. In armour: hauberk of mail, surcoat, conical helmet and nasal, sword, long convex shield. Horse galloping.

SIGILLVM . . . .

Robertus de Paveli, [*son of* ROBERT DE PAVELI, *of Sulby, co. Northt.*]

6282. [A.D. 1258.] Green: very fine and sharp. $1\frac{1}{8}$ in. [Add. ch. 22,434.]

To the r. In armour: hauberk, surcoat, flat-cap or helmet, with fan plume of feathers, sword, shield of arms. Horse galloping. Arms indistinct, but perhaps: ermine on a fess three crosses moline.

S' ROBERTI · DE PAVELI.

The letters AV conjoined.

Beaded borders.

6283. Dark-green: fine and sharp, pressed in places. [Add. ch. 22,422.]

6284. Dark-green: rubbed in places, but the heraldic bearings of the caparisons clearly shown. [xxxvii. 81.]

Ricardus del Pec, [*of Witham, co. Linc.*]

6285. [12th cent.] Light-brown, varnished: fine, but very imperfect. About $2\frac{1}{2}$ in. when perfect. [L. F. C. xv. 1.]

To the r. In armour: hauberk, surcoat, conical helmet, sword, convex shield. Horse galloping.

Legend wanting.

Galfridus Pecche, [*of Morhale, co. Staff.*]

6286. [A.D. 1161–1183.] Creamy-white: indistinct, and flaked off in parts. [xxviii. 56.]

To the r. In armour: hauberk, surcoat, conical helmet and nasal, sword, convex shield. Horse galloping.

SIG . . . . . . LV . . . . . ALF . . . . Є . . .

Gilbertus [? *fil.* HAMONIS] Peche, *Miles.*

6287. [Late 13th, or 14th cent.] Plaster east from fine impression with imperfect edges. 2 in. [lxxx. 37.]

To the r. In armour: hauberk of mail, surcoat, flat-topped

helmet with vizor down, sword, shield of arms slung by a
broad strap over the shoulder. Horse galloping, caparisoned.
Arms: a fess betw. two chevrons, PECCHE. In the foreground,
below, a wyvern contourné reguardant, with expanded wings.

SIGILLVM : GILEB .... HE .... AMONIS.

Gilbertus Peche.
Secretum.

6288. [Late 13th cent.] Sulph. cast from good impression.
1 in. [D.C., E. 267.]

To the r. In armour: hauberk, flat helmet, sword, shield
of arms. Horse galloping, caparisoned. Arms: a fess betw.
two chevrons, PECCHE.

⊕ SECRETV · GILEBERTI · PECHE.

Willelmus de Percy, [*of Berewell in Petworth, co. Suss.*]

6289. [*circ.* A.D. 1245.] Creamy-white: fair, edge imperfect. About 1¾ in. when perfect. [Harl. ch. 54 G. 13.]

Ø. To the r. In armour: hauberk, surcoat, sword, shield
of arms. Horse galloping. Arms: [five?] fusils in fess,
PERCY.

... IGILLVM WILLELMI DE PER ....

℞. A small oval counterseal. ⅝ × ½ in. Impression of an
antique oval intaglio gem, a stork or pelican, to the r.

⊕ SIGILL' SECRETI.

6290. Sulph. east of *obv.* only. [D.C., E. 219.]

6291. Plaster cast of fine impression of *obv.* only. [lxxx.
39.]

SIGILLVM WILLELMI DE : PERCY :

Beaded borders.

Willelmus de Percy, [*son of* WALTER DE PERCY,] *of Kyldale*, [*co. York.*]

6292. [13th cent.] Green: indistinct in places, with mark
of handle, raised rim. 1¾ in. [Add. ch. 20,565.]

To the r. In armour: hauberk, surcoat, flat helmet, crest
of a plume of feathers, sword, shield of arms. Horse galloping,
caparisoned. Arms: [five] fusils in fess, PERCY. In the
base, some branches of conventional foliage, and the field
replenished with groups of pellets arranged three by three.

⊕ S' WILELMI : DE : PERCY : DE : KYLDALE·

Willelmus de Percy, [*of Lang Ludford Manor, co. Linc.*]

6293. [13th cent.?] White: very imperfect and indistinct;
app. by a green thread cord. About 2 in. when perfect.
[Harl. ch. 54 G. 14.] *

To the r. In armour: sword, shield. Horse galloping.
Legend wanting.

---

* The writing of this charter is of doubtful date.

Henricus de Perci, [*Lord of Topclive,* 1*st Baron Percy.*]
6294. [A.D. 1301.] Plaster casts from fine impressions.
2¾ in. [lxxx. 40, 41.]

∅. To the r. In armour: hauberk of mail, surcoat, conical helmet with vizor down, and having fan plume and lambrequins, sword, shield of arms. Horse galloping, caparisoned and plumed. Arms: a lion rampant, PERCY.

Legend in ornamental capitals :—

SIGILLUM · HEN[R]ICI · DE · PERCI. ⋈ ❀

℞. Within a finely carved gothic rosette of eight points, trefoiled, and with countersunk trefoils in the spandrils, a shield of arms: a lion rampant. The background replenished with branching foliage.

Legend in ornamental capitals.

⋈ SIGILLUM : HE[NR]I[C]I : DE : PERCI.

See *Vetusta Monumenta,* vol. i., pl. xxx., fig. 1.

Algernon [**Percy,**] 10*th Earl of Northumberland, K.G.*
[A.D. 1632–1668.]

6295. Plaster casts from matrix in Department of Antiquities. 2⅞ in. [lxxx. 43, 44.]

∅. To the l. In plate armour: crest or plume of ostrich feathers on a helmet with vizor raised, sword, scabbard, oval shield of arms as in the 1st quarter of the shield of the *rev.* Horse springing, with diapered saddle, on a mount replenished with herbage and flowers. In the background the sea, thereon several war-vessels, and on the r. a mountainous country. On the l. the sun, as a human face in an eight-pointed star, with radiancy appearing through the clouds. On the r. a crescent, the badge of PERCY, encircled with an inscribed garter, and surrounded by an earl's coronet of five pearls.

No legend.

℞. An ornamentally carved shield of arms of sixteen quarterings. 1. quarterly i. iv. a lion rampant, ANCIENT DUKES OF BRABANT AND LOUVAIN, ii, iii, the lucies or pikes, haurient, two and one, LUCY ; 2. Five fusils conjoined in fess, PERCY, etc. The shield within an inscribed garter of the order, ensigned with an earl's coronet, on which is the crest, on a jewelled helmet, with very extensive mantling or lambrequins, on a chapeau turned up ermine a lion statant the tail extended. Supporters, *dex.,* a lion rampant ; *sin.,* a lion rampant guardant, ducally crowned, collared gobony. In base on a riband, with split ends intertwined, the motto :—

❀ ESPERANCE ❀ ❀ EN ❀ DIEV ❀

Legend on a riband :—

◡ ⚜ ✿ SIGILLVM ✿ ⚜ ALGERNONI ⚜ COMITIS ⚜ ⚜ NORTHVMB ⚜
RIÆ ⚜ ✿ DECIMI ⚜ ✿ ⚜ ✿

Carved borders. The workmanship of this seal is remarkably fine.

Thomas de Peritone.

6296. [13th cent.] Plaster cast from a good impression. 1⅜ in. [lxxx. 38.]

To the r. In armour : hauberk of mail, surcoat, cap-like helmet, sword, shield. Horse galloping.

✠ SIGILL' THOME DE PERITONE.

Normannus, [*fil.* RAD.] de Pesehale, [*of Peasenhall, co. Suff.*]

6297. [Late 12th or early 13th cent.] Pale-green, covered with a dark-brown varnish : edge chipped. [Harl. ch. 84 A. 10.]

To the r. In armour : hauberk, surcoat, helmet with nasal, sword, convex shield. Horse galloping.

✠ SIGILLUM NORMAN DE . . . SHALLE.

6298. Sulph. cast. [D.C., D. 143.]

Cf. Norman de Peschale, of co. Suff. in the *Rotuli de Oblatis temp. Joh.*, ed. Hardy, p. 300, A.D. 1205.

Willelmus Peuerel, *of Dover,* [*co. Kent.*]

6299. [*Temp.* Hen. II., *ante* A.D. 1166.] Green : very indistinct and imperfect ; app. by a closely woven cord of green silk. About 1⅞ in. when perfect. [Harl. ch. 54 G. 56.]

To the r. In armour. Horse galloping.

Legend wanting.

Elias de Pidele.

6300. [12th cent.] Plaster east from fine but chipped impression. 2¼ in. [lxxviii. 91.]

To the r. In armour : hauberk of mail, conical helmet and nasal, long lance with large triangular head and flag with three streamers, convex kite-shaped shield with central spike and numerous radiating lines. Horse galloping.

✠ SIGILL' ELIE DE PIDELE.

Galfridus Pigot, [*of Gamlingay, co. Cambr.*]

6301. [End of 12th cent.] Greenish-brown, mottled : fair, indistinct in places. 1¾ in. [Harl. ch. 83 B. 41.]

To the r. In armour : hauberk, round-topped helmet, sword. Horse galloping.

✠ SIGILLVM GALFRIDI PIGOT.

6302. Sulph. east. [D.C., D. 144.]

Willelmus Pincerna de Hocherton, [*or* **William Le Butilèr,**
of Hokerton, co. Nott.]

6303. [13th cent.]   Dark - green : fine.   1⅜ in.   [Harl.
ch. 83 D. 38.]

To the l.   In armour : hauberk of mail, surcoat, flat-topped·
helmet, sword, shield.   Horse springing.

✠ SIGILL' · WILL'I · PINCERNE · DE · HOCH'TON.

Beaded borders.

Cf. Will. Pincerna de Hocreton, early 13th cent. Harl. chs. 83 F. 25 ;
112 I. 13.

6304. Sulph. cast.   [D.C., E. 221.]

Hasculfus de Pincheni, [*of Englefield, co. Berks.*]

6305. [*Temp.* Joh.]   Pale greenish-white : fair.   1¼ in.
[Add. ch. 7201.]

To the r.   A hawk on the r. hand.   Horse standing.

✠ SIGILL' HASCVLFI DE PINCHENI.

Cf. Add. ch. 21,890, *circ.* A.D. 1200.

Henricus de Pincheni, [*Lord of Wedon, etc., co. Northt.*]

6306. [*circ.* A.D. 1200.]   Pale-green : very imperfect and
defaced ; app. by a plaited cord or riband of silk strands,
green and white.   About 1¾ in. when perfect.   [Add.
ch. 21,890.]

To the r.   In armour : hauberk, surcoat, sword.   Horse
galloping.

Legend wanting.

Edmundus [**Plantagenet,** *son of* RICHARD PLANTAGENET,
king of the Romans, Earl of Cornwall.]

6307. [A.D. 1275.]   Bronze-green : very fine, only centre
remaining.   About 3 in. when perfect.   [Harl. ch. 84 C. 9.]

∅.   To the r.   In armour ; hauberk of mail, surcoat, sword,
shield of arms slung by the strap over the shoulder.   Horse
galloping.   Arms as on *rev.*

Legend wanting.

℞.   A shield of arms : a lion rampant crowned, within a
bordure, charged with fourteen roundles.   Fine Italian workmanship.

Legend wanting.

Sandford, *Geneal. Hist.,* p. 94 ; Todd, *History of Ashridge College.*

6308. [A.D. 1275.]   Bronze-green : very fine, only centre
remaining.   [Harl. ch. 84 C. 11.]

∅.   As before.

℞.   Part of the eagle on which the shield of arms is slung
by the strap may be seen in this example.

6309. Sulph. casts of *obv.* and *rev.*   [D.C., E. 269, 270.]

Edwardus [Plantagenet,] *son of King Henry III.,*
[and afterwards King Edward I.]

6310. [A.D. 1259.] Green: originally fine, now only the
centre remaining ; app. by plaited cords of faded red thread.
About 3⅛ in. when perfect. [Add. ch. 20,442.]

∅. To the r. In armour : hauberk of chain mail, surcoat,
[cap-shaped helmet,] sword, shield of arms. Horse galloping,
with ornamental breast-band, crossed girths, and saddle
diapered and bordered. Arms as in *rev.*
Legend wanting.

℞. A shield of arms : ENGLAND, with a label of five points.
Fine workmanship.
Legend wanting.

6311. [A.D. 1262.] Creamy - white : fine, but imperfect,
only centre remaining. [Harl. ch. 43 C. 42.]

∅. . . . . RE . . . . . .

℞. . . . . [F]ILII HE . . . .

6312. [A.D. 1266.] Creamy - white : fine, imperfect, only
centre remaining. [Harl. ch. 43 C. 49.]

6313. [A.D. 1269.] Dark bronze-green : imperfect, only
centre remaining. [Egert. ch. 255.]

6314. [A.D. 1272.] Creamy - white : fine, but imperfect.
[Harl. ch. 43 C. 48.]

∅. The head of the prince, with flat-topped helmet and
vizor closed, remaining.

6315. Plaster casts from fine impression. [lxxx. 59, 60.]

∅. ♣ EADWARDVS ⦂ PRIMOGENITVS ⦂ ET ⦂ HERES ⦂ DOMINI ⦂
REGIS ⦂ ANGLIE.

The letters AR of *Edwardus* conjoined.

℞. ✠ SIGILLVM ⦂ EADWARDI ⦂ FILII ⦂ HENRICI ⦂ ILLVSTRIS ⦂
REGIS ⦂ ANGLIE.

The engraving in Sandford, *Geneal. Hist.,* p. 120, gives the legends :—

∅. ♣ EDWARDVS . . . . . NES . . . . REGIS ANGLIE.

℞. SIGILLVM · EDWARDI · FILII · HENRICI . . . .
REGIS · ANGLIE.

The letters AN in *Anglie* conjoined.

Edwardus [Plantagenet,] *Duke of Aquitaine, Earl of Chester,*
Ponthieu, etc., [afterwards King Edward III.]

6316. [A.D. 1325.] Plaster casts from fine impression ; the
legend injured in places. 3¼ in. [lxxx. 69.]

∅. To the l. In armour : hauberk of mail, surcoat of
arms, helmet with closed vizor, rectangular shoulder-piece,
chained sword, shield of arms. Horse caparisoned. Arms :
ENGLAND, with a label of three points. All within an inner

border of small cusps, fleury, with carving countersunk in the spandrils.

✠ EDWARDVS PRIMOGENIT' REGIS ANGLIE · DVX · AQVITANIE ·
      COMES · CESTRIE · PONTIVI · ʒ · MŌTISSROLII.

The letters AN in *Aquitanie* conjoined.

℞. A shield of arms : ENGLAND, with a label or file of five points. The inner border as in *obv*.

S' EDWARDI · P'MOGENITI · REGIS · ANGLIE · DVCIS ·
      AQVITANNIE : COMITIS : CESTRIE · PONTIVI · ʒ ·
      MONTISSOROLLII.

Cf. Douët d'Arcq, *Collection de Sceaux*, No. 10,092.

Geoffrey Plantagenet, *Count of Anjou, father of Henry II.,*
ob. A.D. 1150.

6317. Plaster casts from imperfect impression. About 3⅛ in. when perfect. [lxxx. 46, 47.]

∅. To the r. In armour : hauberk, conical helmet, kite-shaped shield held by an enarme, and showing the interior side, sword.

Legend wanting.

℞. Same style, in the r. h. a long lance-flag with three streamers in place of sword.

Legend wanting.

Gaufridus [Plantagenet,] *son of King Henry* [*II.*]
[*Duke of Brittany and*] *Earl of Richmond.*
[A.D. 1168–1186.]

6318. Dark-green, mottled : imperfect and indistinct ; app. by strands of green silk. 3¼ in. [Harl. ch. 43 C. 35.]

∅. To the r. In armour : long convex shield, lance with flag and streamers. Horse galloping.

✠ GAVFRIDVS · HENRICI · REGIS · FILIVS . . . . NIE.

To the r. In armour : hauberk of mail, surcoat, helmet with nasal, sword, shield showing interior side. Horse galloping.

GA . . . . ICI · REGIS · FILIVS · COMES · RICHEMVNDE.

Hamelinus [Plantagenet, *natural son of* GEOFFREY, *Count of Anjou,*] *Earl of Warenne.*

6319. [A.D. 1163–1202.] Dark-green : fine, but very imperfect. About 3 in. when perfect. [Harl. ch. 43 C. 14.]

∅. To the r. In armour : hauberk, surcoat, sword, long convex shield with ornamental star and central spike. Horse galloping, with ornamental breast-band and saddle diapered and bordered.

. . . . GIL . . . . NI · C . . . .

℞. Small oval counterseal. 1 × ⅞ in. Impression of an antique oval intaglio gem. An Imperial bust in profile to the r., filleted.

. . . . . E : LEGE : A TEGE : ⁓

Henricus, *Dux Normannorum, etc.,* A.D. 1147–1154.
(*Afterwards King Henry II.*)

6320. Greenish-brown : fine fragment, showing only the centre. About 3¼ in. when perfect. [Harl. ch. 84 C. 3.]

∅. To the r. In armour: hauberk of mail, spear. Horse with ornamental saddle.

℞. To the r. In armour : hauberk of mail, kite-shaped shield showing the interior side. Horse with ornamental breast-band and saddle; the ring-like stirrup hangs from a chain. Legend wanting.

6321. Green, with dark varnish. [xxxv. 19 N.]

A small detached fragment, showing the body covered with hauberk of mail, the coif, the conical helmet, and the shield, of the *ob.* and *rev.* Fine workmanship.

Cf. Sandford, *Geneal. Hist.,* p. 54.

6322. Plaster casts from fine impression, very imperfect at the edges. [lxxx. 63, 64.]

∅. To the r. In armour: hauberk of mail, conical helmet and nasal, kite-shaped shield held by the strap and showing interior side only, long lance flag with three streamers. Horse with ornamental saddle and breast-band.

⚜ HEN . . . . DEGAVORV.

℞. To the r. In armour: hauberk of mail and continuous coif, conical helmet and nasal, kite-shaped shield held by the strap and showing interior side only, sword. Horse with ornamental breast-band and saddle, ring-like stirrup hanging from a chain.

⚜ HENRICV . . . . ORVM.

Johannes, [*Count of Mortaigne, afterwards King John.*]

6323. [*circ.* A.D. 1188.] Very dark green: fine, edge chipped ; app. by a closely woven cord or bobbin of light coloured threads. 3¼ in. [Harl. ch. 83 A. 27.]

∅. To the r. In armour: hauberk of mail, coif, surcoat, belt, cap-shaped helmet and nasal, sword, convex shield of arms slung round the neck by a strap. Horse galloping, with ornamental breast-band, saddle and stirrup. Arms: two lions passant in pale.

⟋ ⚜ SIGILLV[M : IOH]ANNIS : FILII : REGIS : ANGLIE : D[OMINI :
HIB'NIE.]

℞. A small oval counterseal. $\frac{13}{16}$ × ¾ in. Impression of an antique oval intaglio gem set in a ring. Bust of a female, to the r.
⚜ SECRETVM IOHANNIS.

6324. Sulph. cast of *obv.* only. [D.C., D. 116.]

6325. [*ante* A.D. 1188.] Dark-green, speckled: edge very imperfect. [Harl. ch. 83 A. 26.]

∅. . . . GIL . . . . HANNIS . . . . . . AN . . . . . DO . . . .

℞. As before.

VOL. II.   Z

6326. [*circ. A.D.* 1188.] Greenish-brown, varnished: the face flaked away in parts; app. by a cord of hollow bobbin, of green and white threads. [Harl. ch. 43 C. 32.]

Ø. ✠ SIGI . . . . OMINI HIB'NIE.

R̶. Imperfect.

✠ SEOR . . . . HANNIS.

6327. Sulph. cast of *obv.* only. [D.C., D. 117.]

Sandford, *Geneal. Hist.*, p. 55; cf. p. 81.

Ricardus [**Plantagenet,**] *Earl of Cornwall, Count of Poictou;* [*afterwards king of the Romans, second son of King John,* A.D. 1209–1272.]

6328. Green: fine, chipped; originally app. by plaited cords of silk to a charter. 3⅛ in. [xxxvi. 215.]

To the r. In armour: hauberk of mail, coif, flat-topped helmet with vizor down, sword, shield of arms slung by the strap round the neck. Horse galloping with ornamental breast-band, crossed girths, and embroidered saddle. For arms see the *rev.*

SIGI[LLVM :] RICARDI : COMITIS : PICTAVIE :

R̶. On a background of foliage forming a tree of three branches elegantly designed with fruit in clusters, a shield of arms: a lion rampant crowned, POICTOU, within a bordure bezantée, ANCIENT DUCHY OF CORNWALL.

⌣ SIGILLVM : RICARDI : COMITIS : CORNVBIE.

6329. [A.D. 1226–1257.] Pale bronze green: very fine, imperfect. [Harl. ch. 111 C. 60.]

Ø. SIG . . . . ICT . . . . . .

R̶. SIGILLVM . . . . VBIE.

6329.* Dark green: originally a fine impression, now very imperfect. [Add. ch. 34,104.]

Legend wanting.

Sandford, *Geneal. Hist.*, p. 95.

Another Seal.

6330. [A.D. 1227.] Plaster casts from imperfect impression. 2¾ in. [lxxx. 56, 57.]

Ø. To the r. In armour: hauberk of mail, surcoat of arms, flat-topped helmet, sword, convex shield of arms. Horse galloping, caparisoned. Arms as in *rev.*

SIGILL'M RICARDI FI . . . . . .

R̶. A shield of arms: a lion rampant, crowned, within a bordure charged with nine roundles, RICHARD, *Earl of Cornwall.* The art of this seal is apparently French, and it is of poor workmanship.

✠ . . . . TAVIENSIS.

See Sandford, *Geneal. Hist.*, p. 95; Douët d'Arcq, *Collection de Sceaux*, No. 10,188.

Thomas [Plantagenet, 2*nd*] *Earl of Lancaster,* [A.D. 1295–, 1321,] *Earl of Leicester,* [*Derby, Lincoln, and Ferrers,*] *Steward of England.*

6331. Pale yellowish-brown : fine, cracked and chipped, with marks of the studs used to steady the matrix. 4⅜ in. [Cott. ch. xvi. 7.]

Ø. To the r. In armour : hauberk of mail with continuous coif, surcoat of arms, square shoulder-piece, helmet with vizor closed and surmounted by a lambrequin and the crest, a wyvern with wings ouvert, sword, shield of arms. Horse springing, crested as above, and caparisoned. Arms : ENGLAND, with a label of three points, each charged with as many fleurs-de-lis.

SIGILLVM **:** THOME **:** COMITIS **:** LANCASTRI . . . . . EYCESTRIE **:** SENESCALLI **:** ANGLIE.

℞. Within an elaborately carved gothic rosette of eight cusps, trefoiled, the spandrils enriched with tracery of various styles, trefoil, quatrefoil, cinquefoil, and sixfoil, in circular panels betw. pairs of small countersunk trefoils, and suspended by the strap from a hook, a large shield of arms : *E*NGLAND, with a label of five points, each charged with three fleurs-de-lis.

✠ SIGILLVM **:** THOME **:** COMITIS **:** LANCASTRIE . . . YCESTRIE **:** SENESCALLI **:** ANGLIE ✠

Carved borders.

Sandford, *Geneal. Hist.*, p. 102.

Small Seal.

6332. [A.D. 1301.] Plaster casts from fine but imperfect impression. 2⅞ in. [lxxx. 61, 62.]

Ø. To the l. In armour : hauberk of mail, surcoat, helmet with vizor closed and surmounted by a lambrequin and the crest, a wyvern with queue nowy, sword, shield of arms. Horse galloping, crested as above, and caparisoned. Arms : ENGLAND, with a label of three points.

✠ S' THOME . . . . . IS : LAN . . . . . . IE : LEYCESTRIE : ET : FERRARIIS.

℞. A shield of arms, as in the *obv.*, suspended by the guige or strap from a trifurcated oak-tree, and betw. two wyverns with tails ornamented with three slipped trefoils and a ball at the end.

. . . S' : THOME : COMITIS · LANCAST . . . . TRIE : E . . . . ARIIS.

Beaded borders.

Thomas [Plantagenet, *of Brotherton,*] *son of King Edward I.; Earl of Norfolk, Marshal of England.*

6333. [A.D. 1322.] Red : small and beautifully engraved fragment. About 1 in. when perfect. [Add. ch. 21,506.]

To the r. In armour: hauberk of mail, surcoat, helmet and vizor closed, sword, shield of arms. Horse caparisoned. Arms: ENGLAND, with an indistinct label. Background diapered.

. Legend wanting

Cf. Sandford, *Geneal. Hist.*, p. 205, for the arms.

Thomas [Plantagenet, "*of Woodstock*,"] *Duke of Gloucester, Earl of Essex and Buckingham, Lord High Constable of England,* A.D. 1385–1397.

6334. Plaster cast from fine impression. 3¼ in. [lxxx. 65.]

To the r. In armour: coat of arms, helmet with vizor closed, lambrequin, and crest—on a chapeau turned up ermine, a lion statant guardant collared and crowned, the tail lowered—sword chained to the body, shield of arms. Horse springing, caparisoned. Arms: quarterly, FRANCE (ANCIENT), and ENGLAND, within a bordure, THOMAS OF WOODSTOCK. The field diapered with a lozengy reticulation, the spaces charged irregularly, either with an ostrich feather or a swan.

Sig' thome : filii : regis : anglie : ж ❀ ducis : gloucestrie : comit : essexie : ? : buk' : ac : constabularii : anglie .

Beaded borders.

Cf. Sandford, *Geneal. Hist.*, p. 229.

Alanus de Plukenet, [*of co. Heref.*]

6335. [12th cent.] Plaster cast from fine but now indistinct impression. 2 in. [lxxx. 75.]

To the r. In armour: hauberk of mail, conical helmet, sword, kite-shaped shield showing only the interior side. Horse with double breast-band.

✠ SIGILLVM ALANI DE . . . . Є . . .

See *Inq. p. mort.*, vol. 1, p. 326, 19 Edw. II.

Laurentius de Plumberga, [*of Pudsey, co. Essex.*]

6336. [*Temp.* Hen. III., *ante* A.D. 1253.] Greenish-brown : fine. 1¾ in. [Harl. ch. 54 H. 54.]

To the r. In armour: hauberk of mail, surcoat, cap-like helmet and nasal, spear, shield. Horse galloping.

✠ SIGILL' LAVRENTII DE PLVMBERGA.

Cf. Dom. Laurentius de Plumberge, miles, *temp.* Hen. III., Harl. ch. 48 G. 25 ; A.D. 1269, Harl. ch. 55 B. 15 ; and 55 C. 3.

6337. Sulph. cast. [D.C., E. 239.]

Wilam de Pun[t]fol [*or* Pontfol, *of Ingham, co. Linc.*]

6338. [Late 12th cent.] Brown, mottled : good, chipped on the l. h. side. 1¼ in. [Harl. ch. 54 I. 39.]

To the r. In armour: hauberk of mail, conical helmet, sword, long convex shield with central spike.

✠ SIGILLVM · WILAM DE PVN . FOL.

6339. Sulph. cast. [D.C., D. 84.]

Adam de Port, [I., *of Hatley, co. Bedf.*]
6340. [*circ.* A.D. 1140.] Discoloured white : imperfect and indistinct. About 2 in. when perfect. [Harl. ch. 54 I. 44.]

To the r. In armour : hauberk, conical helmet, sword. Horse galloping.

Legend wanting.

Adam de Port, [II., *of Hatley, co. Bedf.*]
6341. [*Temp.* Rich. I.] Discoloured white : imperfect and indistinct. About 2 in. when perfect. [Harl. ch. 54 I. 45.]

To the r. In armour : hauberk, surcoat, flat-topped helmet, sword, shield. Horse galloping.

. . . . ORT.

Ernaldus de Powis, [*of La Hida, co. Heref. ?*]
6342. [A.D. 1140–1150.] Green : indistinct and wormed ; app. by a knotted strand of green twilled bobbin. 2¾ in. [Add. ch. 20,454.]

To the r. In armour: sword, kite-shaped shield showing only interior side. Horse galloping.

✠ SI . . . . . . ERNA . . . . . DE . . . . . ı

Gillebertus Prudume, [*of Ockshot, co. Surr.*]
6343. [*Temp.* Joh.] Dark-green, mottled : fine, edge slightly chipped. 2¼ in. [Add. ch. 5528.]

To the r. In armour: hauberk, surcoat, cap-like helmet and nasal, sword, shield ornamented with bordure and central spike. Horse galloping, with breast-band and bordered saddle.

✠ SIGILLVM : GILLEBERTI : PRVDVME.

Cf. Add. chs. 5529, 5537, 5562.

Henricus de Pusiaco, [*of co. York (?).*]
6344. [Late 12th and early 13th cent.] Plaster cast from fine impression, chipped. 1⅞ in. [lxxx. 76.]

To the r. In armour : hauberk of mail, continuous coif, cap-like helmet with tufted top, sword, convex shield slung round the neck by a strap and ornamented with an escarbuncle and bordure. Horse galloping. In the foreground, in base, a small lion or leopard passant contourné.

SIGILLVM HENRICI [DE] PVSIACO.

Cf. *Rotuli de Oblatis temp. Joh.,* pp. 5, 24, A.D. 1199.

Robertus Putrel, *of Cotes, [co. Leic. ?]*

6345. [*Temp.* Joh.]   Dark-red: edge chipped and imperfect.   2 in.   [Harl. ch. 55 A. 35.] ·

To the r.   In armour: hauberk, surcoat, cap-like helmet and nasal, sword, shield.   Horse galloping.

✠ ꙄIGILL ... ƎRT ..... RƎL.

The letters S and Є reversed.

Cf. Harl. ch. 44 A. 31.

Rogerus de Quincy [*or* **Quency**], *Earl of Winchester, and Constable of Scotland*   [A.D. 1219–1264.]

6346. [*circ.* A.D. 1250.]   Green, mottled: very fine, but cracked and imperfect in several places.   3¼ in.   [Harl. ch. 83 B. 42.]

∅.   To the r.   In armour: hauberk of mail, surcoat, flat-topped helmet with vizor down, sword, shield of arms.   Horse galloping, caparisoned.   Arms: seven mascles, three, three, and one, DE QUINCY.   Below the horse a wyvern.   (See description of *rev.*)

..... LL' ROGERI ...... OM .... S : W ...... :

℞.   The *E*arl in armour, as in the *obv.*, with the wyvern on the helmet for a crest, standing, turned to the l., in combat with a lion springing upon his shield.   In base, a six-foiled rose.

SI ...... OGERI DE QVINC .... ARII : SCO .....

Beaded borders.

6347. Sulph. casts of *obv.* and *rev.*   [D.C., E. 258, 259.]

6348. Sulph. casts, tinted red, of *obv.* and *rev.*, from fine impression ; the r. h. side lower part wanting.   [xlvii. 1053, 1054.]

Laing's *Catalogue of Scottish Seals*, Nos. 681, 682 ; pl. xi., f. 2.

6349. [A.D. 1232–1243.]   Dark-green : fragments.   [Harl. ch. 55 B. 6.]

∅. .... COM ....

℞. .... : QVINC ....

6350. [A.D. 1241.]   Pale-green, mottled : very imperfect.   [Cott. ch. viii. 7.]

∅. .... CI : COMITIS ....

℞. ...... NC ....

6351. [A.D. 1259.]   Brownish - green : fine, but very imperfect.   [Harl. ch. 55 B. 7.]

∅. .. SIG ..... O ....

℞. .... O ..... Є.

6352. [A.D. 1219–1264.]   Creamy-white: fine, but imperfect.   [L. F. C. iv. 10.]

∅. ..... LL' ROG ....,. QVINCI : ÇO .....

℞. .... ET : CONST ..... RII : SCOC ....

Spelman's *Aspilogia ;* notes, p. 105.

Saérus de Quinci II., *afterwards Earl of Winchester.*
6353. [Late 12th cent.] Green, discoloured : indistinct,
edge chipped ; app. by a closely woven bobbin of red thread,
faded. 2¼ in. [Harl. ch. 55 B. 4.]
· To the r. In armour : hauberk of mail, surcoat, sword,
long convex shield with ornamentation and central spike.
Horse galloping.
........GILL........SAERI........
6354. Sulph. cast. [D.C., D. 39.]

Seiherus de Quincy, *afterwards Earl of Winchester,*
A.D. 1210–1219.
(? Same as the previous person.)
6355. [Early 13th cent.] Creamy - white, discoloured :
originally fine, only centre remaining. About 2½ in. when
perfect. [L. F. C., xxii. 9.]
Ø. To the l. In armour : hauberk, surcoat, helmet, banner-
flag, convex shield of arms. Horse galloping, caparisoned.
Arms : a fesse in chief a label of eight points, QUINCI.
Legend wanting.
℞. Small counterseal. 1 in. A kite-shaped shield of arms,
as in the *obv.*, betw. two wavy branches of foliage. (The label
of seven points only.)
Spelman, *Aspilogia*, p. 67.
6356. [*circ.* A.D. 1170.] Sulph. casts, from *obv.* and *rev.*,
of imperfect impression, showing further details. [xlvii. 952,
953.]
Ø. In field above the horse on r. h. side, a small kite-shaped
shield of arms : a fess betw. two chevrons, perhaps for his
wife, FITZ-PARNELL. The end of the long banner also shown.
.....GILL.........NO........
℞. A small counterseal. 1⁷⁄₁₆ in. A shield of arms, DE
QUINCY, as before. · (Seven points.)
....CRETVM COMITIS WINTON...
This is a variant counterseal.
Beaded borders.
Laing's *Catal. of Scottish Seals*, No. 679, 680.

Hugo de Rampan, [*or* **Rampen,** *of Kirby-Bellars, co. Leic.*]
6357. [A.D. 1155–1167.] Green : fine, slightly chipped.
1⅞ in. [Add. ch. 20,567.]
· To the r. In armour : hauberk of mail, surcoat, cap-like
helmet, sword, shield. Horse galloping.
✠ SIGILVM HVGONIS DE RAMPAN.
The S's reversed.
6358. Plaster cast. [lxxxi. 32.]

Adam [*fil.* THOMÆ] de Rainvile.

6359. [Late 12th or early 13th cent.] Plaster cast from chipped and indistinct impression. 1¾ in. [lxxxi. 33.]

To the r. In armour: hauberk and coif, surcoat, conical helmet, sword, convex shield with indistinct ornaments or charges.

✠ SIGILL' A . . . . . RAINVIL . . . .

Willelmus de Reines, [*or* Rednes, *of Kirby-Underwood, co. Linc.*]

6360. [*circ.* A.D. 1150–1160.] Brown: fine, with mark of the handle. 1⅞ in. [Add. ch. 20,865.]

To the r. In armour: hauberk and coif of mail with back ties, conical helmet and nasal, sword, long convex shield with star-like ornament and central spike. Horse with ornamented saddle.

SIGILLVM WILLELMI DE REINES.

Radulfus de Reene..s, [*or* de Raines, *of Stathern, co. Leic.*]

6361. [*circ.* A.D. 1150–1160.] Green: fine, edge chipped, with mark of handle. 2 in. [Add. ch. 21,148.]

To the r. In armour: hauberk and coif of mail, long surcoat, conical helmet and nasal, long convex shield with vertical rib.

SIGILLVM RADVLFI DE REENE . . S

The letters S and N reversed.

6362. Plaster cast. [lxxxi. 31.]

Willelmus [*fil.* ROBERTI] de Reydune, [*of Raydon, co. Suff.*]

6363. [*Temp.* Hen. III.] Discoloured - white: l. h. side wanting. About 1¾ in. when perfect. [Harl. ch. 55 C. 15.]

To the r. In armour: hauberk, sword, convex shield with central spike. Horse galloping.

. . . . . . GILL' WILLE . . . .

Ricardus ———.

6364. [12th cent.] Plaster cast from imperfect impression. 2¼ in. [lxxx. 55.]

To the r. In armour: conical helmet, convex shield, lance flag and streamers.

✠ SIGILLVM RICAR[DI] . . . . . .

Ricardus de ———.

6365. [12th or 13th cent.] Sulph. cast from imperfect impression. 1⅞ in. [D.C., D. 72.]

To the l. In armour: a tunic or surcoat of striped pattern, with hawk on the l. hand. Horse springing.

SIGILLVM · RICARDI · DE · . . . . ? l.

Galfridus Ridel, [*son and heir of* RICHARD,
son of RALPH BASSET *and* MATILDIS RIDEL,
dau. of GEOFFREY RIDEL, *of co. Northt.*]
   6366. [*circ.* A.D. 1168.] Light-brown: imperfect and indistinct. About 2¼ in. when perfect. [Harl. ch. 55 D. 8.]
   To the r. In armour: hauberk, sword, [shield ?]. Horse
galloping.
   . . . GI . . . . . . LFRIDI . . . .

Gillebertus, *fil.* **Herberti** [DE RIGGESBI, *of Rigsby,*
co. Linc.]
   6367. [*Temp.* Steph. or Hen. II.] Dark-green: fine, imperfect at lower edge. 2 in. [Harl. ch. 55 D. 11.]
   To the r. In armour: hauberk, conical helmet with back-
ties and nasal, sword, long convex shield with star-like ornament and central spike. Horse with ornamented breast-band.
   ✠ SIGILLVM . . . . FILII HERBERTI.
   6368. Sulph. cast. [D.C., D. 138.]

Herbertus, *fil.* **Gilleberti** [*fil.* HERBERTI DE RIGGHESBIA,
of Rigsby, co. Linc.]
   6369. [*Temp.* Hen. II.] Light-brown, encrusted with a
kind of efflorescence: indistinct, with mark of handle. 1¾ in.
[Harl. ch. 55 D. 12.]
   To the r. In armour: hauberk, surcoat, conical helmet,
shield, sword.
   ✠ SIGILLVM HERBERTI FIL[II . . .] G . . . . BERT.

Walterus de la Riuere, [*or* de Riparia.]
   6370. [*Temp.* Rich. I.] Green: edge chipped and indistinct,
with mark of handle: app. by a hollow twilled bobbin of
bright green silk. 1⅞ in. [Add. ch. 20,236.]
   To the r. In armour: hauberk, helmet, sword, shield.
Horse galloping.
   ✠ SIGILL . . . . . . LTERI DE LA RIVERE.

Michael, *or* **Milo de Riveshal.**
   6371. [12th cent.] Sulph. cast from chipped and imperfect
impression. 2⅛ in. [D.C., D. 200.]
   To the r. In armour: sword, shield. Horse galloping.
   . . . . ILLVM MIL . . . . DE RIVESAL.
   6372. Plaster cast. [lxxxi. 34.]

Willelmus de Romara, [*Lord of Bolingbroke, afterwards*
Earl of Lincoln, A.D. 1142.]
   6373. [Early 12th cent.] Plaster cast from fine but chipped
impression. 2½ in. [lxxxi. 37.]

To the r. In armour: hauberk and coif of mail, represented by small annulets or cup-like depressions, conical helmet with nasal and back-ties, convex helmet with central boss and vertical rib.

　　　　✠ SI .... LVM .. IL ... MI D ... ROMARA.
Beaded borders.

The same, as Earl of Lincoln.

6374. [*post* A.D. 1142.] Plaster cast from fine impression, chipped at edge. 3 in. [lxxxi. 35.]

To the r. In armour: hauberk and coif of mail represented by small annulets or cup-like depressions, long surcoat, conical helmet with nasal and back-ties, sword, kite-shaped shield held by the strap and showing only the interior side. Horse galloping, with breast-band adorned with pendent ornaments.

　　✠ SIGILLVM WILLELMI DE RO .. MARA COMITIS LINCOL.
The S's reversed.

Willelmus de Roumare, [*of co. Lincoln.*]

? Grandson of Wm. de Romare, 1st Earl of Lincoln.

6375. [Late 12th cent.] Sulph. cast, tinted red, from fine but imperfect impression. 2⅜ in. [lii. 2.]

To the r. In armour: hauberk, long surcoat, conical helmet and nasal, sword, long convex shield with star-like ornament and bordure. Horse with breast-band and saddle.

　　　　✠ SIGILL .... LMI DE [R]OVMARE :

6376. Plaster cast from fine impression. [lxxxi. 36.]

　　　✠ SIGILLVM VVILLELMI DE ROVMARE :

Mattheus, *fil.* Alani [DE ROMEL, *of Helmedon, etc.,*
co. Northt.]

6377. [*circ.* A.D. 1220–1230.] Light brownish-yellow, semi-transparent: fine. 1¼ in. [Harl. ch. 84 D. 30.]

To the r. In armour: hauberk, surcoat, helmet, sword, shield with central spike. Horse galloping.

　　　✠ SIGILLVM : MATƷEI : FILI[I] ALANI.

6378. Dark-green, speckled: fine, slightly chipped. [Harl. ch. 86 D. 15.]

6379. Dark-green, speckled: somewhat indistinct, edge chipped. [Harl. ch. 86 D. 16.]

6380. Dark-green, mottled and speckled: edge slightly chipped. [Harl. ch. 86 D. 17.]

6381. Dark-green: fine, chipped at top. [Harl. ch. 86 D. 18.]

6382. Sulph. cast. [D.C., D. 190.]

6383. Green, mottled: chipped and indistinct in places. [Harl. ch. 86 D. 19.]

6384. Green, encrusted : indistinct. [Harl. ch. 86 D. 20.]
6385. Green, discoloured : indistinct. [Harl. ch. 86 D. 22.]
6386. Green, encrusted : imperfect and indistinct. [Harl. ch. 86 D. 23.]
6387. Reddish-brown : fine. [Harl. ch. 86 C. 23.]
6388. Sulph. cast. [D.C., D. 189.]

Johannes de Ros, *Miles,* [*son of Sir* WILLIAM DE ROS, *Knt.,
of Hamelake, co. York.*]
6389. [A.D. 1332.] Red, embedded in a mass of mottled green. 1 in. [Harl. ch. 55 E. 21.]
Ø. To the r. In armour : hauberk, surcoat, crested helmet, sword, shield of arms. Horse galloping, caparisoned and plumed. Arms : chequy, ROS. Crest; a wyvern. In the field, two slipped trefoils. Within a carved and pointed quatrefoil.

⚷ : SIGILLVM : IOHANNIS : DE : ROS :
Beaded borders.
℞. A small counterseal. ⅜ in. Impression of an antique oval intaglio gem. A bust, in profile, to the right.

⚷ IE : SV : LV : NES : SIGIL : SECREZ :
Beaded borders.
6390. [A.D. 1335.] Red, embedded in a mass of mottled green. [Harl. ch. 55 E. 22.]
6391. Sulph. cast of *obv.* only. [D.C., F. 160.]

Willelmus [*fil.* WILLELMI] **de Ros,** [*of Plumstead, etc., co. Kent.*]
6392. [Early Hen. III.] Green, mottled : fine, very imperfect, only centre remaining. About 1⅞ in. when perfect. [Harl. ch. 55 E. 18.]
To the r. In armour : hauberk of mail, surcoat, sword, shield with ornamental bordure. Horse galloping.

. . . . LEL . . . .
6393. Sulph. cast. [D.C., D. 172.]
6394. [*Temp.* Joh.] Dark-green : only centre remaining. [Harl. ch. 112 C. 41.]
Legend wanting.
6395. Sulph. cast. [D.C., D. 171.]

Roggerius de Rosellis, [*of Easington, co. York.*]
6396. [A.D. 1154–1181.] Uncoloured, varnished a dark-brown : originally fine, edge chipped, with raised rim and mark of handle. 2⅛ in. [Add. ch. 20,534.]
To the r. In armour : hauberk of mail, conical helmet and nasal, sword, long convex shield with central bars. Horse with ornamental breast-band and saddle.

SIGILLVM ROGGERII DE ROSELLIS.

Alanus [*fil.* WILLELMI] **de Rowelle,** [*of Rothwell,*
co. Linc.]

6397. [*Temp.* Hen. III.] Dark-green : fine, with mark of
handle. 1¾ in. [Harl. ch. 55 E. 44.]

To the r. In armour : hauberk, surcoat, flat cap with knob
on top, scabbard of sword, shield with central spike, a hawk
on the r. hand.

✠ SIGILLVM · ALANI · DE · ROWELLE.

' The N reversed.

6398. Sulph. cast. [D.C., E. 226.]

Rogerius de Ru[ha]le ?

6399. [13th cent.] Plaster cast from fine but imperfect
impression. 1¾ in. [lxxxi. 41.]

To the l. In long surcoat, girded at the waist, a falcon on
the r. wrist. Horse with embroidered saddle.

✠ SIGILL . . . . OGERII DE RV . . . . LE.

——— **Salivator.**

6400. [13th cent.] Light-brown, mottled : indistinct in
parts, edge chipped. 2¼ in. [xxxix. 60.]

To the r. In armour : hauberk, cap-like helmet, sword,
shield with star-like ornament.

✠ . . . . . . MW . . . . . SALIVATOR . . . . (?)

Johannes de Sancto Johanne, *Dom. de Hannak,*
[*1st Baron St. John, of Lageham,* A.D. 1299–1316.]

6401. [A.D. 1301.] Plaster cast from fine impression, edge
chipped. 3 in. [lxxxi. 43, 44.]

∅. To the l. In armour : hauberk of mail, surcoat, helmet
with vizor closed, lambrequin, and crest—a lion passant
guardant betw. two palm branches—sword, shield of arms.
Horse galloping, caparisoned and crested. Arms : on a chief
two pierced mullets.

✠ S' IOHANNIS · DE · SCO · IOHANNE · DNI [· DE · HAN]NAK.

R. A small round counterseal. ¾ in. A shield of arms
as in *obv.*, suspended by the strap from a tree of three
branches. Betw. two wyverns.

✠ S' IOH'IS · DE · SCO · IOHANNE.

Beaded borders.

Vetusta Monumenta, vol. i., pl. B.

Galfridus, *fil.* **Galfridi de Saintligier.**

6402. [Early 13th cent.] Plaster cast from good impression. 1⅞ in. [lxxxi. 45.]

To the r. In armour : hauberk, surcoat, conical helmet and
nasal, sword, convex shield. Horse galloping.

✠ SIGILL' GALFRIDI FIL' GALF' D' SAINTLIGIER.

The letters AL in *Galf₃* conjoined.

Symon [de St. Liz, *2nd*] *Earl of Northampton.*

6403. [*circ.* A.D. 1147.] Discoloured, the face flaked off, varnished: very imperfect. About 3 in. when perfect. [Cott. ch. x. 14.]

Ø. To the r. In armour: hauberk, surcoat, long maunch attached to the r. wrist, and flowing to the l., conical helmet and nasal, sword, long convex shield with a lozengy ornament. Horse with heavy caparisons reaching to the ground and diapered saddle.

Legend broken away.

℞. A small oval counterseal. 1¼ × 1 in. A lion passant contourné, the tail passing betw. the hind legs and reflexed over the back.

✠ SIGILL' : COMITIS : SIMONIS.

6404. [*circ.* A.D. 1147.] Dark-brown: edge wanting, but originally fine; app. by a damasked bobbin of faded colours. [Cott. ch. vii. 3.]

Ø. SIGILLVM S . . . . HA . . T . . . . .
℞. ✠ SIGILL' : COMITIS : SIMONIS.

6405. Sulph. cast of *obv.* only. [D.C., D. 61.]

Symon [de St. Liz, *3rd*] *Earl of Northampton.*

6406. [*circ.* A.D. 1160.] Dark, uncoloured, varnished with a rich brown colour: edge chipped, imperfect on the r. side. 3⅛ in. [*E*gert. ch. 430.]

To the r. In armour: hauberk, surcoat, long maunch attached to the r. wrist and fully to the ground, conical helmet, sword, long convex shield.

✠ SIGIL . . . . COMITIS NORHAMTVNIЄ.

Alwredus de Sancto Martino, [*of Canterbury, co. Kent.*]

6407. [*circ.* A.D. 1154.] Light-brown or uncoloured: chipped and indistinct in places. 2⅛ in. [L. F. C., xxii. 5.]

To the r. In armour: hauberk of mail, cap-like helmet and nasal, sword, convex shield.

✠ SIGILLVM · ALW . . . . . SCO · MA . . . . . . O.

Cf. Alured de S. Martino, *ante* A.D. 1171, Harl. ch. 86 G. 42; and late 12 cent., L. F. C., xxv. 20; Alured de S. Martino, Dapifer [Regis], Cott. ch. vii. 12.

Tomas de Sancto Walerico, [*son of* BERNARD *and* AANORA, *of Asthallay, co. Oxon.*, *3rd Baron*, *ob.* A.D. 1219.]

6408. [*Temp.* Joh.] Dark mottled-green: fine, edge slightly chipped; app. by flat bobbins of woven thread of various colours. [Harl. ch. 86 D. 48.]

To the r. In armour: hauberk of mail, cap-like helmet, sword, shield of .arms. Horse galloping, with ornamental breast-band. Arms: two lions passant in pale, ST. WALERY.

✠ SIGILLVM : TOME DE SC̄O WALERICO.

R. A shield of arms as in *obv.*

For legend, see counterseal of next seal.

Cf. Harl. ch. 86 D. 49, 51 ; Add. ch. 2.

Another Seal.

6409. [Early 13th cent.] Dark-brown, semi-transparent: fine, edge chipped. 2⅘ in. [xxxiv. 30.]

Ø. To the r. In armour: hauberk of mail, surcoat, flat-topped helmet with vizor down, sword, shield of arms. Horse galloping, with ornamental breast-band. Arms: two lions passant in pale, ST. WALERY.

✠ SIGILLVM : THOME DE SCO WALERICO.

The letters ER in *Walerico* conjoined.

R. A smaller counterseal. 1⅛ in. A heart-shaped shield of arms, as in *obv.*

✠ S' · TH' · DE · S' · WAL' :

6410. Sulph. casts of *obv.* and *rev.* [D.C., E. 202, 203.]

6411. [*Temp.* Joh.] Dark - green : fine, edge chipped. [Harl. ch. 86 D. 50.]

6412. [A.D. 1204–1219.] Mottled-green : fine, edge chipped. [Harl. ch. 86 D. 51.]

Petrus de Sandiacre, [*of Sandiacre, co. Derb.*]

6413. [*circ.* A.D. 1200–1249.] Dark-green : fine, but imperfect, the r. side broken away. About 1⅞ in. when perfect. [Wolley ch. vi. 1.]

To the l. In long surcoat and flowing robe, [a hawk] in the l. hand. Horse, with ornamental breast-plate. In base, an elegantly designed wavy scroll or branch of foliage.

. . . . PETRI · DE · SANDI . . . . . .

6414. Sulph. cast. [D.C., D. 184.]

Alexander de Santona, [*of Sancton, E. R., co. York.*]

6415. [*Temp.* Steph.–Hen. II.] Faded red : imperfect, with mark of handle. 1⅖ in. [Add. ch. 20,507.]

To the l. In armour: hauberk, conical helmet, lance-flag with three long wavy streamers, long convex shield with central spike.

✠ SIGILLVM ·A · . . . . ONA.

Johannes de Sauferd (?)

6416. [13th cent.] Plaster cast from indistinct impression. 1¾ in. [lxxxi. 48.]

To the r. In armour: surcoat, cap-like helmet, sword, convex shield. Horse galloping.

❀ SIG . . . . . DE SAVFERD (?)

Jordan de Saungville, [*of Helmingham, co. Suff.*]

6417. [*circ.* A.D. 1300.] Pale green, faded: edge chipped away; app. by a hollow woven bobbin of faded colours. About 2 in. when perfect. [Add. ch. 9810.]

∅. To the r. In armour: hauberk, sword, convex shield with barry ornamentation. Horse galloping, with fringed saddle.

Legend wanting.

℞. An oval counterseal. $\frac{9}{16}$ × ¾ in. Indistinct impression of an antique oval intaglio gem.

❀ SECRET' SAVNGVILL'.

The letter N reversed.

Willemmus de Sceldesle.

6418. [Late 12th cent.] Plaster cast from chipped impression. 2¼ in. [lxxx. 79.]

To the r. In armour: hauberk and coif, surcoat, conical helmet, sword, large convex shield with central spike. Horse galloping, with fringed saddle and ornamental breast-band.

❀ SIGILLVM WILLEMMI (*sic*) DE SCELDESLE.

Willelmus Scolant (?)

6419. [Late 12th cent.] Plaster cast from indistinct impression. 1¾ in. [lxxviii. 72.]

To the r. In armour: hauberk, conical helmet, sword, kite-shaped shield bordered and spiked.

❀ SIGILLVM WLM - I SCOLANT (?)

Johannes Le Scot, [*6th Earl of Huntingdon.*]

6420. [A.D. 1224.] Sulph. casts of *obv.* and *rev.* of an imperfect impression. About 2¼ in. when perfect. [xlvii. 1020, 1021.]

To the r. In armour: hauberk of mail, surcoat, sword, shield of arms. Horse galloping. Arms: three piles in point, LE SCOT.

Legend wanting.

℞. A small counterseal. 1¾ in. A shield of arms, as in *obv.*

❀ SIGILLVM ⁑ ⁑ ⁑ ⁑ SECRETI ⁑

Laing's *Catal. of Scottish Seals*, Nos. 1233, 1234.

Rogerus Scot, *Miles, de Kalverleia,* [*Calverley, co. York.*]
6421. [*circ.* A.D. 1200.]   Creamy-white ; imperfect and indistinct.   [Add. ch. 16,580.]
To the r.   In armour : sword, shield.   Horse galloping.
          . . . . GER . . . .

Hugo [*fil.* HUGONIS] **de Scotegni,** *or* **Scotigni,**
          [*of Great Limber, co. Linc.*]
6422. [A.D. 1140.]   Brown : fine, with mark of the handle ; app. by a bobbin of closely woven green stuff.   2⅛ in.   [Harl. ch. 56 A. 9.]
To the r.   In armour : hauberk of mail, conical helmet and nasal, sword, long convex shield.   Horse with ornamental breast-band.
          ✠ SIGILLVM HVGONIS DE SCOTEGNI.
6423. Sulph. cast.   [D.C., D. 69.]

Radulfus, *fil.* **Rad. de Seile** (?)
6424. [Late 12th or early 13th cent.]   Discoloured white : indistinct in places, with mark of the handle.   2¼ in. [xxxvi. 56.]
To the r.   In armour : hauberk, surcoat, conical helmet and nasal, sword, convex shield with ornamental bordure.   Horse galloping, with fringed saddle.
          ✠ SIGILLV RADVLFI FILII RADVLFI DE SEILE (?)
The last four letters in the field.

Robertus de Shirley, *Bart.*
6425. [A.D. 1651.]   Plaster casts from the matrices.   1⅓ in. [lxxx. 89, 90.]
Ø. To the r.   In plate-armour: cap-a-pie, with plume of three ostrich feathers, scimetar, shield of arms.   Horse harnessed, springing on a hilly mount.   Arms : SHIRLEY.
Legend on a raised rim.
          ✠ SIGILLVM · ROBERTI · DE · SHIRLEY · BARONETTI ·
R. A shield of arms (with the date 1651 over it) of nine quarterings :—1. Paly of six, a canton ermine, SHIRLEY, etc.
Legend on a raised rim :—
          ✠ SIGILLVM · ROBERTI · DE · SHIRLEY · BARONETTI.
Beaded borders.

Gwillelmus de Simili, [*or* **William de Semitt,** *of co. Leic.?*]
6426. [A.D. 1199.]   Dark-green : fine, edge chipped.   About 2⅑ in. when perfect.   [xxxix. 62.]

To the ·r. In armour: hauberk, surcoat, conical helmet and nasal, sword, long convex shield with central spike and star-like ornament.

SIGILL GWILLELMI DE SIMILI.

6427. [A.D. 1331.] Dark - green: fine, edge chipped. [xxxix. 63.]

Elgenardus de Seningveam.

6428. [Early 13th cent.] Sulph. cast from fine impression. 2⅞ in. [D.C., E. 207.]

To the ·r. In armour: hauberk, surcoat, flat - topped helmet, sword, shield of arms. Horse galloping. Arms: a lion rampant.

⊕ SIGILLVM EL. ENARDI DE SENINGVEAM.

Simon ———.

6429. [A.D. 1183.] Plaster cast from chipped impression. 2⅛ in. [lxxviii. 90.]

To the r. In armour: hauberk, conical helmet, sword, shield with double border and central spike. Horse galloping.

⊕ SIGILLVM ∴ SIMON . . . . EL (?)

Wilelmus de Sviartbi, [Siwardebi, *or* Sewerby, *of co. York.*]

6430. [*Temp.* Hen. II.] Green: the face rubbed in places, with mark of handle. 1⅞ in. [Add. ch. 20,551.]

To the r. In armour: hauberk, conical helmet, sword, shield with central spike.

⊕ SIGILLVM · WILELMI · DE · SVIARTBI.

Symon Sorel, [*of Lapworth, co. Warw.*]

6431. [Late 12th or early 13th cent.] Light-brown, semi-opaque: the lower part broken off. About 2⅜ in. when perfect. [Harl. ch. 86 E. 27.]

To the r. In armour: hauberk, conical helmet and nasal, sword, shield showing the interior side.

⊕ SIGILLV . . . . . . SOREL . .

6432. Sulph. cast. [D.C., D. 127.]

Willelmus de Sparham, [*of Sparham, co. Norf.*]

6433. [Early Hen. III.] Dark-green: fine, edge slightly imperfect. 1¾ in. [L. F. C. i. 3.]

To the r. In armour: hauberk, cap-like helmet, sword, convex shield with central spike.

⊕ SIGILLVM WILLELMI DE SPARHAM.

Robert de Stafford, [*of Oxhill., co. Warw.*]

6434. [*Temp.* Hen. II., *post* 1183.] Dark brownish-red:

VOL. II.　　　　　　　　　　　　　2 A

originally fine, the l. h. side wanting. About 3 in. when perfect. [Harl. ch. 56 D. 50.]

To the r. In armour: hauberk, surcoat, conical helmet and nasal, sword, long convex shield with central spike. Horse with ornamental breast-band.

✠ SIGILLVM ROBERTI DE . . . . .

6435. Red: cracked and imperfect. [Harl. ch. 56 E. 1.]

· ✠ SIGILL'. . . . . A.

6436. Sulph. cast. [D.C., D. 203.]

Henricus [*fil.* WILLELMI] de Stiengrave, [*or* Stanegrave, *of Bulby, co. Linc.*]

6437. [*circ.* A.D. 1180–1190.] Brown: with mark of the handle. 1⅛ in. [Add. ch. 20,627.]

To the r. In armour: hauberk, conical helmet and nasal, sword, and long convex shield.

✠ SIGILLVM HENRICI DE STIENGRAVE.

Walterus de Stanes.

6438. [13th cent.] Plaster cast from fine impression, injured by pressure in places. 2 in. [lxxx. 82.]

To the r. In armour: hauberk of mail, surcoat, cap-like helmet and nasal, sword, long convex shield with central boss and faint indications of armorial bearings, not sufficiently distinct to be identified. Horse galloping.

✠ SIGILLVM : VVALTERI : DE : STANES.

Radulfus de Stantune, [*or* Stantona, *of Whitfield, co. Northt.*]

6439. [*circ.* A.D. 1168–1170.] Reddish-brown: fine, injured in places, with mark of the carved handle. About 2¼ in. when perfect. [Harl. ch. 86 E. 33.]

To the r. In armour: hauberk of mail, surcoat, conical helmet with nasal, sword, shield with central spike and star-like ornament. Horse prancing.

✠ SIGILLVM R . . . LFI · DE · STANTVNE.

6440. Sulph. cast. [D.C., D. 123.]

Hugo de Steintun.

6441. [12th–13th cent.] Cast in cream-coloured composition. 1⅜ in. [lxxv. 73.]

To the r. In armour: hauberk, surcoat, conical helmet, sword, convex shield.

✠ SIGILLVM HVGONIS DE STEINTVN.

Petrus de Stollega, *or* Stodlega.

6442. [A.D. 1179.] Plaster cast from imperfect impression. About 2 in. when perfect. [lxxx. 85.]

To the r. In armour: hauberk, lance, kite-shaped shield showing only the interior side. Horse galloping.

Legend, on a raised annulus:—

. . . . M : PETRI · DE · S . . . .

Rodbertus de Straford.

6443. [13th cent.] Plaster cast from impression somewhat indistinct in places. 1½ in. [lxxx. 81.]

To the r. In armour: hauberk of mail, conical helmet with nasal, sword, convex shield ornamented with a central spike and radiating lines.

✠ SIGILV̄ RODBERTI DE STRAFORD :

Johannes Le Straungge, [*Lord of Knokyn*, 1*st Baron Strange*, A.D. 1299–1309.]

6444. [A.D. 1301.] Plaster cast from fine impression. 1³⁄₁₆ in. [lxxix. 88.]

To the r. In armour: hauberk and coif of mail, surcoat, baldrick, helmet with fan plume and vizor down, sword, shield of arms. Horse galloping, caparisoned and plumed. Arms: two lions passant, STRANGE.

S' : IOHANNIS LE STRAVNGGE.

Beaded borders.

Herveus de Strettona.

6445. [12th cent.] Plaster cast from fine impression, slightly chipped. 1¹⁵⁄₁₆ in. [lxxx. 87.]

To the r. In armour: hauberk and coif, surcoat, conical helmet and nasal, long lance-flag with three streamers, kite-shaped shield hanging on the arm and showing the interior side. Horse with ornamental saddle.

✠ SIGILLV̄ HERVEI DE STRETTONA.

Henricus ------ hiue, [*or* Henry de Strubi, *of Saleby*, co. *Linc.*]

6446. [Early 13th cent.] Yellowish-brown: fine, injured in places. 2⅜ in. [Harl. ch. 56 F. 32.]

To the r. In armour: hauberk of mail, conical helmet and nasal, sword, long convex shield.

✠ SIGILLVM HENRI . . . . . . HIVE ✠

Cf. Cott. ch. xxix. 72, *temp.* Hen. III.

6447. Sulph. cast. [D.C., D. 136.]

Otuel de Sudleia, [*son of* RALPH DE SUDLE, *of Greet*, co. *Glouc.*]

6448. [Early 13th cent.] Dark-green, mottled : chipped. About 2¼ in. when perfect. [Sloan. ch. xxxiii. 3.]

2 A 2

To the r. In armour : hauberk, surcoat, conical helmet and
nasal, sword, long convex shield with bordure and central
spike.   Horse galloping, with ornamental breast-band.
. . . . . ILLVM OTVELIS . . . . VDLEIA.

Radulfus de Sudleie, [*of Dumbleton, co. Glouc.*]
6449. [Early 13th cent.]   Dark-green : imperfect on the
r. h. side, with mark of the handle.   About 2 in. when
perfect.   [Add. ch. 20,395.]
To the r.   In armour : hauberk of mail, surcoat, conical
helmet, sword, shield with ornamental bordure and central
spike.   Horse galloping, with fringed saddle.
SIGILL' . . . . . . I DE SVDLEIE.

Adam de Summeri, [*of Mora, co. Glam.*]
6450. [12th cent.]   Brown, mottled : edge chipped. $2\frac{1}{8}$ in.
[Harl. ch. 75 D. 7.]
To the r.   In armour : hauberk, helmet, sword, kite-shaped
shield showing the interior side.   Horse with ornamental
breast-band.
✠ SIGILLVM ADAM DE SVMMERI.
6451. Sulph. cast.   [D.C., D. 137.]
6452. Brown, mottled : fine, indistinct in places.   [Harl.
ch. 75 D. 8.]

Adam [*fil.* ROGERI] **de Sumeri,** [*of St. Nicholas, co. Glam.*]
6453. [A.D. 1186–1191.]   Bright-red : fine, cracked, and
edge imperfect ; app. by a woven bobbin.   2 in.   [Harl.
ch. 75 D. 10.]
To the r.   In armour : hauberk of mail and continuous
coif, conical helmet and nasal, sword, convex shield with
bordure, star-like ornament, and central boss.   Horse
galloping.   The details of the various portions of armour,
the stirrup, etc., are well shown.
SIGILL' ADE DE SVMER . . . . .
6454. Sulph. cast.   [D.C., D. 152.]

Radulfus de Sumeri, [*of Merlege, co. Berks. ?*]
6455. [*Temp.* Joh., *ante* 1211, or early 13th cent.]   Green,
mottled : fine originally, now very imperfect.   About 2 in.
when perfect.   [Add. ch. 7205.]
To the r.   In armour : hauberk of mail, surcoat,. cap-like
helmet and large nasal, sword, shield of arms.   Horse
galloping, with ornamental breast-band and saddle.   Arms :
a lion rampant.
Legend wanting.
Cf. Harl. ch. 75 D. 9.

Willelmus de Sumery, [*of Gornall, co. Staff.*]
6456. [*Temp.* Hen. III.] Dark-green: originally fine, now very imperfect. About 1¾ in. when perfect. [Add. ch. 6142.]
To the r. In armour: hauberk, surcoat, flat helmet, [sword], shield of arms. Horse galloping. Arms: ? three roses.

    ✠ SIGILLVM ・ W ⸱ . . . .

Wilelmis de Sumervil.

6457. [Late 12th cent.] Plaster cast from indistinct impression. 1¾ in. [lxxx. 80.]
To the r. In armour: hauberk, conical helmet, sword, convex shield and central spike. Horse galloping.

    ✠ SIGILLVM WILELMIS D' SVMERVIL'.

Samsum Tacel, [**Sanson Takel,** *of Brunham, co. Linc.*]
6458. [Early Hen. III.] Creamy-white: indistinct, edge chipped. 2 in. [Add. ch. 20,687.]
To the r. In armour: hauberk of mail, coif, conical helmet and nasal, sword, shield. Horse galloping.

    ✠ S[IGI]LLVM [SA]MSVM TACEL.

6459. [Early 13th cent.] Creamy-white: indistinct, edge chipped. [Add. ch. 20,681.]

    ✠ SI . . . . LLVM SAMSVM TAOEL.

6460. [Early 13th cent.] Creamy-white: imperfect and indistinct. [Add. ch. 20,684.]

    . . . . MSVM TACEL.

6461. Creamy-white: originally fine, but chipped and injured, with mark of the handle. [Add. ch. 22,567.]

    ✠ SIGILLVM SAMSVM TA . . . .

Hugo Talebot, [*of Feltwell, co. Norf.*]

6462. [A.D. 1162.] Dark-green: injured. 1⅞ in. [Harl. ch. 112 D. 57.]
To the r. In armour: hauberk, surcoat, conical helmet, sword, shield. Horse galloping.

    ✠ SIGILLW ✠ HVGONI TALEBOT.

6463. Sulph. cast. [D.C., D. 97.]

Willelmus Taleboth, [*of Wingham, co. Kent.*]

6464. [Late 12th or early 13th cent.] Mottled-green: fine, imperfect at top. 1⅞ in. [Harl. ch. 112 D. 59.]
. To the r. In armour: hauberk, surcoat, sword, shield with indistinct ornamentation. Horse galloping.

    ✠ S . . . LLVM WILLELMI TALEB . . . . . .

6465. Sulph. cast. [D.C., D. 187.]

Hugo Talemasche, [*of Holegate in Acton, co. Suff.*]
6466. [Early Hen. III.] Dark-green: fragment; app. by a woven bobbin of green thread. About 2 in. when perfect. [Harl. ch. 56 H. 1.]
To the r. In armour.

.. IG ... , ...

Tatersale (Walterus, *fil.* **Walteri de).** *v.* **Walterus** *fil.*
Walteri.

Rogerus de Tilliol.
6467. [Early 13th cent.] Plaster cast from indistinct impression. 1⅞ in. [lxxx. 98.]
To the r. In armour: hauberk, surcoat, helmet, sword, convex shield with central spike. Horse galloping.

✠ SIGILL' ROGERI DE ... LE ....

Another Seal.
Doubtful.
6468. [Early 13th cent.] Plaster cast from fine impression. 1¾ × 2 in. [lxxx. 99.]
Oval. To the r. In armour: hauberk, conical helmet, sword, kite-shaped shield showing the interior side.

SIGILLVM RO .. Є .... DE .....

Radulfus de Toinio, [*of co. Heref.?*]
6469. [A.D. 1140–1150.] Red: fine; app. by a woven braid of faded thread. 2⅜ in. [Add. ch. 20,454.]
To the r. In armour: hauberk, conical helmet and nasal, sword, kite-shaped shield showing interior side.

✠ SIGILLVM : RADVLFI : DE TOINIO.

Cf. Radulfus de Tooney, of co. Norf. in *Rotuli de Oblatis*, A.D. 1214.

Galfridus [*fil.* RADULFI] **de Torp,** [*of Twyford, co. Leic.*]
6470. [*Temp.* Hen. II.] Light-brown, varnished and discoloured: very imperfect. About 2 in. when perfect. [Add. ch. 1048.]
To the r. In surcoat, a hawk on the r. h. Horse galloping. In the field on the l. a tree.
Legend wanting.

Willelmus de Turp (1), [*of Castle-Eden, co. Durh.*]
6471. [*Temp.* Hen. II., *circ.* 1180.] Brown, varnished: indistinct and imperfect. About 2⅛ × 1½ in. when perfect. [Add. ch. 20,516.]
Pointed oval. To the r. In armour: hauberk, conical

helmet and nasal, lance flag with streamers, long convex shield with vertical rib. Horse with ornamental breast-band.

... GILLVM WIL ....

6472. [*circ.* A.D. 1180.] Brown, varnished : very imperfect. [Add. ch. 20,570.]

..... LV .... DE T ...

6473. [*circ.* A.D. 1180.] Brown, varnished : edge very much chipped. [Add. ch. 20,571.]

⚜ SIGILLVIM · W[ILL]ELIMI · DE · TVIRP.

6474. Plaster cast from indistinct impression. [lxxx. 96.]

⚜ SIGILL .... D .. TVRP ...

Willelmus de Turp (II.)

6475. [Late 12th cent.] Plaster cast from fine impression, injured by pressure in places. 2 in. [lxxx. 97.]

To the r. In armour : hauberk, surcoat, conical helmet, sword, kite-shaped shield showing only the interior side.

⚜ SIGILLVM : WILLELMI : DE : ... VRP.

Willelmus, *fil.* Roberti de Toteham.

6476. [13th cent.] Plaster cast from imperfect impression. $1\frac{7}{8}$ in. [lxxx. 100.]

To the r. In armour : hauberk, surcoat, conical helmet, sword, long convex shield with central boss and radiating lines. Horse galloping.

⚜ SIG WILL' FIL' ROBERTI DE TOTEHAM.

Davit de Totigtun.

6477. [Early 13th cent.] Plaster cast from indistinct impression. 2 in. [lxxxi. 28.]

To the r. In armour : hauberk, conical helmet, sword, long convex shield. Horse galloping.

⚜ SIGILLVM ꓷAVIT ꓷE TOTIGTVN ..

Radulfus [*fil. Dom.* ROGERI DE] Trehampton, [*of Leymarsh, co. Linc.*]

6478. [12th cent.] Dark-green : imperfect and indistinct About $1\frac{3}{4}$ in. when perfect. [Harl. ch. 57 A. 42.]

∅. To the r. In armour : hauberk, surcoat, conical helmet, sword, shield of arms. Horse caparisoned and plumed, galloping. Arms : a bend, perhaps for : on a bend three cinquefoils, TREHAMPTON.

S ... ADVL .... TO ..

℞. Small round counterseal. $\frac{7}{10}$ in. A shield of arms, as in *obv.?* supported by two lions rampant, and with a helmet or lion's face above and below.

6479. Sulph. cast of *obv.* only. [D.C., G. 81.]

Robertus Trenč [Trenchard ?, *of Carisbrooke, I. of Wight.*]

6480. [*Early* 13th cent.] White, discoloured and varnished: very imperfect. About 2 in. when perfect. [Harl. ch. 112 E. 15.]

To the r. In armour: hauberk, conical helmet with nasal and back-ties, sword, long lozenge-shaped shield with central spike. Horse galloping, with fringed saddle.

        ✠ SIGILL . . . .

6481. Sulph. cast. [D.C., D. 177.]

Willelmus Trussel de Flore, [*of Flower, co. Northt.*]

6482. [A.D. 1327.] Dark-green: injured by pressure, edge chipped. 1⅛ in. [Add. ch. 22,395.]

To the r. In armour: hauberk of mail, surcoat, plumed helmet, sword chained to neck, shield of arms. Horse galloping, caparisoned and plumed. Arms: a cross formeé flory, TRUSSELL.

        SIGILLVM : WILL'I : TRVSSEL.

Jaspar [Tudor], *Earl of Pembroke, Duke of Bedford, etc.*
        [*ob.* A.D. 1495.]

6483. [A.D. 1459.] Yellowish - brown, discoloured: fine, chipped at top, cracked. 3½ in. [Sloan. ch. xxxii. 20.]

∅. To the r. In plate armour: surcoat, helmet, vizor closed, sword, shield of arms. Horse caparisoned, galloping on a mount. Arms: quarterly, 1, 4, FRANCE (MODERN), 2, 3, ENGLAND within a bordure charged with fourteen martlets of EDWARD THE CONFESSOR, for JASPER TUDOR. Crest broken away. Background replenished with elegantly designed wavy branches of foliage and flowers.

     . . . . . ƀm : ɗomini : jasparis : comitis : . . . . .

℞. On a mount, an angel with wings expanded, and draped, holding in front a shield of arms as in *obv.*, supported by two wolves sejant ducally gorged, chained and tethered by a staple to the mount.

    ✿ ⁑ Sig[illum :] ɗomini : jasparis : comitis : penbrochie.

Beaded borders: betw. the words of the legends are sprigs of oak leaves on the *obv.* and roses on the *rev.*

6484. Sulph. casts of *obv.* and *rev.* [D.C., G. 83, 84.]

Seal as Duke of Bedford and Lord of Bergevenny.

6485. Plaster casts from fine impression. 3¾ in. [lxxx. 77, 78.]

∅. A shield of arms as in the preceding seal, but with the fleurs-de-lis *one and two* instead of *two and one*, surmounted by a cap of estate turned up bezanté, and coronet. Supporters, *dex.* a dragon, langued with two tongues, *sin.* a wolf. The field replenished with bunches of peas-cods, in threes, tied together.

✠ ⸲ Sigillum ⸲ excellentissimi ⸲ principis ⸲ iasperis ⸲

⸲ . . . . patrui ⸲ regum ⸲ .

R̊. To the r. In armour : coat of arms, helmet with vizor open, crest a dragon or wyvern volant, sword, shield of arms as before. Horse springing, plumed with an ostrich feather, and caparisoned ermine, on a mount of herbage and flowers. Background as in *obv.*

⸲ D[ucis] ⸲ bedfordie ⸲ co mitis ⸲ . . . . o . . . .

⸲ Dom . . . . . ⸲ De ⸲ bergeuennp ⸲

For arms see Boutell, *Heraldry*, 2nd edit. 1863, p. 367.

Simon de La Tur, [*of Bourn, co. Cambr.*]

6486. [*Temp.* Hen. II.] Dark-green : fine, with mark of the handle, and raised rim. 2¼ in. [Harl. ch. 83 B. 49.]

To the r. In armour : hauberk and coif of mail, cap-like helmet, sword, convex shield with star-like ornament. Horse galloping.

✠ SIGILLVM SIMONIS DE LA TVR.

6487. Sulph. cast. [D.C., D. 106.]

Stephanus de Turnaham, *Miles,* [*Baron Turnham, of .cos. Kent and Sussex, Seneschal of Anjou,* A.D. 1186, *ob. ante* A.D. 1214.]

6488. [*Temp.* Joh.] Dark-red : fine, slightly chipped at top. 1⅞ in. [xxxvi. 216.]

∅. To the r. In armour : hauberk, cap-like helmet with back-ties, sword, shield of arms. Horse galloping, with ornamental breast-band and diapered saddle. Arms : a bend. Below the horse an ornamental flower.

✠ SIGILLVM : STEPHANI : DE : TVRNAHAM.

The letters AH and AM, in *Turnaham,* conjoined.

· R̊. Small, slightly pointed oval counterseal. 1 × ¾ in. Impression of an antique oval intaglio gem. Bust of an old man to the r. In the field of the gem an inscription in oriental characters, indistinct.

✠ DEVS : SALVET : CVI : TE : MITTO.

Willelmus de Turvilla, [*of Pailton, co. Warw.*]

6489. [*Early* Hen. III.] Dark - green, speckled : fair. 1¾ in. [Add. ch. 21,495.]

∅. To the r. In armour : hauberk, surcoat, conical helmet and nasal, sword, shield of arms Arms : three chevronels.

✠ SIGILL' WILL' DE TVRVILLA. ·

℞. Small pip-shaped counterseal, with mark of handle. 1⅛ × 1 in. A shield of arms: three chevronels, TURVILE.

SCVTO : SECRETA : TEGVTVR.

Cf. Wm. de Turvile, Dominus de Palintona, Cott. ch. iv. 21, *temp.* Hen. III.; and Wm. de Turvile, of Helendon, co. Northt., A.D. 1270–1290, Harl. ch. 84 E. 7, 8 ; 86 C. 45 ; 86 D. 47, etc.

Adomarus de Valencia, [*2nd*] *Earl of Pembroke, Lord of Weysford and Montignac,* A.D. 1308–1324.

6490. Plaster casts from fine impression. 2¾ in. [lxxxi. 4, 5.]

∅. To the r. In armour: hauberk of mail, surcoat, helmet with vizor closed and with fan crest and lambrequins, sword, shield of arms. Horse galloping, crested as above, and caparisoned. Arms : as in *rev.*

ADOMARVS DE VALENCIA · COMES · PEMBROCHIE DN̄S WEYS ET DE MONTINIACO.

℞. A shield of arms: burelé (here represented by seven bars), an orle of nine martlets, AYMER DE VALENCE. Another seal, quoted and drawn by Doyle (*Offic. Baron.,* vol. iii. p. 10), gives six bars and thirteen martlets, but the Earl's signet seal in Add. ch. 19,835, which will be described further on in this catalogue, corresponds with this *rev.*

The shield is suspended by a strap to a tree, and betw. two other trees of conventional form, within a finely carved gothic rosace of eight semi-circular cusps, trefoiled, and ornamented with counter-sunk trefoils betw. triplets of pellets in the spandrils.

✠ S' ADOMARI DE VALENCIA COMITIS PEMBROCHIE. DN̄I WEYS' ET DE MONTINIACO.

See Douët D'Arcq, *Collection de Sceaux,* No. 10,184, for an example of this seal used in A.D. 1308. Another seal of Ademar de Valence in the same work, No. 3810, A.D. 1298, gives burelé, an orle of seven martlets.

William Le Vavassour, 1*st Baron?*

6491. [Late 13th cent.] Plaster cast from fine impression. ¾ in. [lxxxi. 30.]

To the r. In armour: hauberk, plumed helmet, sword, shield of arms. Horse galloping, caparisoned and plumed. Arms : a fess dancettée, VAVASSOUR.

In place of a legend a bordure dancettée, in allusion to the armorial bearings of VAVASSOUR.

Oliverus de Vaus.

6492. [*Temp.* Joh.] Plaster cast from chipped impression. 1⅞ in. [lxxxi. 7.]

To the r. In armour : hauberk, surcoat, flat-topped

helmet, sword, shield of arms with central spike. Horse galloping, with fringed caparisons. Arms appear to be : chequy, VAUX.

SIGIL . . . . . OLIVERI DE VAVS.

Bertram de Verdum, [3*rd Baron de Verdon, of Long Whatton, co. Leic.*]

¯ **6493.** [Early Hen. II.] Creamy-white : only fragment of the centre. About 2½ in. when perfect. [Add. ch. 22,572.]

To the r. In armour : long convex shield.

Legend wanting.

Nicholas de Verdun, [5*th Baron de Verdon, ob.* A.D. 1231.]

6494. [*Early* 13th cent.] Cast in dark-green composition. 2 in. [lxxv. 74.]

To the r. In armour : hauberk, surcoat, flat cap-shaped helmet, sword, convex shield ornamented with a fretty device. Horse galloping, caparisoned. The fretty device has in each space a small pellet or spot, and is used on the surcoat, shield, and horse's caparisons, probably to represent leather strengthened with bands and studs of metal.

⊕ SIGILLV(ŋ · ƝIⅭHOLAI · DE · VERDVN.

Theobaldus de Verdun, [7*th Baron de Verdon,* A.D. 1295–1309,] *Constable of Ireland.*

6495. [A.D. 1301.] Plaster cast from fine impression. 1¾ in. [lxxxi. 12, 13.]

∅. To the r. In armour : hauberk of mail, helmet with vizor closed, sword, shield of arms. Horse caparisoned. Arms : fretty, VERDON.

⊕ SIGILLVM THEOBALDI DE VERDVN.·

R. A shield of arms, as in *obv.*, suspended by the strap from a trifurcated tree, with two smaller trees issuing at the sides from behind the shield. In the field, on each side, a lion passant, arranged pale-wise, forming a kind of early supporter.

⊕ CONSTABVLARII : HYBERNIE.

Beaded borders.

Cf. *Vetusta Monumenta*, vol. i., pl. xxx., f. 21.

Theobaldus de Verdon, [8*th Baron de Verdon,* A.D. 1309–1314,] *Constable of Ireland.*

6496. [A.D. 1313.] Red: fine, imperfect. [Harl. ch. 57 C. 25.]

∅. Same as the *obv.* of the seal of his father, see No. 6495, with addition to the field of a diaper lozengy, with a pellet in each space.

SIG . . LVM THEOBALDI . . . .

℞. Same as the *rev.* of the seal above-mentioned, with addition of a small bird on each side at top of the shield ; that on the r. h. side wanting : and below the shield, on each side, a wavy sprig of foliage.

☩ . . . . . . VLARII : HYBERNIE.

Engr. in *Vetusta Monumenta*, vol. i., pl. xxx., f. 21, for the father's seal, but with the diaper on the *rev.*

Albericus [de Vere], 1*st Earl of Oxford.*

6497. [A.D. 1155–1194.] Creamy-white : fine, very fragmentary. About 2¼ in. when perfect. [Add. ch. 28,329.]

To the l. In armour : hauberk and coif of mail, conical helmet and nasal, sword, long convex shield. Horse with fringed saddle.

Legend wanting.

Another Seal.

6498. Creamy-white : fine, edge chipped away. 2¾ in. when perfect. [Cott. ch. xxix. 77.]

To the r. In armour : hauberk and coif, helmet, back-ties, sword, long convex shield. Horse caparisoned, or with fringed saddle.

. . . . . . LBERICI CO . . . .

6499. Sulph. cast. [D.C., D. 148.]

Albericus de Ver, [*son of* ALBERIC, *Earl of Oxford, afterwards 2nd Earl of Oxford.*]

6500. [A.D. 1191–1194.] Light - brown, or discoloured : very imperfect. 2 in. [Harl. ch. 57 C. 3.]

To the r. In armour : hauberk, surcoat, helmet, sword, convex shield with central boss.

Legend wanting.

Albericus de Vere, [*2nd Earl of Oxford?* A.D. 1194–1214.]

. **6501.** Plaster cast from indistinct impression, chipped at the edges. 2¾ in. [lxxxi. 8.]

To the r. In armour : hauberk and coif of mail, surcoat, conical helmet, sword, convex shield with central boss and bordure. Horse galloping, with ornamental breast-band.

☩ SIG . . . . CI · DE V . . . . E.

Called 1st Earl in *Arch. Journ.*, vol. ix., p. 27, where it is figured.

Hugo de Ver, [*4th*] *Earl of Oxford,* [*Lord Great Chamberlain,* A.D. 1221–1263.]

· **6502.** Plaster cast from fine impression. 2½ in. [lxxxi. 9.]

To the r. In armour : hauberk of mail, surcoat, flat-topped

helmet, sword, shield of arms. Horse galloping, caparisoned. Arms: quarterly, in the first quarter a mullet, DE VERE.

⚜ SIGILL' ⁝ HVGONIS ⁝ DE ⁝ VER ⁝ COMITIS ⁝ OXONIE ⁝ ☆
Arch. Journ., vol. ix., p. 27.

Robertus de Veer, [*5th*] *Earl of Oxford.* [A.D. 1263–1296.]
6503. [A.D. 1284.] Creamy-white, the surface flaked very imperfect. About 2¾ in. when perfect. [Harl. ch. 57 C. 8.]
Ø. To the r. In armour: hauberk, surcoat, sword, shield of arms. Horse caparisoned. Arms: quarterly, in the first quarter a mullet, DE VERE.
Legend wanting.
℞. A small counterseal. 1 in. A shield of arms as in *obv.* betw. two demi-lions sejant addorsed, issuing from behind the shield.
⚜ SIGILLVM SECRETI.
Beaded borders.

Robertus de Veer, [*6th*] *Earl of Oxford.* [A.D. 1296–1331.]
6504. Plaster casts from very fine impression. 2¾ in. [lxxxi. 10, 11.]
Ø. To the r. In armour: hauberk of mail, surcoat, helmet with vizor down and fan crest, sword, shield of arms. Horse galloping, crested and caparisoned. Arms: DE VERE.
SIGILLVM ⁝ ROBERTI ⁝ DE ⁝ VEER ⁝ COMITIS ⁝ OXONIE ⁝
℞. A small round counterseal. ¹¹⁄₁₂ in. Within a pointed gothic quatrefoil a shield of arms, DE VERE.
☆ ⁝ SIGILLVM ⁝ ROBERTI ⁝ DE ⁝ VEER ⁝
The letters ER in *Veer* conjoined.

Ricardus de Vernone.
6505. [Late 12th or early 13th cent.] Plaster cast from fine impression. 2¼ in. [lxxxi. 14.]
To the r. In armour: hauberk and coif of mail, hemispherical helmet, sword, shield of arms with central boss, and crossing lines for fretty, VERNON. Horse galloping, with fringed saddle and ornamental breast-band.
⚜ SIGILLVM RICARDI DE VERNONE.

Paganus Vicecomes de Hamicheford, [*Hemmingford, co. Hunts.*] *? Sheriff of Hunts.*
6506. [*post* A.D. 1150.] Light-brown, varnished: a fragment only of the central part. About 2 in. when perfect. [Add. ch. 28,337.]
To the l. In armour: hauberk, surcoat.
Legend wanting.

Willelmus, [DE CHEYNEY], *fil.* ROBERTI VICECOMIITIS, [*of Wrabton, co. Suff.*]
6507. [*circ.* A.D. 1150.] Pale-red, the face flaked away in

parts : edge imperfect. About 3 in. when perfect. [L. F. C., xxiii. 5.]

To the r. In armour : hauberk and coif, conical helmet and nasal, sword, long convex shield. Horse galloping.

✠ . . . . l.

Cf. Dugd. *Mon. Angl.*, vol. v., p. 558.

Ricardus de Vierli.
(*A doubtful Seal.*)

6508. [12th cent.] Plaster cast from fine impression. $1\frac{7}{8} \times 2\frac{1}{8}$ in. [lxxxi. 18.]

Oval. To the r. In armour : surcoat fretty, pointed helmet and nasal, sword, kite-shaped shield showing only the interior side. Horse with breast-band ornamented with pendants.

✠ SIGILLVM · RICARDI · DE · VIERLI. (?)

Journ. Brit. Arch. Assoc., vol. xiii., p. 169.

Ace Vil de Larun, [*of Hadlow, co. Kent.*]

6509. [Early 13th cent.] Dark-red : fine, edge slightly chipped ; app. by a closely woven bobbin of yellowish-brown stuff. $1\frac{1}{2}$ in. [Add. ch. 20,007.]

To the r. In armour : hauberk, surcoat, cap-like helmet, sword, shield. Horse galloping.

SIGILL' ACE VIL DE LARVN.

Willelmus, *fil.* Aylmeri de Vilgeb', [*or* Wilibi, *of Willoughby, co. Warw., etc.*]

6510. [*Temp.* Hen. III.] Creamy-white : only a fragment of the upper l. h. corner. About $2\frac{1}{4}$ in. when perfect. [Harl. ch. 86 F. 57.]

To the r. In armour : hauberk, conical helmet with nasal and back-ties, sword, convex shield with central spike. Horse galloping.

✠ S . . . . ERI DE VILGEB'.

Williame Wacelin, [*of Broome, co. Norf.*]

6511. [Early Hen. III.] Dark-green : fine, edge chipped. $1\frac{7}{8}$ in. [Add. ch. 22,570.]

To the r. In armour : hauberk, cap-like helmet, sword, shield.

✠ SIGILL' WILLIAME WACELIИ.

The letter N reversed.

Walterus [*fil.* SIMONIS] de Wadellie, [*of Pateshull, co. Northt.*]

6512. [*Temp.* Hen. II.] Dark-red : fine, the l. h. side imperfect ; app. by a woven bobbin of green thread. $2\frac{1}{4}$ in. [Cott. ch. v. 20.]

To the r. In armour: hauberk, surcoat, cap-like helmet, sword, shield. Horse galloping, with ornamental breast-band.

✠ SIGILLVM WALTERI DE W . . . .

6513. Sulph. cast. [D.C., D. 126.]

Hugo [*fil.* BALDEWINI] **Wake,** [*of Haconby, co. Linc.*]
6514. [Early Hen. III.] Dark-green: fine. 1¾ in. [Harl. ch. 57 D. 28.]

Ø. To the r. In armour: hauberk of mail, surcoat, flat-topped helmet, sword, shield of arms. Horse galloping, caparisoned. Arms: two bars in chief three roundles, WAKE.

✠ SIGILLVM : HVGONIS : WAKE ᴀ · :

℞. A small round counterseal, +⅒ in. A shield of arms, as in *obv.*

✠ SIGILL' · HVGONIS · WAKE.

Beaded borders.

6515. Sulph. cast of the *obv.* only. [D.C., E. 274.]

Osbertus Walbertus.

(*A doubtful Seal.*)

6516. [Early 13th cent.] Plaster cast from fine impression. 2¼ in. [lxxxi. 19.]

To the r. In armour: hauberk of mail, surcoat, conical helmet and nasal, convex shield with central spike. Horse galloping.

✠ SIGILLVM · OSBERTI · WALBERTI.

Robbertus de Vals [*or* **Wals,** *of Cheddiston, co. Suff.*]
6517. [Late 12th cent.] Light-brown, encrusted: chipped. 2 in. [Harl. ch. 84 B. 5.]

To the r. In armour: hauberk and coif of mail, conical helmet and nasal, sword, convex shield with ornamental bordure and central spike.

✠ SIGILLVM ROBBERTI DE VALS.

6518. Sulph. cast. [D.C., D. 104.]

Herveus Walterus, [*of Wingfield, co. Suff.*]

6519. [Late Hen. II.] Light-brown, varnished with a dark-brown colour: edge imperfect and indistinct. 2 in. [Harl. ch. 57 E. 2.]

To the r. In armour: hauberk, surcoat, helmet, sword, shield of arms. Horse galloping.

✠ SIGIL . . . . HER . . I W . . . ERI.

6520. Sulph. cast. [D.C., D. 199.]

Asceline de Waltervilla, [*of Cotterstock, co. Northt.*]'
. **6521.** [Early Hen. III.]   Pale greenish-white, the face
flaked, varnished with a reddish-brown colour : very imperfect.
About 2¼ in. when perfect. [Add. ch. 21,683.]
   To the r.   In armour : hauberk of mail, conical helmet
with nasal, sword, convex shield with central spike.
   ✠ SIGI . . . . W . . . .

Thomas de Wapuburi, [*or* **Wapenbyri,** *of Wapenbury ?,*
co. Warw.]
   6522. [*E*arly Hen. III.]   Green, mottled : fine, the lower
part wanting.   About 1½ in. when perfect. [Add. ch. 21,499.]
   To the r.   In armour : hauberk, helmet, sword, shield.
Horse galloping.
   ✠ SIGI . . . . . . WAPVBVRI.

Reginaldus de Warren, [*1st Baron de Warren, of Wirmgay,*
ob. ante A.D. 1184.]
   6523. [A.D. 1171.]   Plaster cast, from very imperfect impression.   About 2¼ in. when perfect. [lxxxi. 23.]
   To the l.   In armour : conical helmet, long kite-shaped
shield.   Horse galloping, with fringed saddle and ornamental
breast-band.
   . . . . VVA . . . .

Willelmus de Warennia, *Count of Warren,*
and [*6th*] *Earl of Surrey.*
   6524. [A.D. 1215–1225.]   Creamy-yellow, varnished : fine,
very artistic, imperfect ; app. by plaited cord of yellow and
red thread.   About 3¼ in. when perfect. [Harl. ch. 57 E. 28.]
   . ∅. To the r.   In armour : hauberk of mail, surcoat, helmet,
sword, convex shield of arms slung by a strap round the neck.
Horse galloping.   Arms : as on *rev.*
   ℞. A pip-shaped shield of arms, WARREN.
   Legends wanting.
   6525. Sulph. casts of *obv.* and *rev.* [D.C., E. 210, 211.]
   6526. Plaster casts from fine impression, edges much
chipped. [lxxxi. 50, 51.]
   ∅. ✠ SIGILL' · WILL'I : DE . . . . RENNIA : COM . . . . RREIA.
   ℞. ✠ SIG . . . · . . . . . COMITIS DE ⋮ WARENNIA.
   Beaded borders.

Johannes de Warennia, *Count of Warren, and*
[*7th*] *Earl of Surrey.*
   6527. [A.D. 1254.]   Red : fine, chipped at the edge ; app.
by a plaited cord of pale red silk.   3⅛ in. [Add. ch. 24,551.]
   ∅. To the r.   In armour : hauberk and coif of mail, sur-

coat, flat helmet with vizor closed, sword, shield of arms. Horse galloping, caparisoned.   Arms : chequy, WARREN.

☽ S' . . . . DE WAREN . . . . DE SVRREIA.

The letters AR conjoined.

℞. Within a carved gothic border, with eight semicircular cusps, having a countersunk trefoil in each spandril, a shield of arms as in *rev.* betw. three elegantly designed wavy branches of ivy-leaf foliage.

✠ SIGILLVM : IOH . . . . OMITIS : DE : WARENNIA ⋈

Beaded borders.

6528. [A.D. 1254.]   Red: fine, chipped and imperfect at the lower part ; app. by a plaited cord of red silk.   [Add. ch. 24,551.]

∅. ☽ . . . . . . S : DE WAR . . . . VRREIA.

℞. ⋇ SIGILLVM : IOH . . . . E : WARENNI . . . . . .

Cf. J. Watson, *Memoirs of the Ancient Earls of Warren and Surrey*, 1782, vol. i., pp. 293, 295.

6529. Plaster casts of fine impression, edges chipped in places. · [lxxx. 66, 67.]

∅. ☽ S' IOH'IS : DE WARENNIA : COMIT[IS :] DE : SVRREIA.

℞. ⋇ SIGILLVM : IOHANNIS [: C]OMITIS : DE : WARENNIA.

6530. [A.D. 1243–1257.]   Light-brown, varnished : very imperfect.   [Harl. ch. 57 E. 31.]

℞. . . . . DE : WA . . . . .

6531. Sulph. casts of *obv.* and *rev.*   [D.C., E. 247, 248.]

6532. Sulph. casts of *obv.* and *rev.*   Another set.   [D.C., E. 249, 250.]

Johannes de Warrennia, [8*th ?*] *Earl of Surrey.*

6533. [A.D. 1281.]   Creamy-white, the face flaked : very imperfect.   About 3 in. when perfect.   [Harl. ch. 57 E. 33.]

∅. Resembles *obv.* of No. 6527, but with variant dimensions.

℞. Resembles *rev.* of No. 6527, but with variant dimensions. Legends wanting.

6534. Sulph. casts of *obv.* and *rev.*   [D.C., F. 151, 152.]

6535. Sulph. cast of *rev.* only.   [D.C., F. 153.]

Gaufridus de Watervilla, [*of Thimbleby, co. Linc.*], " *Dapifer Consulis*," [*i.e. of* WILLIAM DE ROMARE, *E. of Lincoln ?*].

6536. [A.D. 1154.]   Light-brown, semi-opaque : fine.   2¼ in. [Harl. ch. 57 F. 14.]

To the r. In armour: hauberk of mail, conical helmet and nasal, sword, oval shield ornamented with a bordure.

✠ SIGILLV GAVFRIDI · DE · WATERVILLA DAPIFERI C̃SVLIS.
Cf. Harl. ch. 55 E. 10.

6537. Sulph. cast. [D.C., D. 75.]

Wathford (Eustacius, *fil.* EUSTACII DE).
v. Athde (Eustacius, *fil.* Eustacii de).

Willelmus de Watevile.

6538. [13th cent.] Plaster cast from fine but chipped impression. 1¾ in. [lxxxi. 24.]

To the r. In armour: hauberk, surcoat, flat helmet, sword, shield of arms. Horse galloping. Arms: two (? for three) chevrons, WATEVILE.

✠ SIGILL' WILLEL . . . . . . ATEVILE.

Robertus [*fil.* WILLELMI] de Wavre, [*of Long-Lawford, co. Warw.*]

6539. [*circ.* A.D. 1200.] Light-red: edge chipped. 1⅘ in. [Cott. ch. xi. 31.]

To the r. In armour: hauberk of mail, surcoat, conical helmet with nasal, sword, shield. Horse galloping.

✠ SIGILL' ROBERT . . . E · WAVRE.

6540. Sulph. cast. [D.C., E. 204.]

Willelmus de Wavere, [*son of* ROBERT, *son of* WILL. DE WAVERE, *of Long Lawford, co. Warw.*]

6541. [Late 12th cent.] Dark-green: fine, injured on l. h. side. 1⅞ in. [Add. ch. 21,456.]

To the r. In armour: hauberk and coif of mail, round-topped helmet with nasal, sword, convex shield with star-like ornament. Horse galloping.

SIGILLVM : WILLELMI : DE : WA . . . .

Wilelmus, *fil.* Allani de Wdehale, [*or* Wudehalle, *of Roughton, co. Linc.*]

6542. [Late 12th cent.] Green, mottled: fine, edge chipped in places. 1⅞ in. [Harl. ch. 58 B. 43.]

To the l. In long surcoat, with a hawk in the l. hand held by the jesses. Horse with ornamental breast-band.

✠ SIGILL' WILELM . . . . . . ALL . . N DE WDEHAL'

6543. Sulph. cast. [D.C., D. 204.]

Willelmus de Wedona, [*or* Weduna, *of Weedon, co. Northt.*]

6544. [13th cent.] Brown, a thick mass: with mark of

the handle; app. by plaited strings. $1\frac{7}{8}$ in. [Harl. ch. 86 F. 38.]

To the r. In armour: hauberk, conical helmet and nasal, sword, convex shield with central spike.

❋ SIGILL' WILLELMI DE WEDONA.

6545. Sulph. cast. [D.C., D. 178]

Alan de Whitchereche, [or Witcherche, of Sheffield, co. Berks.]

6546. [A.D. 1202?] Dark-green: fine, with mark of the handles. $1\frac{1}{2}$ in. [Add. ch. 7203.]

To the r. In armour: hauberk, conical helmet, sword, convex shield with bordure and central spike. Horse galloping, with large ears.

❋ SIGILL' : ALANI : DE WHITCHERECH'.

6547. [A.D. 1202?] Dark-green: fine. [Add. ch. 7204.]

6548. [Early 13th cent.] Green, mottled: edge chipped, with mark of the handle. [Add. ch. 20,592.]

6549. [Early 13th cent.] Dark-green: fine, with raised rim and mark of the handle. [Add. ch. 20,593.]

6550. [Early 13th cent.] Creamy-white: fine. [Add. ch. 20,595.]

Johannes, fil. Walteri de Wighal, [or Wygehale, of Lynn, co. Norf.]

6551. [circ. A.D. 1286.] Bronze-green: fine, chipped and cracked. $1\frac{3}{4}$ in. [Add. ch. 7910.]

To the l. In armour: hauberk, surcoat, helmet with vizor closed, sword, shield of arms. Horse galloping, with ornamental breast-band. Arms: a lion rampant debruised by a fess.

❋ SIGILLVM · IOHANNIS · FILI · WALTERI · DE WIGHAL'.

Beaded borders.

6552. Bronze-green: very imperfect, indistinct. [Add. ch. 7911.]

.... WALTERI · DE ....

6553. [13th cent.] Plaster cast from fine but chipped impression. $1\frac{5}{8}$ in. [lxxxi. 25.]

❋ SIGILLVM : IOHANNIS : FILI : WALTERI : DE : WIGHA ....

Walterus de Winlesores, [? of co. Bucks.]

6554. [A.D. 1212.] Sulph. cast from fine impression. $2\frac{1}{4}$ in. [D.C., E. 199.]

To the r. In armour: hauberk, surcoat, cap-like helmet, sword, long convex shield with central spike. Horse galloping.

❋ SIGILL' WALTERI DE WINLESORES.

The N reversed.

Cf. Rot. de Oblatis, p. 173, A.D. 1201, etc.

2 B 2

Willelmus de Windesòriis, "*filius.***"**

6555. [*E*arly 13th cent.] Plaster cast from. fine but chipped impression. 2¼ in. [lxxxi. 27.]

To the r. In armour: hauberk or tunic, lance held horizontally in the r. hand, kite-shaped shield showing the interior side.

✠ SIGILLVM WILLELMI DE WINDESORIIS FILII.

Robert Wysdom, de Charewelton, [*co. Northt.***]**

6556. [A.D. 1315.] Light-brown: indistinct, edge imperfect. 2⅛ in. [Harl. ch. 84 E. 42.]

To the l. In armour: hauberk, surcoat, conical helmet and nasal, long kite-shaped shield.

✠ SIGILL' . . . . . TI · DE . . . . . THNI. ?

This seal is of the 13th cent., attached to a later charter.

6557. Sulph. cast. [D.C., F. 150.]

A · · · · · · de · · · · · · · · el.

6558. [12th cent.] Sulph. cast from injured impression. 2 in. [D.C., D. 163.]

To the r. In armour: hauberk of mail, conical helmet, sword, kite shield showing interior side.

✠ SIGILLVM A . . . . . . DE . . . . . EL.

John · · · · · · · · el.

6559. [12th cent.] Sulph. cast from chipped impression. 1⅞ in. [D.C., D. 183.]

To the r. In armour: hauberk, surcoat, cap-likc helmet, sword, shield.

✠ SIGILL . . . . . HIS T . . . . . EL (?)

Richardus de · · · · estona.

6560. [12th cent.] Light-brown or uncoloured, partly oxidised: imperfect. 1¾ in. [xxxii. 63 A.]

To the r. In armour: a spear? Horse galloping.

. . . RICHARDI . . . . . . ESTONA.

Uncertain Seals.

6561. [12th cent.] Sulph. cast from indistinct impression. 1⅜ in. [D.C., D. 165.]

To thc r. In armour: hauberk, conical helmet with nasal, sword, shield. Horse standing.

✠ SIGILLVM . . . . R . . .

6562. [12th cent.] White or cream-coloured: injured and detached from an original charter. [xxxvi. 53.]

To the r. In armour: hauberk of mail, coif, conical helmet and nasal, sword, convex shield with central spike and star-like ornament. Horse galloping.

SIGILLV . . . . . EI . . . . .

6563. [12th cent.] Light-brown or uncoloured : very imperfect, only the centre remaining. About $1\frac{1}{2}$ in. when perfect. [xxxix. 74.]

To the r. In armour : hauberk and coif of mail, conical helmet and nasal, sword, long pointed shield with central spike and ornamental border.

Legend wanting.

6564. [12th cent.] Gutta percha impression from a matrix belonging to the Society of Antiquaries of Scotland. $2\frac{3}{8}$ in. [xlvii. 994.]

To the r. In armour : hauberk and coif of mail, surcoat, conical helmet and nasal, sword, convex bordered shield with central spike. Horse galloping, with ornamental breast-band.

      ✠ SIGILL BENEDICVMAS DCI VNNN FIIト.

Beaded borders.

H. Laing's *Suppl. Catal.*, No. 1293.

6565. [12th cent.] Uncoloured, varnished dark - brown : only a fragment of the centre. About $1\frac{3}{4}$ in. when perfect. [xxxv. 19 D.]

To the r. In armour : long pointed convex shield. Horse galloping.

Legend wanting.

FIGURES OF NOBLE AND OTHER LADIES.

Aewis, Comitissa Albama[ra], [*dau. of Earl* WILLIAM.]
6566. [*Early temp.* Joh.] Green : fine originally, now very imperfect and injured. About 2⅞ × 2 in., when perfect. [Add. ch. 20,559.]
Ø. Pointed oval. **To the r.** Standing, wearing a long transparent dress closely fitting.
Legend wanting.
℞. A small round counterseal. 1⅜ in. An early-shaped shield of arms : gyronny of fourteen (?), an escutcheon.
✠ S' . : AEWIDIS COMIT' A[LB]AMA . . . . .
The letters MA in *Albama* conjoined.

Hawis de · · · · fort, [*wife of* HELIAS DE ALBENIACO,*
of Saxilby, co. Linc.]
6567. [*circ.* A.D. 1150–1182.] White, varnished : edge imperfect ; app. by plaited threads. 2 × 1¾ in. when perfect. [Harl. ch. 45 B. 27.]
Pointed oval. **To the l.** standing, wearing a long dress, with maunches at the wrists, in the r. h. a fleur-de-lis.
✠ SIGILLVM : HAW . . . . DE . . . . . FORT.
6568. Sulph. cast. [D.C., D. 212.]

Matildis de Albervilla, [*or* **Auberville,** *of Sandwich,
co. Kent.*]
6569. [*Early* 13th cent.] Mottled - green : fine, edge chipped ; app. by a woven cord of faded bobbin. 2⅛ × 1½ in. [Harl. ch. 45 E. 33.]
Pointed oval. **To the l.** standing, with long dress, and a maunch at each wrist, on the r. wrist a hawk. The field diapered with very elegant scroll-work of foliage and flowers.
✠ SIGILLVM · MATILDIS : DE : ALBERVILLA.
The S's reversed.
6570. Sulph. cast. [D.C., D. 217.]

---

* Burke, *Extinct Peerage*, 1866, p. 160, places the death of Helias de Albeniaco in 1305.

Ysabella de Albigniaco, [*wife of Baron* ROBERT DE ROS, *of Cotes, co. Bedf.*]

6571. [*Temp.* Edw. I.] Dark-green : somewhat indistinct. 1¼ × ⅞ in. [Harl. ch. 45 B. 30.]

Pointed oval. To the r. Standing, wearing a fur cloak and head-dress, in her l. h. a falcon with long jesses.

⚘ S' YSABELLE · DE · ALBIGNIACO.

6572. Sulph. cast. [D.C., E. 290.]

Ela de Audeleḡ, [*or* **Alditheleya,** *dau. of* WILLIAM LONGESPEE II., *widow of* JAMES DE ALDITHELEYA, *of Wretchwick, co. Oxon.*]

6573. [A.D. 1274.] Light-brown : fine. 1⅝ × 1 in. [Add. ch. 10,619.]

Pointed oval. To the r. Standing on a small dog, wearing a long cloak and head-dress, in each hand a shield of arms : r. indistinct, perhaps six mascles, three, two, and one ; l. fretty. In the field on each side a wavy branch of foliage.

★ SIGILLVM ELE DE AVDELEG'.

Issabella, [*widow of* JAMES] **de Appelbi,** [*Miles, and wife of* WILLIAM LE BRET, *of Appleby, co. Leic.*]

6574. [A.D. 1290.] Mottled-green : fine. 1¼ × 1 in. [Harl. ch. 47 B. 24.]

Pointed oval. Standing on a carved corbel, with cloak and head-dress, a falcon on her r. wrist. In the field on each side a shield of arms : r. three garbs ; l. barry of six.

S' ISSABELL' DE : APPELBI.

The letters AP conjoined.

6575. Sulph. cast. [D.C., E. 289.]

Johanna, [*dau. of* JOHN] **atte Berne,** [*of Suthamyngfeld, co. Ess.*]

6576. [A.D. 1335.] Green : a fragment. About 2 × 1 in. when perfect. [Harl. ch. 76 C. 14.]

Pointed oval. Standing on a carved corbel. In the field some roses.

. . . . DE BE . . . .

Johanna, [*wife of* WILLIAM] **Aumbesas,** [*of Carshalton, co. Surr.*]

6577. [A.D. 1307.] Green : fine, edge chipped. The field of the seal raised. About 1⅝ × 1⅛ in. when perfect. [Add. ch. 23,355.]

Pointed oval. To the l. Standing, with a small dog or

brachet at her feet, in the r. hand a shield, of arms : three dice, two and one, AUMBESAS.

.　...GIL..........　AVMBESA..

Beaded borders.

6578. [A.D. 1319.]　Green : fine, edge chipped. [Add. ch. 23,365.]

⚹ SIGIL..... HANNE ⚹ AVMBESAS.

Ela Basset, [*dau. of* WILLIAM LONGESPEE I.],.
Countess of Warwick, [*widow of* THOS. DE NEWBURGH,
Earl of Warwick, and wife of. PHILIP BASSET, *of Hedendon,*
ob. A.D. 1297.]

6579. [*post* A.D. 1242.]　Plaster casts from fine impression. 3 × 1¾ in.　[lxxviii. 19, 20.]

∅. Pointed oval.　In flat cap, tightly-fitting dress, mantle. In the l. h. a shield of arms.　Standing on a carved corbel or platform, beneath an elaborately carved canopy like a cathedral church, with central tower and transept.　Arms : six lioncels, three, two, and one, for her father WILLIAM LONGESPEE, *E*arl of Salisbury.　On the l., in the field, a similar shield of arms : chequy, a chevron erm., WARWICK.

✠ S' ELE · BASSET · COMITISSE · WAREWYKIE.

℞. Pointed oval counterseal, same size.　Within a circular panel, with quatrefoil opening and trefoils in the spandrils, a shield of arms : three bars wavy, BASSET.　In the field two lioncels rampant, derived from her paternal arms (see *obv.*), one above, one below the panel.

SIGILLVM : ELE : BASSET : COMITISSE : WAREVYKIE.

Beaded borders.

W. L. Bowles, *Annals of Lacock Abbey*, 1835, pl. iii., p. 162.

Another Seal.

6580. Pale-green : fine, fragmentary.　About 2 × 1¼ in. when perfect.　[Harl. ch. 54 D. 15.]

Pointed oval.　In dress and cloak, betw. two shields of arms. Standing.　Arms : r. three bars wavy, BASSET ; l. wanting.

Legend wanting.

See Hoare, *Wilts, Old and New Sarum*, p. 40.

Eustachius [Eustachia] Basset, [*wife of* RICHARD DE
CAMPVILLA, *of Bicester, co. Oxon.*]

6581. [*Temp.* Joh.]　Greenish-yellow, mottled : fine, imperfect.　With mark of the handle.　2 × 1¼ in.　[Add. ch. 10,594.]

Pointed oval.　To the l.　Standing, wearing ·a long dress, in the r. h. a fleur-de-lis.

✠ SIGILLVM EVSTACHIVS (*sic*) BASSET.

The S's are reversed.

6582. [*circ.* A.D. 1205–1215.] Dark-green: chipped. [Add. ch. 10,601.]

6583. [*circ.* A.D. 1200.] Green: cracked and indistinct. [Add. ch. 10,605.]

6584. [A.D. 1205–1215.] Mottled-green: imperfect and indistinct. [Add. ch. 10,607.]

Johanna Basset.

6585. [13th cent.] Plaster cast from impression. $1\frac{1}{4} \times \frac{3}{4}$ in. [lxxviii. 21.]

Pointed oval. Standing on a corbel, with flat cap, girdled dress and cloak, a hawk on the r. wrist.

✠ SECRETVM TEGO IOHANNE.

Beaded borders.

Margaret Basset, *Widow,* [*of Quorndon, co. Leic.*]

6586. [*Temp.* Hen. III. or Edw. I.] Light-brown: chipped. $1\frac{1}{2} \times 1$ in. [Cott. ch. xxiii. 2.]

Pointed oval. Standing on a carved corbel, with cloak and long head-dress, in each hand a shield of arms: r. indistinct; l. a bend and chief.

[✠ S]IGILLVM SECRETI.

6587. Sulph. cast. [D.E., E. 288.]

Isabella, [*widow of* WARIN] **de Bassingburne,**
[*of Brettenham, cos. Norf. and Cambr.*]

6588. [*Temp.* Edw. I.] Light-brown, mottled: fine. $1\frac{1}{2} \times \frac{7}{8}$ in. [Add. ch. 22,566.]

Pointed oval. To the r. Standing on a carved corbel, with long dress and head-dress, on the r. wrist a hawk, in the l., over her arm, by the strap a shield of arms: gyronny of eight, BASSINGBOURNE.

✠ S' ISABELLE DE BASSINGBVRNE.

Alexandria *fil.* **Radulphi Bernardi,** [*of Hundington or Honington, co. Linc.*]

6589. [12th cent.] Red: chipped, with mark of the handle. $2\frac{1}{4} \times 1\frac{1}{2}$ in. [Egert. ch. 428.]

Pointed oval. Standing, with long dress and maunches, lifting up the hands. Her hair long.

✠ SIGILLVM · ALEXANDRIE · FILIE · RADVLFI · BERNARDI.

6590. [*circ.* A.D. 1172.] Green, varnished: chipped. [Egert. ch. 434.]

Agatha La Bernarde, [*widow of Sir* RALPH LE FITZ BERNARD.]

6591. Red: fine originally, now chipped and imperfect. $1\frac{3}{4} \times 1\frac{1}{8}$ in. [Add. ch. 19,989.]

Pointed oval. In long flowing dress charged with crosslets, fur cloak, flat head-dress with hanging folds, in each hand a shield of arms. Standing on a carved corbel. Arms: r. vairé on a chief two mullets, FITZ-BERNARD; l. a cross chequy, DE LA LEE? In the field on each side a fleur-de-lis.

S' ... ATHE LA ᴬᴿ B ...... RDE.

Beaded borders.

Matilda Bigot, *Countess of Norfolk and Warren;* [*daughter of* WILLIAM MARESCHAL, *Earl of Pembroke, and widow of* HUGH BIGOT, *Earl of Norfolk; wife of* WILLIAM DE WARREN, *Count of Warren and Earl of Surrey.*]

6592. [A.D. 1241–1245.] Pale greenish-white: only fine fragment of the centre part. About $2\frac{1}{8} \times 1\frac{3}{4}$ in. when perfect. [Harl. ch. 46 D. 41.]

∅. Pointed oval. Standing, wearing a long dress and cloak, betw. two elegantly designed scrolls of foliage.

Legend wanting.

℞. A shield of arms: chequy, WARREN. Remainder of the design and legend wanting.

Cf. Harl. ch. 46 D. 38.

Ysabela [*fil.* WALTERI] **de Bolebec,** [*wife of* ALBERIC DE VER, *of Wavenden, co. Buck.*]

6593. [*Temp.* Joh.] Yellowish-brown, varnished: edge chipped. $1\frac{7}{8} \times 1\frac{1}{4}$ in. [Add. ch. 6026.]

Pointed oval. Standing, with a long dress, in the r. h. a wavy branch.

✠ SIGILL' YSABELE · DE · BOLEBE[C.]

Cf. Harl. ch. 57 C. 3.

Constance, [*dau. of Count* CONAN,] *Duchess of Brittany, Countess of Richmond.*

6594. [A.D. 1190–1198.] Pale greenish-white: points broken and edge chipped; originally fine. About $3\frac{1}{3} \times 2\frac{1}{4}$ in. when perfect. [Cott. ch. xi. 45.]

Pointed oval. To the r. Standing, with tightly-fitting dress, long fur-lined cloak fastened at the throat, in the r. h. a lily-flower, on the l. h. a hawk with long jesses.

...... C]ONSTANCIA DVCIS ....

The N's reversed.

6595. Sulph. cast. [D.C., D. 214.]

Eva de Broc.

6596. [Late 12th cent.] Plaster cast from fine but chipped impression. $2 \times 1\frac{1}{4}$ in. [lxxviii. 48.]

Pointed oval. To the r., with girdled dress and mantle, on the l. wrist a large falcon.

✠ SIGILL' · EVE · [D]E · BROC.

Ysabella de Brus, [*dau. of Earl* DAVID.]

6597. [Early 13th cent.] . Dark - green, mottled : fine.
1⅞ × 1⅝ in. [Add. ch. 28,479.]

Pointed oval. Standing on an elegantly carved corbel,
with long dress, cloak, and head-dress, in the r. h. a fleur-
de-lis, the l. h. on the breast. In the field on each side a
wavy sprig of foliage.

✠ SIGILLVM : YSABELLE : DE : BRVS :

Beaded borders.

See Laing's *Suppl.,* No. 145, where an engraving is given, but the
description is erroneous. Cf. xlvii. 1197.

Cecilia, [*dau. of* SABELINA, *and wife ? of*] **Laurencius
Bucuinte,** [*of Southwark, co. Surr.*]

6598. [13th cent.] Green : edge chipped ; app. by a
woven cord of faded stuff. About 3 × 1¾ in. when perfect.
[Harl. ch. 50 B. 33.]

Pointed oval. To the r. Standing, with tightly - fitting
dress, long maunches, head-dress, in the r. h. a fleur-de-lis on
a stem, the l. h. resting on the hip.

SIGILLVM CECILIE . . . . RENCII BVCVINTE.

· Anastasia de Burgate.

6599. [13th cent.] Plaster cast from fine impression.
1¼ × ¾ in. [lxxviii. 54.]

Pointed oval. Standing, with flat-cap and long dress, short
sleeves, on the l. wrist a falcon by the jesses.

S' : ANASTASIE D' BVRGAT'.

Burgesia, sister of Walter Burre.

6600. [12th cent.] . Plaster cast from chipped impression.
2⅜ × 1⅞ in. [lxxix. 63.]

' Oval. Standing full-face, with pleated petticoat, in the l. h.
a fleur-de-lis on a long stem.

✠ SIG[I]LLVM · BVR · ESIE . . . . . I · BVRRE.

Margaret, dau. of WILLIAM, king of Scotland ;
[<i>Countess of Kent, widow of</i> HUBERT DE BURGH,
Earl of Kent.]

6601. [*circ.* A.D. 1250.] Creamy - white : cracked and
imperfect. Originally fine. About 2⅛ × 1½ in. when perfect.
App. by a plaited cord of red silk strands. [Harl. ch. 43 B. 7.]

Pointed oval. Standing on . a carved corbel, with long
dress and cloak, in the l. h. a hawk.

. . . . FILI . . . . . .

Sibilla de Calna, [*or* **Caune,** *of Burnham, co. Ess.*]

6602. [*Temp.* Hen. III.] Creamy-white: fine, with mark of the handle. 1¾ × 1 in. [Harl. ch. 47 H. 37.]

Pointed oval. Standing on a carved corbel, with tight dress and cloak, on the r. h. a lily flower, the l. h. on the breast.

⌣ SIGLL' · SIBILLE : DE · CALNA.

The N reversed.

6603. Dark-green : fine. [Harl. ch. 52 C. 48.]

6604. Sulph. cast. [D.C., E. 287.]

Miramonda de Calnby, [*seal used by* ALICE DE LANGELE, *widow, of co. Oxon.*]

6605. [*circ.* A.D. 1275.] Red : chipped, indistinct in places. 1⅛ in. [Add. ch. 10,606.]

Within a carved gothic quatrefoil. Standing, with long dress and head-dress, holding in front a shield of arms : a fess betw. three indistinct charges. In the field, on each side a shield of arms : r. on a cross some indistinct charges ; l. three escallops, two and one.

✜ S' MIRAMONDA · DE · CALNBY.

Alicia Capra.

6606. [12th cent.] Plaster cast from fine but imperfect impression. 2¾ × 1⅝ in. [lxxviii. 61.]

Pointed oval. To the r. In a tightly-fitting dress, with long maunches, conical head-dress. Standing on a small *goat* to the r., in allusion to the surname.

✠ SIGILLVM : ALICIE : CAPRE.

Matillis de Chauz, [*of cos. Linc. and Nott.*]

6607. [13th cent.] Yellowish - brown : very fine, with marks of the handle. 1¼ × ¾ in. [Harl. ch. 112 G. 53.]

Pointed oval. To the r. In tightly-fitting dress, standing, in the l. h. by the jesses a small hawk.

✠ SIGILLVM MATILLIDIS DE CHAVZ.

The legend on a raised or bevelled rim.

Matillis, *Countess of Chester,* [*wife of* RANDLE DE GERNONS, *Earl of Chester,* A.D. 1128, *daughter of* ROBERT THE CONSUL, *Earl of Gloucester.*]

6608. [Mid. 12th cent.] Creamy-white, with dark-brown varnish : very imperfect and indistinct. About 2¼ × 1¾ in. when perfect. [Stowe Collection : Repingdon charter, 2.]

Pointed oval. In tight-fitting dress and a long maunch, standing.

Legend wanting.

Bertrea [*or* **Brettya**], *Countess of Chester,* [*wife of* HUGH
KEVELIOC, *3rd Earl, ob.* A.D. 1181, *dau. of* SIMON,
Count of Evereux.]
6609. [End of 12th cent.] Plaster cast from indistinct
impression. 2¾ × 1¾ in. [lxxix. 74.]
Pointed oval. Full-face, tightly-fitting dress with long
maunches at the wrists, standing.
✠ SIGILL' BERTREE COMITISSE CESTRIE.

Matillis de Chissindone, [*widow of* ROBERT
DE CHISSENDUNE, *of Beddington, co. Surr.*]
6610. [*post* A.D. 1228.] Brownish-green: fine, fragment
only. About 1⅝ × 1 in. when perfect. [Add. ch. 23,021.]
Pointed oval. To the r. Tightly-fitting dress and long
cloak, in the l. h. a hawk. Standing.
✠ S' M . . . . SINDONE.
The N's are reversed.

Lucia de Chokefeld, [*or* **Cockefeld,** *of Charwelton,*
co. Northampton.]
6611. [*circ.* A.D. 1200–1208.] Dark-green: fine. 2 × 1¼ in.
[Harl. ch. 85 B. 17.]
Pointed oval. To the l. Tightly-fitting dress, long head-
dress, in the r. h. a lily flower or fleur-de-lis. Standing.
✠ SIGILL' . LVCIE DE CHOKEFELD'.
6612. Sulph. cast. [D.C., D. 215.]
6613. [Early 13th cent.] Discoloured - yellow: edge
chipped. [Harl. ch. 85 B. 18.]

Matillis, *Countess of Clare,* [*dau. of* JAMES DE ST. HILLARY,
and wife of ROGER DE CLARE, *3rd Earl of Hereford.*]
6614. [A.D. 1170–1174.] Pale brownish-green, varnished
red: very imperfect. About 2¾ × 1½ in. when perfect. [Add.
ch. 21,703.]
Oval. To the l., and her attendant to the r., standing. The
attendant is handing to the countess a hawk with jesses on
a staff.
. . . . ILLVM COMI . . . .

Floria de Cleford, [*or* **de Prestone,** *widow of* ROGER
FOLIOT, *of Thornborough, co. Buck.*]
6615. [A.D. 1282.] Dark-green: fair, well preserved.
[Harl. ch. 86 C. 7.]
Pointed oval. In long dress, head-dress, holding before her
an uncertain object. Standing on a corbel.
✠ S' FLORIE DE CLEFORD.
Cf. Harl. ch. 86 C. 6, A.D. 1282.

Cecilia, *uxor* Radulfi Cofinel.

6616. [12th cent.] Plaster cast from fine impression, chipped at points. 1⅝ × 1 in. [lxxviii. 71.]

Pointed oval. To the l. In tightly-fitting dress. Standing on a corbel or pedestal.

[✠ S'] CECIL' VXORI[S R]ADVL' COFINEL.

The OR in *vxoris* conjoined ; the N reversed.

Elizabeth [*wife of* SIR HUGH] de Coleworth, [*of Horndon-on-the-Hill, co. Essex.*]

6617. [*Temp.* Hen. III. or Edw. I.] Dark-green : fine. 2 × 1⅛ in. [Add. ch. 19,976.]

Pointed oval. In long dress, fur cloak, flat head-dress, in the r. hand a shield of arms: vairé, a bend. Cf. the arms of COLTWORT (vairé). On the l. h. a hawk with bells and jesses. Standing on a carved corbel. In the field, on each side, a wavy branch of flowers.

✠ S' ELIZABETH DE COLEWORTHE.

Beaded borders.

6618. [*Temp.* Hen. III.] Brownish-green : upper point broken off. [Harl. ch. 48 G. 25.]

6619. [*Temp.* Hen. III.] Light-brown, semi-opaque : fine, upper point broken off. [Harl. ch. 48 G. 26.]

6620. Sulph. cast. [D.C., E. 279.]

Johanna de Coruhill' (? Cornhill.)

6621. [Early 13th cent.] Plaster cast from fine impression, points slightly chipped. 1¾ × 1⅛. [lxxviii. 74.]

Pointed oval. To the r. In tightly-fitting dress, flat head-dress, long mantle, a falcon on the l. wrist. Standing on a cushion.

✠ SIGILLVM IOHANNE : DE CORVHILL'.

Beaded borders.

Petronilla [de] Crou[n.]

6622. [*ob.* 46 Hen. III.] Plaster cast from fine but imperfect impression. [lxxix. 33.]

Pointed oval. In dress of heraldic bearings : lozengy, CROUN, flat head-dress, and mantle, in the r. h. a shield of arms : three crescents, LONGCHAMPE. Standing on a carved corbel.

. . . LLVM : PETRO[NI]LLE . . OROV . .

Petronilla de Creoun was dau. of Guy, Baron Creon, and married (1) Henry de Mora, (2) Oliver Vaux, (3) William de Longchamp. She died in 46 Hen. III. (Nichols, *Hist. of Leic.*, vol. ii., p. 28.)

A lady's seal used by
Thomas Cursoun, [*cf Byntre, co. Norfolk.*]
6623. [A.D. 1370.] Brownish-green : edge chipped, cracked.
⅝ in. [Harl. ch. 58 C. 5.]
To the r. Standing within a carved and pointed gothic
quatrefoil, holding out her arms to a small hound or *brachet,*
leaping up to her. In the field three small quatrefoil "flowers
of love."
✠ VN · BRACHET · OV · MOVN · QVER · EST.
The N's are reversed.
6624. [A.D. 1370.] Brownish-green : chipped and indistinct in places. [Harl. ch. 58 C. 6.]

P Matildis Donet, *or* **Ronet,** [*wife of* JOHN WINCHESTER.]
6625. [A.D. 1313.] Plaster cast from fine impression.
1⅜ × ⅞ in. [lxxxi. 52.]
Pointed oval. Full-face. In long dress, fur-lined cloak,
low pointed head-dress, in each hand a shield of arms.
Standing on a corbel. Arms : r. a lion rampant ; l., chequy,
on a chief two estoiles.
S' MATILDIS · DONET or RONET. (?)

Letia, [*dau. of* PETER] **de Edisfeld,** (*son of* WILLIAM, *son of*
PETER DE EDISFELD), [*of Ridlington, co. Norf*]
6626. [Early 13th cent.] Green, mottled : fine, imperfect,
chipped at the top. About 2⅜ × 1₁₆⁵ in. when perfect. [Harl.
ch. 49 G. 21.]
Pointed oval. To the r. In tight-fitting dress, holding,
with both hands before her, an indistinct object. Standing.
In the field, on each side, an estoile of eight points.
. . . IG ; . . M : LECIE : DE : . . . . GES . . . .
Beaded borders.

A lady's seal used by
Thomas Elyngham, *Esq.,* [*of Weldon, co. Northt.*]
6627. [A.D. 1454.] Red : from a ring. ₁₆⁹ in. [Add. ch.
808.]
To the l. With peculiar mitre-shaped head-dress, in each
hand, a branch of three quatrefoil "flowers of love." Standing. In the field a motto :—
LA . . . IR . . . . A D . . . S (?)

Johanna, [*widow of* SIR JOHN] **Engayne,** [*of Blatterwick,
co. Northt.*]
6628. [13th cent.] Green : fine, imperfect. About
1¾ × 1⅛ in. when perfect. [Add. ch. 21,545.]
Pointed oval. In tightly-fitting dress, cloak, flat head-dress,

in the l. h. a shield of arms. Standing on a corbel. Arms:
eight martlets, four, three, and one : the corresponding shield
or other object in the r. h. is wanting.

SIGILL' IOHANNE . . . .

Beaded borders.

Emma de Etuna, [*wife of* REGINALD HARANG.]
6629. [*Temp.* Hen. II.] Plaster cast from fine but chipped
impression. $2\frac{1}{8} \times 1\frac{3}{8}$ in. [lxxix. 34.]
In girdled dress, long mantle, in the r. h. a fleur-de-lis on a
long stem, on the l. h. a falcon by the jesses. Standing.

[✠ S]IGI[L]LVM : EMΩE : DE ETVN[A].

Johanna Ferrers?
6630. [13th cent.] Sulph. cast from fine impression.
$1\frac{5}{8} \times 1$ in. [D.C., F. 616.]
Pointed oval. In tightly-fitting dress, cloak, flat head-
dress, in each hand by the strap a shield of arms. Standing
on a carved corbel. Arms: r. a cross moline ; l. vairé, a
bordure charged with nine horseshoes.

☽ ⚜ SIGILLYM ✖ IOHANNE ✖

Beaded borders.

Margreta, [*fil.* YSABEL,] *fil.* **Alulfi** [DE MERCH, *wife of*
ROGER DE BRAY, *of Whitfield, co. Northt.*]
6631. [Early 13th cent.] Creamy-white, with a yellow
varnish : edge chipped. $3 \times 1\frac{3}{4}$ in. [Harl. ch. 84 I. 22.]
Pointed oval. Standing, with long tightly-fitting dress
having long maunches, in each hand an ornamental fleur-
de-lis.

⚜ HOC ≈ SIGILLVM MARGRETE FIL . . . . I.

The use of the sign for *est* is remarkable in the legend.
6632. Sulph. cast. [D.C., D. 213.]

Avicia, *fil.* **Herberti,** [*widow of* ROBERT BLUND,
of Southwark, co. Surr.]
6633. [Early 13th cent.] Brown : fine, with mark of
handle. $1\frac{5}{8} \times 1$ in. [Harl. ch. 83 D. 30.]
Pointed oval. To the l. In long dress, cloak, in the r. h.
a fleur-de-lis. Standing.

⚜ SIGILL' · AVICIE · FILIE · HERBERTI.

6634. Sulph. cast. [D.C., E. 286.]

Maria *fil.* **Laurencii** [ROTOMAGENSIS, *of Southwark,
co. Surr.*]
6635. [12th cent.] Green, mottled : fine, edge chipped.
$2\frac{1}{4} \times 1\frac{5}{8}$ in. [Cott. ch. v. 11.]

Pointed oval. To the r. In tightly-fitting dress with maunch on the l. wrist, fibula at neck, necklace, long riband from the back of the head or neck (perhaps the hair), in the l. h. an ornamental fleur-de-lis, the r. h. on the hip. Standing.

.. IGILL' · MARIE ... LIE LAVRENCI ...

6636. Sulph. cast. [D.C., D. 210.]

Liece, *fil.* **Radulfi** [ROTOMAGENSIS, *dau. of*
RALPH OF ROUEN *and of* MARIA, *dau. of*
LAWRENCE OF ROUEN,* *of Southwark, co. Surr.*]
6637. [12th cent.] Dark-green: fine, edge chipped. About
$2\frac{1}{2} \times 1\frac{5}{8}$ in. [Harl. ch. 50 B. 23.]
Pointed oval. To the r. In tightly-fitting dress, with ornamental maunches, long riband plaited from the back of the head (perhaps the hair) tied in three tails at the end, in the l. h. an ornamental fleur-de-lis. Standing.

.. GILLVM · LIECE .... LIE · RADVLFI.

6638. Plaster cast. [lxxxi. 38.]
6639. Sulph. cast. [D.C., D. 209.]

Cristina, *fil.* **Rogeri de ... ail (?)**
6640. [Late 12th cent.] Sulph. cast from good impression, indistinct in places. $1\frac{7}{8} \times 1\frac{1}{4}$ in. [D.C., D. 216.]
Pointed oval. In tightly-fitting dress, girdled at the waist, in the r. h. an ornamental fleur-de-lis or lily flower, in the l. h. a hawk with long jesses. Standing.

SIGILL' CRISTINE FIL' RO[GE]RI D' · · · IL'. (?)

The NE in Christine conjoined.
6641. Plaster cast. [lxxxi. 21.] !

SIGILL' CRISTINE FIL' · ROG D' · · · AIL'. (?)

Emma, *fil.* **Rogeri.**
6642. [13th cent.] Plaster cast from fine impression, chipped at points. $1\frac{1}{2} \times 1$ in. [lxxix. 15.]
Pointed oval. To the r. In dress, mantle, long hair, in the r. h. a fleur-de-lis. Standing.

✠ SIGILL' EMME FILIE ROGERI.

Mahaut de [Luv]etot, [*or* **Matildis,** *dau. of*
WILLIAM DE LUVETOT, *widow of* GERARD DE FURNIVAL,
2nd Baron, of Grassthorp, co. Nott.]
6643. [*circ.* A.D. 1254–1268.] Green: fine, sharp, edge chipped; app. by a woven cord of red silk. About $2\frac{1}{4} \times 1\frac{3}{8}$ in. [Harl. ch. 112 I. 55.]
Pointed oval. To the r. In tightly-fitting dress, brooch at

---

* See previous seal.

the throat, girdle, mantle of fur, flat head-dress, in her l. h. a lily flower. Standing on a platform.

✠ SIGILLVM : MAHAVT : DE : . . . ETOT · FILIE : WILELMI.

Johanna Gacelin.
(*A doubtful seal.*) ·

6644. [13th cent.] Plaster cast from somewhat indistinct impression. 1⅜ × ⅞ in. [lxxviii. 57.]

Pointed oval. In girdled dress, long cloak, head-dress, in the l. h. a shield of arms ; indistinct. Standing on a corbel. In the field on each side a wavy branch in flower.

✠ S' IOHANNE GACELIN.

Rohais, *uxor* Gilleberti de Gant, [*Earl of Lincoln ; dau. of* WILLIAM DE ROMARA, *Earl of Lincoln.*]

6645. [A.D. 1149–1156.] Red : fine, well preserved. 2¾ × 1⅞ in. [Harl. ch. 50 F. 32.]

Pointed oval. In long dress with ornamental pattern on it, in the r. h. a lily, in the l. h. a fleur-de-lis.. Standing. In the field on the r. a waved sprig, on the l. a quatrefoil.

✠ SIGILL . . . . HAIS. VXORIS GILLEBER . . . . . E GANT.

The letters OR in *uxoris*, and NT in *Gant* conjoined.

6646. Sulph. cast. [D.C., D. 207.]

Sibilla, [*widow of* HUGH] Gargate [*al.* SIBILLA DE KAUERSFELD, *of Stratton Audley, co. Oxon.*]

6647. [A.D. 1226–1232.] Dark - green, mottled : fine, chipped at top. 1¾ × 1⅞ in. [Add. ch. 10,608.]

Pointed oval. In long dress, cloak, flat head-dress, in the r. h. a lily flower, the l. h. on the breast. · Standing on a carved corbel.

✠ SIGILLVM SIBILLE GARGATE.

Mabilia de Gattona.

6648. [13th cent.] Light brownish-green : fine, edge chipped. 2 in. [xxxvi. 218.]

To the l. In long dress, head-dress, a hawk on the l. hand. Riding sideways.* Horse with ornamental breast-band and fringed saddle.

✠ SIGILLV . . MABILIE : DE : GATTONA.

Matildis, *uxor* Godefridi.

· **6649.** [*Temp.* Hen. III.] Dark-green : fine, upper point chipped. 1⅛ × 1 in. [xxxv. 295.]

---

* See *Egert. MS.* 1994, f. 164, b, for introduction of the side-saddle by Anne of Bohemia in 1382.

. Pointed oval. To the r. In the l. h. a fleur-de-lis. Standing.

S' MATILDIS · WX · GODE[F'.]

6650. Plaster cast. [lxxxix. 24.]

Isolda de Grai, [*wife of* REGINALD DE MENDRY, *of Calver, co. Derb.*]

6651. [A.D. 1239.] Creamy-white : imperfect, indistinct. About $1\frac{3}{4} \times 1\frac{1}{8}$ in. when perfect. [Lansd. ch. 584.].

Pointed oval. In tightly-fitting dress, flat head-dress. in the r. h. a lily flower. Standing.

.... Є · DЄ · GRAI.

Alicia, *uxor* Willelmi Grandorge.

6652. [A.D. 1218.] Plaster cast from fine impression. $1\frac{1}{2} \times 1$ in. [lxxix. 25.]

· Pointed oval. · To the l. · With long queue of hair, in the r. h. a branch of foliage. Standing.

✿ ꙄIGILL' ALIϹIЄ VXORIꙄ WILL'I GRAИDORGЄ.

The S's and N reversed ; the letters DOR in the last word conjoined.

Paulina, [*widow of* JOHANNES DE GRAS, *Miles, of Stanford Rivers, co. Essex.*]

6653. [A.D. 1348.] Green : faded. $1\frac{1}{4} \times \frac{11}{16}$ in. [Add. ch. 19,986.]

Oval. In long dress, fur cloak, in the r. h. a hawk, in the l. h. a lure. Standing on a corbel. In the field the initials of the lady, P. M., and two wavy sprigs each with as many roses.

S' AMORIS ✿ DVLCЄDINЄ ✿ ж

6654. [A.D. 1348.] Green : faded. [Add. ch. 19,987.]

Hadewisa Gumin.

6655. [Early 12th cent.] Plaster cast from chipped and indistinct impression. $3 \times 1\frac{1}{2}$ in. . [lxxix. 31.]

Pointed oval. Full-length. In tightly-fitting dress, long maunches, on the l. wrist a falcon drinking from a saucer (?). Standing.

Legend indistinct.

[V]NDA ...... VS ..... W .. ЄVA ...

Elizabeth, Dame de Gunstorp P [*wife of* W. GUNSTORP.]·

6656. [A.D. 1342.] Plaster cast from fine impression, indistinct in places. $\frac{7}{8} \times \frac{3}{4}$ in. [lxxix. 29.]

Oval. Full-face, within a carved border. In dress, head-dress, mantle, betw. two shields of arms set upon the carving.

2 C 2

Standing. Arms: r. a stag lodged, on a chief two buckles : l. four fusils in fess within a bordure engrailed, NEVILLE ?

S' ELIZABET DÃE DE G ... STOR ..

Sibilla de Gurnai, [*of co. Somers.*]

6657. [13th cent.] Plaster cast from fine impression. 1¾ × ⅞ in. [lxxix. 32.]

Pointed oval. To the r. In flat head-dress, girdled dress, long mantle, on the l. wrist a falcon, by the jesses. Standing on a carved corbel.

✠ SIGILL' ꞉ SIBILLE : D' : GVRNAI :

Beaded borders.

Collectanea Archæologica, vol. ii., p. 210.

Matildis, [*widow of* D. WILL.] de Hardredeshilla, [*Miles, of Westleton, co. Suff.*]

6658. [*Temp.* Edw. I.] Brown : imperfect. [Harl. ch. 83 F. 12.]

Pointed oval. [At her feet a small dog, statant,] another in her arms. Standing.

✠ KI : ME RE[C]EIT : SEIT ꞉ BE]NEIT.

Gundrea L'Hausard, [*of Caterham, co. Surr.*]

6659. [13th cent.] Creamy-white : fine, cracked, chipped. 1½ × 1 in. [Add. ch. 20,037.]

Pointed oval. In long dress, cloak, flat head-dress, in the l. h. a hawk, the r. h. on the breast. Standing on a corbel.

✠ SIGILL GVNDREE L'HAVSARD.

The letters ND in *Gundree* conjoined.

Idonia, *fil.* Ricardi .. He .. nest .. [*wife of* HENRY DE COCHE, *of London.*]

6660. [A.D. 1243.] Dark-green : imperfect and indistinct. About 1½ × 1 in. [Harl. ch. 48 F. 27.]

Pointed oval. To the l. In the l. h. a flower, the r. h. on the breast. Standing.

..... NIE · FIL' · RIC[A]RDI · HE · · NEST ..

6661. Sulph. cast. [D.C., E. 280.]

Idonia de Herst, [*Lady of Promhill, co. Kent.*]

6662. [Late 12th cent.] Pale, semi-opaque brown : fine, edge chipped. 2¾ × 1¾ in. [L. F. C. xxv. 20.]

Pointed oval. In long tightly-fitting dress, long maunches, heart-shaped brooch, in the r. h. a lily flower or double fleur-de-lis, on the l. h. a hawk with long jesses. Standing.

✠ SIGILLVM IDONIE DE HERST.

Matildis de Hohtune, [*dau. of* PAGAN DE HOHTUN, *wife of* ROB. GRIMBALD, *of Houghton, co. Northt.*]

6663. [*circ.* A.D. 1170.] Creamy-white : the points broken off ; app. by a plaited cord of woven bobbins diapered of several colours. About 2⅜ × 1⅝ in. [Harl. ch. 86 C. 40.]

Pointed oval. In tightly-fitting dress, long maunches, hair or head-dress, on the r. h. a hawk, in the l. h. a fleur-de-lis or lily flower. Standing.

SIGILLVM MA . . . . DE HOHTVNE.

6664. Sulph. cast. [D.C., D. 218.]

Another Seal.

6665· [Late Hen. II.] Pale brownish-white with dark-brown varnish : very imperfect. About 2¼ × 1¼ in. when perfect. [Add. ch. 6025.]

Pointed oval. In long dress, cloak. Standing.

. . . . . GILL' . . . . . DIS · FILIE . . . . . .

Cf. Harl. ch. 84 D. 1 (*circ.* A.D. 1150–1160) ; 86 C. 41.

Matilda de Hosdeng, [*dau. of* CRISTINA, *of Ham, co. Ess.*]

6666. [12th–13th cent.] Light-green : imperfect and indistinct ; app. by a thick piece of leather. [Harl. ch. 51 G. 41.]

Pointed oval. To the r. In tightly-fitting dress, and long maunches, on the l. h. a hawk. Standing.

SIGILLVM MA . . . . DEN . . .

Amica, *fil.* **Hugonis de Huesd'n.**

6667. [13th cent.] Plaster cast from chipped impression. 1⅝ × 1 in. [lxxix. 43.]

Pointed oval. To the l. In tightly-fitting dress, in the r. h. a flower on a long stalk. Standing.

SIGILL' AMICE · FIL' · HVG : D'HVESD'N.

Sibilla de Ikelesham, [*of Icklesham, co. Suss.*]

6668. [*Temp.* Edw. I.] Dark-green : indistinct in parts. 1⅝ × 1⅛ in. [Add. ch. 20,093.]

Pointed oval. In long dress, cloak, head-dress, in the l. h. a fleur-de-lis. Standing on a corbel. In the field on the l. a word, EVA (?).

⚜ SIGILL' : SIBILLE : DE : IKELESHAM.

Petronella de Kemesek, [*wife of* EDMUND DE KEMESEK ; *dau. and coheir of* HUGH DE POLESTED, *of co. Norf.*]

6669. [*Temp.* Edw. I.] Red : fine, edge slightly chipped. 1½ × ⅝ in. [xxxv. 277.]

Pointed oval. In long dress, fur cloak, head-dress, in each

hand a shield of arms: r. fretty, POLSTODD; l. a chief
indented, KEMESEK. (Cf. per fess indented, KEMELICKE.)
Standing on a dog or lion couchant to the l. In the field on
each side a wyvern sans wings.

S' PETRONELLE DE KEMESEK.

Cf. Blomefield, *Hist. of Norfolk*, vol. vii., p. 33.

Hawisia, *Domina de* KEVEOLOC, *co. Merioneth.* (?) [*dau. of*
OWEN DE LA POLE, *wife of Sir* JOHN CHARLTON,
of Powys.]

6670. [Early 14th cent.] Plaster cast from fine impression.
$1\frac{7}{8} \times 1\frac{1}{8}$ in. [lxxix. 73.]
Pointed oval. Full-face, on a corbel, flat head-dress with
hair in a network, wimple, girdled dress, long cloak, standing;
round the neck a necklet with pendent jewel, in each hand a
shield of arms: r. a lion rampant; l. two lions passant in pale.

✸ S' HAWISIE DNE DE KEVEOLOC.

Beaded borders.

6671. Another, very fine. [lxxix. 73 B.]

Aliscia de Langgelee.

6672. [13th cent.] Plaster cast from fine impression.
$1\frac{3}{8} \times \frac{7}{8}$ in. [lxxix. 86.]
Pointed oval. Full-face, in long dress. In the r. h. a
shield of arms held by a strap: a bar or fess, in chief a label.
On the l. h. a falcon. Standing on a corbel.

✸ SIGILLVM ALISCIE D' · LANGGELEE.

Alesya de Lascy, [*or* Aleis de Lasci, *widow of*
EDMUND DE LASCI, *2nd Earl of Lincoln;*
dau. of the Marquis DE SALUCES.]

6673. [A.D. 1310.] Red: fine, chipped. $2\frac{1}{8} \times 1\frac{3}{4}$ in.
[Add. ch. 20,568.]
Pointed oval. In long dress, girdle, cloak, flat cap or
head-dress, in her r. h. a jewel, the l. touching a shield of
arms. Standing on an elaborately carved corbel. In the
field, on each side, on a tree, a shield of arms, slung by the
strap: l. three garbs, two and one, LACY OF CHESTER; r. a
chief, SALUCES.

✸ SIGILLV ALESYE DE LASCY.

6674. [A.D. 1310.] Red: very fine, imperfect and discoloured in parts. [Add. ch. 7677.]

6675. Plaster cast from fine impression. $2\frac{1}{8} \times 1\frac{1}{4}$ in.
[lxxix. 83.]

✸ SIGILLV · ALESYE DE LASCY.

Beaded borders.

Margareta de Lascy, *Countess of Lincoln and Pembroke,*
dau. of ROB. QUINCY, *Earl of Winchester, widow of*
JOHN, *Earl of Lincoln, and* WALTER, *Earl of Pembroke.*
 6676. [*post* : A.D. 1245.] Green, mottled : fine, edge
chipped. About 2¾ × 1¾ in. when perfect. [L. F. C., v. 4.]
 Pointed oval. In long dress, fur cloak, flat head-dress, the
l. h. on the breast, in the r. h. a shield of arms. Standing.
Above her head a carved canopy, consisting of a round-headed
arch, enriched with battlements. In the field on the r. a shield
of arms: a lion rampant, LACY; on the l., held by the countess,
another, indistinct.
 . . . . [MA]RGARETE : . . . .

Sibilla de Lundonie.

 6677. [Late 12th cent.] Plaster cast from a fine impression or from the matrix. Edge bevelled. Mark of the
handle remaining. 2⅛ × 1⅜ in. [lxxxvi. 42.]
 Pointed oval. In long tight dress, short cloak, long
maunches at the wrists. Long hair. In the r. h. a flower,
in the l. h. a hawk.
 ✠ SIGILLV · SIBILLE · DE LVNDONIE.
 The N's reversed.

Ela, *Comitissa Saresberie,* [*dau. of* WILLIAM D'EVREUX,
2nd Earl of Salisbury ; widow of WILLIAM LONGESPEE I.,
son of Henry II. and " Fair Rosamond."]
 6678. [*post* A.D. 1226.] Dark-green, mottled : fine, imperfect, upper part wanting. About 3 × 1⅞ in. when perfect.
App. by plaited cords of green silk. [Harl. ch. 53 B. 12.]
 Ø. Pointed oval. In long dress, girded at the waist, cloak,
the r. h. on the breast, in the l. h. an object now wanting.
Standing on an elegantly carved corbel. In the field on each
side a lioncel rampant reguardant, in allusion to the arms of
LONGESPEE.
 . . . . . LVM : ELE : COMI . . . S . . . . . . · . .
 ℞. A small shield-shaped counterseal. 1⅝ × 1⅜ in. A
shield of arms : six lioncels rampant, three, two, and one,
LONGESPEE.
 ✠ SECRETV ELE COMITISSE SARESBERIE.
 6679. Sulph. casts of *obv.* and *rev.* [D.C., E. 282, 283.]

Emelina Lungespeie, [*dau. and heir of·*
Sir WALTER DE RIDELSFORD, *Baron of Bray ;*
widow of HUGH DE LACY, *Earl of Ulster ;*
wife of STEPHEN DE LONGESPEE, *Justiciary of Ireland.*]
 6680. [A.D. 1250.] Plaster casts from fine impression.
2⅜ × 1⅜ in. [lxxix. 99, 100.]

Ø. Pointed oval. In flat head-dress, wimplē, long tightly-fitting dress, fur cloak, in each hand a shield of arms. Full-face, standing on a finely carved corbel, under a carved gothic canopy with three pinnacled turrets. Arms : r. a saltire, in chief over all a label of five points ; l. six lioncels, three, two, and one, a label of four points, LONGESPEE. In the field on each side a sword erect, point upwards, for LONGESPEE, or. for the office of JUSTICIARY OF IRELAND. Above the sword. a lion from the arms of *England*.

⦂ S'. EMELINE : LVNGESPEIE. ·

R. A small round counterseal. A shield of arms : as in *obv.*, betw. two swords at the sides, and a lion over the shield, as before.

✠ FOL : EST : KI : ME : BRISERA :
FOR : CELI : A KI : LA : LETTRE : VA.

Maheut de ———.

6681. [Early 12th cent.] Green, mottled : fine, imperfect. 2 × 1⅓ in. when perfect. [xxxix. 67.] Cut from a deed to which it was appended by a curiously woven flat bobbin with damask patterns, green and yellow, upon it.

Pointed oval. In long dress girded at the waist, in the r. h. a wavy branch of foliage, in the l. h. a seeded fleur-de-lis. Standing. In the field on the l. a tree elegantly designed.

. . . . ILLVM · MAHEVT · DE . . . .

Isabel [de Clare], *Comitissa Pembroc*, [*wife of* WILLIAM MARESCHAL, *Earl of Pembroke.*]

6682. [Before A.D. 1219.] Plaster cast from indistinct impression. 2 × 1⅛ in. [lxxx. 9.]

Pointed oval. Full-face. In tightly-fitting dress, pointed head-dress, long mantle, the r. h. laid on the breast, in the l. h. a falcon held on the wrist by the jesses. Standing,

. . . SIGILL' · ISABEL · COMITISSE · PEMBROC · VXORIS ·
WILL'I · MARESCA . . .

Alizia Mauduit, [*of London, widow of* WILLIAM THE CHAMBERLAIN, *son of* FULCRED DIVES, *of London.*]

6683. [*Temp.* Rich. I.] Dark-green : injured, imperfect. About 2¼ × 2 in. when perfect. [Harl. ch. 47 I. 7.]

Pointed oval. In tightly-fitting dress girded at the waist, long maunches, plaited hair, in the r. h. a fleur-de-lis. Standing.

SIGILLVM AL . . . , . E MAVD ... T.

Milisenta de Monte Alto, [*widow, of Barby, co. Northt.*]
     [*dau. of* WILLIAM DE CANTILUPE, *2nd wife of*
        JOHN DE MONTALT, *seneschal of Chester.*]

6684. [*Temp.* Edw. I.] Dark-green: fine, very imperfect.
$1\frac{3}{4} \times 1$. App. by a green silk plaited cord. [L. F. C.
viii. 10.]

For description see next seal, No. 6684*.

. . . . . . ISENTE · DE MONTE . . . . .

6684*. Plaster cast from a fine impression, slightly chipped.
[lxxxvii. 42.]

Pointed oval. In tightly-fitting dress, fur cloak, in each
hand a shield of arms. Standing on a carved corbel. Arms :
r. h. a lion rampant, MONTALT ; l. h. three leopards' heads
jessants-de-lis, CANTILUPE. In the field on each side a wavy
sprig of foliage.

S' MILISENTE · [DE] MONTE ALTO.

The letters A L in *Alto* are conjoined.

Cf. Ormerod, *Hist. of Cheshire*, vol. i., p. 55.

Dionisia de Monte Canisy, [*Domina de Anesty, co. Surr.*,
ob. A.D. 1313.]

6685. [Late 13th cent.] Plaster cast from a fine impression.
$1\frac{3}{4} \times 1\frac{1}{8}$ in. [lxxx. 14.]

Pointed oval. Full-face. In tightly-fitting dress, fur-lined
mantle, flat head-dress, in the r. h. a shield of arms. Standing
on a carved corbel. Arms : three escutcheons vairé, two and
one. Below the shield a squirrel ; on the r. in the field a
cinquefoil and a lion passant.

S'. DIONISIE : DE : MONTE CANISY.

Beaded border.

Cf. Manning and Bray, *History of Surrey*, vol. ii., p. 268.

Alianora, *Comitissa Leycestrie,* [*dau. of King John ;
Countess of Pembroke and Leicester ; widow of*
SIMON DE MONTFORT, *Earl of Leicester, who ob.* A.D. 1264.]

6686. Plaster cast from fine impression. $2\frac{1}{2} \times 1\frac{1}{3}$ in.
[lxxx. 18.]

Pointed oval. To the r. In long dress, mantle, flat head-
dress, at her feet a small dog. Standing on a carved corbel.
On the r. a branching tree, on which is a shield of arms : a
lion rampant queue fourchée, MONTFORT.

SIGILLVM : ALIANORE : COMITISSE : LEYCESTRIE.

Beaded borders.

Johanna, [*widow of* D. RICHARD DE MUNDEVILE,
of Thornborough, co. Buck.]

6687. [A.D. 1263.] Dark-green : well preserved. 1⅜ × 1¾ in.
[Harl. ch. 86 A. 26.]

Pointed oval. In tightly-fitting dress, cloak, flat head-dress,
on the l. h. a hawk. Standing on a platform.

✠ IE SV SEL A AMI LEL.

Dame **Nichola de Mundevile.**

6688. [13th cent.] Plaster cast from fine impression.
1⅛ × ⅞ in. [lxxx. 93.]

Pointed oval. Full-face. In long dress, flat head-dress,
in the r. h. a falcon by the jesses, in the l. hand a shield of
arms. Standing on a pedestal or cushion. Arms : a fret,
MUNDEVILE, debruised by a fess.

✠ S' DAME NICH DE MVNDEVILE

The N's are reversed.

Agnes - - - - - ete. [*or* **Agnes de Muntpinsun** ? *of co. Norf*]

6689. [12th cent.] Plaster cast from imperfect impression.
2¼ × 1¾ in. [lxxx. 91.]

Pointed oval. Full-face. In tightly-fitting dress, having
a long bag maunch attached to each wrist, in the r. h. a branch
or sceptre, in the l. h. an uncertain object. Standing.

✠ SIGILLVM X AGNET . . . . ETE.

Agnes, dau. and heir of Ralph Fucatus, was wife of Fulk de
Munpinzun, cf. Blomefield, *History of Norfolk*, vol. x., p. 335. She or
another of the same name also appears in *Liber Niger Scaccarii*, vol. i.,
p. 245, as a subtenant of Rob. de Valoniis in Hertfordshire.

[*Dame*] **Margareta de Nevyle,** [*of London.*]

6690. [A.D. 1315.] Bronze-green : fine originally, but
fragmentary. About 1¾ × 1⅛ in. [L. F. C. xxiii. 16.]

Pointed oval. In dress with heraldic bearings, viz., three
lions passant in pale, fur cloak, head-dress. Standing. In
the field on each side a shield of arms, suspended from a tree
by a strap : r. a lion rampant, l. three lions passant in pale.

S' MARGA . . . .

6691. Plaster cast from fine impression. [lxxx. 32.]

This shows the feet of the lady resting on a hound couchant,
and in her l. h. a small lap-dog.

S' MARGARETE DE NEVYLE.

Beaded borders.

Engr. in Drummond, *Hist. of Noble-Families, Neville*, p. 7.

Juliana, [*widow of* RICHARD DE NORTON, *of Long Itchington,*
co. Warw.]

6692. [A.D. 1344.] Light-brown, uncoloured. 1¼ × 1 in.
[Add. ch. 21,451.]

Pointed oval. In the hands a brachet or lap-dog. Standing on corbel. In the field on each side a shield of arms, the armorial bearings very indistinct: r. vairé, a bend (?).

❋ IE SV SEL DAMOR LEL.

Pernila, *fil.* **Alfre[de] Parve,** [*i.e.* **Petronilla,** *dau. of* ALFREDA PARVA, *of Berkhampstead, co. Herts.*]
6693. [Early 13th cent.] Dark-green: fine. 1¾ × 1⅛ in. [Harl. ch. 86 B. 5.]
Pointed oval. To the l. In long dress, in the r. h. a fleur-de-lis, the l. h. on the hip.

⚜ SIGILL' · PERNILE · FILIE : ALFRE . PARVE.

The letter N reversed.
6694. Sulph. cast. [D.C., D. 219.]

Agnes de Perecy, [*of Great Steeping, co. Linc.*]
6695. [*Temp.* Edw. I.] Dark-green: fine, chipped. 1⅜ × 1 in. [Harl. ch. 54 G. 12.]
Pointed oval. In dress charged with the following armorial bearings: billetté a fess dancettée. In each hand the strap of a shield of arms: l. a saltire, r. five fusils in fess, PERCY. Standing on a carved corbel.

SIGILL' AGNETIS DE PERECY.

The letters NE conjoined.
6696. Sulph. cast. [D.C., D. 220.]

Petronilla, [*dau. of* ANDREW BRUNSTAKE.]
6697. [12th cent.] Plaster cast from indistinct impression. 2 × 1¼ in. [lxxviii. 49.]
Pointed oval. In girded dress, in the l. h. a fleur-de-lis on a long stem. Standing.

⚜ SIGILLV PETRONILLE.

Sibilla de Plugenet.
6698. [13th cent.] Plaster cast from a fine impression. 1⅞ × 1⅛ in. [lxxviii. 86.]
Pointed oval. To the l. In a long queue of hair, tightly-fitting dress with pleated skirt, a fleur-de-lis on a long stalk in the r. h. Standing.

⚜ SIGILLVM : SIBILLE DE PLVGENET.

Cf. Sibilla uxor Alani Plukenet, *Inq. p. mort., temp.* Edw. III., vol. ii. p. 181.

Beatricia de Pok'lingt', [*wife of* ROBERT DE PERCY, *Miles, of Sutton-upon-Derwent, co. York.*]
6699. [A.D. 1317.] Red. ¾ in. [Harl. ch. 54 G. 18.]
To the l. Kneeling in prayer, with a demi-angel before

her, issuing from the outer border of the legend, touching her hands.

S' BEATCIE' D' POK'LINGT'.

Margareta, *Comitissa Wintoniæ,* [*widow of* SAER DE.
QUINCY, 1*st Earl of Winchester, and dau. of*
ROBERT, *Earl of Leicester.*]

6700. [*circ.* A.D. 1220.] Green : originally fine, very imperfect. About 3¼ × 2 in. when perfect. [Harl. ch. 112 C. 27.]

Pointed oval. To the l. In tightly-fitting dress, charged with the following armorial bearings : masculy, QUINCY ; fur cloak, flat head-dress. In the l. h. a fleur-de-lis. Standing. Above her head a round-arched doorway, elaborately masoned and embattled, the centre point charged with a cinquefoil in allusion to the paternal arms of BELLOMONT. The doorway is supported, on the r. h. side only, by a masoned jamb or tower. On the l. a wavy tree with trefoiled foliage and spikes of flowers, with two shields of arms suspended from it. The upper shield : seven mascles, three, three, and one, QUINCY ; the lower shield : a fess betw. two chevrons, FITZ WALTER ? In the field on the r. an estoile of six points.

GILL . . . . . . OMITISSE : W . . . . .

Cf. Harl. ch. 55 B. 5.

6701. Sulph. cast. [D.C., E. 281.]

Helewisa, *fil.* **Albredæ Roding,** [*or* **Helewisa Blundt.**]

6702. [12th cent.] Plaster cast from fine but chipped impression. 1¾ × 1¼ in. [lxxviii. 33.]

Pointed oval. To the r. In girdled dress and mantle, in the l. h. a fleur-de-lis, the r. h. on the breast. Standing.

S' HELEWISE · FIL' · ALBREDE · RODING . . .

Desirea, *fil.* **Ernaldi Ruffi.**

6703. [A.D. 1204.] Plaster cast from fine impression. 1¼ × ⅞ in. [lxxix. 3.]

Pointed oval. Full-face. In girdled dress, flat head-dress, in the l. h. a fleur-de-lis on a long stem. Standing.

✠ S' DESIREE FIL' ERNALDI RVFFI.

Aliz de Rumeli, [? ROMELY, *of Skipton-in-Craven,*
co. York.]

6704. [Late 12th cent.] Plaster cast from chipped impression. 2 × 1¾ in. [lxxxi. 42.]

Pointed oval. In tightly-fitting dress, long hair or head-

dress, in the r. h. a fleur-de-lis on a long stalk, the l. h. resting
on the hip. On her breast a large cinquefoil. Standing.

⚜ SIGILLVM . . . . . . IZ DE RVMELI.

Matildis, [*fil.* HUG. DE DIVA, *vid.* D. SAHER] **de Sancto
Andrea** [*of Holdenby, co. Northt.*]

6705. [*circ.* A.D. 1270.] Green: fine, well preserved.
1¾ × 1 in. [Add. ch. 21,896.]

Pointed oval. In long dress, flat head-dress, in the r. h. a
fleur-de-lis, in the l. h. a large shield of arms. Standing on a
corbel. Arms: seven mascles, three, three, and one, a label
of four points, ST. ANDREW.

⚜ S' MATILDIS : DE : SANOTO : ANDREA.

Beaded borders.

Matillis, [*fil.* SIMONIS] **de Sancto Licio,** [*of co. Essex
and London, wife of* (1) ROB. *fil.* RICARDI, *and* (2) *of*
S. DE QUINCI.]

6706. [*Temp.* Hen. II.] Light-green : imperfect, indistinct ;
app. by a woven bobbin with damasked pattern of various
colours. [Harl. ch. 55 G. 9.]

Pointed oval. To the l. In tightly-fitting dress with long
maunches, in the r. h. a fleur-de-lis. Standing.

Legend wanting.

Cf. Cott. ch. xi. 25.

Maria de Sancto Paulo, [*dau. of* GUY DE CHASTILLON,
Comte de St. Pol ; 3rd wife of AYMER DE VALENCE,
2nd Earl of Pembroke.]

6707. [*ante* A.D. 1347.] Plaster casts from very fine impression. 3³⁄₁₆ × 1⅞ in. [lxxxi. 46, 47.]

∅. Pointed oval. Full-face. In long dress, mantle, head-
dress, wimple, the hands crossed in front. Standing on an
elaborately carved corbel of foliage, in a carved niche, with
trefoiled canopy enriched with tabernacle work at the top and
sides. At each side, on the window tracery, a shield of arms :
r. VALENCE, l. CHASTILLON. Background of the niche and
lower part of the field diapered lozengy.

⚭ ⚭ S' MARIE DE SC̄O PAVLO COMITISSE PEMBROCH'
DN̄E D' WEYS' D' MONTIGNAC' ET D' BELLAC'. ⚭ ⚭

℞. A small round counterseal. 1¹⁄₁₆ in. Within a very
elaborately carved and traced gothic triangle, enclosing a six-
foil betw. three small countersunk circles and quatrefoiled, a
shield of arms : per pale, *dex.* VALENCE, *sin.* CHASTILLON.
The triangle is flanked on each side with a large six-foil betw.
two small quatrefoiled circles. In each six-foil, a circular

shield of arms: (1) ENGLAND, and (2) FRANCE (ANCIENT),
for HENRY III., her great-grandfather; (3) Chequy, a canton
ermine.

☒ S' MARIE DE SEYN POVL COMITISSE PE .... HIE.
See No. 6490.

Agnes, [*widow of* D. ROBERT] **de Sandcroft,** [*Miles,
of Sandcroft, co. Suff.*]

6708. [A.D. 1301.]   Dark-green: a fragment.   About
1 × ⅝ in. when perfect.   [L. F. C. i. 26.]

Oval.   In tightly-fitting dress charged with armorial bearings: two chevrons (?), in the r. h. a shield of arms: a saltire;
in the l. h. a pierced mullet.   Standing.

器 . . . . FT.

Beaded borders.

Dame **Laura,** [*or* LORETTA] **de Sanford,**
[*in Great Hormead, co. Hertf.*]

6709. [*Temp.* Hen. III.]   Light-brown: cracked, the points
wanting.   About 1¾ × 1⅛ in. when perfect.   [Harl. ch. 50
C. 17.]

Pointed oval.   To the r.   In tightly-fitting dress, cloak,
head-dress, in the l. hand a shield of arms (indistinct), the
r. h. on the breast.   Standing.

SIGILL' LAVRE : DE : SANFORD.

6710. Sulph. cast.   [D.C., E. 285.]

Alicia, [*wife of* ARNULF LE SAUUAGE, *of Stambridge,
co. Essex.*]

6711. [*circ.* A.D. 1233.]   Dark-green: fine, fragmentary.
About 1¾ × 1 in. when perfect.   App. by a woven cord of
plaited threads.   [Harl. ch. 55 G. 21.]

Pointed oval.   In dress, cloak, in the l. h. a lily flower.
Standing.

. . . . . . LICIE . . . .

Christina de S[eg]rave, [*dau. of* HUGH DE PLESSETS, *Miles,
wife of* JOHN DE SEGRAVE,
afterwards 5*th Baron de Segrave.*]

6712. [A.D. 1280.]   Plaster cast from imperfect impression.
1¼ × ¾ in.   [lxxxi. 49.]

Pointed oval.   Full-face.   In girdled dress, mantle, head-
dress, wimple, in the l. h., by the strap, a shield of arms.
Standing on a corbel.   Arms: a lion rampant, SEGRAVE.
In the field on the l. a shield of arms on a tree: a lion
rampant, queue fourchée, SEGRAVE.

. S . . . . . . DE · S . : RAVE.

Ismania La Sor, [*widow of* JOHN LE SOR, *Miles,*
Lord of Shennington, co. Glouc.]

6713· [*Temp.* Hen. III. or Edw. I.]   Green : fine, fragmentary.   About 1⅛ × ¾ in.   [Cott. ch. xxix. 52.]

Oval.   In long dress charged with armorial bearings :
chequy.   In the r. h. a hawk and a fleur-de-lis.   Standing on
a carved corbel.   In the field on the r. a squirrel.

.... LA SOR ..

Matildis de Stafford, [*of Ted-lauetorp, co.* ——— ?]

6714. [Late 12th cent.]   Light-brown : a fragment.   About
2¼ × 1⅛ in. when perfect.   [Harl. ch. 56 E. 2.]

Pointed oval.   To the l.   In tightly-fitting dress and long
maunches, an uncertain object in the r. h.   Standing.

Legend wanting.

Cf. Harl. ch. 56 G. 2, 3 (late 12th cent.).

Milisenta de Sta[fford, *dau. and heiress of*
ROBERT DE STAFFORD, *and wife of*
HERVI BOGOT, *of Coates, co. Glouc.*]

6715. [Early 13th cent.]   Creamy-white, with yellowish-
brown varnish : archaic style, imperfect.   About 1⅞ × 1⅛ in.
when perfect.   [Harl. ch. 46 E. 54.]

Pointed oval.   To the r.   Standing, with narrow waistband,
long tight dress, sash, long hair or head-dress, on the r. wrist
a hawk.

...... LWM . MIL .. ENTE : DE : STA ....

Baker, *Hist. of Northt.*, i. 532.

Rameta de Staunford.

6716. [13th cent.]   Plaster cast from fine impression,
chipped at the top.   About 1⅞ × ³⁄₁₆ in.   [lxxx. 84.]

Pointed oval.   To the r.   In girdled dress, cloak, flat head-
dress, the r. h. laid on the breast, in the l. h. a falcon held on
the wrist by the jesses.   Standing on a carved corbel.   In the
field, on each side, three fleurs-de-lis, perhaps in allusion to the
arms of one of the families of STAMFORD, viz. a fess wavy
between three fleurs-de-lis.

S' RAMETE ⋈ DE : STAVNFORD.

Perunel de Statun.

6717. [12th cent.]   Plaster cast from indistinct impression.
2 in.   [lxxx. 94.]

To the r.   In veil or head-dress, and long maunches, on the
l. wrist a falcon by the jesses.   Standing.

⊕ SIGILL PERVNEL DE STATVN.

The letters S, G, E, N, and D, reversed.

Isbella [de **Patissille**, *dau. of* JOHN] de
Staynesgreve, [*of Waterholm, co. York.*]

6718. [*Temp.* Hen. III.] Creamy-white: imperfect, indistinct. 1 × ¾ in. [Harl. ch. 112 C. 6.]

Oval. In tightly-fitting dress, fur cloak, flat head-dress.
Standing on a carved corbel betw. two wavy sprigs of foliage.

ISBELLE : DE : ST . . . . . . AVE.

Johanna de Stutevile, [*widow of* (1) HUGH WAKE,
(2) *of* HUGH LE BIGOD, *of Hessle, co. York.*]

6719. [A.D. 1265–1275.] Red: originally fine, now very
imperfect. About 2¼ in. when perfect. [Cott. ch. xxix. 63.]

To the l. In loosely-fitting cloak, head-dress, gloves. In
the r. h. a goad, in the l. h. a shield of arms: barruly. Horse
with ornamental breastband and fringed saddle.

. . . . EVIL . . .

Beaded borders.

6720. Sulph. cast. [D.C., E. 271.]

Agnes, [*wife of* PHILIP DE CROILI, *and dau. of* GISLEBERT]
de **Truleriis**, [*of Headley, co. Surr.*]

6721. [*Temp.* Rich. I.] Dark-green, mottled: indistinct ;
app. by an ornamental cord of diapered taffeta. 2¼ × 1¼ in.
[Add. ch. 5526.]

Pointed oval. To the l. In long dress, flat head-dress,
and maunches, in the r. h. an indistinct object, the l. h. on the
hip. Standing.

⚜ SIGILL' · AGNETIS · DE TRVLERIIS.

6722. Pale-green: very imperfect, l. h. side wanting.
[Add. ch. 5527.]

Petronilla, [*widow of* SYMON] de **Turvile**, *of Helmedon,
co. Northt.*]

6723. [*Temp.* Hen. III.] Green, mottled: fine. 1⅝ × 1 in.
[Harl. ch. 86 F. 6.]

Pointed oval. To the r. In dress girdled at waist, fur
cloak, flat head-dress, in the l. h. a sceptre fleur-de-lizé, in the
r. h., on the breast, a bird rising, or a branch. Standing.

⚜ SIGILL' PETRONILLE DE TVRVILE :

6724. Sulph. cast. [D.C., E. 284.]

Dame **Ramette La Tyeyze**.

6725. [13th cent.] Plaster cast from fine impression.
1⅝ × 1¼ in. [lxxxi. 2.]

Pointed oval. Full-face. In girdled robe, fur-lined mantle, flat cap or head-dress, wimple, the hair curled at the sides, the r. h. laid on the breast ; in the l. h. a falcon rising, held by the jesses. Standing on a corbel.

⚜ DAME RAMETTE · LA TYEYZE.

Beaded borders.

Cf. Dugdale, *Baronage*, vol. ii., p. 21.

Agnes de Vesey, [*dau. of* WILLIAM DE FERRERS, *Earl of Derby; and 2nd wife of* EUSTACE DE VESCY, *4th Baron, ob.* A.D. 1216.]

6726. Plaster cast from fine but very imperfect seal. About 2⅝ × 1¾ in. when perfect. [lxxxi. 16, 17.]

Ø. Pointed oval. Full-face. In girdled dress, fur-lined mantle, flat head-dress, in the r. h. a shield of arms : a cross flory, VESCY. Standing on a carved corbel. On the l., in the field, a shield of arms : vairé, FERRARS. Above her head a semicircular canopy, with embattled carving. On each side, in the field, an elegantly designed wavy scroll of foliage and flowers.

. . . . . I ♠ S ⚜ DE . . . .

℞. On a branching tree, a shield of arms hung by a strap, VESCY. Below this another shield of arms, three garbs, two and one, CHESTER. The branch on the l. h. side destroyed ; on that on the r. h. side a similar shield of arms : a lion rampant, contourné, MARESCHAL.

. . . . .IBUNT : P . . . .

Beaded borders.

Dame **Isabella** [de Beaumont, *widow of Sir* JOHN] de Vescy, *Senior, of Scorby, co. York.*

6727. [A.D. 1289-1311.] Red : fine originally, very imperfect. About 2½ × 1⅝ in. when perfect. [Harl. ch. 43 I. 48.]

Pointed oval. To the l. In flowing dress, fur cloak, in the r. h. a shield of arms : a cross, VESCY ; the l. h. on the breast, holding a jewelled pendant suspended round the neck. Standing. In the field on the r. a shield of arms : a lion rampant, BEAUMONT. In the field on each side an oak sapling.

SI . . . L . . . . LE · D . . . . . C . . . .

Beaded borders.

Cf. Harl. ch. 54 G. 19, A.D. 1299 ; and 45 I. 38.

6728. Sulph. cast. [D.C., F. 615.]

Alianora [de Vitrei, *dau. of* TIRREL DE MAINERS,
wife of WILLIAM D'EVEREUX,
Earl of Salisbury], *Countess of Salisbury.*
6729. [A.D. 1222.] Plaster cast from an imperfect impression. About 2¼ × 1¾ in. when perfect. [lxxviii. 94.]
Pointed oval. In long dress, head-dress and cloak. Standing, turned slightly to the left, on a platform. In the r. h. a fleur-de-lis. The l. h. lifted before the breast. In the field on the r. a quatrefoil.

..... LVM : ALIENOR ... MITISSE DE SALESBIR ..

Isabella, *Countess of Warenne,* [*dau. of* WILLIAM DE WARENNE, *3rd Earl; wife of* HAMELIN PLANTAGENET.]
6730. [A.D. 1163–1198.] Creamy-white : originally fine, very indistinct and imperfect ; app. by cords of damasked bobbin, various colours. About 3¼ × 2 in. [Harl. ch. 43 C. 15.]
Pointed oval. In tightly-fitting head-dress, girdle, mantle, coronet, in the r. h. a fleur-de-lis, in the l. h. some indistinct charges. Standing.
Legend destroyed.
6731. [Late 12th cent.] Pale green : imperfect in places. [Add. ch. 24,634.]
This impression shows the mantle, fleur-de-lis, and hawk held in the l. h. by the jesses, very distinctly.

.... OMITISS ...... ET · MO ....

Gundreia de Warenne, [*of Fakenham, co. Suff.*]
6732. [A.D. 1200–1225.] Creamy-white : imperfect, indistinct. About 2 × 1½ in. App. by a woven bobbin of diapered stuff. [Harl. ch. 57 E. 24.]
Pointed oval. To the r. On the l. h. a hawk, in the r. h. a branch. Standing.

.... DE ....

Sarra, *fil.* **Ricardi de Warw ...** , [*wife of* SIMON, *son of* GILBERT DE HALTON, *co. Linc.*]
6733. [13th cent.] Sulph. cast from fine impression. 1⅞ × 1¼ in. [lii. 18.]
Pointed oval. To the r. In flowing dress, in each hand an ornamental flower. Standing on a corbel.

⚜ SIGILL' SARRE FILIE RICARDI DE WARW ....

The letters AR in *Sarre, Ricardi,* and *Warw ...,* are conjoined.

Alicia de Watervile, [*widow of* WILLIAM .DE BANDUN,
Clerk, of Beddington, co. Surr.]
. **6734.** [*post* A.D. 1228.]   Dark-green : fine. $1\frac{5}{8} \times 1$ in.
[Add. ch. 23,018.]
Pointed oval.   To the' r.   Standing, with long dress and
maunches, in l. h. a fleur-de-lis.
⚜ S ALICIE D' WATERVILE.
Cf. Lansd. ch. 409

[**Deonisia Watevile.**]
Seal used by ROGER DE FELBREGGE, *of Howe,* [*co. Norf*]
6735. [A.D. 1391 or 1392.]   Green : $1\frac{1}{16} \times \frac{13}{16}$ in.   [L.F.C.,
I. 24.]
· Oval.   In loosely-fitting dress, head-dress, in each hand a
shield' of arms.   Standing on a platform.   Arms : r. h. three
chevrons, WATEVILLE, l. h. an eagle displayed.
✳ S' DEONISIE WATEWILE.

Mahalt de Watevila, [*widow of* DREU POER, *of Colesbourn,*
co. Glouc.]
6736. [Early Hen. II.] . Red : indistinct in. places.
$2\frac{1}{4} \times 1\frac{1}{4}$ in.   [Add. ch. 20,394.]
Pointed oval.   In tightly-fitting dress, mitre-shaped cap, in
the l. h. a fleur-de-lis, the· r. h. on the hip.   Standing.
SIGILLVM MA[H]ALT DE WATEVILA.

Deonisia, *fil:* **Willelmi Le Well'.**
6737. [13th cent.]   Plaster cast from chipped impression.
$1\frac{1}{4} \times 1\frac{1}{4}$ in. [lxxix. 89.]
Pointed. oval. . To the l.   In tightly-fitting dress, with long
cloak.   In her r. h. a branch of flowers.   Standing on a corbel.
⚜ S'. DEONISI .... LIE WILL'I LE WELL'.
. **6738.** Plaster cast from an indistinct and imperfect impression. . [lxxix. 18.]
⚜ S' DEO .... LL'I LE WELL.

[**Sibbilla de Worth.**]
Seals used by WILLIAM *and* .AGNES HOOG, *of Winchelsea,*
co. Suss.
6739. [A.D. 1364.]   Red : injured.   About $\frac{7}{8} \times \frac{3}{4}$ in. when
perfect.   [Add. ch. 20,186.]
Oval.   To the r.   On the l. h. a hawk.   Standing.
✳ S' SIBBILL' · D' · WORTH'.
6740. Another.   [Add. ch. 20,186.]
2 D 2

Alicia, *fil.* **Philippi de Ykamme,** [*or* ALICE DE
WINCHELSEA.]

. **6741.** [13th cent.] Plaster cast from fine impression.
1½ × ⅞ in. [lxxxi. 26.]

Pointed oval. To the r. In girdled dress, mantle, flat
head-dress, the r. h. on the breast, in the l. h. a falcon held by
the jesses. Standing on a carved corbel.

✠ S' ALICIE · FIL' . PHILIPPI · DE · YKAMME.

Beaded borders.

Dame **Ela,** *or* **Eleina de la Zouche,** [*dau. of* ROGER DE
QUINCI, *Earl of Winchester, wife of* ALAN, *Lord La Zouche
of Ashby*].

6742. [*circ.* A.D. 1298.] Sulph. cast, tinted red : from fine
impression. 1¾ × 1⅛ in. [xlvii. 1198.]

Pointed oval. In tightly-fitting dress, fur cloak, flat head-
dress, in each hand a shield of arms. Standing on a carved
corbel. Arms : r. ten bezants, four, three, two, and one,
LA ZOUCHE, l. a cinquefoil, FITZ-PARNELL, of Leicester.

✠ SIGIL' DN̄E ELE INE (*or* DN̄E) LA ZOCHE.

Laing's *Suppl. Catal. of Scottish Seals*, No. 609.

6743. Plaster cast. [lxxxi. 29.]

Uncertain Seals.

6744. [Early 14th cent.] Sulph. cast from good impression. 1⅛ × ¾ in. [D.C., F. 617.]

Pointed oval. In long dress, a hawk on the l. h. Standing.

✠ IE SV SEL A AMI LEL.

6745. [14th cent.] Recent impression in black sealing-
wax, from a matrix. 1⅙ in. [xxxiv. 79.]

In long dress, head-dress, in each hand a shield of arms.
Standing. ·Arms : r. h. three cocks, two and one, those in
chief combatant or respectant ; l. h. a church.

✠ SOVRABLA ✲ DE VS OLER ✲

Inner border beaded.

6746. Another, black. [xxxiv. 79 k.]
6747. Another, red. [xxxv. 49.]
6748. Another, red. [xlvii. 2417.]

Laing's *MS. Catal.*, No. 579.

HERALDIC SEALS.

A

I——— A———.
Seal used by Richard Champernowne, Esq.
6749. [A.D. 1584 or 1594.] Red. $\frac{3}{4} \times \frac{7}{12}$ in. [Harl. ch. 77 G. 3.]
Oval: a lion rampant, collared and chained, the end of the chain ringed, betw. the initial letters I. A.
Cabled border.

Richard Abberbury, *of Newbury, co. Berks, Gentl.*
6750· [A.D. 1473.] Red: imperfect. 1 in. [Add. ch. 15,764.]
A shield of arms: a fess embattled, ABBERBURY. Upon a branching tree.

𝔖𝔦𝔤𝔦𝔩𝔩ū 𝔯𝔦𝔠𝔞𝔯𝔡𝔦 𝔞𝔟𝔟𝔢𝔯𝔟𝔲𝔯𝔶.

Isabella, *widow of* Richard Abbot, *Tailor,*
of Carshalton, co. Surr.
6751. [A.D. 1362.] Red: fine, chipped at the lower part. 1 × $\frac{3}{4}$ in. [Add. ch. 23,388.]
Oval: Our Lord crucified on a cross raguly. Betw. two wavy rose-trees, each bearing four flowers. Below is a square headed niche, with carved round-headed arch, containing a shield of arms: three animals of uncertain kind, passant, two and one, within a bordure compony. All within a carved gothic rosace or panel with eight cusped points.

HEC · PRO : TE . . . . GIOR : CAVE : TIBI.

Beaded border.
6752. Another; fragmentary. [Add. ch. 23,382.]

Lady Johanna de Abernun, *widow of* INGERAM DE ABERNUN, *of Albury, co. Surr.*
6753. [A.D. 1235–1236.] Discoloured white: edge chipped. 1¼ in. [Add. ch. 5562.]
A fleur-de-lis, betw. two small shields of arms: a chevron

betw. three indistinct charges. Cf. the arms of JOHN DE ABBERNUN, Add. ch. 5543.

+ S' IOHANNE DE AB' NVN.

The N's are reversed.

John de Abbernun, *of Stoke D'Abernon, co. Surr.*

6754. [Late Hen. III.] Green: fine. 1 in. [Add. ch. 5543.]

A shield of arms: a chevron. ABERNON.

+ S' IOHANNIS D' AVBERNOVN.

Beaded borders.

William Dabernoun, *of Stoke Dabernon, co. Surr., Knt.*

6755. [A.D. 1351.] Green: fine. ¾ in. [Add. ch. 5603.]

Within a carved gothic panel, finely traced, a shield of arms: a chevron, in chief a label of three points (?), DABERNON. Above the shield the legend:—

WILL'S.

John Abindone.

6756. [A.D. 1343.] Plaster cast from fine impression. ⅞ in. [lxxxii. 3.]

A shield of arms: ermine, on a chevron three cushions (?) Within a carved and traced gothic six-foil.

✡ SIGILL' + IOH'IS + ABINDONE. (?)

Thomas Dabitott, *of Ridmarley Dabitott, co. Worc.*

6757. [A.D. 1644.] Red: *en placard.* Imperfect. ⅝ × ¾ in. [Add. ch. 24,800.]

Oval: a shield of arms: per pale, three roundles counterchanged, DABITOTT. Above the shield the legend:—

DABITOT.

Cabled border.

Another Seal.

6758. [A.D. 1650.] Red: *en placard.* Imperfect. ⅝ × ¾ in. [Add. ch. 24,801.]

Oval: a shield of arms: per pale; three roundles counterchanged, DABITOT. Legend in the field:—

DE AB TOT.

Beaded border.

Robert de Acastris, *or* **Acastre,** *of Kneeton, co. Nott.*

6759. [Hen. III.] Green: fine, with the mark of the handle at the top, and raised rim chipped. 1 3/16 in. [Harl. ch. 45 B. 4.]

A shield of arms : ermine ? a chief.

. + S' ROBERTI : DE : AEASTRIS. (*sic.*)

6760. Sulph. cast. of No. 6759. [D.C., E. 369.]

Joseph Le Katur, *or* Acatur.

6761. [A.D. 1286–7.] Plaster cast from fine impression, injured in parts. $1\frac{1}{10}$ in. [xcii. 50.]

˙A shield of arms : a cross moline betw. four cranes.

☆ : S' IOSEPH LE ACATVR.

· Beaded borders. ·

Jonathan Acklom, *of Bawtry, co. York, Esq.*

· **6762.** [A.D. 1711.] ˙Red : *en placard* on a label. $\frac{3}{8} \times \frac{1}{4}$ in.˙ [Add. ch. 29,597.]

Oval : a shield of arms : a maunch within a bordure of eight cinquefoils in orle, ACHYM. Crest on a helmet, mantling, and wreath, a cinquefoil.

6763. [A.D. 1711.] Another. [Add. ch. 29,598.]

John de Acton, *son of* ODO DE ACTON, *of Bristol, co. Glouc.* ·

6764. [A.D. 1361.] Red : very imperfect. About $\frac{3}{4}$ in. when perfect. [Harl. ch. 45 B. 8.]

A shield (of arms ?) : three estoiles, two and one, on the chief and base points a cross pattée. Betw.˙ three sprigs ; and above the shield, the initial letters E. I. ·

☆ . . . . ER TIS. (?)

Richard de Actona.

6765. [13th or early 14th cent.] Red : fine, detached˙ from a charter. $\frac{3}{4}$ in. [xxxvi. 115.]

A shield of arms : quarterly per fess indented, in the first quarter an estoile, ACTON. The first and fourth quarters are finely diapered lozengy˙ Above˙ the shield the initial letters R.E. enclosed in small cusps.

S RICARDI DE ACTONA.

Richard de Actone.

6766. [14th cent.] ˙Plaster cast from fine impression˙ 1 in. [lxxxii. 3.]

A shield of arms : quarterly per fess indented, in the first quarter a mullet for difference. Betw. two small slipped flowers. Within a carved gothic panel of two interlaced six-foils.

☆ SIGILLVM : RICARDI : DE : ACTONE. ·

John Adderley, *of Derby,* co *Derb., Gentl.*

6767. [A.D. 1694.]   Red : *en placard* on ;a label.   Imperfect at the bottom.   ¾ × ⅝ in.   [Woll. ch. xii. 40.]

Oval : a shield of arms : on a bend three mascles.   Crest, on a helmet and mantling, on a chapeau, turned up ermine, a stork, ADDERLEY.

Beaded border.

Henry Adis, *al.* **Adys,** *of Westminster, Esq.*

6768. [A.D. 1625.]   Red : imperfect.   ¾ × ⅝ in.   [Add. ch. 6004.]

Oval : a shield of arms : per pale, *dex.*, erm., on a fess three lions rampant ; *sin.*, a fleur-de-lis.

Another Seal.

6769. [A.D. 1631.]   Red : fine.   ⅝ in.   [Add. ch. 6008.]

Slightly oval : a shield of arms : a chevron betw. three crosses pattées, ADIS.

Adolphus-Frederic, *Duke of Cambridge.*
See CAMBRIDGE, *Duke of.*

Charles Agard, *of Foston, co. Derby, Esq.*

6770. [A.D. 1661.]   Red : indistinct.   ⅔ × ½ in.   [Add. ch. 19,434.]

Oval : a shield of arms : quarterly, 1, 4, a chevron (engrailed ?) betw. three (boars' heads ?) AGARD ; 2, 3, indistinct, perhaps HUNDERHILL and MIDDLEMORE.   Cf. Egerton MS. 996, f. 60.   Crest on a wreath, a bugle-horn, stringed and garnished.

Beaded border.

Agard, *arms of.*
See ROGER HAGARTHE.

Richard Aghton, *of Mutford, co. Suff.*

6771. A.D. 1429.   Red : fine, now fragmentary.   About 1 in. when perfect.   [Harl. ch. 43 H. 9.]

A shield of arms, couché : three garbs, AIGHTON.   Crest on a helmet and ornamental mantling, destroyed.

Legend on a ribbon, very fragmentary.

• • • • • • • • **ag** • • • • • • • •

6772. [A.D. 1429.]   Red : cracked and imperfect.   [Harl. ch. 43 I. 50.]

This impression shows the crest, a dexter hand erased, holding up a garb.

S' RICARDI AGHTON.

6773. Sulph. cast from No. 6772, before it was rendered so imperfect. [D.C., G. 182.]

Thomas de Agnis, *or* Aygneus, *of Chalfont St. Giles and St. Peter, co. Buck.*

6774. [A.D. 1286.] Mottled green. ¾ in. [Harl. ch. 84 G. 48.]

A shield of arms: three lambs, statant, two and one. Above the shield a looped strap.

✠ S' THOME DE AGNIS.

6775. Sulph. cast from No. 6774. [D.C., E. 424.]

William, *son of* Ingram Agvillun, *of Cathwait, co. York, E. R.*

6776. [*Temp.* Joh.] Pale green: originally fine, now fragmentary. About 1¼ in. when perfect. [Add. ch. 20,553.]

A shield of arms: quarterly.

.... IGILL' WI ....

James Ainsworthe, *al.* Aynesworth, *son of* RICHARD, *of Southwark, co. Surr.*

6777. [A.D. 1596.] Wafer: *en placard,* the paper of the deed folded over. ⅝ in. [Harl. ch. 76 A. 22.]

Slightly oval: a shield of arms: quarterly, 1, chevronelly, 2, 3, 4, indistinct.

Robert Aischeleghe, *of Hilperton, co. Wilts.*

6778. [A.D. 1405.] Red: impression from a chased ring. ½ × ⁵⁄₁₂ in. [Add. ch. 5688.]

Oblong octagonal: a shield of arms: a fess within an engrailed bordure bezantée. Within an invecked border.

Robert de Aisshefeld, *of Little Haugh Manor, Livermere, co. Suff.*

6779. [A.D. 1382.] Red: fine, chipped. 1 in. [Harl. ch. 45 G. 61.]

A shield of arms: a fess engrailed betw. three fleurs-de-lis, ASHFIELD, suspended by a loop or strap from a lion's face. Within a carved gothic panel.

𝖘𝖎𝖌𝖎𝖑𝖑' : [r]𝖔𝖇𝖊𝖗𝖙𝖎 : 𝖉𝖊 : 𝖆𝖎𝖘𝖘𝖍𝖊𝖋𝖊𝖑𝖉.

6780. Sulph. cast from No. 6779. [D.C., F. 538.]

6781. [A.D. 1394.] Bright red: fine. [Harl. ch. 45 D. 27.]

𝖘𝖎𝖌𝖎𝖑𝖑' : 𝖗𝖔𝖇𝖊𝖗𝖙𝖎 : 𝖉𝖊 : 𝖆𝖎𝖘𝖘𝖍𝖊𝖋𝖊𝖑𝖉.

6782. Sulph. cast from No. 6781. [D.C., F. 590.]

6783. [A.D. 1398.] Red: indistinct. [Harl. ch. 45 D. 28.]

John Akehurst, *of Crawley in Warbleton, co. Suss., Gentl.*

6784. [A.D. 1659.] Red: injured by pressure, indistinct.
⅝ × ¼ in. [Add. ch. 30,170.]
Oval: a shield of arms: per pale, *dex.* three fleurs-de-lis?; *sin.*, uncertain. Crest, on a helmet and mantling, a fleur-de-lis?

John de Akeny.

6785. [A.D. 1367.] Plaster cast from fine impression.
1 in. [lxxxv. 14.]
A shield of arms: a cross betw. four lions rampant, AKENEY. Betw. three roses. Within a carved and pointed gothic quatrefoil ornamented with small ball-flowers along the inner edges.

       ⋇ · S' · ✱ IOHANNIS : ✱ DE : ✱ : AKENY.

Richard de Aketon ?

6786. [A.D. 1330.] Plaster cast from chipped impression.
⅞ in. [lxxxii. 4.]
A shield of arms: ermine, a lion rampant. Suspended by a strap from a hook. Within a pointed gothic panel.

       S' R[ICA]RDI D' ACTO . . . (?)
Beaded border.

Aunays, *dau. of* THOMAS ALAYN, *of Wakefield, co. York.*

6787. [A.D. 1353.] White: a fragment. [Harl. ch. 55 G. 26.]
A shield of arms: a bend cotised (?). Over the shield a loop or strap.
  Legend indistinct.

       . . . . CA . . .

William Alanby, *of Combwell Manor, co. Kent, Gentl.*

6788. [A.D. 1574.] Red. ¾ in. [Harl. ch. 79 F. 10.]
A shield of arms: a chevron engrailed, ALENBY.

       ✱ SIGILLA + AD ⋇ ARMA + A.
Cabled border.

Thomas de Alba . . aria.
Seal used by JOHN HOPE *or* MATILDA, *his wife,*
of Frome, co. Somerset.

6789. [A.D. 1373.] Red: good, chipped. ¾ in. [Harl. ch. 76 E. 3.]

A shield of arms : three (griffins' ?) heads erased, over all a bendlet.

S' THOME DE ALBA . . ARIA.

William de Albinggetone, *of co. Cambridge, Knt.*
6790. [A.D. 1255–6.] Green. ¾ × ⅝ in. [Add. ch. 6293.]
A shield of arms : on a bend three eagles displayed, ABBINGTON and ABINGTON.
. Cf. Harl. ch. 111 E. 44.

. **Elias Daubeneye,** *of Twigworth, co. Glouc.*
6791. [A.D. 1344.] Mottled green : fine. 1 × ¾ in. [Add. ch. 6028.]
Oval : within a cusped gothic rosette or bordure, carved, of eight cusps or points, and suspended by a strap from a tree of three branches, a shield of arms : three helmets, two and one.

⚹ SIGILLVM ✱ ELIE ✱ DAVBENY ⚘ ⚹ ⟨.

Giles Dawbney, *Knt., Lord* **Dawbney,** *and* **Reginald Bray,** *Knt., Justices in Eyre of all the forests, etc., citra Trentham.*
*Official Seal.***
6792. [A.D. 1497.] Green : fine, very imperfect. About 1⅜ in. when perfect. [Add. ch. 22,399.]
A stag's head cabossed, supporting betw. the attires a large shield of arms : per pale, *dex.*, four fusils in fess, DAUBNEY ; *sin.*, a chevron betw. three eagles' legs erased, BRAY.

[𝕾igillu]m : 𝕵usticiarior :
Cabled border.

Philip de Aubigne, *or* **Albynico,** *of co. Linc., Knt.*
6793. [A.D. 1292.] Light brown : indistinct. ¾ in. [Harl. ch. 44 H. 4.]
A shield of arms : four fusils in fess, in chief a label of three points, DAUBNEY.

+ S' : PHILIP : DE : AVBIGNE :
Beaded borders.

Philip de Albiniaco, [? *3rd Baron Daubeney, ob.* A.D. 1293.]
6794. [*Temp.* Hen. III.] Green : very fine, slightly chipped. App. by a faded red woven cord. 1¾ in. [Harl. ch. 83 A. 19.]
Four fusils in fess, betw. a cross pattée fitchée in chief, and

---

* This seal should precede No. 1005, in vol. i., p. 129.

a pierced cinquefoil in base. This device is of considerable interest for its allusion to the arms :—four fusils in fess,—for DAUBNEY.

✠ SIGILL' : PHILIPPI : DE : ALBINIACO.

Beaded borders.

Ysobélla, *relict of* RANULF DE ALBO-MONASTERIO,
of Exe Manor, co. Devon.

6795. [*Temp.* Edw. I.] Green : shrivelled. 1 in. [Add. ch. 29,032.]

A shield of arms : three round buckles, two and one.

. . . . BE . . . .

Roger Albryghton, *Clerk,* [*of London.*]

6796. [A.D. 1404.] Red : fine, sharp, very imperfect. ⅞ in. [Harl. ch. 47 B. 10.]

A shield of arms : per pale, two lions rampant, queue fourchée, in fess, in chief three escallops. Suspended by a loop from a tree, within a finely carved gothic panel.

S' ⚜ rogeri ⚜ albr . . . .

Cf. Harl. ch. 55 H. 3.

6797. Sulph. cast from No. 6796. [D.C., G. 110.]

6798. [A.D. 1404.] Red : fine but fragmentary. [Harl. ch. 47 B. 14.]

. . . . albryghton.

William de Aldeburghe,
of Kirkby Overblow Manor, co. York., Knt.

6799. [A.D. 1363.] Red : very fine. 1⅙ in. [Add. ch. 8311.]

A shield of arms : a lion rampant. Within a finely carved and traced gothic pointed cinquefoil and betw. two leaves, slipped.

✤ Sigillum : willelmi : de : aldeburgh' : militis.

The letters DE in *de Aldeburgh* are conjoined.

Beaded border.

6800. [A.D. 1368.] Red : fine but fragmentary. [Add. ch. 26,770.]

Legend wanting.

Elizabet, *wife of* WILLIAM DE ALDEBURGH.

6801. [A.D. 1368.] Red : fine but fragmentary. [Add. ch. 26,770.]

An angel, half-length, wearing an embroidered robe, supporting before him two small shields of arms : *dex.,* a lion rampant, ALDEBURGH (see previous seal), *sin.,* a lion rampant. Within a carved gothic panel.

Legend wanting.

Aldersey, *family of.*
See DOROTHY CAPELL.

Ralph de Aldham.
See REGINALD PASTOR.

Thomas Aldridge, *Clerk, Prebendary of the Prebend of Trallonge, co. Brecknock.*
6802. [A.D. 1573.] Red: much injured by pressure. $\frac{1}{2} \times \frac{9}{16}$ in. [Add. ch. 1837.]
A shield of arms: on a fess a bull passant, in chief a mullet for difference? ALDRICH.
Beaded border.

John Aleyn, *of Wonford, co. Devon.*
6803. [A.D. 1355.] Green: a fragment. About 1 in. when perfect. [Harl. ch. 45 C. 17.]
A shield of arms: a fess? Within a traced gothic quatrefoil.

John Aleyn, *of Tacolneston, co. Norf.*
6804. [A.D. 1375.] Green: fine, the edge chipped. $\frac{3}{4}$ in. [Add. ch. 14,911.]
A shield of arms: per pale, *dex.*, a bend lozengy, *sin.*, six eagles displayed, three, two, and one, on a canton an indistinct charge. Within a finely carved and pointed gothic quatrefoil, with counter-sunk trefoils in the spaces outside the cusps.
Beaded border.
Blomefield's *Norfolk* (MS. Dept.) vol. v., p. 169.

Robert Aleyn, *of Croydon, co. Surr.*
6805. [A.D. 1392.] Red: much injured by pressure. $\frac{3}{4}$ in. [Add. ch. 24,568.]
A shield of arms: three fusils in fess.
Legend indistinct:—
S . . . . A . . . .

Edward Alford, *of Offington, co. Suss.*
6806. [A.D. 1617.] Red: fine. $\frac{11}{16} \times \frac{13}{16}$ in. [Harl. ch. 79 G. 9.]
Oval: a shield of arms: six pears, three and three, a chief, charged with a crescent in intaglio, for difference, ALFORD.
Crest, on a helmet, mantling, and wreath, a boar's head.
Beaded borders.

6807. [A.D. 1601.] Red: good. [Harl. ch. 79 D. 6.]
6808. [A.D. 1604.] Red: chipped at the top. [Harl. ch. 75 G. 52.]
6809. [A.D. 1617.] Red: much injured by pressure. [Harl. ch. 75 G. 57.]
6810. [A.D. 1620.] Red: blundered. [Harl. ch. 76 F. 36.]

Francis Alford, *of London, Esq.*

6811. [A.D. 1570.] Red: injured by pressure. About ¼ in. when perfect. [Harl. ch. 79 E. 40.]
On a wreath a boar's head, in his mouth three feathers of a pheasant's tail. Crest of ALFORD.

John Alford, *of Offington, co. Suss., Esq.*

6812. [A.D. 1631.] Red: from a ring, showing the mark of the ornamental setting. ⅜ × ½ in. [Harl. ch. 76 F. 39.]
Oval: on a wreath a boar's head, with a broken spear-handle thrust down the mouth. Crest of ALFORD.
Cabled border.
6813. [A.D. 1631.] Red: injured by pressure. [Harl. ch. 77 H. 12.]

John Alford, *Esq.*

6814. [A.D. 1641.] Red: cracked. ⅜ in. [Harl. ch. 77 H. 13.]
A shield of arms: six pears reversed, three and three barwise, a chief, ALFORD. Within a wreath composed of two laurel sprigs, slipped, and tied above and below the shield.

Seal used by JOHN FETTIPLACE, *Esq.*

6815. Red: fine. [Harl. ch. 77 H. 13.]

Roger Alford.
See JOHN LEE.

William Alford, *of Bilton, co. York.*

6816. [A.D. 1614.] Red: fine, from a ring, showing the mark of the ornamental setting. ⅜ × ½ in. [Harl. ch. 79 G. 5.]
Oval: on a wreath a boar's head, in his mouth three feathers of a pheasant's tail. Crest of ALFORD. Cf. Harl. ch. 79 E. 40. No. 6811.
Cabled border.

Giles Alington, *of Horsheath, co. Cambr., Knt.*
6817. [A.D. 1620.] Red: fine. $\frac{1}{4} \times \frac{7}{16}$ in. [Harl. roll Z. 25.]
A shield of arms: a bend engrailed betw. six billets, ALINGTON.
Cabled border.

John Allen.
See JOHN ISTED.

Arms of DAWE, *of cos. Dorset and Somerset, used by*
Nicholas, *son of* BARBARA **Allen,**
of Woodhouse, co. Derby, Gentl.
6818. [A.D. 1600.] Red: fine. $\frac{3}{4} \times \frac{11}{16}$ in. [Woll. ch. xii. 33.]
A shield of arms: on a pile, a chevron betw. three crosses crosslet, DAWE. Crest on a helmet and mantling, a lion's gamb, erased and erect, holding a fleur-de-lis, DAWE.
Cabled border.

Another Seal.

6819. [A.D. 1602.] Red: cracked and imperfect. About $\frac{3}{4}$ in. when perfect. [Woll. ch. xi. 64.]
A shield of arms: a fess betw. three leaves, ALLEN. Cf. Harl. MS. 1537, fo. 1, where the arms occur as a bend betw. three leaves.
Ornamented border.

Richard Allen.
See ANTHONY BLAGRAVE.

John Allott, *of Somersby, co. Linc.*
6820. [A.D. 1616.] Red: indistinct. About $\frac{5}{8} \times \frac{1}{2}$ in. [Add. ch. 32,837.]
Oval: a lion rampant. Perhaps a crest.

Thomas de Alnewick,
of Estchickley super Langacres, co. Durham.
6821. [A.D. 1331.] Light brown: imperfect and indistinct. About $\frac{3}{8}$ in. when perfect. [Egert. ch. 558.]
A shield of arms: a fleur-de-lis épanoui.
Legend broken off:—

......ЄG......

John Alsopp.
Seal used by CHARLES HUNT, *of Alderwasley, co. Derby, Esq.*
6822. [A.D. 1746.]   Red: *en placard.* ¾ × ⅘ in. [Woll. ch. xi. 117.]
Oval : a shield of arms : three doves rising. Crest, on a helmet and mantling, a dove rising, ALSOPP.
The field of the shield powdered with small dots or spots.

Walter Alysaundre.
See WALTER DE CHALFHUNTE.
WALTER DE DENHAM.

Alicia, *widow of* WALTER DE AMBRESLEYE
of Colleshulle, [Coleshill, co. Warw.]
6823. [A.D. 1383.]   Brown, semi-opaque. 1¹⁄₁₆ in. [Add. ch. 21,436.]
Within a finely carved gothic panel, an oval or egg-shaped shield of arms : on a chevron betw. three roundles, some indistinct charges.   Supporters : two lions.   Perhaps a German seal.
✠ SIGILLVM : . . . CODIENIEN : DE : COLONIA (?)

Amelia, *Princess of England, daughter of* GEORGE II.
6824. [A.D. 1761.]   Black : *en placard.*   Cracked.   ⅞ in. [Birch MS. 4271, art. 31.]
A lozenge-shaped shield of arms : ROYAL ARMS OF GEORGE II., see No. 644 (without the escutcheon in the fourth quarter), a label for difference, PRINCESS AMELIA. Ensigned with the coronet and cap of a Princess ; supporters of GREAT BRITAIN, upon a carved device of floral scrolls springing from a cherub's head.

John Améry, *Citizen and Stationer of London.*
6825. [A.D. 1669.]   Red : indistinct, covered with paper previous to impression. ⁷⁄₁₆ × ½ in. [Harl. ch. 111 H. 36.]
A shield of arms : the charges very indistinct.

Ph[ilip] Amherst.
Seal used by ROGER PALMER, *Esq.,*
Cupbearer to CHARLES, *Prince of Wales.*
6826. [A.D. 1624.]   Red : injured. ¾ × ⁹⁄₁₆ in. [Add. ch. 29,559.]
Oval : a shield of arms : three tilting spears, two and one, erect, AMHERST. Crest on a helmet, mantling and wreath, on a mount three tilting spears headed, environed with a chaplet of laurel.
Beaded border.

Ralph de Amundeville, *al.* Mundevile, *of co. Durham.*
6827. [13th cent.] Green: fair. 1 in. [Egert. ch. 519.]
A shield of arms: two bars, each surcharged with a barrulet, in chief three estoiles.

+ S' RADVLFI D' MVNDEVIL'

Cf. Rad. de Amundavilla, witness to a charter of Sulby Abbey, co. Northt., in A.D. 1207–1217. Add. ch. 22,563.

Richard de Amundevile, *of Thorney, co. Suff., Knt.*
6828. [A.D. 1316.] Bronze-green: fine. ⅞ in. [Harl. ch. 45 C. 35.]
A shield of arms: fretty. Probably for a fret, MUNDEVILL, or AMUNDEVILL.

✸ : S' RICARDI : DAMVNDVIL' :

6829. Sulph. cast from No. 6828. [D.C., F. 190.]

Richard, *son and heir of* RICHARD de Amundeville,
of Warwick, co. Warw.
6830. [Early 13th cent.] Light-brown. 1⅛ in. [Harl. ch. 45 C. 34.]
A shield of arms: fretty over all a fess. On the fess an uncertain addition, perhaps a crescent, on the dexter side. The shield is placed over three bars wavy.

⚜ SIGILL' RICARDI DE AMVNDEVILE.

Beaded borders.
6831. Sulph. cast from No. 6830. [D.C., E. 377.]

John de Amyas, *Jun.,*
Receiver of D. ROBERT DE SWYLLINGTON, *Chev. in co. York.*
6832. [A.D. 1386.] Red: injured by pressure. ¾ in. [Add. ch. 20,547.]
Within a carved gothic panel, a shield of arms: [on] a bend cotised three [roses], in chief a label of as many points, AMYAS.

✸ Sigillum : iohanis : de : amyas.

The letters D E, in *de*, are conjoined.

Cf. Add. ch. 20,603, A.D. 1359; and 20,556, A.D. 1362.

Richard Amyas, *of co. York., Gentl.*
6833. [A.D. 1500.] Red: fragmentary. [Add. ch. 17,055.]
Small rectangular-shaped seal, perhaps from a signet ring: a stag's head erased? Crest of AMYAS.

William de An . . . . eld.

6834. [A.D. 1359.]   Brownish-green mixed with red. $\frac{7}{8}$ in.
[Harl. ch. 86 E. 39.]

A shield of arms : a fleur-de-lis.   Betw. three small quatrefoil flowers.   In a carved and pointed gothic six-foil.

✠ S' WILLELMI · DE · AN . . . . ELD.

The L's are of peculiar shape, formed with a heel or serif
on the left of the down stroke.

Edmund Anderson, *Knt.*,
Lord Chief Justice of the Court of Common Pleas,
A.D. 1582–1605.

6835. [A.D. 1586.]   Red : fair, not perfectly stamped.
$\frac{7}{8}$ × $\frac{3}{4}$ in.   [Add. ch. 13,085.]

A shield of arms : quarterly, 1, 4, a chevron betw. three
crosses flory, or crosslet, ANDERSON ; 2, 3, five estoiles in
saltire, ANDERSON.   Crest on a helmet, ornamental mantling,
and wreath, a water-spaniel passant.
Beaded border.

6836. [A.D. 1586.]   Red : fair, but not perfectly stamped.
[Harl. ch. 78 I. 11.]

6837. [A.D. 1588.]   Red : fine, but imperfect.   [Add. ch.
13,655.]

6838. [A.D. 1594.]   Red : very imperfect.   [Add. ch.
15,818.]

6839. [A.D. 1597.]   Red : imperfect and indistinct.   [Add.
ch. 15,819.]

6840. [A.D. 1597.]   Red : the wax rolled up after receiving the impression.   [Harl. ch. 77 C. 3.]

6841. [A.D. 1598.]   Red : fair, the crest very indistinct.
[Harl. ch. 77 C. 10.]

6842. [A.D. 1600.]   Red : good, chipped.   [Woll. ch. xii.
33.]

6843. [A.D. 1602.]   Red : somewhat indistinct.   [Harl. ch.
77 C. 33B.]

6844. [A.D. 1604.]   Red : detached from the charter, indistinct.   [Add. ch. 14,795.]

Francis Anderson, *of Newcastle-upon-Tyne,*
co. Northumb., Knt.

6845. [A.D. 1650.]   Red : the upper half broken off.
About $\frac{3}{4}$ × $\frac{5}{8}$ in. when perfect.   [Egert. ch. 307.]

A shield of arms : three bucks lodged, two and one,
ANDERSON.

William Andrew, *of Estbarry, co. Glamorgan.*
6846. [A.D. 1418.] Red. $\frac{11}{16} \times \frac{5}{8}$ in. [Add. ch. 20,509.]
- A shield of arms: three bars. Suspended by a strap
from a forked tree.

$\mathfrak{S}^r$ **will'i ⚜ ⚜ andrew.**

Beaded border.

Thomas Andrews, *of co. Suff.*
6847. [A.D. 1577.] Red: indistinct. $\frac{11}{16} \times \frac{13}{16}$ in. [Add.
ch. 32,907.]
Oval: on a wreath a dove rising, holding in the beak an
olive branch. Crest of ANDREWS. Within a garland of
foliage and flowers.

Geoffrey de Anesty.
6848. [A.D. 1288–9.] Plaster cast from indistinct impression. $\frac{3}{4}$ in. [lxxxii. 7.]
A shield of arms: on a bend betw. two birds, three bulls
passant (?). Suspended by a strap from a hook. Betw. two
wyverns.

✠ SIGILL' GALFRIDI DE ANESTY.

Thomas de . . . . . .
Seal used by ROBERT ANESTY, *of co. Essex.*
6849. [A.D. 1363.] Dark green: imperfect. About $\frac{7}{8}$ in.
when perfect. [Harl. ch. 76 A. 1.]
A shield of arms: three roundles within a bordure engrailed. (Cf. arms of PINCHYON of Writtle, Essex.)

S' THOME DE . . . .

William de Anesty.
6850. [A.D. 1319–20.] Plaster cast from good impression.
$\frac{3}{4}$ in. [lxxxii. 6.]
A shield of arms: three eagles, two and one, betw. four
estoiles irregularly disposed.

✠ S' WILLELMI DE ANESTY.

Robert Angetelle, *of Bungay, co. Suff.*
6851. [A.D. 1429.] Red: fine. $\frac{1}{2}$ in. [Add. ch. 15,719.]
A shield of false arms: a fess betw. in chief a cross pattée
inter the letters **r. a.,** (Robert Angetelle,) in base a chevron,
in base point an estoile. Within a trilobe.
Cabled border.

2 E 2

Henry de Anna, *Knt., son of* ODO DE CHELWARTONE, *of Quarley, co. Hants.*

6852. [A.D. 1219.]   White: imperfect and indistinct. 1⅛ in. [Toph. ch. 45.]

A shield of arms: three estoiles of eight points?

.... ICI : DE ANN ....

Alexander de Anne, *of co. York.*

6853. [A.D. 1395.]   Dark-green: somewhat injured by pressure.   1 in.   [Add. ch. 17,060.]

A shield of arms: on a bend betw. two cotises, three martlets, in sinister chief a pierced mullet.   Within a carved gothic rosace of six semicircular cusps with three outer ogee points.

✠ 𝔖𝔦𝔤𝔦𝔩𝔩ū . 𝔞𝔩𝔢𝔵𝔞𝔫𝔡𝔢𝔯 𝔡𝔢 𝔞𝔫𝔫𝔢.

6854. [A.D. 1395.]   Dark-green: injured.   [Add. ch. 17,061.]

6855. [A.D. 1395.]   Dark-green: fair, indistinct in places. [Add. ch. 17,062.]

Hugh de Annesley.

6856. [A.D. 1398-9.]   Plaster cast from fine impression. 1 in.   [lxxxii. 8.]

A shield of arms: paly of six, over all a bend, ANNESLEY. With an annulet? for difference.   Suspended by a strap from a forked tree on a mount.   Within a gothic panel.

𝔖𝔦𝔤𝔦𝔩𝔩𝔲𝔪 : 𝔥𝔲𝔤𝔬𝔫𝔦𝔰 : 𝔡𝔢 : 𝔞𝔫𝔫𝔢𝔰𝔩𝔢𝔭.

William de Anstan, *or* Austan, *Rector of the Church of St. Nicholas, Durham, co. Durham.*

6857. [A.D. 1369.]   Mottled-green: semi-opaque.   ⅞ in. [Add. ch. 20,555.]

A shield of arms: a fess.   Within a star of six points bordered with ball-flowers.

Legend betw. the points:—

✠ 𝔖 * _𝔚𝔦𝔩𝔢𝔩_𝔪𝔦 * _ * 𝔡𝔢 * _ 𝔞𝔫 _ ſ𝔱𝔞𝔫, *or* 𝔞𝔲ſ𝔱𝔞𝔫.

John Ansty, *Jun., Gentl.*

6858. [A.D. 1440.]   Red: fine, from chased signet ring. ¾ in.   [Add. ch. 33,547.]

A dexter *hand*, couped at the wrist, vested, grasping a bunch of three holly leaves, fructed ; betw. the letters 𝔤 . 𝔱 𝔭. The whole forming a rebus on the name of the owner.   The holly leaves perhaps a crest of the family.

Cabled border.

Cf. John Ansty, Jun., of Thenford Manor, co. Northt., A.D. 1449, Add. ch. 7569.

Ithel Ap-Bledyn, *of Wales.*

6859. [14th cent. ?] Red: recent impression from the matrix. 1 in. [xxxv. 27.]

A shield of arms, *couché:* quarterly, two lions rampant addorsed, the tails intertwined. Crest on a helmet, lambrequin, and wreath, a maiden's head, coroneted and draped. Within a finely carved gothic panel with six cusps; from the l. h. side spring two pierced cinquefoil roses, slipped, from the r. h. side, one.

𝕾𝖎𝖌𝖎𝖑𝖑𝖚 : 𝕴𝖙𝖍𝖊𝖑 : 𝖆𝖕 : 𝕭𝖑𝖊𝖉𝖞𝖓.

Beaded border.

6860. Gutta percha impression. [xlvii. 1422 B.]

Laing's *MS. Catal.*, No. 14.

6861. Sulph. cast. [D.C., F. 314.]

Gruff ap Gwlad vch Edū ap Ḹi . . , *of Dwygyfylchi,* *co. Caernarvon.*

6862. [A.D. 1444.] Red: cracked and imperfect. ½ × ¼ in. [Add. ch. 17,702.]

Oblate octagonal: a shield of arms: on a bend three small birds or animals reguardant. In the field a very indistinct legend or motto.

Cabled border.

Howel Ap-Hichecok, [*of Bryngwyn, co. Radn. ?*]

6863. [A.D. 1379.] White: imperfect, and very indistinct. 1 in. [Harl. ch. 85 F. 45.]

A shield of arms: the bearings flaked away. Within a carved gothic panel.

Legend destroyed.

Robert Ap-Howelle Ap-Eynone, *of Hodenak, co. Salop.*

6864. [A.D. 1446.] Red: imperfect and indistinct. About 1 in. when perfect. [Add. ch. 7708.]

A shield (of arms?): a lion rampant queue fourchée, debruised by a bend lozengy (?). Over the shield a bird, on the r. a man's bust, in profile to the l., couped at the neck; the corresponding object on the l. wanting. Within a quatrefoil with countersunk trefoil in each spandril.

✠ ICEST SEAL SI . . . . . . AL.

Janckyn Ap-Morgan Ap-John, *of Llanvrenach,* *co. Brecon., Gentl.*

6865. [A.D. 1545.] Red. ⅔ in. [Harl. ch. 111 B. 37.]

Shield-shaped: a shield of arms: a chevron betw. three spear-heads or pheons reversed, MORGAN.

Roger de Appleby.

6866. [14th cent.] Plaster cast from fine but chipped impression. 1⅛ in. [lxxxii. 9.]

A shield of arms. *couché:* a chevron betw. three pine-apples? Crest on a helmet, and lambrequin, a pine-apple. Betw. two wavy sprigs of foliage and flowers. Within a carved gothic panel of six cusps, ornamented along the inner edge with ball-flowers.

SIGILL' ROGERI DE APPLEB .. (?)

Cf. Roger f. Simonis de Appylby, A.D. 1314, Cott. ch. xxvi. 22.

Thomas de Appelby.

6867. [A.D. 1420–1.] Plaster cast from indistinct impression. ⅞ in. [lxxxii. 11.]

A shield of arms; six martlets, three, two, and one, APPLEBY. Within an engrailed panel.

+ Sigillum + thome + de + appelby. (?)

Edmund Apreece, *of Wollaston, co. Northt., Gentl.*

6868. [A.D. 1580.] Red. ₇⁄₁₃ in. [Add. ch. 23,883.]

A shield of arms: three spear-heads, APREECE, a crescent for difference. Burke describes the spear-heads as *guttées de sang.*

Beaded border.

6869. [A.D. 1580.] Red : a fragment. [Add. ch. 23,883.]

Philip Apries *or* Ap-Rees.

See PHILIP HAPRIES.

Rees Ap Rees, *al.* Apries, *[of co. Lincoln.]*

6870. [A.D. 1362.] Red : fine originally, now cracked and very imperfect. 1 in. [Coll. ch. v. 18.]

A shield of arms : paly of six, on a chief a lion passant. Suspended by the strap from a forked tree. Within a finely carved and pointed gothic rosace.

Sigillum ⚜ Ries ⚜ Apries.

Cf. the seal and arms of Philip Hapries.

William Apsley, *Gentl., kinsman and heir of John Apsley, Esq., of Warnham, co. Suss.*

6871. [A.D. 1513.] Red : imperfectly impressed. 1¼ in. [Add. ch. 8927.]

A shield of arms, *couché:* a cross lozengy. Crest, on a helmet and chapeau, uncertain, perhaps a bird on a tree-stump fretty. Within a carved and traced gothic panel.

S' · WILL'I ⚜ . ; . . AO . . . .

John Ap Thomelin, *Lord of Lanlonell and Talevañ, Wales.*
 6872. [A.D. 1432.] Red: a fragment. [Add. ch. 7148.]
 A shield of arms: very imperfect, only a stag's head. cabossed, in the sinister chief.
 Legend wanting.

James Arblaster, *of Longedon, co. Staff.*
 6873. [A.D. 1402.] Red: fine. [Add. ch. 24,242.]
 A shield of arms: erm., a cross-bow, or arbaleste, in pale, ARBLASTER. Suspended by a strap from a forked tree on a mount. Within a carved panel.
   𝕾igillum : iacobi : arblaster.
 Cabled border.
 6874. Plaster cast from No. 6873. [lxxxii. 12.]

John Archer, *Sheriff of Berks, Esq.*
 6875. [A.D. 1693.] Red: *en placard*, on a label, imperfect. ⅞ in. [Add. ch. 19,235.]
 A shield of arms: Erm., a cross, ARCHER.
 Beaded border.

Michael Archer.
See FRANCIS WOLRICHE.

Nicholas Archer, *of co. Kent.*
 6876. [A.D. 1336.] Green: fine originally, now imperfect. 1⅜ in. [Add. ch. 20,173.]
 A shield of arms: a rose, slipped and leaved, in chief three arrows palewise in fess, points downwards, for ARCHER. Within a carved gothic panel.
   . . . . . . NICH [OL] AI ARCHER.
 The letters A, R, and E, R, conjoined.

Robert Le Archer.
 6877. [14th cent. ?] Plaster cast from fine impression or matrix. 1⅝ in. [lxxxii. 13.]
 A shield of arms: ermine, on a bend sinister betw. two cotises, an arrow bendwise, the point in base. Background diapered. Within a carved gothic trefoil ornamented with ball-flowers along the inner edge.
   ✠ SIGILVM ✶ ROBERTI · LE · ARCHER.
 Some of the letters reversed.
 Beaded border.

.Thomas Archer, *of Whitehall, co. Midd., Esq.*

6878. [A.D. 1735.]   Red: *en placard* on a tape, imperfect. About ⅞ × ¾ in. when perfect.   [Add. ch. 17,817.]

A shield of arms : per pale, *dex.*, three arrows, barbed and, feathered, ARCHER ; *sin.*, erm. on a chief three animals' heads erased. Crest on a helmet and mantling, out of a mural coronet a dragon's head (?).   Crest of ARCHER.

John **Darcy**, *Chivaler.*

? SIR JOHN DARCY, *Knt.*, " *Le Cousin*," *Chief Governor of Ireland.*

6879. [A.D. 1322.]   Red: the edge imperfectly impressed. 1 in.   [Add. ch. 19,838.]

On a ship, beaked at each end with an animal's or bird's head, a shield of arms, *couché*: three cinquefoils pierced, betw. seven crosses crosslet (for semé?), DARCY.   Crest, on a helmet and mantling, out of a mural crown, an animal's head (?). On the l. h. side a flag charged with a small indistinct animal *contourné*, perhaps a bull.   Crest of DARCY.

Legend wanting.
Beaded border.

John **Darcy**, *Lord of Knayth, co. Lincoln,* *2nd Baron Darcy.*

6880. [A.D. 1349.]   Red: very fine, edge imperfect.   1⅓ in. [Harl. ch. 49 D. 2.]

A shield of arms : three roses betw. seven crosses crosslet. Suspended by a strap from a forked oak tree.   Background ornamented with a diaper papilone.

𝕾𝖎𝖌𝖎𝖑𝖑𝖚 𝕵𝖔𝖍𝖆𝖓𝖓𝖎𝖘 𝕯𝖆𝖗𝖈𝖞 𝖉𝖓𝖎 𝖉𝖊 𝕶𝖓𝖆𝖞𝖙𝖍.

Beaded border.

6881. Sulph. cast from No. 6880.   [D.C., F. 306.]

Normann de Aresci, *of co. Lincoln,* *? afterwards 5th Baron D'Arcy.*

6882. [A.D. 1219.]   Dark-green: very fragmentary.   About ·1¼ in. when perfect.   [Harl. ch. 49 C. 40.]

A shield of arms : three six-foils or roses, DARCY.

. . . . RMAN' DE A . . . .

Normann de Arcy, *Knt., 2nd Baron D'Arcy,* (*by writ*) ; *Lord of Nocketon, co. Lincoln.*

6883. [A.D. 1334.]   Semi-opaque light-brown: fine ; app. by a finely woven cord of green stuff.   ½½ in.   [Harl. ch. 49 C. 49.]

Four shields of arms arranged in cross with points meeting in the centre: 1. Three roses or six-foils, pierced, DARCY; 2. Three roses betw. seven crosses crosslet (for semé), DARCY; 3. As 1 with label of three points; 4. On a bend betw. six martlets, three roundles (?) Within a carved and pointed gothic quatrefoil panel.

For the 4th shield of arms: cf. on a bend betw. six martlets, three *bezants*, WORTELL, or *roses*, RUSSHAM.

In place of the legend a wavy scroll of foliage with roses.

6884. [A.D. 1334.] Semi-opaque light-brown: fine; app. by another piece of the same kind of cord as in No. 6883. [Harl. ch. 49 C. 50.]

6885. Sulph. cast from No. 6884. [D.C., F. 248.]

6886. [*s. d.*] Semi-opaque pale-green: fine, but a fragment only. [Harl. ch. 49 C. 48.]

Philip, Sire de Arcy, *Lord of Kneyth, 4th Baron D'Arcy, Admiral of the North.*

6887. [A.D. 1386.] Red: very fine, edge imperfect. $1\frac{3}{16}$ in. [Harl. ch. 49 D. 3.]

A shield of arms: three roses betw. seven crosses crosslet. Suspended by a strap from a forked tree, and within a finely carved and traced gothic panel.

⚲ 𝕾𝖎𝖌𝖎𝖑𝖑ū : ꝺn̄i : p𝖍𝖎𝖑𝖎𝖕𝖕𝖎 : ꝺarcꝑ : m𝖎𝖑𝖎𝖙𝖎𝖘 ✱ᴀᴇ
Carved border.

6888. Sulph. cast from No. 6887. [D.C., F. 559.]

6889. [A.D. 1375.] Pale-green: fine. [Add. ch. 20,718.]

Thomas Darci, *al.* **de Areci,**
son and heir of Thomas de Areci, 4th Baron de Arcy by tenure.

6890. [*Temp.* Ric. I.] Dark-green: fine, with raised rim; app. by a closely woven cord of various coloured stuff. $2\frac{1}{8}$ in. [Harl. ch. 49 C. 20.]

Ø. A finely designed rose or pierced six-foil, in allusion to the arms of DARCY.

+ SIGILLVM · THOME DE DARCI.

℞. A small oval counterseal. $\frac{7}{8} \times \frac{3}{4}$ in. Impression of an antique oval intaglio gem: Victory, driving a quadriga, to the r.

+ SIGILL' TOMAS DARCI.

6891. [*Temp.* Ric. I.] Dark-green: fine but imperfect. [Harl. ch. 49 C. 21.]

Ø. .... OM ..... E DAR ....

℞. As in No. 6890.

Nicholaus de Ardena.

Seal used by William Darderne, Clerk, of Offord, co. Warwick.
6892. [A.D. 1366.] Faded green. ¾ in. [Add..ch. 21,492.]
A shield of arms: three crosses crosslet fitchées, on a chief a lion passant. Betw. three small flowers, slipped; and within a carved and pointed gothic quatrefoil.

✠ S' * ИICHOLAI * DE * ARDEИA.

Beaded border.

Peter Arden, *or* Arderne.

6893. [14th cent.] Plaster cast from imperfect impression. ¾ in. [lxxxii. 14.]
A shield of arms: three crosses crosslet pattées, a chief, ARDERNE.

✠ FRANGE · LEGE · TEGE.

Beaded borders.

Cf. Peter fil. Hugonis Arderne, A.D. 1372, Add. ch. 20,492.

Thomas de Ardene, *son of* RALPH DE ARDENE, *of co. Essex, Knt.*

6894. [Late 13th cent.] Green: cracked, but fine. ⅞ in. [Add. ch. 19,967.]
A shield of arms: two trumpets, or horns, mouthpieces in base, betw. nine crosses crosslet in fess, 3, 3, and 3, in pale.

✠ S' THOME · DE · ARDENE.

Beaded borders.

Thomas de Arderne.

6895. [A.D. 1286.] Plaster cast from fine impression. 1 in. [lxxxii. 15.]
A shield of arms: chequy, a chevron.

✠ SIGILL' · THOME · DE · ARDERNE.

William de Ardena, *of Hamtune* [*Hampton-in-Arden, co. Warw.*]

6896. [*c.* A.D. 1188–1198.] Light-brown: very imperfect. About 1⅛ × 1⅛ in. when perfect. [Cott. ch. xi. 36.]
Pointed oval: a lion rampant contourné, in allusion to the arms of ARDEN.

.. GILL' WILL . . . .

John, *son and heir of* ADAM de Arderne, *Knt., of co. Linc.*

6897. [A.D. 1312.] Light-brown, varnished very dark: fine, but a fragment. About ⅚ × ⅔ in. [Harl. ch. 45 D. 9.]

A shield of arms : ermine, on a bend (three crosses crosslet ?).
Suspended by a strap from a tree of three small branches.
.... E : DE : ARDERN ....

Peter, *son of* HUGH de **Arderne,** [*of Macclesfield, co. Ches.*]
6898. [A.D. 1372.] Green : fair. $\frac{11}{16}$ in. [Add. ch. 20,492.]
A shield of arms : three crosses crosslet, fitchées, a chief,
ARDEN, or ARDERNE. Within a carved gothic cinquefoil
with triangle points.
¤ SIGILLVM · PETRI · DE · ARDERN.
Beaded borders.

Ralph de Arderne, [*of Horndon, co. Ess.*] *Knt.*
6899. [Late 13th cent.] Bronze-green : fine. $\frac{9}{10}$ in.
[Harl. ch. 45 D. 8.]
A shield of arms : a fess chequy betw. two roundles, one
in chief and one in base (?) Cf. A fess chequy, ARDEN.
+ SIGILL' RADVLFI DE ARDERNE.
Beaded borders.
6900. Sulph. cast from No. 6899. [D.C., E. 352.]

Robert de Arderne, *of co. Norf*
6901. [A.D. 1315.] Red : fine, edge chipped. 1 in. [Add.
ch. 8069.]
Two shields of arms side by side in fess. *Dex.,* Ermine, a
fess chequy, ARDEN. *Sin.,* on a fess three (garbs ?). Over
the shield the word AGLA, betw. two small trefoils, one at each
side, and over it a wavy scroll. Below them, the sacred
name :—IHC, surmounted by a trefoil or quatrefoil, from which
springs a slipped flower, betw. two small birds.
Legend of initial letters :—
S' ❋ ❋ ❋ [ ] ❋ ❋ ❋ I ❋ ❋ ❋ S ❋ ❋ ❋ E ❋ ❋ ❋ O ❋ ❋ ❋ R ❋ ❋ ❋
Beaded borders.
For the cabalistic use of the words *Agla,* the name of the Almighty
which Lot heard, and *Jhesus,* see Rev. W. Sparrow Simpson, *On a
Magical Roll,* in *Journ. Brit. Arch. Assoc.,* vol. xl., 1884, p. 317, and
pl. 1, 11, ff. 4, 6, 11, 19, etc. For date of this charter see list of Mayors
of King's Lynn in Blomefield's *Hist. of Norfolk,* vol. viii., p. 533.

Thomas de Arderne, [*of Newton, co. Warw.*]
6902. [A.D. 1280–1290.] Green : edges chipped. $\frac{7}{10}$ in.
[Cott. ch. xxii. 5.]
A shield of arms : a fesse chequy, ARDERN.
+ SIGILLVM · SECRETI.
Beaded borders.

Thomas de Arderne, *or* Ardena, *Lord of Peddymore, co. Warw.*

6903. [A.D. 1281.]   Bronze-green: fine.·   1$\frac{1}{16}$ in.   [Egert. ch. 368.]

A shield of arms : chequy, a chevron.

✠ SIGILL' THOME DE ARDERNE.

Beaded border.

Giles de Argenten, *or* Argentein, *of Newmarket, co. Suff., Knt.*

6904. [Late 13th cent.]   Dark green: fine, chipped at the r. h. side.   1$\frac{1}{2}$ in.   [Harl. ch. 45 D. 13.]

∅. A shield of arms : three covered cups, two and one, ARGENTINE.

✠ SIGI[LLVM :] EGIDII : DE : ARGENTEN.

The letters AR and EN of *Argenten* are respectively conjoined.

Beaded borders.

℞. A small shield-shaped counter-seal.   1 × $\frac{4}{5}$ in.   A shield of arms as in the *obv.* within a guilloche border.

6905. Sulph. cast of the *obv.*   [D.C., E. 366.]
6906. Sulph. cast of the *rev.*   [D.C., E. 394.]

John de Argentein, *of Uggeshall Manor, co. Suff.*

6907. [A.D. 1378.]   Red: fine, somewhat injured by· pressure.   ˙1 in.   [Add. ch. 10,376.]

A shield of arms : three covered cups, ARGENTINE. Betw. three small quatrefoils, and within a finely carved gothic six-foil or rosace.

The space or annulus for the legend is filled with a wavy scroll of foliage and quatrefoils.

Reginald de Argentein, *of West Bergholt, co. Essex, Knt.*

6908. [A.D. 1289.]   Discoloured white, or light brownish grey: chipped.   [Harl. ch. 45 D. 14.]

Shield shaped : from the same matrix as the *rev.* of the seal of Giles de Argentein, No. 6904.

William Argentein, *of Ubbeston Manor, co. Suff., Knt.*

6909. [A.D. 1404.]   Red: very imperfect.   About 1 in. [Harl. ch. 45 D. 15.]

˙ A shield of arms : (three) covered cups, ARGENTEIN. Within a carved gothic panel.

⋯⋯⋯ mí argentein.

Beaded border.

David de Armentirs, *or* Armenteriis, *of Hundigton, or Honington, co. Linc.*

6910. [*circ.* A.D. 1150.] Red: originally fine, chipped and ·imperfect, with deep mark of a handle. 2 in. [Eg. ch. 427.]

Three swords fesswise in pale, alternately arranged, that in the middle with hilt downward, those at the side with hilts upward. Perhaps in allusion to a shield of arms.

+ SIGILLVM . . . . DE ARMENTIRS.

Cf. Eg. ch. 430 ; Add. ch. 22,743 ; Harl. ch. 85 D. 49.

6911. Plaster cast, tinted, from No. 6910. [xci. 55.]

Henry de Armenteres, *or* Ermenters, *of Witefeld, or Whitfield, co. Northt.*

6912. [Late Hen. II.] Light brown: chipped. A curious mass or cake of wax. 2¼ × 2⅛ in. [Harl. ch. 84 G. 11.]

Irregular oval: a sword with curved quillons, and spherical ·boss, handle upwards, the grip ornamented.

+ SIGILLVM · HENRICI DE ARMENTERES.

Cf. Harl. ch. 84 D. 13 ; 84 H. 20 ; 85 E. 33 ; 84 G. 12 ; 86 C. 36 ; 86 A. 3 (all late in the 12th cent.).

6913. Sulph. cast from No. 6912. [D.C., D. 294.]

Walter de Armenteres, *also called* Walter filius Emme de Insula, *of Witefeld, co. Northt.*

6914. [Late Hen. II.] Light brown, varnished: with mark of the handle. 1⅝ in. The vellum label is curiously plaited. [Harl. ch. 86 C. 62.]

Two swords of early shape with short transverse bar and hemispherical knob, palewise in fess. The handle of the sword on the r. upwards, the other downwards.

+ SIGILLVM WALTERRI DE ARMENTERES.

6915. Sulph. cast from No. 6914. [D.C., D. 284.]

Arnald, *Vicar of the Church of Ecclesfield, co. York.*

6916. [A.D. 1408.] Red: somewhat indistinct in parts. ¾ × ⁹⁄₁₀ in. [Harl. ch. 112 F. 31.]

A shield of arms: a lion rampant, on a chief, a lion passant guardant. Above the shield two half-length saints, r., an archbishop with mitre, lifting up the r. h. in benediction, in the l. a crozier ; l. the Virgin, crowned, holding the Infant Saviour, overhead a small dove. All within a carved gothic rosace of ten points.

⚹ SIG . . . RV . . . . ETWI . . STELLA · MARIA (?)

6917. Sulph. cast from No. 6916. [D.C., F. 146.]

John Arnold, *Esq.*

6918. [15th cent.] Plaster cast from fine impression. 1⅛ in. [lxxxii. 16.]

A shield of arms, *couché :* per pale, a chevron betw. three :billets, counterchanged. Crest on a helmet, lambrequin and wreath, a unicorn's head, holding in the mouth a blank label, tasselled ends. In the background a sprig of foliage..

⚜ ſigíllū ✱ Joḣaníˢ ⚜ arnolð ⚜ leſqír.

Beaded border.

Cf. Add. ch. 9730, A.D. 1462.

Perhaps foreign.

Robert de Arsic, *of Coges, co. Oxon.*

6919. [A.D. 1212–3.] Dark green: fine, edge chipped. 2³⁄₁₀ in. [Harl. ch. 45 D. 18.]

A shield of arms; quarterly, on a bordure twelve bulls' heads couped, ARSIC. The 1st and 4th quarters diapered with a kind of papilone pattern.

[. . SIG]ILLVM[⋅ ⋅ R]OBERTI ⋅ DE ⋅ ARSIC.

6920. Sulph. cast from No. 6919. [D.C., E. 311.]

Isabella Arthur.

6921. [A.D. 1383–4.] Plaster cast from indistinct impression. 1 in. [lxxxii. 19.]

A shield of arms, per pale : *dex.* a chevron betw. three rests, ARTHUR, *sin.* a fess betw. three birds. Suspended by a strap from a forked tree. Within a carved gothic panel.

Sigill' ⁊ Iſabelle ⁊ artḣur.

Richard Artur.

6922. [A.D. 1368.] Plaster cast from indistinct impression. ⅞ in. [lxxxii. 17.]

A shield of arms : a chevron betw. three rests, ARTHUR. Within a pointed quatrefoil panel.

✠ Sigillum ⚜ ricarðı ⚜ ⚜ artur ⚜

Beaded border.

Cf. Richard Arthur, *al.* Artur, in Portbury, co. Somers., A.D. 1340, Add. ch. 7820, 7821 ; Richard Artur in Wraxall, co. Somers., A.D. 1363, Add. ch. 7837 ; Sir Richard Arthur of Clapton-in-Gordano, co. Somers., A.D. 1368, Slo. ch. xxxii. 4.

Thomas Artur.

6923. [A.D. 1383–4.] Plaster cast from good impression. 1 in. [lxxxii. 19.]

A shield of arms : a chevron betw. three rests, ARTHUR,

over all a label of three points.　Betw. three sprigs of foliage.

ß' . Domini ⚜ thome . artur ⚜

Inner border carved with small quatrefoils or ball-flowers, outer border cabled.

Cf. Thomas Arthur in Portbury, co. Somers., A.D. 1399, Add. ch. 7851.

William Arthur, *of Wadworth, co. York., Gentl.*

6924. [A.D. 1707.]　Red : *en placard* on a label. $\frac{3}{8} \times \frac{1}{2}$ in. [Add. ch. 29,592.]

A shield of arms : a chevron betw. three Irish brogues, ARTHURE.

Beaded border.

6925. [A.D. 1707.]　Another.　[Add. ch. 29,593.]

Arundel Family?

6926. [16th cent.]　Plaster cast from fine impression. $\frac{7}{8} \times \frac{3}{4}$ in.　[lxxxii. 20.]

Oval : a shield of arms : six swallows, three, two, and one. Cabled border.

Alianora de Arundel.
See ALIANORA DE FITZALAN.

Edmund de Arundelle,
2nd son of EDMUND FITZALAN, *8th Earl of Arundel.*

6927. [A.D. 1368.]　Red : very fine but edge imperfect. $1\frac{1}{4}$ in.　[Harl. ch. 53 E. 11.]

A shield of arms : quarterly, 1, 4, a lion rampant, for FITZ-ALAN ; 2, 3, chequy, WARRENNE (the alternate squares powdered, perhaps for *or*), over all a label of three points. Suspended by a strap from a tree, with small side-branches of wavy design and enriched with flowers, springing from the root, and supporting on each side a helmet on which is the crest of a plume of feathers out of a ducal coronet.

ß' : Edmūdi . . . aru . . el.

Beaded border.

6928. Sulph. cast from No. 6927.　[D.C., F. 459.]

Frances Arundell, *of Lanheron, co. Cornw.*

6929. [A.D. 1729.]　Red : *en placard*, on a tape. $\frac{3}{4} \times \frac{5}{8}$ in. [Add. ch. 29,503.]

An oval shield of arms, carved with foliage and arabesques : a lion passant, and chief indented (or, in chief three piles).

John Arundel, *al.* Aroundell,
son of JAMES DE PEYTONE, *of co. Suff.*

6930. [A.D. 1349.] Red: fine, injured, edge chipped. $\frac{9}{10}$ in. [Harl. ch. 48 A. 17.]

A shield of arms: ermine, on a canton a cross lozengy, ARUNDEL. Within a carved and pointed gothic cinquefoil.

✠ · SIGILLVM · · IOH'IS · · ARVNDEL.

For arms cf. Harl. MS. 380, f. 123 *b.*

John Arundelle, *al.* Darondell, *Knt.*; A.D. 1365–1391,
son and heir of Sir JOHN ARUNDELLE, *Knt.*,
[Marshal of England, and ELEANOR, *coheir of* JOHN, *Lord Maltravers].*

6931. [A.D. 1388.] Red: very fine, but imperfect. About $1\frac{1}{8}$ in. when perfect. [Add. ch. 24,553.]

A shield of arms: quarterly, 1, 4, a lion rampant, for FITZ-ALAN of Arundel; 2, 3, a fret, MALTRAVERS. Suspended by a strap from a forked tree. Within an elegantly carved and traced gothic panel, bordered with ball-flowers.

. . . . . . nis Darondell.

Beaded border.

Richard de Arondell, *of Brandon Manor. co. Warw.,*
and Wychampton Manor, co. Dors., Knt.

6932. [A.D. 1415.] Red: fine but very imperfect. About $1\frac{1}{4}$ in. when perfect. [Harl. ch. 45 C. 55.]

A shield of arms, *couché*: quarterly, 1, 4, a lion rampant, FITZ-ALAN of Arundel; 2, 3, a fret, MALTRAVERS. Crest on a helmet, diapered lambrequin and wreath, an eagle's head and wings, charged on the neck with a crescent for difference. Within a carved and traced gothic panel.

. . . gi . . . . Dar . . . . . .

6933. [A.D. 1415.] Red: fine, but edge imperfect. [Harl. ch. 45 C. 56.]

This impression shows portions of the design wanting in No. 6932.

. . . . arD . . . . arondell ʃ Ɱ

. **6934.** [A.D. 1415.] Red: very fine, but imperfect. [Harl. ch. 45 C. 57.]

: **6935.** Sulph. cast from No. 6934. [D.C., G. 146.]

Sibilla Darundell, [*dau. of* WILLIAM DE MONTACUTE,
Earl of Salisbury, and KATHARINE, *dau. of*
WILLIAM *Lord* GRANDISON, *his wife*],
Wife of Sir EDMUND DE ARUNDELLE, 2*nd son of*
EDMUND FITZ-ALAN, 8*th Earl of Arundel.*

6936. [A.D. 1350.] Red : fine, elaborately designed ; edge
chipped. 1 in. [Harl. ch. 83 E. 36.]

A shield of arms : a lion rampant, and label of three
points, for FITZ-ALAN of Arundel, betw. two lozenge-shaped
shields of arms : *dex.*, three fusils in fess, MONTACUTE ; *sin.*,
paly of six, on a bend three eagles displayed, GRANDISON.
In the field on each side of the central shield at the lower
part of it, a slipped leaf. Within a finely carved and traced
gothic panel, bordered with ball-flowers.

✿ S' : SI[BIL]LE : D[ARV]N[D]EL.

Beaded border.

Cf. Harl. ch. 53 E. 11. No. 6938.

6937. Sulph. cast from No. 6936. [D.C., F. 310.]

Second Seal.

6938. [A.D. 1368.] Red : fine, somewhat injured by pressure, edge wanting. About 1¼ in. when perfect. [Harl.
ch. 53 E. 11.]

A shield of arms : per pale, *dex.*, quarterly, 1, 4, FITZ-
ALAN ; 2, WARRENNE (as in the seal of her husband, Sir
Edmund de Arundelle, see No. 6927) ; *sin.*, three fusils in
fess, MONTACUTE. Within an arabesque design of branches,
foliage, and flowers, containing [four] small circular panels in
cross, each charged with armorial bearings, *viz.*, 1 (top),
wanting, but probably same as that below ; 2 (l. h. side),
GRANDISON, see No. 6936 ; 3 (r. h. side), very imperfect, but
apparently same as 2 ; 4 (base), quarterly, in the 2nd and 3rd
quarters a fret, over all a bend, DESPENCER (?).

Legend wanting.

The explanation of this seal will be better understood by
the following pedigree :—

Edmund FITZ-ALAN, 8th Earl of ARUNDEL	=	Alice Planta-genet, sister and sole heir of John, E. of WARRENNE and Surrey.	William MONTACUTE, Earl of Salisbury	=	Katharine, dau. of Wil-liam, Lord GRANDISON.
		Sir Edmund d'Arundel	=		Sibilla.

William de Arundelle, *Chivaler, son of* JOHN DE ARUNDELLE,
Chivaler, of Brandon Manor, co. Warw.

6939. [A.D. 1397.] Red : originally fine, now very imperfect, in parts injured by pressure. About 1³⁄₁₀ in. when perfect.
[Harl. ch. 45 C. 50.]

A shield of arms, *couché*: quarterly, 1, 4, FITZ-ALAN of Arundel ; 2, 3, MALTRAVERS. Crest on a helmet, lambrequin, and wreath (an eagle's head), betw. two wings erect. Within a carved and traced gothic panel.

. . . . **De arundel** . . . . . .

6940. Sulph. cast from No. 6939, [D.C., G. 209.]

William Asshe, *of St. Albans, co. Herts.*
6941. [A.D. 1409.]   Red: indistinct. $\frac{7}{10}$ in.   [Add. ch. 18,185.]
A shield (of arms ?): perhaps a hand couped at the wrist in bend, holding a flower or other uncertain charge, betw. three estoiles.   Within a pointed gothic trefoil.
✠ . . . . IE . SPORIENE . . . (?)

Sir **Denny Ashburnham,** *of Broomeham, co. Suss., Bart.*
6942. [A.D. 1678.]   Red, covered with paper before impression. $\frac{5}{8} \times \frac{1}{2}$ in.   [Egert. ch. 499.]
Oval: a shield of arms, very indistinct : a fess betw. some uncertain charges.   For a fess betw. six mullets, ASHBURNHAM.
Cf. Add. ch. 17,619 ; 17,620.

Another Seal.

6943. [A.D. 1676.]   Red, covered with paper before impression, very indistinct. $\frac{1}{2} \times \frac{7}{16}$ in.   [Add. ch. 17,619.]
Oval signet : out of a ducal coronet an ash-tree, crest of ASHBURNHAM.

John Ashbornham, *of Ashburnham, co. Suss., Esq.*
6944. [A.D. 1595.]   Red: injured by pressure. $\frac{3}{4} \times \frac{5}{8}$ in. [Add. ch. 29,747.]
Oval: a shield of arms : a fess betw. six mullets, ASHBURNHAM.
Beaded border.

Roger Ashburnham, *of cos. Kent, Surr., etc.*
6945. [A.D. 1363.]   Red: fine, apparently from a matrix with the annulus of the legend partially drawn back by a screw. $\frac{11}{10}$ in.   [Add. ch. 16,473.]
A shield of arms : a fess betw. six pierced mullets, ASHBURNHAM.   Within a carved gothic cinquefoil with points in triangle, bordered with ball-flowers.
✠ **Sigillum : rog[eri : de : ashburnham.**

6946. [A.D. 1375.] Red: very fine, but fragmentary.
[Add. ch. 23,626.]

¤ **Sig** . . . . **rnham.**

6947. [A.D. 1375.] Red: imperfect, nearly defaced by
pressure. [Add. ch. 23,625.]

¤ **Sigillum : rogeri** . . . .

Another Seal.

6948. [A.D. 1380.] Red: fine. $\frac{1}{2}$ in. [Harl. ch. 48 E. 35.]
A pierced mullet, derived from the arms of ASHBURNHAM,
see No. 6945. Within a carved trefoil with ogival points.
Legend betw. the points :—

✳ **alche** ⚘ **burne ham** ⚜

Thomas Assheboneham, *of Guestlyng, co. Suss., Gentl.*
6949. [A.D. 1535.] Red: fine but imperfect impression
from a ring. About $\frac{4}{5} \times \frac{1}{2}$ in. when perfect. [Add. ch. 20,113.]
Ornamental shape: on a mount, out of a ducal coronet,
an ash tree eradicated. Crest of ASHBURNHAM.
Cabled border.

William Ashbournham, *al.* **Ashburnham,**
Cofferer of the Royal Household, Esq.
6950. [A.D. 1665.] Red: very indistinct, covered with
paper before impression. $\frac{1}{4}$ in. [Harl. ch. 77 H. 1.]
Slightly oval: a shield of arms: per pale, *dex.*, five
lozenges in bend ; *sin.*, paly of six, a bend.

George Ashby, *Gentl.*
Seal used by JOHN ROGERS, *of Denham, co. Bucks.*
6951. [A.D. 1509.] Red: good. $\frac{1}{2}$ in. [Harl. ch. 86 D. 13.]
A shield of arms: a chevron betw. three eagles displayed,
ASHBY.

Thomas Assheby, *of Lowesby, co. Leic., Esq.*
6952. [A.D. 1444.] Red: chipped. $\frac{1}{4}$ in. [Add. ch. 26,925.]
An eagle rising, in its beak a trefoil slipped. For a crest of
ASHBY?
Cabled border.

Robert de Asshedon.
6953. [A.D. 1381-2.] Plaster cast from chipped impression. 1 in. [lxxxii. 23.]
A shield of arms: two bars, over all a bendlet. Suspended

2 F 2

by a strap from a tree of three branches. Within a carved gothic panel, 'ornamented with small quatrefoils along the inner edge.

Sigill' . Roberti . d' . alſhedon.

Thomas Assheman.

6954. [15th cent.]   Plaster cast from indistinct impression. 1⅛ in. [lxxxii. 22.]

A shield of arms : on a bend two lions passant.

⋈ sigillum ⋈ ✱ thome ⋈ ✱ alſheman ⋈ ✱.

Michael Asshfelde, *of Wadley, co. Berk., Gentl.*

6955. [A.D. 1598.]   Red : fine. ¹¹⁄₁₂ × ⅝ in. [Harl. ch. 79 F. 40.]

A shield of arms : a slipped trefoil, betw. three mullets, ASHFIELD.

Carved border.

Sir Richard Ashfield, *General in the Army of the Commonwealth.*

6956. [A.D. 1653.]   Recent impression in red sealing wax. ⅝ × ½ in. [xlvii. 2384.]

Oblate octagonal : a shield of arms : a slipped trefoil betw. three mullets, ASHFIELD. Crest, on a helmet, mantling, and wreath, a dexter hand grasping a battle-axe, enfiled with a wreath of laurel.

Laing's *MS. Catal.*, No. 53.

Robert de Aisshefelde, Aysshefelde, *or* Asshefeld, *of co. Suff.*

6957. [A.D. 1394.]   Red : fine.   1 in. [Harl. ch. 45 D. 27.]

A shield of arms : a fess engrailed betw. three fleurs-de-lis, ASHFIELD. Suspended by a strap from a lion's face. Within a carved gothic panel.

Sigill' : roberti : de : aiſſhefeld.

Beaded border.

6958. [A.D. 1383.]   Red : somewhat injured by pressure. [Harl. ch. 47 A. 28.]

6959. [A.D. 1386.]   Light-brown or uncoloured, and somewhat opaque : indistinct. [Harl. ch. 51 E. 25.]

6960. [A.D. 1398.]   Red : indistinct. [Harl. ch. 45 D. 28.]

6961. [A.D. 1400.]   Red : cracked, and very indistinct. [Harl. ch. 54 H. 2.]

Robert Ashefylde, *or* Ashefeld,
of Stow-Langtoft, co. Suff.

6962. [A.D. 1553.]   Red : good.   ⅛ × ¼ in.   [Add. ch. 35,212.]

Oval : an ornamental shield of arms : a fess engrailed betw. three fleurs-de-lis, ASHFIELD.   Above the shield, a wolf's head.

Cabled border.

6963. [A.D. 1577.]   Red : indistinct, and injured.   [Add. ch. 19,376.]

6964. [A.D. 1586.]   Red.   [Harl. ch. 111 D. 2.]

Elyanora (Ashwell), *widow of* HENRY DE LACY,
of Aschedon, co. Essex.

6965. [A.D. 1368.]   Red : somewhat indistinct in places. ¾ in.   [Harl. ch. 52 H. 52.]

A shield of arms : a lion passant.   Within a carved gothic panel bordered with ball-flowers.

¤ S' 'ALIANORE : ASCHWELL'.

6966. Sulph. cast from No. 6965.   [D.C., F. 456.]

Alice de Aspale, *widow of Sir* ROBERT DE ASPALE, *Knt.,*
of Great Cressingham, co. Norf

6967. [A.D. 1342.]   Red : fragment only, from fine seal. About 1¼ in. when perfect.   [Harl. ch. 45 D. 24.]

A shield of arms : per pale, *dex.*, three chevrons, ASPALL ; *sin.*, destroyed.   Above the shield a fleur-de-lis.

Legend wanting.

Elizabeth de Aspale, *widow of Sir* JOHN ASPALE, *Knt.,*
of Great Cressingham, co. Norf.

6968. [A.D. 1371.]   Red : fine, edge chipped.   About 1 in. [Harl. ch. 45 D. 23.]

A shield of arms : per pale, *dex.*, three chevrons, ASPALL ; *sin.*, a fess betw. two chevrons, over all in chief a label of seven points.   Within a finely carved and traced panel, with ten outward points.

Legend betw. the points :—

SIG_ILL'_[ELI]_ZA_BE_[THE]_DE_AS_PA_LE.

6969. Sulph. cast from No. 6968.   [D.C., F. 477.]

Tomnas de Asteley.

6970. [*Temp.* Edw. III.]   Red : fine, chipped in places. ¾ in.   [xxxvi. 101.]

A shield of arms : a cinquefoil within a bordure engrailed,

ASTLEY of cos. Stafford; Kent, &c. (The engrailing is somewhat different to the usual style and is enriched with an
inner border or line resembling an escutcheon.) Within a
pointed trefoil bordered with ball-flowers.

S[gï]llū + tomne + de + asteley.

Beaded border.

Thomas, *Lord of Astele, Sir* **Thomas de Asteleye,**
of co. Linc., Knt.

6971. [A.D. 1364.] Red: originally fine, now chipped,
edge bent. 1½ in. [Harl. ch. 52 A. 37.]

A shield of arms: a cinquefoil, ermine, ASTLEY. On a
tree. Within an elaborately carved and traced gothic rosette
of eight double points, the inner series of points bordered
with ball-flowers.

✠ SIGILLVM : THOME : DOMINI : DE : ASTELE.

Beaded border.

6972. Sulph. cast from No. 6971. [D.C., F. 432.]

William de Asteleye, *of Whitace, co. Warw., Knt.*

6973. [A.D. 1399.] Red: fine, from matrix with moveable
legend. 1½ in. [Add. ch. 21,504.]

A shield of arms: a cinquefoil pierced, ermine, ASTLEY.
Betw. five small roses, and within a gothic rosette of eight
points, bordered with ball-flowers.

✠ Sigillum : dñi : Will'i : de : asteleye : militis.

William Asthille, *of Gamlingay, co. Camb., Clerk.*

6974. [A.D. 1412.] Red: good, perhaps from a ring.
½ in. [Harl. ch. 83 A. 41.]

A lion couchant guardant, betw. four trefoiled sprigs,
issuing from a cabled border. Perhaps in reference to the
armorial bearings: a lion passant betw. four crosses crosslet,
etc., ASTELL.

William Aston, *of Unstone, co. Derby.*

6975. [A.D. 1431.] Red: indistinct. ⅔ in. [Woll. ch.
viii. 41.]

A shield of arms, *couché*: two lions' gambs, issuing in
chevron from the sides of the shield, between three annulets,
two in chief and one in base. Crest on a helmet of large
dimensions and mantling, a talbot, or other animal passant.

Motto in the field above :—

ever weri. (Ever wary.)

6976. [A.D. 1431.] Red: indistinct, injured by pressure.
[Woll. ch. viii. 42.]

Raffe Astrye, *of Harlington, co. Bedf., Esq.*
6977. [A.D. 1595.] Red : indistinct. $\frac{5}{8} \times \frac{1}{2}$ in. [Add. ch. 35,846.]
. Oval : a shield charged with an animal's head erased, holding (a ring ?) in its mouth.
6978. [A.D. 1596.] Another. [Add. ch. 35,850.]

James Astyn, *of Westerham, co. Kent, Gentl.*
6979. [A.D. 1593.] Red: $\frac{5}{8} \times \frac{1}{2}$ in. [Add. ch. 23,736.] .
Oval : a shield of arms : a chevron betw. three (eagles' ?) heads erased.
Beaded border.

Gregory Athow, *late of Bytchamwell, co. Norf, Gentl.*
6980. [A.D. 1639.] Red: injured by pressure. $\frac{1}{2} \times \frac{5}{8}$ in. [Add. ch. 30,825.]
Oval : on a wreath, five ostrich-feathers labelled.
Cabled border.

John Athow, *of Beachamwell, co. Norf , Esq.*
Son of THOMAS ATHOW.
(See No. 6983.)
6981. [A.D. 1625.] Red : injured. $\frac{3}{4} \times \frac{5}{8}$ in. [Add. ch. 30,815.]
Oval : a shield of arms : quarterly 1. on a bend cotised three uncertain charges ; 2. quarterly ; 3. a lion rampant ; 4. chequy.
Crest on a helmet, mantling, and wreath, a helmet betw. a pair of wings erect.
Cabled border.
6982. [A.D. 1625.] Another. Red : injured. [Add. ch. 30,817.]

Thomas Athow, *Serjeant-at-the-law.*
6983. [A.D. 1617.] Red. [Add. ch. 30,813.]
The seal is the same as in No. 6980 used by Gregory Athow.
6984. [A.D. 1625.] Red : injured. [Add. ch. 30,815.]
6985. [A.D. 1625.] Red. [Add. ch. 30,817.]

Robert Atkinson, *of Stowell, co. Glouc., Esq.*
6986. [A.D. 1604.] Red : fine. $\frac{3}{4} \times \frac{5}{8}$ in. [Add. ch. 15,157.]
A shield of arms : a cross voided betw. four lions rampant, ATKINSON. Crest, on a wreath, an eagle with wings expanded.

Roger Attebroke.

6987. [A.D. 1296–7.] Plaster cast. ⅞ in. [lxxxii. 24.]

A shield of arms: per pale a chevron counterchanged. Above the shield a long cross, pattee, betw. two pierced sixfoils. Within a carved panel.

S' ROGERI · ATTEBROKE.

Thomas Atte Broke, *of Ivelchester, co. Somer.*

6988. [A.D. 1325.] Red: imperfect. ⅗ in. [Add. ch. 15,460.]

A shield of arms: on a chevron an (eagle?) displayed. Betw. three small trefoils slipped. Within a pointed gothic quatrefoil.

Legend wanting.

Laurence Attebrome ?

6989. [A.D. 1356.] Plaster cast from chipped impression. 1 in. [lxxxii. 27.]

A shield of arms: a chevron engrailed betw. three uncertain charges. Within a carved trefoil panel.

✠ Sigill' : laurencii : de : . . . .

Robert Attebrome.

6990. [14th cent.] Plaster cast from fine impression. 1¾₆ in. [lxxxii. 5.]

The owner, kneeling to the l. h. before the B. Virgin holding the child, and lifting up in his hands a trefoil branch of flowers. In a carved gothic niche of two arches. In base, under an arch a shield of arms: a broom plant?

S' ROBERTI ATTE BROME (?)

Thomas Atte Crouche, *of Sonth Denchworth, co. Berks.*
(? *Serjeant Porter of the Royal Household.*)

6991. [A.D. 1367.] Red: fine, well preserved. 1 in. [Add. ch. 6096.]

A shield of arms: a cross cantoned with four estoiles. Above the shield a cross pattée. Within an elegantly carved gothic rosette of eight double points.

✠ S' THOME ATE CROVCH S' PORTER'.

The latter part of the legend seems to signify "serviens portarius," or serjeant porter.

John Atte ffelde, *of Beddington, co. Surr.*

6992. [A.D. 1324.] Green: chipped, imperfect. ¾ in. [Add. ch. 22,845.]

A shield of arms : per pale, two griffins segreant in fess (? counterchanged), on a chief a fish naiant. On each side of the shield a sprig of foliage.

✠ [S' : I]OH'IS : ATE : FELDE ✶.

Beaded borders.

John Atte ffelde, *of Beddington, co. Surr.*
6993. [A.D. 1324.] Green : edge chipped. About ⅞ × ¾ in. [Add. ch. 22,845.]

Oval : a shield of arms : per pale, two griffins segreant in fess, on a chief a pike fish (or other fish) naiant. Betw. two sprigs of foliage.

✠ . . . . . OH'IS ✶ ATE ✶ FELDE ✶·

Beaded borders.

Willemus Atte ffan.
6994. [A.D. 1436.] Red : much injured by pressure. ¾ in. [Add. ch. 28,847.]

A shield of arms : indistinct. Betw. three small quatrefoil flowers, slipped. Within a carved gothic quatrefoil.

✠ SIG . . . . . VM . . . . LES.

William Atte ffen, *fil.* **Johannis Atteffen,**
of Southwark, etc., co. Surr.
6995. [A.D. 1360.] Red : fragmentary. About 1 in. when perfect. [Add. ch. 1314.]

A lozenge-shaped shield of arms : charges defaced, within an engrailed bordure. Within a carved and traced gothic rosette.

Legend wanting.

Ricardus Atte Hamme.
See JOHAN LE B . . . R . . .

William Atte Homwode, *of Westmeston, co. Suss.,*
and JULIANA, *his wife.*
6996. [A.D. 1381.] Green ; injured by· pressure. ¾ in. [Add. ch. 24,686.]

(i.) An eagle or bird of prey, striking a duck.

✠ ALAS IE SV PRIS.

(ii.) A shield of arms : the charges defaced.

. . . . . M . . . . DE . . (?)

Ralph Atte Lee, *of Theydon Garnon, etc., co. Ess., Gentl.*
6997. [A.D. 1446.] Red : very indistinct, and injured by pressure ; encircled by a twisted rush. [Add. ch. 28,864.]

For description see next No.
6998. [A.D. 1458.] Red : good.　[Add. ch. 28,874.]
Rectangular signet, an eagle rising.　Cabled border.
6999. [A.D. 1458.] Red : good.　[Add. ch. 28,875.]

John Ate Lhude, *or* **Atte Lude,** *of Beckenham, co. Kent.*
7000. [Early 13th cent.] Dark green : fine. ⅜ in. [Harl.
ch. 112 B. 10.]
A shield of arms : three bugle-horns stringed, two and one.
⚹ S' IOH'IS · ATE LHVDE.
7001. Sulph. cast from No. 7000. [D.C., F. 208.]

Richard Atte Moor, *of Chalfont St. Peter, co. Buck.*
7002. [A.D. 1409.] Red : injured by pressure. ⅞ in.
[Harl. ch. 86 A. 7.]
Within a carved gothic cinquefoil, a shield of arms : a
sword in bend, point downward.
⚹ SIGILLVM . . . . . . EARD (?)

William Attemore.
7003. [A.D. 1343.] Plaster cast from indistinct impression.
⅞ in. [lxxxii. 28.]
A shield of arms : diapered lozengy, a bend, ATTEMORE.
Suspended by a strap from a forked tree.　Within a carved
gothic panel.
𝕾𝖎𝖌𝖎𝖑𝖑𝖚𝖒 . 𝖂𝖎𝖑𝖑'𝖎 . 𝖆𝖙𝖙𝖊 𝖒𝖔𝖗𝖊.

John Atte Nassche, *of Merden, co. Kent.*
7004. [A.D. 1451.] Red : cracked, injured by pressure.
⅝ in. [Harl. ch. 79 D. 31.]
A shield of arms : a chevron.　Within an indistinct carved
gothic panel.
. . . . MI . . . . R . . . . . . (?) .

Robert ate Noke, *Wax-chaundiller and Citizen of London.*
·**7005.** [A.D. 1366.] Red : chipped.　About ¾ in. when
perfect. [Harl. ch. 49 I. 28.]
A shield of arms : a cross flory.
⚹ . . . A . . EVER . . . . . T. (?)

John Atte Thele.
See JOHN BURGEYS.

Agnes Atte Thorne.
See JOHN DE SCHURBURNE.

Elena, *wife of* ROBERT Atte Welle, *of Denham, co. Buck.*

7006. [A.D. 1362.] Discoloured white : very indistinct. ¾ in. [Harl. ch. 86 F. 43.]

A shield of arms : charges indistinct. Betw. two wyverns. Within a gothic rosette of eight points.

Legend defaced. ·

Johannes Atte Welle, *of Maidwell, co. North.*

7007. [A.D. 1319.] Green : a fragment, very indistinct. About ⅞ in. when perfect. [Add. ch. 22,150.]

A shield of arms : per pale and per saltire, in chief two roundles, all within an engrailed bordure.

...... STR .

Johannes Atte Welle, *of Pudsay, co. York.*

7008. [A.D. 1394.[Creamy-white : cracked, indistinct. ⅘ in. [Add. ch. 16,875.]

A shield of arms : uncertain charges.

+ S' .... ℇ.

John Ropere, *of Westgate, near Canterbury, or*
Thomas Atte Welle, *of Burstrete in Hierne, or Herne, co. Kent.*

7009. [A.D. 1389.] Red : imperfect. About ¾ in. when perfect. [Toph. ch. 38.]

Within a finely carved gothic rosette, a shield of arms : the charges uncertain.

✠ PENSET DE ....

For legend compare No. 7417.

Robert Atte Wenstalle.
See JOHN COUMSCU .....

Harman Attwoodde, *of Saunderstead, co. Surr., Gentl.*

7010. [A.D. 1614.] Red : imperfect. ¾ × ⅝ in. [Add. ch. 23,496.]

A shield of arms : per pale, *dex.*, field replenished with acorns, a lion rampant, ATTWOODE, *sin.*, quarterly, 1, 4. Three uncertain charges, 2, 3, indistinct, apparently, on a bend betw. three ——, as many martlets.

John Attewode.

7011. [A.D. 1416-7.] Plaster cast. +¾ in. [lxxxii. 33.]

A shield of arms: a lion rampant, ATWOOD. Within a carved gothic panel.

✠ SIGILL' · IOHANNIS · ATTEWODE.

William Atte Wode.
See VINCENT FINCH.

William de Aubeni, *of Belvoir, co. Leic.*

7012. [Early 13th cent.] Dark green : chipped ; app. by a woven silk cord of various colours. 2⅜ in. [Add. ch. 22,576.]

∅. An embattled ship or barge, with a tower of two storeys of arcading, embattled at the top. Two men looking out, one with a flag.

✠ SIGIL[LVM :] WILLELMI : DE : AVB . . . . . . VVER.

℞. A small counterseal. 1¼ in. A shield of arms of early shape : two chevrons, within a bordure, DAUBENY. Betw. a small cross above a cinquefoil on the l. h. side and a sprig of foliage on the r. h. side.

✠ SIGILLVM SALVTIS.

7013. Plaster casts of No. 7012. [lxxxv. 22, 23.]

Agatha, *wife of* WILLIAM de Aubeny.
See AGACA TRUSBUT..

Andrew Aubrey.

7014. [A.D. 1352.] Plaster cast from fine impression. 1⅛ in. [lxxxii. 29.]

A shield of arms : a saltire betw. four griffins, head erased, AUBREY. Within an elaborately traced gothic rose panel.

· ✿ · SIGILLVM ✿✠✿ ANDREE ✼ AVBREY.

Beaded border.

Thomas Aubrey, *of Walton, co. Surr.*

7015. [*Temp.* Edw. I.] Mottled green : imperfect. About ⅜ in. when perfect. [Add. ch. 22,959.]

Three small shields of arms, arranged two and one : 1, chevronelly ; 2, a lion rampant ; 3, fragmentary.

✠ S' PH . . . . O . . VN'.

Henry de Audithelega,
of Chorsbure, in Weston, co. Salop, Knt.

7016. [A.D. 1228.] Pale brownish-white, varnished : a fragment. About 1 in. when perfect. [Add. ch. 20,441.]

A shield of arms : fretty, AUDELEY.

Legend wanting.

Another seal, with counterseal of WILLIAM DE BRUMLE.

7017. [*c.* A.D. 1233.] Dark-green : fine, imperfect ; app. by a plaited cord of coloured silks. About 2½ × 2 in. when perfect, [Cott. ch. xi. 38.]

∅. Shield-shaped : a shield of arms : fretty, on a canton a cross pattée.

⊞ SIGILLVM : HENRICI : DE : ALDIT . . . . . . E.

℞. A small oval counterseal. ⅘ × ⅜ in. Impression of an antique oval intaglio gem. A sea-horse (?)

⊞ S' . WILL'I : DE : BRVML'.

7018. Sulph. cast of the *obv.* only. [D.C., E. 327.]

Hugh Daudelee, *or* de Audeleghe,
of Horseheath, co. Camb., Knt.

7019. [A.D. 1305.] Red : very fine, injured by casting. 1 in. [Harl. ch. 45 E. 36.]

A shield of arms : fretty, for a fret, AUDLEY, a label of three points. On a background diapered lozengy with a small quatrefoil in each space.

Legend betw. four human heads, couped at the neck, and with side-hair curled :—

S'HVG — ONIS — DAVD — ELEE.

Beaded borders.

7020. Sulph. cast from No. 7019. [D.C., F. 177.]

Hugh de Audele, 1st *Baron.*

7021. [A.D. 1330.] Plaster cast from chipped impression. 1 in. [lxxxii. 31.]

A shield of arms : fretty, within a bordure, AUDLEY. Sus-pended by a strap. Betw. two wavy sprigs on each of which is a bird.

⊞ SIGI . . . . : DE : AVDELE.

Beaded borders.

Hugh de Audele, *or* Daudele,
2nd Baron, Earl of Gloucester. A.D. 1337–1347.

7022. [A.D. 1344.] Cast in red composition from fine im-pression. 1¼ in. [xlii. 79.]

A shield of arms, *couché* : three chevrons, for CLARE. The Earl married Margaret de Clare, sister and coheiress of Gilbert de Clare, 8th and last *E*arl. Crest, on a helmet with grating closed, and mantling crusily, out of a ducal coronet a swan's head and wings erect. Within a carved gothic panel.

• SIGILLVM • HVGONIS • DE • AVDELE •

7023. [A.D. 1342.] Red : fragmentary. [Add. ch. 20,402.] This contains only the shield, helmet, and lower part of the crest.

Legend wanting.

Hugh Awdeley, *of the Inner Temple, London, Esq.*

7024. [A.D. 1628.] Red : indistinct. $\frac{3}{4} \times \frac{5}{8}$ in. [Add. ch. 30,822.]

Oval : a shield of arms : quarterly, in the first quarter an indistinct animal. Crest on a helmet, mantling, and wreath, uncertain.

Cabled border.

James de Audedelega, *al.* Audeley,
2nd Baron. Ob. A.D. 1271.

7025. [A.D. 1259.] Plaster, cast from chipped impression. $1\frac{3}{4}$ in. [lxxxii. 30.]

A shield of arms : fretty. Background diapered with a double reticulated pattern.

⌣ SIGILL' : IACOBI : DE : AVDEDELEGA.

James de Audeleye,
" Seigneur de Rouge Chaustell et de Heleye," co. Salop.

7026. [*Temp.* Edw. III.] Green : very imperfect. About ct. [Harl. ch. 45 E. 38.]

A f arms, *couché* : fretty, for a fret, AUDLEY. Crest on a helmet, with grating, and lambrequin, a (griffin's ?) head and wings erect. Background diapered fretty with a small annulet at each intersection, and a quatrefoil in each space.

Legend wanting.

7027. Sulph. cast from No. 7026. [D.C., G. 245.]

James de Audithele, *or* Audelega,
of Berkhampstead, co. Herts.
Secretum.

7028. [*Temp.* Hen. III.] Mottled green : fine, well preserved. 1 in. [Add. ch. 15,469.]

A shield of arms : fretty, for a fret, AUDLEY. On a tree betw. two wavy branches of elegant design.

+ LE SECRE : IAMES : DE AVDITHELE.

Beaded border.

John Avinel, *or* Auenel, *"Chivaler de com' Cantebr."*

7029. [A.D. 1337.] Red : fine, chipped on the r. h. side. $\frac{4}{5}$ in. [Harl. ch. 45 E. 49.]

A lozenge-shaped shield of arms : a fess betw. six annulets,

AUENELL. Betw. four cinquefóils, and within a carved and
pointed gothic quatrefoil bordered with ball-flowers.

✠ SIGILLVM IJOHAИИIS AVINEL :

Beaded border.

7030. Sulph. cast from No. 7029. [D.C., F. 264.]

John Aumr . . . .

Seal used by RICHARD DE HALLE, *of Lullynton, co. Suss.*
7031. [A.D. 1343.] Red: edges chipped. ¾ in. [Add.
ch. 30,208.]

A shield of arms : a fess, over all nine estoiles, three, three,
two and one. The óuter border of the shield invecked.
Within a cordon of estoiles.

IOHANЄS AVMR . . . .

Jane, *dau. of Sir* EDW. ONSLOW,
wife of Lord Gerald Aungier, *2nd Baron Aungier.*
7032. [A.D. 1641.] Red: fine. ¼ × ⁹⁄₁₆ in. [Harl. ch. 77
H. 13.]

A shield of arms : ermine, a lion rampant.
Beaded border.

Rob. Au₀n'.
See ROBERT HARDY.

John Austelle, *of Axbridge and Wells, co. Somer., Esq.*
7033. [A.D. 1439.] Red: fine, injured on the r. h. side.
1¼ in. [Harl. ch. 111 D. 5.]

A shield of arms : per pale, *dex.*, a saltire engrailed betw.
four lions' faces ; *sin.*, a pair of wings in lure. Suspended by
a strap from a forked tree and betw. two pairs of sprigs of
foliage and flowers.

. . . . . . **um** ⚮ . . **annis** ⚮ **auſtell.**

Cabled borders.

7034. Sulph. cast from No. 7033. [D.C., G. 206.]
7035. Red : fine, injured by pressure. [xxxvi. 123.]

Sigillum ⚮ **iohannis** ⚮ **austell.**

Sir John Austen, *of Stagnoe, co. Herts., Bart.*
7036. [A.D. 1686.] Red, covered with paper before impression : very indistinct. ⅝ × ⁷⁄₁₆ in. [Add. ch. 35,413.]

Oval : an ornamental shield of arms : a chevron emballed.

Seal used by Dame Rose, wife of the above.

7037. [A.D. 1686.] Another: as above. [Add. ch. 35,413.]

J. Austen.
Seal used by THOMAS BRIGGS, *of Ticehurst. co. Suss.*
7038. [A.D. 1717.]   Red : *en placard*, on tape.   ¾ × ⅜ in.
[Add. ch. 30,840.]
Oval : a shield of arms : per pale, *dex.*, a chevron betw.
three lions gambs, erased, AUSTEN ; *sin.*, a chevron betw.
three birds, AUSTEN (another coat).   Crest, on a helmet,
mantling, and wreath, a lion's gamb.

Seal used by EDWARD BRITTON,
of Crowhurst, co. Suss., Carpenter.
7039. [A.D. 1710.]   Red : imperfect, *en placard*.   [Add.
ch. 29,981.]

Johan Austyn, *Chev.*
See WILLIAM DE HETT . . S.

Robert Austen.
See SIR ROBERT CHESTER.

Robert Austen, *of Ringmere, co. Suss.*
7040. [A.D. 1577.]   Red : injured.   ¾ in.   [Add. ch.
30,739.]
A stag.   Perhaps in allusion to the crest of AUSTEN, on a
mural crown a stag lodged.

John de Avene,
of co. Glamorg., son of Sir LEYSON DE AVENE.
7041. [A.D. 1341.]   Cast in green composition from a fine
but imperfect impression.   1¾₀ in.   [xcvi. 73.]
A shield of arms : three chevrons, AVENE.   The arms
derived by way of imitation, from those of CLARE, the lords
of Glamorgan and Morgan.   Above the shield an Agnus Dei :
at each side a wyvern.
⚜ S' ✽ IOH'IS ✿ DE ✽ AVENE ⚜ ✽ ✽

` **Thomas Awdeley.**
7042. [A.D. 1618.]   Red : very indistinct and imperfect.
About ⅛ × ¾ in. when perfect.   [Add. ch. 33,108.]
Oval : on a wreath a demi-lion rampant.

Thomas Awdeley, *of London, Gentl.*
7043. [A.D. 1621.]   Red.   ⅞ × ¾ in.   [Add. ch. 36,385.]
Oval : a shield of arms : a fess cotised, betw. three conies,

AUDLEY. Crest on a helmet, ornamental mantling and wreath, a martlet.

Beaded border.

Thomas de Awill?

7044. [14th cent.] Plaster cast from good impression. $\frac{7}{8}$ in. [lxxxii. 32.]

A shield of arms : a fess indented betw. three birds (parrots?). Suspended by a strap from a tree of three branches.

In place of a legend, a wavy scroll of foliage and flowers.

Beaded borders.

John de Ayllesbury, *or* Aylesbury,
of Beaconsfield, co. Buck., Knt., son of
Sir THOMAS DE AYLESBURY, *of Milton-Keynes, co. Buck.,*
and JOAN, *dau. and coheir of* RALPH BASSETT,
Baron Bassett of Weldon.

7045. [A.D. 1376.] Mottled green : good, injured by pressure in places. $1\frac{1}{8}$ in. [Harl. ch. 45 E. 57.]

A shield of arms : quarterly, 1, 4, a cross, AYLESBURY ; 2, 3, barry of six nebulée, BASSETT. Suspended by a strap from a forked tree. Within a finely carved and traced gothic panel with six circular holes pierced with quatrefoils.

$\mathfrak{Sigillum : iohannis : de : ayllefbury :}$

Cf. Baker, *History of Northamptonshire*, vol. 1, p. 355.

7046. Sulph. cast from No. 7045. [D.C., F. 502.]

Thomas Ayres.

7047. [A.D. 1653.] Red : covered with paper before impression. $\frac{9}{16} \times \frac{1}{2}$ in. [Add. ch. 27,328.]

Oval : a shield of arms, quarterly, indistinct.

William de Ayrmynne, *of Keisby, co. Linc., Chevaler.*

7048. [A.D. 1393.] Creamy-white : very indistinct. $\frac{7}{8}$ in. [Add. ch. 21,025.]

A shield of arms : ermine a saltire engrailed, on a chief a lion passant, AYREMINNE. Cf. arms of Will. de Ayreminne, Bishop of Norwich, A.D. 1325, in Add. MS. 12,443. Betw. three small sprigs. Within a carved and pointed gothic quatrefoil.

☆ LE SIEL WILLIAM DE . . . .

Cf. Add. ch. 21,026 ; 21,027 ; 21,028. Cf. also Bedford, *Blazon of Episcopacy*, p. 79.

Edward Ayscoghe, *or* **Ascough,** *of Swinhope, co. Linc., Esq.*
  7049. [A.D. 1575.[Red. ⅟₉ in. [Egert. ch. 483.]
Oval signet : a shield of arms : three mullets pierced, two
and one, a crescent for difference.
Beaded border.

B

Johan Le B——— r———.
Seal used by RICHARD ATE HAMME,
of Goudhurst, co. Kent.
  7050. [A.D. 1367.] Red : injured by pressure. ⅘ in.
[Harl. ch. 78 E 40.]
A shield of arms : a lion rampant. Betw. three small
sprigs, and within a carved and pointed gothic quatrefoil.
  ✠ S' IOHAN LE B . . . . . R . . . (?)

Thomas de B . . . . . .
Seal used by JOHN GRYFFYN, *Chev., or* JOHN DE
  WHYTEMORE, *of Wych Maubanc, co. Chesh.*
  7051. [A.D. 1356.] Brownish-green : imperfect and in-
distinct. [L. F. C. xxviii. 7.]
A shield of arms : two fishes hauriant in fess, in chief a
crown.
  . . . . THOME · DE · B . E . . . EY. (?)

W——— B———.
  7052. [A.D. 1454.] Red. ⅜ in. [Add. ch. 29,535.]
A swan on water. Betw. the initial letters W. B. Perhaps
a crest.

Robert Baa, *of co. Hunt.*
  7053. [A.D. 1391.] Red. ⅟₁₆ in. [Add. ch. 33,516.]
A shield of arms : a chevron betw. three pierced mullets,
BAA, or BAO. Within a carved trefoil panel.
  : **Sigillum : roberti : baa : ⚭ :**

Anthony Babington, *of Dethick, co. Derb., Esq.*
  7054. [A.D. 1586.] Red : imperfect, and injured by
pressure. ¼ in. [Woll. ch. ii. 86.]
A shield of arms : on a fess, betw. three garbs, a martlet
for difference.
Beaded border.

Hugh, *son of* RICHARD DE **Babington,** *of co. York.*
7055. [A.D. 1326.] Creamy-white : very indistinct. ¾ in.
[Add. ch. 16,692.]
A shield of arms : uncertain charges, perhaps a chevron.
S' TH . . . . ÉTON.

William Babyngton.
7056. [A.D. 1424.] Plaster cast from good impression,
injured by pressure. 1 in. [lxxxii. 78.]
A shield of arms : field diapered with sprigs of foliage,
ten roundles, four, three, two, and one, in pile, over all in
chief a label of three points, BABINGTON. Suspended by a
strap from a tree. Within a carved border engrailed and
ornamented with small ball-flowers or quatrefoils.
$igillū : will'i : babyngton : ⚭
Beaded border.

Richard de Bachesworth, *Lord of Herefeld, co. Midd.*
7057. [A.D. 1313.] Uncoloured. ¾ in. [Harl. ch. 84 G.
50.]
A shield of arms : a chevron within a bordure engrailed.
⚭ S' RICARDI : DE : BACHESWORTHE.

Sa[muel ?] Backhouse, [*of co. Buck. ?*]
7058. [A.D. 1620.] Red. ¾ × ⅝ in. [Harl. ch. 76 F. 36.]
Oval : on a wreath, an eagle displayed with inverted
wings, on a snake embowed, nowed at the tail. Crest of
BACKHOUSE.
Cabled border.

John, *son and heir of* EDWARD **Backwell,** *of London, Esq.*
7059. [A.D. 1698.] Red : *en placard* on a label. ½ × 7/16 in.
[Harl. ch. 111 H. 35.]
Oval : on a wreath a bull's head erased. Crest of BACK-
WELL. Cf. Burke, *Armory, s. v.,* out of a mural crown a
demi-bull.

Richard, *son of* EDWARD **Backwell,** *of London, Esq.*
7060. [A.D. 1698.] Red : *en placard* on a label. [Harl.
ch. 111 H. 35.]
Same as for John Backwell, see No. 7059.

Edmund Bacon, *of Redgrave, co. Suff., Bart.*
7061. [A.D. 1657.] Red : injured by pressure. ½ × 7/16 in.
[Add. ch. 19,265.]

2 G 2

Oval: a shield of arms: charges defaced, but apparently not the arms of BACON of Redgrave, *viz.* on a chief two pierced mullets.

Elizabeth Bacon.
See AMBROSE COPINGER.

John Bacon, *Clerk of the Wardrobe to King Richard II.*
7062. [A.D. 1377.] Plaster cast from imperfect impression. 1⅛ in. [lxxxii. 79.]
An angel, issuing from clouds, and with expanded wings, holding up in front betw. two brooms? a shield of arms: field diapered with sprigs of foliage, on a chief three roses.

𝕾igill : ioh'is : bacoun .... gin ....

John Bacon, *of cos. Norf and Suff., Esq.*
7063. [A.D. 1435.] Red: originally fine, encircled with a twisted rush, now injured by pressure. 1 in. [Cott. ch. v. 3.]
A shield of arms, *couché*: three boars passant, two and one, BACON. Crest on a helmet, mantling, and wreath, a plume of feathers in two rows. The field replenished with sprigs of foliage.
Legend on a scroll :—

𝕾igillum ⚜ ioh'is ⚜ bacon ⚜

7064. Sulph. cast from No. 7063. [D.C., G. 198.]
7065. [A.D. 1435.] Red: much injured and imperfect. [Cott. ch. v. 22.]

Thomas Bacoun, *of Methwold, co. Norf*
7066. [A.D. 1366.] Red: fine, imperfect. 1 in. [Stowe ch. 195.]
A shield of arms: three bacon pigs or boars, passant, two and one, BACON. Within a carved panel.
SIGILL' THOM ....

Edward Badby.
See EDMUND FETIRPLACE.

Alianora, *widow of Sir* WILLIAM **Bagot.**
See ALIANORA DE FERRARIIS.

William Bagot,
Lord of the Manor of Allesleye, co. Warw., Knt.

7067. [A.D. 1396.] Red: fine. $1\frac{1}{16}$ in. [Harl. ch. 111 G. 40.]

A shield of arms: on a chevron betw. three martlets a crescent for difference, BAGOT. Suspended by a strap from a forked oak-tree. Within a carved gothic panel.

𝕾𝖎𝖌𝖎𝖑𝖑𝖚𝖒 : 𝖜𝖎𝖑𝖑𝖊𝖑𝖒𝖎 : 𝖇𝖆𝖌𝖔𝖙 : ⚬

Beaded border.

7068. Plaster cast of No. 7067. [lxxxii. 80.]

7069. Sulph. cast of No. 7067. [D.C., F. 597.]

7070. [A.D. 1396.] Red: fine, edge chipped. [Harl. ch. 111 G. 41.]

𝕾𝖎𝖌𝖎 ... 𝖒 : 𝖜𝖎𝖑𝖑𝖊𝖑𝖒𝖎 : 𝖇𝖆𝖌𝖔𝖙 : ⚬

7071. [A.D. 1399.] Red: imperfect, injured by pressure. [Add. ch. 21,504.]

.... 𝖑𝖊𝖑𝖒𝖎 : 𝖇𝖆𝖌𝖔𝖙 : ⚬

Valentine Bailif, *of Pesemersshe, co. Suss., Esq.*

7072. [A.D. 1422.] Red: fine, encircled with a twisted rush. 1 in. [Add. ch. 20,144.]

A shield of arms: on a chevron betw. three human hearts enflamed, as many martlets, BAYLIFF. Within a finely carved gothic pointed trefoil and cusped cinquefoil combined, and having the inner edge ornamented with ballflowers.

Legend betw. the points:—

𝕾𝖎𝖌𝖎𝖑𝖑𝖚𝖒 .. 𝖛𝖆𝖑𝖊𝖓𝖙𝖎𝖓𝖎 .. 𝖇𝖆𝖎𝖑𝖑𝖞𝖋. (or 𝖇𝖆𝖎𝖑𝖑𝖎𝖋𝖋.)

John Bais.
See JOHN DE SANCTO LAUDO.

Emma de Bakepus.
Seal used by ALICIA ADAM, *dau. of* THOMAS ADAM, *of Ashbourne, co. Derb.*

7073. [A.D. 1391.] Red: very fine. $\frac{7}{8}$ in. [Woll. ch. vi. 27.]

A shield of arms: per pale, *dex.*, paly of six, over all a bend, *sin.*, two bars, in chief three horse-shoes, BAKEPUCE. Within a carved and pointed gothic trefoil, having the inner border enriched with ball-flowers, and betw. two small slipped flowers.

✠ SIGILLVM : EMME : DE : BAKEPVS.

Dame **Johanna Bakepuiz,** *of Boilston, co. Derb.*

7074. [A.D. 1383.] Red: imperfect edge, indistinct in places. $1\frac{1}{4}$ in. [Woll. ch. vi. 10.] ...

A shield of arms : per pale, *dex.*, two bars, in chief three horse-shoes, BAKEPUZ, *sin.*, a chevron betw. three (garbs ?). Within a coarsely carved gothic trefoil, enriched with ball-flowers,

.... ᴬᴹ **ioḣa** .... **bakepuʐs.** ᴬᴹ

Beaded borders.

Johannes de Bakepuz, *of Allexton, co. Leic.*
7075. [Early Hen. III.] Green, mottled: imperfect. About 1¾ in. when perfect. [Harl. ch. 45 F. 24.]
A shield of arms, early shape : a lion rampant.
+ SI[GIL]LVM IOH[A]NNI .... Z.
7076. Sulph. cast from No. 7075. [D.C., E. 319.]

Gregorie Baker, *of New Windsor, co. Berk., Gentl.*
7077. [A.D. 1631.] Red : imperfect, indistinct. ¾ in. [Harl. ch. 79 F. 44.]
A shield of arms : uncertain.
Engrailed border.

John Baker, *Citizen and Mercer of London, Servant of* ANTHONY DENNY, *Gentleman of the Privy Chamber.*
7078. [A.D. 1544.] Red : chipped. $\frac{7}{16} \times \frac{1}{4}$ in. [Harl. ch. 77 F. 24.]
Oval : a shield of arms : on a saltire engrailed five escallops, on a chief a lion passant, BAKER.

Thomas Baker, *of Middle-Aston, co. Oxon., Knt.* •
7079. [A.D. 1627.] Red. $\frac{1}{2} \times \frac{3}{8}$ in. [Add. ch. 23,290.]
Oval signet : on a wreath a swan's head and neck, gorged with a ducal coronet. Crest of BAKER ? Cf. arms of BAKER of Worcestershire, three swans' heads erased, ducally gorged.

William Baker, *of Walkeringham, co. Nott.*
7080. [A.D. 1728.] Red : *en placard*, on a tape. $\frac{3}{8} \times \frac{11}{16}$ in. [Add. ch. 29,613.]
Oval : a shield of arms : charges indistinct, per pale, *dex.*, three water bougets, two and one ; *sin.*, three chevrons. Crest on a helmet and ornamental mantling, a peacock.
7081. [A.D. 1728.] Another. [Add. ch. 29,614.]

Seal used by ANNE, *wife of the above.*

7082. [A.D. 1728.] Another. [Add. ch. 29,613.]
7083. [A.D. 1728.] Another. [Add. ch. 29,614.]

Maut, *wife of* JOHN Bakon, *Esq., dau. of*
Sir THOMAS BEDYNGFELD, *Knt.*

7084. [A.D. 1449.] Red: imperfect. $\frac{4}{8} \times \frac{3}{8}$ in. [Add.
ch. 19,861.]

Oblong octagonal signet. A pig, or boar, statant. Crest
of BACON.

John Balden, *of co. Kent.*

7085. [A.D. 1570.] Red: fine. $\frac{1}{2} \times \frac{3}{8}$ in. [Harl. ch. 79
B. 27.]

Oval signet from a ring: an ornamental shield of arms:
three fleurs-de-lis.

Richard de Balderstone, *of Preston, co. Lanc.*

7086. [A.D. 1429.] Red. $\frac{3}{8}$ in. [Add. ch. 17,131.]

Octagonal signet: a lion sejant affronté, in allusion to
the arms of BALDERSTON, of Lancashire, viz., a lion rampant.
Legend in the field :—

ℜ. balderſton.

Cabled border.

Nicholas Sherryer Baldwin, *of Chichester, son of*
N. SHERRYER, *late of Harting, co. Suss.*

7087. [A.D. 1707.] Red: *en placard.* $\frac{4}{8} \times \frac{1}{2}$ in. [Add.
ch. 19,038.]

Oval: on a wreath, a wyvern or cockatrice issuing, for
crest of BALDWIN.
Beaded border.

7088. [A.D. 1707.] Another. [Add. ch. 19,039.]
7089. [A.D. 1707.] Another. [Add. ch. 19,040.]

The same used by RICHARD SCARDEFIELD, *of Harting.*

7090. [A.D. 1707.] Another. [Add. ch. 19,039.]

The same, used by MARY, *widow of* NICH. SHERRYER
aforesaid, wife of RICHARD SCARDEFIELD.

7091. [A.D. 1707.] Another. [Add. ch. 19,039.]

The same used by TIMOTHY LUFF, *of Harting, Yeoman.*

7092. [A.D. 1707.] Another. [Add. ch. 19,039.]
7093. [A.D. 1707.] Another. [Add. ch. 19,040.]

The same used by JOHN PESCOD, *of Harting.*

7094. [A.D. 1707.] Another. [Add. ch. 19,039.]

Abraham Baley, *of St. Clement's, London, Gentl.*
Another Seal.

7095. [A.D. 1766.] Red: *en placard*, on green tape.
1 × ¾ in. [Add. ch. 29,524.]

Oval: an ornamental shield of arms: a chevron betw.
three mullets, on a chief a crescent. Over the shield a
cherub's head and carved foliage and flowers.

7096. [A.D. 1770.] Another: well preserved. [Add. ch.
29,475.]

Another Seal.

7097. [A.D. 1766.] Red: *en placard* on paper. ¾ × ⅝ in.
[Add. ch. 29,525.]

Oval: a carved shield of arms: per fess. Supported on
the *sin.* side by a lion rampant reguardant on a carved scroll.

Thomas Ballard, *Esq.*

7098. [15th cent.] Plaster cast from fine impression.
1¼ in. [lxxxii. 81.]

A shield of arms, *couché*: a griffin segreant, BALLARD:
crest on a helmet and mantling, on a wreath a demi-griffin
wings erect.

Legend on a scroll or ribbon :—

Sigillũ · thome · ballard · armig'i.

Beaded border.

Thomas Balle, *of Flicham, co. Norf.*

7099. [A.D. 1386–7.] Cast in red composition from good
impression. ⅞ in. [lxxvi. 80.]

A shield of arms : a chevron betw. three Katharine wheels.
Within a carved gothic panel.

S : T : B : Amor : bincit : omnia.

John Ballett, *Citizen and Goldsmith of London.*

7100. [A.D. 1594.] Red: cracked, indistinct. ¾ × 11⁄16 in.
[Harl. ch. 57 H. 22.]

Oval: a shield of arms : a lion rampant, on a chief three
cinquefoils, BALLETT. Crest, on a helmet and mantling, out
of a mural coronet a demi-eagle displayed.

Walter de Baltherby.

7101. [15th cent.] Red: indistinct in places. Detached
from a charter. 1 in. [xxxvi. 117.]

A shield of arms, *couché*: three bulls' heads cabossed, two

and one. Crest on a helmet, and mantling, on a chapeau a
goat's head (?) In the field on each side a flowering tree or
branch.

S WALTERI D' BALTHERBY(?)

Walter . . . .,
(seal used by WILLIAM BALTRIP, *Receiver of*
Lord HENRY DE PERCY *in cos. Ess. and Norf*)
7102. [A.D. 1335.] Red: fine, imperfect. About ¾ in.
when perfect. [Harl. ch. 45 F. 32.]
A shield of arms : a chevron betw. three roundles. Within
a carved and pointed gothic trefoil, the inner edge enriched
with ball-flowers.
✪ S . . . . . . WALT . . . .
7103. Sulph. cast from No. 7102. [D.C., F. 253.]

Reginald de Balun, *Lord of Magna Markeleya, co. Heref.*
7104. [A.D. 1294.] Green: fine. 1 in. [Egert. ch. 352.]
A shield of arms: three bars dancettées ; BAALUN and
BALUN : see MS. Cott., Tiberius D. x.
ı ✪ S' REGINALDI DE BALVN.
Beaded borders.

Warwick Bampfield,
Lord of the Manor of Porlock, co. Somers., Esq.
7105. [A.D. 1691.] Red: *en placard*, on a folded paper.
¾ × 1¹⁄₈ in. [Add. ch. 7704.]
A shield of arms: quarterly, 1, a tiger (?) rampant ;
2, *Ermine*, a chevron, on a chief a lion passant ; 3, three
scaling ladders, two and one, bendwise, and betw. the two
uppermost a spear's head, on a chief a castle, triple-towered ;
4, a lion rampant. Crest, on a helmet, mantling, and wreath,.
a tiger (?) passant.
Beaded borders.
The 3rd quarter is borne by LLOYD, JONES, PARRY, OWEN,
etc.

Agnes, *widow of* THOMAS **Banastre,** *Knt.,*
of Singleton, etc., co. Lanc.
7106. [A.D. 1392.] Red: chipped. ⅞ in. [Add. ch.
20,511.]
A shield of arms : per pale, *dex.,* a cross fleury, BANASTRE ;
sin., three bars, or barry of six.
Sigillum ✱ agnetis ✱ banaſtre.
7107. [A.D. 1392.] Red: indistinct. [Add. ch. 20,522.]

Gunnora, *relict of* WILLIÀM **Banastre,**
of Waletun, or Wallington, co. Surr.

7108. [*post* A.D. 1228.]   Green, mottled.   1¾ in.   [Add. ch. 23,674.]

A mermaid, embowed, facing to the r., holding a flower slipped, or cross crosslet, fitchée.   Probably preheraldic.

+ S' GVNNORE RITTE WILL'I.

7109. [*post* A.D. 1228.]   Light brown: imperfect, indistinct.   [Add. ch. 23,673.]

William Banastre, *of Sulhampstead, co. Berks.*

7110. [*circ.* A.D. 1230–1240.]   Green: fine.   1 1⁄16 in.   [Add. ch. 20,267.]

A mermaid, with long spiral tail of a floral character, enclosing a horse.

+ SIGILLV : WILLELMI BANASTRE.

Wyllems Le Banester, *or* **William Le Banester,**
Escheator of Salop.

7111. [A.D. 1335.]   Recent impression in gutta-percha from fine impression or the matrix.   1 in.   [xlvii. 1279.]

A shield of arms: a maunch.   Betw. three porcupines or wyverns.   Within a carved and pointed gothic quatrefoil.

+ S' Wyllems ᛉ le ᛉ banester.

At the end of the legend a wyvern or dragon, with open mouth, and tail flory.

William Banastre, *of Hadenhale, or Hadnall, co. Salop.*

7112. [A.D. 1359.]   Plaster cast from indistinct impression. ⅞ in.   [lxxxii. 82.]

A shield of arms: a maunch.   Betw. five small flowers slipped.   Within a carved gothic panel of eight points.

S' WILL'I BANASTRE DE HADENHALE.

Cf. Harl. ch. 48 A. 53 ; Add. ch. 9356.

William Banaster, *of Quernmore, co. Lanc., Gentl.*

7113. [A.D. 1529.]   Red.   ¼ × ⅜ in.   [Harl. ch. 56 E. 18.]

Oval signet: a shield of arms: three chevrons, BANASTER. Within a trefoil.

Beaded border.

Allen Bancks, *Citizen and Stationer of London.*

7114. [A.D. 1669.]   Red: imperfect, indistinct, covered with paper before impression.   About ¾ × ⅝ in. when perfect. [Harl. ch. 111 H. 36.]

. A shield of arms : a cross engrailed betw. four fleurs-de-lis, BANKS. Crest on a helmet and ornamental mantling, wanting.

Henry Banyarde, *seal used by* EDW. KEMPE, *of Hereford, co. Heref., Gent.*

.7115. [A.D. 1610.] Red. $\frac{3}{8} \times \frac{1}{2}$ in. [Harl. ch. 75 G. 56.]
Oval: a shield of arms : on a fess betw. two chevrons as many links of a chain interlinked in fess, BAYNARD.
Cabled border.

Thomas Barantyn, *seal used by* RICHARD WESTON, *of Clayore, co. Oxon. ?*

7116. [A.D. 1398.] Red : injured, indistinct in places..
$\frac{7}{8}$ in. [Add. ch. 20,334.] .
A shield of arms : three eagles displayed, BARANTINE. Within a carved and pointed gothic quatrefoil, and suspended by a strap from a tree.

S' . thome . barantyn.

Thomas Barantyn, *of Chalgrave, Watlington, etc., co. Oxon.*

7117. [A.D. 1393.] Red : imperfect. [Add. ch. 20,384.]
Seal as described in No. 7116.

S . . . ome . barantyn.

7118. [A.D. 1399.] Dark green : indistinct in places. [Add. ch. 20,387.]

S' . thome . barantyn.

Roger Barber, *of co. Suff.*

7119. [A.D. 1577.] Red : indistinct. $\frac{5}{8} \times \frac{1}{2}$ in. [Add. ch. 32,907.]
Oval: out of a ducal coronet a bull's head. Crest of BARBER.
Beaded border.

William Barber, *of co. Hertf.*

7120. [A.D. 1619.] Red : indistinct. $\frac{1}{2}$ in. [Add. ch. 35,866.]
A griffin's head erased : betw. the initial letters **w. b.** (?)
7121. [A.D. 1619.] Another : indistinct. [Add. ch. 35,867.]

. Robert Barbot, *of Ernell Manor, co. Southt., Esq.* .

7122. [A.D. 1424.] Red : fine, imperfect. About $1\frac{1}{8}$ in. when perfect. [Add. ch. 17,429.]

A shield of arms, *couché*: a chevron betw. three quivers. Crest on a helmet and ornamental mantling, a fox's head.

𝔖' + roberti . . . .

Beaded borders.

Renaud Barbottle.

7123. [A.D. 1265.] Plaster cast from chipped impression. 1¾ × ¾ in. [lxxxii. 86.]

Pointed oval : a carved quatrefoil panel containing five escallops in cross, not on a shield. Below this, a trefoil panel containing three fleurs-de-lis, one and two, not on a shield. At each side, by way of supporters, a demi-angel with wings erect, holding a hand on each panel. In base a countersunk trefoil.

[+ SIIGILLVM · RENAVDI · BARBOTTL'.

Beaded borders.

Perhaps a foreign seal.

William Le Barbour, *or* Barbur, *of Southwark, co. Surr.*

7124. [A.D. 1276–7.] Dark green : fine. 1 × ¾ in. [Add. ch. 15,505.]

Shield shaped : a shield of arms : a cross compony countercompony.

+ S' · WILL'I · LE : BARBOVR :

Robert Bardewelle, *of Garboldesham Manor, co. Norf.*

7125. [A.D. 1446.] Red : injured by pressure. ⅝ × ½ in. [Add. ch. 14,672.]

Octagonal signet : on a helmet a goat's head. Perhaps the crest of BARDEWELLE. In the field an indistinct legend in gothic letters.

Drawn in Blomefield's *Hist. of Norfolk* (Dept. copy), vol. i., p. 257.

William Bardewelle, *or* Berdwell, *of Gasthorpe,*
co. Norf, Thelvetham, co. Suff., etc., Knt.

7126. [A.D. 1404.] Red : fine, slightly chipped at base. 1⅕ in. [Add. ch. 14,674.]

A shield of arms : a goat salient, BARDWELL. Suspended by a strap from a forked tree. Within a carved gothic panel.

: 𝔖igillum : will'i : berdwell' : м

. Cabled border.

Drawn in Blomefield's *Hist. of Norfolk* (Dept. copy), vol. i., p. 253.

7127. Sulph. cast from No. 7126. [D.C., G. 108.]

7128. [A.D. 1401.] Red : imperfect and indistinct. [Harl. ch. 53 E. 31.]

: 𝔖igillum : will'i : . . . .

7129. [A.D. 1404.]   Red : fine.   [Add. ch. 15,537.]
: 𝔖𝔦𝔤𝔦𝔩𝔩𝔲𝔪 : 𝔴𝔦𝔩𝔩'𝔦 : 𝔟𝔢𝔯𝔡𝔴𝔢𝔩𝔩' : ♠

7130. [A.D. 1410.]   Red : imperfect.   [Harl. ch. 51 G. 54.]
:˙𝔖𝔦𝔤𝔦𝔩𝔩𝔲 . . . . : 𝔟𝔢𝔯𝔡𝔴𝔢𝔩𝔩' : ♠

7131. [A.D. 1422.]   Red : imperfect.   [Stowe ch. 232.]
𝔖 . . . . 𝔩𝔩'𝔦 : 𝔟𝔢𝔯𝔡𝔴𝔢𝔩𝔩' : ♠

Hugh Bardolf, *Lord of Wirmegaye, or Wormegay, co. Norf.*
  7132. [Early 14th cent.] Plaster cast from fine impression.
1 in.   [lxxxii. 84.]
  A shield of arms : three cinquefoils, two and one, BARDOLF.
Suspended by a strap from a tree. Betw. two trees. Within
a sixfoil panel, having a small sunk trefoil opening in each
spandril.
  Cf. Harl. ch. 43 D. 6, A.D. 1300.

  John Bardolf, *Lord of Wirmegeye, co. Norf*
  7133. [A.D. 1354.]   Red : fine, dinted and slightly
chipped.   1 3/16 in.   [Harl. ch. 45 F. 52.]
  A shield of arms : three cinquefoils two and one, BARDOLF.
The points of the triangles project into the annulus of the
legend, and are floreated.   Within a very elaborately and
minutely carved and traced gothic double triangle, having
the inner edge cusped and enriched with ball-flowers.
  S' IOHANNIS BARDOLF DÑ[I] DE WYRMEGEYE ♠
  7134. Sulph. cast from No. 7133.   [D.C., F. 390.]

  Thomas Bardolf, *of South Elmham, co. Suff., Knt.*
Secretum.
  7135. [A.D. 1315.]   Red : fine, cracked.   1 in.   [Stowe
ch. 368.]
  A shield of arms : three cinquefoils, two and one, BARDOLF.
Suspended by a strap, from a tree of three branches, and
betw. two lions passant.
  SECRETVM THOME BARDOLF.
  Beaded borders.
  7136. [A.D. 1315.]   Another : fine, slightly chipped at the
base.   [Stowe ch. 369.]

  William Bardolf.
  7137. [A.D. 1368.]   Plaster cast from chipped impression.
1 1/8 in.   [lxxxii. 85.]
  A shield of arms : per pale, *dex.* three cinquefoils, two and
one, BARDOLF ; *sin.* paly a chief indented (dimidiated).
Within a carved gothic panel.
  𝔖𝔦𝔤𝔦𝔩𝔩' : [𝔴𝔦𝔩𝔩]𝔢𝔩𝔪𝔦 : 𝔟𝔞𝔯𝔡𝔲𝔩𝔣:

Thomas [de] Barentyn, *of Berwick-upon-Tweed.*

7138. [A.D. 1360.]   Light brown : somewhat indistinct.
⅞ in. [Harl. ch. 45 F. 53.]

A shield of arms : an eagle displayed, over. all a bendlet.
Within a carved and pointed gothic quatrefoil.

🏵 SIGILLV̄ · THOME · BARENTYN.

7139. Sulph. cast from No. 7138. [D.C., F. 411.]

William Baret.

7140. [A.D. 1331.]   Plaster cast from chipped impression.
⅞ in. [lxxxii. 89.]

A shield of arms : barry of eight per pale countercharged.
Suspended by a strap from a lion's face, and betw. two
wyverns sans wings.

[S]IGILLVM WI[LL]ELMI BARET.

John de Bargothow, *co. Cornw.*

7141. [A.D. 1372.]   Dark red : indistinct.   ¾ × ⅝ in.
[Add. ch. 19,505.]

Slightly oval : a shield of arms : a chevron betw. three
hares' heads couped.

. . . . REV . . . .

7142. [A.D. 1372.]   Dark red : indistinct.   [Add. ch.
19,504.]

Bartholomew Barham, *of London.*

7143. [A.D. 1519.]   Red.   ½ in. [Add. ch. 828.]

A shield of arms : three fleurs-de-lis, two and one. Ensigned with a coronet of five points fleury.

Henry Barkere, *of Langham, co. Suff.*

7144. [A.D. 1369.]   Dark green : sharp, imperfect.   ⅞ in.
[D.C., F. 463.]

A shield (of arms ?) : a crescent enclosing a human heart
from which spring three small slipped quatrefoil flowers,
within a border engrailed.   Betw. the initial letters R.B. at the
sides, and [.˙.] W at [the top and] bottom.   Within a carved
and pointed gothic quatrefoil, enriched with ball-flowers on
the inner edge.

Beaded border.

7145. Sulph. cast from No. 7144.   [D.C., F. 463.]

John Barlowe, *of Denham, co. Buck.*

7146. [A.D. 1457.]   Red : from a signet ring with mark of
the setting.   Injured by pressure.   ⅜ in.   [Harl. ch. 84 H. 9.]

A helmet and mantling. In the field the legend:

iohes : barlow.

Cabled border.

7147. [A.D. 1457.] Red, discoloured: injured by pressure. [Harl. ch. 84 H. 11.]

The same, used by HENRY BERAKER *of Denham.*

7148. [A.D. 1457.] Red: fine, with mark of the setting. [Harl. ch. 84 H. 25.]

John Barlow, *of Denham, co. Buck.*

7149. [A.D. 1468.] Red: imperfect, originally encircled with a twisted rush. $\frac{1}{2}$ in. [Harl. ch. 111 D. 20.]

A greyhound's head, erased, and muzzled. In the field an illegible motto in gothic letters.

Thomas Barnard,
Seal used by MATTHEW BUSH, *Sen., of Bishop-Stortford, co. Herts.*

7150. [A.D. 1695.] Red: *en placard.* $\frac{5}{8} \times \frac{1}{2}$ in. [Add. ch. 27,088.]

An ornamentally-carved oval shield of arms: a bear passant, BARNARD (for a bear rampant or salient).

Beaded border.

Thomas Barnard, *of Lincoln's Inn, co. Midd., Gent.*

7151. [A.D. 1769.] Red: *en placard,* on a green tape. About $\frac{7}{8} \times \frac{3}{4}$ in. [Add. ch. 29,627.]

An ornamentally carved oval shield of arms: quarterly, 1, 4, on a bend three crosses crosslet fitchées; 2, 3, three crosses pattées. Crest on a wreath, a demi-lion, holding in its dexter paw a crosslet as in the arms. Cf. arms of WOODCOCK, of Essex, on a bend engrailed three crosses botonnées fitchées. Elbro' Woodcock signs as a witness to this charter. The seal was also used by Thos. Blackman, *q.v.*

George Barnardiston, *of Caldecoate in Northill parish, co. Bedf., Gentl.*

7152. [A.D. 1612.] Red. About $\frac{3}{4} \times \frac{5}{8}$ in. [Add. ch. 23,870.]

Oval: a shield of arms: a fess dancettée, ermine, betw. six crosses crosslet, BARNARDISTON.

John Barnardistone, *of Northill, co. Bedf., Esq.*
7153. [A.D. 1579.]   Red : cracked, indistinct.   ⅝ in. [Harl.
ch. 45 G. 4.]
. A shield of arms of irregular shape : a fess dancettée betw.
six crosses crosslet, BARNARDISTON.

Nathanael Barnardiston.
See M. DALTON.

George Barne, *Citizen and Haberdasher of London,*
[*Lord Mayor,* 1586.]
7154. [A.D. 1573.]   Yellowish-red. $\frac{7}{12} \times \frac{1}{2}$ in. [Add.
ch. 886.]
· An ornamental shield of arms : on a chevron wavy, betw.
three Cornish choughs, as many trefoils, BARNE.

John Barne, *Citizen and Haberdasher of London.*
7155. [A.D. 1573.] · Yellowish red. $\frac{7}{12} \times \frac{1}{2}$ in. [Add.
ch. 886.]
· Oval : a shield of·arms : quarterly 1, 4, on a chevron engrailed, betw. three Cornish choughs, as many trefoils ; 2, 3,
on a fess engrailed, betw. three goats' heads erased and
collared, a cinquefoil betw. two fleurs-de-lis.   Crest, on a
helmet, mantling and wreath, an eagle displayed.   For these
arms of Sir Geo. Barne, Haberdasher, Lord Mayor of London,
1552, see Harl. MS. 1349, p. 29.

William Barnebye, *Escheator of co. York., Esq.*
· **7156.** [A.D. 1573.]   Red : imperfect, indistinct. [Harl.
ch. 83 D. 47.]
An ornamental shield of arms : an escallop, in allusion to
the arms of BARNBY of co. York, *viz.*, a lion rampant hung
·about with escallop shells.   Betw. the initial letters W.B.
Cabled border.
7157. [A.D. 1573.] Red : imperfect. [Harl. ch. 83 E. 8.]

R. Barnett,
Seal used by HANNAH CONLEY, *of Lewes, co. Suss., Widow.*
. **7158.** [A.D. 1734.]   Red : *en placard* on a tape, imperfect.
About $\frac{7}{8} \times \frac{3}{4}$ in. [Add. ch. 30,680.]
·.· Oval : a carved oval shield of arms : three bars, in chief a
crescent for difference, for BARNETT.

Ralph Barney, *al.* Berney, *Esq.*

7159. [A.D. 1509.] Red: indistinct. $\frac{7}{16} \times \frac{3}{8}$ in. [Add. ch. 28,935.]

. Oval: a bear passant. Perhaps a crest, or in allusion to the name.

7160. [A.D. 1509.] Another: indistinct. [Add. ch. 28,936.]

Beatrice de Barre.
See BEATRICE DE VALENCE.

Paul Barrett, *of Canterbury, co. Kent, Esq.*

7161. [A.D. 1670.] Red, covered with paper before impression: injured by pressure. $\frac{5}{8} \times \frac{1}{2}$ in. [Add. ch. 8465.]

A shield of arms: per pale, *dex.*, on a chevron. betw. three mullets as many lions passant guardant, BARRETT: *sin.*, on a bend, betw. some indistinct charges, three birds, a chief.

Barrett, Arms of.
See EDWARD FLOWERDEW.

Joseph Barshom.
See ROBERT CASTLETON.

John Bartelot, *of Stopham, co. Suss.*

7162. [A.D. 1433.] Red: originally encircled by a twisted rush. $\frac{11}{16}$ in. [Add. ch. 8877.]

A shield of arms: quarterly per fess indented, four crescents counter-changed, BARTLET. Suspended by a strap from a forked tree.

𝔖𝔦𝔤𝔦𝔩𝔩𝔲 𝔦𝔬𝔥𝔦𝔰 𝔟𝔞𝔯𝔱𝔢𝔩𝔬𝔱 𝔡𝔢 𝔰𝔱𝔬𝔭𝔥𝔞𝔪.

Cabled border.

John de Bartoun

7163. [A.D. 1348.] Plaster cast from fine impression. $\frac{7}{8}$ in. [lxxxvii. 94.]

A shield of arms: ermine, on a chief two boars' heads. Betw. five small flowers. Within a cusped border of eight points.

✠ SIGILLVM · IOHANNIS · DE · BARTOVN (?)

John Barton.

7164. [17th cent.] Recent impression in red sealing-wax from the matrix. 1 in. [xxxv. 26.]

A shield of arms : a fess betw. three bucks' heads, BARTON. Within a pointed trefoil.

+ SIGILLVM + IOHANES + BARTON.

The letters NE of *Johanes* are conjoined.

7165. Plaster cast of No. 7164. [lxxxii. 91.]

7166. [17th cent.] Sulph. cast. [D.C., H. 133.]

Robert de Bartone.

7167. [A.D. 1338.] Plaster cast from good impression. $\frac{7}{8}$ in. [lxxxii. 92.]

A shield of arms : a bend betw. two cotises dancettées (field diapered lozengy). Bctw. five small flowers slipped. Within a carved gothic panel of eight points, ornamented along the inner edge with small quatrefoils or ball-flowers.

✠ LE · SEAL · ROBERT · DE · BARTONE ⚜ ❀ ⚜ ❀ ⚜ ❀

Samuel Barton, *of Hellingley, co. Suss., Gentl.*

7168. [A.D. 1654.] Red : indistinct. $\frac{3}{4} \times \frac{5}{8}$ in. [Add. ch. 30,157.]

Oval : a shield of arms, ornamental mantling, helmet and crest, very indistinct.

Thomas Barton, *Canon of the Cathedral Church of St. Peter, Exeter, co. Devon.*

7169. [A.D. 1414.] Red : fine. $\frac{4}{5}$ in. [Add. ch. 27,607.]

A shield of arms : a chevron indented, betw. three scrolls, each charged with a cross pattée. Within a carved and pointed gothic trefoil, ornamented with small ball-flowers on the inner edge.

Legend betw. the points :—

Sigill' : thome : barton :

Cabled border.

7170. [A.D. 1414.] Red : fine. [Add. ch. 27,608.]

7171. [A.D. 1415.] Red : fine. [Add. ch. 27,610.]

7172. [A.D. 1416.] Red : fine. [Add. ch. 27,612.]

John de Barry, *son and heir of* DAVID DE BARRÝ, *of Pennaly or Penally, co. Pembroke.*

7173. [A.D. 1301.] Uncoloured : imperfect. About $1\frac{1}{4}$ in. when perfect. [Harl. ch. 45 G. 13.]

A shield of arms : two bars gemels. Suspended from a hook by a strap, and betw. two small birds, of which that on the r. only remains.

.... IGILLVM ....

John de Barwe ? *or* Barnes ?
7174. [A.D. 1352.] Plaster cast from indistinct impression. $\frac{13}{16}$ in. [lxxxii. 93.]

A shield of arms : quarterly, BARNES ? Within a carved gothic panel.

✠ SIGILL' IOHANES DE BARWE (?)

Elizabeth Baryngge, *(dau. of* —— ZOUCHE ?), *wife of* OLIVER MAULEVERER, *of Creton Manor, co. Linc.*
7175. [A.D. 1401.] Red : originally fine, and encircled with a twisted rush, now chipped. 1 in. [Cott. ch. xii. 29.]

A shield of arms : per pale, *dex.*, a fess (diapered) betw. two barrulets in chief and four in base, BARYNGGE ? ; *sin.*, fourteen roundles, 4, 4, 3, 2, and 1, a canton ermine, ZOUCHE? Suspended by a strap from a forked tree on a mount, and within a carved gothic panel.

𝔖' : elizabeth · [b]aryngge :

7176. Sulph. cast from No. 7175. [D.C., G. 91.]
7177. Another, tinted pink. [xlvii. 1477.]

Laing's *MS. Catal.*, No. 487.

7178. [A.D. 1401.] Red : originally fine, and encircled with a twisted rush. [Cott. ch. xxvii. 79.]

.... elizabeth · baryngge :

Gilebert de Baseville, *of Reading, co. Berks.*
7179. [Late 12th cent. ?] White, flaked away in several places : very indistinct and tender. About $1\frac{3}{4}$ in. [Add. ch. 19,612.]

Ø. A shield of arms of early shape : barry of six, a chevron.

+ SIGIL .... I DE BASEVILE.

℞. A small pointed oval counterseal. $1\frac{1}{16} \times \frac{3}{4}$ in. Impression of an antique oval intaglio gem. An Agnus Dei.

+ ECCE ANGNVS DEI.

Beaded borders.

Robert Basham ?
Seal used by THOMAS BRET, *of Norton, co. Suff.*
7180. [A.D. 1379.] Red : chipped. $\frac{3}{4}$ in. [Harl. ch. 47 B. 25.]

A shield of arms : a chevron betw. three roundles. Within a border ornamented with small ball-flowers on the inner edge.

⚹ S' ROBERTI BASH'A.

Robert de Basinges, *of London.*

7181. [A.D. 1290.] Green: a fragment. About ¾ in. when perfect. [Harl. ch. 48 H. 17.]

A shield of arms: a cross (moline?) BASINGES.

⚹ S . . . . GES.

Ralph de Baskerville, *of Bredwardine, co. Heref.*

7182. [*Temp.* Hen. III.] Dark green: somewhat indistinct. ¾ in. [Add. ch. 20,409.]

A shield of arms: a chevron betw. three annulets (for hurts), BASKERVILLE.

✠ SIG' RADVLFI D' BASK⁊V'.

Beaded borders.

Thomas de Baskervile.

7183. [A.D. 1400.] Red: originally fine, and encircled by a twisted rush. ⅞ in. [L. F. C. xxviii. 10.]

A shield of arms: a chevron betw. two roundles in chief, a crescent in base. Within a carved gothic rosette of eight points.

⚹ SIGILLṼ · THOME · DE · BASKERVIL'.

Alan Basset, *of co. Wilts.*

7184. [*circ.* A.D. 1225.] Green: somewhat indistinct. App. by a piece of finely-woven tape of brownish green stuff. 1⅛ in. [Add. ch. 10,596.]

A shield of arms: two bars undées or dancettées, for BASSET.

✠ SIGILL : ALANI : BASSET.

7185. Plaster cast of No. 7184. [lxxxii. 95.]

Anselm Basset, *of Jakindene, co. Somers.*

7186. [A.D. 1268.] Creamy-white, partly flaked off. 1 in. [Harl. ch. 45 G. 29.]

A shield of arms: erm., on a chief indented three annulets, pierced cinquefoils, or estoiles, BASSET.

✠ SIGILLṼ : . . . .

Arthur Basset, *of Heanton, co. Devon, Esq.*

7187. [A.D. 1660.] Red, covered with paper before impression: very indistinct. ¾ × ⅔ in. [Harl. ch. 85 H. 59.]

Oval: a shield of arms: barry wavy of six, BASSET. Crest on a helmet, mantling, and wreath, an unicorn's head.

7188. [A.D. 1660.] Another: nearly illegible. [Harl. ch. 111 E. 36.]

John Bassett, *son and heir of* ARTHUR BASSET, *of Heanton, Esq., Gentl.*

7189. [A.D. 1660.] Red, covered with paper before impression. [Harl. ch. 85 H. 59.]

Apparently from the same signet as the seal of his father, see No. 7187.

7190. [A.D. 1660.] Another, red: imperfect, indistinct. [Harl. ch. 111 E. 36.]

Philip Basset.

7191. [A.D. 1258.] Plaster cast from imperfect impression. $1\frac{7}{8}$ in. [lxxxii. 97.]

A shield of arms: barry wavy of six, for BASSET.

✠ SIGIL . . . . HILIPPI · BASSET.

Philip Basset, *of Parva Stambridge, co. Essex.*

7192. [A.D. 1257.] Green: originally fine, now imperfect. About $\frac{7}{8}$ in. when perfect. [Harl. ch. 45 G. 26.]

A shield of arms of early shape with beaded edge: three bars wavy, BASSET. Over the shield a crescent for difference. [At each side an estoile.]

✠ S . . . . T.

Bearded borders.

7193. [A.D. 1260.] Plaster cast from good impression. [lxxxii. 96.]

✠ SIGILL' : PHILIPPI : BASSET.

7194. [A.D. 1258.] Plaster cast from chipped impression. [lxxxii. 98.]

. . . IGILL' : PHILIPPI : BAS . . . . .

Ralph Basset.

7195. [A.D. 1328.] Plaster cast from chipped impression. 1 in. [lxxxii. 94.]

A shield of arms: three piles meeting in point, a canton ermine, BASSET. Suspended by a strap from a tree of three branches.

✠ SIGILLVM · RADVLPHI · BASSET.

Cf. Harl. ch. 53 G. 57, A.D. 1319 ; Cott. ch. xxvii. 54, A.D. 1321 ; Harl. ch. 43 D. 30, A.D. 1331, etc.

Ralph, *son of* RALPH, *son of* RÁLPH BASSET, *of Drayton.*
7196. [A.D. 1355.] Red: very fine. 1 in. [Add. ch. 19,895.]
A shield of arms : three piles meeting in one point in base (diapered), a canton ermine, BASSET. Within an elaborately carved and traced gothic panel.

    ✠ SIGILLVM : RAD̄I : BASSET : DE : DRAYTOV̄ :
Beaded border.
7197. [A.D. 1355.] Red: very fine. [Add. ch. 19,896.]

Ralph Basset, *of Welledone, co. Northt.*
7198. [*Temp.* Edw. III.] Dark green : fine, cut from a charter. ⅞ in. [xxxvi. 74.]
A shield of arms , three pales, within a bordure bezantée, BASSET. Suspended by a loop, and betw. two wyverns sans wings.

    ✠ S' RADVLFI BASSET DE WELLEDONE.
Beaded borders.

Cf. Slo. ch. xxxi. 4 (29), A.D. 1330; Add. ch. 719, A.D. 1333 ; Add. ch. 758, A.D. 1341.

Symon Basseth, *son of* RALPH BASSETH,
of Sapcote, co. Leic.
7199. [*Temp.* Hen. III.] Dark green : fragments. About ⅞ in. when perfect. [Harl. ch. 45 G. 30.]
A shield of arms : three bars undées, BASSET.

    . . . . . SIMON' · B . . . .

Family of **Bassingborne,** *or* **Rand.**
7200. [14th cent.] Red. ¾ in. [xxxvi. 84.]
A shield of arms : gyronny of twelve, borne by BASSING-BORNE, and RAND.
In place of the legend a wavy scroll of foliage within beaded borders.

John de Bassingbourne, *Lord of Badelingham,*
[co. Camb.] Knt.
7201. [A.D. 1348.] Red: fine. [Harl. ch. 45 G. 36.]
A shield of arms: quarterly, in each quarter a crescent, BASSINGBORNE. Within a pointed gothic quatrefoil, with the inner edge ornamented with small ball-flowers.

    ✠ M · S' IOHANNIS · DE · BASSINGBOVRN.
The letters M.S. probably signify *Magnum sigillum.*
Beaded border.
7202. Sulph. cast from No. 7201. [D.C., F. 300.]

Maheu de Bassingburne, [*of Badlingham, co. Camb.*]

7203. [A.D. 1332.] Red : a fragment containing only the central part. About ⅞ in. when perfect. [Harl. ch. 45 G. 35.]

A shield of arms : quarterly, in each quarter a crescent, BASSINGBORNE. Suspended by a strap from a hook, and betw. two wyverns sans wings.

.... ING ......

Beaded border.

Maria, *widow of* HUMFREY DE BASSINGBURNE, *Knt., dau. of* MATTHEW DE THORNTONE, *of Fordham, co. Camb.*

7204. [A.D. 1298.] Green, mottled : fine, injured at the points. 1¼ × ¾ in. [Harl. ch. 45 G. 34.]

A shield of arms : gyronny of twelve, BASSINGBORNE. Suspended by a strap from a hook, and on a forked oak tree. Within a cusped panel of eight points. In the place for a legend a wavy scroll of foliage.

Beaded borders.

7205. Sulph. cast from No. 7204. [D.C., E. 490.]

Thomas de Bassingb[orne].

7206. [14th cent.] Plaster cast from fine impression. [lxxxiii. 13.]

A shield of arms : a bend betw. three birds contourné.

+ S' THOME DE BASSINGB'.

Cf. Add. ch. 22,666, A.D. 1364.

John Bastard, *Warden of the Chapel of Holy Cross without the walls of Colchester, co. Essex.*

7207. [A.D. 1331.] Red : imperfect, indistinct. About ¾ in. when perfect. [Harl. ch. 44 C. 55.]

A shield of arms : a lion rampant debruised by a bend.

✠ S' .... STARD.

Master **Robert Le H. ......, *and* Lucia de ....**

Seals used by JOHN DE BASTWYKE, *citizen of Norwich,* *and* RICHARD GILBERT, *of Wroxham, co. Norf.*

7208. [A.D. 1355.] Dark green : fine, imperfect. About ¾ in. [Add. ch. 14,928.]

(1.) A shield of arms : on a cross betw. four eagles displayed, five cinquefoils. Background diapered lozengy with a small cinquefoil in each space. Within a quatrefoil.

Legend betw. the points :—

S' MA ... ROB' L HE ......

7209. (2.) A shield of arms : on a cross five escallops, within a pointed gothic quatrefoil.

[S'] LVCIE DE B ......

Blomefield's *Hist. of Norfolk,* vol. v., p. 458 (Dept. copy).

R. B., *used by* JOHN BATE *de Donkastre,* [*Doncaster, co. York*],
Chaplain of Lincoln.
    7210. [A.D. 1408.]   Red: fine, somewhat injured by pres-
sure. ⅛ in. [Harl. ch. 112 G. 6.]
    A shield of arms: on a fess betw. three talbots' heads (or
bête's heads), or three dexter hands couped bendwise at the
wrist, a quatrefoil, between two roundles, BATE? Betw. the
letters S'. R. B.   Within a carved gothic quatrefoil.
    Cf. Bates' arms.

Edmund Bateman.
See WILLIAM PETTITT.

John Bathe, *of Wallington, co. Surr., or* MATILDIS, *his wife.*
    7211. [A.D. 1390.]   Red: imperfect, indistinct.   ¾ in.
[Add. ch. 23,156.]
    A shield of arms: a lion rampant.   Within a pointed
gothic trefoil.
                 . . . . IV . . H . . . CI . . .
Beaded border.

Thomas Bathe.
See RALPH DE HARYNGTON.

Richard Battelle, *al.* **Battely,** *of Redgrave, co. Suff.*
    7212. [A.D. 1657.]   Red: indistinct.   ⅓ × ¼ in.   [Add.
ch. 19,265.]
    Oval: a shield of arms: on a chevron engrailed betw.
three roundles, as many cinquefoils.
    Cf. the seal of Robert French in the same charter.

Ralph Battell, *al.* **Battle,** *Clerk, Master of the Free School,*
Hertford, co. Hertf.
    7213. [A.D. 1670.]   Red: injured by pressure, very indis-
tinct.   About ¾ × ⅝ in. [Add. ch. 35,491.]
    Oval: a shield of arms: a griffin segreant, BATTELL.
Crest on a helmet and mantling, indistinct.

William Battell, *of co. Hertf.*

    7214. [A.D. 1716.]   Red: *en placard* on a tape. 1⅟₁₆ × ⁹⁄₁₆.
An oval shield of arms: a griffin segreant, BATTELL.
Crest, on a helmet, ornamental mantling and wreath, a
demi-griffin.

    Used by SAMUEL HASSELL, *of Digswell, co. Hertf., Clerk.*
    7215. [A.D. 1716.]   Another: indistinct. [Add. ch. 35,469.]

William Battesford, *Rector of the Church of St. Mary, Maidwell, co. Northt.*

7216. [A.D. 1397.] Red: injured by pressure. ⅞ in [Add. ch. 22,236.]

A shield of arms : a chevron engrailed betw. three mullets. Within a carved gothic trefoil.

𝕾𝖎𝖌𝖎𝖑𝖑 ⚭ ⚭ 𝖜𝖎𝖑𝖑𝖎' ⚭ 𝖇𝖆𝖙𝖊𝖋𝖋𝖔𝖗𝖉.

7217. [A.D. 1397.] Red : imperfect, injured by pressure. [Add. ch. 22,237.]

7218. [A.D. 1397.] Red: originally fine, now imperfect. [Add. ch. 22,238.]

John, *fil.* **Rob. Baudri.**

See EDMUND DE CA . . . . .

Thomas Bawde, *of co. Essex, Knt.*

7219. [A.D. 1498.] Red : injured by pressure. ⅝ × ⅓ in. [Add. ch. 27,438.]

Rectangular : a shield of arms : three chevrons, BAWDE.

Another Seal.

7220. [A.D. 1504.] Red. ⅜ in. [Add. ch. 27.441.]

A wing erect. In the field the initial letter 𝖜.

William Bayfforde, *Lord of the Manor of Estmylne, in the Parish of Fordingbridge, co. Southt.*

7221. [A.D. 1388.] Bronze-green: fine. ⅞ in. [Lansd. ch. 688.]

A shield of arms: an eagle displayed in bend, debruised by a bendlet, and within an engrailed border. Suspended by a loop from a forked tree. Within a carved and pointed gothic panel.

𝕾𝖎𝖌𝖎𝖑𝖑𝖚𝖒 : 𝖜𝖎𝖑𝖑'𝖎 : 𝖇𝖆𝖞𝖋𝖋𝖔𝖗𝖉.

Carved border.

7222. [A.D. 1388.] Another: edge chipped. [Lansd. ch. 689.]

Anna Bayly, *of Havant, co. Southt., Widow.*

7223 [A.D. 1686.] Red : *en placard.* ¼ in. [Add. ch. 9442.]

A shield of arms : a double-headed eagle displayed.

Robert Baynarde, *of Lachkam, co. Wilts.*

7224. [A.D. 1430.] Red: imperfect, injured by pressure. About ¾ in. when perfect. [Add. ch. 1534.]

A shield of arms : a double-headed eagle displayed.   Suspended by a loop from a forked tree.

. . . . **m roberti bayna** . . . . . .

Carved borders.

Edward Bayntone, *of Benfield, co. Berks, Knt.*
7225. [A.D. 1538.]   Red : from a ring with mark of the chasing. $\frac{4}{8}$ × $\frac{1}{2}$ in.   [Add. ch. 13,649.]
Oval : a griffin's head erased.   Crest of BAYNTON.
Beaded border.

John de Baynton.
7226. [*Temp.* Edw. III.]   Red : fine, edge slightly chipped.   Cut from a charter. $\frac{7}{8}$ in.   [xxxvi. 87.]
A shield (? of arms) : a chevron engrailed betw. three Katharine wheels.   In chief a crosslet fitchée, united to the apex of the chevron.   Within a finely carved and traced gothic panel or cinquefoil.
✠ SIGILL' · IOHANNIS · DE · BAYNTON.

John Bayspoole, *or* **Thomas Bayspoole.**
Seals used by JAMES CLERKE, *Rector of Toft Monks, co. Norf*,
THOMAS BAYSPOOLE, JOHN BUCKINGHAM, THOMAS SPORE,
THOMAS DAVEY, STEPHEN HOBSON, *and* EDWARD DENTON,
of Toft Monks.
7227–7233. [A.D. 1706.]   Red : *en placard* on tape.
About $\frac{1}{4}$ in.   Seven impressions.   [Add. ch. 14,921.]
Out of a ducal coronet, a stag's head.   Crest of BAYSPOOLE.

George Beare, *of the Middle Temple, London, Esq.*
7234. [A.D. 1636.]   Red : indistinct. $\frac{7}{16}$ × $\frac{1}{3}$ in.   [Harl. ch. 86 I. 55.]
Oval : a shield of arms : three bears' heads erased (and muzzled), in chief an annulet for difference, BEARE.
Cabled border.

Guy de Beauchamp, *9th Earl of Warwick.*
7235. [A.D. 1305.]   Green : fine, well preserved. $\frac{7}{8}$ in.
[Cott. ch. xxii. 9.]
A shield of arms : a fess betw. six crosses crosslet, BEAUCHAMP.   Suspended by a strap, from a tree of three branches, and betw. two wavy scrolls of foliage and flowers.
. . . . .   S' GVYDONIS : COM' : DE · WARR'.
Beaded borders.

7236. Sulph. cast from No. 7235. [D.C., F. 178.]

7237. [A.D. 1299.] Plaster cast. [lxxxii. 99.]

7238. [A.D. 1307.] Green: a fragment. [Harl. ch. 45 I. 8.]

. . . . IS : CO . . . .

Johanna Beauchamp, *Lady of Bergeveny, dau. of* RICHARD FITZALAN, *sister and coheir of* THOMAS FITZALAN, *Earl of Arundel.* (*ob.* A.D. 1435.)

7239. [A.D. 1424.] Red: finely designed; now fragmentary, the r. h. side wanting. About $1\frac{7}{8}$ in. when perfect. [Harl. ch. 45 I. 11.]

A shield of arms: per pale, *dex.*, on a fess betw. six crosses crosslet, a crescent for difference, BEAUCHAMP; *sin.*, quarterly, 1, 2, 4, wanting, 3, chequy, WARREN. Supporters, *dex.*, a squirrel, *sin.*, wanting. Within a carved gothic quatrefoil, the field contains two small leaves over the supporter.

. . . . [b]ergeuen . . . .

Engraved in Rowland, *Historical Account of the Family of Nevill*, Lond., fol., 1830, p. 70, pl. fig. 3, where the bearing of the first quarter of the impalement is a lion rampant.

7240. Sulph. cast from No. 7239 before it was so fragmentary. [D.C., G. 171.]

. . . . . . om : be : bergeuen . . . .

7241. Plaster cast of a nearly perfect impression of this seal. [lxxxiii. 1.]

The shield of arms, as described above: the quarterings on the *sin.* side being, 1, 4 a lion rampant, 2, 3 chequy; upheld by an angel with open wings. Supporters, two squirrels. Within a finely carved quadrilobe or gothic panel of four cusps, ornamented along the inner edge with small roses or ball-flowers.

Sigillū : iohann[e] : be : bello : campo : dñe : be : bergeuennp.

John de Beauchamp, *of co. Linc.*

7242. [13th cent.] Cast in green composition. $1\frac{1}{4}$ in. From a charter belonging to the Hon. Edw. Stanhope, No. 95. [lii. 21.]

A shield of arms: fretty of six pieces.

. . . . D' BELLOCAMPO.

John de Beauchamp, *of Hache, co. Somers.,* 1*st Baron, ob.* A.D. 1336.

7243. [A.D. 1301.] Plaster cast from fine impression. $1\frac{1}{8}$ in. [lxxxiii. 11.]

An eagle displayed, charged on the breast with a shield of arms : vair, BEAUCHAMP, *of Hache.*

✠ : SIGILL' · IOHANNIS : DE : BELLO : CAMPO : .

John de Beauchamp, *of Somerset, Lord of Hacche Mercatorum, or Hatch-Beauchamp, co. Somers., 3rd Baron Beauchamp, Knt.*

7244. [A.D. 1361.] Dark green : originally fine, injured by pressure, edge chipped. About 1⅛ in. when perfect. [Harl. ch. 45 I. 20.]

A shield of arms : vair, BEAUCHAMP, *of Hache.* Within an elegantly carved and traced gothic sixfoil.

SIGILL' : IO . . . . DE . . . .

7245. Sulph. cast from No. 7244. [D.C., F. 416.]

John de Beauchamp, *of Poywyk, or Powyke, co. Worc., Knt.*

7246. [A.D. 1370.] Red : fine, injured in several places by pressure, chipped at top. 1¾ in. [Add. ch. 20,422.]

A shield of arms, *couché* : a fess (diapered) betw. six martlets, BEAUCHAMP, *of Powick.* Crest on a helmet, out of a ducal coronet, an eagle's head and neck, wings erect. Supporters : two lions sejant affrontés.

𝕾eel : 𝕵e𝖍an 𝖉e bea𝖚c𝖍amp.

The letters DE of *de* conjoined.

John [de Beauchamp], *Lord de Beauchamp,* [*1st Baron Beauchamp, of Powick ?*]

7247. [A.D. 1450.] Red : injured. ¼ in. From a signet ring. [Add. ch. 17,238.]

An uncertain device, perhaps a fetterlock, a beacon, or other badge, ensigned with the coronet of a baron. In the field an indistinct motto or legend.

Beaded border.

Isabella, *dau. of* THOS. DE **Beauchamp.**

See ISAB. DE BEAUCHAMP, widow of WILLIAM DE UFFORD.

Richard de Beauchamp, *14th Earl of Warwick.*

A.D. 1401–1439.

First Seal.

7248. [A.D. 1403.] Red : very finely designed and executed. Edge chipped, lower part wanting. 2¼ in. when perfect. [Add. ch. 20,431.]

A shield of arms : a fess betw. six crosses crosslet (field and fess powdered), BEAUCHAMP. Crest on a helmet and mantling, out of a ducal coronet, ornamented with roses, a swan's head and neck, betw. two flowering branches. Supporters two bears, each with a staff raguly. Within a cusped gothic quatrefoil adorned with roses in place of ball-flowers along the inner edge.

. . . . 𝔡𝔦 : 𝔡𝔢 : 𝔟𝔢𝔩𝔩𝔬 ⚜ ⚜ 𝔠𝔞𝔪𝔭𝔬 : 𝔠𝔬𝔪𝔦𝔱' : 𝔴𝔞 . . . .

The letters DE of *de* are conjoined.

Second Seal.

7249. [A.D. 1412.] Red : very finely designed and executed. Edges chipped. About 2⅛ in. when perfect. [Cott. ch. xi. 22.]

Somewhat similar to the preceding, or first seal. The armorial bearings of the shield are : quarterly 1, 4, chequy, a chevron, GUY OF WARWICK ; 2, 3, BEAUCHAMP, as in No. 7248. The coronet ornamented with quatrefoils instead of roses. The bears collared and ringed. The upper cusps of the enclosing quatrefoil more depressed than in the former seal. Under the shield on the left a small sprig.

𝔖𝔦𝔤𝔦𝔩𝔩𝔲̄ : 𝔯𝔦𝔠 . . . . . : 𝔡𝔢 : 𝔟𝔢𝔩𝔩𝔬 · 𝔠𝔞𝔪𝔭𝔬 . . . .
. . . . . 𝔴 . . . . . . 𝔠𝔥.

Cabled border.

7250. Sulph. cast from No. 7249. [D.C., G. 131.]

7251. [A.D. 1424.] Red : fine, fragments of the central part only. [Harl. ch. 45 I. 11.]

Third Seal.

After his second marriage, viz., with ISABEL, *dau. and coheir of* THOMAS LE DESPENCER, *Earl of Gloucester.*

7252. [A.D. 1426.] Red : a fragment of the central part only, showing portions of the shield of arms and the helmet. [Add. ch. 330.]

This seal closely resembles the fourth, of which the description will be found at No. 7253. The details of the heraldry are slightly different. The fess in the BEAUCHAMP quarter is differently diapered ; the alternate pieces of the chequy arms in the second quarter are diapered but in the fourth seal are plain, the chevron touches the top of the shield but does not go up so far in the fourth seal, and the ermine spots on it are of a different pattern.

This charter records the following titles of the Earl : " Richard de Beauchamp Comte de VVarrevvyke et Daumarle, Seigneur le Despensier et de Lisle Capitaine et lieutenant general du Roy et de mons sieur le Regent sur le fait de la guerre en Normandie Anjou le mayne et es marches de Bretagne." The seal may have been executed in France, and bears some resemblance in points of design to the French seals of this period.

Fourth Seal.

After his second marriage.

7253. [A.D. 1430.]　Red: originally fine, now cracked, imperfect on the r. h. side.　2¾ in.　[Add. ch. 20,432.]

An ornamental shield of arms, *couché*: quarterly, 1, 4, BEAUCHAMP, as in No. 7248 ; 2, 3, chequy a chevron ermine, GUY OF WARWICK.　Over all an escutcheon of pretence, quarterly, 1, 4, three chevrons, CLARE ; 2, 3, quarterly, in the second and third quarters a fret, over all a bend, DESPENSER. Crest on a helmet and ornamental mantling of arabesque foliage which replenishes the whole background of the seal, out of a ducal coronet, a swan's head and neck.　Supporters, *dex.*, a bear, collared, muzzled, and chained ; *sin.*, a griffin, collared.　Within a carved and pointed gothic quatrefoil, ornamented with ball-flowers along the inner edge and with tracery in the spandrils.

Richard[us ⚜ de ⚜ bello ⚜ cāpo ⚜ co]mes ⚜ warrewici ⚜ et ⚜ albe ⚜ marlie ⚜ dn̄s ⚜ despēser ⚜ et ⚜ de ⚜ isula.

Several pairs of letters are conjoined.

7254. [A.D. 1431.]　Red: originally fine, and details very sharply defined, now imperfect in several places.　[Harl. ch. 45 I. 12.]

... ardus ⚜ de ⚜ bello ⚜ capo ⚜ c . . . .

. . . e ⚜ marl . . . dn . . . .

7255. Sulph. cast from No. 7254.　[D.C., G. 186.]

7256. [A.D. 1435.]　Red: imperfect and indistinct fragment of the central part only, showing portions of the shield of arms, helmet, crest, and griffin.　[Add. ch. 2016.]

Richard de Bellocampo.
Seal used by JOHN DONEWYCH, *of co. Hunt.*

7257. [A.D. 1411.]　Red: injured by pressure, matrix injured.　¾ in.　[Add. ch. 34,076.]

A shield of arms: a lion rampant (crowned ?), BEAUCHAMP.

✠ S' RICARDI · DE · BELLO CAMPO. ·

7258. [A.D. 1411.]　Another.　[Add. ch. 34,077.]

Richard *Lord* **Beauchamp,** *of Pouwyk,* 2nd *Baron*

7259. [A.D. 1475–1496.] Plaster cast from fine but chipped impression. 2$\frac{3}{16}$ in. [lxxxiii. 2.]

A shield of arms, *couché*: a fess betw. six martlets, BEAUCHAMP, *of Powick·* Crest, on a helmet and ornamental mantling, out of a ducal coronet a swan's head and neck with wings erect.

Legend on a scroll:—

𝔖igillum · ricardi · dñi · de · beauchamp · de · pouwyk.

Carved border.

Thomas de Beauchamp, 10*th Earl of Warwick,*
[A.D. 1315–1369.] *Marshal of England.*

7260. [A.D. 1340.] Red: fine, somewhat injured by pressure. 1$\frac{1}{4}$ in. [Cott. ch. xxiii. 11.]

A shield of arms: a fess (diapered) betw. six crosses crosslet, BEAUCHAMP. Suspended by a strap from a tree. Within a finely carved and traced gothic panel ornamented with ball-flowers along the inner edge.

I· SIGILLVM · THOME : COMITIS · DE · WARWYK(?)

Beaded border.

Another Seal.

7261. [A.D. 1363.] Red: originally fine, chipped at edge. 1$\frac{1}{4}$ in. [Add. ch. 14,547.]

A shield of arms: BEAUCHAMP, as in No. 7248. Suspended by a strap from a forked oak tree. In base, on each side of the shield a pair of oak-leaves. Within a carved gothic panel with small circles of tracery.

𝔖ig . . . . . 𝔗home : comitis : de : 𝔚arwyk.

See Blomefield's *Hist. of Norfolk.* vol. ii., p. 380 (Dept. copy).

7262. [A.D. 1367.] Red: very imperfect, injured by pressure. [Harl. ch. 45 I. 10.]

. . . . . home . . . . . .

7263. Sulph. cast from No. 7262. [D.C., F. 454.]

Thomas de Beauchamp, [11*th*] *Earl of Warwick, Lord of*
Gower, [A.D. 1369–1401.]

7264. [A.D. 1379.] Red: originally fine, now injured, chipped at the base. 1$\frac{3}{4}$ in. [Harl. ch. 83 D. 26.]

A shield of arms: BEAUCHAMP, as in No. 7248. On a mount, suspended by a strap from a forked tree. Supporters, two bears. Within a carved gothic quatrefoil ornamented on the inner edge with small ball-flowers.

𝔖' thome de bellocāpo co[mitis warwych⁻ dñi gowereye.

Several pairs of letters are conjoined.

Cabled border.

7265. Sulph. cast from No. 7264. [D.C., F. 516.]

7266. [A.D. 1381.] Red: fragment of the shield and part of the *sinister* supporter. [Harl. ch. 76 B. 6.]

7267. [A.D. 1388.] Red: very fine and sharp, chipped, deficient in places. [L.F.C., xxiii. 2.]

S' thome de . . . . comitis warwych- dni . . . . .

Thomas Beauchamp.

7268. [Early 15th cent.] Plaster cast from fine impression. $1\frac{1}{8}$ in. [lxxxiii. 3.]

A shield of arms, *couché*: a chevron betw. three lions' heads erased, crowned, for BEAUCHAMP. Crest on a helmet, short lambrequin and wreath, a lion's head erased crowned. Within a carved gothic bilobe.

sig thome : ✶ . bewchaump.

Carved border.

Walter de Beauchamp.

7269. [13th cent.] Sulph. cast from good impression. $\frac{5}{8}$ in. [D.C., E. 322.]

A shield of arms: a fess betw. six martlets, BEAUCHAMP.

+ S' WALT'I DE BELLOCAMPO.

Beaded borders.

Walter de Beauchamp.

7270. [13th cent.] Plaster cast from indistinct impression. $1\frac{3}{8}$ in. [lxxxiii. 9.]

A shield of arms of early shape: two lions passant guardant in pale.

+ SIGILL' WALTERI DE BELOCAMPO.

Walter de Beauchamp, *Lord of Alecestria, or Alcester, co. Warwick. Steward of the king's household.*

7271. [A.D. 1301.] Plaster cast from fine, large, but imperfect, impression. $2\frac{3}{4}$ in. [lxxxii. 100, 101.]

Ø. A shield of arms: a fess betw. six martlets, BEAUCHAMP. Betw. three lions of England, in allusion to his office of Steward of the Household of Edward I.

. . . . ALTE . . . . ELLO CAMPO · D . . . . . .

Beaded borders.

℞. A small round counterseal. $\frac{3}{4}$ in. A shield of arms as above in the *obv.*

+ S' · WALT'I · DE · BELLO CAMPO.

Beaded borders.

7272. Plaster cast of the *rev.* only. [lxxxiii. 10.]

Walter de Beauchamp, *of Kynewarton, co. Warw., Knt.*
7273. [A.D. 1327.] Light-brown : indistinct. ⅞ in. [Harl. ch. 45 I. 27.]
A shield of arms : a fess betw. six martlets, BEAUCHAMP.

✠ SIGILLVM · WALTERI · DE · BEL .. CO ....

William de Beauchamp, *Brother of* THOMAS DE BEAUCHAMP, 11*th Earl of Warwick, Knt.*
7274. [A.D. 1376.] Red : fine, much injured by pressure, chipped. 1⅛ in. [Cott. ch. xi. 70.]
A shield of arms : BEAUCHAMP, with an uncertain mark of difference, perhaps a crescent, on the fess. Suspended by a strap from a forked tree. Within a carved gothic 8-foil, with ball-flowers along the inner edge.

𝕾𝖎𝖌𝖎𝖑𝖑𝖚 · 𝖜𝖎 ...... 𝖉𝖊 ... 𝖊𝖑𝖑𝖔𝖈𝖆𝖒𝖕𝖔.

William de Beauchamp, 1*st Lord of* [*A*]*bergavenny.*
7275. [A.D. 1396.] Red : originally fine and elegantly designed, now chipped, imperfect at the base. 1¾ in. [Harl. ch. 111 D. 27.]
A shield of arms : on a fess (diapered) betw. six crosses crosslet, a crescent for difference, BEAUCHAMP. Suspended by a strap from a tree on a mount. In the field on each side a columbine (?) betw. two sprigs of foliage.

𝕾𝖎𝖌𝖎𝖑𝖑𝖚𝖒 : 𝖜𝖎𝖑𝖊𝖑𝖒[𝖎 : 𝖉]𝖊 : 𝖇𝖊𝖑𝖑𝖔𝖈𝖆𝖒𝖕𝖔 :

Inner border ornamented with ball-flowers, outer border carved.
7276. Sulph. cast from No. 7275. [D.C., E. 599.]

William Beauchamp, *of Blounham, co. Bed., Knt.*
7277. [A.D. 1432.] Red : cracked, from a chased ring. With marks of the chased setting. [Harl. ch. 45 I. 28.]
On a helmet and mantling, out of a ducal coronet a swan's head and neck betw. a pair of wings, Crest of BEAUCHAMP. In the field a martlet for difference.
Beaded border.

Edmund de Beaufort, *Duke of Somerset,*
Marquess of Dorset, etc., A.D. 1448–1455,
Governor of Normandy, etc.
Seal for the Town of Bayeux.
7278. Sulph. cast from fine impression. 2⅛ in. [xlvii. 1630.]
A ·shield of arms, *couché* : quarterly, 1, 4, FRANCE (MODERN) ; 2, 3, ENGLAND, within a bordure compony,

BEAUFORT. Crest on a helmet, mantling (with foliage re-
plenishing the field), and chapeau turned up ermine, a lion
statant guardant.   Supporters, *dex.*, an eagle rising with
wings ouvertes; *sin.*, an heraldic tiger pelletté, ducally
gorged.

Legend on a scroll :—

: 𝕾 : emunðí : ðucíſ : 𝕾omerſetíe : marchíonís :
ðorſetíe : ē : p : bílla : baíeux.

Outer border ornamented with cinquefoils.

See Sandford, *Geneal. Hist.*, p. 331.

7279. Another.   [D.C., G. 249.]

Henry de Beaufort, *Cardinal of England,*
Governor of Cherbourg Castle, etc.,
Bishop of Winchester, A.D. 1405–1447, *Lord Chancellor.*

7280. [A.D. 1437.]   Red: fine, fragments of the central
part only.   [Add. ch. 5832.]

. The only portion which remains is a shield of arms :
quarterly, 1, 4, FRANCE (MODERN); 2, 3, ENGLAND, within
a bordure compony, BEAUFORT.

Cf. Add. ch. 19,977, A.D. 1414; Harl. ch. 43 E. 19, A.D. 1430; and
43 E. 20, A.D. 1443, for other seals of this personage.

Joan de Beaufort, *2nd wife of* RALPH DE NEVILLE,
4th Baron Neville of Raby.

7281. [A.D. 1435.]   Plaster cast from imperfect impression.
About 1¼ in. when perfect.   [lxxxviii. 66.]

A shield of arms: per pale, *dex.*, NEVILLE, the field diapered
with sprigs of foliage; *sin.*, quarterly, FRANCE and ENGLAND,
within a bordure compony, BEAUFORT.   Betw. two sprigs of
foliage.   Within a carved panel.

Legend imperfect and uncertain.

John de Beaufort, *Earl of Somerset, son of* JOHN OF GAUNT,
Duke of Lancaster ; A.D. 1397–1410.

7282. [A.D. 1408.]   Red: fine, fragments, showing the
shield of arms and a few other details.   About 2¼ in. when
perfect.   [Harl. ch. 43 E. 17.]

A shield of arms: BEAUFORT, as in No. 7280, supported
by a strap round the neck of an eagle contourné.   Crest on a
helmet, [a lion passant guardant.]

Legend on a scroll :—

[𝕾ígí] . . . .   𝕾omerſ . . .

7283. Sulph. cast from No. 7282, but more complete. [D.C., G. 121.]

7284. [A.D. 1408.] Red: fragments of shield of arms only. |Harl. ch. 43 E. 18.]

John de Beaufort, *3rd Earl, [afterwards 1st Duke] of Somerset, and of Kendal, Lord of Corf, etc.,* A.D. 1418–1444.

7285. [A.D. 1443.] Red: small fragments of various parts only. About 3 in. diam. when perfect. [Add. ch. 12,212.]

Ø. Uncertain details. Border ornamented with ball-flowers.

·.·. **ill** .·.·.·.·.·.

℞. A small counterseal of which there only remains the legend.

·.·.·. **i** ⅏

Marguerite de Beaufort, *Duchess of Somerset, Countess of Somerset and Kendal,* widow of JOHN DE BEAUFORT, *2nd Earl of Somerset,* dau. of Sir JOHN DE BEAUCHAMP, *of Bletso.*

7286. [A.D. 1447.] Red: fine originally, now very imperfect. About 2¼ in. when perfect. [Add. ch. 12,347.]

A shield of arms: per pale, *dex.,* BEAUFORT, as in No. 7280; *sin.,* on a fess (diapered lozengy) betw. six martlets, a pierced mullet, BEAUCHAMP. The shield slung by a strap over the neck of an eagle rising. Supporters, *dex.,* an antelope ; *sin.,* wanting.

Legend on a scroll :—

·.·.·. **ete · do** ·.·.·.·. **ciffie · de · Somerfet ·**

An outer border ornamented with small flowering sprigs.

Cf. Sandford, *Geneal. Hist.,* p. 246.

Thomas de Beaufort, *2nd Earl of Dorset,* [*afterw. 2nd Duke of Exeter, etc.*]

7287. [A.D. 1411–1416.] Plaster cast from fine but chipped impression. 2⅜ in. [lxxxiii. 4.]

A shield of arms, *couché* : quarterly 1, 4, FRANCE (MODERN) ; 2, 3, ENGLAND, within a bordure gobony [az. and erm.] This coat was used by the above when Earl of Dorset ; on his accession to the Earldom of Exeter he changed his armorial bearings to those described in Vol. I., No. 1043. Crest on a helmet, lambrequin or mantling, and chapeau, a lion statant guardant. Supporters, two swans.

2 I 2

Background diapered with sprigs of foliage. Within a carved gothic quatrefoil panel, ornamented with small quatrefoils or ball-flowers along the inner edge.

𝕾𝖎𝖌𝖎𝖑𝖑𝖚𝖒 : 𝖙𝖍𝖔𝖒𝖊 : 𝕯𝖚𝖈𝖎𝖘 ⚬ . . . . ⚬ . . . . 𝖙𝖎𝖊 :

Beaded borders.

Sandford, *Geneal. Hist.*, p. 263.

Thomas de Beaufort, *2nd Duke of Exeter,*
Earl of Dorset and Harecourt, Admiral of England and
Captain of Rouen, etc., [A.D. 1416–1426.]
7288. [A.D. 1420.] Red : *en placard,* from a small signet. Very indistinct, fragmentary. [Add. ch. 277.]
Octagonal : a lion sejant guardant.

. . . . . **O** . . . .

Cabled border.

Cf. xliii. 138, 139. Nos. 1043, 1044.

Henry de Bellomonte, *3rd Baron Beaumont,*
Lord of Loughteburgh.
7289. [A.D. 1366.] Red : originally fine, edge imperfect. 1¾ in. [Harl. ch. 45 I. 39.]
A shield of arms, *couché*: semé de lis, a lion rampant, over all a bend, BEAUMONT. Crest on a helmet, short mantling, and chapeau, a lion passant. Within a finely carved and pointed gothic panel, ornamented with ball-flowers on the inner border.

. . . . 𝖗𝖎𝖈𝖎 ⚛ 𝖉𝖊 ⚛ 𝕭𝖊𝖑𝖑𝖔𝖒𝖔𝖓𝖙𝖊 ⚛

Beaded borders.

7290. Sulph. cast from No. 7289. [D.C., F. 446.]

Johanna, *widow of* JOHN **de Beaumont,** *or* **Beamount,**
of Parkham, co. Devon, Knt.
7291. [A.D. 1381.] Red : fine, edge of l. h. side chipped. 1 in. [Add. ch. 13,919.]
A shield of arms : per pale, *dex.,* barry of six, vairé [and gu.], BEAUMONT ; *sin.,* a chevron betw. three crows, CORBET (?) Within a carved gothic cinquefoil with three large points in triangle, ornamented with ball-flowers along the inner edge.
Legend betw. the points.

⚬ 𝕾'. 𝖉𝖓̄𝖊 · ⚬ : 𝖎𝖔𝖍𝖆𝖓𝖓𝖊 : ⚬ · 𝖇𝖊𝖆𝖚 . . . 𝖓𝖙.

Cabled border.

John de Beaumont, *4th Baron Beaumont*,
A.D. 1383–1396.

7292. [A.D. 1383.]　Red : fine, chipped at top.　1½ in.
[Harl. ch. 45 I. 40.]

A shield of arms, *couché* : semé-de-lis, a lion rampant,
BEAUMONT.　Crest on a helmet, with lambrequins or short
mantling and chapeau, semé-de-lis, the chapeau turned up
ermine, a lion passant.　Supporters, two trees, each on a
mount.

　· ᚄᚔᚌᛁᛚᛚū : ᛁᚑᚻᛁᛋ : ᛞᚾᛁ : ᛋᚼ ᛞᛖ : ᛒᛖᛚᛚᚩᛗᚩᚾᛏᛖ :

7293. Sulph. cast from No. 7292.　[D.C., F. 547.]

Richard Beaumont, *of co. York, Esq.*

7294. [A.D. 1459.]　Red : imperfectly impressed, from a
signet, originally encircled by a twisted rush.　⅜ in.　[Add.
ch. 16,951.]

A lion's head erased, above it a crescent, in allusion to the
arms of BEAUMONT.　In the field the initial letters **r. b.**

Thomas Beufou, *or* Beawfoe, *of Empscot, co. Warw., Esq.*

7295. [A.D. 1601.]　Red : indistinct.　¾ in.　[Add. ch.
32,885.]

A shield of arms : a bend betw. six ermine spots.
Cabled border.

Ursula, *wife of* THOMAS **Beawfoe.**

7296. [A.D. 1601.]　Red : indistinct.　½ in.　[Add. ch.
32,885.]

An ornamental shield of arms : a chevron, ermine, betw.
three pairs of links of a chain interlinked.
Cabled border.

Thomas Beawfoe, *of Empscot, co. Warw.*

7297. [A.D. 1601.]　Red : indistinct.　[Add. ch. 32,886.]

On a mount a tree, labelled, the label bears an indistinct
motto.　In the field the initials T. B. at the sides of the tree.
Beaded border.

Henry Becher, *of Weston, co. Hertf., Gentl.*

7298. [A.D. 1653.]　Red : injured by pressure.　[Add. ch.
36,307.]

Oval : a shield of arms, vairé, on a canton a buck's head
cabossed, BECHER.　Crest, on a helmet and mantling, a demi-
lion.
Beaded border.

7299. [A.D. 1653.]　Red : very indistinct.　[Add. ch. 36,306.]

Henry Becher, *of Weston, co. Hertf., Esq.*
7300. [A.D. 1671.] Red, covered with paper before impression. $\frac{5}{8} \times \frac{1}{2}$ in. [Add. ch. 36,315.]
Oval: a shield of arms: vairé, on a canton a buck's head cabossed, BECHER.

John Becher, *of High Laver, co. Essex.*
See JOHN COLEMARSCH.

Walter Beckham, *late of Bytchamwell, now of Castleacre, co. Norf, Gentl.*
7301. [A.D. 1639.] Red: injured. About $\frac{3}{4} \times \frac{1}{2}$ in. [Add. ch. 30,823.]
A shield of arms: quarterly, 1, on a bend cotised, three pairs of wings conjoined in lure; 2, quarterly; 3, a lion rampant; 4. chequy. Crest on a helmet and ornamental mantling, a helmet betw. a pair of wings.
Cabled border.

John Bedale, *of co. Kent, Clerk.*
7302. [A.D. 1480.] Dark red. $\frac{3}{8}$ in. [Harl. ch. 80 G. 13.]
An escallop, in allusion to the arms of BEDELL or BEDLE.
In the field the word t . . . . . Dell.
Cabled border.
7303. [A.D. 1480.] Dark red. [Harl. ch. 80 G. 14.]
7304. [A.D. 1480.] Dark red: indistinct. [Harl. ch. 80 G. 15.]

William de Bedewynde,
Burgess of Reading, co. Berks.
7305. [A.D. 1343.] Red: imperfect, indistinct. $\frac{3}{4}$ in. [Harl. ch. 45 G. 69.]
A shield of arms: an estoile betw. three caltraps, that in base chipped off. Suspended by a strap from a hook.
Beaded border.

James Bedingfield, *alias de Grey, of Gonville and Caius Coll., Cambridge, LL.B.*
7306. [A.D. 1721.] Red: *en placard.* $\frac{7}{12} \times \frac{1}{2}$ in. [Add. ch. 9798.]
An ornamental shield of arms: a fess betw. two chevronels.

Thomas Bedwell, *of St. Clement Danes, co. Midd., Gentl.*
7307. [A.D. 1734.] Red: *en placard,* on tape. $\frac{3}{4} \times \frac{5}{8}$ in. [Add. ch. 29,634.]

Oval: a shield of arms: per saltire lozengy and ermine, BEDEWELL. Crest, on a helmet and ornamental mantling, a griffin's head erased.

John Beek, *of co. Kent.*

7308. [A.D. 1415.] Brown. $\frac{1}{4} \times \frac{3}{8}$ in. [Harl. ch. 76 B. 13.]

Octagonal signet: a shield of arms: on a chevron betw. three eagles' heads erased, an escallop for difference.

Cabled border, partly engrailed on the inner edge.

Nicholas de Beek, *Knt.*

7309. [A.D. 1369.] Red: imperfect. 1 in. [Add. ch. 20,478.]

A shield of arms, *couché*: a cross. Crest, on a helmet, out of a ducal coronet a boar's head and neck. Within a carved gothic panel.

𝕾ig : nicholai : ꝺe : bek :

William de Beestun,

Seal used by RALPH DE BEESTON, *of Pudsay, co. York.*

7310. [A.D. 1398.] Red: injured by pressure on l. h. side. $\frac{3}{4}$ in. [Add. ch. 16,883.]

A shield of arms: a lion rampant crowned, debruised by a bend, BEESTON. On a tree of three branches, and betw. two wyverns sans wings.

✠ SIGILLVM · WIL . . . . . . VN.

John de Beggebury, *of Goudhurst, etc., co. Kent.*

7311. [A.D. 1355.] Red: fine originally, injured in places by pressure. $\frac{11}{16}$ in. [Harl. ch. 76 B. 27.]

A shield of arms: (field diapered lozengy) on a bend three martlets. Within a finely carved and traced gothic six-foil.

✠ SIGILL' · IOH'IS : DE : BEGGEBERI.

Beaded border.

7312. [A.D. 1367.] White: imperfect, very indistinct. [Harl. ch. 76 B. 28.]

✠ SI . . . . DE : BEGGEBERI.

John de Beggeberi, *or* Begebery, *of Goudhurst, co. Kent.*

7313. [A.D. 1411.] Discoloured: indistinct. $\frac{1}{4} \times \frac{3}{8}$ in. [Harl. ch. 76 B. 36.]

Oblong octagonal signet: a shield of arms: on a bend three martlets. On a tree or branch with two small roses.

Cabled border.

7314. [A.D. 1412.]   Red: indistinct.   [Harl. ch. 76 B. 37.]
7315. [A.D. 1412.]   Red.   [Harl. ch. 76 B. 38.]
7316. [A.D. 1412.]   Red: injured and indistinct.   [Harl. ch. 76 B. 40.]
7317. [A.D. 1414.]   Red: good.   [Harl. ch. 76 B. 39.]
7318. [A.D. 1414.]   Red: good.   [Harl. ch. 76 C. 44.].
7319. [A.D. 1422.]   Red: fine.   [Harl. ch. 76 B. 41.]

John Beke, *Lord of Eresby, co. Linc.,* *son of* WALTER BEKE.

7320. [*s.d.*]   Brown. $\frac{5}{8}$ in.   [Harl. ch. 45 H. 14.]
A shield of arms: a cross moline, BECK.   On each side of the shield a garb; above it, a sword.
7321. Sulph. cast from No. 7320.   [D.C., E. 487.]
7322. [A.D. 1297.]   Brown.   [Harl. ch. 45 H. 15 B.]
7323. [A.D. 1297.]   Brown.   [Harl. ch. 45 H. 16.]

Thomas de Bekeryng, *of Bolington, co. Linc., Knt.*

7324. [A.D. 1348.]   Creamy-white: imperfect and very indistinct.   1 in.   [Harl. ch. 45 H. 34.]
A shield of arms: chequy, a bend, BECKERING.

....GILLVM ..... ME · DE · B ....
Inner border engrailed.

James Le Bel de Fermesham, *of Westminster, co. Midd.*

7325. [*Temp.* Hen. III.]   Green: a fragment.   1 × $\frac{3}{4}$ in.   [Harl. ch. 45 H. 39.]
Shield-shaped: a shield of arms: three roses.

....ILLVM ....

Henry Belasyse, *al.* Belassis, *of Coxwould, co. York, Esq.*

7326. [A.D. 1647.]   Red: indistinct. $\frac{9}{16}$ × $\frac{7}{16}$ in.   [Add. ch. 35,523.]
Oval: a shield of arms of eight quarterings.   I. A chevron betw. three fleurs-de-lis, BELASIS, etc.
Beaded borders.
7327. [A.D. 1647.]   Another.   [Add. ch. 35,525.]

Jane, *wife of* JOHN *Lord* Belasyse, *al.* Belassis.

7328. [A.D. 1647.]   Red: injured. $\frac{1}{2}$ × $\frac{7}{16}$ in.   [Add. ch. 35,525.]
Oval: a shield of arms: very indistinct.
7329. [A.D 1647.]   Another.   [Add. ch. 35,523.]

John de Belasise,

Seal used by CECILIA, *daughter and heir of* THOMAS DE BRUNTOFT, *of Bruntoft,* [*co. Durh. ?*]

7330. [A.D. 1380.] Dark red : indistinct in places. 1 in. [Egert. ch. 576.]

A shield of arms : an eagle displayed. Within an estoile of six points or two triangles interlaced, with tracery in the points.

Legend betw. the points :—

S' IO_HAN_NIS_BEL_ASY_IS.

Rt. Hon. **John Belasyse,** *al.* **Belassis,** *Esq.,* *al.* JOHN *Lord* **Belassis.**

7331. [A.D. 1647.] Red : injured. $\frac{3}{8} \times \frac{1}{4}$ in. [Add. ch. 35,523.]

Oval : a shield of arms of ornamental shape : on a chevron betw. three fleurs-de-lis, BELASIS, a crescent for difference. Beaded border.

Another Seal.

7332. [A.D. 1657.] Red. $\frac{1}{4}$ in. [Add. ch. 30,945.]

Small octagonal signet : a shield of arms : a chevron betw. three fleurs-de-lis, BELASIS. Enclosed in a pair of palm-branches.

Another Seal.

7333. [A.D. 1658.] Red : injured by pressure. [Add. ch. 30,950.]

Small octagonal signet : a shield of arms : ermine, on a canton a crescent. Arms of STRODE.

Mary Belasyse, *dau. of the Protector,* OLIVER CROMWELL, *wife of* THOMAS BELASYSE, *Viscount Fauconberge.*

7334. [A.D. 1657.] Red. [Add. ch. 30,952.]

Oval : a shield of arms of ornamental shape : BELASIS, ensigned with a coronet of pearls. Betw. two palm branches.

Thomas Belasyse, *Baron of Yarram,* *and 2nd Viscount Fauconberge,* A.D. 1652–1700.

7335. [A.D. 1658.] Red : injured. $\frac{1}{2} \times \frac{4}{10}$ in. [Add. ch. 30,951.]

Oval : a shield of arms : a chevron betw. three fleurs-de-lis, BELLASIS. Betw. two palm-branches ; and ensigned with a viscount's coronet.

7336. [A.D. 1658.] Another : indistinct. [Add. ch. 30,952.]
7337. [A.D. 1657.] Another. [Add. ch. 30,964.]

Another Seal.

7338. [A.D. 1679.] Red, covered with paper before impression. $\frac{3}{8}$ × $\frac{1}{2}$ in. [Add. ch. 30,955.]
Oval : crest as in No. 7339. Viscount's coronet.

Seal as EARL OF FAUCONBERG, A.D. 1689–1700.

7339. [A.D. 1693.] Red : en placard on a label. [Add. ch. 6076.]
Oval : on a wreath, a lion couchant guardant, crest of BELASYSE. *E*nsigned with an earl's coronet.
Cabled border.
7340. [A.D. 1699.] Another : imperfect, indistinct. [Add. ch. 6152.]

Isolda de Belhous, *dau. and coheir of Lady* ALICIA DE
 BEAUMONT, *widow of* JOHN DE BELHOUS, *Knt.,*
 of Barnwell, co. Northt., Rayleigh, co. Essex, etc.
7341. [A.D. 1336.] White : indistinct. $\frac{3}{4}$ in. [Add. ch. 21,534.]
Two shields of arms, suspended by loops from a tree of three branches : *dex.* quarterly per fess dancettée, over all a bend, BEAUCHAMP ? *sin.*, three lions rampant, BELHOUSE.
,⚹ SIGILLV · ISEVDE DE BELHOVS.
7342. [A.D. 1339.] Red : indistinct. [Harl. ch. 45 H. 50.]
7343. [A.D. 1353.] Red : indistinct. [Harl. ch. 45 H. 53.]
7344. Sulph. cast from No. 7343. [D.C., F. 382.]
Cf. Harl. ch. 44 C. 55, A.D. 1331 ; 45 H. 51, A.D. 1336 ; 45 H. 49, A.D. 1339 ; 45 E. 58, A.D. 1345 ; and 45 G. 51, A.D. 1353.

John Bell, *of London, Clerk.*
7345. [A.D. 1607.] Red : injured by pressure. $\frac{11}{16}$ × $\frac{9}{16}$ in. [Add. ch. 29,575.]
Oval : a bell, in allusion to the arms of BELL. Betw. the initial letters I. B.

John Bellardi ?
7346. [A.D. 1328.] Plaster cast from good impression. 1 × $\frac{7}{8}$ in. [lxxxiii. 7.]
Oval : a shield of arms : a chief. Suspended by a strap from a hook. Within a lozenge. of which the inner edge is engrailed. In four lobes on the sides of the lozenge, the customary emblems of the four Evangelists.
⚹ S' IOH'IS · BELLARDI(?)
Perhaps a foreign seal.

Abigail, *wife of* THOMAS **Bellchamber,** *of London, Gentl.*
7347. [A.D. 1716.]   Red: *en placard,* on a tape. [Add.
ch. 35,469.]
Seal of arms as described for THOS. BELLCHAMBER. *q.v.*

Thomas Bellchamber, *of London, Gentl.*
7348. [A.D. 1716.]   Red: *en placard,* on a tape. $\frac{3}{4} \times \frac{5}{8}$ in.
[Add. ch. 35,469.]
Oval: a shield of arms: three hawks' bells, two and one,
BELLCHAMBER.   Crest on a helmet and mantling, on a
wreath a demi-lion rampant, holding in the forepaws a bell.
7349. Plaster cast of No. 7348. [xcviii. 38.]

Sir **Richard Bellings,** *Knt., Principal Secretary and*
Master of Requests to CATHARINE,
Queen Dowager of CHARLES II.
7350. [A.D. 1693.]   Red: *en placard,* on a label. $\frac{5}{8} \times \frac{1}{2}$ in.
[Add. ch. 6076.]
Octagonal signet: a shield of arms: on a cross, betw. four
crosses-crosslet fitchées, a crescent for difference.   Crest on a
helmet and ornamental mantling, a demi-lion rampant, holding in its dexter paw a cross crosslet fitchée.
7351. Plaster cast of No. 7350. [xcviii. 39.]
7352. [A.D. 1680.]   Another impression: very indistinct.
[Harl. ch. 111 H. 11.]
7353. [A.D. 1698.]   Another. [Add. ch. 6152.]

Simon de Beltone.
7354. [14th cent.]   Red: recent impression from the
matrix. [xxxv. 223.]
A shield of arms: on a chevron betw. three pierced cinquefoils, five quatrefoils; surmounted by a merchant's mark incorporating the initial letter: S.   Within a carved and traced
gothic trefoil.
Legend betw. the points :—
S : SIMO_NIS · DE : _BELTONE.

Ramonil' Benbo,
Seal used by ROBERT LUCAS, *of Ipswich, co. Suff.*
7355. [A.D. 1399.]   Red: somewhat indistinct. $\frac{1}{2} \times \frac{3}{8}$ in.
[Stowe ch. 393.]
Octagonal: a shield of arms, *couché*: a chevron betw.

three estoiles. Crest on a helmet, mantling and wreath, a pair
of arms, embowed, holding up an uncertain object.

S' RAMONIL' : BENBO :

Perhaps a foreign seal.

William Bendes, *of Ipswich, co. Suff., Clerk.*

7356. [A.D. 1615.]   Red: injured. $\frac{5}{12} \times \frac{1}{4}$ in.   [Add. ch.
9783.]

Oval : a shield of arms : a tower.

Peter de Bendinges, *of Benchesham Manor, in Croydon,*
co. Surr.

7357. [*circ.* A.D. 1230.]   Dark green : imperfect, indistinct.
$1\frac{3}{8}$ in.   [Add. ch. 23,323.]

A shield of arms of early shape : a fess cotised.

...IG ... PETRI · DE · BENDIN ...

7358. Plaster cast from fine impression.   [lxxxiii. 12.]

✠ SIGILL' PETRI · DE · BENDINGIES.

Cf. Add. ch. 23,326 ; 16,383, A.D. 1237 ; 16,384, A.D. 1236–7.

Walter, *son of* MATTHEW **de Beningwrd,** *of co. Linc.*

7359. [Late 12th cent.]   Cast in green composition from
original impression. $1\frac{3}{8}$ in.   [lii. 34.]

A shield of arms of early convex shape : a lion rampant.

✠ SIGILL' WAL[TE]RI D' BENINGEWRD.

7360. Plaster cast.   [lxxxiii. 14.]

Cf. Harl. ch. 48 I. 51 ; and 54 E. 7, *temp.* Hen. II.

Isabella [Bennet], *Duchess of Grafton, widow of*
HENRY FITZROY, *Duke of Grafton.*

7361. [A.D. 1693.]   Red : *en placard,* on a label.   [Add. ch.
6151.]

Two oval shields of arms conjoined : *dex.,* quarterly,
1, 4, FRANCE and ENGLAND quarterly ; 2, SCOTLAND ;
3, IRELAND over all a baton sinister compony, for FITZROY,
Duke of Grafton : *sin.,* a bezant betw. three demi-lions rampant, BENNET.   Surmounted by a ducal coronet.

John Bennet, *or* Benet, *of Harlington, co. Midd., Knt.*

7362. [A.D. 1654.]   Red : injured. $\frac{5}{8} \times \frac{1}{2}$ in.   [Add. ch.
18,976.]

Oval : a shield of arms : a bezant betw. three demi-lions
rampant, in chief a crescent for difference, BENNET.

Beaded border.

Sir **John Bennet,** *or* **Benet,** *of St. Martin's-in-the-Fields,*
co. Midd., K.B.

7363. [A.D. 1670.] Red, covered with paper before impression: indistinct. ⅞ × ¾ in. [Add. ch. 19,006.]

Oval: an ornamental shield of arms: a mullet betw. three demi-lions, BENNET. Encircled with the Collar of the Order of the Bath. Crest on a helmet, mantling, and wreath, a lion's head issuant.

7364. [A.D. 1670.] Another: indistinct. [Add. ch. 19,009.]

John Bennet.
See JOHN CARYLE.

Robert Bennett, *or* **Benett,** *of Hereford, co. Heref., Gentl.*

7365. [A.D. 1618.] Red, covered with paper: *en placard,* very indistinct. ¾ × ½ in. [Add. ch. 1913.]

Oval: a shield of arms: on a cross betw. four demi-lions rampant couped, a bezant, BENNETT.

Edmund de Benstede, *son and heir of*
JOHN DE BENSTEDE, *of Ermyngton, co. Devon.*

7366. [A.D. 1333.] Red: injured. ⅞ in. [Harl. ch. 46 A. 13.]

A shield of arms: three bars gemel, BENSTED. Betw. three small pierced roses. Within a cusped and traced gothic six-foil.

Cabled border.

John de Benstede.

7367. [A.D. 1310.] Plaster cast from chipped impression. ¾ in. [lxxxiii. 15.]

A shield of arms: two bars gemel, for BENSTED. Within a carved gothic panel of six cusped points.

Beaded border.

John de Bensted, *of co. Glouc.*

7368. [A.D. 1342.] Red: originally fine, now chipped, imperfect on l. h. side. ⅞ in. [Add. ch. 28,754.]

A shield of arms: (diapered lozengy) three bars gemel, in dexter chief a martlet, for BENSTED. Suspended by a strap from a hook, and betw. two slipped leaves. Within a carved and pointed gothic panel of three points in triangle and five cusps, ornamented with small ball-flowers along the inner edge.

✠ SIGILL' IOHI'S . . . . ED'.

Beaded border.

Pernella, *wife of* JOHN DE **Benstedé.**

7369. [A.D. 1359.] Plaster cast from fine but chipped impression. $1\frac{1}{16}$ in. [lxxxiii. 16.]

A shield of arms : three bars gemel, for BENSTED. Within a very elaborately traced gothic panel, having four small carved compartments in saltire, each enclosing a lozenge-shaped shield of arms : 1, three fusils in fess ; 2, bendy ; 3, ermine ? three fusils in fess ; 4, uncertain, perhaps an escutcheon.

S' PETRONELI · DE · BENSTEDE (?)

William Bentinck, *5th Earl of Portland, K.G.*

7370. [A.D. 1702.] Red : *en placard*, on a label. $\frac{5}{8} \times \frac{1}{2}$ in. [Egert. ch. 104.]

An ornamental shield of arms : a cross moline, BENTINCK. Encircled with a garter inscribed with the motto of the order, and ensigned with an earl's coronet.

Hon. **William Bentinck,** *son of* WILLIAM BENTINCK,
Earl of Portland.

7371. [A.D. 1728.] Red : *en placard*, on a tape. $\frac{5}{8} \times \frac{9}{16}$ in. [Egert. ch. 111.]

Oval : an ornamental shield of arms : a cross moline, BENTINCK. Ensigned with the coronet (of a marquess ?)

Cabled border.

Jeremy Bentley, *of Eland, co. York., Gentl.*

7372. [A.D. 1659.] Red : imperfect at base. $\frac{5}{8} \times \frac{1}{2}$ in. [Harl. ch. 112 D. 6.]

Oval : a shield of arms : three bends, and a cross crosslet, BENTLEY. Crest on a helmet and mantling, a spaniel passant.

Beaded border.

John Ber', *of Stowlangtoft.*
See THOS. WATTONE.

Henry, *fil.* **Rad. de Berdewelle,** *of co. Suff.*

7373. [A.D. 1293–1304.] Green : originally fine, now imperfect. $\frac{3}{4} \times \frac{5}{8}$ in. [Harl ch. 46 A. 26.]

Shield-shaped : a shield of arms : three piles barwise, or per pale indented, on a chief a demi-lion rampant issuing.

+ NE SVI . . . . ISY QVE IE DE LE AMIE_:

Beaded border.

7374. Sulph. cast from No. 7373. [D.C., F. 175.]

Cf. Hen. f. Rad. de Berdewell, Harl. ch. 54 D. 5, A.D. 1300; Hen. de Berdewelle, Harl. ch. 54 A. 30, A.D. 1305; 46 A. 27, A.D. 1307; and 56 E. 15, A.D. 1310.

Kynard de la Bere, *Knt.*

7375. [A.D. 1387.] Red: cracked, imperfect. 1 in. [Cott. ch. xxiii. 13.]

A shield of arms : a bend betw. two cotises and six mart-lets, DE-LA-BERE. Betw. three pairs of leaves, those over the shield surmounted by a pierced mullet. Inner border carved.

☆ :—: 𝕾𝖎𝖌𝖎𝖑𝖑𝖚𝖒 ☆☆☆ 𝕽 . . . . 𝖉𝖊 ☆ 𝖑𝖆 ☆ 𝖇𝖊𝖗.

7376. Sulph. cast from No. 7375. [D.C., F. 563.]

Henry de Bereford, *Parson of Costone, co. Leic. ?*

7377. [A.D. 1327.] Creamy-white ; very indistinct. ¾ in. [Add. ch. 26,603.]

A shield of arms : defaced. Within a carved gothic panel.

. . . . ENRICI · FIL' W . . . .

Simon de Bereford, *of Wysshawe, co.·Warw.*

7378. [A.D. 1329.] Creamy-white: indistinct. ⅞ in. [Add. ch. 26,604.]

A shield of arms: uncertain charges. Within a cusped gothic six-foil.

☆ CEO EST LE SEL SIMOND DE BEREFORD (?)

Hugh de Berewyk, *of Beaconsfield, co. Buck., Knt.*

7379. [A.D. 1375.] Dark-green: fine. 1¼ in. [Harl. ch. 46 D. 18.]

A wild man, holding up before him a shield of arms: a lion rampant, BERWICK. Betw. two wyverns sans wings.

SIGILL · HVGONIS · DE · BEREWYK.

Beaded borders.

7380. Sulph. cast from No. 7379. [D.C., F. 492.]

Margaret Berewyk.

See ARTHUR DE GREY.

Baldewyne de Berford, *of Wysshawe, co. Warw., Knt.*

7381. [A.D. 1372.] Greenish-brown : originally fine, edge chipped. 1 in. [Add. ch. 26,606.]

A shield of arms, *couché*: three fleurs-de-lis, betw. seven crosses crosslets fitchées, BEREFORD.   Crest on a helmet, mantling, and chapeau, a bear statant.   Background diapered with wavy sprigs or tendrils.   Within a carved gothic panel of oval form.

𝕾 : bauⅾewyn : berforⅾ.

The letters DE in *baudewyn* are conjoined.

Cf. Dom. Baudewyn Bereford, Knt., Harl. ch. 49 G. 37, A.D. 1377 ; D. Baldwyn Berford, Knt., Add. ch. 23,859, A.D. 1379 ; B. de Bereforde, Knt., Harl. ch. 58 D. 9, A.D. 1392 ; also Add. ch. 7379, A.D. 1393; 20,311, A.D. 1394 ; 20,386, A.D. 1396 ; and 14,677, A.D. 1399.

Alexander de Bergh.

7382. [A.D. 1303.]   Plaster cast from fine impression. $1\frac{5}{6}$ in. [lxxxiii. 20.]

A shield of arms : on a bend betw. two cotises three roundles.   Betw. two small leaves.   Within a pointed gothic trefoil panel, ornamented along the inner edge with small quatrefoils or ball-flowers.

✠ S' ALEXANDRI : DE : BERGH'.

Richard, *fil.* Joh. de Bergholte, *of Fordham, co. Essex.*

7383. [A.D. 1346.]   Bronze-green: imperfect. $\frac{7}{8}$ in. [Harl. ch. 51 F. 15.]

A shield of arms : an estoile of six points wavy, betw. three roses.   Betw. the initial letters R. I.   Within a carved gothic quatrefoil.

Legend uncertain :—

✠ I H H . . . . Є . . . LYLY (?)

John de Berkeley, *or* Bercley, *of Sockes Denys Manor, co. Somers., Knt.*

7384. [A.D. 1389.]   Red : originally fine, very imperfect. About 1 in. when perfect.   [Harl. ch. 46 A. 45.]

A shield of arms : BERKELEY, as in No. 7392 within a bordure.   Suspended by a diapered strap from a forked tree. Within a traced and carved gothic panel ornamented with ball-flowers along the inner edge.

. . . . ⅾe : berkelee :

7385. Sulph. cast. from No. 7384.   [D.C., F. 572.]

John de Berkeley (?)

7386. [A.D. 1422.]   Plaster cast from imperfect impression. $1\frac{3}{4}$ in. [lxxxiii. 21.]

A shield of arms, *couché*: BERKELEY.   Crest on a helmet

a mitre. Supporters, two mermaids. In the background on the l. h. side a sprig of foliage.

$$\text{Sigillum} \ldots \ldots \ldots \text{\textit{∗} Dne} \ldots \ldots \text{le \textit{∗}}$$

Cf. the seal of Moricius de Berkeley.

John de Berkeley, [1st] *Baron Berkeley, of Stratton,* [A.D. 1650–1678.]

7387. [A.D. 1665.] Red, covered with paper before impression : very indistinct. About $\frac{5}{12} \times \frac{1}{4}$ in. when perfect. [Harl. ch. 77 H. 1.]

A shield of arms : BERKELEY, as in No. 7392. Crest [on a helmet] a mitre.

Moricius de Berkeley, *Lord of Beverston and Bettesthorn, co. Hants, Knt.*

7388. [A.D. 1428.] Red : very fine, imperfect at top and bottom. About $1\frac{3}{4}$ in. when perfect. [Harl. ch. 46 A. 47.]

A shield of arms, *couché* : quarterly, 1, 4, BERKELEY, as in No. 7392 ; 2, 3, on a saltire five mullets of six points, or roses, BEVERSTONE. Crest, on a helmet and mantling, a mitre, diapered with foliage. Supporters, two mermaids. Within a carved gothic panel, the inner edge ornamented with ball-flowers.

$$\text{S' mauricij de berkeley milit} \ldots \ldots \text{[beuerf]ton et bettefthorn.}$$

7389. Sulph. cast from No. 7385. [D.C., G. 178.]

7390. [A.D. 1428.] Another : not so perfect. [Harl. ch. 46 A. 46.]

$$\ldots \ldots \text{m} \ldots \ldots \text{beuerfton et bettef} \ldots \ldots$$

Thomas de Berkele, [? 1st *Baron,* A.D. 1295–1321.]

7391. [Early 14th cent.] Sulph. cast. from fine impression. 1 in. [D.C., E. 317.]

A shield of arms : BERKELEY, as in No. 7392. Suspended by a strap from a hook, and betw. two wyverns.

$$\text{✠ SIGLLVM : THOME DE BERKELE.}$$

Beaded borders.

Thomas de Berkele, *Lord of Berkeley,* 3rd Baron, A.D. 1326–1342.

7392. [A.D. 1335.] Light-red : fine, edge chipped. 1 in. [Cott. ch. xxiii. 17.]

A shield of arms, *couché* : a chevron betw. ten crosses crosslet, six in chief four in base, BERKELEY. Crest on a helmet, a mitre, stringed and garnished, charged on either side with the arms of BERKELEY, as above described. Supporters, two mermaids, each with comb and mirror. All within a cusped border.

SIGILLVM ❋ THOME ❋ DE ❋ BERKELE ❋

Beaded border.

7393. Sulph. cast of No. 7392. [D.C., F. 255.]

7394. Plaster cast. [lxxxvii. 43.]

. **7395.** Another: from fine impression. [xciv. 57.]

. **7396.** [A.D. 1327.] Red: originally fine, now imperfect. [Harl. ch. 46 A. 43.]

. . . . THOME . . . .

7397. [A.D. 1354.] Dark - green: somewhat indistinct, edge chipped. [Harl. ch. 46 A. 44.]

SIGILLVM ❋ TH . . E ❋ DE ❋ BERKELE ❋

Thomas de Berkeley, *5th Baron* [A.D. (1368) 1381–1416.]

7398. Red: originally fine, now injured, imperfect. 1¼ in. [xxxvi. 135.]

On a tree-stump set on a mount of herbage, a shield of arms, *couché*: BERKELEY, as in No. 7392. Crest, on a helmet and mantling, a mitre stringed and garnished, charged with cross crosslets derived from the above arms. Supporters, two mermaids. Background replenished with small sprigs of foliage. Within a carved gothic quatrefoil of elegant design, ornamented with small ball-flowers along the inner edge.

Legend betw. the lobes of the quatrefoil :—

[Sigi]ll' thome dñi de berkley.

The letters HO of *thome*, and BE of *berkley* are conjoined.

Another Seal?

7399. [A.D. 1385.] Plaster cast from chipped impression. 1⅝ in. [xciv. 58.]

A shield of arms: BERKELEY. Suspended by a strap from a forked tree on a mount. Supporters, two mermaids. Within a carved gothic quatrefoil panel or quadrilobe, ornamented along the inner edge with small quatrefoils.

Sigillu : . . . me : ⚜ dñi : de : berkele :

Cf. Sir John Maclean's *Lives of the Berkeleys*, by J. Smyth, 1883, vol. ii., p. 33.

Th₀mas Berkeley, *of co. York, Knt.*

. **7400.** [A.D. 1516.] Red: injured. ₁⁵₂ in. [Harl. ch. 111 D. 31.]

Octagonal signet: a shield of arms: a lion rampant. Betw. the initial letters [. .] B.

William de Berkeley, 7*th Baron,* [1*st Marquess*] *of Berkeley,*
Ob. A.D. 1492.

7401. [A.D. 1470.] Plaster cast from chipped impression.
About 2 in. when perfect. [lxxxiii. 22.]

A shield of arms, *couché*: per pale, *dex.*, three lions passant
guardant in pale, in chief a label of three points over all,
BROTHERTON; *sin.*, BERKELEY. Crest on a helmet [and
mantling, a mitre]. Supporters, *dex.*, (a unicorn?); *sin.*,
wanting (a unicorn).

Legend wanting.

Engraved in Sir J. Maclean's *Lives of the Berkeleys*, by J. Smyth,
1883, vol. ii., p. 146. With the legend :—

S' HONORABILIS · DŇI · WILL'I · DE · BERKELEY ·
ET · WOTTON :

William de Berkeley, *Baron Berkeley, of Stratton.*

7402. [A.D. 1702.] Red: *en placard*, on a label. $\frac{5}{8} \times \frac{1}{2}$ in.
[Egert. ch. 104.]

Oval: a shield of arms: BERKELEY, as in No. 7392. On
an ermine mantle, and ensigned with a baron's coronet.

Beaded border.

Elizabeth, *wife of* LAURENCE **Berkerolles.**

7403. [A.D. 1392.] Plaster cast from good impression.
$\frac{7}{8}$ in. [lxxxiii. 17.]

A shield of arms : per pale, *dex.*, a chevron betw. three
crescents, BERKEROLLS ; *sin.*, a lion rampant. Suspended
by a strap from a forked tree. Within a carved gothic panel
ornamented along the inner edge with small quatrefoils or
ball-flowers.

𝕾𝔦𝔤𝔦𝔩𝔩ū . 𝔢𝔩𝔦𝔰𝔞𝔟𝔢 . . . . 𝔟𝔢𝔯𝔠𝔯𝔬𝔩𝔰 :

Carved border.

Cf. G. T. Clark, *Cartæ de Glamorgan*, vol. ii., p. 36.

Laurence de Berkerolles, *al.* **Bercrols,** *of South Wales.*

7404. [A.D. 1392.] Plaster cast from fine but chipped
impression. $\frac{15}{16}$ in. [lxxxiii. 17.]

A shield of arms: a chevron betw. three crescents,
BERKEROLLS. Betw. two small slipped flowers. Within a
carved cinquefoil panel.

𝔁 : 𝖘' ⚘ ⚘ 𝔩𝔞𝔲[𝔯𝔢𝔫𝔠]𝔦𝔦 ⚘ ⚘ 𝔇𝔢 ⚘ ⚘ 𝔟𝔢𝔯𝔠𝔯𝔬𝔩𝔰:

Cf. G. T. Clark, *Cartæ de Glamorgan*, vol. ii., pp. 16-19, etc., engr.,p. 36.

John de Berland (?).

7405. [A.D. 1357.] Plaster cast from indistinct impression.
1 in. [xcii. 74.]

2 K 2

A shield of arms : on a bend a bear passant. Within a carved trefoil panel.

S' IOHANNIS · DE · BERLAND (?)

Stephen de Berlynde, *of Peasmarsh, co. Suss.*
7406. [A.D. 1338.] Red. ⅝ × ⅜ in. [A.D. 20,133.]
Oval : on a shield (? not heraldic), a chevron betw. three demilozenges.

Fulk de Burmigham, *or* **Bermyngham,** *Chev., of Tamworth, cos. Warw. and Staff.*
7407. [A.D. 1342.] Red : originally fine; now chipped. ¾ in. [Egert. ch. 463.]
A shield of arms : a bend lozengy or five lozenges in bend, in chief a label of five points. Above the shield a lion's face : at each side a wyvern. Within a pointed gothic quatrefoil, ornamented with small quatrefoils along the inner edge.

✠ S[IGILL]VM · FOVKE · DE · BVRMIGHAM.

John Bermingham (?).
7408. [*Temp.* Edw. III.] Red : edge chipped. ¾ in. [xxxvi. 88.]
A shield of arms : three escallops in bend betw. two cotises. Suspended by a strap over the neck of an owl.

✠ S'. IOHANNIS : BE'MINGHAM : (?)

Beaded borders.

Walter de Bermyngham, *of co. Linc.*
7409. [A.D. 1341.] Red : originally fine, now repaired. About 1 in. when perfect. [Harl. ch. 46 A. 49.]
A shield of arms : per pale indented, a bordure bezantée. Crest, on a helmet a wyvern betw. two bulls' horns. Within a finely carved gothic panel with small ball-flowers along the inner edge.

.... DE BERMYNGEHAM.

7410. Sulph. cast of No. 7409. [D.C., F. 278.]

Elizabeth de Multon, *wife of* WALTER DE BERMYNGHAM.
7411. [A.D. 1341.] Red : very fine, edge injured. 1¼ in. [Harl. ch. 46 A. 49.]
In the centre a shield of arms : BERMYNGHAM, as in No. 7409. Betw. three small roses, and within a finely carved gothic rose of six cusped points, ornamented with small cinquefoil ball-flowers along the inner edge. All within an elaborately traced estoile of six points, containing

as many tricusped countersunk panels, with small cinquefoils along the inner edge ; each panel contains a circular shield or roundle of arms : (1) a cross ; (2) three bars, MULTON ; (3) a fret, or fretty of six pieces, in chief, over all, a label of three points, MORVILLE ?   Each repeated in the transversely opposite panels.   The whole design forms one of the most interesting and remarkable specimens of heraldic seals.

Legend betw. the panels :—

        SIGI＿LLVM＿ELIZ＿ABET＿DE　MV＿LTON.

Beaded border.

7412. Sulph. cast from No. 7411.   [D.C., F. 238.]

William de Bermyngeham, *or* Bermygham, *Lord of Bermyngeham, co. Warw.*

7413. [A.D. 1399–1412.]   Red : fine,   edge   imperfect. 1⅓₀ in. [Cott. ch. xxiii. 38.]

A shield of arms, *couché* : quarterly, 1, 4, per pale indented, BERMYNGHAM ; 2, 3, a bend lozengy, BIRMINGHAM.   Crest on a helmet, mantling, and wreath, a tall chapeau betw. a pair of wings erect.   Within a carved gothic panel.

    𝕾 . . . . lelmí : bermpgłam :

7414. Sulph. cast from No. 7413.   [D.C., G. 128.]

Edmund Bernak.

7415. [14th cent.]   Plaster   cast   from   fine   impression: [lxxxiii. 23.]

A shield of arms : three horse-barnacles, two and one, BERNAKE.   Within a carved gothic panel.

    ✶ 𝕾ígíllum : edmundí : bernak,

Beaded border.

John Bernake, *of co. Hunt., Knt.*

7416. [A.D. 1409.]   Red : fine, well preserved.   1 in. [Add. ch. 33,350.]

A shield of arms : quarterly, 1, 4, a barnacle, BERNAKE, 2, 3, a fess dancettée betw. six crosses crosslet.   Within a finely carved gothic trefoil panel, ornamented along the inner edge with small quatrefoils or ball-flowers.

    ✶ 𝕾ígíllum · íołannís : ᴀᴋᴊᴀ : bernak : ᴀᴋ

Beaded border.

Cf. Barrett, *Memorials of Attleborough*, p. 182.

Richard. *son of* Gervase de Bernak, *of co. Northt., Knt.*

7417. [A.D. 1297.]   Red, faded : fine, edge chipped.   ¾ in. [Add. ch. 21,584.]

A shield of arms : three horse-barnacles, BERNAK.

PENSET DE LI [PAR] KI IE SV CI.

I.e., *Pensez de lui par qui je suis ici.* Cf. Harl. ch. 49 C. 5, and 56 D. 31. *" Penset de li par ky su ci."*

William Bernak, of cos. Essex, Hertf., etc.

7418. [A.D. 1372.] Red: injured. $\frac{3}{8}$ in. [Add. ch. 19,979.]
A shield of arms : three horse-barnacles, BERNACK. Betw. an agnus Dei on the r. h., and an obliterated device on the l. h.

CREEZ LI BERNA . . . .
I.e., Croyez le Bernak.

William Bernard, of Ecton, co. Northt., Esq.

7419. [A.D. 1678.]   Red, covered with paper before impression. $\frac{3}{4} \times \frac{5}{8}$ in. [Add. ch. 24,141.]
A shield of arms : charges uncertain.

Pyno Bernardini, Citizen of London.

7420. [A.D. 1292.] Dark green: imperfect, very indistinct.
$\frac{7}{8}$ in. [Harl. ch. 46 D. 5.]
A shield of arms : uncertain charges.   Within a carved gothic six-foil.

✠ . . . . NI.

John Berner.

7421. [A.D. 1337.] Plaster cast from fine impression. $\frac{7}{8}$ in.
[lxxxiii. 24.]
A shield of arms : a lion rampant, debruised by a bendlet. Suspended by a strap from a hook. Betw. two wyverns sans wings.

✠ SIGILLVM ❀ IOHANNIS ❀ BERNER ❀

Beaded border.
Cf. Add. ch. 7607, A.D. 1338.

Richard Berners.

7422. [A.D. 1405.] Plaster cast from fine impression. 1 in.
[lxxxiii. 25.]
A shield of arms : quarterly, BERNERS.   Suspended by a strap from a forked tree.   Within a carved gothic panel.

𝕾igillum : ricarɗi : berneris : ⚜

John Bernewell.

(Seal used by RICHD. GLOOS, Citizen of Norwich, son of ·
THOMAS GLOOS.)

7423. [A.D. 1385.] Red: fine. $\frac{7}{8}$ in. [Add. ch.
A shield of arms : per pale, ten billets, four, four, and two.

❀ 𝕾' · iohanis bernewell ⚜

William Bernewelle, *Citizen of London.*

7424. [A.D. 1441.] Red: indistinct, originally encircled by a twisted rush. $\frac{7}{8}$ in. [Add. ch. 5315.]

A shield of arms: defaced. Within a cusped rosette of six points.

.... N LO LE PYR ... (?)

John Berneye, *of Reedham, co. Norf., Esq.*

7425. [A.D. 1434.] Red: fine, only fragments. About $1\frac{3}{8}$ in. when perfect. [Add. ch. 17,738.]

A shield of arms, *couché*: [quarterly], a cross engrailed ermine, BERNEY, *of Reedham.* Crest, on a helmet, a plume of ostrich feathers.

Legend wanting.

7426. [A.D. 1434.] Red: only a fragment, showing the shield of arms, and portions of the tracery in which it is enclosed. [Stowe ch. 176.]

Robert de Berney, *of cos. Norf., Linc., etc., Knt.*

7427. [A.D. 1403] Red: fine, very imperfect. About $1\frac{1}{8}$ in. when perfect. [Harl. ch. 46 D. 8A.]

A shield of arms, *couché*: [quarterly,] a cross engrailed ermine, in the first quarter a crescent, BERNEY. Crest on a helmet, mantling, and wreath a plume of ostrich feathers. Betw. two wavy sprigs of foliage. Within a carved gothic panel ornamented with small ball-flowers on the inner edge.

𝕾𝖎𝖌 . . . . 𝖇𝖊𝖗𝖙 . . . .

Cf. Harl. ch. 49 G. 45.

Nicholas Beroun, *or* Byrroñ, *of Çadney, near Glamford Bridge, co. Linc.*

7428. [A.D. 1486.] Red: injured by pressure. $\frac{3}{4}$ in. [Add. ch. 20,708.]

A shield of arms: three bends, BERON. Suspended by a strap from a forked tree, betw. the initial letters N.B. Within a cusped quatrefoil.

𝕾' · 𝖓𝖎𝖈𝖔𝖑𝖆𝖎 · 𝖉𝖊 · 𝖇𝖊𝖗𝖔𝖚𝖓.

The letters DE are conjoined.

Edmund Berri, *or* Berry, *of East Dereham, co. Norf., Knt.*

7429. [A.D. 1428.] Red: fine, injured by pressure in places. 1 in. [Add. ch. 14,637.]

A shield of arms: a chevron betw. three bears' heads, couped, muzzled, and collared, BARRÉ, or BARREY. Suspended by a strap from an oak tree.

𝕾 · 𝖊𝖉𝖒𝖚𝖓𝖉𝖎 ⚜ ⚜ 𝖇𝖊𝖗𝖗𝖞 ⚜

Cabled borders.

John Berrington, *or* **Berington,** *of co. Heref., Esq.*
7430. [A.D. 1634.] Red: imperfect. About ¾ in. when perfect. [Add. ch. 1936.]
A shield of arms: three greyhounds courant in pale, collared, BERINGTON.

Elizabeth Bertie, *Countess of Lindsey, etc.*
7431. [A.D. 1634.] Red: injured by pressure. 1 × ¾ in. [Add. ch. 29,969.]
Oval: a shield of arms: quarterly of six pieces. I. BERTIE, etc. Ensigned with an earl's coronet.

Francis Bertye, *of London, Gentl.*
7432. [A.D. 1576.] Red. ⅝ × ½ in. [Add. ch. 24,493.]
A shield of arms: quarterly, 1, 4, a griffin segreant, 2, 3, per pale *dex.*, per fess, in chief chequy, in base an estoile, *sin.*, barry of eight, or four bars. Crest on a helmet, mantling, and wreath, an eagle's head erased.

Mountague Bartye, *i.e.* BERTIE, K.B., *Lord Willoughby,*
son and heir of ROBERT, *Earl of Lindsey.*
7433. [A.D. 1634.] Red: injured. ¾ × ⅝ in. [Add. ch. 29,656.]
Oval: on a wreath, a Saracen's head, ducally crowned, on the breast a label of three points for difference. Crest of WILLOUGHBY.
7434. [A.D. 1634.] Another. [Add. ch. 29,969.]

Montague [**Bertie-Venables,** *2nd*] *Earl of Abingdon, etc.*
7435. [A.D. 1715.] Red, covered with paper before impression. [Add. ch. 13,644.]
A shield of arms, etc., as described at No. 5703, where the seal is used as a *rev.* to an equestrian seal.

Rt. Hon. **Peregrine Bertie,** *Knt., Lord Willoughby of Willoughby and Eresby.*
7436. [A.D. 1583.] Red: indistinct. 1 1/16 × 13/16 in. [Add. ch. 32,819.]
Oval: a shield of arms: quarterly of eight pieces:—1. three battering rams, barwise in pale, BERTIE, etc. Crest on a helmet, ornamental mantling and wreath, a lion's head, affrontée, betw. two bats' wings, each charged with a fret?
✳ S' ✿ PEREGRINI ✿ DOMINI ✿ WILLVGHBY ✿ DE ✿ ERESBY ✿
Beaded border.

Another seal.

7437. [A.D. 1585.] Red : fine, edge chipped. 2 in. [Add. ch. 32,820.]

A shield of arms : quarterly of eight pieces : 1, BERTIE ; 2, Fretty, WILLOUGHBY OF ERESBY ; 3, a cross moline ; 4, a cross engrailed ; 5, quarterly, i. iv. a lion rampant, ii. iii. a fret ; 6, a lion rampant ; 7, a fess dancettée betw. six crosses crosslets ; 8, barry of six, — and erm., three crescents, two and one. Crest on a helmet and ornamental mantling, on a wreath, cf. No. 5703.

Supporters, *dex.* a monk or friar, *sin.* a wild-man.

In base on scroll the motto :—

NATVRA : VADO : VIRTVTE : VOLO.

Legend :—

SIGILLVM : PEREGRINI : DOMINI : ET : BARONIS : WILVGHBY : ET : ERESBY.

Carved border.

Robert Bertie, 1st *Earl of Lindsey,* *Lord Great Chamberlain, K.G.*

7438. [A.D. 1634.] Red : very indistinct. About $1\frac{3}{8} \times \frac{5}{8}$ in. [Add. ch. 29,656.]

Shaped : a shield of arms : quarterly of six pieces. 1, 6. Three battering rams fesswise in pale, BERTIE, etc. Encircled with a Garter inscribed with the usual motto. Ensigned with a coronet.

7439. [A.D. 1634.] Red : injured by pressure. [Add. ch. 29,969.]

Johannes de Bery.

7440. [A.D. 1364.] Faded red : chipped. $\frac{7}{8}$ in. [Harl. ch. 111 G. 60.]

A shield of arms : two arrows in saltire, points downwards, betw. in chief an estoile, in base a hunting-horn, at each side a roundle, all within an engrailed border. Within a carved border.

☆ [S'.] IOHANNIS DE BERY ⋈

7441. Sulph. cast from No. 7440. [D.C., F. 438.]

Henry de Beston.

7442. [14th cent.] Plaster cast from indistinct impression. [lxxxiii. 27.]

A shield of arms : a. bend betw. six (bees ?), BESTON. Betw. three small quatrefoil flowers. Within a carved panel of eight cusped points.

⊕ 𝔖𝔦𝔤𝔦𝔩𝔩𝔲𝔪 ⁖ 𝔥𝔢𝔫𝔯𝔦𝔠𝔦 ⁖ 𝔡𝔢 ⁖ 𝔟𝔢𝔰𝔱𝔬𝔫 ⁖ ⋈ ⁖

William Besyles, *of* [*Hilperton*], *co. Wilts.*

7443. [A.D. 1405.] Red : imperfect, injured by pressure.
1 in. [Add. ch. 5688.]

A shield of arms : three torteaux, two and one, BESILLE,
or BESILLS. Within a carved gothic panel.

. . . . . **Sigillum** . . . . **lelmi · befi** . . . . .

John Bette, *of Bury, etc., co. Suff.*

7444. [A.D. 1401.] Red : imperfect, indistinct ; originally
encircled by a twisted rush. ½ in. [Cott. ch. xxvii. 128.]

A shield (of arms ?) : a chevron, betw. the initial letters
I. D. H.

H . . . . IH . . . . (?)

Stephen Bettenham, (*of co. Kent ?*)

7445. [A.D. 1411.] Red : good ; from a ring. ½ in.
[Add. ch. 16,464.]

A bear's head erased, muzzled and ringed. Crest of
BETENHAM.

Cabled border.

Stephen Bettenham, *son and heir of* JOHN BETTENHAM,
Gentl., late of Cranbrook, co. Kent.

7446. [A.D. 1468.] Red : fine ; from a ring, with mark of
the chasing. $\frac{5}{12}$ in. [Harl. ch. 76 C. 28.]

A bear's head erased, muzzled. Crest of BETENHAM.
Betw. the initial letters—**S. b.**

Cabled border.

Peter Bettesworth, *of Milland, co. Suss., Knt.*

7447. [A.D. 1631.] Red : very indistinct. $\frac{7}{12} \times \frac{5}{12}$ in.
[Add. ch. 6008.]

Oval : a shield of arms : per chevron in chief three mullets,
in base a garb, (CHETMULL ?)

Another seal.

7448. [A.D. 1631.] Red. $\frac{1}{2} \times \frac{3}{8}$ in. [Add. ch. 6009.]

Oval : on a wreath, out of a ducal coronet, a stag's head.

Bestney Betts, *Commissioner of Sewers, Esq.*

7449. [A.D. 1611.] Red : imperfect. About $\frac{11}{16} \times \frac{5}{8}$ in.
[Add. ch. 33,093.]

Oval : a shield of arms : quarterly, 1, 4. On a bend
cotised, three pierced cinquefoils, BETTES ; 2, 3, a lion
rampant.

Beaded border.

Joseph Betts, *of Bentley, co. Hants.*
7450. [A.D. 1698.] Red : *en placard.* [Add. ch. 19,032.]
A shield of arms : *v.* seal of THOMAS GAWEN, Add. ch.
19,031.
7451. Another. [Add. ch. 19,032.]
See also RICHARD PEPPER.

Hugh de Bibbisworthe.
7452. [Early 14th cent.] Plaster cast from indistinct
impression. 1 in. [lxxxiii. 32.]
A shield of arms : three eagles displayed, two and one,
BIBBESWORTH. Suspended by a strap, betw. two wyverns
addorsed.
+ S' · HVGONIS · DE · BIBBISWORTHE :
Beaded border .

Walter, *son of* WALTER **de Bibbeworthe,** *or* **Bibbeswrth,**
of co. Herts, Knt.
7453. [A.D. 1249.] Green : fine, now imperfect. 1 in.
[Egert. ch. 405.]
Shield shaped : a shield of arms : an eagle displayed.
⚜ S' WALTER . . . .
7454. Plaster cast from fine impression. [lxxxiv. 20.] ·
⚜ S' WALTERI · DE · BIBBEWORTHE.
The letters BB, and OR, conjoined.

Philip Bickerstaffe, *al.* **Bickerstathe,**
of Chirton, co. Northumb.
7455. [A.D. 1697.] Red : *en placard,* on a label. $\frac{7}{16}$ in.
[Add. ch. 26,392.]
Octagonal signet : a shield of arms : a cross crosslet, in the
dexter chief a crescent for difference, BICKERSTAFFE. Crest,
on a helmet and mantling, a dexter hand holding an arrow
in bend.
Cf. Add. ch. 13,621, A.D. 1692.

Thomas de Bifeld, *or* **Byfeld,** *used by his son* WILLIAM,
of Thornby, co. Nortlt. ?
7456. [A.D. 1358.] Red : from injured matrix. 1 in.
[Add. ch. 21,670.]
A shield of arms : ermine, a fess fretty, or a fess fretty
betw. six ermine spots. Betw. two wyverns.
✣ SIGILLVM THOME DE BIFELD.
Beaded borders.

Huntley Bigg, *of St. Martin's in the Fields,*
co. Midd., Scrivener.

7457. [A.D. 1687.]   Red, on a dark red mass. $\frac{3}{4} \times \frac{5}{8}$ in.
[Harl. ch. 111 H. 33.]

Oval: an ornamental shield of arms: on a chevron betw. three cinquefoils, a mullet for difference. Over the shield a helmet affronté, mantling and wreath, but no crest.

Beaded border.

Richard Biggs, *of King's-Walden, co. Hertf., Gentl.*

7458. [A.D. 1695.]   Red: *en placard,* on a tape. $\frac{5}{8} \times \frac{1}{2}$ in.
[Add. ch. 35,911.]

Oval: on a wreath, a stag's head. Betw. two palm-branches, tied.

Richard Bigg, *of King's-Walden, co. Hertf., Gentl.*

7459. [A.D. 1729.]   Red: *en placard,* on a tape. $\frac{5}{8} \times \frac{1}{2}$ in.
[Add. ch. 35,916.]

Oval: on a wreath, five arrows in a sheaf, entwined with a serpent.

7460. [A.D. 1729.]   Another.   [Add. ch. 35,917.]

Seal used by FRANCES, *wife of the above.*

7461. [A.D. 1729.]   Another.   [Add. ch. 35,916.]
7462. [A.D. 1729.]   Another.   [Add. ch. 35,917.]

Seal used by LISTER, *son and heir of the above.*

7463. [A.D. 1729.]   Another.   [Add. ch. 35 916.]
7464. [A.D. 1729.]   Another.   [Add. ch. 35,917.]

Ralph Bigot, *Lord of Stokton, etc., cos. Norf and Suff., Knt.*

7465. [A.D. 1368.]   Dark green: fine.   1 in.   [Harl. ch. 46 D. 45.]

A shield of arms: on a cross engrailed five escallops, BYGOD. Betw. eight small cinquefoils or roses, and within a cusped border or rosette of ten points, ornamented with ball-flowers along the inner edge.

✯ : Sigillum : ⚜ ❀ : radulfi : ⚜ ❀ : bigot : ⚜ ❀ ⚜ ❀ ⚜ ❀

7466. Sulph. cast from No. 7465.   [D.C., F. 460.]

7467. [A.D. 1388.]   Red: imperfect, injured by pressure.
[Harl. ch. 46 D. 46.]

✯ : Sigillum : . . . . : bi . . . ⚜ ❀ ⚜ ❀ ⚜ ❀

7468. [A.D. 1404.]   Red: fragmentary.   [Harl. ch. 46 D. 47.]

. . . . bigot : ⚜ ❀ ⚜ ❀ ⚜ ❀

Roger Bigot, *Earl of Norfolk, Marshal of England.*
7469. [Late Henry III.] Dark green: originally fine.
About 1½ in. when perfect. [Add. ch. 19,823.]
A shield of arms of early shape: a cross, BIGOT.

.... I : COMITIS : N ....

Inner border beaded.

Roger le Bygod, *Earl of Norfolk, Marshal of England.*
7470. [A.D. 1291.] Red: small fragment. [Add. ch.
5736.]
Legend only remains.

.... ALV ....

Beaded border.

Roger Bigod, *6th Earl of Norfolk,* A.D. 1270–1307.
7471. [A.D. 1301.] Plaster cast from fine impression.
1⅚ in. [lxxxiii. 33.]
A shield of arms: per pale, a lion rampant.

✧ SIGILLVM · ROGERI · BIGOD.

Beaded borders.

John de Bilindone (Billington), *of Leighton-Buzzard,*
co. Bedf.
7472. [A.D. 1349.] Creamy-white: very indistinct. ¾ × ⅝ in.
[Add. ch. 19,948.]
Oval: a shield of arms: a chevron betw. three fleurs-de-
lis? Suspended by a strap from a hook.

✧ S' IOH .... ON (?)

See next Nó. 7473.

John de Bilindone.
7473. [A.D. 1471.] Red: originally fine, injured by
pressure. ¾ × ⅝ in. [Slo. ch. xxxii. 42.]
Oval: a shield of arms: a chevron betw. three fleurs-
de-lis, or slipped trefoils. Suspended by a strap from a
hook.

✧ S' IOHANNIS D' BILINDON'.

Beaded borders.

Cf. with No. 7472, which may perhaps be from the same matrix as
this, notwithstanding the difference of the dates.

John Bill, *al.* **Byll,** *Gentl.*
7474. [A.D. 1554.] Red: cracked, indistinct. ½ × ⅜ in.
[Add. ch. 35,395.]
Oval: a shield of arms: a demi fleur-de-lis. Above the
shield a sprig of foliage.

Eudo, *fil.* **Will. de Billesby,** *of Bilsby, co. Linc., Knt.*
7475. [*Temp.* Henry III.]   Dark green: fine.   1 × ⅞ in.
[Harl. ch. 46 D. 56.]
Shield shaped: a shield of arms: three hammers, two
and one.
¤ S' · EVDONIS · DE BILLESBI.
Cf. Harl. ch. 46 E. 1.

Family of Billingham ?

7476. [13th cent.]   Recent impression in red sealing-wax
from the matrix.   ⅞ in.   [xxxv. 355.]
A shield of arms: three ducal crowns, two and one, in the
fess point an estoile or rose of six points for difference, cf.
arms of CROWNER, BILLINGHAM, see of ELY, etc.
+ SIGILLVM + RECTVM.
Beaded borders.

Thomas Billyng, *Lord Chief Justice of the King's Bench.*
7477. [A.D. 1473.]   Red: from signet ring with mark of
chased setting.   ⅜ in.   [Add. ch. 22,413.]
A talbot passant, perhaps the crest of the Lord Ch. Justice.
In the field the initial letter **t.**

John de Billyngham.

7478. [A.D. 1348.]   Plaster cast from imperfect impression,
l. h. side broken off.   ⅞ in.   [lxxxiii. 35.]
A shield of arms: on a bend three cushions. Within a
carved gothic panel.
¤ S . . . . DE · BILLYNGHAM.

Adam de Bilokebi.

7479. [A.D. 1337.]   Brown: opaque.   11/16 in.   [Harl. ch.
58 A. 46.]
On a cross, a man's head, couped at the neck, in profile,
betw. four buckles.   Not on a shield.   Within a pointed
quatrefoil panel.
+ S' ADE · DE · BILOKEBI.

Thomas de Birchovere, *of Birchover, co. Derb.*
7480. [A.D. 1350.]   Discoloured red: originally fine, now
chipped on the edge.   ¼ in.   [Woll. ch. ii. 17.]
A shield of arms: a fess dancettée betw. three indistinct
charges, perhaps eagles displayed.   Suspended by a strap
from a lion's face, and betw. two small trees.   Within a
carved and pointed gothic quatrefoil.
. . . . LLVM : THOME : DE : BVRCHOV . . . . .

Henry Birkheved, *of Waltham St. Cross, co. Essex.*

7481. [A.D. 1480.] Red. $\frac{3}{8} \times \frac{1}{4}$ in. [Harl. ch. 78 I. 47.]

Octagonal signet: a garb, in allusion to the arms of BIRKENHEAD, viz.: three garbs within a bordure.

John de Birstalle.

See JOHN DE WALTON.

Isabella de Birtley, *of Silkesworde, &c., co. Durham.*

7482. [A.D. 1376.] Red: injured by pressure. $\frac{3}{4}$ in. [Egert. ch. 574.]

A shield of arms: charges uncertain and indistinct. Within a carved gothic panel.

Legend betw. the points:—

[S'] IOH'IS DE . . . .

William Biscet.

7483. [A.D. 1292.] Sulph. cast from fine impression. $\frac{7}{8}$ in. [D.C., E. 415.]

A shield of arms: a bend, over all in chief a label of five points.

+ S' WILLELMI : BISCET.

Beaded borders.

Probably Scottish, cf. Harl. ch. 47 F. 27.

7484. Another. [xlvii. 1098.]

Richard de Biskele, *of Frostenden, co. Suff.*

7485. [A.D. 1349.] Green, mottled: fine. $\frac{3}{4}$ in. [Harl. ch. 46 E. 8.]

A shield of arms: quarterly, over all a bend, BISKELL. Within a carved and pointed gothic quatrefoil, ornamented with small ball-flowers along the inner edge.

✠ SIGILL' · RICARDI · D' · BISKEL'.

7486. Sulph. cast from No. 7485. [D.C., F. 307.]

Thomas de Bischoplegh, *of Turwick, co. Bucks?*

7487. [A.D. 1336.] Dark green: fine, well preserved, edge chipped. 1 in. [Harl. ch. 46 E. 4.]

A shield of arms: a fess betw. two saltires in chief and a cross in base. In chief point a roundle for difference. Within a carved gothic panel.

✠ SV · THOME · DE · BISCHOPLEGH.

7488. Sulph. cast of No. 7487. [D.C., F. 259.]

Thomas de Bitilisgate.

Seal used by WENTELINA, *wife of* JOHN DE RALEGH, *Chev.*

7489. [A.D. 1381.] Red: fine. $\frac{7}{8}$ in. [Cott. ch. xxix. 3.]

A shield of arms: a bend ermine. Betw. two slipped flowers. Within a carved gothic cinquefoil and triangle, ornamented with small ball-flowers along the inner edge.

✠ SIG · THOME · DE · BITILISGATE'

7490. Sulph. cast of No. 7489. [D.C., F. 535.]

Thurston Blackman.

7491. [A.D. 1769.] Red: *en placard.* [Add. ch. 29,627.]

See description under THOMAS BARNARD.

William de Blaetoft.

7492. [A.D. 1336.] Plaster cast from fine impression. [lxxxiii. 40.]

A shield of arms: a cross engrailed. Above the shield a tree of three branches. At each side a wyvern.

✠ S' WILLELMI · DE · BLAETOFT.

Anthony Blagrave, *of Southcott, co. Berks, Esq.*

Seal used by RICHARD ALLEN, *of Sulham, co. Berks, Esq.*

7493. [A.D. 1751.] Red: *en placard.* $\frac{2}{3} \times \frac{7}{12}$ in. [Add. ch. 19,252.]

A shield of arms: on a bend three legs in armour couped at the thigh and erased at the ancle, in chief a crescent for difference, BLAGRAVE.

Beaded border

Philadelphia Blagrave, *of Sunning, co. Berk., Widow.*

7494. [A.D. 1731.] Red: *en placard,* on a tape. Imperfect. $\frac{1}{2} \times \frac{5}{8}$ in. [Add. ch. 19,250.]

Oval: a shield of arms: per fess and pale counterchanged, three trefoils slipped, a mullet for difference. Perhaps SIMEON or SYMONDS.

Beaded border.

Jacob de Blake.

Seal used by THOMAS COLUMBELL, *of Thorp in Glebis, co. Nott., Esq.*

✠ **7495.** [A.D. 1429.] Red: indistinct. $\frac{3}{4}$ in. [Woll. ch. iv. n. 17.]

A shield of arms: three eagles' heads erased.

✠ IACOB ⚜ DE ⚜ BLAKE.

John de Blakeborne, *seal used by* JOHN FRENSSHE,
of Chiddingley, co. Suss.

7496. [A.D. 1487.] Red: indistinct. $\frac{7}{8}$ in. [Add ch. 29,831.]

A shield of arms: a stag at speed, in the sinister chief an escallop. Within a carved quatrefoil panel.

-Legend betw. the points :—

S' IOH' ⏤ IS DE B ⏤ LAKEB ⏤ ORNE.

John Blaket.

7497. [14th cent.] Sulph. cast from good impression. $\frac{3}{4}$ in. [D.C., F. 347.]

A shield of arms: a chevron betw. three trefoils slipped. Within a carved gothic quatrefoil.

Legend between the points :—

S' IO ⏤ HI'S ⏤ BLA ⏤ KET.

Beaded border.

Thomas Blast, *of cos. Suss. and Hertf.*

7498. [A.D. 1401.] Red: fine, chipped. $\frac{7}{8}$ in. [Add. ch. 35,731.]

A shield of arms: three arbalests or cross-bows, two and one. Within a carved gothic trefoil panel, ornamented with small quatrefoils along the inner edge.

✠ 𝕾igillum : 𝕿home : blaſt *

Thomas Blaunfrount, *of Ramenham, co. Berk.*

7499. [A.D. 1340.] Red: edge injured by pressure. $\frac{3}{4} \times \frac{5}{8}$ in. [Cott. ch. xxiii. 21.]

Oval: a shield of arms: a lion passant, a chief. Betw. three sprigs of foliage.

In place of a legend a wavy scroll of foliage.

Beaded borders.

Roger de Blaykeston, *or* **Blackstone.**

7500. [A.D. 1353.] Plaster cast from fine impression. $\frac{15}{16}$ in. [lxxxiii. 41.]

A shield of arms: two bars, in chief three cocks, BLACK-STONE. Betw. two slipped trefoils. Within a carved trefoil panel.

S' ROGERI DE -BLAYKESTON : *

Beaded border.

VOL. II.   2 L

Raynold Blechenden.
Seal used by TIMOTHY, *son of* PAUL JOHNSON,
of Fordwich, co. Kent, Esq.
7501. [A.D. 1586.] Red : injured. About $\frac{1}{2} \times \frac{5}{8}$ in. when
perfect. [Harl. ch. 78 I. 6.]
A shield of arms : a fess crenellée betw. three lions' heads
erased and collared, BLECHENDEN.
Beaded border.

William Bloome, *of Swaffham, co. Norf.*
7502. [A.D. 1639.] Red : injured. $\frac{3}{4}$ in. [Add. ch.
30,826.]
A bull's head, couped.

Thomas Blosse, *of Little Belstead, co. Suff., Esq.,*
son and heir of THOMAS BLOSSE, *of Norwich.*
7503. [A.D. 1638.] Red : much injured by pressure.
$\frac{3}{4} \times \frac{5}{8}$ in. [Add. ch. 10,551.]
A shield of arms : per pale, *dex.* three dragons passant in
pale, BLOSS ; *sin.* per pale, a saltire. Crest on a helmet,
mantling, and wreath a demi-dragon.
Carved border.

Edward Le Blount.
7504. [A.D. 1354.] Plaster cast from indistinct impression.
1 in. [lxxxiii. 43.]
A shield of arms : three griffins or winged lions passant in
pale. On sprigs of foliage. Within a carved gothic panel of
eight points.
⚹ SIGILLVM · EDWARDI · LE BLOVNT.
Beaded borders.

[Felipa Blount.]
Seal used by HENRY ENGEHERST, *of Merden, co. Suss.*
7505. [A.D. 1428.] Red. $\frac{3}{4}$ in. [Harl. ch. 78 A. 13.]
A shield of arms : barry of eight, BLOUNT. Betw. a trefoil
and two estoiles of six points, that on the l. h. side wanting.
– S' FELIPE BL . . . T.

John Le Blount.
7506. [*Temp.* Edw. III.] Sulph. cast from fine impression. $\frac{3}{4}$ in. [xlvii. 1424.]
A shield of arms : three fleurs-de-lis. Betw. three roses
and within a carved and pointed gothic quatrefoil.
⚹ SIGILLVM · IOH'IS · L' · BLOVNT.
Laing's *MS. Catal.*, No. 461. Cf. John, son of Hugh le Blount, Add.
ch. 24,067, A.D. 1365 ; and John Blount, Add. ch. 24,066, A.D. 1368.

· **John Le Blount,** *of Sheprigge,* *? co. Wilts.* ·

· **7507.** [A.D. 1343.] Red : fine, imperfect. ¾ in. [Add. ch. 17,409.]

A shield of arms, *couché* : barry nebuly of six, BLOUNT. Crest on a helmet and mantling a fan-shaped plume. In the field a wyvern, by way of *dex.* supporter.

· · Cf. Add. MSS. 5937, f. 119, and 6046, f. 50*b*. Add. ch. 17,396. A.D. 1324.

FRANGE · LIEGE · TIEGE.
Beaded borders.

Michaell Blount, *of Iver, co. Buck.*
(*afterwards* Sir MICHAEL BLOUNT).

7508. [A.D. 1578.] Red. ¾ × ⅜ in. [Harl. ch. 86 B. 22.]

A shield of arms : barry nebuly of eight ? BLOUNT. Crest on a helmet, and ornamental mantling, out of a ducal coronet, two horns.

Cf. Harl. MS. 1533, f. 102.

Richard Blownte, *of London, Gentl.*

7509. [A.D. 1571.] Red : much injured by pressure. About ⅞ × ¾ in. when perfect. [Harl. ch. 111 H. 15.]

A shield of arms : barry nebuly of six, BLOUNT. Crest on a helmet and ornamental mantling, an armed foot in the sun ? Cabled border.

Thomas Le Blount.

7510. [*Temp.* Edw. III.] Sulph. cast from fine impression. ¾ in. [xlvii. 1425.]

A shield of arms : a fess betw. six martlets, BLOUNT. Suspended by a strap from a hook, and betw. two wyverns.

✠ SIGILL' : THOME : LE : BLOVNT.
Beaded borders.

Th₀mas Blount.

Seal used by HUGH MORGAN APRICE, *of co. Cardigan.*

7511. [A.D. 1641.] Red : injured by pressure. About ½ × ¾ in. [Harl. ch. 86 I. 51.]

A shield of arms : barry nebuly of eight, a bordure, BLOUNT. Crest on a helmet and ornamental mantling, an armed foot in the sun.

Beaded border.

William Blounte, *of Halden Place, co. Kent., Esq.*

7512. [A.D. 1586.] Red : imperfect, indistinct. ¾ × ⅞ in. [Harl. ch. 77 B. 49.]

A shield of arms: quarterly, 1, two bars, over all an escarbuncle of eight rays, pomettée and florettée, BLOUNT; 2, 3, 4, defaced; in fess point a mullet (?) for difference.
Cabled border.

Fraunceys Bluet, *of St. Coolan, co. Corn., Esq.*

7513. [A.D. 1558.]   Reddish-brown.   ⅓ in.   [Add. ch. 13,081.]

Octagonal signet bearing the arms: a chevron betw. three eagles displayed, BLUET.

Walter Bluett, *of Chard, co. Somers., Knt.*

7514. [A.D. 1363.]   Light brown: ˉchipped on r. h. side. ¾ in.   [Harl. ch. 46 E. 29.]

A shield of arms: a chevron betw. three eagles displayed, BLUET.   Betw. three pairs of leaves, slipped.   Within a carved and pointed gothic quatrefoil.

¤ ❀ SIGILL' ❀ WALTERI ❀ BLEVET.

7515. Sulph. cast. from No. 7514.   [D.C., F. 429.]

John Le Blund.

7516. [Late 13th or early 14th cent.]   Plaster cast from indistinct impression.   ⅞ in. [lxxxiii. 42.]

A shield of arms: quarterly, in the first [and fourth?] quarters a bird?

¤ S' · IOHANNIS · LE · BLVND·

Beaded border.

William Le Blund.

7517. [*Temp.* Edw. II.]   Sulph. cast from indistinct impression.   ⅞ × ¾ in.   [D.C., F. 205.]

Oval: a shield of arms: barry wavy of six, BLOUNT, etc. Suspended by a strap from a tree of three branches.

S' WILL'I · LE · BLVND.

7518. Plaster cast from No. 7517.   [lxxxiii. 46.]

John Blundel.

Seal used by WILLIAM WETHERYNGSETE,
Chaplain of Yarmouth, co. Norf.

7519. [A.D. 1396.]   Red: imperfect, indistinct.   About ⅞ in. when perfect.   [Add. ch. 2006.]

A shield of arms (diapered): on a fess a crescent, in chief a fleur-de-lis (?)

+ Si . . . . iohanis + blundel.

Ranulph Blundeville, *6th Earl of Chester.*
[A.D. 1180–1231.]

7520. Cast in composition painted dark reddish-brown, from imperfect impression. About 2¼ in. [lii. 9.]

A shield of arms of early shape: a lion or wolf rampant.

✠ SI . . . . ANVLFI COMITI . . . . IЄ.

Ralph de Bockyngge, *of Helmingham, co. Suff.*

7521. [A.D. 1318.] Red: fine. ¾ in. [Add. ch. 9904.]

A shield of arms: a cross moline. Cf. a cross botonnée, BOCKINGHAM of Suffolk. Within a carved and pointed gothic quatrefoil.

✠ PRIVЄ SVY : Є BЄN CONV.

Beaded border.

Cf. Add. ch. 10,279; 10,280.

Ralph de Bockyngge, *of Helmingham, co. Suff.*

7522. [A.D. 1376.] Red: originally very fine, now imperfeet on l. h. side. 1 in. [Add. ch. 10,279.]

A shield of arms: a fess nebuly, betw. six crosses crosslet fitchées, BOCKING. In the fess point an annulet for difference. Suspended by a strap from a forked tree. Within a carved gothic panel.

• Sigillum : radulphi : de : . . . . e.

Carved border.

7523. [A.D. 1394.] Red: very fine, edge chipped. [Add. ch. 10,280.]

• Sigillum : radulphi : de : [b]ockyngge.

Cf. Add. ch. 9904.

John de Bodel, *or* **Boydele,** *of Burwell, co. Linc.*

7524. [*Temp.* Hen. III.] Dark green: cracked, imperfect. 1¾ in. [Harl. ch. 47 A. 7.]

A shield of arms of early shape: a bend sinister and fess.

✠ SIG . . . . IOHANNIS DЄ BODЄL.

7525. Sulph. cast from No. 7524. [D.C., D. 233.]

Cf. Harl. ch. 50 D. 47, and 55 D. 15, *temp.* Hen. III.

Thomas Bogheleghe, *of Boycomb in Fareweye, co. Devon.*

7526. [A.D. 1386.] Dark green: indistinct. ¾ in. [Add. ch. 13,009.]

A shield of arms: a bend vairé, betw. seven lozenges, four in chief and three in base.

S' R . . . .

Beaded border.

Edmund de Booun [Bohun],
of Barton-Seagrave, co. Northt., Knt.

7527. [*Temp.* Edw. II.]	Green, mottled : somewhat indistinct, edge chipped.	⅞ in.	[Harl. ch. 83 D. 34.]

A shield of arms : a bend cotised betw. six lions rampant, BOHUN.

S' EADMVNDI DE BOVN.

Beaded border.

7528. Sulph. cast from No. 7527.	[D.C., F. 392.]

Humphrey de Buhun.

7529. [A.D. 1238.]	Plaster cast from fine impression. 1⅛ in.	[lxxxiii. 53.]

A shield of arms : a bendlet betw. six lions rampant, BOHUN.

⚜ SIGIL' : HVИFRIDI DE BVHVИ :

Beaded borders.

Humphrey de Buun, *al.* Bohun.

7530. [A.D. 1260.]	Plaster cast from chipped impression. 1¹⁄₁₆ in.	[lxxxiii. 54.]

A bend charged with fleur-de-lis betw. six lions rampant, for BOHUN, not on a shield.

⚜ SIG . . . . VNFRIDI DE BVVN.

Beaded borders.

Humphrey de Bohun,
4th Earl of Hereford, and of Essex.
Secretum.

7531. [A.D. 1300.]	Plaster cast from fine impression. 1¹⁄₁₆ in.	[lxxxiii. 55.]

A shield of arms : a bend cotised betw. six lions rampant. On a tree of five slipped leaves.	Betw. two trees.

⚹ SECRET · H · DE · BOHVN · COMITIS ·
 HEREFORD · ET · ESSEXIE.

Beaded borders.

Another Secretum.

7532. [A.D. 1320.]	Plaster cast from fine but imperfect impression.	1¹⁄₁₆ in.	[lxxxiii. 56.]

A shield of arms : a bend cotised betw. six lions rampant, BOHUN. At the top and at each side of the shield three slipped trefoils.

⚹ SECRETV : H : DE : BOHVN : COMITIS :
 HEREFORD : ET : ESSEXIE.

Beaded borders.

Another Seal.

7533. [A.D. 1319.] Plaster cast from fine but chipped impression. 1$\frac{1}{16}$ in. [lxxxiii. 59.]

A shield of arms of BOHUN as before.

    ✠ S' HVMFRIDI · DE · BOHVN · COMITIS · HEREFORD' · ET · ESSEXIE.

Beaded borders.

Humphrey de Bohun, *6th Earl of Hereford,*
Earl of Essex, etc., Lord High Constable.
A.D. 1335–1361.

7534. [A.D. 1349.] Red: fragment only of fine seal. About 1$\frac{3}{8}$ in. when perfect. [L.F.C., xviii. 1.]

A shield of arms: BOHUN, as in No. 7532. Within an elaborately carved and traced gothic panel, nearly all broken away, but enclosing over the shield a small circular counter-sunk compartment in which is a lion passant guardant.

    . . . . SSE . . . .

7535. [A.D. 1337.] Plaster cast from fine but chipped impression. 1$\frac{3}{8}$ in. [lxxxiii. 62.]

    S' HVMFRIDI · DE · BOHVN · COMITIS · HEREFORD' · ET · ESSEX.

7536. [A.D. 1342.] Plaster cast from fine impression, slightly chipped. [lxxxiii. 64.]

Another Seal.

7537. [A.D. 1355.] Plaster cast from impression injured in places by pressure. 1$\frac{3}{4}$ in. [lxxxiii. 69.]

A shield of arms: BOHUN, as before. Within a finely carved gothic panel enriched with open tracery and ornamented along the inner edge with small ball-flowers.

    S' hūfr' : De : bohū : coms : heref' : effex : . . . . coftabul' ang'.

Johanna de Bohun.

7538. [A.D. 1313.] Plaster cast from indistinct impression. 1$\frac{1}{4}$ in. [lxxxiii. 57.]

Pointed oval: a shield of arms: a bend cotised betw. six lions rampant. Suspended by a strap from a tree of three branches on a mount.

    ✠ SIGILL' IOHANNE · DE · BOHVN.

Johanna de Bohun,
Countess of Hereford, Essex and Northampton,
dau. of RICHARD FITZ-ALAN, *Earl of Arundel,*
and widow of HUMPHREY DE BOHUN, *Earl of Hereford, etc.*

7539. [A.D. 1389.]   Red: fragmentary.   1¼ in.   [Harl. ch. 46 F. 6.]

For description see below, No. 7540.

✿ S' · iohanne · de · bohun · com . . . . . . mt.

7540. [A.D. 1393.]   Red : originally fine, chipped at edge, injured by pressure.   [Add. ch. 15,602.]

A shield of arms: per pale, *dex.*, BOHUN, as in No. 7538 ; *sin.*, quarterly 1, 4, a lion rampant, FITZ-ALAN ; 2, 3, chequy, WARRENNE.   Suspended by a strap from a forked tree on a mount.   Supporters, two swans, each holding the shield in the beak.   Within a carved gothic panel or rosette.

✿ S' · ioh . . . . . . ohun · comitiffe · herfordie · effexie · et · norhamt.

7541. [A.D. 1406.]   Red: fine, edge injured.   [Harl. ch. 46 F. 7.]

✿ S' · iohanne · de · bohun · co . . . .

7542. [A.D. 1407.]   Red: fine, edge chipped.   [Harl. ch. 111 D. 43.]

. . . ohanne · de · bohun · comitiffe · herfordie · effex . . . . mt.

7543. Sulph. cast of No. 7542.   [D.C., G. 119.]

7544. Plaster cast from good impression.   [lxxxiii. 70.]

✿ S' · iohanne · de · bohun · comitiffe · herfordie · effexie · et · norhamt' (?)

John de Boun, Bouhon [*or* Bohun], *of co. Nott., Knt.*
7545. [A.D. 1286.]   Dark green.   1 in.   [Harl. ch. 43 G. 50.]
A shield of arms : a bend cotised betw. six lioncels rampant, BOHUN.

✠ : SIGILLVM : IOHAN · DE : BOVN :

Beaded borders.
7546. Sulph. cast from No. 7545.   [D.C., E. 425.]

John de Bohun, *5th Earl of Hereford,*
, *4th Earl of Essex, Lord High Constable of England, etc.*
A.D. 1321–1335.
7547. [A.D. 1326.]   Red : originally very fine, now chipped at edges.   1¼ in.   App. by a plaited cord of red silk strands. [Add. ch. 28,574.]

BOHUN. Betw. three slipped trefoils. Within a carved gothic six-foil panel, ornamented along the inner edge with small quatrefoils or ball-flowers, and inscribed in an equilateral triangle of open tracery with a small circular countersunk compartment in each corner. Along each outside length of the triangle is a circular six-foil panel carved and ornamented, bearing a plaque or circular shield of arms of BOHUN as above.

S' · IOH'IS · DE · BOHVN · CO . . . . ER . . ORD' · ET · ESSEX'.
Beaded border.

7548. [A.D. 1334.] Red: originally fine, now the central part only remaining. [Harl. ch. 46 F. 5.]

. . . . ORD E . . . .

7549. Sulph. cast from No. 7548. [D.C., F. 249.]

7550. Plaster cast from indistinct impression. [lxxxii. 58.]

S' IOH'IS · DE · BOHVN · COMITIS · HEREFORD' · ET · ESSEX'.

John Bohun, *of Midhurst Manor, etc., co. Suss., Knt.*

7551. [A.D. 1430.] Red: chipped, injured by pressure. 1⅛ in. [Add. ch. 20,114.]

A shield of arms, *couché*: a cross, BOHUN. Crest on a helmet and mantling the head of an uncertain animal? Within a carved gothic panel ornamented with ball-flowers along the inner edge.

𝕾𝖎𝖌𝖎𝖑𝖑𝖚𝖒 : 𝖎𝖔𝖍𝖆𝖓𝖓𝖎𝖘 : 𝖇𝖔𝖍𝖚𝖓 ·

Beaded border.

Margaret de Bohun, *Countess of Hereford, etc.,* dau. of RALPH LORD BASSET, *widow of* JOHN DE BOHUN.

7552. [A.D. 1339.] Plaster cast from imperfect impression. 1¼ in. [lxxxiii. 63.]

A shield of arms: BOHUN. Within elaborately traced and carved panel as described in No. 7547. The small circular compartments contain, instead of shields of arms, sprigs of foliage and flowers.

. . . MARGARETE · COMITISSE . . . . . .

Oliver de Bohun, *or* **Bohoun.**

7553. [A.D. 1334.] Plaster cast from chipped impression. 1 in. [lxxxiii. 61.]

A shield of arms: on a bend cotised betw. six lions rampant, three escallops, BOHUN. Betw. three swans or pelicans. Within a carved and pointed gothic quatrefoil panel, ornamented along the inner edge with small quatrefoils or ball-flowers.

✠ S[IG]ILLVM : OLIVERI : DE : BOHOVN.

Richard de Bohun, *al.* Bohun.

7554. [A.D. 1343.] · Plaster cast from indistinct impression.
$\frac{7}{8}$ × $\frac{13}{16}$ in. [lxxxiii. 67.]

Oval: a shield of arms: a bend cotised betw. six lions
rampant, BOHUN.

S' RICARDI · DE · BOVN.

Savaric de Bohun, *or* Boun, *of Midhurst, co. Suss.*

7555. [Early Hen. III.]   Green, mottled: fine.   1$\frac{5}{8}$ in.
[Harl. ch. 46 F. 1.]

A shield of arms of early shape: a crescent within a
bordure.

+ SIGILL' : SAVARI : DE : BOVИ.

Cf. Harl. ch. 46 F. 2.   Savaric de Bohun.   Early 13th cent.

7556. Sulph. cast from No. 7555.   [D.C., E. 376.]

William de Bohun, *Earl of Northampton.*
A.D. 1337–1360.

7557. Plaster cast from fine but chipped impression.   1$\frac{1}{4}$ in.
[lxxxiii. 60.]

A shield of arms: on a bend cotised betw. six lions rampant,
three estoiles, for BOHUN.   Within a carved gothic panel.

✠ S' WILL'I ✿ D . . . . . OHVN ✿ COMITIS ✿ NORHAMPTONIE.

Another Seal.

7558. [A.D. 1342.]   Plaster cast from chipped impression.
1$\frac{1}{16}$ in. [lxxxiii. 65.]

Similar to the foregoing, but from a different matrix.

✠ S' WILL'I ✿ DE ✿ BOHVN ✿ COM . . . . ORHAMPTONIE.

Another Seal.

7559. Similar, from another matrix.   [lxxxiii. 66.]

Another Seal.

7560. [A.D. 1353.]   Plaster cast from imperfect impression.
1$\frac{3}{8}$ in. [lxxxiii. 68.]

A shield of arms: BOHUN as before.   Within a carved
gothic trefoil panel.

✠ 𝕾' · guillelmi · de · boҍ . . . . itis · norҍamptone.

John de Bokelee, *of Langeton, co. Linc., Knt.*

7561. [A.D. 1268-9.]   Cast in green composition from
original impression: very imperfect, central part only remaining.   About 1$\frac{3}{4}$ in. when perfect.   [lii. 36.]

A shield of arms: a fess betw. six lions rampant.
Legend wanting.

Henry Bokenham, *of Great Thornham, co. Suff., Knt.*
7562. [A.D. 1625.]   Red: indistinct. $\frac{5}{8} \times \frac{1}{2}$ in.   [Harl.
ch. 57 H. 42.]

A shield of arms: a lion rampant, BOKENHAM.   Over it a
helmet and mantling, without crest.

Cabled border.

Hugh de Bokenham, *of Snyterton, co. Norf, Knt.*
7563. [A.D. 1325.]   Dark green: fine, edge chipped. $\frac{7}{8}$ in.
[Harl. ch. 46 F. 10.]

A shield of arms: a lion rampant, on a bend three bezants.
Background engraved with parallel lines.

✠ S' : HVGONIS : [DE :] BOKEИHAM :

7564. Sulph. cast from No. 7563.   [D.C., F. 217.]

John de Bokyngham.

7565. [A.D. 1384.]   Plaster cast from indistinct impression.
$1\frac{1}{8}$ in.   [lxxxiii. 51.]

A shield of arms: a cross crosslet or botonnée, BOKENHAM.
Within a carved panel of six cusped points.

S · ioḧ'is · ꝺe · buckḧinḧam (?)

John Bokenham.

7566. [A.D. 1423.]   Plaster cast.   About $\frac{5}{8} \times \frac{3}{8}$ in.
[lxxxiii. 50.]

Octagonal: a shield of arms: fretty, BOKENHAM.   Suspended by a strap from a tree of two branches.

William, *son of* **Ralph de Bokenham,**
of Waleole Manor, etc., co. Norf.
7567. [A.D. 1344.]   Red: fine.   [Harl. ch. 46 F. 11.]

A shield of arms: a cross compony countercompony,
BOKENHAM.   Betw. two slipped trefoils.   Within a carved
and·pointed gothic quatrefoil ornamented with ball-flowers
along the inner edge.

✠ SIG' · WILLELMI · DE · BOKEИHAM.

Beaded border.

7568. Sulph. cast from No. 7567.   [D.C., F. 287.]

Thomas de Boketone, *or* .Buctone,
of Great Harrowden, co. Northt.
7569. [A.D. 1324.]   Light-greenish white: indistinct. $\frac{7}{8}$ in.
[Add. ch. 22,004.]

A shield of arms: three bucks, two and one.   .Betw. two
wyverns, and suspended by a strap from a hook.

+ SIGILLVM ·.THOME · DE BVCTON'.

Alan, *son and heir of* **John de Bokysselle,** *or* **Bokeselle,**
of Icklesham, co. Suss., etc.

7570. [*Temp.* Edw. I.]   Green : fine, chipped at the top.
I in. [Add. ch. 20,091.]

A lion couchant, fretty, supporting three shields of arms
meeting in base :—I, three crescents a canton ; 2, quarterly, a
bend vairé ; 3. fretty. Cf. the arms of BUCKSHALL of Sussex,
a lion rampant fretty.

⚹ S' · ALANI : DE · BVKESHILLE.

7571. [A.D. 1312.]   Green : imperfect, injured by pressure.
[Add. ch. 20,115.]

. . . . ALANI' · DE . . KE . . . HIL . . . .

Thomas Bold.

7572. [15th cent.]   Sulph. cast from fine impression.
I⅛ in. [D.C., G. 230.]

A shield of arms : a chevron betw. three roundles. Crest
on a helmet and wreath, a plume of three feathers. Betw.
two wavy sprigs.

⚹ thomas ⚹ bolD ⚹

Geoffrey Boleyn, *of Denham, co. Buck., etc.*

7573. [A.D. 1442.]   Red : indistinct. From a ring. ⅜ in.
[Harl. ch. 111 G. 31.]

A bull's head cabossed, in allusion to the arms of BOLEYN.
In the field above, the initial letters G. B. The field replenished
with sprigs of foliage.

Cabled border.

William Boleyn, *of Sele and Kemsing, co. Kent, Clerk.*

7574. [A.D. 1526.]   Red : fine. ½ in. [Harl. ch. 86 G. 54.]
Lozenge-shaped, from a signet ring. A bull's head couped :
crest of BULLEN. In the field below, the initial letter W.

Cabled border.

John de Boleyng?

7575. [A.D. 1389.]   Green, mottled : indistinct. ¾ in.
[Add. ch. 15,718.]

A shield of arms : a bend cotised betw. six roundles. Suspended by a strap from a three-branched tree. Betw. two
wingless wyverns.

S' IOHANNIS DE BOLEYNG (?)

The E in Boleyng is very obscure and conjectural.

Thomas de Bollesdune.

7576. [13th cent.] Plaster cast from indistinct impression. 1¼ × 2⅛ in. [lxxviii. 35.]

A shield of arms of early shape : six lozenges, three, two and one.

✠ SIGILLVM · TOMAS · DE · BOLLESDVNE.

Another Seal.

7577. Plaster cast from similar seal : nearly, but not quite identical with above, slightly larger. 2¼ × 1⅜ in. [lxxxiii. 88.]

Bartholomew Bolney, *of Chiddingley, co. Suss.*

7578. [A.D. 1459.] Red : indistinct. ⅝ × ½ in. [Add. ch. 30,337.]

A shield of arms : a crescent, and in chief two mullets of six points, BOLNEY.

Cabled border.

7579. [A.D. 1466.] Red : chipped. [Add. ch. 29,815.]

John Bolney.

7580. [A.D. 1378.] Red : cracked, somewhat indistinct. ¾ in. [Add. ch. 23,144.]

A shield of arms : on a chevron betw. three escallops, as many indistinct charges. Betw. two oak-leaves, slipped. Within a carved and pointed gothic trefoil.

✠ SIGILL' · IOH'IS · BOLNEY.

Thomas Bolour, *of co. Somerset.*

7581. [A.D. 1420.] Red : fine, slightly chipped. 1 in. [Harl. ch. 83 D. 32.]

A shield of arms : a butterfly or harvest-fly, BOLOURD or BOLOURE. Suspended by a strap from a forked tree. Within a carved gothic panel.

Sigillum : thome : bolour :

7582. Sulph. cast from No. 7581. [D.C., G. 161.]

Robert Bolton, *of co. Suff., Clerk.*

7583. [A.D. 1430.] Red : imperfect. 1 in. [Harl. ch. 54 I. 10.]

A shield of arms : (diapered) on a bend engrailed some indistinct charges. Within a carved gothic cinquefoil.

✠ Sigillū : dñi : rob . . . . . . bolton : cl'ici.

Cabled border.

Johanna, *wife of* SIMON **Bonde,** *Citizen of London.*
7584. [A.D. 1362.] Red: small fragment. [Harl. ch. 46 F. 24.]

Part of a shield of arms: a fess nebulée betw. three in-distinct charges.

Simon Bonde, *Citizen of London.*
7585. [A.D. 1362.] Red: very imperfect, r. h. side broken away. About 1 in. when perfect. [Harl. ch. 46 F. 24.]

A shield of arms: a lion rampant. Within a garved gothic panel ornamented with ball-flowers along the inner edge.

. . . . onis ⚜ ⚜ ⚜ bonde ⚜ ⚜ ⚜

Thomas Bonde, *of Gretyngham, etc., co. Suff.*
7586. [A.D. 1361.] Red: fine, chipped at the edge. $\frac{7}{8}$ in. [Add. ch. 10,199.]

A shield of arms: (diapered lozengy) a fess, BOND. Within an elaborately carved and traced gothic trefoil with eight circular panels.

✿ SIGILLVM ⚜ THOME ⚜ BOИDE ⚜

7587. [A.D. 1359.] Green: injured by pressure, imperfect. [Add. ch. 10,198.]

SIGI . . . . . H . ME.

Dame **Wenefrid Bonde,**
widow of Sir GEORGE BONDE, *Knt., of London.*
7588. [A.D. 1596.] Red. $\frac{9}{16} \times \frac{7}{16}$ in. [Add. ch. 35,848.]
Oval: a shield of arms: a cross engrailed, in the dexter chief a lozenge. Arms of LEIGH.

Beaded border.

Robert Boneres, *of Merchewod Valley,* [*Marshwood*] *co. Dorset, Priest.*
7589. [A.D. 1338.] Red: originally fine, now chipped, edge wanting. About $\frac{5}{8}$ in. when perfect. [Harl. ch. 46 F. 26.]

A shield of arms: an anchor betw. three leopards' heads jessants-de-lys, within a bordure engrailed. Within a finely carved gothic rosette of eight cusped points, ornamented with small ball-flowers along the inner border; and betw. three pairs of slipped quatrefoils.

Legend betw. the points :—

S'R __ OB' __ TI __ BO __ NE __ RS · __ PE __ SB.

7590. Sulph. cast from No. 7589. [D.C., F. 274.]

William Boneville, *Knt.*

7591. [15th cent.] Plaster cast from indistinct impression. 1 in. [xcii. 70.]

A shield of arms, *couché*: quarterly, 1, 4, six mullets, BONVILE, 2, 3, three lions rampant. Crest on a helmet and ornamental mantling an old man's head wearing a long cap. Betw. two initial letters, 𝔲 𝔢 (?)

[𝔖'] ⚜ 𝔴𝔦𝔩𝔩𝔢𝔩𝔪𝔦 · 𝔟𝔬𝔫𝔢𝔟𝔦𝔩𝔩𝔢 · 𝔪𝔦𝔩𝔦𝔱𝔦𝔰 (?)

Robert de Bonham,
son and heir of JOHN DE BONHAM, *Knt.*,
of the Manor of Great Wychford, co. Wilts.

7592. [A.D. 1356.] Red: indistinct in places, or badly impressed. 1 in. [Add. ch. 17,754.]

A shield of arms: a chevron wavy, betw. three crosses pattées fitchées at the foot, BONHAM. Betw. two pairs of leaves slipped. Within a carved and pointed gothic cinquefoil.

✠ SIGILLVM : ROBERTI : BONHAM.

Beaded border.

7593. [A.D. 1351.] Dark green: originally fine, now imperfect. [Add. ch. 15,081.]

✠ SIGILLVM : RO . . . . ONHAM.

Thomas Bonham, *Esq., of Great Wychford, co. Wilts.*

7594. [A.D. 1449.] Red: originally very fine, now fragmentary. About 1⅛ in. when perfect. Enclosed in a piece of damask of the same date. [Add. ch. 15,089.]

∅. A shield of arms, *couché*: a chevron wavy, betw. three crosses pattées fitchées at the foot, BONHAM. Crest, on a helmet, mantling, and chapeau, broken away.

. . . . . 𝔬𝔪𝔢 . . . . . .

℞. A small round counterseal, ⅜ in. A label or mitre-like escrol; in the field a motto: 𝔖 . . . . . 𝔠𝔥 . . . .(?)

Agnes Bonkede, *kinswoman and coheiress of*
THOMAS HUSCARL, *Knt., of Estbrightwell Manor, co. Oxon.*

7595. [A.D. 1379.] Red. ¾ in. From ring with marks of chased setting. [Add. ch. 23,859.]

A shield charged with pseudo-heraldic devices: a chevron, plain on the under and nebuly on the upper side, betw. two saltires in chief, and an estoile of eight points in base. Betw. three willow sprigs.

Capt. **James Bonnell,** *of Ratcliffe, co. Midd., Mariner.*
7596. [A.D. 1672.]   Red, covered with paper before impression : indistinct and imperfect.   About $\frac{5}{8}$ × $\frac{1}{2}$ in.   [Add. ch. 13,675.]
    Oval : a shield of arms : a saltire cotised.

Adam de Bont . . . ell.

7597. [A.D. 1417.]   Red : imperfect, indistinct.   About $\frac{7}{8}$ in. when perfect.   [Harl. ch. 51 E. 55.]
    A shield of arms : a fess betw. three lions' gambs erect ? Betw. three small quatrefoils slipped.   Within a carved and traced gothic ornamental panel of three semicircular and five pointed cusps.

✠ S' · ADE · DE · BONT . . . . . ELL.

Barton Booth.
See JOHN HODSON.

John Boothe, *of St. Waynardes, co. Heref., Gentl.*

7598. [A.D. 1634.]   Red : indistinct. $\frac{1}{2}$ in.   [Add. ch. 1933.]
    A shield of arms : three boars' heads erect and erased, in chief a crescent for difference, BOOTHE.
    Beaded border.
7599. [A.D. 1634.]   Red : imperfect.   [Add. ch. 1934.]

Used by WILLIAM BODENHAM, *of co. Heref.*

7600. [A.D. 1634.]   Red : very indistinct.   [Add. ch. 1934.]
7601. [A.D. 1634.]   Red : very indistinct.   [Add. ch. 1936.]

John Booth, *of Braynton, co. Heref., Esq.*

7602. [A.D. 1660.]   Red : imperfect.   About $\frac{1}{4}$ in.   [Add. ch. 1959.]
    A shield of arms : three boars' heads erect and erased, BOOTHE.

Thomas Bordale, *of St. Alban's, co. Hertf.*

7603. [A.D. 1409.]   Red. $\frac{1}{2}$ in.   [Add. ch. 18,192.]
    Octagonal : a shield of arms : a chevron betw. two crosses patty in chief and an annulet in base.   Cf. the arms of TWYCROSS, WOTTON, etc.
    Cabled border.
7604. [A.D. 1446.]   Red : injured by pressure.   [Add. ch. 18,193.]

William Borestalle, *of Colmorde Manor, co. Bedf., etc., Clerk.*

7605. [A.D. 1389.] Red: fragmentary. About ¾ in. when perfect. [Harl. ch. 46 F. 35.]

A shield of arms: charged apparently with a fess betw. three crowns, that in base broken off. Within a carved inner border.

✠ SI WILL' . . . . TE.

Robert de Borgate, [*of Borgate, or Burgate, co. Suff.*]

7606. [Late 12th or early 13th cent.] Creamy-white: originally fine, now chipped at edge. 1⅞ in. [Add. ch. 28,354.]

A shield of arms of early shape: paly of six, (the pales bend in slightly towards the base), on a canton or quarter a lion passant (or perhaps rampant). Cf. the arms of BORGAT, BURGATE, etc., paly of six. This is an interesting example of early heraldry.

⚜ S . . . . . OBER . . . DE . . . GATE.

Robert de Burgate, [*of Burgate, co. Suff.*]
Perhaps same as the previous person.

7607. [Late 12th or early 13th cent.] Creamy white: very fine. 1⅝ in. [Add. ch. 28,355.]

A· shield of arms of early shape: three piles converging towards the base (but not quite meeting), on a canton or quarter a lion rampant. See No. 7606. This is an interesting example of early heraldry. The canton is probably an honourable augmentation.

⚜ SIGILL' ∴ ROBERTI ∴ DE ∴ BVRGATE.

Beaded borders.

7608. Plaster cast from a chipped impression. [lxxxiv. 70.]

John Borlas, *or* **Burlase,** *of Marlow, co. Buck.*

7609. [A.D. 1553.] Red: injured. ⁷⁄₁₂ × ½ in. [Harl. ch. 76 E. 12.]

On a wreath a boar's head, couped at the neck. Crest of BORLASE.

Beaded border.

John Borlase, *or* **Burlacey,** *of Little Marlow, co. Bucks, Esq.*

7610. [A.D. 1561.] Red. ⅝ × ¹⁄₁₆ in. [Lansd. ch. 577.]

Oval: on a wreath a boar's head couped at the neck. Crest of BORLASE.

Beaded border.

7611. [A.D. 1561.] Another. [Lansd. ch. 578.]

Ernald de Bosco.

7612. [*Circ.* A.D. 1216–1236.] Dark green, speckled : fine originally, now chipped at top. 1⅓ in. [Harl. ch. 84 H. 55.]
. A shield of arms of early shape : two bars, on a canton or quarter a lion passant.

✚ SIGILL' : ERNALDI : DE : BO . . . . . .

7613. Sulph. cast from No. 7612. [D.C., E. 326.]

John de Bosco, *Knt., son of* ARNULPH DE BOSCO, *of Assington, co. Suff.*

7614. [*Temp.* Edw. I.] Green, mottled : fine. 1 in. [Harl. ch. 47 A. 17.]
A shield of arms : two bars, and a quarter or canton. BOSCO, or BOYS. Suspended by a strap from a hook, and betw. two wavy sprigs of foliage.

☼ SIGILLVM· IOHANNIS D' BOSCO.

Beaded borders.

John de Bosco, *son and heir of* ERNALD DE BOSCO, *of co. Buck.*

7615. [*Temp.* Edw. I.] Dark green : a fragment. About 1 in. when perfect. [Harl. ch. 84 H. 56.]
A shield of arms : charges obliterated, but apparently a canton remains, cf. No. 7614. Suspended by a strap from a hook.

SI . . . . OSCO.

Probably same person and seal as in No. 7614.

7616. Sulph. cast from No. 7615. [D.C., F. 341.]

William Bosenho, *of Watlyngton, etc., co. Oxon.*

7617. [A.D. 1443.] Red : cracked, imperfect, indistinct. ¾ in. [Add. ch. 20,389.]
A shield of arms : per pale, *dex.,* a chevron betw. two bird- . bolts in chief, and a mullet in base ; *sin.,* uncertain.

☼ S . . . . fll'i ☼ ☼ bofeħo ☼

Cf. Will. Bozenho, witness at Chalgrove, co. Oxon., A.D. 1432, in Add. ch. 20,313 ; 20,314.

Jacobus de Boseville, [*of Wickersley, co. York*], *Knt.*

7618. [A.D. 1322.] Red : imperfect, injured by pressure. About 1 in. [Harl. ch. 112 G. 25.]
. A shield of arms : three fig-leaves slipped, two and one. Suspended by a strap from a hook, and betw. two wyverns. The. arms do not agree with those usually borne by BOSVILLE.

☼ : S' I . . . . BI : DE : BOSEVILE :

Beaded borders.

Hugh Bossard, *Lord of Knotinge, co. Bedf., Knt.*
7619. [*Temp.* Hen. III.] Dark green: very fine.
1¼ × 1 in. [Harl. ch. 111 D. 45.]
Shield-shapèd : a shield of arms : three estoiles of many
points wavy, one and two, betw. as many horse-shòes, two and
one.
✠ SIG HVGONIS BOSSARD.
7620. Sulph. cast from No. 7619. [D.C., E. 357.]
Cf. Hugh, son of D. John Bossard, A.D. 1272, Harl. ch. 49 I. 41.

Henry Bostocke, *Merchant of the Calais Staple.*
7621. [A.D. 1551.] Red : cracked, injured by pressure.
About ⅝ × ½ in. [Harl. ch. 46 I. 27.]
An ornamental shield of arms : a fess humettée, in chief a
crescent for difference, BOSTOCK.

Philip de Boston.
7622. [15th cent.] Plaster cast from chipped impression.
1¼ in. [lxxxiii. 75.]
A shield of arms, *couché* : quarterly, 1, 4, a chevron betw.
three griffins' heads erased, 2, 3, three bars over all a bend
engrailed. Crest on a helmet and mantling a griffin's head
erased. Betw. two sprigs in the background.
Legend on a scroll :—

𝕾𝖎𝖌𝖎𝖑𝖑𝖚𝖒 : 𝕻𝖍𝖎𝖑 . . . . ᴀᴿ ✿

John Boswell, *Rector of the Moiety of the Church*
of Darfield, co. York·
7623. [A.D. 1460.] Red : fragmentary. About ½ in. when
perfect. [Add. ch. 17,050.]
Octagonal signet : perhaps bearing a shield of arms and
motto, very indistinct, and doubtful.

William del Bothe, *Burgess of the Town of*
Newcastle-on-Tyne, co. Northumb.
7624. [A.D. 1394.] Red : chipped. ⅝ in. [Add. ch.
20,530.]
A shield of arms : three horse-shoes betw. six crosses
crosslet fitchées, three, two, and one, BOOTH. Within a carved
gothic trefoil ornamentèd with small ball-flowers along the
inner edge.

Hawisia la Botelere,
Seal used by RALPH LE BOTELER, *Lord of Polrebech, or Pulverbatch, co. Salop.*

7625. [A.D. 1314.] Red: fine. 1 in. [Add. ch. 20,444.]

Three shields of arms, meeting at their bases: 1. a cross flory, in chief a label of three points; 2. Paly of six; 3. a fess betw. six crosses crosslet, BOTELER. Background replenished with small trefoils and quatrefoils.

✠ : S' . HAWISIE : LA : BOTELERE : ✠

Beaded borders.

Henry Boteler, *of Lekhamsted Manor, co. Berks.*

7626. [A.D. 1459.] Red: injured by pressure. $\frac{9}{16} \times \frac{3}{8}$ in. From a ring. [Harl. ch. 54 I. 16.]

Oval: a shield of arms: on a fess betw. three covered cups, a small cross for difference, BUTLER. Inner border partly engrailed or cusped.

Johanna le Boteler, *or* **Botillere,** *of Baggebere, or Bagborough Manor, co. Som.*

7627. [*Temp.* Edw. I.] Green: edge chipped, app. by a plaited hollow tape of greenish-brown stuff. $1\frac{3}{8} \times \frac{3}{4}$ in. [Harl. ch. 55 B. 42.]

Pointed oval: a covered cup, in allusion to the arms of BUTLER.

+ S IOHANNE LE BOTELER.

John Botiller, *of Wick, co. Worc.*

7628. [A.D. 1357–1377.] Red: injured by pressure. $\frac{5}{8} \times \frac{1}{2}$ in. [Add. ch. 9239.]

A shield of arms: on a chief three covered cups, BUTLER.

John Le Botteler, *of Penbray* [*? co. Carmarth.*], *Esq.*

7629. [A.D. 1438.] Dark red: originally fine, now chipped. About 1 in. when perfect. [Harl. ch. 46 I. 37.]

A shield of arms: three covered cups, BUTLER. Betw. a lion's face, enraged, at top, and two wyverns sans wings reguardant addorsed at the sides.

✠ S . . . . IOHANNIS B . . . LER.

Beaded borders.

7630. Sulph. cast from No. 7629. [D.C., G. 204.]

John Boteler, *of Higham Gobion, co. Bedf., Knt.*

7631. [A.D. 1609.] Red: indistinct. $\frac{5}{16} \times \frac{1}{4}$ in. [Add. ch. 35,338.]

A shield-shaped signet, bearing a shield of arms : a fess counter-compony betw. six crosses crosslet ? BOTELER.

Another Seal.

7632. [A.D. 1609.] Red. $\frac{5}{8}$ × $\frac{3}{4}$ in. [Add. ch. 35,341.]
Oval : on a wreath a dexter arm embowed, in armour, holding a sword. Crest of BOTELER.
Cabled border.

John Boteler, *of Woodhall in Watton, co. Hertf.*
7633. [A.D. 1651.] Red : indistinct. $\frac{11}{16}$ × $\frac{9}{16}$ in. [Add. ch. 35,510.]
Oval : a shield of arms : a fess counter-compony betw. six crosses crosslet, BOTELER. Crest on a helmet and ornamental mantling, a dexter hand and arm embowed, holding a sword.

Ralph Botiller, *of Theydon Gernon, etc., co. Essex, Knt.*
7634. [A.D. 1446.] Red : imperfect, cracked ; from chased signet ring with mark of setting, encircled with a twisted rush. About $\frac{1}{2}$ × $\frac{3}{8}$ in. [Add. ch. 28,864.]
Small oval signet : a greyhound sejant, ducally gorged and chained, beneath a tree. In allusion to the crest of BUTLER.
Cabled border.
Cf. Add. ch. 17,238.

7635. [A.D. 1458.] Red : fine. [Add. ch. 28,874.]
7636. [A.D. 1458.] Red : injured by pressure. [Add. ch. 28,875.]

Ralph [Boteler], *Lord of Sudley, co. Glouc.*
7637. [A.D. 1450.] Red : fine, from chased signet ring, with mark of setting. $\frac{1}{2}$ in. [Add. ch. 17,238.]
A greyhound sejant, ducally gorged, and chained, beneath a tree. In allusion to the crest of BUTLER.
Cabled border.

Robert le Boteleyr ?
7638. [A.D. 1303.] Plaster cast from fine impression. [lxxxiii. 76.]
A shield of arms : three lions rampant, two and one, within a bordure ermine. Suspended by a strap betw. two pairs of leaves.
In place of legend a wavy border of pierced six-foil roses.
Beaded borders.

Walter Le Botyler, *of Hemmingeston, co. Suff.*

7639. [A.D. 1285.]   Green : lower part ·only remaining, very indistinct.   ¾ in.   [Add. ch. 9834.]

A shield of arms : perhaps a chevron betw. three covered cups.   That in base can only be distinguished.

[+ S'. WAJLTERI · L' · BOT . . . .

Ralph Botreaux, *of Bossulyan, etc., co. Cornw., Knt.*

7640. [A.D. 1426.]   Red : injured by pressure.   From chased ring,· with mark of setting.   ½ × ¾ in.   [Add. ch. 12,986.]

Rectangular : a helmet with a plume or indistinct crest. Motto in the field :—

✠ grace fait honur.

Cabled border.

7641. [A.D. 1426.]   Another.   [Add. ch. 12,987.]

Ralph Botreaux, *of cos. York, Linc., Warw., etc., Knt.*

7642. [A.D. 1427.]   Red : originally fine and sharp, edge chipped.   1½ in.   [Add. ch. 13,977.]

A shield of arms,· *couché* : quarterly, 1, 4, a ·griffin segreant, BOTREAUX, 2, 3, four fusils in fess.   Crest on a helmet mantling and chapeau, turned up ermine, a griffin statant. This armorial design rests on a *buttress* (in allusion to the name of the owner) partly behind the shield.   In the field on each side a wavy branch of flowers and foliage.

✾ Sigillum ⚜ radulphi ✾ [botreaux ✾ ⚜] ✾ ⚜

Carved borders.

7643. [A.D. 1430.]   Red : indistinct from shifting during impression.   [Add. ch. 12,990.]

✾ Sigillum ⚜ radulphi ✾ botreaux ✾ ⚜ ✾ ⚜

7644. [A.D. 1431.]   Red : imperfect at top.   [Add. ch. 12,993.]

. . . gillum ⚜ radulphi ✾ botreaux ✾ ⚜ ✾ ⚜

7645. [A.D. 1431.]   Red : indistinct, injured by pressure. [Add. ch. 12,994.] ·

✾ Sigillum ⚜ radulphi ✾ botreaux ✾ ⚜ ✾ ⚜

7646. [A.D. 1431.]   Red : fine, injured.   [Add. ch. 12,995.]

. . . . . gill . . . radulphi ✾ botreaux ✾ ⚜ ✾ ⚜

William de Botriaux.

7647. [Late 14th cent.]   Red : fine.   Perhaps from matrix, with the ring removable, on which the legend is engraved.   1¼ in.   [xxxvi. 118.]

A shield of arms: a griffin segreant, BOTREAUX. Betw. five small cinquefoils, and within a finely carved gothic rosette or star of eight points ornamented with ball-flowers along the inner edge.

✠ Sigillum : • : Willelmi : • : de : • : Botriaux.

Carved borders.

7648. Plaster cast from No. 7647. [lxxxiii. 78.]

William, *Sire* de Botreaux,
Keeper of the Forest of Exmoor, etc., co. Somers.

7649. [A.D. 1435.] Red: fine, very imperfect at top. 1¼ in. [Harl. ch. 43 E. 47.]

A shield of arms, *couché*: a griffin segreant, BOTREAUX. Crest, on a helmet mantling and chapeau, destroyed, but from remaining traces it appears to have been a griffin. Supporters on a mount two buttresses. Above the shield a ring or annulet. The inside edge of the field enriched with small sprigs of foliage.

. . . . . lliam • botreaux ✠

Border carved with small ball-flowers.

John Botyld, *of Hatfield Regis, co. Essex.*

7650. [A.D. 1345.] Brown: indistinct. ¹¹⁄₁₆ in. [Add. ch. 28,597.]

A shield (of arms?): two hands, couped at the wrist, holding up a human heart.

✠ MOVN QVER AVET.

(*Mon cœur avez.*)

Simon Boulet.

7651. [A.D. 1335.] Plaster cast from fine impression. ⅞ in. [lxxxiii. 52.]

A shield (of arms?): a heart-shaped device voided, enclosing a cross betw. two estoiles in pale. Betw. three sprigs of foliage.

✠ SIGILL' SIMONIS BOVLET.

Beaded borders.

John de Boulton.

7652. [A.D. 1353.] Plaster cast from indistinct impression. 1 in. [lxxxiii. 82.]

A shield of arms: on a chevron three lions passant guardant, BOLTON. On a tree of three branches. Betw. two sprigs of foliage. Within a cusped gothic panel of eight points.

✠ SIGILLVM · IOHANNIS · DE · BOVLTON.

Alianora, *widow of* WILLIAM **Bourgchier,** *Knt.*
(ob. A.D. 1365), *2nd son of* ROBERT DE BOURGCHIER,
of Halsted and Stansted, co. Essex; dau. and heiress
of JOHN DE LOUVAINE *or* LOVAYNE.
7653. [A.D. 1389.] Red: originally fine, now very imperfect, and r. h. side broken off. 1$\frac{1}{16}$ in. when perfect. [Add. ch. 7906.]
A shield of arms: per pale, *dex.,* a cross engrailed betw. four water bougets, BOURGCHIER; *sin.,* billety a fess, LOVAYNE. Suspended by a strap from a rose-tree in flower on a mount, and within a finely-carved gothic panel.

※ ﹩ . . . . **nore** ※ ﹩ ﹙ ※ **bourchere** ※ ﹩

Bartholomew Bourchier, *al.* **Boucher.**
7654. [14th cent.] Plaster cast from indistinct impression. [lxxxiii. 39.]
A shield of arms: a cross engrailed betw. four water bougets, BOURCHIER. Within a carved gothic panel.

※ **﹩igill'** · **bartholomei** · **boucher :** ﹙

Edward Bourchier, *Lord Fitzwarren, son of*
WILLIAM BOURCHIER, *Earl of Bath.*
7655. [A.D. 1605.] Red: fragmentary. [Harl. ch. 78 B. 5].
Oval: a Bourchier's knot.
Beaded border.

Lady Frances Bourchier, *dau. of* WILLIAM BOURCHIER,
Earl of Bath.
7656. [A.D. 1605.] Red: fine. $\frac{3}{16}$ in. [Harl. ch. 78 B. 5.]
A Bourchier's knot.

Henry Bourghchier, *2nd Earl of Ewe, in Normandy.*
7657. [A.D. 1430.] Red: fine fragment. About 1$\frac{3}{4}$ in. when perfect. [Harl. ch. 56 E. 4.]
A shield of arms, *couché*: quarterly, 1, 4, a cross engrailed betw. four water bougets, BOURGHCHIER; 2, 3, billety a fess, LOVAYNE. Crest on a helmet, and ornamental mantling, wanting.
Legend wanting.

Henry Bourschier, *Earl of Essex, Earl of Ewe, etc.*
[A.D. 1461–1483.]
(Same person as the preceding.)
7658. [A.D. 1476.] Red: indistinct. With marks of a twisted rush round it. $\frac{9}{16}$ × $\frac{1}{2}$ in. [Add. ch. 30,437.]

A badge, apparently a breastplate or piece of armour. In
the field some uncertain letters of a motto.

Humfrey Bourgchier, *Lord Cromwell, Knt.*

7659. [A.D. 1469.] Red: fine fragments. About 2¼ in.
when perfect. [Add. ch. 20,504.]

Ø. A shield of arms, *couché*: quarterly. 1, 4, quarterly, i. iv.,
BOURGCHIER, ii. iii., LOVAYNE?, as in No. 7657, with a label
of three points: 2, 3, quarterly, i. iv., chequy a chief ermine?;
ii. iii., a chief, over-all a bend, CROMWELL? Crest on a
helmet and ornamental mantling (a head in profile?) crowned.

. . . ḫum . . . .

℞. A small round counterseal from matrix with reversible
design, ⅜ in. Uncertain design. A hand grasping a tree or
weapon? and other details.

John Burgcher, *al.* Bourgchier.

7660. [14th cent.] Plaster cast from fine but chipped
impression. 1⅛ in. [lxxxiii. 80.]

A shield of arms, *couché*: a cross engrailed betw. four
water bougets, BOURGCHIER. Crest on a helmet, an old
man's head in profile, couped at the shoulders, habited,
collared, on his head a ducal coronet, out of which a long cap,
conical, topped with a knob. Betw. two trefoiled sprigs of
foliage. Within a carved gothic quatrefoil panel.

Sigíllū : íoḫannís : burgcḫer ᴀᴋ ᴀᴋ

John Bourghcher, *Knt.*

7661. [A.D. 1357.] Plaster cast from fine impression. 1 in.
[lxxxiii. 81.]

Similar to the previous seal, with a few points of detail
treated differently. The sprigs of foliage at the side are
omitted.

S' íoḫannís · bourgḫcḫer.

Beaded border.

John de Bourgchier, *of Stanstede Manor, etc., co. Essex, Knt.*

7662. [A.D. 1383.] Red: originally fine, now cracked and
chipped. 1¾ in. [Add. ch. 8052.]

A shield of arms, *couché*: a cross engrailed betw. four
water bougets, BOURGCHIER. Crest on a helmet and short
mantling, an old man's head in profile couped at the shoul-

ders,. habited, collared, on his head a ducal coronet, out of which a long cap tasselled. Supporters: two eagles ·rising.

       Sigillũ : Domini : iohannis : De : bourgcher : ⚮

The letters DO of *domini*, and DE of *de* are conjoined.
.Beaded border.

7663. [A.D. 1390.] Red: fine, imperfect on the r. h. side. [Harl. ch. 46 I. 52.]

        . . . . . ini : iohannis : De : bourgcher : ⚮

7664. Sulph. cast from No. 7663. [D.C., F. 575.]

John Bourchier, 1st *Baron Berners.* A.D. 1455–1474.
. **7665.** Red: fine fragments. About 2⅛ in. when perfect. [xxxvi. 151.]

A shield of arms, *couché*: quarterly, 1, 4, quarterly, i. iv., BOURCHIER; ii. iii., LOVAYNE, as in No. 7657, over all a label of three points; 2, 3, quarterly, BERNERS. Crest on a helmet, ornamental mantling, and wreath, an old man's head couped at the shoulders, habited, collared, and ducally crowned, with a long cap hanging forward, tasselled: on the neck a label as before.

Legend on a strap or ribbon running round the seal :—

       Sigillu : . . . . erners :

7666. Sulph. cast from No. 7665. [D.C., G. 200.]

              Another seal.

7667. [A.D. 1459.] Red. From a signet ring. $\frac{7}{16}$ in. [Add. ch. 30,416.]

Three axes or mallets, one in pale, two in saltire, interlaced, the handles ringed. Betw. the letters **I · e · el.**

Perhaps a badge of BOURGCHIER.
Cabled border.

7668. [A.D. 1459.] Another. [Add. ch. 30,417.]

John Bourgchier, 2nd *Baron Berners, Knt.*

7669. [A.D. 1513.] Red: indistinct. ½ in. [Add. ch. 28,628.]

Shield-shaped: on a branch an eagle rising. Perhaps for a crest.

John Bourne, *of the Holte, co. Worc., Knt.*

7670. [A.D. 1571.] Red. ¾ × ⅝ in. [Harl. ch. 77 H. 10.]

An ornamental shield of arms: a chevron betw. three lions rampant, a chief ermines, BOURNE.
. Cabled border.

Isabella de Bourne, *widow of* THOMAS DE BOURNE, *Knt.,*
of Stanford Ryvers Manor, co. Essex, etc.

7671. [A.D. 1346.] Green, mottled: faded. 1 in. [Add.
ch. 19,985.]

Two shields of arms: *dex.,* a lion rampant, queue fourchée,
within a bordure engrailed; *sin.,* a bend lozengy, or five
fusils in bend, betw. six billets. Suspended by straps, from a
forked tree, and within a carved border.

✠ SIGILLVM ISABELLE DE BOVRNE.

Margaret Bousherste.
See JOHN PELHAM.

William de Bouse, (Bowes?)

7672. [A.D. 1388.] Plaster cast from fine impression. Injured by pressure. ⅞ in. [lxxxiii. 87.]

A shield of arms: on a bend, three uncertain charges.
Within a pointed quatrefoil panel, ornamented with small
quatrefoils along the inner edge.

Sigillum · willelmi · de · bouse ·· (?)

John de Bouthin.

7673. [14th cent.] Sulph. cast from good impression.
1 in. [D.C., F. 336.]

A shield of arms: a bull or *bouquetin,* in allusion to the
name of the owner, statant in a ford under a tree. Suspended
by a strap from a forked tree, and within a carved gothic
panel.

Sigillum ⚜ iohannes ⚜ De ⚜ Bouthin ⚜

The letters DE of *de* are conjoined.
Beaded border.

John Bouttourt, *of Halstead, co. Essex, Lord of Mendlesham,*
co. Suff.

7674. [A.D. 1310.] Dark green: originally fine, now imperfect and indistinct. ⅞ in. [Harl. ch. 47 F. 11.]

A cinquefoil, having each leaf charged with the arms: a
saltire engrailed, BUTTOURT, or BOTATORT.

✠ S'· IO[HÀN]NIS · BOVTTOVRT.

Beaded borders.

7675. Sulph. cast from No. 7674.   [D.C., F. 180.]
7676. Plaster cast.   [lxxxiii. 77.]

John Botourte, *of Mendlesham Manor, co. Suff.*

7677. [A.D. 1355.]   Red : originally fine, chipped, injured by pressure.   ⅞ in.   [Harl. ch. 47 F. 15.]

A shield of arms, *couché* : bendy of six a canton, BOUTE-TOURT or BOTATORT.   Crest on a helmet, mantling or lambrequin diapered, and wreath, a bell (?) betw. two wings erect.   Within a carved gothic panel.

: 𝕾𝖎𝖌' : 𝖎𝖔𝖍'𝖎𝖘 : : 𝖇𝖔𝖙𝖔𝖚𝖗𝖙 :

7678. Sulph. cast from No. 7677.   [D.C., F. 393.]

John Bottourt, *al.* Buttourt.

7679. [A.D. 1358.]   Red : originally fine, now chipped, injured by dust.   About 1¾ in.   [Add. ch. 27,178.]

A shield of arms : a saltire lozengy or engrailed, in chief an annulet for difference, BOTATORT, BOTETOURT, etc. Within an elaborately carved and traced gothic triangle with inner cusped rosace of eight points and inside edge enriched with small ball-flowers.   The points of the triangle enclose each a countersunk quatrefoil with a quatrefoil, four-leaved rose, or other flower within it ; and the segmental spaces betw. the sides of the triangle and the inner circle are filled with triangles and other details of tracery.

Legend betw. the points :—

⚓ SIGI . . . . . . HANNIS : ✿ : : ✿ : BUTTOURT : ✿ :

7680. Plaster cast of No. 7679.   [xcviii. 40.]

John Buttetourt, *Chevr., Lord of Welegh, or Weoleye, co. Worc. ?*

(Same as the previous person ?)

7681. [A.D. 1363.]   Red : originally fine, now wanting edge.   [Harl. ch. 47 F. 16.]

Same as No. 7679, but the annulet for difference in the field of the shield above the saltire engrailed, has been apparently removed from, or filled up in, the matrix before impression ; and faint traces of it remain.   Some of the details in this are more clear than in No. 7679.

⚓ SIGIL . . . .

7682. [A.D. 1370.] .   Red : originally fine, now imperfect. [Harl. ch. 47 F. 17.]

The annulet has been removed from the matrix before impression, but faint traces of it still remain.

. . . . IOHA . . . .

7683. Sulph. cast from No. 7682. [D.C., F. 472.]

Cf. Harl. ch. 46 B. 25*b*, A.D. 1357 ; 46 F. 19, A.D. 1377.

Matilda, *wife of* **John Bouttourt,** *of Halstead, co. Essex.*

7684. [A.D. 1310.] Red : fine fragment. About 1⅛ in. when perfect. [Harl. ch. 47 F. 13.]

A shield of arms : per pale, *dex.*, bendy of six, a canton, BOTATORT or ·BOUTETORT, *sin.*, a saltire engrailed, BUT-TOURT, etc.

Legend wanting.

Beaded borders.

Matillis, *widow of* **John Buteturte,** [*of co. Suff. ?*], *Knt.*
(Probably same person as the preceding.)

7685. [A.D. 1327.] Red : very fine and sharp. 1 in. [Harl. ch. 47 F. 13.]

A shield of arms, as in No. 7684. Suspended by a strap from a small tree of two branches, and betw. two small falcons by way of supporters.

In place of a legend, a cusped border of nineteen·points, ornamented with carved ball-flowers along the inner edge, and having a roundle betw. each of the points. The roundles appear to have very indistinct designs, either letters or armorial details on them.

Thomas Boutetourte, *son of* JOHN BOUTETOURTE,
of co. Essex.

7686. [A.D. 1322.] Dark green : a fragment. About ⅞ in. when perfect. [Harl. ch. 47 F. 12.]

On a branching tree, a shield of arms : a saltire engrailed, and label of three points, BOTATORT.

Legend wanting.

William de Bovile, *of Pesenhale Manor, co. Suff., Knt.*

7687. [*Temp.* Edw. I.] Dark green : very indistinct. ⅞ in. [Harl. ch. 83 D. 41.]

Ø. A shield of arms : quarterly, BOVILE. Betw. two wyverns. Above the shield an indistinct design. Within a quatrefoil.

✠ S' WIL . . . .

R. A smaller counterseal. ¾ in. A shield of arms as in the *obv.*

✿ TVT EN TOV . . . . . . RITO . . . (?)

Cf. Harl. ch. 45 C. 35, A.D. 1316 ; Harl. ch. 46 I. 48, A.D. 1317.

Henry Bovingdon, *of Denham, co. Buck.*

7688. [A.D. 1491.] Faded red : injured by pressure. ⁷⁄₁₆ in. [Harl. ch. 84 I. 2.]

A dog or other small animal courant beneath a tree. In the field the motto :—

. nul : autre.

Beaded border.

William Boway, *of Lutton, co. Bedf.*

7689. [A.D. 1452.] Red : indistinct. From a ring. ⁷⁄₁₆ × ⁹⁄₁₆ in. [Add. ch. 26,172.]

Octagonal : a griffin segreant coutourné.

Beaded border.

John Boweles, *of Colmorde, co. Bedf.*

7690. [A.D. 1374.] Red : imperfect on l. h. side, injured by pressure. About ⅞ in. when perfect. [Harl. ch. 46 I. 56.]

A shield of arms : ermine, a lion passant. Within a carved border.

✿ **Sigillū : iohan . . . .**

7691. [A.D. 1374.] Red : cracked, indistinct. [Harl. ch. 46 I. 57.]

. . . igillū : . . . . nif : bowels :

William Le Bower.

See JOHN DE KEVIRDALE.

Adam de Bowes.

7692. [A.D. 1351.] Plaster cast from fine impression. ¾ in. [lxxxiii. 83.]

A shield of arms : on a fess betw. three crosses moline, as many trefoils slipped. Suspended by a strap from a hook. Betw. two wyverns sans wings.

✿ SIGILLVM ADE DE BOWES.

Beaded borders.

Paul Bowes, *of the Middle Temple, Esq.*

7693. [A.D. 1688.] Red : *en placard*, on a label. Imperfectly impressed. About ¾ × ⅝ in. [Add. ch. 9301.]

A shield of arms: three bows in fess strung palewise,
BOWES. Crest, on a helmet, ornamental mantling and
wreath, a sheaf of arrows bound in a girdle.

Robert de Bowes.

7694. [15th cent.] Plaster cast from fine impression. 1 in.
[lxxxiii. 84.]

A shield of arms: ermine, three bows bent in pale, two
and one, BOWES. Above the shield a Katharine wheel; at
each side a wyvern addorsed reguardant. Within a carved
gothic trefoil panel ornamented along the inner edge with
small ball-flowers.

SIGLLV ROBERTI DE BOWES.

Beaded border.

Edmund Bowyer, *of Camberwell, co. Surr., Knt.*

7695. [A.D. 1646.] Red: indistinct in places. About
$\frac{3}{4} \times \frac{5}{8}$ in. [Add. ch. 1629.]

Oval: a shield of arms of nine quarterings, three, three,
and three:—I. a bend vairé cotised, BOWYER; 2. on a fess
three leopards' faces, BRABANT; 3. a chevron betw. three
acorns, BOYS; 4. on a fess betw. three annulets a mullet betw.
two covered cups, DRAPER; 5, two chevrons [on each three
martlets], betw. as many escallops, DRAPER; 6. on a chief
three lions rampant, AGER; 7. a fess chequy, URSWICK;
8. on a bend engrailed, three cinquefoils, FIFIELD, *al.* LOWE;
9, on a chevron three crosses crosslet.

Cf. Harl. MS. 1561, f. 29*b*.

William Bowyer, *of Denham, co. Buck., Esq. and Knt.*

7696. [A.D. 1597.] Red: with mark of chased setting.
$\frac{5}{8} \times \frac{1}{2}$ in. [Harl. ch. 84 I. 4.]

A shield of arms: quarterly, 1, 4, a bend vairé cotised,
BOWYER; 2, 3, three spades, KNYPERSLEY.

Beaded border.

7697. [A.D. 1601.] Another. [Harl. ch. 84 I. 8.]
7698. [A.D. 1605.] Another. [Harl. ch. 83 H. 20.]
7699. [A.D. 1607.] Another. [Harl. ch. 111 D. 48.]
On the *rev.* a monogram: L S., from a stamp.

Richard Boyce, *of Westfurles and Ripe, co. Suss., Gentl.*

7700. [A.D. 1558.] Red. $\frac{3}{4} \times \frac{5}{8}$ in. [Add. ch. 30,777.]

Oval: an ornamental shield of arms: a stag's head couped
at the neck, in a bush or *bois*.

Cf. Harl. ch. 77 C. 52, Samuel Boys, A.D. 1616.

John de Boydéle.
See JOHN DE BODEL.

I. Boyle.
Seal used by ROBERT CLYTTERBOOKE, *of Remneham,*
co. Berks., Gentl.
7701. [A.D. 1588.] Red : injured. ⅞ in. [Add. ch. 13,655.]
A shield of arms : per bend embattled, in chief a crescent
for difference, BOYLE. Crest on a helmet and mantling, a
lion's head erased per pale embattled. Betw. the letters I. B.

John Boys, *of Felmingham. co. Norf.*
7702. [A.D. 1396.] Red : imperfect, r. h. side wanting.
I in. [Add. ch. 14,665.]
A shield of arms : two bars, and a canton or quarter, over
all a bend, BOYS. Within a carved gothic trefoil ornamented
with ball-flowers along the inner edge.

𝕾igillū . . . . . . 𝖘 : 𝖒 : bops : 𝖆
Cabled border.

John Boys, *of co. Kent.*
7703. [A.D. 1540.] Red. ⅜ × ½ in. [Harl. ch. 78 G. 29.]
Lozenge-shaped : on a wreath a demi-dog holding an oak-
branch leaved and fruited. Crest of BOYS.
Beaded border.

Richard du Boys, *of La Seete Manor, Ludlow, co. Salop, Knt.*
7704. [A.D. 1292.] Dark bronze-green : fine, well preserved. App. by plaited bobbins of green stuff. I in.
[L. F. C. xxiii. I.]
A shield of arms : barry of eight, in chief a pale betw. two
squires, over all an escutcheon. Betw. three oak branches
each having an acorn betw. two leaves.
       ✿ SIGILLVM : RICARDI · DV BOIS ⚜.
Beaded borders.

Robert de Boys.
7705. [A.D. 1360.] . Plaster cast from fine impression.
¾ in. [lxxxiii. 86.]
A shield of arms : a tree eradicated, BOYS, debruised by a
bar. Background hatched.
       ✿ S' ROBERTI DE BOYS.
Beaded borders.

Roger de Boys, *of Farnham, co. Suff., Chivaler.*
7706. [A.D. 1383.]   Red: fine, the sides injured.   1⅛ in.
[Harl. ch. 47 A. 28.]
A shield of arms, *couché*: two bars and a canton or quarter,
over all a bend, BOYS.   Crest on a helmet and short mantling,
an old man's head in profile to the l.   Supporters, two trees
on a mount, in allusion to the name.
. . . . DE · B . . . .
Beaded border.
7707. Sulph. cast from No. 7706.   [D.C., F. 542.]

Samuel Boys, *of Goathurst, co. Kent.*
7708. [A.D. 1616.]   Red: very indistinct.   [Harl. ch.
77 C. 52.]
An ornamental shield of arms: out of a ducal coronet a
buck's head.   Crest of BOYSE (?)
Cf. Add. ch. 30,777, Richard Boyce, A.D. 1558.

Thomas Boys, *of Heth, or Hythe, co. Kent.*
7709. [A.D. 1583.]   Dark green: imperfect at bottom.
¾ × ⅜ in.   [Add. ch. 19,996.]
Oval: a shield of arms: a griffin segreant, BOYS.
Beaded border.
7710. [A.D. 1583.]   Dark green: a fragment of r. h. side
only.   [Add. ch. 19,997.]

Walter Boys, *of East Audeham, Aldham, or Yaldham Manor,*
co. Kent, Knt.
7711. [A.D. 1275.]   Dark green: fine, well preserved.
1⅛ in.   [Add. ch. 16,183.]
A shield of arms: a lion rampant.   Suspended by a strap
from a tree, and betw. two wingless wyverns addorsed.
✳ S WALTERI · BOIS DE MVSSĒDEN.
7712. [*Temp.* Edw. I.]   Dark green: fine, chipped at top
and bottom.   [Add. ch. 16,505.]
. . . . ALTERI · B . . . . E MVSSĒD . .

John del Boythe, *of Wytwelle.*
See GUILL. DE GRESYER.

John Bozoun, *of Exeter, co. Dev.*
7713. [A.D. 1366.]   Red: fine; chipped a little at top.
⅞ in.   [Harl. ch. 46 F. 33.]

A shield of arms : three bird-bolts, BOZUN. Within a finely-carved and traced gothic rosette of sixteen points.

   ✿ SIGILLVM I:I IOHANNIS I:I BOZON I:I
7714. Sulph. cast from No. 7713. [D.C., F. 452.]

Roger de Brabazone.
7715. [Late 13th or early 14th cent.]   Plaster cast from imperfect impression.   1 in. [lxxxiii. 89.]
A shield of arms : on a bend three martlets, BRABAZON.

   ✿ . . . . **one.**

Cf. Add. ch. 6337, A.D. 1293 ; Add. ch. 16,175, A.D. 1294 ; Add. ch. 21,584, A.D. 1297 ; Add. ch. 21,701, 21,702, A.D. 1309.

Roger, *son of* William Le Brabanzon.
7716. [14th cent.]   Sulph. cast. $\frac{7}{8}$ in.   [D.C., F. 351.]
A shield of arms : on a bend three martlets, BRABAZON.

   ✿ S' · ROGI · FIL' · WILL'I · LE BRABANZON.
Beaded borders.

Thomas Brace, *of co. Herts.*
7717. [A.D. 1686.]   Red : *en placard.*   About $\frac{1}{2} \times \frac{3}{8}$ in. when perfect. [Add. ch. 26,581.]
Oval : a shield of arms, and crest, very indistinct.

John de Bracebrigge, *of Lincoln, Knt.*
7718. [Early Edw. I.]   Dark green : somewhat indistinct. $1\frac{1}{8}$ in. [Add. ch. 19,990.]
A shield of arms : *vairé* a fess, BRACEBRIDGE.

   ✠ SIGILL' : IOH'IS : DE : BRACEBRVG :
Beaded borders.

John de Bracebrug, *Lord of Kynesbure, or Kingsbury Manor, co. Warw.*
7719. [A.D. 1311.]   Red : chipped on r. h. side. $\frac{3}{4}$ in. [Cott. ch. xi. 37.]
A shield of arms : *vairé* a fess, BRACEBRIDGE. Suspended by a strap from a tree, in the branches of which is a long-eared squirrel or other animal.   Betw. two branches of foliage.

   . . . . Ȳ : SAVN : GYL'.
Beaded borders.

William Brad.
Seal used by WILLIAM DE FELMYNGHAM, *co. Norf.*
7720. [A.D. 1346.]   Green : fine. $\frac{7}{8}$ in. [Add. ch. 22,565.]

A shield of arms : on a fess betw. six martlets three fleurs-de-lis. Within a carved and pointed gothic quatrefoil.

    ⚹ SIGILLVM WILLELMI BRAD.

At the end of the legend a small bird.

Roger de Bradburne, *of Ashbourne, co. Derb.*

7721. [A.D. 1392.] Red : originally fine, injured in places by pressure. 1 in. [Wol. ch. xi. 31.]

A shield of arms : on a bend cotised three mullets. (Cf. on a bend three mullets, BRADBURNE.) Suspended by a strap from a tree, and within a carved gothic panel.

    𝖘𝖎𝖌𝖎𝖑𝖑𝖚 : 𝖗𝖔𝖌𝖊𝖗𝖎 : 𝖉𝖊 : 𝖇𝖗𝖆𝖉𝖇𝖚𝖗𝖓𝖊 : ⚹

Cf. Rog. de Bradburn, of Plaistow. co. Derb., A.D. 1381, in Woll. ch. vi. 57.

7722. Plaster cast from No. 7721. [lxxxiii. 90.]
7723. Sulph. cast. from No. 7721. [D.C., F. 584.]

Geoffrey, *son of* William de Braddene, *of Thornborough, co. Buck., and Blakesley, co. Northt., Knt.*

7724. [*Temp.* Edw. II.–III.] Red : injured in places. ¾ in. [Add. ch. 19,923.]

A shield of arms : five fusils or lozenges in bend. Betw. two wyverns. Cf. a bend engrailed, BRADDENE, or BRADDEN.

    ⚹ S' GALFRIDI · DE · BRADDENE.

Beaded border.

Cf. Add. ch. 21,856, Geoffrey de Braddene, of Easton-Neston, co. Northt., A.D. 1301 ; Add. ch. 21,857, A.D. 1308.

John de Bradefeld, *son of* ROBERT DE BRADEFELD, *of Stanningfield, co. Suff.*

7725. [A D. 1329.] Green, mottled : indistinct, chipped. ⅞ in. [Add. ch. 24,655.]

A circular shield of arms : per pale, *dex.*, three crescents ; *sin.*, crusily two bird-bolts palewise in fess, over all a fess.

In place of a legend, a wavy garland of flowers.

7726. [A.D. 1329.] Green, mottled : indistinct. [Add. ch. 24,656.]

Thomas de Bradeford.

7727. [A.D. 1366.] Plaster cast from fine but chipped impression. 1⅚ in. [lxxxiii. 91.]

A shield of arms, *couché* : a cross engrailed, BRADFORD.

    2 N 2

Crest on a helmet and short mantling diapered, a wolf's head (?) Betw. two wavy sprigs of foliage and small cinquefoil flowers.

$ . . . . brabeford.

Beaded borders.

Roger, *fil.* D. HENR. de **Bradeleghe,** *Lord of La Bache and of Thonglande,* [*co. Salop.*], *Knt.*

7728. [Late 13th cent.] Dark green : somewhat indistinct. ⅞ in. [Add. ch. 8330.]

A shield of arms : a fess betw. three round buckles. Above the shield a crescent, at each side a small fleur-de-lis.

⁜ S' ROGERI D' BRADELEYE.

Beaded borders.

7729. [Late 13th cent.] Another : indistinct. [Add. ch. 8332.]

Robert de Bradenham, *of Nottingham, co. Nott.*

7730. [A.D. 1364.] Red : chipped, imperfectly impressed in places. ⅞ in. [Harl. ch. 83 E. 35.]

A shield of arms : a chief barry nebuly of four. Suspended by a strap from a forked tree, and within a carved gothic panel.

· SIGILL' · ROBERTI · BRADENHAM.

7731. Sulph. cast from No. 7730. [D.C., F. 436.]

Mabilia de Bradesshawe.

7732. [A.D. 1376.] Plaster cast from indistinct impression. 1¾/16 in. [lxxxiii. 92.]

A shield of arms : per pale : *dex.* two bends, BRADSHAW, *sin.* three bars. Suspended by a strap from a tree of three branches. Betw. two sprigs of foliage.

S' MABILIE ✸ DE ✸ BRADESSHAWE.

Beaded borders.

Thomas Bradewelle, *of London, Chev.*

7733. [A.D. 1374.] Red : originally fine, chipped at the edge. 1 in. [Add. ch. 7909.]

A shield of arms : three bars gemels in chief a canton (powdered). Betw. two leaves, slipped. Within a carved gothic panel of five cusps and three points, ornamented with ball-flowers along the inner edge.

✸ SIGILLVM : THOME : DE : BRADEVEL.

Thomas Bradshaghe, *of Windley, etc., co. Derb.*
7734. [A.D. 1431.] Red : imperfect, injured by pressure.
⅞ in. [Woll. ch. i. 85.]
A shield of arms : defaced. Suspended by a strap from a
forked tree. Within a carved gothic panel.
: S . . . .
Beaded border.

William de Brakenbery, *of Thirsk, co. York.*
7735. [A.D. 1310.] Light brown. ₁₁⁄₁₆ in. [Harl. ch. 112
G. 31.]
A shield of arms : an eagle displayed. Suspended by a
strap from a hook, betw. a crescent and an estoile of six
points.
In place of the legend, a wavy scroll of flowers and foliage.

William Brakenbury, *or* **Brakenbery,** *of Tottenham Court,*
co. Midd., Gentl., Equerry of the King's Stable.
7736. [A.D. 1552.] Red : imperfect, indistinct. About
¾ × ½ in. [Harl. ch. 76 D. 22.]
Ornamental shape : a lion couchant beneath a tree. Crest
of BRACKENBURY.
Cabled border.

Geoffrey Brampton, *of co. Norf , Gentl.*
7737. [A.D. 1569.] Red : good. ¾ × ⅝ in. [Stowe ch.
178.]
Oval : a shield of arms : a saltire betw. four crosses
crosslet fitchées, BRAMPTON.
Beaded border.

Robert Brampton, *Lord of Brampton Manor,*
co. Norf.
7738. [A.D. 1479.] Red : a fragment. [Stowe ch. 180.]
Octagonal signet : a shield of arms : a saltire, etc., for
BRAMPTON.

Thomas, *son and heir of* **Robert Brampton,**
Lord of Brampton Manor, co. Norf.
7739. [A.D. 1479.] Red : from a ring. ½ in. [Stowe
ch. 180.]
A shield of arms, *couché* : a saltire betw. four crosses
crosslets fitchées, BRAMPTON. Crest not given, the shield
surmounted with a helmet and mantling.
Cabled border.

Jone, *daughter of* **John Bramschote,** *of cos. Camb. and Leic.*
7740. [A.D. 1391.] Red: fine, chipped. Originally encircled with a twisted rush. ¾ in. [Add. ch. 29,511.]
A shield of arms: a fess, in *dexter* chief a crescent, in *sinister* chief a canton. For BRAMSHOTT, and BREMSHETT: usually blazoned, a fess on a canton or crescent. Betw. the letters:—

B ⚜ R ⚜ E ⚜ M ⚜

Within a carved and pointed gothic quatrefoil panel, ornamented along the inner edge with small ball-flowers or quatrefoils.
Legend wanting.

John Bramston, or Brampstone,
Knt., Lord Chief Justice of the King's Bench.

7741. [A.D. 1634.] Red: injured by pressure. About ¾ × ⅝ in. [Egert. ch. 305.]
Oval: a shield of arms: on a fess three plates, BRAMSTON.

William Bramstoon, or Bramston, of Boreham,
co. Essex, Gentl.

7742. [A.D. 1614.] Red. ⁹⁄₁₀ × ½ in. [Harl. ch. 78 I. 33.]
A shield of arms: on a fess three plates, within a bordure engrailed, BRAMSTON.
Beaded border.

Peter Branch, of Oxford, Knt.

7743. [A.D. 1258.] Dark green: a fragment. About 1¼ in. when perfect. [Harl. ch. 47 A. 43.]
A shield of arms of early shape: ermine, fretty, BRANCH.
Legend wanting.
Cf. Add. ch. 14,676, A.D. 1244-8.

Robert Brand.

7744. [A.D. 1370.] Plaster cast from indistinct impression. ¹⁵⁄₁₆ in. [lxxxiii. 92.]
A shield of arms: crusily a lion rampant. Betw. a slipped flower above the shield and two pairs of slipped flowers at the sides. Within a carved panel of eight cusped points ornamented along the inner edge with small quatrefoils.

✠ SIGILLVM · ROBERTI · · · · · · · · ·
A doubtful seal.

Charles Brandon, 1st Duke of Suffolk, etc., K.G.
A.D. 1514-1545.

7745. [A.D. 1514.] Plaster cast from fine but very imperfect impression. 2⅜ in. [lxxxiii. 94.]

On a mount, a shield of arms: quarterly, 1, 4, barry of ten, over all a lion rampant queue fourchée, crowned, BRANDON; 2, 3, quarterly, i. iv., a cross moline, BRUYN; ii. iii., indistinct, for lozengy, ROKELEY. Encircled with a garter inscribed with the motto of the Order of the Garter, crest and helmet broken away. Supporters, *dexter*, wanting; *sinister*, an eagle or falcon rising, wings open depressed, in the right claw a small bird.

.... BRANDON · DVX · SVFFOLCHIE.
INCLIT ....

7746. [A.D. 1514.] Plaster cast from indistinct impression, wanting at the lower part. [lxxxvii. 30.]

This shows the *dexter* supporter, similar to the *sinister* supporter described above, and the crest: on a helmet mantling, and wreath, a lion's head erased gouttée, crowned.

KAROLVS · BRANDON · DVX .... ERY · MILES · RC̃.

7747. [A.D. 1527.] Red: fragments. About 1½ to 2 in. when perfect. [Harl. ch. 43 F. 23.]

This fragmentary impression shows only the crest, viz.: on a wreath a lion's head erased.

Another seal.

7748. [A.D. 1538.] Faded red: very indistinct. $\frac{9}{16}$ in. [Harl. ch. 55 H. 43.]

A shield of arms: defaced.

Henry Brandon, *2nd Duke of Suffolk.*
Exchequer seal.

7749. [A.D. 1545–1551.] Plaster cast from imperfect impression. 2½ in. [lxxxiii. 95.]

On a mount, a lion passant. Ensigned with an open coronet of five fleurs-de-lis and four crosses alternately disposed. Within an engrailed bordure.

✠ **Sig'** **scctĩ · ḧ̃ericĩ .. p ... De ....**

.... z y ....(?)

Very doubtful.

John, *son of* **John de Brangwen,**
" liber homo de curia de Grosmund," co. Monm.

7750. [A.D. 1249–1250.] Green: fine, chipped. 1 in. [Add. ch. 20,414.]

A shield of arms: a lion rampant contourné, within a bordure charged with six escallops. In the field on the r. a crescent, on the l. an estoile.

·✠ S' IOHANNIS : FILII : IOHANNIS.

Beaded borders.

Lawrence de Brastrete,
of Oteleye, and of Helmingham, co. Suff.

7751. [A.D. 1347.] Red: imperfect. About ⅞ in. when perfect. [Add. ch. 9,992.]

A shield of arms: a chevron betw. two estoiles in chief and a crescent in base. Above the shield a crook or other indistinct device. Within a pointed quatrefoil.

. . . . I · DE · GVR'. . . . . . (?)

Philip Braunche.

7752. [14th cent.] Sulph. cast. 1 in. [D.C., F. 352.]

A shield of arms: a lion rampant, oppressed with a bend, BRANCH. Suspended by a strap from a forked tree, and within an engrailed border.

𝔖igillum :· 𝔓hilippi :· 𝔅raunche :

Cabled borders.

Gilbert de Braye, *Citizen of London.*

7753. [A.D. 1324.] Red. ¾ in· [Harl. ch. 47 A. 56.]

An ass passant. Perhaps in allusion to the name of the owner.

⚜ S' GILBERTI · D' · BRAY.

Henry Bray, *of Laughton, co. Suss.*

7754. [A.D. 1396.] Red: very imperfect. 1⅛ in. [Add. ch. 30,357.]

A shield of arms, *couché*: a chevron betw. three roundles, within a bordure engrailed, BRAY. Crest, on a helmet, an old man's head in profile, bearded, filleted, and with a head-dress ornamented with roundles. On the l. in the field five cinquefoil roses. Within a carved gothic panel.

. . . . enrici : bra . . .

John Le Bray.
Used by Peter Bray, of co. Suff.

7755. [A.D. 1368.] Light brown, discoloured: indistinct. ⅞ in. [Harl. ch. 47 B. 2.]

A shield of arms: a fess betw. three chess-rooks (?) Within a carved gothic trefoil.

SIGILLV̄ · IOHANIS · LEBRAY.

Beaded borders.

Johanna, *filia* Walteri Le Bray.
See NICHOLAS DE LECHEFORD.

Reginald Bray, *Justice in Eyre.*
See GILES DAWBNEY, *Justice in Eyre.*

William de Bray.
7756. [A.D. 1285.]   Plaster cast from fine impression. 1⅛ × ⅞ in. [lxxxiii. 97.]

Lozenge-shaped: a shield of arms: three bends *vair*, BRAY. The shield on the breast of a demi-angel, with wing open and depressed.

✠ S' · WILLELMI : DE : BRAY.

Beaded borders.

Gerard de Braybrok, *of Ickleford, co. Herts.*
7757. [A.D. 1334.]   Creamy-white, discoloured.   ⅞ in. [Harl. ch. 47 B. 9.]

A shield of arms: seven mascles, three, three, and one, BRAYBROKE. Within a carved and pointed gothic trefoil.

✠ S' · GERARDI + DE + BRAYBROK ✠

7758. Sulph. cast from No. 7757. [D.C., F. 250.]

Cf. Add. ch. 15,434, A.D. 1341 ; 15,473, A.D. 1342.

Gerard Braybroke, *of Castle Ashby Manor, co. Northt.*
7759. [A.D. 1392.]   Red: fine, imperfect.   1 in. [Harl. ch. 47 B. 11.]

A shield of arms: per pale, *dex.*, seven mascles, three, three, and one, BRAYBROKE, as in No. 7757, with a label of three points in chief over all; *sin.*, a fess indented betw. six crosses crosslet, LEDET. Within an elegantly-designed curvilinear hexagon with tracery at the points.

Legend betw. the points:—

·|· s ·|· 𝕮erarⅅy braỉbrok.

Cabled border.

Cf. Bridges, *Hist. of Northamptonsh.*, vol. ii., p. 10.

7760. Sulph. cast. from No. 7759. [D.C., F. 582.]

7761. [A.D. 1396.]   Red: injured, imperfect. [Add. ch. 30,357.]

·|· s ·|· 𝕮erar . . braỉ . . . .

Gerard Braybroke, *of cos. Oxon. and Bucks.*
7762. [A.D. 1421.]   Red: fine.   1¾ in. [Add. ch. 20,288.]

A shield of arms: seven mascles, three, three, and one, BRAYBROKE. Suspended by a strap from a forked tree standing on a mount, within a carved gothic panel.   In the field above the shield two cinquefoil roses.

𝕾igillũ : gerarðí ᴍ:ᴀ brapbrok ᴀ✳ ✳ᴍ.

Beaded border.

7763. Plaster cast from fine but imperfect impression. [lxxxiii. 98.]

Legend broken away.

Johanna, wife of REGINALD Braybroke.
See JOHANNA HEMENHALE.

John de Braybroke, *of Colmorde, or Colmworth Manor, co. Bedf.*

7764. [A.D. 1289.]   Dark green, mottled: fine, edge chipped.   ⅞ in.   [Harl. ch. 47 B. 6.]

A shield of arms: six lozenges (for mascles), three, two, and one, for BRAYBROKE.   Suspended by a strap from the top of the background.

✵ S'. IOH'IS DE BRAIBROK'.

Beaded borders.

Cf. Harl. ch. 55 D. 30 c, A.D. 1272; 55 D. 29, A.D. 1273; 47 B. 4, A.D. 1276; 47 B. 6, A.D. 1289; 47 B. 5, *temp.* Edw. I.; and Add. ch. 15,431, A.D. 1293.

7765. Sulph. cast from No. 7764.   [D.C., E. 419.]

Reginald Braybrook, of co. Suff., Chev.

7766. [A.D. 1403.]   Red: originally fine, now very imperfect.   About ⅞ in. when perfect.   [Harl. ch. 47 B. 15.]

A shield of arms: seven mascles, three, three, and one, BRAYBROKE.   On the r. side the branches of a tree [on which the shield appears to be placed.]

. . . . eginalðí . . . .

Cf. Harl. ch. 47 B. 11, A.D. 1392; 47 B. 12, 13, A.D. 1398; Add. ch. 15,501, A.D. 1403; and Harl. ch. 46 E. 42, 43, A.D. 1409.

7767. Sulph. cast from No. 7766.   [D.C., G. 96.]

Henry Brayne, of London, Esq.

7768. [A.D. 1547.]   Red.   ⅝ in.   [Add. ch. 26,495.]

Shield-shaped: a shield of arms: on a chevron betw. two stags' heads erased in chief, and a hunting dog in base, three pierced mullets.   Cf. arms of LETFORD, co. Glouc., on a chevron betw. in chief two bucks' heads erased and in base a talbot passant, three mullets.   Cf. also arms of KELFORD and KETFORD, which are very much the same.

Cf. Add. ch. 7710, 7711, 7712, A.D. 1542, 1545.

Hugh de Braytofte, *of Westirkel,* [*co. Linc.*]

7769. [A.D. 1377.]   Red: chipped at the bottom. $\frac{7}{8}$ in. [Egert. ch. 464.]

A shield of arms, *couché*: an estoile of six points wavy, within an orle of six crosses pattées.   Crest on a helmet and lambrequin or short mantling, a lion's head erased.   Within a carved gothic panel, ornamented with quatrefoils along the inner edge.

S' HVGONI : DE : BRAITOFT.

John Braz, *of Wyke, co. Dors.*

7770. [A.D. 1417.]   Plaster cast from good impression. $\frac{7}{8}$ in.   [lxxxiii. 99.]

A shield of arms : a bend betw. two dexter hand and arms couped (*bras*).   Within a pointed gothic trefoil panel.

Sigill' iohanis ✳ braʒ ✳

Ralph Bre . . . .

7771. [14th cent.]   Recent impression in red sealing-wax from an indistinct mould derived from an original impression. $1\frac{1}{4}$ in.   [xlix. 85.]

A shield of arms : ermine three bugle-horns stringed, two and one.   Suspended by a strap from a forked tree on a mount.   Within a carved gothic panel.   Cf. arms of HAMMON and JEPHSON.

Sigillum · radulphi · bre . . . .

Carved border.

William Bregge, *or* **Brugge,** *Rector of Syresham, co. Northt.*

7772. [A.D. 1389.]   Dark green: cracked. $\frac{7}{8}$ in.   [Add. ch. 84 F. 8.]

A shield of arms : a cross, BRUGGES.   Legend in mixed Roman and Gothic letters :—W ❀ brVGGE.

Adam Brekespere, *of London, Chaplain.*

7773. [A.D. 1408.]   Red: fragmentary. $\frac{3}{4}$ in.   [Harl. ch. 47 B. 29.]

A shield of arms : per pale, *dex.*, a bend cotised ; *sin.*, barry of six, over all a chevron.   Cf. the arms of ESTOUTE-VILLE, barry of eight, ten, or twelve, over all a lion rampant.

S' H . . . . ESTOVTEV . .

Pelice de Brekyndone.

Seal used by THOMAS WARDE, *Rector of Catworth, co. Hunt.*

7774. [A.D. 1399.] Red : indistinct, chipped. $\frac{15}{16}$ in. [Add. ch. 34,071.]

A shield of arms : uncertain.

Suspended by a strap from a hook. Betw. two sprigs of foliage.

✠ S' PELICE DE BREKYNDONE.

Beaded border.

Laurence de Brenlee, *of co. Kent, Knt.*

7775. [A.D. 1365.] Dark green : originally fine, now very imperfect. [Harl. ch. 47 B. 32.]

A shield of arms, *couché* : a griffin segreant, BRENLY. Crest on a helmet, out of a ducal coronet a griffin's head and wings. Within a carved gothic panel. .

S' LAVRENCI . . . . ENLEE.

7776. Sulph. cast from No. 7775. [D.C., F. 441.]

Anne [Brente], *Lady Powlette, wife of* THOMAS, *Lord Poulet.*

7777. [A.D. 1576.] Red : from a ring. $\frac{1}{4}$ in. [Add. ch. 15,107.)

A wyvern : from the arms of BRENT. Betw. the initial letters A. P.

Cabled border.

Sir William Brereton, *of co. Ches., Knt.*

7778. [A.D. 1589.] Light brown, or uncoloured : much injured by pressure. About $\frac{3}{4}$ in. when perfect. [Add. ch. 8489.]

Oval : a shield of arms of seven quarterings, four in chief and three in base : 1, two bars, BRERETON ; 2, three pheons, MALPAS of Cheshire ; 3, a cross flory ; 4, erm. a lion rampant ; 5, two birds (Cornish choughs ?) in pale ; 6, six chevronels and a canton, thereon a lion passant ; 7, two lions passant in pale, in chief a label of three points. Crest, etc., defaced.

Cf. Harl. MS. 1535, f. 69.

John Le Bret, *Rector of Adderley, co. Salop ; or* RICHARD DE ADEKINS, *Chaplain, of co. Ches.*

7779. [A.D. 1400.] Red : originally encircled by a twisted rush (now wanting), which has injured the legend. $\frac{7}{8}$ in. [L. F., C. xxviii. 10.]

A shield of arms: ermine, on a canton a pike-head or bird-bolt. Betw. two pairs of roses slipped, and within a carved gothic rosette of eight points.

¤ PRIVE · SVY Є PVR LЄL CONV.

John de Bretagne, *8th Earl of Richmond, Duke of Bretagne.*
7780. [A.D. 1325.] Plaster cast from chipped impression. I in. [lxxxv. 54.]
A shield of arms: chequy, a bordure of lions passant, and a canton ermine. Within a pointed gothic trefoil.

S' IOH'I . . . . . . RITANIЄ COMITIS RICH . . . . . DIЄ.

Adam Br(e)tel ?
7781. [13th cent.] Plaster cast from fine impression. 2⅛ in. [lxxxiii. 36.]
A shield of arms of early shape: lozengy, a barrulet.

🌼 SIGILLVM · DOMINI · ADAM · BRTEL.

Perhaps a foreign seal.

James Brethenham, *of Gorleston, co. Suff.*
7782. [A.D. 1429.] Red: imperfect, indistinct. ¾ in. [Stowe ch. 211.]
A shield of arms: three escallops, two and one, within a bordure. Within a carved and traced gothic panel.

Elizabeth, *dau. and heir of* THOMAS **Le Breton.**
See JOHN DE PIERRE . . . NT.

John Le Breton, *Lord of Sporle, co. Norf.*
7783. [A.D. 1301.] Plaster cast from fine impression. 11/16 in. [lxxxiii. 100.]
A shield of arms: quarterly, a bordure, LE BRETON. Suspended by a strap from a hook.

ᴙ ❀ ❀ A ❀ TVZ ᴙ ᴙ SALVZ ᴙ

Beaded borders.

Cf. Nicholas, *Synopsis of the Peerage*, p. 771.

Robert Le Breton, *Lord of Walton, co. Derb.*
7784. [A.D. 1347.] Red: injured by pressure. I in. [Harl. ch. 112 G. 37.]
A shield of arms: a chevron betw. three escallops, BRETON. Betw. three pairs of oak leaves slipped together. Within a carved and pointed gothic quatrefoil.

¤ SIGILLVM : ROBERTI : BRETOVN.

7785. Sulph. cast from No. 7784. [D.C., F. 297.]

Sir **Robert Brett,** *of St. Martin-in-the Fields, co. Midd., Knt.*
7786. [A.D.. 1608.] Red: fine. ⅞ × ⅝ in. [Harl. ch. 77 C. 46.]
A shield of arms: a lion rampant betw. nine crosses crosslet fitchées, BRETT.
Beaded border.
7787. Sulph. cast from No. 7786. [D.C., H. 135.]

Johanna Le Breeus.
Seal used by JOHN, *son and heir of* M. JOHN DE BREOUSE,
of Boyton Manor, co. Wilts.
7788. [A.D. 1348.] Red: fine. 1 in. [Harl. ch. 83 D. 44.]
A shield of arms: crusily a lion rampant crowned, BREOUSE or BRAOSE. Within a carved gothic rosette of six cusps, ornamented with ball-flowers along the inner edge. The rosette is inscribed in a triangle with three small circular panels, filled with tracery, in the angles. Outside the triangle, on each side, a circular panel charged with a roundle, bearing the following arms: barry nebuly of six. Each of the circular panels has a smaller one on each side of it.
✠ SIGILL' IOHANNE LE BREEVS.
7789. Sulph. cast from No. 7788. [D.C., F. 301.]
7790. Plaster cast. [lxxxiv. 16.]

Johanna Le Brewse.
Used by RICHARD LE BREWESE, *of co. Suff., Chev.*
7791. [A.D. 1356.] Red: injured, indistinct. ⅞ in. [Add. ch. 10,009.]
A lozenge-shaped shield of arms: a lion rampant queue fourchée, BREWSE (?) Within a gothic quatrefoil.
Legend betw. the points :—
S' IOH'E L' BREWSE.

John de Brewose, *of Hasketon Manor,* [*co. Suff.*] *Knt.*
7792. [A.D. 1335.] Red: fine. ⅞ in. [Add. ch. 22,578.]
A shield of arms: semé of quatrefoils a lion rampant queue fourchée. Betw. three cinquefoil roses, slipped. Within a pointed gothic quatrefoil ornamented with ball-flowers along the inner edge.
✠ : S' · IOHANNIS : DE : BREVSE :
Beaded border.

John de Brewouse, *Lord of Buckingham, Knt.*
7793. [A.D. 1335.] Creamy-white: imperfect, indistinct. ⅞ in. [Harl. ch. 47 B. 50.]

A shield of arms, very indistinct: a lion rampant, BREWOSE. Within a carved gothic panel.

SIG. RO . . . . . . V . . . .

Cf. Harl. ch. 57 E. 35, A D. 1338.

William de Breouse, *Lord of the Honours of Brember, co. Suss., and Gower, co. Glamorg.*

7794. [A.D. 1301.] Plaster cast from indistinct impression. 2¾ in. [lxxxiv. 13, 14.]

∅. A shield of arms: crusily, a lion rampant, for BRAOSE or BREOWSE. Suspended by a strap from a tree of three branches. Betw. two wavy trees.

+ S. WILL'I · DE · BREOVSE · DN'I · HONOR' · DE · BREMBR' ⁊ DE · GOER'.

Beaded borders.

℞. A small oval counterseal. 1 × ¾ in. A lion passant, to the r. h., in combat with a wyvern. Overhead a flying eagle, in base a cross moline.

Another seal.

7795. [A.D. 1322–1326.] Green, mottled: fine. 1¹⁄₁₆ in. [Harl. ch. 56 D. 28.]

A lozenge-shaped shield of arms: semé of crosslets, a lion rampant, BRAOSE. Field or background diapered with hatched lines, on which are four small estoiles.

⚹ S' WILLELMI · DE · BREAVSSE.

7796. [A.D. 1319.] Red: originally fine, edge chipped. [Harl. ch. 47 B. 49.]

⚹ S' . . . . ELMI · DE · BREAVSSE.

7797. [A.D. 1324.] Green, mottled: originally very fine, edge chipped. [Harl. ch. 47 B. 30.]

⚹ S' WILLELMI · DE · BREAVSSE.

7798. Sulph. cast from No. 7795. [D.C., F. 215.]

7799. Plaster cast. [lxxxiv. 15.]

William Brian, *of co. Norf.*

7800: [A.D. 1350.] Pale green: indistinct, chipped. ⅞ in. [Add. ch. 14,862.]

A shield of arms: a fess betw. three boars' heads couped.

S' WILL'I . . . RYAN.

Cf. Blomefield, *Hist. Norf.*, vol. vi., p. 359.

John Briggs.

See GEORGE WESTLEY.

William Brightwell, *of co. Oxon., Clerk.*
7801. [A.D. 1409.] Red. $\frac{5}{8}$ in. [Harl. ch. 47 C. 4.]
A shield of arms : a chevron betw. three slipped quatrefoils. Within a carved and pointed gothic trefoil.
In place of the legend, a wavy scroll of flowers and foliage.

John Briseworth, *son of* JAMES BRISEWORTH, *of Thornham Magna, co. Suff.*
7802. [A.D. 1386.] Red : imperfect on r. h. side. $\frac{7}{8}$ in. [Harl. ch. 47 B. 22.]
A shield of arms : a lion rampant contourné, oppressed by a bend.

✠ **Si . . . . . . annis . . . .**

John Brisko.
Seal used by Dame MAWDLEN, *wife of Sir* ANTHONY BROWN, *Viscount Mountague, K.G., and dau. of* WILLIAM, *Lord Dacres of Gillesland.*
7803. [A.D. 1572.] Red : cracked. $\frac{3}{4} \times \frac{9}{16}$ in. [Harl. ch. 77 H. 37.]
Oval : a shield of arms : quarterly, 1, 4, three greyhounds courant in pale, BRISKO ; 2, 3, on a fess betw. three fleurs-de-lis, a rose or cinquefoil. In the field over the shield the initial letters I. B.
Cf. MS. Harl. 1536, f. 9*b*.

Edward Britton.
See J. AUSTEN.

William de Briv . . .
See JOHANNA LE GENT.

Hugh de Broc, *of Berkhampstead, co. Hertf.*
7804. [*Temp.* Edw. I.] Dark green : a fragment. [Harl. ch. 46 F. 48.]
A shield of arms : charges broken off.
✠ S' H . . . . ROK.
Beaded border.
Cf. Harl. ch. 50 G. 37, A.D. 1277.
7805. [A.D. 1387.] Red : fragments only, of the crest and gothic tracery. [Harl. ch. 47 C. 15.]

Bernard Brocas, *of Little Weldon, co. Northt., etc., Knt.*

7806. [A.D. 1390.] Red: originally fine, now imperfect edge and wanting on r. h. side. About 1¼ in. when perfect. [Harl. ch. 47 C. 16.]

A shield of arms, *couché*: a lion rampant guardant, BROCAS. Crest on a helmet, and short mantling, a Moor's head couped at the shoulders, radiated as the sun. In the field on either side a flowering branch. Within a gothic panel, ornamented with small ball-flowers along the inner edge.

. . . . **brocas : milit'.**

Cabled border.

Cf. Add. ch. 26,559, A.D. 1358; 24,698, 24,700, 24,701, A.D. 1385, 1394, etc.

7807. Sulph. cast from No. 7806. [D.C., F. 574.]

Bernard Brokeys, *of Little Weldon, co. Northt., Knt.*

7808. [A.D. 1397.] Red: fine, perhaps from a ring. ⅜ in. [Add. ch. 856.]

On a helmet and short mantling a head, or other crest, somewhat obscure. Betw. the initial letters **b. b.**

Cabled border.

Cf. Bernard, son of Bernard Brocas, A.D. 1390, Harl. ch. 47 C. 16.

William Brocas, *of Froyle, co. Southt., etc., Esq.*

7809. [A.D. 1430.] Red. About ½ × ⅜ in. [Add. ch. 17,599.]

Octagonal: on a helmet, short mantling and wreath, a Moor's head couped at the shoulders, radiated as the sun, crest of BROCAS. Betw. the initial letters **w. b.**

Cabled border.

7810. [A.D. 1432.] Red: cracked and indistinct. [Harl. ch. 52. G. 9.]

See also Add. ch. 1534, A.D. 1430.

Will. Atte Brooke.
See ROGER DARCK.

Elizabeth Broket, *Widow, of Merston Manor, co. Kent.*

7811. [A.D. 1478.] Red: originally encircled with a twisted rush. ½ in. [Harl. ch. 47 C. 39.]

On a helmet and mantling a brocket or young deer, lodged, perhaps a badger. Crest of BROCKET.

Isabella Brokett, *dau. of* EDWARD BROKETT,
late of Whethampstead, co. Hertf.

7812. [A.D. 1609.] Red: imperfect, injured by pressure. About ⅞ × ¾ in. [Harl. ch. 112 A. 21.]

Oval: a shield of arms of nine quarterings: 1, a cross patonce, BROCKET, or BROKET; 2, a saltire, NEVILLE; 3, FAUCONBRIDGE; 4, HAREWOOD; 5, THORPE; 6, ASHE; 7, FITZ-SYMONS; 8, BENSTED; 9, CROMWELL.

Cf. Harl. MSS. 1504, f. 11; 1546, f. 63.

John Brokett.
Seal used by ROBERT *and* NICHOLAS SMITHE, *of Thuringe, co. Northt.*

7813. [A.D. 1577.] Brown: imperfectly impressed. About ⅞ × 1 in. [Add. ch. 705.]

Oval: a shield of arms: quarterly, 1, a cross patonce, BROCKET; 2, a saltire, NEVILL, or NEVELL; 3, a fess humettée betw. two lions passant guardant, HARWOOD; 4, a lion rampant, CABIGNER; over all a crescent for difference. Crest on a helmet, ornamental mantling and wreath, a stag lodged, ducally gorged, BROCKET.

Carved border.

Cf. Harl. MS. 1546, f. 63.

Seal used by ROBERT BYWORTH, *of Thuringe, cos. Northt. and Hunt., Husbandman.*

7814. [A.D. 1577.] Red: imperfectly impressed. [Add. ch. 705.]

A shield of arms: quarterly: the 2nd quarter only remains. Mantling, etc. as above.

John Brockett, *of Hatfield, co. Hertf.*
7815. [A.D. 1578.] Red: indistinct. ⅜ × ¾ in. [Add. ch. 35,512.]

Oval: a shield of arms: quarterly: 1, a cross patonce, BROCKETT; 2, a saltire, NEVILL; 3, 4, indistinct. Crest on a helmet and mantling uncertain.

7816. [A.D. 1578.] Another. [Add. ch. 35,513.]

Thomas Brokhull.
7817. [A.D. 1380.] Red: fine, from a ring. ¼ in. [Harl. ch. 48 E. 35.]

A *brock* or badger, on a mount or *hull*, in allusion to the name of the above. In the field the letters: **s'. t. b.**

Edward Brooke, *4th Baron Cobham.* A.D. 1445–1464.
7818. [A.D. 1449.] Red: fragmentary, originally fine. About 1¼ in. when perfect. [Harl. ch. 46 H. 25.]

[A shield of arms: wanting.] Crest on a helmet and

ornamental mantling, a Saracen's head in profile to the r.
wearing a turban. Supporters, two lions rampant.

Legend on a liston or scroll running round the seal :—

Sigillu . . . . ham.

John Broke, *of Stisted, co. Essex.*

·7819. [A.D. 1389.] Brownish-green. ⅞ in. [Harl. ch.
46 G. 19.]

A shield of arms : an eaglé rising. Betw. three wavy sprigs
of foliage and flowers.

✠ Sigillum ✤:✤ iohannis ✤:✤ broke. ✤

Nicholas Brooke, *of co. Wilts, Gentl.*

7820. [A.D. 1568.] Red. ¼ × ⅝ in. [Add. ch. 5710.]

On a wreath, a brock or badger passant, crest of BROKE.

❀ NVLLA   MOTVS   FORTVNA.

With two escallops for stops.

Thomas Broke, *of Holditch, co. Devon, etc.*

7821. [A.D. 1356.] Red : a fragment. About 1 in. when
perfect. [Harl. ch. 46 G. 12.]

A shield of arms : a chevron, etc. Within a carved gothic
panel.

Legend wanting.

Thomas de Brook, *Lord of Holditch, co. Devon.*

7822. [A.D. 1362.] Red : imperfect, indistinct. About
¾ in. when perfect. [Harl. ch. 46 G. 14.]

A shield of arms : a lion rampant and in chief a label of
three points. Suspended by a strap from a hook, and betw.
two wavy sprigs of foliage and flowers.

❀ S' ✤ THOME ✤ DE . . . .

Thomas Brook, *of co. Somers., Knt.*

7823. [A.D. 1415.] Red : fine. From a ring. ½ in.
[Harl. ch. 46 H. 1.]

A greyhound (or perhaps a brock ?) standing on a mount,
beneath a tree.

Motto on a liston or scroll running round the seal :—

i atens : imortalite.

Cabled border.

Johanna, *wife of* THOMAS **Brook,** *Knt.*
of co. Somers.

7824. [A.D. 1415.] Red : originally fine, now chipped at
l. h. lower corner. 1¼ in. [Harl. ch. 46 H. 1.]

A shield of, arms : per pale, *dex.*, on a chevron a lion rampant crowned, BROOKE ; *sin.*, erm. on a chief three bucks' heads cabossed. Suspended by an embroidered strap from a forked tree ; within a carved gothic panel.

𝕾 : iohanne . . . . . . ke : ⱳ

7825. Sulph. cast from an imperfect impression, or from No. 7824, before the bottom was so much broken : showing the mount on which the tree stands, and two ermine spots or slipped trefoils below the shield. [D.C., G. 148.]

Thomas Brooke, *6th Baron Cobham.* A.D. 1509–1529.
7826. [A.D. 1512.] Red. $\frac{5}{8} \times \frac{1}{4}$ in. [Harl. ch. 46 H. 42.]
On a helmet and mantling a Saracen's head wearing a cap. In the field on r. h. side the initial letter 𝕴, on l. h. side a tree. Inner border partly engrailed at the base.

Another seal.

7827. [A.D. 1528.] Red : originally fine, now very fragmentary. About $1\frac{1}{2}$ in. when perfect. [Harl. ch. 46 H. 50.]
A shield of arms : on a chevron a lion rampant [crowned], BROOKE. Crest on a helmet and mantling, on a wreath a Saracen's head. Supporters, two lions rampant.
Legend on a scroll running round the seal, wanting.

. . . . a . . . .

Cf. Harl. ch. 46 H. 25.

William de Brok, *of Haldenby, co. Northt.*
7828. [A.D. 1296.] Dark green : originally sharp, now chipped. $\frac{3}{4}$ in. [Add. ch. 21,905.]
A shield of arms : on a chief a lion passant. Betw. two sprigs of foliage.

⊞ . . WILLELMI . . . ROK' .

Beaded borders.

William de Brok.
Seal used by HUGH, *son and heir of* JOHN NOTE, *of Warwick, co. Warw.*
7829. [A.D. 1335.] Light brown : fine. $\frac{7}{8}$ in. [Cott. ch. xxviii. 21.]
A shield of arms : three mortars and pestles, two and one, BROKE. Within a carved and traced gothic trefoil.
Legend betw. the points :—

· S' · WI · ⎯ LL'I : D ⎯ Є BROK.

7830. Sulph. cast from No. 7829. [D.C., F. 252.]

William, *fil.* WILL. **Broke,** *of Thourstone,* [*co. Suff.*]
7831. [A.D. 1335.] Dark green: slipped in making the impression. ¾ in. [Harl. ch. 46 F. 54.]
A shield of arms: three castles, triple-towered, two and one. Suspended by a strap, and betw. two sprigs of foliage.
 ᴗ IE SV SEEL DE AMVR LEAL.

William de Broke; MATILDIS, *his sister;* RICHARD DE WALDEN; ALICE, *his wife; of Haldenby, co. Northt.*
[A.D. 1339.] Red: only fragments of the central part. About ¾ in. when perfect. [Add. ch. 21,917.]
7832. (1.) A shield of arms: a cross lozengy. Cf. arms of BROOKE.
 . . . . MI ✦ S . . . . . .
7833. (2.) Red: fragmentary. An acorn, slipped and leaved.
Legend wanting.

Robert de Brokesborne, *son of* D. JOHN DE BROKESBORNE, *Knt., of Misteleghe, etc., co. Essex.*
7834. [A.D. 1349.] Light brown: a fragment. About 1 in. when perfect. [Harl. ch. 47 C. 40.]
A shield of arms: [six] eagles displayed, three, two, and one. BROXBORNE and BROKESBORNE.
Legend wanting.

Henry de Brom, *of Ditchingham, co. Norf., and* IRRACLEA, *his wife.*
7835. [A.D. 1400.] Red. ⅞ in. [Add. ch. 14,641.]
A shield of arms: ermine, a chief indented, BROME.
 ✠ ș + ⸑enricuſ + brom ⸑
7836. [A.D. 1400.] Another: injured by pressure. [Add. ch. 14,641.]
7837. [A.D. 1401.] Another. [Add. ch. 14,642.]
7838. [A.D. 1401.] Another: injured by pressure. [Add. ch. 14,642.]

William Brome, *Vicar of Bakewell, co. Derb., Receiver there for the Dean and Chapter of Lichfield.*
7839. [A.D. 1428.] Dark green: indistinct, imperfectly impressed. ⅝ × ⅜ in. [Woll. ch. iii. 24.]
Oblong octagonal signet: a shield of arms: ermine, two barrulets, or a bar gemel. Over the shield the initials. ꟿ. ḅ.

Henry Bromflet, *Chevr.* [*? afterwards Baron Bromflete
of Vescy.* A.D. 1449–1468.]

7840. [A.D. 1434.] Red : originally fine, now very imperfect.
About 1¼ in. when perfect. [Harl. ch. 47 C. 44.]

A shield of arms, *couché*: quarterly, 1, a bend flory
counterflory, BROMFLET ; 2, a cross, VESCY ; 3, three bars
on a canton a cross patonce, ATON ; 4, per fess dancetty,
? ST. JOHN.   Crest on a helmet and mantling, out of a ducal
coronet [a wolf's head].   Supporters, *dex.*, a wolf, collared ;
sin., wanting.

. . . . ᴀ **bromflet** ᴀ

7841. Sulph. cast from No. 7840. [D.C., G. 196.]

Johanna, (*wife of* HENRY **Bromflet,** *Chevr., dau. of*
THOMAS HOLAND, *Earl of Kent,*
and widow of EDMUND PLANTAGENET, *Duke of York*),
Duchess of York, Countess of Cambridge.

7842. [A.D. 1434.] Red : injured by pressure, indistinct.
About 1⅞ in. [Harl. ch. 47 C. 44.]

A shield of arms : per pale, *dex.* quarterly, 1, 4, FRANCE,
(ANCIENT) 2, 3, ENGLAND ; with a label of three points
charged with illegible bearings for PLANTAGENET ; *sin.*,
HOLAND. Suspended by a strap from a tree on a mount.
Supporters, *dex.*, an eagle, *sin.*, a bear. Within a carved
border ornamented along the inner edge with small ball-
flowers.

⚜ : ioḣ'e : ꝺuciſſe : ꝫbora . . : et : comitiſſe : cantebr . .

7843. Sulph. cast from No. 7842. [D.C., G. 197.]

Henry Bromley, *son and heir apparent of*
THOMAS BROMLEY, *Knt., Lord Chancellor of England.*
7844. [A.D. 1584.] Red.   11⁄16 × ⅞ in. [Add. ch. 33,695.]
Oval: a shield of arms, *couché*: quarterly per fess indented,
in the first quarter a crescent for difference, over all a label of
three points, BROMLEY.   Crest on a helmet, ornamental
mantling and wreath, a pheasant cock.
Cabled border.

Thomas Bromley, *Esq., Solicitor General, afterw.*
Sir THOMAS BROMLEY, *Knt., Lord Chancellor of England.*
7845. [A.D. 1570.] Red : injured by pressure. ¾ × ⅝ in.
[Add. ch. 30,786.]

An ornamental shield of arms : quarterly per fess dancettée, in the *dexter* chief a crescent, BROMLEY.

Later seal of the above as Sir THOMAS BROMLEY.

7846. [A.D. 1584.]   Red. $1\frac{1}{16} \times \frac{7}{4}$ in.   [Add. ch. 33,695.]
Oval: a shield of arms: as above.   Crest on a helmet, ornamental mantling and wreath, a pheasant cock.
Cabled border.

Cecilia de Bromtone.
7847. [14th cent.]   Red: injured by pressure. $\frac{3}{4} \times \frac{5}{8}$ in. [xxxvi. 83.]
A shield of arms: two lions passant in pale.   Suspended by a strap.

⚹ S' CECILIE [DE] BROMTONE.

Beaded border.

John Broughton, *of co. Bedf.*
7848. [A.D. 1443.]   Red: from a signet ring with mark of the setting. $\frac{7}{16}$ in.   [Add. ch. 35,243.]
A talbot sejant, in reference to a crest of BROUGHTON, on a *tun*, which with the letters **brougᵺ** in the field make up a rebus on the name of the owner.
Cabled border.

Thomas de Broughton, *Lord of Broughton, co. Staff.*
7849. [A.D. 1361.]   Red: a fragment.   About $\frac{7}{8}$ in. when perfect.   [Harl. ch. 47 C. 49.]
A shield of arms: a cross engrailed, BROUGHTON.   Suspended by a strap, and within a carved and traced gothic panel.
Legend wanting.

William Brouncker, *2nd Viscount Brouncker,*
Chancellor and Keeper of the Great Seal to Qu. CATHARINE,
and President of the Royal Society.   Ob. A.D. 1684.
7850. [A.D. 1680.]   Red: very indistinct.   About $\frac{5}{8} \times \frac{1}{4}$ in. [Harl. ch. 111 H. 11.]
Oval: on a wreath a cubit arm, the crest of BROUNCKER.
The details are too indistinct to be described.

Hugh Brouwe.
7851. [A.D. 1376.]   Plaster cast from fine but chipped impression. $1\frac{3}{16}$ in.   [lxxxiv. 10.]
A shield of arms, *couché*: on a chevron three cinquefoils or roses, for BROW.   Crest on a helmet and short mantling, out of a ducal coronet a rabbit's head and neck.   Betw. two

wavy sprigs of trefoil foliage. Within a carved gothic panel
or bilobe, ornamented along the inner edge with small quatrefoils or ball-flowers.

𝔖igillū : ɧugonis : brouwe ⚜ ❀

John Broue ?

7852. [A.D. 1375.]   Plaster cast from indistinct impression.
⅞ in.   [lxxxiv. 11.]

A shield of arms : a chevron betw. three (leopards' ?) heads
erased.   Within a carved gothic panel.

[𝔖i]gillum + + ioɧannis + + broue + +

John Browe ?

7853. [A.D. 1430.]   Plaster cast from indistinct impression.
⅞ in.   [lxxxiii. 44.]

A shield of arms: diapered with sprigs, on a chevron three
cinquefoils or roses, a chief ermine, for BROW.   Suspended
by a strap from a forked tree.

𝔖igillum : ioɧannis : browe.

John Browe, *of Lyfeld,* [*co. Northt.*] *Esq.*

7854. [A.D. 1462.]   Red : injured in places by pressure.
1¾ in.   [Add. ch. 5365.]

A shield of arms, *couché* : on a chevron three roses, BROW.
Crest on a helmet, mantling, and wreath, a goat's head and
neck.   Supporters, two apes.   In background on each side a
cinquefoil flower on a wavy branch of foliage.

𝔖 + ioɧan ⚜ browe ⚜ ⚜ ⚜

Cf. Add. ch. 810, 811, A.D. 1455.

Robert Browe.

7855. [A.D. 1409.]   Plaster cast from fine impression.
1¼ in.   [lxxxiv. 9.]

A shield of arms, *couché*: on a chevron three roses, BROWE.
Crest on a helmet, short mantling and wreath, a rabbit's
head and neck.   Supporters, two wild-men.   The background replenished with sprigs of foliage, and on each side a
cinquefoil or rose of the arms.

𝔖' roberti ⚜ browe ⚜

John de Browescumbe, *of Chert Parva, co. Kent.*

7856. [A.D. 1342.]   Green, mottled : indistinct.   ⅞ × ¾ in.
[Add. ch. 16,403.]

A shield of arms: a saltire betw. four uncertain charges. Suspended by a strap from a tree. Within a cusped border.

Agnes Brown, *wife of* EDMUND BROWN, *of Capelle, [co. Suff.] and dau. of* ALEXR. OLDHAWE.

7857. [A.D. 1438.] Red: indistinct. ½ in. [Add. ch. 8385.]

Octagonal: a shield of arms (?): quarterly, 1, 4, a cross (?); 2, 3, uncertain, apparently a cup inverted, in bend sinister betw. two cotises. Above the shield two indistinct initial letters.

Sir **Anthony Browne,** *Viscount Mountague, K.G.*

A'D. 1554–1592.

7858. [A.D. 1567.] Red: originally fine, now much injured. 1⅛ in. [Harl. ch. 76 D. 51.]

An ornamentally-carved shield of arms: quarterly, 1, quarterly, i., iv., BROWNE, ii., iii., quarterly, *a.*, *d.*, MALTRAVERS, *b.*, *c.*, FITZ-ALAN, over all a cinquefoil: 2, quarterly, i., iv., NEVILLE, ii., fretty, iii., an eagle displayed: 3, quarterly, i., PLANTAGENET, ii., iii., a saltire engrailed, iv., a lion rampant crowned; 4, quarterly, i., INGLETHORP, ii., INGLETHORP (another coat-of-arms), iii., on a fess betw. three lions' faces an annulet, iv., MONTAGU. The bearings of some of the quarterings are indistinct and uncertain. Encircled by a garter inscribed with the Motto of the Order of the Garter, and ensigned with a viscount's coronet of seven pearls. Supporters, two wolves collared and chained, ducally gorged. Above each a wavy sprig of foliage. In base, on a liston, the motto:—SVIVEZ RAISON.

7859. Sulph. cast from No. 7858. [D.C., H. 115.]

Another Seal.

7860. [A.D. 1569.] Red: imperfect at bottom, indistinct. 1 × ⅞ in. [Harl. ch. 77 H. 33.]

Oval: an eagle displayed, crest of BROWNE. Encircled with a garter inscribed with the Motto of the Order of the Garter.

7861. [A.D. 1567.] Red: imperfect. [Harl. ch. 86 H. 1.]

7862. [A.D. 1569.] Red: indistinct. [Harl. ch. 111 E. 58.]

Another Seal.

7863. [A.D. 1574.] Dark red: imperfect, indistinct. ⅞ in. [Harl. ch. 76 D. 53.]

On a wreath, an eagle displayed. Crest of BROWNE. En-

circled with a garter inscribed with the Motto of the Order of
the Garter.   The seal is ensigned with a viscount's coronet.

7864. [A.D. 1578.]   Red: fine.   [Harl. ch. 77 H. 4.]

7865. [A.D. 1582.]   Red: indistinct, injured by pressure.
[Harl. ch. 77 H. 6.]

Another Seal.

7866. [A.D. 1576.]   Red: fine.   1⅛ in.   [Harl. ch. 76 D.
54.]

This seal resembles that in No. 7863, Harl. ch. 76 D. 53,
but is larger.

7867. [A.D. 1580.]   Red: imperfect.   [Harl. ch. 76 D. 55.]

Anthony **Browne,** *2nd Viscount Mountague.*
A.D. 1592–1629.

7868. [A.D. 1601.]   Red: struck doubly.   [Add. ch.
30,305.]

A shield of arms : of sixteen quarterings closely resembling
that of Anthony Browne, 1st Viscount, in No. 7858, but
in the 2nd quarterly subdivision of the 2nd grand quarter the
fretty bearing appears to have been replaced by some other
charge not now decipherable.   The shield is ensigned with a
coronet.   Crest on a helmet, ornamental mantling and wreath,
an eagle displayed.   Supporters, two wolves, collared and
chained.   In base, on a liston, the motto:— .. IS RA ....

Charles **Brown.**
See ROB. TUNSTALL.

Edmund **Browne,** *of Lavenham, co. Suff., Brewer.*
7869. [A.D. 1623.]   Red: *en placard,* the paper of the
charter being cut and folded over the seal previous to impression.   ⅘ in.   [Harl. ch. 58 F. 40.]

A shield of arms : on a bend three (eagles ?) displayed.

Francis **Browne,** *Esq., brother of Sir* ANTHONY BROWNE,
Viscount Mountague.
7870. [A.D. 1569.]   Red: ⅘ × ½ in.   [Harl. ch. 111 E. 58.]
Oval : a griffin's head erased.
Pearled border.

John **Broun,** *Citizen of Canterbury, Lord of*
Bekesbourne Manor, co. Kent.
7871. [A.D. 1405.]   Red: indistinct.   ⅘ × ½ in.   [Harl. ch.
76 D. 48.]

Oblong octagonal : a shield of arms : a chevron betw. three squirrels. Suspended by two loops or straps.

Cabled border.

Another seal.

7872. [A.D. 1416.] Red: fine. ⅜ in. [Harl. ch. 76 D. 50.]

A shield of arms, *couché* : a chevron betw. two (roses ?) in chief, and the letter s in base, within a bordure charged with eight martlets. Over the shield a triple-towered castle. In the field on each side a wavy sprig of foliage.

John Browne, *of Boston, co. Linc., Gentl.*

7873. [A.D. 1565.] Red: injured by pressure. ¾ × ⅝ in. [Harl. ch. 78 A. 16.]

Oval : a crane rising, with wings inverted, in allusion to the arms and crest of BROWNE.

Beaded border.

Thomas Broun, *of co. Cornwall.*

7874. [A.D. 1434.] Red: imperfect. From a ring. About ½ × 5/16 in. when perfect. [Harl. ch. 57 A. 35.]

A shield of arms (?) : a drake swimming in water, regardant contourné. In the field above the shield the initial letters **t. b.**

Beaded border.

John Brownyng, *al.* **Brounyng,** *Lord of Legh, near Deerhurst, co. Glouc., and of co. Dorset.*

7875. [A.D. 1412.] Red: chipped at bottom, injured by pressure. 1 in. [Slo. ch. xxxiii. 59.]

A shield of arms : three bars wavy, BROWNING. Suspended by a strap from a forked tree on a mount. Within a carved gothic panel.

𝕾𝖎𝖌𝖎𝖑𝖑' : 𝖎𝖔𝖍'𝖎𝖘 : 𝖇𝖗𝖔𝖚𝖓𝖕𝖓𝖌 ⚜

7876. Sulph. cast from No. 7875. [D.C., G. 138.]

7877. [A.D. 1415.] Another: injured by pressure. [Slo. ch. xxxiii. 60.]

𝕾𝖎𝖌𝖎𝖑𝖑' : 𝖎𝖔𝖍'𝖎𝖘 : 𝖇𝖗𝖔𝖚𝖓𝖕𝖓𝖌 ⚜

7878. Plaster cast of No. 7877. [xcviii. 41.]

Thomas de Broyk ?

7879. [? A.D. 1303.] Plaster cast from indistinct impression. 1⅛ in. [lxxxiii. 45.]

A shield of arms, *couché* : on a bend, six crosses crosslet fitchées (?) Crest on a helmet, out of a coronet an eagle's head and wings erect. Within a carved gothic pánel, having on each side a small circular panel, bearing a crowned 𝕾.

𝕾igillū ⚜ tҕome ꝺe ⚜ 𝕭roꝓk ⚜ (?)

Edmund Brudenell, *of Stoke Mandeville, co. Buck., Esq.*
7880. [A.D. 1613.] Red : fine. $\frac{7}{8} \times \frac{5}{8}$ in. [Add. ch. 24,000.]
Oval : a shield of arms : a chevron betw. three steel caps, BRUDENELL. Crest on a helmet, ornamental mantling, and wreath, an arm embowed [covered with leaves], in the hand a spiked club slung to the arm.
Beaded border.
7881. [A.D. 1613.] Red : indistinct, imperfect. [Add. ch. 24,004.]

William Bruly, *al.* **Bruyly,** *of Waterpury Manor, co. Oxon.*
7882. [A.D. 1409.] Red : fine. $\frac{7}{8}$ in. [Add. ch. 6101.]
A shield of arms : ermine, on a bend three chevrons, BRULEY or BRULY. Within a carved gothic panel of five cusps, and three points in triangle.
Legend betw. the points :—

𝕾ig'. 𝖂illelmi : bruꝓlꝓ ⚜

William de Brumle.
See HENRY DE AUDITHELEGA, No. 7016.

Alice Brun, *dau. and coheir of* RICHARD LACER, *or* LAZER ;
widow of WILLIAM BRUN, *Knt., wife of* ROBERT
DE MARNY, *of London, Knt.*
7883. [A.D. 1365.] Red : fine, sharp. $\frac{3}{4}$ in. [Cott. ch. xxvii. 55.]
A shield of arms : per pale, *dex.,* a cross moline over all in chief a label of three points, BRUN ; *sin.,* on a cross five roses, LAZER. Within a gothic trefoil ornamented with small ball-flowers along the inner edge.
Legend betw. the points :—
SIGILL' ✷ ALICIE ✷ ✷ BRVN ✷
Cf. Harl. MS. 1541, f. 9.
7884. Sulph. cast from No. 7883. [D.C., F. 443.]

Robert Brundishe, *of Chelmondeston, co. Suff.*
7885. [A.D. 1637.] Red : indistinct fragment. About $\frac{3}{4} \times \frac{1}{2}$ in. when perfect. [Add. ch. 10,161.]
Oval : a shield of arms : defaced. Over the shield a helmet.

John Brunne, *of Wyvelingham* [*Willingham, co. Cambr.*]
.⸴ **7886.** [A.D. 1397.] Red : originally fine, now chipped at
edge. 1 in. [Harl. ch. 47 D. 18.]

A shield of arms : a lion rampant. Betw. two small cinquefoil roses. Within a carved and traced gothic rosette of five
cusped points.

SIGILLVM : IOHANNIS : BRVNNE :

7887. Sulph. cast from No. 7886. [D.C., F. 602.]

Cecilia de Bruntoft.
See JOHN DE BELASISE.

Philip, *son of* ROBERT **de Bruntoft,** *of Bruntoft,* [*co. Durh.?*]
. **7888.** [13th cent.] Green : fine, sharp. 1⅛ in. [Egert.
ch. 529.]

A shield of arms : a lion rampant contourné.

✠ S'. PHILIPI : DE : BRVNTOFT.

John Bruyn, *of Bridgnorth, co. Salop.*
7889. [A.D. 1434.] Plaster cast from indistinct impression.
1¼ in. [lxxx. iv. 17.]

On a mount a shield of arms : an eagle displayed, for
BRUYN. Suspended by a strap from a tree. Within a
cusped gothic panel.

𝕾igill' : ioh'is ᴥ : bruyn :

Cf. John Le Bruyn, A.D. 1431, Add. ch. 6282.

Maurice Bruyn, *of Beckenham, co. Kent.*
7890. [A.D. 1408.] Red : injured by pressure, indistinct.
1⅛ in. [Harl. ch. 47 D. 23.]

A shield of arms, *couché* : quarterly, 1, 4, a cross cercellée,
BRUVIN ; 2, 3, six lozenges. Crest on a helmet affrontée,
mantling,· and tall hat or chapeau, a pair of wings erect.
Within a carved gothic panel.

𝕾 : mauricii : de : bruyin : ᴀᴋ

Cf. Harl. MS. 1137, f. 17 *b*.

7891. Sulph. cast from No. 7890. [D.C., G. 120.]

John Bryan, *of East Hoathley, co. Sussex.*
7892. [A.D. 1668.] Red : imperfect. ⅜ × ½ in. [Add.
ch. 30,159.]

Oval : a shield of arms : lozengy, a pale

Guy de Bryene.

7893. [A.D. 1345.]   Plaster cast from injured impression.
$1\frac{1}{16}$ in.   [lxxxiv. 18.]

A shield of arms, *couché*: three piles conjoined in base,
BRYAN, over all a label of three points.   Crest on a helmet,
short mantling and chapeau diapered, a horn.   Within a
carved gothic panel.

☒ LE • S[EAL • GV]Y • [DE •] BRYENE • ☒ •

Beaded borders.

Guy de Briene, *or* Bryene, *of Wroxhale-Deneys Manor,*
co. Dors., Knt.

7894. [A.D. 1369.]   Red: fine, sharp, slightly chipped at
edge. $1\frac{1}{4}$ in.   [Add. ch. 29,247.]

A shield of arms: three piles conjoined in base, BRYAN.
Suspended by a strap from an elaborately-carved tree springing from a mount in the base part of the annulus of the
legend.   On this mount a triple branch of foliage with three
small cinquefoil flowers.   Within a cusped gothic panel
ornamented with ball-flowers along the inner edge.

: 𝕷𝖊 : 𝕾𝖊𝖆𝖑 : 𝕲𝖚𝖞 . : 𝖉𝖊 : 𝕭𝖗𝖞𝖊𝖓𝖊 :

Beaded border.

7895.   Red: originally fine, now imperfect along the edge.
[xxxvi. 120.]

: 𝕷𝖊 : 𝕾𝖊𝖆𝖑 : 𝕲𝖚𝖞 . : 𝖉𝖊 : 𝕭𝖗𝖞 . . . :

Another Seal.

7896.   Red: originally fine and sharp, now chipped in
places. $1\frac{1}{4}$ in.   [xxxvi. 121.]

This is a very careful copy of the previous type, No. 7894.
But the foliage varies, the ball-flowers along the inner edge
of the carving are omitted; and the inside annulus or border
of the legend is beaded.

: 𝕷𝖊 : 𝕾𝖊𝖆𝖑 : 𝕲𝖚𝖞 : 𝖉𝖊 : 𝕭𝖗𝖞 [𝖊] 𝖓𝖊 :

Another Seal.

7897. [A.D. 1378.]   Light brown: originally fine, now imperfect, and r. h. side wanting.   About $1\frac{3}{8}$ in.   [Egert. ch. 253.]

Somewhat similar to the two preceding types, but with
several differences of detail.   In the field on the l. h. side a
small cinquefoil has been introduced; that on the r. h. side
broken off.

. . . . ✿ 𝕭𝖗𝖞𝖊𝖓𝖊 ✿ ᴍ ᴍ✿

Beaded border.

7898. [A.D. 1378.] Red: only small fragment of the legend. [Harl. ch. 43 G. 31.]

· · · · · · · · · · · · · **ꝑene** ❀ ᴎ ᴀᴇ · ·

7899. Sulph. cast from imperfect impression of this type. [D.C., F. 528.]

In this example the corresponding cinquefoil on the r. h. side is shown.

❀ **Le** ❀ **Seal** ❀ **Guy** ❀ **De** ❀ **Bryene** ❀ ᴎ ᴀᴇ · ·

Guy de Bryene, (*Junior ?*), *Knt.*

7900. [A.D. 1381.] Red: fine, sharp, injured at top part. $1\frac{5}{16}$ in. [Add. ch. 20,283.]

A shield of arms: three piles conjoined in base, BRYAN. Suspended by a strap from a tree on a mount. Supporters, two monsters, reguardant addorsed, each grasping the strap in its beak. The monster is composed of the head, wings and body of an eagle, coupled to the hinder part of a lion, and differs from the griffin in not having the forelegs of the eagle, and from the griffin-male which has legs but not wings.

Sigillum : guydonis : De : bryene :

The letters DO of *Guydonis* are conjoined.

Cabled border.

7901. [A.D. 1384.] Red: fine, chipped in several places. [Add. ch. 29,250.]

· · · · · · · · **guydonis : De : bryene :**

7902. [A.D. 1387.] Red: very fine. The legend injured by pressure. [Harl. ch. 47 D. 27.]

Sigillum : guydonis : De : bryene :

7903. Sulph. cast from No. 7902. [D.C., F. 530.]

7904. Sulph. cast from fine but imperfect impression. [xlvii. 1275.]

· · · · · · **m : guydo** · · · · · · · · · · **ne.**

Laing's *MS. Catal.*, No. 326.

7905. Sulph. cast from the same. [D.C., F. 529.]

William Brygges, *of Sanderstede, etc., co. Surr.*

7906. [A.D. 1439.] Red: injured by pressure, very indistinct. 1 in. [Add. ch. 24,618.]

A shield of arms: uncertain charges. Within a six-foil.

❀ S' W · · · · · · · · BR · · · · · · · (?)

Henry Brystowe.

See PAULL FOX.

John de Bucton.

7907. [14th cent.]   Red, embedded in a. mass of dark green. ⅞ in. [xxxv. 264.]

A shield of arms : a goat salient, BUCKTON. Within a carved panel of six cusped points.

✠ SIGILLVM · IOHANNIS · DE · BVCTON · ᴗ

Beaded border.

7908. [14th cent.] Plaster cast from No. 7907. [lxxxiv. 19.]

Robert Buktone, *or* Bucton, *of Newenton, co. Suffolk.*

7909. [A.D. 1403.]   Red: slightly chipped.   1 in. [Harl. ch. 53 E. 35.]

A shield of arms : three bars gemel, on a canton a crescent, BUCKTON. Suspended by a strap from a tree, and betw. two wavy sprigs of foliage.

Sigillum : roberti : buktone :

7910. [A.D. 1403.]   Red : fine, imperfect. [Harl. ch. 53 E. 36.]

Sigillum : robert . . . .

Thomas Buggs.
See J. AUSTEN.

William Bugges, *Chaplain, of co. Staff.*

7911. [A.D. 1396.] Red: indistinct in places. ⅞ in. [Stowe ch. 94.]

A shield of arms : a fleur-de-lis. Within a panel of eight points.

✠ SEEL NICHOLE DE (VNSVIC?) CHR.

William Le Buk, *of East Bergholt, co. Suff.*

7912. [A.D. 1346.]   Creamy-white : imperfect, indistinct. ⅜ in. [Add. ch. 9608.]

A shield of arms : a fret.

+ S' BO . . . . . . (?)

Cf. Add. ch. 9609, 9615.

John de Bukynham, *of West-Wittenham, co. Berks, Clerk.*

7913. [A.D. 1381.]   Red: originally fine, now chipped at lower part. 1 1/16 in. [Add. ch. 20,282.]

A shield of arms : two chevrons betw. three bucks' heads cabossed, for BUCKINGHAM (?) Above the shield the B. Virgin Mary, half length, crowned, in the r. h. the Infant Saviour, and in the left hand a sceptre or branch of foliage. Within

a carved gothic bilobe, ornamented with small quatrefoils or
ball-flowers along the inner edge.

𝕾𝖎𝖌𝖎𝖑𝖑 : 𝖎𝖔𝖍'𝖎𝖘 : 𝖉𝖊 : . . . . 𝖍𝖆 : 𝖈𝖑'𝖎𝖈𝖎.

Carved border.

7914. [A.D. 1384.] Red : originally fine, imperfect. [Add.
ch. 24,322.]

𝕾𝖎𝖌 . . . . 𝖎𝖘 : 𝖉𝖊 : 𝖇𝖚 . . . . 𝖌𝖍𝖆 : 𝖈𝖑'𝖎𝖈𝖎.

Matildis, *dau. of* NORMAN,
widow of OSBERT DE **Bulingtona,** *of co. Linc.*

7915. [13th cent.] Dark green. 1⅜ × ¾ in. [Harl. ch.
47 D. 47.]

A shield of arms of early style, diapré (?) : a bend. Indistinct. The bend appears to be charged with some fur or
other uncertain marks.

S' MATILDE · FILIE · NORMAN.

Elizabeth Bull, *of Sprowton, co. Suff.,*
widow of ANTHONY BULL.

7916. [A.D. 1629.] Red : indistinct. 9/16 × ½ in. [Add.
ch. 9790.]

Oval : on a wreath, a bull's head and neck, in the mouth
an acorn.

Cabled border.

Cf. Add. ch. 9785, A.D. 1617.

Richard Bull.
See GEORGE PERYENT.

Thomas Bull, *of Flowton, co. Suff., Gentl.*

7917. [A.D. 1629.] Red : injured by pressure. ½ in. [Add.
ch. 9790.]

A bull's head cabossed, crest of BULL.

John Bulloke, *of co. Lanc.*

7918. [A.D. 1650.] Black : *en placard.* ½ × ⅜ in. [Add.
ch. 5303.]

Oval : a shield of arms : very obscure, apparently three
griffins' heads couped, two and one.

Beaded border.

George Bulstrode, *of Wreysbury, co. Buck., Esq.,*
son and heir of EDW. BULSTRODE, *Esq.*

7919. [A.D. 1532.] Red : indistinct, with marks of the
setting. ⅝ × ½ in. [Harl. ch. 84 I. 41.]

Oval : a shield of arms : a stag's head cabossed, betw. the
attires a cross, in the mouth fesswise an acorn.

7920. [A.D. 1533.] Another. [Harl. ch. 84 I. 54.]

7921. [A.D. 1533.] Another. [Harl. ch. 84 I. 55.]

William de Burcestre.

7922. [14th cent.]   Sulph. cast.   ⅞ in.   [D.C., F. 370.]

A shield of arms : three (wolves'?) heads erased, two and one.   Within a carved gothic triangle with eight cusped points.   Cf. three lions' heads erased, BURCETRE ; and three bears' heads erased, BURCETUR.

Legend betw. the points :—

Sigill' · willelmi · de · burcestre ⚜

The letters D E conjoined.

Cf. Cott. ch. xxvii. 190, A.D. 1328 ; Cott. ch. xii. 43, A.D. 1383 ; Add. ch. 8885, A.D. 1400.

George Burden, *of London, Gentl.*

7923. [A.D. 1570.]   Red.   ¾ in.   [Harl. ch. 76 F. 45.]

A shield of arms : quarterly, in the second and third quarters three bells, two and one, over all on a bend six annulets.   The straps of the shield hang at the sides.

George Burden.
Seal used by EDMUND, *son of* WILLIAM,
son of ALEXR. FETIPLACE, *of Childrey, co. Berks.*

7924. [A.D. 1581.]   Red: injured.   About ¾ × ⅝ in. when perfect.   [Harl. ch. 78 A. 48.]

Oval : an ornamental shield of arms : quarterly, 1, 4, on a bend three bezants, BURDEN ; 2, 3, three (lozenges?) two and one.   Over the shield the initials G. B.

Beaded border.

Nicholas Burdun, *of co. Glouc., Knt.*

7925. [A.D. 1261.]   Green, mottled : a fragment.   About 1 × ⅞ in. when perfect.   [Harl. ch. 44 H. 52.]

∅. Shield-shaped : a shield of arms : five barrulets engrailed.

...... VM : NICHOL ....

℞. Pointed oval : a lady, standing on a carved corbel, wearing a long close-fitting dress, on her r. h. a falcon, her l. h. laid on the breast.

.... FORTESCVT ....

Beaded border.

Andrew de Bures, *of Raydon, co. Suff., Knt.*

7926. [A.D. 1358.]   Light brownish-white : very indistinct. ¾ in.   [Harl. ch. 47 E. 10.]

A shield of arms : quarterly.   Betw. two leaves ; suspended by a strap from a hook, and within a carved gothic quatrefoil.

.... DREE BVRE ..

Cf. Harl. ch. 47 E. 9.

Michael de Bures, *of Raydon, co. Suff.*

7927. [A.D. 1338.] Red: perhaps from a matrix with moveable legend. ⅝ in. [Harl. ch. 47 E. 9.]

A shield of arms: ermine, two lions rampant in fess, BURES. Betw. three small cinquefoil flowers slipped, and within a carved and pointed gothic quatrefoil, ornamented with small ball-flowers along the inner edge.

7928. Sulph. cast from No. 7927. [D.C., F. 269.]

Michael de Bures; MARIA, *his wife;* JOHN DE VERE, *Earl of Oxford;* or MATILDIS, *his wife.*

7929. [A.D. 1349.] Creamy-white: indistinct, edge imperfect. About ⅞ × ¾ in. when perfect. [Harl. ch. 47 E. 12.]

Oval: a shield of arms: a fess. Suspended by a strap from a hook.

Legend very obscure:—

✠ . . BON . . . . Є (?)

Robert de Bures, *of Cokefeld, etc., co. Suff., Knt.*

7930. [A.D. 1316.] Creamy-white: an indistinct fragment. About ⅝ in. when perfect. [Harl. ch. 47 E. 7.]

A shield of arms: charges uncertain.

. . . . RTI · B . . . . . .

Robert de Burgate.

See ROBERT DE BORGATE.

John Burgeys.

Seal used by JOHN ATTE THELE, *of Hontyngton,* [*Hunton, co. Kent.*]

7931. [A.D. 1370.] Red: injured by pressure, indistinct in places. ¾ in. [Add. ch. 8841.]

A shield of arms: a bird holding in its beak a long branch of foliage reflexed over its head. Within a pointed gothic quatrefoil.

✠ S' · IOH[A]NNI[S · B]VRGEYS ✠

7932. [A.D. 1370.] Red: injured by pressure, indistinct in places. [Add. ch. 8842.]

✠ S' · IOHANNIS · BVRGE . . .

Family of **Burgh, Guy,** *or* **Guise.**

7933. Plaster cast, from good impression. 1 × ⅞ in. [lxxxix. 15.]

Oval: a shield of arms: quarterly; 1, 4, seven lozenges, three, three and one, *vair.* BURGH, or GUY, or GUISE ; 2, 3, ermine, on a fess three pheons.

2 P 2

Elizabeth de Burgo, *Lady of Clare* (*ob.* A.D. 1360) ; *dau. of*
　　GILBERT DE CLARE, *Earl of Hertford, and* JOAN,
　　dau. of EDWARD I., *King of England, and* ELEANOR
　　of Castile; wife of (1) JOHN DE BURGO (*ob.* A.D. 1313) ;
　　(2) THEOBALD DE VERDON, *Lord* VERDON (*ob.* A.D. 1316) ;
　　　　　　(3) *Sir* ROGER DAMORY (*ob.* A.D. 1321.)

7934. [A.D. 1333.]　Red : very fine.　1¼ in.　[Harl. ch.
47 E. 38.]

A shield of arms : barry nebuly of six, over all a bend,
SIR ROGER DAMORY.　Betw. three lions passant guardant,
ENGLAND, in reference to her grandfather Edward I.; and
within a square panel ornamented with tracery consisting of
two interlaced quatrefoils, cusped and pointed.　Outside this
square are the lobes of two other quatrefoils ; those in cross
lancet-shaped, those in saltire segmental.　Each of the
lancet-shaped lobes contains a roundle charged with the
following heraldic bearings : 1, a cross, and label of three
points, JOHN DE BURGO ; 2, 3, three chevrons, CLARE ; 4, a
fret, THEOBALD DE VERDON.　Each of the segmental lobes
encloses a countersunk trefoil, which in turn contains a castle,
CASTILE, and a lion rampant, LEON.　The spandrils outside
all these lobes contain countersunk trefoils.

Beaded border.

7935. Sulph. cast from No. 7934.　[D.C., F. 240.]

7936. [A.D. 1331.]　Red : originally very fine, now imperfect at r. h. lower part. [Harl. ch. 47 E. 37.]

7937. [A.D. 1335.]　Red: very fine.　[Harl. ch. 47 E. 39.]

7938. [A.D. 1337.]　Red: very fine, edge imperfect.　[Harl.
ch. 47 E. 40.]

7939. [A.D. 1352.]　Red : injured, imperfect.　[Add. ch.
22,580.]

Another Seal.

7940. [A.D. 1353.]　Red: originally fine, now injured by
pressure in places and chipped at the bottom.　1¼ in.　[Top-
ham ch. 25]

A shield of arms : per pale, *dex.*, CLARE ; *sin.*, DE BURGO ;
all within a bordure guttée.　Betw. three lions guardant for
ENGLAND ; and within a lozenge-shaped panel ornamented
with small ball-flowers along the inner edge.　Outside this
lozenge are the lancet-shaped lobes of a quatrefoil, in saltire ;
each with tracery and containing a trefoil-shaped compartment in which is a bordered roundle charged with the following heraldic bearings : 1, 4, CASTILE ; 2, 3, LEON.　The
intervening spaces betw. the lobes are filled in each instance
with a roundle betw. two small circular countersunk compart-

ments, and other intermediate details of tracery. These roundles are charged with the following heraldic bearings: 1, 2 (at top and bottom), CLARE; 2, VERDON (l. h.); 3, DAMORY (r. h.).

Over the lion of ENGLAND, which is placed above the central shield, is a small ꝿ; and in the four small circular countersunk compartments, betw. which the two roundles of CLARE are placed, at top and bottom of the design, are minute letters which appear to be:—T. O. A. S., thus constituting the name of T(H)OMAS, perhaps in reference to Thomas Hessey or Thomas Raynham, goldsmiths to Edward III., 1360, 1366 (see W. Chaffers, *Gilda Aurifabrorum*, 1883, p. 31).

7941. Sulph. cast from No. 7940. [D.C., F. 239.]

7942. [A.D. 1360.] Red: very imperfect, and discoloured. [Harl. ch. 47 F. 41.]

Cf. Sandford, *Geneal. Hist.*, p. 141·

Hubert de Burgo, *King's Chamberlain.*
[Earl of Kent, A.D. 1226–1243.]
Secretum.

7943. [A.D. 1200–1215.] Creamy-white or uncoloured: originally fine, now very imperfect. About 1¼ in. when perfect. [L.F., C. xxiii. 3.]

Ø. A shield of arms: three lions passant in pale, DE BURGO.

Legend wanting.

℞. A small oval counterseal. 1 × ¾ in. Impression of an antique oval intaglio gem:—Mercury holding a caduceus, and other uncertain attributes.

⚜ . . . . LO : SECRETVM.

(*Celo secretum.*)

John de Burgo, *of Banstead, co. Surr.*

7944. [A.D. 1261.] Green, mottled: fine, much injured, imperfect. About 1 in. when perfect. [Harl. ch. 47 E. 34.]

A shield of arms: lozengy [gu. and] *vairé*, DE BURGO.

⚜ SIGIILLVM · SEICRETI MEI.

7945. Sulph. cast from No. 7944. [D.C., E. 384.]

John Burgh.

7946. [15th cent.] Red: recent impression from brass matrix. 1¼ in. [xxxv. 368.]

A shield (of arms?): a saltire humettée cantoned with an

estoile and a crescent in pale, and two small crosses crosslet in fess. Betw. three rudely-carved sprigs of foliage.

S ☸ IOHAИИES ☸ BVRGH ☸

Simon de Burghe, *of co. Hunt.*
7947. [A.D. 1372.]   Red: fine, imperfect.   1 in.   [Add. ch. 33,331.]

A shield of arms: a fess indented betw. three crescents. Within a pointed gothic quatrefoil.

. . . . NAM . .

Simon de Burgh.
7948. [A.D. 1388–9.]   Plaster cast from fine impression. 1⅚ in.   [xcii. 73.]

A shield of arms: per fess, three fusils in fess counter-changed.   Betw. the letters of a motto:

la — bo — [re?]

Within a pointed trefoil panel, ornamented along the inner edge with small quatrefoils or ball-flowers.

• **Sigillū** ☸ **simonis :** ☸ ☸ **De burgh :** ☸

Beaded border.

Walter de Burgo.
7949. [*Temp.* Hen. III.]   Plaster cast from good impression.   1³⁄₁₆ in.   [xciv. 54.]

A shield of arms of early shape: a chief indented, BURGH.

✠ S' WALTERI DE BVRGO.

Cf. L.F.C., ii. 12, A.D. 1227.

William Burghe, *Knt., 4th Lord* BURGHE *or* BOROUGH.
7950. [A.D. 1576.]   Red.   11⁄16 in.   [Add. ch. 35,817.]

A gauntlet and arm-piece of armour, suspended by a bowed ribbon.   Perhaps a badge.

7951. [A.D. 1576.]   Another.   [Add. ch. 35,819.]

Margaret de Burghersh.
7952. [A.D. 1339.]   Plaster cast from indistinct impression. 1⅛ in.   [xcii. 72.]

A shield of arms: per pale; *dex.*, a lion rampant queue fourchée, BURGHERSH; *sin.*, billet ce or cruzily, a lion rampant, BREOUSE?   Within a carved trefoil gothic panel with ogee points.

Sigillum : margarete : de : burgherſh.

Margaret, sister of Bartholomew, Lord Badlesmere, married Bartholomew de Burghersh, 4th Baron Burghersh, but the arms on the *sin.* side of the shield are not those of Badlesmere.

John de Burghfeld, *son and heir of*
JOHN DE BURGHFELD, *of Burghfield, co. Berks.*
7953. [A.D. 1361.] Dark reddish-brown : imperfect. ¾ in.
[Harl. ch. 47 E. 44.]
A shield of arms : three roses, on a chief a demi-lion rampant issuing. Within a carved curvilinear hexagon or rosette
of six cusps.
Legend betw. the points :—
...... IOHA—N DE—BVR—EFE—LD.

Rowland Burghill, *of co. Heref., Esq.*
7954. [A.D. 1594.] Light-brown: very indistinct, injured
by pressure. About ⅜ in. [Add. ch. 1869.]
On a mount, a stag statant, collared and lined. Betw. the
initial letters D. D. (?)
Beaded border.

Roger de Burghulle, *of Carey, etc., co. Heref.*
7955. [*Temp.* Edw. I.] Dark-green: fragmentary. About
1 in. when perfect. [Add. ch. 1309.]
A shield of arms : paly of ten a bend sinister.
✠ S .... OR .. VLLE.
Beaded borders.

George Burgoyne.
7956. [A.D. 1557.] Red. ¾ × ½ in. [Add. ch. 33,271.]
Shaped : two cramps or chapes. Perhaps for a badge.

George Burgoyne.
See G—— HORSEY.

Roger *f.* **Johannis,** *Lord of* **Buyrleye.**
7957. [A.D. 1316.] Dark green: top broken off. [Harl.
ch. 111 E. 15.]
A shield of arms : a bend gobony. Betw. two sprigs of
foliage.
..... OGERI ✤ DE ✤ BVRLE .....
Beaded borders.

William de Burl, *or* **Burleya,** *son of* JOHN DE BURL,
of Bearley, co. Warw.
7958. [Late 13th cent.] Dark green: fine, with mark of
the handle. 1⅛ in. [Add. ch. 20,421.]
A shield of arms : three garbs, two and one, on a chief as
many fleurs-de-lis.
✠ SIGILL' WILLI DE BVRLEYA.

Odo Burnard, *of co. Essex.*

7959. [*Temp.* Hen. III.] Dark green : indistinct. [Add. ch. 32,985.]

A shield of arms : three stirrups (?) two and one.

✠ SIGILL' : ODONIS BVRNARD.

Beaded borders.

Thomas *and* **Fina de Burnebi.**

See SIMON DAVY.

Stephen Burnei.

Seal used by JOHN GILBERT, *of Bandone, co. Surr.*

7960. [A.D. 1409.] Red. $\frac{7}{8}$ in. [Add. ch. 22,877.]

A shield of arms: three chevrons, ermine, over all a bendlet. Cf. arms of BAYNHARD, and BAYNHAM.

✠ S' STEFANVS BVRNEI.

Hugh Burnelle, *of Magna Bradeleghe* [*Gt. Bradley, co. Suff.*], *Knt.*

7961. [A.D. 1390.] Red: originally fine, now very imperfect, edge broken away. About $1\frac{1}{3}$ in. when perfect. [Harl. ch. 47 E. 46.]

A shield of arms : quarterly, 1, 4, a lion rampant crowned, BURNELL ; 2, 3, a saltire engrailed. Suspended by a strap from a forked tree. Within a carved gothic panel ornamented with small ball-flowers along the inner edge.

: Sigillum : hug . . . .

7962. Sulph. cast from No. 7961. [D.C., F. 573.]

Thomas de Burnetone,

of Newcastle-upon-Tyne, co. Northumb.

7963. [A.D. 1320.] Red: originally fine, now chipped. 1 in. [Egert. ch. 563.]

A shield of arms: a chevron betw. three griffins passant. Within a carved gothic star of eight points.

. . IGILLVM ✡ THOME ✡ . . . RNET . . . . . .

Margaret Burroughs.

See JAMES MANNING.

Edward Burtoun, *of Eastbourne, co. Suss., Knt.*

7964. [A.D. 1612.] Red: indistinct. About $\frac{11}{16} \times \frac{5}{8}$ in. [Add. ch. 29,991.]

A shield of arms: a tau-cross betw. three roses in chief, and two indistinct charges in fess. Perhaps in allusion to the arms of BURTON.

John de Eurtone.

7965. [14th cent.] Dark bronze-green: fine. $\frac{11}{12}$ in. [xxxv. 318.]

A shield of arms : a chevron betw. three roses, on a chief a lucy or pike-fish naiant. Within a carved and pointed gothic quatrefoil ornamented with small ball-flowers along the inner edge. Each of the four points of the quatrefoil is finished with a knop or poppy-head which divides the legend into four parts.

✤ SIG—ILLVM IO—HANNIS—DE BVRT—ONE.

7966. Plaster cast of No. 7965. [xcii. 75.]

Richard Burton, *of Karsalton, co. Surr., Gentl.*

7967. [A.D. 1540.] Red. $\frac{1}{2}$ in. [Harl. ch. 112 D. 41.]

A fleur-de-lis, perhaps in reference to the arms of BURTON, several families of this name bearing fleurs-de-lis.

Thomas Burton, *of Tolethorp, co. Rutland (?), Knt.*

7968. [15th cent.] Red: fine, well-preserved. $1\frac{1}{2}$ in. [xxxvi. 133.]

A shield of arms, *couché*: a chevron betw. three owls crowned, BURTON. Crest on a helmet and mantling, an owl's head, affrontée, crowned. Betw. two wavy sprigs of foliage. Within a carved and traced gothic panel, ornamented with ball-flowers along the inner edge.

𝖘𝖎𝖌𝖎𝖑𝖑𝖚 : 𝖙𝖍𝖔𝖒𝖊 𝖆 𝖇𝖚𝖗𝖙𝖔𝖓 : 𝖒𝖎𝖑𝖎𝖙𝖎𝖘.

7969. Plaster cast from impression injured by pressure. [xcii. 76.]

William de Burton, *of co. Rutland (?) Knt.*

7970. [A.D. 1348.] Red: imperfect, indistinct. $1\frac{1}{4}$ in. [Add. ch. 33,603.]

A shield of arms, *couché*: a chevron betw. three owls crowned, BURTON. Crest on a helmet and mantling, an owl's head, affrontée, crowned. Background replenished with estoiles. Within a carved and traced gothic panel, ornamented with ball-flowers along the inner edge.

SIGILLVM ✤ WILLELMI ✤ DE ✤ . . . .

Edward Bury, *of Farleigh, co. Wilts.*

7971. [A.D. 1544.] Red: cracked. $\frac{5}{8} \times \frac{1}{2}$ in. [Add. ch. 5700.]

An ornamental shield of arms: a bend sinister raguly, betw. the initial letters :—E. B.

John Buscre,
son of HENRY BUSCRE DE MALYNS, *of London*.

7972. [A.D. 1332.]   Red : originally fine, now cracked, imperfect.   ⅘ in.   [Harl. ch. 47 F. 2.]

A shield of arms : a bend, in sinister chief a leopard's face. Over the shield a fleur-de-lis, perhaps part of a crown, on the r. h., the remainder being broken off. Within a cusped gothic compartment of irregular shape, ornamented with ball-flowers along the inner edge.

SIGILL' . . HIS : DE : B . . . . . .

Beaded border.

See No. 7973.

Henry Buskre, *al.* Henry de Malynes.

7973. [A.D. 1315.]   Green : fine, slightly chipped.   ⅞ × ¾ in. [Add. ch. 20,350.]

Oval : a shield of arms : an orle debruised by a bend. Above the shield a demi fleur-de-lis, and two small saltires each attached to a corner of the shield.

✠ : S' . HENRICI : BVSKRE :

Beaded borders.

See No. 7972.

Oliver de Buscy *or* Buzci, *of cos. Nott., York, etc.*

7974. [*Temp.* Henry III.]   Light brown : chipped.   1 in. [Harl. ch. 47 F. 6.]

A shield of arms : a lion rampant, over all a bend.

✠ SIGILL' · OLIVERI · DE : BVZCI :

Cf. Harl. ch. 83 G. 53, *temp.* Joh. ; Add. ch. 20,838, early Hen. III. ; Add. ch. 7465, A.D. 1232–1240.

7975. Sulph. cast from No. 7974.   [D.C., E. 368.]

Matthew Bush.
See THOMAS BARNARD.

Thomas Bushell, *of Enstone, co. Oxon., Esq.*

7976. [A.D. 1638.]   Red : injured by pressure.   ⅝ × ½ in. [Harl. ch. 111 E. 6.]

Oval :- a shield of arms : a chevron betw. three water bougets, BUSHELL.

Beaded border.

7977. [A.D. 1637.]   Red : imperfect.   [Harl. ch. 111 E. 9.]

Another Seal.

7978. [A.D. 1648.] Red: injured by pressure. About
⅝ × ½ in. [Harl. ch. 111 H. 20.]
: Oval : a shield of arms : three birds, two and one. Above
the shield a sprig of foliage.

John Bussy, *of Bernardeston and Kedyngton Manors,*
cos. Suff. and Essex, Knt.

7979. [A.D. 1397.] Red : originally fine, now imperfect on
l. h. side. 1 in. [Harl. ch. 47 F. 9.]
A shield of arms, *couché*: three bars, BUSSEY. Crest, on a
helmet and short mantling, a griffin's head, couped and
collared. Supporters, two lions, sejant guardant.

⚘ **sigillum** ⚜ ⚜ **io . . . . ſſy.**

Carved borders.

Francis Butler, *of Croydon, co. Surr., Esq.*

7980. [A.D. 1627.] Red: injured by pressure in places.
⅝ × ½ in. [Add. ch. 23,499.]
Oval : a shield of arms: quarterly, 1, 4, chequy ; 2, 3, a
sword in bend, hilt downwards. Crest, on a helmet, ornamental mantling, and wreath, a cubit arm holding a sword.
(Cf. arms of HAWARD, whose name occurs among the witnesses.)
. Cabled border.

George Butler, *late of Beddington, co. Surr., Gentl.*

7981. [A.D. 1567.] Red: injured by pressure. ¾ × ⅝ in.
[Add. ch. 23,598.]
On a wreath, an arm embowed, in armour, holding a sword ;
in the field a mullet for difference.
Cabled border.

7982. [A.D. 1561.] Red: a fragment. [Add. ch. 23,422.]

James Butler, *Duke of Ormonde, K.G.*

7983. [A.D. 1690.] Red: *en placard,* on a label, injured
by pressure. $\frac{15}{16}$ × ¾ in. [Add. ch. 19,522.]
A carved shield of arms : a chief indented, BUTLER. Encircled with a Garter inscribed with the Motto of the Order.
Ensigned with the coronet of a Duke.

Another seal as Duke, Marquess, and Earl of Ormonde, K.G.

7984. [A.D. 1697.]   Red: *en placard,* imperfect.   2 × 1¹³⁄₁₆ in. [Add. ch. 24,472.]   .

A shield of arms: quarterly, 1, 4, a chief indented, BUTLER; 2, three covered cups, two and one, BUTLER; 3, a saltire engrailed, DESMOND; over all an escutcheon, three unicorns' heads erased (?) Encircled with a Garter inscribed with the Motto of the Order. Ensigned with the coronet of a Duke. Supporters, *dex.,* a falcon beaked and membered; *sin.,* a griffin-male.

Motto on a liston :—
• COME • IE • TROVE •
Carved border.

Another seal as Lieutenant-General of Ireland.

7985. Leaden impression.   2¹⁄₈ × 2³⁄₈ in.   [xxxiv. 41.]
Oval: similar to the seal in No. 7984, Add. ch. 24,472. With legend on a scroll :—

SIGILL' ✿ IACOBI ✿ DVCIS ✿ ORMONDIÆ ✿ LOCVMTENENTIS ✿
        GENERALIS ✿ HIBERNIÆ ✿

Carved border.

James Butler, *Knt., Attorney General of Qu. Catharine, Dowager Queen of Charles II.*

7986. [A.D. 1693.]   Red : *en placard,* on a label, imperfect. ⁷⁄₈ × ¾ in. [Add. ch. 6076.]
Oval: a shield of arms: quarterly, 1, 4, apparently a fess dancettée for a chief indented, BUTLER; 2, 3, three covered cups; on the fess point a crescent for difference. Crest upon a helmet and mantling, out of a coronet of five pearls an eagle rising.

Another Seal.

7987. [A.D. 1698.]   Red: *en placard,* on a label.   ⅜ × ½ in. [Add. ch. 6152.]
Similar to the previous seal, but smaller.

John Butteler.

7988. [Early 14th cent.]   Plaster cast from indistinct impression.   ⅞ in. [xcii. 77.]
A shield of arms: on a chief three cups, BUTLER.
✠ S' DÑI · IOHIS · BVTTELER.

John Button, *of Lewes, co. Suss.*

7989. [A.D. 1645.]   Red: indistinct.   ½ × ⅜ in.   [Add. ch. 30,644.]

Oval: a dexter hand and couped arm, bent at elbow, holding a few ears of corn. Within a bordure of foliage.

John Button.
See WILLIAM WEST.

Samuel Button, *of Staple Inn, London.*
7990. [A.D. 1682.] Red: *en placard* on a label, imperfect. About ¾ × ⅝ in. [Add. ch. 30,654.]
Oval: a shield of arms: ermine, a fess.

John Buttourt.
See BOUTTOURT.

John Buttetourt.
See BOUTTOURT.

Richard Byddell, *of the Inner Temple, London, Gentl.*
7991. [A.D. 1567.] Red. $\frac{11}{16}$ × $\frac{9}{16}$ in. [Add. ch. 35,332.]
Oval: an ornamental shield of arms: a chevron indented (?) betw. three crosses crosslet fitchées, in the dexter chief a mullet for difference.
Beaded border.

Sir Thomas Byde, *of St. Leonard's, Shoreditch, co. Midd., Knt.*
7992. [A.D. 1668.] Red, covered with paper before impression: very indistinct. ⅝ × ½ in. [Add. ch. 29,533.]
Oval: on a wreath an arm erect, holding an anchor. Crest of BYDE.

Anthony de Bydyk̃, *Parcener of the Manor of Selton, or Silton, co. Dors.*
7993. [A.D. 1314.] Bronze-green: imperfect, injured by pressure. ¾ in. [Add. ch. 13,014.]
A shield of arms: a bend betw. pierced cinquefoils or other indistinct charges.
In place of the legend, a wavy sprig of foliage and flowers.

John Bygot.
7994. [A.D. 1347.] Plaster cast from fine impression. ⅞ in. [lxxxiii. 34]
A shield of arms: on a cross five escallops, BYGOT, in chief a label of three points. Within a finely-carved gothic trefoil

panel, or rosette, ornamented along the inner edge with small roses or ball-flowers.

✠ SIGILLVM · ❀ · IOHANNIS · ❀ · BYGOT.

Beaded border.

Lucia de B. . . . [Bygod?]

7995. [A.D. 1355.] Dark green: fine, imperfect. $\frac{4}{5}$ in. [Add. ch. 14,928.]

A shield of arms: on a cross five escallops, BYZOD, BAGOT, BURNAVILL, or BEAUVAIS, etc. Within a pointed gothic quatrefoil, with small ball-flowers along the inner edge.

✠ S' LVCIE DE B . . . . . .

Ralph Bygod, *of co. York, Knt.*

7996. [A.D. 1513.] Red. $\frac{5}{8}$ in. [Add. ch. 5778.]

A dolphin embowed, in reference to the crest of BYGOD, on a chapeau a dolphin embowed and devouring the cap. The field replenished with sprigs of foliage.

Bygod.

See also BIGOT.

John Byllyng?

7997. [A.D. 1376.] Red: very indistinct. $\frac{3}{4}$ in. [Add. ch. 22,417.]

A shield of arms: on a cross five roundles. Within a carved gothic panel.

✠ Sigill . . . . annis · byllyng (?)

Robert Byng, *of Wrotham, co. Kent, Gentl.*

7998. [A.D. 1558.] Red. $\frac{3}{4} \times \frac{9}{16}$ in. [Harl. ch. 78 F. 2.]

Oval: cut with a bevelled edge. A shield of arms, a fox or wolf salient. Over the shield the initial letters R. [B.?]

John Byrch, *of Gray's Inn, co. Midd., Gentl.*

7999. [A.D. 1591.] Red: good. $\frac{7}{8} \times \frac{13}{16}$ in. [Add. ch. 19,544.]

A shield of arms: a chevron wavy betw. three eagles displayed. Crest on a helmet and mantling, out of a mural crown a demi-boar issuing, with a snake in its mouth.

Beaded borders.

John . . . . , *seal used by* ALIANORA, *wife of* WILLIAM BYS, *of London.*

8000. [A.D. 1383.] Red: imperfect. $\frac{3}{4}$ in. [Add. ch. 23,149.]

A shield of arms : on a bend three uncertain charges, in sinister chief a mullet pierced. Within a carved gothic trefoil.

SIGILL' IOH'I[S] . . . .

Johanna Byroñ, *Lady of Colwyke, co. Notts., widow of Sir* RICHARD BYRON.

8001. [A.D. 1415.] Red: originally fine, now chipped at edge. 1 in. [Add. ch. 21,173.]

A shield of arms : per pale, *dex.*, three bends, BYRON ; *sin.*, on a bend three annulets, in chief a cross crosslet fitchée, CLAYTON. Within a carved gothic panel comprising three points in triangle, and five cusps, ornamented with small ball-flowers along the inner edge.

Sigillū ⚜ ⚜ : ⚜ iohanne ⚜ ⚜ : ⚜ byrone ⚜ : ⚜

Carved border.

Cf. MS. Harl. 1555, f. 6.

Richard de Byronn, *of Durham, Knt.*

8002. [A.D. 1316.] Green: indistinct. ¾ in. [Egert. ch. 553.]

A shield of arms: three bends, over all a label of three points, BYRON.

✠ S' RICARDI : BERVN. (?)

John Bysshop, *of Hobury, etc., co. Kent.*

8003. [A.D. 1379.] Red: fine. ⅞ in. [Slo. ch. xxxii. 45.]

A shield of arms (field diapered) : on a fess three escallops. Within a carved gothic panel of three pointed and five semicircular cusps, ornamented with small ball-flowers along· the inner edge.

⚜ : Sigill' : ⚜ ⚜ : iohannis : ⚜ ⚜ : byſſhop : ⚜

Beaded border.

William Bythemore, *of Nailesey, co. Somerset.*

8004. [A.D. 1484.] Red: very indistinct. 1¼ in. [Add. ch. 5474.]

A shield of arms : per pale, *dex.*, a lion rampant ; *sin.*, per fess, in chief a chevron, in base barry of six. Betw. three sprigs.

sigillu[m] ⚜ will'i ⚜ by ✠ the ⚜ [m]ore.

Beaded borders.

Robert Byworth.

See JOHN BROKETT.

C

Edmund de Ca . . . .

Seal used by JOHN, *son of* ROBERT BAUDRI DE LA WODECOTE,
of co. Surr.

8005. [A.D. 1355.]   Red : originally fine, now chipped.
¾ in. [Add. ch. 23,125.]

A shield of arms : on a bend three stags tripping (field
diapered lozengy with hatched lines).   Betw. two wyverns
sans wings. Cf. on a bend three bucks tripping, CHEVERCOT ;
and on a bend three goats, CHEVERESTON, etc.

. . . . . . DMVNDI · DE · CA . . . .

Beaded borders.

8006. Plaster cast of No. 8005.   [xcviii. 42.]

John Cable, *or* Gable, *of Frome, co. Somers.*

8007. [A.D. 1381.]   Red : imperfect.   About ¾ in. when
perfect.   [Harl. ch. 76 E. 23.]

A shield of arms : two bars nebuly.   Suspended by a strap
from a hook.   Within a carved gothic quatrefoil.

. . . . MERTRS (?)

Reginald Cabus, *or* Kabus, *of Denham, co. Buck.*

8008. [13th cent.]   Green, mottled : edge chipped, app. by
a plaited cord of purple silk.   1⅛ in.   [Harl. ch. 85 F. 55.]

A shield of arms of early shape : on a canton two bars.

✠ SIGILL' REGINALD' CABVS.

The letter N is reversed.

8009. Sulph. cast from No. 8008.   [D.C., E. 360.]

William Cadel.

8010. [A.D. 1285.]   Green : a fragment.   About ¾ in. when
perfect.   [Harl. ch. 43 B. 18.]

A shield of arms : fretty.

Legend wanting : + ...

Beaded borders.

Richard Caily, *Rector of the Church of Sampfford Parva, co. Essex.*

8011. [A.D. 1368.]   Green : imperfect, very indistinct.   1 in.
[Harl. ch. 47 G. 1.]

A shield of arms : a bend dancettée. Within a carved gothic panel.

Legend betw. the points :—

.... RICA (?) .....

John de Cakistrete, *al.* Caccestrut.

Seal used by WILLIAM REYNBURTH, *of Helmingham, co. Suff.*

8012. [A.D. 1307.] Brown, mottled : somewhat indistinct. ⅞ in. [Add. ch. 9873.]

A shield of arms : a crescent (?). Within a cusped ·or curvilinear hexagon.

Legend betw. the points :—

. S. — IOH' — DE — CAC — CES — TRVT (?)

The letters TR appear to be conjoined.

Ralph de Calais.

Seal used by JOHANNA, *widow of* RALPH CALY (*i.e.* CALAIS), *of Shymplyngge, [? Shimpling, co. Norf. and Suff.]*

8013. [A.D. 1373.] Light red : indistinct. $1\frac{1}{16}$ in. [Harl. ch. 47 G. 4.]

A shield of arms of early date : a fess or bar.

⚘ SIGILL' : RADVLFI DE CALAIS. ✲

8014. Sulph. cast from No. 8013. [D.C., F. 486.]

Family of Caldecot.

See JOHN PEIRCE.

Hugh de Calfoure, *of Bathequelle (Bakewell), co. Derb.*

8015. [*Temp.* Edw. I.] Red : fine.. ¾ in. [Harl. ch. 83 D. 57.]

A shield of arms : a lion rampant.

✲ S' HVGONIS DE CAL .. OVER.

The letters ER are conjoined.

8016. Sulph. cast from No. 8015. [D.C., E. 348.]

Phelipe de Calin, *Clericus ?, or* Calincle.

Seal used by ROBERT FYNCH, *son of* WILLIAM FINCH, *of Snapes, co. Suff.*

8017. [A.D. 1372.] Dark green : indistinct. ⅞ in. [Add. ch. 26,259.]

A shield of arms : a bend, and label of five points.

⚘ S' PHELIPE DE CALINCLE (?)

8018. [A.D. 1372.] Dark green : indistinct. [Add. ch. 26,260.]

Perhaps a foreign seal.

Philip, *son of* EUDO de **Caletoft,** *of Thoresby,* [*co. Linc.*]

8019. [*Temp.* Edw. I.] Bronze-green : fine, edge chipped. 1⅛ in. [Harl. ch. 47 F. 42.]

A shield of arms : four bars, a chief chequy of ten pieces.

✠ S' DNI' FILIPPI DE CALETOH'.

The letter N in *Dni'* is reversed.

Beaded borders.

8020. Sulph. cast from No. 8019. [D.C., D. 246.]

8021. [*Temp.* Edw. I.] Creamy-white : indistinct. [Harl. ch. 47 F. 41.]

✠ S . . NI' FILIPPI DE CALETOH'.

Cf. Harl. ch. 47 D. 30, A.D. 1249; 54 B. 31, late 13th cent.; 56 C. 23, and 57 A. 25, late Hen. III.

Yvo de Caletoft Calitot, *or* **Kaletot,** [*of Aby, co. Leic.*]

8022. [*Temp.* Hen. III.] Brown. 1 in. [Harl. ch. 47 F. 40.]

A shield of arms : barry of twelve, a chief chequy of six pieces.

SIGILL' YVONIS DE CALITOT.

8023. Sulph. cast from No. 8022. [D.C., E. 314.]

8024. [*Temp.* Hen. III.] Brown : fine. [Harl. ch. 52 C. 46.]

8025. Sulph. cast from No. 8024. [D.C., E. 313.]

William Calhoun, *and other creditors of* KING WILLIAM III.

8026-8262. [A.D. 1717.] Red : *en placard*, on tapes. ⅝ × ¹⁹⁄₁₆ in. [Add. ch. 6292.]

Oval : a carved lozenge-shaped shield of arms : two bars, in chief three escallops.

Two hundred and thirty-seven impressions.

Elizabeth, *widow of Sir* WILLIAM **Calley,** *of Burdropp, in Cheseldon, co. Wilts.*

8263. [A.D. 1677.] Red, covered with paper before impression. ⅝ × ¼ in. [Add. ch. 17,456.]

Oval : a shield of arms : indistinct.

William Callowe, *of Holbeach, co. Linc., Gentl.*

8264. [A.D. 1568.] Red : a fragment. About ⅞ in. when perfect. [Harl. ch. 79 A. 12.]

A shield of arms : a lion rampant. On the r. h. side in the field the initial letter . B. The corresponding initial letter on the l. h. side is broken away.

Beaded border.

Calthorp, *of Ashwellthorp, co. Norf.*
8265. [*Temp*. Edw. II.]   Green: fine.   ⅞ in.   [xxxv. 328.]
A shield of arms: chequy, a fess ermine, CALTHORP.
Betw. two wyverns sans wings.

✠ FETES : PVR · MOI · E · GE · PVR · WS.
(Faites pour moi et je pour vous.)

Cf. Blomefield, *Hist. of Norfolk*, vol. v., p. 143.

8266. Plaster cast.   [lxxxiv. 27.]

Christopher Calthropp, *of Starston. co. Norf., Esq.*
8267. [A.D. 1610.]   Red: fine.   ⅜ × ½ in.   [Add. ch.
14,655.]
Oval: a shield of arms: chequy, a fess ermine, CALTHROP.

Maud Calthropp.
See WILLIAM DE GREY.

Oliver de Calthorp, *Lord of Sythyng* [*Seething, co. Norf.*],
Knt., son of WILLIAM DE CALTHORP, *Knt.*
8268. [A.D. 1466.]   Dark green: somewhat indistinct.   1 in.
[Harl. ch. 83 D. 58.]
A shield of arms: chequy, a fess ermine, CALTHROP.
Within a carved and pointed gothic trefoil, ornamented with
ball-flowers along the inner edge.

✠ S' ✿ HOLEVERI ✿ DE ✿ CALTHORP ✿
Beaded border.

8269. Red: fine, chipped.   [xxxv. 333.]

✠ S' . . . . . VERI ✿ DE ✿ CALTHORP ✿
Cf. Blomefield, *Hist. of Norfolk*, vol. viii., pp. 333-5.

William de Calthorp, *son of* WALTER DE CALTHORP,
of Calthorpe, co. Norf. [*ob. circ.* A.D. 1360.]
8270. Red on a mass of opaque self-coloured wax: originally fine.   1 in.   Cut from a charter to which it has been
appended by a label.   [xxxv. 266.]
A shield of arms: chequy, a fess ermine, CALTHORP.
Within a carved and traced gothic panel or star of eight
points ornamented with ball-flowers along the inner edge.

✠ SIGILL'V ✿⚜ WILELMI ✿ DE ✿⚜ CALTHORP.
Beaded border.

8271. Plaster cast.   [lxxxiv. 22.]

William Calthorp, *of Calthorpe, co. Norf., Esq.*
8272. [A.D. 1443.]   Red: originally fine, now cracked,
imperfect.   1⅛ in.   [Add. ch. 16,543.]

2 Q 2

A shield of arms, *couché*: quarterly, 1, 4, chequy, a fess ermine, CALTHORP ; 2, 3, on a chief, two mullets.   Crest on a helmet and ornamental mantling, a boar's head and neck, couped, betw. two savages wreathed about the head and .waist with oak leaves, each holding ·a club.
     Legend on a scroll :—

          𝕎𝕚𝕝𝕝'𝕞𝕤 ⸫ 𝕮𝕒𝕝𝕥 . . 𝕣𝕡.

John de Calverlay, *of Calverley, co. York·*
     8273. [A.D. 1324.]   Dark green: fine, app. by a plaited cord of green silk.   ¾ in. ·[Add. ch. 16,794.]
     A shield of arms : a lion rampant debruised by a fess. ·
          ✠ AMOVRS AHOVRS (?)

John de Calverlay, *of co. York, Chev.*
     8274. [A.D. 1352–3.]   Red : indistinct, injured by pressurè.
¾ in. ˍ[Add. ch. 16,803.]
     A shield of arms, *couché*: an inescutcheon within an orle of owls, CALVERLEY.   Crest on a helmet and chapeau, an owl. In the field the initial letters ı. c.   Within a carved gothiç quatrefoil ornamented with ball-flowers along the inner edge.

Walter de Calverlay, *of Pudsey, co. York.*
     8275. [A.D. 1318.]   Creamy-white : imperfect, indistinct. About ¾ in. when perfect.   [Add. ch. 16,816.]
     An inescutcheon within an orle of six owls, a variant form of the arms of CALVERLEY, and not on a shield.

Walter, *son of* JOHN DE CALVIRLAI, [*of co. York*] *Knt.*
     8276. [A.D. 1357.]   Creamy-white : imperfect, very indistinct.   About ⅞ in. when perfect.   [Add. ch. 16,804.]
     A shield of arms : CALVERLEY (?)
     Legend defaced.

Walter de Calverley, *al.* Calverlay, *Chev.,*
Lord of Calverley, co. York.
     8277. [A.D. 1401.]   Red : fine.   1¾ in.   [Add. ch. 16,890.]
     A shield of arms : of large dimensions : an inescutcheon within an orle of six owls, CALVERLEY.   Betw. the initials :—

          ⬩𝕤⬩   ⬩𝕨⬩   ⬩𝕔⬩

     8278. [A.D. 1401.]   Red : fine, imperfect.   [Add. ·ch. 16,887.]

8279. [A.D. 1401.] Red : indistinct in places. [Add. ch. 16,888.]

8280. [A.D. 1401.] Red : fine, chipped in places. [Add. ch. 16,893.]

8281. [A.D. 1402.] Red : imperfect. [Add. ch. 16,894.]

Walter Calverley, *of co. York, Esq.*

8282. [A.D. 1434.] Brown : good. About $\frac{3}{8} \times \frac{5}{16}$ in. [Add. ch. 16,935.]

Octagonal signet : a stag springing, winged. In the field the motto :—

ie matens.

(*Je m' attends.*)

(This may be the seal of THOMAS DE CLIFFORD, Lord de Clifford, one of the grantees mentioned in the deed.)

Cabled border.

Walter Calverley, *of co. York, Esq.*

8283. [A.D. 1442.] Red : imperfectly impressed. [Add. ch. 16,932.]

Seal as described for THOMAS CLAPEHAM, *q.v.*

Walter Calverley, *of Stanley, co. York.*

8284. [A.D. 1568.] Red : indistinct. $\frac{5}{8}$ in. [Add. ch. 17,029.]

An ornamental shield of arms : a fox or other animal salient.

Beaded border.

Walter Calverley, *of Calverley, co. York, and* FRANCES, *his wife, dau. of* HENRY THOMPSON, *of Brumfield.*

8285. [A.D. 1668.] Red, covered with paper before impression : very indistinct. $\frac{5}{8} \times \frac{1}{2}$ in. [Add. ch. 17,174.]

Oval : a shield of arms : an inescutcheon within an orle of owls, CALVERLEY. Crest on a helmet and ornamental mantling, an owl.

8286. [A.D. 1668.] Another. [Add. ch. 17,174.]

Walter Calverley, *of Calverley, co. York, Esq.*

8287. [A.D. 1695.] Red : *en placard*, imperfect. $\frac{5}{8} \times \frac{1}{2}$ in. [Add. ch. 17,193.]

Oval : a shield of arms : an inescutcheon within an orle of six owls, CALVERLEY. Crest on a helmet and mantling, an owl.

Cf. No. 8285, which it resembles.

Sir **Walter Calverley,** *of Calverley. co. York, Bart.*
8288. [A.D. 1721.]　Red: *en placard*, on a tape, imperfect.
¾ × ⅝ in.　[Add. ch. 25,921.]
Oval: on a wreath an owl.　Crest of CALVERLEY.

William Calverley, *of co. York, Knt.*
8289. [A.D. 1437.]　Red: indistinct.　¼ × ⅜ in.　[Add. ch.
17,053.]
Rectangular: an owl: from the shield of arms of CAL-
VERLEY.
Beaded border.

William Calverley, *of co. York, Knt.*
8290. [A.D. 1499.]　Red: injured.　⅝ × ¼ in.　[Add. ch.
16,985.]
Lozenge-shaped: an owl, in allusion to the arms of
CALVERLEY.

Robert Caly, *Citizen and Stationer of London.*
8291. [A.D. 1564.]　Light-brown: injured.　⅝ in.　[Add. ch.
5324.]
An animal's head and neck erased.

William Caly, *of Scratby, co. Norf., Knt.*
8292. [A.D. 1372.]　Red: fine, imperfect.　¾ in.　[Harl. ch.
47 G. 3.]
A shield of arms: quarterly a bend, over all in chief a label
of three points, CALLEY.　The full armorial bearings are:
quarterly on a bend three mullets.　Within a finely-carved
gothic rosette.　In the field round the shield the initial
letter I, five times repeated, one broken away.
☆ S' · WILLELMI · . . . . Y.

Adolphus Frederic, *Duke of* **Cambridge,**
7th son of George III.
Letter Seal.
8293. [A.D. 1800–1850.]　Black.　1¼ × 1⅛ in.　[xlix. 36.]
Oval: an oval shield of arms of GEORGE III., after the
union with Ireland, with a label of three points for difference.
Encircled with a Garter inscribed with the Motto of the Order,
and with two collars of military orders, viz. of the Bath and
of the Guelphs of Hanover, with the George and the badges
of the orders hanging below the shield.　Crest on a duke's
coronet, a lion statant on an open coronet of five points.

Supporters of England each with a label for difference, on carved scrolls.

In base a ribbon with illegible motto.

Hugh de Camera, *of Kersaulton, or Carshalton, co. Surr.*

8294. [A.D. 1311.] Green: chipped. 1 × ¾ in. [Add. ch. 23,358.]

Shield-shaped: two keys palewise in fess, handles downward and interlaced, addorsed, debruised by a bend, betw. a crescent on the *dex.,* and an estoile on the *sin.* side. The keys seem to indicate the duties of a Chamberlain, and to be used by way of a rebus on the name of the owner.

⚹ S' HVGONIS DE CAMERA.

Beaded border.

Roger Camoys, *of Broadwater Manor, etc., co. Suss., Knt.*

8295. [A.D. 1433.] Red: fine, much injured, imperfect. 1⅞ in. [Add. ch. 20,055.]

A shield of arms, *couché*: on a chief three roundles, CAMOYS. Crest on a helmet and ornamental mantling, out of a coronet a plume of feathers.

Legend on a scroll :—

⁕ ⁕ ⁕ ⁕ ⁕ ⁕ ⁕ ⁕ ⁕ ⁕ **geri** ⁕ ⁕ ⁕ ⁕ ⁕ ⁕ ⁕

8296. Plaster cast from No. 8295. [lxxxiv. 26.]

Robert de Campania, *or* **Canpannie,**
of Croft, co. Leic., Knt.

8297. [*circ.* A.D. 1240–1250.] Green, mottled: fine. [Add. ch. 21,690.]

A shield of arms: fretty of six pieces.

⚜ S' ROBERTI DE CANPANNIE.

Beaded border.

Robert de Campania, *or* **Canpanie,**
son of ALEIS DE CRAFT, *or* CROFT, *co. Leic.*

8298. [Early Hen. III.] Green: chipped. 1½ in. [Add. ch. 21,691.]

A shield of arms of early kite shape: fretty of six pieces.

⚜ SIGILL . . . . . TI DE C . . . PANIE.

Cf. Woll. ch. ix. 18, early Henry III.; Harl. ch. 45 G. 27, *temp.* Hen. III.; and the previous seal, No. 8297.

Robert de Campanniis, *or* **Champaigne,**
of Stoke Golding, co. Leic.

8299. [Early Hen. III.] Green: very fine. 1⅜ in. [Add. ch. 19,920.]

A shield of arms : fretty of six pieces.
> ✠ SIGILL' ROBERTI : DE : CHAMPAIGNE.
Beaded border.

Wiliam de Campaniis, *or* Champaine,

son of ROBERT DE CAMPANIIS, *of cos. Northt. and Leic.*
  8300. [Late Hen. III.] Pale red: fine, chipped. 1¼ in.
[Add. ch. 22,311.]
A shield of arms of early shape : fretty of six pieces.
> [✠] SIGILL' WILLELMI DE CHAMPAINE.
  8301. [Late Hen. III.] Green : fine, chipped. [Add. ch.
21,693.]

Edward Campion.

Seal used by ROGER SHOYSWELL, *of Shoyswell, co. Suss., Esq.*
  8302. [A.D. 1637.] Red: injured by pressure, partly in-
distinct. ⅜ × ½ in. [Harl. ch. 112 D. 21.]
Oval : a shield of arms : on a chief an eagle displayed,
CAMPION.   In fess point a mullet for difference.
Carved border.

Philip Canbellanus, *or* Le Chambellene.

  8303. [Cut from a charter, with label dated A.D. 1249.]
Green : injured in places. 1⅛ in. [xxxix. 70.]
A shield of arms : a lion rampant contourné.
> ✠ S PHILIPI CANBELLANI . . . LES.
Perhaps a foreign seal.

Henry de Candela, *of co. Linc.*

  8304. [A.D. 1254.] Dark green : indistinct in places.
1⅛ × ⅞ in. [Harl. ch. 47 G. 21.]
Shield-shaped : a shield of arms : three mullets.
> ✠ SIGILL' HENRICI DE CANDELA.

John de Cantulupo, *Knt., Lord of Snytenfeld,*
[*Snitterfield, co. Warw.*]

  8305. [A.D. 1315.] Green: fine. 1 in. [Add. ch. 21,421.]
A shield of arms : three leopards' heads inverted jessant-
de-lis, CANTILUPE.   Suspended by a strap from a hook, and
betw. two wavy sprigs of trefoiled foliage.
> ✠ S' IOH'IS : DE : CANTVLVPO :
Beaded border.

John de Cantilupo, *al.* Cauntelo,
Valet to WILLIAM DE MONTAGUE, *Earl of Salisbury and Lord of Man.*

8306. [A.D. 1363.] Red: originally fine, injured by pressure. 1 in.· [Cott. ch. v. 29.]

A shield of arms: three leopards' faces jessant-de-lis, CÀNTILUPE. Betw. five small cinquefoil flowers. Within a finely-carved and traced gothic panel.

ജ SIGILLVM IOHANNIS CANTILVP . . .

Beaded border.

8307. Sulph. cast from No. 8306. [D.C., F. 428.]

Nicholas, *son of* WILLIAM de Cantulupo, *of co. Linc.*

8308. [13th cent.] Cast in composition coloured green, from original impression. 1¼ in. [lii. 37.]

A shield of arms: three leopards' heads jessant-de-lis, betw. as many crosses crosslet. Background powdered.

✠ SIGILLVM : NICOLAI : DE : CANTULVPO.

Beaded borders.

Walter de Chantelupo.

8309. [Late 12th or early 13th cent.] Plaster cast from chipped and indistinct impression. 2 in. [lxxxiv. 28.]

A *wolf* leaping on a hind and biting its neck. Perhaps a preheraldic device, similar to the use of the corresponding devices used by the family of Redvers, Earls of Devon.

✠ SIGILLVM W . . . . Є · CHANTELVPO.

W[illiam] de Cantelupo, *Steward of the King's Household.*

8310. [Early *temp.* Hen. III.] Yellowish-white: originally fine, now imperfect at top and on l. h. side. About 2 in. when perfect. [Harl. ch. 47 G. 35.]

A shield of arms of early shape: three fleurs-de-lis, two and one, CANTELUPE. Betw. an estoile with a crescent over it on the l. h. side, and a crescent enclosing an estoile on the r. h. side. The arms as used by Sir William de Cantelupe, Knt., of Aston Cantelupe, co. Warwick, Sheriff of Worcester in the time of King John.

. . . . GILL' W . . . . .

Beaded borders.

8311. Sulph. cast from No. 8310. [D.C., E. 337.]

Cf. Add. ch. 20,578, A.D. 1233 (?) ; 19,826, A.D. 1237.

William, *son of* WILLIAM de Cantelupe, *of co. Warw.*

8312. [A.D. 1228–9 ?] Discoloured brownish-white: originally fine, now fragmentary. About 1¼ in. when perfect. [Add. ch. 20,508.]

A large shield of arms of early shape : three fleurs-de-lis, two and one, CANTELUPE.

✠ SIGILLVM . . . .

Cf. Dugdale, *Hist. of Warwicksh.*, p. 287.

William de Cantilupo, *Lord of Ravensthorpe, co. Northt., 1st Baron.*

8313. [A.D. 1301.] Plaster cast from fine impression. 1 in. [lxxxiv. 29.]

A shield of arms : a fess *vair* betw. three fleurs-de-lis, CANTILUPE.

✠ S' WILLELMI · DE · CANTILVPO.

William Cantrell, *Gentl.*

8314. [A.D. 1577.] Red : indistinct. $\frac{5}{8} \times \frac{1}{2}$ in. [Add. ch. 29,272.]

Oval : a shield of arms : a cinquefoiled rose, slipped and leaved.

Algernon Capel, *2nd Earl of Essex·* [A.D. 1683–1709.]

8315. [A.D. 1707.] Wafer, covered with paper before impression : *en placard.* $1\frac{1}{4} \times 1\frac{1}{8}$ in. [Add. ch. 13,639.]

Oval : a shield of arms : quarterly, 1, 4, a lion rampant betw. three crosses crosslet fitchées, CAPEL ; 2, on a chief three chaplets, MORRISON ; 3, on a chevron three garbs, CRADOCK. Above the shield an earl's coronet. Supporters, two lions ducally crowned. In base, on a liston the motto :—

FIDE : ET : FORTITVDINE :

Arthur Capel, *2nd Baron Capel, 1st Earl of Essex, Visct. Maulden, Baron of Hadham, Lord Lieut. of the County of Hertford.*

8316. [A.D. 1662.] Red : indistinct. App. by plaited strands of red and white silk. $\frac{3}{4} \times \frac{1}{2}$ in. [Add. ch. 35,308.]

Oval : a shield of arms : quarterly, 1, 4, a lion rampant betw. three crosses crosslet fitchées, CAPEL ; 2, on a chief three chaplets, MORRISON ; 3, on a chevron three garbs, CRADOCK. Ensigned with a coronet of five pearls for an earl.

Later Seal.

8317. [A.D. 1680.] Wafer, covered with paper before impression : *en placard.* $1\frac{1}{8} \times 1\frac{3}{16}$ in. [Add. ch. 35,311.]

Oval : a shield of arms, etc., as described above in No. 8315.

8318. [A.D. 16—.] Another : indistinct. The deed's date not completed. [Add. ch. 35,305.]

Dorothy Capell, *widow of* HENRY CAPELL, *of Rayne,*
co. Essex, Knt., formerly wife of THOMAS HOSKINS,
late of Oxted, co. Surr., Knt.
8319. [A.D. 1627.] Red. $\frac{3}{4} \times \frac{1}{2}$ in. [Add. ch. 36,415.]
Oval: a shield of arms: on a bend betw. two cinquefoils,
three leopards' faces, ALDERSEY. Crest on a helmet, ornamental mantling and wreath, a demi-griffin segreant (?)
Beaded border.

Edward Capell, *of Bevilham Manor, etc., co. Suss., Esq.*
8320. [A.D. 1533.] Red. $\frac{5}{8} \times \frac{1}{2}$ in. [Add. ch. 29,978.]
Ornamental shield-shaped: a lion rampant contourné. Cf.
crusily a lion rampant, CAPELL, and a lion rampant betw.
three crosses crosslet fitchées, CAPEL.
Beaded border.

Margaret Capell, *of Little Hadham, co. Hertf., Spinster.*
8321. [A.D. 1654.] Red: cracked, imperfect. About
$\frac{5}{8} \times \frac{1}{2}$ in. [Add. ch. 6213.]
A shield of arms: charges uncertain.

Henricus de Capella, *of Denham, co. Buck.*
8322. [*Temp.* Hen. III.] Green, partially discoloured:
imperfect. $1\frac{1}{8}$ in. [Harl. ch. 85 A. 11.]
A shield of arms: two bars and in chief a label of five
points.
    SIGILL' HENRICI DE CAPELL....
Beaded border.
8323. Sulph. cast from No. 8322. [D.C., E. 373.]
    Cf. Harl. ch. 85 A. 9, 85 A. 12, 85 F. 56, *temp.* Hen. III.; Add. ch.
9160, A.D. 1213–22; Harl. ch. 58 H. 38, 39, 40, A.D. 1227, etc.

John de la Capella.
Seal used by MICHAEL MARCHAL, *of Bridgwater, co. Somers·*
8324. [A.D. 1398.] Red, on a mass of green: injured by
pressure. $1\frac{1}{8}$ in. [Cott. ch. xv. 17.]
A shield of arms, *couché*: a goat salient. Crest on a
helmet and mantling, a fox's head. Supporters, two full-
length figures, *dex.*, a woman, *sin.*, a woodman. In the field
two sprigs.
    S' IOHAN DE LA CAPELLA. ⋈
Apparently a foreign seal.
8325. Sulph. cast from No. 8324. [D.C., F. 610.]

Harrington Capper, *Citizen and Dyer of London.*
8326. [A.D. 1656.]   Red : injured by pressure. $\frac{5}{8}$ in.
[Harl. ch. 111 E. 21.]
Octagonal : a shield of arms : (a fret ?) HARRINGTON.
Crest on a helmet and ornamental mantling, a lion's head
erased, HARRINGTON.
Cabled border.

Nicholaus Capperon, *of Huntingdon, co. Hunt.*
8327. [A.D. 1354.]   Discoloured green : imperfect, indistinct. ·$\frac{3}{4}$ in. [Add. ch. 33,488.]
A shield of arms : chequy, a fess.
Legend uncertain.

George Capstack, *and* ANN, *his wife.*
·*See* SAMUEL MASON.

Leo Capwel, *son of* ELIGIUS DE HOSE (?)
Seal used by THOMAS COTTERE, *of Tanyntone,* [*Thanington,*
co. Kent.]
8328. [A.D. 1363.]   Dark green : indistinct. $\frac{7}{8}$ in.. [Harl.
ch. 77 E. 14.]
A shield of arms : a cross within a bordure engrailed, over
·all a bendlet, in dexter chief an estoile.
S' LEO CAPVVEL [FIL'] ELIGII DE HOSE (?)
8329. Sulph. cast of No. 8328.   [D.C., F. 425.]

Johanna Carbonel, *widow of* WILLIAM DE NEKETONE,
of West Beckham, co. Norf.
8330. [A.D. 1306.]   Green : fine. $\frac{3}{4}$ in. [Add. ch. 19,304.]
Octagonal : a pierced cinquefoil, each leaf of which is
charged, as a shield, with a cross, CARBONELL.
✻ PREVE : SV : E : POY : CONV.
(*Privé suis et peu connu.*)
Beaded borders.
8331. [A.D. 1306.]   Green : fine. [Add. ch. 19,305.]

John, *son of* ROBERT **Carbonel,** *of co. Suff., Knt.*
8332. [*Temp.* Edw. I.]   Dark green : fine. $\frac{3}{4} \times \frac{5}{8}$ in.
[Harl. ch. 47 G. 47.]
A shield of arms : a cross fretty, CARBONEL.
✻ IE SV SEL DE AMVR LEL ✿
(*Je suis sceau d'amour loyal.*)
At the end of the legend, a small bird or dragon.
8333. Sulph. cast from No. 8332.   [D.C., F. 343.]

John Carbonel, *of Benetleye, co. Suff., Knt.*
8334. [A.D. 1275.]   Bronze-green: good.   ⅞ in.   [Add. ch. 9516.]

A shield of arms : a fess and in chief three martlets.

✠ S' IOH'IS CARBVNEL.

Another Seal.

8335. [A.D. 1276.]   Bronze-green, mottled : edge chipped in places.   ¾ in.   [Add. ch. 9517.]

A shield of arms : as above.   Not from the same matrix.

✿ S' IOH'IS CARBVNEL.

Elizabeth Carew, *widow of Sir* NICHOLAS CAREW,
late of Beddington, co. Surr., Bart.
8336. [A.D. 1728.]   Red : *en placard*, on a tape.   ⅝ × ¾ in. [Add. ch. 22,690.]

Oval : a shield of arms : three lioncels passant in pale, armed and langued, ensigned with an escutcheon of pretence, on a bend cotised three uncertain charges.   In dexter chief on a canton the hand of ULSTER.   Crest, a mainmast, the round top set off with palisadoes, a lion issuing therefrom. Supporters, two antelopes.   On a liston in base the motto :—

NIL CONSCIRE SIBI.

Sir **Francis Carew,** *of Beddington, Knt.*
8337. [A.D. 1578.]   Red : chipped.   ¾ × 11⁄16 in.   [Add. ch. 23,599.]

Slightly oval : a shield of arms : three lions passant in pale, CAREW.   Crest on a helmet and mantling of foliage filling the background, a lion statant.

Cabled border.

Another Seal.

8338. [A.D. 1592.]   Red : indistinct in places.   ¾ × ⅝ in. [Add. ch. 23.486.]

Oval : a shield of arms : three lions passant in pale, CAREW. Crest on a helmet and ornamental mantling, a mainmast, the round top palisadoed, therefrom a demi-lion issuing.

Cabled border.

Another Seal.

8339. [A.D. 1608.]   Red : very imperfect.   About ¾ × ⅝ in. when perfect.   [Add. ch. 23,606.]

An ornamental shield of arms : three lions passant in pale, CAREW.

8340. [A.D. 1608.]   Red : cracked and indistinct.   [Add. ch. 23,491.]

Sir **Francis Carewe,** *or* **Darcye,** *of Brameforde,·co. Midd., Knt.*
  8341. [A.D. 1615.]   Red: injured by pressure, very indistinct.   About ¾ × ⅝ in. when perfect.   [Add. ch. 23,720.]
  An ornamental shield of arms : CAREW.

Sir **Francis Carew,** *of Beddington, co. Surr., K.B.*
  8342. [A.D. 1626.]   Red: indistinct, injured by pressure.
About ½ in. when perfect.   [Add. ch. 23,283.]
  An ornamental shield of arms : CAREW.

Sir **Francis Carew,** *of Beddington, co. Surr., K.B.*
      (*Perhaps same as F. C. of Brameforde.*)
  8343. [A.D. 1627.]   Red: imperfect.   About ⅝ × ½ in.
when perfect.   [Add. ch. 23,290.]
  Oval: a shield of arms : three lions passant in pale,
within a bordure compony, CAREW.
  Carved border.
  8344. [A.D. 1627.]   Red: imperfect, indistinct.   [Add.
ch. 23,286.]
                    Another Seal.

  8345. [A.D. 1637–8.]   Red: fragmentary, very indistinct.
About ¾ × ⅝ in. when perfect.   [Add. ch. 23,304.]
  An ornamental shield of arms : CAREW (?)

Sir **Francis Carew,** *of Beddington, co. Surr., K.B.*
  8346. [A.D. 1644.]   Red.   ½ × ₁⁹₆ in.   [Add. ch. 23,310.]
  Oval signet : on a wreath a demi-female figure, draped, and
wearing a bag-shaped head-dress : in the l. h. a staff.

Francis Carew, *of Beddington, co. Surr., Esq.*
  8347. [A.D. 1688.]   Red: *en placard,* on a label.   ¾ × ⅝ in.
[Add. ch. 23,320.]
  Oval: a shield of arms : CAREW.   Crest on a helmet,
ornamental mantling, and wreath, a mainmast, the round top
palisadoed, thereout a demi-lion issuing.
  Beaded border.

Gawinus Carewe, *of Whitwell and Farway Manors,*
            co. Devon, Knt.
  8348. [A.D. 1545.]   Red: fine.   ⅞ in.   [Add. ch. 13,795.]
  A mainmast, the round top set off with palisadoes, therefrom
a demi-lion rampant issuing.   Crest of CAREW.
  Beaded border.

John de Carru.
8349. [*Temp.* Edw. III.] Red : fine, edge chipped. ⅞ in.
[xxxv. 22 E.]
A shield of arms : three lions passant in pale, CAREW.
Suspended by a strap from a hook, and betw. two wyverns,
sans wings.

✠ SIGILLVM · IOHANNIS DE CARRV.

Beaded borders.

Matthew Carewe, *of Horley, co. Surr., Esq.*
8350. [A.D. 1593.] Red : indistinct. ⅝ × ½ in. [Harl.
ch. 111 E. 23.]
Oval : a shield of arms : CAREW. Crest on a helmet, and
ornamental mantling, indistinct.

Nicholas de Carreu, *Lord of Muleford.*
8351. [A.D. 1301.] Plaster cast from fine impression.
1⅝ in. [lxxxiv. 32.]
A shield of arms : three lions passant in pale, CAREW.

✠ S' NICHOLAI · DE · CARREV.

Beaded borders.

Nicholas Carrew, *of Nutfield Manor and Beddington, etc.,*
co. Surr.
8352. [A.D. 1420.] Red : originally fine, encircled with a
twisted rush, now cracked, imperfect. 1 in. [Add. ch. 23,632.]
A shield of arms : three lions passant in pale, CAREW.
Within a finely-carved and traced gothic rosette of nine
points, ornamented with ball-flowers along the inner edge.
·Legend betw. the points :—

SIG — ILL — VM — NIC — HOL — [AI] — DE — CAR — REV.

Beaded border.
8353. Plaster cast. [lxxxiv. 33.]

Sir Nicholas Carew, *of Miccham and Mordon, co. Surr., Knt.*
8354. [A.D. 1530.] Red : fine. 1⅝ in. [Cott. ch. xii., 24.]
A shield of arms : three lions passant in pale, CAREW.
Background diapered with flowers.
Beaded border.
8355. Sulph. cast from No. 8354. [D.C., H. 91.]

Nicholas Carew, *of West Lulham, in Laughton, etc.,*
co. Suss., Knt.
8356. [A.D. 1534.] Red : defaced. ⅝ × ½ in. [Add.
ch. 30,480.]
Oval : a shield of arms : the charges obliterated.

Sir **Nicholas Carewe**, *or* **Throckmorton**, *of Beddington,*
co. Surr., Knt.

8357. [A.D. 1624.]   Red: imperfect, indistinct.   ¾ × ⅝ in.
[Add. ch. 23,587.]

Oval: an ornamentally-carved shield of arms: CAREW.

Nicholas Carew, Jun., *of Beddington, co. Surr.*

8358. [A.D. 1709.]   Red: *en placard*, on tape; imperfect.
About ¾ × ⅝ in.   [Add. ch. 23,965.]

Oval: a shield of arms of ornamental shape: per pale, *dex.*,
three lions in pale, CAREW; *sin.*, a fess chequy betw. six
crosses crosslet, BOTELER.   Above the shield a cherub's head
and wings.

8359. [A.D. 1712.]   Red: *en placard*; imperfect.   [Add.
ch. 23,968.]

Sir **Nicholas Hackett Carew**, *of Beddington, co. Surr., Bart.*

8360. [A.D. 1757.]   Red: *en placard*, on a tape; imperfect.
About ⅞ in.   [Add. ch. 22,917.]

A shield of arms of ornamental shape: three lions passant
in pale, CAREW; in the dexter chief a canton of baronetcy.
Crest on a helmet, ornamental mantling and wreath, a mainmast, the round top set off with palisadoes, therefrom a lion
rampant issuing.   Supporters, two antelopes.   On a liston
in base the motto:—

NIL CONSCIRE SIBI.

Sir **Nicholas Hackett Carew.**
See THOMAS HARRIS.

Nicholas de Carreu.
See JOHAN DE NOVE.

William Carewe, *of London, Clothworker.*

8361. [A.D. 1566.]   Red: cracked, imperfect.   ⅝ in.   [Harl.
ch. 76 E. 31.]

On a wreath a greyhound's head, erased, in the mouth an
uncertain object.   In the field on the r. the initial letter F.,
the corresponding letter on the l. wanting.

Cabled border.

Henry Carey, *Baron Hunsdon.*

8362. [A.D. 1559.]   Plaster cast from indistinct impression.
⅞ × ¾ in.   [lxxxiv. 34.]

Oval : a shield of arms of six quarterings ; I, quarterly, i. iv., on a bend three roses, CAREY, etc. Crest on a helmet, ornamental mantling and wreath, a horse's head.

John Carey, *Knt., 3rd Baron of Hunsdon.*
A.D. 1603–1617.

8363. [A.D. 1607.] Red : fine. ¾ in. [Add. ch. 30,537.] On a wreath a swan rising. Crest of CAREY.
Beaded border.

8364. [A.D. 1607.] Reddish-brown : injured. [Add. ch. 29,560.]

Adam Carles, *of Manchester, co. Lanc., Clerk.*

8365. [A.D. 1355.] Bronze-green : originally fine, now chipped all round the edge. About ¾ in. when perfect. [Add. ch. 29,246.]

A lozenge-shaped shield of arms : on a bend three pierced cinquefoils, CHARLES, or CHARELES. Within a carved and traced gothic quatrefoil.

S . . . . . HIS DE : . . . RLES (?)

8366. Plaster cast. [lxxxiv. 30.]

Richard Carles, *of Estnor, co. Heref. ; or*
John Hopley, *of the same.*

8367. [A.D. 1569.] Red : fine. From a signet ring with mark of the chased setting. ¼ × ₇⁄₁₆ in. [Add. ch. 5284.]

Oval : a shield of arms : three palets, over all a chevron ermine.
Beaded border.

William de Carleton (?)

8368. [A.D. 1356.] Plaster cast from indistinct impression. [lxxxiv. 31.]

A shield of arms : five estoiles, two, two, and one, on a canton a griffin segreant. Within a carved gothic panel.
Legend uncertain.

John de La Carnayl, *or* Carnell,
Escheator of the King in co. Northt.

8369. [A.D. 1377.] Bronze-green : injured by pressure. 1 in. [Harl. ch. 85 A. 26.]

A shield of arms : three bends, on a canton a triple-towered castle. Within a carved and traced gothic trefoil, ornamented with ball-flowers along the inner edge.

✠ 𝕾𝖎𝖌𝖎𝖑𝖑𝖚𝖒 : 𝕵𝖔𝖍'𝖎𝖘 : 𝖉𝖊 𝖑𝖆 𝕮𝖆𝖗𝖓𝖆𝖞𝖑 :

8370. Sulph. cast. from No. 8369. [D.C., F. 611.]

John Carpenter, *of Dilwyn, co. Heref., Gentl.*
8371. [A.D. 1634.] Red: fragmentary. About ¼ in. when perfect. [Add. ch. 1933.]
A shield of arms: paly of six, on a chevron three crosses crosslet, in chief a crescent for difference.

Philadelphia, *dau. and coheiress of* EDWARD **Carre,** *Knt.*
Seal also used by JOHN CLERK, *Esq., son and heir of*
FRANCIS CLERK, *Knt.*
8372. [A.D. 1641.] Red: injured. $\frac{7}{16} \times \frac{5}{16}$ in. [Harl. ch. 77 H. 13.]
Oval signet: a griffin segreant.
8373. [A.D. 1641.] Another. [Harl. ch. 77 H. 13.]

Charles Carrington, *of Hornsey, co. Midd.*
8374. [A.D. 1663.] Red, covered with paper before impression. $\frac{3}{4} \times \frac{5}{8}$ in. [Add. ch. 18,990.]
Oval: a shield of arms, helmet, and crest, too indistinct to be deciphered.

Sir **Henry Carye,** *of Great Berkhampstead, co. Hertf.,*
Lord of Snettisham, co. Norf.
8375. [A.D. 1614.] Red: indistinct. $\frac{3}{4} \times \frac{5}{8}$ in. [Add. ch. 19,387.]
Oval: a shield of arms: on a bend three roses, in chief a label of three points, CAREY. Crest on a helmet and mantling, a swan with wings endorsed.

Henry [Cary,] [*4th Baron*] *Hunsdon, Viscount Rochford, etc.,*
Lord of the Royal Manor and Liberty of Wye, co. Kent.
[A.D. 1617–1668.]
8376. [A.D. 1623.] Red. $\frac{3}{4} \times \frac{5}{8}$ in. [Add. ch. 20,026.]
Oval: a shield of arms: a chevron ermine betw. three cinquefoils. Crest on a helmet, ornamental mantling and wreath, indistinct, apparently a demi-eagle rising with expanded wings.
Beaded border.
The arms of CARY, Baron Hunsdon, are on a bend three roses. The above shield of arms may, perhaps, be a variation of this.

Johanna, *widow of* JOHN **Cary,** *Knt.*
8377. [A.D. 1409.] Red: injured, originally encircled with a twisted rush. ¼ in. [Harl. ch. 47 H. 10.]
A swan, crest of CARY.
Cf. Add. ch. 15,447.

Johanna Cary.
See ALIS DE LA ROUS.

Sir **Philip Cary**, *of London, Knt.*
8378. [A.D. 1619.]   Red : injured.   About ¾ × ⅝ in.
[Add. ch. 19,390.]
Oval : on a shield : a swan with wings endorsed, crest of
CAREY.
8379. [A.D. 1619.]   Red : an indistinct fragment.   [Add.
ch. 19,391.]

Robert Cary.
Seal used by Sir LEWES POLLARDE, *Bart.*
8380. [A.D. 1636.]   Red : injured by pressure, indistinct.
[Harl. ch. 86 I. 55.]
Oval : a shield of arms : very indistinct, apparently ; on a
bend three roses, on a canton an anchor, CARY.
Carved border.

Thomas de Cary, *Knt., son and heir of* THOMAS DE CARY ;
or, Alicia, *widow of* THOMAS DE CARY, *of co. Dors.*
8381. [A.D. 1358.]   Red : chipped.   ⅞ in.   [Harl. ch. 47
H. 8.]
A quatrefoiled flower, and on it a swan.   In allusion to
the arms of CARY, viz., on a bend three roses, and to the crest
of the same family, viz., a swan.   Within a carved quatrefoiled border.

Edward Carill, *or* Caryll, *of Shipley, co. Suss., Esq.*
8382. [A.D. 1587.]   Red : indistinct.   ⅞ in.   [Add. ch.
30,031.]
A shield of arms : on a plain bend within a bordure engrailed, a rose betw. two griffins' heads erased, a crescent
for difference.   CARRIL, or CARRELL.
8383. [A.D. 1587.]   Red : very indistinct.   [Add. ch.
30,032.]

Edward Caryll, *of Harting, co. Suss., Esq.*
8384. [A.D. 1591.]   Red : chipped at top.   About ⅝ × ⅞ in.
[Add. ch. 18,870.]
Oval : a shield of arms : three bars, in chief as many
martlets, CARRILL.   Crest, on a helmet and ornamental
mantling, on a mount a stag lodged reguardant.
Beaded border.

John Carell.
See RICHARD GARTON.

John Caryll, *Gentl., cousin and heir to* RICHARD COLYAR,
      Citizen and Mercer of London.
8385. [A.D. 1540.]   Red : very indistinct. $\frac{3}{8}$ in.   [Add.
ch. 18,822.]
An ornamental shield of arms : apparently a chevron chequy
betw. three animals' heads.
Legend obscure.

John Caryll, *of Horsham, etc., co. Suss., Esq.*
8386. [A.D. 1557.]   Red : fine. $\frac{3}{8} \times \frac{1}{4}$ in.   [Add. ch.
8942.]
Oval : an ornamental shield of arms : on a plain bend, a
rose betw. two griffins' heads erased, within a bordure engrailed, CARYLL.
Cabled border.
8387. [A.D. 1562.]   Red.   [Add. ch. 18,850.]

John Caryll, *of Warnham, co. Suss.*
8388. [A.D. 1600.]   Red : imperfect, very indistinct.
$\frac{3}{4} \times \frac{5}{8}$ in.   [Add. ch. 8969.]
Oval : a shield of arms : three bars, in chief as many
martlets, CARILL.   Crest on a helmet, ornamental mantling
and wreath, imperfect, but apparently on a mount, [a stag
tripping reguardant.]
Cabled border.
8389. [A.D. 1602.]   Red ; slightly injured by pressure.
[Add. ch. 18,896.]
8390. [A.D. 1607.]   Red : fragmentary.   [Add. ch. 8973.]
8391. [A.D. 1621.]   Red : injured by pressure.   [Add. ch.
18,928.]

John Caryll, *of Harting, co. Suss., Esq.*
8392. [A.D. 1658.]   Red : very indistinct.   [Add. ch.
18,982.]
Oval : an ornamental shield of arms : indistinct.

John Caryll, *Senr., of Harting, co. Suss.*
Seal used by Sir JOHN BENNET, *or* BENET,
      of St. Martin's-in-the-Fields.
8393. [A.D. 1670.]   Red, covered with paper before impression.   About $\frac{1}{4} \times \frac{7}{16}$ in.   [Add. ch. 19,005.]

A shield of arms: three bars, in chief as many martlets, CARRILL. Crest on a helmet, ornamental mantling and wreath, a stag.

Carved border.

8394. [A.D. 1681.] Red: [Add. ch. 19,018 c.]

Oval: similar to the preceding (?)

John Caryll, *of Lady-Holt, co. Suss., Esq.*

8395. [A.D. 1697.] Red: *en placard* on paper, imperfect. About ¾ × ⅝ in. [Add. ch. 19,034.]

Oval: a shield of arms: three bars, in chief as many martlets, CARRILL. Crest on a helmet, ornamental mantling and wreath, a stag (?)

Cabled border.

John de Castelacre, *Citizen and Goldsmith of London.*

8396. [A.D. 1319.] Red: injured by pressure. ⅞ in. [Harl. ch. 45 B. 34.]

A shield of arms: a fess betw. three triple-towered castles. Betw. three slipped quatrefoil flowers. Within a carved and pointed gothic quatrefoil.

Legend imperfectly impressed:

¤ S' . . . .

8397. Sulph. cast. from No. 8396. [D.C., F. 173.]

Robert Castell, *or* **Castle,** *of East Hatley, co. Camb., Esq.*

8398. [A.D. 1640.] Red: injured. About ¾ × ⅝ in. [Harl. ch. 86 I. 34.]

Oval: a shield of arms: on a bend three castles, CASTELL. In chief a label of three points.

Another Seal.

8399. [A.D. 1641.] Red: fine. ⅝ × ½ in. [Harl. ch. 112 D. 27.]

A shield of arms: quarterly, 1, on a bend three castles, CASTELL; 2, on a cross fleury five annulets; 3, a bend wavy betw. two horse-shoes, HODSDON; 4, on a quarter sinister, two lions passant in pale, crowned.

Cf. Harl. MS. 1534, f. 39.

8400. [A.D. 1649.] Red: *en placard,* imperfectly impressed. [Harl. ch. 56 C. 8.]

Gregory de Castello, [*son of* NICHOLAS DE CASTELLO,
of Rumburg, etc., co. Suff.]

8401. [A.D. 1300.]   Dark green : fine. $\frac{7}{8}$ × $\frac{3}{4}$ in.   [Harl.
ch. 47 H. 13.]

Oval : a shield of arms : three castles triple-towered, two
and one.   Suspended by a strap from a tree.   Within a
cusped border of ten points.

　　　✠ SECRETṼ : GREGORII : DE : CASTELLO
Beaded border.

8402. Sulph. cast from No. 8401.   [D.C., E. 416.]

William de Castello, [*son of* GEORGE DE CASTELLO,
of Wishaw, co. Warw.]

8403. [A.D. 1323.]   Green : fine. $\frac{7}{8}$ in.   Add. ch. 26,602.]

A shield of arms : two bars, on a quarter over all a double-
towered castle.   Within a carved and pointed gothic quatrefoil.

　　　✠ S' WILL'I · DE CASTELLO.
At the end of the legend a martlet or small bird to the r.
Beaded border.

Philip Castelmartin, [*of co. Pembr. ?*]

8404. [A.D. 1341.]   Plaster cast from injured impression.
$\frac{7}{8}$ in.   [lxxxiv. 36.]

A shield of arms : a fess betw. three castles.   Within a
carved trefoil panel, ornamented with small quatrefoils or
ball-flowers along the inner edge.

　　　✠ S' · PHILIPPI · CASTELMARTIN.

Geoffrey, *son of* GEOFFREY, *son of* RICHARD **de Casterton,**
of Wyketofte, co. Linc.

8405. [A.D. 1376.]   Red : imperfect, indistinct. $\frac{5}{8}$ in.
[Harl. ch. 47 H. 15.]

Hexagonal : three shields of arms, conjoined at the base in
triangle : 1, Barry, indistinct.; 2, indistinct ; 3, a saltire.
Betw. the shields, a griffin, a lion rampant, and a third uncertain heraldic animal.

　　　✠ EN .... ORE .... D'AMOVR.
The letters VR in *amour* conjoined.

Johanna, *widow of* GEOFFREY, *son of* RICHARD **de
Casterton,** *of Marton-near-Horncastle, co. Linc.*

8406. [A.D. 1376.]   Red. $\frac{7}{8}$ in.   [Harl. ch. 47 H. 15.]

Two shields of arms : *dex.,* three bends, in chief over all a
label of as many points, *sin.,* crusily a chevron.   Betw.

the shields a roundle. Within a carved and pointed gothic quatrefoil.

⚹ : SIGILLVM · IOHE · DE · CASTERTON.'

8407. Sulph. cast from No. 8406. [D.C., F. 499.]

.Robert Castleton.

Seal used by parishioners of Toft-Monks, co. Norf.

Seal used by JOSEPH BARSHOM.

8408. [A.D. 1706.] Red: *en placard* on tapes and labels, imperfect, indistinct. [Add. ch. 14,921.]

A shield of arms: on a bend three adders nowed, CASTLE-TON. Crest on a helmet and ornamental mantling, a dragon's head betw. two wings expanded.

Seal used by BENJAMIN EDMONDS.

8409. [A.D. 1706.] Another: as above. [Add. ch. 14,921.]

Seal used by JOSEPH EDMONDS.

8410. [A.D. 1706.] Another: as above. [Add. ch. 14,921.]

Seal used by THOMAS SHERMAN.

8411. [A.D. 1706.] Another: as above. [Add. ch. 14,921.]

John de Castone, *of Bresete parva and magna, co. Suff.*

8412. [A.D. 1350.] Red: injured by pressure at edge. 1 in. [Add. ch. 10,004.]

A shield of arms : a chevron betw. three eagles displayed, CASTON. Betw. three slipped flowers, and within a carved and pointed gothic quatrefoil.

⚹ SIGILLVM · IOHANNIS · DE · CASTONE ⚹

Katerina, *wife of* JOHN DE Castone.

8413. [A.D. 1350.] Red: somewhat indistinct. $\frac{7}{8}$ in. [Add. ch. 10,004.]

Three shields of arms conjoined at the base in triangle: 1, three (escallops?) two and one; 2, a saltire engrailed or lozengy; 3, a chevron betw. three eagles displayed, CASTONE. Within a carved and pointed gothic trefoil.

⚹ : S' : KATERINE : DE : CASTONE :

Beaded border.

William Caston, *of Calais.*

8414. [A.D. 1460.] Red. From a ring. $\frac{1}{2}$ in. [Stowe ch. 130.]

. An eagle's head erased. For a crest (?) or in allusion to arms. In the field the initial letters, **w. r.**

Bartholomew Castre.
See G. DE LA GARDA.

Robert Castrie, *or* Robert de Cestria,
of Kilvingholm, co. Linc.

8415. [*Temp.* Hen. III.]   Green : chipped. $\frac{7}{8}$ in.   [Harl. ch. 47 H. 19.]

A shield of arms of early shape : quarterly, over all a bend.

✠ SIGILL' R . . . . TI CASTRIE ♣

William de Castro-Radulphi.
See WILLIAM DE CHASTEL . . . .

Anthony Catesbye, *and* Eliz., *his wife.*
See JOHN IRELAND.

William Caton.
See ROB. HARDY.

Thomas Caus, *of Hokham, co. Norf.*

8416. [A.D. 1375.]   Red : indistinct. $\frac{7}{8}$ in.   [Harl. ch. 53 E. 45.]

A shield of arms : a griffin segreant, CAUSEY.   Suspended by a strap from a tree, and within a carved gothic panel.

𝕾igillum : thome . . . . uſ.

William Causton.
Seal used by HUMFREY STYLE, *of Norwich, Grocer, or* THOS. HOWLETT, *of North Tuddenham, co. Norf*, *Yeoman.*

8417. [A.D. 1626.]   Red : chipped at the edges, originally encircled by a twisted rush. $\frac{7}{8}$ in.   [Add. ch. 14,931.]

A shield of arms : on a fess three quatrefoils, field diapered lozengy.

✠ S' ✠ WILL'I · CAVSTON ·

Drawn in Blomefield's *Hist. of Norfolk*, vol. x., p. 266.   (*Dept. Copy.*)

8418. [A.D. 1422.]   Red : injured, encircled with à twisted rush.   [Add. ch. 20,144.]

The date is thus given : "primo die mensis Septembris anno regni regis Henrici quinti post conquestum decimo." On this day Henry VI. ascended the throne.

Richard Cave, *of Stanford, co. Northt., Gentl.*

8419. [A.D. 1522.]   Red : fair. $\frac{3}{4} \times \frac{5}{8}$ in.   [Harl. ch. 47 H. 33.]

Oval: out of a flower, stalked and leaved, a greyhound's head per pale ermine and ermines, crest of CAVE.
Beaded border; from a ring with mark of the setting.

William Cavell, *of Butley, co. Suff., Clerk.*

8420. [A.D. 1696.] Red: *en placard* on a label. $\frac{3}{8} \times \frac{1}{2}$ in. [Add. ch. 10,290.]

Oval: a shield of arms: three cinquefoils, pierced two and one, in the fess point a roundle. Above the shield a sprig. Carved border.

Henry [Cavendish],
Duke, Marquess, and Earl of Newcastle, Earl of Ogle, Viscount Mansfield, Lord Lieut. of co. York, etc., K.G.

8421. [A.D. 1688.] Red: *en placard* on tape, imperfect. About $\frac{11}{16} \times \frac{3}{4}$ in. when perfect. [Add. ch. 1806.]

Oval: out of a ducal coronet a (boar's ?) head. Encircled with a Garter inscribed with the Motto of the Order. Beaded border.

John de Cavendysh, *of Walsham Manor, co. Suff., etc.*

8422. [A.D. 1358.] Green: injured, indistinct in places. $\frac{7}{8}$ in. [Add. ch. 15,747.]

A shield of arms: indistinct, three crosses crosslet, in fess point a roundle. Above the shield a slipped flower. Within a carved gothic rosette of eight points, ornamented with small quatrefoils along the inner edge.

      ✠ S'. IOHANNIS : DE : CAVENDYSH (?)

Beaded border.

8423. [A.D. 1363.] Red: originally fine, now injured by pressure. [Harl. ch. 76 E. 45.]

      ✠ S' IOHANNIS : DE : CAVENDYSH.

8424. Sulph. cast from No. 8423. [D.C., F. 426.]

William Cavendishe, *of Chatsworth, co. Derb., Knt.*

8425. [A.D. 1557.] Red. $\frac{3}{8} \times \frac{1}{2}$ in. [Woll. ch. ii. 42.]

An ornamental shield of arms: three stags' heads cabossed, CAVENDISH. In fess point a crescent for difference.

William Cavendish, *3rd Earl of Devonshire.*

8426. [A.D. 1670.] Red, covered with paper before impression. $\frac{3}{4} \times \frac{5}{8}$ in. [Add. ch. 8465.]

Oval: on a wreath a stag statant attired, gorged [with a garland of roses]. Above, an earl's coronet.

William de Cavereswel,
Lord of Kavereswelle, of co. Northt.

8427. [Late Hen. III.]   Green: fine.   1 in.   [Add. ch. 20,457.]

A shield of arms of early shape : fretty, over all a fess.

✠ S' DOMINI · WILL' · D'. CAVERESWEL.

The letters ER and EL in the last word are conjoined.

Cf. Add. ch. 877, A.D. 1280–1290.

William Caunvile, *Esq., son and heir of* WILLIAM CAUNVILE
and ALICE, *his wife, of Pesemerssh, co. Suss.*

8428. [A.D. 1422.]   Red : injured, originally encircled with a twisted rush.   1 in.   [Add. ch. 20,145.]

A shield of arms : on a fess three (lions'?) heads erased.

✠ Sigillu ⚜ will'i ⚜ caunvile ⚜

Inner border cusped and cabled, outer border cabled.

William Cawley, *of Chichester, co. Suss., Esq.*

8429. [A.D. 1647.]   Red : *en placard,* imperfectly impressed.   About ¾ × ⅝ in. when perfect.   [Add. ch. 18,968.]

Oval : a shield of arms : per pale, *dex.,* a chevron ermine betw. three swans' heads erased at the neck, CAWLEY ; *sin.,* three bulls' heads, two and one.   Crest on a helmet and ornamental mantling, an eagle rising.

Edward Cecil, *Viscount Wimbledon,*
Lord Lieut. of Surrey, etc.

8430. [A.D. 1627.]   Red.   1 × ⅞ in.   [Add. ch. 22,700.]

Oval : a carved shield of arms : quarterly, 1, 4, barry of ten, over all six escutcheons, three, two, and one, [each charged with a lion rampant], CECIL ; 2, 3, a saltire, NEVILLE, with an annulet for difference.   Ensigned with a viscount's coronet of seven pearls.

Robert Cecil, *Earl of Salisbury, Lord High Treasurer.*

8431. [A.D. 1610.]   Reddish-brown.   1½ × ⅞ in.   [Add. ch. 18,205.]

Shaped : a shield of arms : of six quarterings, 1, barry of ten, over all six escutcheons, three, two, and one, CECIL. The remaining quarterings very indistinct.   Encircled with a Garter inscribed with the Motto of the Order ; and ensigned with an earl's coronet.

Cf. Harl. ch. 86 G. 56 ; and MS. Harl. 1442, f. 57 b.

Thomas Cecil, *Earl of Exeter.*

8432. [A.D. 1605–1622.] Red. $\frac{7}{8}$ × $\frac{3}{4}$ in. [xxxvi. 162.]
Oval: a shield of arms: quarterly of six pieces: 1, 6, CECIL, etc.
Cf. the seal of William Cecil.
Ensigned with a coronet.
8433. Plaster cast from good impression. [lxxxiv. 39.]

Thomas Cicill, *of Burghley, co. Northt., Esq.*

8434. [A.D. 1575.] Red. 1 × $\frac{7}{8}$ in. [Add. ch. 9270.]
Oval: on a wreath a garb supported by two lions, crest of CECIL.
Beaded border.

Sir William Cecill, *Knt.,* *Master of the Court of Wards and Liveries.* (*Lord Burghley.*)

8435. [A.D. 1561.] Red: very indistinct, much injured by pressure. [Add. ch. 29,642.]
Oval: a shield of arms: quarterly, 1, 4, CECIL; 2, 3, a plate betw. three towers, WINSTONE or ECHINGTON (?) Crest, etc., of difficult identification, on a helmet and mantling.

Another seal for WILLIAM CECIL, *Lord Burghley,* *Lord High Treasurer,* *K.G., etc.*

8436. [A.D. 1574.] Red: injured and indistinct in places. $1\frac{1}{8}$ × $\frac{3}{4}$ in. [Harl. ch. 86 G. 56.]
Slightly oval: a shield of arms: of six quarterings, 1, 6, CECIL; 2, WINSTON; 3, HOWELL, WINSTON, or ECHINGTON; 4, ECKINGTON; 5, DICKENS; 6, CECIL.*
Encircled by a Garter inscribed with the Motto of the Order.
Cf. MS. Harl. 1442, f. 57 b.

8437. Plaster cast from a good impression originally, now injured by pressure. [lxxxiv. 38.]
8438. Sulph. cast from No. 8436. [D.C., H. 117.]

Another Seal.

8439. [A.D. 1579.] Red: indistinct, injured by pressure, imperfect. [Add. ch. 9272.]

---

* From a roll in possession of Lord Fitzhardinge, the following names for the quarterings are derived:—
2. *Sir* Gilbert Winston, Knt., *temp.* Edw. II.
3. Howell ap Owen, of Lacelleon, Esq., *temp.* Edw. III.
4. John Eckington, Esq., *temp.* Henry VII.
5. John Dicones, Esq., *temp.* Edw. IV.

Oval: this resembles the previous seal, but is from a different matrix.

8440. [A.D. 1585.] Red: fragments. [Add. ch. 29,645.]

8441. [A.D. 1594.] Red: very indistinct. [Add. ch. 5371.]

Another Seal.

8442. [A.D. 1584.] Red: imperfect on the r. h. side. About 1 × ⅝ in. when perfect. [Add. ch. 15,816.]

Oval: on a wreath a garb betw. two lions rampant, crest of CECIL. Within a Garter inscribed with the Motto of the Order.

8443. [A.D. 1594.] Red: very indistinct. [Harl. ch. 57 H. 21.]

Perhaps same as No. 8442.

William de Cervyngton, *of Buckland-Filleigh, co. Devon.*

8444. [A.D. 1380.] Red: much injured. [Add. ch. 29,100.]

A shield of arms: on a chevron three uncertain charges. Within a pointed gothic six-foil. The arms of CERVINGTON are: erm. on a chevron, three bucks' heads cabossed.

⚘ S .... DI ..... VN .... IL (?)

Robert de Cestria.
See ROBERT CASTRIE.

Richard de Chaddesle.

8445. [A.D. 1407.] Plaster cast from fine impression. 1 in. [lxxxiv. 40.]

A shield of arms: ermine on a bordure six bezants. Within a carved six-foil panel.

⚜ SIGILL ⚜ RICARDI · DE · CHADDESLE.

Michael Chadwell, *of Chipping Norton, co. Oxon., Gentl.*

8446. [A.D. 1598.] Red: well preserved. ⅞ in. [Harl. ch. 76 E. 50.]

On a wreath, a talbot statant.

Michael Chadwell.
See WILLIAM FOSTER.

Sir **Walter de Chalfhunte** (?), *Knt.*
Seal used by WALTER ALYSAUNDRE, *of Denham, co. Buck.*

8447. [A.D. 1339.] Brown, discoloured: edge injured by pressure. ¾ in. [Harl. ch. 84 G. 4.]

A shield of arms: on a chevron betw. three crosses crosslet fitchées, as. many (fleurs-de-lis ?) Betw. two small leaves,
and within a carved and pointed gothic quatrefoil.

⚹ S' WALTERI · DE · CHALFH .. TE · M.

William Chaloner.
See JOHN LYVET.

John Chaloner, *of Lyndfeld, co. Suss.*
8448. [A.D. 1567.] Red: injured by pressure. ⅝ in.
[Add. ch. 20,085.]

An ornamental shield of arms: a chevron betw. three
lozenges, a crescent for difference. Betw. the initial letters
I. C.
Cabled border.

Henry de Chalphur.
Seal used by THOMAS YONGGE, *Vicar of Cratfield.*
8449. [A.D. 1378.] Yellow: fair. 1 in. [Add. ch. 19,317.]

A shield of arms: erm. a fess chequy. Suspended by a
strap from a hook, and betw. two slipped flowers.· Within a
pointed quatrefoil.

⚹ S' HENRICI DE CHALPHVR.

John del Chambre, *of Newcastle-upon-Tyne, co. Northumbr.*
8450. [A.D. 1373.] Dark green: imperfect, indistinct.
About 1 in. when perfect. [Harl. ch. 47 I. 5.]

A shield, perhaps of arms: a chevron betw. two pierced
mullets of six points in chief, in base a key. Within a carved
gothic panel ornamented with ball-flowers along the inner
edge.

. . . . 𝕮amer . .

John Chamber, *of Radmell, co. Suss., Gentl.*
8451. [A.D. 1595.] Brown. ⅝ × ½ in. [Add. ch. 30,530.]
Oval: an ass's head erased. Crest of CHAMBERLAYN. In
base the initial letters I. D. C.
Cabled border.

Symon Chamber,
Gentl. Farmer of the Fines set by the Clerk of the Market.
8452. [A.D. 1636.] Red: *en placard.* Imperfectly impressed. About ⅜ × ½ in. [Cott. ch. xxiv. 60.]
Oval: a shield of arms: a chevron betw. three trefoils
slipped, CHAMBER.

Edmund Chamberleyne,
of Compton Abdalle, co. Glouc., Esq.

8453. [A.D. 1604.]   Reddish-brown. $\frac{15}{16}$ × $\frac{7}{8}$ in.   [Add. ch. 15,158.]

Oval: a shield of arms of six quarterings: 1, 6, an ines-cutcheon within an orle of mullets, CHAMBERLAYN; 2, a chevron betw. three mullets, CHAMBERLAYN; 3, six demi-lions in pile, three, two, and one; 4, ermine, a chief indented; 5, two lions passant guardant in pale, a label of three points. In fess point a crescent for difference.

Cabled border.

Edward Chamberleyn, *of co. Kent.*

8454. [A.D. 1529.]   Red: indistinct. $\frac{1}{4}$ × $\frac{3}{8}$ in.   [Harl. ch. 76 H. 19.]

Rectangular: three lions rampant, two and one.

8455. [A.D. 1529.]   Red: cracked, imperfect.   [Harl. ch. 76 H. 20.]

Ralph Chamberleyn *or* Chamberlein,
of Hadleigh, etc., co. Suff.

8456. [A.D. 1398.]   Red: fine, well preserved.   [Add. ch. 10,571.]

A shield of arms: fretty, on a chief three plates, CHAMBER-LAYN. Suspended by a strap from an eradicated tree, and within a pointed gothic quatrefoil ornamented with small ball-flowers along the inner edge.

𝔖' · raðulpþi · cþãberlepn.

8457. [A.D. 1399.]   Red: injured by pressure.   [Add. ch. 10,047.]

𝔖' · raðulpþi · cþa . . . pn.

Richard Chaumbirleyn, [*of Denford, co. Northt.*] *Knt.*

8458. [A.D. 1358.]   Creamy-white, discoloured: indistinct, imperfect, edge chipped. $\frac{7}{8}$ in.   [Harl. ch. 47 I. 27.]

A shield of arms: a chevron betw. three escallops. Betw. two small quatrefoil flowers, that on the l. wanting. Within a carved gothic panel of three cusps and two points in triangle, ornamented with small ball-flowers along the inner edge. See next No.

SIG + RICARDI + CHA . . . .

Beaded border.

8459. [A.D. 1371.]   Red: fine, injured in places by pressure.   [Cott. ch. xxix. 8.]

This shows parts wanting in the preceding No., *viz.*, the small flower on the l. h. and the legend :—

☆ SIG' + RICARDI + CHAMBERLAYN.

8460. Sulph. cast from No. 8459. [D.C., F. 475.]

Richard Chaumberleyne de Cotes,
of Denford, co. Northt., Esq.

8461. [A.D. 1428.] Red: imperfect, indistinct. 1¼ in. [Harl. ch. 47 I. 29.]

A shield of arms : on a chevron, betw. three escallops, as many roses slipped, or other uncertain charges.

S RICARDV . . . . N . . . . .

Richard Chamberlayn, *of Astley, co. Warw., Esq.*

8462. [A.D. 1652.] Red, covered with paper before impression : *en placard*. Imperfect. About ⅝ × ½ in. [Add. ch. 13,324.]

Oval : out of a ducal coronet an ass's head, crest of CHAMBERLEYN.

Seal of Arms.

8463. [A.D. 1653.] Black : *en placard.* ⅝ × ½ in. [Add. ch. 13,327.]

Oval : a shield of arms : per pale, *dex.*, a chevron betw. three escallops, CHAMBERLAYN ; *sin.*, ermine a bend lozengy, (PLUMLEY ?). Crest on a helmet and ornamental mantling, out of a ducal coronet an ass's head.

Carved border.

Richard Chaumberlayn.
See RICHARD DE WARWYK.

Robert Le Chamberleyn, *son and heir of* GEOFFREY LE CHAUMBERLEIN, *of Dunton, co. Bedf.*

8464. [*Temp.* Hen. III.] Dark green : originally fine, chipped at the l. h. top corner. [Harl. ch. 83 A. 50.]

Shield-shaped : a fess betw. six billets.

☆ S' ROBERTI : LE : CHAMBER . . . N.

8465. Sulph. cast from No. 8464. [D.C., E. 329.]

Robert Chaumberleyn.
See JOHAN DATHENAISE.

Thomas Chamberlayn, *of Froyle, co. Southt.*
8466. [A.D. 1462.] Red: much injured. About $\frac{3}{8}$ × $\frac{1}{4}$ in.
when perfect. [Add. ch. 17,600.]
Oval signet: an ornamental shield of arms: a chevron
betw. three mullets(?) CHAMBERLAYN.. In the field the initials
T. C.

Sir **Thomas Chamberlayne,**
of Wickham in Banbury, co. Oxon, Bart.
8467. [A.D. 1660.] Red, covered with paper before impression: very indistinct. About $\frac{7}{16}$ × $\frac{1}{4}$ in. [Harl. ch.
111 E. 37.]
Oval signet: a shield of arms: a chevron betw. three cinquefoils (?) CHAMBERLAYNE.

Robert, *son of* ROBERT de **Champayne,** *of co. Surr., Knt.*
8468. [A.D. 1294.] Dark green. $\frac{3}{8}$ in. [Harl. ch. 76 E. 55.]
A lozenge-shaped shield of arms: three bars wavy, CHAM-
PAYNE.
    ✠ SIGILLVM · SECRETI.
Beaded borders.
8469. [A.D. 1294.] Green : chipped. [Harl. ch. 76 E. 56.]
    ✠ SIG . . . M · SECRETI.

Richard de Champernon.
8470. [A.D. 1404.] Plaster cast from imperfect impression.
About 1¼ in. when perfect. [lxxxiv. 41.]
A shield of arms: quarterly, 1, 4, two chevrons, on a
canton a mullet ; 2, 3, CHAMPERNON. Within a carved panel
composed of a triangle and cinquefoil interwined.
   . . . . rð . . . . : chaumperno . . .

Richard Champneys, *of Bexley, co. Kent, Esq.*
8471. [A.D. 1601.] Reddish-brown. 1 × $\frac{3}{4}$ in. [Add. ch.
29,625.]
Oval: a shield of arms: quarterly, 1, a lion rampant within
a bordure engrailed, CHAMPNEYS ; 2, a fess betw. six annulets ; 3, a griffin segreant ; 4, a chevron betw. (three eagles
displayed ?). Crest on a helmet, ornamental mantling and
wreath, a demi man side-faced, wreathed about the head, in
the dexter hand a gem ring, CHAMPNEYS.
Cabled border.

Richard Chapell, *of Preston, co. Northt., Husbandman.*
8472. [A.D. 1506.] Red: somewhat injured by pressure.
[Harl. ch. 85 A. 30.]

Hexagonal: an escallop, in allusion to the arms of
CHAPELL, *i.e.*, a chapel betw. four escallops.
Cabled border.

Edward Chapman, *of Scothorne, co. Linc., Yeoman.*
8473. [A.D. 1682.] Red, covered with paper before impression: very indistinct. $\frac{9}{16} \times \frac{7}{16}$ in. [Add. ch. 29,590.]
Oval: a shield of arms: uncertain. Crest on a helmet and ornamental mantling a tree (?)

Jane Chapman, *wife of* EDWARD CHAPMAN,
of Scothorne, co. Linc.
8474. [A.D. 1682.] Red, covered with paper before impression. [Add. ch. 25,590.]
Same as described for EDWARD CHAPMAN, see No. 8473.

John, *son and heir of* JOHN **Chargge,** *of Windsor,*
co. Berks., Husbandman.
8475. [A.D. 1521.] Red. $\frac{5}{8} \times \frac{1}{2}$ in. [Harl. ch. 85 A. 31.]
Ornamental shield-shaped: an eagle rising with inverted
wings. In the field the motto :—
IN · DÑO · CŌFIDO (?)
8476. [A.D. 1521.] Another. [Harl. ch. 85.A. 32.]

Adam Charles, *Clerk.*
8477. [A.D. 1355.] Recent impression in red composition
from original seal: imperfect. $\frac{7}{8} \times \frac{3}{4}$ in. [xlv. 48.]
Oval: a lozenge-shaped shield of arms: on a bend three
cinquefoils pierced, CHARLES. Within an elaborately-carved
gothic quatrefoil, ornamented with small ball-flowers along
the inner edge.
Legend betw. the points :—
S . . . . . . NIS : DE : C . . RLES (?)

Edmund, *son of* EDWARD **Charlis,** *or* **Charles,**
of Wangeford, etc., co. Suff., Knt.
8478. [A.D. 1329.] Red: fine, well preserved. $\frac{7}{8}$ in.
[Harl. ch. 48 A. 10.]
A shield of arms: ermine, on a chief five lozenges, CHARLES.
Betw. three escallop shells. Within a pointed gothic quatrefoil ornamented with small ball-flowers along the inner edge.
☿ SIGILLVM ✠ EDMVNDI ✠ CHARLIS.
8479. Sulph. cast from No. 8478. [D.C;, F. 234.]
8480. [A.D. 1336.] Red: fine. [Add. ch. 9602.]

Richard Charles,
Lord of Ikeleshamme Manor, co. Suss.

8481. [A.D. 1367.] Red : fine, somewhat injured by pressure. ⅞ in. [Add. ch. 20,096.]

A shield of arms : on a chevron betw. three eagles' heads erased as many estoiles (?). Within a carved gothic six-foil.

☆ 𝕾𝖎𝖌𝖎𝖑𝖑𝖚𝖒 ✲ ᴧ 𝕽𝖎𝖈𝖆𝖗𝖉𝖎 ✲ ᴧ 𝕮𝖍𝖆𝖗𝖑𝖊𝖘.

8482. [A.D. 1374.] Red : edge chipped, indistinct in places. [Add. ch. 20,037.]

Cf. Harl. ch. 76 F. 7.

William, *son of* EDWARD Charles, *Knt.,*
of Dodenash Manor, [co. Suff.]

8483. [A.D. 1309.] Dark green : somewhat indistinct. ¾ in. [Add. ch. 9567.]

A shield of arms : a bend, with some indistinct charges, perhaps ermine spots on it.

Legend :—

I ☆ I S' W C H .

With an escallop in each space betw. the letters.

Cf. Add. ch. 9592–9594, A.D. 1331.

Thomas de Charletone, *of Appeleye, co. Salop.*

8484. [A.D. 1384.] Red : indistinct, much injured by pressure. 1 in. [Cott. ch. V. 8.]

A shield of arms : uncertain. Suspended by a strap from a forked tree. Within a carved gothic panel.

𝕾𝖎𝖌𝖎𝖑𝖑𝖚𝖒 . . . .

Thomas Charltoun, *of co. Midd.*

8485. [A.D. 1404.] Red : fine, well preserved. 1⅛ in. [Add. ch. 19,891.]

A shield of arms : a chevron betw. three swans, CHARLTON. Suspended by a strap from a finely-designed tree. Within a border of cusped lines.

𝕾𝖎𝖌𝖎𝖑𝖑𝖚𝖒 ᴧ 𝖙𝖍𝖔𝖒𝖊 ᴧ 𝖈𝖍𝖆𝖗𝖑𝖙𝖔𝖚𝖓.

Beaded borders.

8486. Plaster cast. [lxxxiv. 42.]

Thomas Charlton, *Esq.*

8487. [A.D. 1450.] Red : indistinct. ⅜ in. [Add. ch. 19,894.]

Small round signet from a ring : a lion's head erased, in

allusion to the arms of CHARLTON. In the field an indistinct legend :—

. . . . I . . n . . .

Cabled borders.

Edmund de Charneles, *of Bilston, co. Leic.*
8488. [A.D. 1369.] Green, mottled: fine. 1 in. [Add. ch. 15,484.]

A shield of arms : a cross engrailed, CHARNELLS, with a bend over all for difference.

✠ S' · EDE : CHARNELES.

The two S's are lying down, and the letters EL conjoined.

John de Charnels, *of Rugby Manor, co. Warw., Clerk.*
8489. [A.D. 1350.] Red: imperfect. [Add. ch. 20,585.]

A shield of arms : a cross lozengy or engrailed, a ring at the crossing of the limbs for CHARNELLS. Betw. the letters I. O. H.' Within a carved and pointed gothic six-foil ornamented with small ball-flowers along the inner edge. This is comprised in a carved and similarly ornamented gothic six-foil, containing in each leaf or cusp a design, viz. at top, the Agnus Dei ; in base the owner, half-length to the r. in prayer ; at the sides the emblems of the four Evangelists (?) Betw. each pair of cusps a small countersunk circular panel, carved : outside these in the spaces round the edge, single letters of the legend.

. . . . [CH]AR[NE]LES.

Cf. Add. ch. 26,916, A.D. 1361 ; Cott. ch. xvi. 62, A.D. 1365.

8490. Plaster cast. [lxxxiv. 54.]

John Charnels (?)
8491. [A.D. 1364.] Plaster cast from indistinct impression, chipped. 1 1/16 in. [lxxxiv. 44.]

A shield of arms : three pales, over all a bend lozengy. Betw. a bird over the shield and four uncertain emblems at the sides. Within a cusped panel of six points.

Legend indistinct.

John Charnele.
8492. [A.D. 1384.] Plaster cast from indistinct impression. 15/16 in. [lxxxiv. 45.]

A shield of arms, *couché* : a cross engrailed, CHARNELL. Crest on a helmet, out of a ducal coronet an old man's head, with long hair, in profile. Within a carved panel.

𝕾' iohannis · charnele.

Beaded border.

Nicholas de Charneles,
[of Little Lawford, co. Warw.] Knt.

8493. [A.D. 1350.]   Red : the impression appears to have slipped in the matrix while it was being made.   1 in.   [Add. ch. 20,541.]

A shield of arms, *couché*: a cross engrailed or lozengy, CHARNELLS.   Crest on a helmet and short lambrequin or cappiline, an old man's head, wearing a pointed chapeau, turned up edge.   Across the field, betw. two parallel lines, the motto :—

IHESV HELPE.

Within a carved gothic panel.

SIGILLVM : NICHOLAI : DE : CHARNELES.

Thomas de Charnels, *of Rugby Manor, co. Warw., Knt.*

8494. [A.D. 1350.]   Red : originally fine, injured by casting, edge chipped.   1⅛ in.   [Cott. ch. xxiv. 9.]

A shield of arms : a cross engrailed, or lozengy, CHAR-NELLS.   In chief a label of (three?) points.   Betw. two small flowers.   Within a carved and pointed gothic trefoil ornamented with small ball-flowers along the inner edge.

·[⚜·S]IGILL ✠ THO[M]E ✠ CHARNELS.

Cabled border.

8495. Sulph. cast from No. 8494.   [D.C., F. 311.]

William, *son of* D. HENRY le Charnel,
of Bedeworth, [co. Warw.]

8496. [A.D. 1328.]   Green, discoloured : indistinct in places. ⅞ in.   [Harl. ch. 48 A. 14.]

A shield of arms : a cross engrailed, CHARNELL.   In chief a label of five points.   Betw. two leaves slipped.   Within a carved and pointed gothic quatrefoil.

⚜ S' WI[LL]ELMI CH . . . .

William de Chartris, *or* Chartres, *of Lesbury, co. Northumb.*

8497. [A.D. 1314.]   Dark green : fine.   ¾ × ⅝ in.   [Add. ch. 20,540.]

Oval : two shields of arms : *dex.*, a cross fleury ; *sin.*, a fess, CHARTERS, or CHARTRES.   Above, a wyvern, in the beak a strap to which the sinister shield is slung.   In base an estoile of six points.

⚜ S' WILL'I DE CHARTRIS.

Sire Richard Chastil(e)t, *or* Chistelet, *of Cobham,*
co. Kent, Clerk.

8498. [A.D. 1383.]   Red : cracked, imperfect.   About ⅞ in. when perfect.   [Harl. ch. 48 F. 15.]

A shield of arms: a triple-towered castle, embattled, betw. a crescent in the dexter and an estoile in the sinister chief. Within a carved gothic trefoil, ornamented with small ball-flowers along the inner edge.

✠ S' RICAR . . . . CHASTIL . T.

William de Chastel . . . . , *or* **de Castro Radulphi,**
Lord of Colrithe, co. Linc.

8499. [A.D. 1323.] Dark green: imperfect at top, injured by pressure. $1\frac{1}{8} \times \frac{7}{8}$ in. [Add. ch. 10,662.]

Oval: a shield of arms: three fleurs-de-lis, two and one, COLRITH, of co. Lincoln, and CHATELLERAULT. On a tree of five branches.

. . . . WILL'I DE CHASTEL . . . . . .

William de Chasteliet, *of Sawtrey, co. Hunt.*

8500. [A.D. 1412.] Red: injured in places. $\frac{3}{4}$ in. [Harl. ch. 83 A. 41.]

A shield of arms, *couché*: a chief, over all a triple-towered castle, betw. four escallops, two on the chief, two on the field. Crest on a helmet and short lambrequin or cappiline, a triple-towered castle. Background diapered lozengy with a pellet in each interstice.

S' WILLMI DE CHASTELIET.

Beaded borders.

Thomas Chaucer, *of Great Milton, co. Oxon., Esq.*

8501. [A.D. 1416.] Red: fine. $\frac{1}{2}$ in. [Harl. ch. 54 I. 34.]

From a signet ring: a pierced cinquefoil. In the field the legend:—

my · trew · crest.

Hugh de Chaucumb.

8502. [*Temp.* Joh.] Plaster cast from fine impression. $1\frac{5}{8}$ in. [lxxxiv. 46.]

A shield of arms of early shape: chequy?. Above the shield a crescent. At each side an estoile of five points wavy betw. two pellets.

✠ SIGILL' HVGONIS : DE : CHAVCVMB.

Cf. Add. ch. 21,405, late Hen. II.; Harl. ch. 52 A. 15, A.D. 1200; "Hugh de Chaucumb, Justiciarius Regis"; Cott. ch. xxiii. 15, 16, *temp.* Joh.

Margerie, *Dame* **de Chaumpaigne,** *of co. Kent.*

8503. [A.D. 1336.] Red: originally fine, only central part remaining. About 1 in. when perfect. [Harl. ch. 47 I. 39.]

A lozenge-shaped shield of arms: three bars nebuly, CHAMPAINE. Within a lozenge-shaped panel ornamented with small ball-flowers along the inner edge.   On each of the sides of the lozenge a circular lobe or compartment, similarly ornamented, containing an ornamental round buckle.

Legend betw. the four lobes, in two concentric circles ·—

[MAR] [RIA] [CHA] PAG
[GE]   DE   VM   NE.

Cf. Harl. ch. 47 I. 40, A.D. 1333.

8504. Sulph. cast from No. 8503. [D.C., F. 262.]

Ralph Chaumpayn, *of Cotton Manor, co. Suff.*

8505. [A.D. 1367.] Red: a fragment. About $\frac{7}{8}$ in. when perfect. [Harl. ch. 47 I. 41.]

A shield of arms: a fess ermine betw. (two mullets in chief ?) and other destroyed charges.

¤ S . . . . AYN . .

Thomas Chauncei, *of co. Glouc., etc.*

8506. [A.D. 1424.] Red: well preserved. $\frac{1}{2}$ in. [Harl. ch. 45 I. 11.]

A griffin's or eagle's leg and wing conjoined.   Within a circular chain.   In allusion to the arms and crest of CHAUNCEY.

Thomas Chaundeler, *Clerk.*

8507. [A.D. 1483.] Red. $\frac{9}{16}$ in. [Harl. ch. 43 I. 51.]

A shield of arms: a saltire.   Surmounted by a cap or coronet ; and betw. two sprigs.

John Chaundos.

Seal used by JOHN DE OLDECASTEL, *of co. Heref.*

8508. [A.D. 1376.] Red: fine, chipped. $\frac{13}{16}$ in. [Harl. ch. 112 B. 56.]

A shield of arms: a pile, CHANDOS.   Within a pointed gothic trefoil ornamented with ball-flowers along the inner edge.

¤ Sigillum : iohan . . . . . chaundos ᴀᴜ

Beaded border.

8509. Sulph. cast from No. 8508. [D.C., F. 504.]

William Chaunsy, *of Skirpenbeck Manor, co. York, Chivaler.*

8510. [A.D. 1398.] Red: originally fine, imperfect and indistinct. I in. [Slo. ch. xxxiii. 50.]

A shield of arms: a cross botonée, on a chief a lion passant guardant, CHAUNCEY.   Suspended by a strap from a hook.

. . . . wilelmi ♦ chau . . . . ♦ . miles ♦

Thomas Chaunterel, *of West Wittenham, co. Berks.*

8511. [A.D. 1331.]   White : imperfect, indistinct.   About
¾ × ⅝ in.   [Add. ch. 20,279.]

Oval : a shield of arms : a chevron betw. three estoiles of
six points. ˙ Suspended by a strap from a hook.   Betw. two
wyverns.

✠ S' THOME CHAVN[TE]REL.

Cf. Add. ch. 20,277, A.D. 1325 ; 20,278, A.D. 1331 ; 20,280, A.D. 1332.

Patrick de Chaworth, *6th Baron ?*

8512. [A.D. 1280.]   Plaster cast from chipped impression.
⅞ in.   [lxxxiv. 47.]

A shield of arms lozenge-shaped : nine barrules, or barruly,
four martlets in cross or orle, for CHAWORTH.   Betw. four
small quatrefoil panels.

✠ S' PATRICI DE CHAW . . ORZ ↗

Thomas de Chaworthe, *or* **Chawrthe,** *Knt.*

8513. [A.D. 1284.]   Light brown : well preserved, edge
chipped.   1⅜ in.   [Woll. ch. I. 21.]

A shield of arms : two chevrons, CHAWORTH.   Suspended
by a strap, from a hook, with the point in base resting on the
back of a lion couchant. ˳ Betw. two wyverns sans wings.

✠ SIGILLVM : THOME : DE : CHAWORTHE.

Beaded borders.

8514. Sulph. cast from No. 8513.   [D.C., F. 203.]

Thomas Chaworth, *of Pyghteslay Manor, co. Northt.*

8515. [A.D. 1419.]   Red : fine, very imperfect.   About
1⅜ in. when perfect.   [Add. ch. 22,388.]

An angel supporting in front with both arms a square-
shaped shield of arms : quarterly, 1, 4, two chevrons, CHA-
WORTH ; 2, 3, an escutcheon betw. eight cinquefoiled roses in
orle, DARCY (?)   At each side a shield of arms : *dex.,* broken
away ; *sin.,* barry of sixteen, three martlets, for CHAWORTH.
In base a third shield of arms : two lions passant guardant in
pale.   This last shield betw. two monograms, that in the l.
broken away, r. 𝕻 with curled tail.

𝔖igill[um] ✱ th . . . .

8516. Plaster cast.   [lxxxiv. 48.]

Johanna Chedder.

8517. [A.D. 1333.]   Plaster cast from fine impression.
1⅟₁₆ in.   [lxxxiv. 50.]

A shield of arms : per pale, *dex.,* a chevron ermine betw.

three escallops, CHEDDER ; *sin.*, ermine on a chief three bucks' heads cabossed.   Within a cusped panel.

✠ Sigillum ✱ iohanne ✱ Chedder ✿

Robert de Cheddre.

8518. [A.D. 1331.]   Plaster cast from fine impression. $1\frac{1}{16}$ in. [lxxxiv. 49.]

A shield of arms: a chevron ermine betw. three escallops, CHEDDER. Suspended by a strap from a forked tree on a mount. Within a finely-carved gothic panel.

S : rob'ti : de : cheddre :

Robert Cheddre, *or* William Cheddre, *of Bristol, co. Glouc.*

8519. [A.D. 1380.]   Red: well preserved. $\frac{5}{8} \times \frac{9}{16}$ in. [Harl. ch. 48 A. 22.]

Oval: a lion sejant, on its head a helmet and chapeau. Apparently a variant from the crest of CHEDDER, on a chapeau a lion passant guardant ducally crowned. Within a carved oval panel of tracery, ornamented along the inner edge with small quatrefoils.

Richard de Chelleray, *of Yedon, co. York.*

8520. [A.D. 1571.]   Red : very imperfect, centre only remaining. About $\frac{3}{4}$ in. when perfect. [Add. ch. 17,092.]

A shield of arms : a bend betw. two (rams' ?) heads. In a cusped panel.

. . . . .' T . . . .

Richard de Chelleray, *or* Chelray.
See THOMAS DE THWAYTE.

John de Chelsham.
See HUGH DE GORGES.

John Chene.
Seal used by WILLIAM CHENE, *of Boxford, etc., co. Suff., Knt.*

8521. [A.D. 1376.]   Brownish-green, semi-opaque : originally fine, imperfect at bottom and along edge. $1\frac{1}{16}$ in. [Harl. ch. 47 H. 48.]

A shield of arms, *couché*: quarterly a bend lozengy, CHEYNEY. Crest on a helmet and chapeau with lambrequins, two proboscides, crested and feathered.   Within a carved and traced gothic bilobe ornamented with small ball-flowers along the inner edge.

.. **S . Ioh'is .... ⊛ chene ⊛**

Carved border.

8522. Sulph. cast from No. 8521. [D.C., E. 497.]

Richard (dil) Cherche, *of Gislingham, co. Suff.*

8523. [A.D. 1391.] Red: edge imperfect. 1 in. [Harl. ch. 47 E. 13.]

A shield of arms: a fess betw. three martlets. Suspended by a strap from a tree.

: Sigillum ⚜ ricardi ⚜ cherche ⚜

Beaded border.

8524. Sulph. cast from No. 8523. [D.C., F. 580.]

Cf. next seal.

Richard dil Cherche, *of Gislingham, co. Suff.*

8525. [A.D. 1391.] Red: fine. 1 in. [Harl. ch. 48 F. 43.]

A shield of arms: a fesse betw. three fleurs-de-lis. Suspended by a strap from a tree. Inner border engrailed.

Sigillum ⚜ ricardi ⚜ cherche ⚜

Beaded borders.

Cf. Harl. ch. 47 E. 13, No. 8523, for a different coat of arms.

8526. Sulph. cast of No. 8525. [D.C., F. 581.]

John de Cherletone, *Lord of Powys, co. Montgom.*

8527. [A.D. 1368.] Red: originally fine, chipped along edge. 1¼ in. [Harl. ch. 48 A. 50.]

A shield of arms: a lion rampant, CHARLTON *of Powys.* Betw. two pairs of oak leaves slipped. Within a gothic panel of three points in triangle and five semicircular cusps ornamented with small ball-flowers along the inner edge.

⚜ Sigillu : ioh'is : de : cherletone : dni : powisie.

Carved border.

8528. Sulph. cast from No. 8527. [D.C., F. 458.]

Robert de Cherlton, *of West Wittenham, co. Berks.*

8529. [A.D. 1381.] Red: cracked, imperfect. ⅞ in. [Add. ch. 20,282.]

A shield of arms: a bend embattled counter-embattled. Within a cusped rosette of eight points.

Ranulph, *Earl of* Chester.

8530. [A.D. 1180–1231.]   Green : a fragment.   About 2¼ in. when perfect.   [Add. ch. 20,397.]

A shield of arms of early shape : a lion or wolf rampant.

✠ SIG.

See *Journ. Brit. Arch. Ass.,* vol. v., p. 235.

Sir John Chester, *of Chichley, co. Bucks., Bart.*

8531. [A.D. 1702.]   Red: *en placard.* 1⁴⁄₁₆ × ⅝ in.   [Add. ch. 23,896.]

Oval : a shield of arms : per pale, a chevron engrailed, betw. three rams' heads erased, in fess point on an escutcheon the hand of ULSTER, CHESTER.

Robert Chester, *of Royston, co. Hertf., Esq.*

8532. [A.D. 1599.]   Red : very indistinct.   ⅞ × ¾ in. [Add. ch. 36,371.]

Oval : a shield of arms : quarterly, 1, a griffin passant, CHESTER.   The other quarters very indistinct.

Robert Chester, *of Royston, co. Hertf., Knt.*

8533. [A.D. 1617.]   Red. 1¹⁄₁₆ × 1⁹⁄₁₆ in.   [Add. ch. 36,282.] Oval : a lion rampant.

Another Seal, used by ROBERT AUSTEN.

8534. [A.D. 1617.]   Red. ⅞ in.   [Add. ch. 36,282.]

A griffin passant.   The bearing of the shield of arms of CHESTER.

George Chettinge.
Seal used by ANDREWE RYVET, *of Brandeston, co. Suff., Gentl.*

8535. [A.D. 1563.]   Red : chipped, imperfect.   ⅝ × ½ in. [Harl. ch. 111 E. 51.]

Oval : a shield of arms : quarterly, on a bend, betw. two talbots' heads erased, three quatrefoils, CHITTINGE.

Beaded border.

John Chetewode, [*of Warkworth, co. Northt.*], *Knt.*

8536. [14th cent.]   Red : edge chipped.   1 in.   [xxxvi. 125.]

A shield of arms : a lion rampant, CHETWOOD.   Within three pairs of thyrsi or palm-branches.

✠ S'. ioħ'is : rɥetewoðe : militis.

Cf. John de Chetwode, Knt., A.D. 1305, in Syresham, co. Northt. Harl. ch. 84 E. 37.

———— **Wodyll,** *wife of* THOMAS Chethewod, *of Reyse or Rees, co. Chest., Esq.*

8537. [Mid. 15th cent.] Recent impression in red sealing-wax, from the matrix. 1⅜ in. [xxxv. 172.]

A shield of arms, *couché*: per pale, *dex.*, quarterly, four crosses pattées, CHETWODE; *sin.*, a lion rampant, WOODALL. Crest on a helmet and mantling, out of a ducal coronet a demi-lion rampant issuing.

𝔖𝔦𝔤𝔦𝔩𝔩𝔲𝔪 : . . . . :· 𝔴𝔬𝔡𝔶𝔩𝔩' : . 𝔲𝔯𝔬𝔯' : 𝔱𝔥𝔬𝔪𝔢 : 𝔠𝔥𝔢𝔱𝔥𝔢𝔴𝔬𝔡.

Cabled borders.

Cf. Harl. MSS. 1424, f. 34; 5868, f. 42.

8538. [A.D. 1438.] Plaster cast from imperfect impression. [xci. 40.]

. . . . . . 𝔴𝔬𝔡𝔶𝔩𝔩 . . . . . . 𝔱𝔥𝔬𝔪𝔢 : 𝔠𝔥𝔢𝔱𝔥𝔢𝔴𝔬𝔡 .

Robert de Chetwynde, *son of* D. PHILIP DE CHETEWYNDE, *of Ingestre, co. Staff.*

8539. [A.D. 1323.] Red: cracked, imperfect. ¾ in. [Add. ch. 20,458.]

A circular shield of arms: a chevron betw. three mullets, CHETWYND.

✠ . . . . . . I · DE CHETEWYND'.

Roger de Chetwynd, *of Shenston Manor, co. Staff.*

8540. [A.D. 1344.] Red: fine, edge chipped. ⅞ in. [Cott. ch. xxv. 11.]

A shield of arms, *couché*: a chevron betw. three mullets, CHETWYND. Crest on a helmet and short mantling or lambrequin, two hands and arms in armour holding the letter I, crowned. In the field on the l. a wavy sprig of foliage and flowers.

In place of the legend the initial letter I, repeated twelve times with as many roses alternately disposed.

Beaded borders.

8541. Sulph. cast of No. 8540. [D.C., F. 289.]

William Chetewynd.
Seal used by ROBERT WYLLIAMS, *al.* CROMWELL, *of Hinchingbrook, co. Hunt., Gentl.*

8542. [1570.] Red: edge imperfectly impressed. ⅞ in. [Add. ch. 34,101.]

A shield of arms: a fess lozengy or five lozenges in fess

betw. three mullets. Within a pointed gothic trefoil, ornamented with ball-flowers along the inner edge.

✠ S' : WILLI' : CHETEWYND ⚜

This seal is of the 14th century.

John de Cheverstun.

Seal used by JOHN HENDE, *Citizen and Clothier of London,*
or KATHARINE, *his wife;* THOMAS DE ST. EDMUND,
or ISABELLA, *his wife.*

8543. [A.D. 1385.]   Red: fine.   ¾ in.   [Harl. ch. 86 H. 25.]
A shield of arms : a lion rampant. Within a carved and
pointed gothic trefoil, ornamented with ball-flowers along
the inner edge.

✠ S' : IOH'IS : DE : CHEVERSTVN.

Beaded borders.
8544. Sulph. cast from No. 8543.   [D.C., F. 557.]

John de Cheverestone, *Knt.*

8545. [*Temp.* Edw. III.]   Red : fine, cut from a charter.
$1\frac{3}{16}$ in.   [xxxvi. 110.]
A shield of arms: on a bend three goats passant, bendwise.
Within a carved and traced gothic six-foil, or hexagon of six
curvilinear points.

✠ · S ✱ Johis ✱ De ✱ Cheuereſtone ✱ Militis ✱ ⚜

Beaded border.
8546. [*Temp.* Edw. III.]   Red : another.   [xxxvi. 111.]
8547. Plaster cast.   [lxxxiv. 55.]

Hugh de Cheyne.

8548. [A.D. 1363.]   Recent impression in gutta-percha
from fine but imperfect impression. $1\frac{1}{8}$ in.   [xlvii. 1309A.]
A shield of arms : chequy a fess fretty. Suspended by a
strap from a forked rose tree in full-bloom. Within a carved
and traced gothic panel with small ball-flowers along the
inner edge.

: Sigillum ⚜ hugoni . . . . cheyne :

Beaded borders.
Laing's *MS. Catal.*, No. 537.
Cf. Harl. ch. 43 E. 3, A.D. 1368.

8549. Gutta-percha mould from the same seal.   [xlv.ii.
1309 B.]

John Cheyne, *Parson of the Church of Hanbury,*
co. Stafford.

8550. [A.D. 1383.] Red: fragmentary. About ⅞ in. when perfect. [Woll. ch. 3. 1.]

A shield of arms : uncertain. Perhaps on a bend betw. six crosslets, CHEYNE. Within a carved gothic panel.

⋯⋯⋯⋯⋯ HEYNE ⋯⋯⋯⋯

Cf. Add. ch. 4859, A.D. 1365.

John Cheyne, *Knt.*

8551. [A.D. 1410.] Plaster cast from fine impression. 1¼ in. [lxxxiv. 53.]

A shield of arms, *couché* : chequy a fess fretty, CHEYNE. Crest on a helmet and chapeau a tree. Within a carved gothic panel.

𝕾𝖎𝖌𝖎𝖑𝖑𝖚 : 𝖎𝖔𝖍𝖎𝖘 : 𝖈𝖍𝖊𝖞𝖓𝖊 : 𝖒𝖎𝖑𝖎𝖙𝖎𝖘.

John Cheyne, *of Fen Ditton, co. Camb., Knt.*

8552. [A.D. 1475.] Red. ⅝ in. [Add. ch. 9190.]

A goat's head erased, ducally gorged. In the field an uncertain motto.

Cabled border.

Cf. Add. ch. 5470, 5471, A.D. 1467 ; Add. ch. 13,066, 18,769, A.D. 1476 ; and Add. ch. 8101, A.D. 1489.

8553. [A.D. 1471.] Red: indistinct. [Add. ch. 18,769.]

8554. [A.D. 1476.] Red. [Stowe ch. 228.]

John Cheyne.

8555. [A.D. 1476.] Red. ½ in. [Add. ch. 13,066.]

A shield (of arms ?) : a helmet, on which is a bull's scalp ; betw. the attires a small cross. For the crest of CHEYNEY, viz., a bull's scalp.

John Cheyne, *of co. Suss.*

8556. [A.D. 1484.] Red. From a ring. ½ × ⅜ in. [Add. ch. 29,829.]

Oval : a mermaid, with a mirror and comb.

Border engrailed.

8557. [A.D. 1484.] Another. [Add. ch. 29,830.]

Roger Cheyne.

8558. [A.D. 1358.] Plaster cast from fine impression. ⅞ in. [lxxxiv. 51.]

A shield of arms : chequy, a fess fretty, CHEYNE. Suspended by a strap.   Betw. two palm branches.

※ Sigillum : rogeri : cheyne.

Beaded borders.

Thomas Cheyne, *or* **Cheinie,** *of Goldehangre,*
co. Essex., Knt.

8559. [A.D. 1372.] Red: fine. ⅞ in. [Cott. ch. xxiv. 12.]
A shield of arms : a fess wavy betw. three crescents, CHEYNEY.   Betw. two sprays of foliage.   Suspended by a strap from a forked tree.   Within a carved and cusped gothic panel.

: Sigillum : thome : cheyne :

Beaded borders.
8560. Sulph. cast from No. 8559. [D.C., F. 483.]

John Cheyny, *or* Cheyne, *son of* WILLIAM CHEYNE, *Knt.,*
late Lord of the Manor of Broke, co. Wilts., Esq.

8561. [A.D. 1467.] Red: fine, somewhat injured by pressure. 1 1/16 in. [Add. ch. 5470.]
A shield of arms : four fusils in fess, on each an escallop, in dexter chief a mullet for difference, CHEYNEY.   Suspended by a strap from a tree.   Within a cusped border.

Sigillum ✠ iohannis ✠ cheyny ✠

8562. [A.D. 1467.] Red : fine, indistinct in places. [Add. ch. 5471.]

William Cheini, *or* **Cheyney,** *of Hulpryngton,*
co. Wilts., Knt.

8563. [A.D. 1405.]   Red, speckled : fine, edge chipped. 1¾ in. [Add. ch. 5687.]
A shield of arms : four fusils in fess, on each an escallop, CHEYNEY.   Suspended by a strap from a forked tree.   Within a carved gothic bilobe, ornamented with ball-flowers along the inner edge.

Sigillu : will'mi : cheini : militis :

Cabled border.

William Cheyne, *of Sheppy, co. Kent.*

8564. [A.D. 1435.]   Red : fragmentary, indistinct.   About 1¼ in. when perfect. [Harl. ch. 47 H. 49.]
A shield of arms, *couché*: (six) lioncels rampant, (three,

two, and one,) a canton, CHEYNEY. Crest (on a helmet) a
bull's scalp. Within a gothic panel.

$$\mathfrak{S}' \quad \mathfrak{will} \ldots \ldots \quad \mathfrak{the} \ldots \ldots$$

8565. [A.D. 1408.] Plaster cast from imperfect impression.
[lxxxiv. 52.]

$$\mathfrak{S} \ldots \mathfrak{ill} \ldots \ldots \mathfrak{cheyne} \; \text{\tiny M}$$

Beaded borders.

Ralph Chiche, *of co. Kent, Gentl.*
8566. [A.D. 1488.] Red: injured. About ½ × ⅜ in. when
perfect. [Harl. ch. 86 G. 57.]
Oval: a lion rampant. In allusion to the arms of CHICHE,
viz., three lions rampant.

Thomas Chiche, *or* Chicche, *of the I. of Thanet, co. Kent.*
8567. [A.D. 1418.] Red: originally fine, and encircled by
a twisted rush, now missing, injured in places by pressure.
1⅛ in. [Add. ch. 16,489.]
A shield of arms: three lions rampant, two and one, within
a bordure, CHICHE. Suspended by a strap from a forked
tree, and within a carved gothic panel ornamented with ball-
flowers along the inner edge.

$$\mathfrak{Sigill'} : \mathfrak{th\bar{e}} : \mathfrak{chiche} : \mathfrak{De} : \mathfrak{bo} \ldots \ldots \text{\tiny M}$$

The letters DE are conjoined.
Cabled border.

Sir John Chichester, *of Hale, co. Devon, Knt.*
8568. [A.D. 1637.] Red: injured. About $\frac{9}{16}$ × ½ in.
[Harl. ch. 83 H. 39.]
Oval: a shield of arms: chequy, a chief vairé, CHICHESTER.
Beaded border.
8569. [A.D. 1660.] Red, covered with paper before impression: indistinct. [Harl. ch. 85 H. 59.]
8570. [A.D. 1660.] Red, covered with paper before impression: indistinct. [Harl. ch. 111 E. 36.]

John Chichester, *son and heir of* JOHN CHICHESTER, *Knt.,*
of Hale, co. Devon., Esq.
8571. [A.D. 1660.] Red, covered with paper before impression: indistinct. [Harl. ch. 85 H. 59.]
Oval: a shield of arms: per pale, *dex.*, chequy, a chief
vairé, CHICHESTER; *sin.*, quarterly, I, 4, indistinct; 2, 3, a
cross.
8572. [A.D. 1660.] Red, covered with paper before impression: indistinct. [Harl. ch. 111 E. 36.]

Sir **John Chichester,** *of Rawleigh, co.. Devon, Bart.*
8573. [A.D. 1656.]   Red: very indistinct.   About ¾ × ⅝ in.
[Harl. ch. 83 H. 40.]
Oval: a shield of arms: chequy, a chief *vairé*, CHICHESTER.
Crest on a helmet, ornamental mantling and wreath, a heron
rising with an eel in its beak.
8574. [A.D. 1657.]   Red, covered with paper before impression: very indistinct.   [Harl. ch. 83 H. 42.]
8575. [A.D. 1660.]   Red, covered with paper before impression: injured.   [Harl. ch. 83 H. 38.]
8576. [A.D. 1660.]   Red, covered with paper before impression: somewhat indistinct.   [Harl. ch. 111 E. 36.]
8577. [A.D. 1660.]   Red, covered with paper before impression: indistinct.   [Harl. ch. 85 H. 59.]

Another Seal.

8578. [A.D. 1660.]   Red, covered with paper before impression: indistinct.   About ⅝ × ½ in.   [Harl. ch. 111 E. 37.]
Oval: a shield of arms: three uncertain charges within a
bordure.

Mary, *wife of* JOHN **Chichester,** *of Rawleigh, co. Devon.*
8579. [A.D. 1662.]   Red: fragmentary.   [Add. ch. 1637.]
A shield of arms: charges too imperfect to ascertain.
Perhaps chequy, a chief *vairé*, CHICHESTER.

John de Chidiok, *of co. Dorset. Knt.*
8580. [A.D. 1351.]   Red: fragments.   About 1 in. when
perfect.   [Harl. ch. 48 B. 5.]
A shield of arms: [an escutcheon betw. eight martlets in
orle, of which there remains only] one martlet in sinister chief,
CHIDIOK.   Suspended by a strap from a hook.
Legend in the field :—
              . . . . . IOH' . . . . IOK.
The annular space for the usual legend is filled with a
carved border of countersunk quatrefoils.

John Chidiock, *of co. Dorset.*
8581. [A.D. 1425.]   Recent impression in gutta-percha
from fine impression.   1⅛ in.   [xlvii. 1523.]
A shield of arms, *couché*: an escutcheon betw. eight
martlets in orle, CHIDIOK.   Crest on a helmet, ornamental
mantling and wreath, a garb.
          𝕾𝖎𝖌𝖎𝖑𝖑'𝖚 ⚜ : ⚜ 𝖎𝖔𝖍𝖎𝖘 ⚜ : ⚜ 𝖈𝖍𝖎𝖉𝖎𝖔𝖐 : ⚜
Cabled borders.

Henry de Childerwyk, *of Haldenby, co. Northt.*
8582. [A.D. 1363.] Creamy-white : imperfect on l. side.
¾ in. [Add. ch. 21,927.]
A shield of arms : a chevron betw. three fleurs-de-lis.
Within a carved gothic panel.

¤ **Sigi : henrei : de : chil . . . . . .**
Beaded border.

William de Chirchehull, *one of the executors of the will of*
WILLIAM DE CLYNTON, *Earl of Huntingdon.*
8583. [A.D. 1357.] Red : originally fine, very imperfect.
About ⅞ × ¾ in. when perfect. [Harl. ch. 76 F. 28.]
Oval : a shield of arms : ermine, on a fess two estoiles of
six points. Within a carved gothic panel with two cusped
and two ogee points, ornamented with ball-flowers along the
inner edge.

S' wilell : de . . . .
The letters D E of *de* conjoined.

William de Chishulle, *of Grant Lawefare*
[? *Great Laver, co. Essex.*]
8584. [*Temp.* Edw. I.] Green : fine, chipped at lower
part. About 1 in. when perfect. [Add. ch. 28,446.]
A shield of arms : a lion rampant.

¤ **S' WILL . . . . HVLLE.**

Richard Chokke, *Knt., Chief Justice of the Common Pleas,*
A.D. 1462.
8585. [A.D. 1472.] Red : fine, from a ring. ½ in. [Add.
ch. 5473.]
On a helmet a stork's head and ornamental mantling, crest
of CHOKE. In the field two small sprigs. Inner edge of field
engrailed or cusped.
Cabled border.

John, *fil.* HERBERTI **de Cholingham,**
of Chesterfield, co. Derb.
8586. [*Late* 13*th cent.*] Green, mottled. 1 in. [Harl.
ch. 83 G. 39.]
A shield : charged with a crescent enclosing a roundle.
Above it, a cross ; and on each side three roundles. Coarse
workmanship.
8587. Sulph. cast from No. 8586. [D.C., E. 398.]

George Cholmondeley, *2nd Earl of Cholmondeley.*
A.D. 1725–1733.

8588. [A.D. 1725.]   Plaster cast from fine impression.
$1\frac{7}{16}$ in. [lxxxiv. 56.].

A shield of arms : two helmets in chief and a garb in base.
CHOLMONDELEY.   Ensigned with an earl's coronet.   Supporters, *dex.*, a griffin, *sin.*, a wolf.

On an escrol in base, the motto :—
　　　　CASSIS · TVTISSIMA · VIRTVS.
Beaded or carved border.

Sir **Henry Cholmeley,** *of Newhouse, co. York, Knt.*

8589. [A.D. 1658.]   Red : indistinct. $\frac{1}{2} \times \frac{3}{8}$ in.   [Add. ch. 30,946.]

Octagonal signet : a shield of arms : two helmets in chief, and a garb in base, within a bordure, CHOLMELEY. Legend around on a bevelled edge.
　　　· ✠ · BONVS · AMICVS ·BONVS · ANGELVS.

8590. [A.D. 1658.]   Red : injured, indistinct. [Add. ch. 30,947.]
　　　... BONVS · AMICVS · BONV...... ,

8591. [A.D. 1658.]   Red : indistinct.   [Add. ch. 30,948.]
Legend as above.

8592. [A.D. 1658.]   Red : somewhat injured by pressure. [Add. ch. 30,949.]
Legend as above.

Sir **Hugh Cholmeley,** *of Whitby, co. York, Knt.*

8593. [A.D. 1642.]   Red : indistinct.   About $\frac{1}{2} \times \frac{3}{8}$ in. [Add. ch. 30,936.]

Oval : a shield of arms : quarterly, 1, 4, two helmets in chief, and a garb in base, CHOLMELEY ; 2, 3, a fess with uncertain charges on it, cf. No. 8600.   In fess point a mark of difference.

8594. [A.D. 1655.]   Red : very indistinct.   [Add. ch. 30,940.]

8595. [A.D. 1655.]   Red : very indistinct.   [Add. ch. 30,941.]

Hugh Cholmeley, *Esq., 2nd son of Sir* HUGH CHOLMELEY, *late of Whitby, co. York, Knt. and Bart.*

8596. [A.D. 1658.]   Red : somewhat injured. $\frac{2}{8} \times \frac{1}{4}$ in. [Add. ch. 30,946.]

Oval : on a wreath a demi-griffin segreant holding a helmet. Crest of CHOLMELEY.

8597. [A.D. 1658.] Rēd : indistinct. [Add. ch. 30,947.]
8598. [A.D. 1658.] Red : indistinct. [Add. ch. 30,948.]

John Cholmley, of co. Monm.

8599. [A.D. 1691.] Red : *en placard*, imperfect. $\frac{11}{16} \times \frac{9}{16}$ in.
[Add. ch. 5349.]
Oval : an ornamental shield of arms : two helmets in chief,
and a garb in base, CHOLMELEY.

William Cholmeley, son and heir of Sir HUGH CHOLMELEY,
of Whitby, co. York, Bart.

8600. [A.D. 1658.] Red : indistinct. About $\frac{1}{2} \times \frac{3}{4}$ in.
[Add. ch. 30,946.]
Oval : a shield of arms : quarterly, 1, 4, two helmets in
chief, and a garb in base, CHOLMELEY ; 2, 3, on a fess three
roundles.
Beaded border.
8601a. [A.D. 1658.] Red : indistinct. [Add. ch. 30,947.]
8601b. [A.D. 1658.] Red : indistinct. [Add. ch. 30,948.]

Philip Chowte, of Sextrey, al. Natyngton Manor,
co. Kent, Esq.

8602. [A.D. 1564.] Red : indistinct. $\frac{2}{8} \times \frac{3}{8}$ in. [Harl. ch.
76 F. 30.]
Ornamental-shaped seal from a signet ring : on a wreath
a dexter arm and hand grasping a broken sword. Cf. crest
of CHUTE.

William Chusulden, Receiver of the Honour of Leicester.

8603. [A.D. 1392.] Red : fine, chipped. $\frac{7}{8}$ in. [Add. ch.
21,453.]
A shield of arms : three estoiles wavy within a bordure
engrailed. Betw. two trefoils. Within an elegantly carved
gothic cinquefoil ornamented with ball-flowers along the inner
edge.

✠ 𝕾 . . . . . . 𝖜𝖎𝖑𝖑𝖊𝖑𝖒𝖎 . . . . 𝖋𝖚𝖑𝖉𝖊𝖓.
Beaded border.

Colley Cibber.
See JOHN HODSON.

Walter de Cilvinghu.
See WALTER DE KILVINGHOLM.

2 T 2

Thomas Clapeham, *of Bemysley,* [*Beamsley, co. York*], *Esq.*
8604. [A.D. 1442.] Red: imperfectly impressed. About
$\frac{5}{8} \times \frac{1}{2}$ in. when perfect. [Add. ch. 16,931.]
A shield of arms: a fess betw. three pierced mullets. In
the field a flowering sprig (?)

(?) Honour *of* **Clare,** *used by* THOMAS CLOYDON, *Esq.,*
Eschaetor in co. Norf.
8605. [A.D. 1612.] Brownish-red. $\frac{1}{2}$ in. [Add. ch. 9276.]
A shield of arms: three chevronels, CLARE. Over it the
inscription :—CLARE.
Beaded border.

Gilbert de Clare, *7th Earl of Hertford and Gloucester.*
[A.D. 1261–1295.]

Privy Seal.

8606. [A.D. 1276.] Plaster cast from chipped impression.
$\frac{13}{16}$ in. [lxxxiv. 59.]
A shield of arms: three chevrons, CLARE. Suspended by
a strap from a hook.
[✠ S]IGILLVM · SECRETI.
Beaded borders.

Another.

8607. [A.D. 1290.] Plaster cast from indistinct impression.
1 in. [lxxxiv. 58.]
A shield of arms: CLARE. Suspended by a strap. Betw.
two lions rampant reguardant addorsed. In the field, on
each side, a mullet or cinquefoil.
✠ SECRETVM · GILEBERTI · DE · CLARE ᴀ
Beaded borders.

Clarence, *Dukes of.*
See LIONEL PLANTAGENET.
See THOMAS PLANTAGENET.

Thos. Clark.
See CLIFFORD.

William Clark, *of Chisfeild, co. Hertf., Esq.*
8608. [A.D. 1626.] Red: indistinct and imperfect. About
$\frac{9}{16} \times \frac{7}{16}$ in. [Add. ch. 35,442.]
Oval: a shield of arms: a chevron betw. uncertain charges.
8609. [A.D. 1626.] Another: injured. [Add. ch. 35,443.]

Alexander de Claveringe, *of co. Essex.*

8610. [A.D. 1318–9.] Green: fine, cut from a charter.
$\frac{7}{8}$ in. [xxxv. 320.]

A shield of arms: quarterly, on a bend three mullets,
CLAVERING.

⚹ S'.: ALEXANDRI DE CLAVERINGE.

Eva, *dau. of* JOHAN **de Clavering,** *2nd Baron Clavering.*

8611. [A.D. 1334.] Red: originally fine, very imperfect.
About $1\frac{1}{8}$ in. when perfect. [Harl. ch. 48 B. 34.]

A shield of arms: per pale, *dex.*, a cross lozengy, dimidiated,
over all a bend, UFFORD, for Ralph de UFFORD, her first
husband; *sin.*, fretty of six pieces for AUDLEY, for Thomas
de AUDLEY, her second husband. Within a carved gothic
panel of three points and five semicircular cusps, ornamented
with ball-flowers along the inner edge. Outside this the
carving and tracery, which is very elaborate, contains three
cusped countersunk panels in triangle, in each of which
is a lozenge-shaped shield of arms: quarterly a bendlet,
CLAVERING.

. . . . € ❀ DE ❀ . . . .

John de Claveryngge.
See WALRAN DE HOYCOURT.

Isabella, *wife of* WILLIAM **de Clavyle,** *of Yetminster,*
co. Dors.

8612. [A.D. 1351.] Red: imperfect, badly impressed.
About $\frac{7}{8}$ in. when perfect. [Harl. ch. 48 B. 37.]

A shield of arms, *couché*: a saltire. Crest, on a helmet and
lambrequin or short mantling, a Katharine wheel. Supporter
on the *dexter* side only, a wyvern sans wings tail nowy.

KATERI[NE · C]ES MEYNTEYNE.

Beaded borders.

Nicholas de Claytone, *of co. Derb., etc.*

8613. [A.D. 1424.] Brown. $\frac{3}{8}$ in. [Woll. ch. x. 56.]

A shield of arms: a cross flory, for CLAYTONE (?) in sinister
chief a fleur-de-lis. Within a carved six-foil.

Mary Claxton, *wife of* HAMOND CLAXTON, *of St. Giles,*
co. Midd.

8614. [A.D. 1638.] Red: injured by pressure. $\frac{9}{16} \times \frac{3}{8}$ in.
[Add. ch. 14,757.]

On a wreath a stag lodged reguardant gorged with a ducal coronet. Perhaps crest of CLAXTON, or in reference to the arms, viz., a chevron betw. three bucks.

William de Claxton, *or* Clauxton, *of co. York, Knt.*
8615. [A.D. 1379.]　Dark green : indistinct, partially injured by pressure.　1 in.　[Egert. ch. 575.]
···'A· shield of· arms, '*couché*: a fess betw. three hedgehogs, CLAXTON.　Crest on a helmet and lambrequin or short mantling, a garb.　Within a carved and traced gothic panel ornamented with ball-flowers along the inner edge.

$\mathfrak{S}'$　willelmi · de : claxton.

8616. Plaster cast from chipped impression.　[lxxxiv. 61.]

$\mathfrak{S}'$　willelmi . d . . laxton.

Edmund *dictus* Clay.
8617. [14th cent.]　Sulph. cast from imperfect impression, injured by pressure.　$1\frac{1}{8}$ in.　[D.C., F. 357.]
A shield of arms, *couché*: a chevron betw. three uncertain charges.　Cf. a chevron betw. three trefoils slipped, for CLAY. Crest on a helmet, lambrequin, and chapeau, a ball betw. two buttresses (?)　Within a carved gothic panel.

$\mathfrak{S}igil'$: edmundi : dci : clay.

John Claymond, *President of Magdalen College, Oxford.*
8618. [A.D. 1513.]　Red : injured.　About $\frac{5}{8} \times \frac{4}{8}$ in.　[Add. ch. 20,363.]
Octagonal signet : on a shield of peculiar and arbitrary shape : an escallop.

Thomas Claymond, *of Littlington, co. Cambr.*
8619. [A.D. 1379.]　Red : fine.　1 in.　[Add. ch. 25,945.]
A shield of arms : a fess betw. three mounts. Suspended by a strap from a forked tree.　Within a cusped border of six carved points ornamented with ball-flowers along the inner edge.

$\mathfrak{S}igillum$: thome : Claymond :

Beaded border.

Thomas Claymond.
See W—— S——.

John Clayton.
Seal used by THOMAS INGRAM, *of Thistleworth, co. Midd., Knt.*
8620. [A.D. 1658.] Red. ⅛ × ⅚ in. [Add. ch. 30,952.]
Oval: a shield of arms: a cross engrailed betw. four
roundles, CLAYTON.
Above the shield a label inscribed:—
FORTITER.

Nicholas de Claytonè, *of Pinxton, etc., co. Derb.*
8621. [A.D. 1424.] Reddish-brown: indistinct. ¾ in.
[Woll. ch. x. 56.]
A shield of arms: a cross flory, for CLAYTON. In sinister
chief, a fleur-de-lis. Within a gothic panel of six cusps of
irregular dimensions.

Richard Clederowe.
8622. [A.D. 1417–8.] Plaster cast from fine impression,
much injured, and imperfect. 1⅛ in. [lxxxiv: 72.]
A shield of arms, *couché*: on a bend three mullets, in chief
a martlet, CLIDEROWE. Crest, on a helmet, mantling or
lambrequin, and wreath, a bird's head, imperfect. Betw. two
wavy sprigs. Within a carved panel with tracery at the sides
and ornamented with small ball-flowers along the inner edge.
[Sig]illū : ricardi ✠ . . ✠ : clederowe : ✠
Cf. No. 1042, vol. I.

Richard Cletherow, *or* **Clyderow,** *of the Isle of Thanet,*
co. Kent.
8623. [A.D. 1418.] Red. ⅛ in. [Add. ch. 16,489.]
On a field semé of trefoils, a martlet, in allusion to one of
the charges in the arms of CLYDEROWE.
Legend in the field above.
r : cletherow.

E—— Cleland (?)
Seal used by GEORGE WAUTON, *or* JOHN PEETE,
of Muche Stoughton, co. Hunt.
8624. [A.D. 1569.] Red: imperfect. [Add. ch. 34,089.]
An ornamental shield of arms: a hare or rabbit sejant,
contourné, CLELAND. Betw. the initials E. C.

John Clemens.
See R—— GOLDESBURGH.

Edmund Clenche, *of Great Bealings, co. Suff., Gentl. ;*
and ELIZABETH, *his wife.*

8625. [A.D. 1668.] Red : very imperfect, injured by
pressure. About ¾ × ⅝ in. when perfect. [Add. ch. 5114.]

Oval : a shield of arms : quarterly, 1, 4, six annulets conjoined in pairs, two pairs in chief and one in base, a chief,
CLENCH ; 2, a bend cotised, CLENCH ; 3, a chevron betw.
three estoiles. Crest on a helmet and mantling, out of a
Saxon crown an arm erect, couped at the elbow, holding in
the hand a club, CLENCH.

8626. Another. [Add. ch. 5114.]

Elizabeth Clenche, *wife of* EDMUND CLENCHE,
of Greate Bealings, co. Suff.

8627. [A.D. 1661.] Light red : indistinct. ⅝ × ½ in.
[Add. ch. 5112.]

Oval : a shield of arms : quarterly, 1, 4, a cross flory ; 2, 3,
a chevron betw. three garbs.

Cabled border.

William Clenche, *of Ipswich, co. Suff., Merchant.*

8628. [A.D. 1690.] Red : *en placard,* on a label. About
¾ × ⅝ in. [Add. ch. 5120.]

Oval : a shield of arms and crest. See seal of Edmund
Clenche, Nos. 8625, 8626.

8629. [A.D. 1690.] Another. [Add. ch. 5121.]

William Clenche.
Seal used by FRANCES CLIATT, *or* CLYATT, *of Butley,*
co. Suff., Widow.

8630. [A.D. 1697.] Red : *en placard,* on a label ; cracked,
imperfect. [Add. ch. 10,290.]

Seal as described for William Clench, No. 8628.

Robert Clere, *of Sele and Kemsing, co. Kent, Knt.*
8631. [A.D. 1525.] Red. ½ in. [Harl. ch. 86 H. 16.]

An eagle displayed with inverted wings ; in allusion to the
arms of CLERE.

Cabled border.

Walter, *dictus* **Clericus** *de Lynleye,* [? *co. Herts.*]
8632. [A.D. 1346.] Creamy-white, discoloured. ¾ in.
[Add. ch. 28,756.]

A shield of arms : uncertain, perhaps quarterly a bend.
Legend indistinct.

Elizabeth, *widow of* NICHOLAS CLERCK, *Esq., son and heir of* JOHN CLERCK, *of cos. Oxon. and Bucks., Knt.*
8633. [A.D. 1552.] Red. $\frac{5}{8} \times \frac{1}{2}$ in. [Harl. ch. 79 G. 29.]
Shield-shaped: a ram's head erased, crest of CLERK.
Betw. the initial letters E. C.

Sir **Frauncis Clerke,** *or* **Clarke,** *of Hicham, co. Buck., Knt.*
8634. [A.D. 1631.] Red: injured by pressure. About $\frac{1}{2} \times \frac{3}{8}$ in. [Harl. ch. 76 F. 38.]
Oval signet: on a wreath a ram's head couped, crest of CLARKE. Cf. Harl. ch. 75 H. 49.
Cabled border.

Dame **Grissell,** *widow of Sir* FRANCIS **Clerke** *or* **Clarke,** *of Hitcham, co. Buck., Knt.*
8635. [A.D. 1634.] Red: fine. $\frac{1}{2} \times \frac{3}{8}$ in. [Harl. ch. 75 H. 49.]
Oval signet: as described for Sir Fr. Clerke or Clarke in No. 8634.
8636. [A.D. 1634.] Red. [Harl. ch. 76 F. 40.]
8637. [A.D. 1634.] Red. [Harl. ch. 76 F. 41.]
8638. [A.D. 1634.] Red. [Harl. ch. 76 F. 42.]
8639. [A.D. 1634.] Red. [Harl. ch. 76 F. 43.]
8640. [A.D. 1634.] Red: injured by pressure. [Harl. ch. 76 F. 44.]
8641. [A.D. 1634.] Red. [Harl. ch. 77 H. 15.]

James Clerke, *Rector of Toft Monks, co. Norf.*
Seals used by the Parishioners of Toft Monks.
8642–8645. [A.D. 1706.] Red: *en placard* on a tape. About $\frac{5}{8}$ in. [Add. ch. 14,921.]
A shield of arms: a saltire betw. four horses' heads couped, CLERKE.
Four impressions.

John Clerk, *of Plecy, co. Essex.*
8646. [A.D. 1472.] Red: indistinct, edge imperfect. $1\frac{1}{8}$ in. [Add. ch. 18,133.]
A shield of arms, *couché*: three animals' heads, or castles. Crest on a helmet, a pair of wings erect. Supporters, two lions sejant guardant.
Legend uncertain.

John Clerk.
See PHILADELPHIA CARRE.

Stephen Clerk, *of Kenilworth, co. Warw.*
8647. [A.D. 1414.] Red : very indistinct. ⅜ in. [Woll. ch. v. 14.]
A shield of arms : a cross voided.
Legend indistinct.

William Clerke, *or* **Clarke,** *of Hitcham, co. Buck., Esq.*
8648. [A.D. 1620.] Red : fine. ¼ in. [Harl. ch. 86 I. 61.]
An escallop : in reference to the arms of CLARKE.

Richard Cletherow.
See RICHARD CLEDEROWE.

John de Clevedone.
8649. [A.D. 1350.] Plaster cast from fine impression. 1⁵⁄₁₆ in. [lxxxiv. 62.]
A shield of arms, *couché* : three escallops, two and one, for CLEVEDON. Crest on a helmet and mantling, a fan plume. In the field on l. h. side a wavy sprig of foliage. Within a carved gothic panel of eight points.
✠ SIGILLVM · IOHANNIS · DE · CLEVEDONE.

Frances Cliatt.
See WILLIAM CLENCHE.

Clifford, *Family of.*
Seal used by
CHARLES ROSS, *of St. James', Westminster, Carpenter.*
THOS. CLARK *and* WM. PERRITT,
of St. George's, Hanover Square, Plasterers.
GEO. MERCER, *of London, Mason.*
RALPH CRUTCHER, *of St. James', Westminster, Bricklayer.*
EDW. IVES, *of St. George's, Bloomsbury, Plumber.*
FRANCIS SHEFFIELD, *of St. James', Westminster, Smith.*
8650–8655. [A.D. 1749.] Red : *en placard,* imperfectly impressed. ⅞ × ¾ in. [Add. ch. 13,748.]
Oval : an ornamental shield of arms : per pale, *dex.,* chequy, on a fess three leopards' faces, CLIFFORD ; *sin.,* semé of billets, a lion rampant. Crest on a wreath, out of a ducal coronet, a griffin's head.
Six impressions.

Alexander Clyfford, *son of* LODEWIC CLYFFORD,
of Shorne Manor, etc., co. Kent.
8656. [A.D. 1452.] Dark-red: originally good, cracked,
and 'l. side wanting. 1⅛ in. [Harl. ch. 48 C. 36.]
A shield of arms, *couché*: per pale, *dex.*, chequy a fess,
CLIFFORD ; *sin.*, six lioncels rampant, three, two, and one.
Crest on a helmet and tasselled mantling or lambrequins, a
lion's gamb erect, erased.
S alexand' clifford.
Beaded borders.
8657. Sulph. cast of No. 8656. [D.C., G. 246.]

Alexander Clyfford, *of Goutherst, co. Kent., Armiger.*
8658. [A.D. 1491.] Dark-brown: chipped. About $\frac{9}{16} \times \frac{1}{4}$ in.
[Harl. ch. 76 H. 6.]
Small signet : a lion's gamb couped at the knee.

Rt. Hon. **Anne Clifford,** *Countess of Cumberland,*
[*dau. of* WILLIAM, *Lord Dacres ;*
widow of HENRY CLIFFORD, *2nd Earl of Cumberland.*]
8659. [A.D. 1574.] Red, discoloured: injured. About
$\frac{3}{8}$ in. [Harl. ch. 76 D. 53.]
On a wreath, an antelope passant, collared and lined, the
line reflexed over the back and betw. the legs. Cf. Harl. ch.
76 G. 8.
8660. [A.D. 1577.] Red: indistinct. [Harl. ch. 76 G. 8.]

Euphemia Clifford,
widow of ROBERT CLIFFORD, *Lord Westmorland.*
See EUPHEMIA DE LUCY.

John Clifford, [*7th Baron Clifford.*]
8661. [A.D. 1417.] Red: originally fine, very imperfect.
About 1¾ in. when perfect. [Harl. ch. 48 C. 35.]
A shield of arms, *couché*: quarterly, 1, 4, chequy a fess,
CLIFFORD ; 2, 3, quarterly, i., iv., six annulets, VIPONT (?)
ii., iii., indistinct, perhaps three water bougets, ROSS, of
Hamlake. Crest on a helmet and lambrequins, a wyvern
rising with wings expanded. Supporters two wyverns.
Legend destroyed.
8662. Sulph. cast of No. 8661. [D.C., G. 149.]

John, *Bastard of* Clyfforde, *Esq.*

8663. [15th cent.] Plaster cast from fine impression.
1¼ in. [lxxxiv. 65.]

A shield of arms : chequy, a bend, and over all a fess,
CLIFFORD. Supporters two wyverns.

✠ 𝔖𝔦𝔤𝔦𝔩𝔩𝔲𝔪 ⚜ 𝔦𝔬𝔥𝔦𝔰 ⚜ 𝔟𝔞𝔩𝔱𝔞𝔯𝔡𝔦 ⚜ 𝔡𝔢 ⚜ 𝔠𝔩𝔶𝔣𝔣𝔬𝔯𝔡𝔢 ⚜ 𝔞𝔯𝔪𝔦𝔤'.

Loys de Clyffort, *Chevalier,*
Lord of Lantyan Manor, co. Cornw.

8664. [A.D. 1395.] Red : injured by pressure. ⅞ in.
[Cott. ch. xxiv. 22.]

A wyvern rising with expanded wings, contourné, crest of
CLIFFORD. Charged on the neck with a small shield of
arms : chequy a fess, CLIFFORD.

Legend in the field :—

𝔩𝔬𝔶𝔰 𝔠𝔩𝔦𝔣𝔣𝔬𝔯𝔡.

Margaret Clifford, *widow of* GEORGE CLIFFORD,
Earl of Cumberland ;
dau. of FRANCIS RUSSELL, *Earl of Bedford.*

8665. [A.D. 1609.] Red : a fragment. About ⅞ in. when
perfect. [Harl. ch. 76 G. 9.]

Oval : an indistinct crest on a wreath, perhaps an antelope
passant. Ensigned with a coronet.

Carved borders.

Cf. Harl. ch. 76 D. 53, 76 G. 8.

Robert de Clifort.

8666. [A.D. 1301.] Plaster cast from fine impression.
1¼ in. [lxxxiv. 64.]

A shield of arms : chequy, a fess, CLIFFORD. Betw. six
annulets. Within a six-foil rosette.

Legend betw. the lobes :—

S' R—OBE—RTI—DE C—LIF—ORT.

Roger de Clifford, *Sen.,*
of Bruges, and Lulham, co. Heref.

8667. [Late Hen. III.] Dark-green : fine, chipped. App.
by green cords plaited. 1 in. [Harl. ch. 48 C. 32.]

A shield of arms : chequy a fess, CLIFFORD. Betw. two
wavy scrolls of foliage.

✠ SIGI[LL' : RO]GERI : DE CLIFFORD.

Beaded borders.

8668. Sulph. cast of No. 8667. [D.C., E. 375.]

8669. [*Temp.* Edw. I.] Dark-green : cracked, injured by pressure. [Harl. ch. 48 C. 33.]

[✠ SIIGILL' : ROGERI : DE CLIIFFORD.]

Walter de Cliford, *al.* Clifford, *al.* Clyford,
son of WALTER DE CLIFORD *and* AGNES DE CUNDI,
Lord of Buckingham. [*ob.* A.D. 1264.]

8670. Bronze-green : fine, now chipped ; app. by a plaited cord of blue and white threads to a charter now wanting. 1⅜ in. [xl. 15.]

Ø. A pip-shaped shield of arms : chequy a bendlet, for CLIFFORD.

✠ SIGILL'M WA . . . . FORD ⦂

The L L in *sigill'm* are conjoined.
℞. A smaller counterseal. 1⅛ in.
A shield of arms: chequy a bend.

✠ SECRET . . . . WALTERI : D' · CLIFFOℝ.

The letters O R in *Cliffor'* are conjoined.

8671. Dark-green : chipped, indistinct in places ; app. by a diapered bobbin of black and white thread. [Harl. ch. 48 C. 26.]

✠ SIGILL'M : WALTERI : D . . . . . ORD.

No counterseal.

8672. Dark-green : edge chipped. [Harl. ch. 48 C. 30.]

✠ SIGILL'M : WALTERI : DE ⸱ . . . . FFORD.

No counterseal.

8673. Bronze-green : fine, sharp, edge chipped, cracked ; app. by a bobbin as in No. 8671. [Harl. ch. 48 C. 27.]

Ø. ✠ SIGILL'M : WALTERI : DE : CLIFFORD.

℞. ✠ SECRETVM WALT . . . . D' CLIFF . . . . .

8674. Sulph. cast of No. 8673. [D.C., E. 388.]
8675. Plaster cast of No. 8673 (*rev.*). [lxxxiv. 63.]
8676. Creamy-white : chipped, indistinct. [Harl. ch. 85 B. 14.]

SIGILL'M . . ALTE . . D . . . . FORD.

No counterseal.
8677. Sulph. cast of No. 8676. [D.C., E. 389.]

John de Clifton, *Knt.*

8678. [15th cent.] Plaster cast from fine impression, now chipped. 1⅓ in. [lxxxiv. 66.]

A shield of arms, *couché*: quarterly, 1, 4, five bendlets, CLIFTON ; 2, 3, chequy, a bend ermine, CLIFTON. Crest on a helmet, lambrequin, and wreath a plume of feathers betw. two bulls' horns. Supporters two stags.

Legend on a scroll :—

$$\text{Sigillū : iohannis : ⚬ Cl . . . . armig'. ✳}$$

John Clifton, *of Topcroft, co. Norf., Knt.*

8679. [A.D. 1427.] Red : a fragment. ⅛ in. [Add. ch. 16,542.]

A shield of arms, *couché*: quarterly, 1, 4, five bendlets; 2, 3, chequy a bend, CLIFTON. Crest on a helmet, wanting. Supporters, *dex.*, a lion rampant; *sin.*, wanting. Within a wreath.

Legend in the field :—

$$\text{clyfto . . . .}$$

T—— de Cliftun.

Seal used by GALFRIDUS, *fil.* ROGERI COCI DE HUNTINGDON.

8680. [A.D. 1351.] Dark-red : indistinct. [Add. ch. 33,487.]

A shield of arms, *couché*: a lion rampant within an orle of cinquefoils, CLIFTON. Crest on a helmet and lambrequin or short mantling, a swan's head (?) Within a carved quatrefoil panel.

Legend betw. the cusps.

$$\text{T' · DE · CL IF TV̄.}$$

Henry Fiennes Clinton,
al. **Henry Fiennes Pelham Clinton.**
Earl of Lincoln, Duke of Newcastle, K.G.

8681. [A.D. 1769.] Red : *en placard*, on a green tape. ¾ × ½ in. [Add. ch. 29,580.]

Oval : an ornamental shield of arms : six crosses crosslet, fitchées, three, two, and one, on a chief two mullets, CLINTON, Encircled with a Garter inscribed with the Motto of the Order of the Garter. Ensigned with a coronet.

John de Clynton, *of Rolvynden, co. Kent, Knt.*

8682. [A.D. 1383.] Red : fine, edge chipped. 1¼ in. [Harl. ch. 48 C 41.]

A shield of arms, *couché*: field hatched with lines crossing lozengy, on a chief two estoiles, CLINTON. Crest on a helmet and lambrequin, a plume of feathers. In the field two sprigs of foliage. Within a carved panel with ogee moulding, ornamented along the inner edge with small ball-flowers.

𝕾𝖎𝖌𝖎𝖑𝖑' : 𝖎𝖔𝖍'𝖎𝖘 : 𝖉𝖊 : 𝖈𝖑𝖞𝖓𝖙𝖔𝖓 :

8683. Sulph. cast from No. 8682. [D.C., F. 546.]

Juliana de Clintone, *dau. of* THOMAS DE LEYBOURNE,
wife of (i.) JOHN DE HASTINGS,
(ii.) WILLIAM DE CLINTONE, *Earl of Huntingdon.*

8684. [After A.D. 1330.] Sulph. cast from fine impression. 1¼ in. [D.C., F. 335.]

A shield of arms : per pale, *dex.*, a maunch, HASTINGS ; *sin.*, six lioncels rampant, three, two, and one, LEYBOURNE. Betw. two slipped roses. Within a carved six-foil, in the centre of elaborate tracery in form of an estoile of six points enriched with countersunk circular panels. Betw. the points, six ogee panels, ornamented with carved ball-flowers along the inner edge, each bearing a lozenge-shaped shield of arms : three crosses crosslets fitchées, on a chief two mullets, for CLINTON.

Thomas de Clyntone, *Lord of Huntyngton, co. Hunt, Knt.*

8685. [A.D. 1407.] Red : very imperfect. About ⅞ in. when perfect. [Harl. ch. 48 C. 42.]

A shield of arms broken off : crest on a helmet a ram's head (?) Supporters, two lions sejant guardant.

⊕ '𝕾𝖊𝖊𝖑 . . . . 𝖊 ᴀᴎ

William de Clinton, *Earl of Huntingdon.*

8686. [A.D. 1340.] Red : fine, cracked, edge chipped. 1¼ in. [Harl. ch. 48 C. 40.]

A shield of arms : six crosses crosslet fitchées, three, two, and one, on a chief two mullets of six points, pierced, CLINTON. Betw. six lions rampant in allusion to the arms of his wife Juliana de LEYBOURNE, see No. 8684, and two small oak-sprigs. Within a finely carved rosette of nine ogee points, elegantly traced, and ornamented with ball-flowers along the inner edge.

✠ SIGILLVM ✿ WILLELMI ✿ DE ✿ CLINTVN.

The second N in *Clintun* reversed.

8687. Sulph. cast from No. 8686. [D.C., F. 449.]

8688. [A.D. 1349.] Red : imperfect, much injured by pressure. [Add. ch. 19,843.]

. . IGILLVM ✿ WILLEL . . . . VN.

William de Clinton *and* **de Say,** *Knt.*

8689. [A.D. 1408–9.] Plaster cast from fine but imperfect impression. 1½ in. [lxxxiv. 68.]

A shield of arms, *couché*: quarterly, 1, 4, *diapré*, on a chief two estoiles, CLINTON ; 2, 3, quarterly, for SAY. Crest on a helmet and lambrequin, a bifurcated plume of feathers. Supporters, two greyhounds sejant, collared and ringed. Over each of their heads a cusped point.

·𝔖 𝔴𝔦 . . . . 𝔡𝔢 . . . . . . 𝔱𝔬𝔫 : 𝔷 . 𝔢 : 𝔰𝔞𝔶.

Inner border cabled.

John Clodder, *of Oving, co. Suss.*

8690. [A.D. 1560.] Dark-red : injured. ⅜ × ¼ in. [Add. ch. 8946.]

A wolf's head erased.

John Clopton, *of co. Essex.*

8691. [A.D. 1479.] Red : very indistinct. ½ in. [Harl. ch. 52 A. 3.]

A shield of arms : a bend betw. two cotises dancettées, CLÓPTON. Border engrailed.

Thomas de Cloptone, *Knt.,*

[*son of* WALTER DE CLOPTON, *of co. Suff.*]

8692. [A.D. 1349.] Pale-green : injured by plaster casting. ¾ in. [Harl. ch. 48 D. 9.]

A shield of arms : a bend betw. two cotises dancettées, CLOPTON. Betw. three slipped roses. Within a carved and pointed quatrefoil ornamented with ball-flowers along the inner edge.

✠ S' : THOME : DE : CLOPTONE :

8693. Sulph. cast. [lxxxiv. 76.]

8694. [A.D. 1379.] Red : very imperfect, and indistinct. [Harl. ch. 48 D. 2.]

. . . . OPTONE :

8695. [A.D. 1382.] Red : a fragment. [Harl. ch. 48 D. 3.]

. . . . E : DE : CLOP . . . .

Thomas Clopton, *of Melford, co. Suff., Esq.*

8696. [A.D. 1591.] Faded red : indistinct. ¾ × ¾ in. [Harl. ch. 57 H. 19.]

A shield of arms: six quarterings; 1, CLOPTON; 2, MYLDE; 3, FRAUNCIS (?) 4, KNYVETT; 5, KYRKHAM; 6, indistinct. Cf. No. 8715. Crest on a helmet, mantling and wreath, a wolf's head.

Thomas Clopton, *of Kentwell Hall, co. Suff., Esq.*
Seal used by BRIDGETT STAFFORD,
widow of JOHN STAFFORD, *of Blatherwicke, co. Northt.*

8697. [A.D. 1596.] Red: indistinct. About $\frac{5}{8} \times \frac{1}{2}$ in. [Harl. ch. 48 D. 44.]

A shield of arms: a bend betw. two cotises dancettée, CLOPTON.

Walter de Clopton,
of Selverleye, etc., co. Cambr. and Clopton, co. Suff.

8698. [A.D. 1319.] Red: imperfect, indistinct. About $\frac{3}{4}$ in. [Harl. ch. 48 C. 47.]

A shield of arms: on a cross five leopards' heads, or other charges, uncertain.

Legend obliterated.

William de Clopton, *of co. Suff.*

8699. [A.D. 1338.] Light-brown: originally fine, chipped along edge. $\frac{7}{8}$ in. [Harl. ch. 50 I. 48.]

A shield of arms: a bend betw. two cotises, indented, CLOPTON. Suspended by a strap from a hook. Betw. six slipped oak-leaves, three on each side. The inner border ornamented with small ball-flowers.

✠ SIGILL' : WILL'I : DE : CL . . . ONE

8700. Plaster cast of No. 8699. [xcviii. 43.]

William de Clopthon, *al.* **Cloptone,** *sen.,*
of Newenham Manor in Ashdon, co. Essex, Knt.

8701. [A.D. 1364.] Red: originally fine, injured by pressure. $\frac{7}{8}$ in. [Harl. ch. 48 C. 53.]

A shield of arms: a bend betw. two cotises indented, CLOPTON. Betw. two wings erect. Within a carved and pointed gothic trefoil, ornamented with small ball-flowers along the inner edge.

✠ SIGILL' I ❀ I WILL'I ❀ DE ❀ CLOPTHON.

8702. Sulph. cast from No. 8701. [D.C., F. 434.]

8703. [A.D. 1350.] Red: injured, imperfect. [Harl. ch. 48 C. 50.]

✠ SIGILL' I ❀ I W . . . . THON.

8704. [A.D. 1359.] Red: fine, fragmentary. [Harl. ch. 48 C. 51.]

. . . . . . WI . . . . CLOPTH . . .

William Clopton, *Knt., or* **Walter Clopton,** *Knt.,*
of co. Suff.

8705. [A.D. 1394.] Creamy-white : very indistinct. ⅞ in.
[Harl. ch. 48 D. 11.]

A shield of arms : CLOPTON, as before. Within a pointed
gothic quatrefoil.

In place of the legend, a wavy scroll of foliage.

William, *son and heir of* EDMUND **Clopton,**
of Newenham halle Manor in Asshedon, co. Essex.

8706. [A.D. 1412.] Red : fine. ⅞ in. [Harl. ch. 48 D. 5.]

A shield of arms : a bend betw. two cotises indented,
CLOPTON. Within an orle or border of quatrefoils.

❖ **Sigillu' + will'mi + clopton +**

8707. Sulph. cast of No. 8706. [lxxxiv. 74.]

8708. [A.D. 1412.] Red : fine, slightly chipped. [Harl.
ch. 48 D. 6.]

William de Cloptone, *son of* WILLIAM CLOPTONE, *Knt.*

8709. [A.D. 1414.] Plaster cast from fine impression, edge
chipped. [lxxxiv. 69.]

A shield of arms, *couché* : a bend betw. two cotises indented,
CLOPTON. Crest on a helmet, mantling and wreath, a wolf's
head. Within a carved gothic ogee panel with open tracery
at the sides.

Sig : willelmi : de : cloptone :

The letters DE are conjoined.

8710. [A.D. 1415.] Red : fine, imperfect. [Harl. ch.
48 D. 13.]

Sig : willelmi . . . .

8711. Sulph. cast of No. 8710. [D.C., G. 145.]

William Clopton, *Esq.*

8712. [A.D. 1430.] Red : injured, imperfect. 1 in. [Harl.
ch. 56 E. 4.]

A shield of arms : a bend betw. two cotises indented,
CLOPTON. Suspended by a strap from a hook. Inner
border partly cusped.

Sigillū : w . . . . . clopton : armig' :

8713. Sulph. cast from good impression. [D.C., G. 183.]

Sigillū: w ill'mi: clopton : armig' :

8714. Plaster cast. [lxxxiv. 71.]

William Clopton, *of Kentwell, co. Suff., Esq.*

8715. [A.D. 1584.] Red: indistinct. ¾ × ⅝ in. [Harl. ch. 48 D. 48.]

Oval: a shield of arms: six quarterings, 1, CLOPTON; 2, MYLDE; 3, ROYDON? 4, KNYVETT; 5, KYRKHAM; 6, FRANCIS. Cf. Harl. MSS. 1103, f. 5*b*, and 1449, f. 16. Crest on a helmet, ornamental mantling and wreath, on wolf's head.

8716. Sulph. cast of No. 8715. [D.C., H. 122.]

8717. [A.D. 1575.] Dark brown: imperfect. [Harl. ch. 48 D. 49.]

William Clopton, *of Groton, co. Suff., Gentl.*

8718. [A.D. 1591.] Faded red: indistinct. About ⅝ × ½ in. [Harl. ch. 57 H. 19.]

Oval: a shield of arms: quarterly, 1, 4, CLOPTON; 2, 3, KNYVETT.

William Clyff, *son and heir of* THOMAS CLYFF, *late of Lokyngtone, co. York.*

8719. [A.D. 1521.] Red. About ⅝ in. [Add. ch. 5791.]

A shield bearing a human heart transfixed by an arrow in bend. Betw. two initial letters, **t. l.** (?) and two sprigs of foliage.

Henry, *son of* WILLIAM **de Clympesfolde,** *of co. Surr.*

8720. [A.D. 1362.] Greenish, mottled: very indistinct. 1 in. [Add. ch. 18,655.]

A shield of arms: apparently a chevron betw. three animals' heads. Within a carved trefoil.

Legend obscure.

Edmund de Clypesby, *of co. Norf.*

8721. [A.D. 1370.] Green: indistinct. ⅞ in. [Add. ch. 14,867.]

A shield of arms: indistinct. A Trinity (?) Suspended by a strap from a tree, and within a carved gothic panel.

𝔖 · 𝖊𝖉𝖒𝖚𝖓𝖉𝖎 · 𝖉𝖊 · 𝖈𝖑𝖞𝖕𝖊𝖘𝖇𝖞.

The letters DE conjoined.

See Blomefield's *Hist. of Norfolk.*, vol. xi., p. 189 (Dept. copy).

Robert Clytterbooke.
See I—— BOYLE.

Johanna de Cobeham.

8722. [A.D. 1364.] Plaster cast from fine but chipped impression. 1 in. [lxxxiv. 79.]

An eagle displayed, charged on the wings with two shields of arms: *dex.*, on a chevron three mullets, COBHAM, *sin.*, a lion rampant. Within a finely-carved gothic panel, ornamented with eighteen crocketted finials, with one letter of the following legend betw. each pair.

☆ S' · IO[HA]NNE · DE · C[OB]EHAM.

John de Cobbeham.

8723. [13th cent.] Plaster cast from fine impression, chipped at the edges. 1 in. [lxxxiv. 77.]

Shield-shaped: a shield of arms: two bends, on the upper one, two, on the lower, three fleurs-de-lis.

✠ SIGILL' IOHANNI[S] DE COBBEHAM.

John de Cobeham, *of co. Kent, Knt.*

8724. [A.D. 1345.] Red: fine. 1 in. [Harl. ch. 45 C. 24.]

A shield of arms: on a chevron three lions rampant, COBHAM. Field diapered lozengy. Within a finely-carved gothic rosette.

☆ SIGILLVM : IOHANNIS : DE : COBEHAM :

8725. Plaster cast of No. 8724. [lxxxiv. 78.]

8726. Sulph. cast of No. 8724. [D.C., F. 291.]

8727. [A.D. 1345.] Red: a small fragment. [Harl. ch. 48 E. 11.]

8728. [A.D. 1348.] Red: originally fine, injured, imperfect. [Harl. ch. 48 F. 20.]

☆ SIGILLVM : IOHANN . . . . . . EHA . . .

John de Cobeham, *of Kent, Knt.*
(*Perhaps same person as the last.*)

8729. [A.D. 1357.] Red: originally fine, very imperfect. About 1⅛ in. [Add. ch. 19,846.]

A shield of arms, *couché*: on a chevron three lions rampant, COBHAM. Crest on a helmet, and lambrequin or mantling charged with the arms as described above, an old man's head, in profile, couped at the neck [with a cap turned up fretty]. In the field on the left a wavy sprig of foliage. Within a carved gothic panel ornamented along the inner edge with ball-flowers.

. . . iohannif de ⚜ ✿ [cobeh]am ✿ ⚜ ⚜ ✿

The letters DE conjoined.

8730. [A.D. 1358.] Red: fine, cracked, and edge chipped. [Harl. ch. 48 E. 17.]

Sig ⚜ ✿ iohannif de ⚜ ✿ cobeham ✿ ⚜ ⚜ ✿

8731. Sulph. cast from No. 8730. [D.C., F. 478.]

8732. [A.D. 1372.] Red : fine, l. h. imperfect. [Harl. ch. 48 E. 28.]

Sig' ⚜ ☸ iohannif . . . . . am ☸ ⚜ ☸

8733. Sulph. cast from No. 8732. [D.C., F. 479,]

8734. [A.D. 1377.] Red : very imperfect, l. h. side wanting. [Harl. ch. 48 E. 32.]

Sig' ⚜ ☸ iohannif . . . .

8735. [A.D. 1381.] Red : a small fragment. [Harl. ch. 48 E. 36.]

. . . . De ⚜ ☸ co . . . . .

John de Cobham, *son of* MARY, *Countess of Norfolk,*
Countess La Marescall,
widow of THOMAS BROTHERTON, *Earl of Norfolk.*

8736. Plaster cast from fine but chipped impression. 1¼ in. [lxxxiv. 75.]

A shield of arms : a lion rampant chequy, COBHAM. Within an elaborately-carved double six-foil rose of gothic tracery, ornamented with ball-flowers along the inner edge. In the points of the tracery a series of initial letters :—
T. I. L. B. E. Y. M. A. Y. B. C. A. Perhaps indicative of a sentence or text.

✠ · SIG[I L]LVM ⚜ ☸ IOHANNI[S] ⚜ ☸ DE ☸ ⚜ COBHAM ⚜ ☸
The N's reversed.

8737. [A.D. 1359.] Red : fine, fragmentary. [Add. ch. 23,615.]

. . GIL . . . . NIS ⚜ ☸ DE . . . .

8738. [A.D. 1359.] Red : only a small fragment. [Add. ch. 23,616.]

. . . . ⚜ ☸ COBH . . .

8739. [A.D. 1359.] Red : fine, r. side broken away. [Add. ch. 23,618.]

✠ · SI . .   NNIS ⚜ ☸ DE ⚜ ☸ COBHAM ⚜ ☸

8740. [A.D. 1359.] Red : fine, imperfect. The legend entirely broken away. [Add. ch. 23,619.]

8741. [A.D. 1363.] Red : an indistinct fragment. [Add. ch. 23,621.]

John de Cobham, *Knt., 2nd Baron Cobham.*

8742. [A.D. 1380.] Red : good. About ⅜ × ⁵⁄₁₆ in. [Harl. ch. 48 E. 35.]

From a signet ring : a shield of arms : on a chevron three lions, COBHAM.

Carved border.

8743. [A.D. 1391.] Red : imperfect. [Harl. ch. 48 E. 40.]

Reginald de Cobeham, *Clerk,*
Parson of Coulyng Church, co. Kent.

8744. [A.D. 1372.] Red : fine. ⅞ in. [Cott. ch. 53 A. 48.]

A shield of arms : on a chevron three crescents, in dexter chief an annulet. Suspended by a strap from a tree, and within a carved six-foil ornamented with small ball-flowers along the inner edge, and a pair of small slipped flowers on each side springing from the middle cusp.

𝔖' : reginaldi : cobeham : cl'ici.

Beaded border.

8745. Sulph. cast from No. 8744. [D.C., F. 480.]

8746. [A.D. 1369.] Red : fine, edge imperfect. ⅞ in. [Harl. ch. 48 F. 8.]

𝔖' : reginaldi : cobeham : cl'ici .

8747. [A.D. 1370.] Dark red, discoloured : cracked. [Harl. ch. 48 F. 9.]

𝔖' : reginaldi : cobeham : cl'ici.

8748. [A.D. 1377.] Plaster cast from fine impression. [lxxxiv. 80.]

𝔖' : reginaldi : cobeham : cl'ici.

Reginald [de] Cobham,
of Newham-juxta-Elyngham, co. Northumb., Knt.

8749. [A.D. 1412.] Red : fine, edge chipped. 1⅜ in. [Harl. ch. 111 C. 61.]

A shield of arms, *couché*: field diapered lozengy, on a chevron three estoiles, COBHAM. Crest, on a helmet an old man's head, bearded and wearing a cap, COBHAM of KENT. In the field two estoiles of six points. Background replenished with flowers slipped and leaved. Within a carved quadrilobe, ornamented with small ball-flowers along the inner edge.

: 𝔖' : reginaldi : ⚜ : de cobham :

8750. Plaster cast from No. 8749. [lxxxiv. 82.]
8751. Sulph. cast from No. 8749. [D.C., G. 133.]

Reginald Cobham, *Lord of Sterbourghe, co. Kent, Knt.*

8752. [A.D. 1437.] Dark red : originally fine, now only the central part remaining. About 2¼ in. when perfect. [Harl. ch. 79 A. 19.]

A shield of arms, *couché*: on a chevron three estoiles wavy, COBHAM. Crest on a helmet, mantling, and wreath : a head imperfect and uncertain. Supporters : *dex.*, wanting ; *sin.*, a talbot, in the mouth a scroll enriched with sprigs.

Legend wanting :—

. . . . ↄ : t . . . .

Richard de Cobham.

8753. [A.D. 1370.] Plaster cast from chipped impression. 1¾ in. [xcii. 80.]

Very similar to No. 8752, the seal of Sir Reginald Cobham, but from a different matrix.

. . . . . . : De : cobham . . :

Thomas de Cobeham.

8754. [A.D. 1378.] Plaster cast from fine impression. 1⅚ in. [lxxxiv. 81.]

A shield of arms: a cross engrailed, field diapered with sprigs of foliage, Suspended by a strap from a tree of three branches. Within a carved panel ornamented along the inner edge with small quatrefoils or ball-flowers.

S' · Thome · De · Cobeham.

Beaded border.

J[ohn] de C[obham.]

8755. [*Temp.* Hen. IV.] Red: very indistinct, *en placard* on an original letter addressed to his cousin Sir Reynald de Cobeham, Canon of Sarum. ⁷⁄₁₆ × ⅜ in. [Harl. ch. 43 B. 24.]

Oval: a shield of arms: a chevron charged with some uncertain animals (? lions), COBHAM.

Carved border.

Family of Cobham (?)

8756. [16th cent.] Red. ⅞ in. [xxxvi. 159.]

A shield of arms: a chevron charged illegibly. Ensigned with a small cross. Betw. two wavy sprigs, COBHAM (?)

William de Cocburn.

8757. [14th cent.] Red, on a mass of uncoloured wax. 1 in. [Cott. ch. xvi. 9 (B.)]

A shield of arms, *couché*: three cocks, two and one, COCK-BURN. Crest on a helmet and mantling, a cock. Supporters, two lions sejant guardant, each with a mantling round the neck charged with three round buckles. In the field two branches of three roses each, slipped and leaved.

S' · GVILL'I · D' · COCBVRN.

Perhaps a Scottish seal.

8758. Sulph. cast of No. 8767. [D.C., F. 435.]

Galfridus *fil.* Rogeri Coci.

See T——— DE CLIFTUN.

John Cocus.
See ADAM DE HODYNTONE.

Richard Cocus, *of Hochton, co. Derby.*
8759. [A.D. 1310.] Opaque brown. ¾ in. [Lansd. ch. 599.]
A shield of arms : three flesh-hooks pale-wise in fess.

· S' · RIC' COK'.

William de Codyngton (?)
8760. [A.D. 1368.] Plaster cast. 1 × ⅜ in. [lxxxv. 83.]
Oval : a shield of arms : a lion rampant crowned, debruised by a bend. Suspended on a branching tree.
Legend, apparently a rhyming verse in Norman-French, but undecipherable.

William de Codyngton,
of Rokenham in Wodynton, and Okkelegh, co. Surr.
Seal used by RALPH CODYNGTON.
8761. [A.D. 1418.] Dark green : fine, well preserved. 1 in.
[Add. ch. 18,702.]
A shield of arms : a cross fretty, CODINGTON. Betw. two small cinquefoils, and within a carved gothic border of five cusps, enclosing three circular countersunk openings, and ornamented with small ball-flowers along the inner edge.

✠ Sigillum ✠ willelmi ✠ De ✠ codyngton.

Beaded border.
8762. [A.D. 1419.] Another : fine, well preserved. [Add. ch. 9063.]

Thomas Coggeshale, *al.* Coggyssale, *of co. Suss.*
8763. [A.D. 1396.] Red : fine, somewhat injured by pressure. 1⅛ in. [Add. ch. 30,357.]
A shield of arms, *couché* : on a cross betw. four escallops, COGGESHALL, a crescent for difference. Crest on a helmet and mantling, out of a ducal coronet an heraldic tiger's head. In the field the letters or motto **a p.** Background diapered with wavy sprigs of foliage. Within a carved gothic panel of four cusps, ornamented along the inner edge with small ball-flowers.

Sigil' : Thome : Coggyssale.

Beaded border.

William de Coggeshale, *of Tilbury, co. Essex, Knt.*
8764. [A.D. 1389.] Red : fine, edge wanting. About 1¼ in. when perfect. [Harl. ch. 48 F. 50.]

A shield of arms, *couché*: a cross betw. four escallops, COGGESHALL. Crest on a helmet and mantling, out of a ducal coronet an heraldic tiger's head. In the field on each side a scroll inscribed :—𝔖𝔲𝔣𝔣𝔯𝔞𝔲𝔫𝔠𝔢 · 𝔟𝔞𝔲𝔱. Within a carved gothic panel, ornamented with small ball-flowers along the inner edge.

Legend wanting.

8765. Sulph. cast of No. 8764. [D.C., F. 568.]

William Coggyshale, *al.* Coggissale, *of East Tilbury Manor, co. Essex, Knt.*

8766. [A.D. 1396.] Red: fine, slightly slipped in making, well preserved. 1⅛ in. [Harl. ch. 48 F. 6.]

A shield, of arms, *couché*: a cross betw. four escallops, COGGESHALL. Crest on a helmet and mantling, out of a ducal coronet an heraldic tiger's head. Within a carved gothic panel or bilobe, and circle, ornamented with small ball-flowers along the inner edge.

𝔖' : 𝔴𝔦𝔩𝔩𝔦 : 𝔠𝔬𝔤𝔤𝔦𝔰𝔰𝔞𝔩𝔢 : 𝔪𝔦𝔩𝔦𝔱'.

Beaded border.

8767. Sulph. cast from No. 8766. [D.C., F. 594.]

Edward Cockayne, *of Powley, co. Warw., Esq.*

8768. [A.D. 1597.] Green. From a ring. ⅜ × ⅜ in. [Woll. ch. xi. 58.]

Shield-shaped : a cock crowing, for the crest of COCKAYNE, or in allusion to the arms of the family, viz. three cocks.

Beaded border.

John Cokayn, *Knt.*

8769. [A.D. 1421–2.] Plaster cast from chipped impression. 1⅜ in. [lxxxiv. 84.]

A shield of arms, *couché*: two bars. Crest on a helmet a cock's head erased. On an escroll in the field the motto :—

𝔄 . . . 𝔬𝔫 . : 𝔢𝔰𝔭𝔬𝔶𝔢𝔯 :

Probably for *En bon Espoyr*, the motto of COCKAYNE.

𝔖𝔦𝔤𝔦𝔩𝔩𝔲𝔪 : 𝔦𝔬𝔥'𝔦𝔰 ⋈ 𝔠𝔬𝔨𝔞𝔶𝔫 : 𝔪𝔦𝔩𝔦𝔱𝔦𝔰.

Elizabeth, *wife of* WILLIAM COKAYNE, *of Manceter, co. Warw.*

8770. [A.D. 1683.] Red : *en placard.* ¾ in. [Add. ch. 24,143.]

A shield of arms : a lion rampant (?)

Sir **Edward Coke,** *Knt.,*
Chief Justice of the Court of Common Pleas.
8771. [A.D. 1610.] Red: a fragment. About ¾ × ⅜ in.
when perfect. [Harl. ch. 78 I. 26.]

Oval: a shield of arms: per pale, three eagles displayed,
COKE. Crest and helmet wanting, only part of the mantling
remains.

Thomas Coke, *of London?*
8772. [A.D. 1650–1.] Red, covered with paper before
impression. ⅜ × ½ in. [Add. ch. 12,629.]

Oval: a shield of arms: three bends, COOKE.

John de Cokefeld, *son and heir of* JOHN DE COKEFELD,
of co. Norf., Knt.
8773. [A.D. 1316.] Dark green: fine, the shield somewhat injured. 1 in. [Add. ch. 29,243.]

A shield of arms, *couché*: diapered chequy, on a cross,
some indistinct charges. Crest on a helmet and lambrequin,
a fan-plume. Betw. a wyvern on the *dexter*, as a round
buckle on the *sinister* side, by way of supporters.

        S'. IOH'IS · FILII · IOH'IS · DE · COKEFELD.
Beaded border.
8774. Cast in composition tinted green, from No. 8773.
[xlv. 45.]

Robert de Cokefeld, *of Charwelton, co. Northt., Knt.*
8775. [Late 13th cent.] Creamy-white: indistinct in
parts, edge chipped. 1¾ in. [Harl. ch. 85 B. 19.]

A shield of arms of early shape: a cock crowing, contourné. Between three crosslets.

        ✠ SIGILL' · ROB'TI · D' · COKEFELD · MIL . . . .
8776. Sulph. cast of No. 8775. [D.C., E. 431.]

William de Cokeleya, *al.* **Cukele,** *al.* **William,** *son of*
WILLIAM DE CUKELEYE, *of Cookley, co. Suff.*
8777. [*Temp.* Hen. III.] Green, mottled: fine, well preserved. 1 in. [Harl. ch. 83 E. 29.]

A shield of arms: two chevrons betw. five pierced cinquefoils, two, two and one.

        ⚜ SIGILLVM : WILLELMI : DE : COKELEYA ⚜
8778. Sulph. cast of No. 8777. [D.C., E. 341.]
8779. [Late 13th cent.] Green, mottled, covered with a
dark-coloured varnish: somewhat indistinct. [Harl. ch. 83
E. 30.]

8780. Green : imperfect, detached from a charter. [xxxv. 322.]

🏵 SIG . . . . ELMI : DE : COKEL . . A ᴬᴷ

John de Cokerington, *Knt.*

8781. [14th cent.] Plaster cast, from fine impression. 1 in. [lxxxiv. 85.]

A shield of arms : on a cross a mullet, field diapered, COCKERINGTON. Suspended by a strap from a forked tree. Within a carved gothic panel, ornamented along the inner edge with small quatrefoils or ball-flowers.

⚬ 𝔖𝔦𝔤𝔦𝔩𝔩𝔲𝔪 : 𝔡𝔬𝔪𝔦𝔫𝔦 : 𝔦𝔬𝔥'𝔦𝔰 : 𝔡𝔢 . 𝔠𝔬𝔨𝔯𝔦𝔫𝔤𝔱𝔲'.

John, *son of* THOMAS Cokes, *of Westwell, co. Kent.*

8782. [A.D. 1362.] Green : imperfect, indistinct. ⅞ in. [L. F., C. ii. 17.]

A shield of arms : per pale, three round buckles in bend ?

S' RICAR . . . . VL . . .

Walter de Cokeseye, *of Eyton-super-Doune, or Eaton-Dovedale, co. Derby, etc., Knt.*

8783. [A.D. 1381.] Red : originally fine, imperfect. 1 in. [Woll. ch. ix. 68.]

A shield of arms : diapered lozengy with a small annulet in each interstice : on a bend three cinquefoils, for COOKSEY. Betw. two roses, and within a finely-carved and pointed gothic trefoil ornamented with small ball-flowers along the inner edge.

𝔖𝔦𝔤𝔦𝔩𝔩'. 𝔴𝔞𝔩𝔱𝔢𝔯𝔦 : 𝔡𝔢 : 𝔠𝔬𝔨𝔢𝔰𝔢𝔶𝔢 :~

8784. [A.D. 1399.] Red : originally fine, very imperfect, in parts indistinct. [Add. ch. 21,504.]

. . . . . . l' 𝔴𝔞𝔩𝔱𝔢𝔯𝔦 : 𝔡𝔢 : 𝔠𝔬𝔨 . . 𝔶𝔢.

Nicholas Cokworthy, *of Bokeland-Fillegh, co. Devon.*

8785. [A.D. 1498.] Red : cracked, indistinct. ⅜ × ¼ in. [Add. ch. 29,146.]

Rectangular : a cock, in its beak an escroll inscribed illegibly :—

𝔴𝔬𝔯𝔱𝔥𝔶 (?)

Crest of COCKWORTHY.

Border engrailed and beaded.

Matthew Cokyr, *of Caundle-Haddon Manor, co. Dorset.*
8786. [A.D. 1419.]   Red : imperfect, indistinct, originally encircled with a twisted rush.   ¾ in.   [Harl. ch. 57 G. 39.]
A shield of arms : on a bend three leopards' faces, COKER.

James Colbron, *of London, Gentl.*
8787. [A.D. 1608.]   Red: injured.   From a ring.   About ¾ × ⅝ in.   [Harl. ch. 75 H. 40.]
Oval : on a wreath or torse a tiger sejant.   Crest of COL-
BRAND.
Beaded border.

Robert Colbran, *of Wartling, co. Suss.*
8788. [A.D. 1583.]   Red.   ⅝ in.   [Add. ch. 30,190.]
A reindeer passant.   In allusion to the crest of COLBRAND,
etc., *viz.,* out of a ducal coronet a reindeer's head.

Thomas Colchester, *of St. Clement-Danes, co. Midd.*
8789. [A.D. 1627.]   Red : indistinct.   ⅜ × ¼ in.   [Add.
ch. 29,585.]
Oval : a lion rampant.   Perhaps for a crest.

Andrew Cole, *of Hoddesdon, co. Herts.*
8790. [A.D. 1672.]   Red: injured.   About ⅝ × ¼ in. when perfect.   [Add. ch. 35,492.]
Oval : a shield of arms : a chevron betw. three indistinct charges in chief.   Crest on a helmet and ornamental mantling indistinct.

Joan Cole.
See RALPH MERIFEILD.

John Cole.
8791. [A.D. 1425.]   Plaster cast from chipped impression.
1⅛ in.   [lxxxiv. 87.]
A shield of arms, *couché* : a bull passant within a bordure bezantée, COLE.   Crest on a helmet, a bull passant betw. a pair of wings erect.   Within a carved gothic panel, ornamented along the inner edge with pellets and ball-flowers.

$\mathfrak{Sigill}'$: iohannis : cole.

John Colemarsch (?)

Seal used by JOHN BECHER, *of High Laver, co. Essex.*

8792. [A.D. 1430.]   Red: fine, somewhat indistinct in parts.   ⅞ in.   [Add. ch. 15,463.]

A shield·of arms: per pale, *dex.*, a fess betw. two swords palewise, points in chief, *sin.*, dimidiating three crescents. Betw. two sprigs of foliage, and suspended by a strap from a hook within a double gothic quatrefoil.

S' IOH' — IS · CO — LEMA — RSCH. (?)

William Colet, *of Shorne, co. Kent.*

8793. [A.D. 1384.]   Red.   ¾ in.   [Harl. ch. 48 G. 12.]

A shield of arms (?): three quatrefoils or flowers of love, slipped, two and one.   Betw. the letters I. O. N.   The inner circle of the seal ornamented with small ball-flowers.

✠ LENSEYNE DE LEL AMOVR.

8794. Sulph. cast. of No. 8793.   [D.C., F. 549.]

Same seal used by JOHN WEBBE, *of Shorne.*

8795. [A.D. 1383.]   Red: fine.   [Harl. ch. 57 F. 34.]

John Colin, *of Bristol, co. Glouc.*

Used by RICHARD FLETTOÑ, *Clerk, of Ramsey, co. Hunt.*

8796. [A.D. 1397.]   Red, embedded in a mass of dark green: fine, chipped, imperfect.   ⅞ in.   [Add. ch. 33,938.]

A shield of arms: a cross, fretty, betw. four sixfoils pierced. Suspended by a strap from a forked tree.   Within a carved gothic panel, ornamented with ball-flowers or small quatrefoils along the inner edge.

𝖘' ioh'is colin de briſtolle.

Cabled border.

8797. Cast from No. 8796.   ·[xcviii. 44.]

Roger, *son of* JOHN de Colkok.
See JOHN DE NOVE.

Alianora de Hastings, *wife of* PHIL. DE Columbers.
See ALIANORA DE HASTYNGHES.

John Colville, *of Dale, Knt.*

8798. [A.D. 1418.]   Cast in a composition tinted red, from good impression injured in places.   1 in.   [xlix. 17.]

A shield of arms, *couché*: a fess, and in chief three roundles, COLVILLE.   Crest on a helmet and mantling, and wreath, a peacock or cock-pheasant (?), in the beak a scroll inscribed :—

droit de . . . . .

In the field a pair of oak-leaves, slipped, on a branch.

$' : ioһ'is : colupll' · ɒe : ɒale : milit'.

Inner border cabled.

Richard Colvile.

8799. [A.D. 1619.] Red: imperfect, indistinct. [Add. ch. 33,117.]

Oval: a shield of arms: quarterly, 1, 4, a lion rampant, COLVILLE; 2, indistinct; 3, a bend. Crest on a helmet and mantling, uncertain.

Roger de Colevile, *son of* ROBERT DE COLEVILE, *of Carleton, co. Suff., Knt.*

8800. [A.D. 1297.] Dark green: fine, well preserved. 1 in. [Harl. ch. 48 G. 17.]

Ø. A shield of arms: a lion rampant, and label of three points. Suspended by a strap from a tree of three branches, and betw. two trees.

    ⚜ S' ROG'I DE COLEVILLE D' CARLETON.

The letters DE conjoined.

Beaded borders.

R. A small oval counterseal. $\frac{3}{4} \times \frac{5}{8}$ in. Impression of an antique oval intaglio gem. A draped bust in profile to the r.

    ⚜ LON ⚜ DO ⚜ NE ⚜ STO ⚜ NE.

8801. Sulph. casts of the *obv.* and *rev.* of No. 8800. [D.C., E. 488, 489.]

8802. Dark green: chipped, indistinct in parts. [Harl. ch. 48 G. 15.]

8803. [A.D. 1296.] Dark green: fine, edge of the *obv.* chipped. [Harl. ch. 48 G. 16.]

Another Seal.

8804. Creamy-white: the surface chipped away. [Harl. ch. 48 G. 13.]

A shield of arms hanging on a tree, cf. No. 8800.

    .... ROGERI DE COLEVILE .....

William de Colevile, *Knt.*

8805. [A.D. 1273.] Plaster cast from fine impression, chipped. 1 × $\frac{3}{4}$ in. [lxxxiv. '91.]

Shield-shaped: a shield of arms, *vairé.*

    ⚜ S' : WILLELMI · DE : COLE .. LE.

Hugh de Coleworthe, *of Horndon-on-the-Hill,*
co. Essex., Knt.

8806, [*Temp.* Hen. III.] Green. ⅞ in. [Harl. ch. 48
G. 26]

A shield of arms: *vairé,* a bend. Suspended by a strap
from a hook.

⊕ S' HVGONIS DE COLEWORTHE.

8807. Sulph. cast of No. 8806. [D.C., E. 393.]

8808. [*Temp.* Hen. III. *or* Edw. I.] Green: indistinct.
[Add. ch. 19,976.]

Johanna de Coleworthy.
See —— TALWORTHE.

Laurence Colgrym, *of Watyndon, or Whattingdon, co. Surr.;*
or **Richard Atten Okette.**

8809. [A.D. 1319.] Discoloured green: a fragment. [Harl.
ch. 48 G. 19.]

A shield of arms: an ox passant guardant.
Legend wanting.

Edmund de Colle, *al.* **Colne,** *of Englefield, co. Berks.*

8810. [A.D. 1335.] Red: fine, injured by pressure. ¾ in.
[Add. ch. 20,256.]

A shield of arms (?): a chevron, on it and over the field a
flower-pot with three slipped quatrefoils springing therefrom,
two in chief and one in base. Within a carved gothic panel
of three points and five cusps.

⋇ SIGILLVM : EADMVNDI : DE : COLNE.

The N in *Colne* is reversed.

John Colle, *of Chester, Knt.*

8811. [A.D. 1361.] Plaster· cast from good impression.
⅝ in. [lxxxiv. 88.]

A shield of arms: *vairé.*

⊕ SEEL DE MENSECRE (?)

John Colle, *of Chester* (?)

8812. [A.D. 1364.] Plaster cast from chipped impression.
1¼ in. [lxxxiv. 89.]

A shield of arms: quarterly, 1, 4, on a bend sinister three
indistinct charges; 2, 3, a cross raguly or engrailed. Within
a carved gothic panel.

𝖘' ioħ . . . . . . 𝖘𝖈𝖍𝖆𝖚𝖙 . . . . . (?)

Beaded borders.

Humphrey Colles, *Superintendent of Shevyock Manor,*
co. Cornw., Esq.
8813. [A.D. 1528.]   Red : imperfect, indistinct.   ¼ in.
[Slo. ch. xxxiii. 80.]
Lozenge-shaped : a chevron betw. two acorns and as many
oak-leaves, in cross.
Cabled border.

John Collys, *of Huntingdon, co. Hunt.*
8814. [A.D. 1426.]   Red.   ¼ × ₁₆⁵ in.   [Add. ch. 33,533.]
Octagonal : a shield of arms : a fer-de-moline (or perhaps
a merchant's mark), in sinister chief a crescent.
Cabled border.

William Colman, *of Bury St. Edmund's, co. Suff., Gentl.*
8815. [A.D. 1663.]   Red : imperfect, indistinct.   About
¾ × ⅝ in. when perfect. [Add. ch. 10,528.]
Oval : a shield of arms : quarterly, 1, 2, and 4, illegible ;
3, a cross betw. four mullets COLMAN (?).   Crest on a helmet
and ornamental mantling, destroyed.

Alexander Colepepyr, *of Goutherst, co. Kent, Esq.,*
afterw. ALEXANDER COLEPEPYR, *Knt.*
8816. [A.D. 1512.]   Red : injured.   ¼ × ₁₆⁷ in.   [Harl. ch.
76 H. 14.]
Rectangular : a shield of arms : per pale, *dex.,* a chevron
betw. [eight] martlets, HARDYSHULL, *sin.,* a bend engrailed,
COLEPEPER.
Pearled border.
8817. [A.D. 1529.]   Red : fair.   [Harl. ch. 76 H. 19.]
8818. [A.D. 1529.]   Red : fair.   [Harl. ch. 76 H. 20.]
8819. [16th cent.]   Red : detached from a charter.
¼ × ₁₆⁷ in. [xxxv. 19A.]
Rectangular : a shield of arms : per pale, *dex.,* a chevron
betw. eight (?) martlets, five in chief, three in base ; *sin.,* a
bend engrailed, COLEPEPER.
Pearled border.

Alexander Culpeper, *al.* **Colepepyr,** *of Bedgebury,*
co. Kent, Esq.
8820. [A.D. 1569.]   Red: good.   About ⅞ × ¾ in.   [Harl.
ch. 77 A. 27.]
Oval : on a stump of a tree shooting with leaves, a falcon
rising with wings inverted.   Crest of COLPEPPER.
8821. [A.D. 1569.]   Red: good.   [Harl. ch. 77 A. 29.]
8822. [A.D. 1573.]   Red: injured.   [Harl. ch. 77 A. 35.]

8823. [A.D. 1573.] Red : injured, indistinct. [Harl. ch. 77 A. 36.]

8824. [A.D. 1574.] Red : fine. [Harl. ch. 77 A. 38.]

Another Seal.

8825. [A.D. 1569.] Light-brown. $\frac{7}{8}$ in. [Harl. ch. 77 H. 29.] .

A goat's head erased.

Sir Alexander Colepeper *or* Colepepyr,
of Bedgebury, co. Kent, Knt.
(Same person as the last.)

8826. [A.D. 1577.] Red : fine. $1\frac{1}{4} \times 1\frac{1}{8}$ in. [Harl. ch. 77 A. 47.]

A shield of arms of six quarterings : 1, 6, a bend engrailed, COLEPEPER ; 2, a fess betw. ten martlets, HARDYSHULL ; 3, a cross engrailed, HAWTE, or MISSENDEN ; 4, a lion rampant queue fourchée, SHELVING (?) ; 5, uncertain, apparently a fess betw. two chevrons, WIGSHALE. Cf. Harl. MS. 1548, ff. 153, 154. Crest on a helmet, ornamental mantling and wreath, a falcon rising, COLEPEPER.

SIGILLÑ : ALEXANDRI : COLEPEPIR : MILITIS.

Beaded border.

8827. [A.D. 1578.] Red : imperfect, originally fine. [Harl. ch. 77 A. 48.]

8828. [A.D. 1578.] Red : cracked, indistinct. [Harl. ch. 77 A. 49.]

8829. [A.D. 1578.] Red : imperfect at lower part. [Harl. ch. 85 H. 8.]

8830. [A.D. 1582.] Red : cracked across, imperfect. [Harl. ch. 77 H. 6.]

8831. [A.D. 1595.] Red, discoloured : cracked, imperfect. [Harl. ch. 77 B. 25.]

8832. [A.D. 1598.] Red : good. [Harl. ch. 77 B. 32.]

8833. [A.D. 1598.] Red : cracked, imperfect. [Harl. ch. 77 B. 33.]

8834. [A.D. 1599.] Red : very indistinct. [Harl. ch. 77 B. 35.]

8835. [A.D. 1600.] Red : fine, well preserved. [Harl. ch. 77 C. 21.]

Another Seal.

8836. [A.D. 1578.] Brownish-red, discoloured. $\frac{3}{4} \times \frac{4}{8}$ in. [Harl. ch. 77 B. 45.]

Oval : on a wreath a falcon rising with inverted wings. Crest of COLEPEPER.

2 X

8837. [A.D. 1578.]   Red.   [Harl. ch. 77 H. 3.]
8838. [A.D. 1582.]   Red.   [Harl. ch. 77 B. 9.]

Sir **Alexander Colepeper,** *of Bedgebury, co. Kent, Knt.*
(Different Signature.)
8839. [A.D. 1630.]   Red.   [Harl. ch. 111 E. 61.]

Seal used by his son, ANTHONY COLEPEPER, *of Bedgebury,*
co. Kent, Esq.

8840. [A.D. 1597.]   Red : imperfect.   [Harl. ch. 77 C. 3.]
8841. [A.D. 1598.]   Red.   [Harl. ch. 77 C. 10.]
8842. [A.D. 1600.]   Red.   [Harl. ch. 77 B. 37.]
8843. [A.D. 1600.]   Red.   [Harl. ch. 77 C. 17.]
8844. [A.D. 1600.]   Red.   [Harl. ch. 77 C. 18.]
8845. [A.D. 1600.]   Red.   [Harl. ch. 77 C. 19.]
8846. [A.D. 1601.]   Red.   [Harl. ch. 77 C. 25.]
8847. [A.D. 1602]   Red.   [Harl. ch. 77 D. 3.]
8848. [A.D. 1605.]   Red : injured.   [Harl. ch. 77 C. 38.]
8849. [A.D. 1606.]   Red : imperfect.   [Harl. ch. 77 C. 41.]

Sir **Alexander Colepeper,** *Knt.*
See —— DAWE.

Anne, *wife of* ANTHONY **Colepeper,** *of Bedgebury, co. Kent.*
8850. [A.D. 1583.]   Red, discoloured : indistinct.   [Harl.
ch. 77 B. 48.]
A falcon rising reguardant, with jesses on the legs.
Cf. No. 8859, Harl. ch. 77 B. 12.

Anna, *widow of* WALTER **Colepepyr,** *of co. Kent.*
(dau. of JAMES AUCHER, *of co. Kent.)*
8851. [A.D. 1529.]   Red : somewhat indistinct. $\frac{3}{4} \times \frac{1}{2}$ in.
[Harl. ch. 76 G. 58.]
Ornamental shape : a shield of arms : a lion rampant queue
fourchée.
Legend in an oval band :—

 Sigill' martin ȝercebop (?)
See Harl. MS. 1548, f. 154.

Anthonye, *son and heir of* ALEXANDER **Colepepyr,**
of Bedgebury, co. Kent,
   afterw. Sir ANTHONYE COLEPEPER, *Knt.*
8852. [A.D. 1569.]   Red : imperfect.   About $\frac{2}{8}$ in.   [Harl.
ch. 77 A. 28.]
A falcon.   Crest of COLEPEPYR.

Another Seal.

8853. [A.D. 1578.]   Red.   [Harl. ch. 85 H. 7.]
As described for Sir ALEXANDER COLEPEPYR in No. 8836.
8854. [A.D. 1598–9.]   Red: chipped.   [Harl. ch. 76 C. 22.]
8855. [A.D. 1599.]   Red, discoloured: badly impressed.
[Harl. ch. 80 D. 34.]
8856. [A.D. 1600.]   Red: fine.   [Harl. ch. 77 B. 37.]
8857. [A.D. 1603.]   Red: injured in parts.   [Harl. ch.
80 H. 38.]
8858. [A.D. 1606.]   Red.   [Harl. ch. 111 E. 60.]

Another Seal.

8859. [A.D. 1582.]   Red: indistinct in places. $\frac{5}{8}$ in.
[Harl. ch. 77 B. 12.]
A falcon, rising reguardant, with jesses on the legs.
Cf. No. 8850, Harl. ch. 77 B. 48.

Another Seal.

8860. [A.D. 1595.]   Red: indistinct. $\frac{1}{2}$ in.   [Harl. ch.
77 H. 47.]
A falcon rising.

Barbara, *wife of Sir* THOMAS **Colepepper,** *of Bedgebury,
co. Kent, Knt.; dau. of* ROBERT SYDNEY, *Earl of Leicester,
widow of* THOMAS SMYTHE, *K.B., Viscount Strangford.*
8861. [A.D. 1637.]   Red: cracked. $\frac{1}{2}$ in.   [Harl. ch.
112 D. 49.]
A shield of arms: a pheon, SYDNEY.   Ensigned with a
viscount's coronet.
Cabled border.
8862. [A.D. 1638.]   Red: fine.   [Harl. ch. 77 D. 17.]

Cheney Culpeper, *of Revenllice, co. Radn., Esq., (afterw.*
1719, *4th Baron Culpeper of Thoresway.*)
8863. [A.D. 1687.]   Red: *en placard,* on a label, imperfectly impressed. $\frac{3}{4} \times \frac{5}{8}$ in.   [Add. ch. 1781.]
Oval: a shield of arms: a bend engrailed, CULPEPER, in
dexter chief a mullet for difference.   Crest on a helmet,
ornamental mantling and wreath, a falcon rising.

Elizabeth Culpeper, *widow of* NICHOLAS CULPEPER,
of Wakeherst, co. Suss.
8864. [A.D. 1517.]   Dark red. $\frac{3}{8} \times \frac{5}{16}$ in.   [Harl. ch.
76 H. 3.]

2 X 2

Rectangular : a falcon rising reguardant, contournée, for crest of CULPEPER.

8865. [A.D. 1517.]　Dark red : fine.　[Harl. ch. 76 H. 4.]

Elizabeth, *wife of* THOMAS **Culpeper,** *of Greenway Court, co. Kent, Knt.*

.**8866.** [A.D. 1629.]　Red : indistinct.　About ⅝ × ½ in. [Add. ch. 30,643.]

Oval : a falcon rising.

Geoffrey Colpepir, *of Peckham parva, co. Kent.*

8867. [A.D. 1369.]　Red, embedded in a mass of green. ⅞ in.　[Harl. ch. 49 B. 5.]

A shield of arms : a bend engrailed, CULPEPER ; with an annulet for difference.　Betw. two oak-leaves, and within a carved gothic panel consisting of a cinquefoil and triangle, ornamented with small ball-flowers along the inner edge.

        ✠ · SIG : GALFRIDI : COLPEPIR.

Beaded border.

8868. Sulph. cast of No. 8867.　[D.C., F. 467.]

8869. [A.D. 1378.]　Plaster cast, from imperfect impression, showing the difference of the annulet.　[lxxxiv. 90.]

John Colepeper, *son and heir of* THOMAS COLEPEPER, *Knt.*

8870. [A.D. 1399.]　Red : cracked, imperfect.　½ in.　[Harl. ch. 76 G. 48.]

Rectangular : a shield of arms : a saltire engrailed (?) Cabled border.

Another Seal.

8871. [A.D. 1429.]　Red.　₇⁄₁₆ in.　[Harl. ch. 76 G. 49.]

Octagonal : within a ducal coronet the letters

                𝕮𝕴𝕮

From a ring.

John Colepepir, *of co. Northt., Knt.*

8872. [A.D. 1430.]　Red : fine, fragmentary.　About 1¾ in. when perfect.　[Harl. ch. 76 G. 50.]

A shield of arms, *couché* : quarterly, [1,] 4, a bend engrailed, CULEPEPER ; 2, [3,] a chevron betw. nine martlets, HARDY-SHULL or HARDRESHULL, over all in chief a label of three points for difference.　Crest, on a helmet, ornamental mant-ling and wreath, the head and wings of a bird.

     · · · · · · · is · · · · · · · · · ·

Peter Colepeper, *of co. Kent.*

8873. [A.D. 1411.] Red: fine. r in. [Add. ch. 16,464.]
A shield of arms: a bend engrailed, field diapré of sprigs,
COLPEPER. Suspended by a strap from a tree, and within a
carved gothic panel or bilobe, with tracery at the sides and
small ball-flowers along the inner edge.

$\mathfrak{Sigillum}$ ⚜ $\mathfrak{petri}$ ⚜ $\mathfrak{colepeper}$ ⚜

Beaded border.

Thomas Colpepir, *Lord of Hardreshull, co. Warw., Knt.*

8874. [A.D. 1407.] Red: fine, slightly chipped at edge.
1⅛ in. [Harl. ch. 76 G. 40.]
A shield of arms: quarterly, 1, 4, a chevron betw. nine
martlets, six in chief, three in base, HARDYSHULL or HARDE-
SHULLE; 2, 3, a bend engrailed, COLPEPER. Cf. Harl. MS.
1548, f. 152 *b*. On the breast of an eagle displayed, with
the strap slung over its neck, and within a carved and traced
gothic panel ornamented with ball-flowers along the inner
edge.

$\mathfrak{Sigillum}$: $\mathfrak{Thome}$: $\mathfrak{Colpepir}$ ⚜

8875. Sulph. cast of No. 8874. [D.C., G. 116.]

8876. [A.D. 1407.] Red: imperfect, indistinct. [Harl.
ch. 76 G. 39.]

• • • • • • • : $\mathfrak{Thome}$ ⚜ • • • • • • • • • •

8877. [A.D. 1407.] Red: chipped, indistinct. [Harl. ch.
76 G. 41.]

$\mathfrak{S}[i]\mathfrak{gill}$ • • • • • • • • • • • • • • • • •

8878. [A.D. 1407.] Red: originally good, imperfect.
[Harl. ch. 76 G. 42.]

• • • • • • • • • • • • $\mathfrak{ome}$ ⚜ • • • $\mathfrak{lpepir}$ ⚜

Thomas Colepeper, *of Bedgebury, co. Kent, Esq.*

8879. [A.D. 1551.] Red. ⅞ × ¾ in. [Harl. ch. 76 I. 6.]
Oval: on a stump of a tree shooting with leaves, a falcon
rising with inverted wings. Crest of COLPEPER. See Harl.
MS. 1106, f. 72 *b*.
From a chased ring.

Another Seal.

8880. [A.D. 1557.] Red. ⅜ in. [Harl. ch. 76 I. 27.]
A falcon rising contourné, on a branch. Crest of COLPEPER.
Coarse style of work, from a stamp?

Thomas Colepeper, *of Aylesford, co. Kent, Esq.*
8881. [A.D. 1557.]   Red : fine.   ⅜ in.   [Harl. ch. 76 I. 29.]
A falcon rising, with inverted wings.   Crest of COLPEPER.

Sir **Thomas Culpeper,** *of Greenway Court, co. Kent, Knt.*
8882. [A.D. 1629.]   Red : very indistinct. · ¾ × ¼ in.
[Add. ch. 30,643.]
Oval : an illegible shield of arms.

Thomas Culpeper, *2nd Baron Culpeper, of Thoresway.*
8883. [A.D. 1687.]   Red : *en placard* on a label.   ⁹⁄₁₀ in.
[Add. ch. 1781.]
A shield of arms : a bend engrailed.   On a mantle doubled
ermine, ensigned with a baron's coronet.

Thomas Colepepyr.
See Sir THOMAS SMYTHE, *Knt.*

Walter Colepepÿr, *of Goutherst, co. Kent, Esq.*
8884. [A.D. 1425.]   Red : fine, very imperfect.   Only
shield of arms remaining.   [Harl. ch. 80 B. 51.]
Ø. For description see next No. 8885. ·
R. A small oval counterseal.   ½ × ⅜ in.   A slipped trefoil.
8885. [A.D. 1444.]   Red : chipped, indistinct.   1⅛ in.
[Harl. ch. 76 G. 54.]
Ø. A shield of arms : quarterly, 1, 4, HARDYSHULL, see
No. 8874 ; 2, 3, COLEPEPER ; over all a label of three points.
Within an engrailed border.
     [✠ ᵃ] **Sigillum :** ᵃ : **walteri :** ᵃ : **colpepyr** ᵃ
Beaded borders.
No counterseal.
8886. [A.D. 1432.]   Red : very imperfect, indistinct.   [Harl.
ch. 78 E. 50.]
No counterseal.

Counterseal only.
8887. [A.D. 1433.]   Red : indistinct.   [Harl. ch. 76 G. 51.]
8888. [A.D. 1449.]   Red : injured.   [Harl. ch. 76 G. 55.]

William Colepepyr, *Esq.,*
2nd son of Sir ANTHONY COLEPEPYR, *of co. Kent, Knt.*
8889. [A.D. 1621.]   Red : indistinct.   ⁹⁄₁₆ × ⅜ in.   [Harl.
ch. 77 F. 33.]
A shield of arms : three chevrons.
Beaded border.

A member of the Family of COLÉPEPER.

8890. [16th cent.] Red : fine, detached from a charter. $\frac{6}{8} \times \frac{4}{8}$ in. [Box with Harl. ch. 77 A. 1–20.]

Oval : an ornamental shield of arms : quarterly, 1, 4, a bend engrailed, COLEPEPER ; 2, 3, a chevron betw. three martlets, HARDRESHALL. In fess point a mullet for difference.

Beaded border.

Thomas de Colt (?)
Secretum.

8891. [14th cent.] Plaster cast from indistinct impression. $\frac{7}{8}$ in. [xc. 87.]

A shield of arms : on a chevron some indistinct charges.

✠ SECRETA : TH : DE : COLT' :

John Colquhon.

8892. [A.D. 1558.] Sulph. cast from good impression. $1\frac{1}{4}$ in. [lxxxiv. 93.]

A shield of arms, *couché* : a saltire engrailed, COLQUHOUN. Crest on a helmet and mantling, a stag's head. Supporters two greyhounds.

S' iohanni colquhon.

Probably a Scottish seal.

Alianora, *wife of* PHELIPPE de Columbers.
See ALIANORA DE HASTYNGHES.

Robert de Colvil.

8893. [A.D. 1324.] Plaster cast from fine impression. $\frac{3}{4}$ in. [lxxxiv. 92.]

A shield of arms : a cross moline, COLVIL. Within a pointed trefoil with letters at each side of the points.

✠ S' · ROBERTI · DE · COLVIL.

Beaded borders.

Probably a Scottish seal.

Thomas Colvyle.

8894. [14th cent.] Plaster cast from fine impression, injured by pressure. 1 in. [xcii. 82.]

A shield of arms : on a fess three lions rampant, COLVILE. Within a gothic cinquefoil with three points in triangle, ornamented with small ball-flowers along the inner edge.

✠ Sigillum : thome : colvyle.

William Combe, *Burgess of Bristol.*
8895. [A.D. 1386–87.]   Red : a fragment.   [Add. ch. 16,206.]

A shield of arms : the charges destroyed.   Within a gothic panel.

✠ S . . . . RT.

John Comber.
Seal used by WILLIAM GRATWICKE, *of Cowfold,*
co. Suss., Yeoman.
8896. [A.D. 1587.]   Red. $\frac{5}{8}$ in.   [Add. ch. 8959.]

A shield of arms : a fess dancettée, betw. three estoiles of six points, COMBER.

William Comber, *of Shoraumbury, co. Suss., Gentl.*
8897. [A.D. 1605.]   Brown : indistinct. $\frac{5}{8} \times \frac{1}{2}$ in.   [Add. ch. 30,037.]

Oval : on a wreath a greyhound's head, for crest of COMBER. From a ring.

Edward Combes, *of Hayes and West Wickham,*
co. Kent, Gentl.
8898. [A.D. 1600.]   Red: indistinct. $\frac{5}{8} \times \frac{9}{16}$ in.   [Harl. ch. 111 F. 15.]

Oval : a shield of arms : three lions rampant, in chief a crescent for difference, COMBE.
Beaded border.

George Compton, *Earl of Northampton, Baron Compton*
of Compton, Constable of the Tower, Ld.-Lieut. of Warwick,
the Tower Hamlets, etc., P.C.
8899. [A.D. 1712.]   Red wafer covered with paper before impression : very imperfect.   About 1¾ in.   [Add. ch. 13,643.]

A shield of arms, destroyed, [a lion passant guardant betw. three helmets], of which only the helmet in sinister chief remains.   Ensigned with an earl's coronet.   Supporters, *dex.* wanting, *sin.* a dragon.   Behind the arms a festoon.
Cabled border.

Spencer Compton, *2nd Earl of Northampton.*
8900. [A.D. 1639.]   Plaster cast, tinted red, from fine impression.   1 × ¾ in.   [lxxv. 70.]

Oval : a shield of arms of twelve quarterings : 1, a lion passant guardant betw. three helmets, COMPTON, etc.   Ensigned with an earl's coronet.

Thomas de Comptone.

8901. [14th cent.] Recent impression in gutta-percha from fine impression. ⅞ in. [xlvii. 1429.]

A shield of arms: on a chevron three quatrefoils. Background roughly diapered lozengy, and within a border ornamented with small ball-flowers along the inner edge.

⚹ S' THOME DE : COMPTONE.

Beaded border.

Laing's *MS. Catal.*, No. 532.

8902. Plaster cast from fine impression. [lxxxiv. 94.]

Compton Family.
See NICHOLAS GWATKYN.

Elizabeth Comyn, *of Goodrich Castle, co. Heref.*

8903. [A.D. 1322–1326.] Red: fine, well preserved. 1 in. [Harl. ch. 48 G. 39.]

A shield of arms: three garbs, two and one, COMYN. Suspended by a strap from a hook; betw. two small slipped quatrefoils; and within a carved and pointed gothic quatrefoil ornamented with ball-flowers along the inner edge.

⚹ · SIGILLVM · ELIZABETH · COMYN ⚹

Beaded border.

8904. Sulph. cast from No. 8903. [D.C., F. 221.]

8905. Plaster cast from No. 8903. [lxxxiv. 95.]

John Comyn, *of Kyllebryde [Kilbride], Lord of Fakenham Magna, co. Suff.*

8906. [A.D. 1289.] Creamy-white: somewhat indistinct. ⅞ in. [Harl. ch. 48 G. 34.]

A shield of arms: three garbs, two and one, COMYN. Suspended by a strap from the beak of the crest, an eagle's head erased.

: S' · IOH'IS · COMYN · DE · KILBRYD'.

Beaded borders.

John Comyn, *al.* Komin, *Lord of Ulseby in Lindsey, co. Linc.*

8907. [A.D. 1313.] Dark green: fine. ⅜ in. [Harl. ch. 48 G. 36.]

A shield of arms: three garbs betw. as many trefoils slipped.

∴ S' :· IOH'IS · KOMIN.

Beaded border.

8908. Green: injured in places. [Harl. ch. 48 G. 35.]

John Comyn, *of Ulseby, co. Linc., son of* JOHN COMYN,
of Scotland, Knt.

8909. [Early 14th cent.]   Dark green : fine.   ¾ in.   [Harl.
ch. 48 G. 37.]

A shield of arms : on a bend betw. three garbs, as many
water-bougets.

        · CET · ERT · ESTABEL ⋈

Beaded borders.

Sir **Ralph Coningsby,** *of North Mimms, co. Hertf., Knt.*

8910. [A.D. 1610.]   Red : indistinct.   ⅜ × ¼ in.   [Add.
ch. 35,341.]

Oval : a shield of arms : quarterly, 1, three conies sejant
within a bordure engrailed, CONINGSBY ; 2, a chevron betw.
three animals' heads ; 3, three pelicans in piety, two and one ;
4, a cross moline voided (?).

8911. [A.D. 1612.]   Another.   [Add. ch. 35,342.]

John Conocke, *or* **Connocke,** *of Treworgye, co. Cornw., Gentl.*

8912. [A.D. 1588.]   Discoloured red : indistinct in parts.
¾ × ⅝ in.   [Add. ch. 15,373.]

A shield of arms : a fess indented betw. three eagles displayed, CONNOCK.   Crest on a helmet and mantling, out of
a ducal coronet, a demi-griffin segreant.

Beaded border.

Nicholas Conyers, *Esq.*

8913. [A.D. 1421.]   Red : imperfect, indistinct.   About
⅞ in. when perfect.   [Harl. ch. 48 G. 46.]

A shield of arms : on a chevron three cinquefoils.   Betw.
three eagles.

        . . . . uíaſ ⋈ ⋈

Humfrey Conyngesby, *of Hampton, co. Heref., Esq.*

8914. [A.D. 1554.]   Red : imperfect, indistinct.   ¼ in.
[Add. ch. 6367.]

A cony sejant, for crest of CONINGSBY.

John de Conyngesholm, *of co. Linc.*

8915. [A.D. 1355.]   Red : fine, well preserved.   ⅞ in.
[Harl. ch. 57 G. 11.]

A shield of arms : a chevron.   Within a carved gothic
pentagonal panel.

        ⋈ S' · IOH'IS · DE · CONINGISHOLM.

Beaded border.

8916. Sulph. cast of No. 8915. [D.C., F. 419.]

8917. [A.D. 1362.] Red: originally fine, cracked. [Harl. ch. 56 E. 28.]

✡ S' · IOH'IS · DE · CONINGISHOLM.

John Coo, *or* **Koo,** *of Stetchworth, co. Camb., Esq.*

8918. [A.D. 1440.] Red: fine, well preserved. $1\frac{1}{8}$ in. [Add. ch. 15,674.]

A shield of arms: on three piles wavy, ten martlets, three, three, three, and one, for COO. Suspended by a strap from a forked tree, and within a carved gothic panel.

· Sigillum : iohannis : coo :

Beaded border.

8919. [A.D. 1428.] Red: very imperfect, only centre remaining. [Harl. ch. 52 G. 2.]

8920. Sulph. cast of No. 8918. [D.C., G. 180.]

Cornelius Cooke, *al.* **Coke,** *Esq.*

8921. [A.D. 1650.] Red, covered with paper before impression. $\frac{3}{4} \times \frac{5}{8}$ in. [Add. ch. 12,629.]

Oval: a shield of arms: a maunch, over all a bend. Crest, on a helmet and ornamental mantling, a maiden's head.

Another Seal.

8922. [A.D. 1653.] Red: injured in parts by pressure. $\frac{5}{8} \times \frac{1}{2}$ in. [Add. ch. 27,328.]

Oval: a shield of arms: uncertain. Crest on a helmet and mantling, indistinct.

John Cooke, *of East Acton, co. Midd., Esq., son and heir of Sir* THOMAS COOKE, *Knt.*

8923. [A.D. 1688.] Red: *en placard,* on a label. About $\frac{5}{8} \times \frac{1}{2}$ in. [Add. ch. 23,856.]

Oval: a shield of arms: a fess betw. two lions passant, COOKE.

8924. [A.D. 1688.] Another. [Add. ch. 23,857.]

8925. [A.D. 1688.] Another. [Add. ch. 23,858.]

Richard Cook.

See THOMAS GERARD.

Thomas Cook, *of Carshalton, co. Surr., Clerk.*

8926. [A.D. 1362.] Red: originally fine, cracked, imperfect. 1 in. [Add. ch. 23,386.]

A shield of canting arms : on a cross, hatched or diapered lozengy, betw. four cinquefoils pierced, another cinquefoil, (these five cinquefoils represent the *Wlnera quinque* of the legend below), in the base point the initial letter T for Thomas. Betw. two slipped flowers and within a carved gothic panel composed of a triangle and cinquefoil, ornamented with small ball-flowers along the inner edge.

⚜ 𝕮𝕬𝖑[𝖓𝖊𝖗𝖆 : 𝖖𝖚𝖎𝖓𝖖𝖚𝖊] : 𝖉𝖊𝖎 : 𝖘[𝖎𝖓𝖙] : 𝖒𝖊𝖉𝖎𝖈𝖎𝖓𝖆 : 𝖒𝖊𝖎.

8927. [A.D. 1362.]   Red : imperfect, indistinct.   [Add. ch. 23,387.]

𝕮𝕬𝖑𝖓𝖊𝖗𝖆 : 𝖖𝖚 . . . . 𝖊 : 𝖉𝖊𝖎 : . . . . 𝖒𝖊 . . . . 𝖓𝖆 : 𝖒𝖊𝖎.

Dowse, *dau. of* JOHN **Cooper,** *of Ditcham, co. Suss.*

8928. [A.D. 1659.]   Red, covered with paper before impression : indistinct.   About ⅞ × ¾ in.   [Add. ch. 18,986.]

Oval : a shield of arms : quarterly, with the charges indistinctly impressed.   Crest on a helmet and mantling, uncertain, betw. two wings.

William Cooper, *of Bury-cum-Hepmangrove,*
co. Hunt., Yeoman.

8929. [A.D. 1660.]   Red : indistinct.   ½ in.   [Add. ch. 33,994.]

A shield of arms : a bend betw. two cotises engrailed (?)

Ambrose Copinger.
Seal used by ELIZABETH, *wife of* DANIELL BACON,
of Bury St. Edmunds, co. Suff.,
dau. of Sir THOS. SKINNER, *Knt.*

8930. [A.D. 1631.]   Red : indistinct.   ⅞ × ¾ in.   [Harl. ch. 111 D. 12.]

A shield of arms : bendy of ——— ? pieces, over all on a fess some uncertain charges, for three bendlets a fess, COPINGER. Crest on a helmet and ornamental mantling, a bull's (?) head. Beaded border.

Roger de Coplond.

8931. [14th cent.]   Sulph. cast.   ¾ in.   [D.C., F. 348.]

A shield of arms : a cross betw. four escallops,. or two escallops in the 1st and 4th, and two roses in the 2nd and 3rd quarters.   Within a pointed gothic trefoil.

⚜ SIGILLVM · ROGERI · DE · COPL'OND :

John Coppendale, *Senr., of Beverley, co. York.*
8932. [A.D. 1336.]   Creamy - white : indistinct.   ¾ in.
[Harl. ch. 45 A. 28.]
A shield of arms : on a bend three mullets.
✠ S' I . . . . . . OPPENDALE.

Agnes de Coppidok.
See JOHN DE LANGL . . .

Stephyn Copping, *of Norwich, co. Norf., Gentl.*
8933. [A.D. 1595.]   Red : injured.   About ⅜ × ½ in.
[Stowe ch. 215.]
Oval : a shield of arms : three bears' heads, two and one,
for COPPIN.
Beaded border.

Allan Corance, *of London, Esq.*
8934. [A.D. 1648.]   Red : injured by pressure.   ½ × ⅜ in.
[Add. ch. 26,512.]
Oval : a shield of arms : on a chevron betw. three ravens,
as many leopards' faces, CORRANCE.   Crest, on a helmet
mantling and wreath, a raven, in his dexter claw an escutcheon
charged with a leopard's face.

Agnes, *wife of* JOHN **Corbet,** *son of* ROGER CORBET,
of Hadley, co. Salop.
8935. [A.D. 1334.]   Red : fine, well preserved.   ⅞ in.
[Harl. ch. 48 H. 1.]
Two shields of arms : *dex.*, two bars, on a canton or
quarter a lion rampant (cf. seal of John CORBET appended to
this charter), *sin.*, ermine, a chevron.   Suspended by a strap
from a forked tree on which is perched a *corbeau*, in allusion
to the name of the owner.
✠ SIGILL' AGNETIS CORBET ✠
Beaded border.
8936. Sulph. cast of No. 8935.   [D.C., F. 251.]

Sir **Andrew Corbett,** *of Moreton Corbett, co. Salop, Bart.*
8937. [A.D. 1636.]   Red : chipped, indistinct.   ½ × ⅜ in.
[Add. ch. 9423.]
A shield of arms : a *corbeau* or raven, CORBETT.
Cabled border.

John Corbet, *son of* ROGER CORBET,
of Hadley, co. Salop.

8938. [A.D. 1334.]　Red: fine, well preserved.　¾ in.
[Harl. ch. 48 H. 1.]

A shield of arms: two bars, on a canton or quarter a lion
passant.　Betw. two wyverns sans wings.

✠ ✿ SIGILLVM ✿ IOHANNIS ✿ CORBET ✿

Peter Corbet, *Lord of Caus, co. Salop.*

8939. [A.D. 1280.]　Red: originally fine, chipped at top.
⅞ in. [Add. ch. 20,437.]

A shield of arms: two crows in pale, for CORBET and
CAUS.　Betw. two wyverns sans wings.　[Suspended by a
strap from a forked tree.]

SIGILLVM : PETRI : CORBET.

Beaded border.

8940. [A.D. 1315.]　Red: originally fine, wanting l. h. side.
[Add. ch. 20,438.]

SIGILLVM : PET . . . .

8941. Plaster cast from fine impression.　[lxxxiv. 97.]

Robert, *son of* ROBERT Corbet, *Lord of Hadley, co. Salop.*

8942. [A.D. 1380.]　Red, embedded in a mass of dark
green.　¾ in. [Harl. ch. 111 F. 19.]

A shield of arms: two bars, in chief a label of three points.
Suspended by a strap from a forked tree, and within a gothic
panel.

S' ROBERTI · CORBET.

8943. Sulph. cast of No. 8942,　[D.C., F. 519.]

Roger Corbet, *Knt., Lord of Hadley, co. Salop.*

8944. [A.D. 1332.]　Red: injured, imperfect.　About 1 in.
when perfect. [Harl. ch. 48 G. 50.]

A shield of arms: two bars, on a canton or quarter [a lion
passant], CORBETT.　Suspended by a strap from a forked
tree, sprouting at the sides.　Within a carved gothic star or
rosette of eight points.

Legend betw. the points.

✠ S' RO__GE__RI . . . .

Robert Corbet, *of Hadley, co. Salop, Knt.*

8945· [A.D. 1363.]　Red: injured, indistinct in parts.
1 in. [Harl. ch. 85 B. 37.]

A shield of arms: two bars, on a quarter or canton a
destroyed charge, CORBET.　Within a finely-carved and

traced gothic panel, of three principal points, ornamented with small ball-flowers along the inner edge.

Legend betw. the points.

SIGILL'V · __ ROBERTI __ · CORBET.

Beaded border.

8946. Sulph. cast of No. 8945. [D.C., F. 427.]

8947. [A.D. 1380.] Red, embedded in a mass of dark green wax: injured. [Harl. ch. 84 F. 5.]

8948. Sulph. cast of No. 8947. [D.C., F. 518.]

8949. [A.D. 1380.] Green: originally fine, indistinct in parts. [Harl. ch. 85 B. 40.]

Robert Corbet, *of Eberton* [*Ebrington*], *co. Glouc., Chev.*

8950. [A.D. 1371.] Red, imbedded in a mass of green wax: good, indistinct in places. 1⅛ in. [Harl. ch. 85 B. 39.]

A shield of arms: two bars, on a canton or quarter an illegible charge, perhaps a lion passant, CORBETT. Within a carved gothic panel composed of two triangles, with tracery in the spaces.

𝕾igillum ROBERTI CORBET:

The form of the R is unusual.

8951. [A.D. 1371.] Red, embedded in a mass of green wax: injured by pressure, indistinct. [Harl. ch. 85 B. 38.]

William Corby, *of Weldon, co. Northt.*

8952. [A.D. 1380–1.] Red: imperfect, indistinct at places. ⅞ in. [Add. ch. 13,917.]

A shield of arms: a fess dancettée betw. three crows. Within two concentric circlets or wreaths; the inner one charged with four crosslets in cross; the outer one ornamented along the inner edge with small carved ball-flowers.

✠ S . . . . . . VM . . . . C . . . . . .

Another Seal.

8953. [A.D. 1396.] Red: a fragment. [Add. ch. 854.]

. . . . ILLELM . . . . RBY.

8954. [A.D. 1396.] Red: originally fine, chipped edge, encircled with a twisted rush. [Add. ch. 855.]

As before, but the crow in base has been replaced by a crescent.

✠ SIGILLVM : WILLELMI : CORBY.

Beaded border.

8955. [A.D. 1402.] Red: indistinct. [Add. ch. 776.]

8956. [A.D. 1402.] Red; fair, injured in parts by pressure. [Add. ch. 777.]

✠ SIGILLVMI : WILLELMI : CORBY.

.8957. [A.D. 1404.]   Red : chipped, indistinct in places.
[Harl. ch. 48 H. 3.]
⚹ SIGILLVM : WILLELMI : CORBY.
8958. Sulph. cast of. No. 8957.   [D.C., G. 104.]

John Corbyn (?)

8959. Plaster cast from chipped impression.   About ⅞ in.
[lxxxiv. 98.]
A shield of arms : field diapered lozengy, a raven.   Probably
for TRENETHIN.   The families of TRENOTHEN, TRENETHYN,
and TREVETHIN, bear a Cornish chough.   Suspended by a
strap from a forked tree, and within a carved gothic panel.
𝕾'. iot̨ . . . . ortt̨ɲn.

Sir William Cordell, Knt., Master of the Rolls.

8960. [A.D. 1578.]   Red : fine.   ⅞ × ¾ in.   [Add. ch. 13,938.]
Oval : a shield of arms : quarterly, 1, 4, a chevron engrailed
betw. three griffins' heads erased, for CORDELL ; 2, 3, a chevron
b'etw. three lions passant guardant.   Crest on a helmet and
mantling, a cockatrice, wings close, collared, combed, wattled,
and legged, CORDALL.

Another Seal.

8961. [A.D. 1579.]   Red : indistinct, imperfect.   ¾ in.
[Harl. ch. 76 D. 55.]
On a wreath a cockatrice.   Crest of CORDELL.
8962. [A.D. 1579.]   Red: imperfect, very indistinct.   [Add.
ch. 32,946.]
8963. [A.D. 1579.]   Red : injured, indistinct.   [Add. ch.
32,947.]

Elizabeth de Cornubia, al. Cornewaile, and Cornewayle, widow of ESMOND DE CORNEWAILE, Lady of Kynlet, co. Salop.

8964. [A.D. 1355.]   Red : fine, edge compressed.   About
⅞ in.   [Add. ch. 20,435.]
A shield of arms : per pale, dex., a lion rampant within a
bordure charged with seven roundles, for CORNWALL ; sin.,
two lions passant in pale, dimidiated.
⚹ S' ELIZABET · DE · CORNVBIA.
Beaded border.
8965. [A.D. 1355.] Red : fine.   [Add. ch. 20.439.]
8966. [A.D. 1357.]   Red : chipped, indistinct.   [Add. ch.
28,645.]
⚹ S' ELIZABET . . . . BIA.
8967. [A.D. 1373.]   Red : chipped, indistinct in places.
[Add. ch. 20,440.]
⚹ S' ELIZABE . . . . VBIA.
8968. Plaster cast of imperfect impression.   [lxxxiv. 99.]

——— **Cornwall** *or* **Cornewayle,** *perhaps*
John de Cormailles, *Knt.*
Seal used. by JOHN DE SANCTO MANEFEO.
· **8969.** [A.D. 1325.] ·Brown ; cracked, imperfect. ¾ in.
[Add. ch. 23,835.]
An eagle displayed with lion's face, in allusion to the arms
and crest of CORNWALL,· charged · on the breast with a
shield of arms : five. fusils in fess betw. six crosses crosslet,
CORNWALL or CORNEWAYLE.

Geoffrey Cornewayle.
Seal used by
. JOHANNA, *widow of* JAMES DE NEVILE, *Knt.,*
· *of the Manor of· Magna Brampton juxta Norhampton.*
. **8970.** [A.D. 1366.] Greenish-brown : good. . ⅜ in. [Add.
ch. 21,607.]
A shield of arms : a lion rampant (queue fourchée ?) within
a bordure engrailed, CORNEWALL. Suspended by a strap
from a forked tree. Within a border ornamented with ball-
flowers along the inner edge,
S' : galfridi : cornewayle :
Beaded border.

John Cornwayll, Cornewaille, *or* Cornoaille, *Chev.*
8971. [A.D. 1418.] Red : indistinct in parts. 1⅜ in. [Add.
ch. 11,448.]
A shield of arms, *couché* : a lion ·rampant within a bordure
engrailed· bezantée, CORNWALL. Crest on a helmet and
chapeau turned up ermine, a lion statant ducally crowned.
Within a carved gothic panel or bilobe, with the inner edge
ornamented with small ball-flowers and rows of slipped
quatrefoils springing to the centre.
Sigillum : ioh'is : cornewaille :
8972. [A.D. 1416.] Red : chipped, indistinct. [Add. ch.
11,434.]
Sigillum : ioh'is : . . . .

John Cornwaille, *Chev., Lord of Fairehölp.*
8973. [A.D. 1440.] Red : fine, fragmentary. About 1¼ in.
[Add. ch. 12,074.]
A shield of arms, *couché* : of ornamental shape : ermine, a
lion rampant ducally crowned, within a bordure bezantée,

CORNWALL.   Crest on [a helmet] and elegantly designed mantling, a lion statant [ducally crowned].

𝖲𝖎𝖌 . . . . 𝖓𝖓𝖎𝖘 ᴍ ᴍ 𝖈𝖔𝖗𝖓𝖊𝖜𝖆 . . . . . . 𝖙𝖎𝖘 ᴍ

Inner border cabled ; outer border ornamented with small ball-flowers.

Charles Cornwaleys, *of Norwich, co. Norf, Esq.*

8974. [A.D. 1597.]   Reddish-brown : very indistinct.   ¾ in. [Add. ch. 10,238.]

On a mount a stag lodged reguardant [gorged with a chaplet of laurel, and vulned on the shoulder].   Crest of CORNWALLIS.

John Cornewalys, *of London, Knt.*

8975. [A.D. 1523.]   Red.   About ⅛ × ⅜ in.   [Harl. ch. 111 F. 20.]

Ornamental shape : a cornish chough, betw. the initial letters G. I.

Beaded border.

William Cornewalleis, *Esq.,*
son and heir of CHARLES CORNEWALLEIS, *Esq.,*
of Trimley-Martyn, co. Suff.

8976. [A.D. 1594.]   Red : very much injured by pressure. About ⅜ in.   [Add. ch. 10,236.]

A large helmet, betw. two sprigs of foliage.   The crest indistinct.

John Corve, *or* **Alice,** *his wife, of co. Suss.*

8977. [A.D. 1425.]   Red : imperfect, indistinct.   About ⅞ in.   [Add. ch. 18,710.]

A shield of arms : three leopards' heads, two and one. Within a carved gothic panel.

Legend indistinct.

William Cory, *or* **Matilda,** *his wife,*
of Spearhay, co. Devon.

8978. [A.D. 1398.]   Red : edge injured.   ⅞ in.   [Harl. ch. 48 H. 16.]

A shield of arms : a chevron betw. three slipped trefoils. Within a finely traced gothic rose of eight points, the inner panel, which is circular, is ornamented along the edge with small ball-flowers.

Legend betw. the points :—

LEL LIOVN(?)

8979. Sulph. cast of No. 8978.   [D.C., F. 609.]

Peter Cosen, *al.* **Cosin,** *Citizen of London.*
8980. [A.D. 1290.]   Green: indistinct, edge chipped.   ¾ in.
[Harl. ch. 48 H. 17.]
A shield of arms: a mallet (?) on a chief an uncertain charge.

...... ILL' PETRI COSEN.

John de Cosyngtone,
brother of STEPHEN DE COSYNGTONE, *co. Kent., Knt.*
8981. [A.D. 1374.]   Red: injured, indistinct in parts.   ⅞ in.
[Harl. ch. 48 H. 28.]
A shield of arms: three roses or six-foils, pierced, within a bordure, for COSINGTON.   Within a carved gothic cinquefoil panel with three points and ornamented along the inner edge with small ball-flowers.

...IOH .... COSYNG ....

William de Cosyngtone,
son and heir of M. STEPHEN DE COSYNGTONE, *of co. Kent.*
8982. [A.D. 1376.]   Red: originally fine, cracked, fragmentary.   1 in.   [Harl. ch. 48 H. 27.]
A shield of arms [*couché,* wanting], cf. Harl. ch. 48 H. 28.
Crest, on a helmet, a bull's scalp, betw. (three?) roses, in allusion to the arms of JOHN DE COSYNGTON, *q.v.*   Within a carved and traced gothic panel.

𝕾'. **wíllel** .... **pngtone.**

Beaded border.
See No. 8981.

Alan, *son of* WALTER **de Cotes,** *of Habrough, co. Linc.*
8983. [A.D. 1269.]   Dark-green: fine.   1¼ in.   [Harl. ch. 48 H. 31.]
A cross in saltire betw. four fleurs-de-lis in cross.   Probably a form of the shield of arms of a cross moline engrailed, borne afterwards by COTES.

✠ S'. ALANI : F'LI WALTER D' COT'.
8984. Another: fine.   [Harl. ch. 48 H. 32]
8985. Another: fine.   [Harl. ch. 48 H. 33.]

Walter, *son of* WILLIAM de Cotes,
of Habrough, co. Linc.
8986. [Late Hen. III.]   Light-brown, varnished.   1⅛ in.
[Harl. ch. 48 H. 30.]
A shield of arms of early shape: a chevron and a chief indented.

✠ SIGILL WALTERI DE COTES.
8987. Sulph. cast of No. 8986.   [D.C., E. 320.]

John, *son of* RICHARD de Cotewyke,
of Over-Stretton, co. Norf

8988. [A.D. 1383.]   Red: chipped.   ¾ in.   [Add. ch. 14,904.]

Two shields of arms conjoined in fess : Dex., per pale, *dex.*, a fess betw. (six ?) martlets, *sin.*, barry-nebuly of six.   Sin., three crescents, two and one, the field diapered.   On a small tree or branch.

In the place for a legend, a wavy scroll of foliage.
Beaded borders.

Thomas Cotiere.
See LEO CAPWEL.

John de Cotteleghe, *or* Cottele,
of Cottelegh Manor, co. Dorset.

8989. [A.D. 1350.]   Light-brown : indistinct.   ⅞ in.   [Harl. ch. 48 H. 48.]

A shield of arms : a saltire.   Suspended by a strap from a spear or branch, and within a pointed gothic quatrefoil orna-mented with small ball-flowers along the inner edge.

✠ S' : IOHANNIS ᛗ DE ᛗ COTTELE · ᛗ

8990. Sulph. cast of No. 8989.   [D.C., F. 294.]

Lawrence Cotton.

8991. [A.D. 1654.]   Red : *en placard,* imperfect.   About $\frac{7}{16} \times \frac{5}{16}$ in.   [Cotton ch. III. 7 (7).]

An eagle displayed.   Crest of COTTON.
Beaded border.

8992. Black : *en placard.*   [Cotton ch. III. 7 (7).]

Robert Cotton, *of Multon, co. Suff.*

8993. [A.D. 1499.]   Red : faint.   About ½ in.   [Stowe ch. 248.]

A lion's face.
Legend uncertain.

Thomas Cotton, *of Multon, co. Suff., Esq.*

8994. [A.D. 1499.]   Red : fine.   From a ring (?)   ⅝ in.   [Stowe ch. 248.]

A griffin's head erased.   Crest of COTTON.   The field re-plenished with flowers.

Beaded border.

Thomas Cotton, *of Panfyld, co. Essex, Esq.*
8995. [A.D. 1602.]   Red.   ⅜ in.   [Harl. ch. 48 I. 3.]
An eagle displayed.   Crest of COTTON.

William de Cottune, *Knt., son of* ROGER DE COTTUNE,
of Wickham Skeith, co. Suff.
8996. [*Temp.* Hen. III.]   Creamy-white: edge chipped.
1¼ in.   [Add. ch. 13,933.]
A shield of arms, of early shape : a fess betw. two chevrons.
Betw. three wavy sprigs of foliage.
✠ SIGILL' : WI[L]L'I : DE CO[TT]VN M'.

Francis Couchman, *al.* **Crouchman,** *of Stoke,*
co. Kent, Gentl.
8997. [A.D. 1621.]   Red : indistinct.   11/16 × 9/16 in.   [Harl.
ch. 77 E. 16.]
Oval : on a wreath two lions combatant, supporting a
crescent.

Ingelram* **de Coucy,** *Lord of Coucy, 2nd Earl of Bedford,*
son-in-law of Edward III., K.G.   [A.D. 1366–1397.]
8998. [A.D. 1369.]   Red : fine.   1½ in.   [Harl. ch. 48 I. 6.]
A shield of arms : barry of six, vairé [and gu.], COUCY.
Crest on a helmet affrontée, and lambrequin, ermine, a plume
of feathers.   Within a carved oval panel ornamented with
ball-flowers along the inner edge ; and at each side in the
tracery two quatrefoiled compartments each enclosing a
lozenge-shaped shield of arms : a fess, for AUSTRIA.
✱ S' engeram : counte : de : bedeford : et :
fire : de : coucy :
The letters D E in the first *de* are conjoined.
Outer border ornamented with ribbons intertwined, and
with pellets in the interstices.
8999. Sulph. cast of No. 8998.   [D.C., F. 447.]
9000. Another.   [D.C., F. 448.]

Hannah Couley.
See R. BARNETT.

---

* Son of Ingelram by Katharine, dau. of the Duke of Austria ; Lord of
Coucy and Count of Soissons ; and nephew of Peter, Archduke of
Austria.   *v.* Sandford, *Geneal. Hist.*, p. 178.   He married Isabel, eldest
dau. of Edw. III.   Cf. Add. ch. 7483.

Johannes Coumscu.
Seal used by ROBERTUS ATTE WENSTALLE, *of Chartham,*
co. Kent.

9001. [A.D. 1382.] Discoloured green: imperfect at top.
About ⅞ in. when perfect. [Harl. ch. 80 I. 6.]

A shield of arms: indistinct, apparently a cross, and chief.
Within a carved and pointed gothic panel. .

..... IOHANIS COVMSCV .... (?)

Giles, *son of* HENRY Le Coupere, *of London, Baker.*
9002. [A.D. 1329.] Dark-green: cracked, imperfect. [Harl.
ch. 48 I. 16.]

A shield [of arms ?]: a rose branch with two roses in chief.

✠ S' · EGIDII · L[E · C]OVPERE.

Beaded borders.

Alan de Coupland.
9003. [13th cent.] Plaster cast from good impression.
1 in. [lxxxiv. 100.]

A shield of arms: two bars and a quarter or canton, over
all a bend, COUPLAND.

✠ SIG' · ALANI : DE COVPLAND'.

Beaded border.

John *and* Elizabeth Court.
See WILLIAM PELLATT.

Anne Courtenay, *Countess of Devon, wife of*
HUGH COURTENAY, *Earl of Devon, and dau. of* RICHARD,
Lord Talbot.

9004. [A.D. 1428.] Red: originally fine, chipped, large
portion of edge wanting. About 2¾ in. when perfect. [Add.
ch. 13,925.]

On a mount, a shield of arms: per pale, *dex.*, field diapered
with sprigs of delicate foliage, COURTENAY, with a label of
three points, *sin.*, a lion rampant within a bordure engrailed,
TALBOT of Shrewsbury. The shield is slung by a strap over
the neck of an angel with arms resting at length on the
upper edge of the shield. Supporters, two lions reguardant
addorsed, the tails betw. the hind legs.

.... [courte]nag : [c]omitif[f] ....

The inner border ornamented with small ball-flowers
along the inner edge. Outer border cabled.

9005. Sulph. cast from No. 9004. [D.C., G. 179.]

9006. Another. [xlvii. 1524.]

Cf. Laing's *MS. Catal.*, No. 323, where the description is erroneous.

Edward Courtenay, *3rd Earl of Devon,*
Lord of Okhampton, etc.

9007. [A.D. 1396.] Red: originally fine, very imperfect. About 2 in. when perfect. [Add. ch. 13,922.]

A shield of arms, *couché*: three roundles, two and one, COURTENAY; in chief a label of three points. Crest on a helmet and lambrequin, out of a ducal coronet a plume of ostrich feathers. Supporters, two swans, ducally gorged. All within a carved gothic quatrefoil, ornamented with small ball-flowers along the inner edge.

. . . ꝺwarꝺí : courtena . . . . [com]ítís : ꝺeboní . .

9008. [A.D. 1414.] Red: a fragment only of the shield and helmet. [Harl. ch. 48 I. 25.]

9009. Plaster cast from fine but imperfect impression, showing parts that are wanting in the previous numbers. [lxxxv. 1.]

⚔'. eꝺw . . . . : comí . . . . : ꝺebouíe : *

Hugh de Cortenay, *of co. Devon.*

9010. [A.D. 1298.] Dark-green : originally fine, edge injured. ¾ in. [Harl. ch. 48 I. 21.]

A rose of five leaves, or cinquefoil, betw. three small shields of arms, conjoined in triangle at the angular points of their chiefs: (1.) COURTENAY; (2.) Three bars wavy, BASSET; (3.) DESPENSER or LE DESPENCER. With a small rose or cinquefoil in each space betw. two shields.

Legend betw. the base points :—
⚔ FRANGE LEGE TEGE.
Cabled borders.

9011. Sulph. cast of No. 9010. [D.C., E. 491.]

Hugh de Courtenay, *2nd Earl of Devon.*
First Seal.

9012. [A.D. 1341.] Red: originally fine, chipped at edge 1¹⁄₁₆ in. [Harl. ch. 48 I. 22.]

A shield of arms : COURTENAY, with a label of three points, enclosed in a design of elaborate gothic tracery ; the centre is a six-foil, ornamented with ball-flowers along the inner edge. This is inscribed in a triangle with small circular countersunk panels at the angles. Outside the triangle a circular panel, six-foiled and enclosing a seeded rose, betw. two small circular panels, on each of the three sides. Very fine work.

S' · HVGONIS · DE · COVRTENAY · COMITIS · DEVONIE.
Beaded border.

9013. Sulph. cast of No. 9012. [D.C., F. 211.]

Second Seal.

9014. [A.D. 1349.]   Red: fine, somewhat injured by pressure in parts.   1¼ in.   [Harl. ch. 48 I. 23.]

A copy of, but slightly larger than, the first seal of arms,
see No. 9013.   The position of the label on the shield and a
few details of the tracery differ from the seal already
described.

S' HVGONIS · DE · COVRTENAY · COMITIS · DEVONIE.
Beaded border.

9015. Sulph. cast of No. 9014.   [D.C., F. 282.]

Hugh Courtenay.

9016. [A.D. 1391-1392.]   Plaster cast from chipped impression.   1⅛ in.   [lxxxv. 2.]

A shield of arms: COURTENAY, with a label of three points.
Suspended by a strap from a tree, and within a carved gothic
panel ornamented with ball-flowers along the inner edge.

𝕾igillum ℥ hugonis ℥ courtenap ℥ ⚊

Hugh Courtenay, 4*th Earl of Devon.*

9017. [A.D. 1421.]   Red: fine, chipped, wanting in places
along edge.   2 in.   [Add. ch. 13,923.]

A shield of arms, *couché*: COURTENAY, with a label of
three points.   Crest on a helmet and mantling, out of a ducal
coronet a plume of feathers.   Supporters, two swans ducally
gorged, wings expanded.   Within a carved gothic quatrefoiled
panel or quadrilobe, ornamented with small ball-flowers along
the inner edge.

𝕾igillū · hugonis courtenap ⚊ comitis ⚊ Deuonie ⚊
Cabled borders.

9018. Sulph. cast of No. 9017.   [D.C., G. 160.]
9019. Sulph. cast, tinted red, of No. 9017.   [xxxv. 157.]
9020. Sulph. cast, cracked, of No. 9017.   [xlvii. 1516.]
Cf. Laing's *MS. Catal.*, No. 322.

9021. Plaster cast of No. 9017.   [lxxxv. 4.]

Katharine Courtney, *wife of* WILLIAM COURTNEY *or*
COURTENAY, *Earl of Devonshire, dau. of King Edward IV.*

9022. [A.D. 1514.]   Red: imperfect, indistinct in places.
About 2¼ in.   [Harl. ch. 43 F. 7.]

A shield of arms: per pale, *dex.*, quarterly, 1, 4, three
roundles, COURTENAY; 2, 3, a lion rampant, REDVERS; *sin.*,
quarterly, 1, quarterly, i., iv., FRANCE (MODERN); ii., iii.,
ENGLAND; 2, 3, a cross, BURGH; 4, MORTIMER.   Over the

shield a rising sun and quatrefoil or. demi-rose in radiance.
At the l. h. side of the shield a dolphin hauriant. The corresponding symbol on the r. h. side is wanting.

∴ KATERINA · [COMITISSA · DEVON · FILIA · S]OROR · Z ·
AMITA · RE[GVM.]

Engraved in Sandford, *Geneal. Hist.*, pp. 372, 419.

Peter de Courtenay, *K.G., standard-bearer to Edward III.,*
Constable of Windsor Castle,
Governor of Calais, Chamberlain of Richard II.,
7th son of Hugh, 2nd Earl of Devon. [*ob.* A.D. 1409.]

9023. [A.D. 1399.] Plaster cast from fine but imperfect
impression. 1¾ in. [lxxxv. 3.]

A shield of 'arms : COURTENAY, with a label of three
points each charged with as many annulets. Suspended by
a strap from a forked tree and within a carved gothic panel,
ornamented with ball-flowers along the inner edge.

𝕾𝖎𝖌𝖎𝖑𝖑𝖚𝖒 : 𝖕𝖊𝖙𝖗𝖎 ⚜ 𝖉𝖊 ⚜ 𝖈𝖔𝖚𝖗𝖙𝖊𝖓𝖆𝖕. ⚜

Cabled borders.

Philip de Courtenay.

9024. [A.D. 1499.] Plaster cast from indistinct impression.
2 in. [lxxxv. 6.]

A shield of arms, *couché* : COURTENAY, with a label of
three points. Crest on a helmet and ornamental mantling,
out of a ducal coronet a plume of feathers. Supporters, *dex.*,
a swan, *sin.*, a wild boar.

Philip de Courtenay, *Lord of Molland, co. Devon.*

9025. [17th cent.] Sulph. cast from fine impression.
1⅜ × 1¹³⁄₁₆ in. [D.C., H. 156.]

Oval : a shield of arms, *couché* : three roundles, two and
one, COURTENAY, a label of three points each charged with
three roundles in pale, for difference. Crest on a helmet,
damascened, and ornamental mantling, out of a ducal coronet;
a triple-tiered plume of ostrich feathers. Supporters, *dex.*, a
swan, *sin.*, a wild boar. Behind the shield a dolphin naiant
embowed, for the crest of COURTENAY, Earls of Devon.

· S' : PHI : DE : COVRTENIE ✿ DO' : DE : MOLLAND ⦂

Border of carved foliage.

9026. Plaster cast from fine impression. [lxxxv. 5.]

Thomas de Courtenay, *of co. Devon.*

9027. [A.D. 1371.] Brown : fine. ½ in. [Harl. ch. 54 C. 54.]

A shield of arms: three roundles, a bend, COURTENAY.
Betw. the initial letters N ^L_T S : the shield being suspended by
a strap from the letter L. Within a carved gothic quatrefoil,
ornamented with ball-flowers along the inner edge.
The signification of the initials L. N. S. T. is not clear.
The seal of Martin de Ferrers, attached to the same charter,
has these four letters in a similar position.

Richard Couper, *of Sawtre, co. Hunt.*
9028. [A.D. 1472.]   Red: indistinct.   ¼ × ⅜ in.   [Add.
ch. 34,087.]
Oval: a griffin (?) perhaps a crest.

Peter Courthope, *of Cranbrook, co. Kent, Gentl.*
9029. [A.D. 1610.]   Red: cracked.   ⅜ × ¼ in.   [Harl. ch.
79 F. 1.]
Oval: a shield of arms: a fess betw. three estoiles,
COURTHOPE.
Cabled border.

John de Cove, *of co. Suff.*
9030. [A.D. 1301.]   Dark-green.   ⅞ in.   [Add. ch. 10,362.]
A shield of arms: a bend cotised.   Indistinct.   Betw.
two wyverns.
✠ S' : IOHANNIS : DE : COVE :

Francis Coventry, *of Carshalton, co. Surr., Esq.*
9031. [A.D. 1687.]   Red: *en placard,* on a label.   ¹¹⁄₁₆ × ⅜ in.
[Add. ch. 15,164.]
Oval: a shield of arms: a fess ermine betw. three crescents,
in chief a mullet for difference, COVENTRY.
9032. [A.D. 1697.]   Red: *en placard,* on a tape.   [Add.
ch. 15,183.]

John de Coventre, *Citizen of London, or* JOHANNA, *his wife.*
9033. [A.D. 1343.]   Dark-green: a fragment.   [Harl.
ch. 48 I. 11.]
A shield of arms: on a flowering branch, two birds respecting, on a chief a lion passant guardant.
Legend wanting.

Henry Coventry, *son of* THOMAS COVENTRY, *one of the Privy Council, Secretary of State.*
9034. [A.D. 1667.]   Red: *en placard.* Injured.   About
1⅜ × ¾ in.   [Sloane ch. xxxii. 56.]

Oval : a shield of arms : a fess ermine betw. three crescents, COVENTRY. Crest on a helmet and mantling, on a garb lying fess-wise a cock.

Beaded border.

Richard de Coventre, *Executor of the Testament of* JOHN DE COVENTRE, *late Archdeacon of Llandaff.*

9035. [A.D. 1361.] Dark-green: fine. $\frac{3}{4}$ in. [Harl. ch. 75 B. 42.]

A shield of arms : a fess, in chief three mullets, COVENTRY. Within a carved gothic trefoil with five points, ornamented along the inner edge with small ball-flowers.

• S' • RICARDI • DE • COVENTRE •

Beaded border.

9036. Sulph. cast of No. 9035. [D. C., F. 412.]

Thomas Coventrye, *Recorder of London.*

9037. [A.D. 1617.] Red: a fragment. [Add. ch. 24,178.]

Oval : a shield of arms : a fess ermine betw. three annulets, COVENTRY (?) Crest on a helmet and mantling, wanting.

Cabled border.

Richard Covert, *of East Sutton, co. Kent, Esq.*

9038. [A.D. 1549.] Green. $\frac{1}{2}$ in. [Harl ch. 77 E. 18.]

A lion rampant, in allusion to the arms of COVERT or COURT.

John Cox, *of Gray's Inn, co. Midd., Esq.*

9039. [A.D. 1677.] Red, covered with paper before impression. $\frac{9}{16} \times \frac{7}{16}$ in. [Add. ch. 5098.]

Oval : a shield of arms : a chevron (? engrailed) betw. three uncertain charges. Crest on a helmet and mantling, uncertain.

Sir **Richard Cox,** *Knt.*

9040. [A.D. 1608.] Red: indistinct. $\frac{3}{4} \times \frac{5}{8}$ in. [Add. ch. 33,083.]

A shield of arms : ermine, a fess betw. three birds (?) Crest on a helmet, mantling and chief, an uncertain bird (?).

Cabled border.

Another Seal.

9041. [A.D. 1608.] Red, discoloured. $\frac{1}{2}$ in. [Add. ch. 33,084.]

A shield of arms : three cocks, two and one, crowned, on a chief a pale charged with a rose, betw. two ostrich feathers.

9042. [A.D. 1608.]' Red : indistinct. [Add. ch. 33,085.]
9043. [A.D. 1609.] . Red : good. [Add. ch. 33,087.]

Thomas Cox, *of Gillingham, co. Dors., Yeoman.*
9044. [A.D. 1642.] Red : injured. ⅜ in. [Egert. ch. 491.]
A thistle, perhaps a crest, on a wreath (?)

Roger Coyes, *of London, Gentl.*
9045. [A.D. 1557.] Red.. ⅜ in. [Add. ch. 5319.]
Hexagonal : an ornamental shield of arms : a goat's head, couped. In the field over the shield the initial letters R. C.
Beaded border.

Hugh Crane, *al.* Craan, *Citizen of Winchester.*
9046. [A.D. 1385.] Red : fine. 1 in. [Add. ch. 24,700.]
A shield of arms : three cranes. Suspended by a strap from a tree and within a carved and pointed gothic quatrefoil, ornamented along the inner edge with small ball-flowers.
𝔖igillu ɥugonis crane.
Cabled border.

John de Cranesley.
See JOH. DE KRANESLE.

Lionel Cranfield, *3rd Earl of Middlesex.*
9047. [A.D. 1657.] Red. ¼ in. [Add. ch. 30,952.]
Octagonal : a shield of arms : quarterly, 1, on a pale three fleurs-de-lis, CRANFIELD ; 2, 3, 4, indistinct. Ensigned with an earl's coronet.
From a ring.

John Cranlegh.
9048. [14th cent.] Plaster cast. ¾ in. [lxxxv. 7.]
A shield of arms : chequy on a bend some indistinct charges. Within a carved gothic trefoil.
x 𝔖igillum : ioɥannis · cranlegɥ ⚬

William Cranmer, *of Canterbury, co. Kent.*
9049. [A.D. 1625.] Red : indistinct. [Add. ch. 24,020.]
Oval : a shield of arms, helmet mantling and crest, illegible.

William Crassell (?)
9050. [A.D. 1362.] Plaster cast from imperfect impression.
About 1 in. when perfect. [lxxxv. 9.]

A shield of arms, *couché*: fretty. Crest on a helmet, and mantling out of a coronet, a hind's head. Background diapered with an ornamental, reticulated pattern, having in each interstice a small quatrefoil.

..... ETVM I .... DE CV ....

Perhaps a foreign seal.

Thomas Cravene, *of Henham and Frostenden, co. Suff.*
9051. [A.D. 1396.] Red: good, injured by pressure in parts. 1 in. [Harl. ch. 48 I. 39.]
A shield of arms: a fess betw. six crosses crosslet fitchées, CRAVEN.

✠ S' · Thome ⚭ · crauene ⚭ .

9052. Sulph. cast of No. 9051. [D.C., G. 142.]
9053. [A.D. 1413.] Red: cracked. [Harl. ch. 45 F. 44.]

✠ S' · Thome ⚭ · crauen · ⚭ .

Sir **William Craven,** *Knt., Alderman of London.*
9054. [A.D. 1608.] Red: indistinct. ⅞ × ¾ in. [Add. ch. 35,463.]
Oval: a shield of arms: five fleurs-de-lis in cross, a chief wavy, ANCIENT CRAVEN. Crest on a helmet, ornamental mantling, and chapeau, an eagle rising.
Beaded border.

William Craven,
Lord Craven, of Hampstead-Marshall, co. Berks,
Lord Lieut. and Custos Rotulorum of co. Berks.
9055. [A.D. 1702.] Wafer, covered with paper before impression. 1⅜ in. [Add. ch. 13,632.]
A shield of arms: quarterly, 1, 4, a fess betw. six crosses crosslet fitchées, CRAVEN ; 2, 3. five fleurs-de-lis in cross, a chief wavy, ANCIENT CRAVEN. Ensigned with a baron's coronet. Supporters, two griffins.
In base, on a scroll the motto :—
VIRTVS · IN · ACTIONE · CONSISTIT.
Carved border.

Another Seal.

9056. [A.D. 1706.] Dutch wax, semi-transparent with gold foil mingled in it. ⅝ × ½ in. [Add. ch. 15,012.]
Octagonal: on a griffin sejant affronté, in place of crest and supporters, a shield of arms: quarterly, as in No. 9055. Ensigned with a baron's coronet.
From a ring.

Richard Crawley, *of Luton Hoo, co. Bedf., Gentl.*
9057. [A.D. 1606.]   Red : ¾ × ⅜ in.   [Add. ch. 35,201.]
Oval : a shield of arms : a chevron betw. three boars'
heads.

Thomas Crawley, *Junr., Gentl.,*
cousin and heir of THOMAS CRAWLEY, *Senr.,*
of Wendon Lofts, co. Essex.
9058. [A.D. 1557.]   Red : indistinct.   [Harl. ch. 79 G. 19.]
An ornamental shield of arms : on a fess betw. three
storks, as many crosses crosslet, CRAWLEY.   Betw. the initial
letters T. C.
9059. [A.D. 1558.]   Red : cracked, imperfect, indistinct.
[Harl. ch. 77 E. 27.]

———— Crecroft.
Seal used by GEORGE MONTAGU DUNK,
3rd Earl of Halifax, K.G.
9060. [A.D. 1760.]   Red : *en placard*, on tape.   ⅞ × 1¾₆ in.
[Add. ch. 5977.]
Oval : a carved shield of arms : per pale, *dex.*, on a bend
dancettée, three martlets, CRECROFT ; *sin.*, per fess a fess, in
chief three escallops in fess.   Crest, on a wreath, a stork, in
its dex. claw an axe.   Crest of CRECROFT or CRACROFT, of
co. Linc.
Carved border.

Geoffrey de Creke, *of Helmingham, co. Suff.*
son of BARTHOLOMEW *and* MARGERY DE CREK.
9061. [13th cent.]   Green : indistinct.   ⅜ in.   [Stowe
ch. 376.]
A shield of arms : a maunch, for CREKE.
✠ S' GALFRIDI · DE · CREK.

Margery de Crek, *Widow, of Flixton, co. Suff.*
9062. [A.D. 1257–1265.]   Green-mottled : fine, imperfect.
App. by strands of red silk.   2¼ in.   [Stowe ch. 291.]
A large shield of arms, of early form : quarterly an orle of
twelve roundles, over all a bend.
⟨ SIGILLVM · : MARGERIE . . . . . DE . . . . .
9063. [A.D. 1280.]   Green-mottled : edge chipped.   [Stowe
ch. 308.]
· SIGILLVM · : MARG . . . E : ⋈ ⋈ : DE C · EC :

Hugh, *son of* WILLIAM de Cressingham.

9064. [*Early* 14th cent.] Sulph. cast from good impression. 1¾ in. [D.C., F. 655.]

A swan, with wings expanded, in a ford. In the background a tree. In allusion to the arms of CRESSINGHAM, viz. three swans in pale.

 ✠ S' HVGONIS · FILII · WILLELMI · DE · CRESSINGHAM.

Beaded borders.

Roger de Cressy, *of Norwich, co. Norf.*

9065. [Before A.D. 1246.] Dark-green, mottled: fine, imperfect. 1¾ in. [Harl. ch. 83 E. 19.]

Ø. A shield of arms, of early form: seven crescents, three, three, and one.

 ✠ SIGILLV[M : R]OGERI : DE : CRESSI :

℞. A small oval counterseal with mark of the handle. 1⅛ × 1 in. Impression of an antique oval intaglio gem. Bust in profile to the r., hair tied in a fillet.

 ✠ SIGILLVM : PRECEPTI :

9066. Sulph. casts of *obv.* and *rev.* [D.C., E. 370, 371.]

Walter Creswell.
Seal used by ROBERT UNDERWODE,
of Worplesdon, co. Surr., Carpenter.

9067. [A.D. 1568.] Red: a fragment. About ⅝ × ½ in. when perfect. [Harl. ch. 80 H. 13.]

Oval: a sinister arm in armour, in the hand a cross bottonée fitchée. Crest of CRESWELL.

Cabled border.

Edward de Cretyngge, *of Kedington, co. Suff.*

9068. [A.D. 1338.] Pale-brown: a fragment. About 1 in. when perfect. [Harl. ch. 50 I. 48.]

A shield of arms: a chevron betw. three mullets pierced, within a bordure, CRETINO.

Legend wanting.

Margeria de Criel, *al.* Kyriel,
of Easton-Neston Manor, co. Northt.

9069. [A.D. 1301.] Bronze-green: fine, upper point chipped. 1⅜ × 1 in. [Add. ch. 21,856.]

Pointed oval: a shield of arms: two chevrons and a canton, over all a label of three points each charged with as many roundles, CRIOLL, etc. Suspended by a strap from a tree of three branches.

 [✠ S]IGILLVM : MARGERIE : DE CRIE . . . . .

Margeria de Kyriel, *of Cherry-Hinton, co. Cambr.*
· **9070.** [*Temp.* Edw. II.] Light-brown : a fragment. About
1¼ in. when perfect.   [Harl. ch. 52 G. 11.]
· A shield of arms : two chevrons, over all a label of three
points, each charged with as many roundles. KYRIEL, CRIOLL,
or KERRIELL.
.....·LVM : M ....
Cf. No. 9069, Add. ch. 21,856, A.D. 1301.

George de Criketot, *or* **Roger,** *his son,*
Dominus de Webbetone, co. Heref.
9071. [A.D. 1342.] Dark-green. ¾ in. [Add. ch. 4594.]
A shield of arms : a fess, and in chief some illegible charges.
Within a pointed trefoil panel, ornamented along the inner
edge with small quatrefoils or ball-flowers.

Humfrey de Creketokes, *al.* **Criketot,**
of Ousden, co. Suff.
9072. [A.D. 1302.] Light-green : good. [Harl. ch. 48 I. 43.]
Shield-shaped : a shield of arms : a cross, with, perhaps,
uncertain charges.
✠ S' VMFRIDI DE CRIKETOT ✻

Humfridus de Criketot, *al.* **Umfridus**
filius **Willelmi de Criketot,** *of Westleton, co. Suff.*
9073. [*Temp.* Edw. I.]   Pale-green : good.   1 × ¾ in.
[Harl. ch. 83 E. 20.]
Shield-shaped : a shield of arms : on a cross five escallops,
CRIKETOFT.
✠ S' VMFRIDI DE CRIKETOT ✻
9074. Sulph. cast from No. 9073. [D.C., E. 372.]
9075. [*Temp.* Edw. I.]   Another. [Harl. ch. 83 E. 21.]

Henry Cryspe, *of Whitstable, co. Kent, Esq.*
9076. [A.D. 1551.]   Red.   ½ × ⅜ in.   [Harl. ch. 49 A. 50.]
Octagonal : an ostrich's head erased, in the beak a mill-
rind.   Crest of CRIPPS (?).
Beaded border.

Henry Crispe, *of Gouthurst, co. Kent.*
9077. [A.D. 1606.]   Red : fair.   ⅚ × ¼ in.   [Harl. ch.
77 C. 42.]
Oval : a shield of arms : quarterly, 1, ermine a fess chequy,
CRISPE ; 2, on a chevron five horse-shoes, CRISPE (another

coat) ; 3, two flaunches, each charged with a leopard's face,
DENNE ; 4, on a fess dancettée, three leopards' faces, and on
a chief as many hazel-trees, HASELHURST.
Beaded border.
Cf. Harl. MS. 1432, f. 230.

Henry Crispe, *of Quex in Birchington, co. Kent, Esq.*
9078. [A.D. 1643.]   Red : indistinct. $\frac{3}{8} \times \frac{1}{4}$ in.   [Harl.
ch. 79 F. 8.]
Oval : on a wreath, a camelopard, pelletté, collared and
lined.   Crest of CRISPE.

John Cryspe, *of Canterbury, co. Kent.*
9079. [A.D. 1577.]   Red : injured by pressure. $\frac{3}{4}$ in.
[Harl. ch. 86 H. 6.]
A shield of arms : on a chevron five horse-shoes, CRISPE.
Beaded border.
9080. [A.D. 1577.]   Another.   [Harl. ch. 86 H. 7.]

Sir Nicholas Crispe, *of Quex in Birchington, co. Kent, Knt.*
9081. [A.D. 1645.]   Red : injured by pressure.   [Harl. ch.
83 H. 45.]
Octagonal : on a wreath a camelopard, collared and chained.
Crest of CRISPE.   From a ring (?)

John Crocker, *of Plympton, co. Devon, Knt.*
9082. [A.D. 1505,]   Red : indistinct. $\frac{1}{4} \times \frac{7}{16}$ in.   [Add.
ch. 29,150.]
Rectangular : an uncertain animal.   Crest of CROKĖR (?)

Edward Croft, *Knt.,*
Lieut. of GEORGE TALBOT, *Earl of Shrewsbury,*
King's Steward of Wigmore Manor, co. Heref.
9083. [A.D. 1529.]   Red : imperfect. $\frac{5}{8} \times \frac{1}{2}$ in.   [Cott.
ch. xxvi. 13.]
Shield-shaped : a shield of arms : quarterly per fess indented, in the first quarter a lion passant guardant, CROFT.
9084. Another, imperfect.   [Cott. ch. xxvi. 13.]

James Croft, *of Craft, co. Heref., Knt.*
9085. [A.D. 1566.]   Red. $\frac{7}{8}$ in.   [Harl. ch. 79 G. 21.]
An ornamental shield of arms : quarterly per fess indented,
in the first quarter a lion passant guardant, CROFT.
Beaded border.

George Croke, *of the Inner Temple, London, Esq.*
9086. [A.D. 1606.]   Red :   imperfect at lower part.
¾ × ⅞ in.   [Add. ch. 19,545.]
Oval : a shield of arms : quarterly, 1, 4, a fess betw. six
martlets, CROKE ; 2. 3, a fess nebuly with each bend pierced,
betw. three annulets, (?) BLOUNT.
Beaded border.
Cf. Harl. MS. 1102, ff. 7, 68 *b.*

Sir **Henry Croke,** *of Hampton Poyl, co. Oxon., Knt., and Bart.*
9087. [A.D. 1647.]   Red : much injured.   About ⅜ in.
[Add. ch. 29,532.]
Oval : a shield of arms : very indistinct.

Thomas Crompton, *of co. Heref., Esq.*
9088. [A.D. 1591.]   Red : very much injured.   About
⅞ × ¾ in.   [Harl. ch. 79 F. 39.]
A shield of arms : a fess wavy betw. three lions rampant,
CROMPTON.   Crest on a helmet and mantling, illegible.
Beaded border.

Sir **Henry Wylliams,** *al.* **Cromwell,** *Knt.,*
of Hinchingbrooke, co. Hunt.
9089. [A.D. 1590.]   Red : imperfect on l. h. side.   About
1⅛ × 1 in. when perfect.   [Add. ch. 34,102.]
Oval : a shield of arms : of seven quarterings, four in chief,
three in base : 1, a lion rampant, CROMWELL ; 2, three spear-
heads, two and one, CARADOC VREICHFRAS ; 3, a chevron
betw. three fleurs-de-lis, COLLWYN AP TANGNO, LORD OF
EFIONYDD ; 4, three chevrons, JESTYN AP GWRGANT, PRINCE
OF GLAMORGAN ; 5, a lion rampant, MADOC AP MEREDITH,
PRINCE OF POWYS ; 6, on a chevron a mullet, MURFYN ;
7, uncertain : an animal, within an orle of fleurs-de-lis.   Crest
on a helmet, ornamental mantling, and wreath, a demi-lion
rampant, in his dexter gamb a gem ring.
Cabled border.
Cf. Henfrey, *Numismata Cromwelliana,* pl. vi.

9090. [A.D. 1603.]   Red : very fragmentary, indistinct.
[Add. ch. 33,159.]

Henry Cromwell, *of Uppwood, co. Hunt., Esq.*
9091. [A.D. 1608.]   Red.   ⁹⁄₁₆ × ⁷⁄₁₆ in.   [Add. ch. 33,164.]
Oval : on a wreath a demi-lion, in the dexter gamb a gem
ring.   Crest of CROMWELL.
Beaded border.
9092. [A.D. 1608.]   Another.   [Add. ch. 33,165.]

Seal used by HENRY CROMWELL, *junr.,*
son and heir of Sir OLIVER CROMWELL, *Knt.*

9093. [A.D. 1610.] Red: a small fragment. [Add. ch. 33,166.]

9094. [A.D. 1618.] Red: imperfect. [Add. ch. 33,107.]

9095. [A.D. 1618.] Red: indistinct. [Add. ch. 33,108.]

John de Crumwell, *of Arnold Manor, co. Nott., Knt.*

9096. [A.D. 1316.] Red: injured at edges. About ⅞ in. when perfect. [Add. ch. 15,251.]

A shield of arms: six annulets, three, two, and one, CROM-WELL. Suspended by a strap from a hook. Betw. two wyverns.

    ✠ . . . IOHANNI . . . . CRVMWEL . .

Matildis, *dau. of* JOHN BARNACK,
wife of Sir RALPH de **Crumwelle,** *al.* **Cromwelle,**
Lord of the Manor and Castle of Tateshale, co. Linc., 2nd Baron.

9097. [A.D. 1370.] Red: fine. 1⅛ in. [Harl. ch. 49 A. 43.]

A shield of arms : per pale, *dex.,* ermine, a fess, BARNACK, *sin.,* a chief (*diapré*) and baton, CROMWELL, *of co. Lincoln.* (Note the impalement is reversed by error of the engraver.) Within a carved and pointed gothic quatrefoil with three shields of arms thereon : viz., 1, chequy, a chief ermine, with a label of four points, TATTERSHALL, or TATSHALE ; 2, three cinquefoils and a canton, DRYBY ; vairé, a fess, MARMYON.

Legend betw. the three small shields :—

    Sigill' _ matilỗf ỗe cro_mỗelle.

Beaded border.

Cf. Harl. MS. ch. 1190, f. 70.

9098. Sulph. cast from No. 9097. [D.C., F. 469.]

9099. [A.D. 1417.] Red: fine, edge injured. [Harl. ch. 49 A. 44.]

    Sigill' _ matilỗs ỗe cro_mỗelle.

Oliver Wylliams, *al.* **Cromwell,**
of Hinchingbrook, co. Hunt., Esq.

9100. [A.D. 1590.] Red: fine. ¾ × ⅞ in. [Add. ch. 34,101.]

Oval: on a wreath a demi-lion rampant, in the dexter gamb a gem ring. Crest of CROMWELL.

Beaded border.

9101. [A.D. 1602.] Red, discoloured: imperfect. [Add. ch. 33,158.]

Sir **Oliver Williams,** *alias* **Cromwell,**
of Hinchingebrooke, co. Hunt., Knt.
(*Same as last.*)

9102. [A.D. 1607.] Red: injured. About $\frac{3}{4} \times \frac{5}{8}$ in. when perfect. [Add. ch. 33,697.]

Oval: a shield of arms: a lion rampant, CROMWELL. Crest on a helmet and ornamental mantling, destroyed.

Small Seal.

9103. [A.D. 1605.] Red. About $\frac{7}{16} \times \frac{3}{8}$ in. [Add. ch. 33,160.]

Oval: a shield of arms: a lion rampant, CROMWELL.

9104. [A.D. 1607.] Red: injured. [Add. ch. 33,163.]

9105. [A.D. 1608.] Red: fine. Beaded border. [Add. ch. 33,164.]

9106. [A.D. 1608.] Red: indistinct. [Add. ch. 33,165.]

9107. [A.D. 1618.] Red: a fragment. [Add. ch. 33,101.]

9108. [A.D. 1618.] Red: good. [Add. ch. 33,105.]

9109. [A.D. 1618.] Red: good. [Add. ch. 33,109.]

Ralph de Cromwell, *Knt., 2nd Lord Cromwell,*
Lord of the Castle and Manor of Tattershall, co. Linc.

9110. [A.D. 1370.] Red: fine. 1 in. [Harl. ch. 49 A. 43.]

A shield of arms: a chief (diapered) and bendlet, CROMWELL. Within a carved and traced gothic cinquefoil, ornamented along the inner edge with small ball-flowers.

☆ Si' : Radulphi : de : cro͞uwelle : Milit'.

Beaded border.

9111. Sulph. cast from No. 9110. [D.C., F. 468.]

Ralph de Cromwell, *4th Lord Cromwell.*

9112. [A.D. 1437.] Red: originally fine, imperfect. About $1\frac{1}{2}$ in. when perfect. [Harl. ch. 45 A. 35.]

A shield of arms, *couché*: quarterly, [1,] 4, a chief, over all a bend, CROMWELL of Tattershall; 2, [3,] chequy, a chief ermine, TATTERSHALL, *al.* TATERSHALE. Crest on a helmet and ornamental mantling, on a chapeau, a garb. Supporters two wild-men. In the field on the r. h. side, over the sinister supporter, a leathern bouget. Background replenished with sprigs.

. . . . hi cramuell . . .

9113. Sulph. cast of No. 9112. [D.C., G. 203.]

Signet.

9114. [A.D. 1450.] Red. $\frac{1}{2}$ in. [Add. ch. 17,238.]

Small round signet: a lion's head erased, perhaps in

allusion to the arms of CROMWELL. Betw. the initial letters **i. l.** ?

Cabled and cusped border.

Richard Cromwell, *Knt., Lord of the Demesne of the late Abbey of Ramsey, co. Hunt.*

9115. [A.D. 1544.] Red. ⅜ in. [Add. ch. 33,691.]

On a wreath a demi-lion, queue fourchée, in the paws a javelin. Crest of CROMWELL.

Richard Cromwell, *of Hinchinbrooke, co. Hunt, Esq.*

9116. [A.D. 1602.] Red: imperfect. About ⅜ × ¼ in. [Add. ch. 33,158.]

Oval: a lion rampant, in allusion to the arms of CROMWELL.

Beaded border.

[*Sir*] Robert Cromwell, [*Knt. ?*]

9117. [A.D. 1609.] Red: indistinct. About ⅜ × ¼ in. [Add. ch. 35,091.]

Oval: a shield of arms: of six quarterings, as Nos. 1–6, on the shield described for Sir Henry Wylliams, *al.* Cromwell, in No. 9089, Add. ch. 34,102, *q.v.*

Robert Cromwell.
See WILLIAM CHETEWYND.

Thomas Crumwell, *Esq., Chief Secretary to the King, afterwards Sir* Thos. Crumwell.
(*See next Seal.*)

9118. [A.D. 1536.] Red: somewhat injured. ⅞ in. [Harl. ch. 57 H. 3.]

An ornamental shield of arms as in No. 9119. Betw. the initial letters T. C.

Beaded border.

Thomas Crumwell, *Knt., Lord Crumwell,*
1*st Baron Cromwell, of Okeham, and afterw. Earl of Essex.*

9119. [A.D. 1538.] Red: fine. ¾ × ⅜ in. [Harl. ch. 49 A. 46.]

Oval: an ornamental shield of arms: on a fess betw. three lions rampant a rose betw. two Cornish choughs, CROMWELL. Above the shield a fleur-de-lis.

9120. Sulph. cast of No. 9119. [D.C., H. 94.]

9121. [A.D. 1539.] Red: fair. ⅞ in. [Harl. ch. 47 A. 50.]

An ornamental shield of arms as before.¹ Betw. the initial letters T. C.
Beaded border.
Cf. No. 9118, Harl. ch. 57 H. 3.
9122. Sulph. cast of No. 9121.   [D.C., H. 95.]

John de Crosho . . . (P) *perhaps of co. Linc.*
9123. [A.D. 1322.]   Brown : indistinct, imperfect.   ¾ in. [Harl. ch. 45 I. 26.]
A shield of arms : a cross flory.   Betw. two wyverns sans wings.
   S' SIGNVM · D . . . IOH' x DE OROSHO . . (?)

John Crosland, *of London.*
Seal used by JEAN SAMUEL PAULY, *of London.*
9124. [A.D. 1816.]   Red : *en placard* on tape, imperfect. About 1 × ¾ in. [Add. ch. 17,263.]
Rectangular with rounded corners : a shield of arms : quarterly a cross flory, CROSLAND.   Crest on, a wreath a dexter hand and arm in armour, embowed, grasping a battle-axe.

William Crosse, *Chaplain, of Norwich, co. Norf*
9125. [A.D. 1478.]   Red : injured.   ₇⁄₁₆ in.   [Stowe ch. 197.]
A quatrefoil, perhaps used as an heraldic bearing for a cross botonnée, one of the charges of CROSSE.
Beaded border.

Robert Crossyñg, *of Englebourne, co. Devon.*
9126. [A.D. 1453.]   Red.   ⅝ in.   [Add. ch. 26,175.]
Shield-shaped : a shield of arms : a chevron.

John Crowe, *Citizen and Fishmonger of London.*
9127. [A.D. 1628.]   Red.   ¼ in.   [Add. ch. 30,822.]
A fleur-de-lis, perhaps used as an heraldic device.

John Crow.
See JOHN THURLBY.

William Crowe, *of Chiddingley, co. Suss., Esq.*
9128. [A.D. 1612.]   Red : fine.   ¾ × ⅝ in.   [Harl. ch. 111 F. 26.]
Oval : a shield of arms : quarterly, 1, 4, a chevron betw. three dunghill-cocks, CROW ; 2, 3, a lion rampant.
Beaded border.

9129. Sulph. cast of No. 9128. [D.C., H. 136.]
9130. [A.D. 1612.] Red: imperfect. [Harl. ch. 86 I. 36.]
9131. [A.D. 1615.] Red: injured. [Add. ch. 30,138.]
9132. [A.D. 1618.] Red: much injured. [Add. ch. 29,653.]

Hamond de Croxtune.

9133. [A.D. 1385.] Red: indistinct in parts. ⅜ in. [Harl. ch. 56 A. 35.]
A shield of arms : indistinct.

✠ S' · Ꝑamonꝺ : ꝺe : croxtune.

John Croylboys, *of Rochester, co. Kent.*

9134. [A.D. 1397–8.] Red: good, injured in parts by pressure, formerly encircled with a twisted rush. 1 in. [Harl. ch. 78 F. 28.]
A shield of arms : on a fess betw. three bugle-horns as many talbots passant (?) The arms of CROYLBOYS are described as three bugle-horns (Burke, *Gen. Arm.*). Within a pointed trefoil, ornamented with small ball-flowers along the inner edge.

Sigillu : iohannis : croylboys.

William Croyser, *of Yelden, co. Bedf.*

9135. [A.D. 1357.] Red: injured in parts by pressure. ⅞ in. [Add. ch. 5154.]
A shield of arms : a cross betw. two flies, in the 1st, and 4th, and three [―――?] in the 2nd and 3rd quarters, for CROYSIER. Within a pointed gothic quatrefoil.

SIGILLVM WILLELMI CROYZE...

William Croyser,
son and heir of WILLIAM CROYSER, *Chevr.,*
of · Great Bookham, co. Surr.

9136. [A.D. 1394.] Red: injured, imperfect. About 1⅛ in. [Add. ch. 5609.]
A shield of arms : quarterly, 1, 4, a cross betw. four flies, CROYSIER ; 2, 3, a chevron.

✠ S' WILL'I...

William Croyser, *of Great Bookham, co. Surr.*

9137. [A.D. 1401.] Red: imperfect, very indistinct in parts, originally encircled by a twisted rush. 1 in. [Add. ch. 5612.]
A shield· of arms : per pale, *dex.,* a cross betw. four flies,

CROYSIER; *sin.*, a chevron, on which are some uncertain charges. Suspended from a tree.

&' wilelmi : [cr]ouser.

Beaded border.

9138. [A.D. 1415.]   Red: very indistinct.   [Add. ch. 5616.]

Ralph Crutcher.
See CLIFFORD.

Sir **Thomas Crymes,** *of Peckham, co. Surr., Knt.*

9139. [A.D. 1620.]   Red : chipped, distorted.   About ¾ × ⅜ in.   [Add. ch. 23,636.]
Oval: a shield of arms: three bars, on the first bar two martlets, and on the third, a chief barry nebuly of four, CRYMES.   (Incorrectly engraved.)

Ernest-Augustus, *Duke of* **Cumberland,**
(King of Hanover, 1837), *5th son of George III.*

9140. [A.D. 1837–1851.]   Red.   1¾ × 1⅛ in.   [xlix. 33.]
Oval: a circular shield of arms: ROYAL ARMS OF GREAT BRITAIN, as used by George III. after the union with Ireland, without the label for difference.   Encircled with a Garter incribed :—

NEC ₐSPERₐ TERRENT.

Ensigned with a foreign royal crown.   Supporters of Great Britain, with labels for difference.   In base a ribbon, entwined with a branch of oak and a branch of laurel, and inscribed :—

SUSCIPERE ET FINIRE.

Another seal.

9141. Red.   1 × ⅞ in.   [xlix. 34.]
Quadrilateral with rounded corners: a circular shield of arms : ROYAL ARMS OF GREAT BRITAIN, with label for difference.   Encircled with a Garter inscribed with the motto of the Order, and with a collar of the Order of the Bath. Ensigned with the coronet of a duke.   Supporters of Great Britain, each with a label for difference, on carved scrolls. From the collar depend four stars or badges of orders.   In base, on a ribbon, the motto :—

SUSCIPERE ET FINIRE.

Margaret, *Duchess of Cumberland.*
See MARGARET CLIFFORD.

Thomas de Cumberworth, *of co. Linc.*

9142. [A.D. 1355.]   Red: fine.   ⅞ in.   [Harl. ch. 57 G. 11.]

A shield of arms: chequy on a chief a lion passant. Betw. two pierced cinquefoils, and suspended by a strap from a flowering tree. Within a carved gothic cinquefoil, ornamented along the inner edge with small ball-flowers.

$\mathfrak{S}$igill' · tfjome · ð' · cüberʇvortfje.

Beaded border.

9143. Sulph. cast of No. 9142. [D.C., F. 397.]

Cf. Harl. ch. 57 A. 28, A.D. 1359; 57 G. 12, 13, A.D. 1359; 55 B. 21, A.D. 1361; 56 E. 28, A.D. 1362.

John Cursun *or* Cursoun,
son of JOHN CURSON, *Knt., of co. Suff.*

9144. [A.D. 1412.] Red: fine. 1 in. [Harl. ch. 49 B. 26.]

A shield of arms, *couché*: quarterly, 1, 4, two lions passant; 2, a bend chequy betw. two annulets (?); 4, ermine, a bend chequy, CURSON. Crest on a helmet and lambrequins, out of a ducal coronet a pair of wings erect.

$\mathfrak{S}$' iofjannis cursoun.

Cabled border.

9145. Sulph. cast of No. 9144. [D.C., G. 129.]

9146. [A.D. 1417.] Red: fine fragments. 1 in. [Add. ch. 7381.]

A shield of arms, *couché*.

· · · · · · · · $\mathfrak{s}$ cu · · · · ·

Richard Curzon.

9147. [A.D. 1499.][1] Plaster cast from fine impression. $\frac{7}{8}$ in. [lxxxx. 11.]

A shield of arms: three lions passant in pale. The field replenished with sprigs of foliage.

Beaded border.

William Cursoun, *of Byntre, co. Norf.*

9148. [A.D. 1370.] Green: fragmentary. About $\frac{7}{8}$ in. when perfect. [Harl. ch. 58 C. 5.]

A shield of arms: ermine, a bend, chequy, CURSON. Within a carved gothic panel.

Legend wanting.

· · · · ʇvil · · · · ·

9149. [A.D. 1370.] Green: a fragment. [Harl. ch. 58 C. 6.]

Sir George Curteis, *of Otterden, co. Kent, Knt.*

9150. [A.D. 1671.] Red: indistinct. [Harl. ch. 86 I. 37.]

Oval: a shield of arms: a chevron betw. three bulls' heads cabossed, CURTEIS.

Hugh Curteys.

9151. [A.D. 1409–10.]   Plaster cast from fine impression.
1 in. [lxxxv. 10.]

A shield of arms : three estoiles within a bordure engrailed.
Suspended by a strap from a forked tree.   Within a carved
gothic cinquefoil ornamented with small ball-flowers along
the inner edge.

Sigillũ : ḥugonis : curteys.

Richard, *son of* ROBERT **Le Curteys,** *of Normanby, co. Linc.*

9152. [*Temp.* Edw. I.]   Dark-green : indistinct in places.
⅞ in. [Harl. ch. 49 B. 41.]

A shield of arms : a chevron betw. three uncertain charges,
perhaps bulls' heads cabossed, for CURTEIS.

✠ S' RICARDI COVRTAIS.

Beaded borders.

Alice Cutler, *widow of* ROBERT CUTLER, *of Ipswich,*
co. Suff., Esq.

9153. [A.D. 1625.]   Red : very indistinct. [Add. ch. 10,160.]
Oval : a shield of arms, helmet, mantling and crest, too
much injured by pressure to be made out.

John Cutte, *Knt., Under-Treasurer of England.*

9154. [A.D. 1507.]   Red : well preserved. $\frac{9}{16} \times \frac{7}{16}$ in.
[Add. ch. 17,744.]

Lozenge-shaped signet : a greyhound sejant contourné.
Above, in the field, the initial letters :—I. C.

Cabled border.

D

M— D—.
Seal used by THOMAS BARENTYN, *of Chalgrave, co. Oxon.*

9155. [A.D. 1394.]   Red : much injured by pressure.   ⅞ in.
[Add. ch. 20,311.]

A shield (of arms ?) : a dexter hand couped at the wrist.
Betw. the initial letters M. D., and two sprigs.   Within a
gothic panel.

. . . . ℂ . . . . 𝔰 ᴀ ᴕ 𝔇𝔬 . . . . ᴀ

John Dabridgecourt.

9156. [A.D. 1409 ?]   Plaster cast from good impression.
1¼ in. [lxxxv. 12.]

A shield of arms : ermine, three bars humettée, DABRIDGE-

COURT. On the second bar an annulet for difference. Suspended by a strap from a forked tree and within a carved panel, ornamented with ball-flowers along the inner edge.

Sigillum : ioḣaniſ : ḋabrichcourt.

Robertus de Dachet, *of Dachet, co. Bucks.*
9157. [A.D. 1343.] Red : imperfect. About ¾ in. when perfect. [Add. ch. 5185.]

A shield of arms : on a bend betw. two square mascles (?) three animals' heads erased. Within a pointed gothic quatrefoil, having in each cusped space an eagle's head.

Legend wanting.

Edward Dacre, *of Croglyn, co. Cumber., Esq.*
9158. [A.D. 1566.] Red. ¼ × ⅜ in. [Harl. ch. 77 F. 1.]

Oval : a bull statant contourné, for the crest of DACRE.

Francis Dacre, *Lord Dacres (?) son of* WILLIAM, *3rd Lord.*
9159. [A.D. 1606.] Red : injured. ⅝ in. [Harl. ch. 77 F. 2.]

On a wreath a bull statant, collared and chained. Crest of DACRE.

Beaded border.

William de Dacre, *Lord of Holbeiche, co. Linc.*
9160. [A.D. 1357.] Red : originally fine, much chipped at edge. About 1¼ in. when perfect. [Add. ch. 19,846.]

A shield of arms, *couché* : three escallops, two and one, DACRE. Crest on a helmet and lambrequin chequy, out of a ducal coronet, a bull's head chequy. Within an elaborate gothic panel, ornamented along the inner edge with small ball-flowers, and having on each side two circular openings in the tracery in each of which is a pierced quatrefoil.

. . SIGILL . . . ILLEL . . . . . RE.

William Dacre, *3rd Baron Dacre, of Greystock.*
9161. [A.D. 1530–1531.] Plaster cast from good impression, injured in places by pressure. 2 in. [lxxxv. 13 A.]

A shield of arms : quarterly of six pieces ; 1, three escallops, DACRE ; 2, 3, GREYSTOCK, etc. Crest on a helmet, ornamental mantling and wreath, a bull couchant. Supporters : *dex.*, a bull (?), *sin.*, a griffin.

✠ SIGILLVM : WILLMI : ᵈ DÑI : DE : DACRE : . . . . . GRAYSTOK.

9162. Another. [lxxxv. 13 B.]

Christopher Dacres, *of Lanercost, co. Cumber.*
9163. [A.D. 1562.]　Red: injured by pressure, imperfect.
[Harl. ch. 77 E. 57.]
A bull statant, collared, chained and ringed.　Crest of
DACRE.

Henry Dade (?)
Seal used by JOHN DE STODHAGH, *of Laxfield, co. Suff.*
9164. [A.D. 1355.]　Green, discoloured: indistinct.　⅞ in.
[Add. ch. 9625.]
A shield of arms: a chevron betw. three garbs, DADE.
⚹ S' HENRICI · DADE ♠ ❀

John de Daekerqe (?)
9165. [14th cent.]　Plaster cast from chipped impression.
⅞ in.　[lxxxv. 15.]
A shield of arms: a chevron, and chief diapered lozengy
with a small roundle or other device in each space.
. . . . . . OH'IS D' DAEKERQE (?)
Probably a foreign seal.

Johanna, *widow of* ROGER **Dakeneye,** *Chivr. of Clophill,*
co. Bedf.
9166. [A.D. 1354.]　Green: originally fine, edge injured.
About 1 in. when perfect.　[Harl. ch. 49 B. 48.]
A lozenge-shaped shield of arms: a cross betw. four
lioncels rampant, DAKENEY.　Within a carved and pointed
gothic quatrefoil, ornamented with small ball-flowers along
the inner edge.
. . . . . . IOH'E ❀ VX'IS ❀ ROGERI ❀ DE . . . . EN . . . .
9167. Sulph. cast from No. 9166.　[D.C., F. 389.]

Robert Dallison, *of St. Faith's, London, Mercer.*
9168. [A.D. 1685.]　Red: *en placard.*　¾ × ⅝ in.　[Add.
ch. 10,540.]
Oval: a shield of arms: an heraldic antelope passant.
Cabled border.
9169. [A.D. 1685.]　Another.　[Add. ch. 10,500.]
9170. [A.D. 1685.]　Another, used by THOS. PLUME.
[Add. ch. 10,500.]
9171. [A.D. 1685.]　Another, used by ANN PLUME.　[Add.
ch. 10,500.]

M. Dalton (?)
Seal used by NATHANAEL BARNARDISTON, of Ketton, al. Keddington, co. Suff., Knt.
9172. [A.D. 1620.] Red. $\frac{1}{16} \times \frac{1}{16}$ in. [Harl. roll. Z. 25.]
Oval: a shield of arms: a lion rampant guardant, DALTON (?)
Cabled border.

John Dameron.
See THOMAS HATTCHETT.

Elizabeth, *widow of Sir* ROGER **Damory**.
See ELIZABETH DE BURGO.

Richard Damory, *Chevr., of co. Bucks.*
9173. [A.D. 1340.] Red: fine. $\frac{1}{12}$ in. [Harl. ch. 49 C. 3.]
A shield of arms: barry nebuly of six. Within a carved
and traced double trefoil or trilobe.
☿ SIGILLVM · RICARDI · DAMORI.
Beaded border.
9174. Sulph. cast from No. 9173. [D.C., F. 453.]

Galiena de Dammar[tin].
9175. [13th cent.] Plaster cast from chipped impression.
$1\frac{3}{8} \times 1\frac{1}{8}$ in. [lxxxv. 16.]
Pointed oval: a shield of arms of early shape: per pale,
dex., pily of (six?) on a chief a lion passant; *sin.*, barry, or
three bars, a chief vairé? Over the shield an estoile of seven
points wavy.
SIGILL' GALIENE DE DAMMAR . . . .
Probably a foreign seal.

Christopher Danby, *of Thorp-pirroo, co. York, Knt.*
9176. [A.D. 1548.] Red: much injured by pressure.
[Add. ch. 17,024.]
A shield (of arms?): a crab erect, charged on the shell with
the text-letter Ɗ for DANBY, crest.
Cf. Add. ch. 17,112.

Sir Robert Danby, *Lord Chief Justice of the Common Pleas, Knt.*
9177. [A.D. 1464.] Red: cracked, indistinct. $\frac{1}{2}$ in. [Harl.
ch. 77 F. 6.]
A martlet, in the field a flowering sprig, and a mullet in
allusion to the arms of DANBY.

William Danby, *of Stoke Daubeny, co. Northt.*
9178. [A.D. 1400.]   Red: much injured by pressure.
About 1 in.   [Add. ch. 21,807.]
A shield of arms : per pale, *dex.,* barry, a bend (?), *sin.,*
uncertain.   Within a carved gothic trefoil.

[𝔖𝔦]𝔤𝔦𝔩𝔩' : 𝔴𝔦𝔩𝔩' : 𝔡𝔞𝔫𝔟𝔦.

Simon Daniel.
9179. [*Temp.* Rich. II.]   Plaster cast from fine impression.
1 in.   [lxxxv. 17.]
A shield of arms : on a bend some illegible charges ; in *sin.*
chief a mullet.   Over the shield the initial letter M. crowned.
Within a carved gothic panel of eight points ornamented
with two slipped leaves, and along the inner edge with
ball-flowers.

· SIGILLVM + SIMONIS + DANIEL ·

Beaded border.

———— Daniel (?)
9180. [14th cent.]   Plaster cast from fine impression.
¾ in.   [lxxxviii. 46.]
A shield of arms : on a bend three martlets, DANIEL.
Suspended on a forked tree.   Within a carved gothic panel.

𝔖𝔦𝔤𝔦𝔩𝔩𝔲𝔪 : . . . 𝔢𝔫𝔰 : 𝔡𝔞𝔫𝔦𝔢𝔩.

Roger Danney, *Parson of the Church of All Saints,*
Snetirton, co. Norf.
9181. [A.D. 1385.]   Red: fine, imperfect.   1⅛ in.   [Harl.
ch. 56 I. 1.]
A shield of arms : a fesse engrailed betw. three leaves or
pineapples.   Within a finely carved gothic trefoil with
elaborate tracery.
Legend betw. the points :—

𝔖𝔦𝔤' 𝔯𝔬𝔤' _ 𝔢𝔯𝔦   𝔡𝔞𝔫𝔫𝔞𝔶 _ 𝔰𝔢𝔯𝔲𝔫𝔡𝔦.

Beaded border.
9182. Sulph. cast from No. 9181.   [D.C., F. 558]

Sir **John Danvers,** *of Chelsea, co. Midd., Knt.*
9183. [A.D. 1652.]   Red: indistinct, imperfect.   About
⅝ × ½ in.   [Add. ch. 5717.]
An ornamental shield of arms : a chevron betw. three
mullets of six points, DANVERS.
Legend illegible.

Another Seal.

9184. [A.D. 1652.] Red : indistinct in parts. 1⅜ × ⅞ in. [Add. ch. 5716.]

Oval : a shield of arms : quarterly, 1, 4, a chevron betw. three mullets of six points, DANVERS ; 2, 3, a saltire betw. some indistinct charges. The shield supported in front by a wyvern, sejant, for the crest. Field diapered with crosslets arranged in a reticulated pattern.

Legend on a scroll :

BONOS · AMO · RELIQVOS · . . AME . . · CVPIO · BONOS ·

William Danvers, *of co. Berk., Esq.*

9185. [A.D. 1427.] Red : fine. 1⅛ in. [Harl. ch. 49 C. 16.]

A shield of arms : a chevron betw. three mullets pierced, DANVERS. Suspended by a strap from a tree, and within a carved gothic panel.

𝕾𝖎𝖌𝖎𝖑𝖑𝖚𝖒 : 𝖜𝖎𝖑𝖑𝖊𝖑𝖒𝖎 : 𝖉𝖆𝖚𝖓𝖚𝖊𝖗𝖘.

9186. Sulph. cast of No. 9185. [D.C., G. 175.]

George Danyell, *Esq., of Denham, co. Buck.*

9187. [A.D. 1468.] Red : injured, originally encircled with a twisted rush. ⅞ in. [Harl. ch. 111 F. 28.]

A garb tied with a tasselled cord : in the field the initial letters 𝖌. 𝖉.

Cabled border.

John Danyllys, *of Bokeland-Fillegh, co. Devon.*

9188. [A.D. 1498.] Red : cracked, imperfect. About ⅞ × ½ in. [Add. ch. 29,146.]

Lozenge-shaped : a bull (?) reguardant, contourné, for crest of DANIELL.

Beaded border.

John Dapphale (?), *of Kedington, co. Suff.*

9189. [A.D. 1338.] Red : injured at edges. ⅞ in. [Harl. ch. 50 I. 48.]

A shield of arms, *couché* : on a bend some uncertain charges. Crest on a helmet and lambrequin, a plume. Background diapered lozengy with an annulet in each space. Within a finely carved gothic rosette of eight points with ball-flowers along the inner edge.

John Darbye (?)

9190. [14th cent.] Plaster cast from good impression, indistinct in parts. 1 in. [lxxxv. 20.]

A shield of arms: a chevron betw. three garbs, DARBY. Suspended by a strap from a forked tree, and within a carved gothic rosette ornamented with a pair of slipped flowerets on each side, and along the inner edge with small ball-flowers.

𝕾𝖎𝖌𝖎𝖑𝖑𝖚𝖒 : 𝕴𝖔𝖍𝖆𝖓𝖓𝖎𝖘 : 𝕯𝖆𝖗 . 𝖞𝖊.

John Darby.
See ——— RHODES.

Roger Darck (?)
Seal used by WILLIAM ATTE BROKE, *of Shoreham, co. Suss.*
9191. [A.D. 1345.] Discoloured white: indistinct. ⅞ in. [Add. ch. 17,308.]
A shield of arms: a squirrel. Within a carved gothic rosette of eight points.

✠ S' ROGERI · DAROK ⌣ .

Perhaps a foreign seal.

John Darcye, *of Lincoln's Inn, co. Midd., Esq.*
9192. [A.D. 1598.] Red: imperfect. ₁₁⁄₁₆ × ¼ in. [Harl. ch. 77 G. 8.]
Oval: a hare sejant, collared, lined and ringed, perhaps for a crest. Betw. the initial letters I. [D?]
Beaded border.

John Darcy, *4th Baron Darcy, of Aston, co. York.*
9193. [A.D. 1625.] Red: a fragment. [Add. ch. 5813.]
On a wreath, a tilting spear broken in three pieces, the head in pale, the others in saltire, banded. Crest of DARCY.

Elias Dardebroun, *of Croydon, co. Surr.*
9194. [A.D. 1357.] Red: fragmentary. About ¾ in. when perfect. [Add. ch. 23,328.]
A shield of arms: three lozenge-buckles, two and one. Betw. three sprigs of foliage.

✠ . . . . Q : REMERD (?)

9195. [A.D. 1359.] Red: fragmentary. [Add. ch. 23,330.]
. . . . . . MI . . . . . Q. REM . . . .

Elias *and* Agnes Dardebroun.
See JOHN GEREBERD.

Marmaduke Darelle, *Lord of Sesay, co. York.*
9196. [A.D. 1401.] Red: edge chipped. 1 in. [Add. ch. 16,892.]

A shield of arms, *couché*: a lion rampant, armed langued, and crowned, DARELL. Crest on a helmet and lambrequin, a Saracen's head in profile, couped at the shoulders, bearded, the temples wreathed, on the head a cap fretty tasselled. Within a cusped border having a pellet in each cusp.

𝕾 . . . . . . aⰆuci : Ɗarell'.

Cabled border.

Thomas Darell, *Esq.*

9197. [15th cent.] Plaster cast from fine impression. 1¾ in. [lxxxv. 19.]

A shield of arms, *couché*: barry of six, (for, on three bars) six cinquefoils, three, two, and one. Crest on a helmet, ornamental mantling of foliage, and wreath, a goat's head.

𝕾igillū tɧome Ɗarell armigir.

Beaded border.

Robert Darkenall, *of co. Kent, Esq.*

9198. [A.D. 1551.] Red: injured, indistinct. ¼ in. [Harl. ch. 86 H. 2.]

Lozenge-shaped: a wolf's head erased, for crest. Betw, the initial letters R. D.

Beaded border.

Thomas Darknoll, *of Beddington, co. Surr., Gentl.*

9199. [A.D. 1654.] Red: *en placard.* About ⅜ × $\frac{9}{16}$ in. [Add. ch. 23,314.]

Oval: a shield of arms: three trees eradicated, two and one, in fess point a crescent for difference. Betw. two myrtle branches, tied above and below the shield.

Cf. Add. ch. 23,608, A.D. 1645 ; 23,500, A.D. 1647 ; 23,501, A.D. 1653.

Sir James Dashwood, *of Northbrook, co. Oxon., Bart.*

9200. [A.D. 1744.] Red: *en placard,* on a tape. About 1 × ¾ in. [Add. ch. 10,292.]

Oval: an ornamental shield of arms: on a fess double-cotised, three griffins' heads erased, in chief point the escutcheon of baronetcy, DASHWOOD; over all an inescutcheon, quarterly, in the 2nd and 3rd, a fret ; on a bend over all three escallops, in the 1st quarter in sinister chief point a mullet for difference, SPENSER. The carving of the shield carries sprigs of foliage.

The same: used by ELIZABETH, *his wife, dau. of* EDW. SPENSER, *of Rendlesham, co. Suff.*

9201. [A.D. 1744.] Another. [Add. ch. 10,292.]

Richard Dashwood, *of the Inner Temple, Esq.,*
Frederic Frankland, *of London, Esq., or*
Edward Ventris, *son of* EDWARD VENTRIS, *of Sproughton,*
co. Suff.

9202. [A.D. 1744.]   Red: *en placard,* on a tape.   ⅝ × ¼ in.
[Add. ch. 10,292.]

Oval: an ornamental shield charged with the crest , as
follows : on a wreath an elephant and castle.

9203. [A.D. 1745.]   Another: imperfectly impressed.   [Add.
ch. 10,292.]

9204. [A.D. 1745.]   Another: imperfectly impressed.   [Add.
ch. 10,292.]

Jehan Dathenaise ?

Seal used by ROBERT CHAUMBERLEYN, *of co. Corn., Esq.*

9205. [A.D. 1426.]   Red: indistinct.   ⅞ in.   [Add. ch.
12,984.]

A shield of arms : a leopard's face.   Supporters, two wild
men.   In the background two sprigs of foliage.

𝔦𝔢𝔥𝔞𝔫 𝔡𝔞𝔱𝔥𝔢𝔫𝔞𝔦𝔰𝔢 (?)

Elias Daubeney, *of co. Linc.*

9206. [*Temp.* Edw. III.]   Discoloured, green: fine.
1 1⁄16 × ⅞ in.   [xxxvi. 90.]

Oval : a shield of arms : three plumed bassinets, two and
one.   Suspended by a strap from a tree of three branches.
Within a cusped border of eight points ornamented along the
inner edge with ball-flowers.

🟆 SIGILLVM • ELIE • DAVBENY ⋈ ❀ ⋈ ⊂

9207. [A.D. 1343.]   Plaster cast.   [lxxxv. 24.]

Giles Daubeney, *1st Baron Daubeney, K.G.*

9208. [A.D. 1499.]   Plaster cast from imperfect and somewhat indistinct impression.   2 in.   [lxxxv. 25.]

A shield of arms : four fusils in fess, DAUBENY.   Encircled with a Garter inscribed with the Motto.   Crest on a
helmet affronté, mantling and wreath, indistinct, perhaps a
plume of feathers.   Supporters two lions, collared and
chained.

SIGILLVM DÑI . . . AWBN . . . . MILITIS.

Edward Davenant, *D.D., Vicar of Gillingham, co. Dorset.*

9209. [A.D. 1640.]   Red: indistinct.   From a ring.
About ¼ × ¼ in.   [Egert. ch. 490.]

Oval : a shield of arms : three escallops betw. six crosses
crosslet fitchées, DAVENANT.

Philip de Daventre.

9210. [Late 14th cent.] Red: óriginally fine, edge chipped. ¾ in. [xxxvi. 75.]

A shield of arms: ermine a cross, DAVENTRE.

S' PHILIPPI : DE : DAUENTR'.

Beaded borders.

9211. Plaster cast from No. 9210. [xcii. 83.]

Robert, *son of* WALTER de Davintre, *of co. Northt.*

9212. [*Temp.* Hen. III.] Dark green: fine. 1 in. [Harl. ch. 49 D. 9.]

Square: a shield of arms: two chevrons, DAVENTER or DAVENTREE. Edge of shield beaded.

SIGILLVM : ROBERTI : FIL' : WALTERI.

Beaded borders.

9213. Sulph. cast of No. 9212. [D.C., F. 206.]

Simon de Daventre, *of co. Northt.*

9214. [*Temp.* Edw. III.] Red: chipped. ¾ in. [Add. ch. 21,514.]

A shield of arms: three crescents, and a canton ermine, within a bordure engrailed. Suspended by a strap from a hook, and betw. two wyverns addorsed.

. . . . .MONIS · DE · . ,. YNTRE.

William de Davintre, *of co. Northt.,*
"*Dom.* WILLELMUS MILES DE DAVINTRE."

9215. [A.D. 1231–1250.] Red: fine. 1¼ in. [Add. ch. 21,699.]

A shield of arms of early shape: a. chevron and a chief indented.

SIGILL' WILL'MI DE DAVINTRE :

William Davison.
See ROBERT ELLISON.

John Davy, *of Multon, co. Suff.*

9216. [A.D. 1499.] Red. ¾ × ½ in. [Stowe ch. 248.]

Oval: a lion rampant, perhaps in allusion to the arms of DAVY.

Simon Davy.
Seal used by THOMAS DE BURNEBI, *and* FINA, *his wife, of Scaldwell, co. Northt.*

9217. [A.D. 1360.] Red: indistinct in places. ⅞ in. [Add. ch. 22,408.]

A shield of arms : per pale, *dex.*, a triple-towered castle, *sin.*, three escallops, two and one.

✠ S' SIMONIS DAVY.

9218. [A.D. 1360.]   Red : injured, but the legend plainer. [Add. ch. 22,408.]

William Davy (?)

9219. [14th cent.]   Plaster cast from fine impression. 1 in. [lxxxv. 18.]

A shield. of arms : three crescents.   Within two gothic triangles interlaced to form a star of six points, elaborately carved and traced.

No legend.

Nicholas Dawbrichcourt.

9220. [15th cent.]   Plaster cast.   1 in.   [lxxxv. 56.]

A shield of arms, *couché*: ermine, three bars humettée, DAWBRICHCOURT, or DABRIDGCOURT.   Crest on a helmet and mantling, two flaming braziers or pans, one on the other, dropping with gouttes.   Within an elegantly carved gothic panel with scroll ends.

𝕾' nicholai : dawbrichcourt ✠

Beaded border.

——— Dawe.

Seal used by Sir ALEXANDER COLEPEPER, *of Begebury, co. Kent, Knt.*

9221. [A.D. 1607.]   Red.   About $\frac{3}{4} \times \frac{5}{8}$ in.   [Harl. ch. 77 D. 7.]

A shield of arms : on a pile a chevron betw. three crosses crosslet, DAW, or DAWE.   Crest on a helmet ornamental mantling, and wreath, a lion's gamb erect, holding a fleur-de-lis.

Beaded border.

Another, used by NICHOLAS ALLEN, *of Woodhouse, co. Derb., Gentl.*

9222. [A.D. 1600.]   Red.   [Woll. ch. xii. 33.]

Another, used by EDWARD KEMP, *of Hereford.*

9223. [A.D. 1610.]   Red.   [Harl. ch. 78 I. 26.]

Dawe.

See NICHOLAS ALLEN.

Philip Dawe.
See WILLIAM HUISH.

Robert Dawe, *of London, Gentl.*
9224. [A.D. 1599.] Red: fine. $\frac{3}{4} \times \frac{5}{8}$ in. [Add. ch. 36,268.]

Oval: a shield of arms: on a pile a chevron betw. three crosses crosslet, DAW.

Beaded border.

Bridget Day, *or* Daye, *widow of* JOHN DAY, *of Chiddingley, co. Suss., Yeoman.*
9225. [A.D. 1620.] Red. $\frac{5}{8} \times \frac{1}{2}$ in. [Add. ch. 30,139.]

Oval: a shield of arms: two bars, and a canton.

Beaded border.

George Day, *of Lincoln's Inn, Esq.*
9226. [A.D. 1676.] Red: very indistinct. $\frac{3}{4} \times \frac{9}{16}$ in [Add. ch. 1646.]

Oval: a shield of arms: per chevron three mullets counterchanged, DAY. Crest, on a helmet, mantling and wreath, two hands conjoined, fixed to a pair of wings, each charged with a mullet.

Counterseal (?) illegible.

Thos. Day.
See R———— W—————.

William Day, *of Wing, co. Buck., Gentl.*
9227. [A.D. 1573.] Red: very indistinct. About $\frac{3}{4} \times \frac{5}{8}$ in. [Add. ch. 22,692.]

Oval: a shield of arms: quarterly, 1, 4, a lion rampant (?) 2, 3, uncertain. Crest on a helmet, mantling and wreath, out of a coronet, uncertain.

William, *son of* JOHN DAY, *of Chiddingley, co. Suss.*
9228. [A.D. 1620.] Red: imperfect. $\frac{1}{2}$ in. [Add. ch. 30,139.]

A stag's head erased.

Arms of Deach.
See RICHARD MOORE.

Thomas Deacon, *Citizen and Clothworker of London.*
9229. [A.D. 1641.] Red : injured by pressure. $\frac{3}{4} \times \frac{1}{2}$ in.
[Harl. ch. 85 H. 37.]
Oval : a shield of arms : a chevron chequy or counter-compony, betw. three roses, slipped and leaved, DEACQN.
Crest, (without helmet, mantling, or wreath) a demi-eagle displayed.
Cabled border.

John Dear, *of Chichester, co. Suss.*
9230. [A.D. 1748.] Red : *en placard*, on a tape. $\frac{3}{8}$ in.
[Add. ch. 19,054.]
On a wreath a deer's head erased, pierced with an arrow : for a crest (?)

Richard Decons, *Esq., Receiver Gen. of Elizabeth of York,*
Queen of King Henry VII.
9231. [A.D. 1509.] Red : imperfect. About $\frac{1}{2}$ in. when perfect. [Harl. ch. 49 D. 23.]
Hexagonal : a shield of arms : a chevron engrailed betw. three quatrefoils. In the field above, a sprig.
Cabled border.

Simon Dedene, *or* **de Dene.**
Seal used by ROBERT, *son of* PAULINUS, *son of* GEOFFREY, *Lord of Westacle, Great Oakley, co. Northt.*
9232. [12th cent.] Bright red : fine, chipped at edge.
$2\frac{1}{4}$ in. [Add. ch. 21,183. (Late 13th cent. handwriting.)]
A shield of arms of early shape : fretty ; or per pale, fretty and—
✠ SIGILLVM : SIMONIS : DE DENE.

Peter Delavale, *Citizen and Clothworker, of London.*
9233. [A.D. 1588.] Red. $\frac{7}{8} \times \frac{3}{4}$ in. [Harl. ch. 79 F. 17.]
Oval : a shield of arms : quarterly, 1, 4, barry of six ermine [and gu. ?], LAVALL ; 2, three eagles displayed, two and one ; 3, a lion rampant. Crest on a helmet, ornamental mantling and wreath, a ram's head attired.
Cabled border.
Cf. Harl. MS. 1554, f. 23.

Henry De . . . . (*perhaps* HENRY DELVÈS ?)
9234. [A.D. 1385.] Plaster cast from fine but imperfect impression. 1 in. [xcii. 85.]
A shield of arms, *couché* : a chevron betw. three delves,

DELVES. Crest on a helmet, out of a coronet, only a wing ·remains. Within a carved gothic panel.·

𝕾𝖎𝖌𝖎𝖑' · 𝖍𝖊𝖓𝖗𝖎𝖈𝖎 : 𝖉𝖊 . . . . . .

John Delves.

9235. [A.D. 1367.] Plaster cast from chipped impression. 1⅛ in. [lxxxv. 32.]

A shield of arms: a chevron fretty betw. three delves, DELVES. Suspended by a strap from a tree of three branches. Within a carved gothic panel, ornamented with ball-flowers along the inner edge.

𝕾𝖎𝖌𝖎𝖑𝖑𝖚𝖒 . . . . 𝖎𝖘 * 𝖉𝖊 * 𝖉𝖊𝖑𝖚𝖊𝖘.

Alanus le . . . sier.

Seal used by ALICE, *widow of* WILLIAM DENEMEDE, *of Bandon, co. Surr.*

9236. [A.D. 1386.] Red: cracked, imperfect. ¾ in. [Add. ch. 22,874.]

A shield (of arms?): a saltire betw. four crosslets; in fess point an annulet (not heraldic). The shield surmounted with a merchant's mark.

S' ALANI · LE . . . . SIER.

Beaded borders.

John Deneys, *of co. Suff.*

9237. [A.D. 1359.] Dark-green: indistinct, chipped at edge. ⅞ in. [Add. ch. 10,198.]

A shield of arms: a chevron betw. three estoiles (or pierced mullets of six points) within a bordure engrailed, for DENYS. Within a carved gothic trefoil ornamented with ball-flowers along the inner edge.

SIGILLV : __ IOH'IS : LE : __ DENEYS :

9238. [A.D. 1361.] Red: very indistinct, injured by pressure. [Add. ch. 10,199.]

SIGILLV : __ IOH'IS : LE : __ DENEYS.

9239. [A.D. 1367.] Dark-green: imperfect, indistinct. [Add. ch. 8378.]

SIG . . . . . . H'IS : LE : __ DENEYS.

Philip Deneys, *of co. Suff., Knt.*

9240. [A.D. 1375.] Red: fine, chipped at edge. 1. in. [Harl. ch. 49 D. 33.] .

· A shield of arms: on a chevron betw. three estoiles a crescent, or annulet, for difference, DENYS. Round .the shield an illegible motto in small gothic letters. Within a carved annulus ornamented with ball-flowers along the inner edge.

¤ Sigillum ⚜ Philippi ⚜ ⚜ Deneys.

9241. Sulph. cast from No. 9240. [D.C., F. 465.]

9242. [A.D. 1367.] Dark-green : chipped. [Add. ch. 8378.]

Sigillum ⚜ Phili . . . . eneys.

Thomas Deneys, *of co. Suff.*

9243. [A.D. 1367.] Dark-green: fine. ¾ in. [Add. ch. 8378.]

A shield of arms : a chevron betw. three estoiles of six points, DENYS. Within a carved and pointed gothic trefoil ornamented along the inner edge with small ball-flowers.

¤ SIGILLV • THOME ◆ LE DENEYS.

Beaded border.

John de Denham, *Citizen and Fishmonger of London.*

9244. [A.D. 1336.] Red : injured. 1 × ⅞ in. [Harl. ch. 85 C. 13.]

Oval : a shield of arms : three Katharine wheels, two and one. Suspended by a strap from a crowned head and betw. two flowers. Within a cusped or engrailed border of eight points ornamented with ball-flowers along the inner edge.

¤ KATERINA · BEATA · ORA · PRO · ME (?)

9245. Sulph. cast of No. 9244. [D.C., F. 254.]

John de Denham, *of Denham, co. Suff.*

9246. [A.D. 1380.] Red : imperfect. ⅞ in. [Add. ch. 5500.]

A shield of arms : quarterly, the 2nd and 3rd chequy, in the first quarter a martlet. Suspended by a strap from a rosette, and betw. two sprigs. Within a carved gothic rosette of six points, ornamented with ball-flowers along the inner border.

. . . . M · [I]OHANNIS DE . . . M.

9247. [A.D. 1383.] Red : injured in places by pressure. [Add. ch. 5502.]

¤ SIGILLVM · IOHANNIS · DENHAM.

Hubert . . . . iol.

Seal used by RICHARD, *son of* NICHOLAS DE DENHAM, *of Denham, co. Buck.*

9248. [A.D. 1367.] Dark-green : fine, imperfect. ¼ in. [Harl. ch. 85 C. 16.]

A hound couchant, collared and lined, above in the field a bugle-horn. Within a cusped rosette of eight points.

S' HVBE . . . . IOL.

Walter de Denham.
Seal used by WALTER ALYSSAUNDRE, *of Denham, co. Buck.*
9249. [A.D. 1349.] Discoloured white : fair. ¾ in. [Harl. ch. 84 G. 5.]
A shield of arms : on a chevron betw. three crosses crosslet fitchées, as many (fleurs-de-lis). Cf. seal of WALTER DE CHALFHUNTE, No. 8447, Harl. ch. 84 G. 4. Betw. two small roses, and within a carved and pointed gothic quatrefoil.

S' WALTERI DE · DENHAM ⋈

James Deniel, *al.* Daniell.
9250. [14th cent.] Sulph. cast from fair impression. ¾ in. [D.C., F. 358.]
A shield of arms : on a bend three martlets, suspended from a forked tree and within a carved gothic panel.

𝕾igillum : iaſ · Deniel.

The letters DE of *deniel* are conjoined.

Sir Anthony Denney, *Knt., one of the Gentlemen of the King's Privy Chamber.*
9251. [A.D. 1546.] Red. ¾ × ⅝ in. [Harl. ch. 77 F. 39.]
Oval : an ornamental shield of arms : quarterly, 1, 4, a saltire betw. twelve crosslets (or ermine spots ?), DENNEY; 2, a fess indented, in chief three martlets ; 3, three trouts fretted in triangle, tête-à-la-guise, TROUTBECK. Over all in fess point a·crescent for difference.
Cf. Harl. MS. 1177, f. 169.

Henry Denny, *al.* Deny, *Esq.*
9252. [A.D. 1559.] Red. From a ring with mark of the setting. ⅝ × 9/16 in. [Harl. ch. 80 F. 12.]
Oval : an ornamental shield of arms : quarterly, as in the seal of Sir ANTHONY DENNEY, No. 9251, *q.v.*

Henry Denny, *of Dalaunce, co. Essex, Esq.*
9253. [A.D. 1561.] Red. ⅞ in. [Harl. ch. 79 F. 13.]
A shield of arms : quarterly, see seal of Sir ANTH. DENNEY, No. 9251. Crest on a helmet a cubit-arm holding a bunch of twelve ears of corn.

Elizabeth Denton, *of Ixworth Abbey, co. Suff., Widow.*

9254. [A.D. 1647.] Red : imperfect, *en placard,* the paper of the charter cut *en triangle,* and folded over before impression. About ¼ × ⅜ in. [Harl. ch. 58 F. 54.]

Oval : an ornamental shield of arms : two bars and in chief three martlets, DENTON.

9255. [A.D. 1647.] Another. [Harl. ch. 58 F. 54.]
9256. [A.D. 1648.] Another. [Harl. ch. 58 F. 54.]
9257. [A.D. 1649.] Another. [Harl. ch. 58 F. 54.]
9258. [A.D. 1649.] Another. [Harl. ch. 58 F. 54.]

William Denton, *of London, Gentl.*

9259. [A.D. 1565.] Red, discoloured. ¾ in. [Harl. ch. 77 A. 11.]

An ornamental shield of arms : two bars, in chief three martlets, on the bar in chief a mullet for difference, DENTON. Betw. the initials W. D.

Edmund de Denum (?)

9260. [A.D. 1338.] Plaster cast. 1 in. [lxxxv. 33.]

A shield of arms : a fess betw. three mallets. Betw. three slipped quatrefoils ; and within a pointed gothic quatrefoil ornamented with ball-flowers along the inner edge.

✠ SIGILLVM EDMVNDI DE DENVM (?)

Gilbert Depenham *or* **Debenham,** *of cos. Essex and Suff.*

9261. [A.D. 1413.] Red : fine, fragmentary. About ⅞ in. when perfect. [Harl. ch. 49 D. 37.]

A shield of arms : a bend betw. two crescents, DEBENHAM. Suspended by a strap from a forked tree ; and within a carved gothic panel.

Legend broken away.

Richard Deram, *of Stamford Bridge* (?)

9262. [A.D. 1485–6.] Plaster cast from indistinct impression. ⅞ in. [lxxxv. 35.]

A shield of arms : bendy of eight. Suspended by a strap from a forked tree ; and within a roughly-formed quatrefoil panel.

S' ricardi de.... ro ....

Hugh Derderne (?)

9263. [13th cent.] Plaster cast from indistinct impression.
1 in. [lxxxv. 67.]
A shield of arms of early shape.

✠ SEC͠T (*secretum*) VGHONIS DERDERNE (?)

John Derham, *late Prior of Hatfield Regis, co. Essex.*
9264. [A.D. 1434.] Red. About ½ in. [Add. ch. 28,615.]
A griffin's or eagle's head erased, in the beak a slipped
trefoil, perhaps a crest.
Cabled border.

Thomas Derham, *Jun., of co. Suff.*
9265. [A.D. 1426.] Red: very imperfect, indistinct. Ori-
ginally encircled by a twisted rush. $\frac{9}{16} \times \frac{3}{8}$ in. [Harl. ch.
56 B. 17.]
Oval signet: a buck's head cabossed: in allusion to the
arms of DERHAM. In the field the motto :—

en Dieu ma . . . e.

Thomas Derham, *Esq.,*
Commissioner of Sewers in co. Norf.
9266. [A.D. 1639.] Red: imperfect. $\frac{5}{8} \times \frac{1}{2}$ in. [Add. ch.
14,604.]
Oval: a shield of arms: three Katharine wheels, two and
one, within a bordure engrailed.

Henry Deringe, *or* **Deeringe**, *of Liss, co. Southt., Gentl.*
9267. [A.D. 1606.] Reddish-brown: imperfect. About
$\frac{5}{8} \times \frac{1}{2}$ in. [Add. ch. 8974.]
Oval: a shield of arms: a saltire engrailed betw. four
escallops, on a canton some uncertain charges.

Nicholas Derynge, *of Liss, co. Southt., Gentl.*
9268. [A.D. 1539.] Red. ½ in. [Egert. ch. 282.]
Ornamental shape: a *deer's* head erased, in the nose a *ring*,
a canting crest of the DEERING family.
Beaded border.

Nicholas Derynge, *or* **Deeringe**,
of Eastley, co. Southt., Gentl.
9269. [A.D. 1606.] Reddish-brown. ½ in. [Add. ch.
8974.]
On a wreath, a roebuck's head, charged with a crescent for

difference, for a crest, or allusion to the arms of DEERING,
viz. three bucks' heads couped.
9270. [A.D. 1606.]   Another.   [Add. ch. 8975.]

Dering.

See RICHARD, *son of* DERING DE HAUT.

William de Derlethorp.

9271. [14th cent.]   Plaster cast from fine impression.   1 in.
[lxxxv. 34.]
A shield of arms: three birds (doves?), two and one.
Suspended by a strap from a forked tree.   Within a carved
gothic panel.

𝔖𝔦𝔤𝔦𝔩𝔩𝔲𝔪 : 𝔴𝔦𝔩𝔩'𝔪𝔦 : 𝔡𝔢 : 𝔇𝔢𝔯𝔩𝔢𝔱𝔥𝔬𝔯𝔭.

John de Derlyngtone.

9272. [A.D. 1380.]   Plaster cast from fine impression.
1 in.   [lxxxv. 21.]
A shield of arms: on a cross five eagles displayed.   In a
gothic rosette of eight cusps ornamented along the inner edge
with small ball-flowers.

✠ 𝔖𝔦𝔤𝔦𝔩𝔩ū : 𝔦𝔬𝔥'𝔦𝔰 : 𝔡𝔢 : 𝔇𝔢𝔯𝔩𝔶𝔫𝔤𝔱𝔬𝔫𝔢.

Margeria Derneden, *of Beaconsfield, co. Buck.*

9273. [A.D. 1381.]   Light-brown.   ¾ in.   [Harl. ch. 49 D.
45.]
A shield of arms: a chevron betw. three cinquefoils pierced.
Above the shield a triple-towered castle, masoned.   Perhaps
an official seal of a sheriff.   The sides of the seal filled with
tracery.

Elizabeth, *Lady* Despencer,
dau. of BARTHOLOMEW, *4th Baron Burghersh,*
and widow of EDWARD, *Baron Despencer.*

9274. [A.D. 1401.]   Red: originally fine, very imperfect.
1½ in.   [Harl. ch. 56 D. 30.]
A shield of arms: per pale, *dex.*, DESPENSER; *sin.*, a lion
rampant, queue fourchée, BURGHERSH.   Above the shield a
griffin couchant.   At the sides the initial letters [E.] S.
Within a finely carved gothic panel ornamented with small
ball-flowers along the inner edge.

✠ 𝔩𝔢 . . . .
9275. Sulph. cast from No. 9274.   [D.C., G. 86.]

9276. Plaster cast from fine impression [lxxxv. 39.]
This shows the initials є. ꜱ. and gives the complete legend.

· le : Seal : eliȝabet : Dame : la : Despenſere.

Hugh le Despensier, *Knt.*

9277. [A.D. 1304.] Dark-green : fine. ⅞ in. [L. F. C. vii. 12.]
A shield of arms : quarterly, in the 2nd and 3rd quarters a fret, over all a bend, DESPENSER.
✠ SIGILLVM HVGONIS LE DESPENSER.
Beaded borders.
9278. Plaster cast from fine impression. [lxxxv. 37.]

Hugh Le Despencer.

9279. [A.D. 1318.] Plaster cast from chipped impression. 1 in. [lxxxv. 35.]
A shield of arms : DESPENSER, with a label of five points. Betw. two wyverns. Suspended by a strap from a lion's face betw. two branches of a tree.
S' HVGONIS LE DESPE[NC]ER.
Beaded borders.

Hugh Le Despencer, *of Solihull, co. Warw., Knt.*

9280. [A.D. 1385.] Red : imperfect. About 1¼ in. [Cott. ch. xxv. 12.]
A shield of arms *couché* : quarterly, in the 2nd and 3rd quarters a fret, over all a bend, in the 1st quarter a martlet for difference, DESPENCER. Crest on a helmet and lambrequin, on a wreath a griffin's head (?) and wings erect. Background enriched with sprigs of foliage. Within a carved gothic panel.

Sigillũ : ḥug . . . . . . e : Spencer.

Hugh Le Despenser.

Seal used by WILLIAM HARYNGTONE, *of co. York, Knt.*
9281. [A.D. 1436.] Red : originally fine, edge chipped. 1 in. [Add. ch. 8325.]
A shield of arms : quarterly, in the 2nd and 3rd quarters a fret, over all a bend, DESPENSER. Suspended by a strap from a tree. Betw. two wyverns.
S' HVGONIS : LE : DESPENSER.
Beaded borders.

Philip Le Despenser, *Chev.*

9282. [A.D. 1396.]   Red, discoloured: very imperfect. About 1¼ in. when perfect.   [Cott. ch. v. 21.]

A shield of arms, *couché*: destroyed.   Crest on a helmet a wing erect (?) with a tasselled plait hanging down on the l. h. side.   On the r. h. a rose, slipped and leaved.   Within a carved gothic quatrefoil.

Legend wanting.

Thomas Le Despenser, *Earl of Gloucester.*

9283. [A.D. 1397.]   Plaster cast from good impression, indistinct in places.   1⅞ in.   [lxxxv. 40.]

A shield of arms, *couché*: quarterly, in the 2nd and 3rd quarters a fret, over all a bendlet, DESPENSER.   Crest on a helmet and mantling, out of a ducal coronet a griffin's head and wings erect.   Betw. two trees eradicated, on each, suspended by a strap, a lozenge-shaped shield of arms: *dex.*, three chevrons, CLARE ; *sin.*, a lion rampant, queue fourchée, BURGHERSH.   All within a carved gothic quadrilobe ornamented with ball-flowers along the edge.

⁂ 𝕾𝖎𝖌𝖎𝖑𝖑𝖚𝖒 : 𝖙𝖍𝖔𝖒𝖊 : ⁂ ⁂ : 𝕯𝖓𝖎 : 𝖑𝖊 𝕯𝖊𝖘𝖕𝖊𝖓𝖘𝖊𝖗 : ⁂

Edmund Dethicke, *of Bechamwell, co. Norf., Esq.*

9284. [A.D. 1558.]   Red: imperfect.   About ¾ × ⅝ in. [Add. ch. 14,551.]

Oval: a shield of arms: per pale, *dex.,* a. fess vairé betw. three water-bougets, DETHICKE ; *sin.*, indistinct, a saltire betw. four flies (?)

Cf. Harl. MS. 6093, f. 66 *b.* ; Add. ch. 10,336, A.D. 1560.

Richard Devenyshe, *Esq., of co. Suss.*

9285. [A.D. 1533.]   Dark-green.   ¾ × ⅝ in.   [Add. ch. 30,479.]

Ornamental shape: a tiger (?) passant, for a crest of DEVENISH.

Beaded border.

John Devereux,
Steward of the King's (Rich. II.) Household.

9286. [A.D. 1392.]   Red: very imperfect.   About 1¾ in. when perfect.   [Harl. ch. 49 D. 54.]

A shield of arms: diapered, a fess, and in chief three roundles, DEVEREUX.   Suspended by a strap from a forked tree on a mound.

Legend wanting.

Robert Devereux, *2nd Earl of Essex, K.G.*

9287. [A.D. 1576–1600.] Plaster cast from indistinct impression. 1 in. [xcii. 86.]

A shield of arms: a fess, in chief three torteaux, DEVEREUX. Ensigned with a coronet, and encircled with the Garter inscribed with the Motto of the Order.

William Deyncourt.
See WILLIAM DE EYNCOURT.

William Deyster.
See IEHEN DE STAUBERT.

William Dickinson.
See G—— (?) FAUNE.

John Digby, *1st Earl of Bristol.*

9288. [A.D. 1631.] Red: indistinct. $\frac{9}{16} \times \frac{7}{16}$ in. [Add. ch. 6006.]

Oval: a shield of arms: quarterly, 1, a fleur-de-lis, DIGBY; 2, on a fess betw. three martlets some illegible charges; 3, on a bend three martlets (?) 4, ermine a bendlet. Crest on a helmet mantling and wreath, uncertain, perhaps an ostrich.

9289. [A.D. 1631.] Red: indistinct. [Add. ch. 6007.]

9290. [A.D. 1631.] Red: very indistinct. [Add. ch. 6008.]

Philip Digby, *of London, Esq.*

9291. [A.D. 1631.] Red. About $\frac{7}{16}$ in. [Add. ch. 6006.]

A shield of arms: a fleur-de-lis, DIGBY. Crest on a helmet mantling and wreath, an ostrich (in the beak a horse-shoe).

Simon Digby, *of London, Esq.*

9292. [A.D. 1631.] Red. About $\frac{7}{16}$ in. [Add. ch. 6006.]

Seal of arms as described for PHILIP DIGBY, No. 9291.

Humphrey Digges, *of Hereford, co. Heref.*

9293. [A.D. 1660.] Red: imperfect, indistinct. About $\frac{5}{8}$ in. [Add. ch. 1957.]

A shield of arms: on a cross [five eagles displayed with two heads], DIGGS.

Cabled border.

9294. [A.D. 1660.] Red: imperfect. [Add. ch. 1959.]

Everard Dighby, *al.* **Digby,** *of Maidwell, co. Northt.*
· **9295.** [A.D 1458.] Red : indistinct. About ⅝ × ½ in.
[Add. ch. 22,285.]
Octagonal : a plume of three ostrich feathers, with a label.
Cf. the arms of Digby. In the field an indistinct motto.

fp . . . . pen . . . ? sus.

Cabled border.
Cf. Add. ch. 21,839 ; 22,286, A.D. 1458.

Johanna, *dau. of* RICHARD **Digun,** *of Rya, Rye, co. Suss.*
9296. [A.D. 1304.] Dark-green. ¼ × ⅜ in. [Add. ch.
20,147.]
Oval : a shield (of arms ?) : a chevron betw. three sugar-
loaves, hatched field. Ensigned with a roughly-cut cross,
betw. four sprigs.

Sir **Wolston Dixie,** *of Normanton, co. Derby, Bart.*
. .**9297.** [A.D. 1650.] Red : *en placard*, on a label. ⅝ × $\frac{9}{16}$ in.
[Add. ch. 5244.]
Oval : a shield of arms : quarterly, 1, 4, a lion rampant, and
a chief, DIXIE ; 2, a saltire engrailed betw. four escallops ;
3, on a saltire five crosses crosslet. Over all an escallop (?)
Crest on a helmet, ornamental mantling and wreath, an ounce
sejant, ducally gorged.
Cabled border.

Richard Doget, *of Weybrede, co. Suff.*
9298. [A.D. 1455.] Red. $\frac{9}{16}$ × ½ in. [Stowe ch. 273.]
Octagonal signet : a bird. In the field a sprig of foliage.
Perhaps a crest.

Walter Doget.
9299. [A.D. 1383.] Plaster cast from impression indistinct
in places. ⅞ in. [lxxxv. 48.]
A shield of arms : ermine, on a bend three talbots' heads
erased, DOGET, *of Kent.*

⚜ S ⚜ walteri ⚜⚜ Doget ⚜

Cf. Harl. roll, S. 23, *temp.* Ed. III. ; Harl. rolls, Z. 2, 5, A.D. 1365–
1384 ; Walter Doget, Sheriff of London, Harl. ch. 56 C. 22, A.D. 1380.

Robert, *son of* RICHARD **de Dokinfeld,**
Lord of Stanton in the Peak, co. Derb.
9300. [*Temp.* Edw. I.] Reddish-brown : imperfect. ⅝ in.
[Woll. ch. ii. 7.]

A shield of arms : quarterly, on a bend three eagles displayed.

In place of a legend, a scroll of foliage.

Peter Domenguez.
See AGNES, *widow of* JOHN ESTBROK.

Thomas de Doncastre.
9301. [A.D. 1398–9.]   Plaster cast from good impression.
⅞ in. [lxxxii. 77.]

A shield of arms : a triple-towered castle, DONCASTER.
Within a carved and pointed gothic trefoil ornamented with
ball-flowers along the inner edge.

⚹ 𝕾𝖎𝖌 : 𝖙𝖍𝖔𝖒𝖊 : 𝖉𝖊 : 𝖉𝖔𝖓𝖈𝖆𝖋𝖙𝖗𝖊.

Beaded border.

William de Doncastre, *of Chester*.
9302. [A.D. 1340.]   Cast in plaster, tinted red, from impression chipped at edge.   ⅝ in. [lxxxi. 66.]

, A triple-towered castle, in allusion to the arms of
DONCASTER.

⚹ S' WILL'I DE DONCASTRE (?)

William, *son of* ELIAS de Doncastre (?)
Seal used by JOHN ATTILBURGHE, *Chaplain, of Norwich,*
co. Norf.

9303. [A.D. 1430.]   Red : indistinct in places.   ⅝ in.
[Add. ch. 14,790.]

A shield of arms : three cinquefoils, over all a bend (?), or a
bend betw. two castles (?)

S · WILL'I · F · ELIE · DE · D . . CASTRE.

John Donewych.
See RICHARD DE BELLOCAMPO.

John, *son of* WILLIAM Doreward, *of Bocking, co. Norf.*
9304. [A.D. 1383.]   Red : injured by pressure.   1 in.
[Add. ch. 14,868.]

A shield of arms : ermine, on a chevron three crescents,
DURWARD.   Suspended by a strap from a tree, and within
a gothic panel.

𝕾𝖎𝖌𝖎𝖑𝖑𝖚𝖒 : 𝖎𝖔𝖍'𝖎𝖘 : 𝖉𝖔𝖗𝖊𝖜𝖆𝖗𝖉.

Cabled border.

9305. [A.D. 1383.] Red: injured by pressure, indistinct in places. [Harl. ch. 77 F. 47.]

𝕾𝖎𝖌𝖎𝖑𝖑𝖚𝖒 : 𝖎𝖔𝖍'𝖎𝖘 : ... 𝖜𝖆𝖗𝖉.

9306. [A.D. 1409.] Plaster cast from fine impression. ⅞ in. [lxxxv. 36.]

𝕾𝖎𝖌𝖎𝖑𝖑𝖚𝖒 : 𝖎𝖔𝖍'𝖎𝖘 : 𝖉𝖔𝖗𝖊𝖜𝖆𝖗𝖉 :

Cf. on a chevron three crescents, DURWARD.

Ralph Doreward.

9307. [14th cent.] Plaster cast. ¾ in. [lxxxv. 46.]

A lozenge-shaped shield of arms: gutté, on a bend betw. two crescents, three roundles. Betw. four slipped roses (?) and within a carved gothic quatrefoil ornamented with small ball-flowers along the inner edge.

⚹ S' : RADVLPHI : DOREWARD :

Beaded border.

Robert Dormer, *of Peterley in Missenden, co. Bucks.*

9308. [A.D. 1640.] Red: a fragment. [Add. ch. 18,956.]

A shield of arms: ten billets, four, three, two, and one, [on] a chief [a demi-lion rampant issuing], DORMER.

William Double, *Smith, of Waltham Holy Cross, co. Essex.*

9309. [A.D. 1423.] Red: a fragment. About 1 × ⅞ in. when perfect. [Harl. ch. 77 F. 48.]

A shield of arms: three horse-shoes, two and one, etc. Legend indistinct.

A——— Douglas.

Seal used by RICHARD MUSGRAVE, *of Norton, co. York.*

9310. [A.D. 1590.] Red. ⅞ in. [Add. ch. 19,543.]

Shield-shaped: an ornamental shield of arms: a human heart, on a chief three mullets, DOUGLAS. Above the shield the initials A. D.

Beaded border.

Probably a Scottish seal.

John Doune, *of Wynton.*

9311. [A.D. 1445.] Plaster cast from fine impression. 1 in. [lxxxv. 44.]

A shield of arms: two bars, on a bend, three arrows, DONE and DONNE. Suspended by a strap from a forked tree, and within a carved gothic panel.

𝕾𝖎𝖌𝖎𝖑𝖑𝖚 : 𝖎𝖔𝖍𝖆𝖓𝖓𝖎𝖘 : 𝖉𝖔𝖚𝖓𝖊 :

Margareta, *widow of* PETER **Dounerdale** (?)
9312. [*Temp.* Edw. III.] Plaster cast of fine impression.
1⅛ in. [lxxxv. 45.]
An eagle displayed, charged on the breast with a shield of
arms : four fusils in fess, on each an ermine spot. Within a
carved gothic quatrefoil, ornamented with ball-flowers along
the inner edge, and with eight outside points cusped. Betw.
each alternate pair of cusps a mill-rind or cross moline.
Legend betw. the other alternate pairs :—
MAR_GA_RE_TA.

John Dounwile.

9313. [A.D. 1377.] Plaster cast from good impression.
[lxxxv. 51.]
A shield of arms : a lion rampant. Suspended by a strap
from a hook, and betw. two pairs of leaves, slipped.
✿ S' IOHIS : DOVNWILE .

Robert Douer, *of Diss, co. Norf., Gentl.*

9314. [A.D. 1630.] Red : somewhat indistinct. ¾ × ⅟₁₆ in.
[Stowe ch. 187.]
Oval : a shield of arms : ermine, a cinquefoil pierced,
DOVER. Crest on a helmet and mantling, a demi-eagle with
wings erect.

Anne Downing, *of White Friars, London, widow of* EDM. DOWNING, *Gentl.*

9315. [A.D. 1608.] Red : fine. ⁹⁄₁₀ × ½ in. [Harl. ch.
77 G. 9.]
Oval : a shield of arms : a fess chequy (for vairé ?) betw.
two lions passant guardant, DOWNING.
Cabled border.

Richard Dowsynge, *of North Walsham, co. Norf.*

9316. [A.D. 1391.] Dark-green, mottled : injured. ¾ in.
[Add. ch. 14,933.]
A shield of arms : fretty, on a chief a lion passant. Sus-
pended from a tree of three branches ; and betw. two wyverns.

John Doyly.

Seal used by WILLIAM WINLOWE, *of Notley, co. Buck., Gentl.*
9317. [A.D. 1570.] Red : injured at top. 1⅟₁₀ × ⅞ in.
[Harl. ch. 80 I. 40.]
Oval : a shield of arms : quarterly, 1, 4, two bends,
D'OYLY ; 2, 3, a raven, MORE. or MOORE. Over all in fess

3 B 2

point a crescent for difference. Crest, on a helmet, ornamental mantling, and wreath, a demi-dragon.
Beaded border.
Cf. Harl. MSS. 1556, f. 108 *b*, etc. ; 1557, f. 94.
9318. [A.D. 1570.]   Red : injured.   [Harl. ch. 79 E. 40.]

Robert Doyly, *or* **Doyle,** *of Marton, co. Oxon., Esq.*
9319. [A.D. 1570.]   Red.   ¾ in.   [Harl. ch. 77 G. 11.]
On a wreath a demi-dragon.   Crest of DOYLY or D'OYLY.
Beaded border.
9320. [A.D. 1570.]   Another.   [Harl. ch. 79 E. 40.]

Maurice Draghswerd, *al.* **Drawswerd,** *of Denham, co. Buck.*
9321. [A.D. 1334.]   Dark-green : injured by pressure in places.   ⅞ in.   [Harl. ch. 85 C. 35.]
A shield of arms : two swords in saltire, points in base, betw. two leopards' faces in pale, and as many crosses crosslet fitchées in fess.   Suspended by a strap from a hook and betw. two wyverns sans wings.
✠ S' MAVRICII : DRAWSWERD.
9322. Sulph. cast from No. 9321.   [D.C., F. 247.]

John Drake, *of Wyrmegey, co. Norf*
9323. [A.D. 1434.]   Red. $\frac{9}{16}$ in.   [Add. ch. 28,615.]
A drake or wyvern, for DRAKE (arms or crest), forming with the initial I an heraldic monogram, I. D.
Bordure of roughly made chevronels.

Ankaretta Drakelow, *wife of* JOHN RUSSHALE,
of Karlton, etc., co. Bedf.
9324. [A.D. 1400.]   Red : fragmentary.   1 in.   [Add. ch. 8126.]
A shield of arms : per pale, *dex.*, on a chevron three escallops, RUSSHALE (?), *sin.*, a chevron betw. three griffins' heads erased, DRAKELOW (the two in chief respecting). Within a carved gothic panel.
𝔖𝔦𝔤𝔦𝔩𝔩𝔲 ~ : 𝔞𝔫𝔨𝔞𝔯𝔢𝔱𝔢 ~ : 𝔡𝔯𝔞𝔨𝔢𝔩𝔬𝔴.
9325. Plaster cast of No. 9324.   [lxxxv. 52.]

Edward Draper, *of Bubnell, co. Warw.*
9326. [A.D. 1660.]   Red : indistinct. $\frac{9}{16} \times \frac{1}{4}$ in.   [Add. ch. 18,033.]
Oval : a shield of arms : three combs, two and one, on a chief a lion passant guardant.

George Draper, *of Hitchin, co. Hertf., Gentl.*
9327. [A.D. 1707.]   Red : *en placard,* on a tape, imperfect.
¾ × ⅝ in.   [Add. ch. 35,913.]
Oval : an ornamental shield of arms : on a pile three trefoils slipped, two and one, for NODES or NOADS.
Beaded border.

William Draper, *of Sternefeld, co. Suff., Chaplain.*
9328. [A.D. 1368.]   Green : fragmentary.   [Stowe ch. 256.]
A shield of arms : illegible, perhaps quarterly.
Legend indistinct.

Robert Drax, *of co. York.*
9329. [A.D. 1434.]   Red : encircled with a twisted rush.
[Add. ch. 17,048.]
Octagonal : a demi-dragon, out of its mouth an uncertain motto, **. . . be war,** for DRAX.
9330. [A.D. 1434.]   Red.   [Add. ch. 17,049.]

Henry Drewry, *of Ardleigh Manor, co. Essex, Esq..*
9331. [A.D. 1430.]   Red. From a ring (?) ⅛ × ⅜ in. [Harl. ch. 56 E. 4.]
Oblong octagonal : on a helmet and wreath, the attires of a bull.
In the field the motto :—**Dieu aide.**
Cabled border.

William de Dronsfeld, *of co. York, Knt.*
9332. [A.D. 1402.]   Red : cracked, indistinct. $\frac{7}{16}$ in.
[Harl. ch. 54 C. 14.]
Octagonal signet : a pierced mullet.   Betw. the points the legend :—
D_ro_nf_fe_ld.
Cabled border.

John-Druel, *al.* **Deruel,** *Sheriff of Northampton.*
9333. [A.D. 1300.]   Green : fine, edge chipped.   ¾ in.
[Add. ch. 19,833.]
Two shields of arms : *dex.,* a lion rampant, *sin.,* quarterly, in the first quarter a crescent, in the third an indistinct charge.   Suspended by straps from a branching tree.
[C]EST LE SEAL IOH LE FIZ IOH DERVEL.
Beaded border.

R—— Drury (?)

9334. [A.D. 1597.] Plaster cast from fine impression.
$\frac{5}{8} \times \frac{1}{2}$ in. [lxxxv. 60.]
Oval: a shield of arms: two bars ermine betw. six mart-
lets. Not the arms of DRURY.
Beaded borders.
Very doubtful.

Robert Drury (?)

9335. Plaster cast from fine impression. $\frac{1}{2} \times \frac{7}{16}$ in.
[lxxxv. 59.]
A shield of arms: a fess, in chief two pierced mullets.
Not the arms of DRURY.
Beaded border.

Roger Drury.

9336. [15th cent.] Plaster cast from indistinct impression.
$1\frac{1}{8}$ in. [lxxxv. 69.]
A shield of arms, *couché*: diapered with a sprig of foliage,
on a chief two mullets, DRURY.   Crest on a helmet and
mantling, out of a ducal coronet, a dog (talbot) collared and
lined.   Within a carved gothic panel.

S rogeri ⚬ ⚬ drury ⚬

9337. Another   [xcii. 87.]

Roger Drury.

9338. [A.D. 1505.] Plaster cast. $\frac{1}{4}$ in. [lxxxv. 57.]
A shield of arms: on a chief a cross tau betw. two pierced
mullets, DRURY.
Border engrailed and beaded.

Thomas Drury, *Esq., of Rougham, co. Suff.*

9339. [A.D. 1464.]   Red: imperfect. $\frac{1}{4}$ in. [Harl. ch.
49 F. 39.]
A greyhound's head couped, collared and ringed, in the
mouth a pierced mullet, in allusion to the arms of DRURY.
In the field are four roses, the initial letter T in base, and in
the upper part the motto :—**remember.**
Cabled border.
9340. [A.D. 1466.]   Red: injured by pressure. [Harl. ch.
49 F. 40.]

William Drury.

9341. [A.D. 1535.] · Plaster cast.   1 in. [lxxxv. 58.]
A shield of arms: on a chief a cross tau betw. two mullets,

DRURY. Crest on a helmet, ornamental mantling of foliage and wreath, a talbot statant. Within a carved gothic triangle ornamented along the inner edge with ball-flowers.

Motto betw. the points :—

IAMES _ AVL_TER. (*Jamais autre.*)

William Drury, *of Watergate, co. Suss., Esq.*
9342. [A.D. 1621.] Red : cracked, imperfect. ⅛ in. [Add. ch. 18,928.]

A shield of arms : on a fess three lions rampant, in chief a, label of as many points.

John Dryden.
See JACOB TONSON.

John Dubu . . .
Seal used by JOHANNA, *wife of* JOHN FAWNCHALL, *Senr.,*
of Holmesfeld, co. Derb.
9343. [A.D. 1454.] Green: chipped. ⅝ in. [Woll. ch. viii. 21.]

A shield of arms, *couché*: three bars, over all a bend. Crest on a helmet a tree or branch of foliage.

𝕴𝔢𝔥𝔞𝔫 : 𝔡𝔲𝔟𝔲 . . .

Perhaps a foreign seal.

Jane, *wife of Sir* JOHN **Dudley,** *of Halden, co. Kent, Knt.,*
afterwards Duke of Northumberland, etc.,
dau. of EDWD. GUILFORD, *Knt.*
9344. [A.D. 1537.] Red: injured by pressure. ⅝ × ½ in. [Harl. ch. 77 G. 17.]

Oval: a shield of arms: quarterly, 1, 4, per fess, a bull's head cabossed (?) OXNEY (?); 2nd and 3rd, a cross pattée voided betw. eight crosses crosslet, over all an escutcheon of pretence, on a chevron engrailed some indistinct charges.

John Dudley, *Duke of Northumberland, Earl of Warwick,*
Earl Marshal, Viscount Lisle, K.G., etc.
9345. [A.D. 1521.] Plaster cast from fine impression. 2⅛ in. [lxxxv. 62.]

A shield of arms: quarterly of five pieces, two in chief and three in base, 1, quarterly, i. iv., two lions passant in pale, SOMERY; ii. iii., a cross flory, MALPAS, over all a crescent for difference ; 2, per pale, *dex.* a fess between six crosses crosslet, BEAUCHAMP, *sin.* chequy, a chevron ermine, NEWBURGH ; 3, a chevron between ten crosses pattées, BERKELEY ; 4, a fess between two chevrons, LISLE ; 5, a lion passant crowned, GERARD, or perhaps rampant, DUDLEY (but should be *queue fourchée*) ; over all an escutcheon, quarterly ; 1, 4, a saltire between four martlets, GUILFORD ; 2, 3, per chief a bend engrailed, HALDEN.

Crest on a helmet, and ornamental mantling of foliage, out of a coronet, a lion's head charged with a crescent. Supporters, *dex.*, a lion rampant guardant, *sin.*, a swan, gorged, with a coronet, chained and ringed.

Legend on a scroll.

+ : VNG : + : DIEV : + : VNG : + : ROY : + : SERVIR : + :
IE : + : DOY : + :

Another Seal.

9346. [A.D. 1537.] Red. $\frac{3}{8} \times \frac{1}{2}$ in. [Harl. ch. 77 G. 17.] Oval : an ornamental shield of arms : a lion passant guardant crowned, tail flory, GERARD (?)

Beaded borders.

Another Seal.

9347. [A.D. 1539.] Red : injured. $\frac{5}{8} \times \frac{1}{2}$ in. [Harl. ch. 49 F. 49.] Oval : an ornamental shield of arms. See No. 9346. But not from the same matrix.

Cabled border.

Another Seal, as Duke of Northumberland, etc., K.G,

9348. [A.D. 1552.] Red : fine, injured by pressure in places. $1\frac{3}{8} \times 1\frac{1}{4}$ in. [Harl. ch. 77 G. 18.] An ornamental shield of arms : quarterly of eight pieces. 1, SOMERY ; 2, barry of six, a label of three points, GREY ; 3, a lion rampant, *queue fourchée*, DUDLEY ; 4, NEWBURGH ; 5, BEAUCHAMP ; 6, BERKELEY ; 7, LISLE ; 8, GERARD. See No. 9345. Ensigned with a coronet and encircled with the Garter inscribed with the Motto of the Order.

John Duddeley, *of Stoke Newington, co. Midd., Gentl.*

9349. [A.D. 1579.] Red : indistinct. $\frac{3}{4} \times \frac{11}{16}$ in. [Harl. ch. 76 D. 44.] Oval : out of a coronet, pearled, a lion's head, collared, charged on the neck with a crescent for difference. Crest of DUDLEY.

Richard Dudley, *Esq.*

9350. [15th cent.] Plaster cast from fine impression. $1\frac{1}{8}$ in. [lxxxv. 61.]

A shield of arms : quarterly, 1, 4, a chevron betw. three lions' heads, DUDLEY ; 2, 3. a cross pattée betw. four roses. Suspended by a strap from a forked tree.

Sigillum ricardi Dudley : armigeri.

Inner border cabled ; outer border carved with ball-flowers.

Richard Dudle, *or* Dudley, *of London.*

9351. [A.D. 1395.] Red : originally fine, cracked, imperfect. $\frac{3}{4}$ in. [Harl. ch. 57 E. 37.]

A shield of arms : a chevron betw. three lions' heads erased, DUDLEY. Within a carved gothic trefoil ornamented along the inner edge with small ball-flowers.

Legend betw. the points :—

Sigill : ricardi : Dudley :

Robert Dudley, 11*th Earl of Leicester, K.G., etc.*

9352. [A.D. 1566.] Red : fine, chipped at edge. $2\frac{1}{2}$ in. [Harl. ch. 83 E. 26.]

Ø. A shield of arms : quarterly of sixteen pieces : 1, SUTTON ; 2, DUDLEY ; 3, PAGANELL ; 4, GREY ; 5, MALPAS ; 6, HASTINGS ; 7, VALENCE ; 8, CHARLEY (?) ; 9, DE QUINCY ; 10, CHESTER ; 11, TALBOT, *of L'Isle ;* 12, BEAUCHAMP ; 13, GUY *of Warwick ;* 14, BERKELEY ; 15, DE L'ISLE ; 16, LYSLE. Ensigned with an earl's coronet, and encircled with (1) a garter inscribed with the Motto of the Order, and (2) a collar of the Order of St. Michael.

ROBERTVS · COMES · LECESTRIE · BARO · DE ·
DENBIGHE · VTRIVSQVE · ORDINIS · GARTERII · ET · SCI ·
MICHIS · MILES.

Some of the letters are conjoined.

R. A smaller counterseal. 1 in. diam. On a wreath, a bear, erect upon its hind feet, collared, chained, and ringed, grasping with its fore paws the trunk of a tree raguly.

+ VNIVS (*sic.*) · PRIVATI · CONSILII · DNE ·
REGINE · AC · MAGISTER · EQVI · DICTE ·
DNE · REGINE.

Cf. No. 5886 for the armorial bearings. Shield engraved in Palliot, *Science des Armoiries,* p. 305.

9353. Sulph. cast of *obv.* and *rev.* of No. 9352. [D.C., H. 123, 124.]

Another Seal.

9354. [A.D. 1566.] Red : indistinct. $1\frac{3}{8} \times 1$ in. [Harl. ch. 77 G. 19.]

Shaped seal : a shield of arms : quarterly of eight pieces.

Encircled with a Garter inscribed with the Motto of the Order, and ensigned with an earl's coronet.

Cf. No. 5886 for the armorial bearings.

9355. Sulph. cast from No. 9354. [D.C., H. 125.]

Another Seal.

9356. [A.D. 1574.]   Red: imperfect, indistinct.   1 in [Harl. ch. 86 G. 56.]

A shield of arms : quarterly of eight pieces. Ensigned with an earl's coronet, and encircled with a Garter inscribed with the Motto of the Order.

Cf. No. 5886 for the armorial bearings.

9357. Sulph. cast of No. 9356. [D.C., H. 126.]
9358. Plaster cast of No. 9356. [lxxxv. 63.]

Richard Duffeld, *Dominus del Northall in Coryngham,*
co. Linc.

9359. [A.D. 1383.]   Red : very imperfect.   ⅞ in. [Add. ch. 20,699.]

A griffin, having round its neck a cord from which is suspended a shield of arms: a chevron ermine betw. three doves, DUFFIELD.

. . . . . **ffil** . . .

9360. Plaster cast of No. 9359.   This shows more of the body of the griffin. [lxxxv. 64.]

Philip Dugdale, *of Henton Martell, co. Dors., Clerk.*
9361. [A.D. 1639.]   Red : indistinct.   ½ in. [Eg. ch. 489.]
A griffin segreant, for crest of DUGDALE.

Richard de Duinre.

9362. [A.D. 1344.]   Plaster cast from good impression. ⅞ in. [lxxxv. 68.]

A shield of arms : a chief compony counter-compony, over all a bend.   Within a carved gothic hexagonal panel.

✠ SIGILLVM · RICARDI · DE · DVINRE ✱

Cf. No. 9371.

Richard Duke, *of London, Gentl.*

9363. [A.D. 1668.]   Red, covered with paper before impression.   ⅝ × 9/16 in. [Add. ch. 29,533.]

Oval : a shield of arms : a chevron betw. three birds close, DUKE.   Crest on a helmet, ornamental mantling and wreath, [a sword stuck in] a plume of five feathers.

John de Dukworth, *of Huntingdon, co. Hunt.,*
John Yonge, *Chapl.,* or **Rich. Porter.**

9364. [A.D. 1389.] Green: a fragment. About 1 in. when perfect. [Add. ch. 33,513.]

A shield: charged with a pentacle in outline, between five pellets.

Legend uncertain.

Another Seal.

9365. Red: imperfect. [Add. ch. 33,513].

Shield-shaped: an eagle rising reguardant, on a chief
BON. SV.

John de Dumfries (?)

9366. [A.D. 1400.] Plaster cast from indistinct impression. ⅞ in. [lxxxv. 65.]

A shield of arms, *couché*: fretty, on a chief a cross betw. two mullets. Crest on a helmet, mantling, and wreath a Moor's head, couped at the neck, wearing a cap.

Legend on a scroll:—

$ ... o .... is de dun .. reis (?)

Perhaps a Scottish seal.

Richard de Dummere, *son of* JOHN DE DUMMERE, *of co. Somers., Knt.*

9367. [A.D. 1323.] Dark green: injured by pressure. ⅞ in. [Harl. ch. 49 F. 54.]

A shield of arms: two bars betw. nine quatrefoils, four, two, two, and one. Within a pointed gothic trefoil.

SIGILLṼ · RICARDI · DOMMERE.

Edward Duncombe, *of Monks Risborough, co. Bucks., Gentl.*

9368. [A.D. 1613.] Red: chipped. ¾ × ⅝ in. [Add. ch. 24,005.]

Oval: a shield of arms: per chevron engrailed three talbots' heads erased, an annulet for difference, DUNCOMBE.

Beaded border.

9369. [A.D. 1621.] Red: very indistinct. [Add. ch. 24,014.]

John Duncombe, *of Battlesden, co. Bedf.*

9370. [A.D. 1683.] Red: *en placard.* About ⅝ × ½ in. when perfect. [Add. ch. 19,268.]

Out of a ducal coronet a horse's leg erect. Crest of DUNCOMBE.

Geo. Montagu-Dunk, *Earl of Halifax.*
See —— CRECROFT.

Richard de Dunre, *Lord of Dunre* (?) *Dinedor, co. Heref.*
9371. [A.D. 1345.]   Red : indistinct in places. $\frac{11}{16}$ in.
[Add. ch. 20,411.]
A shield of arms : a bend, over all a label of three points.
Betw. three small roses, and within a carved and pointed
quatrefoil, ornamented with ball-flowers along the inner edge.
In place of a legend a wavy scroll of roses.
Cf. No. 9362.

John, *son of* ROGER **de Donewyco,** *or* **Dunwich,** *co. Suff.*
9372. [A.D. 1344.]   Red : very fragmentary.   [Add. ch.
10,372.]
A shield of arms : a lion rampant.
Legend uncertain.

Rosa Durant.
Seal used by THOMAS MIDDLETON, *son of* JOHN MIDDLETON,
of Horsham, co. Suss.
9373. [A.D. 1619.]   Red : indistinct. $\frac{5}{8} \times \frac{1}{2}$ in.   [Add.
ch. 30,901.]
Oval : a shield of arms : a cross crosslet, DURANT.

SIG' · AD · ARMA · ROSA · DVRANT.

Lewis de Duras, *2nd Earl of Feversham, Lord Chamberlain
to Catharine, Qu. Dowager of Charles II., K.G.*
9374. [A.D. 1693.]   Red : *en placard,* on a label, imperfect. $\frac{3}{8}$ in.   [Add. ch. 6076.]
A circular shield of arms : quarterly, 1, 4, a lion rampant,
DURAS ; 2, 3, a bend.   Encircled with a Garter inscribed
with the Motto of the Order, and surmounted with an earl's
coronet.   Supporters, two angels.
9375. [A.D. 1698.]   Another : imperfect.   [Add. ch. 6152.]
9376. [A.D. 1703.]   Another : good, edge imperfect.   [Add.
ch. 13,634.]

Margaret Duraud.
Seal used by WILLIAM, *son of* ADAM LE WARD,
of Wolflay, co. York.
9377. [A.D. 1349.]   Green, mottled : indistinct in places.
1 × $\frac{3}{4}$ in.   [Add. ch. 8297.]

Oval : a shield of arms : three fleurs-de-lis within a bordure charged with three (?) lucies or pikes. Above the shield a head. Within a carved and pointed quatrefoil.

⊕ S' MARGARETE DVRAVD.

Richard Duraunt, *of Burton, co. Buck.*

9378. [A.D. 1325.] Red : injured by pressure. ¾ × ⅝ in. [Harl. ch. 84 E. 52.]

Oval : a shield of arms : three boars' heads, in the fess point an indistinct charge.

✠ S' RICARDI DVRAVNT.

Richard Duraunt, *of Kepston.*

9379. [A.D. 1369.] Discoloured green : a fragment. [Add. ch. 8840.]

A shield of arms : a chevron betw. three crosses crosslet fitchées.

. . . Є . HЄ.

Hugh Durburgh, *of Dunster, co. Som., Chevr.*

9380. [A.D. 1384.] Red : imperfect, indistinct. ¾ in. [Harl. ch. 49 G. 6.]

A shield of arms : on a bend three (? nags' heads). Within a gothic cinquefoil.

Legend wanting.

Ralph Durburgh.

9381. [14th cent.] Recent impression in red sealing-wax. I in. [xxxv. 346.]

A shield of arms : on a bend three nags' heads bridled, in chief an annulet. Within a composite gothic panel formed with a triangle and cinquefoil, ornamented with ball-flowers along the inner edge.

𝔖𝔦𝔤𝔦𝔩𝔩𝔲̄ ⚹ ⚹ : 𝔯𝔞𝔡𝔲𝔩𝔭𝔥𝔦 ⚹ ⚹ : 𝔡𝔲𝔯𝔟𝔲𝔯𝔤𝔥 ⚹

Cabled border.

Philip Durdent, *of Denham, co. Buck.*

9382. [A.D. 1347.] Creamy-white : very indistinct. ⅞ in. [Harl. ch. 85 C. 54.]

A shield of arms : a cross (?) indistinct. Suspended by a strap from a hook.

. . . . . PPI . . . .

John Dureward, *of Bromley, etc., co. Kent.*
9383. [A.D. 1407.] Red: fine. ¼ in. [Harl. ch. 111 D. 43.]
A crescent enclosing an escallop. In allusion to the arms of DURWARD.

𝕾oli : 𝕯eo : honor : 𝔞 : gloria.

The letters EO in *deo* are conjoined.
Cabled border.

Adam de Durem *or* **Durham (?).**
Seal used by JOHN, *son and heir of* JOHN VACHE,
of Waltham Holy Cross, co. Essex.

9384. [A.D. 1398.] Red: fine, cracked, injured by pressure. [Harl. ch. 80 H. 2.]
A shield of arms of lozenge-shape: on a cross betw. four slipped quatrefoils five indistinct charges. Cf. DURESME and DURHAM. Within a carved lozenge, ornamented with ball-flowers along the inner edge; inscribed in a quatrefoil of similar style, having in each lobe in base an arrow, in the upper lobe a wolf and a couped head, probably in allusion to the legend of St. *E*dmund, king and martyr.
Legend betw. the lobes.

+ S.' A +__+ L Є · D +__+ Є · DV +__+ RЄM +

John Durem, *al.* **Durham.**

9385. [14th cent.] Plaster cast from fine impression. 1 in. [lxxxv. 70.]
A shield of arms: three crescents, two and one, betw. nine crosses crosslet, DURHAM. Within a carved gothic cinquefoil ornamented along the inner edge with ball-flowers.

� 𝕾igillum : iohannis : Durem : 𝔪

Beaded border.

Jolanus de Dunolmia, *or* **Durham.**

9386. [14th cent.] Plaster cast from good impression. ¾ in. [lxxxv. 66.]
A shield of arms: on a cross five [fleurs-de-lis?], DURHAM.

𝔪 S'. IOLANI DE DVNOLMIA.

Beaded border.

John Dutton, *of Shirborn, co. Glouc., Esq.*
9387. [A.D. 1715.] Red: *en placard*, on a tape. 11/16 × 9/16 in. [Add. ch. 13,746.]
Oval: an ornamental shield of arms: quarterly, in the second and third quarters a fret, for DUTTON.

Elizabeth Dyer, *widow of* LAURENCE DYER, *Pewterer, of London.*

9388. [A.D. 1692.]   Red : on a label.   ⅛ in.   [Add. ch. 1975.]

A bull head attired, couped, contournée, for a crest.

James Dyer, *Knt.,*
Lord Chief Justice of the Court of Common Pleas.

9389. [A.D. 1566.]   Red : a fragment.   From a ring. [Harl. ch. 80 H. 80.]

For description see No. 9390.

9390. [A.D. 1569.]   Red.   ⅝ in.   [Harl. ch. 80 H. 83.]

A goat's head erased, holding in the mouth a rose slipped and leaved.   Crest of DYER.   Betw. the initial letters I. D. Beaded border.

9391. [A.D. 1578.]   Red : with marks of the setting of the ring.   [Add. ch. 13,938.]

William Dygher.
See BRIAN DE SANTUN.

Thomas Dyke, *Jun., of Waldron, co. Suss., Gentl.*
9392. [A.D. 1611.]   Red.   ¼ in.   [Add. ch. 29,968.]

A wolf passant, perhaps for a crest.

Charles Dymoke, *Sen., of Cranfield, co. Bedf., Gentl.*
9393. [A.D. 1703.]   Red : *en placard.*   ½ × 7⁄10 in·   [Add. ch. 24,092.]

Oval : an ornamental shield of arms : two lions passant in pale, crowned, DYMOCK.   Betw. two cornucopiæ, labelled, and united at the base ; and over the shield a cherub.

9394. [A.D. 1703.]   Another.   [Add. ch. 24,093.]

John Dymmok, *Tailor and Citizen of London.*
9395. [A.D. 1379.]   Red : fine, (from a ring ?)   ½ in.   [Harl. ch. 78 B. 47.]

A lion statant guardant crowned.   Crest of DYMOKE.   In the field above, the legend.

J. Dymmok.

The letters DY are conjoined.

Carved border ornamented with ball-flowers along the inner edge.

John Dymock, *Citizen and Clothmaker of London.*
9396. [A.D. 1564.] Red. ⅜ in. [Add. ch. 5323.]
An ornamental shield of arms : four bars undée, over all a sword in pale, point upwards. This is probably a variant form of the arms of DYMOCK.
Beaded border.

Thomas Dymocke.
9397. [A.D. 1408.] Plaster cast from good impression. 1 in. [lxxxv. 71.]
A shield of arms, *couché*: two lions passant in pale, crowned betw. three swords : for DYMOCK. Crest on a helmet and lambrequin and out of a ducal coronet, the scalp of a hare, ears erect. Betw. two sprigs of foliage and within a gothic panel ornamented with ball-flowers along the inner edge.

S : tɧome : м : Dymmok м
Beaded border.

Richard de Dynelay, *Clerk.*
9398. [A.D. 1368.] Red : injured, indistinct. ⅞ in. [Add. ch. 16,826.]
A shield of arms : a fess or barrulet, on a chief some uncertain charges, for DYNELEY. Within a carved gothic panel.

x S' R . . . . AY + CL'ICI.

Robert Dynelay, *of cos. Wilts and Southt.*
9399. [A.D. 1394.] Red : somewhat indistinct, injured by pressure. 1¹⁄₁₆ in. [Add. ch. 24,701.]
A shield of arms, *couché*: a fess, in chief a mullet betw. two pellets, DYNELEY. Crest on a helmet, mantling, and chapeau, a hare's scalp and pair of ears erect. In the field two wavy branches of foliage.

S' : roberti : ᶳ Deynelay : м
Cabled borders.
9400. [A.D. 1419] Red : fine. [Harl. ch. 77 G. 29.]
9401. Sulph. cast of No. 9400. [D.C., G. 155.]

John Dynham, *Knt.*
9402. [A.D. 1428.] Plaster cast from fine impression. 1⅜ in. [lxxxv. 42.]
A shield of arms : four fusils in fess, ermine, DYNHAM.

Within a carved gothic panel, ornamented with ball-flowers along the inner edge.

⚹ 𝕾𝖎𝖌𝖎𝖑𝖑𝖚𝖒 : 𝖎𝖔𝖍𝖆𝖓𝖓𝖎𝖘 : 𝖉𝖞𝖓𝖍𝖆𝖒 : 𝖒𝖎𝖑𝖎𝖙𝖎𝖘.

Beaded borders.

John Dynham, *Lord of Carr-Dynham, co. Cornw.*

9403. [A.D. 1478.] Plaster cast from fine but imperfect impression. 1⅞ in. [lxxxv. 43.]

A shield of arms of ornamental form, *couché*: four fusils in fess, ermine, DYNHAM. Crest on a helmet, ornamental mantling and wreath, an otter between two [trees?].

Supporters, *dex.*, a stag, *sin.*, a unicorn. The field replenished with sprigs.

. . . . . 𝖍𝖆𝖓𝖓𝖎𝖘 : 𝖉𝖓̄𝖎 : . . . 𝖞𝖓𝖍𝖆̄ : 𝖉𝖊 : 𝖈𝖆𝖗𝖗 : 𝖉𝖞𝖓𝖍𝖆̄.

Outer border ornamented with quatrefoils or ball-flowers.

Edmund Dyve, *of Maidwell, co. Northt.*

9404. [A.D. 1458.] Red. ½ × ⅜ in. [Add. ch. 21,839.]

Octagonal: an escallop, in allusion to the arms of DYVE, betw. the initial letters **𝖊. 𝖉.**

Carved border.

9405. [A.D. 1458.] Red. [Add. ch. 22,285.]

Laurence Dyve, *son and heir of* HENRY DYVE,
of Harleston, co. Northt.

9406. [A.D. 1385.] Red: fine, edge chipped. ⅞ in. [Add. ch. 22,217.]

A shield of arms: (field diapered lozengy with a small pellet in each space) on a bend three martlets. Within a carved gothic cinquefoil, ornamented along the inner edge with small ball-flowers.

⚹ 𝕾𝖎𝖌𝖎𝖑𝖑𝖚𝖒 : 𝖑𝖆𝖚𝖗𝖊𝖓𝖈𝖎𝖎 : 𝖉𝖞𝖚𝖊 : ⚹

Beaded border.

9407. [A.D. 1385.] Red: fine, edge slightly chipped. [Add. ch. 22,223.]

9408. [A.D. 1385.] Another. [Add. ch. 22,218.]

9409. [A.D. 1386.] Red: fine, well preserved. [Add. ch. 22,220.]

9410. [A.D. 1391.] Red: injured by pressure, indistinct in places. [Add. ch. 21,634.]

9411. [A.D. 1409.] Red: indistinct. [Add. ch. 21,639.]

William Dyx, *Esq.*

9412. [A.D. 1577.] Red: injured. About $\frac{7}{8} \times \frac{5}{8}$ in. [Add. ch. 29,272.]

Oval: on a wreath a greyhound's head erased, ducally gorged, betw. two wings. Crest of DYX.

Bevelled border.

Cf. Add. ch. 14,937, A.D. 1578; 26,346, A.D. 1582.

E

T—— E——.

Seal used by GEO. SMYTHE, *of Weston, co. Hertf., Laborer.*

9413. [A.D. 1564.] Red. $\frac{3}{4}$ in. [Add. ch. 36,238.]

A shield of arms: on a fess, betw. three birds as many cinquefoils or roses. Betw. the initial letters T. E.

John Earlie, *Clothworker and Citizen of London.*

9414. [A.D. 1561.] Red: well preserved, from a ring, with mark of the setting. $\frac{7}{16} \times \frac{3}{8}$ in. [Harl. ch. 77 G. 34.]

On a wreath, a tiger's head.

Beaded border.

Richard de Echebregge, *al.* **Echebrugge,**
son of JOHN LE CHAUNDELER, *of co. Suff.*

9415. [A.D. 1326.] Creamy-white: very imperfect. [Add. ch. 9586.]

For description see next seal.

9416. [A.D. 1331.] Dark-green: good. $\frac{3}{4}$ in. [Add. ch. 9595.]

A shield of arms: two swords in saltire, points downwards, betw. four cinquefoils. Within a carved gothic six-foil.

✠ S' RICARDI DE ECHEBREGGE.

James de Echingham, *al.* **Ecchingehamme,** *of co. Kent.*

9417. [A.D. 1333.] Dark-green: fine. $\frac{3}{4}$ in. [Add. ch. 16,346.]

A shield of arms: per pale, *dex.*, fretty, ECHINGHAM, *sin.*, a fess betw. two lions rampant. Suspended by a strap from a hook, and betw. two sprigs of foliage.

✠ S' IACOBI [D]E ECHINGHAM.

Beaded borders.

9418. Plaster cast from indistinct impression. [lxxxv. 76.]

Cf. Add. ch. 20,117, A.D. 1349.

Thomas Echyngham, *of co. Suss., Esq.*

9419. [A.D. 1454.]   Red: injured by pressure.   From a , ring, with marks of the setting.   ⅜ in.   [Harl. ch. 49 G. 18.]

A helmet, or flower (?) in the field an illegible motto:—

... ecorwo .. (?)

Beaded border.

William de Echyngham, *of co. Kent.*

9420. [A.D. 1376.]   Red: a fragment.   [Harl. ch. 78 A. 23.]

For description see next seal.

9421. [A.D. 1377.]   Red: originally fine, chipped, imperfeet.   1⅛ in.   .[Harl. ch. 78 A. 24.]

A shield of arms: fretty, ECHINGHAM.   Suspended by a strap from a tree, and betw. two small talbots sejant, by way of supporters.   Within a finely carved gothic panel with three points, ornamented with small ball-flowers along the inner edge.

Legend betw. the points:—

+ Sigillum +_+ willelmi · d ....

9422. Sulph. cast from fine but chipped impression. [D.C., F. 512.]

+ Sigillum +_+ willelmi · de   ech .. gh'm.

Robert de Eccleshale.

9423. [A.D. 1328.]   Plaster cast from fine impression. ⅞ × ¾ in.   [lxxxv. 75.]

Oval: a lozenge-shaped shield of arms: a bend betw. six martlets, ECCLESHALL.   Betw. four small wyverns.

✠ S' ROBERTI DE ECCLESHALE.

Philip Eden, *of Lincoln's Inn, Esq.*

9424. [A.D. 1626.]   Red: injured by pressure.   About ⅝ × ½ in.   [Add. ch. 29,587.]

Oval: a shield of arms: on a fess three garbs, betw. two chevrons each charged with three escallops, EDEN.   Crest on a helmet, mantling, and wreath, a demi-dragon sans wings, holding a rose branch.

Cabled border.

9425. [A.D. 1638.]   Red.   [Add. ch. 30,934.]

William Eden, *of Wendlebury, co. Oxon., Esq.*

9426. [A.D. 1597.]   Red.   ⅝ × ½ in.   [Add. ch. 28,965.]

Oval: a shield of arms: quarterly, 1, 4, on a chevron betw.

three birds or martlets, some illegible charges ; 2, 3, quarterly, a saltire, and in the fess point over all an annulet for difference. Crest on a helmet, mantling, and wreath, a goat's head erased.

Another Seal.

9427. [A.D. 1597.]   Red : imperfect.   About ¼ in.   [Add. ch. 28,966.]

Three helmets, two and one (not on a shield), *E*DEN.
Beaded border.

Roger de Ederikthorp,
of Edderthorpe, in Darfield, co. York.

9428. [A.D. 1345.]   Brown.   ⅝ in.   [Add. ch. 22,610.]
A shield of arms : fretty.

+ S AMAL VI . . . . CA PORT (?)

John, *son of* GEOFFREY de Edintone, *Knt.*

9429. [Late Edw. I.]   Dark green : good.   ¾ in.   [Cott. ch. xxv. 16.]

A shield of arms : quarterly, in chief a label of five points.

✠ S' IOH'IS · FIL' · GALFRIDI.

9430. Sulph. cast of No. 9429.   [D.C., E. 405.]

Benjamin Edmonds.
See ROBERT CASTLETON.

Joseph Edmonds.
See ROBERT CASTLETON.

William Edlyngton, *of co. Linc.*

9431. [A.D. 1420.]   Red : indistinct.   ¼ in.   [Harl. ch. 58 B. 15.]

Octagonal signet : on a helmet, the attires of a stag.   In the field the legend :—

ꞓ . . yngton.

Cabled border.

John Edolf, *of Cherlewode [Charlwood], co. Surr.*

9432. [A.D. 1330.]   Creamy-white : imperfect, indistinct. [Add. ch. 18,591.]

A shield of arms : indistinct.
Legend broken away.

S' . i . . . .

Cf. Add. ch. 18,589 ; 15,560 ; 24,561 ; Harl. ch. 111 G. 3, A.D. 1314–1349.

Bartholomew Edrich.

9433. [14th cent.] Sulph. cast from fine impression. $\frac{7}{8}$ in. [D.C., F. 331.]

A pilgrim with flat cap and staff, holding before him a shield of arms : three wolves' heads erased. Within a gothic panel ornamented with ball-flowers along the inner edge. Cf. the arms of EDRIDGE.

☆ SIGILL' · BARTHOLOMEI · EDRICH.

Beaded border.

John Edward.
See WALTER LE SCOT.

Edward Augustus, *Duke of Kent.*
See DUKE OF KENT.

Thomas Edwards, *of Weston, co. Herts.*

9434. [A.D. 1470.] Red : indistinct. Encircled with a twisted thong of vellum. $\frac{3}{4}$ in. [Add. ch. 36,109.]

A boar's head couped.

Legend in gothic letters, indistinct.

William Edwards.
See ROBERT HARDY.

John Eeles, *of Aynho-on-the-Hill, co. Northt., Esq.*

9435. [A.D. 1689.] Red : *en placard*, on a label, imperfect. About $\frac{5}{8} \times \frac{1}{2}$ in. [Add. ch. 24,147.]

Oval : a shield of arms : goutty, on a chief a lion passant guardant.

John Egerton, *2nd Earl of Bridgwater.*
A.D. 1649–1686.

9436. Plaster casts from good impression, indistinct in places. $2\frac{3}{8}$ in. [lxxxv. 77, 78.]

∅. A shield of arms of eight quarterings : 1, a lion rampant, betw. three pheons, EGERTON ; 2. BASSETT ; 3. CAVENDISH ; 4. HARDWICK ; 5. STANLEY, with crescent for difference ; 6. MAN ; 7. OGLE ; 8. indistinct. Ensigned with the coronet of an earl. Crest on a helmet, ornamental mantling, and wreath, a lion rampant supporting an arrow erect. Supporters, *dex.,* a horse gorged with a ducal coronet, *sin.,* a bull, gorged with a ducal coronet. Motto on a ribbon in base :—

SIC · DONEC.

Within a carved border.

R̵. On a wreath, the crest as described in the *Obv.* ensigned with an earl's coronet.
Within a carved border.

Thomas Egerton, *Baron Ellesmere, Lord Chancellor of England.*
9437. [A.D. 1610.] Red: injured by pressure, 1 × ⅞ in. [Add. ch. 18,205.]
Oval: on a wreath a lion rampant supporting a pheon or arrow. Crest of *EGERTON.*
Carved border.

Otuell Eir, *of co. Somers.*
9438. [A.D. 1517.] Red: imperfect. ⅓ in. [Add. ch. 13,079.]
A shield of arms : a chevron with illegible charges, perhaps three cinquefoils, for *EYRE.*
Engrailed border.

John de Eland, *of Wrenthorpe Manor, co. York, Knt.*
9439. [A.D. 1350.] Red,. on a mass of pale green : edge imperfect. ⅞ in. [Add. ch. 20,602.]. .
A shield of arms, *couché*: two bars betw. eight martlets, three, two, and two and one (or an orle of eight), *ELAND.* Crest on a helmet and lambrequin, a plume of feathers. In the field a sprig of foliage.
S' IOH'IS DE ELAND.

Thomas Eld, *of Scropton, co. Derb.*
9440. [A.D. 1686.] Red: *en placard,* on a label. ⅓ × ⅜ in. [Add. ch. 19,436.]
Octagonal : a double-headed eagle displayed, for the crest of ELD, which is an eagle with wings expanded.
Beaded border. ·
9441. [A.D. 1686.] Another. [Add. ch. 19,437.]

Sir **William Eliott,** *al.* **Elyott,** *of Busbridge, co. Surr., Knt.*
· **9442.** [A.D. 1621.] Red: somewhat indistinct. ⅞ × ⅘ in. [Harl. ch. 57 H. 43.]
· Oval: a shield of arms : a fess, *ELIOTT.* Crest on a helmet, ornamental mantling, and wreath, a griffin's head couped, wings endorsed, collared.

Cabled border.
9443. [A.D. 1622.] Another. [Harl. ch. 57 H. 44.]

Princess **Elizabeth,** *Landgrave of Hesse-Homberg.*
See HESSE-HOMBERG.

Robert de Elkyngton, *of Edgefield Manor, etc., co. Norf*
9444. [A.D. 1366.] Red: injured when being impressed.
[Harl. ch. 58 B. 1.]
A shield of arms: three ducks, two and one, within a
bordure charged with ten crosses crosslets. Within a pointed
gothic quatrefoil.
✠ S' ROBERTI DE ELKYNTON :
Cf. Add. ch. 21,012, A.D. 1366; Lansd. ch. 411, A.D. 1366.

Gilbert de Ellesfeld, *of co. Hants, Chev.*
9445. [A.D. 1335.] Dark-green, edge very imperfect.
1 in. [Add. ch. 15,466.]
An eagle displayed: on its breast a shield of arms: barry
wavy of six, ELLESFIELD.
D' . . . . . FELD.

John Ellis, *Esq.*
9446. [A.D. 1724.] Red: *en placard,* on a tape. $\frac{5}{8} \times \frac{1}{2}$ in.
[Add. ch. 25,967.]
Oval: a shield of arms: on a cross five crescents, in dexter
chief a fleur-de-lis for difference.

William Ellis.
See WILLIAM NEVILE.

Robert Ellison, John Stevenson, William Davison,
or **Robert Sutton,** *of co. Durham.*
9447. [A.D. 1712.] Red: *en placard,* imperfect. $\frac{1}{4} \times \frac{3}{8}$ in.
[Add. ch. 13,308.]
Oval: an oval shield of arms: on a bend three martlets.
Crest on a helmet, mantling, and wreath, a lion's head erased.
9448. Another. [Add. ch. 13,308.]
9449. Another. [Add. ch. 13,308.]
9450. Another. [Add. ch. 13,308.]

Henry Elsynge.
Seal used by ANTHONIE MAYNARD, *of Westminster,*
co. Midd., Esq.

9451. [A.D. 1615.] Red : injured. $\frac{11}{16} \times \frac{9}{16}$ in. [Cott. ch. xxvii. 85.]

Oval : a shield of arms : two bars, betw. three fleurs-de-lis, ELSING.

Beaded border.

William de Elsyngge, *Citizen of London.*
9452. [A.D. 1331.] Dark-green : fine. App. by cords of plaited red silk. 1 in. [Cott. ch. v. 2.]

A shield of arms : Our Lord on the cross, betw. two demi-angels issuing, holding instruments of the Passion, and two estoiles. In chief a sword lying fesswise, handle to the *dexter* side ; in base a half-length figure praying. Betw. three sprigs of foliage.

IESVS · NAZARENVS · REX · IVDAEORVM.

Beaded borders.

9453. Sulph. cast of No. 9452. [D.C., F. 236.]

For an account of shields of the Passion, see *Journ. Brit. Arch. Assoc.* vol. xxxi, p. 92.

William de Eltoft, *of Yedone, co. York.*
9454. [A.D. 1358.] Dark-green : imperfect, indistinct. [Add. ch. 17,084.]

A shield of arms : three chessrooks, two and one, ELTOFT. Within a pointed gothic quatrefoil ornamented with ballflowers along the inner edge.

✠ S' WILELMI . . . . . . TOFT'.

Ambrose Elton, *of Le Hazell, co. Heref., Esq.*
9455. [A.D. 1668.] Red, covered with paper before impression. $\frac{7}{8} \times \frac{3}{8}$ in. [Add. ch. 5287.]

Oval : a shield of arms : a cross, charged with illegible bearings. Crest on a helmet, ornamental mantling, and wreath, a lion passant, in the dexter foreleg an uncertain object.

John Eluet, *Clerk.*
9456. [A.D. 1440.] Plaster cast from fine impression. $1\frac{1}{4}$ in. [lxxxv. 79.]

An angel, with expanded wings, holding before him a shield of arms : *diapré*, a saltire compony, in the fess point an annulet, in chief a mullet for difference. Within a carved gothic panel.

⚓ : iohannis : eluet : clerici :

Jeremy Elwes, *of Broxborne, co. Hertf., Esq.*
9457. [A.D. 1655.] Red : indistinct. $\frac{5}{8} \times \frac{1}{2}$ in. [Add. ch. 35,904.]
Oval : an ornamental shield of arms : a sun in splendour.
9458. [A.D. 1656.] Red: much injured. [Add. ch. 35,432.]
9459. [A.D. 1658.] Red : almost illegible. [Add. ch. 35,433.]

Alexander de Elyngham, *of Rockland, co. Norf*
9460. [A.D. 1370.] Dark-green : indistinct. $\frac{7}{8}$ in. [Add. ch. 14,832.]
A shield of arms : per pale, *dex.*, semé of fleurs-de-lis ; *sin.*, three escutcheons, two and one. Betw. three slipped roses.
$\dots$ S' A $\dots$ RE $\dots$ ELIN $\dots$
Detached from the charter, in a box.

Ralph de Elyngham,
Parson of Elyngham Magna, co. Norf
9461. [A.D. 1360.] Red : chipped and indistinct in places. $1\frac{3}{16}$ in. [Harl. ch. 49 G. 42.]
On a chevron, betw. three escutcheons each barry of six, five fleurs-de-lis.
$\dots$ RADVLFI $\dots$ ELINGHAM.
9462. Sulph. cast of No. 9461. [D.C., F. 464.]

Thomas Elys, *of Kenyngton, co. Kent, Esq.*
9463. [A.D. 1431.] Dark-green. $\frac{7}{16} \times \frac{3}{8}$ in. [Add. ch. 20,012.]
A nag's head, bridled, derived from the arms of ELLEIS or *E*LLES.
Beaded border.

Thomas Emerson, *of London, Esq.*
9464. [A.D. 1617.] Red: injured. $\frac{5}{8} \times \frac{1}{2}$ in. [Harl. ch. 79 G. 9.]
A shield of arms : on a bend three torteaux, EMERSON.
Beaded border.
9465. [A.D. 1617.] Red : good. [Harl. ch. 79 G. 10.]

John Enderby, *of Stratton, co. Bedf., Esq.*
9466. [A.D. 1427.] Red : imperfect. $1\frac{3}{16}$ in. [Add. ch. 35,237.]

A shield of arms : three bars dancettée, in chief a pale ermine, ENDERBY. Suspended by a strap from a tree. Betw. some rose-flowers.

$$\mathfrak{Sig} \ldots \ldots \mathfrak{o\mathfrak{h}annis} * \mathfrak{en\mathfrak{d}erb\mathfrak{y}} : \mathfrak{m}$$

Beaded borders.

9467. [A.D. 1428.]   Red : chipped.   [Add. ch. 35,238.]

$$\ldots \mathfrak{gillum} \mathfrak{m} \ldots \mathfrak{nis} * \mathfrak{en\mathfrak{d}erb\mathfrak{y}} : \mathfrak{m}$$

9468. [A.D. 1436.]   Red : indistinct in parts.   [Add. ch. 35,242.]

$$\mathfrak{Sigillum} \mathfrak{m} \mathfrak{io\mathfrak{h}annis} * \mathfrak{en\mathfrak{d}erb\mathfrak{y}} : \mathfrak{m}$$

9469. [A.D. 1450.]   Red : imperfect, injured by pressure. [Add. ch. 35,245.]

John Enderby, *of Stratton, co. Bedf., Esq.*
9470. [A.D. 1431.]   Red : indistinct, originally encircled with a twisted rush. $\frac{1}{4} \times \frac{3}{8}$ in.   [Add. ch. 35,241.]
Oblong octagonal signet : a swan.   Crest of ENDERBY. In the field, some erminée spots, and the legend :—

$$\mathfrak{en\ \mathfrak{d}er\ b\mathfrak{y}.}$$

John, *son of* JOHN **Engayne,**
of Wood-Newton Manor, etc., co. Northt.
9471. [*circ.* A.D. 1300.]   Green : imperfect, cracked, indistinct. $\frac{7}{8}$ in.   [Add. ch. 22,081.]
Four shields of arms, united in cross at their base points : 1, ENGAYNE ; 2, 3, 4, indistinct.   Within a carved gothic quatrefoil.

$$\ldots \text{OHANN} \ldots \ldots \text{AIN} \ldots$$

Beaded borders.

John Enganye [? **Engaine**], *of Blatherwycke, co. Northt., Knt.*
9472. [A.D. 1307.]   Discoloured : indistinct. $\frac{7}{8}$ in.   [Add. ch. 21,541.]
A shield of arms : a fess dancettée, with some obliterated charges, for ENGAYNE.

$$\maltese \text{S' I} \ldots \ldots \ldots \text{N} \ldots$$

John Engayne.
9473. [A.D. 1356.]   Plaster cast from fine impression. $1\frac{3}{16}$ in.   [lxxxv. 81.]
A shield of arms : a fess dancettée, betw. four crosses crosslet in chief, and three, two, and one in base, for ENGAYNE.

Above the shield a fox statant. The background replenished
with sprigs and foliage. Within a finely carved gothic panel
ornamented with ball-flowers along the inner edge.

SIGILLVM ❀ IOHANNIS ❀ ENGAYNE.

Beaded borders.

John Engayn, *of Grafham, co. Hunt.*

9474. [14th cent.]   Creamy - white : indistinct.   1 in.
[Add. ch. 33,298.]

A shield of arms : a fess dancettée betw. (three crosses ?)
ENGAINE. Betw. two fleurs-de-lis on stalks on each side.
Above the shield a rose of five leaves betw. two slipped
trefoils.

❦ SIGILLVM : IOHANNIS : ENGAYNE.

Beaded borders.

Katharine, *dau. of* HUGH DE COURTENAY, *Earl of Devon,*
widow of THOMAS **Dengayne,** *al.* **Engayne,** *Knt.,*
of co. Northt.

9475. [A.D. 1384.]   Red : originally fine, very imperfect.
1 in. [Harl. ch. 49 G. 54.]

For description see next seal.

. . . . . 𝕳ate . . . . 𝕘aρn.

9476. [A.D. 1397.]   Red : fine, edge chipped.   [Harl. ch.
49 H. 1.]

A shield of arms : per pale, *dex.*, a fess dancettée betw.
four crosslets in chief, and in base three, two, and one,
ENGAYNE, *sin.*, three roundles, two and one, over all in chief
a label of as many points, COURTENAY.   Above this, a
smaller shield of arms : ENGLAND, and on the *dex.* and *sin.*
sides other shields of similar size, BOHUN.   Within a carved
gothic quadrilobe, ornamented with ball-flowers along the
inner edge.

𝕾igill'. : katerine : engaρn.

9477. Sulph. cast from No. 9476.   [D.C., F. 605.]

John Engehame, *of co. Kent, Esq.*

9478. [A.D. 1475.]   Red. ⅝ in. [Harl. ch. 78 A. 10.]

A shield of arms : per chevron three roundles, on a chief a
lion passant guardant, for ENGHAM, *al.* EDINGHAM.

Beaded and engrailed border.

Thomas Engeham, *of Goodnestone, co. Kent, Gentl.*
9479. [A.D. 1547.]   Red : injured in places by pressure.
⅞ in. [Add. ch. 8615.]

An ornamental shield of arms: quarterly 1, 4, a chevron
betw. three pellets, on a chief a lion passant guardant, for
ENGHAM or EDINGHAM ; 2, 3, semé of crosses crosslets, three
birds, GOODNESTONE.
Beaded border.

Durand Le Enginnur, *of co. Suff.*
9480. [*Temp.* Hen. III.]   Pale green or uncoloured : very
indistinct, chipped.   1¼ in. [Harl. ch. 49 H. 9.]
A shield of arms of early form : a cross betw. some uncertain charges.
⊕ S . . . . VRANDI G . . NNVR.
Cf. No. 9493.

John England,
of Aldermill, in Tamworth, co. Staff., Millwright.
9481. [A.D. 1719.]   Red : *en placard,* imperfect.   ⅞ in.
[Add. ch. 23,854.]
A shield of arms : per pale, *dex.,* an uncertain charge
within an orle of six martlets, *sin.,* a bend betw. two cotises.
Crest, on a helmet, mantling, and wreath, a lily-flower.

Seal used by WILLIAM PALMER, *of Lichfield.*
9482. [A.D. 1719.]   Red : *en placard,* imperfect.   [Add. ch.
23,854.]

John, *son of* PHILIP **de Englefeld,**
of Dunsden, co. Oxon.
9483. [A.D. 1368.]   Red, enclosed in mass of creamy-
white : fine.   1 in. [Add. ch. 20,248.]
A shield of arms : barry of six, a lion passant, over all a
label of three points, ENGLEFIELD. Betw. two oak leaves,
slipped. Within a carved gothic panel composed of a cinquefoil and triangle interlaced and ornamented with ball-flowers
along the inner edge.
✠ Sigillū : iohannis : de : englefeld.
Beaded border.

Sir **Thomas Engleffeld,** *Knt.*
9484. [A.D. 1512.]   Red : indistinct.   ⅞ in. [L.F.C., v. 1.]
Shield-shaped : a shield of arms : on a chief a lion passant.

In the field of the shield the initial letters ɢ. ᴛ. ʀ. united by a knot.

Cabled border.

William de Englefeld, *al.* Englesfeld, *of Englefield, etc., co. Berks.*

9485. [*circ.* A.D. 1230.] Creamy-white : fine. 1¼ in. [Add. ch. 20,250.]

A shield of arms of early shape : barry of eight, in chief a lion passant contourné, for *E*NGLEFIELD.

✠ SIGILL' : WILLELMI : DE ENGLESFELD.

9486. [*Temp.* Hen. III.] Green, pale and mottled : imperfect at lower part. [Add. ch. 20,596.]

✠ SIGILL' : WILLEL . . . . . . GLESFELD.

Richard Englys, *al.* Le Engleys, *al.* Lenglis.

9487. [A.D. 1361.] Red : originally fine, edge chipped. 1⁵⁄₁₆ in. [Harl. ch. 49 H. 8.]

A shield of arms, *couché* : ermine on a chief a demi-lion rampant issuing. Crest on a helmet, mantling or lambrequin, and wreath, a plume of three feathers. In the field on each side two roses, slipped and leaved. Within a carved gothic panel, ornamented along the lower edge with small ballflowers.

S' RICARDI LE ENGLEYS.

9488. Sulph. cast from No. 9487. [D.C., F. 415.]

9489. [A D. 1356.] Green : a fragment, showing only the shield of arms. [Harl. ch. 49 H. 5.]

9490. [A.D. 1357.] Green : a fragment. [Harl. ch. 49 H. 6.]

. . . . LE EN . . . .

9491. [A.D. 1357.] Green : imperfect, edge broken off. [Harl. ch. 49 H. 7.]

Richard Englisch.

9492. [14th cent.] Dark-green : fine. 1⁵⁄₁₆ in. [xxxvi. 107.]

A shield of arms : a chevron betw. three lions' heads erased. Betw. two small slipped flowers, and within a carved gothic panel composed of a cinquefoil and triangle interlaced, ornamented with ball-flowers along the inner edge.

✠ SIGILL'. RICARDI · ENGLISCH.

Beaded border.

Robert Le Engynnour, *of Westone, co. Suff.*

9493. [A.D. 1331.] Red : indistinct. ⅞ in. [Harl. ch. 49 H. 2.]

A shield of arms : a fess betw. six fleurs-de-lis. Betw. a crescent and an estoile, and within a pointed gothic quatrefoil.

✠ SINGNETṼ · CH . . SCHEL . . . R . . . (?)

9494. Sulph. cast of No. 9493. [D.C., F. 237.]

Cf. No. 9480.

Hugh Erdiswicke, *al.* Erdyswyke, *of Sandon, co. Staff., Esq.*

9495. [A.D. 1553] Red : imperfect. ⅘ in. [Add. ch. 225.]

A chevron betw. three eagles' heads erased, not on a shield.

Thomas de Erdeswyke, *of co. Staff.*

9496. [A.D. 1407.] Red : originally fine, edge very imperfect. About 1 in. [Woll. ch. v. 31.]

A shield of arms : on a chevron five roundles, ERDESWIKE. Within a carved starlike panel of six points, each having in the cusped interspaces a circular countersunk opening bearing one of the following letters in order N · A · V · T · A · L.

. . . . : erðiistw . . . . . .

Beaded border.

John de Erle, *al.* Erleghe, *Knt.,* son of JOHN DE ERLEGHE, *of co. Linc.*

9497. [A.D. 1334.] Creamy-white, discoloured : indistinct. ⅞ in. [Harl. ch. 44 G. 8.]

A shield of arms : three escallops, two and one, within a bordure engrailed, ERLE. Betw. three estoiles, and within a pointed quatrefoil.

✠ SIGILLVM IOHANNIS DE ERLE.

Beaded borders.

John de Erleghe, *al.* Erleye, *Knt.*

9498. [A.D. 1368.] Red : fine. 1 in. [Add. ch. 29,249.]

A shield of arms : three escallops, two and one, within a bordure engrailed, ERLE. Suspended by a strap from a tree, and within a carved and cusped border.

LE ⦚ SEAL ⦚ IOHAN ⦚ DE ⦚ ERLEGHE.

Carved border.

Another seal.

9499. [A.D. 1373.] Red : injured. ⅞ in. [Harl. ch. 49 H. 15.]

Similar to the preceding seal, No. 9498, but not from same matrix.

Sigill' · Dñs · ioh'is · erleŋe · milit'.

Cabled border.

Ernest-Augustus, *Duke of Cumberland.*
See DUKE OF CUMBERLAND. Nos. 9140, 9141.

John de Erpyngham.

9500. [A.D. 1366.] Green: fine, injured in places. 1 in. [xxxv. 323.]

A shield of arms: an inescutcheon, (perhaps *diapré,* or with illegible charges), within an orle of eight martlets, over all in chief a label of three points, ERPYNGHAM. Betw. two small slipped quatrefoils, and suspended by a strap from a forked tree. Within a carved and traced gothic panel of six points, ornamented with ball-flowers along the inner edge.

Sigill' : ioh'is · De · erpŋngham.

Beaded border.

9501. Plaster cast from No. 9500. [lxxxvi. 33.]

John Erpyngham, *son of* BEATRICE ERPYNGHAM,
of Thornham Parva, co. Suff.

9502. [A.D. 1409.] Green: a small fragment. About ⅞ in. when perfect. [Harl. ch. 49 H. 23.]

A shield of arms: illegible. Within a pointed gothic panel.

. . . . . NES . . .

Thomas, *son of* JOHN **de Erpyngham,** *of co. Norf, Knt.*

9503. [A.D. 1386.] Red: fine, edge injured. 1 in. [Harl. ch. 49 H. 20.]

A shield of arms: an inescutcheon within an orle of eight martlets, in chief over all a label of three points, ERPINGHAM. Betw. two small slipped quatrefoils, and suspended by a strap from a forked tree. Within a carved and traced gothic panel of six points, ornamented with ball-flowers along the inner edge.

Sigill' · thomas · De · erpŋngham.

Beaded border.

This appears to be from the same matrix as that described for JOHN ERPYNGHAM, No. 9502, with the legend altered.

9504. [A.D. 1388.]   Red: very fragmentary.   [Harl. ch. 49 H. 21.]

. . . gill' thom . . . .

In this example the inescutcheon appears to be powdered to represent *or*.

Thomas Erpyngham, *of Edworth, co. Bedf., Knt.*
9505. [A.D. 1394.]   Red : injured. $\frac{4}{10}$ in.   [Add. ch. 35,043.]
An eagle rising, crowned.   In the field an indistinct initial letter.   Cf. Stowe ch. 177, No. 9506.

Thomas de Erpyngham, *of co. Norf., Knt.*
(Same as previous person ?)
9506. [A.D. 1409.]   Red. $\frac{1}{2}$ in.   [Stowe ch. 177.]
On a mount an eagle rising, crowned, perhaps for a crest. In the field the initial letter :—D (?)
Beaded border.

Jordan de Essebi, *son of* WILLIAM DE ESSEBI,
of Lincoln.
9507. [A.D. 1223–1233.]   Dark-green: imperfect, indistinct. [Harl. ch. 49 H. 29.]
A shield of arms of early shape : a bend ermine.

✠ S' . . . . ANI DE ESEB . .

William, *son of* ROBERT ; *al.* **William de Esseby,**
Dominus Willelmus de Magna Esseby, [*co. Ebor.*]
9508. [*Temp.* Hen. III.]   Dark-green : somewhat indistinct.   [Harl. ch. 49 H. 30.]
A shield of arms of early shape : two lions passant in pale, *contournée.*

✠ SIGILL' WILL'I · FIL' ROBERTI.

9509. Sulph. cast. of No. 9508.   [D.C., F. 502.]
9510. [*Temp.* Hen. III.]   Light-brown : imperfect.   [Harl. ch. 49 H. 31.]

✠ S . . . . TI.

Hugh de Essebroc, *of Brokeleya, co. Warw.*
9511. [A.D. 1240–1250.]   White : injured.   1$\frac{1}{4}$ in.   [Cott. ch. xxv. 19.]
A shield of arms of early shape : illegible.

✠ SIG . . . .

Robert, *son of* ROBERT **de Esselington,** *Chev.*

9512. [A.D. 1323.] Green : very imperfect. $\frac{7}{8}$ in. [Harl. ch. 49 H. 33.]

A shield of arms : two bars, in chief three estoiles of six points, for ESLINGTON.   Betw. two dimidiated fleurs-de-lis.

. . . . ESLINGT . .

Symond de Esshe, *of Seaton and Seaham, co. Durh.*

9513. [A.D. 1348.] Red : indistinct in places. $\frac{7}{8}$ in. [Egert. ch. 568.]

Four shields of arms of ancient shape, arranged in cross, meeting at their bases in the centre : 1, chequy, a fess ; 2, an eagle displayed ; 3, a bend embattled counter-embattled ; 4, a fess betw. two double-cotises.   All within a carved gothic quatrefoil.

✠ PAR · CES · SEIGNOVRS · ATAINDREI · HONOVRS.

9514. [A.D. 1333.] Plaster cast from somewhat indistinct impression, attached to a charter.   [lxxxv. 82.]

Peter Domenguez, *Clerk* (?) (*or* **Homenchs.**)

Agnes, *widow of* JOHN **Estbrõk,**
of Dakenham, co. Essex.

9515. [A.D. 1368.] Dark-green : good. $\frac{7}{8}$ in. [Add. ch. 27,372.]

A shield of arms : a trèe (?) on a mount.   Within a pointed quatrefoil.

✠ S'·PETRE DOMENCHS CL'I.

The D very uncertain, perhaps an H.

Seal used by JOHN BOYLLOND, *of Stapleford Abbot, co. Essex.*

9516. [A.D. 1375.] Light-green : discoloured.   [Add. ch. 27,373.]

Richard, *son of* ROGER **de le Estende,** *of Maidwell, Rector of Cliftone juxta Olneye* [*Clifton-Reynes, co. Bucks.*]

9517. [A.D. 1375.] Red : injured. $\frac{7}{8} \times \frac{4}{8}$ in. [Add. ch. 22,196.]

Oval : a shield (of arms?) : a monogram **𝔍𝔄.** betw. three human hearts, from each of which springs a slipped quatrefoil flower.   Suspended by a strap from a trifurcated· tree.

✠ SV . . . . LE CHASTEL LEAL SVY(?)

William, *son of* WILLIAM **de Estfeld,**
of Haugh, co. York.

9518. [A.D. 1355.] Light-brown, semi-transparent. $\frac{7}{8}$ in. [Harl. ch. 49 H. 38.]

A shield of arms : a chevron betw. two bulls' heads cabossed in chief, and a roundle in base. Betw. two wingless wyverns. Above the shield a branch.

IHESVS NAZARENVS REX IVD'.

Elena, *widow of* WILLIAM de Esthalle, *of co. Warw.*

9519. [A.D. 1329.] Red: fine, edge chipped. ¾ in. [Cott. ch. xxv. 20.]

A shield of arms : per pale, *dex.*, chequy a fess ; *sin.*, a lion rampant. Betw. eight small slipped quatrefoils. Within a carved gothic six-foil.

Legend betw. the points.

· S' ... LA ..... OR.

9520. Sulph. cast of No. 9519. [D.C., F. 235.]

H———— Estoutev[ille].

See ADAM BREKESPERE.

Joh. *fil.* Galfridi de Estnest'.

See JOHN *f.* GEOFFREY DE FRIDAY.

Fulcho Le Estraunge, 1st *Baron.*

9521. [A.D. 1301.] Plaster cast from fine impression. $\frac{13}{16}$ in. [lxxxvi. 99.]

A shield of arms: two lions passant guardant in pale, ESTRANGE.

✠ S' FVLCHONIS · LE · ESTRAVNGE.

John Le Estraunge, *al.* Estrange, *son of* JOHN LE ESTRANGE [*of co. Heref.?*]

9522. [*Temp.* Edw. I.] Dark-green : somewhat indistinct. 1⅛ in. [Add. ch. 8068.]

A shield of arms : two lions passant guardant in pale, ESTRANGE.

⊞ S' IOHANNIS LE ESTRAVNGE.

Beaded border.

Robert Esturmi, *of Frelon* [*Fritton*], *co. Norf.; Knt.*

9523. [*Temp.* Edw. I.] Dark-green : edge injured. [Harl. ch. 56 F. 36.]

A shield of arms : a cross engrailed, in chief over all a label of five points.

Legend wanting.

(This seal has been broken from the charter and is now mislaid.)

Stephen Estwicke, *Citizen of London.*

9524. [A.D. 1649.]   Red, covered with paper before impression. ⅜ in. [Add. ch. 27,327.]

An uncertain crest (?)

William de Etone, *of Shorne, co. Kent.*

9525. [A.D. 1338.]   Creamy-white : indistinct in places. ⅞ in. [Harl. ch. 49 H. 44.]

A shield of arms : a saltire betw. four crosses crosslet fitchées.   Background of foliage.   Within a carved sixfoil, ornamented along the inner edge with small ball-flowers.

✠ S' WILL'I • DE • ETONE ⚜ ⚜ ⚜

Beaded border.

9526. Sulph. cast of No. 9525.   [D.C., F. 270.]

William de Etone, *Senr., of Shorne, co. Kent* (*probably same person as last*).

9527. [A.D. 1357.]   Dark-green : originally fine, injured in places. ⅞ in. [Harl. ch. 49 H. 45.]

A shield of arms : as in No. 9525.   Betw. two slipped leaves.   Within a carved panel composed of a triangle and cinquefoil, ornamented along the inner edge with small ball-flowers.

In place of a legend is a wavy scroll of foliage and flowers. Beaded border.

9528. Sulph. cast from No. 9527.   [D.C., F. 405.]

9529. [A.D. 1365.]   Light-brown : edge chipped, injured in places by pressure.   [Harl. ch. 49 H. 46.]

Arthur Evelin, *of Lynn Regis, co. Norf., Esq.*

9530. [A.D. 1675.]   Red : *en placard,* imperfect. About ⅝ × ½ in. [Add. ch. 19,403.]

Oval : a shield of arms : a griffin passant, on a chief a mullet for difference, EVELYN.   Crest, on a helmet and mantling, a griffin of the arms, ducally gorged.

George Evelyn, *of Wotton, co. Surr., Gentl.*

9531. [A.D. 1588.]   Red : imperfect. $\frac{9}{16}$ × $\frac{7}{16}$ in. [Add. ch. 5634.]

Oval : on a wreath, a demi-hind, vulned on the shoulder. Crest of EVELIN.

John Evelyn, *of Kingston-upon-Thames, co. Surr., Gentl.*

9532. [A.D. 1588.]   Red : imperfectly impressed. About ⅞ × ½ in. [Add. ch. 5634.]

Oval : a shield of arms : a griffin passant, on a chief of the second a crescent for difference, EVELIN. Crest on a helmet and ornamental mantling, a griffin passant.

John Evelyn, *of Godstone, co. Surr.*

9533. [A.D. 1635.] Red : injured. About $\frac{3}{8} \times \frac{1}{4}$ in. [Add. ch. 18,944.]

Oval : a griffin segreant, in allusion to the arms of EVELYN. Cabled border.

Hugh de Euer.

9534. [13th cent.] Plaster cast from good impression. 1 in. [lxxxv. 85.]

A shield of arms of early form : quarterly, over all a bendlet.

    ⚜ SIGILL' : HVGONIS : D' · EVER.

Beaded borders.

Cf. the arms of EVERINGHAM, etc.

John de Euer, *Lord of Stokesley, co. York.*

9535. [A.D. 1317.] Plaster cast from fine impression, edge chipped. $\frac{7}{8}$ in. [lxxxv. 84.]

A shield of arms : quarterly, on a bend three escallops. The shield surrounded by foliage, and within a pointed quatrefoil.

    ✳ S' IOH'IS · DE · EVRE · DOMINI · DE STOKESLE . . .

Beaded border.

Ralph de Eure *al.* Euer, *of Durham (?), Knt.*

9536. [A.D. 1375.] Dark-red : fine, edge chipped. $\frac{7}{8}$ in. [Egert. ch. 572.]

A shield of arms : quarterly, on a bend three escallops, EURE. Suspended by a strap from a forked tree. Within a carved panel ornamented along the inner edge with ball-flowers.

    Sigillu : radulphi : de : euer :

Cabled border.

Richard Everard, *of Wisbech, co. Cambr., Esq.*

9537. [A.D. 1565.] Light-brown : injured. $\frac{7}{8} \times \frac{3}{4}$ in. [Harl. ch. 77 F. 53.]

A shield of arms : a fess nebulée, betw. three estoiles, EVERARD. Crest, (without a helmet or mantling) a man's head couped at the shoulders, wearing a cap. Beaded borders.

Amauricus, *or* **Almaric [D'Evereux],** *4th Earl of Gloucester.*
[*ob. circ.* A.D. 1226.]
9538. Dark-green, mottled : fine, imperfect. About 2¾ in.
when perfect. [Harl. ch. 45 C. 28.]
∅. A shield of arms of early shape : barry pily of six
traverse, EVEREUX *of Normandy.*
. . . . ILLVM ALMAR . . . . .
R̵. A smaller round counterseal. 1½ in. A similar shield
of the arms described above.
✠ SECRETVM · A · COMITIS GLOVERNIE.
Beaded borders.
9539. Sulph. casts of No. 9538. [D.C., E. 323, 324.]
9540. Plaster casts of No. 9538. [lxxxv. 86, 87.]

Walter [Devereux], *Earl of Essex, Viscount Hereford, Lord
Ferrers of Charteley, Lord Bourchier and Lovaine, K.G.*
9541. [A.D. 1572.] Red : good, chipped. 1⅛ × 1 in.
[Add. ch. 5841.]
Oval : a shield of arms : quarterly of sixteen quarterings,
1, DEVEREUX, etc. Ensigned with an earl's coronet, and
encircled with a Garter inscribed with the Motto of the Order.

Jodlan de Evermu, *of Hundington, co. Linc., Knt.*
9542. [*Temp.* Hen. III.] Bronze-green : originally fine,
chipped. 1⅛ × 1 in. [Egert. ch. 447.]
Shield-shaped : a shield of arms : a rose of six leaves,
over all in chief a label of three points.
✠ SIGILLVM IOVLANI DE EVE . . V.

John de Evesham, *of co. Bedf., etc.*
9543. [A.D. 1368.] Red : imperfect, injured in places by
pressure. ¾ in. [Cott. ch. xxiv. 11.]
A shield of arms : three round buckles, two and one.
Within a pointed gothic quatrefoil ornamented along the
inner edge with ball-flowers.
⚹ 𝕾igillum : I[ohan]nis : . . . . . . r.

Thomas Evesham, *Citizen and Merchant, of London.*
9544. [A.D. 1376.] Red : injured, imperfect. About 1 in.
when perfect. [Harl. ch. 84 F. 4.]
A shield of arms : illegible. Within a carved gothic
quatrefoil.
𝕾igill' · Thome · eues . . .

John de Evilla, *of Adlingfleet, co. York.*

9545. [Early 14th cent.] Dark-green : fine, fragmentary. App. by a green silk cord. About $1\frac{3}{8} \times 1\frac{1}{4}$ in. when perfect. [Add. ch. 15,511.]

Ø. Shield-shaped : a shield of arms : of which the charges of two fleurs-de-lis in chief only remain.

ᴁ ✿ ᴍ........... ILL ...

℞. A small oval counterseal. About $\frac{7}{8} \times \frac{5}{8}$ in. A bear passant.

✿ SIGILLVM S ....

Frances Ewen, *of Raydon, co. Suff., Widow.*

9546. [A.D. 1714.] Red: *en placard.* About $\frac{5}{8} \times \frac{1}{2}$ in. [Add. ch. 10,592.]

Oval : an ornamentally carved oval shield of arms : two human hearts in fess. Above the shield, an escallop. Below, two hands and arms, clasped.

FIDE : ET : AMORE.

Adrian D'Ewes, *or* Des Ewes.

9547. [16th cent.] Recent impression in red sealing-wax ($\frac{3}{4}$ in.) from a silver seal attached to the document. [Harl. roll O. 9.]

An ornamental shield of arms : a fess vair betw. three quatrefoils. Crest on a helmet and ornamental mantling, a quatrefoil betw. two griffins' heads addorsed.

Beaded border.

Sir Simonds Dewes, *of Stowlangtoft, co. Suff., afterwards Sir* S. D'Ewes, *Bart.*

9548. [A.D. 1627.] Red: indistinct. $\frac{3}{8} \times \frac{1}{4}$ in. [Harl. ch. 57 H. 33.]

Oval : a shield of arms : per fess a pale counterchanged, over all three quatrefoils slipped, two and one, in chief a crescent for difference. Cf. arms of DEWES, or D'EWES, in the following seal.

Another Seal.

9549. [A.D. 1631.] Red. $\frac{3}{4} \times \frac{5}{8}$ in. [Harl. ch. 111 H. 34.]

Oval : a shield of arms of eight quarterings : 1, three quatrefoils pierced, two and one, D'EWES ; 2, per fess nebulée, VAN HULST ; 3, a bend betw. two cotices indented, CLOPTON ; 4, a saltire betw. four quatrefoils, FRANCIS ; 5, per fess a pale counterchanged, over all three quatrefoils slipped, two and one, in chief a crescent for difference ; 6, uncertain ; 7, ROYDON ; 8, KNYVETT.

Beaded border.

9550. [A.D. 1632.] Red :.imperfect and indistinct. [Harl. ch. 49 E. 33.]

9551. [A.D. 1632.] Red : injured by pressure. [Harl. ch. 111 D. 13.]

9552. [A.D. 1632.] Red : fine. [Harl. ch. 57 H. 37.]

9553. [A.D. 1633.] Red: imperfect, well preserved. [Harl. ch. 111 H. 27.]

9554. [A.D. 1641.] Red: injured. [Harl. ch. 111 H. 16.]

9555. [A.D. 1641.] Red : injured by pressure, very indistinct. [Harl. ch. 111 H. 28.]

9556. [A.D. 1641.] Red: cracked. [Harl. ch. 111 H. 29.]

Uncertain Seal.

9557. [A.D. 1647.] Red: very indistinct. [Harl. ch. 111 F. 43.]

Oval : a shield of arms : illegible.

Perhaps same as the shield described above.

Richard Exfolde.
See WALTER MOILE.

William Exham, *of Ewell, co. Surr., Gentl.*
9558. [A.D. 1499–1500.] Red. ¼ in. [Harl. ch. 84 B. 44.]
A shield of arms : a cross engrailed, voided.
Beaded border.

Nicholas de Exton, *of London.*
9559. [A.D. 1377.] Red, discoloured : a fragment. About 1 in. when perfect. [Harl. ch. 49 I. 9.]
A shield of arms : a fess betw. some illegible charges. Within a carved gothic panel.

. . . . **Extoun.**

Robert Eyer, *al.* Eyre, *of Boughton-under-Blean, co. Kent, Esq.*
9560. [A.D. 1567.] Red. 1 1/16 × 9/16 in. [Harl. ch. 78 A. 33.]
Oval : on a wreath a leg erect, in armour, couped at the thigh, per pale, spurred, on the thigh a crescent for difference.
Crest of *E*YRE.
Beaded border.

9561. [A.D. 1568.] Red. [Harl. ch. 78 A. 34.]

John Eyles, *of Hambledon, co. Southt.*
9562. [A.D. 1638.] Red : injured by pressure. [Add. ch. 18,950.]
A shield of arms : illegible (?)

Edmund de Eyncourt, *or* Deyncourt, *Lord of Thurgarton, co. Nott.*
9563. [15th cent.] Plaster cast from good impression. ¾ in. [lxxxv. 41.]
Square : a shield of arms : billettée of six pieces, three, two, and one, on a chief a fess dancettée, and label of four points, for DEYNCOURT. The shield betw. four lions, one at each corner, passant counterpassant.
Beaded border.

William de Eyncourt.
9564. [A.D. 1343.] Red : fine, injured at parts, imperfect. 1 in. [Harl. ch. 57 G. 9.]
A shield of arms, *couché* : a fess dancettée betw. ten billets, four in chief, and three, two, and one in base. Crest on a helmet, and lambrequin ermine, a tall cap betw. two horns.
SIGILL . . . ILELMI . . EYNC . . . .
Cabled borders.
9565. Sulph. cast of No. 9564. [D.C., F. 283.]

William Deyncourt, *Lord of Granby, co. Notts.*
9566. [A.D. 1363.] Red : fine fragment. [Harl. ch. 49 F. 7.]
A shield of arms : a fess dancettée betw. ten billets, four in chief, and three, two, and one in base. Suspended by a strap from a boss, and betw. a series of small roses. Within a carved eight-foil, ornamented with small ball-flowers along the inner edge.
Legend wanting.

Edmund Eyre, *of King's Swynford, co. Staff.*
9567. [A.D. 1579.] Red : a fragment. About ¾ in. when perfect. [Add. ch. 24,483.]
An armed leg, couped at the thigh, wearing a spur-rowel. Betw. the initial letters E. [E.]

William Eyr, *of cos. Essex and Suff.*
9568. [A.D. 1488.] Red. ½ × ¾ in. [Harl. ch. 48 D. 27.]
Oval : a cinquefoil, in allusion to the arms of EYRE.

Peter de Eitone, *dominus* de Eyton, *co. Salop*.
9569. [*Temp.* Edw. I.] Dark-green: fine. 1 × ⅛ in.
[Stowe ch. 167.]
Shiéld-shaped: a shield of arms: per pale, *dex.*, fretty, *sin.*, two bars, EYTON. (Usually borne quarterly.)

☒ S' PETRI DE EITONE ᴀ

Beaded border.

F

William Faber, *of Charwelton, co. Northt.*
9570. [A.D. 1326.] Dark-green: good. 1⅜/16 × ¾ in. [Harl. ch. 84 E. 48.]
Oval: a shield of arms: a leopard's face, enraged. Suspended by a strap from a trifurcated tree.

☒ S' : IE : SV : TESTE : D' : LVPARD.

Beaded borders.
9571. Sulph. cast of No. 9570. [D.C., F. 222.]

John Faireclough, *Senr., of Weston juxta Baldock,*
co. Herts., Esq.
9572. [A.D. 1628.] Red. About 9/16 × ½ in. [Add. ch. 36,289.]
Oval: a fleur-de-lis, in reference to the arms of FAIRCLOUGH, *q.v.*

John Faireclough, *son of* THOMAS FAIRECLOUGH,
of Fairclough Hall, in Weston, co. Herts., Esq.
9573. [A.D. 1628.] Red: very imperfect. About ⅝ × ½ in. when perfect. [Add. ch. 36,288.]
Oval: a shield of arms: a lion rampant betw. three fleurs-de-lis, FAIRCLOUGH. Crest on a helmet, ornamental mantling, and wreath, a demi-lion rampant, holding betw. the paws a fleur-de-lis.
Cabled border.
Another Seal.
9574. [A.D. 1637.] Red: imperfect. ⅝ × ½. in. [Add. ch. 36,292.]
Oval: a shield of arms: a lion rampant, betw. [three] fleurs-de-lis, FAIRCLOUGH.
9575. [A.D. 1652.] Red. [Add. ch. 36,303.]
9576. [A.D. 1652.] Red: injured. [Add. ch. 36,305.]
9577. [A.D. 1660.] Red: very indistinct. [Add. ch. 36,314.]

Litton, *or* Lytton, Fairclough, *son of* THOMAS FAIRCLOUGH, *of Fairclough Hall, in Weston, co. Herts.*

9578. [A.D. 1637.] Red. $\frac{3}{8} \times \frac{1}{2}$ in. [Add. ch. 36,292.]
Oval : a shield of arms : a lion rampant betw. three fleurs-de-lis, FAIRCLOUGH. Cf. the somewhat similar seal of JOHN FAIRCLOUGH, on this deed, No. 9574.
Cabled border.

9579. [A.D. 1642.] Red : very indistinct. [Add. ch. 36,298.]

Mary, *wife of* THOMAS Faireclough.

9580. [A.D. 1628.] Red. [Add. ch. 36,289.]
Seal as described for THOMAS FAIRECLOUGH, q.v.

Sarah, *wife of* JOHN Fairclough.

9581. [A.D. 1652.] Red. [Add. ch. 36,303.]
Oval : shield of arms. See seal of JOHN FAIRECLOUGH in the same charter.

Thomas Faireclough, *son of* JOHN FAIRECLOUGH, *of Weston, co. Herts.*

9582. [A.D. 1628.] Red. $\frac{1}{4} \times \frac{3}{8}$ in. [Add. ch. 36,289.]
Oval : a shield of arms : a fleur-de-lis. In reference to the arms of FAIRCLOUGH.

Another Seal.

9583. [A.D. 1631.] Red. $\frac{3}{8} \times \frac{1}{2}$ in. [Add. ch. 36,291.]
Oval : a shield of arms : a lion rampant betw. three fleurs-de-lis, FAIRCLOUGH.
Cabled border.

Nicholas de Faireforde.

9584. [A.D. 1353.] Plaster cast from fine impression. $\frac{7}{8}$ in. [lxxxv. 91.]
A shield of arms : paly of four ——— and ermine, on a chief three roundles. Within a carved gothic triangle with ogee points.

⚬ S' ⚬ NICH'I__I$I ⚬ DE ⚬ FAIRE *___$ FORDE ⚬I$I⚬

Brian Fairfax, *of St. Margaret's, Westminster, Esq.*

9585. [A.D. 1703.] Red : *en placard*, imperfectly impressed. About $\frac{3}{4} \times \frac{5}{8}$ in. [Add ch. 13,633.]

Oval: an ornamentally carved shield of arms: three bars gemel, over all a lion rampant, FAIRFAX.
[In the field over the shield the motto:—
FARE · FAO.]
9586. [A.D. 1703.] Red: imperfect. [Add. ch. 13,634.]

Seal used by CHARLOTTE, *wife of the above.*

9587. [A.D. 1703.] Red: imperfect. [Add. ch. 13,633.]
9588. [A.D. 1703.] Another. [Add. ch. 13,634.]

Seal used by BRIAN, *son of the above.*

9589. [A.D. 1703.] Another. [Add. ch. 13,634.]
This shows the motto:—
FARE · FAC.

Seal used by FERDINAND, *son of the above.*

9590. [A.D. 1703.] Another. [Add. ch. 13,634.]

Guy Farefax, *Knt., Justice of the King's Bench.*
9591. [A.D. 1480.] Red: injured by pressure. From a ring with marks of the setting. $\frac{3}{8}$ in. [Harl. ch. 83 H. 17.]
A goat's head erased. Crest of FAIRFAX. Within a cabled border cinquefoiled.
9592. [A.D. 1480.] Red: very indistinct. [Harl. ch. 84 I. 52.]

Sir **Thomas Fairfax**, *of Denton, co. York, Knt.*
9593. [A.D. 1615.] Red: injured by pressure. $\frac{9}{16}$ × $\frac{1}{2}$ in. [Add. ch. 1792.]
Oval: on a wreath, a lion's head erased, etc. Crest of FAIRFAX.

Margery, *widow of* THOMAS **Fairsted,**
of Denham, co. Buck.
9594. [A.D. 1368.] Green. [Harl. ch. 85 D. 28.]
See the seal of the BAILIFFS OF DORCHESTER, No. 4876.

Ralph Fakone, *of Otteley, co. Suff.*
9595. [A.D. 1359.] Green: imperfect, indistinct. About $\frac{3}{4}$ in. [Add. ch. 10,198.]
A shield of arms: a chevron betw. three lozenge buckles. Within a carved gothic quatrefoil, and a cordon of small quatrefoils.
D' DEL F...(?)

Edmond Faldo, *of London, Gentl.*
9596. [A.D. 1621.]   Red : injured by pressure, indistinct.
⅜ × ¼ in. [Add. ch. 35,204.]
Oval : a shield of arms : three bucks' heads cabossed, two
and one, in the fess point a mullet for difference, FALDO.
Cabled border.
Cf. Add. ch. 35,845.

Richard Faldo, *of Cardington, co. Bedf., Gentl.*
9597. [A.D. 1590.]   Red : indistinct.   About ¼ in.   [Add.
ch. 35,841.]
Oval : an uncertain shield of arms (?)

Richard Faldo, *of Cardington, co. Bedf., Gentl.*
9598. [A.D. 1595.]   Red.   ⅜ × ¼ in.   [Add. ch. 35,845.]
Oval : a shield of arms : three stags' heads cabossed, two
and one, in the fess point a mullet for difference, FALDO.
Beaded border.
Cf. Add. ch. 35,204.

Robert Faldo, *of North Mimms, co. Herts., Esq.*
8599. [A.D. 1621.]   Red: injured.   About ¼ × ⅜ in.   [Add.
ch. 35,204.]
Oval : on a wreath, three arrows, two in saltire and one in
pale, enfiled with a ducal coronet.   Crest of FALDO.

James Fale, *of Hildercleye. co. Suff., Yeoman.*
9600. [A.D. 1568.]   Red : very indistinct.   About ¼ in.
[Stowe ch. 282.]
A stag at gaze ; perhaps a crest.

William de Falencurt.
[? Fallencourt, dioc. Rouen, Normandy.]
9601. [13th cent.]   Plaster cast from fine impression.
1¼ in. [lxxxv. 89]
A shield of arms : fretty a chief, in the dexter chief a
mullet.
       ✠ SIGILL' WILL'I : DE FALENCVRT.
Probably a foreign seal.

Nicholas de Falsham, *of Peasenhall, co. Suff., Knt.*
9602. [*Temp.* Edw. I.]   Light-brown, varnished : chipped
at edge, partly flaked.   About 1 × ¾ in.   [Harl. ch. 83 E.
33.]

Oval : a shield of arms : on a bend three martlets. Suspended by a strap from a trifurcated tree.

⚹ S' NICHOLAI D' FALSHAM.

Beaded borders.

Cf. Add. ch. 9831, A.D. 1280.

9603. Sulph. cast. from No. 9602. [D.C., E. 395.]

Sir **Francis Fane,** *of Badsell, co. Kent. Knt.*

9604. [A.D. 1608.]   Red : fine.   ⅜ in.   [Harl. ch. 77 C. 46.]

On a wreath, a bull passant, collared and chained, the chain passing betw. the forelegs, over the back, down betw. the hindlegs, and terminating with two staples.   On the shoulder a label of three points for difference.   Supporter of FANE.

Powdered field.   Beaded border.

9605. Sulph. cast of No. 9604. [xcviii. 45.] ·

Another Seal as Commissioner of Sewers.

9606. [A.D. 1618.]   Red : indistinct, injured by pressure ; cracked.   ⅜ × ¼ in.   [Add. ch. 33,104.]

Oval: out of a ducal coronet (?) a griffin's head and wings erect.

Beaded border.

9607. [A.D. 1618.]   Red : chipped ; imperfect on the r. h. side.   [Add. ch. 33,105.]

9608. [A.D. 1618.]   Red : injured ; indistinct.   [Add. ch. 33,108.]

9609. [*n. d.*]   Red : injured by pressure in the lower part. [Add. ch. 33,134.]

George Fane, *of Tudeley, co. Kent, Esq.*

9610. [A.D. 1569.]   Red.   ¾ × ⅝ in.   [Harl. ch. 77 A. 23.]

Oval : a carved shield of arms : three gauntlets, two, and one, FANE.

Cabled border.

Cf. Harl. ch. 77 H. 22.

9611. Sulph. cast of No. 9610.   [xcviii. 46.]

Thomas Fane.
Seal used by WALTER WALLER,
of Spelhurst, co. Kent, Esq.

9612. [A.D. 1568.]   Dark-brown : imperfect, indistinct. [Harl. ch. 80 H. 45.]

An ornamental shield of arms : three gauntlets, two and one, FANE.

Thomas Fane, *Senr., of co. Kent.*
Seal used by WILLIAM LAWRENCE, *Senr.,*
of Yanworth, co. Glouc.

9613. [A.D. 1568.]   Red : injured by pressure.   ¾ in.
[Harl. ch. 79 A. 10.]

A gauntlet holding a broken sword.   Crest of FANE.
Beaded border.

Thomas Fane, *of Hunton, co. Kent, Esq.*

9614. [A.D. 1578.]   Red : cracked, imperfect.   About
⅝ × ¼ in.   [Harl. ch. 78 A. 42.]

Oval : a shield of arms : three gauntlets, two and one, in
chief a crescent for difference, FANE.   Above the shield a
floral device.

Cabled border.

9615. [A.D. 1578.]   Another : good.   [Harl. ch. 78 A. 43.]

Seal used by HENRY FANE, *of Hadlow, co. Kent, Esq.*

9616. [A.D. 1578.]   Another : good.   [Harl. ch. 78 A. 44.]

Thomas Fane, *of Burston, co. Kent, Esq.,*
Lieut. of Dover Castle.

9617. [A.D. 1580.]   Red : good.   ⅞ × ¾ in.   [Harl. ch. 77
B. 3.]

Oval : a shield of arms of eight quarterings : 1, three
gauntlets, two and one, FANE ; 2, DE LA DENE ; 3, DE LA
LEAKE ; 4, BOWEN ; 5, FITZ-ELLIS ; 6, PERESALL ; 7, BID-
OLPH ; 8, PEDWARDEN *al.* BADESHILL.   Crest on a helmet,
ornamental mantling, and wreath, FANE.

9618. [A.D. 1580.]   Red : indistinct in places.   [Harl. ch.
77 B. 5.]

9619. [A.D. 1589.]   Red : good.   [Harl. ch. 77 H. 46.]

Seal used by THOMAS LAWRENCE,
of Cricklade, co. Wilts., Gentl.

9620. [A.D. 1610.]   Red : imperfect.   [Harl. ch. 77 C.
49.]

⋅ Thomas Fanshawe, *of London, Esq.,*
Remembrancer of the Court of Exchequer.

9621. [A.D. 1572.]   Red : indistinct in places.   ¾ × ⅝ in.
[Harl. ch. 77 F. 59.]

Oval: a shield of arms: two chevrons ermine, betw. three fleurs-de-lis, FANSHAW. Crest on a helmet, ornamental mantling, and wreath, a dragon's head erased, charged with two chevrons.

Thomas Fanshaw, *K.B., Viscount Fanshaw,*
of Donomore, Ireland.
9622. [A.D. 1688.] Red, covered with paper before impression: indistinct, injured by pressure. $\frac{3}{4} \times \frac{5}{8}$ in. [Add. ch. 29,533.]

Oval: a shield of arms: a chevron betw. three fleurs-de-lis, FANSHAW. Ensigned with a viscount's coronet.

William de Farendon, *Chev.,*
of the King's Retinue in Normandy.
9623. [A.D. 1378.] Red: originally fine, very imperfect. [Harl. ch. 49 I. 21.]

For description of this seal see that described for WILLIAM DE HERRYES, Add. ch. 7909. The charge of three cinquefoils is also borne by the family of FARRINGTON.

William de Farlay, *of Uttoxeter, co. Staff.*
9624. [A.D. 1400.] Red: very indistinct. $\frac{15}{16}$ in. [Stowe ch. 116.]

A shield of arms: the implements of the Passion of Our Lord. Suspended by a strap, and betw. two palm branches.
Legend injured by pressure.

✠ D . . . . . . Y . . . . RI . .

See No. 9452 for a shield of the Passion differently displayed.

Hatton Farmer, *of Northampton, co. Northt., Gentl.*
9625. [A.D. 1658.] Red: injured by pressure. About $\frac{1}{2} \times \frac{7}{16}$ in. [Add. ch. 6130.] ·

Oval: a leopard passant guardant. Crest of FARMER.

George Farncombe, *of Lewes, co. Suss., Tailor.*
9626. [A.D. 1660.] Red: very indistinct. About $\frac{11}{16} \times \frac{9}{16}$ in. [Add. ch. 30,645.]

Oval: a shield of arms: three griffins' heads erased, two and one, within a bordure engrailed. Crest on a helmet, mantling and wreath, a (griffin's?) head.

Seal used by BARBARA, *wife of the above.*

9627. [A.D. 1660.]   Another.   [Add. ch. 30,645.]

Another Seal.

9628. [A.D. 1674.]   Red: indistinct.   About $\frac{5}{8} \times \frac{1}{4}$ in. [Add. ch. 30,652.]

Oval: an uncertain shield of arms: a bend, etc.

Robert de Farnham.
Seal used by RICHARD GREGORY,
of Beaconsfield, co. Bucks.

9629. [A.D. 1386.]   Red: indistinct. $\frac{3}{4}$ in.   [Harl. ch. 45 H. 27.]

A shield of arms: a chevron betw. some illegible charges. Within a traced border.

✠ SIGILLVM · RO . . . TI · DE ·FARNHAM.

Robert Farrers.
See ROGER PRYDEAUX.

Michael Farthinge, *of Butterwick, co. York.*

9630. [A.D. 1597.]   Red: very indistinct. $\frac{3}{8} \times \frac{5}{8}$ in. [Add. ch. 18,874.]

Oval: an ornamental shield of arms: illegible.

Arthur Farwell, *of Lincoln's Inn, co. Midd., Esq.*

9631. [A.D. 1651.]   Red: *en placard.* $\frac{9}{16} \times \frac{7}{16}$ in.   [Cott. ch. xxiv. 59. (2).]

Oval: a shield of arms: on a chevron betw. three escallops, a cinquefoil for difference, FARWELL.

9632. [A.D. 1651.]   Black: *en placard.*   [Cott. ch. xxiv. 59 (3).]

Hugh Fastolf.

9633. [14th cent.]   Sulph. cast from fine impression.   1 in. [D.C., F. 366.]

A shield of arms: quarterly, on a bend three escallops, FASTOLF. Within a carved panel composed of three points in triangle and five cusps, ornamented with ball-flowers along the inner edge.

Legend betw. the points.

𝕾𝖎𝖌𝖎𝖑𝖑𝖚𝖒 ⚭ : 𝖍𝖚𝖌𝖔𝖓𝖎𝖘 : ⚭ ⚭ : 𝕱𝖆𝖘𝖙𝖔𝖑𝖋 : ⚭

Cabled border.

John Fastolf, *of cos. Norf. and Suff., Knt.*

9634. [A.D. 1435.]   Red: indistinct. $\frac{1}{2} \times \frac{7}{16}$ in.   [Cott. ch. v. 3.]

Oval signet: on a helmet, an oak-tree.   Crest of FAL-STOFE.   In the field the motto:—

fur · ma · fault ꝫ .(?)

‾Cabled border.

9635. [A.D. 1435.]   Red: very indistinct.   [Cott. ch. v. 22.]

John Fastolfe.
Seal used by JOHN LANE, *of Campsey, co. Suff., Gentl.*

9636. [A.D. 1590.]   Red: a fragment.   About $\frac{1}{2}$ in. when perfect.   [Add. ch. 15,614.]

An ornamental shield of arms: quarterly, [1], 4, quarterly, FASTOLE; 2, [3], a fret.

Beaded border.

Walter Fauconberg, 1*st Baron Fauconberg.*

9637. [A.D. 1301.]   Plaster cast from chipped impression, indistinct in places. $1\frac{1}{8}$ in.   [lxxxv. 90.]

A shield of arms: in chief a label of three points, inverted (?) Betw. three wavy sprigs of foliage.   Within a cusped bordure or rosette of six points.

✠ SIGILLVM : WAL[. . . . D]E FAVCVMB'GE.

Beaded borders.

G. Faune (?)
Seal used by WILLIAM DICKINSON, *al.* DICKENSON,
of Apleton, co. Berks, Clerk.

9638. [A.D. 1624.]   Red. $\frac{11}{16} \times \frac{13}{16}$ in.   [Harl. ch. 75 H. 43.]

A shield of arms: a buglehorn betw. three crescents, FAWNES.

Beaded border.

Richard Fawcett, *of Wirksworth, co. Derb., Gentl.*

9639. [A.D. 1663.]   Red: indistinct. $\frac{3}{4} \times \frac{5}{8}$ in.   [Woll. ch. xi. 107.]

Oval: a shield of arms: on a bend three dolphins embowed, in chief a crescent for difference.   Cf. the arms of MAWLE of Suffolk.

Carved border.

Robert Fawkener, *of co. Leic.*

9640. [A.D. 1395.]   Red. $\frac{7}{8}$ in.   [Add. ch. 24,215.]

VOL. II.   3 E

A shield of arms : three falcons, two and one, in chief a crescent enclosing a mullet, perhaps for a difference. Within a pointed trefoil ornamented with ball-flowers along the inner edge.

Sigill' · roberti · fauconer.

John Faukes, *of Bandon, co. Surr.*

9641. [A.D. 1379.]   Red : a fragment.   About ¾ in. when perfect.   [Add. ch. 22,873.]

A shield of arms : uncertain.   Betw. two oak leaves slipped. Within a carved panel.

SIGILL' · IOH . . . .

Henry Fawkener, *of Westborough Green, co. Suss.*

9642. [A.D. 1592.]   Red.   ¾ in.   [Add. ch. 30,896.]

An ornamental shield of arms : a dexter hand in base, couped at the wrist contournée, on it a falcon.   Betw. two initial letters, H. F.

Beaded border.

Joh. Fawkner.
See NICHOLAS TURNOR.

Thomas Faulkner, *of Lewes, co Suss., Blacksmith.*

9643. [A.D. 1691.]   Red : *en placard.*   ⅜ × ¼ in.   [Add. ch. 30,672.]

Oval : a carved shield of arms : a lion rampant.

9644. [A.D. 1691.]   Another.   [Add. ch. 30,673.]

The same, used by MARY, *wife of the above.*

9645. [A.D. 1691.]   Another.   [Add. ch. 30,672.]
9646. [A.D. 1691.]   Another.   [Add. ch. 30,673.]

William Fawkener, *of Wartling, co. Suss.*

9647. [A.D. 1592.]   Red : a fragment.   About ½ × ⅜ in. [Add. ch. 30,896.]

Oval : on a wreath a man's head, couped at the neck, the hair tied with a fillet.

Johanna Fawnchall.
See JOHN DUBU . . .

Henricus de Feckenham, *of Kidderminster, co. Worc.*

9648. [A.D. 1336.] Green. ¾ in. [Egert. ch. 462.]

A shield of arms: three bars. Cf. arms of FAKENHAM or FECKENHAM, barry of ten, six escutcheons.

✡ S' HENRICI ....

John, *son of* WILLIAM **Feild.**

9649. [A.D. 1621.] Red: injured, indistinct. ½ in. [Add. ch. 35,439.]

On a wreath, a griffin segreant.

William Feild, *Citizen and Merchant-Taylor of London.*

9650. [A.D. 1621.] Red. ⅝ in. [Add. ch. 35,439.]

On a mount or wreath, a horse. In the field above a monogram of the initial letters, W F.

George de Filbrigge, *al.* **Felbrigge,**
of Mildenhale, co. Suff.

9651. [A.D. 1375.] Red: fine, edge injured. 1 in. [Harl. ch. 51 E. 10.]

A shield of arms, *couché*: a lion rampant. Crest on a helmet and lambrequin, out of a ducal coronet a garb. Within a carved gothic panel, ornamented with ball-flowers along the inner edge.

S' : georgii : : Felbrigge.

9652. Sulph. cast of No. 9651. [D.C., F. 491.]

Simon [de] Felebrygge, *al.* **Felbrigg,**
of cos. Linc., Warw., etc., Knt.

9653. [A.D. 1406.] Red: imperfect. About 1 in. when perfect. [Harl. ch. 49 I. 30.]

A shield of arms, *couché*: a lion rampant, FELBRIGGE. Crest on a helmet and lambrequin, out of a ducal coronet, a plume of ostrich feathers. Supporters [two?] demi-lions. Within a carved gothic panel, ornamented with ball-flowers along the inner edge.

Sig' : simonis : de : felbrigg'.

9654. [A.D. 1435.] Red: imperfect. [Harl. ch. 49 I. 31.]

Sig' : simonis : de : felbrigg'.

9655. Sulph. cast of No. 9654. [D.C., G. 199.]

9656. Detached, red: imperfect edges. [xxxv. 325.]

Sig' : s.... nis : de : ...lbrigg'.

Simon Felbrygge, *of Basyngham, etc., co. Norf., Knt.*
9657. [A.D. 1434.]   Red.   From a ring with mark of
the setting. $\frac{5}{8}$ × $\frac{1}{2}$ in.   [Stowe ch. 176.]
Oval: a fetterlock, enclosing the initial letters, **s. f.**   For
a badge.
Beaded border.
9658. [A.D. 1431.]   Red.   [Harl. ch. 56 G. 48.]
9659. [A.D. 1442.]   Red.   [Stowe ch. 192.]

William, *son of* THOMAS **de Fellegh,**
of South Buckland Manor, co. Dev.
9660. [A.D. 1328.]   Green: very indistinct. $\frac{3}{4}$ in.   [Add.
ch. 29,046.]
A shield of arms: a fess vairé betw. six crosses formée,
three, two, and one, FILLEIGH.   Within a carved gothic
quatrefoil.
LE · EINLEVMENT TEINDRA : TVT : LÊT (?)
Beaded border.
9661. [A.D. 1342.]   Green, discoloured: very indistinct.
[Add. ch. 29,059.]

William de Felmyngham.
See WILLIAM BRAD.

Alianora Felton.
See ALIANORA, *widow of* ROBERT DE UFFORD.

Sir **Henry Felton,** *of Playford, co. Suff., Bart.*
9662. [A.D. 1651.]   Red: very indistinct, imperfect.   [Add.
ch. 5111.]
A shield of arms: illegible.

Sir **Henry Felton,** *Bart.*
See CHRISTOPHER MILTON.

Simon de Feltone.
9663. [14th cent.]   Red: from the matrix. $\frac{7}{8}$ in.   [xlvii.
1433.]
A shield of arms: on a chevron betw. three cinquefoils
pierced five quatrefoils.   Above the shield the initial letter s.
and a merchant's mark,   Within two carved trefoils interlaced.

Legend betw. the points :—
> S ⁑ SIMO—NIS • DE ⁑ • FELTONE.

Beaded border.

Laing's *MS. Catal.*, No. 535.

John de Fencotes.

9664. [A.D. 1375.] Plaster cast from chipped impression. 1 in. [lxxxv. 73.]

A shield of arms : on a chevron engrailed, three cinquefoils. Suspended from a forked tree and within a carved gothic panel.

𝕾𝖎𝖌𝖎𝖑𝖑𝖚𝖒 : 𝖎𝖔𝖍'𝖎𝖘 : 𝖉𝖊 : 𝖋𝖊𝖓𝖈𝖔𝖙𝖊𝖘.

Richard Fenrother, *of co. Linc.*

9665. [A.D. 1495.] Red : very imperfect. About $\frac{5}{8} \times \frac{1}{2}$ in. when perfect. [Harl. ch. 51 G. 27.]

Oval : a shield of arms : a chevron betw. three yokes or fetters. In the field the initial letter R . . .

From a ring with mark of the setting.

Thomas de Fentone, *of Thorp-sur-le-Hille, co. York.*

9666. [A.D. 1362.] Green, discoloured : indistinct. $\frac{5}{8}$ in. [Add. ch. 20,556.]

A shield of arms : a cross betw. four fleurs-de-lis, FENTON.
> S' THOM . . . .

Cf. Add. ch. 20,603; A.D. 1359.

D. William de Fentun.

9667. [13th cent.] Plaster cast from fine impression. $1\frac{1}{8} \times \frac{7}{8}$ in. [xcii. 90.]

Shield-shaped : a shield of arms : three crescents, two and one, FENTON.
> ✠ S' DOMINI : WILELMI : DE : FENTVN.

Beaded borders.

Cf. xlvii. 1129.

Thomas Fenys, *Knt., Lord Dacre, of co. Suss.*

9668. [A.D. 1508.] Red. $\frac{1}{4}$ in. [Add. ch. 8107.]

Square signet : an escallop, in allusion to the arms of DACRE.

Beaded border.

Cf. Add. ch. 20,112, A.D. 1529.

William **Fermager**, *Knt.*

9669. [A.D. 1400-1.] Cast in red composition from imperfect impression. 1 in. [lxxv. 78.]

A shield of arms : ermine, two chevrons, FERMER, etc. Within a carved cinquefoil panel.

⚹ 𝔖igïllum : ꡳillelmï : . ermager . . . . .

John **Fermer**, *Chev.*

9670. [A.D. 1353.] Plaster cast from fine impression. 1 in. [lxxxvi. 3.]

. A shield of arms : ermine, a chevron betw. three pierced six-foils, FERMOUR. Within a finely-carved gothic rosette.

✠ SIGILLVM ⚶✦✦ IOHANNIS ⚶✦✦ FERMER.

Walter of the **ffermerye**, *of Saltrey, co. Hunt.*

9671. [A.D. 1343.] Light-brown, discoloured : indistinct. ⅞ in. [Add. ch. 34,062.]

A shield of arms : a chev. betw. three uncertain charges. Legend illegible.

Alianora de **Ferrariis**, *? of Stebbing, co. Essex, widow of* D. WILLIAM BAGOT, *Knt.*

9672. [A.D. 1326.] Red : fine. ⅞ in. [Add. ch. 19,988.]

A shield of arms : per pale, *dex.*, vairé, a bordure semeé of horseshoes, FERRARS ; *sin.*, a fess betw. eight billets, three, two, two and one, LOVAINE (?). Betw. three eagles displayed, in allusion to the arms of BAGOT, viz. a bend betw. three eagles displayed. Within a moulded quatrefoil with a mullet in each of the spandrils.

Henry de **Ferrars**, *Lord of Groby, co. Leic.*

9673. [A.D. 1331.] Plaster cast from fine but chipped impression. 1½ in. [lxxxv. 99.]

A shield of arms, *couché*: seven mascles, three, three, and one. Crest on a helmet and lambrequin, on a chapeau a wing erect. Betw. two wavy sprigs of roses. Within a carved gothic panel ornamented with ball-flowers along the inner edge.

𝔖 : ꡳe . . . . arus : ꝺñi : . . . . . oꝰp.

Beaded border.

Johanna de **Ferres**.

9674. [A.D. 1367.] Plaster cast from fine but chipped impression. 1¼ in. [lxxxv. 97.]

A shield of arms : per pale, *dex.*, vairé, FERRARS ; *sin.*, three (conies ?) passant in pale. Within a carved gothic panel, charged on the tracery with four lozenge-shaped shields of arms in cross, vairé, a mullet for difference.
Legend betw. the points :—
SIGILL'V ⚜ IOHANNE ⚜ . . . . . FERRES.
˙Cf. Johanna, daughter of Lucas, Lord Poynings, Nichols' *Leicestersh.*, vol. iv. p. 633.*

John de Ferrers, *òf Stapelford Manor, co. Leic.*
9675. [*Temp.* Edw. I.]   Red : originally fine, very imperfect. ⅞ in. [Harl. ch. 49 I. 43.]
An eagle displayed, charged on the breast with a shield of arms : vairé, FERRARS.
. . . . Є : FΙЄJRΕRΕS.
9676. Sulph. cast from No. 9675. [D.C., E. 318.]

John de Ferrariis.
9677. [A.D. 1347.]   Plaster cast from chipped impression. 1¼ in. [lxxxv. 96.]
A shield of arms, *couché* : vairé, FERRARS. Crest on a helmet, and lambrequin vairé, out of a ducal coronet. a plume of feathers. In a traced gothic panel.
S' · iohanni . . . . ariis.

Martin de Ferers.
9678. [A.D. 1371.]   Brown : indistinct. ¾ in. [Harl. ch. 54 C. 54.]
A shield of arms : on a bend three horseshoes. Betw. the letters I. s. n. t. In a carved gothic quatrefoil.
Legend betw. the points :—
S martini ferrerf.
Beaded border.

Robert de Ferrariis, *Earl of Derby.*
Secretum.
9679. [A.D. 1254.]   Plaster cast from fine impression. ⅞ in. [lxxxv. 95.]
A shield of arms : vairé, for FERRERS. From a tree, betw. two finely-drawn wavy branches of foliage and flowers.
✠ S' SECRETI DE FERRARIIS.
Beaded borders.
Cf. No. 5908, *rev.*

Thomas de Ferrers, *Knt.* (?)

9680. [A.D. 1278.] Plaster cast from fine impression. ¾ in. [lxxxvi. 2.]

A circular shield of arms: barry of six, ermine and ———, over all a bugle-horn, stringed. Within a cordon or bordure of roses, charged also with two lions passant guardant of ENGLAND and as many castles of CASTILE, in cross.

Thomas de Ferrariis, *son of* WILLIAM DE FERRARIIS, *Lord of Groby.*

9681. [A.D. 1435.] Red: fine, chipped at base. 1⅛ in. [Egert. ch. 473.]

A shield of arms, *couché*: seven mascles, three, three and one. Crest on a helmet, ornamental mantling, and chapeau, a horse statant.

✠ ⚜ ꙅ' tɦome · ferrers · ꝺe · groby ⚜ ✠

Beaded borders.

9682. [A.D. 1447.] Plaster cast from fine but chipped impression. [lxxxvi. 1.]

William de Ferrars, *5th Earl of Ferrars* (?)

9683. [Before A.D. 1191.] Greenish-white, varnished: edge wanting. About 2½ in. when perfect. [Egert. ch. 436.]

A tall early-shaped shield of arms, vairé, FERRARS.

Legend wanting.

Cf. Nos. 5916–5921.

William de Ferariis, *Lord of Groby.*

9684. [A.D. 1307.] Plaster cast from fine impression. [lxxxv. 98.]

A double-headed eagle displayed, charged on the breast with a shield of arms: seven mascles, three, three, and one, FERRERS. Within a pointed gothic quatrefoil.

✠ SIGILL' · WILL'I · DE · FERARIIS.

William de Ferrars, *Lord of Groby.*

9685. [A.D. 1364.] Red: originally fine, very imperfect. 1⅛ in. [Harl. ch. 83 E. 35.]

A shield of arms, *couché*: seven mascles, three, three, and one, FERRARS *of Groby*. Crest on a helmet, lambrequin, and chapeau, a pair of wings erect. Within a carved panel ornamented with small ball-flowers along the inner edge.

[ꙅ'] · ꝺn̄i : will'i ꝺ'ffrariis : ꝺn̄i : ꝺe · ꬶrob[y].

9686. Sulph. cast of No. 9685. [D.C., F. 435.]

William de Ferrars, *Lord of Groby, ob.* A.D. 1445.
9687. Plaster cast from fine but imperfect impression. 2 in. [lxxxv. 100.]
A shield of arms: seven mascles, three, three, and one, FERRERS *of Groby.* Crest on a helmet, ornamental mantling and chapeau, a horse statant.

    .... **will'i : de : .... d[ñi] : de : groby** *w*
Cabled borders.

Cf. Nichols' *Leicestersh.*, vol. iv., p. 633*.

William de Ferrers.
See ROBERT HOLIWOD.

Amphillis Ferrours, *of St. Margaret's, Westminster.*
9688. [A.D. 1630.] Red. $\frac{5}{8}$ in. [Cott. ch. I. 3 (4).]
A shield of arms: on a chevron betw. three crescents a mullet for difference.
Beaded border.
9689. [A.D. 1631.] Red: much injured by pressure. [Cott. ch. xxiv. 37.]

John de Feryng, *Parson of the Church of Great Fransham, co. Norf.*
9690. [A.D. 1332.] Dark-green: imperfect. $\frac{3}{4}$ in. [Add. ch. 57 G. 27.]
A shield of arms: a cross lozengy. Suspended by a strap from a forked tree, and betw. two couped busts, facing each other. Within a carved quatrefoil, with a small ball-flower or quatrefoil in each spandril.

Edmunde Fetiplace.
Seal used by EDWARD BADBY, *of London, Gentl.*
9691. [A.D. 1601.] Red: injured. $\frac{1}{2} \times \frac{3}{8}$ in. [Harl. ch. 76 A. 26.]
Oval: a shield of arms: two chevrons, FETTIPLACE. In dexter chief a mullet for difference.

Edmund Fetyplace.
See Sir WILLIAM WENTWORTH.

George Fettiplace, *of the Middle Temple, London, Esq.*
9692. [A.D. 1683.] Dutch wax: imperfect, *en placard.* $\frac{5}{8} \times \frac{1}{2}$ in. [Add. ch. 13,733.]
Oval: a shield of arms: two chevrons, FETTIPLACE.

John Fettiplace, *al.* **Fetiplace,** *of Childrey, co. Berks., Esq.*
9693. [A.D. 1631.]   Brown: very indistinct, imperfect. About $\frac{5}{8}$ × $\frac{1}{2}$ in.   [Harl. ch. 76 F. 39.]
Oval: a shield of arms: quarterly, 1, 4, two chevrons, FETTIPLACE ; 2, 3, indistinct.

John Ffettiplace.
See JOHN ALFORD.

Richard Feverell', *of Edworth, co. Bedf., Clerk.*
9694. [A.D. 1478.]   Red: injured. $\frac{3}{4}$ in. [Add. ch. 35,080.]
A shield of arms : on a crenellated wall in base, a bird, close, contourné.
Beaded border.
Cf. Add. ch. 35,077.

John de Fideston, *Jun.*
Seal used by ADAM,*fil.* WILL. DE BADDELEGH, *or* BADDILEYE, *of Norton-on-the-Moors, co. Staff.*
9695. [A.D. 1344.]   Green, mottled: fine, cracked. $\frac{7}{8}$ in. [Add. ch. 22,574.]
Within a carved gothic panel of six cusped points, and betw. three small roses, a shield of arms : on a bend three uncertain charges.
  ✠ S' IOH'IS · D' · FIDESTON' · IVNIORIS. (?)
9696. [A.D. 1347.]   Light-brown : imperfect, indistinct. [Add. ch. 22,575.]

Hon. **John Fiennes,** *of Amwell-Bury, co. Hertf.*
9697. [A.D. 1685.]   Red: imperfectly impressed, *en placard*, on a label. $\frac{11}{16}$ × $\frac{5}{8}$ in.   [Add. ch. 5375.]
Oval: a shield of arms: quarterly, 1, per bend, ermine and ermines or erminois, a lion rampant ; 2, per pale, three fleurs-de-lis, two and one ; 3, three lions passant in pale ; 4, three roses, two and one.
  ✠ A · FYNO · DDW · Y · DERFYDD.

Seal used by WILLIAM FIENNES, *son of the above.*
9698. [A.D. 1685.]   Another.   [Add. ch. 5375.]

Another Seal.

9699. [A.D. 1685.]   Red: imperfectly impressed, *en placard.*   About $\frac{5}{8}$ × $\frac{1}{2}$ in.   [Add. ch. 5376.]
Oval : a shield of arms, ornamentally carved : three lions rampant, two and one, FIENNES.

Seal used by WILLIAM FIENNES, *son of the above.*

9700. [A.D. 1685.] Another. [Add. ch. 5376.]

William Fiennes.
See Hon. JOHN FIENNES.

Andr. Fiket.
See WILL. DE SALSOMARISCO.

William de Filgeriis.

9701. [A.D. 1200.] Dark-greenish-brown : fine, large, edge chipped, imperfect ; app. by a woven cord of various colours. 2¼ in. [Harl. ch. 52 A. 15.]

A shield of arms of early shape : diapré with sprigs of fern-like foliage (*fougère*) springing from the base. A bend. In the field on each side an estoile of seven points wavy, pierced.

⳨ SIG . . . . . WILL'I . DE FILGERIIS.

Journ. Brit. Arch. Assoc., vol. vi., p. 137. The bend is considered by J. R. Planché, *l.c.*, to be a difference, and "one of the earliest instances of this mark of cadency."

9702. Sulph. cast from No. 9701. [D.C., D. 243.]

Family of Fitz-Alan.

9703. [16th cent.] Sulph. cast from indistinct impression. 1¼ × 1⅛ in. [D.C., H. 105.]

Oval : an ornamental shield of arms : quarterly, 1, 4, a lion rampant, FITZ-ALAN ; 2, 3, a fret, MALTRAVERS. Ensigned with a coronet of five pearls and four strawberry-leaves, for one of the Earls of Arundel (?)

In the field the motto :—

. . . . VIRTVTI.

Carved border of foliage.

Alianora, *dau. of* JOHN MALTRAVERS, *widow of* JOHN **Fitz-Alan,** *of Arundel, Knt.*

9704. [A.D. 1404.] Red : fine, slightly chipped, edge restored. 1⅛ in. [Harl. ch. 45 C. 51.]

A shield of arms : per pale, *dex.*, a lion rampant, FITZ-ALAN ; *sin.*, a fret, MALTRAVERS. Suspended by a strap from a forked tree. Within a finely-carved gothic panel.

𝖲igillum : alianore : de : arundell : ⱥ

9705. Sulph. cast from No. 9704. [D.C., G. 107.]

9706. [A.D. 1404.] Red : chipped. [Harl. ch. 45 C. 53.]

. . . . . illum : alianore : de : arundell : ⱥ

9707. [A.D. 1404.]   Red : fine, cracked, imperfect.   [Harl. ch. 45 C. 54.]

𝕾igíllu . . . . ne : arundell : ⚜

John Fitz-Alan, 16*th Earl of Arundel, Captain of Rouen, etc.*
9708. [A.D. 1431.]   Red : originally fine, very imperfect. About 2¼ in. when perfect.   [Add. ch. 6330.]
A shield of arms, *couché*: quarterly, 1, 4, a lion rampant, enraged, FITZ-ALAN ; 2, 3, fretty, MALTRAVERS.   Crest on a helmet, ornamental mantling and wreath, a griffin's head and wings erect.   Supporters : two horses.   Within a carved gothic bilobe or panel, ornamented along the inner edge with cinquefoil ball-flowers.

. . . . . ll' : . . . . undell : ℨ : dñi : . . . .
9709. [A.D. 1432.]   Red: fine, imperfect.   [Add. ch. 1449.]
Some parts wanting in No. 9708 are here preserved.

𝕾igi . . . . undell : com . . . .
9710. [A.D. 1434.]   Red : fine, very imperfect.   [L. F.C., xxiii. 12.]
9711. Plaster cast from No. 9710.   [lxxxvi. 6.]
Legend wanting.

Another Seal.

9712. Sulph. cast from imperfect impression, not quite corresponding to the foregoing.   [D.C., G. 222.]
Crest out of a ducal coronet.

𝕾igil . . . . . .
9713. Plaster cast.   [lxxxvi. 7.]

Richard Fitz-Alan, 9*th Earl of Arundel.*
9714. [A.D. 1330–1375.]   Sulph. cast from fine but chipped impression.   1¼ in.   [D.C., F. 493.]
A shield of arms : a lion rampant, FITZ-ALAN.   Within a carved gothic device of a circle inscribed in a triangle, which is again inscribed in a circle.   The inner edge of the small circle ornamented with ball-flowers.   Each of the sides of the triangle is ornamented with a small circular panel carrying a circular shield of arms : chequy or fretty.
Legend betw. the points :—
     ✠ S' RICARDI · COMITIS · DE · ARVNDEL.
Beaded border.

Another Seal.

9715. [A.D. 1359.]   Plaster cast from fine impression, chipped at edges.   1½ in.   [lxxxvi. 4.]

A shield of arms: quarterly, 1, 4, a lion rampant, FITZ-ALAN ; 2, 3, chequy, WARREN. Betw. two slipped roses, and within a finely-carved gothic trefoil ornamented along the inner edge with small ball-flowers.

✠ ⁂ ⅍ **Sigillum : Ricardi : Comitis : De : Arundel : ⁂**

Richard Fitz-Alan, 10*th Earl of Arundel and Surrey.*
9716. [A.D. 1375.]   Plaster cast from fine impression, chipped at edges.   1⅞ in.   [lxxxvi. 5.]
A shield of arms, *couché* : quarterly, 1, 4, a lion rampant ; 2, 3, chequy.   Crest on a helmet, a lambrequin out of a ducal coronet, a griffin's head and wings erect.   Supporters, two griffins sejant.   Within a carved quatrefoil, ornamented with ball-flowers along the inner edge.

Sig ... ricardi ..... itis : arund .. le : et : surreye.
Carved border.

Thomas Fitz-Alan, 11*th Earl of Arundel and Surrey.*
9717. [A.D. 1412.]   Red: originally fine, fragmentary. About 2¼ in. when perfect.   [Add. ch. 5615.]
A shield of arms, *couché*: quarterly, 1, 4, a lion rampant enraged, FITZ-ALAN ; 2, 3, chequy, WARREN. Crest on a helmet, lambrequin, out of a ducal coronet, a griffin's head and wings erect.
Legend wanting.
Cabled border.

Walter *fil.* **Bernardi,** *of Little Stambridge, co. Essex, Knt.*
9718. [A.D. 1273.]   Green: imperfect.   1 in.   [Harl. ch. 50 A. 17.]
A shield of arms: vairé, on a chief a lion passant, for FITZ-BERNARD.

         S' WALTERI · FIL' · BERN . . . . . .
9719. Sulph. cast from No. 9717.   [D.C., E. 391.]
9720. [A.D. 1272.]   Green, discoloured : a fragment.   [Harl. ch. 50 A. 18.]
       . . . WALTERI . . . .

John *fil.* **Galfridi.**
9721. [13th cent.]   Plaster cast from indistinct impression. ¾ in.   [lxxxv. 80.]
A shield of arms : quarterly, a label of (five ?) points.
      ✠ S' IOH'IS · FIL' · GALFRIDI.
Cf. arms of FITZ-GEFFREY, of co. Bedf., quarterly, a bordure vairé.

John *f.* Galfridi de Edintone.
See JOHN, *son of* GEOFFREY DE EDINTONE.

Aucher *fil.* **Henrici,** *Lord of Thorp Darch'.,* (?) *co. York.*
9722. [A.D. 1327.] Red: fine. 1 in. [Add. ch. 20,581.]
A shield of arms : ermine, on a chief three lions rampant,
for FITZ-HENRY. Suspended by a strap from a tree of three
branches, and betw. two wyverns.

S' AVCHÉRI FIL' HENRICI.
Beaded borders.

Hugh *fil.* **Henrici,** *Lord of Ravensworth.*
9723. [Early 14th cent.] Plaster cast from good impression. ¾ in. [lxxxvi. 10.]
A shield of arms : fretty, a chief, FITZ-HENRY. Suspended
from a trifurcated tree.

S' · H' · FIL' · HENRICI.
Beaded border.

Edmund FitzHerberd, *Chevr., of Offyngton, etc., co. Suss.*
9724. [A.D. 1381.] Red: fine, edge chipped. 1⅛ in.
[Harl. ch. 78 B. 2.]
A shield of arms : quarterly, 1, 4, three lioncels, two and
one, within an engrailed bordure, FITZHERBERT ; 2, 3, gyronny of twelve within a bordure bezantée. Suspended by a
strap from a forked tree, and within a carved gothic panel
with small ball-flowers along the inner edge.

Sigillū : edmundi : fçtz : he....d. *w.*
Beaded border.
9725. Sulph. cast of No. 9724. [D.C., F. 533.]
9726. [A.D. 1383.] Red: imperfect. [Add. ch. 30,744.]

. igillū : edmu . . . . . herberd. *w.*

Johanna Fitz-Herberd, *of Rype Manor, co. Sussex.*
9727. [A.D. 1391.] Red: injured. ⅞ in. [Add. ch. 30,747.]
A shield of arms : per pale, *dex.,* three lioncels, two and
one, within a bordure engrailed, FITZHERBERD ; *sin.,* three
clarions, two and one. Suspended by a strap from a lion's
face, and betw. two sprigs of foliage. Within a carved gothic
triangle, ornamented with ball-flowers along the inner edge.
Legend betw. the points :—

Sigillu · Ioh'ne fitz · herberd *w*
`9728·` [A.D. 1391.] Red: imperfect. [Add. ch. 30,746.]

William Fitzherbert, *of Norbury, co. Derb.*
9729. [Late Hen. III.] Pale-green: a fragment. About
1 in. when perfect. [Woll. ch. vi. 39.]
A shield of arms of early form: a chief vairé, over all a
bend, FITZHERBERT.
Legend wanting.

John *fil.* **Jerdrut ?**
9730. [13th cent.] Plaster cast from good impression.
[lxxxiii. 3.]
A shield of arms: six martells or hammers, lying bendwise, three, two, and one.

✠ S' IOH'IS · FIL' : IERDRVT (?)

Beaded borders.
Perhaps a foreign seal.
9731. Another. [xci. 87.]
9732. Another. [lxxxvi. 11.]

Brian, *fil.* **Johannis,** *al.* **Brian de Herdeby,** *Knt.,*
son of JOHN, *fil.* OSBERTI DE LINCOLN, *co. Linc.*
9733. [A.D. 1257.] Dark-green: poor, edge chipped.
⅞ in. [Add. ch. 21,162.]
A shield of arms: a fess dancettée, betw. ten billets, four
and three, two and one, HERDBY.

✠ S' BRIANI FIL . . . . IS.

9734. [A.D. 1275.] Dark-green: gnawed by rats. [Add.
ch. 21,163.]

✠ S' BRIANI F . . . . NNIS.

Geoffrey, *fil* **Johannis,** *fil.* **Hugonis,**
of Fyfield. co. Berks.
9735. [*Temp.* Hen. III.] Green: indistinct. With mark
of the handle. 1¼ in. [Add. ch. 20,594.]
A shield of arms: three bars. Within a bordure engrailed,
for FITZ-JOHN.

✠ S' GALFRIDI FIL' IOHANNIS.

John, *fil.* **Johannis,** *of Little Stambridge, co. Essex.*
9736. [A.D. 1275.] Green: originally fine, imperfect.
1¼ in. [Harl. ch. 50 B. 2.]
A shield of arms: quarterly, a bordure vairé, FITZ-JOHN.
Suspended by a strap from a hook. Betw. two wyverns sans
wings, and on the *dex.* a mullet, on the *sin.*, a rose.

[✠ S]IECRETVM : IOHANNIS : FILII : IOH'IS.

Beaded borders.
9737. Sulph. cast from No. 9735.   [D.C., E. 408.]

Matthew Fitz-John, *Lord of Stokeham.*
9738. [13th cent.] Plaster cast from indistinct impression.
$1\frac{3}{16} \times \frac{3}{4}$ in. [lxxxvi. 12.]
Shield-shaped : a shield of arms : per pale, three lions rampant, two and one, FITZ-JOHN.
             ✠ S' MATHEI FIL' IOHANNIS.

William, *fil.* Willelmi, *fil.* JOHANNIS de Herpetre,
[Harptree, co. Somers.]
9739. [A.D. 1180–1190.]   Green : originally fine, large, very imperfect. [Harl. ch. 51 E. 29.]
A lozenge-shaped shield of arms : a cross flory.
             [SIG]ILLV[M . . . . IOH]ANNIS.
The two NN's conjoined.

Reginald, *fil.* Jordani, *of Great Bradley, co. Suff.*
9740. [A.D. 1306.]   Dark-green : fine, very imperfect.
$\frac{7}{8}$ in. [Harl. ch. 50 B. 5.]
A shield of arms : a fess dancettée.   Betw. three estoiles, and within a quatrefoil.
             . . . . RDANI (?)
9741. Sulph. cast from No. 9740.   [D.C., F. 179.]

Richard, *fil.* Johannis, *fil.* Marmaduci,
of Haughthorn, co. Durh.
9742. [A.D. 1316.]   Dark-red facing on uncoloured wax : very fine, edge and back slightly chipped.   1 in.   [Egert. ch. 551.]
A shield of arms : a fess betw. three birds, apparently papingays or parrots, MARMADUKE ; but perhaps intended for doves or partridges, for FITZ-MARMADUKE.   Suspended by a strap from a hook, and betw. two wyverns.
         ✠ : SIGILL' : RICARDI MARMADVC.
Beaded borders.
9743. Plaster cast from chipped impression.   [lxxxvii. 76.]

Robert, *fil.* Mauricii, *of Ireland.*
Seal used by PATRICK FITZMORICE, *of co. Kildare.*
9744. [A.D. 1454.]   Green : · imperfect. $\frac{7}{8}$ in.   [Cott. ch. iv. 35.]

An eagle displayed, charged on the breast with a shield of arms : on a saltire for FITZ-MAURICE, five uncertain charges. Within a pointed quatrefoil.

Legend betw. the points :—

S' ROB__ERTI · F . . . . . . MAV__RICI.

Beaded border.

9745. Sulph. cast from No. 9744. [D.C., G. 247.]

Robert, *fil.* Melredi.

9746. [13th cent.] Plaster cast from fine impression. 2¾ in. [lxxxvi. 13.]

A shield of arms : a saltire.

✠ SIGILLVM : ROBERTI : FILII : MELREDI :

John, *fil.* Michaelis.

9747. [12–13th cent.] Plaster cast from fine impression. 2 in. [lxxxvi. 14.]

A pip-shaped shield of arms : per pale, a chevron interlaced with another reversed.

✠ SIGILLVM IOHANNIS FILII MICAELIS.

Probably a foreign seal.

Patrick Fitz-Morice.
See ROBERT, *fil.* MAURICE.

Matildis, *filia* Normanni,
widow of OSBERT de Bulingtona, *co. Linc.*
See MATILDIS DE BULINGTONA, No. 7915.

Robert, *fil.* Odonis de Herbyrbuř,
of Rodsley, co. Derb.

9748. [13th cent.] Dark-green : fine. 1⅛ × ¾ in. Woll. ch. ix. 77.]

Pointed oval : a falcon, close, with bells, and jesses, contourné ; perhaps a crest.

✠ S' ROB'TI FIL' ODONIS.

9749. Another. [Woll. ch. ix. 78.]

9750. Another : chipped. [Woll. ch. ix. 79.]

Brian, *fil.* Joh. *fil.* Osberti de Lincoln.
See BRIAN, *fil.* JOHANNIS.

Robert, *fil.* **Pagani**, *Lord of Lammer, etc.,*
1*st Baron Fitz-Payne.*

9751. [A.D. 1301.] Plaster cast from fine impression.
1 × ⅝ in. [lxxxvi. 15.]
Oval : three lions passant guardant in pale, over all a
bendlet (not on a shield), the arms of FITZ-PAYNE.

      ✠ S' ROBERTI FIL' PAGANI.

Beaded borders.

Robert, *fil.* Roberti **Fuiz-Paien,** *al.*
Robert Le **Fitz-Paeyn,** *of cos. Somers. and Dors.*

9752. [A.D. 1316.] Red : fine, fragmentary. [Harl. ch. 50
B. 16.]
For description see next seal.

      .... TI : FIL'I L'A ....

9753. [A.D. 1335.] Red : fine, chipped. About ¾ in.
[Harl. ch. 45 F. 11.]
A shield of arms : three lions passant in pale, depressed by
a bend, FITZ PAYNE. Betw. two wyverns sans wings.

      ✠ S' : ROBERTI : FIL' IL' . . PAYN(?)

Beaded borders.
9754. Sulph. cast from No. 9753. [D.C., F. 256.]

Robert *fil.* **Paulini,** *fil.* **Galfridi.**
See SIMON DEDENE, No. 9232.

Hugh, *fil.* **Radulphi,** *of co. Suff.*

9755. [Early Hen. III.] Dark-green : chipped. 1 in.
[Harl. ch. 43 B. 16.]
A shield of arms of early shape : a fess vair, FITZ-RAULF.

      ✠ SIGILL' · HV[GO]NIS · FIL .... RAD'.

Cf. Cott. ch. xxvii. 96, late 12th cent.

9756. Sulph. cast of No. 9755. [xcviii. 47.]

Ralph, *fil.* **Radulphi.**
See JOHANNA DE LAMBOURNE.

William, *fil.* **Roberti.**
See WILL. DE ESSEBY.

Nicholas, *fil.* **Rogeri,** *of co. Glouc.* (?)
9757. [*Temp.* Hen. III. *or* Edw. I.] Plaster cast from fine impression. 1¼ in. [xciv. 55.]
A shield of arms: quarterly, a bendlet, FITZ-ROGER.
☧ SIGILLVM : NICOLAI : FILII : ROGERI.

Richard, *fil.* **Rogeri.**
9758. [Early 13th cent.] Plaster cast from good impression. 1½ in. [lxxxii. 83.]
A saltire and chief.
☧ SIGILLVM⁻: RICARDI : FILI · ROGERI.

Charles Fitz-Roy, *2nd Duke of Grafton, etc.*
9759. [A.D. 1707.] Red: *en placard,* chipped, on a tape. About ⅞ × ¾ in. [Add. ch. 24,148.]
Oval: a shield of arms: quarterly, 1, 4, quarterly, i. iv. FRANCE, (MODERN); ii. iii. ENGLAND; 2, SCOTLAND; 3, IRELAND, over all a baton sinister, compony, FITZ-ROY. Ensigned with a duke's coronet. Supporters, *dex.,* a lion guardant, crowned with a ducal coronet, and gorged with a collar; *sin.,* a greyhound, gorged as the dexter.

Henry Fitz-Roy, *son of King* HENRY VIII.,
Duke of Richmond and Somerset, Earl of Nottingham, K.G.
9760. [A.D. 1525–1536.] Red: originally fine, very imperfect. 3½ in. [xxxiv. 32.]
A shield of arms: quarterly, 1, 4, FRANCE (MODERN); 2, 3, ENGLAND, within a bordure quarterly, 1, ermine; 2, 3, compony; 4, gobony. Over all a baton sinister; an escutcheon of pretence quarterly, charged with a lion rampant, on a chief a castle betw. two buck's heads cabossed. Encircled with a Garter inscribed with the Motto of the Order. Crest on a helmet, ornamental mantling of foliage, and chapeau turned up ermine and semé of roses, a lion statant guardant, ducally gorged and chained. Supporters, *dex.,* a lion rampant guardant, ducally gorged and chained; *sin.,* an heraldic antelope, bezantée, accorned, unguled, gorged with a ducal coronet, and chained.
· SIGILLVM ⫶ HENRICI ⫶ F . . . . TIS · NOTINGHĀ.
9761. Sulph. cast from No. 9760. [D.C., H. 93.]

George Henry Fitz-Roy,
[*4th Duke of Grafton, etc.*] *Earl of Euston.*
9762. [A.D. 1792.] Red: *en placard,* on green ribbon. Indistinct. ⅜ in. [Add. ch. 10,554.]
A lion statant guardant. In the field above, a duke's coronet.

Edward fitz Symondes,
of Bishop's Hatfield, co. Hertf., Chevr.

9763. [A.D. 1367.] Dark-green: indistinct. 1⅛ in. [Add. ch. 28,778.]

A shield of arms : three escutcheons, two, and one, FITZ-SYMONDS. Suspended by a strap from a tree. Within a carved gothic panel, ornamented with small ball-flowers along the inner edge.

𝔖𝔦𝔤𝔦𝔩𝔩𝔲𝔪 : 𝔈𝔡𝔴𝔞𝔯𝔡 . . . . . . 𝔶𝔪𝔬𝔫𝔡 . .

Cabled border.

Hugh, *fil.* Simonis.

9764. [13th cent.] Plaster cast from indistinct impression. [xcii. 88.]

A shield of arms: a lion rampant, contourné. Betw. a crescent and estoile.

⊞ S' HVGONIS FILII SIMONIS.

Nichol fitz Simond, *of Bengeo, co. Hertf.*

9765. [A.D. 1378.] Red. ¼ in. [Add. ch. 28,789.]

An eagle displayed, charged on the breast with an escutcheon. In the field above, the motto :—

𝔖𝔞𝔫𝔰 : . . 𝔞𝔲 . . . .

Ralph Fitz Simon.

See RALPH, *son of* SIMON DE ORMMESBY.

William, *fil.* Simonis, *of Hatfield, co. Hertf.*

9766. [13th cent.] Dark-green : good, chipped at top. ⅞ in. [Add. ch. 28,694.]

A shield of arms : three escutcheons, two and one, FITZ-SIMONDS.

[⊞ S'] WILL'I FIL' SIMON[IS].

Beaded border.

Richard, *fil.* Thome, *fil.* Hugonis de Wodetone,
co. Norf.

9767. [A.D. 1315.] Dark-red : l. h. side wanting. About 1 in. [Add. ch. 14,957.]

Hexagonal : a shield of arms : three garbs, two and one Within a pointed trefoil.

⊞ SEEL · RICAR . . . . H.

Beaded border.

Drawn in Blomefield's *Hist. of Norfolk*, vol. x., p. 190. (Dept. copy.)

William, *fil.* **Vnfridi,** *of Rode, co. Northt.*

9768. [*Temp.* Edw. I.]   Red : indistinct in places, bent. About ⅞ in. when perfect.   [Add. ch. 6111.]

A shield of arms : on a bend some illegible charges, field diapered lozengy.   Suspended by a strap from a tree.   Betw. two lions addorsed.

𝕾𝖎𝖌𝖎𝖑𝖑𝖚𝖒 : 𝖜𝖎𝖑𝖑'𝖒𝖎 . . . . . . 𝖕𝖓𝖌𝖙𝖔𝖓 (?)

Inner border ornamented with ball-flowers.

Robert Fitz-Walter,

[*3rd Baron Fitz-Walter,* A.D. 1198–1234.]

9769. [*Temp.* Hen. III.]   Self-coloured, varnished : fine, imperfect.   [Add. ch. 21,698.]

Ø. Equestrian, see No. 6016, which it should precede.

✠ SIG . . . . II : WALTERI.

℞. A small round counterseal.   1¾ in.

A shield of arms : a fess betw. two chevrons, FITZ-WALTER.

✠ SECRETVM ROBERTI FILII WALTERI.

Beaded borders.

9770. Plaster cast of the *Secretum* only.   [lxxxvi. 17.]

Another Seal.

9771. [*Temp.* Hen. III.]   Light-brown.   1 in.   [Harl. ch. 50 C. 4.]

A *fede*, or two hands clasped in pale, the arms issuing, vested.   Betw. two shields of arms :   a fess betw. two chevrons, FITZ-WALTER.

✠ FOI · E LIEAIVTE · WS · TENGNE.

(*Foi et loiauté vous tiennent.*)

Beaded borders.

9772. Sulph. cast of No. 9771.   [D.C., F. 216.]

Robert Fitz-Walter, *Lord of Wodeham, co. Essex,*

1st Baron by writ.

9773. [A.D. 1313.]   Dark-green.   ⅞ in.   [Harl. ch. 50 C. 8.]

A shield of arms : a fess betw. two chevrons, FITZ-WALTER.   Suspended by a strap from a forked tree.   Betw. two wyverns sans wings.

In place of a legend is a wavy scroll of foliage and flowers.

9774. [Before A.D. 1303.]   Sulph. cast from good impression, edge chipped.   [xlvii. 1237.]

Laing's *MS. Catal.,* No. 35.

9775. Another. [D.C., G. 234.]
9776. [A.D. 1301.] Plaster cast. [lxxxvi. 18.]

Robert, *fil.* Walteri.
See ROB., *fil.* WALTERI DE DAVINTRE.

Simon, *fil.* Walteri.
9777. [13th cent.] Plaster cast from fine impression. 1¼ in. [lxxxvi. 16.]
Shield-shaped: a shield of arms: a boar's head couped, within a bordure charged with leaves.
☩ S' SIMONIS FIL' WALTERI.

Thomas Fitz-Wauter, *Lord of Davintre, co. Northt., Knt.*
9778. [A.D. 1373.] Red: very indistinct. ⅞ in. [Harl. ch. 50 C. 7.]
A shield of arms: perhaps FITZ WALTER. Within two triangles interlaced, ornamented with tracery.
Legend uncertain.

Wauter fitz Wauter, *Lord of Wodeham,* [*co. Essex.*]
9779. [A.D. 1368.] Red: fine, edge chipped. 1⅛ in. [Harl. ch. 50 C. 9.]
A shield of arms : diapré, a fess betw. two chevrons, FITZ-WALTER. Suspended from a forked tree. Betw. two wavy sprigs of elegant design, enclosed roses.
$\mathfrak{Sigillū}$ ✤ $\mathfrak{walteri}$ ✤ $\mathfrak{fis}$ ✤ $\mathfrak{wautier.}$
Carved border ornamented with small ball-flowers.
9780. Sulph. cast of No. 9779. [D.C., F. 457.]

Another seal, as 4th Baron Fitz-Walter.
9781. [A.D. 1383.] Red: fine, chipped. 1¼ in. [Harl. ch. 50 C. 11.]
A shield of arms, *couché*: a fess betw. two chevrons, FITZ-WALTER. Crest on a helmet and lambrequin, on a chapeau turned up ermine, an estoile of six points, betw. a pair of wings erect. Supporters, two griffins segreant, tails coward. In the field on each side, over the griffins' heads the letters **rtr.** with a sprig over them.
❀ ⚹ : $\mathfrak{Sigillum}$: $\mathfrak{walteri}$: ⚹ ❀ : ❀ ⚹ Dñi : fil₂ : $\mathfrak{wautier}$ ⚹ ❀
Carved borders.
9782. Sulph. cast of No. 9781. [D.C., F. 545.]

9783. [A.D. 1386.] Red: originally fine, imperfect, injured by pressure. [Add. ch. 21,510.]

...... walteri : ⚜ ❀ : ❀ ⚜ ꝺñi : fílȝ : wautier ⚜ ❀

Wauter, *Lord Le* **Fitz-Wauter,** *9th Baron Fitz-Walter.*
9784. [A.D. 1398.] Red: fine, very imperfect. 1¾ in. [Harl. ch. 50 C. 10.]

A shield of arms, *couché*: a fess betw. two chevrons, FITZ-WALTER. Crest on a helmet, on a chapeau turned up ermine, an estoile of six points wavy, betw. two wings erect. Supporters, *dex.,* a lion rampant guardant, *sin.,* wanting.

.... wautier.

Carved borders.

9785. Sulph. cast of No. 9784. [D.C., F. 606.]

Elizabeth, *fil.* **Waryn.**
9786. [A.D. 1392-3.] Plaster cast from chipped impression. ⅞ in. [lxxxvi. 21.]

A shield of arms: per pale, *dex.,* quarterly per fess indented; *sin.,* three leaves, two and one, slipped. Within a carved gothic panel composed of three points and five cusps, ornamented with ball-flowers along the inner edge.

.. ígíllū : elíȝabeth : fíl' : warȝn ⚜ ...

Ivo Fywaryn, *al.* **Fitzwaryn.**
9787. [Late 14th cent.] Plaster cast from good impression. 1¼ in. [lxxxvi. 20.]

A shield of arms: quarterly, per fess indented ermine, and ———, FITZ-WARREN. Suspended by a strap from a tree on a mount. Supporters, two swans.

⚜ : s' : íuonís : ⚜ ⚜ fywarȝn : ⚜

Inner border carved with ball-flowers, outer border cabled.

Peter, *fil.* **Warini,** *al. Pieres le* **fitz Waryn.**
9788. [A.D. 1332.] Red: chipped, indistinct. ⅞ in. [Add. ch. 22,536.]

A shield of arms: a bend compony, the lines in bend sinister being alternately plain and indented. This unusual peculiarity in the charge of the bend is in reference to the armorial bearings of FITZ-WARIN, viz., quarterly per fess indented. Suspended by a strap from a hook, and betw. two small birds (? papingays).

✠ S'IGILL .... TRI · LE · FIZ · WARIN.

9789. Plaster cast of No. 9788. [lxxxvi. 19.]

William, *fil.* **Warini,** *" Royal Valet,"* *of Whatley Manor,*
co. Essex.

9790. [*Circ.* A.D. 1280.]   Dark-red : imperfect, indistinct.
⅞ in.   [Harl. ch. 51 C. 16.]

A shield of arms : quarterly per fess indented, crusily, for
FITZ-WARREN or FITZ-WARIN.

✠ S' · WIL . . . . WARINI :

Beaded border.

William, *fil.* **Warini,** *of Pattishall, co. Northt.*

9791. [A.D. 1277.]   Dark-green : imperfect.   1⅛ in.   [Harl.
ch. 57 F. 24.]

A shield of arms : quarterly per fess indented.   Betw. two
swords, points upwards.

S' WILLEL . . . IL'I WA . . . . .

Beaded borders.

9792. Sulph. cast of No. 9791.   [D.C., E. 411.]

William Fitz-Warin, *of Britzlegh, co. Sussex.*

9793. [A.D. 1363.]   Red : fine.   ⅞ in.   [Add. ch. 20,086.]

A shield of arms : per fess indented (the chief is powdered),
FITZ-WARIN.   Within a border of carved gothic tracery.

✠ S' WILL'I FITZ WARIN DE BRIZTLEGH'.

Beaded borders.

Edmund Fitz-William, *of Darfield, co. York.*

9794. [A.D. 1460.]   Red.   ¼ in.   [Add. ch. 17,050.]

A slipped trefoil, perhaps in allusion to a crest.   Within a
carved border ornamented with small ball-flowers along the
inner edge, and partly cusped.   In the field the legend :—

𝔈 : ffitȝ : : toillyam :

John, *son of* JOHN **Fitz-William,** *of co. York, Knt.*

9795. [A.D. 1398.]   Red : fine, injured in places by
pressure.   1 in.   [Harl. ch. 50 C. 26.]

A shield of arms, *couché* : lozengy, FITZ-WILLIAM.   Crest
on a helmet, and lambrequin : out of a ducal coronet, a plume
of feathers.   In the field on each side a pair of sprigs of
foliage.

𝔖' · iehan : fitȝ toillam ⚜

9796. Sulph. cast from No. 9794.   [D.C., F. 607.]

John Fytzwyllyam, *al.* Fitzwilliams,
of Kyngesley, co. Southt., Esq.

9797. [A.D. 1550.] Red. $\frac{5}{8}$ × $\frac{1}{2}$ in. [Add. ch. 18,831.]
A shield of arms: lozengy, in chief an estoile for difference.
In the field the initial letters I. F.

Ralph, *fil.* Willelmi, *Lord of Grenthorp.*

9798. [A.D. 1301.] Plaster cast from fine impression.
1¼ in. [lxxxvi. 22.]
A shield of arms: barry of eight, three chaplets, two and
one, FITZ-WILLIAM. Over the shield a helmet and fan
plume. At each side a wyvern.
S' RADVLFI · FIL' : WILL'I &

Richard, *fil.* Willelmi.
Seal used by JOHN HALPANY, *son of* JOHN HALPANY,
Burgess of Hertford, co. Hertf.

9799. [A.D. 1392.] Bronze-green: indistinct. 1 in. [L.F. C.,
II. 11.]
A shield of arms: an eagle displayed. Betw. five small
roses, and within a carved gothic panel of eight points.
⚹ S' : RICARDI : FILII : WILLELMI :

Richard, *fil.* Willelmi (de Hatton).
See RICH. *f.* WILL. DE HATTON.

William, *fil.* Willelmi, (Fitz-William) *Lord of Emelay,*
co. York.

9800. [*Temp.* Edw. II.] Dark-reddish-brown: large, very
indistinct. 1 in. [Add. ch. 7469.]
A shield of arms: lozengy, FITZ-WILLIAM. Suspended
from a long cross, and within a carved gothic panel.
Legend illegible.
. . . . . LI. . . . WILLE . . . .
9801. Another: very indistinct. [Add. ch. 7471.]
9802. [A.D. 1324.] Dark-green: very indistinct. [Add.
ch. 7473.]
. . . . WILLELMI.

William, *fil.* William, *Lord of Emelay, co. York, Knt.*

9803. [A.D. 1385.] Red: fine, well-preserved. 1 in.
[Add. ch. 7460.]

A shield of arms : lozengy of seventeen · pieces, FITZ-
WILLIAM. Suspended by a strap from a tree, and within a
carved gothic panel, ornamented with ball-flowers along the
inner edge.

$\mathfrak{S}$' : ẁilli' : fitȝ : ẁill'i : milîtis.

9804. [A.D. 1385.] Red : indistinct. [Add. ch. 7475.]
9805. [A.D. 1385.] Red : indistinct. [Add. ch. 7476.]
9806. [A.D. 1385.] Red : indistinct. Appended by a
plaited hempen cord. [Add. ch. 7479.]

William FitzWyllyams, *of co. Berks, Esq.*
9807. [A.D. 1549.] Red : a fragment. About $\frac{5}{8} \times \frac{1}{4}$ in.
when perfect. [Add. ch. 18,829.]
An ornamental shield of arms : on a bend three martlets,
FITZWILLIAM. In the field the initial letters .... FF.
Beaded border.

John Filliol, *of Ramsey, co. Essex, Knt.*
9808. [A.D. 1326.] Red : a fragment. [Harl. ch. 49 I. 52.]
A shield of arms : vairé, FILLIOL. Within a carved
gothic panel.
Legend wanting.
Cf. Add. ch. 15,599, A.D. 1366.

Elizabeth, *wife of Sir* MOYLE **Finche,**
of Eastwell, co. Kent, Knt.
9809. [A.D. 1605.] Red. $\frac{1}{4} \times \frac{7}{10}$ in. [Add. ch. 19,969.]
Oval signet : a crab, perhaps a crest.
Beaded border.

Francis Finch.
See ROBERT SCUDAMOR.

Heneage Finch, *2nd Earl of Winchilsea,*
Viscount Maidstone, etc., Knt.
9810. [A.D. 1660.] Wafer, covered with paper, cut ornamentally, before impression. $1\frac{3}{8}$ in. [Harl. ch. 86 I. 25.]
A shield of arms : per pale, *dex.*, quarterly, 1, 4, FINCH ;
2, 3, FITZHERBERT ; *sin.*, SEYMOUR. Ensigned with the
coronet of an earl. Supporters, *dex.*, a griffin, *sin.*, a Pegasus,
each ducally gorged. Motto on a scroll in base :—
NEC ELATA NEC DEIECTA.
9811. [A.D. 1660.] Another. [Harl. ch. 86 I. 26.]

Sir **John Finch,** *Lord Chief Justice of the Court of Common Pleas, Knt.*

9812. [A.D. 1637.] Red: indistinct. $\frac{5}{8} \times \frac{1}{2}$ in. [Harl. ch. 77 D. 16.]

A shield of arms: quarterly, 1, FINCH, etc. Crest on a helmet, ornamental mantling and wreath, a griffin passant. Motto on a scroll in base: illegible.

Sir **Moyle Finche,** *of Eastwell, co. Kent, Knt.*

9813. [A.D. 1605.] Red. $\frac{1}{2} \times \frac{7}{16}$ in. [Add. ch. 19,969.]

Oval signet from a ring (?): on a wreath a griffin passant. Crest of FINCH.

Beaded border.

Robert, *son of* JOHN **Fynch,** *of Winchelsea, co. Suss.; or* ALICE TAVERNER, *widow of* RICHARD SMITH, *of Ihamme.*

9814. [A.D. 1361.] Mottled-green. $\frac{5}{8}$ in. [Add. ch. 20,090.]

A shield of arms: a cross engrailed, betw. in the 1st quarter two hearts conjoined; 2, 3, two escallops; 4, a roundle. Betw. two sprigs of foliage; and within a carved gothic panel consisting of a cinquefoil and a triangle.

Vincent Finch, *al.* **Fynch,** *of Winchelsea, co. Suss. son of* HENRY FINCH.

9815. [A.D. 1361.] Red: originally fine, chipped. 1 in. [Add. ch. 20,185.]

A shield of arms: a chevron betw. three griffins, passant, wings endorsed, FINCH. Within a carved gothic panel, ornamented along the inner edge with small ball-flowers.

✠ SIGILLV̄ VINSENCII F . . . . . ✠

9816. [A.D. 1361.] Dark-green: very imperfect. The shield of arms only remains. [Add. ch. 20,183.]

. . . . . VI . . . .

9817. [A.D. 1368.] Red: fine, imperfect. [Add. ch. 20,057.]

✠ SIGIL . . . . . II FINCH ✠

The first seal (Add. ch. 20,185) used by WILLIAM ATTE WODE.

William Fisch, *of Sedlescombe, co. Suss.*

9818. [A.D. 1381.] Red: indistinct. $\frac{7}{8}$ in. [Harl. ch. 49 I. 57.]

A shield of arms (?): perhaps a cross betw. four sprigs. Within two carved equilateral triangles interlaced.

Legend betw. the points:—

. I . PERIS.

Thomas Fissenden, *of Lewes, co. Sussex, Apothecary.*
9819. [A.D. 1689.]   Red: *en placard*, imperfectly impressed.   ¾ × ⅜ in.   [Add. ch. 30,696.]
A shield of arms : a wildman riding on a wyvern (?) Crest on a helmet and ornamental mantling, a wild boar.

Anthonye Fysher, *Commissioner of Sewers.*
9820. [A.D. 1621.]   Red : injured by pressure.   About ⅝ × ½ in.   [Add. ch. 33,120.]
A shield of arms : quarterly, 1, 4, on a chief some illegible charges ; 2, 3, barry of eight (?) a bendlet. Crest on a helmet and ornamental mantling, indistinct.

Clement Fyssher, *of Great Packington, co. Warr., Esq.*
9821. [A.D. 1585.]   Red : indistinct.   ¾ × 11/16 in.   [Harl. ch. 78 C. 29.]
On a wreath a demi sea-dog rampant.   Crest of FISHER.

John Fyssher, *Serjeant-at-Law, of co. Kent.*
9822. [A.D. 1502.]   Red.   ⅜ in.   [Harl. ch. 50 F. 12.]
A demi-lion rampant, queue trifurcated, perhaps for a crest of FISHER.

Richard Fissher, *Clerk, of London* (?)
9823. [A.D. 1459.]   Red : fine, injured.   ¼ in.   [Harl. ch. 50 F. 10.]
A shield of arms : semé of fleurs-de-lis, a cross humettée. Betw. the initials **r. f.**
In the field above, the legend or motto :—
alemeto (?)
Cabled border.

Peter ——.
Seal used by JOHN, *son of* PETER FLAMANK, *of Nanstallan, co. Cornw.* (?)
9824. [A.D. 1366.]   Dark-green : indistinct.   The edge chipped.   1 in.   [Harl. ch. 50 C. 36.]
A shield of arms : crusily, a lion rampant. Within a bordure engrailed. Within a carved panel of five cusps and three points.
Sigill' : petri . . . .

Nicholas Flamanke.

See EUSTACHIUS DE VOLEVILE.

Richard Flamank.

See EUSTACHIUS DE VOLEVILE.

William Flamanke, *of Boscarne, co. Cornw., Esq.*

9825. [A.D. 1576.]   Red.   ⅜ in.   [Harl. ch. 50 C. 46.]

A shield of arms : on a cross betw. four pierced mullets, a saltire, FLAMANK,

Carved border.

Philip Flambard.

9826. [A.D. 1363.]   Plaster cast from good impression, chipped.   ¾ in.   [lxxxvi. 23.]

A shield of arms : a bend betw. six lions' heads erased. Suspended by a strap from a hook. Background slightly hatched.

    ✠ S' : PHILIPPI FLAMBARD.

Perhaps a foreign seal.

Cf. the arms of FLAMBART of Bretagne, three leopards' heads erased.

Johanna Flayneur (?)

Seal used by JOHN NEUBURNE, *of Dachet, co. Bucks.*

9827. [A.D. 1352.]   Red : chipped.   ¾ in.   [Add. ch. 5187.]

A shield of arms : three dolphins embowed, two and one, on a chief a griffin segreant.   Crest or initials above the shield, injured and uncertain.   Supporters, two lions sejant. Within a carved gothic quatrefoil.

    S' IOHANE FLAYNEVR (?)

John Fleming, *al.* Le Flemming,
Lord of Dalton, co. York, Knt.,
Grandson of D. WILLIAM LE FLEMMING.

9828. [*Temp.* Edw. I.]   Red : indistinct.   ¾ in.   [Add. ch. 20,514.]

A shield of arms : barry of six, in chief three lozenges, FLEMING.   Betw. two wyverns.

    ✠ S' IOHANNIS · FLEMING.

John Fleming.

9829. [Late 13th cent.]   Plaster cast from fine impression. 1¾ in.   [lxxxvi. 25.]

A shield of arms : a bend, in sinister chief an estoile or mullet of six points.   Betw. two wyverns.   Above the shield a device of foliage.

✸ S' IOHANNIS FLEMING.

Beaded borders.

Marioria, *dau. of* GILBERT **Flemyng.**
See JOHN DEL CHAMBRE.

Laurence de Flete, *of Wisbeach, co. Cambr., Knt.*

9830. [A.D. 1347.]   Reddish-brown : fine. $\frac{13}{16}$ in.   [Harl. ch. 50 C. 55.]

A shield of arms : a lion rampant debruised by a bendlet, FLEET.   Suspended by a strap from a quatrefoil, and betw. two small slipped quatrefoils.   Within a pointed gothic quatrefoil ornamented with ball-flowers along the inner edge.

✣ SIGILL' · LAVRENCII · DE · FLETE :

Beaded borders.

9831. Sulph. cast from No. 9830.   [D.C., F. 298.]

William Flete, *of Horton, co. Kent., Esq.*

9832. [A.D. 1580.]   Red : injured. $\frac{3}{8} \times \frac{1}{2}$ in.   [Harl. ch. 78 B. 13.]

Oval : on a wreath a sea-lion.   Crest of FLETE.
Beaded border.

Richard Fletton, *Clerk, Rector of Wystowe, co. Hunt.*

9833. [A.D. 1412.]   Red : fragmentary.   About 1 in. when perfect.   [Add. ch. 34,219.]

A shield of arms : a fess betw. six pierced estoiles of eight points.

Cf. Add. ch. 33,938.

Richard Fletton.
See JOHN COLIN.

Florimund, *Lord of Spa . . . . (?)*

9834. [14th cent.]   Plaster cast from chipped impression. $1\frac{1}{4}$ in.   [lxxxviii. 6.]

A shield of arms, *couché* : per pale, *dex.*, a lion rampant, over all a canton sinister, *sin.*, lozengy.   Crest on a helmet and lambrequin, an old man's head with long hair and beard, filletted. Within a carved gothic panel.

𝕾' · florimunði · Domíni · de · spa . . . .

Perhaps a foreign seal.

Guillermus Flote.

9835. [Early 14th cent.]   Plaster cast from somewhat indistinct impression.   1⅛ in.   [lxxxvi. 26.]

A shield of arms: barry of six.   Betw. three eagles rising and two wyverns.   Within a cusped trefoil.

⚜ SIGILLVM · GVILLERMI · FLOTE.

Perhaps a foreign seal.

Edward Flowerdew, *of Stanfield, co. Norf., Serjeant-at-Law;*
  Thomas Flowerdew, *of Hederset, co. Norf., Gentl.;*
  Anthony Flowerdew, *of Hederset, co. Norf., Gentl.;*
  or **John Flowerdew,** *of Cantlow, co. Norf., Gentl.*

9836. [A.D. 1583.]   Red. $\frac{9}{16} \times \frac{1}{2}$ in.   [Add. ch. 14,628: detached in box.]

Oval: on a wreath a griffin's head, erased and wings erect.

Drawn in Blomefield's *Norfolk*, vol. v. p. 37 (Dept. copy).

Edward Flowerdew; Anthony Flowerdew;
or Thomas Flowerdew.

9837. [A.D. 1583.]   Red: indistinct. $\frac{1}{4} \times \frac{7}{16}$ in.   [Add. ch. 14,629: detached in box.]

Oval: a shield of arms: a chevron engrailed betw. three bears (?) BARRETT.   Crest on a helmet and ornamental mant_ ling, a demi-man holding a club.

Beaded border.

9838. [A.D. 1583.]   Red: crushed.   [Add. ch. 14,630: detached in box.]

John Flowerdew, *of Cantlowe, co. Norf., Esq.*

9839. [A.D. 1575.]   Red: fragments.   [Add. ch. 6299.]

Apparently a shield of arms: the charges obliterated.

William Foche.
See WILLIAM HUISH.

D. Richard Fokeram, *al.* **Foqueram,** *of co. Somers., Knt.*
9840. [A.D. 1279.] Dark-green: chipped. $\frac{13}{16}$ in. [Add. ch. 5439.]

A shield of arms: five lozenges in bend, for a bend engrailed, FOKERAM or FOKERHAM.

✠ S' RICARDI FIOKJERAM.

9841. [A.D. 1279.] Dark-green: chipped. [Add. ch. 5440.]

✠ S' RICARDI FOK ... M.

Another Seal.

9842. [A.D. 1279.] Dark-green: indistinct, fragmentary. [Add. ch. 5441.]

Resembles the previous seal, but from another matrix.

✠ SIGILL' RIC . . . . . . AM.

Beaded borders.

Robert Fokeram.

9843. [A.D. 1323.] Plaster cast from good impression, edge chipped. $\frac{3}{4}$ in. [lxxxvi. 27.]

A shield of arms: four lozenges in bend, or a bend lozengy, FOKERHAM. Betw. three sprigs of foliage, and within a pointed quatrefoil ornamented with carved ball-flowers along the inner edge.

✠ S' ROB'TI ⚜ FOKERAM.

At the end of the legend a wyvern.

Beaded borders.

Aubrai . . . .
Seal used by **Adam de Foleford,**
of Newton Abbot, co. Devon.

9844. [A.D. 1354.] Dark-green: very imperfect. 1 in. [Harl. ch. 50 C. 59.]

A shield of arms: a lion rampant, crowned, debruised by a bendlet. Within a carved gothic quatrefoil.

Legend betw. the points:—

IE · SV S' AV BRAI S' RO. (?)

9845. Sulph. cast from No. 9844. [D.C., F. 387.]

Rondolf Foleiambe.

9846. [A.D. 1285.] Green: imperfect, indistinct. $\frac{3}{4}$ in. [Harl. ch. 50 D. 1.]

A shield of arms: illegible. Perhaps a jambe, couped at the thigh.

. . . . . . WAI . . .

Godfrey Foliambe, *of Walton, co. Derb., Esq.*
9847. [A.D. 1583.]   Red : imperfect. $1\frac{3}{16} \times \frac{11}{16}$ in.   [Woll. ch. xii. 54.]
Oval : an ornamental shield of arms : a trefoil, slipped and leaved.   Betw. the initials G. F.
Beaded border.

Jordan Foliot, *of Ingham, co. Linc.*
9848. [Early Hen. III.]   Pale-green, opaque : indistinct, chipped. $1\frac{3}{4} \times 1\frac{3}{8}$ in.   [Harl. ch. 50 D. 8.]
Shield-shaped : an early shield of arms : a bend, FOLIOT.
✠ SIGILLVM : IORDANI · FOLIOT.
9849. [Early Hen. III.]   Creamy-white : indistinct, chipped. [Harl. ch. 50 D. 9.]
✠ SIGILLVM : IORDANI · FOLIOT.
9850. Sulph. cast from No. 9849.   [D.C., D. 236.]

Jordan Foliot.
9851. [13th cent.]   Green composition cast from chipped impression.   1 in.   [lxxvi. 73.]
A shield of arms : a bend, over all a· label of five points, FOLIOT.
✶ SIG[ILLVM] : IORDANI : FOLIOT.

Richard Foliot (?)
9852. [15th cent. ?]   Plaster cast from somewhat indistinct impression. $\frac{11}{16}$ in.   [lxxxvi. 28.]
A shield of arms : a lion rampant.
✶ **S' · armoru · ricar[d]i · foliot** *w* (?)
Beaded border.

Benedict de Folsham.
9853. [A.D. 1338.]   Red : fine, well preserved. $1\frac{3}{16}$ in. [Harl. ch. 57 E. 4.]
A shield of arms : bendy of six, within a bordure charged with eleven martlets.   Within a finely-carved gothic rosette of many points, ornamented along the inner edge with small ball-flowers.
✶ SIGILLVM · BENEDICTI · DE · FOLSHAM.
Beaded border.
9854. Sulph. cast from No. 9853.   [D.C., F. 271.]

Richard de Fontibus, *of Kilwingholm, etc., co. Linc.*
9855. [Early 13th cent.]   Dark-green ; chipped, indistinct.

App. by a woven cord of variegated colours. With mark of the handle. 1⅜ × 1¼ in. [Harl. ch. 49 C. 27.]

A shield of arms of early shape : a bend, and over all a mill-rind lying fesswise.

        ✠ SIGILLM RICARDI DE FONTIB'.

9856. Sulph. cast of No. 9855. [D.C., D. 240.]

Another Seal.

9857. [13th cent.] Dark-green : indistinct. With mark of the handle. 1¾ × 1 in. [Harl. ch. 50 E. 50.]

A shield of arms : as before.

        ✠ SIGILL' · RICARD · DE · FVИTAIИ.

Duncan Forbes.
Seal used by EDMUND DOWNING, *of London.*

9858. [A.D. 1572.] Red. ⅛ × ₇⁄₁₀ in. [Harl. ch. 77 F. 56.]

Oval signet : on a wreath a cock. Crest of FORBES. Beaded border.

Edmund Forde, *of Harting, co. Suss., Esq.*

9859. [A.D. 1560.] Red : chipped. ¹¹⁄₁₆ × ⅝ in. [Add. ch. 18,847.]

Oval : a shield of arms : quarterly, 1, 4, three lions rampant crowned, two and one, FORD ; 2, 3, per fess [or, and] ermine, a lion rampant, FORD. In the field over the shield the initial letters E. F.

Henry de Forde, *son of* JOHN DE FORDE, *of co. Somers.*

9860. [A.D. 1362.] Green, mottled : fine. ⅞ in. [Add. ch. 5458.]

A shield of arms : a fess betw. three pierced mullets. Betw. two loops, and within a carved gothic panel ornamented with small ball-flowers along the inner edge.

        : SIGILL' ☆ : HENRICI : ☆ FORDE ☆

Carved border.

9861. [A.D. 1362.] Green, mottled : indistinct in places. [Add. ch. 5459.]

9862. [A.D. 1368.] Green : fine, sharp, edge chipped. [Add. ch. 5460.]

        : SIGILL' ☆ : HENRICI : ☆ . . . . . . E ☆

9863. [A.D. 1373.] Green, mottled. [Add. ch. 5463.]

9864. [A.D. 1373.] Dark-green : fine, well preserved. [Add. ch. 5464.]

9865. [A.D. 1373.] Green : chipped. [Add. ch. 5465.]

John Forde, *of the Inner Temple, London.*

9866. [A.D. 1568.] Brownish-red: cracked, imperfect, and indistinct. $\frac{3}{4} \times \frac{5}{8}$ in. [Add. ch. 8953.]

Oval: a shield of arms: three lions rampant crowned, two and one, FORD. Crest on a helmet, ornamental mantling and wreath, a demi-lion rampant crowned.

William de Forde, *or* **William de Stoke,**
of cos. Bedf., Buck., Berk., etc.

9867. [A.D. 1368.] Red: fragmentary. About $\frac{7}{8}$ in. when perfect. [Cott. ch. xxiv. 11.]

A shield of arms: the charges broken away. Within a carved gothic panel. Field of the shield diapered.

. . . . [w]illi' : de . . . .

Guaston de Forest.
Seal used by JOHN PHILIP, *of Yundecote, of Exeter, co. Devon.*

9868. [A.D. 1414.] Red. $\frac{7}{8}$ in. [Add. ch. 27,606.]

A shield of arms: per pale, *dex.*, three bars; *sin.*, a bend cotised. Within a cordon of small quatrefoils or ball-flowers. Probably a foreign seal.

✠ S' · GVASTON · DE · FOREST ·

John Le Forester, *of Stony-Stratford, co. Buck.*

9869. [A.D. 1330.] Red. $\frac{3}{4}$ in. [Harl. ch. 84 E. 55.]

A shield of arms: per pale, *dex.*, a lion rampant debruised by a bend *sin.*, a cross fleury dimidiated.

✠ SEEL ✿ ✿ HELOUYS ✿

Reginald Le Forester, *of Bandon in Bedyngton, co. Surr.*

9870. [A.D. 1342.] Red: cracked. $\frac{3}{4}$ in. [Add. ch. 23,090.]

A shield of arms: on a chevron betw. two leopards' faces in chief and a bugle-horn stringed and garnished in base, three escallops for FOSTER. Suspended by two straps from hooks, and betw. two slipped quatrefoils. Within a carved and pointed gothic quatrefoil ornamented with ball-flowers along the inner edge.

✠ S' REGINALDI · LE · FORESTER.

Beaded border.

9871. [A.D. 1349.] Green: indistinct in places. [Add. ch. 22,866.]

Edmund Forster, *son of* JOHN FORSTER,
of Bedyngton, co. Surr.

9872. [A.D. 1375.] Red: fragmentary. $\frac{3}{4}$ in. [Add. ch. 23,137.]

A shield of arms : a rose, *en soleil.* Within a carved and pointed gothic quatrefoil ornamented with ball-flowers along the inner edge.

Legend indistinct.

✠ S . . . . IS · DE · . . . .

Sir **Humphry Forster,** *of Aldermaston, co. Berks, Bart.*

9873. [A.D. 1698.] Red : imperfect, *en placard* on a label. About ¾ in. [Add. ch. 19,238.]

A shield of arms : a chevron engrailed betw. three arrows, FORSTER.

Richard Forster.

9874. [A.D. 1380–81.] Plaster cast from fine impression. [lxxxvi. 30.]

A shield of arms : a fess betw. three jaw-bones (?) Upheld by a woman or angel, betw. two small cinquefoils pierced and within a carved gothic device, ornamented with ball-flowers along the inner edge.

𝕾igillum ✠ Ricardi ✠ Forſter.

William Forster, *of Castle Combe, co. Wilts, Gentl.*

9875. [A.D. 1652.] Red : imperfect, indistinct. About ½ × ⅜ in. [Add. ch. 18,413.]

Oval : a shield of arms : a chevron betw. three pheons, FORSTER. A crescent for difference.

Beaded border.

9876. [A.D. 1656.] Red : imperfect, indistinct. [Add. ch. 18,421.]

The same, used by HELLENA, *wife of the above.*

9877. [A.D. 1652.] Red : imperfect. [Add. ch. 18,413.]
9878. [A.D. 1656.] Red : a fragment. [Add. ch. 18,421.]

Another Seal ?

9879. [A.D. 1659.] Red : indistinct. Perhaps a different type. [Add. ch. 18,426.]

The same, used by HELLENA, *wife of the above.*
9880. [A.D. 1659.] Red : indistinct. [Add. ch. 18,426.]

Henry de Forstesburi.

9881. [14th cent.] Plaster cast from good impression. ¾ in. [lxxxvi. 31.]

A shield of arms: three lions rampant, two and one, a canton ermine. Betw. two wavy sprigs of trefoiled foliage. Suspended by a strap from a hook.

☩ S' HENR DE FORSTESBVRI.

Beaded borders.

Henry Fortescu, *Escheator of Devon, Esq.*

9882. [A.D. 1547.] Red: imperfect, indistinct. About ⅞ in. [Add. ch. 29,187.]

A shield of arms, *couché*: charges indistinct. Crest on a helmet, mantling or lambrequin and chapeau, broken off. Legend on a ribbon :—

. . . . **cur'** . . . .

John Fortescue, *Chief Justice of the King's Bench, Knt.*

9883. [A.D. 1447.] Red, discoloured: injured. From a ring. ¼ in. [Harl. ch. 52 A. 26.]

An ornamental shield of arms: a bend engrailed, plain cotised, FORTESCUE.

Legend in the field :—

iohis : fortescu.

Another Seal.

9884. [A.D. 1450.] Red: from a ring. ⅛ × $\frac{7}{16}$ in. [Add. ch. 17,238.]

Oval: an ornamental shield of arms: a bend engrailed, sinister, for FORTESCUE. Perhaps cut on a gem.

✠ S' · M · D · IOH'IS · FFORTESCHU · M.

The letters C H united.

John Fortescue, *of Buckland Filleigh, co. Devon, Esq.*
9885. [A.D. 1655.] Red: a fragment. [Add. ch. 29,239.]
Oval: a shield of arms: a bend or chevron.

Roger Fortescue, *of Buckland Filleigh, co. Dev.*
9886. [A.D. 1606.] Red: a fragment. [Add. ch. 29,223.]
A shield of arms: a bend (engrailed ?), plain cotised, etc. FORTESCUE.

Sir **William Fortescue,** *Surveyor of the Crown lands in Wilts, Knt.*
9887. [A.D. 1610.] Red: injured. ⅝ in. [Add. ch. 5713.]
An heraldic tiger. Crest of FORTESCUE.

Edward Forth, *or* **Foorthe,** *of Hadleigh, co. Suff., Gentl.*
9888. [A.D. 1578.] Red : chipped. ¾ in. [Add. ch. 24,305.]
On a wreath a bear's head erased, muzzled. Crest of
FORTH.

John Forthey, *of Denham, co. Buck.*
9889. [A.D. 1433.] Red. ⅝ × ½ in. [Harl. ch. 85 E. 4.]
Shield-shaped : a shield of arms (?) : per pale, *dex.*, an eagle
displayed, *sin.*, a lion rampant, perhaps in allusion to the
arms of FORTH. On a quasi chief the legend :—
      L'ERME (?)
9890. [A.D. 1433.] Another. [Harl. ch. 85 E. 5.]
9891. Sulph. cast from No. 9890. [D.C., G. 193.]

Richard de Forthyngton, *Parson*
of Wodehall Church, co. Linc.
9892. [A.D. 1333.] Creamy-white : indistinct fragment.
About ⅞ in. when perfect. [Harl. ch. 47 I. 26.]
A shield of arms : illegible. Within a gothic panel.
     . . . . ENGTON.
Cf. Harl. Ch. 50 D. 34, 35 ; 58 B. 49, 50, A.D. 1332 ; 48 E. 7, A.D. 1335 ;
56 F. 42, A.D. 1338 ; 50 D. 36, A.D. 1340 ; and 58 C. 2, A.D. 1365.

Isabella de Fortibus, *Countess of Albemarle and Devon,*
Domina Insulæ [Vectis] ; *wid. of Earl* WILLIAM ;
dau. of BALDWIN DE REDVERS, *Earl of Devon.*
9893. [A.D. 1276.] Light-red : very fine, chipped and
injured. Appended by a plaited cord of faded red silk.
1⁵⁄₁₆ in. [Harl. ch. 50 D. 40.]
A shield of arms : a cross patonce, vair, ALBEMARLE.
Betw. three lions rampant, in allusion to the armorial charge
of REDVERS.
    [S]ECRET' : ISABELLE : DE FORTIB' :
    COMIT[I]SSE : D[I]EVONIE : ET : INSU . . . . . .
The letters EL in *Isabelle,* and ON in *Devonie* are united.
Beaded borders.
The art of this seal is very fine.
9894. Sulph. cast of No. 9893. [D.C., E. 410.]

Another Seal.

9895. [A.D. 1259-62.] Discoloured-greenish-white : very
indistinct from injury. About 1⅜ × 1 in. [Toph. ch. 27.]
Pointed oval : a shield of arms : illegible. Suspended
from a tree and betw. two wavy scrolls of foliage.
  . . . . FORTIB; COMITISSE ALB . . . .

Avia, *wife of* THOMAS **Foscroft,** *of Westminster, co. Midd.*
9896. [A.D. 1556.]   Red : from a ring (?) ⅜ in. [Add. ch. 9379.]
An ornamental shield of arms : a quatrefoil slipped and leaved.

Edward Foster, *of East Ilseley, co. Berks.*
9897. [A.D. 1693.]   Red : imperfect, *en placard* on a label. About ¾ in. when perfect. [Add. ch. 19,234.]
A shield of arms : quarterly, 1, 4, a chevron, ermine ; 2, 3, two bars.   Crest on a helmet and mantling, destroyed.

Humfrey Foster, *of co. Berks.*
9898. [A.D. 1459.]   Red : from a ring. $\frac{7}{16} \times \frac{5}{16}$ in. [Harl. ch. 54 I. 16.]
Oval : two pheons or arrow-heads in fess, in allusion to the armorial bearings of FOSTER.
Cf. Harl. ch. 43 I. 51, from a larger matrix.
9899. Sulph. cast from No. 9898. [xcviii. 48.]

Humfrey Foster, *Senr., Esq.*
9900. [A.D. 1483.]   Red : from a ring. ½ in. [Harl. ch. 43 I. 51.]
Two arrow-heads, in allusion to the arms of FOSTER ; in the field three sprigs.
Motto :—**thynk.**
Cabled border.

John Foster, *of Elyngton, co. Hunt., Esq.*
9901. [A.D. 1470.]   Red : indistinct. ⅝ in. [Add. ch. 33,260.]
An ornamental shield of arms : a chevron ermine (?) betw. three pheons or broad arrows, FOSTER.   Behind, a strap.

John Foster, *of Grofham, co. Hunt., Esq.*
9902. [A.D. 1470.]   Red. ⅝ in. [Add. ch. 33,400.]
An ornamental shield of arms, with strap and buckle : a chevron ermine betw. three pheons, FOSTER.

John Foster, *of Wynche Hill in Walden Regis,*
co. Herts., Yeoman.
9903. [A.D. 1625.]   Red : indistinct. $\frac{7}{16}$ in. [Add. ch. 35,878.]
A leopard's head erased.

Nicholas Fosterd, *al.* **Foster,** *of Cornwood, co. Dev., Yeoman.*
  9904. [A.D. 1613.]　Red : injured by pressure.　About
¾ × ⅝ in.　[Add. ch. 29,225.]
  Oval : an ornamental shield of arms : a castle.　In base
two sprigs. ·

Robert Foster.
Seal used by MARY HEBDEN, *wife of* THOMAS HEBDEN,
of Burwash, co. Suss., Gentl.
  9905. [A.D. 1620.]　Red : *en placard,* the paper of the
charter cut and folded back over the seal before impression.
¾ × ⅝ in.　[Add. ch. 29,759.]
  Oval : on a wreath, a stag statant.　Crest of FOSTER.

Another seal, of the above, described as of the Inner Temple,
London.
  9906. [A.D. 1626.]　Red.　⅝ × ¼ in.　[Add. ch. 30,546.]
  Oval : on a wreath a stag statant, for the crest of FOSTER.

Another seal, of the above, as Sir **Robert Foster,** *Justice of the*
Court of Common Pleas, Knt.
  9907. [A.D. 1642.]　Red : imperfect.　¾ × ⅝ in.　[Add.
ch. 29,665.]
  Oval : a shield of arms : quarterly, 1, 4, a chevron betw.
three bugle-horns, FOSTER ; 2, 3, on a bend (engrailed ?)
three bucks' heads cabossed, FOSTER ; in fess point a crescent
for difference.　Crest on a helmet, ornamental mantling and
wreath, a stag (?)

Symon Foster, *of Litlebourne, co. Kent.*
  9908. [A.D. 1362.]　Red : imperfect, indistinct.　⅞ in.
[Harl. ch. 80 C. 11.]
  A shield of arms : charges illegible within a bordure
engrailed.　Betw. two flowering sprigs.

Thomas Foster, *of the Inner Temple, London,*
son of Sir ROB. FOSTER, *Knt.*
  9909. [A.D. 1642.]　Red : very imperfect.　¼ × ⅜ in.
[Add. ch. 29,665.]
  A shield of arms : quarterly.　See seal of Sir ROBERT
FOSTER.
  Beaded border.

William Foster.
Seal used by MICHAEL CHADWELL, *of Chipping-Norton,*
co. Oxon., Gentl.
9910. [A.D. 1598.] Red. $\frac{3}{4}$ in. [Harl. ch. 76 E. 50.]
On a wreath, a talbot passant. Crest of FOSTER.

William Foster, *al.* **Forster,** *of Shildon in Chippenham,*
co. Wilts., Gentl.
9911. [A.D. 1669.] Red : *en placard.* $\frac{13}{16} \times \frac{7}{16}$ in. [Add.
ch. 18,436.]
Oval : a shield of arms (?) : per pale, *dex.*, a stag's head
cabossed with a cross betw. the antlers ; *sin.*, a fess and in
chief a mullet betw. two roundles. Crest on a helmet and
ornamental mantling a bull's head betw. a pair of wings.

Thomas Fournival.
9912. [Late 13th cent.] Plaster cast from fine impression.
$\frac{7}{8}$ in. [lxxxvi. 38.]
A shield of arms : a bend betw. six martlets, FURNIVAL.
The shield on a background barry, and betw. two lions
passant by way of supporters.
   ✠ : SIGILLVM : THOME : FOVRNIVAL ✠ :
Beaded borders.

Cf. No. 9977.

John *and* **Mary Fowle.**
See JOSEPH SWIFT.

Johanna, *widow of* RICHARD **Fowler,** *late Pantler*
of the King for the Duchy of Lancaster.
9913. [A.D. 1480.] Red : imperfect. About $\frac{1}{2} \times \frac{3}{8}$ in.
[Harl. ch. 55 B. 1.]
An owl on a branch, betw. two wavy sprigs. Crest of
FOWLER.

Charles Fox, *of Bromfield, co. Salop, Esq.*
9914. [A.D. 1574.] Red : from a ring (?) $\frac{3}{4} \times \frac{5}{8}$ in. [Add.
ch. 23,853.]
Oval : a shield of arms of ornamental shape : quarterly,
1, 4, on a bend three dolphins embowed, FOX ; 2, 3, per pale
dancetty, an organ pipe, STEBINGTON. In the field three
roses, barbed and seeded.
For the arms of FOX, see Papworth ; but cf. Harl. MS.
1396, f. 114 *b*, where the seal is attributed to STOKE, head

of the FOX family. For STEBINGTON, see Harl. MS. 1396, f. 114 b.

9915. [A.D. 1587.] Red. [Add. ch. 1035.]

Henry Fox, 1st Baron Holland.
9916. [A.D. 1764.] Red: *en placard*, on green tape. ¾ × ½ in. [Add. ch. 19,271.]

An ornamental shield of arms: an eagle displayed.

Paull Fox.
Seal used by HENRY BRYSTOWE, *of London, Gentl.*
9917. [A.D. 1592.] Red. ¾ in. [Add. ch. 30,529.]

On a chapeau, turned up ermine, a lion, or perhaps a fox sejant guardant (?). Crest of FOX.

Motto in the field :—

❀ FERENDO FERIO.

Beaded border.

Sir Stephen Fox, *Knt., Clerk of the Green Cloth.*
9918. [A.D. 1674.] Red, covered with paper before impression: very indistinct. [Add. ch. 19,267.]

Oval: a shield of arms: crest on a helmet and mantling, illegible.

William Fox, *of Colde Ascheby, co. Northt.*
9919. [A.D. 1391.] Red: imperfect. ¾ in. [Add. ch. 21,636.]

A shield of arms: per pale, *dex.*, a lion rampant; *sin.*, a crescent betw. two estoiles in pale.

❀ SIGI . . . . . DE . . TAYER . . . T . .

Thomas Foxcote, *of Stanford Manor, co. Berks.*
9920. [A.D. 1420.] Red: good. ¾ in. [Add. ch. 24,708.]

A shield of arms: three lions rampant, crowned, two and one.

✠ : **Sigillum : thome : foxcote** ✠ :

Robert de Foxton, *of Draughton, co. Northt.*
9921. [A.D. 1324.] Red: very imperfect. ⅞ in. [Add. ch. 21,747.]

A shield of arms: a lion rampant crowned, within a bordure engrailed. Within a carved gothic device ornamented along the inner edge with ball-flowers.

. . . . OBE . . . . DE · FOX . . . .

John Fraunceys (?)

9922. [*Temp.* Edw. III.] Plaster cast from impression, indistinct in places. ⅞ in. [lxxxvi. 32.]

A shield of arms: a saltire betw. four quatrefoils, FRAUN-CEYS. Suspended by a strap from a forked tree. Within a carved gothic panel. In base two small flowers.

Sig : . . ic : ffraunceys (?)

Cf. arms of Fraunceys, Lord Mayor of London, a saltire betw. four crosses crosslet.

Frederic Frankland.

See RICHARD DASHWOOD.

Frederic Frankland, *of Old Bond Street, co. Midd., Esq.*

9923. [A.D. 1729.] Red: *en placard,* on a tape, indistinct. About ⅝ × ⁹⁄₁₆ in. [Add. ch. 34,940.]

Oval: an ornamental shield of arms: a dolphin embowed, on a chief two saltires humetté, for FRANKLAND, a crescent for difference. Crest on a helmet, ornamental mantling, and wreath, an anchor enfiled with a dolphin.

The same used by ELIZABETH FRANKLAND, *his wife.*

9924. [A.D. 1729.] Red: as before. [Add. ch. 34,940.]

Peter Franckland, (?) *Commissioner of Sewers.*

9925. [Early 17th cent.] Red: a fragment. [Add. ch. 33,134.]

A shield of arms: per pale, *dex.,* two bars, on a bend three illegible charges, *sin.,* a lion rampant debruised by a bend charged with three mascles.

Sir Thomas Frankland, *of Thirkelby, co. York, Bart.*

9926. [A.D. 1737.] Red: *en placard,* on a tape, cracked, chipped. ⅝ × ½ in. [Add. ch. 30,958.]

A shield of arms: two bars.

9927. [A.D. 1737.] Another. [Add. ch. 30,958.]
9928. [A.D. 1737.] Another. [Add. ch. 30,960.]
9929. [A.D. 1737.] Another. [Add. ch. 30,960.]
9930. [A.D. 1737.] Another. [Add. ch. 30,961.]
9931. [A.D. 1737.] Another. [Add. ch. 30,961.]

John Frampton, *of Mynnyngesby, co. Linc., Knt.*

9932. [A.D. 1434.] Red: imperfect. About 1⅛ in. when perfect. [Add. ch. 5308.]

A shield of arms, *couché*: a chevron betw. three goats' heads erased. Crest on a helmet and lambrequin, destroyed. Legend illegible.

Gilbert de [Fransham ? *al.*] Frausham.
of Skernynge, co. Norf

9933. [A.D. 1366.] Red: edge injured. About ⅞ in. App. by silk cords. [L.F.C., xxiii. 15.]

A shield of arms : per pale indented, six martlets counter-changed, FRANSHAM.

✠ SIGILLV̄ · GILBERTI · DE · FRAVSA.

Adam Fraunceys, *Citizen and Mercer of London.*

9934. [A.D. 1350.] Red : very imperfect. [Harl. ch. 50 D. 53.]

For description see next seal.

SIGILL . . . . FRAVNO . . .

9935. [A.D. 1351.] ⁻Red : fine. [Harl. ch. 50 D. 52.]

A shield of arms : a bend, in sinister chief a lion's face. Field diapered lozengy. Within a finely carved gothic six-foil panel.

✠ SIGILLVM · ADE · FRAVNCEYS.

Beaded borders.

9936. Sulph. cast of No. 9935. [D.C., F. 374.]

Sir Edward Fraunceys, *of Petworth and Wappingthorn, co. Suss., Knt.*
Seal used by Sir JOHN LEEDS, *of the same.*

9937. [A.D. 1620.] Red. ¼ in. [Add. ch. 18,927.]

Out of a ducal coronet, a demi-eagle displayed. Crest of FRANCIS.

9938. [A.D. 1623.] Red : much injured by pressure. [Add. ch. 18,929.]

Hugh Fraunceys, *of Cavendish, co. Suff., Esq.*

9939. [A.D. 1424.] Red : good, from a ring (?) ¼ × ⅜ in. [Add. oh. 29,631.]

Rectangular, with corners cut off: on a mount an eagle rising. In the field the initial letter ɧ.

Beaded border.

The same, as Constable of Clare, co. Suff.

9940. [A.D. 1426.] Red : imperfect ; originally encircled by a twisted rush. [Harl. ch. 56 B. 17.]

Isabella, *widow of* WILLIAM Frounceys, *of Melton, co. Suff.*
9941. [A.D. 1382.] Red: indistinct. ⅝ in. [Add. ch. 9655.]
A shield of arms: three birds, two and one. Betw. the emblems of the four evangelists, as an eagle rising, an Agnus Dei, an ox, and an angel kneeling in prayer. Within a carved quatrefoil.

Nicholaus Le Frounceys, *of Wridelyngton, or Worlington, co. Suff.*
9942. [A.D. 1328.] Red: somewhat indistinct. ⅞ in. [Harl. ch. 50 D. 51.]
A shield of arms: a lion rampant, FRANCIS. Betw. three sprigs. Within a carved gothic rosette of eight points.
S' NICH'I · LE · FRAVNCES. ˙
Beaded borders.

Robert Frounces, *of Allestrey, co. Derb.*
9943. [A.D. 1346.] Red: imperfect. ⅞ in. [Woll. ch. ix. 53.]
A shield of arms: a chevron betw. three eagles displayed. Betw. two small fleurs-de-lis. Above the shield, a human face (?) Within a pointed gothic quatrefoil, ornamented with ball-flowers along the inner edge.
⚹ SIGILL' . . . ERTI · FR . . . . EYS.

Robert Frounceys, *Esq.,*
son and heir of ROBERT FRAUNCEYS, *Knt., of co. Derb.*
9944. [A.D. 1440–1.] Red: very indistinct. ⅞ in. [Woll. ch. x. 28.]
A shield of arms: a chevron betw. three eagles displayed. Cf. Woll. ch. ix. 53. Betw. five small quatrefoils. Within a carved gothic rosette of eight points ornamented with ball-flowers along the inner edge.
⚹ Sigillum : Rob . . . .

Simon Frounces.
See PIETER DE LOOTGHIETRE.

William Frounceys.
See COLIN DE POSSI.

Gilbert de Frousham.
See GILBERT DE FRANSHAM.

Ralph de Frechenvile, *of Cruche.*

9945. [*Temp.* Edw. II.] Dark-green: chipped, indistinct.
⅜ in. [Woll. ch. ix. 31.]

A shield of arms: a bend betw. six escallops, FRESCHE-
VILLE.

CREDE · MICH[I].

Beaded border.

Cf. Harl. ch. 84 A. 3, *temp.* Hen. III.; 86 G. 43, A.D. 1294.

Frederic, *Duke of York and Albany.*
See Duke of YORK AND ALBANY.

John de Freford, *of co. Staff., Knt.*

9946. [A.D. 1345.] Red: imperfect. ⅞ in. [Add. ch.
20,475.]

A shield of arms: five lozenges in bend, in the sinister
chief a martlet, FREFORD. Field powdered.

✠ S' IOHA . . . . ORD.

Inner border carved with ball-flowers; outer border beaded.

Margaret, *wife of* JOHN **de Freford.**
See JOHN DE ROCHEFORD.

John Frelond, *of co. Oxon.*

9947. [A.D. 1330.] Green, mottled: indistinct. ¾ in.
[Add. ch. 20,382.]

A shield of arms: a chevron betw. three animals' heads.
The shield on the breast of an eagle displayed.

✠ S IOHANNIS FRELOND.

Inner border ornamented with ball-flowers.

John Freman, *of Ebryghton [Ebrington], co. Glouc.*

9948. [A.D. 1447.] Red: a fragment. About ¾ × ⅝ in.
when perfect. [Slo. ch. xxxiii. 68.]

Oval: a shield of arms: three lozenges in fess, in chief an
annulet for difference.

Legend illegible.

William Freman, *of Leicester, co. Leic.*

9949. [A.D. 1422.] Green: indistinct. ¾ in. [Harl. ch.
50 E. 18.]

A shield of arms : on a fess betw. two roses some illegible charges.

☿ S'. ∴ WILLELME · FRE . . . .

William Fremlyngham.

9950· [A.D. 1402–3.] Plaster cast from good impression. 1⅚ in. [lxxxv. 94.]

A shield of arms : a fess ermine betw. two weasels, FRE- MINGHAM. Suspended by a strap from a tree ; within a carved device.

𝕾𝖎𝖌𝖎𝖑𝖑𝖚𝖒 : 𝖜𝖎𝖑𝖑'𝖎 : 𝖋𝖗𝖊𝖒𝖑𝖞𝖓𝖌𝖍𝖆.

Carved border.

9951. Another. [lxxxvi. 34.]

William Fremon, *of Eberton [Ebrington], co. Glouc.*

9952. [A.D. 1509.] Red : a fragment. [Slo. ch. xxxiii. 78.]

A shield of arms : three lozenges in fess, in chief a crescent for difference.

John Frensshe, *Spurrier and Citizen of London.*

9953. [A.D. 1400.] Red. ¼ in. [Harl. ch. 78 B. 50.]

The ornamental initial I, and a dolphin hauriant embowed. Surmounted by a ducal coronet. The dolphin in allusion to the arms of FRENCH.

John Frensshe.

See JOHN DE BLAKEBORNE.

Robert Frensh, *of Tacolneston, co. Norf., Gentl.*

9954. [A.D. 1657.] Red : injured. ⅜ × 5⁄16 in. [Add. ch. 19,265.]

A shield of arms : on a chevron engrailed, betw. three roundles, as many cinquefoils.

Richard Frere, *of Harlestone, co. Norf., Esq.*

9955. [A.D. 1596.] Red. ¾ in. [Add. ch. 14,690.]

A shield of arms : on a pale six annulets. In the field the initial letters R. F. A. for RICARDUS FRERE, *Armiger.*

Drawn in Blomefield's *Norf.*, vol. v., p. 355. (Dept. copy.)

Walter Frere, *of Sawbridgworth, co. Hertf.*

9956. [A.D. 1354.] Discoloured-white: indistinct. $\frac{11}{16}$ in. [Add. ch. 4775.]

A shield of arms: on a bend three trefoils in sinister chief point a mullet pierced. Betw. three estoiles (?) Within a carved gothic panel.

✠ S' IOH'IS . . . .

Another Seal.

9957. [A.D. 1370.] Discoloured-white: indistinct. $\frac{11}{16}$ in. [Add. ch. 4778.]

A shield of arms: ermine, two bars. Within a pointed quatrefoil.

S'

Baldewine Frevyle.

9958. [*Temp.* Edw. I.] Cast in green composition, from imperfect impression. $\frac{7}{8}$ in. [lxxvi. 76.]

A shield of arms: a cross, perhaps with charges now illegible.

✠ S . . . . . INI DE FRIVILE.

Baldewine Frevyle.

9959. [A.D. 1368.] Plaster cast from chipped impression. 1 in. [lxxxvi. 35.]

A shield of arms, *couché*: a cross flory. The shield resting on a helmet as if it were a lambrequin. Crest on the helmet out of a ducal coronet a garb. The strap and buckle of the shield below the helmet on the r. h. side. Within a carved gothic panel ornamented with ball-flowers along the inner edge.

S . . . . . . wyni : . . . freuyle.

Baldewine Frevylle, *son of* BALDEWINE FREVYLLE, *Chevr., of Tamworth, cos. Warw. and Staff.*

9960. [A.D. 1393.] Red: good, injured in parts by pressure. $1\frac{3}{8}$ in. [Eg. ch. 580.]

A shield of arms, *couché*: quarterly, 1, 4, barry of ten (?) 2, 3, a cross botonneé. Crest on a helmet and lambrequin a garb. Within a carved gothic device ornamented with ball-flowers along the inner edge.

Sigillū : baldewyni : freuile.

William Frey, *of co. Warwick, etc.*

9961. [A.D. 1406.] Red: from a ring. $\frac{7}{16} \times \frac{5}{16}$ in. [Harl. ch. 49 I. 30.]

Octagonal: a horse courant beneath a tree; alluding to the arms of FREY or FRY.

Cabled border.

John, *son of* GEOFFREY **Friday,** *of Estenestone, co. Northt.*

9962. [*Temp.* Edw. I. *or* II.] Creamy-white: indistinct. 1⅛ in. [Add. ch. 21,852.]

A fess, and in chief a six-foil on the dexter, and a cinquefoil on the sinister side, not on a shield. Perhaps intended for arms.

S' IOH' FIL' GALF' D' ESTNEST'.

9963. Another: very indistinct, chipped. [Add. ch. 21,853.]

John Frodsham.

9964. [A.D. 1369.] Plaster cast. 1 in. [lxxxvi. 36.]

A shield of arms, *couché*: a cross engrailed, for FRODSHAM. Crest on a helmet, lambrequin, and chapeau, the sails of a windmill. Within a carved gothic panel.

S' iohis frodulh̄a.

Thomas Frome, *son and heir of* WILLIAM FROME, *of Bristol.*

9965. [A.D. 1414.] Red: well preserved. From a ring. ½ in. [Add. ch. 26,469.]

A cross crosslet. In allusion to the crest of FROME, a cross crosslet betw. two wings.

Bartholomew Fromonde, *of East Cheam, co. Surr., Esq.*

9966. [A.D. 1639.] Red: indistinct, injured. ⅝ × ⁹⁄₁₀ in. [Add. ch. 5637.]

Oval: a shield of arms: per chevron, ermine (and gules) a chevron betw. three fleurs-de-lis, FROMOND.

Henry de Frowyk, *Citizen of London.*

9967. [A.D. 1368.] Red: cracked, imperfect. ¾ in. Appended by a woven bobbin of green silk. [Harl. ch. 79 G. 38.]

A shield of arms: a chevron betw. three leopards' heads, FROWICKE. Betw. two slipped flowers. Within a carved gothic quatrefoil, ornamented with ball-flowers along the inner edge.

Peter, *son of* GEOFFREY **de Frowik,** *Goldsmith, of London.*

9968. [A.D. 1256.] Dark-green: good, from a matrix,

furnished, apparently, with a screw for withdrawing the part containing the legend. $\frac{1}{16}$ in. [Harl. ch. 50 E. 33.]

A shield of arms : a fess betw. two chevrons each betw. three round buckles, the tongues fesswise. Suspended on a tree of flowers and foliage. Within a countersunk quatrefoil betw. four roses.

✠ S' PETRI : DE : FROVWIK : AVRIFABRI :

Beaded borders.

9969. Sulph. cast from No. 9968. [D.C., E. 380.]

William de Fulburn, *Clerk, of cos. Buck. and Berk.*

9970. [A.D. 1380–1.] Red : fine, very imperfect. 1 in. [Add. ch. 13,917.]

A shield of arms : a saltire betw. four martlets. Suspended (by the strap) from a tree on a mount. Betw. four slipped trefoils, two on each side. Within a carved gothic six-foil, ornamented with ball-flowers along the inner side.

. . . . 𝔤𝔦𝔩𝔩' : 𝔴𝔦𝔩𝔩'𝔦 . . . . . 𝔟𝔲𝔯𝔫 : ✠

9971. [A.D. 1380–1.] Plaster cast from good impression. [lxxxvi. 41.]

This impression shows many details which are wanting in the previous example.

𝔖𝔦𝔤𝔦𝔩𝔩' : 𝔴𝔦𝔩𝔩'𝔦 : 𝔡𝔢 · 𝔣𝔲𝔩𝔟𝔲𝔯𝔫 : ✠

Anne Fuller.

See THOS. HOUGHTON.

Rich. Fuller.

See THOS. HOUGHTON.

Robert Fuller, *of Gumecester, co. Hunt.*

9972. [A.D. 1427.] Red. $\frac{9}{16} \times \frac{7}{16}$ in. [Add. ch. 33,536.]

Octagonal : on a *tun* a swan rising. In the field the motto :—𝔥𝔢𝔩𝔭 𝔤𝔬𝔡.

Cabled border.

Sir **John Fullerton,** *Knt., Gentleman of the Bedchamber to Charles I.*

9973. [A.D. 1625.] Red: fine. $\frac{7}{8} \times \frac{11}{16}$ in. [Egert. ch. 419.]

Oval : a shield of arms, quarterly, 1, 4. Three otters' heads erased, two and one, FULLERTON, 2, 3. On a fess three mullets. An annulet for difference.

Carved border.

Richard Fulmerstone, *of Thetford, co. Norf., Esq.*
9974. [A.D. 1551.] Red : from a ring. $\frac{3}{8} \times \frac{1}{2}$ in. [Add. ch. 15,555.]
Oval : on a wreath an heraldic antelope's head erased, holding in the mouth a rose branch. Crest of FULMERSTONE. Betw. the initial letters R. F.

Roger de Fulthorp.
9975. [A.D. 1330.] Plaster cast from fine impression. $\frac{7}{8}$ in. [lxxxvi. 37.]
A shield of arms, *couché* : a cross moline. Crest on a helmet, lambrequin, and chapeau, charged with a cross as in the arms, a bird. In the field on the l. h. side a sprig of foliage.

S' · ROGERI · D' · FVLTHORP.

Beaded borders.

Rog. fil. Alani de Fulthorp.
See PETER GALUN.

Richard de Funtain.
See RICHARD DE FONTIBUS.

Walter de Furneaus, *of co. Derb., Knt.*
9976. [*Temp.* Edw. I.] Bronze-green : fine, edge chipped. $\frac{3}{4}$ in. [L.F.C., iv. 11.]
A shield of arms : on a chief some uncertain charges. Betw. two wavy sprigs of foliage and flowers.

✠ S' WALTERI : DE : FVRNEWES.

Beaded borders.
See next seal.

Walter de Furnewes.
9977. [A.D. 1272.] Plaster east. $\frac{3}{4}$ in. [lxxxvi. 39.]
A shield of arms : six crosses crosslet, three, two, and one, a chief. Betw. two wavy sprigs of foliage and flowers. Above the shield a flower.

✠ S' WALTERI DE FVRNEWES.

Beaded border.
The charges appear to have been altered, but in other respects this is the same seal as that used by WALTER DE FURNEAUS in L.F.C., iv. 11, *q.v.*

Gerard de Fornivale, *of co. Staff.*

9978. [Late 12th cent.]   Dark-green : edge chipped.
2⅛ in. [Harl. ch. 50 E. 54.]
A shield of arms of early shape : a bend betw. six martlets,
FURNIVAL.   On the bend the word :—

MARIA.

✠ SIG[IL]LVM · GERARDI · DE · FORNIVALE.

9979. Sulph. cast of No. 9978. [D.C., D. 235.]

Dame Johane, *widow of* M. THOMAS **Furnivalle,**
of Hallamshire.

9980. [A.D. 1367.]   Red : fine, chipped, injured by
pressure.   1¼ in. [Woll. ch. v. 32.]
Two shields of arms, side by side, suspended from a tree
on a mount. FURNIVAL.   Within a carved gothic panel
ornamented with ball-flowers along the inner edge.

𝕾𝔦𝔤 . . . . . . ✿ ᴹ ✿ 𝔦𝔬𝔥[𝔞𝔫]𝔫𝔢 ✿ ᴹ ✿ 𝔇𝔢 ✿ ᴹ ✿ 𝔣𝔲𝔯𝔫𝔦𝔟 . . . .

Thomas de Furnivallo, *son of* THOMAS DE FURNIVALLO,
of co. York.

9981. [*Temp.* Hen. III. *or* Edw. I.]   Dark-green : imperfect.
1¼ in. [Add. ch. 8196.]
A lozenge-shaped shield of arms : a bend betw. six
martlets. FURNIVAL.

✠ S' : THOME : [D]E : F . . . .

9982. [*Temp.* Hen. III. *or* Edw. I.]   Dark-green : fragments. [Add. ch. 8164.]

. . . . OME : D . . . .

Thomas de Furnefal, *Lord of Sheffield,* 1st *Baron Furnival.*

9983. [? A.D. 1301.]   Green, mottled : fine, chipped.   1¾ in.
[xxxv. 275.]
A shield of arms : a bend betw. six martlets, FURNIVAL.

✠ SIGILLVM : THOME DE FURNEFAL.

9984. Plaster cast of No. 9983. [lxxxvi. 40.]

Cf. No. 9912.

Thomas de Furnivall, *Lord of Hallamshire.*

9985. [A.D. 1347.]   Red : only a fragment of the central
part. [Woll. ch. i. 17.]
For description see next number.

9986. [A.D. 1361.] Red, embedded in a light-brown or discoloured mass. 1⅜ in. [L.F.C., iii. 20.]

A shield of arms : a bend betw. six martlets, FURNIVAL. Betw. two slipped leaves. Suspended by a strap from a tree, on which is an eagle. Within a carved gothic panel ornamented with ball-flowers along the inner edge.

Legend, the magical* words :—

𝖆𝖌𝖑𝖆 · 𝖇𝖊𝖗𝖔𝖓𝖞𝖝 · 𝖌𝖗𝖆𝖛𝖎𝖊𝖑 · 𝖙𝖊𝖙𝖗𝖆𝖌𝖗𝖆𝖒𝖆𝖙𝖔𝖓.

Beaded borders.

William, *son of* THOMAS de Furnial, *al.* Fornevalle, *Lord of Hallamshire.*

9987. [A.D. 1366.] Red : edge chipped. 1⅜ in. [Woll. ch. ix. 50.]

A shield of arms : a bend betw. six martlets, FURNIVAL. Suspended by an embroidered belt from an oak tree of three branches on a mount. Supporters two lions sejant guardant addorsed, each beneath a small tree.

𝕾𝖎𝖌𝖎𝖑' · 𝖂𝖎𝖑𝖑𝖎 · 𝖉𝖊 𝕱𝖔𝖗𝖓𝖊𝖚𝖆𝖑𝖑𝖊.

John, *son of* HENRY Fynch, *of Winchelsea, co. Suss.*

9988. [A.D. 1349.] Green. ⅞ in. [Add. ch. 20,118.]

A shield of arms : on a bend betw. two combs, or tuns, three martlets. Betw. two slipped trefoils, and within a carved gothic panel composed of a cinquefoil and triangle, ornamented with ball-flowers along the inner edge.

✠ S' IOH'IS · FILL' · HENRICI · FINCH.

Robert Fynch.
See PHELIPPE DE CALIN.

John Fyncham, *Commissioner of Sewers, of co. Camb., etc.*

9989. [A.D. 1608.] Red : imperfect. About ⅞ × ¾ in. [Add. ch. 33,083.]

A shield of arms : per pale, *dex.* three bars, over all a bend, ermine, FINCHAM, *sin.*, a lion rampant, over all, on a bend three mascles.

Beaded border.

9990. [A.D. 1608.] Red : cracked, indistinct. [Add. ch. 33,085.]

---

* See Fran. Barrett, *The Magus*, 1801, 4to., p. 105 *et seq.*

9991. [A.D. 1609.] Red: injured by pressure, indistinct. [Add. ch. 33,086.]

9992. [A.D. 1611.] Red: imperfect. [Add. ch. 33,094.]

Another Seal.

9993. [A.D. 1615.] Red: very indistinct. $\frac{5}{8} \times \frac{1}{2}$ in. [Add. ch. 33.097.]

Same design as the previous seal, but not so large.

9994. [A.D. 1619.] Red: a fragment. [Add. ch. 33,117.]

William de Fynchedene, *Jun.*

9995. [A.D. 1347.] Red: injured by pressure. [Add. ch. 16,737.]

A shield of arms: three finches. Betw. two slipped quatrefoils. In the field over the shield a crowned A. Within a carved gothic panel.

      ⚹ S' WILL' . . . Є FINCHEDONE.

Beaded border.

John, *Lord of* Ffyenĩl, Ffenĩl, *or* Fienles, *of Carshalton, co. Surr.*

9996. [Early 14th cent.] Dark-green: fine, imperfect. 1 in. [Add. ch. 23,344.]

A shield of arms: a lion rampant crowned. Betw. three palm sprigs.

      ✠ S' · IЄH . . . . NLЄS · CHL'R.

John de Fynderne, *of Repyndon, co. Derb.*

9997. [A.D. 1413.] Red: fine. $\frac{7}{8}$ in. [Add. ch. 1537.]

A shield of arms: a chevron engrailed betw. three crosses crosslet fitchées. FINDEʀNE. Betw. three pierced mullets. Within a carved gothic rosette or sixfoil ornamented with ball-flowers along the inner edge

      ⚹ SIGILLVM : IOH'IS : DE : FINDERNE: ⚔

Beaded border.

Sir Thomas Fynes, *8th Baron Dacre, Knt.*

9998. [A.D. 1530.] Red: imperfect. About 2 in. when perfect. [Add. ch. 5797.]

A shield of arms: quarterly, 1, 4, three lions rampant, two and one, FYNES; 2, 3, three escallops, two and one, DACRE. Crest on a helmet and ornamental mantling, out of a ducal coronet, broken off. Supporters, *dex.*, a wolf gorged with a spiked collar, chain, and clog.

. . . . . . :·: DÑI : + : DACRE : + : . . . . . .

Christopher Ffyneux.
See HENRY OXYNDEN.

Christopher Fyneux.
See ROGER MANWOOD.

Sir **John Fyneux,** *Chief Justice of the King's Bench, Knt.*
9999. [A.D. 1525.] Green: from a ring with marks of the setting. $\frac{5}{8} \times \frac{1}{2}$ in. [Harl. ch. 86 H. 16.]
Octagonal: an ornamental shield of arms: a chevron betw. three eagles displayed, FYNEUX.
Cabled border.

John Fyneux, *of Herne, co. Kent, Esq.*
10,000. [A.D. 1592.] Red: indistinct. $\frac{3}{4} \times \frac{5}{8}$ in. [Harl. ch. 78 C. 25.]
Oval: a shield of arms: a phœnix perhaps as a rebus for FYNEUX.

✠ RICVS · BIDVS · AMICVS · FIDVS.
Beaded border.

William Fyneux, *of Herne, co. Kent, Esq.*
10,001. [A.D. 1541.] Red. $\frac{5}{8} \times \frac{1}{2}$ in. [Harl. ch. 78 C. 20.]
Oval: an ornamental shield of arms: a chevron betw. three eagles displayed, crowned, FYNEUX.

William, *son of* JOHN **de Fynhagthe,** *of co. Suss.*
10,002. [A.D. 1356.] Red: injured by pressure, indistinct in parts. $\frac{3}{4}$ in. [Add. ch. 5654.]
A shield of arms: illegible. Within a carved trefoil.
S' IOH'IS . . . . IER.

William Fynne.
See HENRY NASH.

END OF VOL. II.

Lightning Source UK Ltd.
Milton Keynes UK
UKHW050156231118
332792UK00030B/218/P